Lecture Notes in Computer Science 13507

More information about this series at https://link.springer.com/bookseries/558

Yevgeniy Dodis · Thomas Shrimpton (Eds.)

Advances in Cryptology – CRYPTO 2022

42nd Annual International Cryptology Conference, CRYPTO 2022
Santa Barbara, CA, USA, August 15–18, 2022
Proceedings, Part I

Editors
Yevgeniy Dodis
New York University
New York, NY, USA

Thomas Shrimpton
University of Florida
Gainesville, FL, USA

ISSN 0302-9743   ISSN 1611-3349 (electronic)
Lecture Notes in Computer Science
ISBN 978-3-031-15801-8   ISBN 978-3-031-15802-5 (eBook)
https://doi.org/10.1007/978-3-031-15802-5

This Springer imprint is published by the registered company Springer Nature Switzerland AG
The registered company address is: Gewerbestrasse 11, 6330 Cham, Switzerland

Preface

The 42nd International Cryptology Conference (CRYPTO 2022) was held at the University of California, Santa Barbara, California, USA, during August 15–18, 2022. The conference had a hybrid format, with some presentations made in person, and some delivered virtually. CRYPTO 2022 was sponsored by the International Association for Cryptologic Research (IACR). The conference was preceded by two days of workshops on various topics.

The conference set new records for both submissions and publications: 455 papers were submitted, and 100 were accepted. Two papers were merged into a single joint paper. Three pairs of papers were soft-merged, meaning that they were written separately, but only one paper in each pair was given a presentation slot at the conference. This resulted in 96 presentations, a record by some margin for a non-virtual edition of Crypto. It took a Program Committee of 72 cryptography experts working with 435 external reviewers almost three months to select the accepted papers. We Chairs extend our heartfelt gratitude for the effort and professionalism displayed by the Program Committee; it was our pleasure to be your Chairs.

We experimented with some new policies and mechanisms this year. The most important had to do with the quality of reviewing, author feedback and interaction with the authors.

Shortly after the standard doubly-blind reviewing stage, we assigned a unique discussion leader (DL) to every paper. The DL's job was to make sure the paper received a thorough and fair treatment, and to moderate interactive communication between the reviewers and authors (described below). The DL also prepared a "Reviewers' consensus summary", which provided the authors with a concise summary of the discussion, the decision, and overall trajectory of the paper throughout the process. Many authors expressed gratitude for receiving the Reviewers' consensus summary, in addition to the usual reviews and scores. Overall, feedback on our DL experiment was quite positive, and we recommend it to future chairs to adopt this process as well.

We also experimented with an "interactive rebuttal" process. Traditionally, the rebuttal process has consisted of a single round: the authors were provided with the initial reviews, and had one opportunity to respond prior to the final decision. While better than no opportunity to rebut, our opinion is that the traditional process suffers from several important flaws. First, the authors were left to respond in (say) 750 words to multiple reviews that are, each, much longer. Too often, the authors are left to divine what are the *crucial* points to address; getting this wrong can lead to reviewers feeling that the rebuttal has missed (or dismissed) what mattered to them. In any case, the authors had no idea if their rebuttal was correctly focused, let alone convincing, until the decisions and final reviews were released. In many instances, the final reviews gave no signal that the rebuttal had been thoughtfully considered. In our view, and personal experience, the traditional rebuttal process led to frustration on both sides, with reviewers and authors feeling that their time had been wasted. Moreover, it had unclear benefits in terms of helping the PC to pick the best possible program.

To address this, we created a review form that required reviewers to make explicit what were their core concerns and criticisms; and we allowed for multiple, DL-moderated, rounds of communication between the reviewers and the authors.

Our review form had *exactly one* field visible to the authors during the initial rebuttal round. The field was called "Question/Clarifications for Authors", and reviewers were instructed to include *only* those things that had significant bearing upon the reviewer's accept/reject stance. We gave all reviewers detailed guidance on things that *must* be included. For example, any claimed errors, crucial prior work that was not cited, or other objective weaknesses that appeared in the detailed review comments. In addition, the reviewers were instructed to clearly state less objective concerns that factored into their initial score and disposition towards the paper. Thus, the authors should know exactly what to focus upon in their response. While not perfect, the new rebuttal format was a resounding success. Very strong/weak papers typically had very short rebuttals, allowing the PC to focus their time and energy on papers in need of extensive discussion or additional reviews.

In concert with the new review form and detailed review instructions, we also implemented *interactive discussions* between the reviewers and authors. The traditional rebuttal round became the first round of the interactive discussion. One round was enough for a fraction of the papers (primarily papers that were very strong or very weak), but the evaluation of most submissions benefited from numerous rounds: reviewers were able to sharpen their questions, authors were able to address points directly and in greater detail. The whole review process shifted more towards a collegial technical exchange. We did not encounter any problems that we initially feared, e.g., authors spamming the PC with comment. We believe that having the DLs moderate these interactions was important for keeping emotions and egos in check, and for encouraging reviewers to share any significant new concerns with the authors.

A few minor hiccups notwithstanding, the focused review forms and the "interactive rebuttal" mechanism received a lot of positive feedback, and we strongly encourage future chairs to adopt this tradition.

We also mention several smaller details which worked well. First, our review form included a "Brief Score Justification" field that remained reviewer-visible (only) for the entire process. This was a space for reviewers to speak freely, but concisely, about how they came to their scores. As Chairs, we found this extremely useful for getting a quick view of each paper's reviews. Second, we had an early rejection round roughly in the middle of our reviewing process. This allowed us to reject roughly half of submissions, i.e., those that clearly had no chance of being accepted to the final program. The process generally worked, and we tried to err on the side of caution, keeping papers alive if the PC was unsure of their seemingly negative views. For example, we allowed PC members to tag papers that they wanted to keep alive, even to the point of overturning a preliminary decision to early reject. However, we did feel slightly rushed in finalizing the early reject decisions, as we made them after less than two weeks after the initial reviewing round, and less than a week after the initial rebuttal round. Part of this rush was due to late reviews. Thus, we recommend that future chairs give themselves a bit more slack in the schedule, and perhaps add a second (less) early rejection round. Third, we experimented with allowing PC members to have a variable number of submissions, rather than the usual hard limits (e.g., at most one or two). Concretely, at most 4 papers could be submitted; the first paper was "free", but every subsequent paper submitted by the PC member resulted in this PC member getting roughly three more papers to review, and one additional DL appointment. We adopted this policy to make it easier for experts to accept our invitation to join the PC. (As always, the chairs were not allowed to submit papers.) Despite some unexpected difficulties and complaints about this system, most having to do with the logistic difficulty of assigning DLs to PC members with late initial reviews, many PC members told us that they appreciated the flexibility to submit more papers, especially when students were involved. We found no evidence that our system resulted in more accepted papers that were co-authored by the PC members, or any other biases and irregularities. Hence, we found it to be positive, overall.

The Program Committee recognized three papers and their authors for particularly outstanding work

- "Batch Arguments for NP and More from Standard Bilinear Group Assumptions," by Brent Waters and David Wu
- "Breaking Rainbow Takes a Weekend on a Laptop", by Ward Beullens
- "Some Easy Instances of Ideal-SVP and Implications to the Partial Vandermonde Knapsack Problem", by Katharina Boudgoust, Erell Gachon, and Alice Pellet-Mary

We were very pleased to have Yehuda Lindell as the Invited Speaker at CRYPTO 2022, who spoke about "The MPC journey from theoretical foundations to commercial success: a story of science and business".

We would like to express our sincere gratitude to all the reviewers for volunteering their time and knowledge in order to select a great program for 2022. Additionally, we are grateful to the following people for helping to make CRYPTO 2022 a success: Allison Bishop (General Chair, CRYPTO 2022), Kevin McCurley and Kay McKelly (IACR IT experts), Carmit Hazay (Workshops Chair), and Whitney Morris and her staff at UCSB conference services.

We would also like to thank the generous sponsors, all of the authors of the submissions, the rump session chair, the regular session chairs, and the speakers.

August 2022   Yevgeniy Dodis
                                                                              Thomas Shrimpton

Organization

General Chair

Allison Bishop   Proof Trading and City College, CUNY, USA

Program Committee Chairs

Yevgeniy Dodis   New York University, USA
Thomas Shrimpton   University of Florida, USA

Steering Committee

Helena Handschuh   Rambus Inc., USA
Anna Lysyanskaya   Brown University, USA

Program Committee

Shweta Agarwal   IIT Madras, India
Prabhanjan Ananth   University of California Santa Barbara, USA
Saikrishna Badrinarayanan   Visa Research, USA
Lejla Batina   Radboud University, Netherlands
Carsten Baum   Aarhus University, Denmark
Jeremiah Blocki   Purdue University, USA
Alexandra Boldyreva   Georgia Tech, USA
Elette Boyle   IDC Herzliya and NTT Research, Israel
David Cash   University of Chicago, USA
Itai Dinur   Ben-Gurion University, Israel
François Dupressoir   University of Bristol, UK
Nico Döttling   Helmholtz Center for Information Security
      (CISPA), Germany
Dario Fiore   IMDEA Software Institute, Spain
Ben Fisch   Stanford, USA
Marc Fischlin   TU Darmstadt, Germany
Rosario Gennaro   City College of New York, USA
Divya Gupta   Microsoft Research, India
Felix Günther   ETH Zurich, Switzerland
Mohammad Hajiabadi   University of Waterloo, Canada
Helena Handschuh   Rambus Inc., USA

Ni Trieu   Arizona State University, USA
Yiannis Tselekounis   Carnegie Mellon University, USA
Mayank Varia   Boston University, USA
Xiao Wang   Northwestern University, USA
Daniel Wichs   Northeastern University and NTT Research, USA
David Wu   UT Austin, USA
Shota Yamada   AIST, Japan
Kan Yasuda   NTT Labs, Japan
Kevin Yeo   Google and Columbia University, USA
Eylon Yogev   Bar-Ilan University, Israel
Vassilis Zikas   Purdue University, USA

Additional Reviewers

Masayuki Abe   Mihir Bellare
Calvin Abou Haidar   Adrien Benamira
Anasuya Acharya   Fabrice Benhamouda
Divesh Aggarwal   Huck Bennett
Shashank Agrawal   Ward Beullens
Gorjan Alagic   Tim Beyne
Navid Alamati   Rishabh Bhadauria
Martin R. Albrecht   Amit Singh Bhati
Nicolas Alhaddad   Ritam Bhaumik
Bar Alon   Sai Lakshmi Bhavana Obbattu
Estuardo Alpirez Bock   Jean-Francois Biasse
Jacob Alprerin-Shreiff   Alexander Bienstock
Joel Alwen   Nina Bindel
Ghous Amjad   Nir Bitansky
Kazumaro Aoki   Olivier Blazy
Gal Arnon   Alexander Block
Rotem Arnon-Friedman   Xavier Bonnetain
Arasu Arun   Jonathan Bootle
Thomas Attema   Katharina Boudgoust
Benedikt Auerbach   Christina Boura
Christian Badertscher   Pedro Branco
David Balbás   Konstantinos Brazitikos
Marco Baldi   Jacqueline Brendel
Gustavo Banegas   Marek Broll
Fabio Banfi   Chris Brzuska
Laaysa Bangalore   Ileana Buhan
James Bartusek   Benedikt Bunz
Andrea Basso   Bin-Bin Cai
Christof Beierle   Federico Canale
Amos Beimel   Ran Canetti

Ignacio Cascudo
Gaëtan Cassiers
Dario Catalano
Pyrros Chaidos
Suvradip Chakraborty
Jeff Champion
Benjamin Chan
Alishah Chator
Shan Chen
Weikeng Chen
Yilei Chen
Yu Long Chen
Nai-Hui Chia
Lukasz Chmielewski
Chongwon Cho
Arka Rai Choudhuri
Miranda Christ
Chitchanok Chuengsatiansup
Peter Chvojka
Michele Ciampi
Benoît Cogliati
Ran Cohen
Alex Cojocaru
Sandro Coretti-Drayton
Arjan Cornelissen
Henry Corrigan-Gibbs
Geoffroy Couteau
Elizabeth Crites
Jan Czajkwoski
Joan Daemen
Quang Dao
Pratish Datta
Bernardo David
Nicolas David
Hannah Davis
Koen de Boer
Leo de Castro
Luca De Feo
Gabrielle De Micheli
Jean Paul Degabriele
Patrick Derbez
Jesus Diaz
Jack Doerner
Jelle Don
Jesko Dujmovic

Sebastien Duval
Ted Eaton
Nadia El Mrabet
Reo Eriguchi
Llorenç Escolà Farràs
Daniel Escudero
Saba Eskandarian
Thomas Espitau
Antonio Faonio
Pooya Farshim
Serge Fehr
Peter Fenteany
Rex Fernando
Rune Fiedler
Matthias Fitzi
Nils Fleischhacker
Danilo Francati
Cody Freitag
Tommaso Gagliardoni
Chaya Ganesh
Rachit Garg
Lydia Garms
Luke Garratt
Adria Gascon
Romain Gay
Peter Gaži
Nicholas Genise
Marios Georgiou
Koustabh Ghosh
Ashrujit Ghoshal
Barbara Gigerl
Niv Gilboa
Emanuele Giunta
Aarushi Goel
Eli Goldin
Junqing Gong
Jesse Goodman
Lorenzo Grassi
Alex Grilo
Alex Bredariol Grilo
Aditya Gulati
Sam Gunn
Aldo Gunsing
Siyao Guo
Yue Guo

Chun Guo
Julie Ha
Ben Hamlin
Ariel Hamlin
Abida Haque
Patrick Harasser
Ben Harsha
Eduard Hauck
Julia Hesse
Clemens Hlauschek
Justin Holmgren
Alexander Hoover
Kai Hu
Yuval Ishai
Muhammad Ishaq
Takanori Isobe
Tetsu Iwata
Hakon Jacobsen
Aayush Jain
Ashwin Jha
Dingding Jia
Zhengzhong Jin
Nathan Ju
Fatih Kaleoglu
Daniel Kales
Simon Kamp
Daniel M. Kane
Dimitris Karakostas
Harish Karthikeyan
Shuichi Katsumata
Marcel Keller
Thomas Kerber
Mustafa Khairallah
Hamidreza Amini Khorasgani
Hamidreza Khoshakhlagh
Dakshita Khurana
Elena Kirshanova
Fuyuki Kitagawa
Susumu Kiyoshima
Dima Kogan
Lisa Kohl
Stefan Kolbl
Dimitris Kolonelos
Ilan Komargodski
Chelsea Komlo

Yashvanth Kondi
Venkata Koppula
Daniel Kuijsters
Mukul Kulkarni
Nishant Kumar
Fukang Liu
Norman Lahr
Russell W. F. Lai
Qiqi Lai
Baptiste Lambin
David Lanzenberger
Philip Lazos
Seunghoon Lee
Jooyoung Lee
Julia Len
Tancrède Lepoint
Gaëtan Leurent
Hanjun Li
Songsong Li
Baiyu Li
Xiao Liang
Yao-Ting Lin
Han-Hsuan Lin
Huijia Lin
Xiaoyuan Liu
Meicheng Liu
Jiahui Liu
Qipeng Liu
Zeyu Liu
Yanyi Liu
Chen-Da Liu-Zhang
Alex Lombardi
Sébastien Lord
Paul Lou
Donghang Lu
George Lu
Yun Lu
Reinhard Lüftenegger
Varun Madathil
Monosij Maitra
Giulio Malavolta
Mary Maller
Jasleen Malvai
Nathan Manohar
Deepak Maram

Lorenzo Martinico

Christian Matt

Sahar Mazloom

Kelsey Melissaris

Nicolas Meloni

Florian Mendel

Rebekah Mercer

Pierre Meyer

Charles Meyer-Hilfiger

Peihan Miao

Brice Minaud

Pratyush Mishra

Tarik Moataz

Victor Mollimard

Andrew Morgan

Tomoyuki Morimae

Travis Morrison

Fabrice Mouhartem

Tamer Mour

Pratyay Mukherjee

Marta Mularczyk

Marcel Nageler

Yusuke Naito

Kohei Nakagawa

Mridul Nandi

Varun Narayanan

Patrick Neumann

Gregory Neven

Samuel Neves

Ngoc Khanh Nguyen

Hai Nguyen

Luca Nizzardo

Ariel Nof

Adam O'Neill

Maciej Obremski

Kazuma Ohara

Miyako Ohkubo

Claudio Orlandi

Michele Orrù

Elisabeth Oswald

Morten Øygarden

Alex Ozdemir

Elena Pagnin

Tapas Pal

Jiaxin Pan

Giorgos Panagiotakos

Omer Paneth

Udaya Parampalli

Anat Paskin-Cherniavsky

Alain Passelègue

Sikhar Patranabis

Chris Peikert

Alice Pellet-Mary

Zachary Pepin

Leo Perrin

Giuseppe Persiano

Edoardo Persichetti

Peter Pessl

Thomas Peters

Stjepan Picek

Maxime Plancon

Bertram Poettering

Christian Porter

Eamonn Postlethwaite

Thomas Prest

Robert Primas

Luowen Qian

Willy Quach

Srinivasan Raghuraman

Samuel Ranellucci

Shahram Rasoolzadeh

Deevashwer Rathee

Mayank Rathee

Divya Ravi

Krijn Reijnders

Doreen Riepel

Peter Rindal

Guilherme Rito

Bhaskar Roberts

Felix Rohrbach

Leah Rosenbloom

Mike Rosulek

Adeline Roux-Langlois

Joe Rowell

Lawrence Roy

Tim Ruffing

Keegan Ryan

Yusuke Sakai

Louis Salvail

Simona Samardjiska

Katerina Samari
Olga Sanina
Amirreza Sarencheh
Pratik Sarkar
Yu Sasaki
Tobias Schmalz
Markus Schofnegger
Peter Scholl
Jan Schoone
Phillipp Schoppmann
André Schrottenloher
Jacob Schuldt
Sven Schäge
Gregor Seiler
Joon Young Seo
Karn Seth
Srinath Setty
Aria Shahverdi
Laura Shea
Yaobin Shen
Emily Shen
Sina Shiehian
Omri Shmueli
Ferdinand Sibleyras
Janno Siim
Jad Silbak
Luisa Siniscalchi
Daniel Slamanig
Yifan Song
Min Jae Song
Fang Song
Nicholas Spooner
Lukas Stennes
Igors Stepanovs
Christoph Striecks
Sathya Subramanian
Adam Suhl
George Sullivan
Mehrdad Tahmasbi
Akira Takahashi
Atsushi Takayasu
Abdul Rahman Taleb
Quan Quan Tan
Ewin Tang
Tianxin Tang

Stefano Tessaro
Justin Thaler
Emmanuel Thome
Søren Eller Thomsen
Mehdi Tibouchi
Radu Titiu
Yosuke Todo
Junichi Tomida
Monika Trimoska
Daniel Tschudi
Ida Tucker
Nirvan Tyagi
Rei Ueno
Dominique Unruh
David Urbanik
Wessel van Woerden
Prashant Vasudevan
Serge Vaudenay
Muthu Venkitasubramaniam
Damien Vergnaud
Thomas Vidick
Mikhail Volkhov
Satyanarayana Vusirikala
Riad Wahby
Roman Walch
Hendrik Waldner
Michael Walter
Qingju Wang
Han Wang
Haoyang Wang
Mingyuan Wang
Zhedong Wang
Geng Wang
Hoeteck Wee
Shiyi Wei
Mor Weiss
Chenkai Weng
Benjamin Wesolowski
Lichao Wu
Keita Xagawa
Jiayu Xu
Anshu Yadav
Sophia Yakoubov
Takashi Yamakawa
Trevor Yap Hong Eng

Xiuyu Ye
Albert Yu
Thomas Zacharias
Michal Zajac
Hadas Zeilberger

Mark Zhandry
Yupeng Zhang
Cong Zhang
Bingsheng Zhang
Dionysis Zindros

Sponsor Logos

Contents – Part I

Cryptanalysis I

Rotational Differential-Linear Distinguishers of ARX Ciphers with Arbitrary Output Linear Masks

Zhongfeng Niu[1,2,3], Siwei Sun[2,5(✉)], Yunwen Liu[1,2,3,4,5], and Chao Li[4]

[1] State Key Laboratory of Information Security, Institute of Information Engineering, Chinese Academy of Sciences, Beijing, China
niuzhongfeng@iie.ac.cn
[2] School of Cryptology, University of Chinese Academy of Sciences, Beijing, China
sunsiwei@ucas.ac.cn
[3] School of Cyber Security, University of Chinese Academy of Sciences, Beijing, China
[4] College of Liberal Arts and Science, National University of Defense Technology, Changsha, China
[5] State Key Laboratory of Cryptology, P.O. Box 5159, Beijing 100878, China

Abstract. The rotational differential-linear attacks, proposed at EUROCRYPT 2021, is a generalization of differential-linear attacks by replacing the differential part of the attacks with rotational differentials. At EUROCRYPT 2021, Liu et al. presented a method based on Morawiecki et al.'s technique (FSE 2013) for evaluating the rotational differential-linear correlations for the special cases where the output linear masks are unit vectors. With this method, some powerful (rotational) differential-linear distinguishers with output linear masks being unit vectors against FRIET, Xoodoo, and Alzette were discovered. However, how to compute the rotational differential-linear correlations for arbitrary output masks was left open. In this work, we partially solve this open problem by presenting an efficient algorithm for computing the (rotational) differential-linear correlation of modulo additions for arbitrary output linear masks, based on which a technique for evaluating the (rotational) differential-linear correlation of ARX ciphers is derived. We apply the technique to Alzette, SipHash, ChaCha, and SPECK. As a result, significantly improved (rotational) differential-linear distinguishers including *deterministic* ones are identified. All results of this work are practical and experimentally verified to confirm the validity of our methods. In addition, we try to explain the experimental distinguishers employed in FSE 2008, FSE 2016, and CRYPTO 2020 against ChaCha. The predicted correlations are close to the experimental ones.

Keywords: Rotational differential-linear · Correlation · ARX · Alzette · SipHash · SPECK · ChaCha

1 Introduction

Building symmetric-key primitives with modulo additions, rotations, and XORs is a common practice in the community of symmetric-key cryptography. The

© International Association for Cryptologic Research 2022
Y. Dodis and T. Shrimpton (Eds.): CRYPTO 2022, LNCS 13507, pp. 3–32, 2022.
https://doi.org/10.1007/978-3-031-15802-5_1

resulting primitives are collectively referred as ARX designs and their represen-
tatives can be found everywhere, including

- Block ciphers: FEAL [42], Bel-T [38], LEA [24], TEA [16], XTEA [41], HIGHT [25], SPECK [6], SPARX [19];
- Stream ciphers: Salsa20 [11], ChaCha20 [10];
- Hash functions: SHA3 finalists Skein [22] and BLAKE [5];
- Cryptographic permutations: Alzette [7], Sparkle [8];
- MAC algorithms: SipHash [3], Chaskey [35].

Some ARX designs are standardized or widely deployed in real world applications. For example, HIGHT, LEA, and Chaskey are standardized in ISO/IEC
18033-3:2010, ISO/IEC 29192-2:2019, and ISO/IEC 29192-6:2019, respectively.
ChaCha is used with HMAC-SHA1 and Poly1305 in the transport layer security
(TLS) protocol. Chaskey is deployed in commercial products by some auto-
motive suppliers and major industrial control systems. Skein has been added
to FreeBSD and is optionally used for authentication tags in the ZRTP protocol. Variants of BLAKE are included in OpenSSL and WolfSSL. In addition,
instances of SipHash are used in the dnscache instances of all OpenDNS resolvers
and employed as hash() in Python for all major platforms.

The popularity of ARX designs can be attributed to the following reasons.
Firstly, modulo additions provide both diffusion and confusion functionalities,
making it possible to construct secure primitives without relying on the table
look-ups associated with the S-box based designs, which increases the resilience
against timing side-channel attacks. Secondly, the native support of the modulo
additions in modern CPUs allows particularly fast software implementations of
ARX ciphers. Finally, the code describing an ARX primitive is relatively simple
and small, making this approach especially appealing for application scenarios
where the memory footprint is highly constrained. In a systematic work for evaluating the performance and resource consumption of lightweight block ciphers
on three major micro-controller platforms (8-bit AVR, 16-bit MSP, and 32-bit
ARM) [18], Dinu et al. concluded:

> "... state-of-the art ARX and ARX-like designs are not only very fast, but
> also extremely small in terms of RAM footprint and code size."

Cryptanalysis of ARX Primitives. ARX designs hold a special position in
the development of techniques for analyzing symmetric-key primitives. The block
cipher FEAL [42], probably the first ARX cipher presented in the literature,
has acted as a catalyst in the discovery of differential and linear cryptanalysis.
However, compared to S-box based designs, the development of the theories
and tools for the analysis of ARX-like primitives tends to lag behind when the
involved additions operate on n-bit words with $n \geq 16$.

In S-box based designs, typically the employed S-boxes are small permutations
(e.g., permutations over $\mathbb{F}_2^4$ or $\mathbb{F}_2^8$) whose differential property can be computed
by enumerating the input pairs. In contrast, the modulo additions often operate

on large words (e.g., 32-bit or 64-bit words). In such cases, computing the probability of a given differential $(\alpha, \beta) \to \gamma$ by enumeration is computationally infeasible. The first algorithm for computing the differential probabilities of modulo additions efficiently was not available until 2001 [31]. After two years, Wallén showed how to compute the correlations of the linear approximations of modulo additions efficiently [44]. Subsequently, alternative descriptions of the cryptographic properties of modulo additions with S-functions [37] and finite automaton [40] appeared. The development of the tools for constructing or finding differential or linear trails of ARX-like ciphers has gone through multiple stages. At first, tools working as helpers for manual analysis were developed [27–29]. Then, dedicated search algorithms are designed to identify differential trails with high probabilities [12, 13]. Now, we have constraint-based (MILP, SAT, or SMT) tools which are quite powerful and convenient in designing and analyzing ARX primitives [23, 36].

In recent years, we witness remarkable advancement in the cryptanalysis of ARX primitives [2, 9, 15, 26, 30, 32, 33]. Nevertheless, there are full of open problems concerning the cryptanalysis of ARX designs. For example, we do not know how to compute the accurate probabilities or correlations of the differential or linear approximations of a chain of modulo additions [21]. There are attacks published at top crypto conferences relying on experimental distinguishers without a theoretical interpretation [9, 15], and we refer the reader to Supplementary Material H in the extended version of this paper [39] for a systematic summary of these experimental distinguishers. Most recently, Liu et al. presented the so-called rotational differential-linear cryptanalysis and proposed the open problem on computing the (rotational) differential-linear correlations of modulo additions with output linear masks of Hamming weight greater than one [32], which is the major problem we are going to solve in this work.

Contribution. First of all, we solve the open problem proposed in [32]. We present a method for computing the (rotational) differential-linear correlation of the modulo addition for arbitrary output linear masks based on a delicate partition of $\mathbb{F}_2^m \times \mathbb{F}_2^m$ into subsets, where the elements in each subset fulfill certain equations. The method is extremely efficient, and the time complexity of computing the (rotational) differential-linear correlation of $x \boxplus y \mod 2^n$ for a specific rotational differential-linear approximation can be roughly estimated by the complexity of n 4×4 matrix multiplications.

Based on the above method and Morawiecki et al.'s technique [34], we propose a method for computing the generalized (rotational) differential-linear correlation of ARX ciphers with arbitrary output linear masks when the probabilities of $x_{i-t} \neq x_i$ for all relevant i's and a specific t are given. Compared with the formulas given in [32], the new ones are not only applicable for output linear masks whose Hamming weights are greater than one, but also weaken the assumptions required for the formulas to hold. We apply the method to Alzette, SipHash, ChaCha, and SPECK. We identify new and significantly improved (rotational) differential-linear distinguishers. All the new distinguishers are highly biased or even *deterministic*, and all of them are experimentally verified. The results are summarized in Table 1.

Table 1. A summary of the results. R-DL = rotational differential-linear, DL = differential-linear, RD = rotational differential, LC = linear characteristic, DC = differential characteristic. We show differentials with probabilities and LC/DL/R-DL with correlations. Note that the 10-round RD distinguisher for SPECK32 works only for $2^{28.10}$ weak keys, and the constants used in the experiments for Alzette are 0xB7E15162 and 0x38B4DA56.

Permutation	Type	# Round	Probability/Correlation		Ref.
			Theoretical	Experimental	
Alzette	DC	4	2^{-6}	–	[7]
	R-DL	4	$2^{-11.37}$	$2^{-7.35}$	[32]
	DL	4	$2^{-0.27}$	$2^{-0.1}$	[32]
	DC	8	$\leq 2^{-32}$	–	[7]
	DL	4	1	1	Sect. 6.1
	R-DL	4	$2^{-5.57}$	$2^{-3.14}$	Sect. 6.1
	DL	5	$-2^{-0.33}$	$-2^{-0.13}$	Sect. 6.1
	DL	6	$2^{-4.95}$	$2^{-1.45}$	Sect. 6.1
	DL	8	$-2^{-8.24}$	$-2^{-5.50}$	Sect. 6.1
SipHash	DC	4	2^{-35}	–	[20]
	DL	3	$2^{-2.19}$	$2^{-0.78}$	Sect. 6.2
	DL	4	$2^{-12.45}$	$2^{-6.03}$	Sect. 6.2
SPECK32	DC	8	2^{-24}	–	[1]
	LC	9	2^{-14}	–	[23]
	DC	10	$2^{-31.01}$	–	[43]
	RD	10*	$2^{-19.15}$	–	[33]
	DL	8	$2^{-8.23}$	$2^{-6.87}$	Sect. 6.3
	DL	9	$2^{-10.23}$	$2^{-8.93}$	Sect. 6.3
	DL	10	$2^{-15.23}$	$2^{-13.90}$	Sect. 6.3
ChaCha	DL	4	–	$2^{-1.19}$	[14]
	DL	4	$2^{-0.02}$	$2^{-0.98}$	Sect. 6.4

In addition, we attempt to give theoretical interpretations of the experimental distinguishers employed in CRYPTO 2020 [9], FSE 2008 [4], and FSE 2016 [14] against ChaCha. The results of the analysis are summarized in Table 13 in the Supplementary Material G in the extended version [39], from which we can see that the predicted correlations are close to the experimental ones.

2 Notations and Preliminaries

For a finite set $\mathbb{D}$, $\#\mathbb{D}$ denotes the number of elements in $\mathbb{D}$. Let $\mathbb{F}_2 = \{0, 1\}$ be the binary field. We denote by x_i the i-th bit of a vector $\mathbf{x} = (x_{n-1}, \cdots, x_0) \in \mathbb{F}_2^n$. In addition, $\lceil \mathbf{x} \rceil^{(t)} = (x_{n-1}, \cdots, x_{n-t})$ denotes the most significant t bits of $\mathbf{x}$, and $\lfloor \mathbf{x} \rfloor^{(t)} = (x_{t-1}, \cdots, x_0)$ denotes the least significant t bits of $\mathbf{x}$. Concrete values in $\mathbb{F}_2^n$ are specified in hexadecimal or binary notations. For example, we use 0x1F12 or 1F12 to denote the binary string $(0001\ 1111\ 0001\ 0010)_2$. Given two n-bit vectors $\mathbf{x} = (x_{n-1}, \cdots, x_0)$ and $\mathbf{y} = (y_{n-1}, \cdots, y_0)$, the inner product of $\mathbf{x}$ and $\mathbf{y}$ is defined as $\mathbf{x} \cdot \mathbf{y} = x_{n-1}y_{n-1} \oplus \cdots \oplus x_0 y_0$. For a constant vector $\boldsymbol{\lambda} \in \mathbb{F}_2^n$, $\boldsymbol{\lambda}^\perp$ represents the set $\{\mathbf{x} \in \mathbb{F}_2^n : \boldsymbol{\lambda} \cdot \mathbf{x} = 0\}$. Rotation of $\mathbf{x}$ by t bits to the left is denoted by $\mathbf{x} \lll t$, and when t is clear from the context, $\mathbf{x} \lll t$ is written as $\overleftarrow{\mathbf{x}}$ for simplicity. The rotational-xor difference (RX-difference) with offset t of two bit strings $\mathbf{x}$ and $\mathbf{x}'$ in $\mathbb{F}_2^n$ are defined as $(x \lll t) \oplus x'$.

Let $F : \mathbb{F}_2^n \to \mathbb{F}_2^m$ be a vectorial Boolean function. We use $\overleftarrow{F}$ to denote the function mapping $\mathbf{x}$ to $F(\mathbf{x}) \lll t$ for some non-negative integer t. The correlation of the rotational differential-linear approximation of F with rotation offset t, RX-difference $\boldsymbol{\alpha} \in \mathbb{F}_2^n$, and output linear mask $\boldsymbol{\lambda} \in \mathbb{F}_2^m$ is defined as

$$\mathcal{C}_{\boldsymbol{\alpha},\boldsymbol{\lambda}}^{\text{R-DL}}(F) = \frac{1}{2^n} \sum_{\mathbf{x} \in \mathbb{F}_2^n} (-1)^{\boldsymbol{\lambda} \cdot ((F(\mathbf{x}) \lll t) \oplus F((\mathbf{x} \lll t) \oplus \boldsymbol{\alpha}))}. \tag{1}$$

When $t = 0$, Eq. (1) computes the ordinary differential-linear correlation of F, which is denoted by $\mathcal{C}_{\boldsymbol{\alpha},\boldsymbol{\lambda}}^{\text{DL}}(F)$. When F is clear from the context, we may drop F and use $\mathcal{C}_{\boldsymbol{\alpha},\boldsymbol{\lambda}}^{\text{R-DL}}$ and $\mathcal{C}_{\boldsymbol{\alpha},\boldsymbol{\lambda}}^{\text{DL}}$ instead.

Let $\mathbf{M}_i$ for $0 \le i < n$ be $k \times k$ matrices, we use $\prod_{i=0}^{n-1} \mathbf{M}_i$ to denote the product with the specified order $\mathbf{M}_{n-1} \cdots \mathbf{M}_0$.

2.1 Modulo Addition with an Initial Carry Bit

Let $\boxplus_b^{(n)} : \mathbb{F}_2^n \times \mathbb{F}_2^n \to \mathbb{F}_2^n$ be the operation mapping $(\mathbf{x}, \mathbf{y}) \in \mathbb{F}_2^n \times \mathbb{F}_2^n$ to

$$\mathbf{x} \boxplus_b^{(n)} \mathbf{y} = \mathbf{x} + \mathbf{y} + b \mod 2^n,$$

where $b \in \mathbb{F}_2$. For the sake of simplicity, we may omit the subscript b when $b = 0$ or the superscript (n) when n is clear from the context.

Example 1. Let $\mathbf{x} = \text{0xE9} = (11101001)_2$ and $\mathbf{y} = \text{0xA3} = (10100011)_2$ be 8-bit strings. Then, $\mathbf{x} \boxplus \mathbf{y} = \mathbf{x} \boxplus_0^{(8)} \mathbf{y} = \text{0x8C} = (10001100)_2$, and $\mathbf{x} \boxplus_1^{(8)} \mathbf{y} = \text{0x8D} = (10001101)_2$.

For $(\mathbf{x}, \mathbf{y}) \in \mathbb{F}_2^n \times \mathbb{F}_2^n$, the carry vector of $(\mathbf{x}, \mathbf{y})$ with initial carry bit $b \in \mathbb{F}_2$ is defined to be an $(n+1)$-bit vector $\mathfrak{c}_b(\mathbf{x}, \mathbf{y}) = (c_n, c_{n-1}, \cdots, c_0)$ such that

$$c_i = \begin{cases} b, & i = 0 \\ x_{i-1}y_{i-1} \oplus x_{i-1}c_{i-1} \oplus y_{i-1}c_{i-1}, & 1 \le i \le n \end{cases}.$$

We call $c_b(\mathbf{x}, \mathbf{y})[n]$ the *most significant carry* of $\mathbf{x} \boxplus_b^{(n)} \mathbf{y}$, denoted as $\hat{c}_b(\mathbf{x}, \mathbf{y})$. Under these notations, $\mathbf{x} \boxplus_b^{(n)} \mathbf{y} = \mathbf{x} \oplus \mathbf{y} \oplus \lfloor c_b(\mathbf{x}, \mathbf{y}) \rfloor^{(n-1)}$. Moreover,

$$c_b(\lfloor \mathbf{x} \rfloor^{(k)}, \lfloor \mathbf{y} \rfloor^{(k)}) = \lfloor c_b(\mathbf{x}, \mathbf{y}) \rfloor^{(k+1)}$$

is a $(k+1)$-bit vector, and $\hat{c}_b(\lfloor \mathbf{x} \rfloor^{(k)}, \lfloor \mathbf{y} \rfloor^{(k)}) = c_b(\mathbf{x}, \mathbf{y})[k]$.

Example 2. Let $\mathbf{x} = \text{0xE9} = (11101001)_2$ and $\mathbf{y} = \text{0xA3} = (10100011)_2$ be 8-bit strings. Then, $c_0(\mathbf{x}, \mathbf{y}) = (111000110)_2 \in \mathbb{F}_2^9$, $c_1(\mathbf{x}, \mathbf{y}) = (111000111)_2 \in \mathbb{F}_2^9$, $\hat{c}_0(\mathbf{x}, \mathbf{y}) = \hat{c}_1(\mathbf{x}, \mathbf{y}) = 1$, $c_0(\lceil \mathbf{x} \rceil^{(4)}, \lceil \mathbf{y} \rceil^{(4)}) = c_0((1110)_2, (1010)_2) = (11100)_2 \in \mathbb{F}_2^5$, and $c_1(\lfloor \mathbf{x} \rfloor^{(4)}, \lfloor \mathbf{y} \rfloor^{(4)}) = c_1((1001)_2, (0011)_2) = (00111)_2 \in \mathbb{F}_2^5$. Moreover, $\hat{c}_1(\lfloor \mathbf{x} \rfloor^{(4)}, \lfloor \mathbf{y} \rfloor^{(4)}) = 0$, and $\hat{c}_0(\lceil \mathbf{x} \rceil^{(4)}, \lceil \mathbf{y} \rceil^{(4)}) = 1$

Finally, the following lemma is frequently used in the subsequent sections.

Lemma 1. *For* $(a, b) \in \mathbb{F}_2 \times \mathbb{F}_2$, $(-1)^{a \oplus b} = (-1)^a (-1)^b$.

2.2   Useful Partitions of $\mathbb{F}_2^k \times \mathbb{F}_2^k$

We now present some partition schemes of the sets $\mathbb{F}_2^k \times \mathbb{F}_2^k$ for $k \leq n$. Note that *being familiar with these partition schemes is essential for understanding the methodology of this paper.*

Definition 1. *Given* $(a, b) \in \mathbb{F}_2^2$, $(u, v) \in \mathbb{F}_2^2$, *and* $(\boldsymbol{\alpha}, \boldsymbol{\beta}) \in \mathbb{F}_2^n \times \mathbb{F}_2^n$, *for* $1 \leq k \leq n$, *we use* $\mathbb{D}_{\substack{u \blacktriangleleft a \\ v \blacktriangleleft b}}^{(k)}(\boldsymbol{\alpha}, \boldsymbol{\beta}) \subseteq \mathbb{F}_2^k \times \mathbb{F}_2^k$ *to denote the set*

$$\{(\boldsymbol{x}, \boldsymbol{y}) \in \mathbb{F}_2^k \times \mathbb{F}_2^k : (\hat{c}_a(\boldsymbol{x}, \boldsymbol{y}), \hat{c}_b(\boldsymbol{x} \oplus \lfloor \boldsymbol{\alpha} \rfloor^{(k)}, \boldsymbol{y} \oplus \lfloor \boldsymbol{\beta} \rfloor^{(k)}) = (u, v)\}.$$

Under this notation, we have

$$\mathbb{D}_{\substack{u \blacktriangleleft a \\ v \blacktriangleleft b}}^{(n)}(\boldsymbol{\alpha}, \boldsymbol{\beta}) = \{(\mathbf{x}, \mathbf{y}) \in \mathbb{F}_2^n \times \mathbb{F}_2^n : (\hat{c}_a(\mathbf{x}, \mathbf{y}), \hat{c}_b(\mathbf{x} \oplus \boldsymbol{\alpha}, \mathbf{y} \oplus \boldsymbol{\beta})) = (u, v)\}.$$

and $\mathbb{D}_{\substack{u \blacktriangleleft a \\ v \blacktriangleleft b}}^{(1)}(\alpha_i, \beta_i) = \{(x, y) \in \mathbb{F}_2^2 : (\hat{c}_a(x, y), \hat{c}_b(x \oplus \alpha_i, y \oplus \beta_i)) = (u, v)\} \subseteq \mathbb{F}_2^2$, which is the solution set of the following system of equations

$$\begin{cases} xy \oplus xa \oplus ya = u \\ (x \oplus \alpha_i)(y \oplus \beta_i) \oplus (x \oplus \alpha_i)b \oplus (y \oplus \beta_i)b = v \end{cases}.$$

In our notation, $\mathbb{D}_{\substack{u \blacktriangleleft a \\ v \blacktriangleleft b}}^{(k)}(\boldsymbol{\alpha}, \boldsymbol{\beta})$ only depends on the least significant k bits of $\boldsymbol{\alpha}$ and $\boldsymbol{\beta}$, and thus some readers may think it is more natural to always write $\mathbb{D}_{\substack{u \blacktriangleleft a \\ v \blacktriangleleft b}}^{(k)}(\lfloor \boldsymbol{\alpha} \rfloor^{(k)}, \lfloor \boldsymbol{\beta} \rfloor^{(k)})$. However, to make the notations shorter, we prefer the former one.

Example 3. $\mathbb{D}_{\substack{0 \blacktriangleleft 0 \\ 1 \blacktriangleleft 1}}^{(1)}(0, 1) = \{00, 10\}$, $\mathbb{D}_{\substack{1 \blacktriangleleft 1 \\ 1 \blacktriangleleft 1}}^{(1)}(0, 0) = \{01, 10, 11\}$, and $\mathbb{D}_{\substack{0 \blacktriangleleft 0 \\ 0 \blacktriangleleft 1}}^{(1)}(1, 1) = \emptyset$. We refer the reader to Supplementary Material A in the extended version of this paper [39] for $\mathbb{D}_{\substack{u \blacktriangleleft a \\ v \blacktriangleleft b}}^{(1)}(\alpha, \beta)$ with all combinations of $(\alpha, \beta, a, b, u, v) \in \mathbb{F}_2^6$.

Example 4. Let $\boldsymbol{\alpha} = 011$ and $\boldsymbol{\beta} = 100 \in \mathbb{F}_2^3$. Then, $\mathbb{D}_{0\blacktriangleleft0}^{(3)}(\boldsymbol{\alpha}, \boldsymbol{\beta}) \subseteq \mathbb{F}_2^6$ contains
the following twenty elements written as binary vectors:
000000, 000001, 000010, 000011, 001001, 001010, 001011, 010010, 010011, 011011,
100000, 100001, 100010, 100011, 101000, 110001, 101010, 110000, 101001, 111000,

$\mathbb{D}_{1\blacktriangleleft1}^{(2)}(\boldsymbol{\alpha}, \boldsymbol{\beta}) = \{0011, 0110, 0111, 1010, 1011, 1111\}$, and $\mathbb{D}_{0\blacktriangleleft0}^{(2)}(\lceil\boldsymbol{\alpha}\rceil^{(2)}, \lceil\boldsymbol{\beta}\rceil^{(2)}) = \{0010, 0011, 0100, 0110\}$.

Lemma 2. *For any fixed* $(a, b) \in \mathbb{F}_2^2$ *and* $(\boldsymbol{\alpha}, \boldsymbol{\beta}) \in \mathbb{F}_2^n \times \mathbb{F}_2^n$,

$$\mathbb{F}_2^n \times \mathbb{F}_2^n = \bigcup_{(u,v)\in\mathbb{F}_2^2} \mathbb{D}_{v\blacktriangleleft b}^{(n)}{}_{u\blacktriangleleft a}(\boldsymbol{\alpha}, \boldsymbol{\beta}), \tag{2}$$

and the necessary and sufficient condition for

$$\mathbb{D}_{v\blacktriangleleft b}^{(n)}{}_{u\blacktriangleleft a}(\boldsymbol{\alpha}, \boldsymbol{\beta}) \bigcap \mathbb{D}_{v'\blacktriangleleft b}^{(n)}{}_{u'\blacktriangleleft a}(\boldsymbol{\alpha}, \boldsymbol{\beta}) \neq \emptyset$$

is $(u, v) = (u', v')$.

Proof. According to Definition 1, Eq. (2) is obvious. The second part holds
because the solution sets of

$$\begin{cases} \hat{c}_a(\mathbf{x}, \mathbf{y}) = u \\ \hat{c}_b(\mathbf{x} \oplus \boldsymbol{\alpha}, \mathbf{y} \oplus \boldsymbol{\beta}) = v \end{cases} \quad \text{and} \quad \begin{cases} \hat{c}_a(\mathbf{x}, \mathbf{y}) = u' \\ \hat{c}_b(\mathbf{x} \oplus \boldsymbol{\alpha}, \mathbf{y} \oplus \boldsymbol{\beta}) = v' \end{cases}$$

have a common solution if and only if $(u, v) = (u', v')$. □

Lemma 3. *Let* $\mathbb{D}_{v\blacktriangleleft0}^{(t)}{}_{b\blacktriangleleft u} \parallel \mathbb{D}_{a\blacktriangleleft v}^{(n-t)}{}_{u\blacktriangleleft0}(\boldsymbol{\alpha}, \boldsymbol{\beta})$ *be the set of all* $(\mathbf{x}, \mathbf{y}) \in \mathbb{F}_2^n \times \mathbb{F}_2^n$ *such that*

$$\begin{cases} (\lceil\mathbf{x}\rceil^{(t)}, \lceil\mathbf{y}\rceil^{(t)}) \in \mathbb{D}_{v\blacktriangleleft0}^{(t)}{}_{b\blacktriangleleft u}(\lfloor\boldsymbol{\alpha}\rfloor^{(t)}, \lfloor\boldsymbol{\beta}\rfloor^{(t)}) \\ (\lfloor\mathbf{x}\rfloor^{(n-t)}, \lfloor\mathbf{y}\rfloor^{(n-t)}) \in \mathbb{D}_{a\blacktriangleleft v}^{(n-t)}{}_{u\blacktriangleleft0}(\lceil\boldsymbol{\alpha}\rceil^{(n-t)}, \lceil\boldsymbol{\beta}\rceil^{(n-t)}) \end{cases} . \tag{3}$$

Then, the necessary and sufficient condition for

$$\left(\mathbb{D}_{v\blacktriangleleft0}^{(t)}{}_{b\blacktriangleleft u} \parallel \mathbb{D}_{a\blacktriangleleft v}^{(n-t)}{}_{u\blacktriangleleft0}(\boldsymbol{\alpha}, \boldsymbol{\beta})\right) \bigcap \left(\mathbb{D}_{v'\blacktriangleleft0}^{(t)}{}_{b'\blacktriangleleft u'} \parallel \mathbb{D}_{a'\blacktriangleleft v'}^{(n-t)}{}_{u'\blacktriangleleft0}(\boldsymbol{\alpha}, \boldsymbol{\beta})\right) \neq \emptyset \tag{4}$$

is $(a, b, u, v) = (a', b', u', v')$. *Moreover, we have*

$$\bigcup_{(a,b)\in\mathbb{F}_2^2} \bigcup_{(u,v)\in\mathbb{F}_2^2} \left(\mathbb{D}_{v\blacktriangleleft0}^{(t)}{}_{b\blacktriangleleft u} \parallel \mathbb{D}_{a\blacktriangleleft v}^{(n-t)}{}_{u\blacktriangleleft0}(\boldsymbol{\alpha}, \boldsymbol{\beta})\right) = \mathbb{F}_2^n \times \mathbb{F}_2^n.$$

Proof. Equation (4) implies that

$$\begin{cases} \mathbb{D}_{v\blacktriangleleft0}^{(t)}{}_{b\blacktriangleleft u}(\lfloor\boldsymbol{\alpha}\rfloor^{(t)}, \lfloor\boldsymbol{\beta}\rfloor^{(t)}) \bigcap \mathbb{D}_{v'\blacktriangleleft0}^{(t)}{}_{b'\blacktriangleleft u'}(\lfloor\boldsymbol{\alpha}\rfloor^{(t)}, \lfloor\boldsymbol{\beta}\rfloor^{(t)}) \neq \emptyset \\ \mathbb{D}_{a\blacktriangleleft v}^{(n-t)}{}_{u\blacktriangleleft0}(\lceil\boldsymbol{\alpha}\rceil^{(n-t)}, \lceil\boldsymbol{\beta}\rceil^{(n-t)}) \bigcap \mathbb{D}_{a'\blacktriangleleft v'}^{(n-t)}{}_{u'\blacktriangleleft0}(\lceil\boldsymbol{\alpha}\rceil^{(n-t)}, \lceil\boldsymbol{\beta}\rceil^{(n-t)}) \neq \emptyset \end{cases},$$

which in turn implies $v = v'$, $u = u'$, $a = a'$, and $b = b'$ according to Definition 1.
The second part of the lemma comes from the fact that any element in $\mathbb{F}_2^{2n}$ must
satisfy Eq. (3) for some (a, b, u, v). □

Remark 1. To make the description of our methods compact and expressive, the symbols employed in this work are complex. Therefore, we accompany the paper with a `SageMath Notebook` file at https://github.com/ZhongfengNiu/rot-differential-linear to help the readers to familiarize with the notations.

3   Ordinary Differential-Linear Correlation of ⊞

Before diving into the details, we emphasize that this section is the key part of the paper, and there is no essential difference between the methods for computing the ordinary differential-linear correlation and the *rotational* differential-linear correlation. For the ease of the reader, we single out this section to avoid the technical complexities introduced by the rotational differentials. We strongly encourage the reader to go through the details of the proofs in this section. Moreover, we provide a `SageMath Notebook` file at https://github.com/ZhongfengNiu/rot-differential-linear for computing the correlations of ordinary and rotational differential-linear approximations of modulo additions with arbitrary output linear masks.

Definition 2. *The differential-linear correlation of* $S(\mathbf{x}, \mathbf{y}) = \mathbf{x} \boxplus \mathbf{y}$ *with input difference* $(\boldsymbol{\alpha}, \boldsymbol{\beta}) \in \mathbb{F}_2^n \times \mathbb{F}_2^n$, *and output linear mask* $\boldsymbol{\lambda} \in \mathbb{F}_2^n$ *is defined as*

$$\mathcal{C}^{\mathrm{DL}}_{(\boldsymbol{\alpha}, \boldsymbol{\beta}), \boldsymbol{\lambda}}(S) = \frac{1}{2^{2n}} \sum_{(\mathbf{x}, \mathbf{y}) \in \mathbb{F}_2^{2n}} (-1)^{\boldsymbol{\lambda} \cdot (S(\mathbf{x} \oplus \boldsymbol{\alpha}, \mathbf{y} \oplus \boldsymbol{\beta}) \oplus S(\mathbf{x}, \mathbf{y}))}.$$

Let $F^{(k)}_{\boldsymbol{\alpha}, \boldsymbol{\beta}, \boldsymbol{\lambda}}(\mathbf{x}, \mathbf{y}) = (-1)^{\lfloor \boldsymbol{\lambda} \rfloor^{(k)} \cdot (\lfloor S(\mathbf{x} \oplus \boldsymbol{\alpha}, \mathbf{y} \oplus \boldsymbol{\beta}) \rfloor^{(k)} \oplus \lfloor S(\mathbf{x}, \mathbf{y}) \rfloor^{(k)})}$ for $1 \leq k \leq n$. Thus, $F^{(k)}_{\boldsymbol{\alpha}, \boldsymbol{\beta}, \boldsymbol{\lambda}}(\mathbf{x}, \mathbf{y})$ can be fully determined by the least significant k-bits of $\boldsymbol{\alpha}$, $\boldsymbol{\beta}$, $\boldsymbol{\lambda}$, $\mathbf{x}$, and $\mathbf{y}$. Under this notation, we have

$$2^{2n} \mathcal{C}^{\mathrm{DL}}_{(\boldsymbol{\alpha}, \boldsymbol{\beta}), \boldsymbol{\lambda}}(S) = \sum_{(\mathbf{x}, \mathbf{y}) \in \mathbb{F}_2^{2n}} F^{(n)}_{\boldsymbol{\alpha}, \boldsymbol{\beta}, \boldsymbol{\lambda}}(\mathbf{x}, \mathbf{y}), \tag{5}$$

In addition, according to the partition given by Eq. (2),

$$\sum_{(\mathbf{x}, \mathbf{y}) \in \mathbb{F}_2^{2n}} F^{(n)}_{\boldsymbol{\alpha}, \boldsymbol{\beta}, \boldsymbol{\lambda}}(\mathbf{x}, \mathbf{y}) = \sum_{\substack{(u, v) \in \mathbb{F}_2^2}} \sum_{\substack{(\mathbf{x}, \mathbf{y}) \in \mathbb{D}^{(n)}_{u \blacktriangleleft 0}(\boldsymbol{\alpha}, \boldsymbol{\beta}) \\ v \blacktriangleleft 0}} F^{(n)}_{\boldsymbol{\alpha}, \boldsymbol{\beta}, \boldsymbol{\lambda}}(\mathbf{x}, \mathbf{y}),$$

or in the matrix notation, we have

$$\sum_{(\mathbf{x}, \mathbf{y}) \in \mathbb{F}_2^{2n}} F^{(n)}_{\boldsymbol{\alpha}, \boldsymbol{\beta}, \boldsymbol{\lambda}}(\mathbf{x}, \mathbf{y}) = \begin{pmatrix} 1 & 1 & 1 & 1 \end{pmatrix} \begin{pmatrix} \displaystyle\sum_{\substack{(\mathbf{x}, \mathbf{y}) \in \mathbb{D}^{(n)}_{0 \blacktriangleleft 0}(\boldsymbol{\alpha}, \boldsymbol{\beta}) \\ 0 \blacktriangleleft 0}} F^{(n)}_{\boldsymbol{\alpha}, \boldsymbol{\beta}, \boldsymbol{\lambda}}(\mathbf{x}, \mathbf{y}) \\ \displaystyle\sum_{\substack{(\mathbf{x}, \mathbf{y}) \in \mathbb{D}^{(n)}_{0 \blacktriangleleft 0}(\boldsymbol{\alpha}, \boldsymbol{\beta}) \\ 1 \blacktriangleleft 0}} F^{(n)}_{\boldsymbol{\alpha}, \boldsymbol{\beta}, \boldsymbol{\lambda}}(\mathbf{x}, \mathbf{y}) \\ \displaystyle\sum_{\substack{(\mathbf{x}, \mathbf{y}) \in \mathbb{D}^{(n)}_{1 \blacktriangleleft 0}(\boldsymbol{\alpha}, \boldsymbol{\beta}) \\ 0 \blacktriangleleft 0}} F^{(n)}_{\boldsymbol{\alpha}, \boldsymbol{\beta}, \boldsymbol{\lambda}}(\mathbf{x}, \mathbf{y}) \\ \displaystyle\sum_{\substack{(\mathbf{x}, \mathbf{y}) \in \mathbb{D}^{(n)}_{1 \blacktriangleleft 0}(\boldsymbol{\alpha}, \boldsymbol{\beta}) \\ 1 \blacktriangleleft 0}} F^{(n)}_{\boldsymbol{\alpha}, \boldsymbol{\beta}, \boldsymbol{\lambda}}(\mathbf{x}, \mathbf{y}) \end{pmatrix}. \tag{6}$$

For $1 \leq k \leq n$, let $\mathbf{V}^{(k)}$ be the column vector

$$
\begin{pmatrix}
\sum_{\substack{(\lfloor \mathbf{x} \rfloor^{(k)}, \lfloor \mathbf{y} \rfloor^{(k)}) \in \mathbb{D}_{0 \blacktriangleleft 0}^{(k)}(\alpha, \beta) \\ 0 \blacktriangleleft 0}} F_{\alpha, \beta, \lambda}^{(k)}(\mathbf{x}, \mathbf{y}) \\
\sum_{\substack{(\lfloor \mathbf{x} \rfloor^{(k)}, \lfloor \mathbf{y} \rfloor^{(k)}) \in \mathbb{D}_{0 \blacktriangleleft 0}^{(k)}(\alpha, \beta) \\ 1 \blacktriangleleft 0}} F_{\alpha, \beta, \lambda}^{(k)}(\mathbf{x}, \mathbf{y}) \\
\sum_{\substack{(\lfloor \mathbf{x} \rfloor^{(k)}, \lfloor \mathbf{y} \rfloor^{(k)}) \in \mathbb{D}_{1 \blacktriangleleft 0}^{(k)}(\alpha, \beta) \\ 0 \blacktriangleleft 0}} F_{\alpha, \beta, \lambda}^{(k)}(\mathbf{x}, \mathbf{y}) \\
\sum_{\substack{(\lfloor \mathbf{x} \rfloor^{(k)}, \lfloor \mathbf{y} \rfloor^{(k)}) \in \mathbb{D}_{1 \blacktriangleleft 0}^{(k)}(\alpha, \beta) \\ 1 \blacktriangleleft 0}} F_{\alpha, \beta, \lambda}^{(k)}(\mathbf{x}, \mathbf{y})
\end{pmatrix} .
$$

Then, according to Eq. (5) and Eq. (6),

$$
2^{2n} \mathcal{C}_{(\alpha, \beta), \lambda}^{\mathrm{DL}}(S) = (1, 1, 1, 1) \mathbf{V}^{(n)}.
$$

Now, we are going to derive a recursive relationship between $\mathbf{V}^{(k)}$ and $\mathbf{V}^{(k-1)}$.

Lemma 4. *For α, β, λ, $\mathbf{x}$ and $\mathbf{y}$ in $\mathbb{F}_2^n$, Let $\mathbf{z} = \mathbf{x} \boxplus \mathbf{y}$ and $\mathbf{z}' = \mathbf{x}' \boxplus \mathbf{y}'$, where $\mathbf{x}' = \mathbf{x} \oplus \alpha$ and $\mathbf{y}' = \mathbf{y} \oplus \beta$. Then we have*

$$
F_{\alpha, \beta, \lambda}^{(k)}(\mathbf{x}, \mathbf{y}) = (-1)^{\lambda_{k-1} \cdot (\alpha_{k-1} \oplus \beta_{k-1} \oplus u \oplus v)} F_{\alpha, \beta, \lambda}^{(k-1)}(\mathbf{x}, \mathbf{y}),
$$

where $u = \hat{c}_0(\lfloor \mathbf{x} \rfloor^{(k-1)}, \lfloor \mathbf{y} \rfloor^{(k-1)})$ and $v = \hat{c}_0(\lfloor \mathbf{x}' \rfloor^{(k-1)}, \lfloor \mathbf{y}' \rfloor^{(k-1)})$.

Proof. It comes from the fact that

$$
\begin{aligned}
F_{\alpha, \beta, \lambda}^{(k)}(\mathbf{x}, \mathbf{y}) &= (-1)^{\lfloor \lambda \rfloor^{(k)} \cdot (\lfloor \mathbf{z} \rfloor^{(k)} \oplus \lfloor \mathbf{z}' \rfloor^{(k)})} \\
&= (-1)^{\lambda_{k-1} \cdot (z_{k-1} \oplus z'_{k-1})} (-1)^{\lfloor \lambda \rfloor^{(k-1)} \cdot (\lfloor \mathbf{z} \rfloor^{(k-1)} \oplus \lfloor \mathbf{z}' \rfloor^{(k-1)})} \\
&= (-1)^{\lambda_{k-1} \cdot (z_{k-1} \oplus z'_{k-1})} F_{\alpha, \beta, \lambda}^{(k-1)}(\mathbf{x}, \mathbf{y}),
\end{aligned}
$$

and $z_{k-1} \oplus z'_{k-1} = \alpha_{k-1} \oplus \beta_{k-1} \oplus \hat{c}_0(\lfloor \mathbf{x} \rfloor^{(k-1)}, \lfloor \mathbf{y} \rfloor^{(k-1)}) \oplus \hat{c}_0(\lfloor \mathbf{x}' \rfloor^{(k-1)}, \lfloor \mathbf{y}' \rfloor^{(k-1)})$. $\square$

For $(a, b, u, v) \in \mathbb{F}_2^4$, let

$$
\pi_{2a+b, 2u+v}(\alpha_t, \beta_t, \lambda_t) = (-1)^{\lambda_t (\alpha_t \oplus \beta_t \oplus u \oplus v)} \# \mathbb{D}_{\substack{a \blacktriangleleft u \\ b \blacktriangleleft v}}^{(1)}(\alpha_t, \beta_t).
$$

and

$$
\mathbf{M}_{\alpha_t, \beta_t, \lambda_t} = \begin{pmatrix}
\pi_{0,0}(\alpha_t, \beta_t, \lambda_t), & \pi_{0,1}(\alpha_t, \beta_t, \lambda_t), & \pi_{0,2}(\alpha_t, \beta_t, \lambda_t), & \pi_{0,3}(\alpha_t, \beta_t, \lambda_t) \\
\pi_{1,0}(\alpha_t, \beta_t, \lambda_t), & \pi_{1,1}(\alpha_t, \beta_t, \lambda_t), & \pi_{1,2}(\alpha_t, \beta_t, \lambda_t), & \pi_{1,3}(\alpha_t, \beta_t, \lambda_t) \\
\pi_{2,0}(\alpha_t, \beta_t, \lambda_t), & \pi_{2,1}(\alpha_t, \beta_t, \lambda_t), & \pi_{2,2}(\alpha_t, \beta_t, \lambda_t), & \pi_{2,3}(\alpha_t, \beta_t, \lambda_t) \\
\pi_{3,0}(\alpha_t, \beta_t, \lambda_t), & \pi_{3,1}(\alpha_t, \beta_t, \lambda_t), & \pi_{3,2}(\alpha_t, \beta_t, \lambda_t), & \pi_{3,3}(\alpha_t, \beta_t, \lambda_t)
\end{pmatrix} .
$$

Note that $\# \mathbb{D}_{\substack{a \blacktriangleleft u \\ b \blacktriangleleft v}}^{(1)}(\alpha_t, \beta_t)$ can be derived from Table 8 in Supplementary Material A in the extended version [39], and the concrete values for $\mathbf{M}_{\alpha_t, \beta_t, \lambda_t}$ for all possible $(\alpha_t, \beta_t, \lambda_t) \in \mathbb{F}_2 \times \mathbb{F}_2 \times \mathbb{F}_2$ are listed in Supplementary Material C in the extended version [39]. Then, we have the following two lemmas.

Lemma 5. $\mathbf{V}^{(1)} = \mathbf{M}_{\alpha_0,\beta_0,\lambda_0}(1,0,0,0)^T.$

Proof. Since $F_{\alpha,\beta,\lambda}^{(1)}(\mathbf{x},\mathbf{y}) = (-1)^{\lambda_0 \cdot ((x_0 \oplus \alpha_0) \oplus (y_0 \oplus \beta_0) \oplus (x_0 \oplus y_0))} = (-1)^{\lambda_0 \cdot (\alpha_0 \oplus \beta_0)}$, $\mathbf{V}^{(1)}$ is equal to

$$
\begin{pmatrix}
\sum\limits_{\substack{(x_0,y_0)\in\mathbb{D}_{0\blacktriangleleft 0}^{(1)}(\alpha_0,\beta_0)\\ 0\blacktriangleleft 0}} F_{\alpha,\beta,\lambda}^{(1)}(\mathbf{x},\mathbf{y}) \\
\sum\limits_{\substack{(x_0,y_0)\in\mathbb{D}_{0\blacktriangleleft 0}^{(1)}(\alpha_0,\beta_0)\\ 1\blacktriangleleft 0}} F_{\alpha,\beta,\lambda}^{(1)}(\mathbf{x},\mathbf{y}) \\
\sum\limits_{\substack{(x_0,y_0)\in\mathbb{D}_{1\blacktriangleleft 0}^{(1)}(\alpha_0,\beta_0)\\ 0\blacktriangleleft 0}} F_{\alpha,\beta,\lambda}^{(1)}(\mathbf{x},\mathbf{y}) \\
\sum\limits_{\substack{(x_0,y_0)\in\mathbb{D}_{1\blacktriangleleft 0}^{(1)}(\alpha_0,\beta_0)\\ 1\blacktriangleleft 0}} F_{\alpha,\beta,\lambda}^{(1)}(\mathbf{x},\mathbf{y})
\end{pmatrix}
=
\begin{pmatrix}
(-1)^{\lambda_0\cdot(\alpha_0\oplus\beta_0)}\#\mathbb{D}_{\substack{0\blacktriangleleft 0\\0\blacktriangleleft 0}}^{(1)}(\alpha_0,\beta_0) \\
(-1)^{\lambda_0\cdot(\alpha_0\oplus\beta_0)}\#\mathbb{D}_{\substack{0\blacktriangleleft 0\\1\blacktriangleleft 0}}^{(1)}(\alpha_0,\beta_0) \\
(-1)^{\lambda_0\cdot(\alpha_0\oplus\beta_0)}\#\mathbb{D}_{\substack{1\blacktriangleleft 0\\0\blacktriangleleft 0}}^{(1)}(\alpha_0,\beta_0) \\
(-1)^{\lambda_0\cdot(\alpha_0\oplus\beta_0)}\#\mathbb{D}_{\substack{1\blacktriangleleft 0\\1\blacktriangleleft 0}}^{(1)}(\alpha_0,\beta_0)
\end{pmatrix}
= \mathbf{M}_{\alpha_0,\beta_0,\lambda_0}
\begin{pmatrix}1\\0\\0\\0\end{pmatrix}.
$$

□

Lemma 6. *For* $1 \le k < n$, $\mathbf{V}^{(k+1)} = \mathbf{M}_{\alpha_k,\beta_k,\lambda_k}\mathbf{V}^{(k)}.$

Proof. We only need to prove

$$
\mathbf{V}^{(k+1)}[i] = \sum_{j=0}^{3} \mathbf{M}_{\alpha_k,\beta_k,\lambda_k}[i][j]\mathbf{V}^{(k)}[j] = \sum_{j=0}^{3} \pi_{i,j}(\alpha_k,\beta_k,\lambda_k)\mathbf{V}^{(k)}[j] \qquad (7)
$$

for $0 \le i < 4$. Here, we only show that Eq. (7) holds for $i = 0$. For $1 \le i < 4$, the proof is similar. Let $u = \hat{\mathfrak{c}}_0(\lfloor\mathbf{x}\rfloor^{(k)}, \lfloor\mathbf{y}\rfloor^{(k)})$ and $v = \hat{\mathfrak{c}}_0(\lfloor\mathbf{x}'\rfloor^{(k)}, \lfloor\mathbf{y}'\rfloor^{(k)})$. Then, we have

$$
\mathbf{V}^{(k+1)}[0] = \sum_{\substack{(\mathbf{x},\mathbf{y})\in\mathbb{D}_{0\blacktriangleleft 0}^{(k+1)}(\alpha,\beta)\\ 0\blacktriangleleft 0}} F_{\alpha,\beta,\lambda}^{(k+1)}(\mathbf{x},\mathbf{y})
$$

$$
= \sum_{\substack{(\mathbf{x},\mathbf{y})\in\mathbb{D}_{0\blacktriangleleft 0}^{(k+1)}(\alpha,\beta)\\ 0\blacktriangleleft 0}} (-1)^{\lambda_k\cdot(\alpha_k\oplus\beta_k\oplus u\oplus v)} F_{\alpha,\beta,\lambda}^{(k)}(\mathbf{x},\mathbf{y})
$$

$$
= \sum_{(u,v)\in\mathbb{F}_2^2} \sum_{\substack{(x_k,y_k)\in\mathbb{D}_{0\blacktriangleleft u}^{(1)}(\alpha_k,\beta_k)\\ 0\blacktriangleleft v}} \sum_{\substack{(\lfloor x\rfloor^{(k)},\lfloor y\rfloor^{(k)})\in\mathbb{D}_{u\blacktriangleleft 0}^{(k)}(\alpha,\beta)\\ v\blacktriangleleft 0}} (-1)^{\lambda_k\cdot(\alpha_k\oplus\beta_k\oplus u\oplus v)} F_{\alpha,\beta,\lambda}^{(k)}(\mathbf{x},\mathbf{y})
$$

$$
= \sum_{(u,v)\in\mathbb{F}_2^2} (-1)^{\lambda_k\cdot(\alpha_k\oplus\beta_k\oplus u\oplus v)} \left(\sum_{\substack{(x_k,y_k)\in\mathbb{D}_{0\blacktriangleleft u}^{(1)}(\alpha_k,\beta_k)\\ 0\blacktriangleleft v}} 1 \right) \sum_{\substack{(\lfloor x\rfloor^{(k)},\lfloor y\rfloor^{(k)})\in\mathbb{D}_{u\blacktriangleleft 0}^{(k)}(\alpha,\beta)\\ v\blacktriangleleft 0}} F_{\alpha,\beta,\lambda}^{(k)}(\mathbf{x},\mathbf{y})
$$

$$
= \sum_{(u,v)\in\mathbb{F}_2^2} (-1)^{\lambda_k\cdot(\alpha_k\oplus\beta_k\oplus u\oplus v)} \#\mathbb{D}_{\substack{0\blacktriangleleft u\\0\blacktriangleleft v}}^{(1)}(\alpha_k,\beta_k) \sum_{\substack{(\lfloor x\rfloor^{(k)},\lfloor y\rfloor^{(k)})\in\mathbb{D}_{u\blacktriangleleft 0}^{(k)}(\alpha,\beta)\\ v\blacktriangleleft 0}} F_{\alpha,\beta,\lambda}^{(k)}(\mathbf{x},\mathbf{y})
$$

$$
= \sum_{j=0}^{3} \pi_{0,j}(\alpha_k,\beta_k,\lambda_k)\mathbf{V}^{(k)}[j].
$$

□

Theorem 1. *The differential-linear correlation of the modulo addition* $\mathcal{C}^{\mathrm{DL}}_{(\alpha,\beta),\lambda} = \frac{1}{2^{2n}} \cdot \sum_{(\mathbf{x},\mathbf{y}) \in \mathbb{F}_2^{2n}} F^{(n)}_{\alpha,\beta,\lambda}(\mathbf{x},\mathbf{y})$, *can be computed as*

$$\frac{1}{2^{2n}} \left(1, 1, 1, 1\right) \mathbf{V}^{(n)} = \frac{1}{2^{2n}} \left(1, 1, 1, 1\right) \mathbf{M}^{(n-1)}_{\alpha_{n-1},\beta_{n-1},\lambda_{n-1}} \cdots \mathbf{M}^{(0)}_{\alpha_0,\beta_0,\lambda_0} \begin{pmatrix} 1 \\ 0 \\ 0 \\ 0 \end{pmatrix}.$$

Proof. It comes from Lemma 5 and Lemma 6.   □

Next, we present two simple corollaries to show the applications of Theorem 1. Note that these corollaries can also be proved by Definition 2.

Corollary 1. *For any given* $(\alpha,\beta) \in \mathbb{F}_2^n \times \mathbb{F}_2^n$, *and* $\lambda \in \mathbb{F}_2^n$ *such that* $\lceil \lambda \rceil^{(n-1)} = 0^{n-1}$. *The absolute differential-linear correlation of* $\boxplus^{(n)}$ *is* $|\mathcal{C}^{\mathrm{DL}}_{(\alpha,\beta),\lambda}| = 1$.

Proof. Since $(1,1,1,1)\mathbf{M}_{\alpha_t,\beta_t,0} = 2^2 \cdot (1,1,1,1)$ for arbitrary $(\alpha_t,\beta_t) \in \mathbb{F}_2^2$,

$$\left(1, 1, 1, 1\right) \mathbf{V}^{(n)} = \left(1, 1, 1, 1\right) \mathbf{M}_{\alpha_{n-1},\beta_{n-1},0} \cdots \mathbf{M}_{\alpha_1,\beta_1,0} \mathbf{M}_{\alpha_0,\beta_0,\lambda_0} \begin{pmatrix} 1 \\ 0 \\ 0 \\ 0 \end{pmatrix}$$

$$= 2^{2(n-1)} \left(1, 1, 1, 1\right) \mathbf{M}_{\alpha_0,\beta_0,\lambda_0} \begin{pmatrix} 1 \\ 0 \\ 0 \\ 0 \end{pmatrix} = \pm 2^{2n}.$$

□

Corollary 2. *For any* $\lambda \in \mathbb{F}_2^n$, *and* $(\alpha,\beta) \in \mathbb{F}_2^{2n}$ *such that* $\lfloor \alpha \rfloor^{(n-1)} = \lfloor \beta \rfloor^{(n-1)} = 0^{n-1}$, *The absolute differential-linear correlation of* $\boxplus^{(n)}$ *is* $|\mathcal{C}^{\mathrm{DL}}_{\alpha,\beta,\lambda}| = 1$.

Proof. Let r be a real number. Then,

$$\mathbf{M}_{0,0,\lambda_t}(r, 0, 0, 1 - r)^T = 2^2 \cdot (r', 0, 0, 1 - r')^T,$$

for some real number r'. Therefore,

$$\left(1, 1, 1, 1\right) \mathbf{V}^{(n)} = \left(1, 1, 1, 1\right) \mathbf{M}_{\alpha_{n-1},\beta_{n-1},\lambda_{n-1}} \mathbf{M}_{0,0,\lambda_{n-2}} \cdots \mathbf{M}_{0,0,\lambda_0} \begin{pmatrix} 1 \\ 0 \\ 0 \\ 0 \end{pmatrix}$$

$$= 2^{2(n-1)} \cdot \left(1, 1, 1, 1\right) \mathbf{M}_{\alpha_{n-1},\beta_{n-1},\lambda_{n-1}} \begin{pmatrix} p \\ 0 \\ 0 \\ 1-p \end{pmatrix}$$

$$= \pm 2^{2n} \cdot (1, \pm 1, \pm 1, 1) \begin{pmatrix} p \\ 0 \\ 0 \\ 1-p \end{pmatrix} = \pm 2^{2n}.$$

□

Next, we give some concrete analysis of differential-linear approximations of modulo additions over 32-bit integers with output linear masks being $\mathbf{e}_i \oplus \mathbf{e}_{i+1}$ whose Hamming weights are 2, where $\mathbf{e}_i$ denotes the ith unit vector. Note that in this work the least significant bit is indexed by 0, and thus $\mathbf{e}_0 = 00\cdots001$. The analysis of 64-bit and 128-bit modulo additions can be found in Supplementary Material E in the extended version of this paper [39].

Table 2. The correlations of example differential-linear approximations of $\boxplus_0^{(32)}$.

i	0	1	2	3	4	5	6	7	8	9	10	11
$\mathcal{C}^{DL}_{(\alpha,\beta),\mathbf{e}_i\oplus\mathbf{e}_{i+1}}$	0	$\frac{1}{2}$	$\frac{3}{4}$	$\frac{7}{8}$	$\frac{15}{16}$	$\frac{31}{32}$	$\frac{1}{64}$	$-\frac{65}{128}$	0	$\frac{1}{2}$	$-\frac{3}{4}$	0
i	12	13	14	15	16	17	18	19	20	21	22	23
$\mathcal{C}^{DL}_{(\alpha,\beta),\mathbf{e}_i\oplus\mathbf{e}_{i+1}}$	0	$-\frac{1}{2}$	0	0	0	0	$\frac{1}{2}$	$\frac{1}{4}$	$-\frac{5}{8}$	0	0	0
i	24	25	26	27	28	29	30					
$\mathcal{C}^{DL}_{(\alpha,\beta),\mathbf{e}_i\oplus\mathbf{e}_{i+1}}$	$-\frac{1}{2}$	0	0	0	0	0	$\frac{1}{2}$					

Example 5. Consider the 32-bit modulo addition. Let $(\boldsymbol{\alpha}, \boldsymbol{\beta}) \in \mathbb{F}^{32} \times \mathbb{F}_2^{32}$ be the input difference

$$\begin{cases} \boldsymbol{\alpha} = (10111010110001000011011111000001)_2 \\ \boldsymbol{\beta} = (10000100001001111110111011000000)_2 \end{cases}.$$

Then, the differential-linear correlations $\mathcal{C}^{DL}_{(\alpha,\beta),\mathbf{e}_i\oplus\mathbf{e}_{i+1}}$ can be computed with Theorem 1, and the results are listed in Table 2.

4   Rotational Differential-Linear Correlation of $\boxplus$

Definition 3. *According to Eq. (1), the correlation of the modulo addition* $S(\mathbf{x}, \mathbf{y}) = \mathbf{x} \boxplus \mathbf{y}$ *with input difference* $(\boldsymbol{\alpha}, \boldsymbol{\beta})$ *and output linear mask* $\boldsymbol{\lambda}$ *is*

$$\mathcal{C}^{R\text{-}DL}_{(\alpha,\beta),\lambda}(S) = \frac{1}{2^{2n}} \sum_{(\mathbf{x},\mathbf{y})\in\mathbb{F}_2^{2n}} (-1)^{\lambda\cdot\left[(((\mathbf{x}\lll t)\oplus\alpha)\boxplus((\mathbf{y}\lll t)\oplus\beta))\oplus((\mathbf{x}\boxplus\mathbf{y})\lll t)\right]}.$$

Lemma 7. *The rotational differential-linear correlation of* $\boxplus$ *with rotational offset t, rotational difference $(\boldsymbol{\alpha}, \boldsymbol{\beta})$, and linear mask $\boldsymbol{\lambda}$ can be computed as*

$$\frac{1}{2^{2n}} \sum_{(\mathbf{x},\mathbf{y})\in\mathbb{F}_2^{2n}} (-1)^{\lambda\cdot\Delta} = \frac{1}{2^{2n}} \sum_{(\mathbf{x},\mathbf{y})\in\mathbb{F}_2^{2n}} (-1)^{\lceil\lambda\rceil^{(n-t)}\cdot\lceil\Delta\rceil^{(n-t)}} (-1)^{\lfloor\lambda\rfloor^{(t)}\cdot\lfloor\Delta\rfloor^{(t)}},$$

where

$$\begin{cases} \Delta = (((\mathbf{x}\lll t)\oplus\boldsymbol{\alpha})\boxplus((\mathbf{y}\lll t)\oplus\boldsymbol{\beta}))\oplus((\mathbf{x}\boxplus\mathbf{y})\lll t) \\ \lceil\Delta\rceil^{(n-t)} = ((\lfloor\mathbf{x}\rfloor^{(n-t)}\oplus\lceil\boldsymbol{\alpha}\rceil^{(n-t)})\boxplus_v(\lfloor\mathbf{y}\rfloor^{(n-t)}\oplus\lceil\boldsymbol{\beta}\rceil^{(n-t)}))\oplus\left(\lfloor\mathbf{x}\rfloor^{(n-t)}\boxplus\lfloor\mathbf{y}\rfloor^{(n-t)}\right) \\ \lfloor\Delta\rfloor^{(t)} = ((\lceil\mathbf{x}\rceil^{(t)}\oplus\lfloor\boldsymbol{\alpha}\rfloor^{(t)})\boxplus(\lceil\mathbf{y}\rceil^{(t)}\oplus\lfloor\boldsymbol{\beta}\rfloor^{(t)}))\oplus(\lceil\mathbf{x}\rceil^{(t)}\boxplus_u\lceil\mathbf{y}\rceil^{(t)}) \end{cases},$$

and

$$\begin{cases} u = \mathfrak{c}_0(\lfloor \mathbf{x} \rfloor^{(n-t)}, \lfloor \mathbf{y} \rfloor^{(n-t)}) \\ v = \mathfrak{c}_0(\lceil \mathbf{x} \rceil^{(t)} \oplus \lfloor \boldsymbol{\alpha} \rfloor^{(t)}, \lceil \mathbf{y} \rceil^{(t)} \oplus \lfloor \boldsymbol{\beta} \rfloor^{(t)}) \end{cases}.$$

Proof. Let $\mathbf{z} = (\mathbf{x} \boxplus \mathbf{y}) \lll t$ and $\mathbf{z}' = ((\mathbf{x} \lll t) \oplus \boldsymbol{\alpha}) \boxplus ((\mathbf{y} \lll t) \oplus \boldsymbol{\beta})$. Then,

$$\begin{cases} \lceil \mathbf{z} \rceil^{(n-t)} = \lfloor \mathbf{x} \rfloor^{(n-t)} \boxplus \lfloor \mathbf{y} \rfloor^{(n-t)} \\ \lfloor \mathbf{z} \rfloor^{(t)} = \lceil \mathbf{x} \rceil^{(t)} \boxplus_u \lceil \mathbf{y} \rceil^{(t)} \end{cases},$$

where $u = \mathfrak{c}_0(\lfloor \mathbf{x} \rfloor^{(n-t)}, \lfloor \mathbf{y} \rfloor^{(n-t)})$. Similarly,

$$\begin{cases} \lceil \mathbf{z}' \rceil^{(n-t)} = (\lfloor \mathbf{x} \rfloor^{(n-t)} \oplus \lceil \boldsymbol{\alpha} \rceil^{(n-t)}) \boxplus_v (\lfloor \mathbf{y} \rfloor^{(n-t)} \oplus \lceil \boldsymbol{\beta} \rceil^{(n-t)}) \\ \lfloor \mathbf{z}' \rfloor^{(t)} = (\lceil \mathbf{x} \rceil^{(t)} \oplus \lfloor \boldsymbol{\alpha} \rfloor^{(t)}) \boxplus (\lceil \mathbf{y} \rceil^{(t)} \oplus \lfloor \boldsymbol{\beta} \rfloor^{(t)}) \end{cases},$$

where $v = \mathfrak{c}_0(\lceil \mathbf{x} \rceil^{(t)} \oplus \lfloor \boldsymbol{\alpha} \rfloor^{(t)}, \lceil \mathbf{y} \rceil^{(t)} \oplus \lfloor \boldsymbol{\beta} \rfloor^{(t)})$. Consequently,

$$\boldsymbol{\lambda} \cdot \boldsymbol{\Delta} = (\lceil \boldsymbol{\lambda} \rceil^{(n-t)} \cdot \lceil \boldsymbol{\Delta} \rceil^{(n-t)}) \oplus (\lfloor \boldsymbol{\lambda} \rfloor^{(t)} \cdot \lfloor \boldsymbol{\Delta} \rfloor^{(n-t)}).$$

Applying Lemma 1 to $(-1)^{\boldsymbol{\lambda} \cdot \boldsymbol{\Delta}}$ gives the proof.   □

Lemma 8. *Let* $u = \mathfrak{c}_0(\lfloor \mathbf{x} \rfloor^{(n-t)}, \lfloor \mathbf{y} \rfloor^{(n-t)})$ *and* $v = \mathfrak{c}_0(\lceil \mathbf{x} \rceil^{(t)} \oplus \lfloor \boldsymbol{\alpha} \rfloor^{(t)}, \lceil \mathbf{y} \rceil^{(t)} \oplus \lfloor \boldsymbol{\beta} \rfloor^{(t)})$. *Then,*

$$\sum_{(\mathbf{x},\mathbf{y}) \in \mathbb{F}_2^n} (-1)^{\boldsymbol{\lambda} \cdot \boldsymbol{\Delta}} = \sum_{(u,v) \in \mathbb{F}_2^2} \Psi(u,v) \Phi(u,v),$$

where $\Psi(u,v)$ *equals to*

$$\sum_{b \in \mathbb{F}_2} \sum_{\substack{(\lceil \mathbf{x} \rceil^{(t)}, \lceil \mathbf{y} \rceil^{(t)}) \in \mathbb{D}_{b \blacktriangleleft u}^{(t)}(\lfloor \boldsymbol{\alpha} \rfloor^{(t)}, \lfloor \boldsymbol{\beta} \rfloor^{(t)}) \\ v \blacktriangleleft 0}} (-1)^{\lfloor \boldsymbol{\lambda} \rfloor^{(t)} \cdot \lfloor \boldsymbol{\Delta} \rfloor^{(t)}},$$

and $\Phi(u,v)$ *equals to*

$$\sum_{a \in \mathbb{F}_2} \sum_{\substack{(\lfloor \mathbf{x} \rfloor^{(n-t)}, \lfloor \mathbf{y} \rfloor^{(n-t)}) \in \mathbb{D}_{u \blacktriangleleft 0}^{(n-t)}(\lceil \boldsymbol{\alpha} \rceil^{(n-t)}, \lceil \boldsymbol{\beta} \rceil^{(n-t)}) \\ a \blacktriangleleft v}} (-1)^{\lceil \boldsymbol{\lambda} \rceil^{(n-t)} \cdot \lceil \boldsymbol{\Delta} \rceil^{(n-t)}}.$$

Proof. See Supplementary Material B in the extended version [39].   □

Theorem 2. *The rotational differential-linear correlation of* $\boxplus$ *with rotational offset* t, *rotational difference* $(\boldsymbol{\alpha}, \boldsymbol{\beta})$, *and linear mask* $\boldsymbol{\lambda}$ *can be computed as*

$$\mathcal{C}_{(\boldsymbol{\alpha},\boldsymbol{\beta}),\boldsymbol{\lambda}}^{\text{R-DL}} = \frac{1}{2^{2n}} (1,0,1,0) \, \mathbf{C}_{\boldsymbol{\alpha},\boldsymbol{\beta},\boldsymbol{\lambda}} \begin{pmatrix} 1 \\ 0 \\ 0 \\ 0 \end{pmatrix} + \frac{1}{2^{2n}} (0,1,0,1) \, \mathbf{C}_{\boldsymbol{\alpha},\boldsymbol{\beta},\boldsymbol{\lambda}} \begin{pmatrix} 0 \\ 1 \\ 0 \\ 0 \end{pmatrix}$$

where

$$\mathbf{C}_{\boldsymbol{\alpha},\boldsymbol{\beta},\boldsymbol{\lambda}} = \prod_{i=0}^{t-1} \mathbf{M}_{\alpha_i,\beta_i,\lambda_i} \begin{pmatrix} 1 & 1 & 0 & 0 \\ 0 & 0 & 0 & 0 \\ 0 & 0 & 1 & 1 \\ 0 & 0 & 0 & 0 \end{pmatrix} \prod_{j=t}^{n-1} \mathbf{M}_{\alpha_j,\beta_j,\lambda_j}.$$

Proof. Applying similar techniques used in the proof of Theorem 1, for $(u,v) = (0,0)$, we can derive that

$$\begin{cases} \varPsi(0,0) = (1,0,1,0)\mathbf{M}_{\alpha_{t-1},\beta_{t-1},\lambda_{t-1}} \cdots \mathbf{M}_{\alpha_0,\beta_0,\lambda_0}(1,0,0,0)^T \\ \varPhi(0,0) = (1,1,0,0)\mathbf{M}_{\alpha_{n-1},\beta_{n-1},\lambda_{n-1}} \cdots \mathbf{M}_{\alpha_t,\beta_t,\lambda_t}.(1,0,0,0)^T \end{cases}$$

For $(u,v) = (0,1)$, we have

$$\begin{cases} \varPsi(0,1) = (0,1,0,1)\mathbf{M}_{\alpha_{t-1},\beta_{t-1},\lambda_{t-1}} \cdots \mathbf{M}_{\alpha_0,\beta_0,\lambda_0}(1,0,0,0)^T \\ \varPhi(0,1) = (1,1,0,0)\mathbf{M}_{\alpha_{n-1},\beta_{n-1},\lambda_{n-1}} \cdots \mathbf{M}_{\alpha_t,\beta_t,\lambda_t}.(0,1,0,0)^T \end{cases}$$

For $(u,v) = (1,0)$, we have

$$\begin{cases} \varPsi(1,0) = (1,0,1,0)\mathbf{M}_{\alpha_{t-1},\beta_{t-1},\lambda_{t-1}} \cdots \mathbf{M}_{\alpha_0,\beta_0,\lambda_0}(0,0,1,0)^T \\ \varPhi(1,0) = (0,0,1,1)\mathbf{M}_{\alpha_{n-1},\beta_{n-1},\lambda_{n-1}} \cdots \mathbf{M}_{\alpha_t,\beta_t,\lambda_t}.(1,0,0,0)^T \end{cases}$$

For $(u,v) = (1,1)$, we have

$$\begin{cases} \varPsi(1,1) = (0,1,0,1)\mathbf{M}_{\alpha_{t-1},\beta_{t-1},\lambda_{t-1}} \cdots \mathbf{M}_{\alpha_0,\beta_0,\lambda_0}(0,0,1,0)^T \\ \varPhi(1,1) = (0,0,1,1)\mathbf{M}_{\alpha_{n-1},\beta_{n-1},\lambda_{n-1}} \cdots \mathbf{M}_{\alpha_t,\beta_t,\lambda_t}.(0,1,0,0)^T \end{cases}$$

According to Definition 3 and Lemma 8, $2^{2n}\mathcal{C}^{\text{R-DL}}_{\alpha,\beta,\lambda} = \sum_{(u,v)\in\mathbb{F}_2^2} \varPsi(u,v)$ $\varPhi(u,v)$ can be computed as

$$\big(\varPsi(0,0)\varPhi(0,0) + \varPsi(1,0)\varPhi(1,0)\big) + \big(\varPsi(0,1)\varPhi(0,1) + \varPsi(1,1)\varPhi(1,1)\big),$$

which is equal to

$$(1,0,1,0)\,\mathbf{C}_{\alpha,\beta,\lambda}(1,0,0,0)^T + (0,1,0,1)\,\mathbf{C}_{\alpha,\beta,\lambda}(0,1,0,0)^T.$$

$\square$

Next, we give some concrete rotational differential-linear analysis of modulo additions over 32-bit integers, where $\mathbf{e}_i$ denotes the ith unit vector. The analysis of 64-bit and 128-bit addition can be found in **Supplementary Material F** in the extended version of this paper [39].

Example 6. Consider the 32-bit modulo addition. Let $(\boldsymbol{\alpha},\boldsymbol{\beta}) \in \mathbb{F}_2^{32} \times \mathbb{F}_2^{32}$ be the input difference such that

$$\begin{cases} \alpha = (10110000000100100101100000110010)_2 \\ \beta = (10100001011101110100110001110011)_2 \end{cases}.$$

Then, the rotational differential-linear correlations $\mathcal{C}^{\text{R-DL}}_{(\alpha,\beta),\mathbf{e}_i\oplus\mathbf{e}_{i+1}}$ with rotation offset $t = 30$ can be computed with Theorem 1, and the results are listed in Table 3.

Table 3. The correlations of example rotational differential-linear approximations of $\boxplus_0^{(32)}$ with rotation offset $t = 30$.

i	0	1	2	3	4	5	6	7
$\mathcal{C}^{\text{R-DL}}_{(\alpha,\beta),\mathbf{e}_i \oplus \mathbf{e}_{i+1}}$	0	$\frac{1}{2}$	$\frac{1}{4}$	$\frac{5}{8}$	$\frac{3}{16}$	$-\frac{19}{32}$	0	$\frac{1}{2}$

i	8	9	10	11	12	13	14	15
$\mathcal{C}^{\text{R-DL}}_{(\alpha,\beta),\mathbf{e}_i \oplus \mathbf{e}_{i+1}}$	$\frac{3}{4}$	$-\frac{7}{8}$	0	$-\frac{1}{2}$	0	$\frac{1}{2}$	$\frac{1}{4}$	$-\frac{3}{8}$

i	16	17	18	19	20	21	22	23
$\mathcal{C}^{\text{R-DL}}_{(\alpha,\beta),\mathbf{e}_i \oplus \mathbf{e}_{i+1}}$	0	$-\frac{1}{2}$	0	$\frac{1}{2}$	$-\frac{1}{4}$	0	0	$-\frac{1}{2}$

i	24	25	26	27	28	29	30
$\mathcal{C}^{\text{R-DL}}_{(\alpha,\beta),\mathbf{e}_i \oplus \mathbf{e}_{i+1}}$	0	$\frac{1}{2}$	$\frac{3}{4}$	$-\frac{7}{8}$	0	$\frac{1}{4294967296}$	$\frac{1073741825}{2147483648}$

Remark 2. Theorem 1 and Theorem 2 completely generalize the formulas presented in [32]. More importantly, the formulas presented in Theorem 1 and Theorem 2 efficiently compute the *exact* correlations of arbitrary rotational differential-linear distinguishers of modulo additions, while the formulas in [32] can only compute *approximations* of the correlations of rotational differential-linear distinguishers of modulo additions with output linear masks being unit vectors. The formulas given in [32] are not exact since they rely on certain statistical assumptions that may not hold perfectly in practice. This difference can be observed in Example 7.

Example 7. Consider the 32-bit modulo addition. Let $(\alpha, \beta) \in \mathbb{F}_2^{32} \times \mathbb{F}_2^{32}$ be the input difference

$$\begin{cases} \alpha = (01100011101110001111101101010111)_2 \\ \beta = (01010011001111111101001111100111)_2 \end{cases}.$$

Then, the rotational differential-linear correlations $\mathcal{C}^{\text{R-DL}}_{(\alpha,\beta),\mathbf{e}_i}$ with rotation offset $t = 30$ can be computed with the formula presented in [32] or Theorem 1 in this work, and the results are listed in Table 4.

Table 4. The correlations $\mathcal{C}^{\text{R-DL}}_{(\alpha,\beta),\mathbf{e}_i}$ of example rotational differential-linear approximations of $\boxplus_0^{(32)}$ with rotation offset $t = 30$ and output masks being unit vectors

i	0	1	2	3	4	5	6	7
[32]	0	-0.5	-0.75	-0.875	-0.0625	0	0	0.5
This work	0.25	-0.375	-0.6875	-0.84375	-0.078125	0	0	0.5

5   Computing the (Rotational) Differential-Linear Correlation of Iterative ARX Primitives

Previous sections focus on the analysis of the *local* properties of modulo additions. In this section, we show how to efficiently compute the (rotational) differential-linear correlations of ARX primitives based on the theories developed in previous sections and Morawiecki's technique [34].

To extend Morawiecki's technique to evaluate the correlations of arbitrary rotational differential-linear approximations of a cipher, one must be able to compute the rotational differential-linear correlation (with an arbitrary output linear mask) of each building block $F : \mathbb{F}_2^m \rightarrow \mathbb{F}_2^n$ of the cipher being analyzed with the knowledge of $\Pr[x_{i-t} \oplus x_i']$ for all $0 \leq i < m$ and some integer t. In the following, we provide the formulas for accomplishing this task.

Lemma 9. *Let $F : \mathbb{F}_2^m \rightarrow \mathbb{F}_2^n$ be a vectorial Boolean function. Assume that the input pair $(\mathbf{x}, \mathbf{x}') \in \mathbb{F}_2^m \times \mathbb{F}_2^m$ satisfies $\Pr[x_i \oplus x_i' = 1] = \Pr[x_i \neq x_i'] = p_i$ for $0 \leq i < m$, and the events $x_i \neq x_i'$ and $x_j \neq x_j'$ for different i and j are mutually independent. Then, for $\boldsymbol{\lambda} \in \mathbb{F}_2^n$, the differential-linear correlation of F can be computed as*

$$C_{\boldsymbol{\lambda}}^{\mathrm{DL}} = \Pr[\boldsymbol{\lambda} \cdot (F(\mathbf{x}) \oplus F(\mathbf{x}')) = 0] - \Pr[\boldsymbol{\lambda} \cdot (F(\mathbf{x}) \oplus F(\mathbf{x}')) = 1]$$

$$= \sum_{\mathbf{u} \in \mathbb{F}_2^m} \frac{1}{2^m} \sum_{\mathbf{x} \in \mathbb{F}_2^m} (-1)^{\boldsymbol{\lambda} \cdot (F(\mathbf{x}) \oplus F(\mathbf{x} \oplus \mathbf{u}))} \prod_{i=0}^{m-1} ((1 - u_i) - (-1)^{u_i} p_i).$$

Proof. Let $\mathcal{S}_{\mathbf{u}} = \{(\mathbf{x}, \mathbf{x}') \in \mathbb{F}_2^m \times \mathbb{F}_2^m : x \oplus x' = \mathbf{u}\}$ with $\#\mathcal{S}_{\mathbf{u}} = 2^m$. Then

$$C_{\boldsymbol{\lambda}}^{\mathrm{DL}} = \sum_{\mathbf{v} \in \boldsymbol{\lambda}^{\perp}} \Pr[F(\mathbf{x}) \oplus F(\mathbf{x}') = \mathbf{v}] - \sum_{\mathbf{v} \in \mathbb{F}_2^n \setminus \boldsymbol{\lambda}^{\perp}} \Pr[F(\mathbf{x}) \oplus F(\mathbf{x}') = \mathbf{v}]$$

$$= \sum_{\mathbf{v} \in \mathbb{F}_2^n} (-1)^{\boldsymbol{\lambda} \cdot \mathbf{v}} \Pr[F(\mathbf{x}) \oplus F(\mathbf{x}') = \mathbf{v}]$$

$$= \sum_{\mathbf{v} \in \mathbb{F}_2^n} (-1)^{\boldsymbol{\lambda} \cdot \mathbf{v}} \sum_{\mathbf{u} \in \mathbb{F}_2^m} \Pr[F(\mathbf{x}) \oplus F(\mathbf{x}') = \mathbf{v} | (\mathbf{x}, \mathbf{x}') \in \mathcal{S}_{\mathbf{u}}] \Pr[(\mathbf{x}, \mathbf{x}') \in \mathcal{S}_{\mathbf{u}}]$$

$$= \sum_{\mathbf{u} \in \mathbb{F}_2^m} \sum_{\mathbf{v} \in \mathbb{F}_2^n} (-1)^{\boldsymbol{\lambda} \cdot \mathbf{v}} \Pr[F(\mathbf{x}) \oplus F(\mathbf{x}') = \mathbf{v} | (\mathbf{x}, \mathbf{x}') \in \mathcal{S}_{\mathbf{u}}] \Pr[(\mathbf{x}, \mathbf{x}') \in \mathcal{S}_{\mathbf{u}}]$$

$$= \sum_{\mathbf{u} \in \mathbb{F}_2^m} \frac{1}{2^m} \sum_{\mathbf{x} \in \mathbb{F}_2^m} (-1)^{\boldsymbol{\lambda} \cdot (F(\mathbf{x}) \oplus F(\mathbf{x} \oplus \mathbf{u}))} \prod_{i=0}^{m-1} ((1 - u_i) - (-1)^{u_i} p_i).$$

$\square$

Theorem 3. *Let $\mathbf{x}$, $\mathbf{x}'$, $\mathbf{y}$, and $\mathbf{y}'$ be random n-bit strings such that $\Pr[x_i \oplus x_i' = 1] = p_i$ and $\Pr[y_i \oplus y_i' = 1] = q_i$ for $0 \leq i < n$. In addition, the events $x_i \oplus x_i' = 1$ and $y_j \oplus y_j' = 1$ for $0 \leq i, j < n$ are mutually independent. For $\boldsymbol{\lambda} \in \mathbb{F}_2^n$, the differential-linear correlation of $F(\mathbf{x}, \mathbf{y}) = \mathbf{x} \boxplus \mathbf{y}$ can be computed as*

$$C_{\boldsymbol{\lambda}}^{\mathrm{DL}} = \frac{1}{2^{2n}} (1, 1, 1, 1) \prod_{i=0}^{n-1} \mathbf{H}_{\lambda_i}^{p_i, q_i} (1, 0, 0, 0)^T,$$

where $\mathbf{H}_{\lambda_i}^{p_i,q_i}$ *is a* 4×4 *matrix and is defined as*

$$\mathbf{H}_{\lambda_i}^{p_i,q_i} = \sum_{a,b \in \mathbb{F}_2} ((1-a) - (-1)^a p_i)((1-b) - (-1)^b q_i)\mathbf{M}_{a,b,\lambda_i}.$$

Proof. Let $\hat{p}_i(\alpha_i) = ((1-\alpha_i) - (-1)^{\alpha_i} p_i)$ and $\hat{q}_i(\beta_i) = ((1-\beta_i) - (-1)^{\beta_i} q_i)$. According to Lemma 9 and Theorem 1, $2^{2n} \mathcal{C}_\lambda^{\mathrm{DL}}$ can be computed as

$$\sum_{(\alpha,\beta)\in\mathbb{F}_2^{2n}} \sum_{(\mathbf{x},\mathbf{y})\in\mathbb{F}_2^{2n}} (-1)^{\lambda \cdot (S(\mathbf{x}\oplus\alpha,\mathbf{y}\oplus\beta)\oplus S(\mathbf{x},\mathbf{y}))} \prod_{i=0}^{n-1} \hat{p}_i(\alpha_i)\hat{q}_i(\beta_i)$$

$$= \sum_{(\alpha,\beta)\in\mathbb{F}_2^{2n}} (1,1,1,1) \prod_{i=0}^{n-1} \mathbf{M}_{\alpha_i,\beta_i,\lambda_i}(1,0,0,0)^T \prod_{i=0}^{n-1} \hat{p}_i(\alpha_i)\hat{q}_i(\beta_i)$$

$$= (1,1,1,1) \sum_{(\alpha,\beta)\in\mathbb{F}_2^{2n}} \prod_{i=0}^{n-1} \hat{p}_i(\alpha_i)\hat{q}_i(\beta_i)\mathbf{M}_{\alpha_i,\beta_i,\lambda_i}(1,0,0,0)^T$$

$$= (1,1,1,1) \prod_{i=0}^{n-1} \sum_{(a,b)\in\mathbb{F}_2^2} \hat{p}_i(a)\hat{q}_i(b)\mathbf{M}_{a,b,\lambda_i}(1,0,0,0)^T$$

$$= (1,1,1,1) \prod_{i=0}^{n-1} \mathbf{H}_{\lambda_i}^{p_i,q_i}(1,0,0,0)^T.$$

$\square$

Lemma 10. *Let* $F : \mathbb{F}_2^m \to \mathbb{F}_2^n$ *be a vectorial Boolean function and* $0 \le t \le m-1$ *be an integer. Assume that the input pair* $(\mathbf{x},\mathbf{x}') \in \mathbb{F}_2^m \times \mathbb{F}_2^m$ *satisfies* $\Pr[x_{i-t} \oplus x_i' = 1] = p_i$ *for* $0 \le i < m$, *and the events* $x_{i-t} \ne x_i'$ *and* $x_{j-t} \ne x_j'$ *for different* i *and* j *are mutually independent. Then, for* $\boldsymbol{\lambda} \in \mathbb{F}_2^n$ *and rotation offset* t, *the rotational differential-linear correlation of* F *can be computed as*

$$\mathcal{C}_\lambda^{\mathrm{R\text{-}DL}} = \Pr[\boldsymbol{\lambda} \cdot (\overleftarrow{F}(\mathbf{x}) \oplus F(\mathbf{x}')) = 0] - \Pr[\boldsymbol{\lambda} \cdot (\overleftarrow{F}(\mathbf{x}) \oplus F(\mathbf{x}')) = 1]$$

$$= \sum_{\mathbf{u}\in\mathbb{F}_2^m} \frac{1}{2^m} \sum_{\mathbf{x}\in\mathbb{F}_2^m} (-1)^{\boldsymbol{\lambda}\cdot(\overleftarrow{F}(\mathbf{x})\oplus F(\overleftarrow{\mathbf{x}}\oplus\mathbf{u}))} \prod_{i=0}^{m-1} ((1-u_i) - (-1)^{u_i} p_i).$$

Proof. Let $\mathcal{S}_\mathbf{u} = \{(\mathbf{x},\mathbf{x}') \in \mathbb{F}_2^m \times \mathbb{F}_2^m : \overleftarrow{\mathbf{x}} \oplus \mathbf{x}' = \mathbf{u}\}$ with $\#\mathcal{S}_\mathbf{u} = 2^m$. Then,

$$\mathcal{C}_\lambda^{\mathrm{R\text{-}DL}} = \sum_{\mathbf{v}\in\lambda^\perp} \Pr[\overleftarrow{F}(\mathbf{x}) \oplus F(\mathbf{x}') = \mathbf{v}] - \sum_{\mathbf{v}\in\mathbb{F}_2^n\setminus\lambda^\perp} \Pr[\overleftarrow{F}(\mathbf{x}) \oplus F(\mathbf{x}') = \mathbf{v}]$$

$$= \sum_{\mathbf{v}\in\mathbb{F}_2^n} (-1)^{\boldsymbol{\lambda}\cdot\mathbf{v}} \Pr[\overleftarrow{F}(\mathbf{x}) \oplus F(\mathbf{x}') = \mathbf{v}]$$

$$= \sum_{\mathbf{v}\in\mathbb{F}_2^n} (-1)^{\boldsymbol{\lambda}\cdot\mathbf{v}} \sum_{\mathbf{u}\in\mathbb{F}_2^m} \Pr[\overleftarrow{F}(\mathbf{x}) \oplus F(\mathbf{x}') = \mathbf{v}|(\mathbf{x},\mathbf{x}') \in \mathcal{S}_\mathbf{u}] \Pr[(\mathbf{x},\mathbf{x}') \in \mathcal{S}_\mathbf{u}]$$

$$= \sum_{\mathbf{u}\in\mathbb{F}_2^m} \sum_{\mathbf{v}\in\mathbb{F}_2^n} (-1)^{\boldsymbol{\lambda}\cdot\mathbf{v}} \Pr[F(\mathbf{x}) \oplus F(\mathbf{x}') = \mathbf{v}|(\mathbf{x},\mathbf{x}') \in \mathcal{S}_\mathbf{u}] \Pr[(\mathbf{x},\mathbf{x}') \in \mathcal{S}_\mathbf{u}]$$

$$= \sum_{\mathbf{u}\in\mathbb{F}_2^m} \frac{1}{2^m} \sum_{\mathbf{x}\in\mathbb{F}_2^m} (-1)^{\boldsymbol{\lambda}\cdot(\overleftarrow{F}(\mathbf{x})\oplus F(\overleftarrow{\mathbf{x}}\oplus\mathbf{u}))} \prod_{i=0}^{m-1} ((1-u_i) - (-1)^{u_i} p_i).$$

$\square$

Theorem 4. *We use* $\mathbf{x}$, $\mathbf{x}'$, $\mathbf{y}$, *and* $\mathbf{y}'$ *to represent random n-bit strings such that* $\Pr[x_{i-t} \oplus x_i' = 1] = p_i$ *and* $\Pr[y_{i-t} \oplus y_i' = 1] = q_i$ *for* $0 \le i < n$. *In addition, the events* $x_{i-t} \oplus x_i' = 1$ *and* $y_{j-t} \oplus y_j' = 1$ *for* $0 \le i,j < n$ *are mutually statistical independent. Let* $S(\mathbf{x},\mathbf{y}) = \mathbf{x} \boxplus \mathbf{y}$ *and* $\mathbf{W}$ *be*

$$\prod_{i=0}^{t-1}\left(\sum_{(c,d)\in\mathbb{F}_2^2} \zeta(c,d,p_i,q_i)\mathbf{M}_{c,d,\lambda_i}\right)\begin{pmatrix}1&1&0&0\\0&0&0&0\\0&0&1&1\\0&0&0&0\end{pmatrix}\prod_{i=t}^{n-1}\left(\sum_{(a,b)\in\mathbb{F}_2^2} \zeta(a,b,p_i,q_i)\mathbf{M}_{a,b,\lambda_i}\right),$$

where $\zeta(a,b,p,q) = ((1-a)-(-1)^a p)((1-b)-(-1)^b q)$. *Then, for* $\boldsymbol{\lambda} \in \mathbb{F}_2^n$ *and rotation offset t, the rotational differential-linear correlation of $S(\mathbf{x},\mathbf{y})$ can be computed as*

$$\mathcal{C}_{\boldsymbol{\lambda}}^{\text{R-DL}} = (1,0,1,0)\mathbf{W}(1,0,0,0)^T + (0,1,0,1)\mathbf{W}(0,1,0,0)^T.$$

Proof. See Supplementary Material D in the extended version [39]. □

The above theorems only consider *standalone* modulo additions. In practice, we may tweak these theorems to make them suitable for use in specific applications. In what follows, we demonstrate a case where linear and nonlinear operations are considered as a whole. Note that in the remainder of this section, $\mathbf{x} \in \mathbb{F}_2^n$ and $F(\mathbf{x})$ for some vectorial Boolean function $F : \mathbb{F}_2^n \to \mathbb{F}_2^n$ are regarded as *column* vectors. Therefore, a linear transformation of $\mathbf{y} \in \mathbb{F}_2^n$ can be written as $L\mathbf{y}$, where L is an $n \times n$ binary matrix.

Lemma 11. *Let* $F : \mathbb{F}_2^n \to \mathbb{F}_2^n$ *be a vectorial Boolean function mapping* $\mathbf{x} \in \mathbb{F}_2^n$ *to* $L \circ S(\mathbf{x}) \oplus \mathbf{c}$, *where* $\mathbf{c} \in \mathbb{F}_2^n$ *is a constant,* $S : \mathbb{F}_2^n \to \mathbb{F}_2^n$ *is a nonlinear permutation, and L is an $n \times n$ binary matrix such that* $L(\mathbf{y} \lll t) = (L\mathbf{y}) \lll t$ *for all* $\mathbf{y} \in \mathbb{F}_2^n$ *and integer t. Then, the correlation of the rotational differential-linear approximation of F with rotation offset t, RX-difference $\boldsymbol{\Delta}$, and output linear mask* $\boldsymbol{\lambda} \in \mathbb{F}_2^n$ *can be computed as*

$$\mathcal{C}_{\boldsymbol{\Delta},\boldsymbol{\lambda}}^{\text{R-DL}}(F) = (-1)^{\boldsymbol{\lambda}\cdot(\mathbf{c}\oplus\overleftarrow{\mathbf{c}})}\mathcal{C}_{\boldsymbol{\Delta},L^T\boldsymbol{\lambda}}^{\text{R-DL}}(S).$$

Proof. According to the definition of $\mathcal{C}_{\boldsymbol{\Delta},\boldsymbol{\lambda}}^{\text{R-DL}}(F)$, we have

$$\mathcal{C}_{\boldsymbol{\Delta},\boldsymbol{\lambda}}^{\text{R-DL}}(F) = \frac{1}{2^{2n}}\sum_{\mathbf{x}\in\mathbb{F}_2^n}(-1)^{\boldsymbol{\lambda}\cdot(\overleftarrow{F}(\mathbf{x})\oplus F(\overleftarrow{\mathbf{x}}\oplus\boldsymbol{\Delta}))}$$

$$= \frac{1}{2^{2n}}\sum_{\mathbf{x}\in\mathbb{F}_2^n}(-1)^{\boldsymbol{\lambda}\cdot(L(\overleftarrow{S}(\mathbf{x})\oplus S(\overleftarrow{\mathbf{x}}\oplus\boldsymbol{\Delta}))\oplus\overleftarrow{\mathbf{c}}\oplus\mathbf{c})}$$

$$= \frac{1}{2^{2n}}\sum_{\mathbf{x}\in\mathbb{F}_2^n}(-1)^{\boldsymbol{\lambda}\cdot(\overleftarrow{\mathbf{c}}\oplus\mathbf{c})\oplus\boldsymbol{\lambda}\cdot(L(\overleftarrow{S}(\mathbf{x})\oplus S(\overleftarrow{\mathbf{x}}\oplus\boldsymbol{\Delta})))}$$

$$= \frac{1}{2^{2n}}(-1)^{\boldsymbol{\lambda}\cdot(\overleftarrow{\mathbf{c}}\oplus\mathbf{c})}\sum_{\mathbf{x}\in\mathbb{F}_2^n}(-1)^{(L^T\boldsymbol{\lambda})\cdot(\overleftarrow{S}(\mathbf{x})\oplus S(\overleftarrow{\mathbf{x}}\oplus\boldsymbol{\Delta}))}$$

$$= (-1)^{\boldsymbol{\lambda}\cdot(\mathbf{c}\oplus\overleftarrow{\mathbf{c}})}\mathcal{C}_{\boldsymbol{\Delta},L^T\boldsymbol{\lambda}}^{\text{R-DL}}(S).$$

□

In the analysis of `Alzette`, `SipHash`, `ChaCha`, and `SPECK`, we will instantiate the nonlinear permutation S in Lemma 11 with $S(\mathbf{x}, \mathbf{y}) = (\mathbf{x} \boxplus \mathbf{y}, \mathbf{y})$, while for `ChaCha`, we will consider $S(\mathbf{x}, \mathbf{y}, \mathbf{z}, \mathbf{w}) = (\mathbf{x} \boxplus \mathbf{y}, \mathbf{y}, \mathbf{z}, \mathbf{w})$. Next, we only consider $S(\mathbf{x}, \mathbf{y}) = (\mathbf{x} \boxplus \mathbf{y}, \mathbf{y})$, and the generalization to the latter case is trivial.

Lemma 12. *The correlation of the differential-linear approximation of* $S(\mathbf{x}, \mathbf{y}) = (\mathbf{x} \boxplus \mathbf{y}, \mathbf{y})$ *with* $\mathbf{x}$ *and* $\mathbf{y} \in \mathbb{F}_2^n$, *input difference* $(\boldsymbol{\alpha}, \boldsymbol{\beta}) \in \mathbb{F}_2^n \times \mathbb{F}_2^n$, *and output linear mask* $(\boldsymbol{\lambda}, \boldsymbol{\gamma}) \in \mathbb{F}_2^n \times \mathbb{F}_2^n$ *can be computed as*

$$\mathcal{C}^{\mathrm{DL}}_{(\boldsymbol{\alpha}, \boldsymbol{\beta}), (\boldsymbol{\lambda}, \boldsymbol{\gamma})}(S) = \frac{1}{2^{2n}}(1, 1, 1, 1) \prod_{i=0}^{n-1} (-1)^{\gamma_i \beta_i} \mathbf{M}_{\alpha_i, \beta_i, \lambda_i} \begin{pmatrix} 1 \\ 0 \\ 0 \\ 0 \end{pmatrix}.$$

Proof. Let $\mathbf{x}' = \mathbf{x} \oplus \boldsymbol{\alpha}$ and $\mathbf{y}' = \mathbf{y} \oplus \boldsymbol{\beta}$. Then,

$$\mathcal{C}^{\mathrm{DL}}_{(\boldsymbol{\alpha}, \boldsymbol{\beta}), (\boldsymbol{\lambda}, \boldsymbol{\gamma})}(S) = \frac{1}{2^{2n}} \sum_{(\mathbf{x}, \mathbf{y}) \in \mathbb{F}_2^{2n}} (-1)^{(\boldsymbol{\lambda}, \boldsymbol{\gamma}) \cdot (S(\mathbf{x}, \mathbf{y}) \oplus S(\mathbf{x}', \mathbf{y}'))}$$

$$= \frac{(-1)^{\boldsymbol{\gamma} \cdot \boldsymbol{\beta}}}{2^{2n}} \sum_{(\mathbf{x}, \mathbf{y}) \in \mathbb{F}_2^{2n}} (-1)^{\boldsymbol{\lambda} \cdot ((\mathbf{x} \boxplus \mathbf{y}) \oplus (\mathbf{x}' \boxplus \mathbf{y}'))}.$$

Applying Theorem 1 to $\sum_{(\mathbf{x}, \mathbf{y}) \in \mathbb{F}_2^{2n}} (-1)^{\boldsymbol{\lambda} \cdot ((\mathbf{x} \boxplus \mathbf{y}) \oplus (\mathbf{x}' \boxplus \mathbf{y}'))}$ gives the proof. $\square$

Similarly, based on Theorem 2, we can derive the following Lemma.

Lemma 13. *The correlation* $\mathcal{C}^{\mathrm{R\text{-}DL}}_{(\boldsymbol{\alpha}, \boldsymbol{\beta}), (\boldsymbol{\lambda}, \boldsymbol{\gamma})}(S)$ *of the rotational differential-linear approximation of* $S(\mathbf{x}, \mathbf{y}) = (\mathbf{x} \boxplus \mathbf{y}, \mathbf{y})$ *with rotational offset* t, *input RX-difference* $(\boldsymbol{\alpha}, \boldsymbol{\beta}) \in \mathbb{F}_2^n \times \mathbb{F}_2^n$, *and output linear mask* $(\boldsymbol{\lambda}, \boldsymbol{\gamma}) \in \mathbb{F}_2^n \times \mathbb{F}_2^n$ *can be computed as*

$$(1, 0, 1, 0) \, \mathbf{C}_{(\boldsymbol{\alpha}, \boldsymbol{\beta}), (\boldsymbol{\lambda}, \boldsymbol{\gamma})} \begin{pmatrix} 1 \\ 0 \\ 0 \\ 0 \end{pmatrix} + (0, 1, 0, 1) \, \mathbf{C}_{(\boldsymbol{\alpha}, \boldsymbol{\beta}), (\boldsymbol{\lambda}, \boldsymbol{\gamma})} \begin{pmatrix} 0 \\ 1 \\ 0 \\ 0 \end{pmatrix},$$

where

$$\mathbf{C}_{(\boldsymbol{\alpha}, \boldsymbol{\beta}), (\boldsymbol{\lambda}, \boldsymbol{\gamma})} = 2^{-2n} \prod_{i=0}^{t-1} (-1)^{\gamma_i \beta_i} \mathbf{M}_{\alpha_i, \beta_i, \lambda_i} \begin{pmatrix} 1 & 1 & 0 & 0 \\ 0 & 0 & 0 & 0 \\ 0 & 0 & 1 & 1 \\ 0 & 0 & 0 & 0 \end{pmatrix} \prod_{j=t}^{n-1} (-1)^{\gamma_j \beta_j} \mathbf{M}_{\alpha_j, \beta_j, \lambda_j}.$$

Lemma 12 and Lemma 13 lead to the following generalizations of Theorem 3 and Theorem 4.

Corollary 3. *Let* $\mathbf{x}$, $\mathbf{x}'$, $\mathbf{y}$, *and* $\mathbf{y}'$ *be random* n-*bit strings such that* $\Pr[x_i \oplus x_i' = 1] = p_i$ *and* $\Pr[y_i \oplus y_i' = 1] = q_i$ *for* $0 \le i < n$. *In addition, the events* $x_i \oplus x_i' = 1$ *and* $y_j \oplus y_j' = 1$ *for* $0 \le i, j < n$ *are mutually independent. For output linear* mask $(\boldsymbol{\lambda}, \boldsymbol{\gamma}) \in \mathbb{F}_2^n \times \mathbb{F}_2^n$, the differential-linear correlation of $F(\mathbf{x}, \mathbf{y}) = (\mathbf{x} \boxplus \mathbf{y}, \mathbf{y})$ can be computed as

$$\mathcal{C}_{(\boldsymbol{\lambda}, \boldsymbol{\gamma})}^{\mathrm{DL}} = \frac{1}{2^{2n}} (1, 1, 1, 1) \prod_{i=0}^{n-1} \mathbf{H}_{\lambda_i, \gamma_i}^{p_i, q_i} (1, 0, 0, 0)^T,$$

where $\mathbf{H}_{\lambda_i, \gamma_i}^{p_i, q_i}$ is a 4×4 matrix defined as

$$\mathbf{H}_{\lambda_i, \gamma_i}^{p_i, q_i} = \sum_{a, b \in \mathbb{F}_2} (-1)^{\gamma_i b} ((1 - a) - (-1)^a p_i) ((1 - b) - (-1)^b q_i) \mathbf{M}_{a, b, \lambda_i}.$$

Corollary 4. *We use* $\mathbf{x}, \mathbf{x}', \mathbf{y}$, *and* $\mathbf{y}'$ *to represent random n-bit strings such that* $\Pr[x_{i-t} \oplus x_i' = 1] = p_i$ *and* $\Pr[y_{i-t} \oplus y_i' = 1] = q_i$ *for* $0 \leq i < n$. *In addition, the events* $x_{i-t} \oplus x_i' = 1$ *and* $y_{j-t} \oplus y_j' = 1$ *for* $0 \leq i, j < n$ *are mutually statistical independent. Then, for output linear mask* $(\boldsymbol{\lambda}, \boldsymbol{\gamma}) \in \mathbb{F}_2^n \times \mathbb{F}_2^n$, *rotational offset* t, *the rotational differential-linear correlation of* $F(\mathbf{x}, \mathbf{y}) = (\mathbf{x} \boxplus \mathbf{y}, \mathbf{y})$ *can be computed as*

$$\mathcal{C}_{(\boldsymbol{\lambda}, \boldsymbol{\gamma})}^{\mathrm{R\text{-}DL}}(S) = (1, 0, 1, 0) \mathbf{W} \begin{pmatrix} 1 \\ 0 \\ 0 \\ 0 \end{pmatrix} + (0, 1, 0, 1) \mathbf{W} \begin{pmatrix} 0 \\ 1 \\ 0 \\ 0 \end{pmatrix},$$

where $\zeta(a, b, p, q) = ((1 - a) - (-1)^a p)((1 - b) - (-1)^b q)$, *and* $\mathbf{W}$ *is*

$$\prod_{i=0}^{t-1} \left(\sum_{(c,d) \in \mathbb{F}_2^2} (-1)^{\gamma_i d} \zeta(c, d, p_i, q_i) \mathbf{M}_{c, d, \lambda_i} \right) \begin{pmatrix} 1 & 1 & 0 & 0 \\ 0 & 0 & 0 & 0 \\ 0 & 0 & 1 & 1 \\ 0 & 0 & 0 & 0 \end{pmatrix} \prod_{i=t}^{n-1} \left(\sum_{(a,b) \in \mathbb{F}_2^2} (-1)^{\gamma_i b} \zeta(a, b, p_i, q_i) \mathbf{M}_{a, b, \lambda_i} \right).$$

6   Applications to ARX Primitives

In this section, we apply the new technique for (rotational) differential-linear cryptanalysis proposed in Sect. 5 to the ARX primitives `Alzette`, `SipHash`, `SPECK`, and `ChaCha`. The source code for experimental verification is available at https://github.com/ZhongfengNiu/rot-differential-linear.

6.1   Cryptanalysis of `Alzette`

`Alzette` [7] is a 64-bit ARX-based S-box designed by Beierle et al., which is the main building block of the `Sparkle`-suite [8], a collection of lightweight symmetric cryptographic algorithms (AEADs and hash functions) currently in the final round of the NIST lightweight cryptography standardization effort. An instance of `Alzette` with an input $(x, y) \in \mathbb{F}_2^{32} \times \mathbb{F}_2^{32}$ is depicted in Fig. 1. To apply Corollary 3 and Corollary 4 developed in Sect. 5, we convert the `Alzette` round function into its equivalent form illustrated in Fig. 2.

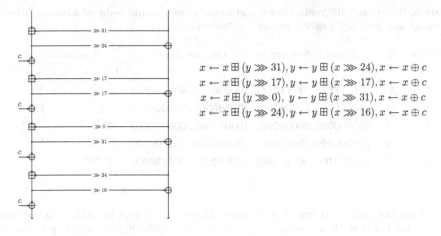

$$x \leftarrow x \boxplus (y \ggg 31), y \leftarrow y \boxplus (x \ggg 24), x \leftarrow x \oplus c$$
$$x \leftarrow x \boxplus (y \ggg 17), y \leftarrow y \boxplus (x \ggg 17), x \leftarrow x \oplus c$$
$$x \leftarrow x \boxplus (y \ggg 0), \ y \leftarrow y \boxplus (x \ggg 31), x \leftarrow x \oplus c$$
$$x \leftarrow x \boxplus (y \ggg 24), y \leftarrow y \boxplus (x \ggg 16), x \leftarrow x \oplus c$$

Fig. 1. The `Alzette` instance with $c = $ `B7E15162`

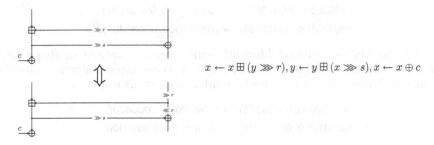

$$x \leftarrow x \boxplus (y \ggg r), y \leftarrow y \boxplus (x \ggg s), x \leftarrow x \oplus c$$

Fig. 2. An equivalent transformation of the round function of `Alzette`

Rotational Differential-Linear Distinguishers. We use the same input RX-difference (`7fffffc`, `3fffffff`) employed in [32]. Then, we evaluate the correlations of the 4-round rotational differential-linear approximations of `Alzette` for all possible output linear masks with Hamming weight 2. The best distinguisher has a theoretical correlation of $2^{-5.57}$ (see the first row of Table 5), whose experimental correlation with 2^{26} random input pairs with the predefined input RX-difference is about $2^{-3.14}$.

Differential-Linear Distinguishers. According to Corollary 2, we choose (`80000000`, `00000000`) to be the input difference. Then, we evaluate the correlations of the differential-linear approximations of 4-, 5- and 6-round `Alzette` for all possible output linear masks with Hamming weight 2.

For 4-round `Alzette`, we identify a *deterministic* differential-linear approximation (see the second row of Table 5). For 5-, and 6-round `Alzette`, the best differential-linear distinguishers have a theoretical correlation of $-2^{-0.33}$ and $2^{-4.95}$, respectively. The experimental correlations given in Table 5 are obtained with 2^{26} random input pairs with the predefined input differences.

Table 5. Rotational differential-linear distinguishers for round-reduced `Alzette`, where the constants used are `0xB7E15162` and `0x38B4DA56`.

#Rnd	$\lll \gamma$	Input Difference	Output Mask	Correlation	
				Theory	Experiment
4	30	$(\text{7fffffc}, \text{3fffffff})$	$(00004000, 40000000)$	$2^{-5.57}$	$2^{-3.14}$
4	0	$(80000000, 00000000)$	$(00080000, 00000008)$	1	1
5	0	$(80000000, 00000000)$	$(00000080, 00008000)$	$-2^{-0.33}$	$-2^{-0.13}$
6	0	$(80000000, 00000000)$	$(00000040, 00200000)$	$2^{-4.95}$	$2^{-1.45}$
8	0	$(80020100, 00010080)$	$(80000000, 00008000)$	$-2^{-8.24}$	$-2^{-5.50}$

Extending the Distinguisher. For 4-round `Alzette`, we can identify two optimal differential trails with a common input difference $(80020100, 00010080)$ whose probabilities are 2^{-6}:

$$(80020100, 00010080) \rightarrow (01010000, 00030101),$$
$$(80020100, 00010080) \rightarrow (03010000, 00030301).$$

Moreover, we find two 4-round differential-linear approximations sharing a common output linear mask $(80000000, 00008000)$ whose input differences are the two output differences of the above two differential trails respectively:

$$(01010000, 00030101) \rightarrow (80000000, 00008000),$$
$$(03010000, 00030301) \rightarrow (80000000, 00008000).$$

The theoretical correlations of the differential-linear approximations are $-2^{-2.90}$ and $-2^{-3.69}$, respectively. Combining the 4-round differential trials with the 4-round differential-linear approximations leads to an 8-round differential-linear distinguisher with theoretical correlation $2^{-6} \cdot (-2^{-2.90} - 2^{-3.69}) \approx -2^{-8.24}$ (see the last row of Table 5). The experimental correlation with 2^{26} random input pairs with the predefined input difference is $2^{-5.50}$.

6.2   Cryptanalysis of SipHash

SipHash [3] is a family of ARX-based pseudorandom functions optimized for short inputs. As mentioned in the introduction, instances of `SipHash` are widely deployed in real-world applications. The round function of `SipHash` is illustrated in Fig. 3.

Aumasson and Bernstein proposed two specific instances for use, which are `SipHash`-2-4 and `SipHash`-4-8. Here we focus on the finalization process of `SipHash`-2-4, where four rounds are applied and the output branches are XORed together. In [20], Dobraunig, Mendel and Schläffer found a 4-round differential distinguisher for the finalization (see the last row of Table 6). According to Corollary 2, we choose 8000000000000000 to be the input difference of branch a. Then, we evaluate the correlations of all 3-round differential-linear approximations of `SipHash` for all possible output linear masks with Hamming weight 2. We

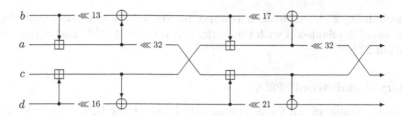

Fig. 3. The round function of SipHash

Table 6. Differential-linear distinguishers for the finalization of SipHash. Note that the 4-round distinguisher from [20] is a differential one.

#Rnd	Input Difference	Mask/Difference	Correlation/probability		Ref.
			Theory	Experiment	
3	0000000000000000	0000400000004000	$2^{-2.19}$	$2^{-0.78}$	Sect. 6.2
	8000000000000000				
	0000000000000000				
	0000000000000000				
4	0000000000040000	2000000020000000	$2^{-12.45}$	$2^{-6.03}$	Sect. 6.2
	0000000080040000				
	0000000000000000				
	0000000000000000				
4	0014002020010000	2011421120010200	2^{-35}	–	[20]
	8010042000010000				
	0402200000000002				
	0402200000000000				

find a 3-round distinguisher given in the first row of Table 6 with theoretical correlation $2^{-2.19}$ and experimental correlation $2^{-0.78}$.

If we choose 8000000000000000 to be the input difference of branch a and branch d, we find the following 3-round differential-linear distinguisher

$$
\begin{matrix}
0000000000000000 \\
8000000000000000 \\
0000000000000000 \\
8000000000000000
\end{matrix}
\rightarrow 2000000020000000
$$

with theoretical correlation $2^{-10.45}$. Extending this distinguisher backwards with the following differential

$$
\begin{matrix}
0000000000040000 \\
0000000080040000 \\
0000000000000000 \\
0000000000000000
\end{matrix}
\rightarrow
\begin{matrix}
0000000000000000 \\
8000000000000000 \\
0000000000000000 \\
8000000000000000
\end{matrix}
$$

with probability 2^{-2}, we obtain a 4-round differential-linear distinguisher for the finalization of SipHash-2-4 with theoretical correlation $2^{-12.45}$ and experimental correlation $2^{-6.03}$.

6.3 Cryptanalysis of SPECK

SPECK [6] is a family of ARX block ciphers designed by the U.S. National Security Agency (NSA). In this work, we focus on the version with a 32-bit block size, whose round function is depicted in Fig. 4.

Fig. 4. The SPECK instance

As discussed in [32], it is difficult to apply rotational differential-linear attacks with nonzero rotation offset on keyed primitives due to the peculiarities of the RX-difference, and thus for SPECK we only consider ordinary differential-linear attacks (rotational differential-linear attacks with zero rotation offset). For SPECK32, we start with a 4-round differential trail:

$$(0211, 0a04) \rightarrow (8100, 8102)$$

with probability 2^{-7}. Then, setting the input difference to $(8100, 8102)$, we evaluate the correlations of the differential-linear approximations of 4-round SPECK32 for all possible output linear masks with Hamming weight 2, and find one: $(8100, 8102) \rightarrow (0008, 0008)$ with correlation $2^{-1.23}$. At this point, we obtain an 8-round differential-linear distinguisher for SPECK32 with theoretical correlation $2^{-8.23}$. By extending this distinguisher forward by a 1-round linear approximation $(0008, 0008) \rightarrow (5820, 4020)$ with correlation 2^{-1} and backwards by a differential trail

$$(0a20, 4205) \rightarrow (0211, 0a04)$$

with probability 2^{-5} we get a 10-round differential-linear distinguisher for SPECK32 with a theoretical correlation of $2^{-15.23}$, while previous best 10-round distinguisher for SPECK32 is a differential one with probability $2^{-31.01}$ [43] (too close to 2^{-32} to be valid in practice). Moreover, experimental results indicate that the actual correlation of our distinguisher is higher than expected. We random chose 100 master keys. For each key, we compute the experimental correlation of the distinguisher by going through the full plaintext space. The average correlation over the 100 keys is about $2^{-13.90}$ (Table 7).

Table 7. Differential-linear distinguishers for round-reduced SPECK32

#Rnd	$\lll \gamma$	Input Difference	Output Mask	Correlation	
				Theory	Experiment
8	0	$(0211, 0a04)$	$(0008, 0008)$	$2^{-8.23}$	$2^{-6.87}$
9	0	$(0211, 0a04)$	$(5820, 4020)$	$2^{-10.23}$	$2^{-8.93}$
10	0	$(0a20, 4205)$	$(5820, 4020)$	$2^{-15.23}$	$2^{-13.90}$

6.4 Cryptanalysis of ChaCha

As the default replacement for RC4 in the TLS protocol, ChaCha [10] is one of the most important ARX primitives. ChaCha operates on a 4×4 matrix of sixteen 32-bit words written as

$$\begin{pmatrix} x_0 & x_1 & x_2 & x_3 \\ x_4 & x_5 & x_6 & x_7 \\ x_8 & x_9 & x_{10} & x_{11} \\ x_{12} & x_{13} & x_{14} & x_{15} \end{pmatrix}.$$

In each round, four parallel applications of a nonlinear transformation depicted in Fig. 5 are performed on four 128-bit tuples formed by the words of the state matrix. Specifically, in odd-numbered rounds, the nonlinear transformation is applied to columns (x_0, x_4, x_8, x_{12}), (x_1, x_5, x_9, x_{13}), $(x_2, x_6, x_{10}, x_{14})$, $(x_3, x_7, x_{11}, x_{15})$. In even-numbered rounds, the nonlinear operation is applied to $(x_0, x_5, x_{10}, x_{15})$, $(x_1, x_6, x_{11}, x_{12})$, (x_2, x_7, x_8, x_{13}), (x_3, x_4, x_9, x_{14}).

Rotational Differential-Linear Distinguishers. In [45], Xu et al. presented a 1-round rotational differential-linear distinguisher for ChaCha (see the first row of Table 13 in Supplementary Material G in the extended version of this paper [39]) with an experimental correlation $2^{-0.01}$. The lower bound of the correlation of this differential-linear distinguisher is estimated to be 2^{-2} in [45]. We re-evaluate the correlation of this distinguisher with the method proposed in Sect. 5, and the obtained theoretical correlation is $2^{-0.01}$, perfectly matching the experimental result.

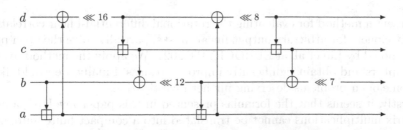

Fig. 5. The quartered round function of ChaCha

Differential-Linear Distinguishers. At CRYPTO 2020, Beierle et al. employed a series of 2.5-round differential-linear distinguishers (starting form even round) to perform key-recovery attacks on ChaCha [9] (see Table 13 in Supplementary Material G in the extended version of this paper [39]) whose experimental correlations are $2^{-8.3}$. With the method presented in Sect. 5, the predicted correlations are $2^{-12.14}$. Concerning this result, we would like to mention that the result obtained by Dey, Dey, Sarkar, and Meier [17] is better than ours. However, if the readers take a look at [17], it is easy to find that our method is more generic. Also, we evaluate the correlation of the 3-round differential-linear approximation used in FSE 2008 [4] and FSE 2016 [14] with an experimental correlation $2^{-5.25}$, and the obtained theoretical correlation is $2^{-9.88}$ (see the last row of Table 13 in Supplementary Material G in the extended version of this paper [39]).

Moreover, for 2.5-round ChaCha, we find a differential-linear distinguisher

$$
\begin{array}{l}
00000000000000000000000000000000 \\
00000000000000000000000000000000 \\
00000000000000000000000000000000 \\
00000000000000000000000020000000
\end{array}
\rightarrow
\begin{array}{l}
00000000000000000000000000000000 \\
00000000000000000000000000000000 \\
00000000000000000000000100000000 \\
00000000000000000000000000000000
\end{array}
$$

whose theoretical correlation is $2^{-0.02}$. Since

$$
\begin{cases}
x_{10}^{2.5}[0] & = x_{10}^{3}[0] \oplus x_{14}^{3}[0] \\
x_{10}^{3}[0] & = x_{6}^{4}[0] \oplus x_{10}^{4}[0] \oplus x_{15}^{4}[0] \oplus x_{15}^{4}[8] \\
x_{14}^{3}[0] & = x_{3}^{4}[0] \oplus x_{3}^{4}[16] \oplus x_{4}^{4}[7] \oplus x_{9}^{4}[0] \oplus x_{14}^{4}[24]
\end{cases},
$$

extending the 2.5-round distinguisher gives a 4-round differential-linear distinguisher

$$
\begin{array}{llll}
00000000 & 00000000 & 00000000 & 00000000 \\
00000000 & 00000000 & 00000000 & 00000000 \\
00000000 & 00000000 & 00000000 & 00000000 \\
00000000 & 00000000 & 00000000 & 20000000
\end{array}
\rightarrow
\begin{array}{llll}
00000001 & 00000000 & 00000000 & 00010001 \\
00000080 & 00000000 & 00000000 & 00000000 \\
00000000 & 00000001 & 00000001 & 00000000 \\
00000000 & 00000000 & 01000000 & 00000101
\end{array}
$$

with a theoretical correlation of $2^{-0.02}$ and experimental correlation of $2^{-0.98}$.

7   Conclusion, Discussion, and Open Problems

We present a method for evaluating the rotational differential-linear correlations of ARX ciphers for arbitrary output linear masks, partially solve the open problem proposed by Liu et al. at EUROCRYPT 2021. We apply the method to some ARX ciphers and obtain significantly improved results. Finally, we would like to give some open problems deserving further investigations.

Firstly, it seems that the formulas presented in this paper involving a chain of matrix multiplications cannot be translated into a compact finite automaton to be modeled with the MILP methodology. Therefore, we feel that the major pain spot of the current development is that there is no effective tool that can automatically search for good (rotational) differential-linear approximations, and thus in practice the search space is severely limited to low Hamming weight output masks. Secondly, can we weaken or avoid the independence assumptions used in the method for evaluating the rotational differential-linear correlations? Remembering that we still have difficulties in explaining the experimental distinguishers listed in Supplementary Material H in the extended version of this paper [39], a solution to the independence problem may completely solve this problem.

Acknowledgment. We thank the reviewers for their valuable comments. This work is supported by the National Key Research and Development Program of China (2018YFA0704704), the Natural Science Foundation of China (62032014), and the Fundamental Research Funds for the Central Universities.

References

1. Abed, F., List, E., Lucks, S., Wenzel, J.: Differential cryptanalysis of round-reduced SIMON and SPECK. In: Cid, C., Rechberger, C. (eds.) FSE 2014. LNCS, vol. 8540, pp. 525–545. Springer, Heidelberg (2015). https://doi.org/10.1007/978-3-662-46706-0_27
2. Ashur, T., Liu, Y.: Rotational cryptanalysis in the presence of constants. IACR Trans. Symmetric Cryptol. **2016**(1), 57–70 (2016)
3. Aumasson, J.-P., Bernstein, D.J.: SipHash: a fast short-input PRF. In: Galbraith, S., Nandi, M. (eds.) INDOCRYPT 2012. LNCS, vol. 7668, pp. 489–508. Springer, Heidelberg (2012). https://doi.org/10.1007/978-3-642-34931-7_28
4. Aumasson, J.-P., Fischer, S., Khazaei, S., Meier, W., Rechberger, C.: New features of Latin dances: analysis of Salsa, ChaCha, and Rumba. In: Nyberg, K. (ed.) FSE 2008. LNCS, vol. 5086, pp. 470–488. Springer, Heidelberg (2008). https://doi.org/10.1007/978-3-540-71039-4_30
5. Aumasson, J.-P., Henzen, L., Meier, W., Phan, R.C.-W.: SHA-3 proposal BLAKE. Submission to NIST (2010)
6. Beaulieu, R., Shors, D., Smith, J., Treatman-Clark, S., Weeks, B., Wingers, L.: The SIMON and SPECK families of lightweight block ciphers. IACR Cryptology ePrint Archive, p. 404 (2013)
7. Beierle, C., et al.: Alzette: a 64-bit ARX-box - (Feat. CRAX and TRAX). In: Advances in Cryptology - CRYPTO 2020–40th Annual International Cryptology Conference, CRYPTO 2020, 17–21 August 2020, Proceedings, Part III, pp. 419–448 (2020)
8. Beierle, C., et al.: Lightweight AEAD and hashing using the SPARKLE permutation family. IACR Trans. Symmetric Cryptol. **2020**(S1), 208–261 (2020)
9. Beierle, C., Leander, G., Todo, Y.: Improved differential-linear attacks with applications to ARX ciphers. In: Micciancio, D., Ristenpart, T. (eds.) CRYPTO 2020, Part III. LNCS, vol. 12172, pp. 329–358. Springer, Cham (2020). https://doi.org/10.1007/978-3-030-56877-1_12
10. Bernstein, D.J.: ChaCha, a variant of Salsa20. In: Workshop Record of SASC, vol. 8, pp. 3–5 (2008)

11. Bernstein, D.J.: The Salsa20 family of stream ciphers. In: Robshaw, M., Billet, O. (eds.) New Stream Cipher Designs. LNCS, vol. 4986, pp. 84–97. Springer, Heidelberg (2008). https://doi.org/10.1007/978-3-540-68351-3_8

12. Biryukov, A., Velichkov, V.: Automatic search for differential trails in ARX ciphers. In: Benaloh, J. (ed.) CT-RSA 2014. LNCS, vol. 8366, pp. 227–250. Springer, Cham (2014). https://doi.org/10.1007/978-3-319-04852-9_12

13. Biryukov, A., Velichkov, V., Le Corre, Y.: Automatic search for the best trails in ARX: application to block cipher SPECK. In: Peyrin, T. (ed.) FSE 2016. LNCS, vol. 9783, pp. 289–310. Springer, Heidelberg (2016). https://doi.org/10.1007/978-3-662-52993-5_15

14. Choudhuri, A.R., Maitra, S.: Significantly improved multi-bit differentials for reduced round Salsa and ChaCha. IACR Trans. Symmetric Cryptol. **2016**(2), 261–287 (2016)

15. Coutinho, M., Souza Neto, T.C.: Improved linear approximations to ARX ciphers and attacks against ChaCha. In: Canteaut, A., Standaert, F.-X. (eds.) EUROCRYPT 2021, Part I. LNCS, vol. 12696, pp. 711–740. Springer, Cham (2021). https://doi.org/10.1007/978-3-030-77870-5_25

16. Wheeler, D.J., Needham, R.M.: TEA, a tiny encryption algorithm. In: Preneel, B. (ed.) FSE 1994. LNCS, vol. 1008, pp. 363–366. Springer, Heidelberg (1995). https://doi.org/10.1007/3-540-60590-8_29

17. Dey, S., Dey, C., Sarkar, S., Meier, W.: Revisiting cryptanalysis on ChaCha from Crypto 2020 and Eurocrypt 2021. IACR Cryptology ePrint Archive, p. 1059 (2021)

18. Dinu, D., Le Corre, Y., Khovratovich, D., Perrin, L., Großschädl, J., Biryukov, A.: Triathlon of lightweight block ciphers for the Internet of things. J. Cryptogr. Eng. **9**(3), 283–302 (2019)

19. Dinu, D., Perrin, L., Udovenko, A., Velichkov, V., Großschädl, J., Biryukov, A.: Design strategies for ARX with provable bounds: SPARX and LAX. In: Cheon, J.H., Takagi, T. (eds.) ASIACRYPT 2016, Part I. LNCS, vol. 10031, pp. 484–513. Springer, Heidelberg (2016). https://doi.org/10.1007/978-3-662-53887-6_18

20. Dobraunig, C., Mendel, F., Schläffer, M.: Differential cryptanalysis of SipHash. In: Joux, A., Youssef, A. (eds.) SAC 2014. LNCS, vol. 8781, pp. 165–182. Springer, Cham (2014). https://doi.org/10.1007/978-3-319-13051-4_10

21. ElSheikh, M., Abdelkhalek, A., Youssef, A.M.: On MILP-based automatic search for differential trails through modular additions with application to Bel-T. In: Buchmann, J., Nitaj, A., Rachidi, T. (eds.) AFRICACRYPT 2019. LNCS, vol. 11627, pp. 273–296. Springer, Cham (2019). https://doi.org/10.1007/978-3-030-23696-0_14

22. Ferguson, N., et al.: The Skein Hash Function Family. Submission to NIST (2010)

23. Fu, K., Wang, M., Guo, Y., Sun, S., Hu, L.: MILP-based automatic search algorithms for differential and linear trails for Speck. In: Peyrin, T. (ed.) FSE 2016. LNCS, vol. 9783, pp. 268–288. Springer, Heidelberg (2016). https://doi.org/10.1007/978-3-662-52993-5_14

24. Hong, D., Lee, J.-K., Kim, D.-C., Kwon, D., Ryu, K.H., Lee, D.-G.: LEA: a 128-bit block cipher for fast encryption on common processors. In: Kim, Y., Lee, H., Perrig, A. (eds.) WISA 2013. LNCS, vol. 8267, pp. 3–27. Springer, Cham (2014). https://doi.org/10.1007/978-3-319-05149-9_1

25. Hong, D., et al.: HIGHT: a new block cipher suitable for low-resource device. In: Goubin, L., Matsui, M. (eds.) CHES 2006. LNCS, vol. 4249, pp. 46–59. Springer, Heidelberg (2006). https://doi.org/10.1007/11894063_4

26. Kim, D., Kwon, D., Song, J.: Efficient computation of boomerang connection probability for ARX-based block ciphers with application to SPECK and LEA. IEICE Trans. Fundam. Electron. Commun. Comput. Sci. **103-A**(4), 677–685 (2020)
27. Leurent, G.: https://who.paris.inria.fr/Gaetan.Leurent/arxtools.html
28. Leurent, G.: Analysis of differential attacks in ARX constructions. In: Wang, X., Sako, K. (eds.) ASIACRYPT 2012. LNCS, vol. 7658, pp. 226–243. Springer, Heidelberg (2012). https://doi.org/10.1007/978-3-642-34961-4_15
29. Leurent, G.: Construction of differential characteristics in ARX designs application to Skein. In: Canetti, R., Garay, J.A. (eds.) CRYPTO 2013, Part I. LNCS, vol. 8042, pp. 241–258. Springer, Heidelberg (2013). https://doi.org/10.1007/978-3-642-40041-4_14
30. Leurent, G.: Improved differential-linear cryptanalysis of 7-Round Chaskey with partitioning. In: Fischlin, M., Coron, J.-S. (eds.) EUROCRYPT 2016, Part I. LNCS, vol. 9665, pp. 344–371. Springer, Heidelberg (2016). https://doi.org/10.1007/978-3-662-49890-3_14
31. Lipmaa, H., Moriai, S.: Efficient algorithms for computing differential properties of addition. In: Matsui, M. (ed.) FSE 2001. LNCS, vol. 2355, pp. 336–350. Springer, Heidelberg (2002). https://doi.org/10.1007/3-540-45473-X_28
32. Liu, Y., Sun, S., Li, C.: Rotational cryptanalysis from a differential-linear perspective. In: Canteaut, A., Standaert, F.-X. (eds.) EUROCRYPT 2021, Part I. LNCS, vol. 12696, pp. 741–770. Springer, Cham (2021). https://doi.org/10.1007/978-3-030-77870-5_26
33. Liu, Y., De Witte, G., Ranea, A., Ashur, T.: Rotational-XOR cryptanalysis of reduced-round SPECK. IACR Trans. Symmetric Cryptol. **2017**(3), 24–36 (2017)
34. Morawiecki, P., Pieprzyk, J., Srebrny, M.: Rotational cryptanalysis of round-reduced KECCAK. In: Moriai, S. (ed.) FSE 2013. LNCS, vol. 8424, pp. 241–262. Springer, Heidelberg (2014). https://doi.org/10.1007/978-3-662-43933-3_13
35. Mouha, N., Mennink, B., Van Herrewege, A., Watanabe, D., Preneel, B., Verbauwhede, I.: Chaskey: an efficient MAC algorithm for 32-bit microcontrollers. In: Joux, A., Youssef, A. (eds.) SAC 2014. LNCS, vol. 8781, pp. 306–323. Springer, Cham (2014). https://doi.org/10.1007/978-3-319-13051-4_19
36. Mouha, N., Preneel, B.: Towards finding optimal differential characteristics for ARX: application to Salsa20. Cryptology ePrint Archive, Report 2013/328 (2013). https://ia.cr/2013/328
37. Mouha, N., Velichkov, V., De Cannière, C., Preneel, B.: The differential analysis of S-functions. In: Biryukov, A., Gong, G., Stinson, D.R. (eds.) SAC 2010. LNCS, vol. 6544, pp. 36–56. Springer, Heidelberg (2011). https://doi.org/10.1007/978-3-642-19574-7_3
38. National Institute of Standards and Technology. Preliminary state standard of republic of Belarus (STBP 34.101.312011) (2011). https://apmi.bsu.by/assets/files/std/belt-spec27.pdf
39. Niu, Z., Sun, S., Liu, Y., Li, C.: Rotational differential-linear distinguishers of ARX ciphers with arbitrary output linear masks (2022). https://eprint.iacr.org/2022/765
40. Nyberg, K., Wallén, J.: Improved linear distinguishers for SNOW 2.0. In: Robshaw, M. (ed.) FSE 2006. LNCS, vol. 4047, pp. 144–162. Springer, Heidelberg (2006). https://doi.org/10.1007/11799313_10
41. Needham, R.M., Wheeler, D.J.: TEA extensions. Report, Cambridge University (1997)

42. Shimizu, A., Miyaguchi, S.: Fast data encipherment algorithm FEAL. In: Chaum, D., Price, W.L. (eds.) EUROCRYPT 1987. LNCS, vol. 304, pp. 267–278. Springer, Heidelberg (1988). https://doi.org/10.1007/3-540-39118-5_24

43. Song, L., Huang, Z., Yang, Q.: Automatic differential analysis of ARX block ciphers with application to SPECK and LEA. In: Liu, J.K., Steinfeld, R. (eds.) ACISP 2016, Part II. LNCS, vol. 9723, pp. 379–394. Springer, Cham (2016). https://doi.org/10.1007/978-3-319-40367-0_24

44. Wallén, Johan: Linear approximations of addition modulo 2^n. In: Johansson, Thomas (ed.) FSE 2003. LNCS, vol. 2887, pp. 261–273. Springer, Heidelberg (2003). https://doi.org/10.1007/978-3-540-39887-5_20

45. Xu, Y., Wu, B., Lin, D.: Rotational-linear attack: a new framework of cryptanalysis on ARX ciphers with applications to Chaskey. In: Gao, D., Li, Q., Guan, X., Liao, X. (eds.) ICICS 2021, Part II. LNCS, vol. 12919, pp. 192–209. Springer, Cham (2021). https://doi.org/10.1007/978-3-030-88052-1_12

Implicit White-Box Implementations: White-Boxing ARX Ciphers

Adrián Ranea[1]([✉])[ID], Joachim Vandersmissen[2], and Bart Preneel[1][ID]

[1] imec-COSIC, KU Leuven, Leuven, Belgium
{adrian.ranea,bart.preneel}@esat.kuleuven.be
[2] Atsec Information Security, Austin, USA
joachim@atsec.com

Abstract. Since the first white-box implementation of AES published twenty years ago, no significant progress has been made in the design of secure implementations against an attacker with full control of the device. Designing white-box implementations of existing block ciphers is a challenging problem, as all proposals have been broken. Only two white-box design strategies have been published this far: the CEJO framework, which can only be applied to ciphers with small S-boxes, and self-equivalence encodings, which were only applied to AES.

In this work we propose implicit implementations, a new design of white-box implementations based on implicit functions, and we show that current generic attacks that break CEJO or self-equivalence implementations are not successful against implicit implementations. The generation and the security of implicit implementations are related to the self-equivalences of the non-linear layer of the cipher, and we propose a new method to obtain self-equivalences based on the CCZ-equivalence. We implemented this method and many other functionalities in a new open-source tool BoolCrypt, which we used to obtain for the first time affine, linear, and even quadratic self-equivalences of the permuted modular addition. Using the implicit framework and these self-equivalences, we describe for the first time a practical white-box implementation of a generic Addition-Rotation-XOR (ARX) cipher, and we provide an open-source tool to easily generate implicit implementations of ARX ciphers.

Keywords: White-box cryptography · Self-equivalence · Implicit implementation · ARX

1 Introduction

In some settings, such as digital rights management (DRM) or mobile banking, an attacker might get full control of the device performing the sensitive cryptographic computations. This extreme case cannot be captured by traditional black-box cryptography, which considers an attacker with only access to the input and output behaviour of the cryptographic algorithm, or even grey-box

© International Association for Cryptologic Research 2022
Y. Dodis and T. Shrimpton (Eds.): CRYPTO 2022, LNCS 13507, pp. 33–63, 2022.
https://doi.org/10.1007/978-3-031-15802-5_2

cryptography, that assumes some leakage from the device can be extracted from an attacker with partial access.

This setting was captured into the so-called white-box model by Chow et al. [13]. In this cryptographic model, it is assumed that the attacker has full control on the device running the cryptographic algorithm. In other words, the attacker can observe and even modify all the intermediate values of the cryptographic computation.

Chow et al. also proposed in this seminal work a design of an implementation of AES with the ambitious goal of preventing key-extraction attacks without relying on secure hardware or on the secrecy of the design. The main idea of this design, later called the CEJO framework, is to represent the cipher as a network of encoded look-up tables, where each table is composed with random perturbations or encodings in such a way that the output encoding of one step cancels the next input encoding. The encodings are small functions such as 4-bit or 8-bit permutations to avoid huge look-up tables and implementations with impractical size. To prevent a trivial attack, the first and last encodings are not cancelled, and due to these external encodings the resulting white-box implementation is not functionally equivalent to the original cipher.

To avoid external encodings and to keep the input-output behaviour of the cipher, some industrial white-box implementations rely on the secrecy of their designs. However, the WhibOx Contest [40] has shown that these white-box implementations can be broken by automated white-box attacks based on side-channel analysis and fault attacks [4,10,35]. This work focuses on the white-box setting proposed by Chow et al. and white-box implementations relying on secret designs [9] are outside the scope of this paper.

Several CEJO implementations [3,14,23,26,27,37,43] have been proposed, but all of them have been broken. These attacks exploit some properties of the underlying cipher (AES in most cases), but efficient generic attacks have also been proposed to the CEJO framework [3,17,29], which can break CEJO implementations of a wide class of ciphers.

Apart from CEJO implementations only one other type of white-box implementations, of existing block ciphers and without relying on secret designs, has been published: self-equivalence implementations [28,34]. In the latter implementations, the round functions are protected by affine self-equivalences of the non-linear layer S, that is, affine permutations (A, B) such that $S = B \circ S \circ A$ [15]. In other words, each round in a self-equivalence implementation is composed of the non-linear layer, which is left unprotected, and the encoded affine layer, which encodes the affine layer containing the round key material with self-equivalences of the non-linear layer.

Whereas CEJO implementations can only use small encodings, self-equivalence implementations can use large encodings and avoid many of the attacks to the CEJO framework. Ranea and Preneel showed in [34] that the affine self-equivalence group of the non-linear layer plays a major role in the security of self-equivalence and CEJO implementations, and they suggest securing a cipher with a non-linear layer that is composed of large S-boxes and that has large affine self-equivalence group, instead of securing AES which was the focus of most earlier work.

Unfortunately and apart from the insecure example for AES [28], no other self-equivalence implementation has been proposed this far. The main difficulty is finding a suitable non-linear layer. Among the functions used in non-linear layers, the power function $x \mapsto x^d$ is one of the few for which a large affine self-equivalence subgroup[1] is known for large bitsizes. However, power functions are used in block ciphers mostly in small S-boxes, with the exception of some algebraic ciphers [1].

One of the most important large non-linear permutations used in block ciphers is the permuted modular addition, $(x, y) \mapsto (x \boxplus y, y)$, but no previous work has studied its affine self-equivalences. However, quadratic functions tend to have many affine self-equivalences, and the modular addition is CCZ-equivalent to a quadratic function [36]. CCZ-equivalence [12] is an equivalence relation between functions based on their graphs that preserves many properties such as differential or linear properties. Thus, the quadratic CCZ-equivalence of the modular addition suggests its affine self-equivalence group can be very large.

1.1 Contributions

In this work we first address the problem of finding the affine self-equivalence group of the permuted modular addition. Schulte-Geers obtained in [36] the differential and linear properties of the modular addition from the differential and linear properties of its simpler CCZ-equivalent quadratic function. Inspired by this approach and the relation between the self-equivalences of two CCZ-equivalent functions, we propose a method to obtain the self-equivalences of a non-linear function from a low-degree CCZ-equivalent function. Our method can find affine but also other types of self-equivalences, such as self-equivalences (A, B) with A being affine and B being quadratic or affine permutations that map the graph of a function to itself.

We provide a new open-source library BoolCrypt[2] that implements the previous method and many functionalities related to vectorial Boolean functions, self-equivalences, and functional equations. We dedicated a significant engineering effort to equip BoolCrypt with plenty of functionalities, a modular structure and an extensive documentation, so that it can be useful and practical for the community.

After running BoolCrypt on the permuted modular addition, we obtained subsets of $3 \times 2^{2n+2}$ linear, $3 \times 2^{2n+8}$ affine, and $3^2 \times 2^{3n+14} - 3 \times 2^{2n+8}$ affine-quadratic self-equivalences for wordsize $n \in \{4, 5 \ldots, 64\}$. It is worth mentioning that the self-equivalence results, the tool BoolCrypt and the generic method to

---

[1] The power function $F(x) = x^d \in \mathbb{F}_{2^n}$ has at least $n(2^n - 1)$ linear self-equivalences of the form $(A(x), B(x)) = (ax^{2^i}, a^{-d2^{n-i}} x^{2^{n-i}})$, where $a \neq 0$ and $i = 0, 1, \ldots, n-1$. The whole linear self-equivalence group has only been found for some exponents [41].

[2] https://github.com/ranea/BoolCrypt.

compute self-equivalences can be of independent interest for other areas apart from white-box cryptography.

Unfortunately, the self-equivalences that we found are too structured and not suitable for self-equivalence implementations. Despite the exponential number of these linear, affine and affine-quadratic self-equivalences, they have a common sparse shape and low-entropy constant vectors. As a result, the round keys are not securely hidden in the constant vectors of the encoded affine layers.

Thus, we propose *implicit implementations*, a new design of white-box implementations that combines large self-equivalences with large affine encodings to prevent attacks exploiting the structure of the self-equivalences. Implicit implementations represent each round function by a low-degree *implicit* function and apply the large encodings on the implicit round functions.

Whereas CEJO implementations can only apply small encodings and self-equivalence implementations can only use self-equivalence encodings, the main advantage of implicit implementations is that they can efficiently encode the low-degree implicit round functions with large affine permutations and even large non-linear self-equivalences.

We analyse the security of implicit implementations against key-extraction attacks and show that implicit implementations that use non-linear encodings or where the non-linear layer of the cipher is not composed of small S-boxes prevent all known generic key-extraction attacks. We also propose a new generic attack for the implicit framework that provides insightful requirements for implicit implementations with affine encodings.

Using the implicit framework and the self-equivalences of the permuted modular addition, we describe an implicit implementation of a generic cipher with the permuted modular addition as the non-linear layer, which captures the well-known family of Addition-Rotation-XOR (ARX) ciphers. We analyse the security of these implicit implementations and provide an open-source tool[3] to generate implicit implementations of ARX ciphers in an automated way.

Designing white-box implementations of existing ciphers is currently the most challenging problem in white-box cryptography. Since the first white-box implementation of AES published twenty years ago [13], no major progress has been made in the design of white-box implementations; only CEJO implementations with small encodings and a toy self-equivalence implementation of AES were proposed thus far. In this work we address this challenging problem by proposing the new design framework of implicit implementations, which not only prevent all known generic key-extraction attacks but also can be applied to ARX ciphers for the first time.

Outline. In Sect. 2 the notation and the preliminaries are introduced. Implicit implementations are presented in Sect. 3, and their security is analysed in Sect. 4. In Sect. 5 we propose a method to obtain self-equivalences based on a low-degree CCZ-equivalent function, and we show the results of this method applied to the permuted modular addition. We then describe an implicit implementation of a

---

[3] https://github.com/ranea/whiteboxarx.

generic ARX cipher in Sect. 6, together with its security analysis and the tool to generate implicit implementations of ARX ciphers. Section 7 presents the conclusions and future work.

2 Preliminaries

Let $\mathbb{F}_2^n$ be the vector space with n-bit values. We denote the addition in $\mathbb{F}_2^n$ by $\oplus$, and the function representing the addition by a constant k by $\oplus_k : x \mapsto x \oplus k$. The identity function in $\mathbb{F}_2^n$ is denoted by Id_n. Functions from $\mathbb{F}_2^n$ to $\mathbb{F}_2^m$ will be called (n, m)-bit functions or just n-bit functions if $m = n$. Given two functions F and G, their composition is denoted by $F \circ G$ and their concatenation by $(F, G)(x, y) = (F(x), G(y))$.

The degree of an (n, m)-bit function F refers in this paper to the algebraic degree of F, that is, the maximum polynomial degree of the m multivariate polynomials uniquely representing the coordinate Boolean functions of F. A function F is affine if its algebraic degree is 1, and it is linear if, in addition, $F(0) = 0$. A non-linear function is a function with algebraic degree greater than or equal to 2. In particular, functions with algebraic degree 2, 3, and 4 are called quadratic, cubic and quartic functions respectively.

In this paper, functions are denoted by capital letters (e.g., F, G), elements of $\mathbb{F}_2^n$ by lowercase letters (e.g., x, y) and sets of functions by calligraphic letters (e.g., $\mathcal{F}, \mathcal{G}$).

2.1 Implicit Functions, Self-equivalences and Graph Automorphisms

In this section we will introduce the three main ingredients of our new design of white-box implementations: implicit functions, self-equivalences, and graph automorphisms.

Let F be an n-bit function. A $(2n, m)$-bit function P is called an *implicit function of F* if it satisfies

$$P(x, y) = 0 \iff y = F(x).$$

Moreover, the n-bit variable vectors x and y will be called the *input* and *output variable vectors*, respectively.

For example, $P(x, y) = y \oplus F(x)$ is an implicit function for any F. An implicit function can also be defined as a function that implicitly defines the graph of a function. Let $\Gamma_F = \{(x, F(x)) : x \in \mathbb{F}_2^n\}$ be the graph of an n-bit function F. Then, P is an implicit function of F if and only if $\Gamma_F = \{(x, y) : P(x, y) = 0\}$. The next lemma describes how the composition of functions translates to their implicit functions and their graphs.

Lemma 1. *Let P be a $(2n, m)$-bit implicit function of an n-bit function F, (A, B) be a pair of n-bit permutations, U be a $2n$-bit permutation and V be an m-bit permutation with $V(0) = 0$.*

(i) $P' = P \circ (A, B^{-1})$ is an implicit function of $F' = B \circ F \circ A$.

(ii) $V \circ P$ is an implicit function of F.

(iii) $U(\Gamma_F) = \{U(x, F(x)) : x \in \mathbb{F}_2^n\}$ is implicitly defined by $P \circ U^{-1}$, that is,

$$U(\Gamma_F) = \{(x', y') : (P \circ U^{-1})(x', y') = 0\}.$$

Proof. The first two statements follows from the definition of P,

$$\big(V \circ P \circ (A, B^{-1})\big)(x, y) = 0 \iff P(A(x), B^{-1}(y)) = V^{-1}(0) = 0$$
$$\iff B^{-1}(y) = F(A(x)) \iff y = B(F(A(x))),$$

and similarly for the last statement,

$$U(\Gamma_F) = \{U(x, y) : P(x, y) = 0\} = \left\{(x', y') : \begin{array}{l} (x', y') = U(x, y) \\ P(x, y) = 0 \end{array}\right\}. \qquad \square$$

In other words, applying a permutation A to the input of F and a permutation B to the output of F corresponds to applying (A, B^{-1}) to the input of an implicit function of F. Moreover, applying any permutation V with the fixed point 0 to an implicit function of F leads to another implicit function of F. The third statement of Lemma 1 shows that applying a permutation U to the points of the graph of F leads to the set of points defined by an implicit function of F composed with the inverse of U.

A *self-equivalence* of a function F is a pair of permutations (A, B) such that $F = B \circ F \circ A$. If (A, B) is a self-equivalence of F, we say that A (resp. B) is a right (resp. left) self-equivalence of F. Moreover, if A and B are affine (resp. linear), we say that (A, B) is an *affine (resp. linear) self-equivalence*. In this work we also consider non-linear self-equivalences; if A is affine and B is quadratic we say that (A, B) is an *affine-quadratic self-equivalence*.

The set of self-equivalences forms a group with respect to the composition, and the subsets of affine and linear self-equivalences are subgroups respectively [19, 25]. Moreover, given a function F and two permutations C and D, the self-equivalence groups of F and $D \circ F \circ C$ are conjugates, that is,

$$(A, B) \text{ is a self-equivalence of } F \iff$$
$$\big(C^{-1} \circ A \circ C, D \circ B \circ D^{-1}\big) \text{ is a self-equivalence of } D \circ F \circ C.$$

A *graph automorphism*[4] of F is a permutation U such that $\Gamma_F = U(\Gamma_F)$. It is easy to show that the set of graph automorphisms is a group with respect to the composition, and its restriction to affine permutations is also a subgroup. The next lemma shows the relation among implicit functions, self-equivalences and graph automorphisms.

Lemma 2. *Let P be an implicit function of F. If (U, V) is a self-equivalence of P with $V(0) = 0$, then U is a graph automorphism of F. Moreover, (A, B) is a self-equivalence of F if and only if $U(x, y) = (A(x), B^{-1}(y))$ is a graph automorphism of F.*

---

[4] Self-equivalences are sometimes called automorphisms in the literature, but in this paper we only use the term automorphism to refer to a graph automorphism.

Proof. From Lemma 1, we have that $P' = V \circ P$ is an implicit function of F. Moreover,

$$0 = (P' \circ U)(x, y) \iff 0 = V(0) = V(P(U(x,y))) = P(x,y) \iff y = F(x).$$

Thus, $P' \circ U$ is an implicit function of F and from Lemma 1, $U^{-1}(\Gamma_F) = \Gamma_F$. Since the set of graph automorphisms is a group, U is also a graph automorphism of F.

To prove the last statement, let A, B and U be three permutations and let P be an implicit function of F. For the forward direction, note that if (A, B) is a self-equivalence of F, then

$$(P \circ (A, B^{-1}))(x, y) = 0 \iff y = B(F(A(x))) = F(x).$$

In other words, $P \circ (A, B^{-1})$ is another implicit function of F. Reasoning as in the previous case, $U = (A, B^{-1})$ is a graph automorphism of F. For the other direction, if $U = (A, B^{-1})$ is a graph automorphism of F, then $P \circ U^{-1}$ and $P \circ U$ are implicit functions of F (Lemma 1), which proves

$$y = F(x) \iff (P \circ (A, B^{-1}))(x, y) = 0 \iff y = B(F(A(x))). \qquad \square$$

In other words, the self-equivalences of a function F and some right self-equivalences of their implicit functions can be embedded in the group of graph automorphisms of F. In general, the group of graph automorphisms of F contains more elements, and some of them do not correspond to self-equivalences of F or self-equivalences of an implicit function of F. The next lemma shows that a function can have multiple implicit functions; its proof is straightforward from Lemmas 1 and 2.

Lemma 3. *Let P be an implicit function of F. If V is a permutation with $V(0) = 0$ and U is a graph automorphism of F, then $V \circ P \circ U$ is an implicit function of F.*

2.2 Encoded Implementations

Given an n-bit iterated block cipher, we denote the encryption function for a fixed key k by $E_k = E_{k^{(n_r)}}^{(n_r)} \circ E_{k^{(n_r-1)}}^{(n_r-1)} \circ \cdots \circ E_{k^{(1)}}^{(1)}$, where $E_{k^{(i)}}^{(i)}$ denotes the ith round function and $k^{(i)}$ denotes the ith round key. For ease of notation, we omit the round-key subscript of the round functions.

CEJO and self-equivalence implementations can be seen as encoded implementations, a class of white-box implementations based on the notion of encoding.

Definition 1 ([13]). *Let F be an (n, m)-bit function and let (I, O) be a pair of n-bit and m-bit permutations, respectively. The function $\overline{F} = O \circ F \circ I$ is called an encoded F with input and output encodings I and O, respectively.*

Definition 2 ([34]). *Let* $E_k = E^{(n_r)} \circ E^{(n_r-1)} \circ \cdots \circ E^{(1)}$ *be the encryption function of an iterated n-bit block cipher with fixed key k. An encoded (white-box) implementation of E_k is an encoded E_k composed of encoded round functions, that is,*

$$\overline{E_k} = \overline{E^{(n_r)}} \circ \cdots \circ \overline{E^{(1)}} = (O^{(n_r)} \circ E^{(n_r)} \circ I^{(n_r)}) \circ \cdots \circ (O^{(1)} \circ E^{(1)} \circ I^{(1)}),$$

where the round encodings $(I^{(1)}, O^{(1)}), (I^{(2)}, O^{(2)}), \ldots, (I^{(n_r)}, O^{(n_r)})$ *are n-bit permutation pairs s.t.* $I^{(i+1)} = (O^{(i)})^{-1}$ *for* $i = 1, 2, \ldots, n_r - 1$.

In other words, an encoded implementation is the composition of encoded round functions where the intermediate round encodings are cancelled out. Thus, $\overline{E_k}$ can also be written as $\overline{E_k} = O^{(n_r)} \circ E_k \circ I^{(1)}$, where the encodings $(I^{(1)}, O^{(n_r)})$ are also called the *external encodings*.

Definition 2 only considers round encodings satisfying the cancellation rule $I^{(i+1)} = (O^{(i)})^{-1}$. However, in this paper we extend the definition of round encodings of an encoded implementation to any n-bit permutations pairs $(I^{(1)}, O^{(1)}), (I^{(2)}, O^{(2)}), \ldots, (I^{(n_r)}, O^{(n_r)})$ that satisfy the cancellation rule

$$\overline{E^{(i+1)}} \circ \overline{E^{(i)}} \circ \overline{E^{(i-1)}} = O^{(i+1)} \circ E^{(i+1)} \circ E^{(i)} \circ E^{(i-1)} \circ I^{(i-1)} \tag{1}$$

for $i = 2, 3, \ldots, n_r - 2$. In Sect. 6 we will describe an example of round encodings satisfying the general cancellation rule given by Eq. (1) but not the cancellation rule $I^{(i+1)} = (O^{(i)})^{-1}$.

3   Implicit White-Box Implementations

In this section we present implicit implementations, a new class of white-box implementations of iterated block ciphers. The main idea of implicit implementations is to represent the high-degree round function of the cipher by a quasilinear implicit function of low degree.

Definition 3. *A $(2n, m)$-bit implicit function P is quasilinear if for all $x \in \mathbb{F}_2^n$ the (n, m)-bit function $y \mapsto P(x, y)$ is affine.*

Informally, an implicit function is quasilinear if it is affine in the output variable vector. For any function F, a trivial quasilinear implicit function is $P(x, y) = y \oplus F(x)$. An example of a non-trivial quasilinear implicit function is the quadratic implicit function $P(x, y) = (x(xy+1), y(xy+1))$ of the finite field inversion over $\mathbb{F}_{2^n}$, i.e., $F(x) = x^{2^n-2}$.

The quasilinear property is necessary to make the implicit evaluation of F practical. Since a quasilinear implicit function becomes an affine function when the input variable vector x is fixed to a constant x_0, one can *implicitly* evaluate $F(x_0)$ by solving the affine system $P(x_0, y) = 0$ for y. Since the affine system $P(x_0, y) = 0$ has a unique y solution due to the definition of an implicit function, a $(2n, m)$-bit quasilinear implicit function of an n-bit function has at least n Boolean components $(m \geq n)$.

With the notions of encoding, implicit and quasilinear function previously defined, we can now present implicit white-box implementations.

Definition 4. *Let $E_k = E^{(n_r)} \circ E^{(n_r-1)} \circ \cdots \circ E^{(1)}$ be the encryption function of an iterated n-bit block cipher with fixed key k, and let $\overline{E_k} = \overline{E^{(n_r)}} \circ \overline{E^{(n_r-1)}} \circ \cdots \circ \overline{E^{(1)}}$ be an encoded implementation of E_k. An implicit (white-box) implementation of $\overline{E_k}$ is a set of quasilinear implicit functions $\{P^{(1)}, P^{(2)}, \ldots, P^{(n_r)}\}$ where $P^{(i)}$ is an implicit function of $\overline{E^{(i)}}$.*

In other words, an implicit implementation is an alternative representation of an encoded implementation where the high-degree encoded round functions are given by low-degree implicit functions.

An implicit implementation is evaluated by implicitly evaluating the encoded round functions. Thus, given the output x_0 of the round $i-1$, the output y of the ith round is computed by finding the solution of the affine system $P^{(i)}(x_0, y) = 0$ for y. Note that an implicit implementation has the same input-output behaviour as its underlying encoded implementation.

The external encodings of an implicit implementation refer to the external encodings of its underlying encoded implementation. In this we work we focus on implicit implementations with non-trivial external[5] encodings.

The size of an implicit implementation mainly depends on the degree of the implicit encoded round functions $P^{(i)}$, which are implemented as binary multivariate polynomials. If the $(2n, m)$-bit functions $P^{(i)}$ have degree d, each one has at most

$$\sum_{i=0}^{d} \binom{n}{i} + n \sum_{i=0}^{d-1} \binom{n}{i}$$

coefficients, and thus the size of an implicit implementation is $\mathcal{O}(n^d)$. The running time of an implicit implementation is dominated by obtaining each affine system, by iterating over the monomials, in $\mathcal{O}(n^d)$ and by solving each affine system with Gaussian elimination in $\mathcal{O}(m^3)$.

3.1   Quasilinear Implicit Round Functions

While it is known how to obtain low-degree implicit functions of small S-boxes [21] and power mappings [7], obtaining a low-degree quasilinear implicit function of an arbitrary function (if it exists) is a hard problem. We will see how we can derive a low-degree quasilinear implicit function of the whole round function from a known low-degree quasilinear implicit function of the non-linear layer.

---

[5] It is worth to mention that all known white-box implementations of existing ciphers that do not rely on secret designs include external encodings in their designs. While external encodings impose severe limitations on the applicability of the white-box implementation, it is currently the only alternative to secret designs.

Assume the encoded ith round function is of the form

$$\overline{E^{(i)}} = O^{(i)} \circ (L \circ S \circ \oplus_{k^{(i)}}) \circ I^{(i)},$$

where L is an affine permutation also called the linear layer, S is a non-linear permutation also called the non-linear layer, $k^{(i)}$ is the round key and $(I^{(i)}, O^{(i)})$ are the round encodings with $O^{(i)}$ being affine. Note that this approach to obtain a quasilinear implicit function of the ith round function applies to all rounds $i = 1, 2, \ldots, n_r$, and thus the affine restriction also applies to the external output encoding.

The output encoding $O^{(i)}$ needs to be affine for the quasilinear property, but there is no degree restriction on $I^{(i)}$. The degree of $I^{(i)}$ can be different from the degree of $O^{(i)}$ if the round encodings satisfy the cancellation rule given in Eq. (1) rather than the one from Definition 2. For example, in Sect. 6 we describe an implicit implementation with quadratic input encodings and affine output encodings.

Given a known quasilinear implicit function T of S and by applying Lemma 1, we can obtain a quasilinear implicit function of $\overline{E^{(i)}}$ as

$$T \circ (\oplus_{k^{(i)}}, L^{-1}) \circ (I^{(i)}, (O^{(i)})^{-1}).$$

Note that the left composition by affine functions and the right composition by diagonal functions $A(x, y) = (A_1(x), A_2(y)))$ with A_2 affine preserves the quasilinear property.

Moreover, we can replace the known implicit function of S with a different implicit function by applying Lemma 3. In particular, if V is a linear permutation and U is an affine graph automorphism of S that preserves the quasilinear property (i.e., $T \circ U$ is quasilinear), then $V \circ T \circ U$ is another quasilinear implicit function of S. However, U should not be a right self-equivalence of T to prevent U from being cancelled. That is, if U is a right self-equivalence of T, then $V \circ T \circ U = V' \circ T$ for some V' affine.

To conclude, given a quasilinear implicit function T of the non-linear layer S, we can build a quasilinear implicit function $P^{(i)}$ of the encoded round function $\overline{E^{(i)}} = O^{(i)} \circ (L \circ S \circ \oplus_{k^{(i)}}) \circ I^{(i)}$ by sampling a linear permutation $V^{(i)}$ and a quasilinear-preserving graph automorphism $U^{(i)}$ that is not a right self-equivalence of T, obtaining

$$P^{(i)} = V^{(i)} \circ T \circ U^{(i)} \circ (\oplus_{k^{(i)}}, L^{-1}) \circ (I^{(i)}, (O^{(i)})^{-1}). \tag{2}$$

Figure 1 depicts a representation of $\overline{E^{(i)}}$ and $P^{(i)}$.

From Eq. (2) it is easy to see that degree of $P^{(i)}$ only depends on the degree of T and the degree of the input encoding $I^{(i)}$, since the other functions are either linear or affine. The function T at least has degree 2 and n components if S is an n-bit non-linear function. Thus, we can consider affine or quadratic $I^{(i)}$ to build a practical implicit implementation.

Whereas CEJO or self-equivalence implementations impose severe restrictions on the encodings, an implicit implementation can use large affine or quad-

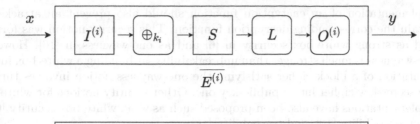

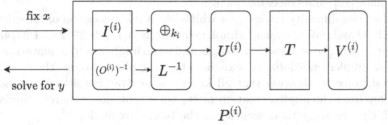

Fig. 1. An encoded round function $\overline{E^{(i)}}$ (top) given by the round function $(L \circ S \circ \oplus_{k(i)})$ and the round encodings $(I^{(i)}, O^{(i)})$, and an implicit function $P^{(i)}$ (bottom) of $\overline{E^{(i)}}$, where T is an implicit function of the non-linear layer S, $U^{(i)}$ is a graph automorphism of S and $V^{(i)}$ is a linear permutation.

ratic encodings and have a practical[6] size and running time. As we will see in the next section, these encodings are the reason why implicit implementations prevent the white-box attacks that break CEJO or self-equivalence implementations.

4   Security Analysis

In this section, we analyse the security of implicit implementations against key-extraction attacks in the white-box model, where it is assumed that the specifications of the block cipher and the specifications of the implicit implementation are public, and the attacker is in possession of an implicit implementation but does not know the encodings or the key.

The security objective to resist key-extraction attacks in the white-box model was proposed by Chow et al. in their seminar work [13], and properly defined by Delerablée et al. as the unbreakability security notion [16]. For simplicity, in this work we will use the informal security objective of key-extraction resistance from [13], but we refer the reader to [16] for the complete definition of the unbreakability notion.

Key-extraction resistance or unbreakability is the minimum security goal a white-box implementation should aim for. In many applications, a white-box

---

[6] We will provide specific numbers for the size of an example of an implicit implementation in Sect. 6.

implementation of an encryption function should also prevent an attacker to obtain the corresponding decryption function. This security notion was formalized as strong white-box security in [6] and as one-wayness in [16]. However, one-wayness is much stronger than unbreakability, as building a white-box implementation of a block cipher satisfying the one-wayness notion involves turning the secret-key cipher into a public-key one. Other security notions for white-box implementations have also been proposed such as weak white-box security [6] or incompressibility [16], and traceability [16].

Due to the huge difficulty to design a white-box implementation of an existing cipher, CEJO and self-equivalence implementations [3,14,23,26–28,34,37,43] only aim at preventing key-extraction attacks and so do implicit implementations.

White-box implementations of existing block ciphers argue their key-extraction resistance by showing that all known key-extraction attacks cannot recover the key from the implementation faster than brute-force search, similar as how block ciphers argue their security in the black-box model.

4.1   Previous Generic Attacks

In this section we will show that all known generic key-extraction attacks, that is, key-extraction attacks to white-box implementations that do not exploit specific properties of the underlying ciphers, cannot recover the key from a generic implicit implementation if quadratic round input encodings are used or the non-linear layer is not composed of smaller S-boxes.

Note that showing that implicit implementations prevent all known generic key-extraction attacks is not sufficient to claim that a specific implicit implementation of a particular cipher is secure for two reasons. First, since the implicit framework is a new method, previous generic attacks were not designed to break implicit implementations. Thus, further research on new generic attacks targeting the implicit framework is needed. Second, for a specific implicit implementation of a particular cipher one still needs to check key-extraction attacks exploiting properties of the underlying cipher. Despite these two remarks, the fact that implicit implementations prevent all known generic key-extraction attacks is noteworthy as all CEJO and self-equivalence implementations have been broken even with generic attacks.

CEJO Attacks. The first generic attack that we will consider is the reduction subroutine that transforms the encodings of a CEJO implementation to self-equivalence encodings. This subroutine was proposed in [34] and combines the three generic CEJO attacks proposed in [3,17,29]; showing that the reduction subroutine does not succeed implies that neither the three generic CEJO attacks do.

Since the reduction subroutine only requires black-box access to three consecutive encoded rounds, it can be applied to an implicit implementation. For an implicit implementation where the non-linear part of the round encodings is composed of m_{nl}-bit functions and the non-linear layer of the underlying cipher is composed of m_s-bit S-boxes, the complexity of the reduction subroutine is roughly $\mathcal{O}(2^{\max(3m_{nl}, m_s)})$ (Proposition 1 of [34]). For example, the reduction subroutine is efficient for an implicit implementation of AES ($m_s = 8$) with affine round encodings. However, the reduction subroutine is not efficient if the implicit implementation uses non-linear encodings or if the non-linear layer of the cipher is not composed of small S-boxes.

The CEJO framework cannot implement large non-linear encodings or such a non-linear layer due to its impractical size; a CEJO implementation requires roughly $\mathcal{O}(2^{\max(2m_{nl}, m_s)})$ bits of memory for each round [3]. On the other hand, the implicit framework can provide practical implementations under these constraints; the size of an implicit implementation is exponential in the degree of the implicit round functions, and not on the bitsize of the encodings or the non-linear layer. An example of a practical implicit implementation with large non-linear encodings and where the non-linear layer is composed of a single S-box will be described in Sect. 6.

Self-equivalence Attacks. The generic attack to self-equivalence implementations proposed in [34] cannot be applied to implicit implementations since it requires access to encoded affine layers where the round encodings are self-equivalences of the non-linear layer. However, implicit implementations use random affine permutations for the round encodings, and the affine layer of the cipher is merged with the non-linear layer in the implicit round functions. Moreover, this attack also assumes the non-linear layer is composed of small S-boxes.

Self-equivalence implementations might also be vulnerable if the self-equivalences of the non-linear layer are very structured, such as having the same coefficient in some monomial terms for all self-equivalences. In this case, some coefficients in the encoded affine layers might directly leak coefficients from the round encodings or even bits from the round keys. Self-equivalence implementations of ciphers where the non-linear layer is the permuted modular addition exhibit this weakness, since the self-equivalences of the permuted modular addition have a common sparse shape and low-entropy constant vectors as we will see in Sect. 5.2. Implicit implementations do not exhibit this weakness since the round encodings use random and large affine permutations.

Automated White-Box Attacks. For white-box implementations not relying on external encodings but on secret designs, several automated white-box attacks have been proposed such as Differential Computational Analysis (DCA) or Differential Fault Analysis (DFA) [4,10,35]. These attacks easily break CEJO implementations in a fully automated way, but they assume the external encodings are the identity functions. The only automated attack successful against non-trivial external encodings is a DFA attack by Amadori et al. [2] to a CEJO implementation of AES where the external output encoding is the composition of 8-bit functions.

Since the implicit framework uses at least large affine permutations for the external encodings, current automated attacks cannot be applied to generic implicit implementations. On top of that, these attacks usually target an intermediate computation where the output is encoded with an small function and depends on a few key bits. However, in implicit implementations the only computations are evaluations of polynomials with large inputs and large encodings, and the outputs of these computations depend on the whole round keys. Finding new automated attacks to implicit implementations is an interesting challenge that we leave as future work.

4.2   Reducing Implicit Implementations to Self-equivalence Implementations

We have shown that implicit implementations that use non-linear encodings or where the non-linear layer of the cipher is not composed of small S-boxes are secure against all known generic key-extraction attacks[7]. For the rest of this section, we will describe a new generic attack for implicit implementations.

The crucial step in most generic key-extraction attacks on encoded implementations is the reduction subroutine, that is, obtaining new encoded rounds with the same round key material but with simpler encodings [34]. Thus, we will not describe a complete key-extraction attack but a reduction subroutine that transforms an implicit implementation to a self-equivalence implementation, similar to the reduction subroutine from [34].

The reasons to consider a reduction to a self-equivalence implementation are three-fold. First, we will see that the self-equivalences of the non-linear layer play an important role in the security of implicit implementations, similar as in self-equivalence implementations. Second, if an implicit implementation is reduced to a self-equivalence one, then the generic attack to self-equivalence implementations [34] can be applied. Third, since a self-equivalence implementation is more efficient than an implicit one, an implicit implementation that can be reduced to a self-equivalence one does not provide any advantage.

Note that both CEJO and self-equivalence implementations can be transformed efficiently into an implicit one. First, any CEJO implementation can be transformed into a self-equivalence one using the techniques from [34]. Second, a self-equivalence implementation can be transformed into an implicit one simply by composing the encoded affine layers with the implicit function of the non-linear layer.

For our reduction subroutine, we will consider an intermediate round of an implicit implementation. Let $E = L \circ S \circ \oplus_k$ be an intermediate round function, $\overline{E} = O \circ E \circ I$ be an encoded function of E, and

$$P = U \circ T \circ V \circ (\oplus_k, L^{-1}) \circ (I, O^{-1})$$

be an implicit function of $\overline{E}$, as defined in Eq. (2). For simplicity, we will drop the round index i. We will assume that the round key k, the encodings I and O,

[7] While not the focus of this work, it is worth mentioning that this type of implicit implementations with trivial external encodings seems less vulnerable than CEJO or self-equivalences implementations with trivial external encodings.

and the functions U and V are unknown to the adversary, but the linear layer L, the non-linear layer S, the implicit function T of S and the implicit function P are known.

The first step in most reduction subroutines is to solve a functional equation involving the round encodings. For an implicit implementation, the adversary can consider the two following functional equations:

$$P = Y \circ T \circ X \tag{3}$$
$$\overline{E} = Y \circ (L \circ S) \circ X. \tag{4}$$

In Eq. (3), P and T are fully known, X is an unknown permutation with the same degree as I and Y is an unknown linear permutation. In Eq. (4), $(L \circ S)$ is fully known, $\overline{E}$ can only be evaluated implicitly, X is an unknown permutation with the same degree as I and Y is an unknown affine permutation.

When the unknowns X and Y are affine permutations, this type of functional equations has received multiple names in the literature: the affine equivalence [8], the Isomorphism of Polynomials (IP) [31] or the affine-substitution-affine (ASA) [6,30] problems. Most algorithms to solve affine equivalence problems exploit the particular structure of the central map. For example: (1) if T is a triangular function, the structural attack by [42] can solve Eq. (3) in polynomial time; (2) for many quadratic T, Gröbner-based attacks have solved Eq. (3) in polynomial time [19]; or (3) if S is composed of small m_s-bit S-boxes, the algorithm by Derbez et al. can solve Eq. (4) in about $\mathcal{O}(2^{2m_s})$ [17].

When the unknown X is a non-linear permutation, this type of functional equations has been less studied in the literature, but some efficient algorithms have been proposed for particular quadratic central maps. Some examples are attacks on public-key schemes with 2 rounds [32], attacks on the ASASA structure [30] or attacks based on the decomposition of multivariate polynomials [20]. For the rest of the attack we will assume that I and X are affine permutations and we will leave the non-linear case for future work.

Obtaining any solution of Eq. (4) allows the reduction from the implicit round function into an encoded affine layer. An arbitrary solution of Eq. (4) for (X, Y) is of the form

$$(A \circ (\oplus_k \circ I), O \circ B),$$

where (A, B) is an affine self-equivalence of $L \circ S$. By combining a solution of that round and of the previous round, one can easily derive an encoded affine layer of that round. Repeating this process for all rounds leads to a complete reduction to a self-equivalence implementation.

On the other hand, not all the solutions of Eq. (3) allow the reduction to an encoded affine layer. Every solution (X, Y) of Eq. (3) is of the form

$$\left(A \circ (U \circ (\oplus_k, L^{-1}) \circ (I, O^{-1})), V \circ B\right),$$

where (A, B) is an affine self-equivalence of T. If (X, Y) is a solution with X diagonal (i.e., $X(x, y) = (X_1(x), X_2(y))$) and Y linear, then $A \circ U$ is diagonal and contains a self-equivalence of S by Lemma 2. Therefore, by combining two solutions of this form for that round and the previous round respectively, an adversary can easily build an encoded affine layer for that round.

As a result, an implicit implementation with affine encodings must ensure that no solution of Eq. (4) can be obtained efficiently. Previously, we showed that an implicit implementation with affine encodings of a cipher with small S-boxes is vulnerable to the reduction subroutine of [34]. Similarly, such an implicit implementation is also vulnerable to this reduction attack as Eq. (4) can be solved by the algorithm of Derbez et al. [17].

Moreover, an implicit implementation with affine encodings must also ensure that no solution (X, Y) with X diagonal and Y linear of Eq. (3) can be obtained efficiently. In particular, if an adversary can obtain efficiently a random solution (X, Y), then the adversary can always try all (A, B) and all U until $X' = U^{-1} \circ A^{-1} \circ X$ is diagonal and $Y' = Y \circ B^{-1}$ affine; an encoded affine layer can easily be derived from (X', Y') afterwards. Thus, the number of affine self-equivalences (A, B) of T and the number of quasilinear-preserving graph automorphisms U that are not self-equivalences of T such be large enough to prevent an exhaustive search.

Our generic reduction subroutine provides insightful requirements for an implicit implementation with affine encodings, but it also leaves several open problems, such as estimating the complexity to obtain a solution of Eq. (4) for a generic implicit implementation or analysing the case where the input encoding is non-linear. Our generic reduction did not cover either the case where additional countermeasures are added to the implicit implementation. In particular, the representation of the implicit round functions as systems of multivariate Boolean polynomials allows applying countermeasures from multivariate public-key cryptosystems (MPKC) such as adding extra variables [24], adding or removing equations [33] or adding perturbations [18]. Understanding the security provided by the implicit framework requires further research, but our generic reduction subroutine together with the algorithms that we mentioned to solve Eqs. (3) and (4) can be used as starting point.

In the next section we will describe the self-equivalences of the modular addition in order to later propose an implicit implementation of a cipher with modular addition as the non-linear layer.

5   Self-equivalences of Modular Addition

In this section we describe a new method to compute self-equivalences of a function from a CCZ-equivalent function of low degree. We applied this method to the permuted modular addition $(x, x') \mapsto (x \boxplus x', x')$, obtaining for the first time the self-equivalences of this operation for wordsize $n \leq 64$. The permuted modular addition is frequently used in the non-linear layers of block ciphers, and we focus on this operation to propose in the next section an implicit implementation of a cipher using the permuted modular addition. However, our new method is of independent interest, and it can also be applied to the non-permuted modular addition or other functions CCZ-equivalent to low-degree functions.

5.1 Computing Self-equivalences from a CCZ-Equivalent Function

CCZ-equivalence is an equivalence relation between functions based on their graphs. It was introduced in [12] by Carlet, Charpin and Zinoviev, and named after these authors.

Definition 5. *A function F is CCZ-equivalent to a function G if the graph of F can be transformed to the graph of G through an affine permutation, that is, if there exists an affine permutation $L_{G,F}$ such that $\Gamma_F = L_{G,F}(\Gamma_G)$.*

To obtain the self-equivalences of a high-degree function F that is CCZ-equivalent to a low-degree function G, the core of this method is to compute a subset of graph automorphisms of G by solving a system of low-degree equations. Our method exploits the relation between the graph automorphisms of two CCZ-equivalent functions and the functional equation that characterizes a graph automorphism, shown in the next two lemmas.

Lemma 4. *Let F and G be two CCZ-equivalent functions. Then, the graph automorphism groups of F and G are conjugates, that is, U is a graph automorphism of F if and only if $L_{G,F}^{-1} \circ U \circ L_{G,F}$ is a graph automorphism of G.*

Proof. If U is a graph automorphism of F, then

$$\Gamma_G = L_{G,F}^{-1}(\Gamma_F) = (L_{G,F}^{-1} \circ U)(\Gamma_F) = (L_{G,F}^{-1} \circ U \circ L_{G,F})(\Gamma_G),$$

which proves the forward direction of the statement. The backward direction can be proven similarly. □

Lemma 5. *Let G be an n-bit function and let $U(x,y) = (U_1(x,y), U_2(x,y))$ be a $2n$-bit affine permutation. Then U is a graph automorphism of G if and only if U satisfies the functional equation*

$$U_2 \circ (\mathrm{Id}_n, G) = G \circ U_1 \circ (\mathrm{Id}_n, G). \tag{5}$$

Proof. From Lemma 1, for any permutation U one has

$$U^{-1}(\Gamma_G) = \{(x,y) : U_2(x,y) = G(U_1(x,y))\}.$$

If U is a graph automorphism, then $\Gamma_G = U^{-1}(\Gamma_G)$. Therefore, $x = G(y)$ is equivalent to $U_2(x,y) = G(U_1(x,y))$. In particular, we have $U_2(x,G(x)) = G(U_1(x,G(x)))$ for all x, which proves the forward direction.

If $U_2(x,G(x)) = G(U_1(x,G(x)))$ for all x, then $\Gamma_G = \{(x,y) : x = G(y)\}$ is contained in

$$\{(x,y) : U_2(x,y) = G(U_1(x,y))\} = U^{-1}(\Gamma_G).$$

Since U^{-1} is a permutation, Γ_G and $U^{-1}(\Gamma_G)$ have the same cardinality. Therefore, $\Gamma_G = U^{-1}(\Gamma_G)$, which implies that U is a graph automorphism of G. □

Our method consists of computing a set $\mathcal{U}$ of solutions of the functional equation given by Eq. (5) with the additional constraints that U is invertible and that $U' = L_{G,F} \circ U \circ L_{G,F}^{-1}$ is diagonal (i.e., $U'(x,y) = (A(x), B(y))$). To reduce the degree of the invertibility constraint, we impose the invertibility constraint over the diagonal blocks of U' instead of over the entire U. After the set $\mathcal{U}$ is obtained, the self-equivalences of F can be extracted from the set $\mathcal{U}' = \{L_{G,F} \circ U \circ L_{G,F}^{-1} : U \in \mathcal{U}\}$ by applying Lemma 2, that is,

$$U'(x,y) = (A(x), B(y)) \in \mathcal{U}' \iff (A, B^{-1}) \text{ is a self-equivalence of } F.$$

A weaker variant of this method is to compute the affine right self-equivalences U of an implicit function P of G such that $U' = L_{G,F} \circ U \circ L_{G,F}^{-1}$ is diagonal. In this variant, Eq. (5) is replaced by the functional equation $P = V \circ P \circ U$, and a third additional constraint is added to ensure that $V(0) = 0$ (Lemma 2). The advantage of this variant is that the degree of the functional equation is the same as the degree of the implicit function P, while the degree of Eq. (5) is upper bounded by $2 \times \deg(G)$. However, not all the self-equivalences of F might be found if the weaker variant is used, since in general not all the graph automorphisms are right self-equivalences of an implicit function.

To obtain the set $\mathcal{U}$ in either of the two variants, we perform in practice the following three steps. First, we represent the functional equation and the additional constraints by a system of binary equations, perform Gaussian elimination on the system of equations, and then find an small set of solutions (e.g., 2^{20}) of the reduced system of equations with a SAT solver. Given the functional equation LHS = RHS, we build the system of equations by creating the vectorial Boolean function LHS $\oplus$ RHS as a system of multivariate polynomials, and then adding the equation $c = 0$ for each monomial coefficient c of LHS $\oplus$ RHS; the invertibility constraint is added to the system of equations using the determinant expression.

Second, we extract a set of candidate affine relations involving the monomial coefficients of U (seen as system of multivariate polynomials) from the small set of solutions previously obtained. For example, if the sum of two coefficients u_i and u_j is always 0 in all the solutions, we include the candidate affine relation $u_i + u_j = 0$. We call them *candidate* relations since they are satisfied for the small set of solutions but they might not be satisfied by the whole solution set. To find out whether a candidate relation $R = 0$ is satisfied by the whole solution set, we add the complementary relation $R = 1$ to the reduced system of equations previously obtained, and we check whether this new system is unsatisfiable with a SAT solver. If the system is unsatisfiable, then the relation $R = 0$ is satisfied by the whole solution set. We repeat this process for all candidate relations, obtaining a list of affine relations satisfied by the whole solution set.

Third, we build the final system of equations from the reduced system previously obtained by using the affine relations to fix coefficients of U and remove variables from the system. We then use a SAT solver to obtain a small number of solutions (e.g., 2^{20}) of the final system. Finally, we create the set $\mathcal{U}$ from these solutions and the affine relations, and we compute the cardinality of $\mathcal{U}$ by also taking into account the free coefficients of U not appearing in any of the equations of the final system nor in the affine relations. While further modifications and optimizations are possible, this practical approach is suitable for functional equations with sparse and quadratic central maps, such as the CCZ-equivalent function of the permuted modular addition.

Implementation. We have implemented this method in a new open-source library BoolCrypt[8]. Our library is written in Python and uses the library SageMath [39]. In particular, it relies on the PolyBori package of SageMath to create and manipulate binary equations, and on the SAT solver CryptoMiniSat [38] to find the solutions of systems of binary equations. Apart from this method, our library also provides many functionalities related to vectorial Boolean functions, self-equivalences and functional equations. We designed BoolCrypt with a modular structure and we documented it extensively, so that it can be useful and it can be adapted to future works.

5.2   Self-equivalences and Graph Automorphisms of the Permuted Modular Addition

Let $\boxplus$ denote the $(2n, n)$-bit function representing the modular addition with wordsize n, i.e., $x \boxplus x' = x + x' \mod 2^n$. The modular addition has degree $n-1$, but Schulte-Geers proved that it is CCZ-equivalent to a quadratic function [36].

Theorem 1 ([36]). *Let $Q(x, x')$ be the $(2n, n)$-bit quadratic function given by*

$$Q(x, x') = (0, x_0 x'_0, x_0 x'_0 \oplus x_1 x'_1, \ldots, x_0 x'_0 \oplus \cdots \oplus x_{n-2} x'_{n-2}).$$

Then Q is CCZ-equivalent to $\boxplus$, and $\Gamma_\boxplus = L_{Q,\boxplus}(\Gamma_Q)$ where $L_{Q,\boxplus}$ is given by the block matrix

$$L_{Q,\boxplus} = \begin{pmatrix} \mathrm{Id}_n & 0_n & \mathrm{Id}_n \\ 0_n & \mathrm{Id}_n & \mathrm{Id}_n \\ \mathrm{Id}_n & \mathrm{Id}_n & \mathrm{Id}_n \end{pmatrix}.$$

Let Q' be the trivial implicit function of Q given by $Q'(x, x', y) = y \oplus Q(x, x')$. From Theorem 1 and Lemma 1, it is easy to see that

$$(Q' \circ L_{Q,\boxplus}^{-1})(x, x', y) = x \oplus x' \oplus y \oplus Q(x \oplus y, x' \oplus y) \tag{6}$$

is a quadratic implicit function of the modular addition.

The modular addition is mostly used in block ciphers in its permuted variant, $S(x, x') = (x \boxplus x', x')$, and this latter function is the focus of our work. The next lemma shows that a right self-equivalence of the permuted modular addition S is also a left self-equivalence up to the addition of some constants.

Lemma 6. *The permutation A is a right self-equivalence of S if and only if $\oplus_{(c_1, c_0)} \circ A \circ \oplus_{(c_1, c_0)}$ is a left self-equivalence of S, where c_0 and c_1 denote the n-bit values $(0, 0, \ldots, 0)$ and $(1, 1, \ldots, 1)$ respectively.*

[8] https://github.com/ranea/BoolCrypt.

Proof. The inverse of the permuted modular addition is $S^{-1}(x, x') = (x \boxminus x', x')$, where $\boxminus = x - x' \bmod 2^n$. Since the modular subtraction $\boxminus$ verifies $c_1 \oplus (x \boxminus y) = ((x \oplus c_1) \boxplus y)$ [22], we have the relation $S^{-1} = \oplus_{(c_1, c_0)} \circ S \circ \oplus_{(c_1, c_0)}$.

On the other hand, if (A, B) is a self-equivalence of S, then $S = B \circ S \circ A$, or equivalently $S^{-1} = A^{-1} \circ S^{-1} \circ B^{-1}$. By applying the previous relation and moving some terms, we have that

$$S = (\oplus_{(c_1, c_0)} \circ A^{-1} \circ \oplus_{(c_1, c_0)}) \circ S \circ (\oplus_{(c_1, c_0)} \circ B^{-1} \circ \oplus_{(c_1, c_0)}).$$

Since the set of self-equivalences is a group, the inverse of $(\oplus_{(c_1, c_0)} \circ A^{-1} \circ \oplus_{(c_1, c_0)})$ is also a left self-equivalence of S, which proves the forward direction of the statement. The other direction can be proven similarly. □

From Eq. (6) and Theorem 1, it is easy to show that the $(2n, 2n)$-bit function $x, x' \mapsto (Q(x, x'), x')$ is CCZ-equivalent to the permuted modular addition S and that the following function is a quadratic implicit function of S:

$$T(x, x', y, y') = (x \oplus x' \oplus y \oplus Q(x \oplus y, x' \oplus y), x' \oplus y'). \tag{7}$$

Using the CCZ-equivalent quadratic function of the permuted[9] modular addition, we applied our method implemented in `BoolCrypt` to obtain the affine and linear self-equivalences for multiple wordsizes n. First, we obtained all the affine and linear self-equivalences for the wordsizes $n \in \{2, 3, 4, 5\}$, for which we could solve Eq. (5) directly. For $n = 2$ we obtained 3×2^{10} affine and 3×2^8 linear self-equivalences, and for $n \in \{3, 4, 5\}$ we obtained $3 \times 2^{2n+8}$ affine and $3 \times 2^{2n+2}$ linear self-equivalences, respectively. For verification purposes, we also ran the affine and linear equivalence algorithms by Biryukov et al. [8], and we obtained the same number of linear and affine self-equivalences. In Appendix A we fully describe the affine self-equivalence groups for $n = 4$.

For $n \geq 6$, we could not directly solve Eq. (5). However, we noticed that the right (and by Lemma 6 also the left) affine self-equivalences for the small wordsizes have a common sparse matrix shape:

$$\left(\begin{array}{cccc|cccc} \star & & & & \star & & & \\ \star & 1 & & & \star & & & \\ \vdots & & \ddots & & \vdots & & & \\ \star & & & 1 & \star & & & \\ \star & & & \star\ 1 & \star\ \star\ \ldots\ \star\ \star & & & \\ \star & & & & \star & & & \\ \star & & & & \star & 1 & & \\ \vdots & & & & \vdots & & \ddots & \\ \star & & & & \star & & & 1 \\ \star & & & & \star & & & \star\ 1 \end{array}\right),$$

---

[9] The self-equivalence group of the permuted modular addition cannot be derived from that of the modular addition, as the permuted variant contains many non-diagonal self-equivalences.

where each of the four blocks denote an n-bit binary matrix, the $\star$ denotes a coefficient that can take the value 0 or 1 and empty spaces denote zero coefficients. In the constant vector of the affine self-equivalences we also noticed a common shape where one value b was repeated in all but 6 positions:

$$(\overbrace{\star\, b\, \cdots\, b\, \star\, \star}^{n}\,|\,\star\, b\, \cdots\, b\, \star\, \star).$$

To make Eq. (5) easier to solve, we pre-emptively fixed some coefficients of U to enforce that the resulting self-equivalences have the previous shape. Thus, we applied our method with wordsizes $n \in \{6, 7, \ldots, 64\}$ and we obtained a subset of affine (resp. linear) self-equivalences with cardinality $3 \times 2^{2n+8}$ (resp. $3 \times 2^{2n+2}$). Note that for $n = 64$ this method takes only a few minutes to obtain these subsets of self-equivalences. Since the number $3 \times 2^{2n+8}$ (resp. $3 \times 2^{2n+2}$) is the cardinality of the whole affine (resp. linear) self-equivalence group for $n \in \{3, 4, 5\}$ and a lower bound of this cardinality for $6 \leq n \leq 64$, we conjecture that the total number of affine (resp. linear) self-equivalences for any wordsize $n \geq 3$ is $3 \times 2^{2n+8}$ (resp. $3 \times 2^{2n+2}$).

Using our method and our library BoolCrypt, we also obtained affine-quadratic self-equivalences (A, B) of the permuted modular addition, that is, with A affine and B quadratic. Affine-quadratic self-equivalences can be used for quadratic input encodings and affine output encodings of implicit implementations, as we will see in the next section. We first computed all affine-quadratic self-equivalences for the small wordsizes $n \in \{2, 4\}$. We obtained $19 \times 3^2 \times 2^{10} - 3 \times 2^{10}$ affine-quadratic self-equivalences for $n = 2$, and $3^2 \times 2^{3n+14} - 3 \times 2^{2n+8}$ for $n = 4$. Our method returned solutions including affine and affine-quadratic self-equivalences, and the factors 3×2^{10} and $3 \times 2^{2n+8}$ are the number of affine self-equivalences in the solutions for $n = 2$ and $n = 4$ respectively.

Affine-quadratic self-equivalences also share a common shape with several quadratic and linear terms that vanish. For example, the coefficients of the linear terms are of the form

$$\begin{pmatrix}
\star & \star &   &   &   &   & \star & \star &   &   &   &   \\
\star & \star &   &   &   &   & \star & \star &   &   &   &   \\
\star & \star & 1 &   &   &   & \star & \star &   &   &   &   \\
\vdots & \vdots &   & \ddots &   &   & \vdots & \vdots &   &   &   &   \\
\star & \star &   &   & 1 &   & \star & \star &   &   &   &   \\
\star & \star &   &   & \star & 1 & \star & \star & \star & \cdots & \star & \star \\
\star & \star &   &   & \star & \star & 1 & \star & \star & \star & \cdots & \star & \star \\
\star & \star &   &   &   &   & \star & \star &   &   &   &   \\
\star & \star &   &   &   &   & \star & \star & 1 &   &   &   \\
\vdots & \vdots &   &   &   &   & \vdots & \vdots &   & \ddots &   &   \\
\star & \star &   &   &   &   & \star & \star &   &   & 1 &   \\
\star & \star &   &   &   &   & \star & \star & \star & \cdots & \star & \star \\
\star & \star &   &   &   &   & \star & \star & \star & \cdots & \star & \star
\end{pmatrix},$$

and the constant vectors contain a repeated value b in all but 7 positions.

$$(\star\ \overbrace{b\ \cdots\ b}^{n}\ \star\ \star\ |\ \star\ b\ \cdots\ b\ \star\ \star\ \star).$$

We used this shape to obtain a subset of affine-quadratic self-equivalences for the larger wordsizes $n \in \{5, 6, \ldots, 64\}$ with cardinality $3^2 \times 2^{3n+14} - 3 \times 2^{2n+8}$. Thus, we conjecture that the number of affine-quadratic self-equivalences is equal or greater than $3^2 \times 2^{3n+14} - 3 \times 2^{2n+8}$ for any wordsize $n \geq 4$.

Finally, we also obtained quasilinear-preserving graph automorphisms U of the permuted modular addition by adapting the method of Sect. 5.1. In this case, the diagonal constraint is replaced by the quasilinear constraint over $T \circ U'$, where T is the implicit function defined in Eq. (7). While in the original method the invertibility constraint is only applied to the diagonal blocks of U', to sample graph automorphisms the invertibility constraint needs to be applied to the entire U. Due to this more complex invertibility constraint, for small wordsizes $n \in \{2, 3, 4\}$ we could find some but not all the quasilinear-preserving graph automorphisms. For large wordsizes $n \in \{5, 6, \ldots, 64\}$, we could sample quasilinear-preserving graph automorphisms by finding some solutions without the invertibility constraint and with some coefficients pre-emptively fixed, and then searching among the solutions for an invertible function. In our experiments, invertible solutions were quickly found after checking few solutions.

We noticed that if the invertibility constraint is not included in the system of equations, many coefficients of U do not appear in any equation. For example, for the wordsizes 3, 4, 5, 6, 7 and 8, we observed $54, 80, 110, 144, 182$ and 244 free coefficients, respectively, and we found at least 2^{20} solutions for each possible assignment of the free coefficients, that is, $2^{74}, 2^{100}, 2^{130}, 2^{174}, 2^{212}$ and 2^{274} solutions respectively. Moreover, all the quasilinear-preserving graph automorphisms that we sampled in our experiments were not right self-equivalences of T. Thus, we conjecture that the number of quasilinear-preserving graph automorphisms that are not right self-equivalences of T is exponential in the input size of the permuted modular addition.

As a summary, using the method described in Sect. 5.1 for the permuted modular addition with wordsize $4 \leq n \leq 64$, we found affine, linear, and affine-quadratic self-equivalence subsets with cardinality $3 \times 2^{2n+8}$, $3 \times 2^{2n+2}$ and $3^2 \times 2^{3n+14} - 3 \times 2^{2n+8}$, respectively. We could not obtain a lower bound on the number of quasilinear-preserving graph automorphisms that are not right self-equivalences of T, but using our method we can sample this type of graph automorphisms for wordsizes $n \leq 64$.

The motivation behind these self-equivalences and graph automorphisms is to propose in the next section an implicit implementation of an arbitrary cipher with the permuted modular addition as the non-linear layer. Since the affine, linear, and affine-quadratic self-equivalence subsets are large enough, we did not focus on finding all the self-equivalences and we leave it as an open problem. On the other hand, finding a lower bound on the number of quasilinear-preserving graph automorphisms that are not right self-equivalences of T would have been useful for the security analysis of the implicit implementation, but we were not able to obtain this bound and we leave it for future work.

6   An Implicit Implementation of an ARX Cipher

In this section we describe how to build an implementation of a generic iterated block cipher with an arbitrary affine layer and with the permuted modular addition as the non-linear layer. Most Addition-Rotation-XOR (ARX) ciphers fall under this description, and our method is the first white-box design that can be applied to ARX ciphers.

Let $E_k = E^{(n_r)} \circ E^{(n_r-1)} \circ \cdots \circ E^{(1)}$ be the encryption function of an n-bit iterated block cipher (n even), and let $E^{(i)} = AL^{(i)} \circ S$ be its ith round function where S is the permuted modular addition[10] with wordsize $n/2$ (i.e., input bitsize n) and $AL^{(i)}$ is an arbitrary n-bit affine layer containing the i-th round key $k^{(i)}$.

To build the quasilinear implicit function $P^{(i)}$ of the ith round, we use the approach described in Sect. 3.1 which defines $P^{(i)}$ as

$$P^{(i)} = V^{(i)} \circ T \circ U^{(i)} \circ \left(\mathrm{Id}_n, (AL^{(i)})^{-1}\right) \circ \left(I^{(i)}, (O^{(i)})^{-1}\right),$$

where $V^{(i)}$ is a linear permutation, T is the quasilinear implicit function of S, $U^{(i)}$ is a quasilinear-preserving affine graph automorphism of S that does not belong to the right self-equivalences of T, and $(I^{(i)}, O^{(i)})$ are the round encodings.

In this case, $T(x, x', y, y')$ is the quadratic implicit function of the permuted modular addition, previously defined in Eq. (7). It is easy to see that T is quasi-linear, as all its quadratic monomials contain an input variable (from the variable vectors x or x'). For $V^{(i)}$ we sample a random linear permutation, and we sample a random $U^{(i)}$ with the method described in Sect. 5.2.

For the round encodings, we sample an affine permutation $C^{(i+1)}$ and an affine-quadratic self-equivalence $(A^{(i)}, B^{(i)})$ of $E^{(i)}$, and we build the round encodings as

$$\left(I^{(i)}, O^{(i)}\right) = \left(A^{(i)} \circ B^{(i-1)} \circ (C^{(i)})^{-1}, \ C^{(i+1)}\right). \tag{8}$$

In the first input round encoding (i.e., the external input encoding), for $B^{(0)}$ we sample a random quadratic permutation.

Since the self-equivalence groups of S and $E^{(i)}$ are conjugates, that is,

$$\left(A^{(i)}, B^{(i)}\right) \text{ is a self-equivalence of } S \iff$$

$$\left(A^{(i)}, AL^{(i)} \circ B^{(i)} \circ (AL^{(i)})^{-1}\right) \text{ is a self-equivalence of } E^{(i)},$$

we can sample an affine-quadratic self-equivalence of $E^{(i)}$ from the subset of affine-quadratic self-equivalences of the permuted modular addition obtained

---

[10] For simplicity we restrict the n-bit non-linear layer to contain a single permuted modular addition with wordsize $n/2$, but our method can easily be extended to non-linear layers composed of smaller permuted modular additions.

in Sect. 5.2. In this construction, the pairs $(A^{(i)}, B^{(i)})$ can also be taken as the identity functions, and the choice of using affine-quadratic self-equivalences leads to a trade-off between security and performance that we will discuss later.

Note that the round encodings do not satisfy the cancellation rule $I^{(i+1)} \circ O^{(i)} = \mathrm{Id}_n$ from Definition 2 but the cancellation rule given by Eq. (1), since

$$E^{(i)} = B^{(i)} \circ (C^{(i+1)})^{-1} \circ C^{(i+1)} \circ E^{(i)} \circ A^{(i)}.$$

Figure 2 depicts how the round encodings are cancelled in two consecutive rounds. The round encodings could also be defined as

$$\left(I^{(i)}, O^{(i)}\right) = \left(B^{(i-1)} \circ (C^{(i)})^{-1}, C^{(i+1)} \circ (B^{(i)})^{-1}\right), \tag{9}$$

which satisfy the cancellation rule $I^{(i+1)} \circ O^{(i)} = \mathrm{Id}_n$. While both Eq. (8) and Eq. (9) define the same encoded round function, we will use Eq. (8) where the output round encoding is affine to preserve the quasilinear property (see Sect. 3.1).

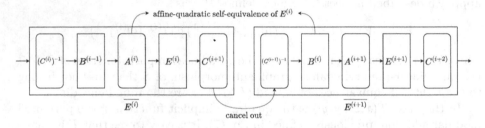

Fig. 2. Two consecutive encoded rounds, $\overline{E^{(i)}}$ and $\overline{E^{(i+1)}}$, with the round encodings defined by Eq. (8). Rounded blocks denote affine functions and rectangular blocks denote non-linear functions.

As a result, we have built an implicit implementation of E_k given by the quasilinear implicit functions $\{P^{(1)}, P^{(2)}, \ldots, P^{(n_r)}\}$. Let $\overline{E_k}$ be the underlying encoded implementation, whose round encodings are given by Eq. (8). Note that $\overline{E_k}$ is not functionally equivalent to E_k since

$$\overline{E_k} = \left(C^{(n_r+1)} \circ (B^{(n_r)})^{-1}\right) \circ E_k \circ \left(B^{(0)} \circ (C^{(1)})^{-1}\right).$$

Thus, the implicit implementation is not functionally equivalent to E_k either.

The degree of the implicit round functions $P^{(i)}$ depends on whether affine-quadratic self-equivalences are used in the round encodings. If they are not used, the functions $P^{(i)}$ are quadratic. Otherwise, the functions $P^{(i)}$ are quartic, or cubic if the affine-quadratic self-equivalences are chosen carefully. Higher degree self-equivalences (e.g., affine-cubic, affine-quartic, etc.) could also be used at the cost of increasing the degree of the implicit round functions.

Table 1 shows an upper bound on the memory required by an implicit round function for different degrees and bitsizes. As shown in the table, implicit implementations with bitsize $n = 64$ are quite practical; for bitsize $n = 128$ implicit implementations are practical with quadratic or cubic rounds.

Table 1. Upper bound on the size in megabytes (MB) of a $(2n, n)$-bit implicit round function $P^{(i)}$ for different degrees and bitsizes n.

Cipher blocksize n	Degree of $P^{(i)}$	Size of $P^{(i)}$
32	2	0.01 MB
32	3	0.09 MB
32	4	0.23 MB
64	2	0.05 MB
64	3	1.42 MB
64	4	6.50 MB
128	2	0.40 MB
128	3	22.50 MB
128	4	193.19 MB

Note that an implementation with multivariate binary polynomials of the underlying encoded implementation would be infeasible (even without affine-quadratic self-equivalences) due to its size, since the permuted modular addition has degree n. A CEJO implementation of the underlying encoded implementation would also have impractical size as the non-linear layer cannot be written as the composition of smaller functions. While an implicit implementation introduces a significant overhead in the running time and a severe overhead in the size as shown in Table 1, the implicit framework is the first method that provides practical white-box implementations of ARX ciphers.

Security Analysis. Let $\mathcal{I}$ be an implicit implementation following the method described in this section, and let E_k be the underlying block cipher with the permuted modular addition as the non-linear operation. In Sect. 4.1 we showed that implicit implementations that use non-linear encodings or where the non-linear layer of the cipher is not composed of small S-boxes are secure against all known generic key-extraction attacks. Therefore, if $\mathcal{I}$ uses quadratic input encodings (i.e., affine-quadratic self-equivalences) or the non-linear layer of E_k is not composed of small permuted modular additions, then known generic key-extraction attacks cannot extract the key from $\mathcal{I}$. Recall that a self-equivalence implementation of E_k has the structural weakness mentioned in Sect. 4.1, but $\mathcal{I}$ does not exhibit this weakness due to the large affine permutations C^i in the round encodings.

For the rest of the analysis, we will restrict $\mathcal{I}$ to have affine round encodings and E_k to have a permuted modular addition with wordsize $n/2$ as the non-linear layer. In Sect. 4.2 we also argued that an implicit implementation with affine encodings must ensure that no solution of Eq. (4) and no diagonal-linear solution of Eq. (3) can be obtained efficiently.

The central map in Eq. (4) is the permuted modular addition, a triangular function with degree n. If an attacker would have access to the coefficients of Eq. (4), the attacker could efficiently obtain a solution using the structural attack by Wolf et al. [42]. This structural attack can solve in polynomial time a functional equation with affine permutations as unknowns and with a non-linear (not necessarily quadratic) triangular central map. However, the attack by Wolf et al. assumes that the coefficients of the functional equation are public. This is not the case since an attacker only has black-box access to Eq. (4), that is, the attacker can only evaluate Eq. (4) by using the implicit round functions.

Regarding Eq. (3), using the method of Sect. 5.1 we obtained that $3^n \times 2^{11n-4}$ is a lower bound on the cardinality of the affine self-equivalence group of T for wordsizes $2 \le n \le 64$. While we were not able to obtain a lower bound on the number of quasilinear-preserving graph automorphisms U that are not right self-equivalences of T, the large number of affine self-equivalences (A, B) of T prevents an attacker from trying all (A, B) and U to transform a random solution (X, Y) into (X', Y') with X diagonal and Y linear.

To conclude, an implicit implementation following the method described in this section prevents all known generic key-extraction attacks if quadratic input encodings are used or the non-linear layer of the underlying cipher is given by a large permuted modular addition. Our new generic attack to the implicit framework based on Eqs. (3) and (4) was also not able to break an implicit implementation with affine encodings. This contribution also leaves several open problems such as the cost of an attack dealing with quadratic input encodings, whether it is possible to extend the structural attack by Wolf et al. to only black-box access or even finding new algorithms to solve Eq. (3) or to obtain a diagonal-linear solution of Eq. (4) without trying all (A, B) and U.

Implementation. As mentioned at the beginning of Sect. 4.1, the implicit framework is a novel design which requires further research on new attacks. Rather than proposing a particular implicit implementation of some ARX cipher, we provide instead an open-source Python script[11] that generates an implicit implementation of any given ARX cipher following the method described in Sect. 6.

Our script can be used for any cipher with the permuted modular addition as the non-linear layer. Given as input the affine layer of each round, the script generates the implicit implementation in an automated way. As an example, we have included an additional script that generates the affine layers of SPECK [5], but other ciphers based on the permuted modular addition can be easily added.

Moreover, the script provides many options that can be enabled or disabled, such as the affine-quadratic self-equivalences, the external encodings, an additional countermeasure based on Bringer et al.'s perturbations [11] or whether to export the implicit implementation to a Python function or to a C source file.

---

[11] https://github.com/ranea/whiteboxarx.

This script can generate many variants of implicit implementations of any ARX cipher, and we hope that these many practical examples encourage further analysis of implicit implementations.

7   Conclusion

Despite the total lack of secure candidates of white-box implementations, many recent works have focused on attack techniques, but only a few on design strategies. That is why in this work we addressed the challenging problem of designing white-box implementations of existing ciphers by proposing implicit implementations. On top of that, we proposed a generic method to obtain self-equivalences and graph automorphisms, which can be of independent interest together with BoolCrypt.

While we analysed the resistance of implicit implementations against the existing generic key-extraction attacks, the implicit framework is a new design that is very different from previous CEJO or self-equivalence implementations; many open problems arise when analysing new attacks. Understanding the security of implicit implementations requires further research, and we encourage the cryptographic community to participate by providing many practical examples with our script.

On the other hand, in this work we focused on implicit implementations with external encodings and with the permuted modular addition as the non-linear layer of the cipher, but future work could explore other non-linear layers such as large power functions or the security of implicit implementations without external encodings against automated white-box attacks based on grey-box techniques.

Acknowledgements. Adrián Ranea is supported by a PhD Fellowship from the Research Foundation - Flanders (FWO). The authors would like to thank the anonymous reviewers for their comments and suggestions.

A   Affine Self-equivalences of the Permuted Modular Addition with Wordsize 4

Let $L(A)$ and $C(A)$ be the linear part and the constant vector, respectively, of an affine function A. Any affine self-equivalence (A, B) of the 8-bit permuted modular addition (wordsize 4) is of the form

$$L(A) = \begin{pmatrix} c_1 + c_8 + c_9 & 0 & 0 & 0 & c_1 + c_8 & 0 & 0 & 0 \\ d_0 + d_2 & 1 & 0 & 0 & d_1 & 0 & 0 & 0 \\ d_0 + d_2 & 0 & 1 & 0 & d_1 & 0 & 0 & 0 \\ d_1 + c_6 + c_{12} + c_{15} & 0 & c_4 + c_7 & 1 & d_1 + c_6 + c_{12} & c_{13} & c_4 + c_7 + c_{16} & c_5 + 1 \\ c_0 + c_8 + c_9 & 0 & 0 & 0 & c_0 + c_1 + c_8 & 0 & 0 & 0 \\ d_0 + d_2 & 0 & 0 & 0 & d_1 & 1 & 0 & 0 \\ d_0 + d_2 & 0 & 0 & 0 & d_1 & 0 & 1 & 0 \\ d_1 + c_2 + c_{12} + c_{15} & 0 & 0 & 0 & d_1 + c_2 + c_6 + c_{12} & c_3 + c_{13} & c_7 + c_{16} & 1 \end{pmatrix}$$

$$C(A) = (c_{10}+c_{11},\ c_{10}c_{11}+c_{11},\ c_4+d_3,\ c_{17}+c_{18},\ c_{11},\ c_{10}c_{11}+c_{11},\ d_3+c_{14}+c_{16},\ d_4)^T$$

$$L(B^{-1}) = \begin{pmatrix}
c_0+c_1 & 0 & 0 & 0 & c_1 & 0 & 0 & 0 \\
d_0+d_2 & 1 & 0 & 0 & d_2+c_1c_{10} & 0 & 0 & 0 \\
d_0+d_2 & 0 & 1 & 0 & d_2+c_1c_{10} & 0 & 0 & 0 \\
d_0+c_2+c_6 & 0 & c_4+c_{14}+c_{16} & 1 & c_1c_{10}+c_6 & c_3 & d_5+c_7 & c_5+1 \\
c_0+c_8+c_9 & 0 & 0 & 0 & c_1+c_9 & 0 & 0 & 0 \\
d_0+d_2 & 0 & 0 & 0 & d_2+c_1c_{10} & 1 & 0 & 0 \\
d_0+d_2 & 0 & 0 & 0 & d_2+c_1c_{10} & 0 & 1 & 0 \\
d_1+c_2+c_{12}+c_{15} & 0 & 0 & 0 & c_6+c_{15} & c_3+c_{13} & c_7+c_{16} & 1
\end{pmatrix}$$

$$C(B^{-1}) = (c_{10},\ c_{10}c_{11}+c_{11},\ c_{10}c_{11}+c_{11}+d_5,\ c_{17},\ c_{11},\ c_{10}c_{11}+c_{11},\ d_3+c_{14}+c_{16},\ d_4)^T$$

where the binary coefficients c_i and d_j satisfy the following constraints

$$0 = d_0 + c_0c_1 + c_0c_8 + c_0c_{10} + c_0c_{11} + c_1 + c_8c_{10} + c_8$$
$$0 = d_1 + d_0 + c_1c_{10}$$
$$0 = d_2 + c_1c_9 + c_1c_{11} + c_9c_{10} + c_9 + 1$$
$$0 = d_3 + c_7 + c_{10}c_{11} + c_{11}$$
$$0 = d_4 + c_4c_7 + c_4c_{14} + c_4c_{16} + c_7c_{14} + c_7c_{16} + d_3 + c_{18}$$
$$0 = d_5 + c_4 + c_{14} + c_{16}$$
$$0 = c_0c_9 + c_1c_8 + c_1 + 1.$$

The coefficients d_j are just short labels to denote large expressions involving coefficients c_i. Among the 19 c_i coefficients, 15 are free variables and (c_0, c_1, c_8, c_9) are restricted by the constraint $c_0c_9 + c_1c_8 + c_1 + 1$. This constraint excludes 10 out of the 2^4 assignments of (c_0, c_1, c_8, c_9). Therefore, the number of affine self-equivalences is $2^{15} \times (2^4 - 10) = 196\,608$, which corresponds to $3 \times 2^{2n+8}$ for $n = 4$.

References

1. Albrecht, M., Grassi, L., Rechberger, C., Roy, A., Tiessen, T.: MiMC: efficient encryption and cryptographic hashing with minimal multiplicative complexity. In: Cheon, J.H., Takagi, T. (eds.) ASIACRYPT 2016. LNCS, vol. 10031, pp. 191–219. Springer, Heidelberg (2016). https://doi.org/10.1007/978-3-662-53887-6_7
2. Amadori, A., Michiels, W., Roelse, P.: A DFA attack on white-box implementations of AES with external encodings. In: Paterson, K.G., Stebila, D. (eds.) SAC 2019. LNCS, vol. 11959, pp. 591–617. Springer, Cham (2020). https://doi.org/10.1007/978-3-030-38471-5_24
3. Baek, C.H., Cheon, J.H., Hong, H.: White-box AES implementation revisited. J. Commun. Networks **18**(3), 273–287 (2016)
4. Banik, S., Bogdanov, A., Isobe, T., Jepsen, M.B.: Analysis of software countermeasures for whitebox encryption. IACR Trans. Symmetric Cryptol. **2017**(1), 307–328 (2017)
5. Beaulieu, R., Shors, D., Smith, J., Treatman-Clark, S., Weeks, B., Wingers, L.: The SIMON and SPECK families of lightweight block ciphers. IACR Cryptology ePrint Archive, p. 404 (2013)

6. Biryukov, A., Bouillaguet, C., Khovratovich, D.: Cryptographic schemes based on the ASASA structure: Black-Box, White-Box, and Public-Key (Extended abstract). In: Sarkar, P., Iwata, T. (eds.) ASIACRYPT 2014. LNCS, vol. 8873, pp. 63–84. Springer, Heidelberg (2014). https://doi.org/10.1007/978-3-662-45611-8_4

7. Biryukov, A., De Cannière, C.: Block ciphers and systems of quadratic equations. In: Johansson, T. (ed.) FSE 2003. LNCS, vol. 2887, pp. 274–289. Springer, Heidelberg (2003). https://doi.org/10.1007/978-3-540-39887-5_21

8. Biryukov, A., De Cannière, C., Braeken, A., Preneel, B.: A toolbox for cryptanalysis: linear and affine equivalence algorithms. In: Biham, E. (ed.) EUROCRYPT 2003. LNCS, vol. 2656, pp. 33–50. Springer, Heidelberg (2003). https://doi.org/10.1007/3-540-39200-9_3

9. Biryukov, A., Udovenko, A.: Attacks and countermeasures for white-box designs. In: Peyrin, T., Galbraith, S. (eds.) ASIACRYPT 2018. LNCS, vol. 11273, pp. 373–402. Springer, Cham (2018). https://doi.org/10.1007/978-3-030-03329-3_13

10. Bos, J.W., Hubain, C., Michiels, W., Teuwen, P.: Differential computation analysis: hiding your white-box designs is not enough. In: Gierlichs, B., Poschmann, A.Y. (eds.) CHES 2016. LNCS, vol. 9813, pp. 215–236. Springer, Heidelberg (2016). https://doi.org/10.1007/978-3-662-53140-2_11

11. Bringer, J., Chabanne, H., Dottax, E.: White box cryptography: another attempt. IACR Cryptology ePrint Archive **2006**, 468 (2006)

12. Carlet, C., Charpin, P., Zinoviev, V.A.: Codes, bent functions and permutations suitable for DES-like cryptosystems. Des. Codes Cryptogr. **15**(2), 125–156 (1998)

13. Chow, S., Eisen, P., Johnson, H., Van Oorschot, P.C.: White-box cryptography and an AES implementation. In: Nyberg, K., Heys, H. (eds.) SAC 2002. LNCS, vol. 2595, pp. 250–270. Springer, Heidelberg (2003). https://doi.org/10.1007/3-540-36492-7_17

14. Chow, S., Eisen, P., Johnson, H., van Oorschot, P.C.: A white-box DES implementation for DRM applications. In: Feigenbaum, J. (ed.) DRM 2002. LNCS, vol. 2696, pp. 1–15. Springer, Heidelberg (2003). https://doi.org/10.1007/978-3-540-44993-5_1

15. De Cannière, C.: Analysis and design of symmetric encryption algorithms. Ph.D. thesis, Katholieke Universiteit Leuven (2007). Bart Preneel (Promotor)

16. Delerablée, C., Lepoint, T., Paillier, P., Rivain, M.: White-box security notions for symmetric encryption schemes. In: Lange, T., Lauter, K., Lisoněk, P. (eds.) SAC 2013. LNCS, vol. 8282, pp. 247–264. Springer, Heidelberg (2014). https://doi.org/10.1007/978-3-662-43414-7_13

17. Derbez, P., Fouque, P., Lambin, B., Minaud, B.: On recovering affine encodings in white-box implementations. IACR Trans. Cryptogr. Hardw. Embed. Syst. **2018**(3), 121–149 (2018)

18. Ding, J.: A new variant of the Matsumoto-Imai cryptosystem through perturbation. In: Bao, F., Deng, R., Zhou, J. (eds.) PKC 2004. LNCS, vol. 2947, pp. 305–318. Springer, Heidelberg (2004). https://doi.org/10.1007/978-3-540-24632-9_22

19. Faugère, J.-C., Perret, L.: Polynomial equivalence problems: algorithmic and theoretical aspects. In: Vaudenay, S. (ed.) EUROCRYPT 2006. LNCS, vol. 4004, pp. 30–47. Springer, Heidelberg (2006). https://doi.org/10.1007/11761679_3

20. Faugère, J., Perret, L.: An efficient algorithm for decomposing multivariate polynomials and its applications to cryptography. J. Symb. Comput. **44**(12), 1676–1689 (2009)

21. Gupta, K.C., Ray, I.G.: Finding biaffine and quadratic equations for s-boxes based on power mappings. IEEE Trans. Inf. Theory **61**(4), 2200–2209 (2015)

22. Warren Jr., H.S.: Hacker's Delight. Addison-Wesley, Boston (2003)
23. Karroumi, M.: Protecting white-box AES with dual ciphers. In: Rhee, K.-H., Nyang, D.H. (eds.) ICISC 2010. LNCS, vol. 6829, pp. 278–291. Springer, Heidelberg (2011). https://doi.org/10.1007/978-3-642-24209-0_19
24. Kipnis, A., Patarin, J., Goubin, L.: Unbalanced oil and vinegar signature schemes. In: Stern, J. (ed.) EUROCRYPT 1999. LNCS, vol. 1592, pp. 206–222. Springer, Heidelberg (1999). https://doi.org/10.1007/3-540-48910-X_15
25. Lin, D., Faugère, J., Perret, L., Wang, T.: On enumeration of polynomial equivalence classes and their application to MPKC. Finite Fields Appl. 18(2), 283–302 (2012)
26. Link, H.E., Neumann, W.D.: Clarifying obfuscation: Improving the security of white-box DES. In: ITCC (1), pp. 679–684. IEEE Computer Society (2005)
27. Luo, R., Lai, X., You, R.: A new attempt of white-box AES implementation. In: SPAC, pp. 423–429. IEEE (2014)
28. McMillion, B., Sullivan, N.: Attacking white-box AES constructions. In: SPRO@CCS, pp. 85–90. ACM (2016)
29. Michiels, W., Gorissen, P., Hollmann, H.D.L.: Cryptanalysis of a generic class of white-box implementations. In: Avanzi, R.M., Keliher, L., Sica, F. (eds.) SAC 2008. LNCS, vol. 5381, pp. 414–428. Springer, Heidelberg (2009). https://doi.org/10.1007/978-3-642-04159-4_27
30. Minaud, B., Derbez, P., Fouque, P., Karpman, P.: Key-recovery attacks on ASASA. J. Cryptol. 31(3), 845–884 (2018)
31. Patarin, J.: Hidden Fields Equations (HFE) and Isomorphisms of Polynomials (IP): two new families of asymmetric algorithms. In: Maurer, U. (ed.) EUROCRYPT 1996. LNCS, vol. 1070, pp. 33–48. Springer, Heidelberg (1996). https://doi.org/10.1007/3-540-68339-9_4
32. Patarin, J., Goubin, L.: Asymmetric cryptography with S-boxes Is it easier than expected to design efficient asymmetric cryptosystems? In: Han, Y., Okamoto, T., Qing, S. (eds.) ICICS 1997. LNCS, vol. 1334, pp. 369–380. Springer, Heidelberg (1997). https://doi.org/10.1007/BFb0028492
33. Patarin, J., Goubin, L., Courtois, N.: C^*_{-+} and HM: variations around two schemes of T. Matsumoto and H. Imai. In: Ohta, K., Pei, D. (eds.) ASIACRYPT 1998. LNCS, vol. 1514, pp. 35–50. Springer, Heidelberg (1998). https://doi.org/10.1007/3-540-49649-1_4
34. Ranea, A., Preneel, B.: On self-equivalence encodings in white-box implementations. In: Dunkelman, O., Jacobson Jr., M.J., O'Flynn, C. (eds.) SAC 2020. LNCS, vol. 12804, pp. 639–669. Springer, Cham (2021). https://doi.org/10.1007/978-3-030-81652-0_25
35. Rivain, M., Wang, J.: Analysis and improvement of differential computation attacks against internally-encoded white-box implementations. IACR Trans. Cryptogr. Hardw. Embed. Syst. 2019(2), 225–255 (2019)
36. Schulte-Geers, E.: On CCZ-equivalence of addition mod 2^n. Des. Codes Cryptogr. 66(1–3), 111–127 (2013)
37. Shi, Y., Wei, W., He, Z.: A lightweight white-box symmetric encryption algorithm against node capture for WSNs. Sensors 15(5), 11928–11952 (2015)
38. Soos, M., Nohl, K., Castelluccia, C.: Extending SAT solvers to cryptographic problems. In: Kullmann, O. (ed.) SAT 2009. LNCS, vol. 5584, pp. 244–257. Springer, Heidelberg (2009). https://doi.org/10.1007/978-3-642-02777-2_24
39. The Sage Developers: SageMath, the Sage Mathematics Software System (Version 9.1) (2021). https://www.sagemath.org

40. Capture the Flag Challenge - The WhibOx Contest (2007). https://whibox.io/contests/2017/
41. Wiemers, A.: A note on invariant linear transformations in multivariate public key cryptography. IACR Cryptology ePrint Archive, p. 602 (2012)
42. Wolf, C., Braeken, A., Preneel, B.: On the security of stepwise triangular systems. Des. Codes Cryptogr. **40**(3), 285–302 (2006)
43. Xiao, Y., Lai, X.: A secure implementation of white-box AES. In: 2009 2nd International Conference on Computer Science and its Applications, pp. 1–6. IEEE (2009)

Superposition Meet-in-the-Middle Attacks: Updates on Fundamental Security of AES-like Hashing

Zhenzhen Bao[2,3] , Jian Guo[2] , Danping Shi[1,4(✉)] , and Yi Tu[2]

[1] State Key Laboratory of Information Security, Institute of Information Engineering, Chinese Academy of Sciences, Beijing, China
shidanping@iie.ac.cn
[2] School of Physical and Mathematical Sciences, Nanyang Technological University, Singapore, Singapore
guojian@ntu.edu.sg, TUYI0002@e.ntu.edu.sg
[3] Institute for Network Sciences and Cyberspace, BNRist, Tsinghua University, Beijing, China
[4] School of Cyber Security, University of Chinese Academy of Sciences, Beijing, China

Abstract. The Meet-in-the-Middle approach is one of the most powerful cryptanalysis techniques, demonstrated by its applications in preimage attacks on the full MD4, MD5, Tiger, HAVAL, and Haraka-512 v2 hash functions, and key recovery of the full block cipher KTANTAN. The success relies on the separation of a primitive into two independent chunks, where each active cell of the state is used to represent only one chunk or is otherwise considered unusable once mixed. We observe that some of such cells are linearly mixed and can be as useful as the independent ones. This leads to the introduction of superposition states and a whole suite of accompanied techniques, which we incorporate into the MILP-based search framework proposed by Bao *et al.* at EUROCRYPT 2021 and Dong *et al.* at CRYPTO 2021, and find applications on a wide range of AES-like hash functions and block ciphers.

Keywords: Whirlpool · Grøstl · AES hashing modes · MITM · MILP

1 Introduction

Hash function is a function mapping a document of arbitrary length into a short fixed-length digest. For a cryptographically secure hash function, it should fulfill three basic security requirements: collision resistance, preimage resistance, and second-preimage resistance. In this paper, we focus on the security notion of preimage and collision resistance, i.e., it should be computationally difficult to invert the function or find two inputs map to the same digest. Specially, for an ideal hash function H with n-bit digest and a target T given at random, it should cost no less than 2^n compression function evaluations to find an input x such that $H(x) = T$. Preimage attack refers to an algorithm achieving this in lesser evaluations. Collision attack refers to an algorithm finding different x and x' such that $H(x) = H(x')$ with lesser evaluations than birthday attack, *i.e.*, $2^{n/2}$ computations.

Y. Dodis and T. Shrimpton (Eds.): CRYPTO 2022, LNCS 13507, pp. 64–93, 2022.
https://doi.org/10.1007/978-3-031-15802-5_3

Traditionally, there are two common methods to construct cryptographic hash functions. One is to convert from block ciphers through mode of operations, and the other is to build from scratch. There are 12 secure PGV modes [23], which enjoy the proof of security reduction of the hash function to the underlying block cipher. This method is especially useful when a block cipher like AES [10] has long-standing security against intensive cryptanalysis. When it is already implemented for other purposes like encryption, the same implementation can be re-used to construct a hash function by implementing the additional mode only. In this way it also leads to performance merits. Particularly, hash function constructed from AES through PGV modes are called AES hashing, and they have been standardized by Zigbee [1] and also suggested by ISO/IEC [17]. Due to the well understood security and high performance, many dedicated block ciphers and hash functions built from scratch follow similar design strategy by using an AES-like round function, such as Whirlpool [7] and Grøstl [13].

THE MEET-IN-THE-MIDDLE (MITM) ATTACK has a long history and an important role in various cryptanalysis on various primitives. It was introduced to preimage attacks on hash functions by Aumasson et al. [3] and Sasaki et al. [25] in 2008. Since then, MITM preimage attack has shown its power on many MD/SHA families of hash functions. That includes the full versions of MD4 [15], MD5 [27], Tiger [15], and HAVAL [25], as well as lightweight block cipher KTANTAN [8].

The basic MITM idea is to find ways to split the cipher into two computational chunks and find the so-called neutral bits from each side, independent of the computation of the state of the other side. Hence, the two chunks can be computed independently but end up at a common state, where previously independent computations are finally pairwise matched. The critical point is that the independence between the two chunks allows their results to be pairwise matchable, enabling this MITM procedure to require fewer computations than a trivial enumeration.

In 2011, MITM was introduced by Sasaki [24] for the first time to preimage attack on AES hashing, invalidating the preimage resistance of the 7-round reduced version. To avoid dealing with the key schedule, the key value of AES was pre-set to a constant, and hence the same number of rounds was attacked for AES hashing based on all three versions of AES (AES-128, AES-192, and AES-256). In 2019, the attack was revisited in [4], and it was found that the degree of freedoms from the key values can be utilized for at least one side of the computation. This observation led to the attack complexity improvements over 7-round AES-128 hashing, and increased the number of attacked rounds from 7 to 8 for the AES-hashing based on AES-192 and AES-256. In 2020, the MITM preimage attack was introduced to meet a popular automatic tool, the Mixed-Integer-Linear-Programming (MILP) [5]. This match with MILP enables the previously invented enhancements for MITM, e.g., the initial structure, the selection and cancellation of neutral bits, to evolve to a more generalized form. The MILP models characterizing the generalized formalization of MITM, produced many improved preimage attacks on AES hashing, penetrated 8-round

AES-128 hashing and full rounds of Haraka v2-512. In 2021, MITM-MILP models find more applications not only in preimage attacks but also in key-recovery and collision attacks on AES-like ciphers [11].

A common practice in all these MITM attacks is the byte-oriented decomposition of states, *i.e.*, each useful byte carries the influence of neutral bits from at most one direction. Once influences of neutral bits from both directions reach the same byte, this byte will be considered unusable for the either chunk. An immediate consequence of this practice is that the information from unusable bytes is lost, and any byte in the subsequent round computed from it becomes unusable too.

1.1 Our Contribution

Superposition Meet-in-the-Middle Attack Framework. In this work, different from the byte-oriented decomposition, we propose SUPERPOSITION MITM attack framework with the help of SUPERPOSITION STATE (SUPP), under which every byte is viewed as a combination of two virtual bytes separately representing the influence of the neutral bits from one direction each. It becomes obvious to see that, the advantage of this representation is the preservation of linearity, *i.e.*, any state which is a linear combination of neutral bits from both directions will be kept so when linear operations such as MixColumns and AddRoundKey are applied. SupP opens up the possibility of new local collisions between/within the encryption and key states, thus maximizes the chances of canceling impacts on independence and enables new MITM attack configurations. Enabled by SupP, a suite of techniques is added into the MILP-based search framework proposed by Bao *et al.* [5] and Dong *et al.* [11], which greatly enlarged the solution space and led to rich results on AES-like ciphers.

GUESS-AND-DETERMINE (GnD) is a popular technique and has countless applications in cryptanalysis against symmetric-key primitives such as stream ciphers [31] and block ciphers [9]. The basic idea is that, in the process of some attack, the gain of guessing some state or key bits is higher than the price, *i.e.*, the guess itself comes with a probability p then the attack needs to repeat at least $1/p$ times in order to have a correct guess. This technique has also been used in the MITM preimage attacks [15,28,30], where the guess allows further computation of more state/message bits which help either extend the attack to more rounds or lower the time complexities. It is noted that GnD has never been incorporated into the MILP models for the MITM attacks in [5,11].

BI-DIRECTION ATTRIBUTE-PROPAGATION AND CANCELLATION (BIDIR). In previous MITM attacks [4,5,11,24,28,30], each computation chunk propagates towards a single direction. Although the idea of adding constraints to some neutral bits in order to cancel their impact on the opposite computation has already appeared, such cancellations are only allowed in one direction in each chunk. In this work, we allow cancellation between neutral bytes in both directions. This led us to attack configurations with lower time complexities.

MULTIPLE WAYS OF AddRoundKey (MULAK). The identical encryption and key-schedule of Whirlpool allows the AddRoundKey to be moved around the MixColumns using an equivalent key state already involved in the key-schedule. We add the flexibility of key-addition at different positions in each round into the model, and make it possible to save the double consumption of freedom degrees between the encryption and key-schedule. This simple yet efficient strategy makes it possible to attack one more round on reduced Whirlpool.

Application Results. The superposition MITM attack framework aided by the additional techniques shows its effectiveness when applied to the popular AES-like hashing Whirlpool (an ISO/IEC standard), Grøstl (a finalist of the SHA-3 competition), AES-hashing modes (widely used, *e.g.*, AES-MMO in Zigbee protocols), and tweakable block cipher SKINNY (in its way to be included in ISO/IEC 18033). Broad improvements upon the previous best results on preimage, collision, and key-recovery attacks were obtained. The updates and a comparison with the state-of-the-art results in literature are summarized in Table 1.

For Whirlpool, the preimage resistance of its 7-round reduced version out of the total 10 rounds gets challenged for the first time, a decade after MITM itself challenging its 5-round [24] for the first time, or GnD joining MITM challenging its 6-rounds [28]. Meanwhile, the complexities of preimage attacks on the 5- and 6-round reduced versions are significantly improved. The new attack on 7-round Whirlpool relies on multiple modeling enhancements, including GnD, BiDir, and MulAK. Noticeably, in terms of preimage resistance, the presented attack reduces one round security margin out of the remaining four for this important target.

For Grøstl, there are two main instances, Grøstl-256 and Grøstl-512, named after the size of their digests. The preimage resistance of their longest attacked variants, 6-round Grøstl-256 and 8-round Grøstl-512, get updated eight years after [32]. Improvements with larger complexity reductions are also found on variants with lesser rounds. The improved attacks are achieved by allowing BiDir, in addition to the GnD. Such improvement is not possible using only MITM-GnD, and MITM-GnD is already considered in [22,32].

In addition, the MILP models for searching preimage attacks can be directly transformed into models searching for collision attacks on hash functions and key-recovery attacks on block ciphers. With the superposition MITM-GnD models, immediate improvements were obtained on many more targets: For Grøstl-256, the collision resistance of its output transformation's longest attacked version, the 6-round, gets updated; For AES-hashing, the collision resistance of hash functions based on AES-128 reduced to 7-round get challenged, more than a decade after rebound attacks challenging its 6-round [14,19], or two years after quantum attacks challenging its 7-round version [16]. For SKINNY, the security in terms of key-recovery attack in the single-key setting of the longest attacked version, 23-round SKINNY-n-$3n$, gets updated. Remarkably, data complexity is drastically reduced, *e.g.*, from 2^{52} to 2^{28} for SKINNY-64-192.

ORGANIZATION. Section 2 briefly introduces the AES-like hashing and MITM preimage attacks. Section 3 describes the details of our enhanced MILP model. The application to Whirlpool and Grøstl is given in Sect. 4 and 5, respectively. Section 6 briefly introduces the applications to collision and key-recovery attack. Please refer to the full version [6] for more details. Relevant source codes can be found via https://github.com/MITM-AES-like.

2   AES-like Hashing and MITM Preimage Attacks

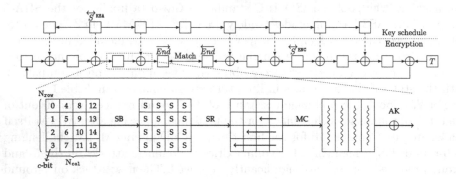

Fig. 1. Overview of AES-like hashing [5]

THE AES-LIKE HASHING in our context refers to those hash functions whose compression function (CF) or output transformation (OT) uses an AES-like round function as depicted in Fig. 1, where the state can be viewed as a $N_{row} \times N_{col}$ matrix of c-bit cells. There are 4 general operations in order:

- SubBytes (SB) applies a non-linear substitution-box operation to each cell.
- ShiftRows (SR) cyclically shifts each row by a pre-defined number of positions.
- MixColumns (MC) mixes every column, e.g., by multiplying an (MDS) matrix.
- AddRoundKey (AK) adds the round key (or round message).

For some designs, the SR and MC may work on the transpose of the matrix, i.e., SR on columns and MC on rows; the SR can be a cell-permutation.

THE MITM PREIMAGE ATTACKS generally cut the entire encryption process into two chunks (forward and backward chunks), and there are few neutral bits from each side, so that the computation of each chunk can be done independently starting from the cutting point (starting point). The two computations end at a common intermediate (partial) state (matching point), and the computed results from the two sides can be pairwise matched via a linear relation.

Since MITM has been applied to preimage attacks on MD4, MD5, and HAVAL [3, 20, 25, 26], it has been developed further and applied to preimage attacks on many

Table 1. Updated results on (pseudo-) preimage attacks

Cipher (Target)	#R	Time-1	Time-2	$(\overrightarrow{d_b}, \overleftarrow{d_r}, \overrightarrow{m}, \overrightarrow{d_{g_b}}, \overleftarrow{d_{g_r}})$	Critical Tech.	Ref.
(Pseudo-) Preimage						
Whirlpool (Hash)	5/10	2^{416}	2^{448}	$(16,12,16,0,0)$	Dedicated	[28]
	5/10	2^{352}	2^{433}	$(20,20,20,0,0)$	MILP, BiDir, MulAK	*Fig. 13
	6/10	2^{448}	2^{481}	$(32,8,32,0,24)$	Dedicated, GnD	[28]
	6/10	2^{440}	2^{477}	$(9,24,24,15,0)$	MILP, GnD	*Fig. 12
	7/10	2^{480}	2^{497}	$(16,4,16,0,12)$	MILP, GnD, MulAK	*Fig. 3, 11
Grøstl-256 (CF+OT)	5/10	2^{192}	$2^{234.67}$	$(8,8,8,0,0)$	Dedicated	‡ [22,32]
	5/10	2^{184}	2^{232}	$(9,9,16,0,0)$	MILP, BiDir	*Fig. 14, 15
	6/10	2^{240}	2^{252}	$(8,2,8,0,6)$	Dedicated, GnD	‡ [22,32]
	6/10	2^{224}	$2^{245.33}$	$(4,20,16,12,0)$	MILP, GnD, BiDir	*Fig. 5, 6
Grøstl-512 (CF+OT)	7/14	2^{416}	2^{480}	$(19,12,19,0,7)$	MILP, GnD, BiDir	*Fig. 16, 17
	8/14	2^{472}	2^{504}	$(10,10,18,5,5)$	Dedicated	† [32]
	8/14	2^{472}	2^{500}	$(9,5,10,0,4)$	MILP, GnD, BiDir	*Fig. 7, 8
AES-192 Hashing	9/12	2^{120}	2^{125}	$(1,1,1,0,0)$	MILP	[5]
	9/12	2^{112}	2^{121}	$(2,2,2,0,0)$	MILP, SupP, BiDir	*Fig. 18
Kiasu-BC Hashing	8/10	2^{120}	2^{123}	$(1,4,4,0,0)$	Dedicated	[4]
	9/10	2^{120}	2^{125}	$(1,1,1,0,0)$	MILP, SupP, BiDir	*Fig. 19

Cipher (Target)	#R	Time	Mem	Setting & Type	Critical Tech.	Ref.
(Free-start) Collision						
Grøstl-256 (OT)	6/10	2^{124}	2^{124}	classic collision	MILP	[11]
	6/10	2^{116}	2^{116}	classic collision	MILP, BiDir	*Fig. 20
Grøstl-512 (OT)	8/14	2^{248}	2^{248}	classic collision	MILP	[11]
	8/14	2^{244}	2^{244}	classic collision	MILP, BiDir	*Fig. 21
AES-128 Hashing	6/10	2^{56}	2^{32}	classic collision	Dedicated	[14,19]
	7/10	$2^{42.5}$	(2^{48})	quantum collision	Dedicated	[16]
	7/10	2^{56}	2^{56}	classic free-start	MILP, BiDir	*Fig. 22

Cipher (Target)	#R	Time	Mem	Data	Critical Tech.	Ref.
Key-recovery						
SKINNY-64-192	23/40	2^{188}	2^{4}	2^{52}	MILP	[11]
	23/40	2^{184}	2^{8}	2^{60}	MILP, SupP	*Fig. 23
	23/40	2^{188}	2^{4}	2^{28}	MILP, SupP	*Fig. 24
SKINNY-128-384	23/56	2^{376}	2^{8}	2^{104}	MILP	[11]
	23/56	2^{368}	2^{16}	2^{120}	MILP, SupP	*Fig. 23
	23/56	2^{376}	2^{8}	2^{56}	MILP, SupP	*Fig. 24

– CF: Compression Function; OT: Output Transformation; Dedicated: Dedicated method;
– Time-1 and Time-2 are complexities of pseudo-preimage and preimage attacks following the notions in [4] when the target is a hash function, and complexities of inverting OT and CF+OT (pseudo-preimage) following the notions in [30] for Grøstl, respectively.
– * Please refer to the full version of this paper [6].
– † The presented complexities for the attacks in [32] are recomputed by removing constant factors (*e.g.*, the cost C_{TL} for lookup table is replaced by 1) and replacing $C_2(2n, b)$ that is lower bounded by $b/2$ in [30] with $\overline{C_2(2n, b)}$ that can be 2^0 considering the amortized complexity. Thus, all complexities are computed follow the same way.
– ‡ The 5- and 6-round attacks in [22] are on the OT of Grøstl-256. To convert to pseudo-preimage, we used the results for the case with no truncation in [22]. However, for the 6-round attack, in which guessing are required, it cannot be directly used. Thus, we combined the attack on OT in [22] with the best previous attack on the CF in [32].

other hash functions. Advanced techniques in MITM preimage attacks were developed, including the *splice-and-cut* [2], (probabilistic) *initial structure* [15, 27], and (indirect) *partial matching* techniques [2,27].

The *splice-and-cut* technique [2] views the input and output of the compression function *connected* through the feedforward operation. The *initial structure* is a few consecutive starting steps, where the two chunks overlap and two sets of neutral words (denoted by $\overrightarrow{\mathcal{N}}$ and $\overleftarrow{\mathcal{N}}$) appear simultaneously at these steps. Typically, one adds *constraints* to the values of $\overrightarrow{\mathcal{N}}$ and $\overleftarrow{\mathcal{N}}$ to limit their impact on the opposite chunk such that steps after the initial structure (forward chunk) can be computed independently of $\overleftarrow{\mathcal{N}}$ and steps before the initial structure (backward chunk) can be computed independently of $\overrightarrow{\mathcal{N}}$. The *(indirect-) partial matching* exploits any easily determined relations between the computed ending states from the two computation chunks instead of requiring values of full states. There may or may not be any *neutral bits* from the message of the compression function (or key of the underlying block cipher).

The Attack Framework. The procedure and complexity of the MITM attack depend on how the computation is decomposed into independent chunks, how neutral bits are selected and constrained, and how to match. Once these configurations have been determined, the basic MITM pseudo-preimage attack on a CF goes as follows (with initial structure and partial matching).

1. Assign arbitrary compatible values to all bytes except those that depend on the neutral bytes.
2. Obtain possible values of neutral bytes $\overrightarrow{\mathcal{N}}$ and $\overleftarrow{\mathcal{N}}$ under the constraints on them. Suppose there are 2^{d_1} values for $\overrightarrow{\mathcal{N}}$, and 2^{d_2} for $\overleftarrow{\mathcal{N}}$.
3. For all 2^{d_1} values of $\overrightarrow{\mathcal{N}}$, compute forward from the initial structure to the matching point to get a table $\overrightarrow{\mathcal{L}}$, whose indices are the values for matching, and the elements are the values of $\overrightarrow{\mathcal{N}}$.
4. For all 2^{d_2} values of $\overleftarrow{\mathcal{N}}$, compute backward from the initial structure to the matching point to get a table $\overleftarrow{\mathcal{L}}$, whose indices are the values for matching, and the elements are the values of $\overleftarrow{\mathcal{N}}$.
5. Check whether there is a match on indices between $\overrightarrow{\mathcal{L}}$ and $\overleftarrow{\mathcal{L}}$.
6. In case of partial-matching exist in the above step, for the surviving pairs, check for a full-state match. In case none of them are fully matched, repeat the procedure by changing values assigned in Step 1 till find a full match.

The Attack Complexity. Denote the size of the internal state by n, the degree of freedom in the forward and backward chunks by d_1 and d_2, and the number of bits for (partial-) matching by m, the time complexity of the attack is [4]:

$$2^{n-(d_1+d_2)} \cdot \left(2^{\max(d_1,d_2)} + 2^{d_1+d_2-m}\right) \simeq 2^{n-\min(d_1,d_2,m)}. \tag{1}$$

3   MILP Model for the Configuration Search

3.1   Basic MILP Model for MITM

For searching MITM attacks using MILP, one should characterize valid attack configurations in MILP language.

To generate MILP models and search for the best MITM attack, the high-level workflow is as follows. Given a targeted cipher, enumerate all possible combinations of starting and matching points (detailed in **Searching Framework**). For each combination, build the MILP model as follows: 1) claim variables indicating the attribute of each state cell in the input/output of each operation in each round, introduce necessary auxiliary variables; 2) define linear equations and inequalities to express relations and constraints among those variables according to the cipher specification and attack principles; 3) write the objective function corresponding to the optimal computational complexity. For each generated MILP model, use an MILP solver to search its optimal solution; Among solutions of various MILP models, select the best one; parse the solution into the attack.

The challenging parts of the modeling are to formalize new attack settings and techniques into explicit rules and then translate into linear inequalities/equations. The linear inequalities/equations should be exact such that the solutions can one-to-one correspond to valid attack configurations.

In the following, we describe the basic modeling method following the framework in [5]. As introducing the basic model, we directly introduce some natural generalizations, while other generalizations and enhancements are deferred to the sequel subsections.

Notations and Encoding. For the ease of notation, the conversational coloring scheme for describing and visualizing MITM attacks [4,5,11,24,28,30] is adopted here to characterize the attributes of state cells. As in the MILP modeling in [5], the attribute of individual state cell is encoded using two binary variables (x, y) and defined as follows. A cell is

- Gray (■) if and only if its value is a predefined constant, thus is known and fixed in *both* forward and backward chunks; Indicating variables $(x, y) = (1, 1)$;
- Blue (■) if and only if its value is determined by forward neutral bytes and predefined constants, thus is known and active in the *forward* chunk but unknown in the backward; Indicating variables $(x, y) = (1, 0)$;
- Red (■) if and only if its value is determined by backward neutral bytes and predefined constants, thus is known and active in the *backward* chunk but unknown in the forward; Indicating variables $(x, y) = (0, 1)$;
- White (□) if and only if its value is determined by both forward and backward neutral bytes, thus can be computed independently in *neither* chunk; Indicating variables $(x, y) = (0, 0)$.

For convenience, Black (■) is used to represent any of the 4 cells (■, ■, ■, □). Additionally, indicating variables β and ω are defined as follows.

$$- \beta = \begin{cases} 1 & \text{is inactive, do not contain degree of freedom; is Gray;} \\ 0 & \text{is active, is Blue, Red or White.} \end{cases}$$

$$- \omega = \begin{cases} 1 & \text{cannot be computed in both forward and backward chunks; is White;} \\ 0 & \text{can be computed in at least one direction; is Blue, Red, or Gray.} \end{cases}$$

Searching Framework. The top-level of a search for the optimal MITM attacks is to enumerate all high-level configurations. A high-level configuration is determined by four parameters, including $\texttt{total}_r$, $\texttt{init}_r^{\text{E}}$, $\texttt{init}_r^{\text{K}}$, and $\texttt{match}_r$, representing the total number of targeted rounds, the location of the initial state in encryption, the location of the initial state in the key-schedule, and the location of the matching point, respectively. For the complete search of $\texttt{total}_r$-round attacks, all possible combinations of values of $\texttt{init}_r^{\text{E}}$, $\texttt{init}_r^{\text{K}}$, and $\texttt{match}_r$ should be tried; each combination corresponds to an independent MILP model; The following description of the modeling method is for an individual model with a fixed ($\texttt{total}_r$, $\texttt{init}_r^{\text{E}}$, $\texttt{init}_r^{\text{K}}$, $\texttt{match}_r$).

When building an MILP model, constraints are imposed on propagation of attributes starting from some initial states (*i.e.*, $\overleftrightarrow{S}^{\text{ENC}}$ and $\overleftrightarrow{S}^{\text{KSA}}$ in round $\texttt{init}_r^{\text{E}}$ and $\texttt{init}_r^{\text{K}}$) and terminating at some ending states (*i.e.*, $\overrightarrow{End}$ and $\overleftarrow{End}$ in round $\texttt{match}_r$) from two directions.

- In all states in both encryption and key-schedule data-paths, constraints are imposed on attribute-indicating variables for state cells. The constraints indicate the relations of cells between consecutive states intra-round and inter-round. The change of attributes of cells from state to state is attribute propagation.

- In the initial states in encryption and key-schedule (*i.e.*, in $\overleftrightarrow{S}^{\text{ENC}}$ and $\overleftrightarrow{S}^{\text{KSA}}$), the attribute of each cell is constrained to be non-White. Thus, its indicating variables can take three assignments, *i.e.*, $(x_i, y_i) \in \{(1,0),(0,1),(1,1)\}$ for $\forall\, i \in \mathcal{N}$, where $\mathcal{N} = \{0, 1, \cdots, \text{N}_{\text{row}} \cdot \text{N}_{\text{col}} - 1\}$. The states in the starting round are called initial because initial degree of freedoms are all contained in these states. Denote the initial degree of freedom for the forward by $\overrightarrow{\iota}$, and that for backward by $\overleftarrow{\iota}$. Accordingly, one has the equations for $\overrightarrow{\iota}$ and $\overleftarrow{\iota}$ as in Eq. (2), where $|\mathcal{BL}^{\text{ENC}}|$, $|\mathcal{RD}^{\text{ENC}}|$, $|\mathcal{BL}^{\text{KSA}}|$, and $|\mathcal{RD}^{\text{KSA}}|$ denote the number of Blue, Red cells in $\overleftrightarrow{S}^{\text{ENC}}$, and Blue, Red cells $\overleftrightarrow{S}^{\text{KSA}}$, respectively.

- In the ending states at the matching round (*i.e.*, $\overrightarrow{End}$ and $\overleftarrow{End}$), each column is associated with a general variable since the matching is performed column-wise. Specifically, for each pair of input/output columns of the states before and after MixColumns, the associated variable $\overrightarrow{m}_i$ indicates the degree of matching in column i and is constrained by the numbers of Blue, Red, and Gray cells. The total degree of matching of the attack, denoted as $\overrightarrow{m}$, is the sum of the degrees of matching from all columns, as shown in Eq. (4).

In order for Blue- and Red-attribute to independently propagate from initial states to ending states and remain matchable, special constraints might be occasionally imposed to indicate whether to cancel impact by consuming degrees of freedom. Concrete constraints on how attributes propagate and how freedom be consumed will be introduced shortly. At this moment, let's denote the accumulated consumed degree of freedom of forward by $\overrightarrow{\sigma}$ and that of backward by $\overleftarrow{\sigma}$. The remaining degrees of freedom in forward and backward (denoted by $\overrightarrow{d_b}$ and $\overleftarrow{d_r}$, respectively) after the occasionally freedom-consuming during attribute-propagation are constrained as in Eq. (3). Note that the $\overrightarrow{d_b}$ and $\overleftarrow{d_r}$ are the essential degrees of freedom for the attack, which determine the attack complexity.

According to the attack complexity in Formula 1, the search for a *valid* attack corresponds to the search for a valid attribute propagation with $\min\{\overrightarrow{d_b}, \overleftarrow{d_r}, \overrightarrow{\overleftarrow{m}}\} \geq 1$; the search of the *optimal* attack corresponds to the search with maximized $\min\{\overrightarrow{d_b}, \overleftarrow{d_r}, \overrightarrow{\overleftarrow{m}}\}$. Thus, the objective of the search model is to maximize a variable τ_{Obj}, which is constrained by Eq. (5).

$$
\begin{cases} \overrightarrow{\iota} = |\mathcal{BL}^{\text{ENC}}| + |\mathcal{BL}^{\text{KSA}}|, \\ \overleftarrow{\iota} = |\mathcal{RD}^{\text{ENC}}| + |\mathcal{RD}^{\text{KSA}}|. \end{cases} \qquad \begin{cases} \overrightarrow{d_b} = \overrightarrow{\iota} - \overrightarrow{\sigma}, \\ \overleftarrow{d_r} = \overleftarrow{\iota} - \overleftarrow{\sigma}. \end{cases} \qquad \overrightarrow{\overleftarrow{m}} = \sum_{i=0}^{N_{\text{col}}-1} \overrightarrow{\overleftarrow{m}}_i . \qquad \begin{cases} \tau_{\text{Obj}} \leq \overrightarrow{d_b}, \\ \tau_{\text{Obj}} \leq \overleftarrow{d_r}, \\ \tau_{\text{Obj}} \leq \overrightarrow{\overleftarrow{m}} . \end{cases}
$$

$$ (2) \qquad\qquad\qquad\qquad (3) \qquad\qquad (4) \qquad\qquad (5) $$

Basic Rules for Attributes to Propagate and to Match. The attribute propagation and the matching are governed by two types of constraints. The first type is due to the specification of the targeted cipher; the second type is due to the principle of the attack. If attacks are technically improved, the second type constraints should be adapted to the improvement. In turn, when the second type constraints are properly relaxed, the attack space is expanded so that improved attacks might be discovered.

Remark 1 (Bi-direction attribute-propagation and cancellation (BiDir)). Previously [4,5,11,24,28,30], the constraints are imposed such that the propagation of Red-attribute can "make a concession" [1] to the propagation of Blue, but Blue never "gives in" to Red for forward computation, and vice versa. Unlike the previous work, in this work, the constraints are relaxed such that the propagation of Blue or Red attribute can make a concession (cancel its impact by consuming its degree of freedom) to the propagation of the opposite attribute in both directions. The reasons are as follows.

---

[1] Here, the use of phrases "make a concession" or "give in" is due to a view of the forward computation and backward computation be in a competition for being able to be propagated unaffected. In previous attacks, for forward computation, propagation of Blue-attribute is of high priority. When unaffected propagation of Blue-attribute becomes not straightforward due to the existence of cells of Red-attribute, we may try to cancel the impact by consuming the freedom of backward to ensure the propagation of Blue-attribute. We say such cancellation of impact by consuming freedom "concede", "make a concession" or "give in".

- In the modeling, we introduce neutral bytes into key states as well as in encryption states to bring more degree of freedom. In attribute propagation through encryption, letting Blue-propagation concede such that a local Red-cell be reserved, that might enable a remote Red-cell introduced from the key state be canceled such that Blue-propagation be possible in that remote point. That also applies to the case of Red-propagation.
- Besides, letting Blue to concede and reserve a local Red-cell might enable this local Red-cell to propagate and combine with other Red-cells at a remote point such that their impacts on a certain cell be mutually canceled through MixColumns and benefit Blue-propagation.
- In addition, once an attribute of Blue or Red propagate to the ending states no matter from which direction, it provides source of degree of matching.

Relaxing the model in this way results in attacks with bi-direction attribute-propagation; the attack space is expanded so that improved attacks are possible. However, this relaxation caused the models to be solved less efficiently. When the efficiency is acceptable, we used such relaxed model for better attacks. Otherwise, we restricted the models such that in certain rounds of the cipher, one attribute can only propagate in one direction and concede in the other direction.

In the following, we describe the MILP modeling with the relaxed model as the basic setting. The difference between this basic modeling and the modeling in [5] and how to get the restricted models will be indicated alongside.

Modeling of the Attribute Propagation through SubBytes and ShiftRows. The Sub-Bytes operation does not change the attribute of the cells, thus is not involved when building the basic model. The ShiftRows operation permutes the state cells, thus can be modeled by a set of equations or hardcoded variable substitution.

Modeling of the Attribute Propagation through AddRoundKey and XOR (*XOR-RULE*). The AddRoundKey operation is involved in the model when the cipher has KeySchedule (message schedule), and the attack exploits freedom from the key state. Basically, the attribute propagation through AddRoundKey is governed by a set of cell-wise constraints under the name XOR-RULE. The high-level principle is that White is the dominant attribute, Gray is the recessive attribute, Blue and Red are mutually exclusive attributes. The concrete rules are as follows.

- A White cell XORed with a cell of any attribute results in a White cell, *i.e.*, $(\square \oplus \blacksquare) \rightarrow \square$;
- a Gray cell XORed with a cell of any attribute results in the cell of the same attribute, *i.e.*, $(\blacksquare \oplus \blacksquare) \rightarrow \blacksquare$;
- a couple of Blue and Red cells results in a cell deteriorated to White, *i.e.*, $(\blacksquare \oplus \blacksquare) \rightarrow \square$;
- a couple of Blue cells can keep the attributes without consuming or evolve to Gray by consuming a degree of freedom of Blue, *i.e.*, $(\blacksquare \oplus \blacksquare) \rightarrow \blacksquare$ or $(\blacksquare \oplus \blacksquare) \xrightarrow{-1 \times \blacksquare} \blacksquare$;

– a couple of Red cells can keep the attributes without consuming or evolve to Gray by consuming a degree of freedom of Red, *i.e.*,

$$(\blacksquare \oplus \blacksquare) \to \blacksquare \text{ or } (\blacksquare \oplus \blacksquare) \xrightarrow{-1 \times \blacksquare} \blacksquare.$$

These propagation rules can be described using only a few variables, thus can be easily translated into inequalities using convex hull computations [29].

Modeling of the Attribute Propagation through MixColumns (MC-RULE). The attribute propagation through MixColumns is governed by a set of column-wise constraints under the name MC-RULE. The MC-RULE constraints are mostly governed by the branch number (Br_n) of the MixColumns. Again, the high-level principle is that White is the dominant attribute, Gray is the recessive attribute, Blue and Red are mutually exclusive attributes. The concrete rules are as follows:

– any White cell in an input column results in all cells in the output column deteriorated to White, *i.e.*,
  $(i \times \square, \ j \times \blacksquare) \to (N_{row} \times \square)$, where $i \geq 1, i + j = N_{row}$;
– the Gray attribute inherits to the output without consuming degrees of freedom only if all cells in the input column are Gray, *i.e.*,
  $(N_{row} \times \blacksquare) \to (N_{row} \times \blacksquare)$;
– existing no White cell, a column of i Blue, j Red, and k Gray cells propagate to a column of i' Blue, j' Red, k' Gray, and ℓ' White cells by consuming $j' + k'$ degree of freedom from Blue, and $i' + k'$ from Red, *i.e.*,

$$(i \times \blacksquare, \ j \times \blacksquare, \ k \times \blacksquare) \xrightarrow[\substack{-(i'+k') \times \blacksquare \text{ if } j \neq 0}]{-(j'+k') \times \blacksquare \text{ if } i \neq 0} (i' \times \blacksquare, \ j' \times \blacksquare, \ k' \times \blacksquare, \ \ell' \times \square), \text{ where}$$

$i + j + k = i' + j' + k' + \ell' = N_{row}$ and $\begin{cases} j' + k' < i \leq N_{row} & \text{if } i \neq 0 \\ j' + k' = N_{row} & \text{otherwise} \end{cases}$,

$\begin{cases} i' + k' < j \leq N_{row} & \text{if } j \neq 0 \\ i' + k' = N_{row} & \text{otherwise} \end{cases}$. Note that when $i \neq 0$, $j' + k' < i \Leftrightarrow$ $N_{row} - i' - l' < i \Leftrightarrow i + i' + l' >= N_{row} + 1$, which is due to the branch number; similarly, $i' + k' < j$ when $j \neq 0$ is due to the branch number.

To formalize these propagation rules into a system of inequalities, the involved number of variables is not small. Concretely, the involved variables include the binary variables that indicate the attribute of each cell in the input and output columns, *i.e.*, (x_i^I, y_i^I), (x_i^O, y_i^O), and ω_i^I for $i \in \{0, 1, \cdots, N_{row} - 1\}$, the general variables c_x and c_y representing the consumed degree of freedom from Blue and Red, respectively. Apart from those variables, three auxiliary binary variables are introduced to indicate the following attributes of the input column:

$$\omega = \begin{cases} 1 & \text{exists White cell,} \\ 0 & \text{otherwise.} \end{cases} \qquad x = \begin{cases} 1 & \text{all are Blue/Gray,} \\ 0 & \text{exists Red/White.} \end{cases} \qquad y = \begin{cases} 1 & \text{all are Red/Gray,} \\ 0 & \text{exists Blue/White.} \end{cases}$$

$$(6) \hspace{4cm} (7) \hspace{4cm} (8)$$

The constraints can then be formalized using inequalities listed in Eq. (15, 16, 17) in the full version [6].

Modeling of the Matching through MixColumns and AddRoundKey (MATCH-RULE).
The modeling for matching also focuses on the MixColumns and AddRoundKey
operations. The matching through MixColumns and AddRoundKey is governed
by a set of column-wise constraints under the name MATCH-RULE.

The involved states are those around MixColumns at the matching round,
including $\overrightarrow{End}$ and $\overleftarrow{End}$ in encryption and $\overrightarrow{End}^{\mathrm{KMC}}$ or $\overleftarrow{End}^{\mathrm{K}}$ in key-schedule.
Note that $\overrightarrow{End}$ and $\overleftarrow{End}$ are states that have not been added with key-state
$\overrightarrow{End}^{\mathrm{KMC}}$ or $\overleftarrow{End}^{\mathrm{K}}$. Since AddRoundKey is linear, the influence of AddRoundKey
for matching can be formalized using simple rules. Concretely, only a White cell
in key state destroy the match-ability of the corresponding cell in encryption
state. The Blue and Red cells in key state do not impact the match-ability but
on the contrary might provide degree of matching.

Remark 2. For specific targeted cipher whose key-schedule is almost identical to
the encryption, *e.g.*, Whirlpool, one can use $\overrightarrow{End} \oplus \overrightarrow{End}^{\mathrm{KMC}}$ as an equivalent key
addition to $\overrightarrow{End} \oplus \overleftarrow{End}^{\mathrm{K}}$. The color pattern (most importantly, the distribution
of White cells) of $\overrightarrow{End}^{\mathrm{KMC}}$ and $\overleftarrow{End}^{\mathrm{K}}$ are different in most cases. Thus, adding
$\overrightarrow{End}^{\mathrm{KMC}}$ or $\overleftarrow{End}^{\mathrm{K}}$, these two ways may have different effects on the degree of
matching. To find the optimal solution, one should consider both ways. However,
we can simply choose to use the key state with fewer White cells. That is because,
known the propagation direction of the key-schedule (*i.e.*, $\mathrm{init}_r^{\mathrm{K}}$), between the
two states $\overrightarrow{End}^{\mathrm{KMC}}$ and $\overleftarrow{End}^{\mathrm{K}}$, the one that is near to the initial key state must
have set of White cells be subset of that in the remote state, thus has less impact.

The condition for the i-th column to have $\overset{\rightarrow\leftarrow}{m}_i$ degree of matching is as
follows: denote the number of known cells (*i.e.*, except White cells) in the input
and output columns by $\overline{m_{ki}}$; when $\overline{m_{ki}} > \mathrm{N_{row}}$, $\overset{\rightarrow\leftarrow}{m}_i = \overline{m_{ki}} - \mathrm{N_{row}}$; otherwise,
$\overset{\rightarrow\leftarrow}{m}_i = 0$. Denote the number of white cells by $\overline{m_{wi}}$; Since $\overline{m_{ki}} = 2 \cdot \mathrm{N_{row}} - \overline{m_{wi}}$, one
have $\overset{\rightarrow\leftarrow}{m}_i = \max(0, \mathrm{N_{row}} - \overline{m_{wi}})$. Accordingly, the concrete system of inequalities
modeling MATCH-RULE can be obtained as explained in Sect. A and as listed
in Eq. (18) in the full version [6].

3.2 Superposition States and Separate Attribute-Propagation

Except for allowing bi-direction attribute-propagation, the above basic modeling
is in line with previous work [4,5,11,24,28,30], where Blue and Red attributes
propagate exclusively and competitively through each operation. Once the two
exclusive attribute propagate into the same cell position, this cell is considered
being White, cannot be independently computed in either forward nor backward.

However, such modeling might miss valid attacks as will be discussed shortly.
In our final modeling, the two exclusive attributes Blue and Red propagate independently as long as it is possible. This is achieved by introducing *superposition
states*. Superposition states are all intermediate states in encryption and key-
schedule being separated into two virtual states. One virtual state carries one
attribute propagation independently of the other attribute propagation. The two

virtual states are combined only when going through non-linear operations. In this way, two exclusive attributes can simultaneously propagate through all linear operations in both encryption and key-schedule. See Fig. 3 for an example. This superposition setting captures the independence of the computation in a more essential way, allows new ways of local collisions between/within the encryption and key states, thus, maximize the chances of canceling impacts on independence and enables new ways of MITM decomposition. Concretely, the reasons and benefits of separating propagation with superposition states are as follows.

- As mentioned above, under certain constraints, Blue propagation can make a concession so that impacts are canceled and Red can propagate unaffected, and vice versa. To cancel impact, it requires consuming degrees of freedom. To be able to consume degrees of freedom, different types of operations impose different requirements on the attribute of input states. Concretely, the XOR-RULE and MC-RULE requires differently for canceling impacts. Attributes of state cells might not meet the individual requirements but it is actually possible to cancel impacts when combining these two linear operations.
  In [5], the propagation through the combination of AddRoundKey and Mix-Columns is characterized using the set of XOR-MC-RULE. In XOR-MC-RULE, the OR of the attribute indicating variables of encryption and key-state cell is used to indicate the attribute of the input cell of MixColumns. In that way, the group of cells of the same attribute in both encryption and key states can jointly cancel their impacts on certain output cells.
  However, using only XOR-MC-RULE, the possibility of the following scenario is missed. That is, an attribute can be completely canceled via XOR-RULE before propagating through MixColumns (refer to Fig. 2a for an illustration). Thus, to find optimal attack configurations, applying XOR-RULE-then-MC-RULE and XOR-MC-RULE should be both considered in the models.
  In this work, we model the combination of AddRoundKey and MixColumns by considering the separation of (Blue and Red) attribute propagation with superposition states. Note that AddRoundKey and MixColumns are linear. Essentially, for linear operations, in the same state, the attributes of Blue and Red can separately propagate through them and then combine by cell-wise XOR upon the non-linear operation (i.e., SubBytes).
  Due to this separation with superposition states, XOR-RULE and MC-RULE without XOR-MC-RULE are sufficient (refer to Fig. 2 for an illustration of the separation of attribute-propagation through AddRoundKey and MixColumns).
- Additionally, the key/message-schedule of the ciphers also has linear operations. It is possible that before going through the non-linear operation in the key-schedule, the attribute of one cell in the round-key is a linear combination of Blue and Red. If not be separately considered, such a linear combination of Blue and Red becomes White. Separately, the Blue component in the linear combination in a key state can be used to cancel impact from the Blue component in another key state or in an encryption state, and same for the Red component. Consequently, impacts that cannot be canceled

in previous models can be canceled now, thus independent propagation gets more chances (see Fig. 22 in the full version [6] for an example.)
- Moreover, at the matching point, if a key state cell is in superposition (a linear combination of Blue and Red), it does not impact the matching ability of the corresponding state cell, and instead, the Blue component and Red component may provide degrees of matching (see Fig. 18 in the full version [6] for an example.)

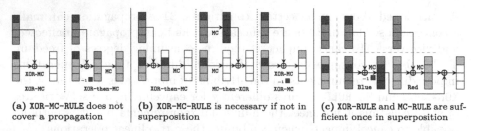

(a) XOR-MC-RULE does not cover a propagation

(b) XOR-MC-RULE is necessary if not in superposition

(c) XOR-RULE and MC-RULE are sufficient once in superposition

- In 2a, using XOR-MC-RULE, a result of full Red attribute can not be achieved, which can be obtained by XOR-then-MC-RULE.
- In 2b, without superposition, (Blue and Red) attribute-propagation ruled by XOR-MC-RULE cannot be obtained directly by XOR-then-MC-RULE and MC-then-XOR-RULE.
- In 2c, with (Blue and Red) attribute-propagation in superposition, XOR-RULE and MC-RULE are sufficient (2c achieve the same results as achieved by XOR-MC-RULE 2b).

Fig. 2. Combination of linear operations and superposition attribute-propagation

3.3   Multiple Ways of AddRoundKey (MulAK)

In Whirlpool, the key-schedule shares the same operations with the encryption except for AddRoundKey. This identity between encryption and key-schedule enables that in encryption, the AddRoundKey can be easily moved around Mix-Columns. Moving around MixColumns is simply switching between adding $\#\text{KMC}$ or adding k, where $\#\text{KMC}$ and k are the states before and after MixColumns in the round function of key-schedule, that is, a switch between adding the real round-key k or an equivalent (up to MixColumns) round-key $\#\text{KMC}$.

Moving AddRoundKey before MixColumns and using $\#\text{KMC}$ can bring more advantages in some cases. Take the case where we need to reserve Blue by consuming Red for example. Let's focus on one column of the state. Suppose there is one Red cell in that column of $\#\text{MC}$ and one Red cell in the same cell-position in $\#\text{KMC}$; the influence of these single Red cells will be diffused into the whole columns in both states if there is no constraint. In such case, adding $\#\text{KMC}$ with $\#\text{MC}$ and letting the Red cell in $\#\text{MC}$ be canceled by the Red cell in $\#\text{KMC}$ achieve the same cancellation effect but consume fewer degrees of freedom than adding $\#\text{AK}$ with k (take using $\#\text{MC}^5 \oplus \#\text{KMC}^4$ vs. $\#\text{AK}^5 \oplus k_5$ in Fig. 3 for an example). Similarly, it is also possible that adding $\#\text{AK}$ with k after the MixColumns has more advantages than adding $\#\text{MC}$ with $\#\text{KMC}$ (take using $\#\text{SB}^4 \oplus k_3$ vs. $\#\text{MC}^5 \oplus k_2$ in Fig. 3 for an example).

Thus, to find optimal attack configurations, both scenarios should be considered. The essential difference between the scenarios is to either firstly use freedom in the key state to directly cancel impacts before diffusion or to postpone the insertion of the key state in order to postpone impacts from the key. We name the choice of applying the first scenario by AK-MC-RULE and the second scenario by MC-AK-RULE. The integration of the two scenarios into one model is in the form of indicator constraints that is available in Gurobi. Note that, for forward computation, AK-MC-RULE corresponds to using $\#\text{MC} \oplus \#\text{KMC}$, MC-AK-RULE corresponds to using $\#\text{AC} \oplus k$; for backward computation, AK-MC-RULE corresponds to using $\#\text{SB} \oplus k$, and MC-AK-RULE corresponds to using $\#\text{MC} \oplus \#\text{KMC}$;

In addition, since the MixColumns is column-wise, different columns can apply different ways (apply AK-MC-RULE or MC-AK-RULE) independently. Besides, since MixColumns is linear, with superposition states, different attributes of Blue and Red can independently apply AK-MC-RULE or MC-AK-RULE.

Integrating such flexibility of choice into the MILP models expand the covered attack space but make the solving less efficient. So, to decide in which way to proceed for each column, we use the heuristic that when the key-schedule has already consumed some degree of freedom in that column, we apply MC-AK-RULE; otherwise, apply AK-MC-RULE.

3.4   Enhanced Model with Guess-and-Determine (GnD)

The Guess-and-Determine Strategy. In MITM attacks, one unfavorable situation is that a single or a few unknown cells in the input column of MC makes all cells in the output column unknown (refer to point 1 of MC-RULE). This is inevitable due to the diffusion of MixColumns, especially the property of the MDS matrix.

To turn things around in such situations, Sasaki *et al.* in [28] invent the following guess-and-determine strategy. That is, guess values of the few unknown cells to continue the propagation of attribute to reach the matching point, after (partial) matching, check the consistency of the few guessed cells. If the gained degree of matching is sufficient and the required guesswork is very little, one can still achieve a better attack complexity than a brute-force attack.

Concretely, denote 2^c by ς (where c is the number of bits in each cell). Let:

- $\overrightarrow{d_{g_b}}$ be the number of cells only guessed to be Blue (forward computation);
- $\overleftarrow{d_{g_r}}$ be the number of cells only guessed to be Red (backward computation);
- $\overleftrightarrow{d_{g_{br}}}$ be the number of cells guessed to be both Blue and Red.[2]

The framework of the MITM attack with GnD is as follows:

1. Assign arbitrary compatible values to all cells except for those depending on the neutral bits, and assign arbitrary values to the constants in pre-defined constraints on neutral bits;

---

[2] Since we allow bi-direction attribute propagation in superposition states, it might bring benefit to guess a superposition cell to be simultaneously Blue and Red. Thus, here is a slight generalization of the previous GnD strategy.

2. Compute values $\{\overrightarrow{v}_i\}$ of forward neutral bits and values $\{\overleftarrow{v}_i\}$ of backward neutral bits fulfilling pre-defined constraints.
3. For all $\varsigma^{\overrightarrow{d_b}}$ values $\{\overrightarrow{v}_i\}$ of forward neutral bits, and $\varsigma^{(\overrightarrow{d_{g_b}}+\overleftrightarrow{d_{g_{br}}})}$ guessed values $\{\overrightarrow{v}_g\}$ for forward, compute forward to the matching point and store all $\varsigma^{\overrightarrow{d_b}+\overrightarrow{d_{g_b}}+\overleftrightarrow{d_{g_{br}}}}$ partial matching values $\{\overrightarrow{v}_m\}$ in a look up table $\overrightarrow{\mathcal{T}}$ (the values are $\overrightarrow{v}_i$ and $\overrightarrow{v}_g$, and the index is $\overrightarrow{v}_m$).
4. For all $\varsigma^{\overleftarrow{d_r}}$ values $\{\overleftarrow{v}_i\}$ of backward neutral bits, and $\varsigma^{(\overleftarrow{d_{g_r}}+\overleftrightarrow{d_{g_{br}}})}$ guessed values $\{\overleftarrow{v}_g\}$ for backward, compute backward to the matching point, obtain the partial matching values $\overleftarrow{v}_m$.
5. For all values of $\overrightarrow{v}_i$ and $\overrightarrow{v}_g$ in entry $\overrightarrow{\mathcal{T}}[\overleftarrow{v}_m]$, use $\overrightarrow{v}_i$ and $\overleftarrow{v}_i$ to compute and check if the guessed values $\overrightarrow{v}_g$ and $\overleftarrow{v}_g$ are compatible. For compatible guesses, compute to the matching point to check if it is a full-state match. If so, use $\overrightarrow{v}_i$ and $\overleftarrow{v}_i$ to compute the preimage, output it, and return; otherwise, repeat from Step 1 by changing values assigned at that step.

In the above framework of the MITM attack with GnD,

- the total degree of freedom for Blue with guessing is $\overrightarrow{d_b}+\overrightarrow{d_{g_b}}+\overleftrightarrow{d_{g_{br}}}$;
- the total degree of freedom for Red with guessing is $\overleftarrow{d_r}+\overleftarrow{d_{g_r}}+\overleftrightarrow{d_{g_{br}}}$;
- the expected number of matched pairs is $\varsigma^{\overrightarrow{d_b}+\overrightarrow{d_{g_b}}+\overleftrightarrow{d_{g_{br}}}+\overleftarrow{d_r}+\overleftarrow{d_{g_r}}+\overleftrightarrow{d_{g_{br}}}-\overleftrightarrow{m}}$;
- the required number of repetitions to get a full match at the guessing cells and a full-state match is $\varsigma^{-(\overrightarrow{d_b}+\overrightarrow{d_{g_b}}+\overleftrightarrow{d_{g_{br}}}+\overleftarrow{d_r}+\overleftarrow{d_{g_r}}+\overleftrightarrow{d_{g_{br}}}-\overleftrightarrow{m})}\cdot\varsigma^{\overrightarrow{d_{g_b}}+\overleftrightarrow{d_{g_{br}}}+\overleftarrow{d_{g_r}}}\cdot\varsigma^{(n-\overleftrightarrow{m})}$, which equals $\varsigma^{n-\overrightarrow{d_b}-\overleftarrow{d_r}-\overleftrightarrow{d_{g_{br}}}}$;

Thus, the complexity of the attack is $\varsigma^{n-\overrightarrow{d_b}-\overleftarrow{d_r}-\overleftrightarrow{d_{g_{br}}}}\cdot(\varsigma^{\overrightarrow{d_b}+\overrightarrow{d_{g_b}}+\overleftrightarrow{d_{g_{br}}}}+\varsigma^{\overleftarrow{d_r}+\overleftarrow{d_{g_r}}+\overleftrightarrow{d_{g_{br}}}}+\varsigma^{\overrightarrow{d_b}+\overrightarrow{d_{g_b}}+\overleftrightarrow{d_{g_{br}}}+\overleftarrow{d_r}+\overleftarrow{d_{g_r}}+\overleftrightarrow{d_{g_{br}}}-\overleftrightarrow{m}})$, which equals

$$\varsigma^n\cdot(\varsigma^{-(\overleftarrow{d_r}-\overrightarrow{d_{g_b}})}+\varsigma^{-(\overrightarrow{d_b}-\overleftarrow{d_{g_r}})}+\varsigma^{-(\overleftrightarrow{m}-\overrightarrow{d_{g_b}}-\overleftarrow{d_{g_r}}-\overleftrightarrow{d_{g_{br}}})})$$
$$\simeq\varsigma^n\cdot\max(\varsigma^{-(\overleftarrow{d_r}-\overrightarrow{d_{g_b}})},\varsigma^{-(\overrightarrow{d_b}-\overleftarrow{d_{g_r}})},\varsigma^{-(\overleftrightarrow{m}-\overrightarrow{d_{g_b}}-\overleftarrow{d_{g_r}}-\overleftrightarrow{d_{g_{br}}})}) \tag{9}$$

Accordingly, the complexity is determined by

$$\min(\overleftarrow{d_r}-\overrightarrow{d_{g_b}},\overrightarrow{d_b}-\overleftarrow{d_{g_r}},\overleftrightarrow{m}-\overrightarrow{d_{g_b}}-\overleftarrow{d_{g_r}}-\overleftrightarrow{d_{g_{br}}}).$$

Building Model for Guessing. To model the mechanism of GnD, three binary variables, g_b, g_r, g_{br}, are introduced for each cell in the input state of MixColumns (invMixColumns for the backward computation).

The variables indicate whether the values of the cells should be guessed to be of one attribute. Concretely, $g_b = 1$ for guessing one White cell to be Blue. $g_r = 1$ for guessing one White cell to be Red. $g_{br} = 1$ for guessing one White cell to be Blue (for forward propagation) and also Red (for backward propagation).

With these guess-indicating variables, attribute-indicating variables of each cell in the input of MixColumns are thus constrained together with attribute-indicating variables of the cell in output state of last operations (*e.g.*, ShiftRows or AddRoundKey). Besides, according to the complexity Eq. (9) of the attack with GnD, the objective should turn from $\min(\overrightarrow{d_b}, \overleftarrow{d_r}, \overleftrightarrow{m})$ to $\min(\overrightarrow{d_b} - \overrightarrow{d_{g_r}}, \overleftarrow{d_r} - \overleftarrow{d_{g_b}}, \overleftrightarrow{m} - \overrightarrow{d_{g_b}} - \overleftarrow{d_{g_r}} - \overleftrightarrow{d_{g_{br}}})$. Thus, the variable that to be maximized is constrained as in Eq. (10) and (11).

$$
\begin{cases}
\overrightarrow{d_{g_b}} = \sum_{r=0,i=0}^{total_r-1,n-1} g_{b_i}^r, \\
\overleftarrow{d_{g_r}} = \sum_{r=0,i=0}^{total_r-1,n-1} g_{r_i}^r, \quad (10) \\
\overleftrightarrow{d_{g_{br}}} = \sum_{r=0,i=0}^{total_r-1,n-1} g_{br_i}^r,
\end{cases}
\qquad
\begin{cases}
\tau_{Obj} \le \overrightarrow{d_b} - \overrightarrow{d_{g_r}}, \\
\tau_{Obj} \le \overleftarrow{d_r} - \overleftarrow{d_{g_b}}, \quad (11) \\
\tau_{Obj} \le \overleftrightarrow{m} - \overrightarrow{d_{g_b}} - \overleftarrow{d_{g_r}} - \overleftrightarrow{d_{g_{br}}}.
\end{cases}
$$

Note that in the starting round, all cells are known and in the matching round, guessing brought no advantage. Thus, for these two rounds, such constraints on guessing can be omitted. Besides, generally, guessing are only required around the matching point. Thus, when trade-off between search quality and search efficiency is needed, these guessing constraints can be added only for rounds around the matching point.

3.5   Transforming to Models for Searching for Collision Attacks

A MITM partial target preimage attack whose matching point is at the last round can be transformed into a collision attack, as described by Li *et al.* in [21]. Thus, the searching of MITM preimage attacks can be constraint to search for such partial target preimage attacks, and then translate into valid collision attack. Concretely, one have the follows.

Definition 1 ((t-bit) partial target pseudo preimage attack on CF [21]). *Given the value v of t bits in T, find (h', m') such that t bits in $T' := CF(h', m')$ at the same position as the t bits in T, take value v.*

Let $\mathcal{A}$ be a random algorithm that can find a t-bit partial target pseudo preimage with a complexity of 2^s. This complexity can be in the average sense, which means that $\mathcal{A}$ can generate 2^r different (h', m', T') in one time with a complexity 2^{r+s}. Additionally, assume $\mathcal{A}$ output different (h', m', T')'s for different calls. Then, a free-start collision attack goes as follows.

- Set t-bit arbitrary value d' to the target. Call $\mathcal{A}$ with d' as the partial target and run it to obtain $2^{(n-t)/2}$ values of (h', m', T').
- From the $2^{(n-t)/2}$ values of (h', m', T'), find a collision on the remaining $(n-t)$ bits of T'.

According to the birthday paradox, with a high probability, the above procedure produces a valid collision pair. The total complexity of this attack is $2^{s+(n-t)/2}$.

The above complexity analysis misses the details of the MITM complexity. In the following, we re-formalize the complexity analysis of the above collision attack using its correspondence with the MITM-GnD preimage attack.

Essentially, the $\mathcal{A}$ can be the core of a MITM pseudo preimage attack on CF. The t-bit partial target corresponds to $c\times \overrightarrow{\overleftarrow{m}}$ bits for partial matching in the MITM attack. Essentially, the t bits for partial matching can be a fixed t-bit linear relations on ℓ bits for $\ell \geq t$, which restrict the values of ℓ bits to a subspace of dimension $\ell - t$. Thus, matching through MixColumns instead of matching at exact same bit positions does not have essential influence on the effectiveness of the attack. The 2^s computational complexity of $\mathcal{A}$ corresponds to

$$\varsigma^{\max\left\{(\overrightarrow{d_b}+\overrightarrow{d_{g_b}}+\overleftrightarrow{d_{g_{br}}}),(\overrightarrow{d_r}+\overrightarrow{d_{g_r}}+\overleftrightarrow{d_{g_{br}}}),(\overrightarrow{d_b}+\overrightarrow{d_{g_b}}+\overleftrightarrow{d_{g_{br}}}+\overrightarrow{d_r}+\overrightarrow{d_{g_r}}+\overleftrightarrow{d_{g_{br}}}-\overrightarrow{\overleftarrow{m}})\right\}}/\varsigma^{\overrightarrow{d_b}+\overrightarrow{d_r}+\overleftrightarrow{d_{g_{br}}}-\overrightarrow{\overleftarrow{m}}},$$

which equals to $\varsigma^{\max\left\{(\overrightarrow{d_{g_b}}-\overrightarrow{d_r}),(\overrightarrow{d_{g_r}}-\overrightarrow{d_b}),(\overrightarrow{d_{g_b}}+\overrightarrow{d_{g_r}}+\overleftrightarrow{d_{g_{br}}}-\overrightarrow{\overleftarrow{m}})\right\}}/\varsigma^{-\overrightarrow{\overleftarrow{m}}}$. Thus, the total complexity is $\varsigma^{\max\left\{(\overrightarrow{d_{g_b}}-\overrightarrow{d_r}),(\overrightarrow{d_{g_r}}-\overrightarrow{d_b}),(\overrightarrow{d_{g_b}}+\overrightarrow{d_{g_r}}+\overleftrightarrow{d_{g_{br}}}-\overrightarrow{\overleftarrow{m}})\right\}}/\varsigma^{-\overrightarrow{\overleftarrow{m}}} \times \varsigma^{\frac{n-\overrightarrow{\overleftarrow{m}}}{2}}$, i.e.,

$$\varsigma^{-\min\left\{(\overleftarrow{d_r}-\overrightarrow{d_{g_b}}),(\overleftarrow{d_b}-\overrightarrow{d_{g_r}}),(\overrightarrow{\overleftarrow{m}}-\overrightarrow{d_{g_b}}-\overleftarrow{d_{g_r}}-\overrightarrow{d_{g_{br}}})\right\}} \times \varsigma^{\frac{n+\overrightarrow{\overleftarrow{m}}}{2}}. \tag{12}$$

For a valid attack (better than birthday attack), the following should be fulfilled

$$\left\{\overrightarrow{d_b} - \overrightarrow{d_{g_r}} > \overrightarrow{\overleftarrow{m}}/2, \quad \overleftarrow{d_r} - \overrightarrow{d_{g_b}} > \overrightarrow{\overleftarrow{m}}/2, \quad \overrightarrow{d_{g_b}} + \overleftarrow{d_{g_r}} + \overrightarrow{d_{g_{br}}} < \overrightarrow{\overleftarrow{m}}/2\right\}. \tag{13}$$

For searching for the best attack, the objective function is the same as that for preimage attack, i.e.,

$$\max\left\{\min\left\{\overrightarrow{d_b} - \overleftarrow{d_{g_r}}, \overleftarrow{d_r} - \overrightarrow{d_{g_b}}, \overrightarrow{\overleftarrow{m}} - \overrightarrow{d_{g_b}} - \overleftarrow{d_{g_r}} - \overrightarrow{d_{g_{br}}}\right\}\right\}. \tag{14}$$

Remark 3. A solution to the MILP model only corresponds to a valid attack configuration but does not formally imply a valid attack. For the attack complexity in Eq. 1, 9, and 12 to be valid, the attacker should be able to generate each value of neutral bytes with (amortized) computational complexity $O(1)$. In some obtained attack configurations, the neutral bytes are constrained in such a sophisticated manner that it is not trivial to efficiently generate their values. For such non-trivial cases, we propose to use local meet-in-the-middle procedures to solve the problem (as done for the pseudo-preimage attack on 7-round Whirlpool in Sect. 4.1). Such local meet-in-the-middle procedures might be found by manual analysis or aided by automatic tools, such as the Automatic-tool from [9]. Sometimes, to achieve amortized computational complexity $O(1)$, it is necessary to pre-compute values of neutral bytes for many fixed bytes (enumerated in the outermost loop of the attack) at once. However, for some very complex cases, even aided by automatic-tools and considering amortized complexity, it might be difficult to find pre-computation procedures with total complexity lower than the main procedure. As a theoretical problem for all attacks under this framework, this problem of efficiently generating values of neutral bits stays open.

3.6 Exploit Symmetry of the Ciphers

Integrating that many technical generalizations, the search space is greatly enlarged but the search is slow down. One needs to make a trade-off between the quality of the searching result and the efficiency of the search. Apart from the ways of trade-off mentioned alongside the introduction of the modeling, one can reduce the problem scale using symmetry of the ciphers. Specifically, in many AES-like designs, the states and operations have symmetric structures and parameters. The symmetry allows projecting attacks on small-size versions to that on large-size versions. Concretely, a state of 8×8 cells can be viewed as a 2×2 matrix of state of 4×4 cells, or a 1×2 matrix of state of 8×4 cells. Suppose the ShiftRows parameters of the 8×8 state version are $\{p_0, p_1, \ldots, p_7\}$ and $(p_{i+4} \mod 4) = p_i$ for $i \in \{0, \ldots, 3\}$, and 2 times the branch number of MixColumns of a 4×4 state version is no less than that of the 8×8 state version. Then, obtaining an attack on the 4×4 state version, cloning the state patterns four times and placing them in a 2×2 matrix, this will result in an attack on the 8×8 state version. Exploiting such symmetry of the ciphers, the search can be efficient, while might lose asymmetric attack configurations.

4   Application to Preimage Attacks on Whirlpool

Whirlpool [7] is a block-cipher based secure hash function designed by Rijmen and Barreto in 2000 and has been adopted as an ISO/IEC standard. It produces a 512-bit hash value using Miyaguchi-Preneel-mode (MP-mode) CF. The CF is defined as $\mathsf{CF}(H_i, M_i) = E_{H_i}(M_i) \oplus M_i \oplus H_i$, where E is a 10-round AES-like block cipher with 8×8-byte internal states. This underlying block cipher takes the 512-bit chaining value H_i as the key material and the 512-bit message block M_i as the input of the encryption. Both the encryption and key-schedule use round functions consisting of four operations:

- SubBytes (SB) applies the Substitution-Box to each byte.
- ShiftColumns (SC) cyclically shifts the j-column downwards by j bytes.
- MixRows (MR) multiplies each row of the state by an MDS matrix.
- AddRoundKey (AK or AddRoundConstants AC) XOR the round key (or round constants in key-schedule) to the state.

Note that the last round is a complete round which is unlike AES; a whiting key is added before the first round of encryption. However, the effect of whitening key will be canceled in the splice-and-cut MITM attacks due to the feed-forward mechanism of MP-mode. Please refer to [7] for a detailed description of Whirlpool.

4.1   New Attacks Resulted from Applying the MILP Modeling

Applying the MILP modeling in Sect. 3 on Whirlpool, improved attacks are found for 5- and 6-round, and first attacks are found for 7-round.

For 5-round attacks, guess-and-determine is not required, but allowing bi-direction attribute-propagation/cancellation is essential to achieve the best complexity. For 6-round attacks, guess-and-determine is the critical technique that enables the improved results. For 7-round attacks, guess-and-determine and multiple ways of AddRoundKey (flexible choices from applying AK-MC-RULE or MC-AK-RULE) are the two critical points.

The remaining of this section describes how to use one of the resulted attack configurations to launch a concrete attack on 7-round Whirlpool. A brief description of the improved 6-round attack is then followed. In the description, ShiftRows and MixColumns instead of ShiftColumns and MixRows are used. Thus, the states should be transposed to correspond with the specification of Whirlpool. This transposition does not influence the attacks.

Please refer to Figs. 11, 12, and 13 in the full version [6] for visualizations of configurations of the 7-, 6-, and 5-round attacks, and refer to Sect. B [6] for a summary of notations.

The Attack on 7-Round Whirlpool can be obtained by searching on a small version with $N_{row} \times N_{col} = 4 \times 4$ states and then projecting to attack on the 8×8-state version. In the sequel, to facilitate readers to find the correspondence between the text description and the code implementation for experimental verification of the attack, we describe it using the small version with $N_{row} \times N_{col} = 4 \times 4$ states that is depicted in Fig. 3. One can quickly project this attack on the small version to the real version of Whirlpool (refer to Sect. 3.6 and the correspondence between Figs. 10 and 11 in the full version [6] for illustrations). The attack complexity on the real version is the fourth power of that on the small version.

The attack configuration in Fig. 3a is found with the MILP models. With this configuration, one can conceive an equivalent configuration shown in Fig. 3b. Following both configurations, one can devise the attack, with different procedures to compute initial values of backward neutral bytes. The latter (Fig. 3b) is more direct for the computation; thus, it will be used in the following description. In the following description, all referred states are actual states that are the combination of two virtual states.

Compute Initial Values of Neutral Bytes in Red. To get the initial values of backward neutral bytes (in Red), one only needs to enumerate all possible values of cell $k_3[15]$, and fix values of cells in the main anti-diagonal of #SB^4. That is due to the following observation. Fixing the values of cells in the first column of #MC^4 to be 0 (equivalently, fixing the values of cells in the main anti-diagonal of #SB^4 to be Sbox$^{-1}[0]$), the values of the first column of #SB^5 equals that of k_4. Note that the operations of the round function in encryption and key-schedule are exactly the same, excepting the former using AddRoundKey and the latter using AddRoundConstants. Thus, the first anti-diagonal of #MC^5 will equal that of #KMC^4. Consequently, the impact brought by adding Red cells in the 4th round (k_4) will be canceled in the next round by adding #KMC^4 without consuming degrees of freedom.

Compute Initial Values of Neutral Bytes in Blue. To get the initial values of forward neutral bytes (in Blue), one focuses on the constraints among states $\{$#MC^2, #AK^2, #SB^3, #MC^3, #AK$^3\}$ (refer to Fig. 3b).

There are five degrees of freedom (in bytes) for the forward (Blue). Using four out of the five, one can keep the same attack complexity because the degree of freedom for backward is the bottleneck. Thus, we fix the value of one Blue cell in $\#AK^3$, *i.e.*, $\#AK^3[3]$, as indicated by ▣.

Note that values of Blue cells are constrained such that they have no impact on the last anti-diagonal of $\#MC^2$ and the first diagonal of $\#AK^3$ (are mapped to constants on these state cells). Denote the constants by $\#MC_C^2[3,6,9,12]$ and $\#AK_C^3[0,5,10]$. The initial values of forward neutral bytes can be computed using a *local meet-in-the-middle procedure* as shown in Algorithm 1 in the full version [6]. In Algorithm 1 [6], the procedure starts from guessing two free cells in the first column of $\#AK^3$ and one cell in each of the columns in $\#SB^3$, computes other undetermined cells column-by-column using predetermined constant-impacts on cells in $\#MC^2$, and compute back pair-wisely to match at constant cells in $\#AK^3$. From Algorithm 1 [6], the computational complexity for obtaining the initial values of neutral bytes in Blue is 2^{32} and the memory required is 2^{32} (blocks).

The Main Procedure (refer to Fig. 3b). Assign arbitrary values to those constant impacts of Blue on Red in $\#MC^2$ (*i.e.*, $\#MC_C^2[3,6,9,12]$) and to $\#AK^3_C[3]$. Set $\#AK^3[0,5,10,12,13,14]$ be 0, $k_3[0,5,10]$ and $\#SB_4[0,5,10,15]$ be Sbox$^{-1}[0]$.

Compute the initial values of backward neutral bytes as described above and as shown in Algorithm 1 [6], store the result in $\overrightarrow{T_{\text{Init}}}$.

1. For a new value of 12 Gray bytes $k_3[1,2,3,4,6,7,8,9,11,12,13,14]$, calculate the values of Gray bytes in k_4 and $\#KMC^4$ (this is expected to repeat ς^{11} times before terminating from Step 1(b)iiiE according to Sect. 3.4).
   (a) For each value $\overrightarrow{v}_i$ of Blue cells in $\#MC^3$ stored in $\overrightarrow{T_{\text{Init}}}$,
       i. start from $\#MC^3$, compute forward (only cells in Blue) with the values of Gray bytes in k_3 and k_4 to $\#MC^5$;
       ii. XOR $\#MC^5$ with the values of Gray bytes in $\#KMC^4$;
       iii. set the first anti-diagonal of $\#MC^5$ to be zero, and compute forward to $\#MC^6$ (without AddRoundKey with k_5 but need to XOR the round constant RC[5], because $\#KMC^4$ is used instead);
       iv. compute $MC(\#MC^6)$ and get the value $\overrightarrow{v}_m$ of the main diagonal
       v. store $\overrightarrow{v}_i$ in a look-up table $\overrightarrow{T}$ with $\overrightarrow{v}_m$ as index;
   (b) For each value $\overleftarrow{v}_i$ of the Red cell in k_3, with the value of Gray cells,
       i. compute all values of the round keys, *i.e.*, $k_2, k_1, k_0, k_m, k_4, k_5, k_6$, where k_m is the master key;
       ii. set the Red cell $\#AK^3[15]$ to be $\overleftarrow{v}_i \oplus$ Sbox$^{-1}[0]$, combine with the constant value in $\#AK^3$, compute backward up to $\#AK^0$;
       iii. For each value $\overleftarrow{v}_g$ of the Pink cells in $\#AK^0$,
           A. with the value of Red cell in the first column of $\#AK^0$, compute backward through feed-forward, XOR the given target T, compute $\#AK^6$;
           B. get the value $\overleftarrow{v}_m$ of the main diagonal of $\#AK^6$.

C. for each value $\overrightarrow{v}_i$ of Blue cells in $\#\text{MC}^3$ stored in $\overrightarrow{T}[\overleftarrow{v}_m]$, combine the values of Red cells, restart the computation from $\#\text{AK}^3$ up to $\#\text{AK}^0$;

D. If the newly computed value $\overrightarrow{v}'_g$ of the Pink cells in $\#\text{AK}^0$ does not equal $\overleftarrow{v}_g$, go to Step 1(b)iii. Else, compute to $\#\text{AK}^6$, denote the value by $\overleftarrow{v}$.

E. Start from $\#\text{AK}^3$ with the combined knowledge of values of both Blue and Red cells, compute to $\text{MC}(\#\text{MC}^6)$, if its value $\overrightarrow{v}$ equals $\overleftarrow{v}$, a full-state match is found, output the state $\#\text{SB}^0$ and the key state k_m, and *terminate*. Otherwise, go to Step 1.

Complexity. As analyzed above, the computational and memory complexity of the precomputation of the initial value of forward neutral bytes is 2^{32}. As for the complexity of the main procedure, the attack configuration on the small version $(n = \text{N}_{\text{row}} \times \text{N}_{\text{col}} = 4 \times 4 = 16)$ is, $\overrightarrow{d_b} = 4$, $\overleftarrow{d_r} = 1$, $\overleftarrow{d_{g_r}} = 3$, $\overrightarrow{m} = 4$, $\varsigma = 2^8$, and $\overrightarrow{d_{g_b}} = \overleftrightarrow{d_{g_{br}}} = 0$. According to Eq. (9), the complexity of the whole attack on the small version is therefore $\varsigma^n \cdot (\varsigma^{-(\overleftarrow{d_r} - \overrightarrow{d_{g_b}})} + \varsigma^{-(\overrightarrow{d_b} - \overleftarrow{d_{g_r}})} + \varsigma^{-(\overrightarrow{m} - \overrightarrow{d_{g_b}} - \overleftarrow{d_{g_r}} - \overleftrightarrow{d_{g_{br}}})}) = \varsigma^{16} \cdot \max(\varsigma^{-1} + \varsigma^{-(4-3)} + \varsigma^{-(4-3)}) = \varsigma^{15} = 2^{120}$.

Projecting to the real version of Whirlpool $(n = \text{N}_{\text{row}} \times \text{N}_{\text{col}} = 16 \cdot 4 = 64)$, the complexity will be $(2^{120})^4 = 2^{480}$. Concretely, the attack configuration will be $\overrightarrow{d_b} = 4 \cdot 4 = 16$, $\overleftarrow{d_r} = 1 \cdot 4 = 4$, $\overleftarrow{d_{g_r}} = 3 \cdot 4 = 12$, $\overrightarrow{m} = 4 \cdot 4 = 16$, $\varsigma = 2^8$, and $\overrightarrow{d_{g_b}} = \overleftrightarrow{d_{g_{br}}} = 0$. Accordingly, the attack complexity on the real version of 7-round Whirlpool is $\varsigma^{64} \cdot \max(\varsigma^{-4} + \varsigma^{-(16-12)} + \varsigma^{-(16-12)}) = 2^{480}$.

The memory required by the main procedure is the memory taken by $\overrightarrow{T}$, whose size is limited by the degree of freedom for forward, that is 2^{32} for the small version and 2^{128} for the real version.

To further verify the attack and its complexity analysis, we implemented the attack on the small version with 4×4 states. The round functions of encryption and key-schedule of small Whirlpool CF is simulated using the round function of AES. To make the verification practical, the experiments aim for partial matching instead of full-state matching, while preserving the complexity gain. Concretely, the goal is to match m bits with complexity $\max\{2^{32}, 2^{m-8}\}$. Please refer to https://github.com/MITM-AES-like/Whirlpool_7R for results on $m \in \{36, 40, 44, 48\}$.

The Attack on 6-Round Whirlpool. When searching on the full-size version $(\text{N}_{\text{row}} \times \text{N}_{\text{col}} = 8 \times 8)$, results with asymmetric patterns were found. One example is depicted in Fig. 12 [6]. Following the configuration, one can devise an attack on 6-round of Whirlpool with better complexity than previous ones. The concrete attack configuration is $\overrightarrow{d_b} = 9$, $\overleftarrow{d_r} = 24$, $\overrightarrow{d_{g_b}} = 15$, $\overrightarrow{m} = 24$, $\varsigma = 2^8$, and $\overleftarrow{d_{g_r}} = \overleftrightarrow{d_{g_{br}}} = 0$. Accordingly, the attack complexity on the full-size version of 6-round Whirlpool is $\varsigma^{64} \cdot \max(\varsigma^{-24-15} + \varsigma^{-(9)} + \varsigma^{-(24-15)}) = 2^{440}$. The memory required is $2^{24 \times 8} = 2^{192}$. The procedures to compute the initial values of neutral bytes for both directions are relatively simpler than that of the above attack on

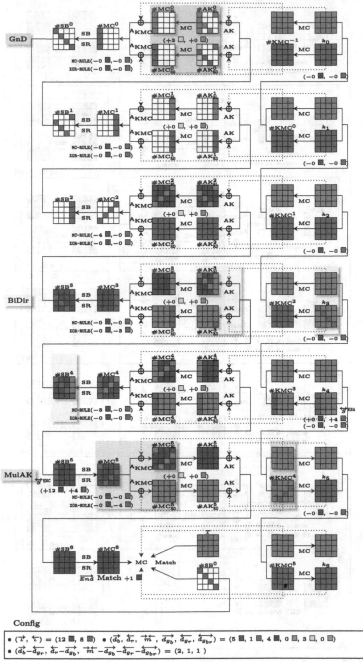

(a) Configuration automatically found

This implies an attack on the full version (8×8) as shown in Fig. 11 with configuration (($\overrightarrow{d_b} - \overleftarrow{d_{g_r}}$, $\overleftarrow{d_r} - \overrightarrow{d_{g_b}}$, $\overleftrightarrow{m} - \overrightarrow{d_{g_b}} - \overleftarrow{d_{g_r}} - \overleftrightarrow{d_{g_{br}}}$) = $(8, 4, 4)$).

Fig. 3. An example of using (2×2 of 4×4) to search the MITM attack on 7-round Whirlpool and an equivalent configuration used in the experimental verification (cont.)

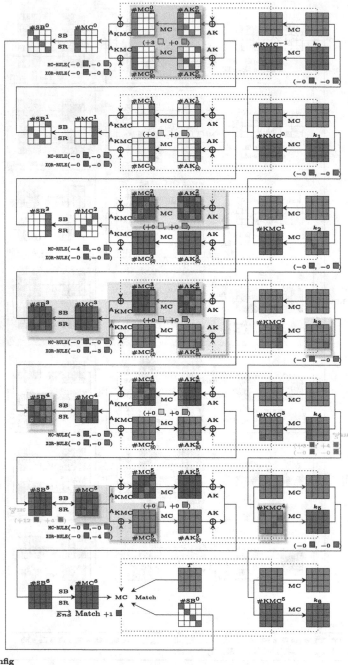

Config

- $(\overrightarrow{r}, \overleftarrow{r}) = (12\ \blacksquare, 8\ \blacksquare)$ • $(\overrightarrow{d_b}, \overleftarrow{d_r}, \overrightarrow{m}, \overrightarrow{d_{gb}}, \overleftarrow{d_{gr}}, \overrightarrow{d_{gbr}}) = (4\ \blacksquare, 1\ \blacksquare, 4\ \blacksquare, 0\ \blacksquare, 3\ \square, 0\ \blacksquare)$
- $(\overrightarrow{d_b} - \overleftarrow{d_{gr}}, \overleftarrow{d_r} - \overrightarrow{d_{gb}}, \overrightarrow{m} - \overrightarrow{d_{gb}} - \overleftarrow{d_{gr}} - \overrightarrow{d_{gbr}}) = (1, 1, 1)$

(b) Equivalent configuration used in the experimental verification

Fig. 3. (*continued*)

7-round. That is because, the cancellation constraints on the Blue is at a single point, *i.e.*, ($\#\text{MC}^2, \#\text{AK}^2$). The cancellation constraints on the Red is also at a single point, *i.e.*, ($\#\text{MC}^4, \#\text{AK}^4$). As for such constraints, column-by-column independent computations can be used to derive the initial values of neutral bytes for both directions.

Conversion from Pseudo-Preimage to Preimage Attacks has been discussed in previous works. Here, we follow the *Two Types of Last Block Attacks* from [28,30]. Denote the time complexity of inverting the reduced-Whirlpool compression function as 2^ℓ. A random message fulfills the padding rule of Whirlpool with probability 2^{-9}, hence it costs $2^{\ell+9}$ to find a right last block. Then an unbalanced meet-in-the-middle is carried out between the initial value and the input chaining value of the last block, which costs $2^{(512+\ell)/2}$ and sums to $2^{(512+\ell)/2} + 2^{\ell+9}$ to find a long and full preimage. Detailed conversion results are summarized in Table 1. We note further complexity optimizations are possible, by finding pseudo-preimages under multi-target scenarios and utilizing them in the "unbalanced meet-in-the-middle" phase as discussed in [15].

4.2 Discussions on the New Attacks

The previous best attack on Whirlpool is up to 6-round [28]. In the 6-round attack in [28], although the freedom degree in the key states is exploited, the computational chunks between the key schedule and the encryption data-path are designed to be almost identical due to the limitation of manual analysis. In contrast, in the new attack, the computational chunks between the key schedule and the encryption data-path are largely different. Thus, the degree of freedom in Blue and Red can be relatively more balanced, and the required number of guessing bytes is relatively less. Consequently, the complexity is better.

Attacking one more round than the previously best attacked, new strategies are required on top of those appeared in [28]. In the new 7-round attack, apart from GnD, flexibly using of equivalent round-keys $\#\text{KMC}$ or the real round keys k (MulAK) is critical to save degrees of freedom. Moreover, complex non-linear constraints must be imposed on Blue cells to let Blue propagates towards backward besides forward (BiDir), and then cancel their impacts on Red-attribute propagation. Thus, efficient procedure (*e.g.*, the *local meet-in-the-middle procedure*) for obtaining initial values of neutral cells fulfilling the non-linear constraints is necessary here.

5 Application to Preimage Attacks on Grøstl

Grøstl, proposed by Gauravaram *et al.* in [13], is one of the five finalists of SHA-3 competition hosted by NIST. Grøstl adopts a double-pipe design, *i.e.*, the size of the chaining value, which is $2n$-bit, is twice as the hash size, which is n-bit. For Grøstl-256, the hash size is 256 bits, and for Grøstl-512, it is 512 bits. Two $2n$-bit AES-like permutations P and Q are employed to build the CF and OT.

5.1   New Attacks Resulted from Applying the MILP Modeling

Applying the MILP modeling approach described in Sect. 3 on the OT (and on the $P(H_i) \oplus H_i$ part of the CF) of Grøstl-256 and Grøstl-512, new attacks are found on 6-round and 8-round, respectively. Besides, many efficient attacks on shorter rounds are found.

For the 6-round attack on the OT of Grøstl-256, GnD is the essential that enables to cover one more attacked round than previous 5-round attacks [30]; BiDir is the essential that enables better complexity than previous 6-round attacks [22]. Besides, many inferior attacks than the presented best one on 6-round Grøstl-256 are found. For those inferior attacks, the computation of initial values of neutral bytes is relatively easier, but the complexity of the entire attack is higher. Thus, a non-trivial procedure to compute the initial structure (initial values of neutral bytes) is essential for achieving the best complexity.

For the 8-round attack on the OT of Grøstl-512, GnD is the essential that enables to achieve better complexity than the previous 8-round attack [30]. Besides, compared to the 8-round attack in [30], in the presented attack, the initial structure covers one more round (4 rounds) by allowing one attribute-propagation conceding to the opposite attribute-propagation in both directions.

The configurations of various attacks can be found in Figs. 5, 6, 7, 8, 16, 17, 14 and 15 in the full version [6]. The concrete attack procedures on 6-round OT of Grøstl-256 and 8-round OT of Grøstl-512 are presented in Sect. C [6].

CONVERSION TO PSEUDO-PREIMAGE ATTACKS. The attacks on the OT of Grøstl can be converted into pseudo-preimage attacks on Grøstl combining with similar attacks on the $P(H) \oplus H$ of the CF using the conversion method in [30]. The complexity of the converted pseudo-preimage attacks are summarized in Table 1. More details about the conversion can be found in Sect. F of the full version [6].

5.2   Discussions on the New Attacks

An interesting feature of the best attack on 6-round Grøstl-256 depicted in Fig. 5 [6] is that, with necessary guessing, the computation of Blue covers the full 6-round. That is, the Blue propagates to backward besides forward and contributes to degrees of matching from both sides. Besides, like the attack on 7-round Whirlpool, it requires a non-trivial local meet-in-the-middle procedure to compute initial values of neutral bytes.

Note that, obtaining the previous best attacks on Grøstl, the work in [30] has already been assisted with automatic searching, and the 5-round attack on Grøstl-256 in [30] was claimed to be optimal. However, the optimality hold only in a restricted search space, apart from lacking the consideration of the GnD technique. In contrast, the presented 5-round attacks on Grøstl-256 in Figs. 14 and 15 [6] achieve better complexity than that in [30] and is optimal in an expanded search space where BiDir and GnD are considered.

6   Applications to Collision and Key-Recovery Attacks

The MILP models for searching for the best preimage attacks can be directly transformed to search for the best collision attacks on hash functions and key-recovery attacks on block ciphers. For collision attacks, according to the analysis in Sect. 3.5, what needs to be done is to simply restrict the matching point to be at the last round and add constraints shown in Eq. 13. Applying to Grøstl's OT, AES-hashing, Kiasu-BC-hashing[3], new and improved attacks were found.

For key-recovery attacks, upon the MILP models for preimage attack, one simply needs to constraint that the degrees of freedom in both forward and backward only source from the key states, relax the degrees of matching such that it is not included in the objective but simply be non-zero[4], and constraint that the plaintext or ciphertext contains only Red and Gray cells or only Blue and Gray cells. Besides, the objective can be set to maximize the number of Gray cells in the plaintext or ciphertext, which can optimize data complexity. Applying to SKINNY-n-$3n$, improvements in terms of time complexity (see Fig. 23 of the full version [6]) or data complexity (see Fig. 24 [6]) upon the attack in [11] on 23-round reduced version were obtained. In Sect. F of the full version, visualizations of representative attack configurations are presented. The complexity of the attacks are summarized in Table 1.

Acknowledgements. We thank anonymous reviewers for their valuable comments. This research is partially supported by the National Natural Science Foundation of China (Grants No. 62172410, 61802400, 61732021, 61802399, 61961146004), the National Key R&D Program of China (Grants No. 2018YFA0704704, 2018YFA0704701), the Youth Innovation Promotion Association of Chinese Academy of Sciences; Nanyang Technological University in Singapore under Grant 04INS000397C230, Ministry of Education in Singapore under Grants RG91/20 and MOE2019-T2-1-060; the Gopalakrishnan – NTU Presidential Postdoctoral Fellowship 2020; the Major Program of Guangdong Basic and Applied Research (Grant No. 2019B030302008), Shandong Province Key R&D Project (Nos. 2020ZLYS09 and 2019JZZY010133).

References

1. Alliance, ZigBee. ZigBee 2007 specification (2007). http://www.zigbee.org/
2. Aoki, K., Sasaki, Yu.: Preimage attacks on one-block MD4, 63-step MD5 and more. In: Avanzi, R.M., Keliher, L., Sica, F. (eds.) SAC 2008. LNCS, vol. 5381, pp. 103–119. Springer, Heidelberg (2009). https://doi.org/10.1007/978-3-642-04159-4_7
3. Aumasson, J.-P., Meier, W., Mendel, F.: Preimage attacks on 3-pass HAVAL and step-reduced MD5. In: Avanzi, R.M., Keliher, L., Sica, F. (eds.) SAC 2008. LNCS, vol. 5381, pp. 120–135. Springer, Heidelberg (2009). https://doi.org/10.1007/978-3-642-04159-4_8

---

[3] Kiasu-BC [18] is a tweakable block cipher, the only difference with AES-128 is XOR-ing a 64-bit tweak value to the first two rows of the state after each AddRoundKey.

[4] In MITM key-recovery attack, the degree of matching can be efficiently increased using simultaneous matching with multiple plaintext/ciphertext pairs [12].

4. Bao, Z., Ding, L., Guo, J., Wang, H., Zhang, W.: Improved meet-in-the-middle preimage attacks against AES hashing modes. IACR Trans. Symm. Cryptol. **2019**(4), 318–347 (2019)
5. Bao, Z., et al.: Automatic search of meet-in-the-middle preimage attacks on AES-like hashing. In: Canteaut, A., Standaert, F.-X. (eds.) EUROCRYPT 2021. LNCS, vol. 12696, pp. 771–804. Springer, Cham (2021). https://doi.org/10.1007/978-3-030-77870-5_27
6. Bao, Z., Guo, J., Shi, D., Tu, Y.: Superposition meet-in-the-middle attacks: updates on fundamental security of AES-like hashing. Cryptology ePrint Archive, Report 2021/575 (2021). https://eprint.iacr.org/2021/575
7. Barreto, P.S.L.M., Rijmen, V.: The WHIRLPOOL Hashing Function (2000). http://citeseerx.ist.psu.edu/viewdoc/download?doi=10.1.1.529.3184&rep=rep1&type=pdf. Revised in 2003
8. Bogdanov, A., Rechberger, C.: A 3-subset meet-in-the-middle attack: cryptanalysis of the lightweight block cipher KTANTAN. In: Biryukov, A., Gong, G., Stinson, D.R. (eds.) SAC 2010. LNCS, vol. 6544, pp. 229–240. Springer, Heidelberg (2011). https://doi.org/10.1007/978-3-642-19574-7_16
9. Bouillaguet, C., Derbez, P., Fouque, P.-A.: Automatic search of attacks on round-reduced AES and applications. In: Rogaway, P. (ed.) CRYPTO 2011. LNCS, vol. 6841, pp. 169–187. Springer, Heidelberg (2011). https://doi.org/10.1007/978-3-642-22792-9_10
10. Daemen, J., Rijmen, V.: The Design of Rijndael: AES - The Advanced Encryption Standard. Information Security and Cryptography. Springer, Heidelberg (2002). https://doi.org/10.1007/978-3-662-04722-4
11. Dong, X., Hua, J., Sun, S., Li, Z., Wang, X., Hu, L.: Meet-in-the-middle attacks revisited: key-recovery, collision, and preimage attacks. In: Malkin, T., Peikert, C. (eds.) CRYPTO 2021. LNCS, vol. 12827, pp. 278–308. Springer, Cham (2021). https://doi.org/10.1007/978-3-030-84252-9_10
12. Fuhr, T., Minaud, B.: Match box meet-in-the-middle attack against KATAN. In: Cid, C., Rechberger, C. (eds.) FSE 2014. LNCS, vol. 8540, pp. 61–81. Springer, Heidelberg (2015). https://doi.org/10.1007/978-3-662-46706-0_4
13. Gauravaram, P., et al.: Grøstl - a SHA-3 candidate (March 2011). http://www.groestl.info/Groestl.pdf
14. Gilbert, H., Peyrin, T.: Super-sbox cryptanalysis: improved attacks for AES-like permutations. In: Hong, S., Iwata, T. (eds.) FSE 2010. LNCS, vol. 6147, pp. 365–383. Springer, Heidelberg (2010). https://doi.org/10.1007/978-3-642-13858-4_21
15. Guo, J., Ling, S., Rechberger, C., Wang, H.: Advanced meet-in-the-middle preimage attacks: first results on full tiger, and improved results on MD4 and SHA-2. In: Abe, M. (ed.) ASIACRYPT 2010. LNCS, vol. 6477, pp. 56–75. Springer, Heidelberg (2010). https://doi.org/10.1007/978-3-642-17373-8_4
16. Hosoyamada, A., Sasaki, Yu.: Finding hash collisions with quantum computers by using differential trails with smaller probability than birthday bound. In: Canteaut, A., Ishai, Y. (eds.) EUROCRYPT 2020. LNCS, vol. 12106, pp. 249–279. Springer, Cham (2020). https://doi.org/10.1007/978-3-030-45724-2_9
17. ISO/IEC. 10118-2:2010: Information technology - Security techniques - Hash-functions - Part 2: Hash-functions using an n-bit block cipher, 3rd edn. International Organization for Standardization, Geneve, Switzerland (October 2010)
18. Jean, J., Nikolić, I., Peyrin, T.: Tweaks and keys for block ciphers: the TWEAKEY framework. In: Sarkar, P., Iwata, T. (eds.) ASIACRYPT 2014. LNCS, vol. 8874, pp. 274–288. Springer, Heidelberg (2014). https://doi.org/10.1007/978-3-662-45608-8_15

19. Lamberger, M., Mendel, F., Rechberger, C., Rijmen, V., Schläffer, M.: Rebound distinguishers: results on the full whirlpool compression function. In: Matsui, M. (ed.) ASIACRYPT 2009. LNCS, vol. 5912, pp. 126–143. Springer, Heidelberg (2009). https://doi.org/10.1007/978-3-642-10366-7_8

20. Leurent, G.: MD4 is not one-way. In: Nyberg, K. (ed.) FSE 2008. LNCS, vol. 5086, pp. 412–428. Springer, Heidelberg (2008). https://doi.org/10.1007/978-3-540-71039-4_26

21. Li, J., Isobe, T., Shibutani, K.: Converting meet-in-the-middle preimage attack into pseudo collision attack: application to SHA-2. In: Canteaut, A. (ed.) FSE 2012. LNCS, vol. 7549, pp. 264–286. Springer, Heidelberg (2012). https://doi.org/10.1007/978-3-642-34047-5_16

22. Ma, B., Li, B., Hao, R., Li, X.: Improved (pseudo) preimage attacks on reduced-round GOST and Grøstl-256 and studies on several truncation patterns for AES-like compression functions. In: Tanaka, K., Suga, Y. (eds.) IWSEC 2015. LNCS, vol. 9241, pp. 79–96. Springer, Cham (2015). https://doi.org/10.1007/978-3-319-22425-1_6

23. Preneel, B., Govaerts, R., Vandewalle, J.: Hash functions based on block ciphers: a synthetic approach. In: Stinson, D.R. (ed.) CRYPTO 1993. LNCS, vol. 773, pp. 368–378. Springer, Heidelberg (1994). https://doi.org/10.1007/3-540-48329-2_31

24. Sasaki, Yu.: Meet-in-the-middle preimage attacks on aes hashing modes and an application to whirlpool. In: Joux, A. (ed.) FSE 2011. LNCS, vol. 6733, pp. 378–396. Springer, Heidelberg (2011). https://doi.org/10.1007/978-3-642-21702-9_22

25. Sasaki, Yu., Aoki, K.: Preimage attacks on 3, 4, and 5-pass HAVAL. In: Pieprzyk, J. (ed.) ASIACRYPT 2008. LNCS, vol. 5350, pp. 253–271. Springer, Heidelberg (2008). https://doi.org/10.1007/978-3-540-89255-7_16

26. Sasaki, Yu., Aoki, K.: Preimage attacks on step-reduced MD5. In: Mu, Y., Susilo, W., Seberry, J. (eds.) ACISP 2008. LNCS, vol. 5107, pp. 282–296. Springer, Heidelberg (2008). https://doi.org/10.1007/978-3-540-70500-0_21

27. Sasaki, Yu., Aoki, K.: Finding preimages in full MD5 faster than exhaustive search. In: Joux, A. (ed.) EUROCRYPT 2009. LNCS, vol. 5479, pp. 134–152. Springer, Heidelberg (2009). https://doi.org/10.1007/978-3-642-01001-9_8

28. Sasaki, Yu., Wang, L., Wu, S., Wu, W.: Investigating fundamental security requirements on whirlpool: improved preimage and collision attacks. In: Wang, X., Sako, K. (eds.) ASIACRYPT 2012. LNCS, vol. 7658, pp. 562–579. Springer, Heidelberg (2012). https://doi.org/10.1007/978-3-642-34961-4_34

29. Sun, S., Hu, L., Wang, P., Qiao, K., Ma, X., Song, L.: Automatic security evaluation and (related-key) differential characteristic search: application to SIMON, PRESENT, LBlock, DES(L) and other bit-oriented block ciphers. In: Sarkar, P., Iwata, T. (eds.) ASIACRYPT 2014. LNCS, vol. 8873, pp. 158–178. Springer, Heidelberg (2014). https://doi.org/10.1007/978-3-662-45611-8_9

30. Wu, S., Feng, D., Wu, W., Guo, J., Dong, L., Zou, J.: (Pseudo) preimage attack on round-reduced Grøstl hash function and others. In: Canteaut, A. (ed.) FSE 2012. LNCS, vol. 7549, pp. 127–145. Springer, Heidelberg (2012). https://doi.org/10.1007/978-3-642-34047-5_8

31. Zhang, B., Feng, D.: New guess-and-determine attack on the self-shrinking generator. In: Lai, X., Chen, K. (eds.) ASIACRYPT 2006. LNCS, vol. 4284, pp. 54–68. Springer, Heidelberg (2006). https://doi.org/10.1007/11935230_4

32. Zou, J., Wu, W., Wu, S., Dong, L.: Improved (pseudo) preimage attack and second preimage attack on round-reduced Grostl hash function. J. Inf. Sci. Eng. 30(6), 1789–1806 (2014)

Triangulating Rebound Attack on AES-like Hashing

Xiaoyang Dong[1,3]([✉]) [ID], Jian Guo[2]([✉]) [ID], Shun Li[2,4]([✉]) [ID],
and Phuong Pham[2]([✉]) [ID]

[1] Institute for Advanced Study, BNRist, Tsinghua University, Beijing, China
xiaoyangdong@tsinghua.edu.cn
[2] School of Physical and Mathematical Sciences, Nanyang Technological University,
Singapore, Singapore
{guojian,shun.li}@ntu.edu.sg, pham0079@e.ntu.edu.sg
[3] National Financial Cryptography Research Center, Beijing, China
[4] Department of Computer Science and Engineering, Shanghai Jiao Tong University,
Shanghai 200240, China

Abstract. The rebound attack was introduced by Mendel *et al.* at
FSE 2009 to fulfill a heavy middle round of a differential path for free, utilizing the degree of freedom from states. The inbound phase was extended
to 2 rounds by the Super-Sbox technique invented by Lamberger *et al.*
at ASIACRYPT 2009 and Gilbert and Peyrin at FSE 2010. In ASI-
ACRYPT 2010, Sasaki *et al.* further reduced the requirement of memory
by introducing the non-full-active Super-Sbox. In this paper, we further develop this line of research by introducing *Super-Inbound*, which
is able to connect multiple 1-round or 2-round (non-full-active) Super-
Sbox inbound phases by utilizing fully the degrees of freedom from both
states and key, yet without the use of large memory. This essentially
extends the inbound phase by up to 3 rounds. We applied this technique
to find classic or quantum collisions on several AES-like hash functions,
and improved the attacked round number by 1 to 5 in targets including
AES-128 and SKINNY hashing modes, Saturnin-Hash, and Grøstl-512. To
demonstrate the correctness of our attacks, the semi-free-start collision
on 6-round AES-128-MMO/MP with estimated time complexity 2^{24} in classical setting was implemented and an example pair was found instantly
on a standard PC.

Keywords: Triangulating Rebound · Quantum Attack · Collision
Attacks · Rebound Attacks · Triangulation Algorithm · Super-Inbound

1   Introduction

Cryptographic hash function compresses a binary string of arbitrary length into
a short fixed-length digest. It is one of the most fundamental cryptographic

The full version of the paper is available at https://eprint.iacr.org/2022/731.

Y. Dodis and T. Shrimpton (Eds.): CRYPTO 2022, LNCS 13507, pp. 94–124, 2022.
https://doi.org/10.1007/978-3-031-15802-5_4

primitives that act as the underlying building blocks in various advanced crypto-graphic protocols, including digital signatures, authenticated encryption, secure multiparty computation and post-quantum public-key cryptography, etc. A cryptographic hash function must fulfill three basic security properties: collision resistance, preimage resistance, and second-preimage resistance. Due to the breakthroughs in collision attacks [74, 76, 77] on the hash functions MD5 and SHA-1, the academic communities advanced new hashing designs, including the best-known SHA-3 [10]. AES-like hashing, inspired by the elegant yet secure and efficient design strategies of Advanced Encryption Standard (AES) [21], is another new hashing design. It adopts block ciphers or permutations with similar features to AES as the underlying building blocks, such as Whirlpool [6], Grøstl [34], AES-MMO, Grindahl [52], ECHO [8], Haraka v2 [53], etc. These hash functions are commonly known as AES-like hashing.

Rebound Attacks [62], introduced by Mendel, Rechberger, Schläffer, and Thomsen at FSE 2009, is one of the most effective tools on the cryptanalysis of AES-like hash functions. It can be applied to both block cipher based and permutation based constructions. The idea of the rebound attack is to divide an attack into two phases, an inbound and an outbound phase. In the inbound phase, degrees of freedom are used to realize part of the differential characteristic deterministically. The remainder of the characteristic in the outbound phase is fulfilled in a probabilistic manner.

In order to penetrate more rounds, at ASIACRYPT 2009, Lamberger et al. [56] proposed the multiple inbound phases and connected them by leveraging the degrees of freedom of the key. Later, Gilbert and Peyrin [35] and Lamberger et al. [56] further extended the inbound phase by treating two consecutive AES-like rounds as the Super-Sbox [20]. At ASIACRYPT 2010, Sasaki et al. [70] reduced the memory cost by exploiting the differential property of non-full-active Super-Sboxes. At CRYPTO 2011, Naya-Plasencia [66] improved the rebound attack by introducing advanced algorithms for merging large lists. At CRYPTO 2012, Dinur et al. [26] further reduced the memory cost of the rebound attack by proposing the dissection technique. The rebound attack has since become a basic cryptanalysis tool to evaluate hash functions against collision attacks or distinguishing attacks [25, 32, 45, 46, 51, 59, 60, 63, 71]. Interestingly, the idea of the rebound attack was in turn used to improve the Demirci-Selçuk MITM attacks [24, 33] and biclique attack [11].

Quantum Cryptanalysis attracts more and more attention due to Shor's quantum attacks [73] breaking the security of public-key crypto-systems RSA and ECC. For symmetric ciphers, the community has also witnessed many important quantum cryptanalysis results recently, such as quantum distinguisher on 3-round Feistel [54], key-recovery attack on Even-Mansour construction [55], key-recovery attacks or forgeries on MACs and authenticated encryption schemes [47], and more [13, 27, 57]. However, most attacks need to query the online quantum oracles with superposition states, which is believed to be an impractical projection for quantum physics. Thereafter, the quantum attacks [12,14,19,36,38,48,67] only using offline quantum computers are considered to be of more practical relevance.

Since hash functions can be implemented in offline quantum circuit, the attackers can freely make offline quantum superposition queries. There are several quantum generic (multi-target) preimage attacks [2,19] and multicollision attacks [41,42,58]. For generic quantum collision attacks, three quantum generic algorithms exist under different assumptions of the availability of quantum and classical memory resources:

- Condition 1: Exponentially large quantum random access memory (qRAM) is available. Brassard, Høyer, and Tapp [15] introduced the generic quantum collision attack (named as BHT algorithm) with $2^{n/3}$ quantum time complexity and $2^{n/3}$ qRAM.
- Condition 2: Neither exponentially large qRAM nor classic RAM is available. The quantum version of parallel rho's algorithm [9,39,75] achieves a time-space trade off of time $\frac{2^{n/2}}{S}$ with S computers.
- Condition 3: Exponentially large qRAM is not available but large classical RAM is. Chailloux, Naya-Plasencia, and Schrottenloher [19] introduced the CNS algorithm to find collision in time $2^{2n/5}$ with classical RAM of size $2^{n/5}$.

At EUROCRYPT 2020, Hosoyamada and Sasaki [39] introduced the first quantum dedicated collision attacks by converting the classical rebound attacks into quantum rebound attacks. This showed that, under their respective bounds of generic algorithms, quantum attacks are able to penetrate more rounds than classical attacks. At ASIACRYPT 2020, Dong et al. [30] reduced the requirement of qRAM in the quantum rebound attack by exploiting non-full-active Super-Sbox technique [70]. At CRYPTO 2021, Hosoyamada and Sasaki [40] introduced the quantum collision attacks on reduced SHA-2. At ASIACRYPT 2021, Dong et al. [31] studied the quantum free-start collision attacks.

1.1   Our Contributions

In order to extend the attacked round by the rebound attack, Lamberger et al. [56] connected two local inbound phases by consuming the degree of freedom in the key. Later, Super-Sbox [35,56] and non-full-active Super-Sbox [70] were proposed. In this paper, we further generalize this idea by bridging multiple inbound phases with available degrees of freedom both from the key and the internal data path, to build the *Super-Inbound*. With the help of Khovratovich et al.'s [50] triangulation algorithm, we identify truncated differential trails for AES hashing modes with sound configurations on the positions of several local inbound parts, as well as relatively low complexity to bridge the multiple local inbound parts. We name this method as *triangulating rebound attack*. With this advanced method in hand, we achieve the following results:

AES-MMO. The MMO-mode (shown in Fig. 2) instantiated with AES [21] is a popular AES-like hashing design, which is standardized by Zigbee [1] and also suggested by ISO [43]. Many advanced cryptographic protocols, e.g., multi-party computation [37,49], adopt AES-MMO due to its high efficiency when implemented with AES-IN. The best classical collision attacks are for 6 rounds [35,56]. At EUROCRYPT 2020, Hosoyamda and Sasaki [39] introduced two 7-round quantum collision attacks better than BHT algorithm [15] or parallel rho's algorithm [75]. At ASIACRYPT 2020, Dong et al. [30] introduced 7-round quantum collison better than CNS algorithm [19].

We extend the previous 2-round inbound phase into 3- or 4-round *Super-Inbound* for AES-128. Thereby, we build the first 7-round semi-free-start collision attack on AES-128-MMO/MP in classical setting, while the previous classical collision attack reaches 6 rounds [35,56]. In addition, a 6-round practical instance of semi-free-start collision and an 8-round quantum semi-free-start collision attack are given. Moreover, the first 8-round quantum collision attack on AES-128-MMO/MP is given, with time complexity better than parallel rho's algorithm [9,39,75].

Saturnin-Hash. It is the hash function among the post-quantum lightweight cipher family Saturnin designed by Canteaut et al. [17]. It is one of the round 2 candidates of the NIST lightweight cryptography competition. The designers of Saturnin introduced the 10-round related-key recovery attack on the Saturnin block cipher [16]. At ASIACRYPT 2021, Dong et al. [31] proposed several quantum and classical collision attacks on Saturnin-Hash and its compression function, including a 7-round semi-free-start quantum collision attack and an 8-round free-start quantum collision attack.

We extend the previous 2-round inbound phase to the 4-round *Super-Inbound*. Finally, the time complexity of the 8-round free-start quantum collision attack is significantly reduce from $2^{122.5}$ to $2^{89.65}$. Further, the first 10-round free-start quantum collision attack is derived with two more rounds than Dong et al.'s result [31].

SKINNY-128-384-MMO. As SKINNY [7] is running for ISO standard, it is natural to build lightweight hash with the ISO suggested hashing mode MMO. At ASIACRYPT 2021, Dong et al. [31] introduced the 16-round quantum free-start collision attack on SKINNY-128-384-MMO. In this paper, by exploring the large degrees of freedom of the key schedule for SKINNY-128-384-MMO, we extend the previous 2-round inbound phase into a 5-round *Super-Inbound*, and finally achieve 5 more rounds on the free-start quantum collision attack. In addition, a 19-round classical free start collision attack is given, which is even better than previous quantum attack.

Grøstl. Grøstl is one of the five finalists of SHA-3. In this paper, by bridging the differences with degrees of freedom from the states, we propose the memoryless method to solve the 3-round non-full-active inbound part for Grøstl-512. Thereafter, the improved semi-free-start collisions with one more round than before for both Grøstl-512 and its predecessor are derived. The results are summarized in Table 1.

1.2 Novelty and Comparison with Previous Works

Both rebound attack [62] and triangulation algorithm [50] are existing techniques. However, combining these two techniques together as one cryptanalysis tool has not appeared before. When using these two techniques together, we can exploit many more degrees of freedom (DoF) from the key schedule algorithm, which greatly extends the inbound part of our rebound attack. Therefore, the number of possible truncated differential trails for the rebound attack increases significantly than before. In previous rebound attacks on AES-MMO (including [30,39]), the authors place a 2-round full/non-full active Super-Sbox in the inbound phase, and extend it forwards and backwards in the outbound phases to find a useful rebound-attack trail. However, in our attack, we have to use 3-/4-round truncated differentials as the multiple inbound phases, which have many more choices than a 2-round Super-Sbox before. Moreover, not all those 3-/4-round inbound can be solved efficiently by triangulation algorithm (actually, it is time consuming to compute a compatible pair for most 3-/4-round truncated differentials), and we have to pick a good trail from many choices.

Therefore, as another contribution, we introduce a heuristic automatic tool (CP-based) to identify good trails for our rebound attacks, which succeeds to find the 7-/8-round collision attacks on AES-MMO and gains 1-round improvement.

We note that the multiple inbound phases technique was already introduced and used many times before, see for instance the rebound attacks on the LANE [59], ECHO [44], JH [68], etc. The additional degrees of freedom were in these cases given by bigger states. The truncated differences affect both the number of rounds covered by the inbound phases, and the differential probabilities of the outbound phases. In the previous works, the choices of these truncated differences are made in ad hoc ways. In our paper, we introduce triangulation algorithm into the rebound attack, as well as the automated search of configuration for the rebound attack with multiple inbound phases, which is the main novelty comparing to previous ad hoc ways.

2 Preliminaries

2.1 AES-like Hashing

AES [21] operates on a 4×4 column-major order array of bytes, whose round function contains four major transformations as illustrated in Fig. 1: SubBytes (SB), ShiftRows (SR), MixColumns (MC), and AddRoundKey (AK). By making changes to the numbers of rows and columns, the sizes of the cells, the order of the transformations, one can produce new designs named as AES-like round functions. Usually, the MixColumns is to multiply an MDS matrix to each column of the state. An exception is SKINNY [7], which uses the non-MDS matrix.

By using (keyed) permutations with AES-like round functions in certain hashing modes (like MD, MMO, and MP hashing modes [64, Section 9.4] in Fig. 2), compression functions (denoted as CF) can be constructed. Plugging such compression functions into the Merkle-Damgård construction [22,65], one arrives at AES-like

Table 1. A summary of the results.

Target	Attack	Rounds	Time	C-Mem	qRAM	Setting	Ref.
AES-128-MMO/MP							
Hash	Collision	5/10	2^{56}	2^4	0	Classic	[62]
		6/10	2^{56}	2^{32}	0	Classic	[35,56]
		7/10	$2^{42.50}$	0	2^{48}	Quantum	[39]
		7/10	$2^{59.5}$	0	0	Quantum	[39]
		7/10	$2^{45.8}$	0	0	Quantum	[30]
		8/10	$2^{55.53}$	0	0	Quantum	Sect. 4.3
	Preimage	7/10	2^{125}	2^8	-	Classic	[69]
		7/10	2^{123}	2^8	-		[3]
		8/10	2^{125}	2^8	-		[4]
Compression function	Semi-free	6/10	2^{24}	-	-	Classic	Sect. 4.2
	Semi-free	7/10	2^{56}	2^{16}	-	Classic	Sect. 4.1
	Semi-free	8/10	2^{34}	-	-	Quantum	Sect. 4.2
	any	any	2^{64}	-	-	any	[9,39,75]
	any	any	$2^{42.7}$	-	$2^{42.7}$	Quantum	[15]
	any	any	$2^{51.2}$	$2^{25.6}$	-	Quantum	[19]
Saturnin-Hash							
Hash	Collision	5/16	2^{64}	2^{66}	0	Classic	[31]
		7/16	$2^{113.5}$	-	-	Quantum	[31]
	Preimage	7/16	2^{232}	2^{48}	-	Classic	[29]
Compression function	Free-start	6/16	2^{80}	2^{66}	-	Classic	[31]
	Semi-free	7/16	$2^{90.1}$	-	-	Quantum	[31]
	Semi-free	7/16	2^{86}	-	-	Quantum	Full Ver. [28]
	Free-start	8/16	$2^{122.5}$	-	-	Quantum	[31]
	Free-start	8/16	$2^{89.65}$	-	-	Quantum	Sect. 5.1
	Free-start	10/16	$2^{127.2}$	-	-	Quantum	Sect. 5.2
	any	any	2^{128}	-	-	any	[9,39,75]
	any	any	$2^{85.3}$	-	$2^{85.3}$	Quantum	[15]
	any	any	$2^{102.4}$	$2^{51.2}$	-	Quantum	[19]
Grøstl-512							
Compression function	Distinguisher	10/14	2^{392}	2^{64}	-	Classic	[45]
		11/14	2^{72}	2^{56}	-	Classic	[18]
	Semi-free	6/14	2^{180}	2^{64}	-	Classic	[72]
		7/14	2^{214}	-	-	Quantum	Full Ver. [28]
Compression function v0	Semi-free	7/14	2^{152}	2^{64}	-	Classic	[61]
		7/14	2^{152}	2^{56}	-	Classic	[70]
		8/14	2^{244}	-	-	Quantum	Full Ver. [28]
	any	any	2^{256}	-	-	any	[9,39,75]
	any	any	$2^{170.7}$	-	$2^{170.7}$	Quantum	[15]
	any	any	$2^{204.8}$	$2^{102.4}$	-	Quantum	[19]
SKINNY-128-384-MMO/MP							
Compression function	Free-start	16/56	$2^{59.8}$	-	-	Quantum	[31]
		19/56	$2^{51.2}$	-	-	Classic	Sect. 6.2
		21/56	$2^{46.2}$	-	-	Quantum	Sect. 6.1
	any	any	2^{64}	-	-	any	[9,39,75]
	any	any	$2^{42.7}$	-	$2^{42.7}$	Quantum	[15]
	any	any	$2^{51.2}$	$2^{25.6}$	-	Quantum	[19]

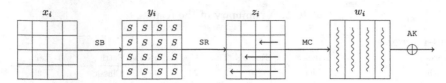

Fig. 1. The round function of AES

hashings. Concrete designs include AES-128-MMO, AES-128-MP, Saturnin-Hash [17], Whirlpool [6] Grøstl [34].

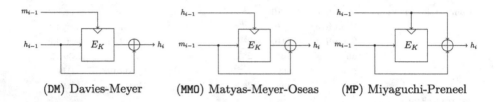

(DM) Davies-Meyer   (MMO) Matyas-Meyer-Oseas   (MP) Miyaguchi-Preneel

Fig. 2. Common Hashing Modes

2.2 The Rebound Attack

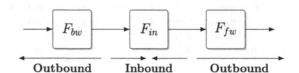

Fig. 3. The Rebound Attack

The rebound attack was first introduced by Mendel et al. in [62]. It consists of an inbound phase and an outbound phase as shown in Fig. 3, where F is an internal block cipher or permutation which is split into three subparts, then $F = F_{fw} \circ F_{in} \circ F_{bw}$.

- **Inbound phase.** In the inbound phase, the attackers efficiently fulfill the low probability part in the middle of the differential trail with a meet-in-the-middle technique. The degree of freedom is the number of matched pairs in the inbound phase, which will act as the starting point for the outbound phase.
- **Outbound phase.** In the outbound phase, the matched values of the inbound phase, i.e., starting points, are computed backward and forward through F_{bw} and F_{fw} to obtain a pair of values which satisfy the outbound differential trail in a bruteforce fashion.

Overall, the rebound attack is essentially a technique to efficiently generate a message pair fulfilling the inbound phase, which utilizes a truncated differential rather than a single differential characteristic. Suppose the probability of the outbound phase is p, then we have to prepare $1/p$ starting points in the inbound phase to expect one pair conforming to the differential trail of the outbound phase. Hence, the degree of freedom should be larger than $1/p$.

2.3 The Super-Sbox Technique

The Super-Sbox technique proposed by Gilbert and Peyrin [35] and Lamberger et al. [56] extends Mendel et al.'s [62] inbound part into 2 S-box layers by regarding them as four Super-Sboxes as shown in Fig. 4 (a). In [70], Sasaki et al. further reduced the the memory complexity by considering non-full-active Super-Sboxes as shown in Fig. 4 (b). In both the two techniques, AK acts as a constant addition operation and does not provide any degree of freedom.

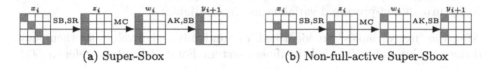

(a) Super-Sbox · · · · · · · · · · · · · · (b) Non-full-active Super-Sbox

Fig. 4. The Two-Round Differential

Super-Sbox Technique. For the jth Super-Sbox SSB_j and given input difference $\Delta x_i^{(j)}$ ($j = 0$ in Fig. 4 (a)), compute $\Delta y_{i+1}^{(j)} = \mathsf{SSB}_j(x \oplus \Delta x_i^{(j)}) \oplus \mathsf{SSB}_j(x)$ for $x \in \mathbb{F}^{32}$. Store the pair $(x, x \oplus \Delta x_i^{(j)})$ in a table $\mathbb{L}^{(j)}[\Delta y_{i+1}^{(j)}]$. Given $\Delta y_{i+1}^{(j)}$, we find a pair conforming the two-round differential with $(\Delta x_i^{(j)}, \Delta y_{i+1}^{(j)})$ by assessing $\mathbb{L}^{(j)}[\Delta y_{i+1}^{(j)}]$. The memory cost is about 2^{32}.

Non-full-active Super-Sbox. In Fig. 4 (b), the Property 1 of MDS in MC is used. Look at $\Delta w_i = \mathsf{MC}(\Delta z_i)$, by guessing the differences of one active byte, we can determine other differences according to Property 1. Then, for a fixed input-output differences $(\Delta x_i^{(j)}, \Delta y_{i+1}^{(j)})$ of SSB_j, we deduce all the input-output differences for the active cells of two S-box layers for each guess and then deduce their values by accessing the differential distribution table (DDT) of the S-box.

Property 1. Suppose MC is an $n \times n$ MDS matrix and $\mathsf{MC} \cdot (z[1], \dots, z[n])^T = (w[1], \dots, w[n])^T$, the knowledge of any n out of $2n$ bytes of (z, w) is necessary and sufficient to determine the rest. (z, w) here can be either value or difference.

2.4 Triangulation Algorithm

At CT-RSA 2009, Khovratovich, Biryukov, and Nikolić [50] introduced the triangulation algorithm tool, an efficient Gaussian-based-algorithm to solve system of bijective equations, to automatically detect a way to solve the nonlinear system. The algorithm models an AES-like block cipher as a system of key schedule and round function equations, and the state bytes and key bytes as variables. At first, the system is determined by n initial state bytes and k initial key bytes. Therefore, when m bytes are fixed, the algorithm will return $n + k - m$ "free variables" to form a basis of the system. The algorithm can output exactly the "free variables" when the system is deterministically solvable, and improve the guessing and checking the "free variables" when the system is probabilistically solvable. The idea of triangulation algorithm is roughly described following.

1. Construct a system of equations whose variables are the bytes. The predefined values are fixed to constants.
2. All variables and equations are marked as non-processed.
3. Mark the variable which is involved in only one non-processed equation as processed. Also mark this equation as processed. If no such variable exist, exit.
4. Return to Step 3 if still have non-processed equations.
5. Return all non-processed variables as "free variables".

After the "free variables" are identified, we randomly assign values for them and deduce a solution for the whole nonlinear system. For details, please refer to [50].

2.5 Collision Attacks and Its Variants

Given a hash function H, a standard collision message pair (m, m') satisfies $H(IV, m) = H(IV, m')$, where the initial vector IV is a fixed initial value. A *semi-free-start collision* is to find a pair (u, m) and (u, m'), such that $H(u, m) = H(u, m')$ $(u \neq IV)$. A *free-start collision* is to find a pair (v, m) and (v', m'), so that $H(v, m) = H(v', m')$ $(v \neq v')$. When the hash function H is built by iterating the compression function (CF) with Merkle-Damgård construction, we can similarly define the semi-free-start collision and free-start collision attack on the compression function. Taking the MMO and MP hashing modes in Fig. 2 as examples, when considering the semi-free-start or free-start collision attack, the attackers can explore the degrees of freedom from the chaining value h_{i-1} through the key schedule algorithm, which may lead to better attacks such as [56, 71]. We would like to emphasize the importance of semi-free-start and free-start collision attacks: The Merkle-Damgård security reduction assumes that any type of collision for the compression function should be intractable for the attacker, including semi-free-start and free-start collisions.

3   Triangulating Rebound Attack

3.1   Solving Non-full-active Super-Sbox by Key Bytes

In previous collision attacks, both Super-Sbox [35, 56] and non-full-active Super-Sbox [70] techniques, the subkeys are prefixed in advance (as shown in Sect. 2.3).

In other words, the degree of freedom of the subkeys was not be utilized. We observe that, by carefully choosing the values of subkeys, state pairs conforming the given differential can be obtained without additional computation only at a cost of memory for storing the differential distribution table (DDT). This observation enables utilization of the degrees of freedom from the corresponding subkeys and leads to collision attacks without the need of building large lists of compatible pairs for Super-Sboxes. Here we describe this new Super-Sbox technique through a concrete example in Fig. 5.

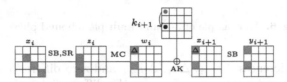

Fig. 5. An example of Super-Sbox with degrees of freedom from the subkey (Color figure online)

Given the pair of non-full difference of $(\Delta x_i, \Delta y_{i+1})$ and zero difference in key of an Super-Sbox (marked as red for the corresponding column), we are to generate state pairs and corresponding subkey k_{i+1} conforming to that difference. First, we randomly assign a difference Δ compatible with $\Delta y_{i+1}[0]$ to $\Delta x_{i+1}[0]$ and asset to DDT to get an actual value for $x_{i+1}[0]$ conforming the difference $(\Delta, \Delta y_{i+1}[0])$. Since there is no difference in the subkey k_{i+1}, the difference $\Delta w_i[0]$ is equal to Δ as well. We use a simple property of maximum distance separable (MDS) matrix to determine all the rest bytes of Δw_i and Δz_i.

With the knowledge of 4 bytes of Δz_i and Δw_i ($\Delta z_i[0] = \Delta w_i[1,3] = 0$ and $\Delta w_i[0] = \Delta$), all bytes of Δz_i and Δw_i are uniquely determined, and so for the entire differential characteristic $(\Delta x_i, \Delta z_i, \Delta w_i, \Delta x_{i+1}, \Delta y_{i+1})$ of the Super-Sbox. By looking up DDT, the byte values before and after the active Sboxes, e.g., $x_i[5, 10, 15], z_i[1, 2, 3], x_{i+1}[0, 2]$ and $y_{i+1}[0, 2]$, are determined as well. Next, we randomly assign a value to $k_{i+1}[0]$, then $w_i[0]$ can be calculated as $w_i[0] = x_{i+1}[0] \oplus k_{i+1}[0]$. Again, Property 1 allows to determine the remaining bytes $z_i[0]$ and $w_i[1, 2, 3]$ since 4 bytes $z_i[1, 2, 3]$ and $w_i[0]$ are known. Finally, the key byte $k_{i+1}[2]$ is determined as $k_{i+1}[2] = w_i[2] \oplus x_{i+1}[2]$. In summary, after randomly assigning (compatible) values to $\Delta x_{i+1}[0]$ and $k_{i+1}[0]$, all the values and differences of the active bytes in the state as well as the subkey bytes corresponding to the active state bytes positions of AK are determined, with time complexity 1.

3.2   Connecting Multiple Inbound Phases by Key Bytes

In this section, we present a 3-round inbound phase by extending the Super-Sbox backward by one round. Since the Super-Sbox and the extended round are not solved in two inbound phases, this technique is also referred to as "multiple inbound phases". These phases are connected by free bytes of the corresponding subkeys, and so one has to ensure the value assignments to the subkeys from different rounds are not over-defined through the key schedule algorithm. This new technique is illustrated through an example of 3-round truncated differential trail depicted in Fig. 6.

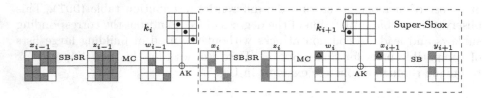

Fig. 6. An example of 3-round multiple inbound phases

Given the differences Δx_{i-1}, Δx_i, Δy_{i+1} and zero difference in key, we are to generate state and key pairs conforming the differential path with low memory requirement by utilizing the degrees of freedom from subkeys k_i and k_{i+1}. First, applying the Super-Sbox technique presented above to the given Δx_i and Δy_{i+1}, both value and difference of $\Delta x_i[5, 10, 15]$ and value of $k_{i+1}[0, 2]$ will be determined. Then, with fixed Δx_{i-1} and Δx_i, standard inbound phase of the original rebound attack can be applied, i.e., lookup DDT with input/output differences $(\Delta x_{i-1}, \mathtt{SR}^{-1}(\Delta z_{i-1} = \mathtt{MC}^{-1}(\Delta x_i)))$, values of the last three columns of z_{i-1} and so w_{i-1} are determined. Hence, $\Delta k_i[5, 10, 15]$ can be calculated as $\Delta w_{i-1}[5, 10, 15] \oplus \Delta x_i[5, 10, 15]$. Note, there is no direct implication between any assignment of $k_i[5, 10, 15]$ and $k_{i+1}[0, 2]$ through the AES key schedule. The whole process costs 17 DDT lookups and memory hosting the DDT lookup table.

3.3   The Triangulating Rebound Attack

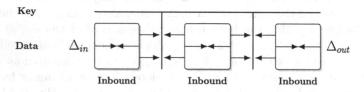

Fig. 7. *Super-Inbound*: bridging multiple local inbound parts

Generally speaking, the development of the rebound attack can be viewed as a continuous process to find as many degrees of freedom (DoF) as possible, to either reduce the overall inbound solving complexity, or to extend for more rounds. As shown in Fig. 7, the multiple local inbound parts form a *Super-Inbound*. Given the input/output differences $(\Delta_{in}, \Delta_{out})$ of the super inbound phase, bridging the multiple local inbound parts is to find the conforming pair for $(\Delta_{in}, \Delta_{out})$, while the exact differentials and values of the internal rounds are up to attacker's control. Usually, $(\Delta_{in}, \Delta_{out})$ are chosen from a truncated differential in the rebound attack. In summary, the source of DoF for the whole rebound attack can come from the choices of

S1 truncated differential of the internal rounds of the *Super-Inbound*,
S2 input/output differences and values of the active Sboxes of the state,
S3 values of the inactive Sboxes of the state,
S4 differences of key bytes,
S5 values of key bytes.

The differences and values of the active Sboxes of the state are listed together, as once differences are fixed, values can be derived from DDT, and vice versa. This is not the case for key bytes, as it is not necessarily for each of the key bytes to pass through Sbox depending on the key schedule algorithm. Then the Super-Sbox technique can be viewed as a way to connect two 1-round inbound parts by fully utilizing the DoF from S2, i.e., the output differences of first round and input differences of the second round. Our techniques presented in Sect. 3.1, 3.2 is from (S2,S5), (S2,S5), respectively. Under this generic view, connecting multiple inbound parts to form a *Super-Inbound* can be seen as a system of nonlinear equations, where all DoF serve as variables and DoF from subkeys are constrained by key schedule, and our goal is to find a procedure to solve this system, efficiently. There are two main considerations.

I. The system of nonlinear equations must have solutions. In other words, the system should not be over-defined. Hence, the number DoF should be larger than the number of equations.
II. The system must be solvable efficiently, which for most of the time can be translated into a procedure of consuming degrees of freedom by fixing certain variables involved, and the final complexity is determined by the number variables which can not be fixed and have to be brute-forced.

We adopt the triangulation algorithm [50] as shown in Sect. 2.4 to solve the nonlinear system and bridge the multiple inbound parts. The algorithm can output exactly the "free variables" when the system is deterministically solvable, and improve the guessing and checking the "free variables" when the system is probabilistically solvable. We name this method as *triangulating rebound attack*.

Heuristic Method to Determine a Trail. So far, we have not mentioned the use of DoF from S1 and S4 yet. While S4 determines whether difference is allowed in key hence resulting in semi-free-start or free-start collision for attacks against hash functions, S1 directly determines the system of nonlinear equations, hence the number of rounds covered by the *Super-Inbound* and complexity as well. For collision attack on n-bit hash, the overall steps to identify a rebound attack trail are as follows:

1. Find a truncated differential trail following the *Constrained Programming* based search model from [5].
2. Choose certain consecutive rounds as the *Super-Inbound* (i.e., S1), which includes several local inbound parts. For example, in Fig. 7 a *Super-Inbound* includes three local inbound parts. Usually, 2 to 4 consecutive rounds are

chosen as possible *Super-Inbound*. Following this search, all the input/output differences of the active Sboxes are fixed, and therefore corresponding values are fixed.

3. Build equation system that connects the inbound parts and through key schedule. Check if the system is solvable by triangulation algorithm.

Before checking the solvability of the system, a potential truncated trail must satisfy the condition that the number of active Sboxes in the *Super-Inbound* does not exceed the DoF from both key and state. This is because the system of state bytes and keys bytes are determined by the initial k key bytes and n plaintext bytes, then for any set of fixed bytes in advance, the system is potentially solvable if the number of fixed bytes is not larger than $n+k$. Our observation shows that the ideal case is when the number of active bytes in the *Super-Inbound* equals to $n+k-1$ and only 1 free byte is left, since the scenario without free byte is likely to form an over-defined system. Therefore, this constraint is also added to our model. For classical collision attacks, after the *Super-Inbound* is fixed, the probability of the outbound phase can be computed and denoted as Pr, which should meet $Pr > 2^{-n/2}$. For quantum collision attacks, let $Pr^1 > 2^{-n}$. Similarly to previous models [39], for the attacks based on the truncated differentials, P_r is the probability for the cancellation of MC operator in the backward and forward trunks, as well as the cancellation for the feed-forward operator of hashing modes. After checking the potential truncated trails satisfying the above conditions for inbound and outbound phases, the triangulation algorithm is applied to detect the free bytes left followed by the step to generate sufficient data pairs for the outbound phase.

4   Improved Collision Attacks on AES-128-MMO

In this section, by applying the *triangulating rebound*, we introduce a 7-round classical semi-free-start collision attack and an 8-round quantum semi-free-start collision attack on AES-MMO. Moreover, we identify the first 8-round quantum collision attack, which is better than parallel rho's algorithm [75].

4.1   Semi-free-start Collision Attack on 7-Round AES-128

New 7-Round AES-128 Truncated Differential Trail. We introduce here our new differential trail in Fig. 8. Our Super-Inbound phase covers 3 middle rounds with 2 inbound phases (marked with red and blue dashed lines), which consumes 31 bytes of degree of freedom for the fixed state bytes, i.e., 16 active bytes in x_3, 9 active bytes in x_4, and 6 active bytes in x_5. Since we have 32 bytes in total (16 bytes in key and 16 bytes in the state), only 1 free byte is left. By triangulating algorithm, the 1 free byte is identified to be $k_5[12]$. The

---

[1] As shown in the introduction, we consider three quantum attack conditions. $Pr > 2^{-2n/3}$ is to be better than the BHT algorithm, $Pr > 2^{-n}$ is to be better than quantum time-space tradeoff, $Pr > 2^{-4n/5}$ is to be better than CNS algorithm. So we let $Pr > 2^{-n}$ to keep all characteristics that may lead to possible attacks.

remaining outbound phase happens with probability $p_{out} = 2^{-56}$ including the MC cancellation in round 1 and 4-byte cancellation for $\Delta P = \Delta C$.

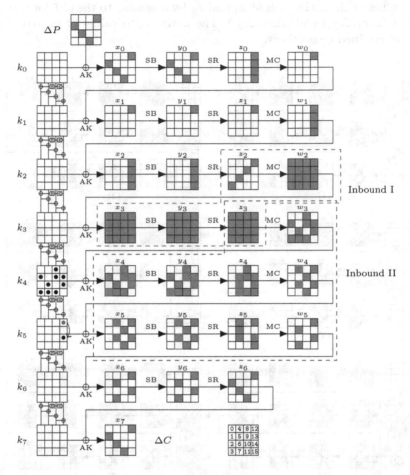

Fig. 8. Semi-free-start collision attack on 7-round AES-128 (Color figure online)

The Super-Inbound Phase. As shown in Fig. 8, the Super-Inbound phase divides into 2 parts, the Inbound II marked with blue dashed line makes use of k_5 to link round 4 and round 5, and the Inbound I marked with red dashed line connects with Inbound II via k_4. To generate a data pair conforming a given difference $(\Delta z_2, \Delta w_3, \Delta w_5)$, assuming $\Delta Z_5 = \text{MC}^{-1}(\Delta w_5)$ keeps the truncated differential in Fig. 8, we perform the following steps:

- Perform the Inbound II:
  1. Randomly assign a difference to $\Delta x_5[4, 9, 12]$. Then $\Delta w_4[4, 9, 12]$ are known accordingly, implies all the differences at these active cells of

z_4 and the remaining active cells of w_4 are determined as a result of the Property 1. From Δz_4, we deduce $\Delta y_4 = \mathrm{SR}^{-1}(\Delta z_4)$.

2. Compute the difference $\Delta y_5 = \mathrm{SR}^{-1}(\mathrm{MC}^{-1}(\Delta w_5))$. Next, we deduce the values of the active cells at x_4 and x_5 by assessing to the DDT for each cell of $(\Delta x_4, \Delta y_4)$ and $(\Delta x_5, \Delta y_5)$. The active byte values of y_4 and y_5 are determined respectively.

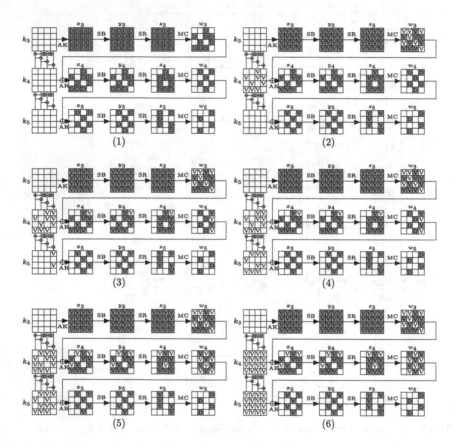

Fig. 9. Steps to recover k_5. The bytes marked by 'D' mean that the differences are known. The bytes marked by 'V' mean that the values are known. In subfigures, the bytes marked by 'V' are deduced from those marked by 'V'.

– Perform the Inbound I:
  1. Compute $\Delta x_3 = \mathrm{MC}(\Delta z_2)$ and $\Delta y_3 = \mathrm{SR}^{-1}(\mathrm{MC}^{-1}(\Delta w_3))$.
  2. Deduce full state values x_3 and y_3 by assessing the DDT. We compute the full state values of w_3 by the action $w_3 = \mathrm{MC}(\mathrm{SR}(y_3))$.
– Connect the phases by the subkeys:

1. Since the full state of w_3 and the active bytes of x_4 are known, we obtain $k_4[1, 3, 6, 7, 8, 9, 11, 13, 14] = x_4[1, 3, 6, 7, 8, 9, 11, 13, 14] \oplus w_3[1, 3, 6, 7, 8, 9, 11, 13, 14]$ (marked as black dots).

2. Add constrains on the related cells of k_5 to the system of equations of the subkeys. We solve the constrains on k_4 and k_5 by triangulation algorithm and obtain a free byte $k_5[12]$.

3. The steps (shown in Fig. 9) to recover k_5 and compute a starting point are shown as follows (equations are also given in Table 2):

   (a) As shown in Fig. 9(1), all the differences marked by 'D' are known. In Fig. 9(2), by assessing the DDT, we know the values of $x_3[V]$, $x_4[V]$, and $x_5[V]$. Then deduce $k_4[V] = w_3[V] \oplus x_4[V]$.

   (b) In Fig. 9(3), randomly assign a value for $k_5[12]$ marked by 'V', compute $w_4[12] = k_5[12] \oplus x_5[12]$. According to Property 1, deduce all the bytes marked by 'V' in z_4 and w_4. Then, $k_5[14] = x_5[14] \oplus w_4[14]$. From $z_4[V]$, we get $x_4[V]$. Then $k_4[V]$ is deduced.

   (c) In Fig. 9(4), following the key schedule of AES-128, compute the $k_5[V]$: $k_5[8] = k_4[12] \oplus k_5[12]$, $k_5[10] = k_4[14] \oplus k_5[14]$, $k_5[11] = k_4[11] \oplus k_5[7]$, $k_5[4] = k_4[8] \oplus k_5[8]$, $k_5[7] = k_5[3] \oplus k_4[7]$, $k_5[1] = k_4[1] \oplus \mathsf{SB}(k_4[14]) \oplus r_c$, $k_5[3] = k_4[3] \oplus \mathsf{SB}(k_4[12]) \oplus r_c$.

   (d) In Fig. 9(5), deduce $w_4[4] = k_5[4] \oplus x_5[4]$ and $w_4[11] = k_5[11] \oplus x_5[11]$, then according to Property 1, all the bytes in w_4 and z_4 marked by 'V' are deduced. Then, two bytes marked by 'V' in k_5 are deduced, i.e., $k_5[6] = w_4[6] \oplus x_5[6]$ and $k_5[9] = w_4[9] \oplus x_5[9]$. Moreover, compute two bytes marked by 'V' in k_4, i.e., $k_4[2] = x_4[2] \oplus w_3[2]$ and $k_4[4] = x_4[4] \oplus w_3[4]$.

   (e) In Fig. 9(6), following the key schedule, deduce the bytes marked by 'V' in k_5, i.e., $k_5[0] = k_4[4] \oplus k_5[4]$, $k_5[2] = k_4[6] \oplus k_5[6]$, $k_5[5] = k_4[9] \oplus k_5[9]$, $k_5[13] = k_4[13] \oplus k_5[9]$, $k_4[15] = \mathsf{SB}^{-1}(k_4[2] \oplus k_5[2])$, $k_5[15] = k_4[15] \oplus k_5[11]$.

4. Finally, full state w_3 and full subkey k_5 are obtained by using 34 DDT assesses.

Due to the probability of the outbound phase is 2^{-56}, we need to check 2^{56} starting points to find the collision. The final complexity is 2^{56} and memory needed is 2^{16} for DDT storing.

Remark. In a rebound attack [62], we typically have a probability $\frac{1}{2}$ to have a solution for each active SBox, so that we have to repeat the attack with new differences, but when the differences are compatible we obtain many solutions and the amortized cost is close to 1. In our attack, when $(\Delta x_3, \Delta y_3)$, $(\Delta x_4, \Delta y_4)$ and $(\Delta x_5, \Delta y_5)$ are fixed, we have 31 active Sboxes. Therefore, one compatible differential characteristic is found in roughly 2^{31} time, which leads to 2^{31} solutions for the active bytes of (x_3, x_4, x_5). Moreover, since we can randomly assign $k_5[12]$ (Step 3 (b)), we totally have about $2^{31+8} = 2^{39}$ starting points, which is lower than the final time 2^{56}. Briefly, for a given $(\Delta x_3, \Delta y_3)$, $(\Delta x_4, \Delta y_4)$, $(\Delta x_5, \Delta y_5)$ and $k_5[12]$, we find one starting point with time complexity of 1 on average.

Table 2. Steps to recover the subkey k_5 from known bytes

1. $w_4[12] = x_5[12] \oplus k_5[12]$	15. $k_5[7] = k_5[3] \oplus k_4[7]$
2. $z_4[12], w_4[13,14,15] = \mathtt{MC}(w_4[12], z_4[13,14,15])$	16. $k_5[11] = k_4[11] \oplus k_5[7]$
3. $k_5[14] = w_4[14] \oplus x_5[14]$	17. $w_4[11] = k_5[11] \oplus x_5[11]$
4. $x_4[12] = \mathtt{SB}^{-1}(z_4[12])$	18. $z_4[10], w_4[8,9,10] = \mathtt{MC}(z_4[8,9,11], w_4[11])$
5. $k_4[12] = w_3[12] \oplus x_4[12]$	19. $k_5[9] = w_4[9] \oplus x_5[9]$
6. $k_5[8] = k_4[12] \oplus k_5[12]$	20. $k_5[13] = k_5[9] \oplus k_4[13]$
7. $k_5[1] = k_4[1] \oplus \mathtt{SB}(k_4[14]) \oplus r_c$	21. $k_5[5] = k_4[9] \oplus k_5[9]$
8. $k_5[10] = k_4[14] \oplus k_5[14]$	22. $k_4[5] = k_5[1] \oplus k_5[5]$
9. $k_5[4] = k_4[8] \oplus k_5[8]$	23. $k_4[4] = w_3[4] \oplus \mathtt{SB}^{-1}(z_4[4])$
10. $w_4[4] = k_5[4] \oplus x_5[4]$	24. $k_5[0] = k_4[4] \oplus k_5[4]$
11. $z_4[4], w_4[5,6,7] = \mathtt{MC}^{-1}(w_4[4], z_4[5,6,7])$	25. $x_4[2] = \mathtt{SB}^{-1}(z_4[10])$
12. $k_5[6] = w_4[6] \oplus x_5[6]$	26. $k_4[2] = w_3[2] \oplus x_4[2]$
13. $k_5[2] = k_4[6] \oplus k_5[6]$	27. $k_4[15] = \mathtt{SB}^{-1}(k_4[2] \oplus k_5[2])$
14. $k_5[3] = k_4[3] \oplus \mathtt{SB}(k_4[12]) \oplus r_c$	28. $k_5[15] = k_5[11] \oplus k_4[15]$

4.2 Semi-free-start Collision Attack on 8-Round AES-128-MMO

As shown in Fig. 10, there are three inbound parts in the Super-Inbound phase. For given fixed differences of Δz_1, Δz_2, Δw_4, and Δw_5, assuming $\Delta w_1 = \mathtt{MC}(\Delta z_1)$ and $\Delta z_5 = \mathtt{MC}^{-1}(\Delta w_5)$ keep the truncated differential of Fig. 10, we perform inbound part I, II, and III without the key information. Then, we connect the three inbound part by determining certain key values and get the starting point for the outbound phase. The probability of the outbound phase is 2^{-64}, including the condition $\Delta P = \Delta C$.

Given fixed differences of Δz_1, Δz_2, Δw_4, and Δw_5, the procedures to get one starting point are as follows:

1. Deduce values $(x_5[0,5,10], x_5'[0,5,10])$ with Δw_4 and $\Delta z_5 = \mathtt{MC}^{-1}(\Delta w_5)$ by accessing the DDT.
2. Deduce values $(x_2[0,1,2], x_2'[0,1,2])$ with $\Delta w_1 = \mathtt{MC}(\Delta z_1)$ and Δz_2 by accessing the DDT. Then $z_2[0,10,13]$ are known as well.
3. For $\mathtt{SSB}^{(0)}$ in Inbound III (marked in red), we compute $\Delta x_3 = \mathtt{MC}(\Delta z_2)$ and $\Delta y_4 = \mathtt{SR}^{-1}(\mathtt{MC}^{-1}(\Delta w_4))$.
4. Randomly choose $\Delta w_3[0,2] \in \mathbb{F}_2^8 \times \mathbb{F}_2^8$,
   (a) Compute other active differences $\Delta z_3[0,2,3]$ and $\Delta w_3[3]$ by Property 1
   (b) Deduce $(z_3[0,2,3], z_3'[0,2,3])$ and $(x_4[0,2,3], x_4'[0,2,3])$ by assessing DDT
5. Repeat Step 4 for random differences $\Delta w_3[4,5], \Delta w_3[8,9], \Delta w_3[13,14]$ to compute all active bytes of x_3 and x_4. Next, we compute $w_4[0,5,10] = \mathtt{MC}(\mathtt{SR}(\mathtt{SB}(x_4)))[0,5,10]$ and then $k_5[0,5,10] = w_4[0,5,10] \oplus x_5[0,5,10]$.
6. Assign random values to $k_3[6]$, $k_4[0]$, and $k_4[4]$. We recover the full key k_5 by the following steps in Table 3. There exists a filter of 2^{-8} in the step to recover $k_3[3]$.

Since Step 6 has a filter of 2^{-8} to meet the condition "$k_3[3] = w_2[3] \oplus x_3[3] \stackrel{?}{=} \mathtt{SB}(k_3[12]) \oplus k_4[3] \oplus r_c$" in Table 3, the time complexity to find a starting point

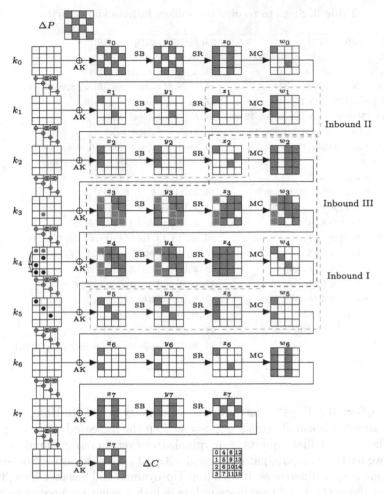

Fig. 10. Quantum semi-free-start collision attack on 8-round AES-128 (Color figure online)

(including a data pair and a key value conforming the inbound parts from Δz_1 to Δw_5) is 2^8. The probability of the outbound phase is 2^{-64}, we need 2^{64} starting points to find one collision. In other words, given 21 bytes of Δz_1, Δz_2, Δw_4, Δw_5, $\Delta w_3[0,2]$, $\Delta w_3[4,5]$, $\Delta w_3[8,9]$, $\Delta w_3[13,14]$ and $k_3[6]$ $k_4[0]$, $k_4[4]$, we get one collision with probability of 2^{-72}. Since $21 \times 8 = 168 > 72$, we have enough degrees of freedom to find one collision.

The Quantum Attack. Given input-output differences of the active Sbox, it is expected to find one pair on average, e.g. (x, x'), satisfying the differences. In inbound phase of the quantum rebound attacks, given a valid input-output differences of l active Sboxes, we obtain about $2^l/2$ choices for starting points. To indicate which starting point to choose among $2^l/2$ choices, Hosoyamda and

Table 3. Steps to recover the subkey k_3 from known bytes

1. $w_3[0] = k_4[0] \oplus x_4[0]$	23. $k_3[10] = k_4[6] \oplus k_4[10]$
2. $w_3[2,3] = \text{MC}^{-1}(w_3[0], z_3[0,2,3])$	24. $k_5[4] = k_5[0] \oplus k_4[4]$
3. $k_4[2,3] = w_3[2,3] \oplus x_4[2,3]$	25. $w_3[10] = x_4[10] \oplus k_4[10]$
4. $k_4[13] = \text{SB}^{-1}(k_4[0] \oplus k_5[0] \oplus r_c)$	26. $w_3[8,9] = \text{MC}^{-1}(w_3[10], z_3[8,9,10])$
5. $w_3[13] = x_4[13] \oplus k_4[13]$	27. $k_4[8,9] = w_3[8,9] \oplus x_4[8,9]$
6. $w_3[14,15] = \text{MC}^{-1}(w_3[13], z_3[12,13,15])$	28. $k_3[9] = k_4[5] \oplus k_4[9]$
7. $k_4[14,15] = w_3[14,15] \oplus x_4[14,15]$	29. $k_3[8] = k_4[4] \oplus k_4[8]$
8. $k_5[14] = k_5[10] \oplus k_4[14]$	30. $w_2[8,9,10] = x_3[8,9,10] \oplus k_3[8,9,10]$
9. $k_4[6] = k_4[2] \oplus k_3[6]$	31. $w_2[11] = \text{MC}^{-1}(w_2[8,9,10], z_2[10])$
10. $w_3[4] = x_4[4] \oplus k_4[4]$	32. $k_3[11] = w_2[11] \oplus x_3[11]$
11. $w_3[5,7] = \text{MC}^{-1}(w_3[4], z_3[5,6,7])$	33. $k_4[11] = k_4[7] \oplus k_3[11]$
12. $k_4[5,7] = w_3[5,7] \oplus x_4[5,7]$	34. $k_3[13] = k_4[9] \oplus k_4[13]$
13. $k_3[4] = k_4[0] \oplus k_4[4]$	35. $k_3[15] = k_4[11] \oplus k_4[15]$
14. $k_3[7] = k_4[3] \oplus k_4[7]$	36. $w_2[13,14,15] = k_3[13,14,15] \oplus x_3[13,14,15]$
15. $k_5[1] = k_4[5] \oplus k_5[5]$	37. $w_2[12] = \text{MC}^{-1}(w_2[13,14,15], z_2[13])$
16. $k_4[1] = k_5[1] \oplus \text{SB}(k_4[14]) \oplus r_c$	38. $k_3[12] = x_3[12] \oplus w_2[12]$
17. $k_3[5] = k_4[5] \oplus k_4[1]$	39. $k_3[0] = \text{SB}(k_3[13]) \oplus k_4[0] \oplus r_c$
18. $k_5[2] = k_4[2] \oplus \text{SB}(k_4[15]) \oplus r_c$	40. $k_3[2] = \text{SB}(k_3[15]) \oplus k_4[2] \oplus r_c$
19. $k_5[6] = k_5[2] \oplus k_4[6]$	41. $w_2[0,1,2] = x_3[0,1,2] \oplus k_3[0,1,2]$
20. $k_4[10] = k_5[6] \oplus k_5[10]$	42. $w_2[3] = \text{MC}^{-1}(w_2[0,1,2], z_2[0])$
21. $k_3[14] = k_4[10] \oplus k_4[14]$	43. $k_3[3] = w_2[3] \oplus x_3[3] \overset{?}{=} \text{SB}(k_3[12]) \oplus k_4[3] \oplus r_c$
22. $k_3[1] = \text{SB}(k_3[14]) \oplus k_4[1] \oplus r_c$	

Sasaki [39, Sect. 6.2, Page 22] introduce $l-1$ auxiliary qubits. In Hosoyamda and Sasaki's attack, l is usually small, e.g. $l = 4$, then the increased time complexity due to the $l - 1$ auxiliary qubits is marginal. However, in our 8-round attack of Fig. 10, we have to compute pairs for $l = 3+3+12+12 = 30$ active Sboxes with given input-output differences. If we follow Hosoyamda and Sasaki's idea [39], we have to introduce $l-1 = 29$ auxiliary qubits, which can not be ignored anymore. To deal with the problem, we introduce a trick in Supplementary Material A in our full version [28], which introduces the auxiliary qubits nearly for free. By our new trick, we perform the 8-round quantum semi-free-start collision attack. According to Equation 5 in [28], we have $l = 3 + 3 + 12 + 12 = 30$, and choose 9 bytes out of the 21 bytes to act as "$|\Delta_{in}| + |\Delta_{out}|$" to find the collision with time complexity roughly $30 \cdot 2^{72/2}/128 \approx 2^{34}$ 8-round AES, which is roughly the square root of 2^{72}.

Practical Semi-free-start Collision Attack on 6-Round AES-128. To prove the correctness of the 8-round semi-free-start collision, we give a 6-round practical semi-free-start collision by cutting the differential characteristic depicted in Fig. 10 to 6 rounds (round 1 to 6). The total complexity to find the collision is 2^{24}, including 2^8 time for solving the Super-Inbound phase and 2^{16} for the condition $\Delta x_1 = \Delta z_6$. We have verified the validity and complexity of the attack by implementing the 6-round attack. One such example collision is presented in Table 4 in Supplementary Material of the full version [28].

4.3   Quantum Collision Attack on 8-Round AES-128

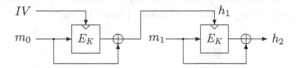

Fig. 11. Matyas-Meyer-Oseas (MMO) hashing mode with two blocks

Remove the Inbound I/II from Fig. 10, we get the trail for 8-round collision attack (also shown in Figure 15 in [28]). The inbound phase covers states z_2 to w_4. The probability of the outbound phase is 2^{-96}. For a random given Δz_2, Δw_4 and the master key, the steps to get one starting point are as follows:

1. Deduce Δx_3 and Δy_4 from Δz_2 and Δw_4.
2. For $\mathrm{SSB}^{(0)}$ marked in red, randomly choose $\Delta w_3[0,2] \in \mathbb{F}_2^{16}$,
   (a) Compute other active differences $\Delta z_3[0,2,3]$ and $\Delta w_3[3]$ by Property 1
   (b) Deduce the values for active bytes by accessing DDT to get $(z_3[0,2,3], z_3'[0,2,3])$ and $(x_4[0,2,3], x_4'[0,2,3])$
   (c) Deduce $(w_4[0,2,3], w_4'[0,2,3])$ by XORing $(x_4[0,2,3], x_4'[0,2,3])$ with k_4
   (d) Check if $\mathrm{MC}(z_3[0,2,3]) \overset{?}{=} w_4[0,2,3]$, which is a 16-bit filter by Property 1
3. Repeat Step 2 in parallel for $\mathrm{SSB}^{(1)}$, $\mathrm{SSB}^{(2)}$, and $\mathrm{SSB}^{(3)}$ to get one starting point on average.

Hence, we need 2^{16} time complexity to get one starting point for a random given a random given Δz_2, Δw_4 and the master key. Since the probability of the outbound phase is 2^{-96}, we need 2^{96} starting points to get one collision. Since $|\Delta z_2| \times |\Delta w_4| = 2^{48} < 2^{96}$, we need two blocks as shown in Fig. 11 to get additional degrees of freedom from the first block. The overall time complexity of the classical time is 2^{112}. According to the quantum analysis by [30,39], we apply Grover's algorithm and get a quantum collision attack with roughly 2^{56} quantum time complexity. Full paper [28] gives a very detailed quantum collision attack on 8-round AES, whose time complexity is $2^{55.53}$ 8-round AES, which is very close to the estimated 2^{56}.

5   Improved Quantum Attacks on Saturnin-Hash

Saturnin is a block cipher with a 256-bit state and 256-bit key that was designed as the derivative of AES with efficient implementation by Canteaut et al. [17]. It is among the round 2 candidates of the NIST lightweight cryptography competition. The composition of two consecutive rounds starting from even round is called super-round, which is very similar to an AES round operating on 16-bit words except that the SR is replaced by a transposition. Saturnin-Hash is built on 16-super-round Saturnin block cipher with the MMO hashing mode.

5.1   Improved 8-Round Quantum Free-Start Collision

The differential trail we use here was found in [31]. As shown in Fig. 12, our new method extends the inbound phase by covering round 0 to round 4 in inbound phase, and the probability of the outbound phase becomes $2^{-135.8}$.

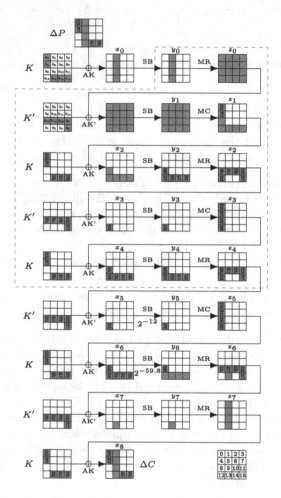

Fig. 12. Free-start collision attack on 8-round Saturnin-Hash

Super-Inbound Phase. In Dong et al.'s [31] attack, the inbound phase covers states from y_0 to x_3. However, our Super-Inbound covers two more rounds from state y_0 to x_5. Hence, the probabilities $Pr(\Delta x_3 \mapsto \Delta y_3) = 2^{-12}$ and $Pr(\Delta x_4 \mapsto \Delta z_4) = 2^{-59.8}$ in Dong et al.'s attack are removed in ours.

To perform the 4-round Super-Inbound phase, we first randomly assign arbitrary differences for all unfixed differences in $\Delta z_0 = \text{MR}(\Delta y_0)$, Δz_1 and Δz_4.

Together with the prefixed differences of Δz_2 and Δz_3, we do the following steps to find a pair to confirm the given differences in the Super-Inbound phase.

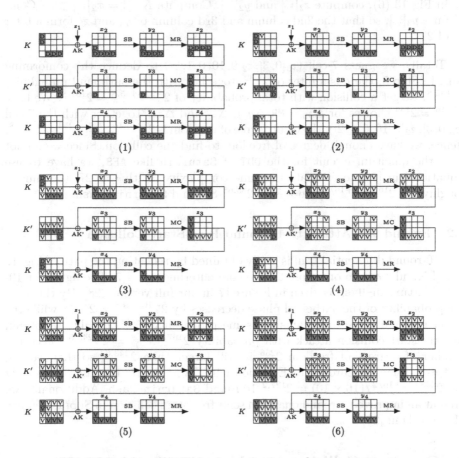

Fig. 13. Solving the inbound part for 8-round Saturnin-Hash

1. Deduce the differences of Δy_1, Δy_4. Compute all the active byte values of $(x_1, y_1), (x_2, y_2), (x_3, y_3)$ and (x_4, y_4) by assessing the DDT. Then z_1 is known. As shown in Fig. 13, we pick out round 2 to round 4 to clarify the steps to compute a conforming pair for the inbound part. As shown Fig. 13 (2), compute $K[V] = z_1 \oplus x_2[V]$. Compute $K'[V] = x_3[V] \oplus z_2[V]$. Similarly, compute all other cells marked by "V" and "V".

2. In Fig. 13 (3), deduce "V" and "V" cells by the "V" cells. **Guess** $z_3[0]$ to compute $y_3[V]$ and $z_3[V]$ by Property 1. Compute $z_2[V] = K'[V] \oplus x_3[V]$. **Guess** $z_2[9, 10]$ to deduce $z_2[V]$ and $y_2[V]$ by Property 1. Then, compute $K[V] = x_2[V] \oplus z_1$ and $x_3[V] = z_2[V] \oplus K'[V]$.

3. In Fig. 13 (4), **guess** $z_2[0, 1, 2]$ to deduce $y_2[V]$ and $z_2[V]$. Deduce $K[V]$ and $K'[V]$. Compute $K'[V] = x_3[V] \oplus z_2[V]$.

4. In Fig. 13 (5), **guess** $z_3[3]$ to deduce $z_3[V]$ and $y_2[V]$. Compute $K'[V] = x_3[V] \oplus z_2[V]$ and $z_2[V] = K'[V] \oplus x_3[V]$. Compute $x_2[V] = K[V] \oplus z_1$.
5. In Fig. 13 (6), compute $z_2[V]$ and $y_2[V]$. Compute $K[V] = x_2[V] \oplus z_1$. Compute $y_3[V]$, so that the 2nd column and 3rd column of y_3 and z_3 form a filter of 2^{-32}.

Totally, we guess 7-cell $(z_3[0,3], z_2[9,10,0,1,2])$ to deduce the conforming pair. In Step 5, there is a filter of 2^{-32}, together with the outbound probability $2^{-135.8}$, we get a collision with total probability of $2^{-32-135.8} = 2^{167.8}$. We have $2^{9 \times 16} = 2^{144}$ choices for $\Delta z_0 = \text{MR}(\Delta y_0)$, Δz_1 and Δz_4. Together with the 7-cell $(z_3[0,3], z_2[9,10,0,1,2])$, the total degree of freedom is $2^{144+16 \times 7} = 2^{256} > 2^{167.8}$. Hence, we have enough degree of freedom to find the collision. Since we do not have the quantum circuit for the DDT of Saturnin like AES, we have to use Equation 4 in [28] to estimate the time complexity. With $l = 27$, the time is roughly $27 \cdot 2^{167.8/2+16/2}/(16 \times 8) = 2^{89.65}$ 8-round Saturnin-Hash.

5.2   Extend the Attack to 10-round Free-Start Collision

The 10-round differential trail is easily obtained by repeating the path of Fig. 12 round 5 and round 6 one more time before entering round 7. The figure for 10-round Saturnin-Hash is given in Figure 17 in our full version [28]. By this way, the probability of the outbound phase decreases by $2^{-16-59.8} = 2^{-75.8}$ while the Super-Inbound phase maintains the same probability 2^{-32}. Finally, we obtain the free-start collision attack with probability $2^{167.8-75.8} = 2^{-243.6}$. Since the number of degrees of freedom 2^{256} is still larger than $2^{243.6}$, so that we can find a collision. According to Equation 4 in [28], $l = 27$, the time is roughly $27 \cdot 2^{243.6/2+16/2}/(16 \times 10) = 2^{127.2}$ 10-round Saturnin-Hash. Additionally, we present an improved 7-round quantum semi-free-start collision in Supplementary Material D in [28].

6   Quantum Collision Attack on SKINNY-128-384-MMO

SKINNY is a family of lightweight block ciphers designed by Beierle et al. [7]. In this section, we focus on the hashing mode of SKINNY-128-384. Please find the structure of SKINNY-n-$3n$ in [7]. The MC operation is non-MDS:

$$\text{MC} \begin{pmatrix} a \\ b \\ c \\ d \end{pmatrix} = \begin{pmatrix} a \oplus c \oplus d \\ a \\ b \oplus c \\ a \oplus c \end{pmatrix} \quad \text{and} \quad \text{MC}^{-1} \begin{pmatrix} \alpha \\ \beta \\ \gamma \\ \delta \end{pmatrix} = \begin{pmatrix} \beta \\ \beta \oplus \gamma \oplus \delta \\ \beta \oplus \delta \\ \alpha \oplus \delta \end{pmatrix}. \tag{1}$$

6.1   21-Round Quantum Free-Start Collision Attack

In quantum setting, we derive the free-start collision attack on hashing modes (MMO/MP) with 21-round SKINNY-128-384 using the differential characteristic shown in Figure 18 in Supplementary Material D in [28]. The new differential trail is found by using the automatic tool in [23]. The 5-round Super-Inbound covers from state w_9 to x_{14}. The outbound phase happens with probability $2^{-103.4}$.

We pick out the 5-round Super-Inbound phase from the whole rebound attack trail of Figure 18 in [28] to get Fig. 14 (a). To launch the rebound attack, we first precompute a pair satisfying the 5-round inbound trail as shown in Fig. 14 (b). Then thanks to the large degrees of freedom from the tweakey, we get enough starting points by changing the 384-bit tweakey.

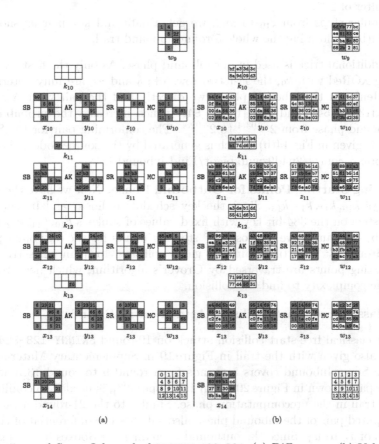

Fig. 14. 5-round Super-Inbound of SKINNY-128-384: (a) Differences, (b) Values. The values of k_i are the XOR of subkeys and constants of AC operator.

Precomputation in the Super-Inbound Phase. We build several steps to compute the conforming data pairs for the Super-Inbound phase.

1. In Fig. 14(a), focusing on states z_{10} to x_{11}, the values in $z_{10}[8,12] = \text{SR}(x_{10}[10,13])$ and all active bytes of w_{10} are deduced by assessing DDT with fixed differences in Fig. 14(a). In the 1st column z_{10} and w_{10}, i.e., $z_{10}^{(0)}$ and $w_{10}^{(0)}$, we have a condition "$w_{10}[4] \oplus w_{10}[12] = z_{10}[8]$" due to Eq. 1, which is a filter of 2^{-8}. In our trail, the differences are dedicatedly

chosen, so that we have enough pairs to verify the filters for the given differences. For example, in the condition "$w_{10}[4] \oplus w_{10}[12] = z_{10}[8]$", we choose $(w_{10}[4], w_{10}[12], z_{10}[8]) \in (\text{DDT}[\text{b0}_x][\text{80}_x] \times \text{DDT}[\text{21}_x][\text{a0}_x] \times \text{DDT}[\text{2f}_x][\text{91}_x])$, where $\text{DDT}[\text{b0}_x][\text{80}_x]$ is the subset of DDT with input-output differences $(\text{b0}_x, \text{80}_x)$. The size $|\text{DDT}[\text{b0}_x][\text{80}_x] \times \text{DDT}[\text{21}_x][\text{a0}_x] \times \text{DDT}[\text{2f}_x][\text{91}_x]| = 48 \cdot 2^5 \cdot 2^3 > 2^8$.

2. With the choice of $w_{10}[12]$, $z_{11}[15]$ is known as well. $z_{11}[8, 9, 10, 12]$ and all active bytes of w_{11} are deduced by DDT. We have similar conditions to fulfill for the 1st column of z_{11} and w_{11} with $w_{11}[0] \oplus w_{11}[12] = z_{11}[12]$, which act as a filter of 2^{-8}.

3. Do similar steps from z_{10} to w_{13}, we get a data and key pair as shown in Fig. 14(b) conforming the whole 5-round inbound trail.

An additional trick is used in our inbound phase. As only the first two rows of x_9 are XORed with k_9, the last two rows of x_9 and w_8 are fully determined by w_9. Hence, in the inbound phase, we directly find the pair with $\Delta w_8[8] = \text{04}_x$, $\Delta w_8[13] = \text{54}_x$, and $\Delta w_8[14] = \text{54}_x$, which increases the probability of the outbound phase from $2^{-103.4}$ to $2^{-92.4}$. The conforming pair for the Super-Inbound is given in Fig. 14(b), which is generated by the source code at https://www.dropbox.com/s/2n4d9zwufkpigqt/Find_inbound.7z

Generating Starting Points for Outbound Phase. Now we have the values of subkeys $k_{10}, k_{11}, k_{12}, k_{13}$. Since the key schedule is linear and by solving a linear system on the 384-bit key with fixed values of subkeys $k_{10}, k_{11}, k_{12}, k_{13}$ in Fig. 14 (b), we can derive at most 2^{128} starting points for the outbound phase. We need only $2^{92.4}$ starting points to get a collision. In quantum setting, the $2^{92.4}$ starting points are traversed by Grover's algorithm, which need roughly $2^{46.2}$ time complexity to find the collision.

6.2 Classic Free-Start Collision Attack on 19-Round

The first classical free-start collision attack on 19-round SKINNY-128-384 hash mode is also given with the trail in Figure 19 in Supplementary Material F in [28]. The Super-Inbound covers 5 rounds from round 9 to round 13, and only one data pair, shown in Figure 20 in our full paper [28], is needed to confirm the inbound trail in the precomputation phase. Similar to the 21-round attack, the pre-computed pair of the inbound phase also satisfies the differential of the last two rows of x_8 to w_7. Since the outbound excluding the Sboxes in the last two rows of x_8 happens with probability $2^{-51.2}$, the final time complexity is $2^{51.2}$.

7   Discussion and Conclusion

7.1   Possible Generalization of Triangulating Rebound

In Sect. 3, we have shown that the multiple inbound phases can be connected by the key bytes. We may describe the idea in a more generalized way. In fact, for active Sbox or Super-Sbox with fixed input/output differences, the values are fixed. For active Sbox without fixed input/output differences, or inactive Sbox, the values are not fixed and up to attacker's control, which are the source of the degree of freedom (DoF). In order to identify a data pair conforming the truncated differential, we may consume the degree of freedom from the unfixed Sbox to bridge several fixed values due to active Sboxes or Super-Sboxes with fixed input/output differences. This intuitive idea implies that not only the key bytes are useful to connect the differences, but also the internal states. In Supplementary Material G in [28], we give an example to connect the differences with DoF from internal states and gain some improved collision attacks on Grøstl.

7.2 Conclusion

In this paper, we extended the number of attacked rounds by the rebound attack by introducing *triangulating rebound attack*. The core idea is to take full advantage of the available degrees of freedom from both the subkeys and the state to greatly extend the number of rounds covered by the inbound phase, which is named as Super-Inbound. As a consequence, multiple improved classic or quantum collision attacks on AES-like hashing were presented. Possible future works are to investigate more ciphers with our method, as well as to find more applications such as distinguishing attacks based the improved rebound attacks.

Acknowledgments. We would like to thank the anonymous reviewers from EURO-CRYPT 2022 and CRYPTO 2022 for their valuable comments. This research is partially supported by Nanyang Technological University in Singapore under Grant 04INS000397C230, Ministry of Education in Singapore under Grants RG91/20 and MOE2019-T2-1-060, and National Natural Science Foundation of China (61961146004). Xiaoyang Dong is supported by National Key R&D Program of China (2018YFA0704701), the Major Program of Guangdong Basic and Applied Research (2019B030302008), Major Scientific and Technological Innovation Project of Shandong Province, China (2019JZZY010133), Natural Science Foundation of China (61902207).

References

1. Alliance, Z.: ZigBee 2007 specification (2007). http://www.zigbee.org/
2. Banegas, G., Bernstein, D.J.: Low-communication parallel quantum multi-target preimage search. In: Adams, C., Camenisch, J. (eds.) SAC 2017. LNCS, vol. 10719, pp. 325–335. Springer, Cham (2018). https://doi.org/10.1007/978-3-319-72565-9_16
3. Bao, Z., Ding, L., Guo, J., Wang, H., Zhang, W.: Improved meet-in-the-middle preimage attacks against AES hashing modes. IACR Trans. Symmetric Cryptol. **2019**(4), 318–347 (2019)
4. Bao, Z., et al.: Automatic search of meet-in-the-middle preimage attacks on AES-like hashing. In: Canteaut, A., Standaert, F.-X. (eds.) EUROCRYPT 2021, Part I. LNCS, vol. 12696, pp. 771–804. Springer, Cham (2021). https://doi.org/10.1007/978-3-030-77870-5_27
5. Bao, Z., Guo, J., Li, S., Pham, P.: Quantum multi-collision distinguishers. Cryptology ePrint Archive, Report 2021/703 (2021). https://ia.cr/2021/703

6. Barreto, P.S., Rijmen, V.: The Whirlpool hashing function. Submitted to NESSIE
7. Beierle, C., et al.: The SKINNY family of block ciphers and its low-latency variant MANTIS. In: Robshaw, M., Katz, J. (eds.) CRYPTO 2016, Part II. LNCS, vol. 9815, pp. 123–153. Springer, Heidelberg (2016). https://doi.org/10.1007/978-3-662-53008-5_5
8. Benadjila, R., et al: SHA-3 proposal: ECHO. Submission to NIST (updated), p. 113 (2009)
9. Bernstein, D.J.: Cost analysis of hash collisions: will quantum computers make SHARCS obsolete. In: SHARCS 2009, vol. 9, p. 105 (2009)
10. Bertoni, G., Daemen, J., Peeters, M., Assche, G.V.: Keccak sponge function family main document. Submission to NIST (Round 2), 3(30), 320–337 (2009)
11. Bogdanov, A., Khovratovich, D., Rechberger, C.: Biclique cryptanalysis of the full AES. In: Lee, D.H., Wang, X. (eds.) ASIACRYPT 2011. LNCS, vol. 7073, pp. 344–371. Springer, Heidelberg (2011). https://doi.org/10.1007/978-3-642-25385-0_19
12. Bonnetain, X., Hosoyamada, A., Naya-Plasencia, M., Sasaki, Yu., Schrottenloher, A.: Quantum attacks without superposition queries: the offline Simon's algorithm. In: Galbraith, S.D., Moriai, S. (eds.) ASIACRYPT 2019, Part I. LNCS, vol. 11921, pp. 552–583. Springer, Cham (2019). https://doi.org/10.1007/978-3-030-34578-5_20
13. Bonnetain, X., Naya-Plasencia, M., Schrottenloher, A.: On quantum slide attacks. In: Paterson, K.G., Stebila, D. (eds.) SAC 2019. LNCS, vol. 11959, pp. 492–519. Springer, Cham (2020). https://doi.org/10.1007/978-3-030-38471-5_20
14. Bonnetain, X., Naya-Plasencia, M., Schrottenloher, A.: Quantum security analysis of AES. IACR Trans. Symmetric Cryptol. 2019(2), 55–93 (2019)
15. Brassard, G., Høyer, P., Tapp, A.: Quantum cryptanalysis of hash and claw-free functions. In: Lucchesi, C.L., Moura, A.V. (eds.) LATIN 1998. LNCS, vol. 1380, pp. 163–169. Springer, Heidelberg (1998). https://doi.org/10.1007/BFb0054319
16. Canteaut, A., et al.: A note on related-key attacks on Saturnin (2020). https://project.inria.fr/saturnin/files/2020/11/Note-RK-1.pdf
17. Canteaut, A., et al.: Saturnin: a suite of lightweight symmetric algorithms for postquantum security. IACR Trans. Symmetric Cryptol. 2020(S1), 160–207 (2020)
18. Cauchois, V., Gomez, C., Lercier, R.: Grøstl distinguishing attack: a new rebound attack of an AES-like permutation. IACR Trans. Symmetric Cryptol. 2017(3), 1–23 (2017)
19. Chailloux, A., Naya-Plasencia, M., Schrottenloher, A.: An efficient quantum collision search algorithm and implications on symmetric cryptography. In: Takagi, T., Peyrin, T. (eds.) ASIACRYPT 2017, Part II. LNCS, vol. 10625, pp. 211–240. Springer, Cham (2017). https://doi.org/10.1007/978-3-319-70697-9_8
20. Daemen, J., Rijmen, V.: Understanding two-round differentials in AES. In: De Prisco, R., Yung, M. (eds.) SCN 2006. LNCS, vol. 4116, pp. 78–94. Springer, Heidelberg (2006). https://doi.org/10.1007/11832072_6
21. Daemen, J., Rijmen, V.: The Design of Rijndael: AES - The Advanced Encryption Standard. Information Security and Cryptography, Springer, Cham (2002). https://doi.org/10.1007/978-3-662-04722-4
22. Damgård, I.B.: A design principle for hash functions. In: Brassard, G. (ed.) CRYPTO 1989. LNCS, vol. 435, pp. 416–427. Springer, New York (1990). https://doi.org/10.1007/0-387-34805-0_39
23. Delaune, S., Derbez, P., Vavrille, M.: Catching the fastest boomerangs. IACR Trans. Symmetric Cryptol. 104–129 (2020)

24. Derbez, P., Fouque, P.-A., Jean, J.: Improved key recovery attacks on reduced-round AES in the single-key setting. In: Johansson, T., Nguyen, P.Q. (eds.) EURO-CRYPT 2013. LNCS, vol. 7881, pp. 371–387. Springer, Heidelberg (2013). https://doi.org/10.1007/978-3-642-38348-9_23

25. Derbez, P., Huynh, P., Lallemand, V., Naya-Plasencia, M., Perrin, L., Schrottenloher, A.: Cryptanalysis results on Spook - bringing full-round Shadow-512 to the light. In: Micciancio, D., Ristenpart, T. (eds.) CRYPTO 2020, Part III. LNCS, vol. 12172, pp. 359–388. Springer, Cham (2020). https://doi.org/10.1007/978-3-030-56877-1_13

26. Dinur, I., Dunkelman, O., Keller, N., Shamir, A.: Efficient dissection of composite problems, with applications to cryptanalysis, knapsacks, and combinatorial search problems. In: Safavi-Naini, R., Canetti, R. (eds.) CRYPTO 2012. LNCS, vol. 7417, pp. 719–740. Springer, Heidelberg (2012). https://doi.org/10.1007/978-3-642-32009-5_42

27. Dong, X., Dong, B., Wang, X.: Quantum attacks on some Feistel block ciphers. Des. Codes Cryptogr. 88(6), 1179–1203 (2020). https://doi.org/10.1007/s10623-020-00741-y

28. Dong, X., Guo, J., Li, S., Pham, P.: Triangulating rebound attack on AES-like hashing. Cryptology ePrint Archive, Paper 2022/731 (2022). https://eprint.iacr.org/2022/731

29. Dong, X., Hua, J., Sun, S., Li, Z., Wang, X., Hu, L.: Meet-in-the-middle attacks revisited: key-recovery, collision, and preimage attacks. In: Malkin, T., Peikert, C. (eds.) CRYPTO 2021, Part III. LNCS, vol. 12827, pp. 278–308. Springer, Cham (2021). https://doi.org/10.1007/978-3-030-84252-9_10

30. Dong, X., Sun, S., Shi, D., Gao, F., Wang, X., Hu, L.: Quantum collision attacks on AES-like hashing with low quantum random access memories. In: Moriai, S., Wang, H. (eds.) ASIACRYPT 2020, Part II. LNCS, vol. 12492, pp. 727–757. Springer, Cham (2020). https://doi.org/10.1007/978-3-030-64834-3_25

31. Dong, X., Zhang, Z., Sun, S., Wei, C., Wang, X., Hu, L.: Automatic classical and quantum rebound attacks on AES-like hashing by exploiting related-key differentials. In: Tibouchi, M., Wang, H. (eds.) ASIACRYPT 2021, Part I. LNCS, vol. 13090, pp. 241–271. Springer, Cham (2021). https://doi.org/10.1007/978-3-030-92062-3_9

32. Duc, A., Guo, J., Peyrin, T., Wei, L.: Unaligned rebound attack: application to Keccak. In: Canteaut, A. (ed.) FSE 2012. LNCS, vol. 7549, pp. 402–421. Springer, Heidelberg (2012). https://doi.org/10.1007/978-3-642-34047-5_23

33. Dunkelman, O., Keller, N., Shamir, A.: Improved single-key attacks on 8-round AES-192 and AES-256. In: Abe, M. (ed.) ASIACRYPT 2010. LNCS, vol. 6477, pp. 158–176. Springer, Heidelberg (2010). https://doi.org/10.1007/978-3-642-17373-8_10

34. Gauravaram, P., et al.: Grøstl - a SHA-3 candidate. In: Symmetric Cryptography, 11–16 January 2009 (2009)

35. Gilbert, H., Peyrin, T.: Super-Sbox cryptanalysis: improved attacks for AES-like permutations. In: Hong, S., Iwata, T. (eds.) FSE 2010. LNCS, vol. 6147, pp. 365–383. Springer, Heidelberg (2010). https://doi.org/10.1007/978-3-642-13858-4_21

36. Grassi, L., Naya-Plasencia, M., Schrottenloher, A.: Quantum algorithms for the k-xor problem. In: Peyrin, T., Galbraith, S. (eds.) ASIACRYPT 2018, Part I. LNCS, vol. 11272, pp. 527–559. Springer, Cham (2018). https://doi.org/10.1007/978-3-030-03326-2_18

37. Guo, C., Katz, J., Wang, X., Yu, Y.: Efficient and secure multiparty computation from fixed-key block ciphers. In: 2020 IEEE Symposium on Security and Privacy, San Francisco, CA, USA, 18–21 May 2020, pp. 825–841 (2020)

38. Hosoyamada, A., Sasaki, Yu.: Cryptanalysis against symmetric-key schemes with online classical queries and offline quantum computations. In: Smart, N.P. (ed.) CT-RSA 2018. LNCS, vol. 10808, pp. 198–218. Springer, Cham (2018). https://doi.org/10.1007/978-3-319-76953-0_11

39. Hosoyamada, A., Sasaki, Yu.: Finding hash collisions with quantum computers by using differential trails with smaller probability than birthday bound. In: Canteaut, A., Ishai, Y. (eds.) EUROCRYPT 2020, Part II. LNCS, vol. 12106, pp. 249–279. Springer, Cham (2020). https://doi.org/10.1007/978-3-030-45724-2_9

40. Hosoyamada, A., Sasaki, Yu.: Quantum collision attacks on reduced SHA-256 and SHA-512. In: Malkin, T., Peikert, C. (eds.) CRYPTO 2021. LNCS, vol. 12825, pp. 616–646. Springer, Cham (2021). https://doi.org/10.1007/978-3-030-84242-0_22

41. Hosoyamada, A., Sasaki, Yu., Tani, S., Xagawa, K.: Improved quantum multicollision-finding algorithm. In: Ding, J., Steinwandt, R. (eds.) PQCrypto 2019. LNCS, vol. 11505, pp. 350–367. Springer, Cham (2019). https://doi.org/10.1007/978-3-030-25510-7_19

42. Hosoyamada, A., Sasaki, Yu., Xagawa, K.: Quantum multicollision-finding algorithm. In: Takagi, T., Peyrin, T. (eds.) ASIACRYPT 2017, Part II. LNCS, vol. 10625, pp. 179–210. Springer, Cham (2017). https://doi.org/10.1007/978-3-319-70697-9_7

43. ISO/IEC. 10118-2:2010 Information technology—Security techniques – Hash-functions – Part 2: Hash-functions using an n-bit block cipher. 3rd edn., International Organization for Standardization, Geneve, Switzerland, October 2010

44. Jean, J., Fouque, P.-A.: Practical near-collisions and collisions on round-reduced ECHO-256 compression function. In: Joux, A. (ed.) FSE 2011. LNCS, vol. 6733, pp. 107–127. Springer, Heidelberg (2011). https://doi.org/10.1007/978-3-642-21702-9_7

45. Jean, J., Naya-Plasencia, M., Peyrin, T.: Improved rebound attack on the finalist Grøstl. In: Canteaut, A. (ed.) FSE 2012. LNCS, vol. 7549, pp. 110–126. Springer, Heidelberg (2012). https://doi.org/10.1007/978-3-642-34047-5_7

46. Jean, J., Naya-Plasencia, M., Peyrin, T.: Multiple limited-birthday distinguishers and applications. In: Lange, T., Lauter, K., Lisoněk, P. (eds.) SAC 2013. LNCS, vol. 8282, pp. 533–550. Springer, Heidelberg (2014). https://doi.org/10.1007/978-3-662-43414-7_27

47. Kaplan, M., Leurent, G., Leverrier, A., Naya-Plasencia, M.: Breaking symmetric cryptosystems using quantum period finding. In: Robshaw, M., Katz, J. (eds.) CRYPTO 2016, Part II. LNCS, vol. 9815, pp. 207–237. Springer, Heidelberg (2016). https://doi.org/10.1007/978-3-662-53008-5_8

48. Kaplan, M., Leurent, G., Leverrier, A., Naya-Plasencia, M.: Quantum differential and linear cryptanalysis. IACR Trans. Symmetric Cryptol. **2016**(1), 71–94 (2016)

49. Keller, M., Orsini, E., Scholl, P.: MASCOT: faster malicious arithmetic secure computation with oblivious transfer. In: Proceedings of the 2016 ACM SIGSAC Conference on Computer and Communications Security, Vienna, Austria, 24–28 October 2016, pp. 830–842 (2016)

50. Khovratovich, D., Biryukov, A., Nikolic, I.: Speeding up collision search for byte-oriented hash functions. In: Fischlin, M. (ed.) CT-RSA 2009. LNCS, vol. 5473, pp. 164–181. Springer, Heidelberg (2009). https://doi.org/10.1007/978-3-642-00862-7_11

51. Khovratovich, D., Nikolic, I., Rechberger, C.: Rotational rebound attacks on reduced Skein. J. Cryptol. **27**(3), 452–479 (2014)

52. Knudsen, L.R., Rechberger, C., Thomsen, S.S.: The Grindahl hash functions. In: Biryukov, A. (ed.) FSE 2007. LNCS, vol. 4593, pp. 39–57. Springer, Heidelberg (2007). https://doi.org/10.1007/978-3-540-74619-5_3

53. Kölbl, S., Lauridsen, M.M., Mendel, F., Rechberger, C.: Haraka v2 - efficient short-input hashing for post-quantum applications. IACR Trans. Symmetric Cryptol. **2016**(2), 1–29 (2016)

54. Kuwakado, H., Morii, M.: Quantum distinguisher between the 3-round Feistel cipher and the random permutation. In: Proceedings of ISIT 2010, Austin, Texas, USA, 13–18 June 2010, pp. 2682–2685 (2010)

55. Kuwakado, H., Morii, M.: Security on the quantum-type Even-Mansour cipher. In: ISITA 2012, Honolulu, HI, USA, 28–31 October 2012, pp. 312–316 (2012)

56. Lamberger, M., Mendel, F., Rechberger, C., Rijmen, V., Schläffer, M.: Rebound distinguishers: results on the full Whirlpool compression function. In: Matsui, M. (ed.) ASIACRYPT 2009. LNCS, vol. 5912, pp. 126–143. Springer, Heidelberg (2009). https://doi.org/10.1007/978-3-642-10366-7_8

57. Leander, G., May, A.: Grover meets Simon – quantumly attacking the FX-construction. In: Takagi, T., Peyrin, T. (eds.) ASIACRYPT 2017, Part II. LNCS, vol. 10625, pp. 161–178. Springer, Cham (2017). https://doi.org/10.1007/978-3-319-70697-9_6

58. Liu, Q., Zhandry, M.: On finding quantum multi-collisions. In: Ishai, Y., Rijmen, V. (eds.) EUROCRYPT 2019, Part III. LNCS, vol. 11478, pp. 189–218. Springer, Cham (2019). https://doi.org/10.1007/978-3-030-17659-4_7

59. Matusiewicz, K., Naya-Plasencia, M., Nikolić, I., Sasaki, Yu., Schläffer, M.: Rebound attack on the full LANE compression function. In: Matsui, M. (ed.) ASIACRYPT 2009. LNCS, vol. 5912, pp. 106–125. Springer, Heidelberg (2009). https://doi.org/10.1007/978-3-642-10366-7_7

60. Mendel, F., Peyrin, T., Rechberger, C., Schläffer, M.: Improved cryptanalysis of the reduced Grøstl compression function, ECHO permutation and AES block cipher. In: Jacobson, M.J., Rijmen, V., Safavi-Naini, R. (eds.) SAC 2009. LNCS, vol. 5867, pp. 16–35. Springer, Heidelberg (2009). https://doi.org/10.1007/978-3-642-05445-7_2

61. Mendel, F., Rechberger, C., Schläffer, M., Thomsen, S.S.: Rebound attacks on the reduced Grøstl hash function. In: Pieprzyk, J. (ed.) CT-RSA 2010. LNCS, vol. 5985, pp. 350–365. Springer, Heidelberg (2010). https://doi.org/10.1007/978-3-642-11925-5_24

62. Mendel, F., Rechberger, C., Schläffer, M., Thomsen, S.S.: The rebound attack: cryptanalysis of reduced Whirlpool and Grøstl. In: Dunkelman, O. (ed.) FSE 2009. LNCS, vol. 5665, pp. 260–276. Springer, Heidelberg (2009). https://doi.org/10.1007/978-3-642-03317-9_16

63. Mendel, F., Rijmen, V., Schläffer, M.: Collision attack on 5 rounds of Grøstl. In: Cid, C., Rechberger, C. (eds.) FSE 2014. LNCS, vol. 8540, pp. 509–521. Springer, Heidelberg (2015). https://doi.org/10.1007/978-3-662-46706-0_26

64. Menezes, A., van Oorschot, P.C., Vanstone, S.A.: Handbook of Applied Cryptography. CRC Press (1996)

65. Merkle, R.C.: A certified digital signature. In: Brassard, G. (ed.) CRYPTO 1989. LNCS, vol. 435, pp. 218–238. Springer, New York (1990). https://doi.org/10.1007/0-387-34805-0_21

66. Naya-Plasencia, M.: How to improve rebound attacks. In: Rogaway, P. (ed.) CRYPTO 2011. LNCS, vol. 6841, pp. 188–205. Springer, Heidelberg (2011). https://doi.org/10.1007/978-3-642-22792-9_11

67. Naya-Plasencia, M., Schrottenloher, A.: Optimal merging in quantum k-xor and k-sum algorithms. In: Canteaut, A., Ishai, Y. (eds.) EUROCRYPT 2020, Part II. LNCS, vol. 12106, pp. 311–340. Springer, Cham (2020). https://doi.org/10.1007/978-3-030-45724-2_11

68. Naya-Plasencia, M., Toz, D., Varici, K.: Rebound attack on JH42. In: Lee, D.H., Wang, X. (eds.) ASIACRYPT 2011. LNCS, vol. 7073, pp. 252–269. Springer, Heidelberg (2011). https://doi.org/10.1007/978-3-642-25385-0_14

69. Sasaki, Yu.: Meet-in-the-middle preimage attacks on AES hashing modes and an application to Whirlpool. In: Joux, A. (ed.) FSE 2011. LNCS, vol. 6733, pp. 378–396. Springer, Heidelberg (2011). https://doi.org/10.1007/978-3-642-21702-9_22

70. Sasaki, Yu., Li, Y., Wang, L., Sakiyama, K., Ohta, K.: Non-full-active Super-Sbox analysis: applications to ECHO and Grøstl. In: Abe, M. (ed.) ASIACRYPT 2010. LNCS, vol. 6477, pp. 38–55. Springer, Heidelberg (2010). https://doi.org/10.1007/978-3-642-17373-8_3

71. Sasaki, Yu., Wang, L., Wu, S., Wu, W.: Investigating fundamental security requirements on Whirlpool: improved preimage and collision attacks. In: Wang, X., Sako, K. (eds.) ASIACRYPT 2012. LNCS, vol. 7658, pp. 562–579. Springer, Heidelberg (2012). https://doi.org/10.1007/978-3-642-34961-4_34

72. Schläffer, M.: Updated differential analysis of Grøstl. Grøstl website, January 2011 (2011)

73. Shor, P.W.: Algorithms for quantum computation: discrete logarithms and factoring. In: 35th Annual Symposium on Foundations of Computer Science, Santa Fe, New Mexico, USA, 20–22 November 1994, pp. 124–134 (1994)

74. Stevens, M., Bursztein, E., Karpman, P., Albertini, A., Markov, Y.: The first collision for full SHA-1. In: Katz, J., Shacham, H. (eds.) CRYPTO 2017, Part I. LNCS, vol. 10401, pp. 570–596. Springer, Cham (2017). https://doi.org/10.1007/978-3-319-63688-7_19

75. van Oorschot, P.C., Wiener, M.J.: Parallel collision search with cryptanalytic applications. J. Cryptol. **12**(1), 1–28 (1999)

76. Wang, X., Yin, Y.L., Yu, H.: Finding collisions in the full SHA-1. In: Shoup, V. (ed.) CRYPTO 2005. LNCS, vol. 3621, pp. 17–36. Springer, Heidelberg (2005). https://doi.org/10.1007/11535218_2

77. Wang, X., Yu, H.: How to break MD5 and other hash functions. In: Cramer, R. (ed.) EUROCRYPT 2005. LNCS, vol. 3494, pp. 19–35. Springer, Heidelberg (2005). https://doi.org/10.1007/11426639_2

Randomness

Public Randomness Extraction with Ephemeral Roles and Worst-Case Corruptions

Jesper Buus Nielsen[1] , João Ribeiro[2(✉)] , and Maciej Obremski[3]

[1] Aarhus University, Aarhus, Denmark
jbn@cs.au.dk
[2] Carnegie Mellon University, Pittsburgh, PA, USA
jlourenc@cs.cmu.edu
[3] National University of Singapore, Singapore, Singapore

Abstract. We distill a simple information-theoretic model for randomness extraction motivated by the task of generating publicly verifiable randomness in blockchain settings and which is closely related to *You-Only-Speak-Once (YOSO)* protocols (CRYPTO 2021). With the goal of avoiding denial-of-service attacks, parties speak only once and in sequence by broadcasting a public value and forwarding secret values to future parties. Additionally, an unbounded adversary can corrupt any chosen subset of at most t parties. In contrast, existing YOSO protocols only handle random corruptions. As a notable example, considering worst-case corruptions allows us to reduce trust in the role assignment mechanism, which is assumed to be perfectly random in YOSO.

We study the maximum corruption threshold t which allows for unconditional randomness extraction in our model:

- With respect to feasibility, we give protocols for t corruptions and $n = 6t + 1$ or $n = 5t$ parties depending on whether the adversary learns secret values forwarded to corrupted parties immediately once they are sent or only once the corrupted party is executed, respectively. Both settings are motivated by practical implementations of secret value forwarding. To design such protocols, we go beyond the committee-based approach that is sufficient for random corruptions in YOSO but turns out to be sub-optimal for chosen corruptions.
- To complement our protocols, we show that low-error randomness extraction is impossible with corruption threshold t and $n \leq 4t$ parties in both settings above. This also provides a separation between chosen and random corruptions, since the latter allows for randomness extraction with close to $n/2$ random corruptions.

1 Introduction

Publicly verifiable randomness is a fundamental resource for many tasks, including contract signing, electronic voting, and anonymous communication and

---

M. Obremski—The author ordering is randomized. A certificate of the randomization procedure can be found here.

Y. Dodis and T. Shrimpton (Eds.): CRYPTO 2022, LNCS 13507, pp. 127–147, 2022.
https://doi.org/10.1007/978-3-031-15802-5_5

browsing [7,10]. However, such sources of randomness are hard to come by in the wild, and so it is imperative to develop protocols which allow multiple mutually distrusting parties, each with access to their own source of randomness, to agree on a public string of nearly unbiased random bits even under adversarial behavior. We propose and study a simple information theoretic model for extracting randomness which is inspired by the problem of generating publicly verifiable randomness in blockchain settings, sometimes also known as blockchain randomness beacons. Our model is in particular motivated by the notions of *player-replacable* protocols as introduced by Micali [16] and *You-Only-Speak-Once* (YOSO) protocols as introduced by Gentry, Halevi, Krawczyk, Magri, Nielsen, Rabin, and Yakoubov [11]. In these classes of protocols, each party only sends messages once, and therefore need not have a mutable secret state. This gives high resilience to Denial-of-Service (DoS) attacks as often desirable in blockchain settings.

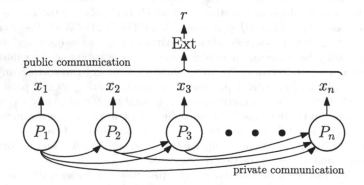

Fig. 1. Illustration of the model. Each party sends a public message and secret messages to future parties. The extracted value r depends deterministically on the public values.

More precisely, we consider a multiparty computation model where n parties $P_1, \ldots, P_n$ are activated sequentially, with each party having access to an internal source of randomness. To begin with, P_1 is executed and it outputs a public value x_1 which we think of as being shown to all parties, including the adversary. Moreover, P_1 also gets to send secret values $s_{1,j}$ to each future party P_j. When a future P_j is executed it receives all previous public values x_i for $i < j$ along with all secret values intended for P_j. We can think of P_i as being described by a distribution D_i defining the conditional probabilities

$$\Pr_{D_i}[x_i, s_{i,i+1}, \ldots, s_{i,n} \mid x_1, \ldots x_{i-1}, s_{1,i}, \ldots, s_{i-1,i}].$$

After all parties speak, the goal is to deterministically extract nearly unbiased public randomness from the public values $(x_1, \ldots, x_n)$. The model is illustrated in Fig. 1. We interpret these parties $P_1, \ldots, P_n$ as *ephemeral roles*. In a practical setting there would be a ground set of N parties, usually with $N \gg n$, and executing each of the n roles entails sampling a party in some manner from the ground set to follow the instructions. This is discussed in more detail in Sect. 1.1.

We study threshold static worst-case corruptions: The adversary is allowed to corrupt an arbitrary unknown subset of up to t parties before the start of the protocol, where we call t the *corruption threshold*. The adversary sees all public outputs when they are produced. Additionally, it also sees all secret inputs for corrupted parties and can determine their outputs. I.e., when a corrupted party P_i is about to be executed, it is the adversary who receives inputs $(x_1, \ldots x_{i-1}, s_{1,i}, \ldots, s_{i-1,i})$ and determines the outputs $(x_i, s_{i,i+1}, \ldots, s_{i,n})$. Note that the adversary also has access to information it gathered in the past. For example, it also has access to the secret values sent to past corrupted parties $P_{i'}$ with $i' < i$.

Information may be revealed to the adversary in different ways. We consider two scenarios, which we term the *sending-leaks* and *execution-leaks* settings. In the sending-leaks setting, if party P_i is honest and sends the secret value $s_{i,j}$ to a corrupted party P_j during its execution, then the adversary learns $s_{i,j}$ immediately. In contrast, in the execution-leaks setting the secret value $s_{i,j}$ would only be revealed to the adversary later when the corrupted party P_j is executed. The motivation behind these settings is related to how the forwarding of the secret values is implemented in practice. We discuss this in more detail in Sect. 1.1.

We consider unconditional security only. More precisely, after the protocol ends and some randomness r has been extracted from $(x_1, \ldots, x_n)$, we require that r is statistically close to uniform over $\{0, 1\}$ given the view of the adversary. Note that this view includes all secret messages sent or received by corrupted parties. Furthermore, we may generate more random bits by running the protocol several times in parallel. The following general question arises naturally:

> *What is the maximum corruption threshold that allows unconditional randomness extraction in each of the corruption models?*

A Naive First Approach via Standard Multiparty Computation. Our setting is closely related to previous multiparty computation (MPC) models. In particular, it can be seen as a special case of information theoretic MPC of a random string in the models of [2,8]. There is, however, one significant difference: In standard MPC a party can have identity over time, while in our case each party speaks only once. This is also related to the notion of proactive security [13] where refreshment is used to decouple future states of a party from previous states.

Naively, a standard r-round MPC protocol tolerating that t out of m parties can be corrupted immediately yields a protocol in our model where t out of $n = rm$ parties $P_{1,1}, \ldots, P_{1,m}, \ldots, P_{r,1}, \ldots, P_{r,m}$ can be corrupted. This is accomplished by implementing the behavior of the i-th party over the r rounds using r distinct parties $P_{1,m}, \ldots, P_{r,m}$ in our model. Then, we use the secret values to pass the current state of $P_{i,\rho}$ to $P_{i,\rho+1}$, and consider party P_i corrupted if *at least one* of the parties $P_{i,1}, \ldots, P_{i,r}$ is corrupted.

In particular, one can generate unbiased randomness using this approach by having all parties run a verifiable secret sharing protocol of a random value, and then reconstruct all values and XOR them. Using, for instance, the protocol from [9] with 2-round sharing and 1-round reconstruction procedures tolerating $t < m/3$ corruptions, we immediately obtain a randomness extraction protocol in our model tolerating $t < n/9$ corruptions. However, this is not very satisfactory. In fact, this approach implies a reduction by a factor of r in the tolerated corruption threshold. This is inevitable because, in our model, the adversary can concentrate all t corruptions wherever it wishes (and this also applies to proactively secure protocols). Therefore, if the original protocol has some notion of "rounds", then the adversary can concentrate all corruptions in a single round. We find it interesting to understand how the ability to "concentrate" corruptions affects the feasibility of MPC. This is in particular interesting in player-replaceable and YOSO style protocols where there is no identity.

The naive approach above does show that we can withstand *some* constant threshold of corruptions. On the other hand, it is easy to see that we cannot tolerate $t \geq n/2$ corruptions. With this in mind along with the loss incurred by translating a round-based protocol to our setting, we are interested in the following concrete question:

Can we improve the lower and upper bounds on the exact maximum corruption threshold that allows for public randomness generation in our model?

1.1 The Motivation Behind Our Setting

Our model is very closely related to the *You Only Speak Once (YOSO)* model proposed in [11], which was in turn inspired by the model from [3] and is related to the *fluid MPC* model in [9]. The YOSO model is also related to the notion of a *player-replaceable* protocol as introduced by Micali [16]. The main difference between player-replaceable and YOSO protocols is that player-replaceable protocols only allow public messages and YOSO protocols allow secret messages.

The YOSO model considers information theoretic MPC where each party speaks only once and has secure channels to future parties. Therefore, our model is a specialisation of the YOSO model to public randomness extraction. The YOSO model is inspired by the problem of doing MPC in an open blockchain setting. In such a setting, once someone sends a message, their IP address becomes known and they are subject to DoS attacks. To mitigate this issue, blockchain protocols are often designed such that each party speaks only once and does not have to keep state.

For instance, in Bitcoin the next block is produced by a random miner, and so the adversary cannot target a DoS attack on the next party to act. However, there are two additional issues to keep in mind when performing MPC in this model: *First, how does a party send a secret value to an unknown future speaker? Second, how impartial is the selection of speakers?*

The Motivation Behind the Sending-Leaks and Execution-Leaks Models. In [3] and [12] so called *role assignment* protocols are proposed to solve the first problem above. In these protocols an ephemeral public key pk for a future role R is made public and at the same time some random party P learns the secret key sk. A role is simply the description of some future part of the protocol, such as "execute the code of party P_{42}". In order to send a secret message s to P, one can then simply broadcast an encryption of s. In the context of a blockchain, the broadcast could for instance be done by posting the ciphertext on the blockchain along with the public value. When it is P's turn to execute the role R in the protocol, it will decrypt the incoming values, compute its outgoing values, and then post them all on the blockchain in one flow. In particular, P speaks only once and does not have to reveal its identity until it sends its values.

A different approach to role assignment is given in [5]. Values to role R are encrypted to identity R in a threshold identity-based encryption scheme, and a rolling committee holds a secret sharing of the master secret key. Once R is about to be executed, the secret key for role R is reconstructed to a random hidden party P which then executes the role.

A role assignment protocol can also be used to implement our model on top of a blockchain to yield public randomness extraction in the YOSO model. Note that the role assignment protocols in [3,12] corresponds roughly to what we call the sending-leaks model. If P is corrupted, then it learns sk once the ephemeral keys pk has been made public. So the adversary learns the secret values forwarded to P as soon as they are sent. The role assignment protocol in [5] corresponds roughly to the execution-leaks model, as P does not learn the identity secret key until execution time. Therefore, both of our models can be motivated by practical settings.

Another important motivation for our model is that it is a clean setting for studying public randomness extraction techniques. This model is simple and detached from its blockchain motivation, and can therefore hopefully draw in researchers from other areas which are not necessarily interested in the nitty-gritty practical details of blockchains. At the same time, it is close enough to its motivating setting that new insights in the model hopefully can lead to better protocols for practical generation of randomness on public blockchains.

Worst-Case vs. Random Corruptions. The YOSO paper [11] studies mainly *random* corruptions (i.e., each party is independently corrupted with some constant probability). The motivation behind this is that, since roles R are assumed to be mapped uniformly to parties P by some perfectly random role assignment mechanism and the adversary in practice can do chosen corruptions of *parties*, then the adversary is *de facto* restricted to random corruptions of roles. As a result, one can morally restrict attention to protocols secure against random corruptions only, and then compile them to practice using role assignment.

However, there are natural motivations for considering worst-case corruptions in this model, as opposed to random corruptions:

1. **Reducing trust in the role assignment mechanism:** The first main reason for considering worst-case corruptions is that the role assignment mechanism might not be perfectly random, in which case the YOSO protocols for random corruptions are no longer secure. Assuming worst-case corruptions in our protocol design allows us to withstand bias on the part of the role assignment mechanism without losing security, and so the required level of trust in this mechanism is greatly reduced. Furthermore, studying chosen corruptions may also inspire more efficient techniques for the intermediate case where role assignment is neither perfect nor extremely biased.

   An example of a role assignment which is highly biased is the *fluid MPC* model in [9]. Here, parties may come and go at will. One motivating setting is parties lending their machines to MPC when they are idle. In this case, honest parties might be seen as registering at random times, but corrupted parties can strategically choose when they join the computation. This is closer to chosen corruptions than random corruptions.

   Another example of imperfect random role assignment is the *A Practically Appealing Weak Batch-RPIR* scheme in [12]. Here, parties are put into small buckets using a known distribution. Then, the next random role is assigned by chosen a random unknown party from the next bucket. This gives a lot of information on which parties could execute which roles, but it is good enough for electing large committees with enough honest parties, which is all that is needed for committee based protocols.

2. **Randomness for small groups:** Another case where it makes sense to consider chosen corruption is when generating randomness for small groups. For instance, this happens naturally in the player simulation technique in secure MPC [14], where a constant sized group carries out a given task. If enough group members are honest, we want the task to be carried out securely. On the other hand, if too many are corrupted we simply count the group as fully corrupted. Overall, security holds if enough groups are honest. In such a setting, random corruptions will have all possible subsets of the group be corrupted with constant probability, and so we might therefore as well study chosen corruptions. We would be interested in under which corruptions the group can generate good joint randomness.

3. **Moving away from established round-based techniques:** Considering only random corruptions as in YOSO [11] ensures that one can stay mostly within established methodologies for round-based MPC, which we have seen do not work well in our setting with worst-case corruptions. Indeed, the following design pattern works for random corruptions: If there is an r-round protocol with committees of size m, then pick m large enough so that if there are less than $(1/2 - \delta)m$ corruptions, for a small constant $\delta > 0$, then also among any m parties in a given committee the frequency of corruption will be below half. Following this, design a protocol tolerating less than half corruptions in each committee. If we assign committees to rounds, this leads to a model with rounds where one can assume honest majority during all rounds. This makes it easier to design protocols as one does not have to deal with the *concentration* problem discussed above.

In [11] there is a YOSO protocol for public randomness generation for *random corruptions* with threshold $t = (1/2 - \delta)n$ for any constant $\delta > 0$. This protocol is obtained by first giving an MPC protocol for this setting and then noting that randomness generation is a special case of MPC. The MPC protocol uses a number of committees linear in the security parameter and all committees need to have honest majority. This means that if the protocol is cast in our model with chosen corruptions, then only a vanishing fraction of corruptions can be tolerated since the adversary could concentrate corruptions on a single committee. This gives a worse bound than the previously discussed naive approach via verifiable secret sharing using [9].

With the above in mind, another main motivation for studying chosen corruptions, as opposed to random corruptions, is that it forces us to develop new techniques beyond the committee-based methodology in order to minimize the total number of parties needed for a given task. We hope that studying our proposed model with chosen corruptions can shed light on the following question:

> Can we develop YOSO extraction/MPC techniques qualitatively different from the ones developed for the committee-based methodology?

As we shall discuss in more detail in Sect. 1.4, we also take the committee-based approach as a starting point for our protocols, but then make additional improvements beyond the naive approach by exploiting the structure of the YOSO model.

1.2 Other Related Work

Some papers have also studied the generation of unbiased randomness from a blockchain based on computational assumptions – see, for instance, ALBATROSS [7] and the citations therein. This protocol again assumes rounds with at least honest majority in each round, and therefore do not have to deal with the concentration problem.

Other works have considered related models where parties publish public values in sequence but future secret values are not permitted, such as Santha-Vazirani sources [17], Bitcoin beacons [4], and SHELA sources [1]. Crucially, in such versions it is not possible to deterministically extract uniformly random bits.

The execution-leaks model is related to the standard model in secure MPC where the adversary is monolithic, i.e., when a corrupted party P_i is about to be executed, it is the adversary who receives input $(x_1, \ldots x_{i-1}, s_{1,i}, \ldots, s_{i-1,i})$ and determines the outputs $(x_i, s_{i,i+1}, \ldots, s_{i,n})$, and the adversary can see what is sent to corrupted parties as soon as the messages are sent. This is opposed to a model where corrupted party is corrupted independently and only can communicate within the model. In such a model a future corrupted party could not send information back to a previous corrupted party as there is no channel for this. Such a model is related to the notion of a local adversary, as introduced in [6], though there are technical differences.

1.3 Our Contributions

We obtain both feasibility and impossibility results for randomness extraction in our models. In the context of feasibility, we improve on the naive VSS- and committee-based approach described above, leading to the following results in the sending-leaks and execution-leaks adversarial models. For formal definitions of the models we consider, we refer the reader to Sect. 2.

Theorem 1 (Feasibility in the sending-leaks model). *There is a zero-error n-party randomness extraction protocol secure against any sending-leaks adversary with corruption threshold t whenever $n \geq 6t + 1$.*

We can improve the theorem above in the execution-leaks model.

Theorem 2 (Feasibility in the execution-leaks model). *There is a zero-error n-party randomness extraction protocol secure against any execution-leaks adversary with corruption threshold t whenever $n \geq 5t$.*

To complement our feasibility results, we also prove an upper bound on the maximum corruption threshold that allows for low-error randomness extraction in our model. This bound also allows us to separate the "random corruptions" regime in YOSO [11], where $t = (1/2 - \delta)n$ random corruptions can be tolerated for any constant $\delta > 0$, from our "worst-case corruptions" regime.

Theorem 3 (Impossibility result). *There is no randomness extraction protocol secure against t corruptions with $n \leq 4t$ parties and bias less than $1/100$ in both the sending-leaks or execution-leaks models.*

For example, combining Theorems 2 and 3 allows us to conclude that the maximal corruption threshold $t^\star$ in the execution-leaks model lies somewhere between $\lfloor n/5 \rfloor$ and $\lceil n/4 \rceil - 1$. Moreover, it follows that $n = 5$ parties are both sufficient and necessary for low-error randomness extraction with $t = 1$ worst-case corruptions in both models.

Extracting Multiple Random Bits. Observe that in order to extract a λ-bit string of unbiased random bits, we can just run our protocols λ times in parallel. This incurs an extra factor of λ in the total communication complexity. We leave it as an interesting open problem to improve on this approach.

Communication Complexity and Scalability. Our protocols incur communication complexity growing exponentially with n, the number of roles to be executed. Moreover, it is also the case that any protocol in our setting requires time and communication complexity $\Omega(n)$. This raises the question of whether protocols in our setting can scale as the number of users increases. We believe this to be the case since the number of roles n is detached from the number of users N in the ground set, and it typically holds that $N \gg n$. Nevertheless, improving the concrete efficiency of protocols is very much relevant and we leave it as an interesting future direction to improve on the communication complexity of our protocols.

1.4   Technical Overview

Protocols for Randomness Extraction. We begin by discussing the app-roach behind the feasibility results in Theorems 1 and 2. Our starting point is an elegant MPC protocol due to Maurer [15] which we modify by taking advantage of the YOSO structure of our models. We present here a sub-optimal version of the protocol for t corruptions and $n = 6t + 2$ parties, and then briefly discuss how we optimize it in the different settings. Divide the set of parties $P_1, \ldots, P_n$ into two consecutive blocks of size $3t + 1$: The *verifiers* $P_1, \ldots, P_{3t+1}$ and the *publishers* $P'_1 = P_{3t+2}, \ldots, P'_{3t+1} = P_{6t+2}$. Intuitively, the protocol proceeds as follows:

1. **Sampling and verification phases:** Do as follows for each set $S \subseteq [3t + 1]$ of size $2t + 1$ in parallel:
   (a) Party $P_{i=\min S}$ samples a value x_S uniformly at random from $\{0, 1\}$ and sends it to P_j for all $j \in S \setminus \{i\}$.
   (b) Each such party P_j then forwards the value it received from P_i to all parties $P_{j'}$ with $j' > j$ and $j' \in S$.
   (c) If a party in this process notices an inconsistency between received secret values, it publicly complains about the set S. Else, it sends the consistent value to all publishers $P'_{j''}$ with $j'' \in S$.
2. **Publishing phase:** For every set S as above which did not receive a com-plaint, each publisher $P'_{j''}$ with $j'' \in S$ publishes the majority of the values it received from verifiers P_j with $j \in S$.

We show that we can obtain an unbiased random bit from this protocol simply by XORing the public values output by all publishers for sets S which did not receive a complaint, even in the stronger sending-leaks setting. The reasons for this are that (i) there exists a set $S^\star$ such that the parties $(P_i, P'_i)_{i \in S^\star}$ are all honest, since $3t + 1 - |S^\star| = t$, and (ii) there is a strict honest majority in all tuples $(P_i)_{i \in S}$ and $(P'_i)_{i \in S}$ for all sets S, since $|S| = 2t + 1$. Roughly speaking, these two properties enforce that an adversary must commit to the final values associated to all sets S *before* the publishing phase, and that at this point the adversary has no knowledge of the value associated to $S^\star$. This ensures that the final XOR is unbiased. In the sending-leaks setting where the adversary learns the secret values sent to corrupted parties as soon as they are sent, we can optimize the protocol above and reduce the number of parties from $6t + 2$ to $6t + 1$, leading to Theorem 1.

In the execution-leaks setting where the adversary only learns the secret values to a corrupted party when it is executed later in the protocol, we optimize the protocol above first by observing that the publishing phase is wasteful. In fact, we can reduce the number of publishers from $3t + 1$ to $2t + 1$ and have each verifier send its value to *all* publishers instead. Exploiting the structure of the execution-leaks setting, it follows that the properties detailed above still hold and so the final XOR is still unbiased. This yields a protocol in the execution-leaks setting for t corruptions and $n = 5t + 2$ parties, which is shy of Theorem 2.

The path towards improving on this result in the execution-leaks setting and finally arriving at Theorem 2 is motivated by the following simple (and, as we show, optimal) protocol for $n = 5$ parties and $t = 1$ corruptions, which does not completely fit the steps above because the set of verifiers is too small:

1. Parties P_1 and P_2 sample uniformly random bits x_1 and x_2, respectively, and send them to parties P_3, P_4, and P_5.
2. Parties P_3, P_4, and P_5 publish all secret values they receive.
3. Extract an unbiased bit by XORing the majority of the values attributed to P_1 and P_2, respectively.

As our final optimization, we show that we can modify the general protocol above and reduce the number of verifiers from $3t + 1$ to $3t - 1$, leading to Theorem 2 and thus obtaining this simple protocol as a natural special case. More details can be found in Sect. 3.

Impossibility Result. We now discuss the approach behind our impossibility result in Theorem 3. For the sake of simplicity, consider a protocol with four parties $P_1, \ldots, P_4$ and one corruption, and assume that a (close to) final output bit is produced if all parties behave honestly. Our proof follows a careful sequential argument where we analyze what would happen if we corrupted parties P_4 through P_1. At a high level, we show that either the behavior of parties $P_1, \ldots, P_{i-1}$ already fully determines the final output of the protocol with high probability, or corrupting P_i allows an adversary to locally control and bias the final output. Care is needed in all stages to ensure the adversary can accurately predict the final output of the protocol locally. We now discuss the main ideas behind each of the four cases:

1. **Corrupt P_4:** In this case, it is easy to see that either the behavior of P_1, P_2, P_3 fully determines the final output with high probability, or there is a decent probability that there are two public values P_4 can publish that would lead to final output 0 and 1, respectively. Therefore, in the latter scenario corrupting P_4 allows us to bias the final output.
2. **Corrupt P_3:** First, we may now assume that the final output is fully determined by P_1, P_2, P_3 with high probability. We use this to show that either corrupting P_3 allows us to bias the final output, or the final output is not only already fully determined by the behavior of P_1 and P_2, *but actually is "independent" of the secret value sent by P_1 to P_3* with high probability. This stronger property will prove useful in the next step where we try to corrupt P_2.

3. **Corrupt P_2:** The goal here is, again, to prove that, assuming it is not useful to bias neither P_3 nor P_4, either we can bias the final output by corrupting P_2 or the final output is fully determined by P_1. However, a main difficulty in this step that is not present elsewhere is that P_2 *does not see the secret value sent from P_1 to P_3.* We exploit the stronger statement we proved for P_3 to argue that this is not problematic.

4. **Corrupt P_1:** Finally, assuming that corrupting one of P_2, P_3, P_4 is not useful, we show that P_1 can locally determine the final output based on its public and secret values with high probability. Since we assumed that an honest execution of the protocol yields a nearly unbiased bit, we can corrupt P_1, simulate several runs of the protocol, and always choose the one that leads to, say, final output 0 with high probability.

The above argument shows that such a protocol cannot possibly be secure, which leads to Theorem 3. More details can be found in Sect. 4.

1.5 Directions for Future Research

Our work leaves open several interesting avenues for future research. We highlight some of them here:

– We have proved, in particular, that the minimum number of parties n required for low-error randomness extraction given a corruption threshold t satisfies $4t + 1 \leq n \leq 5t$ in the execution-leaks model and $4t + 1 \leq n \leq 6t + 1$ in the sending-leaks model. It would be interesting to improve those bounds further towards a complete characterization.
– In this work we did not focus on the efficiency of randomness extraction protocols. Given the practical connections of our models, it would be interesting to design more efficient protocols in this setting. Efficiency could be measured in the number of secret messages and/or the total number of bits sent.
– In line with the previous item, and as already mentioned above, it would be interesting to improve the communication complexity necessary for extracting λ unbiased random bits beyond running our protocols λ times in parallel.
– We considered only static corruptions. However, it also makes sense to consider an active adversary in our model. We leave this as another interesting future modification.

2 Network Models for Randomness Extraction

In this section, we formally define the network models and security notions under which we will be working.

Suppose there are n parties $P_1, \ldots, P_n$. In the first round, party P_1 outputs a public value x_1 and send secret values $s_{1,2}, \ldots, s_{1,n}$ to be received by parties speaking in rounds $i = 2, \ldots, n$, respectively. In the i-th round for $2 \leq i \leq$

n, party P_i outputs a public value $x_i \in \mathcal{X}$ which depends on the previously broadcast public values

$$x^{<i} = (x_1, \ldots, x_{i-1})$$

along with the secret values sent to the party speaking in the i-th round,

$$s^{<i} = (s_{1,i}, \ldots, s_{i-1,i}).$$

Party P_i then sends secret values

$$s^{>i} = (s_{i,i+1}, \ldots, s_{i,n})$$

to be received by parties speaking in rounds $i + 1$ through n, respectively. At the end of the protocol, the goal is to *deterministically* extract from the public values $x_1, \ldots, x_n$ a bit that is statistically close to uniform. More precisely, a *randomness extraction protocol* is specified by a tuple $\Pi = (D_1, \ldots, D_n, \text{Ext})$, where $D_1, \ldots, D_n$ are distributions such that

$$(x_i, s^{>i}) \leftarrow D_i(x^{<i}, s^{<i})$$

and $\text{Ext} : \mathcal{X}^n \rightarrow \{0, 1\}$ is a deterministic function such that the final output of the protocol is given by

$$r = \text{Ext}(x_1, \ldots, x_n).$$

We additionally consider a computationally-unbounded adversary which is allowed to corrupt a subset of parties C of size $|C| \leq t$. We call t the *corruption threshold*. The adversary is taken to be *static*, i.e., the set C is chosen before the start of the protocol. For each party $i \in C$, the adversary is allowed to replace the distribution D_i by an arbitrary malicious distribution M_i of its choice. We study randomness extraction protocols in two natural models depending on the information made available to the adversary when it chooses each M_i, as described next.

2.1   The Sending-Leaks Adversarial Model

In the strongest adversarial model we consider, a *sending-leaks adversary* immediately learns secret values once they are sent. More precisely, for each corrupted party $i \in C$, the adversary may choose the malicious distribution M_i above as a randomized function of the public values $x_1, \ldots, x_{i-1}$ and all values $(s_{j,j'})_{j<i,j'\in C}$. In words, if the adversary corrupts P_i, then it is allowed to see the previously broadcast public values along with all secret values sent by parties 1 through $i - 1$ to *all* corrupted parties $j' \in C$, even when $j' > i$. Given a randomness extraction protocol $\Pi = (D_1, \ldots, D_n, \text{Ext})$ and a sending-leaks adversary $\mathcal{A}$, we denote the output of the extractor Ext under the adversarial corruptions imposed by $\mathcal{A}$ by $R(\Pi, \mathcal{A})$. We now present the associated security definition.

Definition 1 (Security in the sending-leaks model). *We say that a randomness extraction protocol Π is (ε, t)-secure in the sending-leaks model if for all sending-leaks adversaries $\mathcal{A}$ corrupting at most t parties we have*

$$\left| \Pr[R(\Pi, \mathcal{A}) = 1] - \frac{1}{2} \right| \leq \varepsilon.$$

We say that the protocol is zero-error *if we can take $\varepsilon = 0$.*

2.2   The Execution-Leaks Adversarial Model

We also consider a weaker adversarial model where secret values sent to some corrupted party P_i are only revealed to the adversary once P_i is executed. More precisely, an *execution-leaks adversary* $\mathcal{A}$ chooses the malicious distribution M_i as a randomized function of the public values $x_1, \ldots, x_{i-1}$ and only the secret values $(s_{j,j'})_{1 \leq j < j' \leq i}$. As before, we denote the output of the extractor Ext under the adversarial corruptions imposed by $\mathcal{A}$ by $R(\Pi, \mathcal{A})$, and define security as follows.

Definition 2 (Security in the execution-leaks model). *We say that a randomness extraction protocol Π is (ε, t)-secure in the execution-leaks model if for all execution-leaks adversaries $\mathcal{A}$ corrupting at most t parties we have*

$$\left| \Pr[R(\Pi, \mathcal{A}) = 1] - \frac{1}{2} \right| \leq \varepsilon.$$

We say that the protocol is zero-error *if we can take $\varepsilon = 0$.*

3   Zero-Error Randomness Extraction Protocols

We prove our main feasibility results in this section.

3.1   Zero-Error Randomness Extraction in the Sending-Leaks Model

We prove the following feasibility result in the sending-leaks model.

Theorem 4 (Restatement of Theorem 1). *There is a zero-error randomness extraction protocol in the sending-leaks model for corruption threshold t and $n = 6t + 1$ parties.*

We now describe the protocol used to prove Theorem 4, which is a "YOSO-version" of a protocol introduced by Maurer [15]. For the sake of clarity, we first fix a corruption threshold t and $n = 6t + 2$ parties, which we subdivide into consecutive blocks $P_1, P_2, \ldots, P_{3t+1}$, which we call the *verifiers*, and $P'_1, \ldots, P'_{3t+1}$, which we call the *publishers*. We will then show how to optimize this argument so that only $6t + 1$ parties are needed. First, define

$$\mathcal{S} = \{S \subseteq [3t+1] : |S| = 2t + 1\}.$$

The protocol proceeds as follows:

1. **Sampling phase:** For $i = 1, \ldots, t+1$ and all sets $S \in \mathcal{S}$ such that $\min S = i$, party P_i samples x_S uniformly at random from $\{0,1\}$. We call P_i the *leader* of S. Then, P_i sends x_S to every party P_j such that $j \in S$.
2. For each set $S \in \mathcal{S}$ and $j \in S$, let x_S^j denote the value received by P_j from the leader of S. Then, P_j sends x_S^j to every $P_{j'}$ such that $j' > j$ and $j' \in S$.
3. **Verification phase:** For each set $S \in \mathcal{S}$ and $j' \in S$, let $x_S^{j,j'}$ denote the value received by $P_{j'}$ from P_j for $j' > j$ and $j, j' \in S$. Then, every party $P_{j'}$ checks whether $x_S^{j,j'} = x_S^{j'}$ for all $j \in S$ such that $j < j'$. If this does not hold, then $P_{j'}$ broadcasts the public value $(\mathrm{COMPLAIN}, S)$. Otherwise, the verifier $P_{j'}$ sends $x_S^{j'}$ to all publishers $P_{j''}'$ such that $j'' \in S$.
4. **Publishing phase:** For each $S \in \mathcal{S}$ which did not receive a complaint and $j', j'' \in S$, let $y_S^{j',j''}$ denote the value received by the publisher $P_{j''}'$ from the verifier $P_{j'}$. Then, $P_{j''}'$ broadcasts $(S, s_S^{j''})$, where

$$s_S^{j''} = \mathsf{maj}((y_S^{j',j''})_{j' \in S})$$

and maj denotes the majority function with ties broken to 0.

Given the values broadcast by the protocol above, our randomness extractor behaves as follows: First, for all $S \in \mathcal{S}$ which did not receive a complaint, set

$$m_S = \mathsf{maj}((s_S^j)_{j \in S}).$$

For all sets $S \in \mathcal{S}$ which received a complaint, set $m_S = 0$. Then, the output of the extractor is

$$\bigoplus_{S \in \mathcal{S}} m_S.$$

The following statement holds.

Proposition 1. *The value $\bigoplus_{S \in \mathcal{S}} m_S$ is uniformly random whenever at most t out of $n = 6t + 2$ parties are corrupted.*

Proof. Observe that there is a set $S^* \in \mathcal{S}$ such that all verifiers P_j and publishers P_j' with $j \in S^*$ are honest. In particular, this means that the value x_{S^*} sampled by the leader of S^* is uniformly random, that S^* does not receive a complaint, and that $m_{S^*} = x_{S^*}$. Moreover, since all associated publishers $(P_j')_{j \in S^*}$ are honest, the value of x_{S^*} is not leaked to the adversary before the publishing phase. It remains to argue that the values m_S for $S \neq S^*$ are independent of x_{S^*}, which concludes the proof.

Consider any set $S \neq S^*$ in $\mathcal{S}$. Note that whether S receives a complaint or not is independent of the value of x_{S^*} since corrupted parties only learn this value later in the publishing phase. Therefore, it suffices to consider the case where S did not receive a complaint. If this holds, it must be the case that all honest parties P_j for $j \in S$ received the same value x_S' from the leader of S, which is independent of x_{S^*}. Otherwise, if honest parties P_{j_1} and P_{j_2} received different values and $j_1 < j_2$, then P_{j_2} would fail the check and broadcast a complaint during the verification phase. Since a strict majority of verifiers in $(P_j)_{j \in S}$ is honest, it follows that all honest publishers $P'_{j'}$ for $j' \in S$ will broadcast $s^{j'}_S = x'_S$. Therefore, we have $m_S = x'_S$ since a strict majority of publishers in $(P'_{j'})_{j' \in S}$ is honest, which yields the desired claim.   □

In order to obtain Theorem 4 from Proposition 1, it remains to describe how to modify the protocol in order to reduce the number of parties from $6t + 2$ to $6t + 1$. This can be accomplished by merging parties P_{3t+1} and P'_{3t+1} into one party. Since the publishing phase of the protocol is insensitive to the broadcast order and to the fact that each publisher P'_j may share a state with the verifier P_j, the correctness of the protocol still holds.

3.2 Improved Zero-Error Randomness Extraction in the Execution-Leaks Model

The protocol described in Sect. 3.1 is secure in the strong adversarial model where values sent to corrupted parties are immediately displayed to the adversary. However, we can also consider the natural execution-leaks model where parties only learn their values when they are executed. Our impossibility bound also holds in this model, meaning that $n \geq 4t + 1$ parties are necessary in this model as well. Therefore, it is natural to wonder whether a bound better than $n \leq 6t+1$ is achievable in this case. It turns out that in this model we can optimize our protocol above and prove the following result.

Theorem 5 (Restatement of Theorem 2). *There is a zero-error randomness extraction protocol in the execution-leaks model for corruption threshold t and $n = 5t$ parties.*

Our starting point towards proving Theorem 5 is a protocol for $n = 5t + 2$ parties.

Proposition 2. *There is a zero-error randomness extraction protocol in the execution-leaks model for corruption threshold t and $n = 5t + 2$ parties.*

Proof. The protocol proceeds as in Sect. 3.1 except for the following differences:

- There are $2t + 1$ publishers $P'_1, \ldots, P'_{2t+1}$ instead of $3t + 1$;
- In the verification phase (Step 3), the verifier $P_{j'}$ sends $x^{j'}_S$ to *all* publishers $P'_1, \ldots, P'_{2t+1}$;
- In the publishing phase (Step 4), one takes $j' \in S$ and $j'' \in [2t + 1]$ arbitrary.

The correctness of the modified protocol follows as in the proof of Proposition 1, except that we only use the fact that there exists a set $S^\star \in \mathcal{S}$ such that all verifiers $(P_j)_{j \in S^\star}$ are honest and that a strict majority of the verifiers is honest.
    □

We now show how we can improve the protocol above so that $n = 5t$ parties are enough, yielding Theorem 5.

Proof (Theorem 5). The protocol proceeds as in the proof of Proposition 2 except for the following differences:

- There are $3t - 1$ verifiers $P_1, \ldots, P_{3t-1}$ instead of $3t + 1$;
- The family $\mathcal{S}$ is now defined as

$$\mathcal{S} = \{S \subseteq [3t - 1] : |S| = 2t - 1\}.$$

The correctness of the protocol follows by case analysis:

1. **If t verifiers are corrupted:** This implies that all publishers $P'_1, \ldots, P'_{2t+1}$ are honest. Moreover, there is a set $S^\star \in \mathcal{S}$ of fully honest verifiers $(P_i)_{i \in S^\star}$. Since the output of the extractor is fully determined after all verifiers speak and the adversary does not observe $x_{S^\star}$, the output of the extractor is uniformly random.
2. **If at most $t - 1$ verifiers are corrupted:** In this case all sets $S \in \mathcal{S}$ have a strict majority of honest parties (since $2t - 1 > 2(t - 1)$), a strict majority of publishers is honest, and there is a set $S^\star \in \mathcal{S}$ containing only honest parties. Therefore, the argument from the proof of Proposition 2 goes through and shows that the output of the extractor is uniformly random.   □

Combining Theorems 5 and 6 leads to the following exact characterization of the round complexity of randomness extraction for $t = 1$ corruptions in both models.

Corollary 1. *A total of $n = 5$ parties are both sufficient and necessary for low-error randomness extraction with $t = 1$ corruptions (in both the sending-leaks and execution-leaks models).*

4   Low-Error Randomness Extraction Is Impossible with $n/4$ Corruptions

We prove our impossibility result in this section.

Theorem 6 (Restatement of Theorem 3). *There is no $(\varepsilon = 0.01, t)$-secure randomness extraction protocol in both the sending-leaks and execution-leaks models for n parties and corruption threshold $t \geq n/4$.*

Proof. At a high level, we prove this result by dividing the parties into four consecutive blocks $B_1, \ldots, B_4$ and then sequentially arguing that either the behavior of $B_1, \ldots, B_{i-1}$ already fully determines the final output of the protocol with high probability, or corrupting B_i allows an adversary to locally control and bias the final output by consistently resampling B_i's public value and secret values. Care is needed in all stages to ensure the adversary can accurately predict the final output of the protocol locally.

Fix some randomness extraction protocol $\Pi = (D_1, \ldots, D_n, f)$ with corresponding public values $X_1, \ldots, X_n$. Let $f(X_1, \ldots, X_n)$ denote the output of the YOSO extraction protocol, where f is a deterministic function and $t = \lceil n/4 \rceil$

parties may be corrupted by an execution-leaks adversary. With a contradiction in view, suppose that

$$|\Pr[f(X_1,\ldots,X_n) = 1] - \Pr[f(X_1,\ldots,X_n) = 0]| \leq \varepsilon = 0.01, \tag{1}$$

where the probability is taken over the randomness of the protocol. Partition the set of parties $[n]$ into four consecutive blocks B_1, B_2, B_3, B_4 each containing at most $\lceil n/4 \rceil$ parties. Note that the adversary is able to corrupt all parties in one of these blocks. Let Q_i denote the string of public values output by the block B_i and $S_{i \to j}$ denote the set of secret values sent by parties of block B_i to parties of block B_j for $i < j$.

We begin by considering the case where the adversary fully corrupts the block B_4. Sample $(q_1, q_2, q_3) \leftarrow (Q_1, Q_2, Q_3)$. By our assumption, it must be the case that

$$\Pr\left[\exists q_4^{(0)}, q_4^{(1)} : f\left(q_1, q_2, q_3, q_4^{(b)}\right) = b, b \in \{0,1\}\right] \leq \varepsilon, \tag{2}$$

where the probability is taken over the sampling above. In other words, the last block of parties must have little control over the output of the extractor. To see this, note that if (2) did not hold then we could simply have the adversary make block B_4 select $q_4^{(0)}$ as the public value (whenever such choices exist) so that (1) is not satisfied.

We move to the case where the adversary fully corrupts B_3. Suppose blocks B_1 and B_2 output public and secret value sets $(q_1, s_{1 \to 3}, q_2, s_{2 \to 3})$ according to the joint distribution $(Q_1, S_{1 \to 3}, Q_2, S_{2 \to 3})$, which the adversary sees. Set $s_{1 \to 3}^{(1)} = s_{1 \to 3}$ and sample $s_{1 \to 3}^{(2)}$ according to the distribution

$$(S_{1 \to 3} | Q_1 = q_1, Q_2 = q_2, S_{2 \to 3} = s_{2 \to 3}).$$

Then, sample

$$q_3^{(i)} \leftarrow (Q_3 | Q_1 = q_1, Q_2 = q_2, S_{1 \to 3} = s_{1 \to 3}^{(i)}, S_{2 \to 3} = s_{2 \to 3})$$

for $i = 1, 2$. Handling this extra sample from $S_{1 \to 3}$ will be crucial for our argument later on in the case where we corrupt B_2. We define the set of *good* tuples

$$\mathcal{G}_3 = \{(q_1', q_2', q_3') : f(q_1', q_2', q_3', \cdot) \text{ is constant}\}$$

and claim that

$$\Pr\left[(q_1, q_2, q_3^{(1)}) \in \mathcal{G}_3, (q_1, q_2, q_3^{(2)}) \in \mathcal{G}_3, f(q_1, q_2, q_3^{(1)}, \cdot) \equiv f(q_1, q_2, q_3^{(2)}, \cdot)\right]$$
$$\geq 1 - 3\varepsilon, \tag{3}$$

where the probability is taken over the sampling procedures described above. To see this, first note that both $q_3^{(1)}$ and $q_3^{(2)}$ are distributed like a correct public value of B_3 in the protocol, i.e., the tuples $(q_1, q_2, q_3^{(1)})$ and $(q_1, q_2, q_3^{(2)})$ are both distributed according to the joint distribution (Q_1, Q_2, Q_3). Therefore, invoking (2) and the union bound shows that

$$\Pr[(q_1, q_2, q_3^{(1)}) \in \mathcal{G}_3, (q_1, q_2, q_3^{(2)}) \in \mathcal{G}_3] \geq 1 - 2\varepsilon. \tag{4}$$

Moreover, it must be the case that

$$\Pr\left[(q_1, q_2, q_3^{(1)}) \in \mathcal{G}_3, (q_1, q_2, q_3^{(2)}) \in \mathcal{G}_3, f(q_1, q_2, q_3^{(1)}, \cdot) \not\equiv f(q_1, q_2, q_3^{(2)}, \cdot)\right] \leq \varepsilon, \tag{5}$$

since otherwise the adversary could sample $q_3^{(1)}$ and $q_3^{(2)}$ as above, each of which would fully determine the output of the extractor with probability larger than ε, and so bias the extractor appropriately, thus implying that (1) is false. Combining (5) and (4) yields (3), as desired.

Continuing this trend, suppose now that the adversary fully corrupts B_2 and that block B_1 outputs public and secret values $(q_1, s_{1\to2}, s_{1\to3})$. Note, however, that the adversary only has access to q_1 and $s_{1\to2}$. We will exploit (3) to argue that the adversary can still adequately simulate Q_3 and Q_4 for a given choice of its public value Q_2 and predict the output of f with decent probability by simulating the values from B_1 to B_3 locally. First, independently sample pairs

$$(q_2^{(i)}, s_{2\to3}^{(i)}) \leftarrow (Q_2, S_{2\to3} | Q_1 = q_1, S_{1\to2} = s_{1\to2})$$

for $i = 1, 2$. Then, independently sample *simulated* secret value sets

$$\tilde{s}_{1\to3}^{(i)} \leftarrow (S_{1\to3} | Q_1 = q_1, Q_2 = q_2^{(i)}, S_{2\to3} = s_{2\to3}^{(i)})$$

and simulated public values

$$\tilde{q}_3^{(i)} \leftarrow (Q_3 | Q_1 = q_1, Q_2 = q_2^{(i)}, S_{1\to3} = s_{1\to3}^{(i)}, S_{2\to3} = s_{2\to3}^{(i)})$$

for $i = 1, 2$. Denote by

$$f(q_1', q_2', q_3'; m_{1\to3}', m_{2\to3}')$$

the (possibly randomized) output of $f(Q_1, Q_2, Q_3, Q_4)$ conditioned on the joint event

$$(Q_1 = q_1', Q_2 = q_2', Q_3 = q_3', S_{1\to3} = m_{1\to3}', S_{2\to3} = m_{2\to3}').$$

Then, we define the set of good tuples

$$\mathcal{G}_2 = \{(q_1', q_2', q_3', m_{1\to3}', m_{2\to3}') : f(q_1', q_2', q_3'; m_{1\to3}', m_{2\to3}') \text{ is constant}\}.$$

Suppose that $q_3^{(i)}$ is the true public value of B_3 when the corrupted block B_2 outputs $q_2^{(i)}$ and sends values $s_{2\to3}^{(i)}$. For convenience, we set

$$\mathbf{v}^{(i)} = (q_1, q_2^{(i)}, q_3^{(i)}, s_{1\to3}, s_{2\to3}^{(i)}),$$
$$\tilde{\mathbf{v}}^{(i)} = (q_1, q_2^{(i)}, \tilde{q}_3^{(i)}; \tilde{s}_{1\to3}, s_{2\to3}^{(i)}),$$
$$r^{(i)} = f(\mathbf{v}^{(i)}),$$
$$\tilde{r}^{(i)} = f(\tilde{\mathbf{v}}^{(i)}).$$

Using this notation, combining (3) with a union bound over $i = 1, 2$ yields

$$\Pr[\forall i \in \{1, 2\} : \mathbf{v}^{(i)} \in \mathcal{G}_2, r^{(i)} \equiv \tilde{r}^{(i)}] \geq 1 - 6\varepsilon. \tag{6}$$

In words, the adversary can predict the final output of the protocol if he decides on $(q_2^{(i)}, s_{2\rightarrow 3}^{(i)})$ with high probability by locally computing $\widetilde{r}^{(i)}$ for $i = 1, 2$. Moreover, similarly to previous cases, it must be that

$$\Pr[\forall i \in \{1, 2\} : \mathbf{v}^{(i)} \in \mathcal{G}_2, r^{(i)} \equiv \widetilde{r}^{(i)}, \widetilde{r}^{(1)} \not\equiv \widetilde{r}^{(2)}] \leq \varepsilon. \tag{7}$$

In fact, if this did not hold, then the adversary could locally sample the tuples $(q_2^{(i)}, s_{2\rightarrow 3}^{(i)}, \widetilde{q}_3^{(i)}, \widetilde{s}_{1\rightarrow 3}^{(i)})$, compute $\widetilde{r}^{(i)}$, and then choose i such that $\widetilde{r}^{(i)} = 0$ and behave accordingly, thus biasing the output to 0 by more than ε. Therefore, combining (6) and (7) implies that

$$\Pr[\forall i \in \{1, 2\} : \mathbf{v}^{(i)} \in \mathcal{G}_2, r^{(i)} \equiv \widetilde{r}^{(i)}, \widetilde{r}^{(1)} \equiv \widetilde{r}^{(2)}] \geq 1 - 7\varepsilon. \tag{8}$$

This means that we can predict the final output of f with high probability given only $(q_1, s_{1\rightarrow 2})$.

Finally, we consider the case where the adversary corrupts the first block B_1. Consider two independent samples $(q_1^{(1)}, s_1^{(1)})$ and $(q_1^{(2)}, s_1^{(2)})$ according to the joint distribution (Q_1, S_1), where S_1 denotes all values sent by parties in B_1. Then, if (1) holds it must be the case that the output of f differs between the runs of the protocol beginning with $(q_1^{(1)}, s_1^{(1)})$ and $(q_1^{(2)}, s_1^{(2)})$ with some probability $p > 1/2 - \varepsilon^2$. By (2), (3), and (8), the output of f on the respective runs of the protocol is fully determined by knowledge of $(q_1^{(1)}, s_1^{(1)})$ and $(q_1^{(2)}, s_1^{(2)})$ with probability at least $1 - 2 \cdot 7\varepsilon = 1 - 14\varepsilon$. This implies that with probability at least

$$p - 14\varepsilon > 1/2 - 14\varepsilon - \varepsilon^2 \geq \varepsilon$$

the adversary can completely bias the output of f by choosing the run which leads to output 0, which contradicts (1). Since all steps above only involve re-sampling the distributions of honest parties, this strategy can be implemented by a execution-leaks adversary.   □

We also show that we cannot hope to prove a better upper bound using the ideas above, as formalized in the following theorem.

Theorem 7. *There exists a zero-error randomness extraction protocol with $n = 4t + 1$ parties in both the sending-leaks and execution-leaks models when the adversary is only allowed to corrupt at most t consecutive parties.*

Proof. Fix a corruption threshold t and $n \geq 4t + 1$ parties. Consider a protocol where parties $i \in [t + 1]$ (the generators) publish 0 and send a random bit b_i to all parties in $\{2t + 1, \ldots, n\}$. Parties $i \in \{t + 2, \ldots, 2t\}$ are silent (they do not publish public values nor do they send any secret values). Let b_i^j denote the bit received by the j-th party from the i-th party. Then, parties $j \in \{2t + 1, \ldots, n\}$ (the publishers) each output $b^j = \bigoplus_{i=1}^{t+1} b_i^j$. Finally, the extractor computes

$$\mathsf{maj}(b^{2t+2}, \ldots, b^n).$$

Suppose there is an adversary which corrupts a block of t consecutive parties. Note that the adversary cannot corrupt generators and publishers simultaneously, since there are $t - 1$ silent parties in between. Moreover, the adversary gains nothing by corrupting silent parties, since their public values and values may just be ignored. It remains to consider two cases:

- The adversary corrupts at most t generators: Without loss of generality, suppose the first generator is honest. Then, it holds that the adversarial choice of the bits b_i^j for $i \in \{2, \ldots, t+1\}$ is independent of b_1, which is uniformly random, and $b_1^j = b_1$ for all publishers j. It follows that the majority is uniformly random as well.
- The adversary corrupts at most t publishers: Since there are $2t+1$ publishers and all generators are honest, the majority coincides with $\bigoplus_{i=1}^{t+1} b_i$, which is uniformly random.

We conclude that the protocol outputs a uniformly random bit.   □

Acknowledgments. JBN was partially funded by The Concordium Foundation; The Danish Independent Research Council under Grant-ID DFF-8021-00366B (BETHE); The Carlsberg Foundation under the Semper Ardens Research Project CF18-112 (BCM). JR was supported in part by the NSF grants CCF-1814603 and CCF-2107347 and by the following grants of Vipul Goyal: the NSF award 1916939, DARPA SIEVE program, a gift from Ripple, a DoE NETL award, a JP Morgan Faculty Fellowship, a PNC center for financial services innovation award, and a Cylab seed funding award. MO was supported by MOE2019-T2-1-145 Foundations of quantum-safe cryptography.

JR thanks Chen-Da Liu Zhang, Elisaweta Masserova, and Justin Raizes for insightful discussions.

References

1. Aggarwal, D., Obremski, M., Ribeiro, J., Siniscalchi, L., Visconti, I.: How to extract useful randomness from unreliable sources. In: Canteaut, A., Ishai, Y. (eds.) EUROCRYPT 2020, Part I. LNCS, vol. 12105, pp. 343–372. Springer, Cham (2020). https://doi.org/10.1007/978-3-030-45721-1_13
2. Ben-Or, M., Goldwasser, S., Wigderson, A.: Completeness theorems for non-cryptographic fault-tolerant distributed computation (extended abstract). In: Simon, J. (ed.) Proceedings of the 20th Annual ACM Symposium on Theory of Computing, pp. 1–10. ACM (1988). https://doi.org/10.1145/62212.62213
3. Benhamouda, F., et al.: Can a public blockchain keep a secret? In: Pass, R., Pietrzak, K. (eds.) TCC 2020, Part I. LNCS, vol. 12550, pp. 260–290. Springer, Cham (2020). https://doi.org/10.1007/978-3-030-64375-1_10
4. Bentov, I., Gabizon, A., Zuckerman, D.: Bitcoin beacon. CoRR abs/1605.04559 (2016). http://arxiv.org/abs/1605.04559
5. Campanelli, M., David, B., Khoshakhlagh, H., Kristensen, A.K., Nielsen, J.B.: Encryption to the future: a paradigm for sending secret messages to future (anonymous) committees. IACR Cryptology ePrint Archive (2021). https://eprint.iacr.org/2021/1423

6. Canetti, R., Vald, M.: Universally composable security with local adversaries. In: Visconti, I., De Prisco, R. (eds.) SCN 2012. LNCS, vol. 7485, pp. 281–301. Springer, Heidelberg (2012). https://doi.org/10.1007/978-3-642-32928-9_16
7. Cascudo, I., David, B.: ALBATROSS: publicly AttestabLe BATched randomness based on secret sharing. In: Moriai, S., Wang, H. (eds.) ASIACRYPT 2020, Part III. LNCS, vol. 12493, pp. 311–341. Springer, Cham (2020). https://doi.org/10.1007/978-3-030-64840-4_11
8. Chaum, D., Crépeau, C., Damgård, I.: Multiparty unconditionally secure protocols (extended abstract). In: Simon, J. (ed.) Proceedings of the 20th Annual ACM Symposium on Theory of Computing, pp. 11–19. ACM (1988). https://doi.org/10.1145/62212.62214
9. Choudhuri, A.R., Goel, A., Green, M., Jain, A., Kaptchuk, G.: Fluid MPC: secure multiparty computation with dynamic participants. In: Malkin, T., Peikert, C. (eds.) CRYPTO 2021, Part II. LNCS, vol. 12826, pp. 94–123. Springer, Cham (2021). https://doi.org/10.1007/978-3-030-84245-1_4
10. Das, S., Krishnan, V., Isaac, I., Ren, L.: SPURT: scalable distributed randomness beacon with transparent setup. In: 2022 IEEE Symposium on Security and Privacy (SP), Los Alamitos, CA, USA, pp. 1380–1395. IEEE Computer Society, May 2022. https://doi.org/10.1109/SP46214.2022.00080
11. Gentry, C., et al.: YOSO: you only speak once. In: Malkin, T., Peikert, C. (eds.) CRYPTO 2021, Part II. LNCS, vol. 12826, pp. 64–93. Springer, Cham (2021). https://doi.org/10.1007/978-3-030-84245-1_3
12. Gentry, C., Halevi, S., Magri, B., Nielsen, J.B., Yakoubov, S.: Random-index PIR and applications. In: Nissim, K., Waters, B. (eds.) TCC 2021, Part III. LNCS, vol. 13044, pp. 32–61. Springer, Cham (2021). https://doi.org/10.1007/978-3-030-90456-2_2
13. Herzberg, A., Jarecki, S., Krawczyk, H., Yung, M.: Proactive secret sharing or: how to cope with perpetual leakage. In: Coppersmith, D. (ed.) CRYPTO 1995. LNCS, vol. 963, pp. 339–352. Springer, Heidelberg (1995). https://doi.org/10.1007/3-540-44750-4_27
14. Hirt, M., Maurer, U.: Player simulation and general adversary structures in perfect multiparty computation. J. Cryptol. 13(1), 31–60 (2000). https://doi.org/10.1007/s001459910003
15. Maurer, U.: Secure multi-party computation made simple. Discrete Appl. Math. 154(2), 370–381 (2006). https://doi.org/10.1016/j.dam.2005.03.020
16. Micali, S.: ALGORAND: the efficient and democratic ledger. CoRR abs/1607.01341 (2016). http://arxiv.org/abs/1607.01341
17. Santha, M., Vazirani, U.V.: Generating quasi-random sequences from slightly-random sources (extended abstract). In: 25th Annual Symposium on Foundations of Computer Science, pp. 434–440. IEEE Computer Society (1984). https://doi.org/10.1109/SFCS.1984.715945

(Nondeterministic) Hardness vs. Non-malleability

Marshall Ball[1] , Dana Dachman-Soled[2](✉) , and Julian Loss[3]

[1] New York University, New York, USA
marshall@cs.nyu.edu
[2] University of Maryland, College Park, USA
danadach@umd.edu
[3] CISPA Helmholtz Center for Information Security, Saarbrücken, Germany

Abstract. We present the first truly explicit constructions of *non-malleable codes* against tampering by bounded polynomial size circuits. These objects imply unproven circuit lower bounds and our construction is secure provided E requires exponential size nondeterministic circuits, an assumption from the derandomization literature.

Prior works on NMC for polysize circuits, either required an untamperable CRS [Cheraghchi, Guruswami ITCS'14; Faust, Mukherjee, Venturi, Wichs EUROCRYPT'14] or very strong cryptographic assumptions [Ball, Dachman-Soled, Kulkarni, Lin, Malkin EUROCRYPT'18; Dachman-Soled, Komargodski, Pass CRYPTO'21]. Both of works in the latter category only achieve non-malleability with respect to efficient distinguishers and, more importantly, utilize cryptographic objects for which no provably secure instantiations are known outside the random oracle model. In this sense, none of the prior yields fully explicit codes from non-heuristic assumptions. Our assumption is not known to imply the existence of one-way functions, which suggests that cryptography is unnecessary for non-malleability against this class.

Technically, security is shown by *non-deterministically* reducing polynomial size tampering to split-state tampering. The technique is general enough that it allows us to construct the first *seedless non-malleable extractors* [Cheraghchi, Guruswami TCC'14] for sources sampled by polynomial size circuits [Trevisan, Vadhan FOCS'00] (resp. recognized by polynomial size circuits [Shaltiel CC'11]) and tampered by

M. Ball—Part of this work was done while the author was a student at Columbia University and a postdoc at University of Washington. This material is based upon work supported by the National Science Foundation under Grant #2030859 to the Computing Research Association for the CIFellows Project. Any opinions, findings, and conclusions or recommendations expressed in this material are those of the author(s) and do not necessarily reflect the views of the National Science Foundation nor the Computing Research Association.
D. Dachman-Soled—Supported in part by NSF grants #CNS-1933033, #CNS-1453045 (CAREER), and by financial assistance awards 70NANB15H328 and 70NANB19H126 from the U.S. Department of Commerce, National Institute of Standards and Technology.
J. Loss—Part of this work was done while the author was a postdoc at the University of Maryland and Carnegie Mellon University.

© International Association for Cryptologic Research 2022
Y. Dodis and T. Shrimpton (Eds.): CRYPTO 2022, LNCS 13507, pp. 148–177, 2022.
https://doi.org/10.1007/978-3-031-15802-5_6

polynomial size circuits. Our construction is secure assuming E requires exponential size Σ_4-circuits (resp. Σ_3-circuits), this assumption is the state-of-the-art for extracting randomness from such sources (without non-malleability).

Several additional results are included in the full version of this paper [Eprint 2022/070]. First, we observe that non-malleable codes and non-malleable secret sharing [Goyal, Kumar STOC'18] are essentially equivalent with respect to polynomial size tampering. In more detail, assuming E is hard for exponential size nondeterministic circuits, any efficient secret sharing scheme can be made non-malleable against polynomial size circuit tampering.

Second, we observe that the fact that our constructions only achieve inverse polynomial (statistical) security is inherent. Extending a result from [Applebaum, Artemenko, Shaltiel, Yang CC'16] we show it is impossible to do better using black-box reductions. However, we extend the notion of relative error from [Applebaum, Artemenko, Shaltiel, Yang CC'16] to non-malleable extractors and show that they can be constructed from similar assumptions.

Third, we observe that relative-error non-malleable extractors can be utilized to render a broad class of cryptographic primitives tamper and leakage resilient, while preserving negligible security guarantees.

1 Introduction

This work focuses on mitigating polynomial size circuit tampering attacks via constructing two kinds of fundamental objects: *non-malleable* codes (NMC) and seedless *non-malleable* extractors (NME). In the coding setting, non-malleability (roughly) guarantees that the output of the decoding algorithm on a codeword is independent of the output of the decoding algorithm on a tampered version of the codeword. Similarly in the seedless extractor setting, non-malleability guarantees that the output of the extractor on a sample drawn from a high min-entropy source remains uniform random, even conditioned on the output of the extractor on a tampered version of the sample.

A recent thrust of research has focused on constructing explicit (efficient) NMC and NME for broad and natural classes of tampering. Perhaps the most natural class of tampering functions, is tampering by polynomial size circuits. Unfortunately, a simple argument shows that any (seedless) non-malleable code (resp. extractor) resilient to arbitrary polynomial size circuit tampering cannot be decoded (resp. evaluated) in polynomial time. The next best thing would be a non-malleable code (resp. seedless extractor) that can be encoded/decoded (resp. evaluated) in polynomial time that is resilient to *bounded* polynomial size circuit tampering—tampering by circuits of size at most n^c where c is a constant fixed a priori. In this work, we are interested in constructing *explicit* (i.e. computable by polynomial time Turing machines) objects that are resilient to such tampering attacks.

This tampering class has been studied extensively in the non-malleable code literature and prior work constructing NMC for bounded polynomial size circuit tampering can be collected into two categories, both of which fail to provide explicit constructions:

Unconditionally Secure Constructions via the Probabilistic Method. [26,38] show that efficiently computable non-malleable codes for bounded polynomial size circuit tampering exist. These constructions can alternately be cast as explicit codes in an (untamperable) common reference string (CRS) model, or as codes with efficient Monte Carlo style constructions.

Computational assumptions are *needed* for any explicit construction (without a CRS) since security of the non-malleable code implies circuit lower bounds—existence of an explicit hard-on-average problem for circuits of size n^{c1}—a question that is still wide open in the complexity literature.

Unfortunately even under strong assumptions, it is unclear how to derandomize these constructions completely. (See beginning of Sect. 1.4 for further discussion.)

Computationally Secure Constructions via Strong Cryptographic Assumptions. [12,28,29] leverage a variety of non-standard cryptographic assumptions to construct non-malleable codes for bounded polynomial size circuit tampering (no CRS) with computational security guarantees.

While some assumptions are necessary (as mentioned above), these works utilize very powerful computational assumptions. Most importantly, these works (among other assumptions[2]) require the existence of objects that we currently only know how to provably instantiate with random oracles (e.g. [12] uses P-certificates and [28,29] uses keyless multi-collision resistant hash functions).

Consequently, these works only yield explicit constructions of non-malleable codes under heuristic assumptions.[3] Additionally, these works fall short of providing statistical security guarantees.

In summary, none of the prior constructions are fully explicit.

---

[1] If (E, D) is ϵ-non-malleable code for n^c-size tampering, then D is hard-on-average for $n^c - O(n)$ size circuits with respect to the distribution $E(\mathcal{U}_{\{0,1\}})$, encodings of a random bit. In particular if there exists a small circuit C such that $\Pr[C(E(\mathcal{U})) = D(E(\mathcal{U})) = \mathcal{U}] \geq 1/2 + \epsilon$ then consider the C' that on input c outputs a fixed encoding of $0, c_0$, if $C(c) = 1$ and a fixed encoding of 1, c_1 otherwise. Then we have $\Pr[D(C'(E(\mathcal{U}))) = 1 - \mathcal{U}] \geq 1/2 + \epsilon$, breaking ϵ-non-malleability.

[2] In addition to a variety of subexponentially secure variants of standard cryptographic assumptions, the work of [28,29] also crucially requires a specific number-theoretic assumption (the non-uniform subexponential hardness of the repeated squaring assumption), while the work of [12] needs the same derandomization assumption in this work.

[3] E.g. [21] suggests possibly instantiating keyless multi-collision resistant hash with an unstructured hash, such as SHA-2 (extended to arbitrarily large keys), with keys chosen according to digits of π. Establishing the security of any such candidate is well beyond our current techniques, as we cannot even base the security of (extended) SHA-2 with randomly chosen keys to a natural computational problem.

In this work, we employ an assumption from the derandomization literature to construct *explicit* non-malleable codes and seedless non-malleable extractors resilient to bounded polynomial tampering. Our non-malleable codes in particular are secure under a hardness conjecture introduced in the context of derandomizing AM: there is a language that can be computed in exponential deterministic time that requires exponential size nondeterministic circuits.

In Sect. 1.1, we describe the hardness assumptions we use to construct our codes and extractors. In Sect. 1.2, we discuss the main results of this work, and additional results included in the full version of our paper [16]. Finally in Sect. 1.4, we illustrate our primary technique through a simple yet illuminating example and describe how the ideas can be extended to prove our main results.

1.1 Hardness Assumptions for Nondeterministic and Σ_i-Circuits

Definition 1.1 (Nondeterministic Circuit). *A nondeterministic circuit C is a circuit with "non-deterministic" inputs, in addition to the usual inputs. We say C evaluates to 1 on x iff there exists an assignment, w, to the non-deterministic input wires such that the circuit, evaluated deterministically on input (x, w) outputs 1.*

Assumption 1 (E Requires Exponential Size Nondeterministic Circuits). *There is a language $L \in \mathsf{E} = \mathsf{DTIME}(2^{O(n)})$ and a constant γ s.t. for sufficiently large n nondeterministic circuits of size $2^{\gamma n}$ fail to decide L on inputs of length n.*

Informally, the above assumption says that non-uniformity and nondeterminism do not always imply significant speed-ups of uniform deterministic computations. For some of the results in this work, we require assumptions that hold even for (non-deterministic) NP circuits or Σ_i circuits. Before we state the assumption, we provide a formal definition of these objects.

Definition 1.2. *An oracle circuit $C^{(\cdot)}$ is a circuit which in addition to the standard gates uses an additional gate (which may have large fan in). When instantiated with a specific boolean function A, C^A is the circuit in which the additional gate is A. Given a boolean function $A(x)$, an A-circuit is a circuit that is allowed to use A gates (in addition to the standard gates). An NP-circuit is a SAT-circuit (where SAT is the satisfiability function) a Σ_i-circuit is an A-circuit where A is the canonical Σ_i^P-complete language. We take the size of a circuit to be the total number of wires and gates.*[4]

We now state the corresponding set of assumptions:

Assumption 2 (E Requires Exponential Size NP (resp. Σ_i) Circuits). *There is a language $L \in \mathsf{E} = \mathsf{DTIME}(2^{O(n)})$ and a constant γ such that for sufficiently large n, NP (resp. Σ_i) circuits of size $2^{\gamma n}$ fail to compute the characteristic function of L on inputs of length n.*

---

[4] Note that an NP-circuit is different than a nondeterministic circuit. The former is a nonuniform analogue of P^{NP} (which contains coNP) while the latter is an analogue of NP.

Hardness assumptions against nondeterministic/NP/Σ_i circuits appear in the literature in various contexts of complexity theory and derandomization [19,32,39,41,45,51,59,61–64]. As noted in [7], such assumptions can be seen as the nonuniform and scaled-up versions of assumptions of the form $\mathsf{EXP} \neq \mathsf{NP}$ or $\mathsf{EXP} \neq \Sigma_2^\mathsf{P}$. While very strong, falsification of one of these assumptions would yield surprising implications on the relationship between standard complexity classes, thus creating a win-win situation: Either the construction based on these assumptions is secure, or a breakthrough result has been achieved that changes our current understanding of the power of nonuniformity and nondeterminism. Further, since assumptions of the above type on the strength of E are *worst-case assumptions*, we can directly instantiate constructions based on these assumptions with any E-complete problem.

Finally, we highlight that, so far as we know, this assumption is orthogonal to standard cryptographic assumptions such as one-way functions and, consequently, may hold even if cryptography does not exist.

We summarize the main results of this paper in Sect. 1.2, and then discuss additional results contained in the full version [16] in Sect. 1.3. Briefly, included in this work are new constructions of non-malleable codes (Sect. 1.2) and non-malleable extractors. Additional results contained in the full version include barriers to achieving negligible security guarantees, circumventing these barriers in a manner that has applications to tamper and leakage resilient cryptography (with negligible security guarantees), and an equivalence between non-malleable codes and non-malleable secret sharing in the context of polynomial size circuit tampering.

1.2   Our Results–Included in This Work

Non-malleable Codes. Our results are as follows:

Theorem 1.3 (Informal). *If E requires exponential size nondeterministic circuits, then for every constant c, and for sufficiently large k, there is an explicit, efficient, n^{-c}-secure non-malleable code for k-bit messages, with codeword length $n = \mathsf{poly}(k)$, resilient to tampering by n^c-size circuits.*

The formal statement and proof of this theorem can be found in Sect. 3.

We construct our codes by "fooling" non-malleable codes for *split-state tampering* (with special properties).

Split-state tampering functions may manipulate the left and right halves of a codeword arbitrarily, but independently (i.e. functions such that $(c_L, c_R) \mapsto (f_L(c_L), f_R(c_R))$ for some f_L, f_R). Leakage-resilient split-state tampering allows each tampered codeword half to depend on bounded leakage from the opposite codeword half. In addition to a split-state NMC, we also use a pseudorandom generator (PRG) for nondeterministic circuits, where $c' > c$ is a constant. In particular, we require that the PRG, G, is secure even when given the seed (seed extending), i.e. no nondeterministic circuit of bounded polynomial size can distinguish $G(s)$ from uniform *and* s is a prefix of $G(s)$. The existence of such PRGs follows from Assumption 2 [7,46,50,51,61,62].

Given a (leakage-resilient) split-state non-malleable code, with necessary properties and a seed-extending pseudorandom PRG for nondeterministic circuits, G, we encode a message x by sampling the following:

$$(s, c_R) \text{ such that } (G(s), c_R) \text{ is a split-state encoding of } x.$$

While we refer the reader to the technical overview (Sect. 1.4) for a more detailed sketch, we provide here some intuition for security:

1. We assume towards contradiction that (s, c_R) is *malleable* and fix the corresponding poly-size tampering function g which is *not* split-state and violates non-malleability.
2. We transform g into a split-state tampering function f_L, f_R on (c_L, c_R), where (1) f_L is *unbounded*, relies on $|s|$ bits of leakage from c_R and returns some c'_L, (2) f_R is efficient, relies on $|s|$ bits of leakage from c_L and returns c'_R. Crucially, split-state tampering function (f_L, f_R) is guaranteed to break non-malleability when $c_L = (s||y) = G(s)$.
3. Since (c_L, c_R) is a leakage-resilient split-state non-malleable code when c_L is uniform random, then when c_L is random (as opposed to in the construction where codewords are sampled as $(G(s), c_R)$), every tampering function (f'_L, f_R) *fails* to break non-malleability, even when f'_L is unbounded and chooses its output c'_L in the "optimal" way.
4. We construct an Arthur-Merlin protocol (with bounded poly-size Arthur), that distinguishes between input c_L being random or pseudorandom. Such a protocol can then be transformed into a non-deterministic polynomial bounded circuit (this follows from classical results: $\mathsf{IP}[O(1)] \subseteq \mathsf{AM} \subseteq \mathsf{NP/poly}$ [7–9,42]).
5. Intuitively, Arthur can efficiently compute all the values needed to simulate the tampering experiment except for c'_L, which is obtained from Merlin. Specifically, on input c_L, Arthur samples c_R, and computes $c'_R = f_R(c_R)$, as well as the leakage on c_R. Arthur sends c_L and the leakage on c_R to Merlin who responds with c'_L. If c_L is pseudorandom, then an honest Merlin will return $c'_L = f_L(c_L)$, and, with Merlin's help, Arthur can check that non-malleability is violated with this c'_L. If c_L is random, then despite any response $c'_L = f'_L(c_L)$ from Merlin, non-malleability will *not* be violated, and a dishonest Merlin cannot convince Arthur otherwise.

Non-malleable Extractors. We next shift our focus to the case of seedless non-malleable extractors for computational sources with sufficient min-entropy[5] and for tampering with bounded polynomial size circuits. We consider two types of computational sources:

---

[5] Min-entropy measures the unpredictability of a random variable. In particular, X has min-entropy k if $\forall x$ in the support of X, $\Pr[X = x] \leq 2^{-k}$.

Samplable Sources: These are distributions that can be generated by bounded polynomial size circuits that are given uniform random coins as input. Specifically, the source distribution X is equivalent to $C(U_r)$, the distribution generated by some circuit C of size n^c on input uniform randomness of length r bits.

Extracting from this class of sources was first considered by Trevisan and Vadhan [64]. In 1986, Levin [52] argued that this class reasonably captures sources arising in nature.[6]

A non-malleable extractor for this class yields non-malleable cryptography resilient to tampering attacks on the very entropy sources used for key generation.

As an alternate motivation, one can consider a natural, albeit restricted, online extraction setting: imagine a natural source over a time interval as (X_1, X_2) where X_1 is efficiently (and randomly) transformed to X_2 with the promise that X_1 and X_2 have entropy independent of the other. Then any non-malleable extractor for samplable sources with respect to polynomial size tampering, Ext, can extract from such as source online, i.e. $\mathsf{Ext}(X_1), \mathsf{Ext}(X_2)$ is approximately uniform.[7]

Recognizable Sources: These are uniform distributions over the set of inputs accepted by some polynomial sized circuit. Specifically, the source distribution X is uniform over $\{x : C(x) = 1\}$, where C is a circuit of size n^c.

Extracting from this class of sources was first considered by Shaltiel [60] in the context of derandomization. This class corresponds with sources about which some efficiently computable leakage is known.

As we will see, *non-malleable* extractors for recognizable sources and polynomial size tampering provide a natural, generic means constructing non-malleable, leakage-resilient cryptography.

Theorem 1.4 (Informal). *If* E *requires exponential size Σ_4-circuits, then for every constant c, there is an explicit n^{-c}-secure seedless non-malleable extractor for sources $X \in \{0, 1\}^n$ samplable by n^c size circuits with linear min-entropy, that outputs $\Omega(\frac{n \log \log(n)}{\log(n)})$ bits and is resilient to tampering by n^c-size circuits.*

The formal statement and proof are left to the full version [16]. A detailed construction and proof sketch for a weaker type of non-malleable extractor can be found in the technical overview (see Sect. 1.4). The construction and proof sketch in the technical overview contain the main ideas needed for the full result.

Similarly to our non-malleable codes, we construct our non-malleable extractors by "fooling" *(seedless) two-source non-malleable extractors.*

Roughly, a two-source non-malleable extractor, 2NMExt, can extract randomness from two-independent sources (with sufficient min-entropy) even after

---

[6] Sources sampled by polynomial size *quantum* circuits seem a more appropriate model for physical sources of randomness. Nonetheless, (classical) samplable sources are an interesting and important subclass.

[7] Note that with a random seed it is easy to extract from say X_1 conditioned on X_2.

seeing the output of the extractor invoked on input generated by independently (and arbitrarily) tampering each source.

Our construction of a non-malleable extractor for samplable sources and polynomial size tampering follows. Let $\mathsf{Ext}_{\mathsf{samp}}$ be an extractor for samplable sources, 2NMExt an (efficient) two-source non-malleable extractor, and G a PRG for nondeterministic NP-circuits, then given a samplable source X. The idea is to extract a seed with the samplable extractor and then use the seed to "fool" the two-source non-malleable extractor in a similar manner to the non-malleable code construction above.

– Extract a seed $s = \mathsf{Ext}_{\mathsf{samp}}(X)$.
– Output 2NMExt$(G(s), X)$.

The high-level idea of the proof is similar to the outline for the non-malleable code proof. An added difficulty here over our non-malleable code analysis (responsible for the stronger assumption on the PRG) is that Arthur again receives either pseudorandom $(s\|y) = G(s)$ or random $(s\|y)$ as input, but now must sample a source, X, that is consistent with its input, i.e. sample X such that $\mathsf{Ext}_{\mathsf{samp}}(X) = s$. Arthur can do this with a bounded poly-size circuit, given an added level of non-determinism.

The above result is obtained by first constructing "relaxed" seedless non-malleable extractors for $n^{c'}$ samplable sources and n^c tampering (by "relaxed" we mean restricting the tampering function to have no fixed points), and then presenting a generic transformation from relaxed seedless non-malleable extractors for $n^{c'}$ samplable sources and n^c tampering to seedless non-malleable extractors for n^c samplable sources and n^c tampering.

We obtain a similar result for recognizable sources:

Theorem 1.5 (Informal). *If* E *requires exponential size* Σ_3*-circuits, then for every constant* c*, there is an explicit* n^{-c}*-secure seedless non-malleable extractor for sources* $X \in \{0,1\}^n$ *recognizable by* n^c *size circuits with linear min-entropy, that outputs* $\Omega(\frac{n \log \log(n)}{\log(n)})$ *bits and is resilient to tampering by* n^c*-size circuits.*

The formal statement and proof are left to the full version [16]. We note that the assumption that E requires exponential size Σ_4-circuits (resp. E requires exponential size Σ_3-circuits) is inherited from the seedless extractor for samplable (resp. recognizable) sources of [7] that is used as a building block in our construction. Assuming the existence of a seedless extractor for samplable (resp. recognizable) sources, our construction requires only the weaker assumption that E requires exponential size nondeterministic NP circuits.

Before presenting a technical overview of the main ideas of our constructions, we discuss the relationship between our positive results and known negative results from the literature.

On the Feasibility of Explicit Codes from Minimal Assumptions. It is known that explicit non-malleable codes for circuits of size $O(n^c)$ imply explicit languages that are hard on average for circuits of size $O(n^c)$.[8] Due to the limitations in current techniques for proving unconditional circuit lower bounds, it is therefore unlikely to construct explicit codes for such a tampering class, unconditionally. Yet, one might still hope to construct codes by assuming minimal circuit lower bounds (i.e. assuming there exists a language computable in time n^d, for some $d > c$, that is hard on average for $O(n^c)$-size circuits). Unfortunately, Ball et al. [15] showed a barrier to proving such a theorem. In particular, they ruled out constructions of non-malleable codes where the *security proof*–which is a *reduction* from breaking the above assumption to breaking the non-malleable code— makes *black box* usage of the tampering adversary. This implies that either radically different proof approaches are necessary (that make use of non-black box methods) or stronger assumptions (beyond the minimal one discussed above) are needed.

Our present result skirts this lower bound by taking the second approach of stronger assumptions. Specifically, the techniques of [15] rule out non-black box reductions when the constructed non-malleable code is resilient against some class $\mathcal{C}$ and the underlying assumption is hard for the *same* class $\mathcal{C}$ of circuits. In this work, our tampering class consists of small *deterministic* circuits, but our assumption is stronger and requires hardness for small *nondeterministic* circuits.

1.3   Our Results–Included in the Full Version [16]

On the Necessity of $1/\mathsf{poly}$-*indistinguishability.* One could hope to construct non-malleable extractors and non-malleable codes with *negligible* error from the types of assumptions we consider in this work–i.e. that E requires exponential size Σ_i-circuits. Unfortunately, for the case of non-malleable extractors for samplable or recognizable distributions, barriers to achieving such a result were already shown in the work of Applebaum et al. [7]. Specifically, they rule out certain types of black-box reductions from functions that are $(1/2 + \delta)$-hard (where δ is a small constant) for n^d-size Σ_i-circuits to extractors for distributions that are samplable or recognizable by size n^c circuits (where $c \leq d$ are constants), and that achieve negligible error. As a consequence, their results rule out reductions from the assumption that E requires exponential size Σ_i-circuits. In the full version [16], we extend the results of Applebaum et al. [7] to rule out black-box reductions from any function f that is $(1/2 + \delta)$-hard for n^d-size Σ_i-circuits to efficient, 1-bit non-malleable codes resilient to tampering by by size n^c circuits (where $c \leq d$ are constants), and that achieve negligible error.[9] Since f as above can be constructed from the scaled down and padded characteristic function of some (average case hard) language in E, it means that if one can compute the characteristic function of an E-complete language on all inputs (i.e. break the

---

[8] In particular, the Decode function is hard with respect to the distribution formed by encoding a random bit. If this wasn't the case, one could attack by computing the encoded value and outputting a fixed encoding of the opposite bit.

[9] Note that ruling out reductions to 1-bit non-malleable codes also rules out reductions to k-bit non-malleable codes.

worst-case hardness of an E-complete language), then one can compute f on average (with probability $1/2 + \delta$). Thus, our results also rule out reductions from the assumption that E is (worst-case) hard for exponential size Σ_i-circuits.

We note that there are differences in the class of reductions ruled out by our result and the corresponding results of Applebaum et al. [7]: Our result allows *function-specific* and *non*-security parameter-preserving reductions. On the other hand, our results require the assumption that there is a function that is hard for n^d-size Σ_i-circuits and rule out only efficient constructions of non-malleable codes (where encode/decode are polynomial time), while the results of Applebaum et al. [7] are unconditional and rule out even inefficient constructions. Please see the full version for further discussion.

Taken together, the results of Applebaum et al. [7] together with our new results for non-malleable codes in the full version [16], indicate that significantly new proof techniques are necessary to construct non-malleable extractors and non-malleable codes with *negligible* error from the assumption that E requires exponential size Σ_i-circuits.

Partially Bypassing the Impossibility via "Relative Error." The above results indicate that it is inherently difficult to construct non-malleable extractors with negligible error under non-deterministic reductions, where error is measured in terms of *statistical distance*. Another measure of closeness between distributions is known as *relative error*. Specifically, relative error α between a pair of distributions $\mathcal{D}_1, \mathcal{D}_2$ requires that for every element x in the support of $\mathcal{D}_1$,

$$(1 - \alpha)Pr_{\mathcal{D}_2}[x] \leq Pr_{\mathcal{D}_1}[x] \leq (1 + \alpha)Pr_{\mathcal{D}_2}[x].$$

In this case, even if α is *non-negligible*, the above guarantee is still useful for achieving negligible security.

Applebaum et al. [7] introduced a notion of *relative-error* extractors, observing that if the output of the extractor is $1/\mathsf{poly}$-close to uniform with relative error, then every event occurs w.r.t. the output distribution with probability at most $(1 + 1/\mathsf{poly})$ times the probability it occurs w.r.t. the uniform distribution. In particular, events that are negligible under the uniform distributions cannot become noticeable under the distribution outputted by the extractor. This was then sufficient for obtaining leakage resilient cryptosystems with negligible security guarantees.

In this work, we consider applying the relative error notion to the setting of *seedless, non-malleable* extractors. Our notion differs in two ways: First, we need to extend the notion to the case where neither the real nor simulated distribution is uniform. This is because the guarantee of the non-malleable extractor holds with respect to a pair of output values (a, b), where a should be uniform random, but b can come from an arbitrary distribution. Second, due to the above, we slightly relax the notion and incorporate a small additive term, $\beta \ll 2^{-2m}$, where m is the output length of the extractor.

We now parametrize the relative extractor notion by α and β and require that the probability of any untampered/tampered output pair (a, b) under the real distribution is at most $(1+\alpha)p_I(a,b)+\beta$, where $p_I(a,b)$ denotes the probability of output pair (a,b) under the ideal distribution.

Applications to Leakage and Tamper Resilience with Negligible Security. A non-malleable extractor $\mathsf{E} : \{0,1\}^n \to \{0,1\}^m$ with *relative error (α,β)* for a class of recognizable sources $\mathcal{X}$ and tampering family $\mathcal{T}$, can be used to obtain leakage and *tamper* resilient cryptosystems with *negligible* security guarantees. To achieve this, one can store a uniformly random R on a device and use $a = \mathsf{E}(R)$ as the secret key for a symmetric key cryptosystem Π. The attacker is allowed (1) leakage on R with leakage function ℓ from the class of bounded polynomial-size circuits with bounded output length;[10] (2) tampering on R with tampering function t from the class of bounded polynomial-size circuits; (3) oracle access to *both* Π_a, and Π_b, where $b = \mathsf{E}(t(R))$ is the tampered version of the key (Π_a, Π_b denote fixing the secret key of Π to a or b respectively). We show that in several cases, we can still guarantee the *negligible* security of the cryptosystem with respect to the *original* key a, despite this stronger adversarial model.

We consider two types of applications. First, for cryptosystems Π that have an associated *unpredictability* game (such as MAC's), negligible security in the leakage and tampering game described above can be proved from the properties of the relative error non-malleable extractor, assuming the original cryptosystem Π satisfies the standard security notion. Second, for cryptosystems Π that have an associated *indistinguishability* game (such as CPA secure symmetric key encryption), negligible security in the leakage and tampering game described above can be proved in the case that the original cryptosystem Π satisfies a type of "square-security" notion (see for example [18,31], for a discussion of the square-security notion). We note that there are natural examples of cryptosystems that achieve this required notion. For example CPA-secure symmetric key encryption satisfies the "square-security" notion needed for our result.

We emphasize that, for both the unpredictability and indistinguishability applications discussed above, by using *relative error* non-malleable extractors, we are able to prove that the attacker's advantage is *negligible* in the leakage and tampering game.

Non-malleable Secret Sharing and Non-malleable Codes are Equivalent Under Plysize Circuit Tampering. Secret sharing schemes allow a user with a secret to send "shares" to a set of parties such that any "authorized" subset of parties can recover the secret from their collective shares, but "unauthorized" subsets of parties learn nothing about the secret from their collective shares. This relatively simple object, about which many foundational questions remain unanswered, is a critical tool in modern cryptography.

In 2018, Goyal and Kumar [43] introduced the notion of *non-malleable secret sharing*. To understand what it means for a secret sharing scheme to be non-malleable, consider the following experiment: share a secret, jointly tamper all the shares, reconstruct the tampered shares of some authorized subset of

---

[10] In fact, the precise leakage class we can handle is slightly more broad.

parties. Loosely, a secret sharing scheme is non-malleable if the outcome of this experiment returns the original secret or some value independent of the original secret (and which case occurs should also be independent of the original secret).

In the full version [16], we construct non-malleable secret sharing schemes that are resilient to joint tampering of the shares by polynomial size circuits for a wide variety of access structures, any access structure for which an explicit (efficiently computable) secret sharing scheme exists. In fact, we observe that non-malleable secret sharing and non-malleable codes for polynomial size circuit tampering are effectively equivalent. This is a testament to the richness of this tampering class. More precisely, to construct such a non-malleable secret sharing scheme from a non-malleable code, one simply encodes the secret with the non-malleable code and shares the codeword according to a polysize computable secret sharing scheme (to reconstruct the secret, simply reconstruct the codeword and decode). This is safe because composing sharing, tampering, and reconstructing can in turn be performed by a polynomial size circuit, because the secret sharing scheme is efficient. (The reverse direction is immediate.) We go on to construct *adaptive* non-malleable secret sharing schemes resilient to polynomial size circuit tampering for a wide variety of access structures, including any access structure admitting an efficient *linear* secret sharing scheme. In adaptive non-malleable secret sharing, the tampering function can be chosen arbitrarily as a function of any unauthorized set of shares.

1.4   Technical Overview

We demonstrate our techniques by presenting a construction and proofsketch for a simplified case: constructing "relaxed" non-malleable extractors (where the tampering function is guaranteed to have no fixed points) for uniformly random sources and bounded polynomial tampering (i.e. size n^c circuits for some constant c). This simplified case will already provides most of the key ideas of our main results. We conclude the section by discussing how to extend this example and its analysis to achieve our main results.

A Simple Example: (Relaxed) Seedless Non-malleable "Extractor" for Uniform Sources. First, recall that a *relaxed seedless non-malleable extractor* for sources of the form (S, X) is a deterministic function NMExt such that for any n^c size circuit, C *without fixed points* we have

$$(\mathrm{NMExt}(S, X), \mathrm{NMExt}(C(S, X))) \approx (\mathcal{U}, \mathrm{NMExt}(C(S, X))).$$

We reiterate that here we simplify by assuming that the source (S, X) is uniform random. While this trivializes the task of randomness extraction, the question of non-malleable extraction remains interesting for such sources, e.g. it already implies the existence of non-malleable codes for 1-bit messages.[11]

Before describing our construction, we give a brief overview of the necessary building blocks:

---

[11] To see this, recall the characterization of non-malleability for a single bit (see previous footnote). Note that for any tampering function f of size n^c, one can define

Strong Relaxed Two-Source Non-malleable Extractor. Loosely speaking, a function NMExt : $\{0,1\}^n \times \{0,1\}^n \to \{0,1\}^m$ is a relaxed two-source non-malleable extractor for sources (X,Y) if for every split-state tampering function (τ_L, τ_R) for which either τ_L or τ_R has no fixed points, we have

$$(\text{NMExt}(X,Y), \text{NMExt}(\tau_L(X), \tau_R(Y))) \overset{s}{\approx} (\mathcal{U}_m, \text{NMExt}(\tau_L(X), \tau_R(Y))).$$

We say NMExt is a strong two-source non-malleable extractor for no-fixed points tampering if we further have that

$$(X, \text{NMExt}(X,Y), \text{NMExt}(\tau_L(X), \tau_R(Y))) \overset{s}{\approx} (X, \mathcal{U}_m, \text{NMExt}(\tau_L(X), \tau_R(Y))).$$

Two source non-malleable extractors are well-studied in the literature with the current state-of-the-art being extractors for sources $(X,Y) \in \{0,1\}^n \times \{0,1\}^n$ with min-entropy $(1-\gamma)n$ for some constant γ and error $2^{-\Omega(n \log\log(n)/\log(n))}$ [56]. Further, [54] showed that every two source non-malleable extractor is also a strong two source non-malleable extractor for sources with some loss in parameters.

Recalling the notion of a nondeterministic circuit from the introduction, we now introduce a type of pseudorandom generator (PRG) with security against non-deterministic circuits of bounded polynomial size.

Seed-Extending Pseudorandom Generators. A *pseudorandom generator (PRG) for nondeterministic circuits of size* n^d, $\mathsf{G} : \{0,1\}^\ell \to \{0,1\}^n$, allows one to extend a short random seed into a long string that is indistinguishable from random to nondeterministic circuits of size n^d (for constant d). More precisely, for every nondeterministic circuit, C, of size at most n^d,

$$|\Pr[C(\mathsf{G}(\mathcal{U}_\ell)) = 1] - \Pr[C(\mathcal{U}_n) = 1]| \le \frac{1}{n^d},$$

where $\mathcal{U}_m$ denotes a random variable uniformly distributed over $\{0,1\}^m$.

The above type of PRG are different from cryptographic PRG's since the computation time of the PRG is larger than the size of the adversary. These PRG's are secure against nondeterministic circuits of size n^d, but take larger polynomial time to compute. Cryptographic PRG's are computable in some fixed polynomial time but secure against adversaries of arbitrary polynomial size. In the case of seed-extending pseudorandom generators, this gap between honest and adversarial computational resources allows for unintuitive behavior, where the seed of the PRG itself is included as part of the output and the output remains pseudorandom, which is impossible in the cryptographic case.

---

a function f' of size $n^c + O(n)$ that has no fixed points and behaves identically to f on every x that is not a fixed point of f. Because, $\Pr[D(f(\mathsf{E}(b)) = 1 - b] \le \Pr[D(f'(\mathsf{E}(b)) = 1 - b]$ we can deduce that E, D is non-malleable with respect to circuits of size $n^c - O(n)$, where D is NMExt and E simply performs rejection sampling to find a random (s,x) such that $\text{NMExt}(s,x) = b$. Note that the resulting non-malleable code will not have perfect correctness because the rejection sampling procedure might fail.

Indeed, we are interested in exactly such PRGs that remain secure even when given the seed, referred to as "seed-extending" PRGs.[12] A PRG, $G : \{0,1\}^\ell \to \{0,1\}^n$, is said to be seed-extending if $G(s) = (s, G'(s))$ (where G' is the function corresponding to the $n - \ell$ bit suffix). This particular name was introduced by Kinne et al. in the context of derandomizing randomized algorithms on random inputs. [50,53] They observed that PRG constructions based on Nisan and Wigderson's seminal construction [50] can be made seed-extending. Consequently, many constructions of PRGs for nondeterministic circuits can be made seed extending.

Theorem 1.6 ([7,46,50,51,61,62])**.** *If* E *requires exponential size nondeterministic circuits, then for every constant $c > 1$ there exists a constant $\alpha > 1$ such that for every sufficiently large n, and every ℓ such that $\alpha \log n \leq \ell \leq n$ there is a seed-extending PRG, $G : \{0,1\}^\ell \to \{0,1\}^n$, for nondeterministic circuits of size n^c.*

Construction of a Seedless Relaxed Non-malleable Extractor. Our construction of a (relaxed) seedless non-malleable extractor for uniform sources and n^c-size circuit tampering is exceedingly simple. Let 2NMExt be a relaxed, two-source non-malleable extractor (NME). Our seedless relaxed non-malleable extractor, NMExt, is defined as

$$\text{NMExt} : (s, x) \mapsto 2\text{NMExt}(G(s), x)$$

where G is a *seed-extending PRG for nondeterministic circuits of size n^d* for some constant $d > c$.

Sketch of the Security Proof. To prove security of the construction, we need to show that the existence of a size n^c tampering function with no fixed points that breaks the security of the NME, implies the existence of a nondeterministic circuit of size n^d that distinguishes outputs of G from random.

Suppose for the sake of contradiction that there exists a successful tampering function, $\tau : (s, x) \mapsto (\tilde{s}, \tilde{x})$ of circuit size n^c with no fixed points. We will define f to denote the function that computes $(s, x) \mapsto \tilde{x}$ according to τ, and g to denote the function that computes $(s, x) \mapsto \tilde{s}$ according to τ. In other words, $\tau(s, x) = (g(s, x), f(s, x))$ and moreover, for each (s, x) either $g(s, x) \neq s$ or $f(s, x) \neq x$. Note that there is *no* split-state assumption on the tampering function $\tau(s, x) = (g(s, x), f(s, x))$, as both f and g can depend on the entire input (s, x). Now, our assumption on τ (and hence f, g) breaking the NME can be restated as

$$\Delta\Big((2\text{NMExt}(G(S), X), 2\text{NMExt}(G(g(S, X)), f(S, X)));$$

$$(\mathcal{U}_m, 2\text{NMExt}(G(g(S, X)), f(S, X)))\Big) \geq \epsilon. \tag{1}$$

---

[12] We refer the reader to [51] for further discussion.

We will use this assumption to "distinguish" the seed-extending PRG, G, from the uniform distribution via a private constant round interactive proof (i.e. Arthur Merlin protocol). In particular, (private-coin) Arthur will accept pseudorandom inputs (completeness) with polynomially higher probability than he accepts random inputs, regardless of how Merlin behaves (soundness). Then, we can deduce from standard transformations ($\mathsf{IP}[k] \subseteq \mathsf{AM} \subseteq \mathsf{NP/poly}$ [9,42]) that a small non-deterministic distinguisher exists.[13]

Looking ahead (1) which asserts the *malleability* of the constructed extractor when provided pseudorandom inputs will enable us to prove the protocol is complete, i.e. Arthur accepts pseudorandom inputs with high probability. Soundness, i.e. Arthur rejects random inputs with high probability, will ultimately follow from security of the 2-source non-malleable extractor. Furthermore, what ultimately will enable our soundness argument to go through is the fact that to achieve completeness Arthur communicates very little about random variable X and thus X remains entropic, even after conditioning on this communication. We use a standard private coin technique, where Arthur forces Merlin to guess between two samplable distributions [40] to handle the fact that our extractor has relatively long outputs (even though our hardness assumption only holds for boolean distinguishers in a relatively high error regime).

Arthur Merlin Protocol. We next describe the interactive proof for distinguishing G from uniformly random bits. **Both Arthur and Merlin receive (s, y) as input.** Our protocol aims to accept strings from $G(\mathcal{U}_\ell)$ when Merlin plays according to below (completeness) and reject strings from $\mathcal{U}_n$ regardless of the strategy Merlin utilizes (soundness). Because we can amplify by repetition, it suffices for there to be small gap between the two.

Arthur Sample $x \leftarrow \mathcal{U}_n$. Send Merlin $\tilde{s} = g(s, x)$.
Merlin If $(s, y) = G(s)$, respond $\tilde{y}$ such that $(\tilde{s}, \tilde{y}) = G(\tilde{s})$. Otherwise, respond
   arbitrary $\tilde{y}$.
Arthur Sample a random coin $b \leftarrow \mathcal{U}$ and set $\tilde{z} = 2\mathsf{NMExt}((\tilde{s}, \tilde{y}), \tilde{x})$ where
   $\tilde{x} = f(s, x)$.
   – *If $b = 0$:* Sample $z \leftarrow \mathcal{U}_m$ and send $z, \tilde{z}$.
   – *Else if $b = 1$:* Sample $z \leftarrow 2\mathsf{NMExt}((s, y), x)$ and send $z, \tilde{z}$.
Merlin Guess Arthur's bit by guessing whether $(z, \tilde{z})$ was drawn from the first
   or second distribution.
Arthur Accept if $b = b'$, and reject otherwise.

Completeness: Accepting Pseudorandom Inputs. We first argue that Arthur, when playing with Merlin as specified above, accepts pseudorandom inputs, drawn from $G(S)$, with probability significantly greater than $1/2$. Indeed, if the protocol

---

[13] In actuality, this is too naive because these transformations only hold for worst-case notions of soundness and completeness. Thus in the body, we will instead show that there exists a constant round interactive proof for a *promise problem* (Π_Y, Π_N) such that Π_Y is dense in the pseudorandom distribution and Π_N is dense in the uniform distribution, and not vice-versa.

above is given inputs from $G(S)$ (i.e. legitimate outputs of G), then if Arthur chooses $b = 1$, his final message is sampled as:

$$(z, \tilde{z}) \sim (2\text{NMExt}(G(S), X), 2\text{NMExt}(G(g(S, X)), f(S, X))).$$

On the other hand, if $b = 0$, Arthur's final message is sampled according to:

$$(z, \tilde{z}) \sim (\mathcal{U}_m, 2\text{NMExt}(G(g(S, X)), f(S, X))).$$

By our malleability assumption towards contradiction (1), these two distributions are ϵ-far from each other.

Soundness: Rejecting Random Inputs. We must now show that when given uniformly random inputs, Arthur accepts with significantly lower probability than the case above. This case is harder than the previous case, since here Merlin can behave arbitrarily, and we must show that Arthur still rejects w.h.p.

At a high-level, we get around this by observing that although Merlin is computationally unbounded, the fact that the information sent to him by Arthur is limited, essentially constrains Merlin to *split-state* strategies. Specifically, let $G^* : (s, y, \tilde{s}) \mapsto \tilde{y}$ be the function that given Merlin's input (s, y) and the transcript thus far, outputs Merlin's first message. Conditioned on $s, \tilde{s}$, we have that $G^*(s, y, \tilde{s}) = \tilde{y}$ is independent of x (as is $\tilde{s}$). And similarly, $\tilde{x} = f(s, x)$ is independent of (s, y). So conditioned on $s, \tilde{s}$ we can define a *split-state* tampering function as follows:

- $\tau_L^{\tilde{s}} : (s, y) \mapsto (\tilde{s}, \tilde{y})$ where $\tilde{y} = G^*(s, y, \tilde{s})$
- $\tau_R^s : x \mapsto \tilde{x}$ where $\tilde{x} = f(s, x)$

Note that because τ has no fixed points, either $f(s, x) \neq x$ or $g(s, x) \neq s$. So, either $\tau_L^{\tilde{s}}$ or τ_R^s contains no fixed points. Thus, conditioned on $s, \tilde{s}$ and Arthur's coin $b = 0$, Merlin's view is simply

$$T_0^{s, \tilde{s}} \equiv \left((s, y), \mathcal{U}, 2\text{NMExt}(\tau_L^{\tilde{s}}(s, y), \tau_R^s(x))\right).$$

On the other hand, if Arthur's coin is $b = 1$, Merlin's view is

$$T_1^{s, \tilde{s}} \equiv \left((s, y), 2\text{NMExt}((s, y), x), 2\text{NMExt}(\tau_L^{\tilde{s}}(s, y), \tau_R^s(x))\right).$$

Recall that the input (s, y) (left source) and x (right source) are both uniform. Thus, after conditioning on the transcript (or equivalently $s, \tilde{s}$) nearly all the entropy remains in each source (in fact, we can take $s, \tilde{s}$ short enough that the entropy deficiency is just $O(\log(n))$). Then because 2NMExt is a *strong* two-source non-malleable extractor for sources with linear min-entropy, it follows from the security property that $T_0^{s, \tilde{s}} \overset{s}{\approx} T_1^{s, \tilde{s}}$.

Obtaining Our Main Results. We extend the above technique in several ways:

Non-malleable Extractors for Samplable/Recognizable Sources. First, we combine the above construction with a seedless extractor for polynomially samplable (resp. recognizable) sources [7,64] to obtain a *relaxed* seedless *non-malleable* extractor for polynomially samplable (resp. recognizable) sources and polynomially bounded tampering.

In brief, we use a seedless extractor to sample the uniform seed, s, for the PRG in the simple construction above. The main difference relative to the proof above, is that now Arthur must sample the samplable/recognizable source to be consistent with the pseudorandom challenge, i.e. conditioned on the seedless extractor outputting s. This is resolved in both cases by equipping Arthur with an NP-oracle, so he can efficiently sample random satisfying assignments to small circuits [20,47].

The full details of our constructions and their analysis can be found in the full version. Similar to above, we first construct an extractor secure against tampering functions without fixed points (this one by Cheraghchi and Guruswami [27] and first construct an extractor secure against tampering functions without fixed points. Then we show how to remove the requirement of no fixed-points in the tampering functions to obtain seedless *non-malleable* extractor for polynomially samplable sources and polynomially bounded tampering.[14]

Non-malleable Code. The above non-malleable extractors suggest an natural path to non-malleable codes. Cheraghchi and Guruswami [27] show that *invertible* non-malleable extractors for a tampering class C imply non-malleable codes for that C. However, there are two obstacles to applying their approach here. First, it is unclear how to efficiently invert our extractors. Secondly, this transformation has 2^k security loss, where k is the bit length of the messages to be encoded. Given the polynomial security, this means the resulting construction would have exponential length codewords and would not actually be explicit.

We therefore take the route of directly constructing non-malleable codes, with the added benefit that we reduce our hardness assumptions from "E requires exponential size Σ_3-circuits" (required for our non-malleable extractors) to "E requires exponential size nondeterministic circuits."

Our result is obtained by replacing the two-source non-malleable extractor in the simple example above with a split-state non-malleable code: to encode a message m, sample a split-state encoding of the form $(G(S), y)$ and output s, y. To make a similar Arthur Merlin distinguisher work for this construction, we need the split-state code to have some special properties:

Special Encoding: We need to be able to sample pseudorandom split-state code words efficiently in order to encode efficiently at all. To do this we introduce a notion of *special encoding*:

There is an alternate encoding algorithm that receives the value of the first split state along with a message m and samples the second split-state so that the

---

[14] Cheraghchi and Guruswami [27] showed a similar lemma for the case of split-state tampering.

resulting encoding decodes to m. Critically, if the value of the first split-state is sampled uniformly at random, then the outputted encoding is distributed identically to a random encoding of m.

Leakage Resilience: The soundness argument above relied on the fact that two-source extractors remain secure even if there is small amount of leakage on the states (corresponding to the transcript). Note that this leakage is both to the independent components of the split-state tampering function *and* the (possibly inefficient) distinguisher of the non-malleability game. If this is the case, we say a such split-state code is *leakage-resilient*.[15]

"Augmented" NMC: Finally, our soundness argument above additionally required that Merlin could not distinguish the real and ideal experiments even when given the left source in its entirety. For this we relied on the fact that 2NMExt was a *strong* two-source non-malleable extractor. The corresponding notion for split-state non-malleable codes is the *augmented* property: security of the NMC holds even when one half of the codeword is revealed at the end of the experiment to a (possibly inefficient) distinguisher.

The split-state NMC constructions of [2,3] satisfy the necessary properties. In the full version [16] we show how the leakage-resilience transformation of Ball et al. [17] yields comparable codes with better leakage parameters. Details of our NMC construction and its analysis are in Sect. 3. The rate of our code inherits the rate of the NMC of Aggarwal et al. [2], which means that to encode a message of length k one needs a codeword length of $n = O(k^7)$. A better split-state NMC with the above properties will yield a better NMC for polysize tampering, but rate is not our focus here.

1.5   Related Work

Non-malleable Extractors and Codes. There is by now a large body of work on non-malleable extractors (NME) and non-malleable codes (NMC) resilient against various classes of tampering [1,2,4,5,10,11,13,17,24,33,34,48,55,56]. In the NMC case, some constructions not included in the list above rely on cryptographic assumptions [6,14], while others require an untamperable common reference string (CRS) [14,57]. There has also been much work on variants of NME/NMC [23,30,37,49], as well as a relatively new line of work on a related primitive called non-malleable secret sharing [43,44]. We restrict our attention to constructions most relevant to the current work, namely, the prior constructions of NMC (in the CRS and standard models) resilient to bounded polynomial tampering, where "bounded polynomial" can refer to a restriction on (1) circuit size, (2) uniform computation time, or (3) circuit depth. Existence

---

[15] In the literature, leakage-resilient has been alternately used to refer to codes that handle leakage only to the distinguisher as well as code that handle leakage only between the tampering of each state.

of non-malleable codes under all of the above types of tampering was initially shown via the probabilistic method in [35] and they can also be constructed efficiently in the random oracle model [35]. In the following, we additionally restrict our attention to explicit, efficient constructions *without* random oracles. We also mention a somewhat related line of work on variants of non-malleable codes resilient to polynomially *space-bounded* tampering in the random oracle model [25, 36].

NMC Against Bounded Polynomial Sized Circuits in the CRS Model. Faust et al. [38] presented efficient information theoretically secure NMC with negligible error in the CRS model, resilient against tampering function classes F which can be represented as circuits of size $\mathsf{poly}(n)$. The CRS in their construction is a seed s for a $p(n)$-wise independent hash function, where $p(n)$ is a polynomial that is larger than the bound on the tampering circuit size.

NMC Against Uniform, Bounded Polynomial Time in the Standard Model. Ball et al. [12] presented efficient NMC resilient against tampering by functions computable in uniform bounded polynomial time. Their construction is in the standard, no-CRS model and achieves error of $1/\mathsf{poly}$. They require a similar assumption as those used in the current work, as well as cryptographic assumptions of the existence of sub-exponentially hard trapdoor permutations and the existence of P-certificates with sub-exponential soundness. The only known instantiation of P-certificates requires assuming soundness of a non-trivial argument system (Micali's CS proofs [58]), which is true in the Random Oracle model. Due to the use of cryptographic techniques in the construction and proof, the final non-malleable code achieves computational indistinguishability.

NMC Against Bounded Polynomial Depth Circuits (Unbounded Polynomial Size) in the Standard Model. Dachman-Soled et al. [28,29] constructed NMC resilient to all polynomial size tampering functions that have bounded polynomial depth. This tampering class contains all bounded polynomial size functions and contains non-uniform NC. Their construction is in the standard, no-CRS model and achieves negligible error. They require the cryptographic assumptions of the existence of keyless multi-collision resistant hash function, injective one-way function, and non-interactive witness-indistinguishable proofs, as well as the repeated squaring assumption. Keyless multi-collision resistant hash function are known to exist in the auxiliary input random oracle model. Due to the use of cryptographic techniques in the construction and proof, the final non-malleable code achieves computational indistinguishability.

Seedless Extractors for Samplable and Recognizable Sources. Trevisan and Vadhan [64] considered seedless extractors for the class of distributions samplable by bounded polynomial sized circuits. Under the assumption that E requires exponential size Σ_4 circuits, they presented constructions of seedless extractors for linear min-entropy, samplable sources over n bits, that output $\Omega(n)$ bits that are $1/\mathsf{poly}$-close to uniform. Applebaum et al. [7] showed that the $1/\mathsf{poly}$ error is somewhat inherent by ruling out black-box reductions in this setting. They introduced a notion of *relative-error* extractors and showed that if the output of the extractor is 1/poly-close to uniform with relative error, then every event occurs w.r.t. the output distribution with probability at most $(1 + 1/\text{poly})$ times the probability it occurs w.r.t. the uniform distribution. In particular, events that are negligible under the uniform distributions cannot become noticeable under the distribution outputted by the extractor. Under the assumption that E requires exponential size Σ_4 circuits, they constructed relative-error seedless extractors whose outputs are 1/poly-close to uniform with relative error for linear min-entropy, samplable sources. Under the assumption that E requires exponential size Σ_3 circuits, they constructed relative-error seedless extractors whose outputs are 1/poly-close to uniform with relative error for linear min-entropy, recognizable sources.

2   Preliminaries

For $S \subseteq N$, where $S = \{i_1, \ldots, i_\ell : i_1 < \cdots < i_\ell\}$ and any n-ary string of values $x_1, \ldots, x_n$, let x_S denote the string $(x_{i_1}, \ldots, x_{i_\ell})$. For random variables X, Y, we write $\Delta(X; Y) \leq \epsilon$ or $X \approx_\epsilon Y$ if the total variation distance between their distributions is at most ϵ.

2.1   Complexity Classes and Assumptions

We take E to denote $\text{DTIME}[2^{O(n)}]$ the class of languages decidable by deterministic Turing machines in 2^{cn}-time for some constant c. We take circuits to denote circuits over the standard basis $\{\vee, \wedge, \neg\}$. For any language O, an O-oracle aided circuit is a circuit that has special gates that decide O, in addition to the standard-basis. For any circuit, we say it has size s if it contains at most s gates. We say it has depth d if the longest path from any input to any output gate is of size d. A circuit family, $\{C_n\}_{n \in N}$, is a collection of circuits such that C_n takes inputs of length n. We take the $\text{SIZE}[s(n)]$ to denote the function families computable by a circuit family $\{C_n\}_{n \in N}$ such that C_n has size at most $s(n)$, for large enough n. Similarly, we take $\text{SIZE}^O[s(n)]$ to denote the function families computable by an O-oracle aided circuit family $\{C_n\}_{n \in N}$ such that C_n has size at most $s(n)$, for sufficiently large n.

2.2   Non-malleable Codes

Definition 2.1 (Coding Schemes). *A pair of functions* (Enc, Dec), *where* Enc : $\{0,1\}^k \to \{0,1\}^n$ *is a randomized function and* Dec : $\{0,1\}^n \to \{0,1\}^k \cup \{\bot\}$ *is a deterministic function, is defined to be a coding scheme with block length n and message length k if for all $s \in \{0,1\}^k$,* $\Pr[\text{Dec}(\text{Enc}(s)) = s] = 1$.

Definition 2.2 (Tampering Functions). *For any $n > 0$, let $\mathcal{H}_n$ denote the set of all functions $h : \{0,1\}^n \to \{0,1\}^n$. Any subset $\mathcal{G} \subseteq \mathcal{H}_n$ is a family of tampering* *functions. For any class of boolean functions* $\mathcal{F} = \{f : \{0,1\}^n \to \{0,1\}\}$, *we take* $\mathcal{F}^n$ *to denote the class of n-output functions where each output is computed by some function in* $\mathcal{F}$, *i.e.* $\mathcal{F}^n = \{f_{i_1,\ldots,i_n} : x \mapsto f_{i_1}(x),\ldots,f_{i_n}(x) \mid f_{i_1},\ldots,f_{i_n} \in \mathcal{F}\}$.

The particular classes of tampering functions we consider in this work:

- Tampering where each output is computable by an $s(n)$-size circuit, $\mathsf{SIZE}^n[s(n)]$.
- Split-state tampering where two halves of an input are tampered independently and arbitrarily: $\{(\tau_L, \tau_R) : x_1,\ldots,x_{2n} \mapsto \tau_L(x_1,\ldots,x_n), \tau_R(x_{n+1}, \ldots, x_{2n}) \mid \tau_L, \tau_R \in \mathcal{H}_n\}$.

We define a function that will be useful in defining non-malleable codes:

$$\mathrm{Copy}(x,y) = \begin{cases} x & \text{if } x \neq \mathsf{same} \\ y & \text{if } x = \mathsf{same}. \end{cases}$$

Definition 2.3 (Non-malleable codes). *A coding scheme* (Enc, Dec) *on alphabet* $\{0,1\}$ *with block length n and message length k is a ϵ-non-malleable code with respect to a tampering family* $\mathcal{F} \subset \mathcal{H}_n$ *if for every* $f \in \mathcal{F}$ *there is a random variable* D_f *supported on* $\{0,1\}^k \cup \{\mathsf{same}\}$ *that is independent of the randomness in* Enc, *and for any message* $z \in \{0,1\}^k$, *we have*

$$\Delta\left(\mathsf{Dec}(f(\mathsf{Enc}(z))); \mathrm{Copy}(D_f, z)\right) \leq \epsilon.$$

We refer to the parameter ϵ as the "error" of the non-malleable code.

We define the rate of a non-malleable code $\mathcal{C}$ to be the quantity $\frac{k}{n}$. We require split-state codes with special properties.

Leakage-Resilience: Alice and Bob perform the split-state tampering, but can communicate a bounded amount before tampering.

Augmented Split-State Non-malleability: There exists a simulator which can simulate the joint distribution of the left (or right) codeword states in addition to the outcome of non-malleability experiment.

Special Encoding: There exists a special encoding procedure that given a desired left (or right) codeword state and message, outputs a valid encoding of the message. Importantly, if the special encoder is given uniform left codeword states, its output is identically distributed to real encodings of the message.

Theorem 2.4 ([2,3,3,22]). *There is a constant $\gamma \in (0,1]$ such that, there exist efficient n^γ-leakage-resilient $\exp(-n^{\Omega(1)})$-augmented-split-state non-malleable codes with special encoding. Moreover, the codewords are length $(3+o(1))k$ where k is the message length.*

2.3   Seed-Extending Pseudorandom Generators

Definition 2.5 ([50]). *A function* $G : \{0,1\}^\ell \to \{0,1\}^n$ *is said to be an ϵ-pseudorandom generator (PRG) for a class $\mathcal{C}$, if for all $C \in \mathcal{C}$,*

$$\Delta(C(G(\mathcal{U}_\ell)); C(\mathcal{U}_n)) \leq \epsilon$$

A PRG, G, is said to be seed-extending *if the prefix of its output is its input, i.e. $G(s) = s, G'(s)$ for some function $G' : \{0,1\}^\ell \to \{0,1\}^{n-\ell}$.*

We are principally concerned with seed-extending PRGs against various types of circuits of a given size: non-deterministic circuits, non-deterministic NP-circuits, etc. Throughout this paper, we take a PRG for a class of circuits of size s to mean a $1/s$-PRG for that class of circuits. Note that because we are interested in both seed-extending PRGs, as well as PRGs for non-deterministic circuits, so-called "cryptographic" PRGs which can be easily evaluated by the classes they are constructed to fool do not suffice: a distinguisher given the seed, or nondeterminism, can easily determine if a string is in the PRG's image. Thankfully, as observed by Kinne et al. [50], Nisan and Wigderson's seminal construction yields a seed extending PRG, provided one starts with an appropriately hard function. We conclude with the formal theorem statement.

Theorem 2.6 ([7,46,50,51,61,62]). *If E requires exponential size circuits of type $X \in \{deterministic, nondeterministic, \mathsf{NP}, \Sigma_i\}$, then for every constant $c > 1$ there exists a constant $\alpha > 1$ such that for every sufficiently large n, and every r such that $\alpha \log n \leq \ell \leq n$ there is a seed-extending PRG, $\mathsf{G} : \{0,1\}^\ell \to \{0,1\}^n$, for size n^c circuits of type $X \in \{deterministic, nondeterministic, \mathsf{NP}, \Sigma_i\}$.*

Proposition 1. *Let X be a random variable and f a function. Define $Y = f(X)$. For any ϵ and any random variable Y',*

$$\Delta(X; (X|f(X) = Y')) = \Delta(Y; Y').$$

The proof of Proposition 1 can be found in the full version [16].

3   A Non-malleable Code for Small Circuit Tampering

Lemma 3.1. *For any polynomial $s(n)$, there exists a polynomial $s'(n) > s(n)$ such that the following is true. Let $\ell(n) = O(\log n)$ be the function from Theorem 1.6 for $\mathsf{G} : \{0,1\}^{\ell(n)} \to \{0,1\}^n$. If $\mathsf{alrssEnc} : \{0,1\}^{k'} \to \{0,1\}^{2n}, \mathsf{alrssDec} : \{0,1\}^{2n} \to \{0,1\}^{k'}$ is an augmented α-leakage-resilient split-state δ-non-malleable code with special encoding, computable in time $o(s(n))$, and $\mathsf{G} : \{0,1\}^{\ell(n)} \to \{0,1\}^n$ is a seed-extending PRG for nondeterministic circuits of size $O(s(n)^c)$ such that $\ell(n) \leq \alpha(n)$ and $\delta < (s'(n))^2/32$, then the construction, (E, D) in Fig. 3.1 is a $4/s'(n)$-alternate-non-malleable code for k'-bit messages with codeword length $O(n)$, resilient to $\mathsf{SIZE}[s(n)]$-tampering with error $4/s'(n)$.*

Instantiating the above lemma with the alrssEnc presented in Theorem 2.4, and with G given in Theorem 2.6, and using the fact that a $4/s'(n)$-alternate-non-malleable code for k'-bit messages is a $4/s'(n) + 2^{-k'}$-non-malleable code for k'-bit messages we obtain the following corollary:

Theorem 3.2. *If* E *requires exponential size nondeterministic circuits then for any polynomial $s(n)$, and for sufficiently large k, there exists a $1/s(n)$-non-malleable code for k-bit messages with codeword length $(1.5 + o(1))k$ that is resilient to* SIZE$[s(n)]$*-tampering.*

We note that rate 1 seems quite plausible in this setting.

Figure 3.1: Non-Malleable Code

Let (alrssEnc, alrssDec) be an augmented $\alpha(n)$-leakage-resilient δ-split-state non-malleable code with special encoding. Recall that special encoding means that there exists an efficient algorithm alrssEnc* that takes a pattern $p := y||*^n$ as input, in addition to the message m, and outputs alrssEnc$^*(m, p) = (y, X)$ with the property that (alrssEnc$^*(\cdot, \mathcal{U})$, alrssDec) is an augmented leakage-resilient split-state non-malleable code.
Let G be a PRG for nondeterministic circuits of size $O(s(n))$.

Encoding (E) : On input m, do the following
    Sample $s \leftarrow \mathcal{U}_\ell$. Sample $(\mathsf{G}(s), x) \leftarrow$ alrssEnc$^*(m; p = \mathsf{G}(s)||*^n)$.
    Output $\mathsf{E}(m) = (s, x)$.
Decoding (D) : On input $(\tilde{s}, \tilde{x})$, do the following
    Compute $\tilde{m} =$ alrssDec$(\mathsf{G}(\tilde{s}), \tilde{x})$.
    Output $\mathsf{D}(\tilde{s}, \tilde{x}) = \tilde{m}$.

Proof of Lemma 3.1. Let $\epsilon(n) = 4/s'(n)$ (the target error of our non-malleable code). Recall that $1/s'(n)$ is the advantage bound of the PRG, G. And (alrssEnc, alrssDec) is δ-non-malleable (with additional properties).

For the sake contradiction, assume (E, D) does not satisfy ϵ-alternate-non-malleability: namely, there exists $m_0, m_1 \in \{0,1\}^k$ and tampering function τ of size $s(n)$ such that

$$\mathrm{AltNM}_{m_0,m_1}^{\tau,\mathsf{E},\mathsf{D}}(0) \not\approx_{4/\epsilon} \mathrm{AltNM}_{m_0,m_1}^{\tau,\mathsf{E},\mathsf{D}}(1)$$

As before, we will use this fact (as well as the security of the underlying leakage-resilient augmented-split-state non-malleable code) to break the pseudorandomness guarantee of G by designing a constant-round private coin interactive proof that distinguishes with some non-trivial soundness/completeness gap.

Fix any $\tau : (s, x) \mapsto (\tilde{s}, \tilde{x})$ in SIZE$^{\Sigma_k}[s(n)]$. Define f to denote the function that computes $(s, x) \mapsto \tilde{x}$ according to τ, and g to denote the function that computes $(s, x) \mapsto \tilde{s}$ according to τ. In other words, $\tau(s, x) = (g(s, x), f(s, x))$.

Claim 3.1. There exists a set Π_Y such that

1. Π_Y is noticeably dense in G: $\Pr_{s \xleftarrow{u} \{0,1\}^\ell}[\mathsf{G}(s) \in \Pi_Y] \geq \epsilon/2$
2. When Merlin is honest, Arthur accepts $(s, y) \in \Pi_Y$ with prob. $> \frac{1+\epsilon/2}{2}$.

Figure 3.2: Interactive Proof for distinguishing G from uniform random

Recall that $(\mathsf{alrssEnc}, \mathsf{alrssDec})$ is an augmented leakage-resilient split-state non-malleable code with special encoding, $\mathsf{alrssEnc}^*$. Define $\mathsf{alrssEnc}_R^*$ to be the $\mathsf{alrssEnc}^*$ that just outputs the right state, i.e. if $\mathsf{alrssEnc}^*(m, p = y||*^n; r) \mapsto (y, x)$ then $\mathsf{alrssEnc}_R^* : (m, p = y||*^n; r) \mapsto x$. Recall that G is a PRG for nondeterministic circuits of size $O(s(n))$. Finally, recall that f, g correspond to the tampering attack.

Our protocol aims to accept strings from $\mathcal{U}_\ell, G(\mathcal{U}_\ell)$ when Merlin plays according to below (completeness) and reject strings from $\mathcal{U}_{\ell+n}$ regardless of the strategy Merlin utilizes (soundness). Because we can amplify by repetition, it suffices for there to be small gap between the two. Hardcoded into Arthur as non-uniform advice are f, g and m_0, m_1.

On input s, y:

Arthur Sample coin $b \leftarrow \mathcal{U}$. Sample encoding $(y, x) \leftarrow \mathsf{alrssEnc}^*(m_b, p = y||*^n)$. Send Merlin $\tilde{s} = g(s, x)$.

Merlin If $(s, y) = \mathsf{G}(s)$, respond $\tilde{y}$ such that $(\tilde{s}, \tilde{y}) = \mathsf{G}(\tilde{s})$. Otherwise, respond arbitrary $\tilde{y}$.

Arthur Set $z' = \mathsf{alrssDec}(\tilde{y}, \tilde{x})$ where $\tilde{x} = f(s, x)$. If $z' \in \{m_0, m_1\}$, set $z = \mathsf{same}$. Otherwise, set $z = z'$. Send z to Merlin.

Merlin (Guess Arthur's bit.) If

$$\Pr[\mathsf{alrssDec}(\tilde{y}, f(s, \mathsf{alrssEnc}_R^*(m_0, y))) = z | g(s, \mathsf{alrssEnc}_R^*(m_0, y)) = \tilde{s}]$$

is upper bounded by

$$\Pr[\mathsf{alrssDec}(\tilde{y}, f(s, \mathsf{alrssEnc}_R^*(m_1, y))) = z | g(s, \mathsf{alrssEnc}_R^*(m_1, y)) = \tilde{s}]$$

set $b' = 1$. Otherwise, set $b' = 0$. Respond b'.

Arthur Accept if $b = b'$, and reject otherwise.

Proof. If the protocol in Fig. 3.2 is given inputs from $\mathsf{G}(S) = (S, \mathsf{G}'(S))$ (where $S \equiv \mathcal{U}_\ell$), then upon choice of $b = 1$, Arthur's final message is that of the alternate-non-malleability game, $z \sim \mathrm{AltNM}_{m_0, m_1}^\tau(1)$. If $b = 0$, Arthur's final message is sampled according to $(z, \tilde{z}) \sim \mathrm{AltNM}_{m_0, m_1}^\tau(0)$. By our assumption, these two distributions are ϵ-far from each other. From this and a simple combinatorial argument (Proposition 4 in the full version [16]), there exists a set Π_Y s.t. for any $(s, y) \in \Pi_Y$ these distributions are $\epsilon/2$-far, and moreover $\Pr[\mathsf{G}(S) \in \Pi_Y] \geq \epsilon/2$. By a standard argument (Proposition 2 in the full version [16]), this means that for any $(s, y) \in \Pi_Y$ Merlin guesses b correctly and Arthur accepts with probability $\geq \frac{1+\epsilon/2}{2}$. $\square$

Claim 3.2. There exists a set Π_N such that

1. Π_N is large: $\Pr_{(s,y) \xleftarrow{u} \{0,1\}^{\ell+n}}[(s,y) \in \Pi_N] \geq 1 - 8\delta/\epsilon$
2. Arthur accepts inputs in Π_N with probability $\leq \frac{1+\epsilon/4}{2}$ when playing with any (cheating) Merlin (as prescribed in Fig. 3.2).

Proof. Soundness follows from first observing that any Merlin strategy corresponds to some α-leaky split-state tampering on the augmented-leakage resilient split state-code. We conclude soundness because Merlin's view is that of the alternate leakage-resilient augmented-split-state game. We use the existence an optimal strategy M^* (who, for any input (s,y), chooses messages to maximize the distance of his view when Arthur chooses $b = 0$ versus his view when Arthur chooses $b = 1$) to apply the Markov argument to a single distribution.

Fix an optimal Merlin strategy M^* as described and assume s, y are uniformly distributed. We make some observations about the protocol in this case:

Well-Formed Augmented Leakage-Resilient Split-State Encodings. Uniform $y \sim \mathcal{U}$ means our leakage-resilient augmented-split-state codewords are properly distributed, namely for $b = 0, 1$ it is the case that $\mathsf{alrssEnc}^*(m_b, p = \mathcal{U}||*^n) \equiv \mathsf{alrssEnc}(m_b)$. Moreover, s is independent of the split-state codeword (x, y) sampled by Arthur at the beginning.

ℓ-Leaky Split-State Tampering. Arthur's first message to Merlin, corresponding to the random variable $\tilde{s} = g(s, x)$, can be viewed as ℓ-bits of leakage from the right codeword state (to the left tampering function).

Thus, we have $\tilde{x} = f(s, x)$ and $\tilde{y} = M^*(s, y, g(s, x))$ which for any fixed choice of s is an ℓ-leaky split-state tampering, Π^s. Thus when s is random, Π^s is a distribution over ℓ-leaky split-state tampering functions.

Merlin's View is Identical to Augmented Alternate-Non-malleable Game. Recall that Merlin's view corresponds to the variables $(s, y, \tilde{s}, z) = \mathsf{View}^{M^*}(b)$, where b is Arthur's initial coin. Observe that $(y, \tilde{s}, z)$ is sampled identically to $\mathsf{AltANM}^{\Pi^s, \mathsf{alrssEnc}, \mathsf{alrssDec}}(b)$, where b is Arthur's initial coin toss. And s is independent of the initial encoding in the AltANM game, which has worst case guarantees that apply to Π^s for any choice of s.

Putting these observations together, we have by that, because ($\mathsf{alrssEnc}$, $\mathsf{alrssDec}$) is an ℓ-leakage-resilient δ-augmented-split-state non-malleable code, and since (see Lemma A.9 in the full version [16]) this implies that it is also a 2δ-augmented-split-state alternate non-malleable code, $\mathsf{View}^{M^*}(0) \approx_{2\delta} \mathsf{View}^{M^*}(1)$.

Observe that if there existed a strategy M' and input (s, y) such that the distance between the view of M' on $b = 0$ vs $b = 1$ was greater than that of M^*, this would contradict the optimality of M^*. Thus, by a simple Markov argument (Proposition 3 in the full version [16]) there exists a set, Π_N such that $\Pr_{(s,y) \xleftarrow{u} \{0,1\}^{\ell+n}}[(s,y) \in \Pi_N] \geq 1 - 8\delta/\epsilon$ and for each $(s,y) \in \Pi_N$ and any Merlin strategy M', the view when $b = 0$ is $\epsilon/4$-far from the view when $b = 1$. Thus by a standard argument (Proposition 2 in the full version [16]), this means for any $(s, y) \in \Pi_N$, any Merlin strategy outputs b' such that $b' = b$ with probability at most $\frac{1+\epsilon/4}{2}$. □

We conclude from Claim 3.1 and Claim 3.2, that there is a constant round IP protocol where Arthur can be represented by circuit of size $O(s(n))$ that recognizes $\Pi = (\Pi_Y, \Pi_N)$ with completeness/soundness gap $\epsilon/2$. By classical results (Lemma 2.21 in the full version [16]), this implies the existence of an $s'(n)$-size nondeterministic circuit, $\mathcal{C}$, that decides the promise problem, Π. Because Π_Y is $\epsilon/2$-dense under G (i.e. $\Pr_s[G(s) \in \Pi_Y]$) and Π_N is $1 - 8\delta/\epsilon$ dense under the uniform distribution (i.e. $\Pr_z[z \in \Pi_Y] \leq 4\delta/\epsilon$). The nondeterministic circuit $\mathcal{C}$ can distinguish with advantage $|\epsilon/2 - 8\delta/\epsilon| \geq \epsilon/4 = 1/s'(n)$. So, our initial assumption must be false. □

References

1. Aggarwal, D., Dodis, Y., Kazana, T., Obremski, M.: Non-malleable reductions and applications. In: Servedio, R.A., Rubinfeld, R. (eds.) Proceedings of the 47th Annual ACM Symposium on Theory of Computing, Portland, 14–17 June 2015, pp. 459–468. ACM Press (2015)
2. Aggarwal, D., Dodis, Y., Lovett, S.: Non-malleable codes from additive combinatorics. SIAM J. Comput. **47**(2), 524–546 (2018)
3. Aggarwal, D., Kanukurthi, B., Obbattu, S.L.B., Obremski, M., Sekar, S.: Rate one-third non-malleable codes. In: IACR Cryptology ePrint Archive, p. 1042 (2021)
4. Aggarwal, D., Obremski, M.: A constant rate non-malleable code in the split-state model. In: Proceedings of the 61st Annual Symposium on Foundations of Computer Science, Durham, 16–19 November 2020, pp. 1285–1294. IEEE Computer Society Press (2020)
5. Agrawal, S., Gupta, D., Maji, H.K., Pandey, O., Prabhakaran, M.: Explicit non-malleable codes against bit-wise tampering and permutations. In: Gennaro, R., Robshaw, M. (eds.) CRYPTO 2015. LNCS, vol. 9215, pp. 538–557. Springer, Heidelberg (2015). https://doi.org/10.1007/978-3-662-47989-6_26
6. Agrawal, S., Gupta, D., Maji, H.K., Pandey, O., Prabhakaran, M.: A rate-optimizing compiler for non-malleable codes against bit-wise tampering and permutations. In: Dodis, Y., Nielsen, J.B. (eds.) TCC 2015. LNCS, vol. 9014, pp. 375–397. Springer, Heidelberg (2015). https://doi.org/10.1007/978-3-662-46494-6_16
7. Applebaum, B., Artemenko, S., Shaltiel, R., Yang, G.: Incompressible functions, relative-error extractors, and the power of nondeterministic reductions. Comput. Complex. **25**(2), 349–418 (2016)
8. Babai, L.: Trading group theory for randomness. In: 17th Annual ACM Symposium on Theory of Computing, Providence, 6–8 May 1985, pp. 421–429. ACM Press (1985)
9. Babai, L., Moran, S.: Arthur-merlin games: a randomized proof system, and a hierarchy of complexity classes. J. Comput. Syst. Sci. **36**(2), 254–276 (1988)

10. Ball, M., Chattopadhyay, E., Liao, J.-J., Malkin, T., Tan, L.-Y.: Non-malleability against polynomial tampering. In: Micciancio, D., Ristenpart, T. (eds.) CRYPTO 2020. LNCS, vol. 12172, pp. 97–126. Springer, Cham (2020). https://doi.org/10.1007/978-3-030-56877-1_4

11. Ball, M., Dachman-Soled, D., Guo, S., Malkin, T., Tan, L.-Y.: Non-malleable codes for small-depth circuits. In: Thorup, M. (ed.) Proceedings of the 59th Annual Symposium on Foundations of Computer Science, Paris, 7–9 October 2018, pp. 826–837. IEEE Computer Society Press (2018)

12. Ball, M., Dachman-Soled, D., Kulkarni, M., Lin, H., Malkin, T.: Non-malleable codes against bounded polynomial time tampering. In: Ishai, Y., Rijmen, V. (eds.) EUROCRYPT 2019. LNCS, vol. 11476, pp. 501–530. Springer, Cham (2019). https://doi.org/10.1007/978-3-030-17653-2_17

13. Ball, M., Dachman-Soled, D., Kulkarni, M., Malkin, T.: Non-malleable codes for bounded depth, bounded fan-in circuits. In: Fischlin, M., Coron, J.-S. (eds.) EUROCRYPT 2016. LNCS, vol. 9666, pp. 881–908. Springer, Heidelberg (2016). https://doi.org/10.1007/978-3-662-49896-5_31

14. Ball, M., Dachman-Soled, D., Kulkarni, M., Malkin, T.: Non-malleable codes from average-case hardness: AC^0, decision trees, and streaming space-bounded tampering. In: Nielsen, J.B., Rijmen, V. (eds.) EUROCRYPT 2018. LNCS, vol. 10822, pp. 618–650. Springer, Cham (2018). https://doi.org/10.1007/978-3-319-78372-7_20

15. Ball, M., Dachman-Soled, D., Kulkarni, M., Malkin, T.: Limits to non-malleability. In: Vidick, T. (ed.) Proceedings of the ITCS 2020: 11th Innovations in Theoretical Computer Science Conference, Seattle, 12–14 January 2020, vol. 151, pp. 80:1–80:32. LIPIcs (2020)

16. Ball, M., Dachman-Soled, D., Loss, J.: (Nondeterministic) hardness vs. non-malleability. In: IACR Cryptology ePrint Archive, p. 70 (2022)

17. Ball, M., Guo, S., Wichs, D.: Non-malleable codes for decision trees. In: Boldyreva, A., Micciancio, D. (eds.) CRYPTO 2019. LNCS, vol. 11692, pp. 413–434. Springer, Cham (2019). https://doi.org/10.1007/978-3-030-26948-7_15

18. Barak, B., et al.: Leftover hash lemma, revisited. In: Rogaway, P. (ed.) CRYPTO 2011. LNCS, vol. 6841, pp. 1–20. Springer, Heidelberg (2011). https://doi.org/10.1007/978-3-642-22792-9_1

19. Barak, B., Ong, S.J., Vadhan, S.: Derandomization in cryptography. In: Boneh, D. (ed.) CRYPTO 2003. LNCS, vol. 2729, pp. 299–315. Springer, Heidelberg (2003). https://doi.org/10.1007/978-3-540-45146-4_18

20. Bellare, M., Goldreich, O., Petrank, E.: Uniform generation of NP-witnesses using an NP-oracle. Inf. Comput. **163**(2), 510–526 (2000)

21. Bitansky, N., Kalai, Y.T., Paneth, O.: Multi-collision resistance: a paradigm for keyless hash functions. In: Diakonikolas, I., Kempe, D., Henzinger, M. (eds.) Proceedings of the 50th Annual ACM Symposium on Theory of Computing, Los Angeles, 25–29 June 2018, pp. 671–684. ACM Press (2018)

22. Brian, G., Faonio, A., Obremski, M., Simkin, M., Venturi, D.: Non-malleable secret sharing against bounded joint-tampering attacks in the plain model. In: Micciancio, D., Ristenpart, T. (eds.) CRYPTO 2020. LNCS, vol. 12172, pp. 127–155. Springer, Cham (2020). https://doi.org/10.1007/978-3-030-56877-1_5

23. Chattopadhyay, E., Goyal, V., Li, X.: Non-malleable extractors and codes, with their many tampered extensions. In: Wichs, D., Mansour, Y. (eds.) Proceedings of the 48th Annual ACM Symposium on Theory of Computing, Cambridge, 18–21 June 2016, pp. 285–298. ACM Press (2018)

24. Chattopadhyay, E., Li, X.: Non-malleable codes and extractors for small-depth circuits, and affine functions. In: Hatami, H., McKenzie, P., King, V. (eds.) Proceedings of the 49th Annual ACM Symposium on Theory of Computing, Montreal, 19–23 June 2017, pp. 1171–1184. ACM Press (2017)

25. Chen, B., Chen, Y., Hostáková, K., Mukherjee, P.: Continuous space-bounded non-malleable codes from stronger proofs-of-space. In: Boldyreva, A., Micciancio, D. (eds.) CRYPTO 2019. LNCS, vol. 11692, pp. 467–495. Springer, Cham (2019). https://doi.org/10.1007/978-3-030-26948-7_17

26. Cheraghchi, M., Guruswami, V.: Capacity of non-malleable codes. In: Naor, M. (ed.) Proceedings of the ITCS 2014: 5th Conference on Innovations in Theoretical Computer Science, Princeton, 12–14 January 2014, pp. 155–168. Association for Computing Machinery (2014)

27. Cheraghchi, M., Guruswami, V.: Non-malleable coding against bit-wise and split-state tampering. In: Lindell, Y. (ed.) TCC 2014. LNCS, vol. 8349, pp. 440–464. Springer, Heidelberg (2014). https://doi.org/10.1007/978-3-642-54242-8_19

28. Dachman-Soled, D., Komargodski, I., Pass, R.: Non-malleable codes for bounded polynomial depth tampering. Cryptology ePrint Archive, Report 2020/776 (2020). https://eprint.iacr.org/2020/776

29. Dachman-Soled, D., Komargodski, I., Pass, R.: Non-malleable codes for bounded parallel-time tampering. In: Malkin, T., Peikert, C. (eds.) CRYPTO 2021. LNCS, vol. 12827, pp. 535–565. Springer, Cham (2021). https://doi.org/10.1007/978-3-030-84252-9_18

30. Dachman-Soled, D., Liu, F.-H., Shi, E., Zhou, H.-S.: Locally decodable and updatable non-malleable codes and their applications. In: Dodis, Y., Nielsen, J.B. (eds.) TCC 2015. LNCS, vol. 9014, pp. 427–450. Springer, Heidelberg (2015). https://doi.org/10.1007/978-3-662-46494-6_18

31. Dodis, Y., Yu, Yu.: Overcoming weak expectations. In: Sahai, A. (ed.) TCC 2013. LNCS, vol. 7785, pp. 1–22. Springer, Heidelberg (2013). https://doi.org/10.1007/978-3-642-36594-2_1

32. Drucker, A.: Nondeterministic direct product reductions and the success probability of SAT solvers. In: 54th Annual Symposium on Foundations of Computer Science, Berkeley, 26–29 October 2013, pp. 736–745. IEEE Computer Society Press (2013)

33. Dziembowski, S., Kazana, T., Obremski, M.: Non-malleable codes from two-source extractors. In: Canetti, R., Garay, J.A. (eds.) CRYPTO 2013. LNCS, vol. 8043, pp. 239–257. Springer, Heidelberg (2013). https://doi.org/10.1007/978-3-642-40084-1_14

34. Dziembowski, S., Pietrzak, K., Wichs, D.: Non-malleable codes. In: Yao, A.C.-C. (ed.) ICS 2010: 1st Innovations in Computer Science, Tsinghua University, Beijing, 5–7 January 2010, pp. 434–452. Tsinghua University Press (2010)

35. Dziembowski, S., Pietrzak, K., Wichs, D.: Non-malleable codes. J. ACM 65(4), 20:1-20:32 (2018)

36. Faust, S., Hostáková, K., Mukherjee, P., Venturi, D.: Non-malleable codes for space-bounded tampering. In: Katz, J., Shacham, H. (eds.) CRYPTO 2017. LNCS, vol. 10402, pp. 95–126. Springer, Cham (2017). https://doi.org/10.1007/978-3-319-63715-0_4

37. Faust, S., Mukherjee, P., Nielsen, J.B., Venturi, D.: Continuous non-malleable codes. In: Lindell, Y. (ed.) TCC 2014. LNCS, vol. 8349, pp. 465–488. Springer, Heidelberg (2014). https://doi.org/10.1007/978-3-642-54242-8_20

38. Faust, S., Mukherjee, P., Venturi, D., Wichs, D.: Efficient non-malleable codes and key-derivation for poly-size tampering circuits. In: Nguyen, P.Q., Oswald, E. (eds.) EUROCRYPT 2014. LNCS, vol. 8441, pp. 111–128. Springer, Heidelberg (2014). https://doi.org/10.1007/978-3-642-55220-5_7

39. Feige, U., Lund, C.: On the hardness of computing the permanent of random matrices. Comput. Complex. 6(2), 101–132 (1997)

40. Goldreich, O., Micali, S., Wigderson, A.: Proofs that yield nothing but their validity for all languages in NP have zero-knowledge proof systems. J. ACM 38(3), 691–729 (1991)

41. Goldreich, O., Wigderson, A.: Derandomization that is rarely wrong from short advice that is typically good. In: Rolim, J.D.P., Vadhan, S. (eds.) RANDOM 2002. LNCS, vol. 2483, pp. 209–223. Springer, Heidelberg (2002). https://doi.org/10.1007/3-540-45726-7_17

42. Goldwasser, S., Sipser, M.: Private coins versus public coins in interactive proof systems. In: 18th Annual ACM Symposium on Theory of Computing, Berkeley, 28–30 May 1986, pp. 59–68. ACM Press (1986)

43. Goyal, V., Kumar, A.: Non-malleable secret sharing. In: Diakonikolas, I., Kempe, D., Henzinger, M. (eds.) Proceedings of the 50th Annual ACM Symposium on Theory of Computing, Los Angeles, 25–29 June 2018, pp. 685–698. ACM Press (2018)

44. Goyal, V., Kumar, A.: Non-malleable secret sharing for general access structures. In: Shacham, H., Boldyreva, A. (eds.) CRYPTO 2018. LNCS, vol. 10991, pp. 501–530. Springer, Cham (2018). https://doi.org/10.1007/978-3-319-96884-1_17

45. Gutfreund, D., Shaltiel, R., Ta-Shma, A.: Uniform hardness versus randomness tradeoffs for Arthur-Merlin games. Comput. Complex. 12(3–4), 85–130 (2003)

46. Impagliazzo, R., Wigderson, A.: P = BPP if E requires exponential circuits: derandomizing the XOR lemma. In: 29th Annual ACM Symposium on Theory of Computing, El Paso, 4–6 May 1997, pp. 220–229. ACM Press (1997)

47. Jerrum, M., Valiant, L.G., Vazirani, V.V.: Random generation of combinatorial structures from a uniform distribution. Theor. Comput. Sci. 43, 169–188 (1986)

48. Kanukurthi, B., Obbattu, S.L.B., Sekar, S.: Four-state non-malleable codes with explicit constant rate. In: Kalai, Y., Reyzin, L. (eds.) TCC 2017. LNCS, vol. 10678, pp. 344–375. Springer, Cham (2017). https://doi.org/10.1007/978-3-319-70503-3_11

49. Kanukurthi, B., Obbattu, S.L.B., Sekar, S.: Non-malleable randomness encoders and their applications. In: Nielsen, J.B., Rijmen, V. (eds.) EUROCRYPT 2018. LNCS, vol. 10822, pp. 589–617. Springer, Cham (2018). https://doi.org/10.1007/978-3-319-78372-7_19

50. Kinne, J., van Melkebeek, D., Shaltiel, R.: Pseudorandom generators, typically-correct derandomization, and circuit lower bounds. Comput. Complex. 21(1), 3–61 (2012)

51. Klivans, A.R., van Melkebeek, D.: Graph nonisomorphism has subexponential size proofs unless the polynomial-time hierarchy collapses. SIAM J. Comput. 31(5), 1501–1526 (2002)

52. Levin, L.A.: Average case complete problems. SIAM J. Comput. 15(1), 285–286 (1986)

53. Li, F., Zuckerman, D.: Improved extractors for recognizable and algebraic sources. In: Achlioptas, D., Végh, L.A. (eds.) Approximation, Randomization, and Combinatorial Optimization. Algorithms and Techniques, APPROX/RANDOM 2019, 20–22 September 2019, Massachusetts Institute of Technology, Cambridge, volume 145 of LIPIcs, pp. 72:1–72:22. Schloss Dagstuhl - Leibniz-Zentrum für Informatik (2019)

54. Li, X.: Improved non-malleable extractors, non-malleable codes and independent source extractors. Electron. Colloq. Comput. Complex. **23**, 115 (2016)

55. Li, X.: Improved non-malleable extractors, non-malleable codes and independent source extractors. In Hatami, H., McKenzie, P., King, V. (eds.) Proceedings of the 49th Annual ACM Symposium on Theory of Computing, Montreal, 19–23 June 2017, pp. 1144–1156. ACM Press (2017)

56. Li, X.: Non-malleable extractors and non-malleable codes: partially optimal constructions. In: Proceedings of the 34th Computational Complexity Conference, CCC 2019, New Brunswick, 18–20 July 2019, pp. 28:1–28:49 (2019)

57. Liu, F.-H., Lysyanskaya, A.: Tamper and leakage resilience in the split-state model. In: Safavi-Naini, R., Canetti, R. (eds.) CRYPTO 2012. LNCS, vol. 7417, pp. 517–532. Springer, Heidelberg (2012). https://doi.org/10.1007/978-3-642-32009-5_30

58. Micali, S.: CS proofs (extended abstracts). In: 35th Annual Symposium on Foundations of Computer Science, Santa Fe, 20–22 November 1994, pp. 436–453. IEEE Computer Society Press (1994)

59. Miltersen, P.B., Vinodchandran, N.V.: Derandomizing Arthur-Merlin games using hitting sets. Comput. Complex. **14**(3), 256–279 (2005)

60. Shaltiel, R.: Weak derandomization of weak algorithms: explicit versions of Vao's lemma. Comput. Complex. **20**(1), 87–143 (2011)

61. Shaltiel, R., Umans, C.: Simple extractors for all min-entropies and a new pseudorandom generator. J. ACM **52**(2), 172–216 (2005)

62. Shaltiel, R., Umans, C.: Pseudorandomness for approximate counting and sampling. Comput. Complex. **15**(4), 298–341 (2006)

63. Shaltiel, R., Umans, C.: Low-end uniform hardness versus randomness tradeoffs for AM. SIAM J. Comput. **39**(3), 1006–1037 (2009)

64. Trevisan, L., Vadhan, S.P.: Extracting randomness from samplable distributions. In: 41st Annual Symposium on Foundations of Computer Science, Redondo Beach, 12–14 November 2000, pp. 32–42. IEEE Computer Society Press (2000)

Short Leakage Resilient and Non-malleable Secret Sharing Schemes

Nishanth Chandran[1], Bhavana Kanukurthi[2], Sai Lakshmi Bhavana Obbattu[1], and Sruthi Sekar[3(✉)]

[1] Microsoft Research, Bengaluru, India
nichandr@microsoft.com, oslbhavana@gmail.com
[2] Department of Computer Science and Automation, Indian Institute of Science, Bengaluru, India
bhavana@iisc.ac.in
[3] UC Berkeley, Berkeley, CA, USA
sruthi.sekar1@gmail.com

Abstract. Leakage resilient secret sharing (LRSS) allows a dealer to share a secret amongst n parties such that any authorized subset of the parties can recover the secret from their shares, while an adversary that obtains shares of any unauthorized subset of parties along with bounded leakage from the other shares learns no information about the secret. Non-malleable secret sharing (NMSS) provides a guarantee that even shares that are tampered by an adversary will reconstruct to either the original message or something independent of it.

The most important parameter of LRSS and NMSS schemes is the size of each share. For LRSS, in the *local leakage model* (i.e., when the leakage functions on each share are independent of each other and bounded), Srinivasan and Vasudevan (CRYPTO 2019), gave a scheme for threshold access structures with share size of approximately $(3 \cdot \text{message length} + \mu)$, where μ is the number of bits of leakage tolerated from every share. For the case of NMSS, the best known result (again due to the above work) has share size of $(11 \cdot \text{message length})$.

In this work, we build LRSS and NMSS schemes with much improved share size. Additionally, our LRSS scheme obtains optimal share and leakage size. In particular, we get the following results:

- We build an information-theoretic LRSS scheme for threshold access structures with a share size of $(\text{message length} + \mu)$.
- As an application of the above result, we obtain an NMSS with a share size of $(4 \cdot \text{message length})$. Further, for the special case of sharing random messages, we obtain a share size of $(2 \cdot \text{message length})$.

1 Introduction

Secret sharing schemes [Sha79, Bla79] are fundamental cryptographic primitives that allow a dealer to distribute its secret m amongst n parties in such a way that any authorized subset of parties can recover m from their

B. Kanukurthi—Research supported by Microsoft Research, India.
S. Sekar—This work was done while at Indian Institute of Science, Bangalore.

Y. Dodis and T. Shrimpton (Eds.): CRYPTO 2022, LNCS 13507, pp. 178–207, 2022.
https://doi.org/10.1007/978-3-031-15802-5_7

shares (*correctness*), and no unauthorized subset of parties get any information about m (*privacy*). For instance, in a t-out-of-n ($t \leq n$) threshold secret sharing scheme, any subset of t parties or more is an authorized set and can reconstruct the secret, while any subset of fewer than t parties is unauthorized. Secret sharing schemes have found several applications in literature, such as in multiparty computation [GMW87, BGW88, CCD88], leakage-resilient circuit compilers [ISW03, FRR+10, Rot12] and threshold cryptographic systems [DF89, Fra89, SDFY94]. An assumption that secret sharing schemes make is that the adversary, controlling an unauthorized set of parties, gets no information about the shares of the honest parties. However, a rich study on side-channel attacks called *leakage attacks* points to the fact that such an assumption is idealized and may not hold in practice. This has led to much work on *leakage resilient* cryptography [Koc96, BBR88, BBCM95, Riv97, DSS01, CDH+00, MR04, DP07, AGV09]. In the context of secret sharing, leakage attacks allow the adversary to additionally obtain some bounded leakage from the honest party shares, and such a leakage may help an adversary break privacy of the secret sharing.[1] To secure against such attacks, Dziembowski and Pietrzak [DP07] introduced the notion of leakage resilient secret sharing.

LEAKAGE RESILIENT/NON-MALLEABLE SECRET SHARING (LRSS/NMSS). Informally, an LRSS gives a guarantee that the adversary gets no information about the secret, given its shares from an unauthorized set, as well as leakage from the remaining honest shares. In particular, in the *local leakage model* [BDIR18, GK18, SV19, ADN+19], the adversary is allowed to make a non-adaptive query to obtain a complete unauthorized set of shares, along with independent (bounded) leakage on the remaining shares. Privacy is then required to hold against such an adversary. LRSS schemes tolerating local leakage have been shown to have applications to leakage-resilient MPC [BGK11, GIM+16, BDIR18, SV19], leakage-resilient non-malleable secret sharing [GK18, SV19, BS19], and more recently to zero knowledge PCPs [HVW21]. Non-malleable secret sharing (NMSS) was introduced by Goyal and Kumar in [GK18] and provides a guarantee that under a tampering attack by the adversary, the message recovered from the tampered shares will either be the same as the original message or will be independent of it.

SHARE SIZE OF LRSS/NMSS SCHEMES. The most important aspect of secret sharing schemes is their share size, which typically determines the efficiency of the application that relies on it. For example, in an application to MPC, the size of each share affects the overall communication complexity of the MPC protocol. For standard threshold secret sharing schemes, we know construc-

---

[1] In fact, Guruswami and Wooters [GW16] show that Shamir's secret sharing scheme over a field of characteristic 2 is completely insecure if the adversary gets $t-1$ shares and just one-bit of leakage from other shares. Further, Nielsen and Simkin [NS20] show that for larger characteristic fields and large n, Shamir's secret sharing scheme is not leakage resilient for threshold $t \leq cn/\log n$, for constant $0 < c < 1$.

tions [Sha79, LCG+19] with optimal share size (i.e., same as the message length). However, the picture is quite different in the presence of leakage and/or tampering. For a very special case,[2] Benhamouda, Degwekar, Ishai and Rabin [BDIR18] show that the Shamir secret sharing [Sha79] is leakage resilient and can leak upto $1/4$ th fraction of bits from each share.[3] The work of Aggarwal, Damgard, Nielsen, Obremski, Purwanto, Ribeiro and Simkin [ADN+19] constructs – as a stepping stone towards constructing an NMSS – an LRSS scheme; however, this scheme suffers a polynomial (in n) blowup in its share size and additionally obtains optimal leakage ($\approx ((1 - o(1))$message length)) only for the restricted case of constant number of parties. For the general case of arbitrary n and t, Srinivasan and Vasudevan [SV19] constructed an LRSS against the local leakage model with a share size of approximately ($3 \cdot$ message length $+ \mu$), to tolerate μ bits of leakage from each share. Most constructions of NMSS schemes implicitly require an LRSS and hence share size of LRSS schemes directly impact that of NMSS. The best known share size for an NMSS is ($11 \cdot$ message length), achieved by the construction of [SV19] (through the [BS19] compiler).

We remark here that obtaining LRSS/NMSS with short share size while simultaneously tolerating high leakage rate is an important problem noted in several works (e.g.: In [ADN+19], the authors state: *"It would be interesting to give constructions of leakage-resilient schemes (even in the non-adaptive setting) with an improved tradeoff between leakage rate and share length"*).

1.1   Our Results

In this work, we construct the first information-theoretic LRSS scheme for threshold access structures against the local leakage model, with a share size of (message length $+ \mu$), tolerating μ bits of leakage from each share. This result is obtained as a corollary of the following more general statement that we prove:

Result 1. *Given any secret sharing scheme[4] for general monotone access structure $\mathcal{A}$ with share size ℓ/R, where ℓ is the message length and $R \leq 1$, one can construct an LRSS for the same access structure $\mathcal{A}$, against the local leakage model allowing μ bits of leakage per share, with a share size of $\ell/R + \mu + o(\ell/R + \mu)$.*

---

[2] Where the underlying field is a large characteristic field, the number of parties n is large, the threshold t is at least $n - o(\log n)$, and the adversary can only obtain a constant number of full shares.

[3] In [BDIR18], under the same restrictions (on n, the field and the number of full shares allowed), Shamir secret sharing is also shown to allow constant bits of leakage per share, under threshold $t \leq \alpha n$, for $\alpha < 1$. The lower bound of [NS20, Section 4] mentioned in footnote 1 proves that this is the best possible trade-off from Shamir. However, for the LRSS scheme of [SV19] or ours, their lower bound allows for leakage almost as large as the size of a single share.

[4] We require the secret sharing to satisfy an additional property of "local uniformity", which requires every share to individually have (an almost) uniform distribution. We show later that such a property is already satisfied by many natural secret sharing schemes (e.g.: Shamir secret sharing).

Using our LRSS scheme from Result 1, along with the recent 1/3-rate non-malleable code of [AKO+22] in the [GK18] NMSS compiler, we obtain an NMSS with a share size of only (4 · message length). Additionally, we also formalize a natural restriction of NMSS schemes to uniformly random secrets, called non-malleable randomness sharing (NMRS), and show how to construct this with a share size of (2·message length). NMRS is useful in many practical applications of secret sharing that only require uniformly random secrets (e.g., when the secret to be shared and protected against malleability is an encryption key or a digital signature signing key, whose distribution is (typically) uniform). In particular, we show:

Result 2. *There exists a non-malleable secret sharing scheme against the independent tampering model for the threshold access structure, that achieves a share size of 4ℓ, for messages of length ℓ.*
There exists a non-malleable randomness sharing scheme against the independent tampering model for the threshold access structure that achieves a share size of 2ℓ, for messages of length ℓ.

1.2   Technical Overview

One of the initial ideas [ADN+19] to build an LRSS scheme against the local leakage model, was using linear invertible extractors in the following way: a) First, threshold secret share the message m into n shares $m_1, \cdots, m_n$; b) then invert each share m_i under an invertible extractor to get (w_i, s_i); c) Finally, the i-th share contains w_i and all s_j's except for $j = i$. This scheme, even when instantiated with the best known linear extractors, has a share size of $((n-1) \cdot$ message length $+ |w_i|)$, which will not be optimal (even for a constant number of parties). This is because this construction mandates the size of the seeds s_j's to be as long as the message m in order to get a negligible leakage error. Furthermore, this scheme allows a leakage of size $((1 - o(1)) \cdot$ message length$)$ only for a constant number of parties.

In a subsequent work of [SV19], the authors once again rely on the use of randomness extractors, but use a single seed s, across all the shares to get a rate improvement. In particular, they do the following: a) First m is threshold secret shared into $m_1, \cdots, m_n$ (referred to as "simple shares") using a threshold secret sharing scheme b) Next, each m_i is masked using an extractor output $\mathsf{Ext}(w_i, s)$ where s and w_i's are uniformly chosen. Now, let $sh_1, \cdots, sh_n$ denote these masked shares c) r is uniformly chosen to additionally mask each sh_i d) Finally, r and s are together secret shared using a 2-out-of-n secret sharing scheme into shares $(a_1, \cdots, a_n)$ and the ith share of the scheme is then set to be $(w_i, sh_i \oplus r, a_i)$. At a high level, m_i was "doubly masked" in order to cast the leakage on the ith share as leakage on the extractor source w_i. In order to add leakage resilience on top of the simple shares, they needed to be masked twice, and thus, information of both these masks and the masked value (each roughly of size $|m_i|$) is given as part of the final share, resulting in its length being approximately $3|m_i|$, and hence, giving a rate of 1/3.

In our construction, we try to combine the best things from these two constructions, i.e., use of the invertibility of linear extractors with great parameters, and the use of a single seed across all shares to optimize the share size. Our techniques use linear extractors in such a way that we not only remove the dependence of the share size on the number of parties (which in itself is important), but also obtain an optimal rate of 1 while still allowing a leakage of size $((1 - o(1)) \cdot$ message length). We now proceed to describe our approach.

A SIMPLER PROBLEM. Our goal is to compile simple shares m_i into leakage resilient shares in a share size-preserving manner (i.e., the size of the leakage resilient share needs to be about the same as $|m_i|$). As a first step, we relax the problem in two ways a) consider an LRSS only for the (n, n) access structure (i.e., where the set of all n parties is the only authorized set); and b) require that the sharing scheme only works for uniformly random messages.

We first construct an LRSS scheme with the desired share size of message length $+ \mu$, under these two relaxations. For this, we choose extractor sources $w_1, \cdots, w_n$ and a seed s uniformly, secret share s as $(s_1, \cdots, s_n)$ and define $share_i$ to be (w_i, s_i). Now, define reconstruction of $share_i$'s as $m = \oplus_{i \in [n]} \mathsf{Ext}(w_i; s)$, where s is obtained by reconstructing s_i's. Now, first observe that, by extractor security, the reconstructed value m has (almost) uniform distribution. Also, each share supports local leakage resilience as s_i (a share) is devoid of information about s and hence any bounded leakage of the form $f(w_i, s_i)$ is only dependent on w_i and is (almost) independent of the extractor output and hence m too. This scheme infact has a share size of $|m| + \mu$ (for μ bits of leakage per share) as there are explicit extractor constructions with good parameters such that $|s| \ll |w_i| \approx |\mathsf{Ext}(w_i, s)|$.

FINAL CONSTRUCTION OVERVIEW. Unfortunately, the above construction does not extend to either support threshold access structures or for secret sharing a specific message m. In order to reconstruct to a message m, the extractor outputs $\mathsf{Ext}(w_i, s)$'s $(i \in [n])$ would have to be correlated. However, the fact that the extractor outputs $\mathsf{Ext}(w_i, s)$ are uncorrelated is what gives leakage resilience in the scheme above for sharing random messages. The main technical hurdle which we overcome in this work is to ensure correlation in the shares while retaining enough independence (via extractors) so that we can argue leakage resilience.

In our construction, we first generate simple shares of m, denoted $(m_1, \cdots, m_n)$ using a standard secret sharing scheme. Next, we aim to cast each of these simple shares m_i as an extractor output. This, however, has two challenges a) the distribution of m_i could be arbitrary and need not have any entropy; and b) it is not clear how to express m_i's as the output of an extractor. To address (a), we observe that many natural secret sharing schemes (for example, the Shamir secret sharing scheme) satisfy the property that each share individually has (an almost) uniform distribution. We formalize this property as "local uniformity" of a secret sharing scheme and generate simple shares of m using such a locally uniform secret sharing scheme. To solve the challenge (b), we make use of seeded extractors that are linear functions - i.e., where the extractor function is guaranteed to be a linear map (over the source) for any fixed value of the seed, called linear seeded extractors [Tre99, Tre01, RRV02]. We show that such extractors provide an efficient way to find an (entropic sample of an) extractor source such that the extractor output on this source takes a given value under a given seed. With this useful property, each of our simple shares can indeed be expressed as extractor outputs.[5]

To summarize our construction, we a) secret share m into simple shares $m_1, \cdots, m_n$ using any locally uniform secret sharing scheme for the given general access structure; b) choose a seed s uniformly and generate its shares $s_1, \cdots, s_n$ such that s can be reconstructed from any two shares s_i and s_j; c) for each m_i, sample w_i such that $\mathsf{Ext}(w_i, s) = m_i$; d) Finally, each share is set to be (w_i, s_i) for all $i \in [n]$. Leakage resilience of this scheme follows from a careful argument using extractor security and local uniformity. In this scheme, the length of each share (w_i, s_i) is only negligibly larger than the length of m_i as there are explicit constructions of linear extractors that extract out almost all the entropy from the source while only using very short seeds.

NON-MALLEABLE RANDOMNESS SHARING. We obtain a non-malleable secret sharing (NMSS) scheme with a share size of 4(message length) by instantiating the NMSS compiler from [GK18] with our rate-1 LRSS scheme, along with the recent rate-1/3 NMC from [AKO+22]. Hence, our focus in the main section will be in formalizing and building the NMRS scheme with a share size of 2(message length). Our NMRS construction follows the same blueprint as [GK18], but uses a non-malleable randomness encoder (NMRE) (instead of using a non-malleable code) and our LRSS scheme with rate 1. NMREs [KOS18], outputs a random message along with its encoding L, R, with the guarantee that whenever an adversary tampers L, R (in a split-state manner, i.e., tamper L and R independent of each other), the original message looks uniformly random, even given this tampered message. Now, our NMRS construction outputs the random message m output by the NMRE, and to generate its shares: first secret share L using our LRSS scheme for the 2-out-of-n threshold setting and then share R using a t-out-of-n threshold secret sharing scheme.

1.3   Related Work

The problems of leakage resilient and non-malleable secret sharing has seen much research in recent times [DDV10, LL12, BDIR18, GK18, BS19, SV19, ADN+19], [FV19, BFV19, KMS19, LCG+19, CGG+20, BFO+20, CKOS21, MPSW21, MNP+21]. In the information -theoretic setting, majority of these works focus on improving the leakage model, such as allowing the adversary to obtain adaptive (leakage queries dependent on prior leakage responses) and joint (combined leakage from

---

[5] A similar technique of using linear and invertible extractors to get rate optimality has been used in two prior settings before: information-theoretic privacy of communication data in the wiretap channel setting in [BT12, CDS12] and binary secret sharing schemes in [LCG+19].

multiple shares) leakages, and such strong leakage models come at the expense of poor and sub-optimal share size (typically $\omega(\text{message length})$). For the case where the adversary is restricted to be computationally bounded, the works of [BFO+20, FV19] show NMSS and LRSS schemes achieving optimal rate for strong adaptive and joint leakage and tampering models.

1.4   Organization of the Paper

We give the preliminary definitions and lemmata in Sect. 2. Then, we build our leakage resilient secret sharing scheme in Sect. 3. Finally, we define and build our non-malleable randomness sharing scheme in Sect. 4.

2   Preliminaries

2.1   Notation

We begin by describing a few notations that we use. For any two sets S and S', $S \backslash S'$ denotes the set of elements that are present in S, but not in S'. For any natural number n, $[n]$ denotes the set $\{1, 2, \cdots, n\}$. $x \leftarrow X$ denotes sampling from a probability distribution X. $x\|y$ represents concatenation of two binary strings x and y. $|x|$ denotes length of binary string x. U_l denotes the uniform distribution on $\{0, 1\}^l$. All logarithms are base 2. If S is a subset of $[n]$ and $x_1, .., x_n$ are some variables or elements, then x_S denotes the set $\{x_i \text{ such that } i \in S\}$. $\chi(a = b)$ indicates equality of the strings a and b (i.e. $\chi(a = b) = 1$ is an only if a is equal to b). In this paper we assume natural one-to-one correspondence between the set $\{0, 1\}^n$ and the field $GF(2^n)$.

We now give the standard definitions of statistical distance and entropy along with some preliminary lemmata of the same.

2.2   Statistical Distance and Entropy - Definitions and Lemmata

Statistical Distance. Let X_1, X_2 be two probability distributions over some set S. Their *statistical distance* is

$$\mathbf{SD}\,(X_1, X_2) \overset{\text{def}}{=} \max_{T \subseteq S}\{\Pr[X_1 \in T] - \Pr[X_2 \in T]\} = \frac{1}{2}\sum_{s \in S}\left|\Pr_{X_1}[s] - \Pr_{X_2}[s]\right|$$

(they are said to be ε-*close* if $\mathbf{SD}\,(X_1, X_2) \leq \varepsilon$ and denoted by $X_1 \approx_\varepsilon X_2$). For an event E, $\mathbf{SD}_E(A; B)$ denotes $\mathbf{SD}\,(A|E; B|E)$.

Entropy. The *min-entropy* of a random variable W is $\mathbf{H}_\infty(W) = -\log(\max_w \Pr[W = w])$.
For a joint distribution (W, Z), following [DORS08], we define the *(average) conditional min-entropy* of W given Z as

$$\widetilde{\mathbf{H}}_\infty(W \mid Z) = -\log(\underset{z \leftarrow Z}{\mathbf{E}}(2^{-\log(\max_w \Pr[W=w|Z=z])}))$$

(here the expectation is taken over z for which $\Pr[Z = z]$ is nonzero).
For any two random variable W, Z, $(W|Z)$ is said to be an (n, t')-average source if W is over $\{0,1\}^n$ and $\widetilde{\mathbf{H}}_\infty(W|Z) \geq t'$.
We require some basic properties of entropy and statistical distance, which are given by the following lemmata and propositions.

Lemma 1. *[DORS08] Let A, B, C be random variables. If B has at most 2^λ possible values, then*

$$\widetilde{\mathbf{H}}_\infty(A \mid B) \geq \mathbf{H}_\infty(A, B) - \lambda \geq \mathbf{H}_\infty(A) - \lambda$$

and, more generally, $\widetilde{\mathbf{H}}_\infty(A \mid B, C) \geq \widetilde{\mathbf{H}}_\infty(A, B \mid C) - \lambda \geq \widetilde{\mathbf{H}}_\infty(A \mid C) - \lambda$.

Proposition 1. *For any three random variables A, B and C, $\widetilde{\mathbf{H}}_\infty(A|B) \geq \widetilde{\mathbf{H}}_\infty(A|B, C)$.*

Proof. Let A, B, C be random variables over $\mathcal{A}, \mathcal{B}, \mathcal{C}$. Then,

$$\widetilde{\mathbf{H}}_\infty(A|B) = -\log(\underset{b \leftarrow B}{\mathbf{E}}(2^{-\mathbf{H}_\infty(A|B=b)}))$$

$$= -\log \sum_{b \in \mathcal{B}} \max_{a \in \mathcal{A}} \Pr[A = a, B = b]$$

$$= -\log \sum_{b \in \mathcal{B}} \max_{a \in \mathcal{A}} \sum_{c \in \mathcal{C}} \Pr[A = a, B = b, C = c]$$

Similarly,

$$\widetilde{\mathbf{H}}_\infty(A|B, C) = -\log \sum_{b \in \mathcal{B}} \sum_{c \in \mathcal{C}} \max_{a \in \mathcal{A}} \Pr[A = a, B = b, C = c]$$

The proposition follows from the observation that for any $b \in \mathcal{B}$,

$$\sum_{c \in \mathcal{C}} \max_{a \in \mathcal{A}} \Pr[A = a, B = b, C = c] \geq \max_{a \in \mathcal{A}} \sum_{c \in \mathcal{C}} \Pr[A = a, B = b, C = c]$$

Lemma 2. *[Vad12] For any random variables A, B, if $A \approx_\epsilon B$, then for any function f, $f(A) \approx_\epsilon f(B)$.*

2.3   Randomness Extractors

Extractors (introduced by Nissan and Zuckerman [NZ96]) output an almost uniform string from a (η, τ)-entropic source, using a short uniform string, called *seed*, as a catalyst. Average-case extractors are extractors whose output remains close to uniform, even given the seed and some auxiliary information about the source (but independent of the seed), whenever the source has enough average entropy given the auxiliary information. We formally define them as below.

Definition 1. *[DORS08] Let* $\mathsf{Ext} : \{0,1\}^\eta \times \{0,1\}^d \to \{0,1\}^l$ *be a polynomial time computable function. We say that* Ext *is an* **efficient average-case** $(\eta, \tau, d, l, \epsilon)$**-strong extractor** *if for all pairs of random variables* (W, Z) *such that* W *is a random variable over* η-*bit strings satisfying* $\tilde{\mathbf{H}}_\infty(W|Z) \geq \tau$, *we have*

$$\mathsf{Ext}(W; U_d), U_d, Z \approx_\epsilon U_l, U_d, Z$$

LINEAR EXTRACTORS. *Further, the average-case strong extractor* Ext *is said to be linear if for every* $s \in \{0,1\}^d$, $\mathsf{Ext}(\cdot, s)$ *is a linear function.*

In this paper, we instantiate linear extractors with extractors due to Raz et al. [RRV02], which extracts almost all the randomness and is an improvement of Trevisan's extractor [Tre99]. Particularly, we use the following instantiation of the same given in [LCG+19].

Lemma 3. *[LCG+19, Lemma 6] There is an explicit* $(\eta, \tau, d, l, \epsilon)$-*strong linear extractor with* $d = \mathcal{O}(\log^3(\frac{\eta}{\epsilon}))$ *and* $l = \tau - \mathcal{O}(d)$.

In our application of linear extractors we will often require to uniformly sample an extractor source such that the extractor output on this source and a given seed s takes a given value y. Basically, given a seed s and some $y \in \{0,1\}^l$, the inverting function needs to sample an element uniformly from the set $\mathsf{Ext}(\cdot, s)^{-1}(y)$ (which is $\{w : \mathsf{Ext}(w; s) = y\}$). We formalize this procedure[6] as InvExt and show that linear extractors allow such sampling in the following lemma.

Lemma 4. *For every efficient linear extractor* Ext, *there exists an efficient randomized function* $\mathsf{InvExt} : \{0,1\}^l \times \{0,1\}^d \to \{0,1\}^\eta \cup \{\bot\}$ *(termed inverter) such that*

1. $U_\eta, U_d, \mathsf{Ext}(U_\eta; U_d) \equiv \mathsf{InvExt}(\mathsf{Ext}(U_\eta; U_d), U_d), U_d, \mathsf{Ext}(U_\eta; U_d)$
2. *For each* $(s, y) \in \{0,1\}^d \times \{0,1\}^l$,
    (a) $\Pr[\mathsf{InvExt}(y, s) = \bot] = 1$, *if and only if there exists no* $w \in \{0,1\}^\eta$ *such that* $\mathsf{Ext}(w; s) = y$.
    (b) $\Pr[\mathsf{Ext}(\mathsf{InvExt}(y, s); s) = y] = 1$, *if there exists some* $w \in \{0,1\}^\eta$ *such that* $\mathsf{Ext}(w; s) = y$.

Proof. Recall that for a linear extractor, for any seed $s \in \{0,1\}^d$, $\mathsf{Ext}(\cdot, s)$ is a linear map from the vector space $\{0,1\}^\eta$ to the vector space $\{0,1\}^l$. Let $\mathcal{I}_s$ and $\mathcal{K}_s$ denote the image and kernel of this linear map $\mathsf{Ext}(\cdot, s)$. We now define InvExt as follows. Fix any arbitrary input y, s to InvExt. $\mathsf{InvExt}(y, s)$:

– If $y \in \mathcal{I}_s$

---

[6] In literature, invertible (seeded) extractors (see [CDS12] for an exposition on the same) are well-studied which allow efficient sampling of a source w and a seed s such that the extractor output on w and s equals a given value y. Note that our requirement to sample a source w given a seed s and a value y is stronger than the guarantee provided by invertible extractors. Hence we explicitly show that certain extractors allow such sampling.

- Let w be such that $\mathsf{Ext}(w; s) = y$
- Sample z uniformly from $\mathcal{K}_s$
- Output $w + z$

Else output $\perp$

InvExt is efficient because the bases for the linear sub-spaces $\mathcal{K}_s$, $\mathcal{I}_s$ and the preimage space on the value y (corresponding to the linear map $\mathsf{Ext}(\cdot, s)$) can be determined efficiently. By the definition, it is easy to see that InvExt satisfies property (2) of the Lemma statement. We now proceed to prove property (1) about statistical distance. Consider the set $\mathcal{S} = \{(w, s, y) : \mathsf{Ext}(w; s) = y\}$. For any $(w, s, y) \in \mathcal{S}$,

$$\Pr[(\mathsf{InvExt}(\mathsf{Ext}(U_\eta; U_d), U_d), U_d, \mathsf{Ext}(U_\eta; U_d)) = (w, s, y)]$$
$$= \sum_{w' \in \{0,1\}^\eta} \Pr[U_\eta = w', U_d = s] \cdot \Pr[\mathsf{InvExt}(y, s) = w] \cdot \chi(\mathsf{Ext}(w'; s) = y)$$

Since $\mathsf{Ext}(w; s) = y$ by definition of $\mathcal{S}$, we know that w lies in the set of $|\mathcal{K}_s|$ elements from which $\mathsf{InvExt}(y, s)$ chooses its output uniformly. Therefore $\Pr[\mathsf{InvExt}(y, s) = w] = \frac{1}{|\mathcal{K}_s|}$. Further, since $\mathsf{Ext}(\cdot; s)$ is a linear map and $y \in \mathcal{I}_s$, we know that there are exactly $|\mathcal{K}_s|$ number of values $w' \in \{0, 1\}^\eta$ such that $\mathsf{Ext}(w'; s) = y$. With these observations, we conclude that

$$\Pr[(\mathsf{InvExt}(\mathsf{Ext}(U_\eta; U_d), U_d), U_d, \mathsf{Ext}(U_\eta; U_d)) = (w, s, y)] = \frac{1}{2^{\eta+d}}$$

Also for any $(w, s, y) \in \mathcal{S}$, $\Pr[(U_\eta, U_d, \mathsf{Ext}(U_\eta; U_d)) = (w, s, y)] = \frac{1}{2^{\eta+d}}$. For any $(w, s, y) \notin \mathcal{S}$, it holds that $\mathsf{Ext}(w; s) \neq y$. With this we have

$$Pr[(U_\eta, U_d, \mathsf{Ext}(U_\eta; U_d)) = (w, s, y)] = 0$$

and

$$\Pr[(\mathsf{InvExt}(\mathsf{Ext}(U_\eta; U_d), U_d), U_d, \mathsf{Ext}(U_\eta; U_d)) = (w, s, y)] = 0$$

The last equation is true because a) if $y \in \mathcal{I}_s$, then $\Pr[\mathsf{InvExt}(y, s) = w] = 0$ b) if $y \notin \mathcal{I}_s$, then $\Pr[(U_d, \mathsf{Ext}(U_\eta; U_d)) = (s, y)] = 0$. Further note that $\Pr[\mathsf{InvExt}(\mathsf{Ext}(U_\eta; U_d), U_d) = \perp] = 0$ as $\mathsf{Ext}(U_\eta; U_d) \in \mathcal{I}_{U_d}$ with probability 1. Combining these observations, it follows that the statistical distance between the distributions $(\mathsf{InvExt}(\mathsf{Ext}(U_\eta; U_d), U_d), U_d, \mathsf{Ext}(U_\eta; U_d))$ and $(U_\eta, U_d, \mathsf{Ext}(U_\eta; U_d))$ is zero, which concludes the proof.

2.4   Secret Sharing Schemes

Secret sharing schemes provide a mechanism to distribute a secret into shares such that only an authorized subset of shares can reconstruct the secret and any unauthorized subset of shares has "almost" no information about the secret. We now define secret sharing schemes formally.

Definition 2. *Let* $[n]$ *be a set of identities (indices) of* n *parties. A sharing function* Share : $\{0,1\}^l \to (\{0,1\}^{l'})^n$ *is an* $(n, \mathcal{A})$ - ***secret sharing scheme*** *that is* ϵ_s-*private with respect to a monotone access structure[7]* $\mathcal{A}$ *if the following two properties hold:*

1. ***Correctness:*** *The secret can be reconstructed by any set of parties that are part of the access structure* $\mathcal{A}$. *That is, for any set* $T \in \mathcal{A}$, *there exists a deterministic reconstruction function* Rec : $(\{0,1\}^{l'})^{|T|} \to \{0,1\}^l$ *such that for every* $m \in \mathcal{M}$,
$$\Pr[\mathsf{Rec}(\mathsf{Share}(m)_T) = m] = 1$$
   where the probability is over the randomness of the Share *function and if* $(sh_1, .., sh_n) \leftarrow \mathsf{Share}(m)$, *then* $\mathsf{Share}(m)_T$ *denotes* $\{sh_i\}_{i \in T}$. *We will slightly abuse the notation and denote* Rec *as the reconstruction procedure that takes in* $T \in \mathcal{A}$ *and* $\mathsf{Share}(m)_T$ *as input and outputs the secret.*

2. ***Statistical Privacy:*** *Any collusion of parties not part of the access structure should have "almost" no information about the underlying secret. More formally, for any unauthorized set* $U \notin \mathcal{A}$, *and for every pair of secrets* $m, m' \in \{0,1\}^l$,
$$\Delta((\mathsf{Share}(m))_U; (\mathsf{Share}(m'))_U) \le \epsilon_s$$

(Share, Rec) *is said to be perfectly private if* $\epsilon_s = 0$. *An access structure* $\mathcal{A}$ *is said to be* (n, t)-*threshold if and only if* $\mathcal{A}$ *contains all subsets of* $[n]$ *of size atleast* t.

Rate *of a secret sharing scheme is defined as* $\frac{\text{message size}}{\text{share size}}$ *(which would be equal to* l/l').

LEAKAGE RESILIENCE. *A secret sharing scheme* (Share, Rec) *is said to be* ϵ_{lr}-*leakage resilient against a leakage function family* $\mathcal{F}$ *if for all messages* $m, m' \in \{0,1\}^l$ *and every function* $f \in \mathcal{F}$,
$$f((\mathsf{Share}(m))_{[n]}) \approx_{\epsilon_{lr}} f((\mathsf{Share}(m'))_{[n]})$$

We use secret sharing schemes augmented with the following property as a building block to our leakage resilient secret sharing scheme.

LOCAL UNIFORMITY. We say a secret sharing scheme (Share, Rec) satisfies *local uniformity* if the distribution of each individual share given out by the Share function is ϵ_u-statistically close to the uniform distribution in its share space. Formally, any sharing function Share : $\{0,1\}^l \to \{\{0,1\}^{l'}\}^n$ is ϵ_u-locally uniform if for each message $m \in \{0,1\}^l$ it holds that
$$\mathsf{Share}(m)_{\{i\}} \approx_{\epsilon_u} U_{l'}, \ \forall \ i \in [n]$$

---

[7] $\mathcal{A}$ is a monotone access structure if for all A, B such that $A \subset B \subseteq [n]$ and $A \in \mathcal{A}$, it holds that $B \in \mathcal{A}$. Throughout this paper whenever we consider a general access structure, we mean a monotone access structure.

Note that Shamir secret sharing scheme [Sha79, Bla79] and Benaloh-Leichter secret sharing scheme [BL88] are instantiations of a locally uniform secret sharing schemes for threshold access structures and general monotone access structures respectively.[8]

CONSISTENT RESAMPLING. For any $(n, \mathcal{A})$-secret sharing scheme (Share, Rec) which is ϵ_s-private, and for any message m and a subset $\mathcal{L} \subseteq [n]$, when we say "$(sh_1, .., sh_n) \leftarrow \text{Share}(m|sh_{\mathcal{L}}^*)$" we mean the following procedure:

- Sample and output $(sh_1, .., sh_n)$ uniformly from the distribution Share(m) conditioned on the event that $sh_{\mathcal{L}} = sh_{\mathcal{L}}^*$.
- If the above event is a zero probability event then output a string of all zeroes (of appropriate length).

Note that for any $\mathcal{L} \subseteq [n]$, the distributions Share(m) and Share$(m|sh_{\mathcal{L}}^*)$ are identical when $(sh_1^*, \cdots, sh_n^*) \leftarrow \text{Share}(m)$.

3 Leakage Resilient Secret Sharing Schemes

3.1 Local Leakage Family

The local leakage family allows bounded leakage queries $\{f_i : \{0,1\}^{l'} \rightarrow \{0,1\}^{\mu}\}_{i \in \mathcal{K}}$, on each share corresponding to an arbitrary set of indices $\mathcal{K}(\subseteq [n])$, and further allows full share queries corresponding to an unauthorised subset $\mathcal{U}$. Formally, for any access structure $\mathcal{A}$ and leakage amount $\mu > 0$, we define this family as

$$\mathcal{F}_{\mathcal{A},\mu} = \{(\mathcal{U}, \mathcal{K}, \{f_i\}_{i \in \mathcal{K}}) : \mathcal{U} \notin \mathcal{A}, \mathcal{K} \subseteq [n] \text{ and } \forall\ i \in \mathcal{K}, f_i : \{0,1\}^{l'} \rightarrow \{0,1\}^{\mu}\}$$

where for any secret sharing scheme (Share, Rec), the leakage response corresponding to a leakage query $(\mathcal{U}, \mathcal{K}, \{f_i\}_{i \in \mathcal{K}}) \in \mathcal{F}_{\mathcal{A},\mu}$ on any secret m is $(sh_{\mathcal{U}}, \{f_i(sh_i)\}_{i \in \mathcal{K}})$ when $(sh_1, \cdots, sh_n) \leftarrow \text{Share}(m)$.

Remark 1. Consider a leakage family which is the set of all functions $(\mathcal{U}, \mathcal{K}, \{f_i\}_{i \in \mathcal{K}}) \in \mathcal{F}_{\mathcal{A},\mu}$ such that $\mathcal{U} \cap \mathcal{K} = \phi$. Intuitively, this is the leakage query which doesn't ask to reveal a full share and also query bounded leakage on the same share. Though this may seem like a restriction on $\mathcal{F}_{\mathcal{A},\mu}$, we would like to emphasize that leakage resilience against this weaker family guarantees leakage resilience against $\mathcal{F}_{\mathcal{A},\mu}$ itself. This is because leakage response to any function $(\mathcal{U}, \mathcal{K}, \{f_i\}_{i \in \mathcal{K}}) \in \mathcal{F}_{\mathcal{A},\mu}$ can be simulated from leakage response to $(\mathcal{U}, \mathcal{K} \backslash \mathcal{U}, \{f_i\}_{i \in \mathcal{K} \backslash \mathcal{U}}) \in \mathcal{F}_{\mathcal{A},\mu}$, as $\{f_i(sh_i)\}_{i \in \mathcal{K} \cap \mathcal{U}}$ can be trivially computed given $sh_{\mathcal{U}}$(which is part of the leakage response to $(\mathcal{U}, \mathcal{K} \backslash \mathcal{U}, \{f_i\}_{i \in \mathcal{K} \backslash \mathcal{U}})$).

---

[8] This is formally proven in [CKOS21, Claim 2].

3.2 Construction

Building Blocks

- (MShare, MRec) be any ϵ_p-private and ϵ_u-locally uniform secret sharing scheme for the message space $\{0,1\}^l$ and a monotone access structure $(n, \mathcal{A})$. Let l' denote the share size of MShare (that is MShare : $\{0,1\}^l \rightarrow (\{0,1\}^{l'})^n$).
- (SdShare, SdRec) be any ϵ'_p-private secret sharing scheme for the message space $\{0,1\}^d$ and against the $(n, 2)$-threshold access structure with share length d'.
- Ext be an $(\eta, \tau, d, l', \epsilon_{ext})$-strong linear extractor. InvExt be the inverter function corresponding to Ext given by Lemma 4.

Construction Overview

We now build our LRSS scheme. Informally, to share a message m, we first share it using MShare to get $m_1, \cdots, m_n$, pick a random extractor seed s and then use InvExt to get the source w_i corresponding to the extractor output m_i and seed s, for each $i \in [n]$. If any of the w_i is $\perp$, then we output each of the i-th share to be $(\perp, m_i)$. Else, we share s using SdShare to get $s_1, \cdots, s_n$, and set the i-th share to be (w_i, s_i). The reconstruction procedure either directly reconstructs using m_i's (in case of $\perp$), else reconstructs s, evaluates the extractor Ext on w_i and s to get the m_i's and recovers m.

LRShare(m)	LRRec($share_T$) (where $T \in \mathcal{A}$)

- $(m_1, \cdots, m_n) \leftarrow$ MShare(m).
- Sample $s \in_R \{0,1\}^d$.
- $(s_1, \cdots, s_n) \leftarrow$ SdShare(s).
- For $i \in [n]$, $w_i \leftarrow$ InvExt(m_i, s).
- If $w_j = \perp$ for some $j \in [n]$, set $share_i = (\perp, m_i)$ for each $i \in [n]$.
- Else, for each $i \in [n]$, set $share_i = (w_i, s_i)$.
- Output $(share_1, \cdots, share_n)$.
	- If for any $i \in T$, $share_i$ is of the form $(\perp, m_i)$, then parse each $share_j$ as $(\perp, m_j)$ for each $j \in T$
	- Else, for $i \in T$, parse $share_i$ as (w_i, s_i) and do:
	   • $s \leftarrow$ SdRec(s_{i_1}, s_{i_2}), where i_1, i_2 are two indices from T.
	   • For $i \in T$, set $m_i = $ Ext($w_i; s$).
	- Output $m \leftarrow$ MRec(m_T).

Theorem 1. *Let* (MShare, MRec), (SdShare, SdRec) *and* (Ext, InvExt) *be the secret sharing schemes and a strong linear extractor as given in Sect. 3.2. Then* (LRShare, LRRec) *is a leakage resilient secret sharing scheme for messages in* $\{0,1\}^l$ *against the access structure* $(n, \mathcal{A})$ *which is* ϵ_p-private *and* $(6n(\epsilon_{ext} + \epsilon'_p + \epsilon_u) + \epsilon_p)$ *-leakage resilient against the local leakage family* $\mathcal{F}_{\mathcal{A},\mu}$.

Also, for any $l, \mu > 0$ *and every instantiation of* (MShare, MRec) *with rate* $R(l)$[9] *on secrets of size* l, *there exists an instantiation of* (LRShare, LRRec) *with a share size of approximately* $(l/R(l) + \mu)$, *for* μ *bits of leakage per share. In particular, for* $\mu = o(l/R(l))$, *we get the same rate* $R(l)$ *for our LRSS scheme.*

---

[9] Here, we let R denote the function that computes the rate to secret share l-size secrets.

Further, there exists an efficient instantiation of (LRShare, LRRec) *for threshold access structures on secrets of size l, which has a share size of approximately $(l + \mu)$, for μ bits of leakage (and in particular gives rate 1, when $\mu = o(l)$), that is perfectly private and $6n \cdot 2^{-\Omega(\sqrt[3]{(l/\log l)})}$-leakage resilient against $\mathcal{F}_{A,\mu}$.*

3.3   Security Proof

CORRECTNESS AND PRIVACY
Correctness of the scheme follows from the correctness of (MShare, MRec) in case any InvExt outputs $\bot$, else it follows from correctness of both (MShare, MRec), (SdShare, SdRec) and properties of InvExt (property 2(b) of Lemma 4). It is easy to see that (LRShare, LRRec) is ϵ_p-private by ϵ_p-privacy of (MShare, MRec).

LEAKAGE RESILIENCE AGAINST THE LOCAL LEAKAGE FAMILY
Choose an arbitrary leakage function $(\mathcal{U}, \mathcal{K}, \{f_i\}_{i \in \mathcal{K}}) \in \mathcal{F}_{A,\mu}$. Note that by Remark 1, it suffices to show leakage resilience against leakage functions such that $\mathcal{U} \cap \mathcal{K} = \phi$. For the sake of simplicity assume $\mathcal{K} = \{1, 2, \cdots, |\mathcal{K}|\}$.

Our goal is to show that the distributions of leakage response to the query $(\mathcal{U}, \mathcal{K}, \{f_i\}_{i \in \mathcal{K}})$ on shares of two distinct messages m and m' are statistically close. We denote the distribution of these leakage responses on m and m' by Leak_0^m and $\mathsf{Leak}_0^{m'}$ respectively.

In case either of the shares corresponding to m or m' contain $\bot$, then we do not get leakage resilience, however in Claim 1, we show that the shares corresponding to any message m contain $\bot$, only with probability $(n(\epsilon_{ext} + \epsilon_u))$.

Claim 1. *For any message m,* $\mathsf{LRShare}(m) = ((\bot, m_1), \cdots, (\bot, m_n))$ *with probability $\leq (n(\epsilon_{ext} + \epsilon_u))$.*

Proof. Let M_i, W_i, S_i (for $i \in [n]$) and S denote the distributions of the samples m_i, w_i, s_i (for $i \in [n]$) and s respectively in the sharing procedure $\mathsf{LRShare}(m)$. By definition of $\mathsf{LRShare}$, for any m, the probability that $\mathsf{LRShare}(m) = ((\bot, m_1), \cdots, (\bot, m_n))$ is $= \Pr[\exists i \in [n] : W_i = \bot]$. We now analyze this probability. Let $\mathcal{I}_s$ denote the image of the linear map $\mathsf{Ext}(\cdot, s)$ for $s \in \{0,1\}^d$. By Lemma 4, note that $\mathsf{InvExt}(m_i, s)$ outputs $\bot$ if and only if $m_i \notin \mathcal{I}_s$. Therefore,

$$\Pr[\exists i \in [n] : W_i = \bot] \leq \sum_{i \in [n]} \Pr[M_i \notin \mathcal{I}_S]$$

Since Ext is a strong linear extractor, we know

$$\mathsf{Ext}(U_\eta, S), S \approx_{\epsilon_{ext}} U_{l'}, S.$$

By local uniformity of MShare, for each $i \in [n]$ we have $M_i \approx_{\epsilon_u} U_{l'}$. Since S is independent of M_i and $U_{l'}$ it follows that,

$$\forall i \in [n], \ \mathsf{Ext}(U_\eta, S), S \approx_{\epsilon_{ext} + \epsilon_u} M_i, S.$$

By the definition of statistical distance, for each $i \in [n]$

$$\Pr[M_i \notin \mathcal{I}_S] \leq \epsilon_{ext} + \epsilon_u + \Pr[\mathsf{Ext}(U_\eta, S) \notin \mathcal{I}_S] = \epsilon_{ext} + \epsilon_u.$$

The last implication follows because $\mathsf{Ext}(U_\eta, S) \in \mathcal{I}_S$ with probability 1. Therefore,

$$\Pr[\exists i \in [n] : W_i = \bot] \leq n(\epsilon_{ext} + \epsilon_u).$$

∎

Thus, assuming this error of $(2n(\epsilon_{ext} + \epsilon_u))$, we can consider all shares of m and m' to not contain $\bot$, and through a sequence of hybrids $\mathsf{Leak}_0^m, \mathsf{Leak}_1^m, \cdots, \mathsf{Leak}_{|\mathcal{K}|}^m$ we show that the responses to the leakage functions f_i's are (almost) independent of the choice of m in Claim 2. A similar sequence of hybrids is followed for the message m'. Then, we show that the distributions of the shares of the messages m and m' corresponding to the set $\mathcal{U}$ are statistically close in Claim 3. Together, these claims prove leakage resilience. We formally describe these hybrids below (recall we assume the non-$\bot$ case here).

Leak_0^m

- $(m_1, \cdots, m_n) \leftarrow \mathsf{MShare}(m)$.
- Sample $s \in_R \{0,1\}^d$.
- $(s_1, \cdots, s_n) \leftarrow \mathsf{SdShare}(s)$.
- For $i \in [n]$, $w_i \leftarrow \mathsf{InvExt}(m_i, s)$.
- For $i \in [n]$, set $share_i = (w_i, s_i)$.
- Output
  $(\{f_i(share_i)\}_{i \in [|\mathcal{K}|]}, share_\mathcal{U})$

Leak_j^m $(j \in [|\mathcal{K}|])$

- $(m_1, \cdots, m_n) \leftarrow \mathsf{MShare}(m)$.
- Sample $s \in_R \{0,1\}^d$.
- $(s_1, \cdots, s_n) \leftarrow \mathsf{SdShare}(s)$.
- For $1 \leq i \leq j$, $w_i \in_R \{0,1\}^\eta$.
- For $j < i \leq n$, $w_i \leftarrow \mathsf{InvExt}(m_i, s)$.
- For $i \in [n]$, set $share_i = (w_i, s_i)$.
- Output $(\{f_i(share_i)\}_{i \in [|\mathcal{K}|]}, share_\mathcal{U})$

Leak_0^m captures the response to the leakage query $(\mathcal{U}, \mathcal{K}, \{f_i\}_{i \in \mathcal{K}})$ on message m corresponding to the sharing function $\mathsf{LRShare}$. Particularly, in Leak_0^m all responses $f_j(share_j)$ have dependence on m via w_j (as w_j is correlated to m_j, a share of m). Informally, hybrids Leak_j^m and Leak_{j-1}^m differ only in the computation of w_j, where w_j is chosen uniformly in Leak_j^m while it is sampled using InvExt in Leak_{j-1}^m (as in the actual leakage distribution Leak_0^m). We now use the security guarantees provided by $(\mathsf{Ext}, \mathsf{InvExt})$ and local uniformity of MShare to prove that the successive hybrids Leak_{j-1}^m and Leak_j^m are statistically close, for each $j \in [|\mathcal{K}|]$.

Claim 2. *By ϵ_u-local uniformity of* MShare, *ϵ_p'-privacy of* $(\mathsf{SdShare}, \mathsf{SdRec})$ *and security of the strong linear extractor* Ext, *for each* $j \in [|\mathcal{K}|]$, $\mathsf{Leak}_{j-1}^m \approx_{2(\epsilon_{ext} + \epsilon_p' + \epsilon_u)} \mathsf{Leak}_j^m$.

Proof. For any $j \in [|\mathcal{K}|]$, the distributions Leak_{j-1}^m and Leak_j^m only differ in computation of w_j (which in turn influences computation of $share_j$ and $f_j(share_j)$). Let W and S denote uniform distributions on $\{0,1\}^\eta$ and $\{0,1\}^d$ respectively. From Lemma 4 we have,

$$W, S, \mathsf{Ext}(W; S) \equiv \mathsf{InvExt}(\mathsf{Ext}(W; S), S), S, \mathsf{Ext}(W; S)$$

Let $\tilde{S}_j \equiv \mathsf{SdShare}(0^d)_{\{j\}}$. By Lemma 2 we have,

$$f_j(W, \tilde{S}_j), \tilde{S}_j, S, \mathsf{Ext}(W; S) \equiv f_j(\mathsf{InvExt}(\mathsf{Ext}(W; S), S), \tilde{S}_j), \tilde{S}_j, S, \mathsf{Ext}(W; S)$$

Since $\widetilde{\mathbf{H}}_\infty(W | (f_j(W, \tilde{S}_j), \tilde{S}_j)) \geq \eta - \mu \geq \tau$ (by our setting of parameters), we invoke extractor security of Ext to get,

$$f_j(W, \tilde{S}_j), \tilde{S}_j, S, U_{l'} \approx_{\epsilon_{ext}} f_j(W, \tilde{S}_j), \tilde{S}_j, S, \mathsf{Ext}(W; S)$$

By triangle inequality on the above two inequalities,

$$f_j(W, \tilde{S}_j), \tilde{S}_j, S, U_{l'} \approx_{\epsilon_{ext}} f_j(\mathsf{InvExt}(\mathsf{Ext}(W; S), S), \tilde{S}_j), \tilde{S}_j, S, \mathsf{Ext}(W; S) \quad (1)$$

Observe that RHS of the inequality 1 is a randomised function (with randomness being independent of the input) of $(\tilde{S}_j, S, \mathsf{Ext}(W; S))$. Let g_1 denote this function. From Inequality 1 and Lemma 2 we have

$$g_1(\tilde{S}_j, S, U_{l'}) \approx_{\epsilon_{ext}} g_1(\tilde{S}_j, S, \mathsf{Ext}(W; S))$$

Then, by definition of g_1 we have

$$f_j(\mathsf{InvExt}(U_{l'}, S), \tilde{S}_j), \tilde{S}_j, S, U_{l'} \approx_{\epsilon_{ext}} f_j(\mathsf{InvExt}(\mathsf{Ext}(W; S), S), \tilde{S}_j), \tilde{S}_j, S, \mathsf{Ext}(W; S) \tag{2}$$

Applying triangle inequality on inequalities 1 and 2 we have,

$$f_j(W, \tilde{S}_j), \tilde{S}_j, S, U_{l'} \approx_{2\epsilon_{ext}} f_j(\mathsf{InvExt}(U_{l'}, S), \tilde{S}_j), \tilde{S}_j, S, U_{l'} \tag{3}$$

By privacy of $\mathsf{SdShare}$, it holds that $S_j, S \approx_{\epsilon'_p} \tilde{S}_j, S$. Further, by local uniformity of MShare, it holds that $U_{l'} \approx_{\epsilon_u} M_j$. Since (S, S_j), $U_{l'}$ and M_j are mutually independent we get

$$S_j, S, M_j \approx_{\epsilon'_p + \epsilon_u} \tilde{S}_j, S, U_{l'} \tag{4}$$

Note that the LHS and RHS of Inequality 3 can each be expressed as randomised functions of $(\tilde{S}_j, S, U_{l'})$. Formally, a) $g_1(\tilde{S}_j, S, U_{l'}) \equiv (f_j(\mathsf{InvExt}(U_{l'}, S), \tilde{S}_j), \tilde{S}_j, S, U_{l'})$; b) there exists a randomised function (whose randomness is independent of the input) g_2 such that $g_2(\tilde{S}_j, S, U_{l'}) \equiv (f_j(W, \tilde{S}_j), \tilde{S}_j, S, U_{l'})$. Now, by Lemma 2

$$g_2(\tilde{S}_j, S, M_j) \approx_{\epsilon'_p + \epsilon_u} g_2(\tilde{S}_j, S, U_{l'}) \tag{5}$$

$$g_1(\tilde{S}_j, S, M_j) \approx_{\epsilon'_p + \epsilon_u} g_1(\tilde{S}_j, S, U_{l'}) \tag{6}$$

From Inequality 3 we know,

$$g_2(\tilde{S}_j, S, U_{l'}) \approx_{2\epsilon_{ext}} g_1(\tilde{S}_j, S, U_{l'}) \tag{7}$$

Now, with applications of triangle inequality to inequalities 5, 7 and 6 and by definition of g_1 and g_2 we have

$$f_j(W, S_j), S_j, S, M_j \approx_{2(\epsilon_{ext} + \epsilon'_p + \epsilon_u)} f_j(\mathsf{InvExt}(M_j, S), S_j), S_j, S, M_j \tag{8}$$

Note that the distributions (S_j, S, M_j) are identical in both the distributions Leak_{j-1}^m and Leak_j^m. The distribution W on the LHS of inequality 8 is identical to the distribution of w_j in Leak_j^m. The distribution $\mathsf{InvExt}(M_j, S)$ on the RHS of inequality 8 is identical to the distribution of w_j in Leak_{j-1}^m. To compute the output of the distributions Leak_j^m and Leak_{j-1}^m we invoke the following function on the above LHS and RHS respectively.

$func(a, s_j, s, m_j)$

- $(m_1, \cdots, m_n) \leftarrow \mathsf{MShare}(m | m_{\{j\}})$
- Sample $s \in_R \{0,1\}^d$
- $(s_1, \cdots, s_n) \leftarrow \mathsf{SdShare}(s | s_{\{j\}})$
- For $1 \le i < j$, $w_i \in_r \{0,1\}^\eta$
- For $j < i \le n$, $w_i \leftarrow \mathsf{InvExt}(m_i, s)$
- For $i \in [n] \backslash \{j\}$, define (w_i, s_i) as $share_i$ and $a_i = f_i(share_i)$.
- Set $a_j = a$.
- Output $(\{a_i\}_{i \in [|\mathcal{K}|]}, share_{\mathcal{U}})$

By application of Lemma 2 and by the definition of consistent resampling, we have

$$\mathsf{Leak}_j^m \equiv func(f_j(W, S_j), S_j, S, M_j)$$

$$\approx_{2(\epsilon_{ext} + \epsilon_p' + \epsilon_u)} func(f_j(\mathsf{InvExt}(M_j, S), S_j), S_j, S, M_j) \equiv \mathsf{Leak}_{j-1}^m$$

∎

Claim 3. *By* ϵ_p-*privacy of* $(\mathsf{MShare}, \mathsf{MRec})$*, for any two messages* $m \ne m'$*,* $\mathsf{Leak}_{|\mathcal{K}|}^m \approx_{\epsilon_p} \mathsf{Leak}_{|\mathcal{K}|}^{m'}$*.*

Proof. Note that for any message m, the distribution $\mathsf{Leak}_{|\mathcal{K}|}^m$ only depends on shares of the unauthorised set $\mathcal{U}$. By privacy of MShare, for m, m'

$$\mathsf{MShare}(m)_{\mathcal{U}} \approx_{\epsilon_p} \mathsf{MShare}(m')_{\mathcal{U}}$$

Note that given $\mathsf{MShare}(m)_{\mathcal{U}}$, the output of $\mathsf{Leak}_{|\mathcal{K}|}^m$ can be computed by choosing $\{w_i\}_{i \in \mathcal{K}}$ and s uniformly, generating shares of s and performing the remaining computation using f_i's. Similar is the case for $\mathsf{Leak}_{|\mathcal{K}|}^{m'}$ given $\mathsf{MShare}(m')_{\mathcal{U}}$. Therefore, we have

$$\mathsf{Leak}_{|\mathcal{K}|}^m \approx_{\epsilon_p} \mathsf{Leak}_{|\mathcal{K}|}^{m'}.$$

∎

Using Claims 1, 2 and 3, with applications of triangle equality, we get

$$\mathsf{Leak}_0^m \approx_{2n(\epsilon_{ext} + \epsilon_u) + 4|\mathcal{K}|(\epsilon_{ext} + \epsilon_p' + \epsilon_u) + \epsilon_p} \mathsf{Leak}_0^{m'}$$

This gives the leakage error of at most $6n(\epsilon_{ext} + \epsilon_p' + \epsilon_u) + \epsilon_p$.

3.4 Parameters

Recall that $\{0,1\}^l$ is the message space.

- For an (n,t)-threshold access structure
  - We instantiate $(\mathsf{MShare}, \mathsf{MRec})$ with the (n,t)-Shamir secret sharing scheme for messages. $\{0,1\}^l$, which is perfectly private and perfectly locally uniform (that is $\epsilon_p = \epsilon_u = 0$). With this instantiation $|m_i| = l' = l$.
  - We set $\epsilon_{ext} = 2^{-\Omega(\sqrt[3]{\frac{l'}{\log l'}})}$ and instantiate the $(\eta, \tau, d, l', \epsilon_{ext})$-strong linear extractor Ext (as in Lemma 3) with $\eta = l' + \mu + \mathcal{O}(\log^3(\frac{l'}{\epsilon_{ext}}))$, $\tau = l' + \mathcal{O}(\log^3(\frac{\eta}{\epsilon_{ext}}))$ and $d = \mathcal{O}(\log^3(\frac{\eta}{\epsilon_{ext}}))$.
  - We instantiate $(\mathsf{SdShare}, \mathsf{SdRec})$ with the $(n,2)$-Shamir secret sharing scheme for messages $\{0,1\}^d$, which is perfectly private (that is $\epsilon'_p = 0$). With this instantiation we have $|s_i| = d$ (for all $i \in [n]$).
  - With the above instantiations, the size of each share output by $\mathsf{LRShare}$ to support μ bits leakage (for the leakage family $\mathcal{F}_{\mathcal{A},\mu}$) is $\eta + d = l' + \mu + \mathcal{O}(\frac{l'}{\log l'} + \log^3 \mu) = l + \mu + o(l, \mu)$. The scheme is perfectly private and $6n \cdot 2^{-\Omega(\sqrt[3]{l/\log l})}$-leakage resilient against $\mathcal{F}_{\mathcal{A},\mu}$. Therefore rate of the scheme is asymptotically 1 when $\mu = o(l)$.
- For general access structures
  - Suppose R is the function specifying the rate of the scheme $(\mathsf{MShare}, \mathsf{SdShare})$ on a given message length l. Then $l' = \frac{l}{R(l)}$. Instantiate Ext and $(\mathsf{SdShare}, \mathsf{SdRec})$ as done in the above for threshold access structures with $l' = \frac{l}{R(l)}$. With this, we get the share size of $\mathsf{LRShare} = l' + \mu + o(l', \mu)$ and hence results in rate $R(l)$ whenever $\mu = o(\frac{l}{R(l)})$.

4 Non-malleable Secret Sharing Schemes

As we mentioned in the introduction, we can get the NMSS scheme with the improved rate of $1/4$, by directly instantiating the NMSS scheme of [GK18] with our LRSS scheme[10] and the rate-$1/3$ non-malleable code [AKO+22]. Hence, our focus in this section will be on formalizing and building non-malleable randomnesss sharing schemes with the further improved rate. We begin by defining non-malleable randomness sharing, which specially gives secret sharing and non-malleability guarantees for uniform random messages. The sharing procedure outputs a (uniform random) message m along with its shares. The privacy

---

[10] Particularly, instantiating the NMSS sharing scheme of [GK18, Theorem 1] with the NMC of [AKO+22, Theorem 3] and our LRSS would give: First encode the secret m using the NMC to get states L and R. For [AKO+22]'s NMC, one of the states, L is larger than R. Secret share L using our LRSS from Theorem 1 for $(n,2)$-threshold access structure to get $L_1, \cdots, L_n$, and R using an (n,t)-threshold secret sharing scheme to get $R_1, \cdots, R_n$. Set the i-th share as (L_i, R_i).

guarantee is that, given any unautorized set of shares, the message m still looks random. The non-malleability guarantee is that, when the shares are tampered with respect to some tampering family $\mathcal{F}$, the original message m looks random, even given the recovered tampered message (using any authorized (adversarially mentioned) set for reconstruction).

Definition 3 (Non-malleable Randomness Sharing). *Let* RNMShare *be a function such that* RNMShare $: \{0,1\}^{\alpha} \rightarrow \{0,1\}^{\ell} \times (\{0,1\}^{\ell'})^n$ *is defined as* RNMShare$(r) := (\text{RNMShare}_1(r), \text{RNMShare}_2(r)) = (m, (\text{Share}_1, \cdots, \text{Share}_n))$ *We say that* RNMShare *is a (n,t)-non-malleable randomness sharing with ϵ_s-privacy and ϵ_{nm}-non-malleability, message space $\{0,1\}^{\ell}$, shares from $\{0,1\}^{\ell'}$, for the distribution $\mathcal{R}$ on $\{0,1\}^{\alpha}$, and with respect to a tampering family $\mathcal{F}$ if it satisfies the following properties.*

1. **Correctness.** *For any $T \subseteq [n]$ with $|T| \geq t$, there exists a deterministic reconstruction function* RNMRec $: (\{0,1\}^{\ell'})^{|T|} \rightarrow \{0,1\}^{\ell}$ *such that*

$$\Pr_{r \leftarrow \mathcal{R}}[\text{RNMRec}(\text{RNMShare}_2(r)_T) = \text{RNMShare}_1(r)] = 1$$

2. **Statistical Privacy.** *For any unauthorized set $U \subseteq [n]$ such that $|U| < t$,*

$$(\text{RNMShare}_1(\mathcal{R}), \text{RNMShare}_2(\mathcal{R})_U) \approx_{\epsilon_s} (U_{\ell}, \text{RNMShare}_2(\mathcal{R})_U)$$

3. **Non-malleability.** *For each $f \in \mathcal{F}$ and every authorized set $T \subseteq [n]$ containing t indices, there exists a simulator* $\text{Sim}_{f,T}$ *over $\{0,1\}^{\ell} \cup \{same^*, \perp\}$, such that*

$$\text{Tamper}_{f,T} \approx_{\epsilon_{nm}} Copy(U_{\ell}, \text{Sim}_{f,T})$$

where $\text{Tamper}_{f,T}$ *denotes the distribution* $(\text{RNMShare}_1(\mathcal{R}),$ $\text{RNMRec}(f(\text{RNMShare}_2(\mathcal{R}))_T))$ *and $Copy(U_{\ell}, \text{Sim}_{f,T})$ is defined as:*

$$Copy(U_{\ell}, \text{Sim}_{f,T}) := \left\{ \begin{array}{ll} u \leftarrow U_{\ell}; & \tilde{m} \leftarrow \text{Sim}_{f,T} \\ Output: (u, u), & if \ \tilde{m} = same^* \\ Output: (u, \tilde{m}), & otherwise \end{array} \right\}$$

where $\text{Sim}_{f,T}$ *should be efficiently samplable given oracle access to $f(.)$.*

*The **rate** of this random secret sharing scheme is defined as ℓ/ℓ'.*

We specifically consider the independent tampering family, first defined in [GK18], as given below.

INDEPENDENT TAMPERING FAMILY $\mathcal{F}_{ind}$. Specifically, we build non-malleable randomness sharing schemes for the independent tampering family, where each share is allowed to be tampered arbitrarily, but independent of each other. Let RNMShare$_2(r) = (\text{Share}_1, \cdots, \text{Share}_n)$. Formally, $\mathcal{F}_{ind}$ consists of functions $(f_1, \cdots, f_n)$, such that, for each $i \in [n]$, $f_i : \{0,1\}^{\ell'} \rightarrow \{0,1\}^{\ell'}$ is an arbitrary tampering function that takes as input Share$_i$ and outputs a tampered share. Now we proceed to build such non-malleable randomness sharing schemes with respect to $\mathcal{F}_{ind}$, achieving rate $1/2$.

4.1 Building Blocks

We begin by looking at the building blocks needed for the construction. Besides our leakage resilient secret sharing scheme, and any threshold secret sharing scheme, we require non-malleable randomness encoders, defined below.

Non-malleable Randomness Encoders

Non-malleable randomness encoders (NMRE) were introduced in [KOS18] and give non-malleability guarantees for random messages, which we formally define below.

Definition 4 (Non-malleable Randomness Encoders [KOS18]). *Let* $(\mathsf{NMREnc}, \mathsf{NMRDec})$ *be s.t.* $\mathsf{NMREnc} : \{0,1\}^\alpha \to \{0,1\}^\ell \times (\{0,1\}^{\beta_1} \times \{0,1\}^{\beta_2})$ *is defined as* $\mathsf{NMREnc}(r) = (\mathsf{NMREnc}_1(r), \mathsf{NMREnc}_2(r)) = (m, (L, R))$ *and* $\mathsf{NMRDec} : \{0,1\}^{\beta_1} \times \{0,1\}^{\beta_2} \to \{0,1\}^\ell$. *We say that* $(\mathsf{NMREnc}, \mathsf{NMRDec})$ *is an ϵ-non-malleable randomness encoder with message space* $\{0,1\}^\ell$, *codeword space* $\{0,1\}^{\beta_1} \times \{0,1\}^{\beta_2}$, *for the distribution* $\mathcal{R}$ *over* $\{0,1\}^\alpha$, *and with respect to the 2-split-state tampering family* $\mathcal{F}_{split}$ *(consisting of functions (f,g) such that* $f : \{0,1\}^{\beta_1} \to \{0,1\}^{\beta_1}$ *and* $g : \{0,1\}^{\beta_2} \to \{0,1\}^{\beta_2}$ *are arbitrary functions acting on L and R respectively), if it satisfies the following properties.*

1. **Correctness.** $\Pr_{r \leftarrow \mathcal{R}}[\mathsf{NMRDec}(\mathsf{NMREnc}_2(r)) = \mathsf{NMREnc}_1(r)] = 1$.
2. **Non-malleability.** *For each* $(f,g) \in \mathcal{F}_{split}$, $\exists$ *a distribution* $\mathsf{NMRSim}_{f,g}$ *over* $\{0,1\}^\ell \cup \{same^*, \bot\}$ *such that*

$$\mathsf{NMRTamper}_{f,g} \approx_\epsilon Copy(U_\ell, \mathsf{NMRSim}_{f,g})$$

where $\mathsf{NMRTamper}_{f,g}$ *denotes the distribution* $(\mathsf{NMREnc}_1(\mathcal{R}),$ $\mathsf{NMRDec}((f,g)(\mathsf{NMREnc}_2(\mathcal{R}))))$ *and* $Copy(U_\ell, \mathsf{NMRSim}_{f,g})$ *is defined as:*

$$Copy(U_\ell, \mathsf{NMRSim}_{f,g}) := \begin{cases} u \leftarrow U_\ell; & \tilde{m} \leftarrow \mathsf{NMRSim}_{f,g} \\ \text{Output: } (u, u), & \text{if } \tilde{m} = same^* \\ \text{Output: } (u, \tilde{m}), & \text{otherwise} \end{cases}$$

where $\mathsf{NMRSim}_{f,g}$ *should be efficiently samplable given oracle access to* $(f,g)(.)$.

We also require the following secret sharing property of the NMRE, which states that the message of an NMRE looks random, even given one of the states.

Lemma 5. *Let* $(\mathsf{NMREnc}, \mathsf{NMRDec})$ *and an ϵ-non-malleable randomness encoder over the message space* $\{0,1\}^\ell$, *using the distribution* $\mathcal{R}$, *and against the 2-split-state* $\mathcal{F}_{split}$. *Then,* $(\mathsf{NMREnc}_1(\mathcal{R}), L) \approx_{3\epsilon} (U_\ell, L)$, *where* $(L, R) \leftarrow \mathsf{NMREnc}_2(\mathcal{R})$.

The proof of this lemma is very similar to an analogous property satisfied of non-malleable codes, shown in [ADKO15, Lemma 6.1]. For a detailed proof, we refer the readers to our full version.

Instatiations of Our Building Blocks
Specifically, we can now list the building blocks required for our construction.

- (NMREnc, NMRDec) be an ϵ_{nmre}-non-malleable randomness encoder, outputting messages from $\{0,1\}^\ell$ and codewords from $\{0,1\}^{\beta_1} \times \{0,1\}^{\beta_2}$, using randomness from some distribution $\mathcal{R}$, and against the split-state family $\mathcal{F}_{split}$. Further, the NMRE satifies ϵ'_p-secret sharing property (Lemma 5) that $(\mathsf{NMREnc}_1(\mathcal{R}), L) \approx_{\epsilon'_p} (U_\ell, L)$, where $(L, R) \leftarrow \mathsf{NMREnc}_2(\mathcal{R})$.
- $(\mathsf{LRShare}_n^2, \mathsf{LRRec}_n^2)$ be a $(n, 2)$-leakage resilient secret sharing scheme with ϵ_{lr}-leakage resilience against $\mathcal{F}_{2,\mu}$ taking messages from $\{0,1\}^{\beta_1}$, specifically for 2-threshold setting, i.e., the adversary can query independent leakage on $n-1$ shares, non-adaptively (upto μ bits from each share) and get one full share.
- $(\mathsf{Share}_n^t, \mathsf{Rec}_n^t)$ be any (n, t)-secret sharing scheme with ϵ_p-privacy against the (n, t)-threshold access structure, taking messages from $\{0,1\}^{\beta_2}$.

4.2 Our Construction

We now build a non-malleable randomness sharing scheme. Informally, we first use the non-malleable randomness encoder to generate a message m along with its encoding (L, R). Then, we secret share L and R using the leakage resilient and threshold secret sharing schemes respectively, to get the shares $(L_1, \cdots, L_n)$ and $(R_1, \cdots, R_n)$. Finally, we set the i-th share Share_i to be (L_i, R_i). The reconstruction procedure first reconstructs L and R, and subsequently decodes it to recover m.

$\mathsf{RNMShare}(r)$:
1. $(m, (L, R)) \leftarrow \mathsf{NMREnc}(r)$.
2. We further secret share L and R as follows:

$$(L_1, \cdots, L_n) \leftarrow \mathsf{LRShare}_n^2(L)$$
$$(R_1, \cdots, R_n) \leftarrow \mathsf{Share}_n^t(R)$$

3. For each $i \in [n]$, set $\mathsf{Share}_i = (L_i, R_i)$.
4. Output $(m, (\mathsf{Share}_1, \cdots, \mathsf{Share}_n))$.
   $\mathsf{RNMRec}(\mathsf{Share}_T)$: Parse $T = \{i_1, \cdots, i_t\}$ and do the following:

1. For each $j \in T$, parse Share_j as (L_j, R_j).
2. Recover L and R as:

$$L \leftarrow \mathsf{LRRec}_n^2(L_{i_1}, L_{i_2})$$
$$R \leftarrow \mathsf{Rec}_n^t(R_{i_1}, \cdots, R_{i_t})$$

3. Output $m = \mathsf{NMRDec}(L, R)$.

Theorem 2. *Let* (NMREnc, NMRDec), (LRShare$_n^2$, LRRec$_n^2$) *and* (Share$_n^t$, Rec$_n^t$) *be building blocks as in Sect. 4.1. Then, the construction above gives an* (n,t)-*non-malleable randomness sharing scheme with* $2\epsilon_p + \epsilon_p'$-*privacy and* ϵ_{nmre} + $\epsilon_{lr} + \epsilon_p$-*non-malleability against* $\mathcal{F}_{ind}$.

Further, we give an instantiation of the above construction in Sect. 4.3, which achieves an asymptotic rate of $1/2$, *has a privacy error of* $2^{-\Omega(\ell/\log^{\rho+1}(\ell))}$, *and a non-malleablity error of* $6n \cdot 2^{-\Omega(\ell/\log^{\rho+1}(\ell))}$, *for any* $\rho > 0$, *for messages of length* ℓ.

Proof. CORRECTNESS. The correctness of the scheme is straightforward from the correctness of the underlying non-malleable randomness encoder, the threshold secret sharing scheme and the leakage resilient secret sharing.

PRIVACY. We prove the statistical privacy using a hybrid argument. We wish to show that, for any unauthorized set $U \subseteq [n]$ with $|U| < t$, (RNMShare$_1(\mathcal{R})$, RNMShare$_2(\mathcal{R})_U$) $\approx_{2\epsilon_p + \epsilon_p'}$ $(U_\ell, \text{RNMShare}_2(\mathcal{R})_U))$. Let U be any arbitrary unauthorized set. Consider the following sequence of hybrids.

- Hyb$_0$: This hybrid corresponds to the case where the NMRE encoder is used to generate the message m.
  Generate $(m,(L,R)) \leftarrow \text{NMREnc}(r)$, for $r \leftarrow \mathcal{R}$. Further generate $(L_1, \cdots, L_n) \leftarrow \text{LRShare}_n^2(L)$ and $(R_1, \cdots, R_n) \leftarrow \text{Share}_n^t(R)$. Set Share$_i = (L_i, R_i)$, for each $i \in U$ and output $(m, \{\text{Share}_i\}_{i \in U})$.
- Hyb$_1$: Replace the shares of R in the set U with shares of an R' corresponding to a message m' output by the NMRE encoder.
  Generate $(m,(L,R)) \leftarrow \text{NMREnc}(r)$ and $(L', R') \leftarrow \text{NMREnc}_2(r')$, for $r, r' \leftarrow \mathcal{R}$. Further generate $(L_1, \cdots, L_n) \leftarrow \text{LRShare}_n^2(L)$ and $(R_1', \cdots, R_n') \leftarrow \text{Share}_n^t(R')$. Set Share$_i = (L_i, R_i')$, for each $i \in U$ and output $(m, \{\text{Share}_i\}_{i \in U})$.
- Hyb$_2$: Replace the m with a random message u, and use the L corresponding to m, as in Hyb$_1$.
  Generate $u \leftarrow U_\ell$, $(L,R) \leftarrow \text{NMREnc}_2(r)$ and $(L', R') \leftarrow \text{NMREnc}_2(r')$, for $r, r' \leftarrow \mathcal{R}$. Further generate $(L_1, \cdots, L_n) \leftarrow \text{LRShare}_n^2(L)$ and $(R_1', \cdots, R_n') \leftarrow \text{Share}_n^t(R')$. Set Share$_i = (L_i, R_i')$, for each $i \in U$ and output $(u, \{\text{Share}_i\}_{i \in U})$.
- Hyb$_3$: This final hybrid corresponds to the case where L and R are generated corresponding to some message m, but an independent uniform message u is output.
  Generate $u \leftarrow U_\ell$, $(L,R) \leftarrow \text{NMREnc}_2(r)$, for $r \leftarrow \mathcal{R}$. Further generate $(L_1, \cdots, L_n) \leftarrow \text{LRShare}_n^2(L)$ and $(R_1, \cdots, R_n) \leftarrow \text{Share}_n^t(R)$. Set Share$_i = (L_i, R_i)$, for each $i \in U$ and output $(u, \{\text{Share}_i\}_{i \in U})$.

Clearly, Hyb$_0$ $\equiv$ (RNMShare$_1(\mathcal{R})$, RNMShare$_2(\mathcal{R})_U$) and Hyb$_3$ $\equiv$ $(U_\ell,$ RNMShare$_2(\mathcal{R})_U))$. By statistical privacy of (Share$_n^t$, Rec$_n^t$), it follows that Hyb$_0$ $\approx_{\epsilon_p}$ Hyb$_1$ and Hyb$_2$ $\approx_{\epsilon_p}$ Hyb$_3$. By the privacy property of NMRE, it follows that Hyb$_1$ $\approx_{\epsilon_p'}$ Hyb$_2$. Hence, (RNMShare$_1(\mathcal{R})$, RNMShare$_2(\mathcal{R})_U$) $\equiv$

$\mathsf{Hyb}_0 \approx_{2\epsilon_p + \epsilon'_p} \mathsf{Hyb}_3 \equiv (U_\ell, \mathsf{RNMShare}_2(\mathcal{R})_U)).$

NON-MALLEABILITY. We prove this using a hybrid argument. We begin by describing the simulator $\mathsf{Sim}_{f_1,\cdots,f_n,T}$, for arbitrary tampering functions $f_1, \cdots, f_n \in \mathcal{F}_{ind}$ and reconstruction set $T = \{i_1, \cdots, i_t\}$.

$\mathsf{Sim}_{f_1,\cdots,f_n,T}$:
1. Let $(L^*, R^*) \leftarrow \mathsf{NMREnc}_2(r)$, for $r \leftarrow \mathcal{R}$.
2. $(L_1^*, \cdots, L_n^*) \leftarrow \mathsf{LRShare}_n^2(L^*)$
   $(R_1^*, \cdots, R_n^*) \leftarrow \mathsf{Share}_n^t(R^*)$
3. Set $h = (R_{i_1}^*, \cdots, R_{i_{t-1}}^*, \widetilde{R_{i_1}^*}, \cdots, \widetilde{R_{i_{t-1}}^*}, L_{i_t}^*)$, where $(\widetilde{L_j^*}, \widetilde{R_j^*}) = f_j(L_j^*, R_j^*)$, for $j = i_1, \cdots, i_{t-1}$. Define the tampering functions F_h and G_h, acting on inputs L and R respectively as:
   $F_h(L)$:
   – Pick $L_{i_1}, \cdots, L_{i_{t-1}}$ such that the reconstruction using any two shares among $L_{i_t}^*$ and $L_{i_1}, \cdots, L_{i_{t-1}}$ gives L.
   – For each $j \in \{i_1, \cdots, i_{t-1}\}$, evaluate $(\widetilde{L_j}, \widetilde{R_j}) = f_j(L_j, R_j^*)$. Then the sampling should be such that $\widetilde{R_j} = \widetilde{R_j^*}$ for each $j = i_1, \cdots, i_{t-1}$.
   – If such a sampling is not possible then output $\perp$.
     Else output $\widetilde{L} \leftarrow \mathsf{LRRec}_n^2(\widetilde{L_{i_1}}, \widetilde{L_{i_2}})$.
   $G_h(R)$:
   – Pick R_{i_t} such that it is consistent with $R_{i_1}^*, \cdots, R_{i_{t-1}}^*$ and R.
   – If such a sampling is not possible, then output $\perp$.
   – Else evaluate $(., \widetilde{R_{i_t}}) = f_{i_t}(L_{i_t}^*, R_{i_t})$.
   – Output $\widetilde{R} \leftarrow \mathsf{Rec}_n^t(\widetilde{R_{i_1}^*}, \cdots, \widetilde{R_{i_{t-1}}^*}, \widetilde{R_{i_t}})$.
4. Output $\tilde{m} \leftarrow \mathsf{NMRSim}_{F_h, G_h}$.

Now, we describe a sequence of hybrids to show that $\mathsf{Copy}(U_\ell, \mathsf{Sim}_{f_1,\cdots,f_n,T}) \approx_{\epsilon_{nmre} + \epsilon_{lr} + \epsilon_p} \mathsf{Tamper}_{f_1,\cdots,f_n,T}$.

$\underline{\mathsf{Hyb}_1^{f_1,\cdots,f_n,T}}$: This hybrid is the same as $\mathsf{Copy}(U_\ell, \mathsf{Sim}_{f_1,\cdots,f_n,T})$, except that we **change step 4**, using $\mathsf{NMRSim}_{F_h,G_h}$, and use $\mathsf{NMRTamper}_{F_h,G_h}$ to output $m, \tilde{m}$ instead of using $\mathsf{Copy}(U_\ell, \mathsf{NMRSim}_{F_h,G_h})$.

Claim 4. *If* $(\mathsf{NMREnc}, \mathsf{NMRDec})$ *is an* ϵ_{nmre}*-NMRE against* $\mathcal{F}_{split}$, *using the distribution* $\mathcal{R}$, *then* $\mathsf{Copy}(U_\ell, \mathsf{Sim}_{f_1,\cdots,f_n,T}) \approx_{\epsilon_{nmre}} \mathsf{Hyb}_1^{f_1,\cdots,f_n,T}$

Proof. The proof of this claim is straightforward. Clearly, $(F_h, G_h) \in \mathcal{F}_{split}$ and hence, by the non-malleability of the NMRE, we know that $\mathsf{NMRTamper}_{F_h,G_h} \approx_{\epsilon_{nmre}} \mathsf{Copy}(U_\ell, \mathsf{NMRSim}_{F_h,G_h})$. Thus, the reduction can generate h and forward the functions F_h, G_h to the NMRE challenger, and the response directly gives either the distribution $\mathsf{Copy}(U_\ell, \mathsf{Sim}_{f_1,\cdots,f_n,T})$ or $\mathsf{Hyb}_1^{f_1,\cdots,f_n,T}$. Hence, the proof of the claim follows.

$\underline{\mathsf{Hyb}_2^{f_1,\cdots,f_n,T}}$: In this hybrid, we generate $(L, R) \leftarrow \mathsf{NMREnc}_2(r)$ for $r \leftarrow \mathcal{R}$ and use the same R to generate the shares $R_1, \cdots, R_n$, used in h and as an input to the function G_h in $\mathsf{NMRTamper}_{F_h, G_h}$. The remaining steps are exactly same as in $\mathsf{Hyb}_1^{f_1, \cdots, f_n, T}$.

Claim 5. *If* $(\mathsf{Share}_n^t, \mathsf{Rec}_n^t)$ *is an* ϵ_p-*secure* (n, t)-*threshold secret sharing scheme, then* $\mathsf{Hyb}_1^{f_1, \cdots, f_n, T} \approx_{\epsilon_p} \mathsf{Hyb}_2^{f_1, \cdots, f_n, T}$.

Proof. Suppose for contradiction that the statistical distance between $\mathsf{Hyb}_1^{f_1, \cdots, f_n, T}$ and $\mathsf{Hyb}_2^{f_1, \cdots, f_n, T}$ is greater than ϵ_p. Then we describe a reduction below, to break the privacy of $(\mathsf{Share}_n^t, \mathsf{Rec}_n^t)$:

1. The reduction generates $(L^*, R^*) \leftarrow \mathsf{NMREnc}_2(r)$ and $(L, R) \leftarrow \mathsf{NMREnc}_2(r')$, for $r, r' \leftarrow \mathcal{R}$.
2. Further, generate $(L_1^*, \cdots, L_n^*) \leftarrow \mathsf{LRShare}_n^2(L^*)$.
3. Now, the reduction sends R^*, R and receives $t-1$ shares $R_{i_1}^b, \cdots, R_{i_{t-1}}^b$, from the secret sharing challenger, which correspond to either R or R^*.
4. Now, set $h = (R_{i_1}^b, \cdots, R_{i_{t-1}}^b, \widetilde{R_{i_1}^b}, \cdots, \widetilde{R_{i_{t-1}}^b}, L_{i_t}^*)$, where $(\widetilde{L_j^*}, \widetilde{R_j^b}) = f_j(L_j^*, R_j^b)$, for $j = i_1, \cdots, i_{t-1}$.
5. Now, the reduction evaluates $F_h(L) = \widetilde{L}$ and $G_h(R) = \widetilde{R}$ and outputs $(\mathsf{NMREnc}_1(r'), \mathsf{NMRDec}(\widetilde{L}, \widetilde{R}))$.

Clearly, if R^* was used by the secret sharing challenger, then the reduction output is identical to $\mathsf{Hyb}_1^{f_1, \cdots, f_n, T}$ and if R was used, then it is identical to $\mathsf{Hyb}_2^{f_1, \cdots, f_n, T}$. Hence, this breaks the privacy of $(\mathsf{Share}_n^t, \mathsf{Rec}_n^t)$.

$\mathsf{Hyb}_3^{f_1, \cdots, f_n, T}$: In this hybrid, all steps are exactly same as in $\mathsf{Hyb}_2^{f_1, \cdots, f_n, T}$, except that, instead of G_h reverse sampling R_{i_t}, satisfying the consistency condition, we use the same share R_{i_t} generated while setting h.

Claim 6. $\mathsf{Hyb}_2^{f_1, \cdots, f_n, T} \equiv \mathsf{Hyb}_3^{f_1, \cdots, f_n, T}$.

Proof. The reverse sampling of R_{i_t} in $\mathsf{Hyb}_2^{f_1, \cdots, f_n, T}$ uses the same R as used in generating h. Hence, G_h doesn't output $\bot$ and successfully samples R_{i_t}. This directly proves the claim.

$\mathsf{Hyb}_4^{f_1, \cdots, f_n, T}$: In this hybrid, we generate $(L, R) \leftarrow \mathsf{NMREnc}_2(r)$ for $r \leftarrow \mathcal{R}$ and use the same L to generate the shares $L_1, \cdots, L_n$, used in h and as an input to the function F_h in $\mathsf{NMRTamper}_{F_h, G_h}$. The remaining steps are exactly same as in $\mathsf{Hyb}_3^{f_1, \cdots, f_n, T}$.

Claim 7. *If* $(\mathsf{LRShare}_n^2, \mathsf{LRRec}_n^2)$ *is an* ϵ_{lr}-*LRSS against* $\mathcal{F}_{2, \mu}$, *then* $\mathsf{Hyb}_3^{f_1, \cdots, f_n, T} \approx_{\epsilon_{lr}} \mathsf{Hyb}_4^{f_1, \cdots, f_n, T}$.

Proof. Suppose for contradiction that the statistical distance between $\mathsf{Hyb}_3^{f_1, \cdots, f_n, T}$ and $\mathsf{Hyb}_4^{f_1, \cdots, f_n, T}$ is greater than ϵ_{lr}. Then we descirbe a reduction below, to break the leakage resilience of $(\mathsf{LRShare}_n^2, \mathsf{LRRec}_n^2)$:

1. The reduction generates $(L^*, R^*) \leftarrow \mathsf{NMREnc}_2(r)$ and $(L, R) \leftarrow \mathsf{NMREnc}_2(r')$, for $r, r' \leftarrow \mathcal{R}$.

2. Generate $R_1, \cdots, R_n \leftarrow \mathsf{Share}_n^t(R)$.
3. Now, send L, L^* as the two challenge messages to the leakage resilience challenger. Query the i_t-th full share and the leakages $g_{i_1}, \cdots, g_{i_{t-1}}$, each hardcoded with $R_{i_1}, \cdots, R_{i_{t-1}}$ respectively, defined as below. For each $j = i_1, \cdots, i_{t-1}$:

$g_j(L_j^b)$: Evaluate $(., \widetilde{R_j}) = f_j(L_j^b, R_j)$ and output $\widetilde{R_j}$.
4. On receiving $L_{i_t}^b$ and $\widetilde{R_{i_1}}, \cdots, \widetilde{R_{i_{t-1}}}$ from the leakage resilience challenger, the reduction evaluates $(., \widetilde{R_{i_t}}) = f_{i_t}(L_{i_t}^b, R_{i_t})$ and sets $h = (R_{i_1}, \cdots, R_{i_{t-1}}, \widetilde{R_{i_1}}, \cdots, \widetilde{R_{i_{t-1}}}, L_{i_t}^b)$.
5. Now, evaluate $F_h(L) = \widetilde{L}$ and $\widetilde{R} \leftarrow \mathsf{Rec}_n^t(\widetilde{R_{i_1}}, \cdots, \widetilde{R_{i_{t-1}}}, \widetilde{R_{i_t}})$, and output $(\mathsf{NMREnc}_1(r'), \mathsf{NMRDec}(\widetilde{L}, \widetilde{R}))$.

Clearly, if the challenger picks L^*, the reduction output is identical to $\mathsf{Hyb}_3^{f_1, \cdots, f_n, T}$ and if it picks L, then it is identical to $\mathsf{Hyb}_4^{f_1, \cdots, f_n, T}$ and further, the reduction makes queries from $\mathcal{F}_{2,\mu}$, with $\mu = |R_j|$. Hence, this breaks the leakage resilience of $(\mathsf{LRShare}_n^2, \mathsf{LRRec}_n^2)$.

$\mathsf{Hyb}_5^{f_1, \cdots, f_n, T}$: In this hybrid, all steps are exactly same as in $\mathsf{Hyb}_4^{f_1, \cdots, f_n, T}$, except that, instead of F_h reverse sampling $L_{i_1}, \cdots, L_{i_{t-1}}$, satisfying the consistency condition, we use the same share L_j's generated while setting h.

Claim 8. $\mathsf{Hyb}_4^{f_1, \cdots, f_n, T} \equiv \mathsf{Hyb}_5^{f_1, \cdots, f_n, T}$.

Proof. The reverse sampling of $L_{i_1}, \cdots, L_{i_{t-1}}$ in $\mathsf{Hyb}_4^{f_1, \cdots, f_n, T}$ uses the same L as used in generating h. Hence, F_h doesn't output $\bot$, which directly proves the claim.

Note that $\mathsf{Hyb}_5^{f_1, \cdots, f_n, T} \equiv \mathsf{Tamper}_{f_1, \cdots, f_n, T}$. Hence, by Claims 4, 5, 6, 7 and 8, using triangle inequality we get $Copy(U_\ell, \mathsf{Sim}_{f_1, \cdots, f_n, T}) \approx_{\epsilon_{nmre} + \epsilon_p + \epsilon_{lr}} \mathsf{Tamper}_{f_1, \cdots, f_n, T}$, which proves the non-malleability.

4.3 Instantiation of Our Scheme

We instantiate our scheme with the following primitives, where the NMRE message space is $\{0,1\}^\ell$.

- We use the following rate-1/2 NMRE from [KOS18].

Lemma 6 (Theorem 1, [KOS18]). *There exists an NMRE for uniform messages in the two-split-state model* $\mathcal{F}_{split}$, *achieving a constant rate* $1/(2+\zeta)$, *for any* $\zeta > 0$ *and an error of* $2^{-\Omega(\ell/\log^{\rho+1}(\ell))}$, *for any* $\rho > 0$.

Specifically, the above construction has codeword with each block of lengths: $|L| = \beta_1 = \ell(2+\zeta)$ and $|R| = \beta_2 = o(\ell)$.

- We instantiate the threshold secret sharing scheme with a perfectly private t-out-of-n Shamir secret sharing scheme for messages from $\{0,1\}^\beta$, which gives the shares of size $|R_i| = |R| = \beta_2 = o(\ell)$, for each $i \in [n]$.

- Further, we instantiate the LRSS ($\mathsf{LRShare}_n^2, \mathsf{LRRec}_n^2$) against the leakage family $\mathcal{F}_{2,\mu}$ with the scheme from Sect. 3, with $\mu = |R_i| = \beta_2 = o(\ell)$. This gives $|L_i| = |L| + \mu + o(|L|, \mu) = \ell(2 + \zeta')$, for a small $\zeta' > 0$ (ignoring the small order terms). This instantiation has a leakage error ϵ_{lr} of $6n \cdot 2^{-\Omega(\sqrt[3]{(\beta_1/\log\beta_1)})} = 6n \cdot 2^{-\Omega(\sqrt[3]{(\ell/\log\ell)})}$.

Combining these instantiations, we get a rate of $1/(2 + \zeta')$, for any $\zeta' > 0$, a privacy error of $2\epsilon_p + \epsilon_p' = 2^{-\Omega(\ell/\log^{\rho+1}(\ell))}$, for any $\rho > 0$ and non-malleability error of $\epsilon_{nmre} + \epsilon_{lr} + \epsilon_p = 6n \cdot 2^{-\Omega(\ell/\log^{\rho+1}(\ell))}$, for any $\rho > 0$.

References

[ADKO15] Aggarwal, D., Dziembowski, S., Kazana, T., Obremski, M.: Leakage-resilient non-malleable codes. In: Dodis, Y., Nielsen, J.B. (eds.) TCC 2015, Part I. LNCS, vol. 9014, pp. 398–426. Springer, Heidelberg (2015). https://doi.org/10.1007/978-3-662-46494-6_17

[ADN+19] Aggarwal, D., et al.: Stronger leakage-resilient and non-malleable secret sharing schemes for general access structures. In: Boldyreva, A., Micciancio, D. (eds.) CRYPTO 2019, Part II. LNCS, vol. 11693, pp. 510–539. Springer, Cham (2019). https://doi.org/10.1007/978-3-030-26951-7_18

[AGV09] Akavia, A., Goldwasser, S., Vaikuntanathan, V.: Simultaneous hardcore bits and cryptography against memory attacks. In: Reingold, O. (ed.) TCC 2009. LNCS, vol. 5444, pp. 474–495. Springer, Heidelberg (2009). https://doi.org/10.1007/978-3-642-00457-5_28

[AKO+22] Aggarwal, D., Kanukurthi, B., Obbattu, S.L.B., Obremski, M., Sekar, S.: Rate one-third non-malleable codes. In: Proceedings of the Symposium on Theory of Computing, STOC 2022 (2022)

[BBCM95] Bennett, C.H., Brassard, G., Crépeau, C., Maurer, U.M.: Generalized privacy amplification. IEEE Trans. Inf. Theory **41**(6), 1915–1923 (1995)

[BBR88] Bennett, C., Brassard, G., Robert, J.-M.: Privacy amplification by public discussion. SIAM J. Comput. **17**(2), 210–229 (1988)

[BDIR18] Benhamouda, F., Degwekar, A., Ishai, Y., Rabin, T.: On the local leakage resilience of linear secret sharing schemes. In: Shacham, H., Boldyreva, A. (eds.) CRYPTO 2018, Part I. LNCS, vol. 10991, pp. 531–561. Springer, Cham (2018). https://doi.org/10.1007/978-3-319-96884-1_18

[BFO+20] Brian, G., Faonio, A., Obremski, M., Simkin, M., Venturi, D.: Non-malleable secret sharing against bounded joint-tampering attacks in the plain model. In: Micciancio, D., Ristenpart, T. (eds.) CRYPTO 2020, Part III. LNCS, vol. 12172, pp. 127–155. Springer, Cham (2020). https://doi.org/10.1007/978-3-030-56877-1_5

[BFV19] Brian, G., Faonio, A., Venturi, D.: Continuously non-malleable secret sharing for general access structures. In: Hofheinz, D., Rosen, A. (eds.) TCC 2019, Part II. LNCS, vol. 11892, pp. 211–232. Springer, Cham (2019). https://doi.org/10.1007/978-3-030-36033-7_8

[BGK11] Boyle, E., Goldwasser, S., Kalai, Y.T.: Leakage-resilient coin tossing. In: Peleg, D. (ed.) DISC 2011. LNCS, vol. 6950, pp. 181–196. Springer, Heidelberg (2011). https://doi.org/10.1007/978-3-642-24100-0_16

[BGW88] Ben-Or, M., Goldwasser, S., Wigderson, A.: Completeness theorems for non-cryptographic fault-tolerant distributed computation (extended abstract). In: STOC, pp. 1–10 (1988)

[BL88] Benaloh, J., Leichter, J.: Generalized secret sharing and monotone functions. In: Goldwasser, S. (ed.) CRYPTO 1988. LNCS, vol. 403, pp. 27–35. Springer, New York (1990). https://doi.org/10.1007/0-387-34799-2_3

[Bla79] Blakley, G.R.: Safeguarding cryptographic keys. In: Proceedings of the 1979 AFIPS National Computer Conference, Monval, NJ, USA, pp. 313–317. AFIPS Press (1979)

[BS19] Badrinarayanan, S., Srinivasan, A.: Revisiting non-malleable secret sharing. In: Ishai, Y., Rijmen, V. (eds.) EUROCRYPT 2019, Part I. LNCS, vol. 11476, pp. 593–622. Springer, Cham (2019). https://doi.org/10.1007/978-3-030-17653-2_20

[BT12] Bellare, M., Tessaro, S.: Polynomial-time, semantically-secure encryption achieving the secrecy capacity. CoRR arXiv:1201.3160 (2012)

[CCD88] Chaum, D., Crépeau, C., Damgård, I.: Multiparty unconditionally secure protocols (extended abstract). In: STOC, pp. 11–19 (1988)

[CDH+00] Canetti, R., Dodis, Y., Halevi, S., Kushilevitz, E., Sahai, A.: Exposure-resilient functions and all-or-nothing transforms. In: Preneel, B. (ed.) EUROCRYPT 2000. LNCS, vol. 1807, pp. 453–469. Springer, Heidelberg (2000). https://doi.org/10.1007/3-540-45539-6_33

[CDS12] Cheraghchi, M., Didier, F., Shokrollahi, A.: Invertible extractors and wiretap protocols. IEEE Trans. Inf. Theory 58(2), 1254–1274 (2012)

[CGG+20] Chattopadhyay, E., et al.: Extractors and secret sharing against bounded collusion protocols. In: 61st IEEE Annual Symposium on Foundations of Computer Science, FOCS 2020, Durham, NC, USA, 16–19 November 2020, pp. 1226–1242. IEEE (2020)

[CKOS21] Chandran, N., Kanukurthi, B., Obbattu, S.L.B., Sekar, S.: Adaptive extractors and their application to leakage resilient secret sharing. In: Malkin, T., Peikert, C. (eds.) CRYPTO 2021. LNCS, vol. 12827, pp. 595–624. Springer, Cham (2021). https://doi.org/10.1007/978-3-030-84252-9_20

[DDV10] Davì, F., Dziembowski, S., Venturi, D.: Leakage-resilient storage. In: Garay, J.A., De Prisco, R. (eds.) SCN 2010. LNCS, vol. 6280, pp. 121–137. Springer, Heidelberg (2010). https://doi.org/10.1007/978-3-642-15317-4_9

[DF89] Desmedt, Y., Frankel, Y.: Threshold cryptosystems. In: Brassard, G. (ed.) CRYPTO 1989. LNCS, vol. 435, pp. 307–315. Springer, New York (1990). https://doi.org/10.1007/0-387-34805-0_28

[DORS08] Dodis, Y., Ostrovsky, R., Reyzin, L., Smith, A.: Fuzzy extractors: how to generate strong keys from biometrics and other noisy data. SIAM J. Comput. 38(1), 97–139 (2008). arXiv:cs/0602007

[DP07] Dziembowski, S., Pietrzak, K.: Intrusion-resilient secret sharing. In: Proceedings of the 48th Annual IEEE Symposium on Foundations of Computer Science, FOCS 2007, Washington, DC, USA, pp. 227–237. IEEE Computer Society (2007)

[DSS01] Dodis, Y., Sahai, A., Smith, A.: On perfect and adaptive security in exposure-resilient cryptography. In: Pfitzmann, B. (ed.) EUROCRYPT 2001. LNCS, vol. 2045, pp. 301–324. Springer, Heidelberg (2001). https://doi.org/10.1007/3-540-44987-6_19

[Fra89] Frankel, Y.: A practical protocol for large group oriented networks. In: Quisquater, J.-J., Vandewalle, J. (eds.) EUROCRYPT 1989. LNCS, vol. 434, pp. 56–61. Springer, Heidelberg (1990). https://doi.org/10.1007/3-540-46885-4_8

[FRR+10] Faust, S., Rabin, T., Reyzin, L., Tromer, E., Vaikuntanathan, V.: Protecting circuits from leakage: the computationally-bounded and noisy cases. In: Gilbert, H. (ed.) EUROCRYPT 2010. LNCS, vol. 6110, pp. 135–156. Springer, Heidelberg (2010). https://doi.org/10.1007/978-3-642-13190-5_7

[FV19] Faonio, A., Venturi, D.: Non-malleable secret sharing in the computational setting: adaptive tampering, noisy-leakage resilience, and improved rate. In: Boldyreva, A., Micciancio, D. (eds.) CRYPTO 2019, Part II. LNCS, vol. 11693, pp. 448–479. Springer, Cham (2019). https://doi.org/10.1007/978-3-030-26951-7_16

[GIM+16] Goyal, V., Ishai, Y., Maji, H.K., Sahai, A., Sherstov, A.A.: Bounded-communication leakage resilience via parity-resilient circuits. In: Dinur, I. (ed.) IEEE 57th Annual Symposium on Foundations of Computer Science, FOCS 2016, Hyatt Regency, New Brunswick, New Jersey, USA, 9–11 October 2016, pp. 1–10. IEEE Computer Society (2016)

[GK18] Goyal, V., Kumar, A.: Non-malleable secret sharing. In: Proceedings of the 50th Annual ACM SIGACT Symposium on Theory of Computing, STOC 2018, Los Angeles, CA, USA, 25–29 June 2018, pp. 685–698 (2018)

[GMW87] Goldreich, O., Micali, S., Wigderson, A.: How to play any mental game or a completeness theorem for protocols with honest majority. In: Proceedings of the Nineteenth Annual ACM Symposium on Theory of Computing, New York City, 25–27 May 1987, pp. 218–229 (1987)

[GW16] Guruswami, V., Wootters, M.: Repairing reed-solomon codes. In: Proceedings of the Forty-Eighth Annual ACM Symposium on Theory of Computing, STOC 2016, New York, NY, USA, pp. 216–226. ACM (2016)

[HVW21] Hazay, C., Venkitasubramaniam, M., Weiss, M.: ZK-PCPs from leakage-resilient secret sharing. IACR Cryptol. ePrint Arch. 2021 (2021)

[ISW03] Ishai, Y., Sahai, A., Wagner, D.: Private circuits: securing hardware against probing attacks. In: Boneh, D. (ed.) CRYPTO 2003. LNCS, vol. 2729, pp. 463–481. Springer, Heidelberg (2003). https://doi.org/10.1007/978-3-540-45146-4_27

[KMS19] Kumar, A., Meka, R., Sahai, A.: Leakage-resilient secret sharing against colluding parties. In: Zuckerman, D. (ed.) 60th IEEE Annual Symposium on Foundations of Computer Science, FOCS 2019, Baltimore, Maryland, USA, 9–12 November 2019, pp. 636–660. IEEE Computer Society (2019)

[Koc96] Kocher, P.C.: Timing attacks on implementations of Diffie-Hellman, RSA, DSS, and other systems. In: Koblitz, N. (ed.) CRYPTO 1996. LNCS, vol. 1109, pp. 104–113. Springer, Heidelberg (1996). https://doi.org/10.1007/3-540-68697-5_9

[KOS18] Kanukurthi, B., Obbattu, S.L.B., Sekar, S.: Non-malleable randomness encoders and their applications. In: Nielsen, J.B., Rijmen, V. (eds.) EUROCRYPT 2018, Part III. LNCS, vol. 10822, pp. 589–617. Springer, Cham (2018). https://doi.org/10.1007/978-3-319-78372-7_19

[LCG+19] Lin, F., Cheraghchi, M., Guruswami, V., Safavi-Naini, R., Wang, H.: Secret sharing with binary shares. In: Blum, A. (ed.) 10th Innovations in Theoretical Computer Science Conference, ITCS 2019, San Diego, California, USA, volume 124 of LIPIcs, 10–12 January 2019, pp. 53:1–53:20. Schloss Dagstuhl - Leibniz-Zentrum für Informatik (2019)

[LL12] Liu, F.-H., Lysyanskaya, A.: Tamper and leakage resilience in the split-state model. In: Safavi-Naini, R., Canetti, R. (eds.) CRYPTO 2012. LNCS, vol. 7417, pp. 517–532. Springer, Heidelberg (2012). https://doi.org/10.1007/978-3-642-32009-5_30

[MNP+21] Maji, H.K., Nguyen, H.H., Paskin-Cherniavsky, A., Suad, T., Wang, M.: Leakage-resilience of the Shamir secret-sharing scheme against physical-bit leakages. In: Canteaut, A., Standaert, F.-X. (eds.) EUROCRYPT 2021, Part II. LNCS, vol. 12697, pp. 344–374. Springer, Cham (2021). https://doi.org/10.1007/978-3-030-77886-6_12

[MPSW21] Maji, H.K., Paskin-Cherniavsky, A., Suad, T., Wang, M.: Constructing locally leakage-resilient linear secret-sharing schemes. In: Malkin, T., Peikert, C. (eds.) CRYPTO 2021, Part III. LNCS, vol. 12827, pp. 779–808. Springer, Cham (2021). https://doi.org/10.1007/978-3-030-84252-9_26

[MR04] Micali, S., Reyzin, L.: Physically observable cryptography. In: Naor, M. (ed.) TCC 2004. LNCS, vol. 2951, pp. 278–296. Springer, Heidelberg (2004). https://doi.org/10.1007/978-3-540-24638-1_16

[NS20] Nielsen, J.B., Simkin, M.: Lower bounds for leakage-resilient secret sharing. In: Canteaut, A., Ishai, Y. (eds.) EUROCRYPT 2020, Part I. LNCS, vol. 12105, pp. 556–577. Springer, Cham (2020). https://doi.org/10.1007/978-3-030-45721-1_20

[NZ96] Nisan, N., Zuckerman, D.: Randomness is linear in space. J. Comput. Syst. Sci. **52**(1), 43–53 (1996)

[Riv97] Rivest, R.L.: All-or-nothing encryption and the package transform. In: Biham, E. (ed.) FSE 1997. LNCS, vol. 1267, pp. 210–218. Springer, Heidelberg (1997). https://doi.org/10.1007/BFb0052348

[Rot12] Rothblum, G.N.: How to compute under $\mathcal{AC}^0$ leakage without secure hardware. In: Safavi-Naini, R., Canetti, R. (eds.) CRYPTO 2012. LNCS, vol. 7417, pp. 552–569. Springer, Heidelberg (2012). https://doi.org/10.1007/978-3-642-32009-5_32

[RRV02] Raz, R., Reingold, O., Vadhan, S.: Extracting all the randomness and reducing the error in Trevisan's extractors. J. Comput. Syst. Sci. **65**(1), 97–128 (2002)

[SDFY94] De Santis, A., Desmedt, Y., Frankel, Y., Yung, M.: How to share a function securely. In: Leighton, F.T., Goodrich, M.T. (eds.) Proceedings of the Twenty-Sixth Annual ACM Symposium on Theory of Computing, Montréal, Québec, Canada, 23–25 May 1994, pp. 522–533. ACM (1994)

[Sha79] Shamir, A.: How to share a secret. Commun. ACM **22**(11), 612–613 (1979)

[SV19] Srinivasan, A., Vasudevan, P.N.: Leakage resilient secret sharing and applications. In: Boldyreva, A., Micciancio, D. (eds.) CRYPTO 2019. LNCS, vol. 11693, pp. 480–509. Springer, Cham (2019). https://doi.org/10.1007/978-3-030-26951-7_17

[Tre99] Trevisan, L.: Construction of extractors using pseudo-random generators (extended abstract). In: STOC, pp. 141–148 (1999)

[Tre01] Trevisan, L.: Extractors and pseudorandom generators. J. ACM **48**(4), 860–879 (2001)

[Vad12] Vadhan, S.: Pseudorandomness. Foundations and Trends in Theoretical Computer Science. Now Publishers (2012). http://people.seas.harvard.edu/~salil/pseudorandomness/

Cryptography from Pseudorandom Quantum States

Prabhanjan Ananth[1] , Luowen Qian[2](✉) , and Henry Yuen[3]

[1] UCSB, Santa Barbara, USA
prabhanjan@cs.ucsb.edu
[2] Boston University, Boston, USA
luowenq@bu.edu
[3] Columbia University, New York, USA
hyuen@cs.columbia.edu

Abstract. Pseudorandom states, introduced by Ji, Liu and Song (Crypto'18), are efficiently-computable quantum states that are computationally indistinguishable from Haar-random states. One-way functions imply the existence of pseudorandom states, but Kretschmer (TQC'20) recently constructed an oracle relative to which there are no one-way functions but pseudorandom states still exist. Motivated by this, we study the intriguing possibility of basing interesting cryptographic tasks on pseudorandom states.

We construct, assuming the existence of pseudorandom state generators that map a λ-bit seed to a $\omega(\log \lambda)$-qubit state, (a) statistically binding and computationally hiding commitments and (b) pseudo one-time encryption schemes. A consequence of (a) is that pseudorandom states are sufficient to construct maliciously secure multiparty computation protocols in the dishonest majority setting.

Our constructions are derived via a new notion called *pseudorandom function-like states* (PRFS), a generalization of pseudorandom states that parallels the classical notion of pseudorandom functions. Beyond the above two applications, we believe our notion can effectively replace pseudorandom functions in many other cryptographic applications.

1 Introduction

Assumptions are the bedrock of designing provably secure cryptographic constructions. Over the years, theoretical cryptographers have pondered over the precise assumptions needed to achieve cryptographic tasks, often losing sleep over this [24]. The celebrated work of Goldreich [18] shows that most interesting cryptographic tasks (encryption, commitments, pseudorandom generators, etc.) imply the existence of one-way functions, i.e., functions that can be efficiently computed in the forward direction but cannot be efficiently inverted. Thus it appears that the existence of one-way functions is a *minimal* and *necessary* assumption in cryptography.

H. Yuen—Supported by AFOSR award FA9550-21-1-0040 and NSF CAREER award CCF-2144219. L. Qian—Supported by DARPA under Agreement No. HR00112020023.

Y. Dodis and T. Shrimpton (Eds.): CRYPTO 2022, LNCS 13507, pp. 208–236, 2022.
https://doi.org/10.1007/978-3-031-15802-5_8

Quantum information processing presents new opportunities for cryptography. Specifically, in many contexts the assumptions necessary for cryptographic tasks can be weakened with the help of quantum resources. To illustrate, the seminal work of Bennett and Brassard [7] showed that key exchange can be achieved unconditionally (i.e. without any computational assumptions) using quantum communication. In contrast, key exchange is known to require computational assumptions if the parties are restricted to classical communication. More recently, the work of Bartusek, Coladangelo, Khurana, and Ma [4] and that of Grilo, Lin, Song and Vaikuntanathan [19] demonstrate that quantum protocols for secure multiparty computation can be constructed from post-quantum one-way functions. On the other hand classical protocols for secure computation cannot be based (in a black-box fashion) on one-way functions alone [22].

These examples suggest that we revisit our belief about the necessity of certain cryptographic assumptions for quantum cryptographic tasks (tasks that make use of quantum computation and/or quantum communication). Specifically, it is not even clear whether one-way functions are even necessary in the quantum setting—Goldreich's result [18] only applies to classical cryptographic primitives and protocols.

Our work continues the research agenda carried out by our predecessors [4, 7, 8, 19, 29]: *can we achieve cryptographic tasks using quantum communication in a world without one-way functions[1] ?*

Pseudorandom Quantum States. Motivated by the question above, we turn to the notion of pseudorandom quantum states (abbreviated PRS) introduced by Ji, Liu and Song [23]. A *PRS generator* G is a quantum polynomial-time (QPT) algorithm that, given input a λ-bit key, outputs an n-qubit quantum state with the guarantee that it is computationally indistinguishable from an n-qubit Haar random state (i.e. the uniform distribution over n-qubit pure states), even with many copies. Ji, Liu and Song (and subsequently improved by Brakerski and Shmueli [11, 12]) show the existence of PRS assuming post-quantum one-way functions.

This notion is analogous to pseudorandom generators (PRGs) from classical cryptography which take as input a random seed of length λ, and deterministically outputs a larger string of length $n > \lambda$ that is computationally indistinguishable from a string sampled from the uniform distribution. Despite the analogy, it has not been obvious whether pseudorandom quantum states have much cryptographic utility outside of quantum money [23] (unlike PRGs, which are ubiquitous in cryptography). Understanding the consequences of pseudorandom quantum states is particularly important in light of a recent result by Kretschmer [25], who showed that there is a relativized world where $BQP = QMA$ (and thus post-quantum one-way functions do not exist) while pseudorandom states exist. Kretschmer's result motivates us to focus the afore-

---

[1] Both the works [4, 19] explicitly raised the question of basing secure computation on assumptions weaker than one-way functions.

mentioned research agenda on the following question: *what cryptographic tasks can be based solely on pseudorandom quantum states?*

1.1   Our Results

Our contributions in a nutshell are as follows:

- We propose a new notion called *pseudorandom function-like quantum states (PRFS)*.
- Using PRFS, we show how to build (a) statistically binding commitments and (b) pseudo one-time encryption schemes. As a consequence of (a), we obtain maliciously secure computation in the dishonest majority setting.
- Finally, we show that for a certain range of parameters – the same as what is needed for the above applications – we can construct PRFS from a PRS.

Before we present the definition of PRFS, we first highlight the need for defining a new notion by describing the challenges for constructing primitives directly from PRS.

Challenges for Basing Primitives on PRS. Although the closest classical analogue of a PRS generator is a PRG, the analogy breaks down in several critical ways. This makes it challenging to use PRS generators in the same way that PRGs are used throughout cryptography.

Specifically, PRS generators appear very *rigid*, meaning that it seems challenging to take an existing PRS generator and generically increase or decrease its output length. Moreover, it is difficult to use output qubits of a PRS generator independently.

Inability to Stretch the Output. A fundamental result about PRGs is that their *stretch* (the output length as a function of the key length) can be amplified arbitrarily. In other words, given a PRG G that maps λ random bits to at least $(\lambda+1)$ pseudorandom bits, one can construct a PRG with any polynomial output length. This fact is implicitly used everywhere in cryptography; specifically, it gives us the flexibility to choose the appropriate stretch of PRG relevant for the application without having to worry about the underlying hardness assumptions.

If PRS generators are analogous to PRGs, then one would expect that a similar amplification result to hold: the existence of PRS with nontrivial output length would (hopefully) imply the existence of PRS with arbitrarily large output length. The natural approach to amplify the stretch of a PRG by iteratively composing it with itself does not immediately work with PRS for a number of reasons; for one, a PRS generator takes as input a classical key while its output is a quantum state!

Inability to Shrink the Output. To add insult to injury, it is not even obvious how to *shrink* the output length of a PRS generator; this was also observed by Brakerski and Shmueli [9]. Classically, one can always discard bits from the output of a PRG, and the result is still obviously a PRG. However, discarding a single qubit of an n-qubit pseudorandom state will leave a mixed state that is easily distinguishable from an $(n-1)$-qubit Haar-random state.

Inability to Separate the Output. Since the PRS output is highly entangled, it seems difficult to use the individual output qubits. As an example, suppose we want to encrypt a message of length ℓ. In the classical setting, an ℓ-bit output PRG can be used to encrypt a message of length ℓ by xor-ing the ith PRG output bit with the ith bit of the message. Implicitly, we are using the fact that the output of a PRG can be viewed a tensor product of bits and this feature of classical PRGs is mirrored by our notion of PRFS (explained next). On the other hand, if we have a single (entangled) PRS state (irrespective of the number of qubits it represents), it is unclear how to use each qubit to encode a bit; any operations performed on a single qubit could affect the other qubits that are entangled with this qubit.

New Notion: Pseudorandom Function-Like States. Pseudorandom function-like states (abbreviated PRFS) is a generalization of PRS, where the same key k can be used to generate many pseudorandom states. In more details, a (d,n)-*PRFS generator* G is a QPT algorithm that, given as input a key $k \in \{0,1\}^\lambda$ and an input $x \in \{0,1\}^d$, outputs a n-qubit quantum state $|\psi_{k,x}\rangle$, satisfying the following pseudorandomness property: no efficient adversaries can distinguish between multiple copies of the output states $(|\psi_{k,x_1}\rangle, \ldots, |\psi_{k,x_s}\rangle)$ from a collection of states $(|\vartheta_1\rangle, \ldots, |\vartheta_s\rangle)$ where each $|\vartheta_i\rangle$ is sampled independently from the Haar distribution; furthermore, the indistinguishability holds even if the inputs $x_1, \ldots, x_s$ are chosen by the adversary. This is formalized in Definition 2.

An Alternate Perspective: Tensor Product PRS Generators. If PRS generators are analogous to classical pseudorandom generators, then PRFS generators are analogous to classical pseudorandom *functions* (hence the name pseudorandom *function-like*). A PRS generator outputs a single state per key k. On the other hand, we can think of PRFS as a *relaxed* notion of PRS generator that on input k outputs a *tensor product* of states $|\psi_0\rangle \otimes |\psi_1\rangle \otimes \cdots \otimes |\psi_{2^d-1}\rangle$ where each $|\psi_i\rangle$, is indistinguishable from a Haar-random state.

The tensor product feature is quite useful in applications, as we will see shortly.

Additional Observations. Some additional observations of PRFS are in order:

- Assuming one-way functions, we can generically construct (d,n)-PRFS from any n-qubit PRS for any polynomial d,n. To compute PRFS on key k and input x, first compute a classical PRF on (k,x) and use the resulting output as a key for the n-qubit PRS. Since n-qubit PRS can be based on (post-quantum) one-way functions [12,23], this shows that even PRFS can be based on (post-quantum) one-way functions.

- In the other direction, we can construct n-qubit PRS from any (d, n)-qubit PRFS. On input k, the PRS simply outputs the result of PRFS on input $(k, 0)$.
- Another interesting aspect about PRFS is that it too, like PRS, is separated from (post-quantum) one-way functions. This can be obtained by a generalization of Kretschmer's result [2].

Implications. We show that PRFS can effectively replace the usage of pseudorandom generators and pseudorandom functions in many primitives one learns about in "Cryptography 101". Specifically, we focus on two applications of PRFS generators. Later we will show that in fact that we can achieve these two applications from PRS generators only.

Implication 1. One-time Encryption with Short Keys and Long Messages. As a starter illustration of the usefulness of PRFS, we construct from a PRFS generator G a one-time encryption scheme for classical messages. The important feature of this construction is the fact that the message length is much larger than the key length. This is impossible to achieve information-theoretically, even in the quantum setting. This type of one-time encryption schemes, also referred to as *pseudo one-time pad*, is already quite useful, as it implies garbling schemes for P/poly [6] and even garbling for quantum circuits [13].

Theorem 1 (Informal; Pseudo One-time Pad). *Assuming the existence of (d, n)-PRFS with[2] $d = O(\log \lambda)$ and $n = \omega(\log \lambda)$, there exists a one-time encryption scheme for messages of length $\ell = 2^d$.*

We emphasize that in the implication to one-time encryption, we only require PRFS with logarithmic-length inputs.

The construction is simple and a direct adaptation of the construction of one-time encryption from pseudorandom generators. To encrypt a message x of length $\ell \gg \lambda$, output the state $G(k, (1, x_i)) \otimes \cdots \otimes G(k, (\ell, x_\ell))$, where $k \in \{0, 1\}^\lambda$ is the symmetric key shared by the encryptor and the decryptor. The decryptor using the secret key k can decode[3] the message x. The security of the encryption scheme follows from the pseudorandomness of PRFS.

Implication 2. Statistically Binding Commitment Schemes. We focus on designing commitment schemes with statistical binding and computational hiding properties. In the classical setting, this notion of commitment schemes can be constructed from any length-tripling PRG [27]. Recently, two independent works [4, 19] showed that commitment schemes with aforementioned properties imply maliciously secure multiparty computation protocols with quantum communication in the dishonest majority setting. Of particular interest is the work of [4] who

---

[2] Recall that λ is the key length.

[3] In the technical sections, we define a QPT algorithm Test that given a state ρ along with k, x, determines if ρ is equal to the output $G(k, x)$. We show the existence of such a test algorithm for any PRFS.

construct the multiparty computation protocol using the commitment scheme as a *black box*. In particular, their construction works even when the commitment scheme uses quantum communication. They then instantiate the underlying commitment scheme from post-quantum one-way functions.

We design commitment schemes based on PRFS instead of one-way functions. First, we present a new definition of the statistical binding property for commitment schemes that utilize quantum communication. The notion of binding for quantum commitment schemes is more subtle than that for classical commitment schemes and has been extensively studied in prior works [4,9,17,28,30]. Our definition generalizes all previously known definitions of statistical binding for quantum commitments, and suffice for applications such as secure multiparty computation. (Our definition is formally presented in Definition 6).

Then we show, assuming the existence of PRFS with certain parameters, the existence of quantum commitment schemes satisfying our definition.

Theorem 2 (Informal). *Assuming the existence of (d,n)-PRFS[4] where $2^d \cdot n \geq 7\lambda$, there exists a statistically binding and computationally hiding commitment scheme.*

By plugging our commitment scheme into the framework of [4], we obtain the following corollary.

Corollary 1 (Informal). *Assuming the existence of (d,n)-PRFS with $2^d \cdot n \geq 7\lambda$, there exists a maliciously secure multiparty computation protocol in the dishonest majority setting.*

Our construction is an adaptation of Naor's commitment scheme [27]. We replace the use of the PRG in Naor's construction with a PRFS generator and the first message, which is a random string in Naor's construction, instead specifies a random Pauli operator.

Other Implications. Besides the above applications, we show that PRFS (with polynomially-long input length) can also be used to construct other fundamental primitives such as symmetric-key CPA-secure encryption and message authentication codes (see full version). Both primitives guarantee security in the setting when the secret key can be reused multiple times.

Unlike the previous applications (pseudo QOTP and commitments), the straightforward constructions of reusable encryption and MACs require PRFS generators with input lengths $\omega(\log \lambda)$ and ℓ respectively, where ℓ is the length of the message being authenticated. We do not know if such PRFS generators can be constructed from PRS generators in a black box way. Nonetheless, we believe these applications illustrate the usefulness of the concept of PRFS generators.

---

[4] To simplify the analysis, there is an additional technical property of the PRFS not mentioned here that is required by our construction, called *recognizable abort* (Definition 4). All known constructions of PRFS and PRS (including ours) have the recognizable abort property.

Construction of PRFS. Given the interesting implications of PRFS, the next natural step is to focus on constructing PRFS generators. We show that for some interesting range of parameters, we can achieve PRFS from any PRS. In particular, we show the following.

Theorem 3 (Informal). *For $d = O(\log \lambda)$ and $n = d + \omega(\log \log \lambda)$, assuming the existence of a $(d + n)$-qubit PRS generator, there exists a (d, n)-PRFS generator.*

A surprising aspect about the above result is that the starting PRS's output length $d + n = \omega(\log \log \lambda)$ could even be much smaller than the key length λ. In contrast, classical pseudorandom generators with output length less than the input length are trivial.

We remark that if $d \ll \log \lambda$ then it is easy to build PRFS from PRS; chop up the key k into 2^d blocks; to compute the PRFS generator with key k and input x, compute the PRS generator on the xth block of the key. Unfortunately, PRFS with this range of parameters does not appear useful for applications because the seed length is too large. On the other hand, the construction of PRFS generators from PRS generators in Theorem 3 allows for 2^d to be an arbitrarily large polynomial in the key length. Note that this is sufficient for Theorem 1 and Corollary 1. We thus obtain the following corollary.

Corollary 2. *Assuming $(2 \log \lambda + \omega(\log \log \lambda))$-qubit PRS, there exist statistically binding commitment schemes and therefore secure computations. Assuming $\omega(\log \lambda)$-qubit PRS, there exist pseudo one-time pad schemes for messages of any polynomial length.*

We remark that the assumptions of Corollary 2 on the PRS generators are essentially *optimal*, in the sense that it is not possible to significantly weaken them. This is because commitment and pseudo one-time pad schemes require computational assumptions on the adversary; on other hand Brakerski and Shmueli [12] demonstrate the existence a "pseudo"-random state generator with output length $c \log \lambda$ for some constant $c < 1$ that is *statistically secure*: in other words, the outputs of the generator are indistinguishable from Haar-random states by *any* distinguisher (not just polynomial-time ones).

Furthermore, it can be shown that PRS generators with $\log \lambda$-qubit outputs require computational assumptions on the adversary and that generators with $(1 + \varepsilon) \log \lambda$-qubit outputs imply BQP $\neq$ PP [2].

Concurrent Work. A concurrent preprint of Morimae and Yamakawa [26] also construct statistically binding and computationally hiding commitment schemes from PRS, adapting Naor's commitment scheme in a manner similar to ours. We note several differences between their work and ours, with regards to commitment schemes.

1. They show a weaker notion of binding known as *sum-binding*, which roughly says that the *sum* of the probabilities that an adversarial committer can

successfully decommit to the bit 0 and the bit 1 is at most a quantity negligibly close to 1. This notion of binding is not known to be sufficient for general quantum commitment protocols to conclude that PRS implies protocols for secure computation[5]. However, our notion of statistical binding (Definition 6) is sufficient for leveraging the machinery of [4] to obtain quantum protocols for secure computation. Moreover, our definition of statistical binding implies the sum-binding definition[6].

2. For the same level of statistical binding security, that is $O(2^{-\lambda})$, they require the existence of a PRS that stretches λ random bits to 3λ qubits of Haar-randomness (i.e., they require the PRS generator to have *stretch*), whereas our result assumes the existence of a PRS that maps λ bits to $2\log\lambda + \omega(\log\log\lambda)$ qubits. On the other hand, they require the pseudorandomness/indistinguishability of a single copy of PRS state versus Haar random, while we require the pseudorandomness to hold again multiple copies, especially when the output length is short.

3. The state generation guarantee required from the underlying PRS is much stricter in their setting. In our work, we require the underlying PRS to only satisfy recognizable abort (Definition 4) whereas in their work, the underlying PRS needs to satisfy a guarantee that is even stronger than perfect state generation (Definition 3).

4. Their commitment scheme is non-interactive whereas our commitment scheme is a two-message scheme. Furthermore, our protocol has a classical opening message while theirs is quantum. However, these differences are rather minor since we can easily adapt our construction to satisfy these requirements, and vice versa.

We also note that the notion of PRFS, its implications and its construction from PRS is unique to our work.

1.2 Discussion: Why Explore a World Without One-Way Functions?

Before getting into the technical overview we address a common question: *"Sure, it is interesting that one can construct commitment schemes and pseudo one-time pad schemes without one-way functions, but will this still matter if someone proves that (post-quantum) one-way functions exist?"*

Our view is the following: it is *not* our goal to avoid one-way functions because we don't believe that they exist[7]. The main motivation is to gain a *deeper understanding* of fundamental cryptographic primitives such as encryption and commitment schemes. As mentioned previously, it has been understood for many

---

[5] However, in an updated draft of [26], the authors sketch how, for a special form of quantum commitment schemes, sum-binding does imply our notion of statistical binding.

[6] The sum of probabilities that an adversarial decommitter can decommit to 0 and to 1 in the ideal world of our definition (Definition 6) and therefore they sum up to at most negligibly larger than 1 in the real world by our statistical binding guarantee.

[7] The majority of the authors of this paper believe one-way functions exist.

decades that these primitives are inseparable from one-way functions (even in a black box way) in the classical setting. We view our results as revising this understanding in the quantum world: one-way functions are not necessary for these primitives.

Another motivation comes from complexity theory. An oft-repeated storyline is that if P = NP, then one-way functions would not exist and thus most cryptography would be impossible; this scenario has been coined by Impagliazzo as *Algorithmica* as one of his five "complexity worlds" [21]. While most people believe that P $\neq$ NP, it is nonetheless scientifically interesting to study the consequences of other complexity-theoretic outcomes. Our work adds a twist to the usual P = NP storyline: perhaps *QAlgorithmica* – Impagliazzo's *Algorithmica* plus quantum information – can potentially support both an algorithmic *and* cryptographic paradise.

Finally, we believe that studying the possibilities of basing cryptography solely on quantum assumptions is extremely useful for deepening our understanding of quantum information. By restricting ourselves to *not* use one-way functions, we force ourselves to use the unique properties of quantum mechanics to the hilt. For example, our constructions of PRFS generators, pseudo one-time pad and commitment schemes ultimately required us to make use of properties of pseudorandom states such as concentration of measure over the Haar distribution.

Another question that often arises is: *"Is there a candidate construction of PRS generators that do not (obviously) involve one-way functions?"* While Kretschmer [25] showed an oracle separation between pseudorandom states and one-way functions, this is an artificial setting where the oracle is constructed by sampling a Haar-random unitary.

We claim that *random quantum circuits* form natural constructions of pseudorandom states: the generator G interprets the key k as a description of a quantum circuit on n qubits, and G outputs the state $k|0^n\rangle$ (i.e. executes the circuit with the all zeroes input). It has been conjectured in a number of settings that random quantum circuits have excellent pseudorandom properties. For example, the quantum supremacy experiments of Google [3] and UTSC [31] are based on the premise that random n-qubit circuits of sufficiently large depth should generate states that are essentially Haar-random [20]. Random quantum circuits have also been extensively studied as toy models of scrambling in black hole dynamics [10,14,15].

It seems beyond the reach of present-day techniques to prove that polynomialsize random quantum circuits yield pseudorandom states; for one, doing so would separate BQP from PP [25], which would be an incredible result in complexity theory. However, this is a plausible candidate PRS generator, and arguably this construction does not involve one-way functions at all.

1.3   Technical Overview

We first describe the techniques behind the construction of pseudorandom function-like states from pseudorandom quantum states. Then, we will give an overview of the result of statistical binding commitments from PRFS.

PRFS from PRS. To construct a (d, n)-PRFS, we start with an $(n + d)$-qubit PRS. For the purposes of the current discussion, we will assume that PRS has *perfect state generation*. That is, the output of PRS is a pure state.

Main Insight: Post-Selection. The construction proceeds as follows: on input key k and $x \in \{0, 1\}^d$, first generate a $(d + n)$-qubit PRS state by treating k as the PRS seed. As the PRS satisfies perfect state generation, the output is a pure state and we can write the state as $|\psi\rangle = \sum_{x \in \{0,1\}^d} \alpha_x |x\rangle \otimes |\psi_x\rangle$, where $|\psi_x\rangle$ is a n-qubit state. Suppose we post-select (i.e., condition) on the first d qubits being in the state $|x\rangle$, the remaining n qubits will be in the state $|\psi_x\rangle$, which we define to be the output of the PRFS on input (k, x).

   In general, we do not know how to perform post-selection in polynomial-time [1]. However, if the event on which we are post-selecting has an inverse polynomial (where the polynomial is known ahead of time) probability of occurring, then we can efficiently perform post-selection. That is, we repeat the following process $2^d \lambda$ number of times: generate $|\psi\rangle$ by computing the PRS generator on k and then measure the first d qubits in the computational basis. If the first d qubits is x then output the residual state (which is $|\psi_x\rangle$), otherwise continue. If in none of the $2^d \lambda$ iterations, we obtained the first d qubits to be x, we declare failure and output some fixed state $|\bot\rangle$.

   We prove that the above PRFS generator satisfies pseudorandomness by making two observations.

Observation 1: Output of PRFS is close to $|\psi_x\rangle$. We need to argue that the probability that the PRFS generator outputs $|\psi_x\rangle$ is negligibly (in λ) close to 1. This boils down to showing that with probability negligibly close to 1, in one of the iterations, the measurement outcome will be x. Indeed if $|\alpha_x|^2$ is roughly $\frac{1}{2^d}$ then this statement is true. But it is a priori not clear how to argue this.

   Towards resolving this issue, let us first pretend that $|\psi\rangle$ was instead drawn from the Haar measure. In this case, we can rely upon Lévy's Lemma to argue that $|\alpha_x|^2$ is indeed close to $\frac{1}{2^d}$, with overwhelming probability over the Haar measure. Thus, if $|\psi\rangle$ was drawn from the Haar measure, the probability that the PRFS generator outputs $|\psi_x\rangle$ is negligibly close to 1.

   Now, let us go back to the case when $|\psi\rangle$ was a PRS state. Since the PRFS generator is a quantum polynomial-time algorithm, it cannot distinguish whether $|\psi\rangle$ was generated by PRS or whether it was sampled from the Haar measure. This means that the probability that it outputs $|\psi_x\rangle$, when $|\psi\rangle$ was a PRS state, should also be negligibly close to 1.

   While ideally we would have liked the PRFS to have perfect state generation, the above construction still satisfies a nice property that we call *recognizable abort*: the output of the PRFS is either a pure state or it is some known pure state $|\perp\rangle$.

All is left is to show that the post-selected state $|\psi_x\rangle$ is Haar random when $|\psi\rangle$ is Haar random.

Observation 2: Post-selected Haar random state is also Haar random. Haar random states satisfy a property called unitary invariance: applying any unitary on a Haar random state yields a Haar random state. Consider the following distribution $\mathcal{R}$ of unitaries: $R = \sum_{x \in \{0,1\}^n} |x\rangle\langle x| \otimes R_x$, where R_x is a Haar random unitary. Now, applying R, where $R \leftarrow \mathcal{R}$, on a Haar random state $|\psi\rangle = \sum_{x \in \{0,1\}^d} |x\rangle \otimes |\psi_x\rangle$ yields a Haar random state.

Thus, the following two processes yield the same distribution:

– Process 1: Sample $|\psi\rangle = \sum_{x \in \{0,1\}^d} |x\rangle \otimes |\psi_x\rangle$ be a Haar random state. Output $|\psi_x\rangle$.
– Process 2: Sample a Haar random state $|\psi\rangle = \sum_{x \in \{0,1\}^d} |x\rangle \otimes |\psi_x\rangle$. Output $R_x|\psi_x\rangle$.

Notice that the output distribution of Process 2 is Haar random since R_x is a Haar random unitary. From this we can conclude that even the output distribution of Process 1 is also Haar random.

Test Procedure. Classical pseudorandom generators satisfy a verifiability property that we often take for granted: given a value y and a seed k, we can successfully check if y is obtained as an evaluation of a seed k. This feature is implicitly used in many applications of pseudorandom generators. We would like to have a similar feature even for pseudorandom function-like states. More specifically, we would like the following to hold: given a state ρ, a PRFS key k and an input x, check if ρ is close to the output of PRFS on (k, x).

Let us start with a simple case when the PRFS satisfies perfect state generation property and moreover, PRFS generator is a unitary G. We can express PRFS state generation as follows: on input a key k, input x and ancillas $|k\rangle \otimes |x\rangle \otimes |0\rangle$, G outputs $|\psi_{k,x}\rangle \otimes |\phi\rangle$. The state $|\psi_x\rangle$ is designated to be the PRFS state corresponding to input x and the state $|\phi\rangle$ is discarded as the garbage state.

Suppose we need to test if a state ρ is the output of PRFS on k and x. The test procedure is defined as follows:

– Compute $G(|k\rangle \otimes |x\rangle \otimes |0\rangle)$,
– Swap the register containing the PRFS state with ρ,
– Apply $G^\dagger$ on the resulting state and,
– Measure the resulting state and output 1 if the outcome is $(k, x, 0)$. Otherwise, output 0.

Since unitaries preserve fidelity between the states, we can show that the following holds: the above test procedure outputs 1 with probability proportional to $F(\rho, |\psi_{k,x}\rangle\langle\psi_{k,x}|)$. More precisely, the test procedure outputs 1 with probability $\mathrm{Tr}(|\psi_{k,x}\rangle\langle\psi_{k,x}|\rho)$.

The above test procedure can be suitably generalized if the PRFS satisfies the (weaker) state generation with recognizable abort property. If the PRFS generator is a quantum circuit then we designate G, in the above test procedure, to be a purification of this quantum circuit.

Statistical Binding Commitments. We show how to construct statistical binding quantum commitments from PRFS.

Definition. A statistical binding quantum commitment scheme consists of two interactive phases between a sender and a receiver: a commit phase and a reveal phase. In both the phases, the communication between the parties can be quantum. In the commit phase, the sender commits to a bit b. In the reveal phase, the committer reveals b and the receiver either accepts or rejects.

We require that any (even unbounded) sender cannot commit to bit b in the commit phase and then successfully open to $1 - b$ in the reveal phase. Formalizing this can be tricky in the setting where the communication channel is quantum. For example, consider the following attack: an adversarial sender can send a uniform superposition of commitments of 0 and 1 and then open to one of them in the reveal phase. Any definition we come up should handle this attack.

We propose an extractor-based definition. Consider an adversarial sender S^*. Let us define the ideal experiment as follows: execute the commit phase with S^*. After the commit phase, apply an extractor on the receiver's state. The output of the extractor is a bit b^* along with the collapse state σ_R. Execute the reveal phase; let b be the bit opened to by S^*. Output Fail if $b \neq b^*$ and R accepts. Otherwise, output S^*'s final state (after the execution of the Reveal phase) along with R's decision, which is either the decommitted bit of the sender or it is $\perp$. Similarly, we can define real experiment as follows: We execute the commit phase and the reveal phase between S^* and R and then output the final state of S^* along with R's decision.

Going back to the earlier superposition attack, the extractor would, with equal probability, collapse to either commitment of 0 or collapse to commitment of 1.

We say that the quantum commitment scheme satisfies statistical binding if the output distributions of the real and ideal experiments are statistically close. Our definition of statistical binding generalizes all the previous definitions of statistical binding in the context of quantum commitments [4,9,17,28,30]. Refer to Sect. 5.1 for a detailed comparison with prior definitions.

We also require the quantum commitment scheme to satisfy computational hiding: in the commit phase, any quantum poly-time receiver cannot tell apart whether the sender committed to 0 or 1.

Construction. Our construction is a direct adaptation of Naor's commitment scheme [27], i.e. the same protocol but simply replacing PRG with PRFS. We start with a (d, n)-PRFS, where $d = O(\log(\lambda))$ and $n \geq 1$.

- In the commit phase, the receiver sends a random $2^d n$-qubit Pauli $P = P_0 \otimes \cdots P_{2^d-1}$ to the sender, where each P_i is a n-qubit Pauli. The sender on input bit b, samples a key k uniformly at random from $\{0,1\}^\lambda$. The sender then sends the state $\mathbf{c} = \bigotimes_{x \in [2^d]} P_i^b \sigma_{k,x} P_i^b$, where $\sigma_{k,x} = PRFS(k,i)$ to the receiver.
- In the reveal phase, the sender sends (k,b) to the receiver. The receiver accepts if $P^b \mathbf{c} P^b$ is a tensor product of the PRFS evaluations of (k,x), for all $x = 0,\ldots,2^d - 1$.

From the pseudorandomness property of PRFS, hiding follows. To prove that the above scheme satisfies binding, we describe the extractor first. It again helps to think of PRFS as satisfying the perfect state generation property. The extractor applies the following projection $\{\Pi_0, \Pi_1, I - (\Pi_0 + \Pi_1)\}$, where Π_b projects onto the subspace spanned by $T_b = \left\{ \bigotimes_{x \in \{0,1\}^{2^d}} P^b |\psi_{k,x}\rangle\langle\psi_{k,x}| P^b \; : \; \forall k \in \{0,1\}^\lambda \right\}$, where $|\psi_{k,x}\rangle$ is the output of $PRFS(k,x)$. If Π_b succeeds then b is designated to be the extracted bit. At the core of proving the indistinguishability of the real and the ideal world is the following fact: applying a projector that projects onto T_b (as done by the extractor), followed by the projector $\bigotimes_{x \in \{0,1\}^{2^d}} P^b |\psi_{k,x}\rangle\langle\psi_{k,x}| P^b$ (as done by the receiver) is the equivalent to only applying the projector $\bigotimes_{x \in \{0,1\}^{2^d}} P^b |\psi_{k,x}\rangle\langle\psi_{k,x}| P^b$.

While our actual proof is conceptually similar to the proof sketched above, there are some crucial details that we shoved under the rug. Firstly, $I - (\Pi_0 + \Pi_1)$ is not necessarily a projection since the projections Π_0 and Π_1 need not be orthogonal. Secondly, the PRFS generation is not perfect and we need to work with recognizable abort property. Nonetheless we circumvent these issues and show that the above construction still works. We refer the reader to Sect. 5.2 for more details.

1.4   Future Directions

We end this section with some future directions and open questions.

Properties of Pseudorandom States. Given a PRS generator G mapping λ-bit keys to n-qubit states, is it possible to construct in as black-box fashion as possible, a PRS generator G' with longer output length (but same length key)? In other words, it is possible to arbitrarily *stretch* the output of a PRS?

Is it possible to construct PRFS generators (with polynomial-length inputs) from PRS generators in a black-box fashion? Are there separations?

More Applications of Pseudorandom States. One of Impagliazzo's "five worlds" is called *MiniCrypt*, which represents a world where one-way functions exist but we do not have public-key cryptography. In this world, applications such as symmetric-key encryption, commitment schemes, secure multiparty computation, and digital signatures are possible to achieve.

It appears that we can obtain most MiniCrypt primitives from PR(F)S; for example this paper shows that we can get symmetric-key encryption, commitments, and secure multiparty computation. However it is a tantalizing open question of whether we can also build digital signatures from PR(F)S. Morimae and Yamakawa show that an analogue of one-time Lamport signatures can be constructed from PRS [26], but obtaining many-time signatures from PR(F)S seems more challenging.

More generally, what are other cryptographic applications of pseudorandom states?

Other Quantum Assumptions. What are other interesting "fully quantum" assumptions that can we base cryptography on? Can we base cryptography on the assumption BQP $\neq$ PP? We note that Chia, Chou, Zhang, Zhang also suggest the possibility of basing cryptography on the assumption that a quantum version of the Minimum Circuit Size Problem is hard [16, Open Problem 9].

2 Pseudorandom States

The notion of pseudorandom states were first introduced by Ji, Liu, and Song in [23]. We reproduce their definition here:

Definition 1 (PRS Generator [23]). *We say that a QPT algorithm G is a pseudorandom state (PRS) generator if the following holds.*

1. ***State Generation.*** *There is a negligible function $\varepsilon(\cdot)$ such that for all λ and for all $k \in \{0,1\}^\lambda$, the algorithm G behaves as*

$$G_\lambda(k) = |\psi_k\rangle\langle\psi_k|.$$

   for some $n(\lambda)$-qubit pure state $|\psi_k\rangle$.
2. ***Pseudorandomness.*** *For all polynomials $t(\cdot)$ and QPT (nonuniform) distinguisher A there exists a negligible function $\varepsilon(\lambda)$ such that for all λ, we have*

$$\left| \Pr_{k \leftarrow \{0,1\}^\lambda}\left[A_\lambda(G_\lambda(k)^{\otimes t(\lambda)}) = 1\right] - \Pr_{|\vartheta\rangle \leftarrow \mathscr{H}_{n(\lambda)}}\left[A_\lambda(|\vartheta\rangle^{\otimes t(\lambda)}) = 1\right] \right| \leq \varepsilon(\lambda) .$$

We also say that G is a $n(\lambda)$-PRS generator to succinctly indicate that the output length of G is $n(\lambda)$.

Ji, Liu, and Song showed that post-quantum one-way functions can be used to construct PRS generators.

Theorem 4 [12,23]. *If post-quantum one-way functions exist, then there exist PRS generators for all polynomial output lengths.*

2.1 Pseudorandom Function-Like State (PRFS) Generators

In this section, we present our definition of pseudorandom function-like state (PRFS) generators. PRFS generators generalize PRS generators in two ways: first, in addition to the secret key k, the PRFS generator additionally takes in a (classical) input x. The security guarantee of a PRFS implies that, even if x is adversarially chosen, the output state of the generator is indistinguishable from Haar-random. The second way in which this definition generalizes the definition of PRS generators is that the output of the generator need not be a pure state.

Definition 2 (PRFS generator). *We say that a QPT algorithm G is a (selectively secure) pseudorandom function-like state (PRFS) generator if for all polynomials $s(\cdot), t(\cdot)$, QPT (nonuniform) distinguishers A and a family of indices $(\{x_1, \ldots, x_{s(\lambda)}\} \subseteq \{0,1\}^{d(\lambda)})_\lambda$, there exists a negligible function $\varepsilon(\cdot)$ such that for all λ,*

$$\left| \Pr_{k \leftarrow \{0,1\}^\lambda} \left[A_\lambda(x_1, \ldots, x_{s(\lambda)}, G_\lambda(k, x_1)^{\otimes t(\lambda)}, \ldots, G_\lambda(k, x_{s(\lambda)})^{\otimes t(\lambda)}) = 1 \right] \right.$$
$$\left. - \Pr_{|\vartheta_1\rangle, \ldots, |\vartheta_{s(\lambda)}\rangle \leftarrow \mathscr{H}_{n(\lambda)}} \left[A_\lambda(x_1, \ldots, x_{s(\lambda)}, |\vartheta_1\rangle^{\otimes t(\lambda)}, \ldots, |\vartheta_{s(\lambda)}\rangle^{\otimes t(\lambda)}) = 1 \right] \right| \le \varepsilon(\lambda).$$

We also say that G is a $(d(\lambda), n(\lambda))$-PRFS generator to succinctly indicate that its input length is $d(\lambda)$ and its output length is $n(\lambda)$.

Our notion of security here can be seen as a version of *(classical) selective security*, where the queries to the PRFS generator are fixed before the key is sampled. One could consider stronger notions of security where the indistinguishability property holds even when the adversary is allowed to query the PRFS generator adaptively, or even in superposition. We explore these stronger notions in forthcoming work [2].

State Generation Guarantees. As mentioned above, our definition of PRFS generator does not require that the output of the generator is always a pure state. However, we will see later that a consequence of the PRFS security guarantee is that the output of the generator is *close* to a pure state for an overwhelming fraction of keys k.

Nevertheless, for applications it is sometimes more useful to also consider a stronger guarantee on the state generation of a PRFS generator.

Definition 3 (Perfect state generation). *A $(d(\lambda), n(\lambda))$-PRFS generator G satisfies perfect state generation, if for every $k \in \{0,1\}^\lambda$ and $x \in \{0,1\}^{d(\lambda)}$, there exists an $n(\lambda)$-qubit pure state $|\psi\rangle$ such that $G_\lambda(k,x) = |\psi\rangle\langle\psi|$.*

We observe that an $n(\lambda)$-PRS generator defined in Definition 1 is by definition equivalent to an $(0, n(\lambda))$-PRFS generator with perfect state generation.

In general, it may be difficult to construct PR(F)S with perfect state generation as the state generation could occasionally fail; for example, the generator may perform a (quantum) rejection sampling procedure in order to output the state. The scalable PRS generators of Brakerski and Shmueli [12] is an example of this. To capture a very natural class of PRFS generators (including the one constructed in this paper), we define the notion of a PRFS generator where $G(k,x)$ outputs a convex combination of a fixed pure state $|\psi_{k,x}\rangle$ or a known abort state $|\bot\rangle$.

Definition 4 (Recognizable abort). *A $(d(\lambda), n(\lambda))$-PRFS generator G has the recognizable abort property if for every $k \in \{0,1\}^\lambda$ and $x \in \{0,1\}^{d(\lambda)}$ there exists an $n(\lambda)$-qubit pure state $|\psi\rangle$ and $0 \leq \eta \leq 1$ such that $G_\lambda(k,x) = \eta|\psi\rangle\langle\psi| + (1-\eta)|\bot\rangle\langle\bot|$, where $\bot$ is a special symbol[8].*

Note that this definition alone does not have any constraint on η being close to 1. However, the security guarantee of a PRFS generator implies that η will be negligibly close to 1 with overwhelming probability over the choice of k[9]. We also note that a PRFS generator with perfect state generation trivially has the recognizable abort property with $\eta = 1$ for all k, x.

2.2   Testing Pseudorandom States

Given a state ρ, it is useful to know whether it is the output of a PRFS generator with key k and input x. One approach would be to invoke the generator to get some number of copies and perform SWAP tests. Unfortunately, this approach would only achieve polynomially small error, which is undesirable for cryptographic applications where we want negligible security. Another approach is to "uncompute" the state generation. The issue with this approach is that it is not clear how to do it when the state generation is not perfect, or if it outputs some additional auxiliary states that we do not know how to uncompute.

In the following, we will show how to use the generator in a semi-black-box way to test any PRFS states. We first state a general Lemma that shows how to convert any circuit that generates a state ρ into a tester (of sorts) for the state ρ.

Lemma 1 (Circuit output tester). *Let G denote a (generalized) quantum circuit that takes no input and outputs an n-qubit mixed state ρ. Then there exists a circuit Test with boolean output such that:*

1. For all density matrices σ_{EQ} where Q is an n-qubit register, applying the circuit Test on register Q yields the following state on registers EF where F

---

[8] One can think of $|\bot\rangle$ as the $(n+1)$-qubit state $|100\cdots0\rangle$ with the first qubit indicating whether the generator aborted or not. If the generator doesn't abort, then it outputs $|0\rangle \otimes |\psi\rangle$ for some pure state $|\psi\rangle$ (called the *correct output state* of G on input (k,x)). The distinguisher in the definition of PRFS generator would then only get the last n qubits as input.

[9] The argument is as follows: if η were on average noticeably far from 1, then a purity test using SWAP tests would distinguish the outputs from Haar random states which are pure. This is formalized in the full version.

stores the decision bit:

$$(I_E \otimes \text{Test}_Q)(\sigma_{EQ}) = \sum_b \text{Tr}_Q\Big((I_E \otimes M_b)\sigma_{EQ}\Big) \otimes |b\rangle\langle b|_F$$

where $M_1 = \rho^2$ and $M_0 = I - M_1$.

2. *Furthermore,* Test *runs the unitary part[10] of G as a black box, and if the complexity of G is T, the complexity of* Test *is $O(T + n)$.*

Due to space constraints, we defer the proof of this lemma to the full version.

We note that if a PRFS satisfies perfect state generation, then the Test algorithm corresponding to the circuit $G_\lambda(k,x)$ implements a projection onto the state $|\psi_{k,x}\rangle = G_\lambda(k,x)$ in the case that the Test accepts (i.e. outputs 1). If the PRFS satisfies the weaker recognizable abort property, we get that the Test algorithm implements a *scaled* projection onto the correct state $|\psi_{k,x}\rangle$.

Corollary 3 (PRFS tester with recognizable abort). *Let G be a (d,n)-PRFS generator with the recognizable abort property. Then there exists a QPT algorithm* Test *such that for all λ, $k \in \{0,1\}^\lambda$ and $x \in \{0,1\}^{d(\lambda)}$, for all density matrices σ_{EQ} where Q is an $n(\lambda)$-qubit register, applying* Test$(k,x,\cdot)$ *to register Q yields the following state on registers EF where F stores the decision bit:*

$$(I_E \otimes \text{Test}_Q)(k,x,\sigma_{EQ}) = \sum_b \text{Tr}_Q\Big((I_E \otimes M_b)\sigma_{EQ}\Big) \otimes |b\rangle\langle b|_F$$

where $M_1 = \eta^2|\psi\rangle\langle\psi|$ and $M_0 = I - M_1$ with $\eta, |\psi\rangle$ (which generally depend on k,x) are those guaranteed by the recognizable abort property.

Proof. Fix λ and $k \in \{0,1\}^\lambda, x \in \{0,1\}^{d(\lambda)}$. By the recognizable abort property, we know that $G_\lambda(k,x) = \eta|\psi\rangle\langle\psi| + (1-\eta)|\bot\rangle\langle\bot|$. We implement the circuit Test by first testing whether the input state is $|\bot\rangle$ (which we can do since it is a fixed known state), rejecting if so, and otherwise applying the test circuit from Lemma 1 with the circuit $G_{k,x}$ that takes no input and outputs $\rho = G_\lambda(k,x)$. Since we projected the input state to have no overlap with $|\bot\rangle$, we get that

$$\rho\sigma\rho = \eta^2 |\psi\rangle\langle\psi| \sigma |\psi\rangle\langle\psi|$$

as desired.   □

Next we analyze a *product* of Test algorithms run in parallel on different qubits of a (possibly entangled) state.

Corollary 4 (Product of PRFS testers with recognizable abort). *Let G be a (d,n)-PRFS generator with the recognizable abort property and let* Test *denote the corresponding tester algorithm given by Corollary 3. Fix $\lambda, t \in \mathbb{N}$. For all $k_1,\ldots,k_t \in \{0,1\}^\lambda$ and for all $x_1,\ldots,x_t \in \{0,1\}^{d(\lambda)}$, define the QPT*

---

[10] See the full version for a definition of the unitary part of a generalized quantum circuit.

algorithm $\mathsf{Test}^{\otimes t}$ *that given an* $t \cdot n(\lambda)$-*qubit density matrix* σ *behaves as follows: for all* $i = 1, \ldots, t$, *on the* i'*th block of* $n(\lambda)$ *qubits of* σ, *run the algorithm* $\mathsf{Test}_\lambda(k_i, x_i, \cdot)$. *Output* 1 *if and only if all* t *invocations of* Test *output* 1.

Then $\mathsf{Test}^{\otimes t}$ *satisfies the following. For all density matrices* σ_{EQ} *where* Q *is an* $t \cdot n(\lambda)$-*qubit register, applying* $\mathsf{Test}^{\otimes t}$ *to register* Q *yields the following state on registers* EQF *where* F *stores the decision bit:*

$$(I_{\mathsf{E}} \otimes \mathsf{Test}^{\otimes t})(\sigma_{\mathsf{EQ}}) = \sum_b \mathrm{Tr}_{\mathsf{Q}}\Big((I_{\mathsf{E}} \otimes M_b)\sigma_{\mathsf{EQ}}\Big) \otimes |b\rangle\langle b|_{\mathsf{F}}$$

where $M_1 = \eta^2 |\psi\rangle\langle\psi|$ *and* $M_0 = I - M_1$ *with* $|\psi\rangle = |\psi_{k_1, x_1}\rangle \otimes \cdots \otimes |\psi_{k_t, x_t}\rangle$, *and* $\eta = \eta_{k_1, x_1} \cdots \eta_{k_t, x_t}$ *where* $|\psi_{k_i, x_i}\rangle$, η_{k_i, x_i} *for* $i = 1, \ldots, t$ *are the values guaranteed by the recognizable abort property.*

Proof. This follows from the fact that each invocation of $\mathsf{Test}(k_i, x_i, \cdot)$, conditioned on accepting, implements a (scaled) projection $\eta_{k_i, x_i} |\psi_{k_i, x_i}\rangle\langle\psi_{k_i, x_i}|$ on a disjoint register of σ. $\qquad\square$

We note that the previous two Corollaries establish the behavior of the Test procedure for *every* fixed key k (or sequence of keys, in the case of Corollary 4). The next Lemma establishes the behavior of the Test procedure when given outputs of *any* PRFS generator (even ones without recognizable abort); the bounds are stated *on average* over a uniformly random key k.

Lemma 2 (Self-testing PRFS). *Let* G *be a* (d, n)-*PRFS generator and* $\mathsf{Test}(k, x, \cdot)$ *denote the tester algorithm for* $G(k, x)$ *given by Lemma 1. There exists a negligible function* $\nu(\cdot)$ *such that for all* λ, *for all* $x \neq y$,

$$\Pr_k[\mathsf{Test}(k, x, G(k, x)) = 1] \geq 1 - \nu(\lambda),$$

and

$$\Pr_k[\mathsf{Test}(k, x, G(k, y)) = 1] \leq 2^{-n(\lambda)} + \nu(\lambda).$$

Due to space constraints, we defer the proof of this to the full version.

3   Constructing PRFS from PRS

In this section we present our construction of PRFS generators using PRS generators, which are seemingly weaker objects. As mentioned in the introduction, there is a trivial construction of PRFS from PRS. Let G be a PRS generator. Define the PRFS generator G' with input length $d(\lambda) = O(\log \lambda)$, where $G'_{\lambda'}(k, x) = G_\lambda(k_x)$ with $\lambda' = 2^{d(\lambda)}\lambda$ and k_x denoting the x'th block of λ bits in $k \in \{0, 1\}^{\lambda'}$. However, this simple construction is such that the input length is always at most logarithmic in the seed length. This, as far as we can tell, is not very useful for applications.

We are going to present a more interesting construction: we will build a PRFS generator for *any* input length $d(\lambda)$ that is at most constant times $\log \lambda$, as long as the output length of the starting PRS generator is at least $2d(\lambda) + \omega(\log \log \lambda)$. Although the input length may appear modest, such PRFS generators are sufficient for most of the applications we consider in this paper. We find it an intriguing question of whether it is possible to construct PRFS generators with longer input lengths from PRS generators in a black box way.

Theorem 5. *Let* $d(\lambda), n(\lambda)$ *be functions such that* $d(\lambda) = O(\log \lambda)$ *and* $n(\lambda) = d(\lambda)+\omega(\log \log \lambda)$. *Let* G *denote a* $(n(\lambda)+d(\lambda))$-*PRS generator. Then there exists a* $(d(\lambda), n(\lambda))$-*PRFS generator* F *with the recognizable abort property, such that for all* λ *the circuit* F_λ *invokes the* G_λ *as a black box.*

The rest of this section is dedicated to proving the theorem. For notational clarity we use the abbreviations $d = d(\lambda)$ and $n = n(\lambda)$.

The construction of the PRFS generator is given by the following circuit $F_\lambda(k, x)$. On input key $k \in \{0,1\}^\lambda$, input $x \in \{0,1\}^d$, repeat the following $2^d \cdot \lambda$ times:

- Compute the $(d + n)$-qubit state $\rho_k \leftarrow G_\lambda(k)$.
- Measure the first d qubits of ρ_k in the computational basis to obtain a string $y \in \{0,1\}^d$. If $y = x$, then output the remaining n qubits. Otherwise, continue.

If the measurement outcomes was different from x in all the $2^d\lambda$ iterations, set $\sigma_{k,x} = |\bot\rangle\langle\bot|$. Let the output be $\sigma_{k,x}$.

The algorithm $F = \{F_\lambda\}_\lambda$ is uniform QPT because for each λ, the running time of the circuit F_λ is going to be $O(2^d \cdot \lambda)$ times the complexity of running G_λ, which is QPT since $d = O(\log \lambda)$ and G is QPT. It is easy to see that even if G (as a PRFS generator) only satisfies recognizable abort (instead of perfect generation), F still satisfies recognizable abort by construction. Therefore, the construction also works with the PRS generator constructed by Brakerski and Shmueli [12].

Due to space constraints, we defer the proof of security to the full version.

4   Quantum Pseudo One-Time Pad from PRFS

The first application of PRFS we present is the Quantum Pseudo One-Time Pad (QP-OTP). In classical cryptography, a pseudo one-time pad is like the one-time pad except the key length is shorter than the length of the plaintext message. This is often presented in introductory cryptography courses as a basic example of using pseudorandomness to achieve a cryptographic task that is impossible in the information-theoretic setting. Here, we use a PRFS in place of a PRG to encrypt (classical) messages.

We point out that without knowing about the notion of PRFS, it appears difficult and challenging to construct secure quantum one-time pad schemes directly from PRS generators alone.

Definition 5 (Quantum Pseudo One-Time Pad). *We say that a pair of QPT algorithms* (Enc, Dec) *is a* quantum pseudo one-time pad (QP-OTP) *for messages of length* $\ell(\lambda) > \lambda$ *for some polynomial* $\ell(\cdot)$ *if the following properties are satisfied:*

- *Correctness: There exists a negligible function* $\varepsilon(\cdot)$ *such that for every* λ, *every* $x \in \{0,1\}^\ell$,

$$\Pr_{\substack{k \leftarrow \{0,1\}^\lambda, \\ \sigma \leftarrow \mathsf{Enc}_\lambda(k,x)}} [\mathsf{Dec}_\lambda(k,\sigma) = x] \geq 1 - \varepsilon(\lambda).$$

- *Security: There exist a polynomial* $n(\cdot)$ *such that for every polynomial* $t(\cdot)$, *for every nonuniform QPT adversary* A, *there exists a negligible function* $\varepsilon(\cdot)$ *where for every* λ *and* $x \in \{0,1\}^\ell$,

$$\left| \Pr_{\substack{k \leftarrow \{0,1\}^\lambda, \\ \sigma \leftarrow \mathsf{Enc}_\lambda(k,x)}} \left[A_\lambda(\sigma^{\otimes t}) = 1 \right] - \Pr_{|\vartheta_1\rangle, \ldots, |\vartheta_\ell\rangle \leftarrow \mathscr{H}_n} \left[A_\lambda((|\vartheta_1\rangle \otimes \cdots \otimes |\vartheta_\ell\rangle)^{\otimes t}) = 1 \right] \right| \leq \varepsilon(\lambda),$$

where we have abbreviated $n = n(\lambda)$, $\ell = \ell(\lambda)$, *and* $t = t(\lambda)$.

Here the security holds even if the adversary could see multiple copies of the same ciphertexts, which might be useful for certain applications, for example when the communication channel is adversarially lossy. However, when $t = 1$, we can see that the security implies that the ciphertext is computationally indistinguishable to random bit strings of length ℓn (or a maximally mixed state).

To construct such a quantum pseudo one-time pad, let G be a $(d(\lambda), n(\lambda))$-PRFS generator where $d(\lambda) \geq \lceil \log \ell(\lambda) \rceil + 1$ and $n(\lambda) = \omega(\log \lambda)$. We interpret $G_\lambda(k, \cdot)$ as taking inputs of the form (i, b) where $i \in [\ell(\lambda)]$ and $b \in \{0,1\}$. Let Test denote the test algorithm from Lemma 2.

Fix λ and let $\ell = \ell(\lambda)$, $d = d(\lambda)$, and $n = n(\lambda)$.

1. $\mathsf{Enc}_\lambda(k,x)$: on input $k \in \{0,1\}^\lambda$ and a message $x \in \{0,1\}^\ell$, do the following:
    - For every $i \in [\ell]$, compute $\sigma_i \leftarrow G_\lambda(k, (i, x_i))$.
    - Set $\sigma = \sigma_1 \otimes \cdots \otimes \sigma_\ell$.
    - Output the ciphertext state σ.
2. $\mathsf{Dec}_\lambda(k,\sigma)$: on input k, ℓn-qubit ciphertext state σ, perform the following operations:
    - Parse σ as $\sigma_1 \otimes \cdots \otimes \sigma_\ell$.
    - For $i \in [\ell]$, execute $\mathsf{Test}(k, (i,0), \sigma_i)$. If it accepts, set $x_i = 0$. Otherwise, set $x_i = 1$.
    - Output $x = x_1 \cdots x_\ell$.

Lemma 3. (Enc, Dec) *satisfies the correctness property of a quantum pseudo one-time pad according to Definition 5.*

Proof. Fix λ and let $\ell = \ell(\lambda)$. Fix a message $x \in \{0,1\}^\ell$. Let $\sigma_{k,i} = G_\lambda(k, (i, x_i))$ and let $\sigma_k = \sigma_{k,1} \otimes \cdots \otimes \sigma_{k,\ell}$.

Consider the decryption process. Fix an index $i \in [\ell]$. By Lemma 2, the probability that $\mathsf{Test}\big(k, (i, 0), \sigma_{k,i}\big)$ accepts (on average over k) is negligibly close to 1 if $x_i = 0$, and it is negligibly close to 0 if $x_i = 1$, on average over the key k (here we use the fact that the output length of the PRFS generator is $\omega(\log \lambda)$, so that $2^{-n(\lambda)}$ is negligible). Thus the probability that the correct bit x_i gets decoded is negligibly close to 1. Taking a union bound over all indices $i \in [\ell]$, we get that the probability of decoding x is negligibly close to 1, over the randomness of the key k and the decryption algorithm. $\qquad\square$

Lemma 4. $(\mathsf{Enc}, \mathsf{Dec})$ *satisfies the security property of quantum pseudo one-time pad according to Definition 5.*

Proof. We prove the security via a hybrid argument. Let $n(\lambda)$ denote the output length of the PRFS generator G. Fix λ, and let $\ell = \ell(\lambda)$, $n = n(\lambda)$, and $t = t(\lambda)$. Fix a message $x \in \{0,1\}^\ell$. Consider a nonuniform QPT adversary A such that A_λ takes as input t copies of an ℓn-qubit density matrix σ.

Hybrid H_1. Sample $k \leftarrow \{0,1\}^\lambda$. Compute $\sigma \leftarrow \mathsf{Enc}_\lambda(k, x)$. The output of the hybrid is the output of the adversary A_λ on input $\sigma^{\otimes t}$.

Hybrid H_2. Consider the following QPT algorithm B_λ: it takes as input $(i_1, b_1), \ldots, (i_\ell, b_\ell) \in [\ell] \times \{0,1\}$ and a tn-qubit state $\sigma_1^{\otimes t} \otimes \cdots \otimes \sigma_\ell^{\otimes t}$. The algorithm B runs the adversary A_λ on input $(\sigma_1 \otimes \cdots \otimes \sigma_\ell)^{\otimes t}$ and returns A_λ's output.

Sample $k \leftarrow \{0,1\}^\lambda$. Compute t copies of $\sigma \leftarrow \mathsf{Enc}_\lambda(k, x)$. The output of this hybrid is the output of B_λ on input $((1, x_1), \ldots, (\ell, x_\ell))$ and $\sigma^{\otimes t} = \sigma_1^{\otimes t} \otimes \cdots \otimes \sigma_\ell^{\otimes t}$.

Hybrid H_3. Sample t copies of Haar-random states $|\vartheta_1\rangle, \ldots, |\vartheta_\ell\rangle \leftarrow \mathscr{H}_n$. The output of this hybrid is the output of B_λ on input $((1, x_1), \ldots, (\ell, x_\ell))$ and $|\vartheta_1\rangle^{\otimes t} \otimes \cdots \otimes |\vartheta_\ell\rangle^{\otimes t}$.

We now argue the indistinguishability of the hybrids. Clearly, hybrids H_1 and H_2 are identical by construction (the adversary B_λ ignores its first input and runs A_λ on input $\sigma^{\otimes t}$). Hybrids H_2 and H_3 are indistinguishable because of the pseudorandomness property of the PRFS generator G. Notice that, by construction, the output of hybrid H_3 is $A_\lambda((|\vartheta_1\rangle \otimes \cdots \otimes |\vartheta_\ell\rangle)^{\otimes t})$. $\qquad\square$

5   Quantum Bit Commitments from PRFS

5.1   Definition

We consider the notion of quantum commitment scheme with statistical binding and computational hiding property. This is analogous to a classical commitment scheme where the messages are allowed to be quantum states. We in particular focus on bit commitments where the committed message is a single bit.

We can generically achieve commitments of long messages by composing many instantiations of the bit-commitment scheme in parallel.

A (bit) commitment scheme is given by a pair of (uniform) QPT algorithms (C, R), where $C = \{C_\lambda\}_{\lambda \in \mathbb{N}}$ is called the *committer* and $R = \{R_\lambda\}_{\lambda \in \mathbb{N}}$ is called the *receiver*. There are two phases in a commitment scheme: a commit phase and a reveal phase.

- In the (possibly interactive) commit phase between C_λ and R_λ, the committer C_λ commits to a bit, say b. We denote the execution of the commit phase to be $\sigma_{CR} \leftarrow \mathsf{Commit}\langle C_\lambda(b), R_\lambda\rangle$, where σ_{CR} is a joint state of C_λ and R_λ after the commit phase.
- In the reveal phase C_λ interacts with R_λ and the output is a trit $\mu \in \{0, 1, \bot\}$ indicating the receiver's output bit or a rejection flag. We denote an execution of the reveal phase where the committer and receiver start with the joint state σ_{CR} by $\mu \leftarrow \mathsf{Reveal}\langle C_\lambda, R_\lambda, \sigma_{CR}\rangle$.

We define the properties satisfied by a commitment scheme.

Statistical Binding. We start by discussing the statistical binding property. The classical statistical binding property could be rephrased as the following in the quantum setting: for any adversarial (possibly unbounded) committer C_λ^*, we require that at the end of the commit phase, with high probability over the measurement randomness of the receiver, there is a unique bit that C_λ^* can decommit to in the reveal phase. Unfortunately, this idealistic notion is not always possible to achieve: in some quantum commitment protocols where the receiver does not measure everything, it is possible for C_λ^* to send a uniform superposition of commitments of 0 and 1 and later can open to either 0 or 1 with equal probability. This attack was observed and taken into account in many works, including but not limited to [9,17,28,30].

To account for this issue, we consider a notion where an extraction procedure can be applied on the state of the receiver after the commit phase. The output is the receiver's post-extraction state along with the extracted bit b. We revise the statistical binding property guarantee to informally require the following: (a) whether the extractor is applied or not is imperceivable to the committer and (b) the committer can almost never decommit to $1 - b$ if the extracted bit is b.

Definition 6 (Statistical Binding). *We say that a quantum commitment scheme (C, R) satisfies statistical binding if for any (non-uniform) adversarial committer $C^* = \{C_\lambda^*\}_{\lambda \in \mathbb{N}}$, there exists a (possibly inefficient) extractor algorithm $\mathcal{E}$ such that the following holds:*

$$\mathsf{TD}\left(\mathsf{RealExpt}_\lambda^{C^*}, \mathsf{IdealExpt}_\lambda^{C^*, \mathcal{E}}\right) \leq \nu(\lambda),$$

for some negligible function $\nu(\lambda)$, where the experiments $\mathsf{RealExpt}_\lambda^{C^*}$ and $\mathsf{IdealExpt}_\lambda^{C^*, \mathcal{E}}$ are defined as follows.

- RealExpt$_\lambda^{C^*}$: *Execute the commit phase to obtain the joint state* $\sigma_{C^*R} \leftarrow$ Commit$\langle C_\lambda^*, R_\lambda \rangle$. *Execute the reveal phase to obtain the trit* $\mu \leftarrow$ Reveal$\langle C_\lambda^*, R_\lambda, \sigma_{C^*R} \rangle$. *Output the pair* (τ_{C^*}, μ) *where* τ_{C^*} *is the final state of the committer.*

- IdealExpt$_\lambda^{C^*,\mathcal{E}}$: *Execute the commit phase to obtain the joint state* $\sigma_{C^*R} \leftarrow$ Commit$\langle C_\lambda^*, R_\lambda \rangle$. *Apply the extractor* $I \otimes \mathcal{E}$ *on* σ_{C^*R} *(acting only on the receiver's part) to obtain a new joint committer-receiver state* σ_{C^*R}' *along with* $b' \in \{0, 1, \perp\}$. *Execute the reveal phase to obtain the trit* $\mu \leftarrow$ Reveal$\langle C_\lambda^*, R_\lambda, \sigma_{C^*R}' \rangle$. *Let* τ_{C^*} *denote the final state of the committer. If* $\mu = \perp$ *or* $\mu = b'$, *then output* (τ_{C^*}, μ). *Otherwise, output a special symbol* $\mathfrak{E}$ *(unused in the real experiment) indicating extraction error.*

Remark 1. Many prior works consider statistical binding for quantum commitments. We highlight the main differences between our definition and the prior notions.

- Comparison with [17, 28, 30]: the statistical binding property is formalized by requiring the states of the (honest) committer when committing to bits 0 and 1 to be far in trace distance. While their definition is cleaner (and probably equivalent to our notion), in our opinion, it is unwieldy to use their definition for applications. Specifically, one has to either implicitly or explicitly come up with an extractor in the security proofs for applications [17, 30] and moreover, show that the indistinguishability of the real and the ideal world holds against dishonest committers. On the other hand, we incorporate these technical difficulties as requirements in our definition making it easier to use in applications.

  Another downside of the statistical binding property there is that in order for the sum-binding property to be useful in applications, it is common to additionally require the opening phase to follow the "canonical" opening protocol, where the committer sends the purification of the mixed state sent in the committing phase, and the receiver performs a rank-1 projection to check the state. This implies that *both* parties must keep their part of the state coherent between the two phases. However, our definition gives the flexibility of the reveal phase having purely classical communication.

- Comparison with [9]: A related work by [9] considers statistical binding of quantum commitments called classical binding. The main difference is the following. In their notion, the honest receiver applies a measurement that collapses the commitment into a quantum state and a classical string in such a way that the classical string information theoretically determines the message. They then use this feature to show that in some applications, the opening of the commitment can be classical. Our definition is also more general in the sense that the honest receiver is not required to do any measurement and the collapsing happens implicitly in the ideal world during the execution of extractor.

Remark 2. One has to be careful when using quantum commitments in a larger system if the receiver's state is quantum after the commit phase. As an example, suppose we design a protocol where the quantum commitment held by the receiver before the reveal phase is used inside another cryptographic protocol. Then we might not be able to invoke binding if the state is destroyed, whereas classically the state could always be copied. Nevertheless, this is a generic caveat of quantum commitments and is not an artifact of any specific definition of binding.

Computational Hiding. We define the computational hiding property below. This is the natural quantum analogue of the classical computational hiding property. In the literature, this property is also sometimes referred to as quantum concealing.

Definition 7 (Computational Hiding). *We say that a quantum commitment scheme (C, R) satisfies computational hiding if for any malicious QPT receiver $\{R_\lambda^*\}_{\lambda \in \mathbb{N}}$, for any QPT distinguisher $\{D_\lambda\}_{\lambda \in \mathbb{N}}$, the following holds:*

$$\left| \Pr\left[D_\lambda(\sigma_{R^*}) = 1 \; : \; \sigma_{CR^*} \leftarrow \mathsf{Commit}\langle C_\lambda(0), R_\lambda^* \rangle\right] \right.$$

$$\left. - \Pr\left[D_\lambda(\sigma_{R^*}) = 1 \; : \; \sigma_{CR^*} \leftarrow \mathsf{Commit}\langle C_\lambda(1), R_\lambda^* \rangle\right] \right| \leq \nu(\lambda),$$

for some negligible function $\nu(\cdot)$, where σ_{R^*} is obtained by tracing out the committer's part of the state σ_{CR^*}.

5.2   Construction

We now present the main theorem of this section, which shows that statistically binding quantum commitment schemes can be constructed from PRFS.

Theorem 6. *Assuming the existence of $(d(\lambda), n(\lambda))$-PRFS satisfying recognizable abort (Definition 4) with $2^d \cdot n \geq 7\lambda$, there exists a commitment scheme satisfying statistical completeness, statistical binding (Definition 6) and computational hiding (Definition 7).*

We note that, combined with Theorem 5 which constructs PRFS generators with $\Omega(\log \lambda)$ input length and recognizable abort property from PRS generators, we can obtain quantum commitment schemes from PRS generators. We present the construction, which is inspired by Naor's commitment scheme [27].

The main building block is a $(d(\lambda), n(\lambda))$-PRFS, denoted by $G = \{G_\lambda(\cdot, \cdot)\}_{\lambda \in \mathbb{N}}$. Since $n \geq 1$, we assume $d(\lambda) = \lceil \log \frac{7\lambda}{n} \rceil = O(\log \lambda)$ to ensure the efficiency of the algorithm. This is without loss of generality since we can generically shrink the input length for a PRFS by padding zeroes. Let $\mathsf{Test}_\lambda^{\otimes 2^{d(\lambda)}}$ be the product PRFS tester corresponding to G as guaranteed by Corollary 4.

We describe the commitment scheme, (C, R) as follows. For notational convenience, we abbreviate $n = n(\lambda)$, $d = d(\lambda)$.

1. *Commit Phase*:

- The receiver R_λ samples a uniformly random m-qubit Pauli operator P, where $m = 2^d \cdot n$. We write P as $P_0 \otimes \cdots \otimes P_{2^d-1}$, where P_i is an n-qubit Pauli operator[11]. It sends P to the committer.
- The committer C_λ on input a bit $b \in \{0,1\}$, does the following:
  - It samples $k \xleftarrow{\$} \{0,1\}^\lambda$.
  - For every $x \in \{0,1\}^d$, computes $\sigma_{k,x} \leftarrow G_\lambda(k,x)$.
  It sends the commitment $\mathbf{c} = \bigotimes_{x \in \{0,1\}^d} \widetilde{\sigma}_{k,x}$, where $\widetilde{\sigma}_{k,x} = P_x^b \sigma_{k,x} P_x^b$, to the receiver.

2. *Reveal Phase*: The committer sends $(k,b) \in \{0,1\}^\lambda \times \{0,1\}$ as the decommitment to the receiver. The receiver outputs b if and only if $\mathsf{Test}_\lambda^{\otimes 2^d}\left(\{k,x\}_x, P^b \mathbf{c} P^b\right) = 1$ where $P^b = \bigotimes_{x \in \{0,1\}^{2^d}} P_x^b$. Otherwise the receiver outputs $\perp$.

Lemma 5. *If G is a PRFS, then there exists a negligible function $\nu(\cdot)$ such that the probability that the honest receiver accepts the honest committer's opening is at least $1 - \nu(\lambda)$.*

Proof. This follows immediately from Lemma 2 and union bound as 2^d is polynomial in λ. □

Due to space constraints, we defer the security proof of this construction to the full version.

5.3   Application: Secure Computation

In this section, we show how to base secure computation solely on the existence of a PRS. While there are two works [4,19] showing that post-quantum one-way functions and quantum communication suffice to obtain protocols for secure computation, the construction of Bartusek, Coladangelo, Khurana, and Ma [4] has the advantage that it uses the starting commitment scheme as a black box. We recall their main theorem.

Theorem 7 (Implicit from [4]). *Assuming the existence of quantum statistically binding bit commitments, maliciously secure computation protocols (in the dishonest majority setting) for P/poly exist.*

Comparison of the Definitions of statistical Binding. The application of Theorem 7 would be straightforward except for one subtlety, which is that we are using a more general definition of the statistical binding property than required by their work. Their notion of statistical binding is tailored to commitment schemes with classical messages as it suffices for their purposes. We first recall their definition of statistical binding in the full version of their work [5], and show that it seems strictly stronger than our definition.

---

[11] To sample $P = \bigotimes_i P_i$, the receiver can sample uniformly random bits $\alpha_1, \beta_1, \ldots, \alpha_m, \beta_m$, and let $P_i = X^{\alpha_i} Z^{\beta_i}$ where X and Z are the single-qubit Pauli operators.

Definition 8 ([5, **Definition 3.2**]).   *A bit commitment scheme is statistically binding if for every unbounded-size committer C^*, there exists a negligible function $\nu(\cdot)$ such that with probability at least $1 - \nu(\lambda)$ over the measurement randomness in the commitment phase, there exists a bit $b \in \{0,1\}$ such that the probability that the receiver accepts b in the reveal phase is at most $\nu(\lambda)$.*

Lemma 6. *If a commitment scheme satisfies Definition 8, then it also satisfies Definition 6.*

Proof. Since a malicious committer can always "purify" his measurements via the deferred measurement principle, without loss of generality we assume the only measurements in the commit phase are only done by the honest receiver. By Definition 8, there exists a classical function $\mathcal{E}$ that maps the honest receiver's measurement outcomes m to a bit so that the probability that the receiver accepts $1 - \mathcal{E}(m)$ is negligible (also known as the correctness of the extractor). As $\mathcal{E}$ only acts on the measurement outcome that is therefore guaranteed to be classical, $\mathcal{E}$ commutes with the committer's and receiver's operations. Furthermore, the output of $\mathcal{E}$ is also classical by definition. Therefore, the only difference between the real world and the ideal world is introduced by the extraction error in the ideal world, and thus the statistical indistinguishability follows immediately by the correctness of the extractor.   □

Our protocol cannot satisfy this property since the honest receiver does not measure the committer's message in any way, and therefore in general it is possible for the committer to generate an equal superposition of commitment to 0 and commitment to 1, in which case this binding property is violated, as the receiver will open to 0 and 1 with equal probability. Nonetheless, Definition 6 is very similar to Definition 8. In particular, Definition 6 says that there is an implicit measurement that could be done to extract the committed bit in a way unnoticeable to the malicious committer as well as the honest receiver. Intuitively, whenever we would like to invoke Definition 8, we can switch to the ideal world where the bit is extracted, and then this "ideal scheme" essentially satisfies Definition 8. We formalize this intuition with the following lemma.

Definition 9. *We call (C, R) a quantum commitment scheme with an inefficient receiver if it satisfies the requirements of a commitment scheme except that R need not be a QPT algorithm.*

Let (C, R) and (C, R') be two quantum commitment schemes with an inefficient receiver. We call them statistically indistinguishable against malicious committers, if the outcome of any (unbounded) nonuniform experiment described below can only distinguish R from R' with negligible advantage.

- *The algorithm has an arbitrary non-uniform input state $|\psi_\lambda\rangle$, and interacts as a committer with either R or R' via the commitment scheme.*
- *The algorithm can choose to abort the interaction at any stage. Otherwise at the end of the interaction, R or R' outputs his decision as a classical symbol $\mu \in \{0, 1, \perp\}$ to the algorithm.*

– *The algorithm performs an arbitrary channel on his internal state as the output.*

Lemma 7. *If a commitment scheme (C, R) satisfies Definition 6, then there is a commitment scheme $(C, \tilde{R})$ with an inefficient receiver that satisfies Definition 8. Furthermore, these two commitment schemes are statistically indistinguishable against malicious committers; and $\tilde{R}$ is the same as R, except that at the end of the commit phase, the extractor $\mathcal{E}$ of (C, R) is applied on the receiver's state, and its output is saved in a separate register.*

Proof. Note that $(C, \tilde{R})$ is the same receiver as the ideal experiment of Definition 6, except that at the end we always run the honest receiver as usual instead of checking whether the extraction is correct, and therefore this change is statistically indistinguishable to the committer by Definition 6.

To show that it satisfies Definition 8, we notice that assume the extractor's measurement outcome is b (if it is $\perp$ then set b to 0), the probability that the committer can open to $1 - b$ is negligible, as otherwise the ideal world will have a non-negligible weight on extraction error $|\mathfrak{E}\rangle\langle\mathfrak{E}|$, which contradicts Definition 6.   □

It is not hard to see that by leveraging Lemma 6 and 7, we can recover Theorem 7 even with our definition of statistical binding (Definition 6). The proof of this is not very enlightening and we defer the details to the full version. By instantiating the statistically binding bit commitments in Theorem 7 with PRS (Theorem 6 and Theorem 5), we obtain the following corollary.

Corollary 5. *Assuming the existence of $(2 \log \lambda + \omega(\log \log \lambda))$-PRS, there exists maliciously secure computation protocol for P/poly in the dishonest majority setting.*

Acknowledgements. We thank Tomoyuki Morimae, Takashi Yamakawa, Jun Yan, and Fermi Ma for their very helpful feedback and discussions about pseudorandom quantum states.

References

1. Aaronson, S.: Quantum computing, postselection, and probabilistic polynomial-time. Proc.: Math. Phys. Eng. Sci. **461**(2063), 3473–3482 (2005). http://www.jstor.org/stable/30047928
2. Ananth, P., Qian, L., Yuen, H.: Manuscript (in preparation) (2022)
3. Arute, F., et al.: Quantum supremacy using a programmable superconducting processor. Nature **574**(7779), 505–510 (2019). https://doi.org/10.1038/s41586-019-1666-5
4. Bartusek, J., Coladangelo, A., Khurana, D., Ma, F.: One-way functions imply secure computation in a quantum world. In: Malkin, T., Peikert, C. (eds.) CRYPTO 2021, Part I. LNCS, vol. 12825, pp. 467–496. Springer, Cham (2021). https://doi.org/10.1007/978-3-030-84242-0_17

5. Bartusek, J., Coladangelo, A., Khurana, D., Ma, F.: One-way functions imply secure computation in a quantum world. In: Malkin, T., Peikert, C. (eds.) CRYPTO 2021. LNCS, vol. 12825, pp. 467–496. Springer, Cham (2021). https://doi.org/10.1007/978-3-030-84242-0_17

6. Beaver, D., Micali, S., Rogaway, P.: The round complexity of secure protocols (extended abstract). In: Ortiz, H. (ed.) Proceedings of the 22nd Annual ACM Symposium on Theory of Computing, Baltimore, Maryland, USA, 13–17 May 1990, pp. 503–513. ACM (1990). https://doi.org/10.1145/100216.100287

7. Bennett, C.H., Brassard, G.: Quantum cryptography: public key distribution and coin tossing. In: Proceedings of International Conference on Computers, Systems & Signal Processing, Bangalore, India, 9–12 December 1984, pp. 175–179 (1984)

8. Bennett, C.H., Brassard, G., Crépeau, C., Skubiszewska, M.-H.: Practical quantum oblivious transfer. In: Feigenbaum, J. (ed.) CRYPTO 1991. LNCS, vol. 576, pp. 351–366. Springer, Heidelberg (1992). https://doi.org/10.1007/3-540-46766-1_29

9. Bitansky, N., Brakerski, Z.: Classical binding for quantum commitments. In: Nissim, K., Waters, B. (eds.) TCC 2021, Part I. LNCS, vol. 13042, pp. 273–298. Springer, Cham (2021). https://doi.org/10.1007/978-3-030-90459-3_10

10. Bouland, A., Fefferman, B., Vazirani, U.V.: Computational pseudorandomness, the wormhole growth paradox, and constraints on the AdS/CFT duality (abstract). In: Vidick, T. (ed.) 11th Innovations in Theoretical Computer Science Conference, ITCS 2020, LIPIcs, Seattle, Washington, USA, 12–14 January 2020, vol. 151, pp. 63:1–63:2. Schloss Dagstuhl - Leibniz-Zentrum für Informatik (2020). https://doi.org/10.4230/LIPIcs.ITCS.2020.63

11. Brakerski, Z., Shmueli, O.: (Pseudo) random quantum states with binary phase. In: Hofheinz, D., Rosen, A. (eds.) TCC 2019, Part I. LNCS, vol. 11891, pp. 229–250. Springer, Cham (2019). https://doi.org/10.1007/978-3-030-36030-6_10

12. Brakerski, Z., Shmueli, O.: Scalable pseudorandom quantum states. In: Micciancio, D., Ristenpart, T. (eds.) CRYPTO 2020, Part II. LNCS, vol. 12171, pp. 417–440. Springer, Cham (2020). https://doi.org/10.1007/978-3-030-56880-1_15

13. Brakerski, Z., Yuen, H.: Quantum garbled circuits (2020)

14. Brandão, F.G., Chemissany, W., Hunter-Jones, N., Kueng, R., Preskill, J.: Models of quantum complexity growth. PRX Quantum 2, 030316 (2021). https://doi.org/10.1103/PRXQuantum.2.030316

15. Brown, W., Fawzi, O.: Scrambling speed of random quantum circuits (2013)

16. Chia, N., Chou, C., Zhang, J., Zhang, R.: Quantum meets the minimum circuit size problem. In: Braverman, M. (ed.) 13th Innovations in Theoretical Computer Science Conference, ITCS 2022, LIPIcs, Berkeley, CA, USA, 31 January–3 February 2022, vol. 215, pp. 47:1–47:16. Schloss Dagstuhl - Leibniz-Zentrum für Informatik (2022). https://doi.org/10.4230/LIPIcs.ITCS.2022.47

17. Fang, J., Unruh, D., Yan, J., Zhou, D.: How to base security on the perfect/statistical binding property of quantum bit commitment? Cryptology ePrint Archive, Report 2020/621 (2020). http://ia.cr/2020/621

18. Goldreich, O.: A note on computational indistinguishability. Inf. Process. Lett. 34(6), 277–281 (1990). https://doi.org/10.1016/0020-0190(90)90010-U

19. Grilo, A.B., Lin, H., Song, F., Vaikuntanathan, V.: Oblivious transfer is in MiniQCrypt. In: Canteaut, A., Standaert, F.-X. (eds.) EUROCRYPT 2021, Part II. LNCS, vol. 12697, pp. 531–561. Springer, Cham (2021). https://doi.org/10.1007/978-3-030-77886-6_18

20. Harrow, A., Mehraban, S.: Approximate unitary t-designs by short random quantum circuits using nearest-neighbor and long-range gates (2018)

21. Impagliazzo, R.: A personal view of average-case complexity. In: Proceedings of the Tenth Annual Structure in Complexity Theory Conference, Minneapolis, Minnesota, USA, 19–22 June 1995, pp. 134–147. IEEE Computer Society (1995). https://doi.org/10.1109/SCT.1995.514853

22. Impagliazzo, R., Rudich, S.: Limits on the provable consequences of one-way permutations. In: Johnson, D.S. (ed.) Proceedings of the 21st Annual ACM Symposium on Theory of Computing, Seattle, Washington, USA, 14–17 May 1989, pp. 44–61. ACM (1989). https://doi.org/10.1145/73007.73012

23. Ji, Z., Liu, Y.-K., Song, F.: Pseudorandom quantum states. In: Shacham, H., Boldyreva, A. (eds.) CRYPTO 2018, Part III. LNCS, vol. 10993, pp. 126–152. Springer, Cham (2018). https://doi.org/10.1007/978-3-319-96878-0_5

24. Kilian, J.: Founding cryptography on oblivious transfer. In: Simon, J. (ed.) Proceedings of the 20th Annual ACM Symposium on Theory of Computing, Chicago, Illinois, USA, 2–4 May 1988, pp. 20–31. ACM (1988). https://doi.org/10.1145/62212.62215

25. Kretschmer, W.: Quantum pseudorandomness and classical complexity. In: Hsieh, M. (ed.) 16th Conference on the Theory of Quantum Computation, Communication and Cryptography, TQC 2021, Virtual Conference, LIPIcs, 5–8 July 2021, vol. 197, pp. 2:1–2:20. Schloss Dagstuhl - Leibniz-Zentrum für Informatik (2021). https://doi.org/10.4230/LIPIcs.TQC.2021.2

26. Morimae, T., Yamakawa, T.: Quantum commitments and signatures without one-way functions. arXiv:2112.06369 (2021)

27. Naor, M.: Bit commitment using pseudorandomness. J. Cryptol. $4(2)$, 151–158 (1991). https://doi.org/10.1007/BF00196774

28. Unruh, D.: Computationally binding quantum commitments. In: Fischlin, M., Coron, J.-S. (eds.) EUROCRYPT 2016, Part II. LNCS, vol. 9666, pp. 497–527. Springer, Heidelberg (2016). https://doi.org/10.1007/978-3-662-49896-5_18

29. Wiesner, S.: Conjugate coding. SIGACT News $15(1)$, 78–88 (1983). https://doi.org/10.1145/1008908.1008920

30. Yan, J., Weng, J., Lin, D., Quan, Y.: Quantum bit commitment with application in quantum zero-knowledge proof (extended abstract). In: Elbassioni, K., Makino, K. (eds.) ISAAC 2015. LNCS, vol. 9472, pp. 555–565. Springer, Heidelberg (2015). https://doi.org/10.1007/978-3-662-48971-0_47

31. Zhu, Q., et al.: Quantum computational advantage via 60-qubit 24-cycle random circuit sampling. Sci. Bull. $67(3)$, 240–245 (2022). https://doi.org/10.1016/j.scib.2021.10.017

Quantum Cryptography I

Certified Everlasting Zero-Knowledge Proof for QMA

Taiga Hiroka[1]([✉]), Tomoyuki Morimae[1], Ryo Nishimaki[2], and Takashi Yamakawa[1,2]

[1] Yukawa Institute for Theoretical Physics, Kyoto University, Kyoto, Japan
taiga.hiroka@yukawa.kyoto-u.ac.jp
[2] NTT Corporation, Tokyo, Japan

Abstract. In known constructions of classical zero-knowledge protocols for **NP**, either zero-knowledge or soundness holds only against computationally bounded adversaries. Indeed, achieving both statistical zero-knowledge and statistical soundness at the same time with classical verifier is impossible for **NP** unless the polynomial-time hierarchy collapses, and it is also believed to be impossible even with a quantum verifier. In this work, we introduce a novel compromise, which we call the certified everlasting zero-knowledge proof for **QMA**. It is a computational zero-knowledge proof for **QMA**, but the verifier issues a classical certificate that shows that the verifier has deleted its quantum information. If the certificate is valid, even an unbounded malicious verifier can no longer learn anything beyond the validity of the statement.

We construct a certified everlasting zero-knowledge proof for **QMA**. For the construction, we introduce a new quantum cryptographic primitive, which we call commitment with statistical binding and certified everlasting hiding, where the hiding property becomes statistical once the receiver has issued a valid certificate that shows that the receiver has deleted the committed information. We construct commitment with statistical binding and certified everlasting hiding from quantum encryption with certified deletion by Broadbent and Islam [TCC 2020] (in a black-box way), and then combine it with the quantum sigma-protocol for **QMA** by Broadbent and Grilo [FOCS 2020] to construct the certified everlasting zero-knowledge proof for **QMA**. Our constructions are secure in the quantum random oracle model. Commitment with statistical binding and certified everlasting hiding itself is of independent interest, and there will be many other useful applications beyond zero-knowledge.

1 Introduction

1.1 Background

Zero-knowledge [GMR89], which roughly states that the verifier cannot learn anything beyond the validity of the statement, is one of the most important concepts in cryptography and computer science. The study of zero-knowledge has a long history in classical cryptography, and recently there have been many results in quantum cryptography. In known constructions of classical zero-knowledge protocols for **NP**, either zero-knowledge or soundness holds only against computationally bounded adversaries. Indeed, achieving both statistical zero-knowledge

Y. Dodis and T. Shrimpton (Eds.): CRYPTO 2022, LNCS 13507, pp. 239–268, 2022.
https://doi.org/10.1007/978-3-031-15802-5_9

and statistical soundness at the same time with classical verifier is impossible for **NP** unless the polynomial-time hierarchy collapses [For87]. It is also believed to be impossible even with a quantum verifier [MW18].

Broadbent and Islam [BI20] recently suggested an idea of the novel compromise: realizing "everlasting zero-knowledge" by using quantum encryption with certified deletion. The everlasting security defined by Unruh [Unr13] states that the protocol remains secure as long as the adversary runs in polynomial-time during the execution of the protocol. Quantum encryption with certified deletion introduced by Broadbent and Islam [BI20] is a new quantum cryptographic primitive where a classical message is encrypted into a quantum ciphertext, and the receiver in possession of a quantum ciphertext can generate a classical certificate that shows that the receiver has deleted the quantum ciphertext. If the certificate is valid, the receiver can no longer decrypt the message even if it receives the secret key. Broadbent and Islam's idea is to use quantum commitment with a similar certified deletion security to encrypt the first message from the prover to the verifier in the standard Σ-protocol. Once the verifier issues the deletion certificate for all commitments that are not opened by the verifier's challenge, even an unbounded verifier can no longer access the committed values of the unopened commitments. They left the formal definition and the construction as future works.

There are many obstacles to realizing their idea. First, their quantum encryption with certified deletion cannot be directly used in a Σ-protocol because it does not have any binding property. Their ciphertext consists of a classical and quantum part. The classical part is $m \oplus u \oplus H(r)$, where m is the plaintext, u and r are random bit strings, and H is a hash function. The quantum part is a random BB84 states whose computational basis states encode r. The decryption key is u and the place of computational basis states that encode r, and therefore it is not binding: by changing u, a different message can be obtained. We therefore need to extend quantum encryption with certified deletion in such a way that the statistical binding property is included.

Second, defining a meaningful notion of "everlasting zero-knowledge proof" itself is non-trivial. In fact, everlasting zero-knowledge proofs for **QMA** or even for **NP** in the sense of Unruh's definition [Unr13] are unlikely to exist.[1] To see this, recall that the definition of quantum statistical zero-knowledge [Wat09, MW18] requires a simulator to simulate the view of a *quantum polynomial-time* malicious verifier in a statistically indistinguishable manner. Therefore, everlasting zero-knowledge in the sense of Unruh's definition [Unr13] is actually equivalent to quantum statistical zero-knowledge. On the other hand, as already mentioned,

---

[1] We mention that everlasting zero-knowledge *arguments*, which only satisfy computational soundness, can exist. Indeed, any statistical zero-knowledge argument is an everlasting zero-knowledge argument. One may think that the computational soundness is fine since that ensures everlasting soundness in the sense of Unruh's definition [Unr13]. For practical purposes, this may be true. On the other hand, we believe that it is theoretically interesting to pursue (a kind of) everlasting zero-knowledge without compromising the soundness as is done in this paper.

it is believed that quantum statistical zero-knowledge proofs for **NP** do not exist [MW18]. In particular, Menda and Watrous [MW18] constructed an oracle relative to which quantum statistical zero-knowledge proofs for (even a subclass of) **NP** do not exist.

However, we notice that this argument does not go through for *certified everlasting zero-knowledge*, where the verifier can issue a classical certificate that shows that the verifier has deleted its information. Once a valid certificate has been issued, even an unbounded malicious verifier can no longer learn anything beyond the validity of the statement. The reason is that certified everlasting zero-knowledge does not imply statistical zero-knowledge since it does not ensure any security against a malicious verifier that refuses to provide a valid certificate of deletion. Therefore, we have the following question.

*Is it possible to define and construct a certified everlasting zero-knowledge proof for **QMA**?*

1.2 Our Results

In this work, we define and construct the certified everlasting zero-knowledge proof for **QMA**. This goal is achieved in the following four steps.

1. We define a new quantum cryptographic primitive, which we call *commitment with statistical binding and certified everlasting hiding*. In this new commitment scheme, binding is statistical but hiding is computational. However, the hiding property becomes statistical once the receiver has issued a valid certificate that shows that the receiver has deleted the committed information.
2. We construct commitment with statistical binding and certified everlasting hiding. We use secret-key quantum encryption with certified deletion as the building block in a black-box way. This construction is secure in the quantum random oracle model [BDF+11].
3. We define a new notion of zero-knowledge proof, which we call *the certified everlasting zero-knowledge proof for **QMA***. It is a computational zero-knowledge proof for **QMA** with the following additional property. A verifier can issue a classical certificate that shows that the verifier has deleted its information. If the certificate is valid, even an unbounded malicious verifier can no longer learn anything beyond the validity of the statement.
4. We apply commitment with statistical binding and certified everlasting hiding to the quantum Σ-protocol for **QMA** by Broadbent and Grilo [BG20] to construct the certified everlasting zero-knowledge proof for **QMA**.

We have three remarks on our results. First, although our main results are the definition and the construction of the certified everlasting zero-knowledge proof for **QMA**, our commitment with statistical binding and certified everlasting hiding itself is also of independent interest. There will be many other useful applications beyond zero-knowledge. In fact, it is known that binding and hiding cannot be made statistical at the same time even in the quantum world [LC97, May97], and therefore our new commitment scheme provides a nice compromise.

Second, our new commitment scheme and the new zero-knowledge proof are the first cryptographic applications of symmetric-key quantum encryption with certified deletion. Although certified deletion is conceptually very interesting, there was no concrete construction of cryptographic applications when it was first introduced [BI20]. One reason why the applications are limited is that in cryptography it is not natural to consider the case when the receiver receives the private key later. Hiroka et al. [HMNY21b] recently extended the symmetric-key scheme by Broadbent and Islam [BI20] to a public-key encryption scheme, an attribute-based encryption scheme, and a publicly verifiable scheme, which have opened many applications. However, one disadvantage is that their security is the computational one unlike the symmetric-key scheme [BI20]. Therefore it was open whether there is any cryptographic application of the information-theoretically secure certified deletion scheme. Our results provide the first cryptographic applications of it. Interestingly, the setup of the symmetric-key scheme [BI20], where the receiver does not have the private key in advance, nicely fits into the framework of the Σ-protocol, because the verifier (receiver) in the Σ-protocol does not have the decryption key of the first encrypted message from the prover (sender).

Finally, note that certified everlasting zero-knowledge and certified everlasting hiding seem to be impossible in the classical world, because a malicious adversary can copy its information. In particular, certified everlasting zero-knowledge against classical verifiers clearly implies honest-verifier statistical zero-knowledge since an honest verifier runs in polynomial-time.[2] Moreover, it is known that **HVSZK** = **SZK** where **HVSZK** and **SZK** are languages that have honest-verifier statistical zero-knowledge proofs and (general) statistical zero-knowledge proofs, respectively [GSV98]. Therefore, if certified everlasting zero-knowledge proofs for **NP** with classical verification exist, we obtain **NP** $\subseteq$ **HVSZK** = **SZK**, which means the collapse of the polynomial-time hierarchy [For87]. Though the above argument only works for protocols in the standard model, no construction of honest-verifier statistical zero-knowledge proofs for **NP** is known in the random oracle model either. Our results therefore add novel items to the list of quantum cryptographic primitives that can be achieved only in the quantum world.

1.3   Technical Overview

Certified Everlasting Zero-Knowledge. As explained in Sect. 1.1, everlasting zero-knowledge proofs for **NP** (and for **QMA**) seem impossible even with quantum verifiers. Therefore, we introduce a relaxed notion of zero-knowledge which we call

---

[2] A similar argument does not work for quantum verifiers since the honest-verifier quantum statistical zero-knowledge [Wat02] requires a simulator to simulate honest verifier's internal state *at any point* of the protocol execution. This is not implied by certified everlasting zero-knowledge, which only requires security after generating a valid deletion certificate.

certified everlasting zero-knowledge inspired by quantum encryption with certified deletion introduced by Broadbent and Islam [BI20]. Certified everlasting zero-knowledge ensures security against malicious verifiers that run in polynomial-time during the protocol and provide a valid certificate that sensitive information is "deleted". (For the formal definition, see Sect. 4.1.) The difference from everlasting zero-knowledge is that it does not ensure security against malicious verifiers that do not provide a valid certificate. We believe that this is still a meaningful security notion since if the verifier refuses to provide a valid certificate, the prover may penalize the verifier for cheating.

Quantum Commitment with Certified Everlasting Hiding. Our construction of certified everlasting zero-knowledge proofs is based on the idea sketched by Broadbent and Islam [BI20]. (For the details of the construction, see Sect. 4.2.) The idea is to implement a Σ-protocol using a commitment scheme with certified deletion. However, they did not give a construction or definition of commitment with certified deletion. First, we remark that the encryption with certified deletion in [BI20] cannot be directly used as a commitment. A natural way to use their scheme as a commitment scheme is to consider a ciphertext as a commitment. However, since different secret keys decrypt the same ciphertext into different messages, this does not satisfy the binding property as commitment.

A natural (failed) attempt to fix this problem is to add a classical commitment to the secret key of the encryption scheme with certified deletion making use of the fact that the secret key of the encryption with certified deletion in [BI20] is classical. That is, a commitment to a message m consists of

$$(\mathsf{CT} = \mathsf{Enc}(\mathsf{sk}, m), \mathsf{com} = \mathsf{Commit}(\mathsf{sk}))$$

where Enc is the encryption algorithm of the scheme in [BI20], sk is its secret key, and Commit is a statistically binding and computationally hiding classical commitment scheme. This resolves the issue of binding since the secret key is now committed by the classical commitment scheme. On the other hand, we cannot prove a hiding property that is sufficiently strong for achieving certified everlasting zero-knowledge. It is not difficult to see that what we need here is *certified everlasting hiding*, which ensures that once a receiver generates a valid certificate that it deleted the commitment in a polynomial-time, the hiding property is ensured even if the receiver runs in unbounded-time afterwards. Unfortunately, we observe that the above generic construction seems insufficient for achieving certified everlasting hiding.[3] The reason is as follows: We want to reduce the certified everlasting hiding to the certified deletion security of Enc. However, the security of Enc can be invoked only if sk is information-theoretically hidden before the deletion. On the other hand, sk is committed by a statistically binding commitment in the above construction, and thus sk is information-theoretically determined from the commitment. Therefore, we

---

[3] One may think that we can just use statistically hiding commitment. However, such a commitment can only satisfy computational binding, which is not sufficient for achieving certified everlasting zero-knowledge *proofs* rather than arguments.

have to somehow delete the information of sk from the commitment in some hybrid game in a security proof. A similar issue was dealt with by Hiroka et al. [HMNY21b] by using receiver non-committing encryption in the context of public key encryption with certified deletion. However, their technique inherently relies on the assumption that an adversary runs in polynomial-time *even after the deletion*. Therefore, their technique is not applicable in the context of certified everlasting hiding.

To overcome the above issue, we rely on random oracles. We modify the above construction as follows:

$$(\mathsf{CT} = \mathsf{Enc}(\mathsf{sk}, m), \mathsf{com} = \mathsf{Commit}(R), H(R) \oplus \mathsf{sk})$$

where R is a sufficiently long random string and H is a hash function modeled as a random oracle whose output length is the same as that of sk. We give an intuition on why the above issue is resolved with this modification. As explained in the previous paragraph, we want to delete the information of sk from the commitment in some hybrid games. By the computational hiding of commitment, a polynomial-time receiver cannot find R from $\mathsf{Commit}(R)$. Therefore, it cannot get any information on $H(R)$ since otherwise we can "extract" R from one of the receiver's queries. This argument can be made rigorous by using the one-way to hiding lemma [Unr15, AHU19]. Importantly, we only have to assume that the receiver runs in polynomial-time *before the deletion* and do not need to assume anything about the running time after the deletion because we extract R from one of the queries before the deletion. Since sk is masked by $H(R)$, the receiver cannot get any information on sk either. Thus, we can simulate the whole commitment $(\mathsf{CT}, \mathsf{com}, H(R) \oplus \mathsf{sk})$ without using sk, which resolves the issue and enables us to reduce certified everlasting hiding to certified deletion security of Enc.

We remark that quantum commitments in general cannot satisfy the binding property in the classical sense. Indeed, if a malicious sender generates a superposition of valid commitments on different messages m_0 and m_1, it can later open to m_0 or m_1 with probability $1/2$ for each. Defining a binding property for quantum commitments is non-trivial, and there have been proposed various flavors of definitions in the literature, e.g., [CDMS04, DFS04, DFR+07, Yan20, BB21]. It might be possible to adopt some of those definitions. However, we choose to introduce a new definition, which we call *classical-extractor-based binding*, tailored to our construction because this is more convenient for our purpose. Classical-extractor-based binding captures the property of our construction that the randomness R is information-theoretically determined by the classical part $\mathsf{com} = \mathsf{Commit}(R)$ of a commitment, and the decommitment can be done by using the rest part of the commitment and R.[4] In particular, this roughly means that one can extract the committed message with an unbounded-time extractor before the sender decommits. This enables us to prove soundness for our certi-

---

[4] For this definition to make sense, we need to require that $\mathsf{com} = \mathsf{Commit}(R)$ is classical. This can be ensured if the honest receiver measures it as soon as receiving it even if only quantum communication channel is available.

fied everlasting zero-knowledge proofs in essentially the same manner as in the classical case.

The details of the construction and security proofs are explained in Sect. 3.2.

Certified Everlasting Zero-Knowledge Proof for QMA. Once we obtain a commitment scheme with certified everlasting hiding, the construction of certified everlasting zero-knowledge proofs is straightforward based on the idea sketched in [BI20]. Though they only considered a construction for **NP**, we observe that the idea can be naturally extended to a construction for **QMA** since a "quantum version" of Σ-protocol for **QMA** called Ξ-protocol is constructed by Broadbent and Grilo [BG20]. Below, we sketch the construction for clarity. Let $A = (A_{\text{yes}}, A_{\text{no}})$ be a promise problem in **QMA**. [BG20] showed that for any $\text{x} \in A_{\text{yes}}$ and any corresponding witness w, it is possible to generate (in a quantum polynomial-time) so-called the local simulatable history state ρ_{hist} from w, which satisfies the following two special properties (for details, see Definition 2.2):

(LS1) The verification can be done by measuring randomly chosen five qubits of ρ_{hist}.
(LS2) The classical description of any five-qubit reduced density matrix of ρ_{hist} can be obtained in classical polynomial-time.

With these properties, the quantum Σ-protocol of [BG20] is constructed as follows:

1. **Commitment phase**: The prover randomly chooses $x, z \in \{0, 1\}^n$, and sends $(X^x Z^z \rho_{\text{hist}} Z^z X^x) \otimes \text{com}(x, z)$ to the verifier, where $X^x Z^z := \prod_{i=1}^{n} X_i^{x_i} Z_i^{z_i}$, n is the number of qubits of ρ_{hist}, and $\text{com}(x, z)$ is a classical commitment of (x, z).
2. **Challenge phase**: The verifier randomly chooses a subset $S \subset [n]$ of size $|S| = 5$, and sends it to the prover.
3. **Response phase**: The prover opens the commitment for $\{x_i, z_i\}_{i \in S}$.
4. **Verification phase**: The verifier applies $\prod_{i \in S} X_i^{x_i} Z_i^{z_i}$ on the state and measures qubits in S.

The correctness and the soundness come from the property (LS1), and the zero-knowledge comes from the property (LS2). If the classical commitment scheme used in the above construction is the one with statistical binding and computational hiding, the quantum Σ-protocol is a computational zero-knowledge proof for **QMA**, because the unbounded malicious verifier can open the commitment of $\{x_i, z_i\}_{i \in [n] \setminus S}$, and therefore can obtain the entire ρ_{hist}. If more than five qubits of ρ_{hist} are available to the malicious verifier, the zero-knowledge property no longer holds.

We construct the certified everlasting zero-knowledge proof for **QMA** based on the quantum Σ-protocol. Our idea is to use commitment with certified everlasting hiding and statistical binding for the commitment of (x, z) in the above construction of the quantum Σ-protocol. If the verifier issues a valid deletion certificate for the commitment of $\{x_i, z_i\}_{i \in [n] \setminus S}$, even unbounded malicious verifier can no longer learn $\{x_i, z_i\}_{i \in [n] \setminus S}$, and therefore what it can access is only the five qubits of ρ_{hist}. This gives a proof for certified everlasting zero-knowledge. Using classical-extractor-based binding, the proof of statistical soundness can be done almost in the same way as in [BG20]. Recall that classical-extractor-based binding enables us to extract the committed message with an unbounded-time extractor before the sender decommits. Therefore, we can extract the committed (x, z) from $\text{com}(x, z)$. Since the extraction is done before the challenge phase, the extracted values do not depend on the challenge S. Then, it is easy to reduce the soundness of the scheme to that of the original **QMA** promise problem A. The details of the construction are explained in Sect. 4.2.

1.4   Related Works

Zero-Knowledge for QMA. Zero-knowledge for **QMA** was first constructed by Broadbent, Ji, Song, and Watrous [BJSW16]. Broadbent and Grilo [BG20] gave an elegant and simpler construction what they call the Ξ-protocol (which is considered as a quantum version of the standard Σ-protocol) by using the local simulatability [GSY19]. Our construction is based on the Ξ-protocol. Bitansky and Shmueli [BS20] gave the first constant round zero-knowledge argument for **QMA** with negligible soundness error. Brakerski and Yuen [BY20] gave a construction of 3-round *delayed-input* zero-knowledge proof for **QMA** where the prover needs to know the statement and witness only for generating its last message. Chardouvelis and Malavolta [CM21] constructed 4-round statistical zero-knowledge arguments for **QMA** and 2-round zero-knowledge for **QMA** in the timing model.

Regarding non-interactive zero-knowledge proofs or arguments (NIZK), Kobayashi [Kob03] first studied (statistically sound and zero-knowledge) NIZKs in a model where the prover and verifier share Bell pairs, and gave a complete problem in this setting. It is unlikely that the complete problem contains (even a subclass of) **NP** [MW18], and thus even a NIZK for all **NP** languages is unlikely to exist in this model. Chailloux et al. [CCKV08] showed that there exists a (statistically sound and zero-knowledge) NIZK for all languages in **QSZK** in the help model where a trusted party generates a pure state *depending on the statement to be proven* and gives copies of the state to both prover and verifier. Recently, there are many constructions of NIZK proofs or arguments for **QMA** in various kinds of setup models and assumptions [ACGH20, CVZ20, BG20, Shm21, BCKM21, MY21, BM21].

Quantum Commitment. It is well-known that statistically binding and hiding commitments are impossible even with quantum communication [LC97, May97]. On the other hand, there is a large body of literature on constructing quantum commitments assuming some computational assumptions, e.g., see the references in the introduction of [Yan20]. Among them, several works showed the possibility of using quantum commitments in constructions of zero-knowledge proofs and arguments [YWLQ15, FUW+20, Yan20, BB21]. However, they only consider replacing classical commitments with quantum commitments in classical constructions while keeping the same functionality and security level as the classical construction. In particular, none of them considers protocols for **QMA** or properties that are classically impossible to achieve like our notion of the certified everlasting zero-knowledge.

2 Preliminaries

2.1 Notations

Here we introduce basic notations we will use. In this paper, $x \leftarrow X$ denotes selecting an element from a finite set X uniformly at random, and $y \leftarrow A(x)$ denotes assigning to y the output of a probabilistic or deterministic algorithm A on an input x. When we explicitly show that A uses randomness r, we write $y \leftarrow A(x; r)$. When D is a distribution, $x \leftarrow D$ denotes sampling an element from D. Let $[n]$ be the set $\{1, \ldots, n\}$. Let λ be a security parameter, and $y := z$ denotes that y is set, defined, or substituted by z. For a bit string $s \in \{0,1\}^n$, s_i denotes the i-th bit of s. QPT stands for quantum polynomial time. PPT stands for (classical) probabilistic polynomial time. For a subset $S \subseteq W$ of a set W, $\overline{S}$ is the complement of S, i.e., $\overline{S} := W \setminus S$. A function $f : \mathbb{N} \to \mathbb{R}$ is a negligible function if for any constant c, there exists $\lambda_0 \in \mathbb{N}$ such that for any $\lambda > \lambda_0$, $f(\lambda) < \lambda^{-c}$. We write $f(\lambda) \leq \mathsf{negl}(\lambda)$ to denote $f(\lambda)$ being a negligible function.

2.2 Quantum Computation

We assume the familiarity with basics of quantum computation, and use standard notations. Let us denote $\mathcal{Q}$ be the state space of a single qubit. I is the two-dimensional identity operator. For simplicity, we often write $I^{\otimes n}$ as I for any n when the dimension of the identity operator is clear from the context. For any single-qubit operator O, O_i means an operator that applies O on the i-th qubit and applies I on all other qubits. X and Z are the Pauli X and Z operators, respectively. For any n-bit strings $x := (x_1, x_2, \cdots, x_n) \in \{0,1\}^n$ and $z := (z_1, z_2, \cdots, z_n) \in \{0,1\}^n$, $X^x := \prod_{i \in [n]} X_i^{x_i}$ and $Z^z := \prod_{i \in [n]} Z_i^{z_i}$. For any subset S, Tr_S means the trace over all qubits in S. For any quantum state ρ and a bit string $s \in \{0,1\}^n$, $\rho \otimes s$ means $\rho \otimes |s\rangle\langle s|$. The trace distance between two states ρ and σ is given by $\frac{1}{2} \|\rho - \sigma\|_{\mathrm{tr}}$, where $\|A\|_{\mathrm{tr}} := \mathrm{Tr}\sqrt{A^\dagger A}$ is the trace norm. If $\frac{1}{2} \|\rho - \sigma\|_{\mathrm{tr}} \leq \epsilon$, we say that ρ and σ are ϵ-close. If $\epsilon = \mathsf{negl}(\lambda)$, then we say that ρ and σ are statistically indistinguishable.

Let C_0 and C_1 be quantum channels from p qubits to q qubits, where p and q are polynomials. We say that they are computationally indistinguishable, and denote it by $C_0 \approx_c C_1$ if there exists a negligible function negl such that $|\Pr[D((C_0 \otimes I)(\sigma)) = 1] - \Pr[D((C_1 \otimes I)(\sigma)) = 1]| \leq \mathsf{negl}(\lambda)$ for any polynomial k, any $(p + k)$-qubit state σ, and any polynomial-size quantum circuit D acting on $q + k$ qubits. We say that C_0 and C_1 are statistically indistinguishable, and denote it by $C_0 \approx_s C_1$, if D is an unbounded algorithm.

Lemma 2.1 (Quantum Rewinding Lemma [Wat09]). *Let Q be a quantum circuit that acts on an n-qubit state $|\psi\rangle$ and an m-qubit auxiliary state $|0^m\rangle$.*

Let $p(\psi) := \|((\langle 0| \otimes I)Q(|\psi\rangle \otimes |0^m\rangle))\|^2$ and $|\phi(\psi)\rangle := \frac{1}{\sqrt{p(\psi)}}((\langle 0| \otimes I)Q(|\psi\rangle \otimes |0^m\rangle))$. Let $p_0, q \in (0,1)$ and $\epsilon \in (0,\frac{1}{2})$ such that $|p(\psi) - q| < \epsilon$, $p_0(1 - p_0) < q(1-q)$, and $p_0 < p(\psi)$. Then there is a quantum circuit R of size at most $O\left(\frac{\log(\frac{1}{\epsilon})\text{size}(Q)}{p_0(1-p_0)}\right)$ such that on input $|\psi\rangle$, R computes a quantum state $\rho(\psi)$ that satisfies $\langle \phi(\psi)|\rho(\psi)|\phi(\psi)\rangle \geq 1 - -16\epsilon\frac{\log^2(\frac{1}{\epsilon})}{p_0^2(1-p_0)^2}$.

Lemma 2.2 (One-Way to Hiding Lemma [AHU19]). *Let* $S \subseteq \mathcal{X}$ *be a random subset of* $\mathcal{X}$. *Let* $G, H : \mathcal{X} \to \mathcal{Y}$ *be random functions satisfying* $\forall x \notin S$ $[G(x) = H(x)]$. *Let* z *be a random classical bit string. (S, G, H, z may have an arbitrary joint distribution.) Let* $\mathcal{A}$ *be an oracle-aided quantum algorithm that makes at most* q *quantum queries. Let* $\mathcal{B}$ *be an algorithm that on input* z *chooses* $i \leftarrow [q]$, *runs* $\mathcal{A}^H(z)$, *measures* $\mathcal{A}$'s *i-th query, and outputs the measurement outcome. Then we have* $|\Pr[\mathcal{A}^G(z) = 1] - \Pr[\mathcal{A}^H(z) = 1]| \leq 2q\sqrt{\Pr[\mathcal{B}^H(z) \in S]}$.

2.3 QMA and k-SimQMA

Definition 2.1 (QMA). *We say that a promise problem* $A = (A_{\text{yes}}, A_{\text{no}})$ *is in* **QMA** *if there exist a polynomial* p, *a QPT algorithm* V, *and* $0 \leq \beta < \alpha \leq 1$ *with* $\alpha - \beta \geq \frac{1}{\text{poly}(|x|)}$ *such that*

Completeness: *For any* $x \in A_{\text{yes}}$, *there exists a quantum state* w *of* $p(|x|)$-*qubit (called a witness) such that*

$$\Pr[V(x, w) = \top] \geq \alpha.$$

Soundness: *For any* $x \in A_{\text{no}}$ *and any quantum state* w *of* $p(|x|)$-*qubit,*

$$\Pr[V(x, w) = \top] \leq \beta.$$

For any $x \in A_{\text{yes}}$, $R_A(x)$ *is the (possibly infinite) set of all quantum states* w *such that* $\Pr[V(x, w) = \top] \geq \frac{2}{3}$.

A complexity class of k-**SimQMA** is introduced, and proven to be equal to **QMA** in [BG20].

Definition 2.2 (k-SimQMA [BG20]). *A promise problem* $A = (A_{\text{yes}}, A_{\text{no}})$ *is in* k-**SimQMA** *with soundness* $\beta(|x|) \leq 1 - \frac{1}{\text{poly}(|x|)}$, *if there exist polynomials* m *and* n *such that given* $x \in A_{\text{yes}}$, *there is an efficient deterministic algorithm that computes* $m(|x|)$ k-*qubit POVMs* $\{\Pi_1, I - \Pi_1\}, \ldots, \{\Pi_{m(|x|)}, I - \Pi_{m(|x|)}\}$ *such that:*

Simulatable Completeness: *If* $x \in A_{\text{yes}}$, *there exists an* $n(|x|)$-*qubit state* ρ_{hist}, *which we call a simulatable witness, such that for all* $c \in [m]$, $\text{Tr}(\Pi_c \rho_{\text{hist}}) \geq 1 - \text{negl}(|x|)$, *and there exists a set of* k-*qubit density matrices* $\{\rho_{\text{sim}}^{x,S}\}_{S \subseteq [n(|x|)], |S|=k}$ *that can be computed in polynomial time from* x *and* ρ_{hist} *such that* $\|Tr_{\overline{S}}(\rho_{\text{hist}}) - \rho_{\text{sim}}^{x,S}\|_{\text{tr}} \leq \text{negl}(|x|)$.

Soundness: *If* $x \in A_{\text{no}}$, *for any* $n(|x|)$-*qubit state* ρ, $\frac{1}{m}\sum_{c \in [m]} Tr(\Pi_c \rho) \leq \beta(|x|)$.

2.4   Cryptographic Tools

In this section, we review cryptographic tools used in this paper.

Non-interactive Commitment.

Definition 2.3 (Non-interactive Commitment (Syntax)). *Let λ be the security parameter and let p, q and r be some polynomials. A (classical) non-interactive commitment scheme consists of a single PPT algorithm Commit with plaintext space $\mathcal{M} := \{0,1\}^{p(\lambda)}$, randomness space $\{0,1\}^{q(\lambda)}$ and commitment space $\mathcal{C} := \{0,1\}^{r(\lambda)}$ satisfying two properties:*

Perfect binding:*For every $(r_0, r_1) \in \{0,1\}^{q(\lambda)} \times \{0,1\}^{q(\lambda)}$ and $(m, m') \in \mathcal{M}^2$ such that $m \neq m'$, we have that $\mathsf{Commit}(m; r_0) \neq \mathsf{Commit}(m'; r_1)$, where $(\mathsf{Commit}(m; r_0), \mathsf{Commit}(m'; r_1)) \in \mathcal{C}^2$.*

Unpredictability: *Let $\Sigma := \mathsf{Commit}$. For any QPT adversary $\mathcal{A}$, we define the following security experiment $\mathsf{Exp}_{\Sigma, \mathcal{A}}^{\mathsf{unpre}}(\lambda)$.*

1. *The challenger chooses $R \leftarrow \mathcal{M}$ and $R' \leftarrow \{0,1\}^{q(\lambda)}$, computes $\mathsf{com} \leftarrow \mathsf{Commit}(R; R')$, and sends com to $\mathcal{A}$.*
2. *$\mathcal{A}$ outputs R^*. The output of the experiment is 1 if $R^* = R$. Otherwise, the output of the experiment is 0.*

We say that the commitment is unpredictable if for any QPT adversary $\mathcal{A}$, it holds that

$$\mathsf{Adv}_{\Sigma, \mathcal{A}}^{\mathsf{unpre}}(\lambda) := \Pr[\mathsf{Exp}_{\Sigma, \mathcal{A}}^{\mathsf{unpre}}(\lambda) = 1] \leq \mathsf{negl}(\lambda).$$

Note that we assume $\frac{1}{|\mathcal{M}|}$ is negligible.

Remark 2.1. The unpredictability is a weaker version of computational hiding. We define unpredictability instead of computational hiding since this suffices for our purpose.

A non-interactive commitment scheme that satisfies the above definition exists assuming the existence of injective one-way functions or perfectly correct public key encryption [LS19]. Alternatively, we can also instantiate it based on random oracles.

Quantum Encryption with Certified Deletion. Broadbent and Islam [BI20] introduced the notion of quantum encryption with certified deletion.

Definition 2.4 (One-Time SKE with Certified Deletion (Syntax)). *Let λ be the security parameter and let p, q and r be some polynomials. A one-time secret key encryption scheme with certified deletion consists of a tuple of polynomial-time algorithms $(\mathsf{KeyGen}, \mathsf{Enc}, \mathsf{Dec}, \mathsf{Del}, \mathsf{Verify})$ with plaintext space $\mathcal{M} := \{0,1\}^n$, ciphertext space $\mathcal{C} := \mathcal{Q}^{\otimes p(\lambda)}$, key space $\mathcal{K} := \{0,1\}^{q(\lambda)}$ and deletion certificate space $\mathcal{D} := \{0,1\}^{r(\lambda)}$.*

$\mathsf{KeyGen}(1^\lambda) \rightarrow \mathsf{sk}$: *The key generation algorithm takes as input the security parameter 1^λ, and outputs a secret key $\mathsf{sk} \in \mathcal{K}$.*

$\mathsf{Enc}(\mathsf{sk}, m) \to \mathsf{CT}$: *The encryption algorithm takes as input* sk *and a plaintext* $m \in \mathcal{M}$, *and outputs a ciphertext* $\mathsf{CT} \in \mathcal{C}$.

$\mathsf{Dec}(\mathsf{sk}, \mathsf{CT}) \to m'$ *or* $\perp$: *The decryption algorithm takes as input* sk *and* CT, *and outputs a plaintext* $m' \in \mathcal{M}$ *or* $\perp$.

$\mathsf{Del}(\mathsf{CT}) \to \mathsf{cert}$: *The deletion algorithm takes as input* CT, *and outputs a certification* $\mathsf{cert} \in \mathcal{D}$.

$\mathsf{Verify}(\mathsf{sk}, \mathsf{cert}) \to \top$ *or* $\perp$: *The verification algorithm takes* sk *and* cert, *and outputs* $\top$ *to indicate acceptance or* $\perp$.

Definition 2.5 (Correctness for One-Time SKE with Certified Deletion). *There are two types of correctness. One is decryption correctness and the other is verification correctness.*

Decryption Correctness: *There exists a negligible function* negl *such that for any* $\lambda \in \mathbb{N}$ *and* $m \in \mathcal{M}$,

$$\Pr\left[\mathsf{Dec}(\mathsf{sk}, \mathsf{CT}) = m \;\middle|\; \begin{array}{l} \mathsf{sk} \leftarrow \mathsf{KeyGen}(1^\lambda) \\ \mathsf{CT} \leftarrow \mathsf{Enc}(\mathsf{sk}, m) \end{array}\right] \geq 1 - \mathsf{negl}(\lambda).$$

Verification Correctness: *There exists a negligible function* negl *such that for any* $\lambda \in \mathbb{N}$ *and* $m \in \mathcal{M}$,

$$\Pr\left[\mathsf{Verify}(\mathsf{sk}, \mathsf{cert}) = \top \;\middle|\; \begin{array}{l} \mathsf{sk} \leftarrow \mathsf{KeyGen}(1^\lambda) \\ \mathsf{CT} \leftarrow \mathsf{Enc}(\mathsf{sk}, m) \\ \mathsf{cert} \leftarrow \mathsf{Del}(\mathsf{CT}) \end{array}\right] \geq 1 - \mathsf{negl}(\lambda).$$

Definition 2.6 (Certified Deletion Security for One-Time SKE). *Let* $\Sigma = (\mathsf{KeyGen}, \mathsf{Enc}, \mathsf{Dec}, \mathsf{Del}, \mathsf{Verify})$ *be a secret key encryption with certified deletion. We consider the following security experiment* $\mathsf{Exp}_{\Sigma, \mathcal{A}}^{\mathsf{otsk\text{-}cert\text{-}del}}(\lambda, b)$.

1. *The challenger computes* $\mathsf{sk} \leftarrow \mathsf{KeyGen}(1^\lambda)$.
2. $\mathcal{A}$ *sends* $(m_0, m_1) \in \mathcal{M}^2$ *to the challenger.*
3. *The challenger computes* $\mathsf{CT}_b \leftarrow \mathsf{Enc}(\mathsf{sk}, m_b)$ *and sends* CT_b *to* $\mathcal{A}$.
4. $\mathcal{A}$ *sends* cert *to the challenger.*
5. *The challenger computes* $\mathsf{Verify}(\mathsf{sk}, \mathsf{cert})$. *If the output is* $\perp$, *the challenger sends* $\perp$ *to* $\mathcal{A}$. *If the output is* $\top$, *the challenger sends* sk *to* $\mathcal{A}$.
6. $\mathcal{A}$ *outputs* $b' \in \{0, 1\}$. *The experiment outputs* b'.

We say that the Σ *is OT-CD secure if for any unbounded* $\mathcal{A}$, *it holds that*

$$\mathsf{Adv}_{\Sigma, \mathcal{A}}^{\mathsf{otsk\text{-}cert\text{-}del}}(\lambda)$$
$$:= |\Pr[\mathsf{Exp}_{\Sigma, \mathcal{A}}^{\mathsf{otsk\text{-}cert\text{-}del}}(\lambda, 0) = 1] - \Pr[\mathsf{Exp}_{\Sigma, \mathcal{A}}^{\mathsf{otsk\text{-}cert\text{-}del}}(\lambda, 1) = 1]| \leq \mathsf{negl}(\lambda).$$

Broadbent and Islam [BI20] showed that a one-time SKE scheme with certified deletion that satisfies the above correctness and security exists unconditionally.

3   Commitment with Certified Everlasting Hiding and Classical-Extractor-Based Binding

In this section, we define and construct commitment with certified everlasting hiding and statistical binding. We adopt a non-standard syntax for the verification algorithm and a slightly involved definition for the binding, which we call the classical-extractor-based binding, that are tailored to our construction. This is because they are convenient for our construction of certified everlasting zero-knowledge proof for **QMA** given in Sect. 4. We can also construct one with a more standard syntax of verification and binding property, namely, the sum-binding, by essentially the same construction. See the full version [HMNY21a] for details.

3.1   Definition

Definition 3.1 (Commitment with Certified Everlasting Hiding and Classical-Extractor-Based Binding (Syntax)). *Let λ be the security parameter and let p, q, r, s and t be some polynomials. Commitment with certified everlasting hiding and classical-extractor-based binding consists of a tuple of polynomial-time algorithms* (Commit, Verify, Del, Cert) *with message space* $\mathcal{M} := \{0,1\}^n$, *commitment space* $\mathcal{C} := \mathcal{Q}^{\otimes p(\lambda)} \times \{0,1\}^{q(\lambda)}$, *decommitment space* $\mathcal{D} := \{0,1\}^{r(\lambda)}$, *key space* $\mathcal{K} := \{0,1\}^{s(\lambda)}$ *and deletion certificate space* $\mathcal{E} := \{0,1\}^{t(\lambda)}$.

Commit$(1^\lambda, m) \to (\mathsf{com}, \mathsf{d}, \mathsf{ck})$: *The commitment algorithm takes as input a security parameter 1^λ and a message $m \in \mathcal{M}$, and outputs a commitment* com $\in \mathcal{C}$, *a decommitment* $\mathsf{d} := (\mathsf{d}_1, \mathsf{d}_2) \in \mathcal{D}$ *and a key* ck $\in \mathcal{K}$. *Note that* com *consists of a quantum state $\psi \in \mathcal{Q}^{\otimes p(\lambda)}$ and a classical bit string $f \in \{0,1\}^{q(\lambda)}$.*

Verify$(\mathsf{com}, \mathsf{d}) \to m'$ *or* $\bot$: *The verification algorithm consists of two algorithms,* Verify$_1$ *and* Verify$_2$. *It parses* $\mathsf{d} = (\mathsf{d}_1, \mathsf{d}_2)$. Verify$_1$ *takes f and $(\mathsf{d}_1, \mathsf{d}_2)$ as input, and outputs $\top$ to indicate acceptance or $\bot$.* Verify$_2$ *takes* com *and* d_1 *as input, and outputs m'. If the output of* Verify$_1$ *is $\bot$, then the output of* Verify *is $\bot$. Otherwise the output of* Verify *is m'.*

Del(com) $\to$ cert: *The deletion algorithm takes* com *as input, and outputs a certificate* cert $\in \mathcal{E}$.

Cert(cert, ck) $\to \top$ *or* $\bot$: *The certification algorithm takes* cert *and* ck *as input, and outputs $\top$ to indicate acceptance or $\bot$.*

Definition 3.2 (Correctness). *There are two types of correctness, namely, decommitment correctness and deletion correctness.*

Decommitment Correctness: *There exists a negligible function* negl *such that for any $\lambda \in \mathbb{N}$ and $m \in \{0,1\}^n$,*

$$\Pr[m \leftarrow \mathsf{Verify}(\mathsf{com}, \mathsf{d}) \mid (\mathsf{com}, \mathsf{d}, \mathsf{ck}) \leftarrow \mathsf{Commit}(1^\lambda, m)] \geq 1 - \mathsf{negl}(\lambda).$$

Deletion Correctness: *There exists a negligible function* negl *such that for any $\lambda \in \mathbb{N}$ and $m \in \{0,1\}^n$,*

$$\Pr[\top \leftarrow \mathsf{Cert}(\mathsf{cert}, \mathsf{ck}) \mid (\mathsf{com}, \mathsf{d}, \mathsf{ck}) \leftarrow \mathsf{Commit}(1^\lambda, m), \mathsf{cert} \leftarrow \mathsf{Del}(\mathsf{com})] \geq 1 - \mathsf{negl}(\lambda).$$

Definition 3.3 (Classical-Extractor-Based Binding). *There exists an unbounded-time deterministic algorithm* Ext *that takes* $f \in \{0,1\}^{q(\lambda)}$ *of* com *as input, and outputs* $d_1^* \leftarrow \text{Ext}(f)$ *such that for any* com, *any* $d_1 \neq d_1^*$, *and any* d_2, $\Pr[\text{Verify}(\text{com}, d = (d_1, d_2)) = \bot] = 1$.

Definition 3.4 (Computational Hiding). *Let* $\Sigma := $ (Commit, Verify, Del, Cert). *Let us consider the following security experiment* $\text{Exp}_{\Sigma, \mathcal{A}}^{\text{c-hide}}(\lambda, b)$ *against any QPT adversary* $\mathcal{A}$.

1. $\mathcal{A}$ *generates* $(m_0, m_1) \in \mathcal{M}^2$ *and sends them to the challenger.*
2. *The challenger computes* $(\text{com}, d, ck) \leftarrow \text{Commit}(1^\lambda, m_b)$, *and sends* com *to* $\mathcal{A}$.
3. $\mathcal{A}$ *outputs* $b' \in \{0, 1\}$.
4. *The output of the experiment is* b'.

Computational hiding means that the following is satisfied for any QPT $\mathcal{A}$.

$$\text{Adv}_{\Sigma, \mathcal{A}}^{\text{c-hide}}(\lambda) := \left| \Pr[\text{Exp}_{\Sigma, \mathcal{A}}^{\text{c-hide}}(\lambda, 0) = 1] - \Pr[\text{Exp}_{\Sigma, \mathcal{A}}^{\text{c-hide}}(\lambda, 1) = 1] \right| \leq \text{negl}(\lambda).$$

Definition 3.5 (Certified Everlasting Hiding). *Let* $\Sigma := $ (Commit, Verify, Del, Cert). *Let us consider the following security experiment* $\text{Exp}_{\Sigma, \mathcal{A}}^{\text{ever-hide}}(\lambda, b)$ *against* $\mathcal{A} = (\mathcal{A}_1, \mathcal{A}_2)$ *consisting of any QPT adversary* $\mathcal{A}_1$ *and any unbounded adversary* $\mathcal{A}_2$.

1. $\mathcal{A}_1$ *generates* $(m_0, m_1) \in \mathcal{M}^2$ *and sends it to the challenger.*
2. *The challenger computes* $(\text{com}, d, ck) \leftarrow \text{Commit}(1^\lambda, m_b)$, *and sends* com *to* $\mathcal{A}_1$.
3. *At some point,* $\mathcal{A}_1$ *sends* cert *to the challenger, and sends its internal state to* $\mathcal{A}_2$.
4. *The challenger computes* Cert(cert, ck). *If the output is* $\top$, *then the challenger outputs* $\top$, *and sends* (d, ck) *to* $\mathcal{A}_2$. *Else, the challenger outputs* $\bot$, *and sends* $\bot$ *to* $\mathcal{A}_2$.
5. $\mathcal{A}_2$ *outputs* $b' \in \{0, 1\}$.
6. *If the challenger outputs* $\top$, *then the output of the experiment is* b'. *Otherwise, the output of the experiment is* $\bot$.

We say that it is certified everlasting hiding if the following is satisfied for any $\mathcal{A} = (\mathcal{A}_1, \mathcal{A}_2)$.

$$\text{Adv}_{\Sigma, \mathcal{A}}^{\text{ever-hide}}(\lambda) := \left| \Pr[\text{Exp}_{\Sigma, \mathcal{A}}^{\text{ever-hide}}(\lambda, 0) = 1] - \Pr[\text{Exp}_{\Sigma, \mathcal{A}}^{\text{ever-hide}}(\lambda, 1) = 1] \right| \leq \text{negl}(\lambda).$$

Remark 3.1. We remark that it would be incorrect to formulate a definition that conditions on cert being accepted (see discussion in [Unr15].) We also remark that certified everlasting hiding does not imply computational hiding since it does not require anything if the adversary does not send a valid certificate.

The following lemma will be used in the construction of the certified everlasting zero-knowledge proof for **QMA** in Sect. 4. It is shown with the standard hybrid argument. It is also easy to see that a similar lemma holds for computational hiding.

Lemma 3.1. *Let* $\Sigma := (\mathsf{Commit}, \mathsf{Verify}, \mathsf{Del}, \mathsf{Cert})$ *and* $\mathcal{M} = \{0,1\}$. *Let us consider the following security experiment* $\mathsf{Exp}^{\text{bit-ever-hide}}_{\Sigma,\mathcal{A}}(\lambda, b)$ *against* $\mathcal{A} = (\mathcal{A}_1, \mathcal{A}_2)$ *consisting of any QPT adversary* $\mathcal{A}_1$ *and any unbounded adversary* $\mathcal{A}_2$.

1. $\mathcal{A}_1$ *generates* $(m^0, m^1) \in \{0,1\}^n \times \{0,1\}^n$ *and sends it to the challenger.*
2. *The challenger computes*

$$(\mathsf{com}_i(m_i^b), \mathsf{d}_i(m_i^b), \mathsf{ck}_i(m_i^b)) \leftarrow \mathsf{Commit}(1^\lambda, m_i^b)$$

   for each $i \in [n]$, *and sends* $\{\mathsf{com}_i(m_i^b)\}_{i \in [n]}$ *to* $\mathcal{A}_1$. *Here,* m_i^b *is the* i-*th bit of* m^b.
3. *At some point,* $\mathcal{A}_1$ *sends* $\{\mathsf{cert}_i\}_{i \in [n]}$ *to the challenger, and sends its internal state to* $\mathcal{A}_2$.
4. *The challenger computes* $\mathsf{Cert}(\mathsf{cert}_i, \mathsf{ck}_i(m_i^b))$ *for each* $i \in [n]$. *If the output is* $\top$ *for all* $i \in [n]$, *then the challenger outputs* $\top$, *and sends* $\{\mathsf{d}_i(m_i^b), \mathsf{ck}_i(m_i^b)\}_{i \in [n]}$ *to* $\mathcal{A}_2$. *Else, the challenger outputs* $\bot$, *and sends* $\bot$ *to* $\mathcal{A}_2$.
5. $\mathcal{A}_2$ *outputs* $b' \in \{0,1\}$.
6. *If the challenger outputs* $\top$, *then the output of the experiment is* b'. *Otherwise, the output of the experiment is* $\bot$.

If Σ *is certified everlasting hiding,*

$$\mathsf{Adv}^{\text{bit-ever-hide}}_{\Sigma,\mathcal{A}}(\lambda)$$

$$:= \left| \Pr[\mathsf{Exp}^{\text{bit-ever-hide}}_{\Sigma,\mathcal{A}}(\lambda, 0) = 1] - \Pr[\mathsf{Exp}^{\text{bit-ever-hide}}_{\Sigma,\mathcal{A}}(\lambda, 1) = 1] \right| \leq \mathsf{negl}(\lambda)$$

for any $\mathcal{A} = (\mathcal{A}_1, \mathcal{A}_2)$.

3.2 Construction

Let λ be the security parameter, and let p, q, r, s, t and u be some polynomials. We construct commitment with certified everlasting hiding and classical-extractor-based binding, $\Sigma_{\mathsf{ccd}} = (\mathsf{Commit}, \mathsf{Verify}, \mathsf{Del}, \mathsf{Cert})$, with message space $\mathcal{M} = \{0,1\}^n$, commitment space $\mathcal{C} = \mathcal{Q}^{\otimes p(\lambda)} \times \{0,1\}^{q(\lambda)} \times \{0,1\}^{r(\lambda)}$, decommitment space $\mathcal{D} = \{0,1\}^{s(\lambda)} \times \{0,1\}^{t(\lambda)}$, key space $\mathcal{K} = \{0,1\}^{r(\lambda)}$ and deletion certificate space $\mathcal{E} = \{0,1\}^{u(\lambda)}$ from the following primitives:

- Secret-key encryption with certified deletion, $\Sigma_{\mathsf{skcd}} = \mathsf{SKE}.(\mathsf{KeyGen}, \mathsf{Enc}, \mathsf{Dec}, \mathsf{Del}, \mathsf{Verify})$, with plaintext space $\mathcal{M} = \{0,1\}^n$, ciphertext space $\mathcal{C} = \mathcal{Q}^{\otimes p(\lambda)}$, key space $\mathcal{K} = \{0,1\}^{r(\lambda)}$, and deletion certificate space $\mathcal{E} = \{0,1\}^{u(\lambda)}$.
- Classical non-interactive commitment, $\Sigma_{\mathsf{com}} = \mathsf{Classical.Commit}$, with plaintext space $\{0,1\}^{s(\lambda)}$, randomness space $\{0,1\}^{t(\lambda)}$, and commitment space $\{0,1\}^{q(\lambda)}$.
- A hash function H from $\{0,1\}^{s(\lambda)}$ to $\{0,1\}^{r(\lambda)}$ modeled as a quantumly-accessible random oracle.

The construction is as follows.

$\mathsf{Commit}(1^\lambda, m)$:

- Generate ske.sk $\leftarrow$ SKE.KeyGen(1^λ), $R \leftarrow \{0,1\}^{s(\lambda)}$, $R' \leftarrow \{0,1\}^{t(\lambda)}$, and a hash function H from $\{0,1\}^{s(\lambda)}$ to $\{0,1\}^{r(\lambda)}$.
- Compute ske.CT $\leftarrow$ SKE.Enc(ske.sk, m), $f \leftarrow$ Classical.Commit($R; R'$), and $h := H(R) \oplus$ ske.sk.
- Output com $:=$ (ske.CT, f, h), $d_1 := R$, $d_2 := R'$, and ck $:=$ ske.sk.

Verify$_1$(com, d_1, d_2):
- Parse com $=$ (ske.CT, f, h), $d_1 = R$, and $d_2 = R'$.
- Output $\top$ if $f =$ Classical.Commit($R; R'$), and output $\bot$ otherwise.

Verify$_2$(com, d_1):
- Parse com $=$ (ske.CT, f, h) and $d_1 = R$.
- Compute ske.sk' $:= H(R) \oplus h$.
- Output $m' \leftarrow$ SKE.Dec(ske.sk', ske.CT).

Del(com):
- Parse com $=$ (ske.CT, f, h).
- Compute ske.cert $\leftarrow$ SKE.Del(ske.CT).
- Output cert $:=$ ske.cert.

Cert(cert, ck):
- Parse cert $=$ ske.cert and ck $=$ ske.sk.
- Output $\top/\bot \leftarrow$ SKE.Verify(ske.sk, ske.cert).

Correctness. The decommitment and deletion correctness easily follow from the correctness of Σ_{skcd}.

Security. We prove the following three theorems.

Theorem 3.1. *If Σ_{com} is perfect binding, then Σ_{ccd} is classical-extractor-based binding.*

Theorem 3.2. *If Σ_{com} is unpredictable and Σ_{skcd} is OT-CD secure, then Σ_{ccd} is certified everlasting hiding.*

Theorem 3.3. *If Σ_{com} is unpredictable and Σ_{skcd} is OT-CD secure, then Σ_{ccd} is computationally hiding.*

Proof of Theorem 3.1. Due to the perfect binding of $\Sigma_{\mathsf{com}} =$ Classical.Commit, there exists a unique d_1^* such that $f =$ Classical.Commit($d_1^*; d_2$) for a given f. Let Ext be the algorithm that finds such d_1^* and outputs it. (If there is no such d_1^*, then Ext outputs $\bot$.) Then, for any com $=$ (ske.CT, f, h), any $d_1 \neq d_1^*$, and any d_2,

$$\Pr[\mathsf{Verify}(\mathsf{com}, \mathsf{d} = (d_1, d_2)) = \bot] \geq \Pr[f \neq \mathsf{Classical.Commit}(d_1, d_2)] = 1,$$

which completes the proof. $\square$

Proof of Theorem 3.2. For clarity, we describe how the experiment works against an adversary $\mathcal{A} := (\mathcal{A}_1, \mathcal{A}_2)$ consisting of any QPT adversary $\mathcal{A}_1$ and any quantum unbounded time adversary $\mathcal{A}_2$.

$\mathsf{Exp}_{\Sigma_{ccd},\mathcal{A}}^{\mathsf{ever-hide}}(\lambda, b)$: This is the original experiment.

1. A uniformly random function H from $\{0,1\}^{s(\lambda)}$ to $\{0,1\}^{r(\lambda)}$ is chosen. $\mathcal{A}_1$ and $\mathcal{A}_2$ can make arbitrarily many quantum queries to H at any time in the experiment.
2. $\mathcal{A}_1$ chooses $(m_0, m_1) \leftarrow \mathcal{M}^2$, and sends (m_0, m_1) to the challenger.
3. The challenger generates $\mathsf{ske.sk} \leftarrow \mathsf{SKE.KeyGen}(1^\lambda)$, $R \leftarrow \{0,1\}^{s(\lambda)}$ and $R' \leftarrow \{0,1\}^{t(\lambda)}$. The challenger computes $\mathsf{ske.CT} \leftarrow \mathsf{SKE.Enc}(\mathsf{ske.sk}, m_b)$, $f := \mathsf{Classical.Commit}(R; R')$ and $h := H(R) \oplus \mathsf{ske.sk}$, and sends $(\mathsf{ske.CT}, f, h)$ to $\mathcal{A}_1$.
4. $\mathcal{A}_1$ sends $\mathsf{ske.cert}$ to the challenger and sends its internal state to $\mathcal{A}_2$.
5. If $\top \leftarrow \mathsf{SKE.Verify}(\mathsf{ske.sk}, \mathsf{ske.cert})$, the challenger outputs $\top$ and sends $(R, R', \mathsf{ske.sk})$ to $\mathcal{A}_2$. Otherwise, the challenger outputs $\bot$ and sends $\bot$ to $\mathcal{A}_2$.
6. $\mathcal{A}_2$ outputs b'.
7. If the challenger outputs $\top$, then the output of the experiment is b'. Otherwise, the output of the experiment is $\bot$.

What we have to prove is that

$$\mathsf{Adv}_{\Sigma_{ccd},\mathcal{A}}^{\mathsf{ever-hide}}(\lambda) := \left| \Pr[\mathsf{Exp}_{\Sigma_{ccd},\mathcal{A}}^{\mathsf{ever-hide}}(\lambda, 0) = 1] - \Pr[\mathsf{Exp}_{\Sigma_{ccd},\mathcal{A}}^{\mathsf{ever-hide}}(\lambda, 1) = 1] \right| \leq \mathsf{negl}(\lambda).$$

We define the following sequence of hybrids.

$\mathsf{Hyb}_1(b)$: This is identical to $\mathsf{Exp}_{\Sigma_{ccd},\mathcal{A}}^{\mathsf{ever-hide}}(\lambda, b)$ except that the oracle given to $\mathcal{A}_1$ is replaced with $H_{R \to H'}$ which is H reprogrammed according to H' on an input R where H' is another independent uniformly random function. More formally, $H_{R \to H'}$ is defined by

$$H_{R \to H'}(R^*) := \begin{cases} H(R^*) & (R^* \neq R) \\ H'(R^*) & (R^* = R). \end{cases}$$

We note that the challenger still uses H to generate h, and the oracle which $\mathcal{A}_2$ uses is still H similarly to the original experiment.

$\mathsf{Hyb}_2(b)$: This is identical to $\mathsf{Hyb}_1(b)$ except for the following three points. First, the challenger generates h uniformly at random. Second, the oracle given to $\mathcal{A}_1$ is replaced with H' which is an independent uniformly random function. Third, the oracle given to $\mathcal{A}_2$ is replaced with $H'_{R \to h \oplus \mathsf{ske.sk}}$ which is H' reprogrammed to $h \oplus \mathsf{ske.sk}$ on an input R. More formally, $H'_{R \to h \oplus \mathsf{ske.sk}}$ is defined by

$$H'_{R \to h \oplus \mathsf{ske.sk}}(R^*) := \begin{cases} H'(R^*) & (R^* \neq R) \\ h \oplus \mathsf{ske.sk} & (R^* = R). \end{cases}$$

Proposition 3.1. *If Σ_{com} is unpredictable, then*

$$|\Pr[\mathsf{Exp}_{\Sigma_{ccd},\mathcal{A}}^{\mathsf{ever-hide}}(\lambda, b) = 1] - \Pr[\mathsf{Hyb}_1(b) = 1]| \leq \mathsf{negl}(\lambda).$$

Proof. The proof is similar to [HMNY21b, Propositoin 5.8], but note that this time we have to consider an unbounded adversary after the certificate is issued unlike the case of [HMNY21b]. We assume that $|\Pr[\mathsf{Exp}_{\Sigma_{ccd},\mathcal{A}}^{\text{ever-hide}}(\lambda, b) = 1] - \Pr[\mathsf{Hyb}_1(b) = 1]|$ is non-negligible, and construct an adversary $\mathcal{B}$ that breaks the unpredictability of Σ_{com}. For notational simplicity, we denote $\mathsf{Exp}_{\Sigma_{ccd},\mathcal{A}}^{\text{ever-hide}}(\lambda, b)$ by $\mathsf{Hyb}_0(b)$. We consider an algorithm $\widetilde{\mathcal{A}}$ that works as follows. $\widetilde{\mathcal{A}}$ is given an oracle $\mathcal{O}$, which is either H or $H_{R \to H'}$, and an input z that consists of R and the whole truth table of H, where $R \leftarrow \{0, 1\}^{s(\lambda)}$, and H and H' are uniformly random functions. $\widetilde{\mathcal{A}}$ runs $\mathsf{Hyb}_0(b)$ except that it uses its own oracle $\mathcal{O}$ to simulate $\mathcal{A}_1$'s random oracle queries. On the other hand, $\widetilde{\mathcal{A}}$ uses H to simulate h and $\mathcal{A}_2$'s random oracle queries regardless of $\mathcal{O}$, which is possible because the truth table of H is included in the input z. By definition, we have

$$\Pr[\mathsf{Hyb}_0(b) = 1] = \Pr[\widetilde{\mathcal{A}}^H(R, H) = 1]$$

and

$$\Pr[\mathsf{Hyb}_1(b) = 1] = \Pr[\widetilde{\mathcal{A}}^{H_{R \to H'}}(R, H) = 1]$$

where H in the input means the truth table of H. We apply the one-way to hiding lemma (Lemma 2.2) to the above $\widetilde{\mathcal{A}}$. Note that $\widetilde{\mathcal{A}}$ is inefficient, but the one-way to hiding lemma is applicable to inefficient algorithms. Then if we let $\widetilde{\mathcal{B}}$ be the algorithm that measures uniformly chosen query of $\widetilde{\mathcal{A}}$, we have

$$|\Pr[\widetilde{\mathcal{A}}^H(R, H) = 1] - \Pr[\widetilde{\mathcal{A}}^{H_{R \to H'}}(R, H) = 1]| \leq 2q\sqrt{\Pr[\widetilde{\mathcal{B}}^{H_{R \to H'}}(R, H) = R]}.$$

By the assumption, the LHS is non-negligible, and thus $\Pr[\widetilde{\mathcal{B}}^{H_{R \to H'}}(R, H) = R]$ is non-negligible.

Let $\widetilde{\mathcal{B}}'$ be the algorithm that is the same as $\widetilde{\mathcal{B}}$ except that it does not take the truth table of H as input, and sets h to be uniformly random string instead of setting $h := H(R) \oplus \mathsf{ske.sk}$. Then we have

$$\Pr[\widetilde{\mathcal{B}}^{H_{R \to H'}}(R, H) = R] = \Pr[\widetilde{\mathcal{B}}'^{H_{R \to H'}}(R) = R].$$

The reason is as follows: First, $\widetilde{\mathcal{B}}$ uses the truth table of H only for generating $h := H(R) \oplus \mathsf{ske.sk}$, because it halts before $\widetilde{\mathcal{B}}$ simulates $\mathcal{A}_2$. Second, the oracle $H_{R \to H'}$ reveals no information about $H(R)$, and thus h can be independently and uniformly random.

Moreover, for any fixed R, when H and H' are uniformly random, $H_{R \to H'}$ is also a uniformly random function, and therefore we have

$$\Pr[\widetilde{\mathcal{B}}'^{H_{R \to H'}}(R) = R] = \Pr[\widetilde{\mathcal{B}}'^H(R) = R].$$

Since $\Pr[\widetilde{\mathcal{B}}^{H_{R \to H'}}(R, H) = R]$ is non-negligible, $\Pr[\widetilde{\mathcal{B}}'^H(R) = R]$ is also non-negligible. Recall that $\widetilde{\mathcal{B}}'^H$ is an algorithm that simulates $\mathsf{Hyb}_0(b)$ with the modification that h is set to be uniformly random and measures randomly chosen $\mathcal{A}_1$'s query. Then it is straightforward to construct an adversary $\mathcal{B}$ that breaks the unpredictability of Σ_{com} by using $\widetilde{\mathcal{B}}'$. For clarity, let us give the description of $\mathcal{B}$ as follows.

$\mathcal{B}$ is given $\mathsf{Classical.Commit}(R; R')$ from the challenger of $\mathsf{Exp}^{\mathsf{unpre}}_{\Sigma_{\mathsf{com}}, \mathcal{B}}(\lambda)$. $\mathcal{B}$ chooses $i \leftarrow [q]$ and runs $\mathsf{Hyb}_1(b)$ until $\mathcal{A}_1$ makes i-th random oracle query or $\mathcal{A}_1$ sends the internal state to $\mathcal{A}_2$, where $\mathcal{B}$ embeds the problem instance $\mathsf{Classical.Commit}(R; R')$ into those sent to $\mathcal{A}_1$ instead of generating it by itself. $\mathcal{B}$ measures the i-th random oracle query by $\mathcal{A}_1$, and outputs the measurement outcome. Note that $\mathcal{B}$ can efficiently simulate the random oracle H by Zhandry's compressed oracle technique [Zha19]. It is clear that the probability that $\mathcal{B}$ outputs R is exactly $\Pr[\widetilde{\mathcal{B}}'^H(R) = R]$, which is non-negligible. This contradicts the unpredictability of Σ_{com}. Therefore $|\Pr[\mathsf{Hyb}_0(b) = 1] - \Pr[\mathsf{Hyb}_1(b) = 1]|$ is negligible. □

Proposition 3.2. $\Pr[\mathsf{Hyb}_1(b) = 1] = \Pr[\mathsf{Hyb}_2(b) = 1]$.

Proof. First, let us remind the difference between $\mathsf{Hyb}_1(b)$ and $\mathsf{Hyb}_2(b)$. In $\mathsf{Hyb}_1(b)$, $\mathcal{A}_1$ receives $h = \mathsf{ske.sk} \oplus H(R)$. Moreover, $\mathcal{A}_1$ can access to the random oracle $H_{R \to H'}$, and $\mathcal{A}_2$ can access to the random oracle H. On the other hand, in $\mathsf{Hyb}_2(b)$, $\mathcal{A}_1$ receives uniformly random h. Moreover, $\mathcal{A}_1$ can access to the random oracle H' instead of $H_{R \to H'}$, and $\mathcal{A}_2$ can access to the random oracle $H'_{R \to h \oplus \mathsf{ske.sk}}$ instead of H.

Let $\Pr[(h, H_{R \to H'}, H) = (r, G, G') \mid \mathsf{Hyb}_1(b)]$ be the probability that the adversary $\mathcal{A}_1$ in $\mathsf{Hyb}_1(b)$ receives a classical bit string r as h, random oracle which $\mathcal{A}_1$ can access to is G, and random oracle which $\mathcal{A}_2$ can access to is G'. Similarly, let us define $\Pr[(h, H', H'_{R \to h \oplus \mathsf{ske.sk}}) = (r, G, G') \mid \mathsf{Hyb}_2(b)]$ for $\mathsf{Hyb}_2(b)$. What we have to show is that the following equation holds for any (r, G, G')

$$\Pr[(h, H_{R \to H'}, H) = (r, G, G') \mid \mathsf{Hyb}_1(b)] = \Pr[(h, H', H'_{R \to h \oplus \mathsf{ske.sk}}) = (r, G, G') \mid \mathsf{Hyb}_2(b)].$$

Since $h = \mathsf{ske.sk} \oplus H(R)$ in $\mathsf{Hyb}_1(b)$, H is a uniformly random function, and h in $\mathsf{Hyb}_2(b)$ is uniformly generated,

$$\Pr[h = r \mid \mathsf{Hyb}_1(b)] = \Pr[h = r \mid \mathsf{Hyb}_2(b)]$$

holds for any r.

For any classical bit string r and any random oracle G, we have

$$\Pr[H_{R \to H'} = G \mid h = r, \mathsf{Hyb}_1(b)] = \Pr[H' = G \mid h = r, \mathsf{Hyb}_2(b)].$$

This is shown as follows. First, in $\mathsf{Hyb}_1(b)$, from the construction of $H_{R \to H'}$, $H_{R \to H'}(R)$ is independent from h for any $R \in \{0, 1\}^{s(\lambda)}$. Furthermore, since H and H' is random oracle, $H_{R \to H'}(R)$ is uniformly random for any $R \in \{0, 1\}^{s(\lambda)}$. Second, in $\mathsf{Hyb}_2(b)$, from the construction of H', $H'(R)$ is independent from h for any $R \in \{0, 1\}^{s(\lambda)}$. Furthermore, since H' is random oracle, $H'(R)$ is uniformly random for any $R \in \{0, 1\}^{s(\lambda)}$. Therefore, we have the above equation.

For any classical bit string r and any random oracles G and G', we have

$$\Pr[H = G' \mid (h, H_{R \to H'}) = (r, G), \mathsf{Hyb}_1(b)] = \Pr[H'_{R \to h \oplus \mathsf{ske.sk}} = G' \mid (h, H') = (r, G), \mathsf{Hyb}_2(b)].$$

This can be shown as follows. First, in $\mathsf{Hyb}_1(b)$, we obtain $H(R) = r \oplus \mathsf{ske.sk}$, because $h := \mathsf{ske.sk} \oplus H(R)$ and $h = r$. Furthermore, from the definition of $H_{R \to H'}$, we obtain $H(R^*) = G(R^*)$ for $R^* \neq R$. Second, in $\mathsf{Hyb}_2(b)$, from the definition of $H'_{R \to h \oplus \mathsf{ske.sk}}$, we have $H'_{R \to h \oplus \mathsf{ske.sk}}(R) = r \oplus \mathsf{ske.sk}$ and $H'_{R \to h \oplus \mathsf{ske.sk}}(R^*) = G(R^*)$ for $R^* \neq R$.

From all the above discussions, we have

$$\Pr[(h, H_{R \to H'}, H) = (r, G, G') \mid \mathsf{Hyb}_1(b)] = \Pr[(h, H', H'_{R \to h \oplus \mathsf{ske.sk}}) = (r, G, G') \mid \mathsf{Hyb}_2(b)].$$

$\square$

Proposition 3.3. *If Σ_{skcd} is OT-CD secure, then*

$$|\Pr[\mathsf{Hyb}_2(1) = 1] - \Pr[\mathsf{Hyb}_2(0) = 1]| \leq \mathsf{negl}(\lambda).$$

Proof. To show this, we assume that $|\Pr[\mathsf{Hyb}_2(1) = 1] - \Pr[\mathsf{Hyb}_2(0) = 1]|$ is non-negligible, and construct an adversary $\mathcal{B}$ that breaks the OT-CD security of Σ_{skcd}.

$\mathcal{B}$ plays the experiment $\mathsf{Exp}^{\mathsf{otsk\text{-}cert\text{-}del}}_{\Sigma_{\mathsf{skcd}}, \mathcal{B}}(\lambda, b')$ for some $b' \in \{0, 1\}$. First, $\mathcal{B}$ sends $(m_0, m_1) \in \mathcal{M}^2$ to the challenger of $\mathsf{Exp}^{\mathsf{otsk\text{-}cert\text{-}del}}_{\Sigma_{\mathsf{skcd}}, \mathcal{B}}(\lambda, b')$. $\mathcal{B}$ receives $\mathsf{ske.CT}$ from the challenger of $\mathsf{Exp}^{\mathsf{otsk\text{-}cert\text{-}del}}_{\Sigma_{\mathsf{skcd}}, \mathcal{B}}(\lambda, b')$. $\mathcal{B}$ generates $R \leftarrow \{0, 1\}^{s(\lambda)}$, $R' \leftarrow \{0, 1\}^{t(\lambda)}$ and $h \leftarrow \{0, 1\}^{r(\lambda)}$, and computes $f := \mathsf{Classical.Commit}(R; R')$. $\mathcal{B}$ sends $(\mathsf{ske.CT}, f, h)$ to $\mathcal{A}_1$. $\mathcal{B}$ simulates the random oracle H' given to $\mathcal{A}_1$ by itself. At some point, $\mathcal{A}_1$ sends $\mathsf{ske.cert}$ to $\mathcal{B}$, and sends the internal state to $\mathcal{A}_2$. $\mathcal{B}$ passes $\mathsf{ske.cert}$ to the challenger of $\mathsf{Exp}^{\mathsf{otsk\text{-}cert\text{-}del}}_{\Sigma_{\mathsf{skcd}}, \mathcal{B}}(\lambda, b')$.

The challenger of $\mathsf{Exp}^{\mathsf{otsk\text{-}cert\text{-}del}}_{\Sigma_{\mathsf{skcd}}, \mathcal{B}}(\lambda, b')$ runs $\mathsf{SKE.Verify}(\mathsf{ske.sk}, \mathsf{ske.cert}) \to \top/\bot$. If it is $\top$, the challenger sends $\mathsf{ske.sk}$ to $\mathcal{B}$. In that case, $\mathcal{B}$ outputs $\top$, and sends $(R, R', \mathsf{ske.sk})$ to $\mathcal{A}_2$. We denote this event by $\mathsf{Reveal}_{\mathsf{sk}}(b')$. $\mathcal{B}$ simulates $\mathcal{A}_2$, and outputs the output of $\mathcal{A}_2$. On the other hand, if $\mathsf{SKE.Verify}(\mathsf{ske.sk}, \mathsf{ske.cert}) \to \bot$, then the challenger sends $\bot$ to $\mathcal{B}$. In that case, $\mathcal{B}$ outputs $\bot$ and aborts. Note that $\mathcal{B}$ can simulate the random oracle $H'_{R \to h \oplus \mathsf{ske.sk}}$ given to $\mathcal{A}_2$ when $\mathcal{B}$ does not abort, because $\mathcal{B}$ receives $\mathsf{ske.sk}$ from the challenger of $\mathsf{Exp}^{\mathsf{otsk\text{-}cert\text{-}del}}_{\Sigma_{\mathsf{skcd}}, \mathcal{B}}(\lambda, b')$ when $\mathcal{B}$ does not abort.

Now we have

$$\mathsf{Adv}^{\mathsf{otsk\text{-}cert\text{-}del}}_{\Sigma_{\mathsf{skcd}}, \mathcal{B}}(\lambda)$$

$$:= |\Pr[\mathsf{Exp}^{\mathsf{otsk\text{-}cert\text{-}del}}_{\Sigma_{\mathsf{skcd}}, \mathcal{B}}(\lambda, b') = 1 \mid b' = 0] - \Pr[\mathsf{Exp}^{\mathsf{otsk\text{-}cert\text{-}del}}_{\Sigma_{\mathsf{skcd}}, \mathcal{B}}(\lambda, b') = 1 \mid b' = 1]|$$

$$= |\Pr[\mathcal{B} = 1 \wedge \mathsf{Reveal}_{\mathsf{sk}}(b') \mid b' = 0] - \Pr[\mathcal{B} = 1 \wedge \mathsf{Reveal}_{\mathsf{sk}}(b') \mid b' = 1]|$$

$$= |\Pr[\mathcal{A}_2 = 1 \wedge \mathsf{Reveal}_{\mathsf{sk}}(b') \mid b' = 0] - \Pr[\mathcal{A}_2 = 1 \wedge \mathsf{Reveal}_{\mathsf{sk}}(b') \mid b' = 1]|$$

$$= |\Pr[\mathsf{Hyb}_2(b') = 1 \wedge \mathsf{Reveal}_{\mathsf{sk}}(b') \mid b' = 0] - \Pr[\mathsf{Hyb}_2(b') = 1 \wedge \mathsf{Reveal}_{\mathsf{sk}}(b') \mid b' = 1]|$$

$$= |\Pr[\mathsf{Hyb}_2(b') = 1 \mid b' = 0] - \Pr[\mathsf{Hyb}_2(b') = 1 \mid b' = 1]|$$

$$= |\Pr[\mathsf{Hyb}_2(0) = 1] - \Pr[\mathsf{Hyb}_2(1) = 1]|.$$

In the second equation, we have used the fact that $\mathsf{Exp}^{\mathsf{otsk\text{-}cert\text{-}del}}_{\Sigma_{\mathsf{skcd}},\mathcal{B}}(\lambda, b) = 1$ if and only if $\mathcal{B} = 1$ and the challenger of $\mathsf{Exp}^{\mathsf{otsk\text{-}cert\text{-}del}}_{\Sigma_{\mathsf{skcd}},\mathcal{B}}(\lambda, b')$ outputs $\top$. In the third equation, we have used the fact that the output of $\mathcal{B}$ is equal to the output of $\mathcal{A}_2$ conditioned that $\mathsf{Reveal}_{\mathsf{sk}}(b')$ occurs. In the fourth equation, we have used the fact that $\mathcal{B}$ simulates the challenger of $\mathsf{Hyb}_2(b)$ when $\mathsf{Reveal}_{\mathsf{sk}}(b)$ occurs. In the fifth equation, we have used the fact that $\mathsf{Hyb}_2(b) = 1$ only when $\mathsf{Reveal}_{\mathsf{sk}}(b)$ occurs. Since $|\Pr[\mathsf{Hyb}_2(0) = 1] - \Pr[\mathsf{Hyb}_2(1) = 1]|$ is non-negligible, $\mathsf{Adv}^{\mathsf{otsk\text{-}cert\text{-}del}}_{\Sigma_{\mathsf{skcd}},\mathcal{B}}(\lambda)$ is non-negligible. This contradicts the OT-CD security of Σ_{skcd}. $\qquad\square$

By Proposition 3.1 to 3.3, we immediately obtain Theorem 3.2. $\qquad\square$

Proof of Theorem 3.3. This can be shown similarly to Theorem 3.2. $\qquad\square$

4   Certified Everlasting Zero-Knowledge Proof for QMA

In this section, we define and construct the certified everlasting zero-knowledge proof for **QMA**. In Sect. 4.1, we define the certified everlasting zero-knowledge proof for **QMA**. We then construct a three round protocol with completeness-soundness gap $\frac{1}{\mathsf{poly}(\lambda)}$ in Sect. 4.2, and finally amplify the gap to $1 - \mathsf{negl}(\lambda)$ with the sequential repetition in Sect. 4.3.

4.1   Definition

We first define a quantum interactive protocol. Usually, in zero-knowledge proofs or arguments, we do not consider prover's output. However, in this paper, we also consider prover's output, because we are interested in the certified everlasting zero-knowledge. Furthermore, in this paper, we consider only an interactive proof, which means that a malicious prover is unbounded.

Definition 4.1 (Quantum Interactive Protocol). *A quantum interactive protocol is modeled as an interaction between QPT machines $\mathcal{P}$ referred as a prover and $\mathcal{V}$ referred as a verifier. We denote by $\langle \mathcal{P}(x_P), \mathcal{V}(x_V)\rangle(x)$ an execution of the protocol where x is a common input, x_P is $\mathcal{P}$'s private input, and x_V is $\mathcal{V}$'s private input. We denote by $\mathrm{OUT}_\mathcal{V}\langle \mathcal{P}(x_P), \mathcal{V}(x_V)\rangle(x)$ the final output of $\mathcal{V}$ in the execution. An honest verifier's output is $\top$ indicating acceptance or $\bot$ indicating rejection, and a malicious verifier's output is an arbitrary quantum state. We denote by $\mathrm{OUT}_\mathcal{P}\langle \mathcal{P}(x_P), \mathcal{V}(x_V)\rangle(x)$ the final output of $\mathcal{P}$ in the execution. An honest prover's output is $\top$ indicating acceptance or $\bot$ indicating rejection. We also define $\mathrm{OUT}'_{\mathcal{P},\mathcal{V}}\langle \mathcal{P}(x_P), \mathcal{V}(x_V)\rangle(x)$ by*

$$\mathrm{OUT}'_{\mathcal{P},\mathcal{V}}\langle \mathcal{P}(x_P), \mathcal{V}(x_V)\rangle(x)$$
$$:= \begin{cases} (\top, \mathrm{OUT}_\mathcal{V}\langle \mathcal{P}(x_P), \mathcal{V}(x_V)\rangle(x)) & (\mathrm{OUT}_\mathcal{P}\langle \mathcal{P}(x_P), \mathcal{V}(x_V)\rangle(x) = \top) \\ (\bot, \bot) & (\mathrm{OUT}_\mathcal{P}\langle \mathcal{P}(x_P), \mathcal{V}(x_V)\rangle(x) \neq \top). \end{cases}$$

We next define a computational zero-knowledge proof for **QMA**, which is the standard definition.

Definition 4.2 (Computational Zero-Knowledge Proof for QMA). *A c-complete s-sound computational zero-knowledge proof for a **QMA** promise problem $A = (A_{\mathsf{yes}}, A_{\mathsf{no}})$ is a quantum interactive protocol between a QPT prover $\mathcal{P}$ and a QPT verifier $\mathcal{V}$ that satisfies the followings:*

*c-**completeness:** For any $\mathsf{x} \in A_{\mathsf{yes}}$ and any $\mathsf{w} \in R_A(\mathsf{x})$,*

$$\Pr[\mathrm{Out}_{\mathcal{V}}\langle \mathcal{P}(\mathsf{w}^{\otimes k(|\mathsf{x}|)}), \mathcal{V}\rangle(\mathsf{x}) = \top] \geq c$$

for some polynomial k.
*s-**soundness:** For any $\mathsf{x} \in A_{\mathsf{no}}$ and any unbounded-time prover $\mathcal{P}^*$,*

$$\Pr[\mathrm{Out}_{\mathcal{V}}\langle \mathcal{P}^*, \mathcal{V}\rangle(\mathsf{x}) = \top] \leq s.$$

Computational zero-knowledge: *There exists a QPT algorithm $\mathcal{S}$ such that*

$$\mathrm{OUT}_{\mathcal{V}^*}\langle \mathcal{P}(\mathsf{w}^{\otimes k(|\mathsf{x}|)}), \mathcal{V}^*(\cdot)\rangle(\mathsf{x}) \approx_c \mathcal{S}(\mathsf{x}, \mathcal{V}^*, \cdot)$$

for any QPT malicious verifier $\mathcal{V}^*$, any $\mathsf{x} \in A_{\mathsf{yes}} \cap \{0,1\}^\lambda$, any $\mathsf{w} \in R_A(\mathsf{x})$, and some polynomial k. Note that $\mathrm{OUT}_{\mathcal{V}^*}\langle \mathcal{P}(\mathsf{w}^{\otimes k(|\mathsf{x}|)}), \mathcal{V}^*(\cdot)\rangle(\mathsf{x})$ and $\mathcal{S}(\mathsf{x}, \mathcal{V}^*, \cdot)$ are quantum channels that map any quantum state ξ to quantum states $\mathrm{OUT}_{\mathcal{V}^*}\langle \mathcal{P}(\mathsf{w}^{\otimes k(|\mathsf{x}|)}), \mathcal{V}^*(\xi)\rangle(\mathsf{x})$ and $\mathcal{S}(\mathsf{x}, \mathcal{V}^*, \xi)$, respectively.

We just call it a computational zero-knowledge proof if it satisfies $(1 - \mathsf{negl}(|\mathsf{x}|))$-completeness, $\mathsf{negl}(|\mathsf{x}|)$-soundness, and computational zero-knowledge.

We finally define a certified everlasting zero-knowledge proof for **QMA**, which is the main target of this paper.

Definition 4.3 (Certified Everlasting Zero-Knowledge Proof for QMA). *A certified everlasting zero-knowledge proof for a **QMA** promise problem $A = (A_{\mathsf{yes}}, A_{\mathsf{no}})$ is a computational zero-knowledge proof for A (Definition 4.2) that additionally satisfies the followings:*

Prover's Completeness: $\Pr[\mathrm{OUT}_{\mathcal{P}}\langle \mathcal{P}(\mathsf{w}^{\otimes k(|\mathsf{x}|)}), \mathcal{V}\rangle(\mathsf{x}) = \top] \geq 1 - \mathsf{negl}(\lambda)$ *for any $\mathsf{x} \in A_{\mathsf{yes}} \cap \{0,1\}^\lambda$ and any $\mathsf{w} \in R_A(\mathsf{x})$.*
Certified Everlasting Zero-Knowledge: *There exists a QPT algorithm $\mathcal{S}$ such that*

$$\mathrm{OUT}'_{\mathcal{P}, \mathcal{V}^*}\langle \mathcal{P}(\mathsf{w}^{\otimes k(|\mathsf{x}|)}), \mathcal{V}^*(\cdot)\rangle(\mathsf{x}) \approx_s \mathcal{S}(\mathsf{x}, \mathcal{V}^*, \cdot)$$

for any QPT malicious verifier $\mathcal{V}^*$, any $\mathsf{x} \in A_{\mathsf{yes}} \cap \{0,1\}^\lambda$, any $\mathsf{w} \in R_A(\mathsf{x})$, and some polynomial k. Note that $\mathrm{OUT}'_{\mathcal{P}, \mathcal{V}^*}\langle \mathcal{P}(\mathsf{w}^{\otimes k(|\mathsf{x}|)}), \mathcal{V}^*(\cdot)\rangle(\mathsf{x})$ and $\mathcal{S}(\mathsf{x}, \mathcal{V}^*, \cdot)$ are quantum channels that map any quantum state ξ to quantum states $\mathrm{OUT}'_{\mathcal{P}, \mathcal{V}^*}\langle \mathcal{P}(\mathsf{w}^{\otimes k(|\mathsf{x}|)}), \mathcal{V}^*(\xi)\rangle(\mathsf{x})$ and $\mathcal{S}(\mathsf{x}, \mathcal{V}^*, \xi)$, respectively.

Remark 4.1 We remark that certified everlasting zero-knowledge does not imply computational zero-knowledge since it does not require anything if the prover does not output $\top$.

4.2   Construction of Three Round Protocol

In this section, we construct a three round protocol with completeness-soundness gap $\frac{1}{\text{poly}(\lambda)}$. In the next section, we will amplify its completeness-soundness gap by the sequential repetition.

In the following, n, m, Π_c, ρ_{hist}, and $\rho_{\text{Sim}}^{\text{x},S}$ are given in Definition 2.2. Let $S_c \subseteq [n]$ be the set of qubits on which Π_c acts non-trivially. The three round protocol $\Sigma_{\Xi\text{cd}}$ is constructed from commitment with certified everlasting hiding and classical-extractor-based binding, $\Sigma_{\text{ccd}} = (\text{Commit}, \text{Verify}, \text{Del}, \text{Cert})$.

The first action by the prover (commitment phase):
  - Generate $x, z \leftarrow \{0,1\}^n$.
  - Compute

$$(\text{com}_i(x_i), \text{d}_i(x_i), \text{ck}_i(x_i)) \leftarrow \text{Commit}(1^\lambda, x_i)$$
$$(\text{com}_i(z_i), \text{d}_i(z_i), \text{ck}_i(z_i)) \leftarrow \text{Commit}(1^\lambda, z_i)$$

  for all $i \in [n]$.
  - Generate a simulatable witness ρ_{hist} for the instance x and generate $X^x Z^z \rho_{\text{hist}} Z^z X^x$.
  - Send the first message (commitment), $\text{msg}_1 := (X^x Z^z \rho_{\text{hist}} Z^z X^x) \otimes \text{com}(x) \otimes \text{com}(z)$, to the verifier, where $\text{com}(x) := \bigotimes_{i=1}^n \text{com}_i(x_i)$ and $\text{com}(z) := \bigotimes_{i=1}^n \text{com}_i(z_i)$.

The second action by the verifier (challenge phase):
  - Generate $c \leftarrow [m]$.
  - Compute $\text{cert}_i(x_i) \leftarrow \text{Del}(\text{com}_i(x_i))$ and $\text{cert}_i(z_i) \leftarrow \text{Del}(\text{com}_i(z_i))$ for all $i \in \overline{S}_c$.
  - Send the second message (challenge), $\text{msg}_2 := (c, \{\text{cert}_i(x_i), \text{cert}_i(z_i)\}_{i \in \overline{S}_c})$, to the prover.

The third action by the prover (reply phase):
  - Send the third message (reply), $\text{msg}_3 := \{\text{d}_i(x_i), \text{d}_i(z_i)\}_{i \in S_c}$, to the verifier.
  - Output $\top$ if $\top \leftarrow \text{Cert}(\text{cert}_i(x_i), \text{ck}_i(x_i))$ and $\top \leftarrow \text{Cert}(\text{cert}_i(z_i), \text{ck}_i(z_i))$ for all $i \in \overline{S}_c$, and output $\bot$ otherwise.

The fourth action by the verifier (verification phase):
  - Compute $x_i' \leftarrow \text{Verify}(\text{com}_i(x_i), \text{d}_i(x_i))$ and $z_i' \leftarrow \text{Verify}(\text{com}_i(z_i), \text{d}_i(z_i))$ for all $i \in S_c$. If $x_i' = \bot$ or $z_i' = \bot$ for at least one $i \in S_c$, output $\bot$ and abort.
  - Apply $X_i^{x_i'} Z_i^{z_i'}$ on the i-th qubit of $X^x Z^z \rho_{\text{hist}} Z^z X^x$ for each $i \in S_c$, and perform the POVM measurement $\{\Pi_c, I - \Pi_c\}$ on the state.
  - Output $\top$ if the result Π_c is obtained, and output $\bot$ otherwise.

Theorem 4.1. $\Sigma_{\Xi\text{cd}}$ *is a certified everlasting zero-knowledge proof for* ***QMA*** *with* $(1 - \text{negl}(\lambda))$-*completeness and* $\left(1 - \frac{1}{\text{poly}(\lambda)}\right)$-*soundness.*

This is shown from the following Lemmata 4.1 to 4.4.

Lemma 4.1. $\Sigma_{\Xi\mathrm{cd}}$ *satisfies the* $(1 - \mathsf{negl}(\lambda))$-*completeness and prover's completeness.*

Lemma 4.2. *If* Σ_{ccd} *is classical-extractor-based binding, then* $\Sigma_{\Xi\mathrm{cd}}$ *satisfies* $\left(1 - \frac{1}{\mathsf{poly}(\lambda)}\right)$-*soundness.*

Lemma 4.3. *If* Σ_{ccd} *is certified everlasting hiding and computational hiding, then* $\Sigma_{\Xi\mathrm{cd}}$ *satisfies certified everlasting zero-knowledge.*

Lemma 4.4. *If* Σ_{ccd} *is computational hiding, then* $\Sigma_{\Xi\mathrm{cd}}$ *satisfies computational zero-knowledge.*

Proof of Lemma 4.1. It is clear from the definition of k-**SimQMA** (Definition 2.2) and the correctness of Σ_{ccd}. $\quad\square$

Proof of Lemma 4.2. Let us show the soundness by analyzing the case for $\mathsf{x} \in A_{\mathsf{no}}$. The prover sends the first message to the verifier. The first message consists of three registers, RS, RCX, and RCZ. The register RCX further consists of n registers $\{RCX_i\}_{i\in[n]}$. The register RCZ also consists of n registers $\{RCZ_i\}_{i\in[n]}$. If the prover is honest, RS contains $X^x Z^z \rho_{\mathsf{hist}} Z^z X^x$, RCX_i contains $\mathsf{com}_i(x_i)$, and RCZ_i contains $\mathsf{com}_i(z_i)$. Let $\mathsf{com}'_{i,x}$ and $\mathsf{com}'_{i,z}$ be the (reduced) states of the registers RCX_i and RCZ_i, respectively. Let $f'_{i,x}$ and $f'_{i,z}$ be classical parts of $\mathsf{com}'_{i,x}$ and $\mathsf{com}'_{i,z}$, respectively.

The verifier generates $c \leftarrow [m]$, and issues the deletion certificate. The verifier sends c and the deletion certificate to the prover. The verifier then receives $\{\mathsf{d}_1^{x,i}, \mathsf{d}_2^{x,i}, \mathsf{d}_1^{z,i}, \mathsf{d}_2^{z,i}\}_{i\in S_c}$ from the prover. For each $i \in [n]$, let us define $\mathsf{d}_1^{*,x,i}$ and $\mathsf{d}_1^{*,z,i}$ by $\mathsf{d}_1^{*,x,i} \leftarrow \mathsf{Ext}(f'_{i,x})$ and $\mathsf{d}_1^{*,z,i} \leftarrow \mathsf{Ext}(f'_{i,z})$, respectively. Note that each $\mathsf{d}_1^{*,x,i}$ and $\mathsf{d}_1^{*,z,i}$ is independent of c, because $\mathsf{com}'_{i,x}$ and $\mathsf{com}'_{i,z}$ are sent to the verifier before the verifier chooses c.

We have only to consider the case when $\mathsf{d}_1^{x,i} = \mathsf{d}_1^{*,x,i}$ and $\mathsf{d}_1^{z,i} = \mathsf{d}_1^{*,z,i}$ for all $i \in S_c$, because of the following reason: Due to the classical-extractor-based binding of Σ_{ccd}, $\mathsf{Verify}(\mathsf{com}'_{i,x}, (\mathsf{d}_1^{x,i}, \mathsf{d}_2^{x,i})) = \bot$ for any $\mathsf{d}_1^{x,i} \neq \mathsf{d}_1^{*,x,i}$ and any $\mathsf{d}_2^{x,i}$. Similarly, $\mathsf{Verify}(\mathsf{com}'_{i,z}, (\mathsf{d}_1^{z,i}, \mathsf{d}_2^{z,i})) = \bot$ for any $\mathsf{d}_1^{z,i} \neq \mathsf{d}_1^{*,z,i}$ and any $\mathsf{d}_2^{z,i}$. Therefore, the prover who wants to make the verifier accept has to send $\mathsf{d}_1^{x,i} = \mathsf{d}_1^{*,x,i}$ and $\mathsf{d}_1^{z,i} = \mathsf{d}_1^{*,z,i}$ for all $i \in S_c$.

Let us define

$$p(x,z) := \Pr\left[\bigwedge_{i\in[n]} \left(\mathsf{Verify}_2(\mathsf{com}'_{i,x}, \mathsf{d}_1^{*,x,i}) \to x_i \wedge \mathsf{Verify}_2(\mathsf{com}'_{i,z}, \mathsf{d}_1^{*,z,i}) \to z_i\right)\right].$$

Note that $p(x,z)$ is independent of c, because $\{\mathsf{com}'_{i,x}, \mathsf{com}'_{i,z}\}_{i\in[n]}$ and $\{\mathsf{d}_1^{*,x,i}, \mathsf{d}_1^{*,z,i}\}_{i\in[n]}$ are independent of c. Let ψ be the (reduced) state of the register RS. The verifier's acceptance probability is

$$\frac{1}{m} \sum_{c \in [m]} \sum_{x,z \in \{0,1\}^n} p(x,z) \mathrm{Tr}\left[\Pi_c \left(\prod_{i \in S_c} Z_i^{z_i} X_i^{x_i}\right) \psi \left(\prod_{i \in S_c} X_i^{x_i} Z_i^{z_i}\right)\right]$$

$$= \frac{1}{m} \sum_{c \in [m]} \sum_{x,z \in \{0,1\}^n} p(x,z) \mathrm{Tr}\left[\Pi_c \left(\prod_{i \in [n]} Z_i^{z_i} X_i^{x_i}\right) \psi \left(\prod_{i \in [n]} X_i^{x_i} Z_i^{z_i}\right)\right]$$

$$= \frac{1}{m} \sum_{c \in [m]} \mathrm{Tr}\left[\Pi_c \sum_{x,z \in \{0,1\}^n} p(x,z) \left(\prod_{i \in [n]} Z_i^{z_i} X_i^{x_i}\right) \psi \left(\prod_{i \in [n]} X_i^{x_i} Z_i^{z_i}\right)\right]$$

$$\leq 1 - \frac{1}{\mathrm{poly}(\lambda)},$$

where the last inequality comes from Definition 2.2. This completes the proof. □

Proof of Lemma 4.3 Let us show certified everlasting zero-knowledge. For a subset $S_c \subseteq [n]$ and $x, z \in \{0,1\}^n$, let us define $x^{S_c} := (x_1^{S_c}, x_2^{S_c}, \cdots, x_n^{S_c})$ and $z^{S_c} := (z_1^{S_c}, z_2^{S_c}, \cdots, z_n^{S_c})$, where $x_i^{S_c} = x_i$ and $z_i^{S_c} = z_i$ for $i \in S_c$, and $x_i^{S_c} = z_i^{S_c} = 0$ for $i \notin S_c$.

For clarity, we describe how the interactive algorithm $\langle \mathcal{P}(w^{\otimes k(|x|)}), \mathcal{V}^*(\xi)\rangle(x)$ runs against a QPT verifier $\mathcal{V}^*$ with an input ξ, where w is the witness and x is the instance.

$\langle \mathcal{P}(w^{\otimes k(|x|)}), \mathcal{V}^*(\xi)\rangle(x):$

1. $\mathcal{P}$ generates $x, z \leftarrow \{0,1\}^n$, and computes

$$(\mathsf{com}_i(x_i), \mathsf{d}_i(x_i), \mathsf{ck}_i(x_i)) \leftarrow \mathsf{Commit}(1^\lambda, x_i)$$
$$(\mathsf{com}_i(z_i), \mathsf{d}_i(z_i), \mathsf{ck}_i(z_i)) \leftarrow \mathsf{Commit}(1^\lambda, z_i)$$

   for all $i \in [n]$. $\mathcal{P}$ sends $\mathsf{msg}_1 := (X^x Z^z \rho_{\mathsf{hist}} Z^z X^x) \otimes \mathsf{com}(x) \otimes \mathsf{com}(z)$ to $\mathcal{V}^*$.

2. $\mathcal{V}^*$ appends ξ to the received state, and runs a QPT circuit V_1^* on it to obtain $(c, \{\mathsf{cert}_{i,x}', \mathsf{cert}_{i,z}'\}_{i \in \overline{S}_c})$. $\mathcal{V}^*$ sends $\mathsf{msg}_2 := (c, \{\mathsf{cert}_{i,x}', \mathsf{cert}_{i,z}'\}_{i \in \overline{S}_c})$ to $\mathcal{P}$.

3. $\mathcal{P}$ sends $\mathsf{msg}_3 := \{\mathsf{d}_i(x_i), \mathsf{d}_i(z_i)\}_{i \in S_c}$ to $\mathcal{V}^*$.

4. $\mathcal{V}^*$ appends msg_3 to its state, and runs a QPT circuit V_2^* on it. $\mathcal{V}^*$ outputs its state ξ'.

5. $\mathcal{P}$ computes $\mathsf{Cert}(\mathsf{cert}_{i,x}', \mathsf{ck}_i(x_i))$ and $\mathsf{Cert}(\mathsf{cert}_{i,z}', \mathsf{ck}_i(z_i))$ for all $i \in \overline{S}_c$. If all outputs are $\top$, then $\mathcal{P}$ outputs $\top$. Otherwise, $\mathcal{P}$ outputs $\bot$.

Next, let us define a simulator $\mathcal{S}^{(1)}$ as follows.

The simulator $\mathcal{S}^{(1)}(x, \mathcal{V}^*, \xi):$

1. Pick $c \leftarrow [m]$ and $x, z \leftarrow \{0,1\}^n$. Compute

$$(\mathsf{com}_i(x_i^{S_c}), \mathsf{d}_i(x_i^{S_c}), \mathsf{ck}_i(x_i^{S_c})) \leftarrow \mathsf{Commit}(1^\lambda, x_i^{S_c})$$
$$(\mathsf{com}_i(z_i^{S_c}), \mathsf{d}_i(z_i^{S_c}), \mathsf{ck}_i(z_i^{S_c})) \leftarrow \mathsf{Commit}(1^\lambda, z_i^{S_c})$$

   for all $i \in [n]$.

2. Generate $(X^x Z^z \sigma(c) Z^z X^x) \otimes \mathrm{com}(x^{S_c}) \otimes \mathrm{com}(z^{S_c}) \otimes \xi$, where $\sigma(c) := \rho_{\mathrm{sim}}^{\times, S_c} \otimes (\prod_{i \in \overline{S}_c} |0\rangle\langle 0|_i)$. Run V_1^* on the state to obtain $(c', \{\mathrm{cert}'_{i,x}, \mathrm{cert}'_{i,z}\}_{i \in \overline{S}_{c'}})$.

3. If $c' \neq c$, abort and output a fixed state η and the flag state fail.

4. Append $\{\mathsf{d}_i(x_i^{S_c}), \mathsf{d}_i(z_i^{S_c})\}_{i \in S_c}$ to its quantum state, and run V_2^* on the state to obtain ξ'.

5. Compute $\mathsf{Cert}(\mathrm{cert}'_{i,x}, \mathsf{ck}_i(x_i^{S_c}))$ and $\mathsf{Cert}(\mathrm{cert}'_{i,z}, \mathsf{ck}_i(z_i^{S_c}))$ for all $i \in \overline{S}_c$. If all outputs are $\top$, then output the state $(\top, \xi')$. Otherwise, output $(\bot, \bot)$. Also output the flag state success.

Let us also define other two simulators, $\mathcal{S}^{(2)}$ and $\mathcal{S}^{(3)}$, as follows.

The simulator $\mathcal{S}^{(2)}(\mathsf{x}, \mathsf{w}^{\otimes k(|\mathsf{x}|)}, \mathcal{V}^*, \xi)$: It is the same as $\mathcal{S}^{(1)}$ except that $\sigma(c)$ is replaced with ρ_{hist}.

The simulator $\mathcal{S}^{(3)}(\mathsf{x}, \mathsf{w}^{\otimes k(|\mathsf{x}|)}, \mathcal{V}^*, \xi)$: $\mathcal{S}^{(3)}(\mathsf{x}, \mathsf{w}^{\otimes k(|\mathsf{x}|)}, \mathcal{V}^*, \cdot)$ is the channel that postselects the output of $\mathcal{S}^{(2)}(\mathsf{x}, \mathsf{w}^{\otimes k(|\mathsf{x}|)}, \mathcal{V}^*, \cdot)$ on the non-aborting state. More precisely, if we write $\mathcal{S}^{(2)}(\mathsf{x}, \mathsf{w}^{\otimes k(|\mathsf{x}|)}, \mathcal{V}^*, \rho_{in}) = p\rho_{out} \otimes \mathsf{success} + (1-p)\eta \otimes \mathsf{fail}$, where p is the non-aborting probability, $\mathcal{S}^{(3)}(\mathsf{x}, \mathsf{w}^{\otimes k(|\mathsf{x}|)}, \mathcal{V}^*, \rho_{in}) = \rho_{out}$.

Lemma 4.3 is shown from the following Proposition 4.1 to 4.3 (whose proofs will be given later) and quantum rewinding lemma (Lemma 2.1), which is used to reduce the probability that $\mathcal{S}^{(1)}$ aborts to $\mathsf{negl}(\lambda)$. In fact, from Proposition 4.1 and Lemma 2.1, there exists a quantum circuit $\mathcal{S}^{(0)}$ of size at most $O(m \, \mathrm{poly}(n)\mathrm{size}(\mathcal{S}^{(1)}))$ such that the probability that $\mathcal{S}^{(0)}$ aborts is $\mathsf{negl}(\lambda)$, and the output quantum states of $\mathcal{S}^{(0)}$ and $\mathcal{S}^{(1)}$ are $\mathsf{negl}(\lambda)$-close when they do not abort. From Proposition 4.2 and 4.3, $\mathcal{S}^{(0)}$ is $\mathsf{negl}(\lambda)$-close to the real protocol, which completes the proof. $\qquad \square$

Proposition 4.1. *If Σ_{ccd} is computationally hiding, then the probability that $\mathcal{S}^{(1)}$ does not abort is $\frac{1}{m} \pm \mathsf{negl}(\lambda)$.*

Proposition 4.2. $\mathcal{S}^{(1)}(\mathsf{x}, \mathcal{V}^*, \cdot) \approx_s \mathcal{S}^{(2)}(\mathsf{x}, \mathsf{w}^{\otimes k(|\mathsf{x}|)}, \mathcal{V}^*, \cdot)$ *for any $\mathsf{x} \in A_{\mathsf{yes}} \cap \{0,1\}^\lambda$ and any $\mathsf{w} \in R_A(\mathsf{x})$.*

Proposition 4.3. *If Σ_{ccd} is certified everlasting hiding, $\mathcal{S}^{(3)}(\mathsf{x}, \mathsf{w}^{\otimes k(|\mathsf{x}|)}, \mathcal{V}^*, \cdot) \approx_s \mathsf{OUT}'_{\mathcal{P}, \mathcal{V}^*} \langle \mathcal{P}(\mathsf{w}^{\otimes k(|\mathsf{x}|)}), \mathcal{V}^*(\cdot) \rangle(\mathsf{x})$.*

Proof of Proposition 4.1. This can be shown similarly to [BG20, Lemma 5.6]. $\qquad \square$

Proof of Proposition 4.2. It is clear from the local simulatability (Definition 2.2) and the definition of x^{S_c} and z^{S_c} (all $x_i^{S_c}$ and $z_i^{S_c}$ are 0 except for those in $i \in S_c$). $\qquad \square$

Proof of Proposition 4.3. We prove the proposition by contradiction. We construct an adversary $\mathcal{B}$ that breaks the security of the certified everlasting hiding of Σ_{ccd} by assuming the existence of a distinguisher $\mathcal{D}$ that distinguishes two states δ_0 and δ_1,

$$\delta_0 := (\mathsf{OUT}'_{\mathcal{P},\mathcal{V}^*}\langle\mathcal{P}(\mathsf{w}^{\otimes k(|\mathsf{x}|)}),\mathcal{V}^*(\cdot)\rangle(\mathsf{x})\otimes I)\sigma$$
$$\delta_1 := (\mathcal{S}^{(3)}(\mathsf{x},\mathsf{w}^{\otimes k(|\mathsf{x}|)},\mathcal{V}^*,\cdot)\otimes I)\sigma,$$

with a certain state σ. Let us describe how $\mathcal{B}$ works.

1. $\mathcal{B}$ generates $c \leftarrow [m]$ and $x,z \leftarrow \{0,1\}^n$.
2. $\mathcal{B}$ sends $m_0 := \{x_i,z_i\}_{i\in\overline{S}_c}$ and $m_1 := 0^{2n-10}$ to the challenger of $\mathsf{Exp}^{\mathsf{bit-ever-hide}}_{\Sigma_{\mathsf{ccd}},\mathcal{B}}(\lambda,b)$. $\mathcal{B}$ receives commitments from the challenger which is either $\{\mathsf{com}_i(x_i),\mathsf{com}_i(z_i)\}_{i\in\overline{S}_c}$ or $\{\mathsf{com}_i(0),\mathsf{com}_i(0)\}_{i\in\overline{S}_c}$.
3. $\mathcal{B}$ computes

$$(\mathsf{com}_i(x_i),\mathsf{d}_i(x_i),\mathsf{ck}_i(x_i)) \leftarrow \mathsf{Commit}(1^\lambda,x_i)$$
$$(\mathsf{com}_i(z_i),\mathsf{d}_i(z_i),\mathsf{ck}_i(z_i)) \leftarrow \mathsf{Commit}(1^\lambda,z_i)$$

   for $i \in S_c$ by itself.
4. $\mathcal{B}$ generates $X^x Z^z \rho_{\mathsf{hist}} Z^z X^x$. $\mathcal{B}$ appends commitments and σ to the quantum state. If the commitments for $i \in \overline{S}_c$ are $\{\mathsf{com}_i(x_i),\mathsf{com}_i(z_i)\}_{i\in\overline{S}_c}$, $\mathcal{B}$ obtains $(X^x Z^z \rho_{\mathsf{hist}} Z^z X^x)\otimes\mathsf{com}(x)\otimes\mathsf{com}(z)\otimes\sigma$. If the commitments for $i \in \overline{S}_c$ are $\{\mathsf{com}_i(0),\mathsf{com}_i(0)\}_{i\in\overline{S}_c}$, $\mathcal{B}$ obtains $(X^x Z^z \rho_{\mathsf{hist}} Z^z X^x)\otimes\mathsf{com}(x^{S_c})\otimes\mathsf{com}(z^{S_c})\otimes\sigma$.
5. $\mathcal{B}$ runs V_1^* on it to obtain $(c',\{\mathsf{cert}'_{i,x},\mathsf{cert}'_{i,z}\}_{i\in\overline{S}_{c'}})$. $\mathcal{B}$ aborts when $c \neq c'$.
6. $\mathcal{B}$ appends $\{\mathsf{d}_i(x_i),\mathsf{d}_i(z_i)\}_{i\in S_c}$ to the post-measurement state and runs V_2^* on it to obtain σ'.
7. $\mathcal{B}$ sends $\{\mathsf{cert}'_{i,x},\mathsf{cert}'_{i,z}\}_{i\in\overline{S}_c}$ to the challenger of $\mathsf{Exp}^{\mathsf{bit-ever-hide}}_{\Sigma_{\mathsf{ccd}},\mathcal{B}}(\lambda,b)$, and receives $\bot$ or $\{\mathsf{d}_i(x_i),\mathsf{d}_i(z_i)\}_{i\in\overline{S}_c}$ and $\{\mathsf{ck}_i(x_i),\mathsf{ck}_i(z_i)\}_{i\in\overline{S}_c}$ from the challenger.
8. $\mathcal{B}$ passes $(\bot,\bot)$ to $\mathcal{D}$ if $\mathcal{B}$ receives $\bot$ from the challenger, and passes $(\top,\sigma')$ to $\mathcal{D}$ otherwise.
9. When $\mathcal{D}$ outputs b, $\mathcal{B}$ outputs b.

When $\mathcal{B}$ receives $\{\mathsf{com}_i(x_i),\mathsf{com}_i(z_i)\}_{i\in\overline{S}_c}$ from the challenger and it does not abort, it simulates $\mathsf{OUT}'_{\mathcal{P},\mathcal{V}^*}\langle\mathcal{P}(\mathsf{w}^{\otimes k(|\mathsf{x}|)}),\mathcal{V}^*(\cdot)\rangle(\mathsf{x})$. Because $(X^x Z^z \rho_{\mathsf{hist}} Z^z X^x)\otimes\mathsf{com}(x)\otimes\mathsf{com}(z)\otimes\sigma$ is independent of c, the probability that $\mathcal{B}$ does not abort is $\frac{1}{m}$. Therefore, $\mathcal{B}$ can simulate $\mathsf{OUT}'_{\mathcal{P},\mathcal{V}^*}\langle\mathcal{P}(\mathsf{w}^{\otimes k(|\mathsf{x}|)}),\mathcal{V}^*(\cdot)\rangle(\mathsf{x})$ with probability $\frac{1}{m}$.

When $\mathcal{B}$ receives $\{\mathsf{com}_i(0),\mathsf{com}_i(0)\}_{i\in\overline{S}_c}$ from the challenger and it does not abort, it simulates $\mathcal{S}^{(3)}(\mathsf{x},\mathsf{w}^{\otimes k(|\mathsf{x}|)},\mathcal{V}^*,\cdot)$. The probability that $\mathcal{B}$ does not abort is $\frac{1}{m} \pm \mathsf{negl}(\lambda)$ from Proposition 4.1 and 4.2. Therefore, $\mathcal{B}$ can simulate $\mathcal{S}^{(3)}(\mathsf{x},\mathsf{w}^{\otimes k(|\mathsf{x}|)},\mathcal{V}^*,\cdot)$ with probability $\frac{1}{m} \pm \mathsf{negl}(\lambda)$.

Therefore, if there exists a distinguisher $\mathcal{D}$ that distinguishes δ_0 and δ_1, $\mathcal{B}$ can distinguish $\{\mathsf{com}_i(x_i),\mathsf{com}_i(z_i)\}_{i\in\overline{S}_c}$ from $\{\mathsf{com}_i(0),\mathsf{com}_i(0)\}_{i\in\overline{S}_c}$. From Lemma 3.1, this contradicts the certified everlasting hiding of Σ_{ccd}.

$\square$

Proof of Lemma 4.4. Computational zero-knowledge can be proven similarly to [BG20, Lemma 5.3] because our protocol is identical to theirs if we ignore the deletion certificates, which are irrelevant to the computational zero-knowledge property.   □

4.3 Sequential Repetition for Certified Everlasting Zero-Knowledge Proof for QMA

We can amplify the completeness-soundness gap of the three-round protocol constructed in the previous section by sequential repetition. See the full version [HMNY21a] for details.

Acknowledgements. TH is supported by JSPS research fellowship and by JSPS KAKENHI No. JP22J21864. TM is supported by JST Moonshot R&D JPMJMS2061-5-1-1, JST FOREST, MEXT QLEAP, the Grant-in-Aid for Scientific Research (B) No. JP19H04066, the Grant-in Aid for Transformative Research Areas (A) 21H05183, and the Grant-in-Aid for Scientific Research (A) No. 22H00522.

References

[ACGH20] Alagic, G., Childs, A.M., Grilo, A.B., Hung, S.-H.: Non-interactive Classical Verification of Quantum Computation. In: Pass, R., Pietrzak, K. (eds.) TCC 2020. LNCS, vol. 12552, pp. 153–180. Springer, Cham (2020). https://doi.org/10.1007/978-3-030-64381-2_6

[AHU19] Ambainis, A., Hamburg, M., Unruh, D.: Quantum security proofs using semi-classical oracles. In: Boldyreva, A., Micciancio, D. (eds.) CRYPTO 2019. LNCS, vol. 11693, pp. 269–295. Springer, Cham (2019). https://doi.org/10.1007/978-3-030-26951-7_10

[BB21] Bitansky, N., Brakerski, Z.: Classical binding for quantum commitments. IACR Cryptol. ePrint Arch. **2021**, 1001 (2021)

[BCKM21] Bartusek, J., Coladangelo, A., Khurana, D., Ma, F.: On the round complexity of secure quantum computation. In: Malkin, T., Peikert, C. (eds.) CRYPTO 2021. LNCS, vol. 12825, pp. 406–435. Springer, Cham (2021). https://doi.org/10.1007/978-3-030-84242-0_15

[BDF+11] Boneh, D., Dagdelen, Ö., Fischlin, M., Lehmann, A., Schaffner, C., Zhandry, M.: Random oracles in a quantum world. In: Lee, D.H., Wang, X. (eds.) ASIACRYPT 2011. LNCS, vol. 7073, pp. 41–69. Springer, Heidelberg (2011). https://doi.org/10.1007/978-3-642-25385-0_3

[BG20] Broadbent, A., Grilo, A.B.: QMA-hardness of consistency of local density matrices with applications to quantum zero-knowledge. In: 61st FOCS, pp. 196–205. IEEE Computer Society Press (2020)

[BI20] Broadbent, A., Islam, R.: Quantum encryption with certified deletion. In: Pass, R., Pietrzak, K. (eds.) TCC 2020. LNCS, vol. 12552, pp. 92–122. Springer, Cham (2020). https://doi.org/10.1007/978-3-030-64381-2_4

[BJSW16] Broadbent, A., Ji, Z., Song, F., Watrous, J.: Zero-knowledge proof systems for QMA. In: Dinur, I. (ed.) 57th FOCS, pp. 31–40. IEEE Computer Society Press (2016)

[BM21] Bartusek, J., Malavolta, G.: Candidate obfuscation of null quantum circuits and witness encryption for QMA. IACR Cryptol. ePrint Arch. **2021**, 421 (2021)

[BS20] Bitansky, N., Shmueli, O.: Post-quantum zero knowledge in constant rounds. In: Makarychev, K., Makarychev, Y., Tulsiani, M., Kamath, G., Chuzhoy, J. (eds.) 52nd ACM STOC, pp. 269–279. ACM Press (2020)

[BY20] Brakerski, Z., Yuen, H.: Quantum garbled circuits. arXiv preprint arXiv:2006.01085 (2020)

[CCKV08] Chailloux, A., Ciocan, D.F., Kerenidis, I., Vadhan, S.: Interactive and noninteractive zero knowledge are equivalent in the help model. In: Canetti, R. (ed.) TCC 2008. LNCS, vol. 4948, pp. 501–534. Springer, Heidelberg (2008). https://doi.org/10.1007/978-3-540-78524-8_28

[CDMS04] Crépeau, C., Dumais, P., Mayers, D., Salvail, L.: Computational collapse of quantum state with application to oblivious transfer. In: Naor, M. (ed.) TCC 2004. LNCS, vol. 2951, pp. 374–393. Springer, Heidelberg (2004). https://doi.org/10.1007/978-3-540-24638-1_21

[CM21] Chardouvelis, O., Malavolta, G.: The round complexity of quantum zero-knowledge. IACR Cryptol. ePrint Arch. (2021)

[CVZ20] Coladangelo, A., Vidick, T., Zhang, T.: Non-interactive zero-Knowledge arguments for QMA, with preprocessing. In: Micciancio, D., Ristenpart, T. (eds.) CRYPTO 2020. LNCS, vol. 12172, pp. 799–828. Springer, Cham (2020). https://doi.org/10.1007/978-3-030-56877-1_28

[DFR+07] Damgård, I.B., Fehr, S., Renner, R., Salvail, L., Schaffner, C.: A tight high-order entropic quantum uncertainty relation with applications. In: Menezes, A. (ed.) CRYPTO 2007. LNCS, vol. 4622, pp. 360–378. Springer, Heidelberg (2007). https://doi.org/10.1007/978-3-540-74143-5_20

[DFS04] Damgård, I., Fehr, S., Salvail, L.: Zero-knowledge proofs and string commitments with standing quantum attacks. In: Franklin, M. (ed.) CRYPTO 2004. LNCS, vol. 3152, pp. 254–272. Springer, Heidelberg (2004). https://doi.org/10.1007/978-3-540-28628-8_16

[For87] Fortnow, L.: The complexity of perfect zero-knowledge (extended abstract). In: Aho, A. (ed.) 19th ACM STOC, pp. 204–209. ACM Press (1987)

[FUW+20] Fang, J., Unruh, D., Weng, J., Yan, J., Zhou, D.: How to base security on the perfect/statistical binding property of quantum bit commitment? IACR Cryptol. ePrint Arch. **2020**, 621 (2020)

[GMR89] Goldwasser, S., Micali, S., Rackoff, C.: The knowledge complexity of interactive proof systems. SIAM J. Comput. **18**(1), 186–208 (1989)

[GSV98] Goldreich, O., Sahai, A., Vadhan, S.P.: Honest-verifier statistical zero-knowledge equals general statistical zero-knowledge. In: 30th ACM STOC, pp. 399–408. ACM Press (1998)

[GSY19] Grilo, A.B., Slofstra, W., Yuen, H.: Perfect zero knowledge for quantum multiprover interactive proofs. In: Zuckerman, D. (ed.) 60th FOCS, pp. 611–635. IEEE Computer Society Press (2019)

[HMNY21a] Hiroka, T., Morimae, T., Nishimaki, R., Yamakawa, T.: Certified everlasting zero-knowledge proof for QMA. IACR Cryptol. ePrint Arch. **2021**, 1315 (2021)

[HMNY21b] Hiroka, T., Morimae, T., Nishimaki, R., Yamakawa, T.: Quantum encryption with certified deletion, revisited: public key, attribute-based, and classical communication. IACR Cryptol. ePrint Arch. **2021**, 617 (2021)

[Kob03] Kobayashi, H.: Non-interactive quantum perfect and statistical zero-knowledge. In: Ibaraki, T., Katoh, N., Ono, H. (eds.) ISAAC 2003. LNCS, vol. 2906, pp. 178–188. Springer, Heidelberg (2003). https://doi.org/10.1007/978-3-540-24587-2_20

[LC97] Lo, H.-K., Chau, H.F.: Is quantum bit commitment really possible? Phys. Rev. Lett. **78**, 3410–3413 (1997)

[LS19] Lombardi, A., Schaeffer, L.: A note on key agreement and non-interactive commitments. Cryptology ePrint Archive, Report 2019/279 (2019). https://eprint.iacr.org/2019/279

[May97] Mayers, D.: Unconditionally secure quantum bit commitment is impossible. Phys. Rev. Lett. **78**, 3414–3417 (1997)

[MW18] Menda, S., Watrous, J.: Oracle separations for quantum statistical zero-knowledge. arXiv preprint arXiv:1801.08967 (2018)

[MY21] Morimae, T., Yamakawa, T.: Classically verifiable (dual-mode) NIZK for QMA with preprocessing. arXiv preprint arXiv:2102.09149 (2021)

[Shm21] Shmueli, O.: Multi-theorem designated-verifier NIZK for QMA. In: Malkin, T., Peikert, C. (eds.) CRYPTO 2021. LNCS, vol. 12825, pp. 375–405. Springer, Cham (2021). https://doi.org/10.1007/978-3-030-84242-0_14

[Unr13] Unruh, D.: Everlasting multi-party computation. In: Canetti, R., Garay, J.A. (eds.) CRYPTO 2013. LNCS, vol. 8043, pp. 380–397. Springer, Heidelberg (2013). https://doi.org/10.1007/978-3-642-40084-1_22

[Unr15] Unruh, D.: Revocable quantum timed-release encryption. J. ACM **62**(6), 49:1–49:76 (2015)

[Wat02] Watrous, J.: Limits on the power of quantum statistical zero-knowledge. In: 43rd FOCS, pp. 459–470. IEEE Computer Society Press (2002)

[Wat09] Watrous, J.: Zero-knowledge against quantum attacks. SIAM J. Comput. **39**(1), 25–58 (2009)

[Yan20] Yan, J.: Quantum computationally predicate-binding commitment with application in quantum zero-knowledge argument for NP. IACR Cryptol. ePrint Arch. **2020**, 1510 (2020)

[YWLQ15] Yan, J., Weng, J., Lin, D., Quan, Y.: Quantum bit commitment with application in quantum zero-knowledge proof (extended abstract). In: Elbassioni, K., Makino, K. (eds.) ISAAC 2015. LNCS, vol. 9472, pp. 555–565. Springer, Heidelberg (2015). https://doi.org/10.1007/978-3-662-48971-0_47

[Zha19] Zhandry, M.: How to record quantum queries, and applications to quantum indifferentiability. In: Boldyreva, A., Micciancio, D. (eds.) CRYPTO 2019. LNCS, vol. 11693, pp. 239–268. Springer, Cham (2019). https://doi.org/10.1007/978-3-030-26951-7_9

Quantum Commitments and Signatures Without One-Way Functions

Tomoyuki Morimae[1(✉)] and Takashi Yamakawa[1,2]

[1] Yukawa Institute for Theoretical Physics, Kyoto University, Kyoto, Japan
tomoyuki.morimae@yukawa.kyoto-u.ac.jp
[2] NTT Social Informatics Laboratories, Tokyo, Japan

Abstract. In the classical world, the existence of commitments is equivalent to the existence of one-way functions. In the quantum setting, on the other hand, commitments are not known to imply one-way functions, but all known constructions of quantum commitments use at least one-way functions. Are one-way functions really necessary for commitments in the quantum world? In this work, we show that non-interactive quantum commitments (for classical messages) with computational hiding and statistical binding exist if pseudorandom quantum states exist. Pseudorandom quantum states are sets of quantum states that are efficiently generated but their polynomially many copies are computationally indistinguishable from the same number of copies of Haar random states [Ji, Liu, and Song, CRYPTO 2018]. It is known that pseudorandom quantum states exist even if **BQP = QMA** (relative to a quantum oracle) [Kretschmer, TQC 2021], which means that pseudorandom quantum states can exist even if no quantum-secure classical cryptographic primitive exists. Our result therefore shows that quantum commitments can exist even if no quantum-secure classical cryptographic primitive exists. In particular, quantum commitments can exist even if no quantum-secure one-way function exists. In this work, we also consider digital signatures, which are other fundamental primitives in cryptography. We show that one-time secure digital signatures with quantum public keys exist if pseudorandom quantum states exist. In the classical setting, the existence of digital signatures is equivalent to the existence of one-way functions. Our result, on the other hand, shows that quantum signatures can exist even if no quantum-secure classical cryptographic primitive (including quantum-secure one-way functions) exists.

1 Introduction

1.1 Background

Commitments [Blu81] are one of the most central primitives in cryptography. Assume that a sender wants to commit a message m to a receiver. The sender encrypts it and sends it to the receiver. Later, the sender sends a key so that the receiver can open the message m. Before the sender sends the key, the receiver should not be able to learn the message m, which is called *hiding*. Furthermore, the sender should not be able to change the message later once the

Y. Dodis and T. Shrimpton (Eds.): CRYPTO 2022, LNCS 13507, pp. 269–295, 2022.
https://doi.org/10.1007/978-3-031-15802-5_10

sender commits it, which is called *binding*. (Imagine that the sender's message is put in a safe box and sent to the receiver. The receiver cannot open it until the receiver receives the key, and the sender cannot change the message in the safe box once it is sent to the receiver.) In cryptography, there are two types of definitions for security. One is statistical security and the other is computational security. Statistical security means that it is secure against any computationally-unbounded adversary, while computational security means that it is secure against adversaries restricted to polynomial-time classical/quantum computations. It is easy to see that both hiding and binding cannot be statistical at the same time in the classical setting,[1] and therefore one of them has to be based on a computational assumption. In other words, in a computationally hiding commitment scheme, a malicious receiver can learn the message m before the opening if its computational power is unbounded, and in a computationally binding commitment scheme, a malicious sender can change its committed message later if its computational power is unbounded. For the computational assumption, the existence of one-way functions is known to be equivalent to the existence of classical commitments [Nao91, HILL99]. The existence of one-way functions is considered the weakest assumption in classical cryptography, because virtually all complexity-based classical cryptographic primitives are known to imply the existence of one-way functions [LR86, IL89, ILL89].

The history of quantum information has demonstrated that utilizing quantum physics in information processing achieves many advantages. In particular, it has been shown in quantum cryptography that quantum physics can weaken cryptographic assumptions. For example, if quantum states are transmitted, statistically-secure key distribution is possible [BB84], although it is impossible classically. Furthermore, oblivious transfer is possible with only (quantum-secure) one-way functions when quantum states are transmitted [BCKM21, GLSV21, CK88, BBCS92, MS94, Yao95, DFL+09]. Classically, it is known to be impossible to construct oblivious transfer from only one-way functions [IR90].[2]

As we have mentioned, it is classically impossible to realize commitments with statistical hiding and statistical binding. Does quantum physics overcome the barrier? Unfortunately, it is already known that both binding and hiding cannot be statistical at the same time even in the quantum world [LC97, May97]. In fact, all known constructions of quantum commitments use at least (quantum-secure) one-way functions [DMS00, CLS01, KO09, KO11, YWLQ15, Yan20, BB21].

In this paper, we ask the following fundamental question:

Are one-way functions really necessary for commitments?

---

[1] If a commitment scheme is statistically binding, there exists at most one message to which a commitment can be opened except for a negligible probability. This unique message can be found by a brute-force search, which means that the scheme is not statistically hiding.

[2] [IR90] showed the impossibility of *relativizing constructions* of key exchange from one-way functions, and oblivious transfer is stronger than key exchange. Since most cryptographic constructions are relativizing, this gives a strong negative result on constructing oblivious transfer from one-way functions in the classical setting.

It could be the case that in the quantum world commitments can be constructed from an assumption weaker than the existence of one-way functions. This possibility is mentioned in previous works [BCKM21,GLSV21], but no construction is provided.

Digital signatures [DH76] are another important primitive in cryptography. In a signature scheme, a secret key sk and a public key pk are generated. The secret key sk is used to generate a signature σ for a message m, and the public key pk is used for the verification of the pair (m, σ) of the message and the signature. Any adversary who has pk and can query the signing oracle many times cannot forge a signature σ' for a message m' which is not queried. In other words, (m', σ') is not accepted by the verification algorithm except for an negligible probability.

Obviously, statistically-secure digital signatures are impossible, because an unbounded adversary who can access pk and the verification algorithm can find a valid signature by a brute-force search. In the classical world, it is known that the existence of digital signatures is equivalent to the existence of one-way functions. In the quantum setting, on the other hand, digital signatures are not known to imply one-way functions. Gottesman and Chuang introduced digital signatures with quantum public keys [GC01], but they considered information-theoretical security, and therefore the number of public keys should be bounded. Our second fundamental question in this paper is the following:

Are digital signatures possible without one-way functions?

1.2 Our Results

In this paper, we answer the above two fundamental questions affirmatively. The first result of this paper is a construction of quantum commitments from pseudorandom quantum states generators (PRSGs) [JLS18,BS19,BS20]. A PRSG is a quantum polynomial-time algorithm that, on input $k \in \{0,1\}^n$, outputs an m-qubit state $|\phi_k\rangle$ such that $|\phi_k\rangle^{\otimes t}$ over uniform random k is computationally indistinguishable from the same number of copies of Haar random states for any polynomial t. (The formal definition of PRSGs is given in Definition 2.1.)

Our first result is stated as follows:[3]

Theorem 1.1. *If a pseudorandom quantum states generator with $m \geq cn$ for a constant $c > 1$ exists, then non-interactive quantum commitments (for classical messages) with computational hiding and statistical binding exist.*

In [Kre21], it is shown that PRSGs exist even if $\mathbf{BQP} = \mathbf{QMA}$ relative to a quantum oracle. If $\mathbf{BQP} = \mathbf{QMA}$, no quantum-secure classical cryptographic primitive exists, because $\mathbf{BQP} = \mathbf{QMA}$ means $\mathbf{NP} \subseteq \mathbf{BQP}$. In particular, no quantum-secure one-way function exists. Our Theorem 1.1 therefore shows that quantum commitments can exist even if no quantum-secure classical cryptographic

---

[3] Our construction of commitments also satisfies perfect correctness, i.e., the probability that the honest receiver opens the correct bit committed by the honest sender is 1.

primitive exists.[4] In particular, quantum commitments can exist even if no quantum-secure one-way function exists.

As we will see later (Sect. 3), what we actually need is a weaker version of PRSGs where only the computational indistinguishability of a single copy of $|\phi_k\rangle$ from the Haar random state is required. We call such a weaker version of PRSGs *single-copy-secure PRSGs*. (See Definition 2.2. It is the $t = 1$ version of Definition 2.1.) Because a single copy of the Haar random state is equivalent to the maximally-mixed state, the single-copy security means the computational indistinguishability from the maximally-mixed state. It could be the case that the realization of single-copy-secure PRSGs is easier than that of (multi-copy-secure) PRSGs. (For more discussions, see Sect. 2.2.)

Non-interactive commitments are a special type of commitments. (See Definition 3.1.) In general, the sender and the receiver exchange many rounds of messages during the commitment phase, but in non-interactive commitments, only a single message from the sender to the receiver is enough for the commitment. It is known that non-interactive quantum commitments (for classical messages) are possible with (quantum-secure) one-way functions [YWLQ15], while it is subject to a black-box barrier in the classical case [MP12].

As the definition of binding, we choose a standard one, sum-binding [Unr16], which roughly means that $p_0 + p_1 \leq 1 + \mathsf{negl}(\lambda)$, where negl is a negligible function, λ is a security parameter, and p_0 and p_1 are probabilities that the malicious sender makes the receiver open 0 and 1, respectively. (The formal definition of statistical sum-binding is given in Definition 3.4.)

Our first result, Theorem 1.1, that quantum commitments can be possible without one-way functions has important consequences in cryptography. It is known that quantum commitments imply the existence of quantum-secure zero-knowledge proofs (of knowledge) for all **NP** languages [FUYZ20] and quantum-secure oblivious transfer (and therefore multi-party computations (MPC)) [BCKM21, GLSV21]. Thus, those primitives can also exist even if **BQP** = **QMA** (and in particular quantum-secure one-way functions do not exist)[5] while classical constructions of them imply the existence of one-way functions. For more details, see Appendix B.

We also remark that there is no known construction of PRSGs from weaker assumptions than the existence of one-way functions without oracles. Thus, our result should be understood as a theoretical evidence that quantum commitments can exist even if **BQP** = **QMA** rather than a new concrete construction. It is an interesting open problem to construct a PRSG from weaker assumptions than the

---

[4] It actually shows stronger things, because **BQP** = **QMA** also excludes the existence of some quantum-secure *quantum* cryptographic primitives where honest algorithms are quantum.

[5] Indeed, [BCKM21] states as follows: "*Moreover if in the future, new constructions of statistically binding, quantum computationally hiding commitments involving quantum communication are discovered based on assumptions weaker than quantum-hard one-way functions, it would be possible to plug those into our protocol compilers to obtain QOT.*".

existence of one-way functions without oracles. Such a construction immediately yields commitments (and more) by our result.

One might ask the following question: can we remove (or improve) the condition of $m \geq cn$ with a constant $c > 1$ in Theorem 1.1? The answer is no for single-copy-secure PRSGs, because if $m \leq n$, there is a trivial construction of a single-copy-secure PRSG without any assumption: $|\phi_k\rangle := |k_1, ..., k_m\rangle$ for any $k \in \{0, 1\}^n$, where k_j is the jth bit of k. In fact, $\frac{1}{2^n} \sum_{k \in \{0,1\}^n} |\phi_k\rangle\langle\phi_k| = \frac{I^{\otimes m}}{2^m}$. If quantum commitments were constructed from such a single-copy-secure PRSG, we could realize quantum commitments without any assumption, which is known to be impossible [LC97, May97]. We note that [Kre21] considers only the case when $m = n$, but it is clear that the result holds for $m \geq cn$ with constant $c > 1$.

Finally, we do not know whether the opposite of Theorem 1.1 holds or not. Namely, do quantum commitments imply PRSGs (or single-copy-secure PRSGs)? It is an interesting open problem.

Now let us move on to our second subject, namely, digital signatures. Our second result in this paper is the following:

Theorem 1.2. *If a pseudorandom quantum states generator with $m \geq cn$ for a constant $c > 1$ exists, then one-time secure digital signatures with quantum public keys exist.*

One-time security means that the adversary can query the signing oracle at most once. (See Definition 4.2 and Definition 4.4.) In the classical setting, it is known how to construct many-time secure digital signatures from one-time secure digital signatures [Mer90], but we do not know how to generalize our one-time secure quantum signature scheme to a many-time secure one, because in our case public keys are quantum. It is an important open problem to construct many-time secure digital signatures from PRSGs.

Due to the oracle separation by [Kre21], Theorem 1.2 means that (at least one-time secure) digital signatures can exist even if no quantum-secure classical cryptographic primitive exists.[6] In particular, (one-time secure) digital signatures can exist even if no quantum-secure one-way function exists.

Our construction is similar to the "quantum public key version" of the classical Lamport signature [DH76] by Gottesman and Chuang [GC01]. They consider information-theoretical security, and therefore the number of public keys should be bounded. On the other hand, our construction from PRSGs allows unbounded polynomial number of public keys. Quantum cryptography with quantum public keys are also studied in [KKNY12, Dol21].

We do not know whether the condition, $m \geq cn$ with a constant $c > 1$, can be improved or not in Theorem 1.2. Although it is possible to construct PRSGs without this restriction [BS20], this is satisfied in the construction of [Kre21], and therefore enough for our purpose of showing the existence of digital signatures without one-way functions.

As we will see later (Sect. 4), our construction of digital signatures is actually based on what we call *one-way quantum states generators (OWSGs)*

---

[6] Again, it also excludes some quantum-secure *quantum* cryptographic primitives.

(Definition 4.1). Intuitively, we say that a quantum polynomial-time algorithm that outputs an m-qubit quantum state $|\phi_k\rangle$ on input $k \in \{0,1\}^n$ is a OWSG if it is hard to find, given polynomially many copies of $|\phi_k\rangle$ (with uniformly random k), an n-bit string $\sigma \in \{0,1\}^n$ such that $|\phi_\sigma\rangle$ is close to $|\phi_k\rangle$. In other words, what we actually show is the following:

Theorem 1.3. *If a one-way quantum states generator exists, then one-time secure digital signatures with quantum public keys exist.*

We show that a PRSG is a OWSG (Lemma 4.1), and therefore, Theorem 1.2 is obtained as a corollary of Theorem 1.3. The concept of OWSGs itself seems to be of independent interest. In particular, we do not know whether OWSGs imply PRSGs or not, which is an interesting open problem.

Remember that for the construction of our commitment scheme we use only single-copy-secure PRSGs. Unlike our commitment scheme, on the other hand, our signature scheme uses the security of PRSGs for an unbounded polynomial number of copies, because the number of copies decides the number of quantum public keys. In other words, single-copy-secure PRSGs enable commitments but (multi-copy-secure) PRSGs enable signatures. There could be therefore a kind of hierarchy in PRSGs for different numbers of copies, which seems to be an interesting future research subject.

1.3   Technical Overviews

Here we provide intuitive explanations of our constructions given in Sect. 3 and Sect. 4.

Commitments. The basic idea of our construction of commitments is, in some sense, a quantum generalization of the classical Naor's commitment scheme [Nao91].

Let us recall Naor's construction. The receiver first samples uniformly random $\eta \leftarrow \{0,1\}^{3n}$, and sends it to the sender. The sender chooses a uniformly random seed $s \leftarrow \{0,1\}^n$, and sends $G(s) \oplus \eta^b$ to the receiver, where $G : \{0,1\}^n \rightarrow \{0,1\}^{3n}$ is a length-tripling pseudorandom generator, and $b \in \{0,1\}$ is the bit to commit. Hiding is clear: because the receiver does not know s, the receiver cannot distinguish $G(s)$ and $G(s) \oplus \eta$. The decommitment is (b,s). The receiver can check whether the commitment is $G(s)$ or $G(s) \oplus \eta$ from s. Binding comes from the fact that if both 0 and 1 can be opened, there exist s_0, s_1 such that $G(s_0) = G(s_1) = \eta$. There are 2^{2n} such seeds, and therefore for a random η, it is impossible except for 2^{-n} probability.

Our idea is to replace $G(s)$ with a pseudorandom state $|\phi_k\rangle$, and to replace the addition of η^b with the quantum one-time pad, which randomly applies Pauli X and Z. More precisely, the sender who wants to commit $b \in \{0,1\}$ generates the state

$$|\psi_b\rangle := \frac{1}{\sqrt{2^{2m+n}}} \sum_{x,z \in \{0,1\}^m} \sum_{k \in \{0,1\}^n} |x, z, k\rangle_R \otimes P_{x,z}^b |\phi_k\rangle_C,$$

and sends the register C to the receiver, where $P_{x,z} := \bigotimes_{j=1}^{m} X_j^{x_j} Z_j^{z_j}$. It is the commitment phase. At the end of the commitment phase, the receiver's state is $\rho_0 := \frac{1}{2^n} \sum_k |\phi_k\rangle\langle\phi_k|$ when $b = 0$ and $\rho_1 := \frac{1}{2^n} \frac{1}{4^m} \sum_k \sum_{x,z} P_{x,z}^b |\phi_k\rangle\langle\phi_k| P_{x,z}^b$ when $b = 1$. By the security of single-copy-secure PRSGs, ρ_0 is computationally indistinguishable from the m-qubit maximally-mixed state $\frac{I^{\otimes m}}{2^m}$, while $\rho_1 = \frac{I^{\otimes m}}{2^m}$ due to the quantum one-time pad (Lemma 2.1). The two states, ρ_0 and ρ_1, are therefore computationally indistinguishable, which shows computational hiding.

For statistical sum-binding, we show that the fidelity between ρ_0 and ρ_1 is negligibly small. It is intuitively understood as follows: $\rho_0 = \frac{1}{2^n} \sum_{k\in\{0,1\}^n} |\phi_k\rangle\langle\phi_k|$ has a support in at most 2^n-dimensional space, while $\rho_1 = \frac{I^{\otimes m}}{2^m}$ has a support in the entire 2^m-dimensional space, where $m \geq cn$ with $c > 1$, and therefore the "overlap" between ρ_0 and ρ_1 is small.

A detailed explanation of our construction of commitments and its security proof are given in Sect. 3.

Digital Signatures. Our construction of digital signatures is a quantum public key version of the classical Lamport signature. The Lamport signature scheme is constructed from a one-way function. For simplicity, let us explain the Lamport signature scheme for a single-bit message. Let f be a one-way function. The secret key is $sk := (sk_0, sk_1)$, where sk_0, sk_1 are uniform randomly chosen n-bit strings. The public key is $pk := (pk_0, pk_1)$, where $pk_0 := f(sk_0)$ and $pk_1 := f(sk_1)$. The signature σ for a message $m \in \{0,1\}$ is sk_m, and the verification is to check whether $pk_m = f(\sigma)$. Intuitively, the (one-time) security of this signature scheme comes from that of the one-way function f.

We consider the quantum public key version of it: pk is a quantum state. More precisely, our key generation algorithm chooses $k_0, k_1 \leftarrow \{0,1\}^n$, and runs $|\phi_{k_b}\rangle \leftarrow \mathsf{StateGen}(k_b)$ for $b \in \{0,1\}$, where $\mathsf{StateGen}$ is a PRSG.[7] It outputs $sk := (sk_0, sk_1)$ and $pk := (pk_0, pk_1)$, where $sk_b := k_b$ and $pk_b := |\phi_{sk_b}\rangle$ for $b \in \{0,1\}$. To sign a bit $m \in \{0,1\}$, the signing algorithm outputs the signature $\sigma := sk_m$. Given the message-signature pair (m, σ), the verification algorithm measures pk_m with $\{|\phi_\sigma\rangle\langle\phi_\sigma|, I - |\phi_\sigma\rangle\langle\phi_\sigma|\}$ and accepts if and only if the result is $|\phi_\sigma\rangle\langle\phi_\sigma|$.

Intuitively, this signature scheme is one-time secure because sk_b cannot be obtained from $|\phi_{sk_b}\rangle^{\otimes t}$: If sk_b is obtained, $|\phi_{sk_b}\rangle^{\otimes t}$ can be distinguished from Haar random states, which contradicts the security of PRSGs. In order to formalize this intuition, we introduce what we call OWSGs (Definition 4.1), and show that PRSGs imply OWSGs (Lemma 4.1). For details of our construction of digital signatures and its security proof, see Sect. 4.

---

[7] It is not necessarily a PRSG. Any OWSG (Definition 4.1) is enough. For details, see Sect. 4.

1.4   Concurrent Work

Few days after the first version of this paper was made online, a concurrent work [AQY21] appeared. The concurrent work also constructs commitments from PRSGs. We give comparisons between our and their results.

1. For achieving the security level of $O(2^{-n})$ for binding, they rely on PRSGs with $m = 2\log n + \omega(\log\log n)$ and any t, or $m = 7n$ and $t = 1$. On the other hand, we rely on PRSGs with $m = 3n$ and $t = 1$. Thus, the required parameters seem incomparable though we cannot simply compare them due to the difference of definitions of binding. (See also Appendix B.)
2. Our scheme is non-interactive whereas theirs is interactive though we believe that their scheme can also be made non-interactive by a similar technique to ours.
3. They consider a more general definition of PRSGs than us that allows the state generation algorithm to sometimes fail. We do not take this into account since we can rely on PRSGs of [Kre21] whose state generation never fails for our primary goal to show that commitments and digital signatures can exist even if one-way functions do not exist. Moreover, the failure probability has to be anyway negligibly small due to the security of PRSGs, and therefore it would be simpler to ignore the failure.

Besides commitments, the result on digital signatures is unique to this paper. On the other hand, [AQY21] contains results that are not covered in this paper such as pseudorandom function-like states and symmetric key encryption. We remark that our result on digital signatures was added a few days after the initial version of [AQY21] was made online, but the result was obtained independently, and there is no overlap with [AQY21] in this part.

Though most part of this work was done independently of [AQY21], there are two part where we revised the paper based on [AQY21]. The first is the definition of PRSGs. As pointed out in the initial version of [AQY21], the initial version of this work implicitly assumed that PRSGs do not use any ancillary qubits, which is a very strong restriction. However, we found that all of our results can be based on PRSGs that use ancillary qubits with just notational adaptations. Thus, we regard this as a notational level issue and fixed it.

The second is the connection to oblivious transfer and MPC explained in Appendix B. In the initial version of this work, we only mentioned the idea of using the techniques of [FUYZ20] to instantiate oblivious transfer and MPC of [BCKM21] based on quantum commitments. On the other hand, [AQY21] shows it assuming that the base quantum commitment satisfies a newly introduced definition of statistical binding property, which we call AQY-binding. Interestingly, we found that it is already implicitly shown in [FUYZ20] that the sum-binding implies AQY-binding. As a result, our commitment scheme can also be used to instantiate oblivious transfer and MPC of [BCKM21]. See Appendix B for more detail.

2 Preliminaries

In this section, we provide preliminaries.

2.1 Basic Notations

We use standard notations in quantum information. For example, $I := |0\rangle\langle 0| + |1\rangle\langle 1|$ is the two-dimensional identity operator. For notational simplicity, we sometimes write the n-qubit identity operator $I^{\otimes n}$ just I when it is clear from the context. X, Y, Z are Pauli operators. X_j means the Pauli X operator that acts on the jth qubit. Let ρ_{AB} be a quantum state over the subsystems A and B. Then $\mathrm{Tr}_A(\rho_{AB})$ is the partial trace of ρ_{AB} over subsystem A. For n-bit strings $x, z \in \{0,1\}^n$, $X^x := \bigotimes_{j=1}^{n} X_j^{x_j}$ and $Z^z := \bigotimes_{j=1}^{n} Z_j^{z_j}$, where x_j and z_j are the jth bit of x and z, respectively.

We also use standard notations in cryptography. A function f is negligible if for all constant $c > 0$, $f(\lambda) < \lambda^{-c}$ for large enough λ. QPT and PPT stand for quantum polynomial time and (classical) probabilistic polynomial time, respectively. $k \leftarrow \{0,1\}^n$ means that k is sampled from $\{0,1\}^n$ uniformly at random. For an algorithm $\mathcal{A}$, $\mathcal{A}(\xi) \rightarrow \eta$ means that the algorithm outputs η on input ξ.

In this paper, we use the following lemma. It can be shown by a straightforward calculation.

Lemma 2.1 (Quantum one-time pad). *For any m-qubit state ρ,*

$$\frac{1}{4^m} \sum_{x \in \{0,1\}^m} \sum_{z \in \{0,1\}^m} X^x Z^z \rho Z^z X^x = \frac{I^{\otimes m}}{2^m}.$$

2.2 Pseudorandom Quantum States Generators

Let us review pseudorandom quantum states generators (PRSGs) [JLS18, BS19, BS20]. The definition of PRSGs is given as follows.

Definition 2.1 (Pseudorandom quantum states generators (PRSGs) [JLS18, BS19, BS20]**).** *A pseudorandom quantum states generator (PRSG) is a QPT algorithm StateGen that, on input $k \in \{0,1\}^n$, outputs an m-qubit quantum state $|\phi_k\rangle$. As the security, we require the following: for any polynomial t and any non-uniform QPT adversary $\mathcal{A}$, there exists a negligible function negl such that for all n,*

$$\left| \Pr_{k \leftarrow \{0,1\}^n} \left[\mathcal{A}(|\phi_k\rangle^{\otimes t(n)}) \rightarrow 1 \right] - \Pr_{|\psi\rangle \leftarrow \mu_m} \left[\mathcal{A}(|\psi\rangle^{\otimes t(n)}) \rightarrow 1 \right] \right| \leq \mathsf{negl}(n),$$

where μ_m is the Haar measure on m-qubit states.

Remark 2.1. In the most general case, StateGen is the following QPT algorithm: given an input $k \in \{0,1\}^n$, it first computes a classical description of a unitary quantum circuit U_k, and next applies U_k on the all zero state $|0...0\rangle$ to generate

$|\Phi_k\rangle_{AB} := U_k|0...0\rangle$. It finally outputs the m-qubit state $\rho_k := \mathrm{Tr}_B(|\Phi_k\rangle\langle\Phi_k|_{AB})$. However, ρ_k is, on average, almost pure, because otherwise the security is broken by a QPT adversary who runs the SWAP test on two copies.[8] In this paper, for simplicity, we assume that ρ_k is pure, and denote it by $|\phi_k\rangle$. The same results hold even if it is negligibly close to pure. What StateGen generates is therefore $|\Phi_k\rangle_{AB} = |\phi_k\rangle_A \otimes |\eta_k\rangle_B$ with an ancilla state $|\eta_k\rangle$. In this paper, for simplicity, we assume that there is no ancilla state in the final state generated by StateGen, but actually the same results hold even if ancilla states exist. (See Sect. 3 and Sect. 4.) Moreover, [Kre21] considers the case with pure outputs and no ancilla state, and therefore restricting to the pure and no ancilla case is enough for our purpose of showing the existence of commitments and digital signatures without one-way functions.

Interestingly, what we actually need for our construction of commitments (Sect. 3) is a weaker version of PRSGs where the security is satisfied only for $t = 1$. We call them *single-copy-secure PRSGs*:

Definition 2.2 (Single-copy-secure PRSGs). *A single-copy-secure pseudo-random quantum states generator (PRSG) is a QPT algorithm StateGen that, on input $k \in \{0,1\}^n$, outputs an m-qubit quantum state $|\phi_k\rangle$. As the security, we require the following: for any non-uniform QPT adversary $\mathcal{A}$, there exists a negligible function negl such that for all n,*

$$\left| \Pr_{k \leftarrow \{0,1\}^n}\left[\mathcal{A}(|\phi_k\rangle) \to 1\right] - \Pr_{|\psi\rangle \leftarrow \mu_m}\left[\mathcal{A}(|\psi\rangle) \to 1\right] \right| \leq \mathsf{negl}(n),$$

where μ_m is the Haar measure on m-qubit states.

Remark 2.2. Because a single copy of an m-qubit state sampled Haar randomly is equivalent to the m-qubit maximally-mixed state, $\frac{I^{\otimes m}}{2^m}$, the security of single-copy-secure PRSGs is in fact the computational indistinguishability of a single copy of $|\phi_k\rangle$ from $\frac{I^{\otimes m}}{2^m}$.

Remark 2.3. As we have explained in Remark 2.1, in the definition of PRSGs (Definition 2.1), the output state ρ_k of StateGen has to be negligibly close to pure (on average). When we consider single-copy-secure PRSGs (Definition 2.2), on the other hand, the SWAP-test attack does not work because only a single copy is available to adversaries. In fact, there is a trivial construction of a single-copy-secure PRSG whose output is not pure: $\mathsf{StateGen}(k) \to \frac{I^{\otimes m}}{2^m}$ for all $k \in \{0,1\}^n$. We therefore assume that the output of StateGen is pure, i.e., $\rho_k = |\phi_k\rangle\langle\phi_k|$, when we consider single-copy-secure PRSGs.

---

[8] Let us consider an adversary $\mathcal{A}$ that runs the SWAP test on two copies of the received state and outputs the result of the SWAP test. When $\rho_k^{\otimes t}$ is sent with uniformly random k, the probability that $\mathcal{A}$ outputs 1 is $(1 + \frac{1}{2^n}\sum_k \mathrm{Tr}(\rho_k^2))/2$. When the t copies of Haar random states $|\psi\rangle^{\otimes t}$ is sent, the probability that $\mathcal{A}$ outputs 1 is 1. For the security, $|(1 + \frac{1}{2^n}\sum_k \mathrm{Tr}(\rho_k^2))/2 - 1| \leq \mathsf{negl}(\lambda)$ has to be satisfied, which means the expected purity of ρ_k, $\frac{1}{2^n}\sum_k \mathrm{Tr}(\rho_k^2)$, has to be negligibly close to 1.

Remark 2.4. It could be the case that single-copy-secure PRSGs are easier to realize than (multi-copy-secure) PRSGs. In fact, the security proofs of the constructions of [JLS18, BS19] are simpler for $t = 1$. Furthermore, there is a simple construction of a single-copy-secure PRSG by using a pseudorandom generator $G : \{0,1\}^n \to \{0,1\}^m$. In fact, we have only to take $|\phi_k\rangle = |G(k)\rangle$ for all $k \in \{0,1\}^n$.

Remark 2.5. One might think that a single-copy-secure PRSG with $m \geq n+1$ is a pseudorandom generator (PRG), because if the m-qubit state $|\phi_k\rangle$ is measured in the computational basis, the probability distribution of the measurement results is computationally indistinguishable from that (i.e., the m-bit uniform distribution) obtained when the m-qubit maximally mixed state $\frac{I^{\otimes m}}{2^m}$ is measured in the computational basis. It is, however, strange because if it was true then the existence of single-copy-secure PRSGs implies the existence of PRGs, which contradicts [Kre21]. The point is that measuring $|\phi_k\rangle$ in the computational basis does not work as PRGs because the output is not deterministically obtained. (Remember that PRGs are deterministic algorithms.)

3   Commitments

In this section, we provide our construction of commitments, and show its security.

3.1   Definition

Let us first give a formal definition of non-interactive quantum commitments.

Definition 3.1 (Non-interactive quantum commitments (Syntax)). *A non-interactive quantum commitment scheme is the following protocol.*

- **Commit phase:** *Let $b \in \{0,1\}$ be the bit to commit. The sender generates a quantum state $|\psi_b\rangle_{RC}$ on registers R and C, and sends the register C to the receiver. The states $\{|\psi_b\rangle\}_{b \in \{0,1\}}$ can be generated in quantum polynomial-time from the all zero state.*
- **Reveal phase:** *The sender sends b and the register R to the receiver. The receiver does the measurement $\{|\psi_b\rangle\langle\psi_b|, I - |\psi_b\rangle\langle\psi_b|\}$ on the registers R and C. If the result is $|\psi_b\rangle\langle\psi_b|$, the receiver outputs b. Otherwise, the receiver outputs $\perp$. Because $\{|\psi_b\rangle\}_{b \in \{0,1\}}$ can be generated in quantum polynomial-time from the all zero state, the measurement $\{|\psi_b\rangle\langle\psi_b|, I - |\psi_b\rangle\langle\psi_b|\}$ can be implemented efficiently.*

The perfect correctness is defined as follows:

Definition 3.2 (Perfect correctness). *A commitment scheme satisfies perfect correctness if the following is satisfied: when the honest sender commits $b \in \{0,1\}$, the probability that the honest receiver opens b is 1.*

The computational hiding is defined as follows:

Definition 3.3 (Computational hiding). *Let us consider the following security game,* $\mathsf{Exp}(b)$, *with the parameter* $b \in \{0,1\}$ *between a challenger* $\mathcal{C}$ *and a QPT adversary* $\mathcal{A}$.

1. $\mathcal{C}$ *generates* $|\psi_b\rangle_{RC}$ *and sends the register* C *to* $\mathcal{A}$.
2. $\mathcal{A}$ *outputs* $b' \in \{0,1\}$, *which is the output of the experiment.*

We say that a non-interactive quantum commitment scheme is computationally hiding if for any QPT adversary $\mathcal{A}$ *there exists a negligible function* negl *such that,*

$$|\Pr[\mathsf{Exp}(0) = 1] - \Pr[\mathsf{Exp}(1) = 1]| \leq \mathsf{negl}(\lambda).$$

As the definition of binding, we consider sum-binding [Unr16] that is defined as follows:

Definition 3.4 (Statistical sum-binding). *Let us consider the following security game between a challenger* $\mathcal{C}$ *and an unbounded adversary* $\mathcal{A}$:

1. $\mathcal{A}$ *generates a quantum state* $|\Psi\rangle_{ERC}$ *on the three registers* E, R, *and* C.
2. $\mathcal{A}$ *sends the register* C *to* $\mathcal{C}$, *which is the commitment.*
3. *If* $\mathcal{A}$ *wants to make* $\mathcal{C}$ *open* $b \in \{0,1\}$, $\mathcal{A}$ *applies a unitary* $U_{ER}^{(b)}$ *on the registers* E *and* R. $\mathcal{A}$ *sends* b *and the register* R *to* $\mathcal{C}$.
4. $\mathcal{C}$ *does the measurement* $\{|\psi_b\rangle\langle\psi_b|, I - |\psi_b\rangle\langle\psi_b|\}$ *on the registers* R *and* C. *If the result* $|\psi_b\rangle\langle\psi_b|$ *is obtained,* $\mathcal{C}$ *accepts* b. *Otherwise,* $\mathcal{C}$ *outputs* $\perp$.

Let p_b *be the probability that* $\mathcal{A}$ *makes* $\mathcal{C}$ *open* $b \in \{0,1\}$:

$$p_b := \langle\psi_b|_{RC}\mathrm{Tr}_E(U_{ER}^{(b)}|\Psi\rangle\langle\Psi|_{ERC}U_{ER}^{(b)\dagger})|\psi_b\rangle_{RC}.$$

We say that the commitment scheme is statistical sum-binding if for any unbounded $\mathcal{A}$ *there exists a negligible function* negl *such that*

$$p_0 + p_1 \leq 1 + \mathsf{negl}(\lambda).$$

3.2   Construction

Let us explain our construction of commitments.[9] Let $\mathsf{StateGen}$ be a single-copy-secure PRSG that, on input $k \in \{0,1\}^n$, outputs an m-qubit state $|\phi_k\rangle$. The commit phase is the following.

1. Let $b \in \{0,1\}$ be the bit to commit. The sender generates

$$|\psi_b\rangle := \frac{1}{\sqrt{2^{2m+n}}} \sum_{x,z\in\{0,1\}^m} \sum_{k\in\{0,1\}^n} |x,z,k\rangle_R \otimes P_{x,z}^b|\phi_k\rangle_C,$$

and sends the register C to the receiver, where $P_{x,z} := \bigotimes_{j=1}^m X_j^{x_j} Z_j^{z_j}$.

---

[9] Another example of constructions is $|\psi_0\rangle = \sum_{k\in\{0,1\}^n} |k\rangle|\phi_k\rangle$ and $|\psi_1\rangle = \sum_{r\in\{0,1\}^m} |r\rangle|r\rangle$. We have chosen the one we have explained, because the analogy to Naor's commitment scheme is clearer.

The reveal phase is the following.

1. The sender sends the register R and the bit b to the receiver.
2. The receiver measures the state with $\{|\psi_b\rangle\langle\psi_b|, I - |\psi_b\rangle\langle\psi_b|\}$. If the result is $|\psi_b\rangle\langle\psi_b|$, the receiver outputs b. Otherwise, the receiver outputs $\perp$. (Note that such a measurement can be done efficiently: first apply $V_b^\dagger$ such that $|\psi_b\rangle = V_b|0...0\rangle$, and then measure all qubits in the computational basis to see whether all results are zero or not.)

It is obvious that this construction satisfies perfect correctness (Definition 3.2).

Remark 3.1. Note that if we slightly modify the above construction, the communication in the reveal phase can be classical. In fact, we can show it for general settings. We will provide a detailed explanation of it in Appendix A. Here, we give an intuitive argument. In general non-interactive quantum commitments (Definition 3.1), the sender who wants to commit $b \in \{0,1\}$ generates a certain state $|\psi_b\rangle_{RC}$ on the registers R and C, and sends the register C to the receiver, which is the commit phase. In the reveal phase, b and the register R are sent to the receiver. The receiver runs the verification algorithm on the registers R and C. Let us modify it as follows. In the commit phase, the sender chooses uniform random $x, z \leftarrow \{0,1\}^{|R|}$ and applies $\bigotimes_{j=1}^{|R|} X_j^{x_j} Z_j^{z_j}$ on the register R of $|\psi_b\rangle_{RC}$, where $|R|$ is the number of qubits in the register R. The sender then sends both the registers R and C to the receiver. It ends the commit phase. In the reveal phase, the sender sends the bit b to open and (x, z) to the receiver. The receiver applies $\bigotimes_{j=1}^{|R|} X_j^{x_j} Z_j^{z_j}$ on the register R and runs the original verification algorithm. Hiding is clear because the register R is traced out to the receiver before the reveal phase due to the quantum one-time pad. Binding is also easy to understand: Assume a malicious sender of the modified scheme can break binding. Then, we can construct a malicious sender that breaks binding of the original scheme, because the malicious sender of the original scheme can simulate the malicious sender of the modified scheme.

Remark 3.2. We also note that our construction of commitments can be extended to more general cases where ancilla qubits are used in PRSGs. Let us consider a more general PRSG that generates $|\phi_k\rangle \otimes |\eta_k\rangle$ and outputs $|\phi_k\rangle$, where $|\eta_k\rangle$ is an ancilla state. In that case, hiding and binding hold if we replace $|\psi_b\rangle$ with

$$\frac{1}{\sqrt{2^{2m+n}}} \sum_{x,z\in\{0,1\}^m} \sum_{k\in\{0,1\}^n} (|x, z, k\rangle \otimes |\eta_k\rangle)_R \otimes P_{x,z}^b |\phi_k\rangle_C.$$

3.3 Computational Hiding

We show computational hiding of our construction.

Theorem 3.1 (Computational hiding). *Our construction satisfies computational hiding.*

Proof of Theorem 3.1. Let us consider the following security game, $\mathsf{Hyb}_0(b)$, which is the same as the original experiment.

1. The challenger $\mathcal{C}$ generates

$$|\psi_b\rangle = \frac{1}{\sqrt{2^{2m+n}}} \sum_{x,z\in\{0,1\}^m} \sum_{k\in\{0,1\}^n} |x,z,k\rangle_R \otimes P_{x,z}^b |\phi_k\rangle_C,$$

and sends the register C to the adversary $\mathcal{A}$, where $P_{x,z} := \bigotimes_{j=1}^m X_j^{x_j} Z_j^{z_j}$.
2. $\mathcal{A}$ outputs $b' \in \{0,1\}$, which is the output of this hybrid.

Let us define $\mathsf{Hyb}_1(b)$ as follows:

1. If $b = 0$, $\mathcal{C}$ chooses a Haar random m-qubit state $|\psi\rangle \leftarrow \mu_m$, and sends it to $\mathcal{A}$. If $b = 1$, $\mathcal{C}$ generates $|\psi_1\rangle_{RC}$ and sends the register C to $\mathcal{A}$.
2. $\mathcal{A}$ outputs $b' \in \{0,1\}$, which is the output of this hybrid.

Lemma 3.1.

$$|\Pr[\mathsf{Hyb}_0(b) = 1] - \Pr[\mathsf{Hyb}_1(b) = 1]| \leq \mathsf{negl}(\lambda)$$

for each $b \in \{0,1\}$.

Proof of Lemma 3.1. It is clear that

$$\Pr[\mathsf{Hyb}_0(1) = 1] = \Pr[\mathsf{Hyb}_1(1) = 1].$$

Let us show

$$|\Pr[\mathsf{Hyb}_0(0) = 1] - \Pr[\mathsf{Hyb}_1(0) = 1]| \leq \mathsf{negl}(\lambda).$$

To show it, assume that

$$|\Pr[\mathsf{Hyb}_0(0) = 1] - \Pr[\mathsf{Hyb}_1(0) = 1]|$$

is non-negligible. Then, we can construct an adversary $\mathcal{A}'$ that breaks the security of PRSGs as follows. Let $b'' \in \{0,1\}$ be the parameter of the security game of PRSGs.

1. The challenger $\mathcal{C}'$ of the security game of PRSGs sends $\mathcal{A}'$ the state $|\phi_k\rangle$ with uniform random k if $b'' = 0$ and a Haar random state $|\psi\rangle \leftarrow \mu_m$ if $b'' = 1$.
2. $\mathcal{A}'$ sends the received state to $\mathcal{A}$.
3. $\mathcal{A}'$ outputs the output of $\mathcal{A}$.

If $b'' = 0$, it simulates $\mathsf{Hyb}_0(0)$. If $b'' = 1$, it simulates $\mathsf{Hyb}_1(0)$. Therefore, $\mathcal{A}'$ breaks the security of PRSGs. $\qquad\square$

Let us define $\mathsf{Hyb}_2(b)$ as follows:

1. The challenger $\mathcal{C}$ chooses a Haar random m-qubit state $|\psi\rangle \leftarrow \mu_m$, and sends it to the adversary.

2. The adversary outputs $b' \in \{0, 1\}$, which is the output of this hybrid.

Lemma 3.2.

$$|\Pr[\mathsf{Hyb}_1(b) = 1] - \Pr[\mathsf{Hyb}_2(b) = 1]| \leq \mathsf{negl}(\lambda)$$

for each $b \in \{0, 1\}$.

Proof of Lemma 3.2.

$$\Pr[\mathsf{Hyb}_1(0) = 1] = \Pr[\mathsf{Hyb}_2(0) = 1]$$

is clear. Let us show

$$|\Pr[\mathsf{Hyb}_1(1) = 1] - \Pr[\mathsf{Hyb}_2(1) = 1]| \leq \mathsf{negl}(\lambda).$$

To show it, assume that

$$|\Pr[\mathsf{Hyb}_1(1) = 1] - \Pr[\mathsf{Hyb}_2(1) = 1]|$$

is non-negligible. Then, we can construct an adversary $\mathcal{A}'$ that breaks the security of PRSGs as follows. Let $b'' \in \{0, 1\}$ be the parameter of the security game of PRSGs.

1. The challenger $\mathcal{C}'$ of the security game of PRSGs sends $\mathcal{A}'$ the state $|\phi_k\rangle$ with uniform random k if $b'' = 0$ and a Haar random state $|\psi\rangle \leftarrow \mu_m$ if $b'' = 1$.
2. $\mathcal{A}'$ applies $X^x Z^z$ with uniform random $x, z \leftarrow \{0, 1\}^m$, and sends the state to $\mathcal{A}$.
3. $\mathcal{A}'$ outputs the output of $\mathcal{A}$.

If $b'' = 0$, it simulates $\mathsf{Hyb}_1(1)$. If $b'' = 1$, it simulates $\mathsf{Hyb}_2(1)$. Therefore, $\mathcal{A}'$ breaks the security of PRSGs.   □

It is obvious that

$$\Pr[\mathsf{Hyb}_2(0) = 1] = \Pr[\mathsf{Hyb}_2(1) = 1].$$

Therefore, from Lemma 3.1 and Lemma 3.2, we conclude

$$|\Pr[\mathsf{Hyb}_0(0) = 1] - \Pr[\mathsf{Hyb}_0(1) = 1]| \leq \mathsf{negl}(\lambda),$$

which shows Theorem 3.1.   □

3.4   Statistical Binding

Let us show that our construction satisfies statistical sum-binding.

Theorem 3.2 (Statistical sum-binding). *Our construction satisfies statistical sum-binding.*

Proof of Theorem 3.2. Let

$$F(\rho, \sigma) := \left(\text{Tr}\sqrt{\sqrt{\sigma}\rho\sqrt{\sigma}}\right)^2$$

be the fidelity between two states ρ and σ. Then we have

$$\begin{aligned}
p_b &= \langle\psi_b|_{RC}\text{Tr}_E(U_{ER}^{(b)}|\Psi\rangle\langle\Psi|_{ERC}U_{ER}^{(b)\dagger})|\psi_b\rangle_{RC}\\
&= F\left(|\psi_b\rangle_{RC}, \text{Tr}_E(U_{ER}^{(b)}|\Psi\rangle\langle\Psi|_{ERC}U_{ER}^{(b)\dagger})\right)\\
&\leq F\left(\text{Tr}_R(|\psi_b\rangle\langle\psi_b|_{RC}), \text{Tr}_{RE}(U_{ER}^{(b)}|\Psi\rangle\langle\Psi|_{ERC}U_{ER}^{(b)\dagger})\right)\\
&= F\left(\text{Tr}_R(|\psi_b\rangle\langle\psi_b|_{RC}), \text{Tr}_{RE}(|\Psi\rangle\langle\Psi|_{ERC})\right).
\end{aligned}$$

Here, we have used the facts that if $\sigma = |\sigma\rangle\langle\sigma|$, $F(\rho, \sigma) = \langle\sigma|\rho|\sigma\rangle$, and that for any bipartite states ρ_{AB}, σ_{AB}, $F(\rho_{AB}, \sigma_{AB}) \leq F(\rho_A, \sigma_A)$, where $\rho_A = \text{Tr}_B(\rho_{AB})$ and $\sigma_A = \text{Tr}_B(\sigma_{AB})$.

Therefore,

$$\begin{aligned}
p_0 + p_1 &\leq 1 + \sqrt{F\left(\text{Tr}_R(|\psi_0\rangle\langle\psi_0|_{RC}), \text{Tr}_R(|\psi_1\rangle\langle\psi_1|_{RC})\right)}\\
&= 1 + \sqrt{F\left(\frac{1}{2^n}\sum_k|\phi_k\rangle\langle\phi_k|, \frac{1}{2^{2m}}\frac{1}{2^n}\sum_{x,z}\sum_k X^x Z^z|\phi_k\rangle\langle\phi_k|X^x Z^z\right)}\\
&= 1 + \sqrt{F\left(\frac{1}{2^n}\sum_k|\phi_k\rangle\langle\phi_k|, \frac{I^{\otimes m}}{2^m}\right)}\\
&= 1 + \left\|\sum_{i=1}^{\xi}\sqrt{\lambda_i}\frac{1}{\sqrt{2^m}}|\lambda_i\rangle\langle\lambda_i|\right\|_1\\
&= 1 + \sum_{i=1}^{\xi}\sqrt{\lambda_i}\frac{1}{\sqrt{2^m}}\\
&\leq 1 + \sqrt{\sum_{i=1}^{\xi}\lambda_i}\sqrt{\sum_{i=1}^{\xi}\frac{1}{2^m}}\\
&\leq 1 + \sqrt{\frac{2^n}{2^m}}\\
&\leq 1 + \frac{1}{\sqrt{2^{(c-1)n}}}.
\end{aligned}$$

In the first inequality, we have used the fact that for any states ρ, σ, ξ,

$$F(\rho, \xi) + F(\sigma, \xi) \leq 1 + \sqrt{F(\rho, \sigma)}$$

is satisfied [NS03]. In the fourth equality, $\sum_{i=1}^{\xi}\lambda_i|\lambda_i\rangle\langle\lambda_i|$ is the diagonalization of $\frac{1}{2^n}\sum_k|\phi_k\rangle\langle\phi_k|$. In the sixth inequality, we have used Cauchy-Schwarz inequality. In the seventh inequality, we have used $\xi \leq 2^n$. In the last inequality, we have used $m \geq cn$ for a constant $c > 1$.   □

4   Digital Signatures

In this section, we provide our construction of digital signatures and show its security. For that goal, we first define OWSGs (Definition 4.1), and show that PRSGs imply OWSGs (Lemma 4.1).

4.1   One-Way Quantum States Generators

For the construction of our signature scheme, we introduce OWSGs, which are defined as follows:

Definition 4.1 (One-way quantum states generators (OWSGs)). *Let G be a QPT algorithm that, on input $k \in \{0,1\}^n$, outputs a quantum state $|\phi_k\rangle$. Let us consider the following security game, Exp, between a challenger C and a QPT adversary A:*

1. *C chooses $k \leftarrow \{0,1\}^n$.*
2. *C runs $|\phi_k\rangle \leftarrow G(k)$ $t + 1$ times.*
3. *C sends $|\phi_k\rangle^{\otimes t}$ to A.*
4. *A sends $\sigma \in \{0,1\}^n$ to C.*
5. *C measures $|\phi_k\rangle$ with $\{|\phi_\sigma\rangle\langle\phi_\sigma|, I - |\phi_\sigma\rangle\langle\phi_\sigma|\}$. If the result is $|\phi_\sigma\rangle\langle\phi_\sigma|$, the output of the experiment is 1. Otherwise, the output of the experiment is 0.*

We say that G is a one-way quantum states generator (OWSG) if for any $t = poly(n)$ and for any QPT adversary A there exists a negligible function negl such that

$$\Pr[\mathsf{Exp} = 1] \leq \mathsf{negl}(n).$$

Remark 4.1. Note that another natural definition of one-wayness is that given $|\phi_k\rangle^{\otimes t}$ it is hard to find k. However, as we will see later, it is not useful for our construction of digital signatures.

Remark 4.2. The most general form of G is as follows: on input $k \in \{0,1\}^n$, it computes a classical description of a unitary quantum circuit U_k, and applies U_k on $|0...0\rangle$ to generate $|\Phi_k\rangle_{AB} := U_k|0...0\rangle$, and outputs $\rho_k := \mathrm{Tr}_B(|\Phi_k\rangle\langle\Phi_k|_{AB})$. However, because ρ_k plays the role of a public key in our construction of digital signatures, we assume that ρ_k is pure. (It is not natural if public keys and secret keys are entangled.) In that case, $U_k|0...0\rangle = |\phi_k\rangle_A \otimes |\eta_k\rangle_B$, where $|\eta_k\rangle$ is an ancilla state. For simplicity, we assume that there is no ancilla state: $U_k|0...0\rangle = |\phi_k\rangle$. In that case, the measurement $\{|\phi_\sigma\rangle\langle\phi_\sigma|, I - |\phi_\sigma\rangle\langle\phi_\sigma|\}$ by the challenger in Definition 4.1 can be done as follows: the challenger first applies $U_\sigma^\dagger$ on the state and then measures all qubits in the computational basis. The all zero measurement result corresponds to $|\phi_\sigma\rangle\langle\phi_\sigma|$ and other results correspond to $I - |\phi_\sigma\rangle\langle\phi_\sigma|$. Even if ancilla states exist, however, the same result holds. In that case, the verification of the challenger in Definition 4.1 is modified as follows: given σ, it generates $U_\sigma|0...0\rangle = |\phi_\sigma\rangle_A \otimes |\eta_\sigma\rangle_B$ to obtain $|\eta_\sigma\rangle$, applies $U_\sigma^\dagger$ on $|\phi_k\rangle \otimes |\eta_\sigma\rangle$, and measures all qubits in the computational basis. If the result is all zero, it accepts, i.e., the output of the experiment is 1. Otherwise, it rejects.

We can show the following:

Lemma 4.1 (PRSGs imply OWSGs). *If a pseudorandom quantum states generator with $m \geq cn$ for a constant $c > 1$ exists, then a one-way quantum states generator exists.*

Proof of Lemma 4.1. Assume that $\Pr[\mathsf{Exp} = 1]$ of the security game of Definition 4.1 with $G = \mathsf{StateGen}$ is non-negligible. Then we can construct an adversary $\mathcal{A}'$ that breaks the security of PRSGs as follows. Let $b' \in \{0, 1\}$ be the parameter of the security game for PRSGs.

1. If $b' = 0$, the challenger $\mathcal{C}'$ of the security game for PRSGs chooses $k \leftarrow \{0, 1\}^n$, runs $|\phi_k\rangle \leftarrow \mathsf{StateGen}(k)$ $t + 1$ times, and sends $|\phi_k\rangle^{\otimes t+1}$ to $\mathcal{A}'$. If $b' = 1$, the challenger $\mathcal{C}'$ of the security game for PRSGs sends $t + 1$ copies of Haar random state $|\psi\rangle^{\otimes t+1}$ to $\mathcal{A}'$. In other words, $\mathcal{A}'$ receives $\rho^{\otimes t+1}$, where $\rho = |\phi_k\rangle$ if $b' = 0$ and $\rho = |\psi\rangle$ if $b' = 1$.
2. $\mathcal{A}'$ sends $\rho^{\otimes t}$ to $\mathcal{A}$.
3. $\mathcal{A}$ outputs $\sigma \in \{0, 1\}^n$.
4. $\mathcal{A}'$ measures ρ with $\{|\phi_\sigma\rangle\langle\phi_\sigma|, I - |\phi_\sigma\rangle\langle\phi_\sigma|\}$. If the result is $|\phi_\sigma\rangle\langle\phi_\sigma|$, $\mathcal{A}'$ outputs 1. Otherwise, $\mathcal{A}'$ outputs 0.

It is clear that

$$\Pr[\mathcal{A}' \to 1 | b' = 0] = \Pr[\mathsf{Exp} = 1].$$

By assumption, $\Pr[\mathsf{Exp} = 1]$ is non-negligible, and therefore $\Pr[\mathcal{A}' \to 1 | b' = 0]$ is also non-negligible. On the other hand,

$$
\begin{aligned}
\Pr[\mathcal{A}' \to 1 | b' = 1] &= \int d\mu(\psi) \sum_{\sigma \in \{0,1\}^n} \Pr[\sigma \leftarrow \mathcal{A}(|\psi\rangle^{\otimes t})] |\langle\phi_\sigma|\psi\rangle|^2 \\
&\leq \int d\mu(\psi) \sum_{\sigma \in \{0,1\}^n} |\langle\phi_\sigma|\psi\rangle|^2 \\
&= \sum_{\sigma \in \{0,1\}^n} \langle\phi_\sigma| \left[\int d\mu(\psi) |\psi\rangle\langle\psi| \right] |\phi_\sigma\rangle \\
&= \sum_{\sigma \in \{0,1\}^n} \langle\phi_\sigma| \frac{I^{\otimes m}}{2m} |\phi_\sigma\rangle \\
&\leq \frac{2^n}{2^m} \\
&\leq \frac{1}{2^{(c-1)n}}.
\end{aligned}
$$

Therefore, $\mathcal{A}'$ breaks the security of PRSGs.   □

Remark 4.3. For simplicity, Lemma 4.1 considers the case when no ancilla state exists in PRSGs. It is easy to see that Lemma 4.1 can be generalized to the case when PRSGs have ancilla states: on input $k \in \{0, 1\}^n$, a PRSG applies U_k on

$|0...0\rangle$ to generate $U_k|0...0\rangle = |\phi_k\rangle \otimes |\eta_k\rangle$, where $|\phi_k\rangle$ is the output of the PRSG and $|\eta_k\rangle$ is an ancilla state. In that case, we modify Definition 4.1 in such a way that the verification of the challenger is modified as follows: given σ, it generates $U_\sigma|0...0\rangle = |\phi_\sigma\rangle \otimes |\eta_\sigma\rangle$ to obtain $|\eta_\sigma\rangle$, applies $U_\sigma^\dagger$ on $|\phi_k\rangle \otimes |\eta_\sigma\rangle$, and measures all qubits in the computational basis. If the result is all zero, it accepts, i.e., the output of the experiment is 1.

4.2   Definition of Digital Signatures with Quantum Public Keys

We now formally define digital signatures with quantum public keys:

Definition 4.2 (Digital signatures with quantum public keys (Syntax)). *A signature scheme with quantum public keys is the set of algorithms* $(\mathsf{Gen}_1, \mathsf{Gen}_2, \mathsf{Sign}, \mathsf{Verify})$ *such that*

- $\mathsf{Gen}_1(1^\lambda)$: *It is a classical PPT algorithm that, on input the security parameter* 1^λ, *outputs a classical secret key* sk.
- $\mathsf{Gen}_2(sk)$: *It is a QPT algorithm that, on input the secret key* sk, *outputs a quantum public key* pk.
- $\mathsf{Sign}(sk, m)$: *It is a classical deterministic polynomial-time algorithm that, on input the secret key* sk *and a message* m, *outputs a classical signature* σ.
- $\mathsf{Verify}(pk, m, \sigma)$: *It is a QPT algorithm that, on input a public key* pk, *the message* m, *and the signature* σ, *outputs* $\top/\bot$.

The perfect correctness is defines as follows:

Definition 4.3 (Perfect correctness). *We say that a signature scheme satisfies perfect correctness if*

$$\Pr[\top \leftarrow \mathsf{Verify}(pk, m, \sigma) : sk \leftarrow \mathsf{Gen}_1(1^\lambda), pk \leftarrow \mathsf{Gen}_2(sk), \sigma \leftarrow \mathsf{Sign}(sk, m)] = 1$$

for all messages m.

The one-time security is defined as follows:

Definition 4.4 (One-time security of digital signatures with quantum public keys). *Let us consider the following security game,* Exp, *between a challenger* $\mathcal{C}$ *and a QPT adversary* $\mathcal{A}$:

1. $\mathcal{C}$ *runs* $sk \leftarrow \mathsf{Gen}_1(1^\lambda)$.
2. $\mathcal{A}$ *can query* $pk \leftarrow \mathsf{Gen}_2(sk)$ *poly*(λ) *times.*
3. $\mathcal{A}$ *sends a message* m *to* $\mathcal{C}$.
4. $\mathcal{C}$ *runs* $\sigma \leftarrow \mathsf{Sign}(sk, m)$, *and sends* σ *to* $\mathcal{A}$.
5. $\mathcal{A}$ *sends* σ' *and* m' *to* $\mathcal{C}$.
6. $\mathcal{C}$ *runs* $v \leftarrow \mathsf{Verify}(pk, m', \sigma')$. *If* $m' \neq m$ *and* $v = \top$, $\mathcal{C}$ *outputs 1. Otherwise,* $\mathcal{C}$ *outputs 0. This* $\mathcal{C}$'s *output is the output of the game.*

A signature scheme with quantum public keys is one-time secure if for any QPT adversary $\mathcal{A}$ *there exists a negligible function* negl *such that*

$$\Pr[\mathsf{Exp} = 1] \leq \mathsf{negl}(\lambda).$$

4.3   Construction

Let G be a OWSG. Our construction of a one-time secure signature scheme with quantum public keys is as follows. (For simplicity, we consider the case when the message space is $\{0,1\}$.)

– $\mathsf{Gen}_1(1^n)$: Choose $k_0, k_1 \leftarrow \{0,1\}^n$. Output $sk := (sk_0, sk_1)$, where $sk_b := k_b$ for $b \in \{0,1\}$.
– $\mathsf{Gen}_2(sk)$: Run $|\phi_{k_b}\rangle \leftarrow G(k_b)$ for $b \in \{0,1\}$. Output $pk := (pk_0, pk_1)$, where $pk_b := |\phi_{k_b}\rangle$ for $b \in \{0,1\}$.
– $\mathsf{Sign}(sk, m)$: Output $\sigma := sk_m$.
– $\mathsf{Verify}(pk, m, \sigma)$: Measure pk_m with $\{|\phi_\sigma\rangle\langle\phi_\sigma|, I - |\phi_\sigma\rangle\langle\phi_\sigma|\}$, and output $\top$ if the result is $|\phi_\sigma\rangle\langle\phi_\sigma|$. Otherwise, output $\bot$.

It is clear that this construction satisfies perfect correctness (Definition 4.3).

4.4   Security

Let us show the security of our construction.

Theorem 4.1. *Our construction of a signature scheme is one-time secure.*

Proof of Theorem 4.1. Let us consider the following security game, Exp, between the challenger $\mathcal{C}$ and a QPT adversary $\mathcal{A}$:

1. $\mathcal{C}$ chooses $k_0, k_1 \leftarrow \{0,1\}^n$.
2. $\mathcal{A}$ can query $|\phi_{k_b}\rangle \leftarrow G(k_b)$ $poly(n)$ times for $b \in \{0,1\}$.
3. $\mathcal{A}$ sends m to $\mathcal{C}$.
4. $\mathcal{C}$ sends k_m to $\mathcal{A}$.
5. $\mathcal{A}$ sends σ to $\mathcal{C}$.
6. $\mathcal{C}$ measures $|\phi_{k_{m\oplus 1}}\rangle$ with $\{|\phi_\sigma\rangle\langle\phi_\sigma|, I - |\phi_\sigma\rangle\langle\phi_\sigma|\}$. If the result is $|\phi_\sigma\rangle\langle\phi_\sigma|$, $\mathcal{C}$ outputs 1. Otherwise, $\mathcal{C}$ outputs 0. This $\mathcal{C}$'s output is the output of the game.

Assume that our construction is not one-time secure, which means that $\Pr[\mathsf{Exp} = 1]$ is non-negligible for an adversary $\mathcal{A}$ who queries both $\mathsf{Gen}_2(sk_0)$ and $\mathsf{Gen}_2(sk_1)$ $s = poly(n)$ times. (Without loss of generality, we can assume that the numbers of $\mathcal{A}$'s queries to $\mathsf{Gen}_2(sk_0)$ and $\mathsf{Gen}_2(sk_1)$ are the same. An adversary who queries to $\mathsf{Gen}_2(sk_0)$ s_0 times and to $\mathsf{Gen}_2(sk_1)$ s_1 times can be simulated by another adversary who queries to both $\mathsf{Gen}_2(sk_0)$ and $\mathsf{Gen}_2(sk_1)$ $s := \max(s_0, s_1)$ times.) Then, we can construct an adversary that breaks the security of OWSG G as follows. Let $\mathcal{C}'$ and $\mathcal{A}'$ be the challenger and the adversary of the security game of G, respectively.

1. $\mathcal{C}'$ chooses $k \leftarrow \{0,1\}^n$. $\mathcal{C}'$ runs $|\phi_k\rangle \leftarrow G(k)$ $s+1$ times. $\mathcal{C}'$ sends $|\phi_k\rangle^{\otimes s}$ to $\mathcal{A}'$.
2. $\mathcal{A}'$ chooses $r \leftarrow \{0,1\}$. $\mathcal{A}'$ chooses $k' \leftarrow \{0,1\}^n$. $\mathcal{A}'$ runs $|\phi_{k'}\rangle \leftarrow G(k')$ s times. If $r = 0$, $\mathcal{A}'$ returns $(|\phi_k\rangle^{\otimes s}, |\phi_{k'}\rangle^{\otimes s})$ to the query of $\mathcal{A}$. If $r = 1$, $\mathcal{A}'$ returns $(|\phi_{k'}\rangle^{\otimes s}, |\phi_k\rangle^{\otimes s})$ to the query of $\mathcal{A}$.
3. $\mathcal{A}$ sends $m \in \{0,1\}$ to $\mathcal{A}'$.

4. If $r = m$, $\mathcal{A}'$ aborts. If $r \neq m$, $\mathcal{A}'$ sends k' to $\mathcal{A}$.
5. $\mathcal{A}$ sends σ to $\mathcal{A}'$.
6. $\mathcal{A}'$ sends σ to $\mathcal{C}'$.
7. $\mathcal{C}'$ measures $|\phi_k\rangle$ with $\{|\phi_\sigma\rangle\langle\phi_\sigma|, I - |\phi_\sigma\rangle\langle\phi_\sigma|\}$. If the result is $|\phi_\sigma\rangle\langle\phi_\sigma|$, $\mathcal{C}'$ outputs 1. Otherwise, $\mathcal{C}'$ outputs 0.

By a straightforward calculation, which is given below,

$$\Pr[\mathcal{C}' \to 1] = \frac{1}{2}\Pr[\mathsf{Exp} = 1]. \tag{1}$$

Therefore, if $\Pr[\mathsf{Exp} = 1]$ is non-negligible, $\Pr[\mathcal{C}' \to 1]$ is also non-negligible, which means that $\mathcal{A}'$ breaks the security of G.

Let us show Eq. (1). In fact,

$$
\begin{aligned}
\Pr[\mathcal{C}' \to 1] &= \frac{1}{2^{2n}} \sum_{k,k' \in \{0,1\}^n} \frac{1}{2}\Pr[1 \leftarrow \mathcal{A}(|\phi_k\rangle^{\otimes s}, |\phi_{k'}\rangle^{\otimes s})]\Pr[\sigma \leftarrow \mathcal{A}(k')]|\langle\phi_\sigma|\phi_k\rangle|^2 \\
&\quad + \frac{1}{2^{2n}} \sum_{k,k' \in \{0,1\}^n} \frac{1}{2}\Pr[0 \leftarrow \mathcal{A}(|\phi_{k'}\rangle^{\otimes s}, |\phi_k\rangle^{\otimes s})]\Pr[\sigma \leftarrow \mathcal{A}(k')]|\langle\phi_\sigma|\phi_k\rangle|^2 \\
&= \frac{1}{2^{2n}} \sum_{k,k' \in \{0,1\}^n} \frac{1}{2}\Pr[1 \leftarrow \mathcal{A}(|\phi_k\rangle^{\otimes s}, |\phi_{k'}\rangle^{\otimes s})]\Pr[\sigma \leftarrow \mathcal{A}(k')]|\langle\phi_\sigma|\phi_k\rangle|^2 \\
&\quad + \frac{1}{2^{2n}} \sum_{k,k' \in \{0,1\}^n} \frac{1}{2}\Pr[0 \leftarrow \mathcal{A}(|\phi_k\rangle^{\otimes s}, |\phi_{k'}\rangle^{\otimes s})]\Pr[\sigma \leftarrow \mathcal{A}(k)]|\langle\phi_\sigma|\phi_{k'}\rangle|^2 \\
&= \frac{1}{2}\Pr[\mathsf{Exp} = 1].
\end{aligned}
$$

$\square$

Remark 4.4. For simplicity, we have assumed that the OWSG G does not have any ancilla state. We can extend the result to the case when G has ancilla states. In that case, the verification algorithm in our construction of digital signatures is modified as follows: Given σ, first generate $U_\sigma|0...0\rangle = |\phi_\sigma\rangle \otimes |\eta_\sigma\rangle$. Then run $U_\sigma^\dagger$ on $pk_m \otimes |\eta_\sigma\rangle$, and measures all qubits in the computational basis. If all results are zero, output $\top$. Otherwise, output $\bot$. It is easy to check that a similar proof holds for the security of this generalized version.

Acknowledgements. TM is supported by JST Moonshot R&D JPMJMS2061-5-1-1, JST FOREST, MEXT QLEAP, the Grant-in-Aid for Scientific Research (B) No. JP19H04066, the Grant-in Aid for Transformative Research Areas (A) 21H05183, and the Grant-in-Aid for Scientific Research (A) No. 22H00522.

A   Making Opening Message Classical

In this Appendix, we show that general quantum non-interactive commitments can be modified so that the opening message is classical.

Let us consider the following general non-interactive quantum commitments:

- **Commit phase:** The sender who wants to commit $b \in \{0,1\}$ generates a certain state $|\psi_b\rangle_{RC}$ on the registers R and C. The sender sends the register C to the receiver.
- **Reveal phase:** The sender sends b and the register R to the receiver. The receiver runs a certain verification algorithm on the registers R and C.

Let us modify it as follows:

- **Commit phase:** The sender who wants to commit $b \in \{0,1\}$ chooses $x, z \leftarrow \{0,1\}^{|R|}$, and generates the state

$$[(X^x Z^z)_R \otimes I_C]|\psi_b\rangle_{RC},$$

where $|R|$ is the size of the register R. The sender sends the registers R and C to the receiver.
- **Reveal phase:** The sender sends (x, z) and b to the receiver. The receiver applies $(X^x Z^z)_R \otimes I_C$ on the state, and runs the original verification algorithm on the registers R and C.

Theorem A.1. *If the original commitment scheme is computationally hiding and statistically sum-binding, then the modified commitment scheme is also computationally hiding and statistically sum-binding.*

Proof. Let us first show hiding. Hiding is clear because what the receiver has after the commit phase in the modified scheme is $\frac{I^{\otimes |R|}}{2^{|R|}} \otimes \mathrm{Tr}_R(|\psi_b\rangle\langle\psi_b|_{RC})$, which is the same as that in the original scheme.

Next let us show binding. Biding is also easy to understand. The most general action of a malicious sender in the modified scheme is as follows.

1. The sender generates a state $|\Psi\rangle_{ERC}$ on the three registers E, R, and C. The sender sends the registers R and C to the receiver.
2. Given $b \in \{0,1\}$, the sender computes $(x, z) \in \{0,1\}^{|R|} \times \{0,1\}^{|R|}$. The sender sends (x, z) and b to the receiver.
3. The receiver applies $X^x Z^z$ on the register R.
4. The receiver runs the verification algorithm on the registers R and C.

Assume that this attack breaks sum-binding of the modified scheme. Then we can construct an attack that breaks sum-binding of the original scheme as follows:

1. The sender generates a state $|\Psi\rangle_{ERC}$ on the three registers E, R, and C. The sender sends the register C to the receiver.
2. Given $b \in \{0,1\}$, the sender computes (x, z) and applies $X^x Z^z$ on the register R. The sender sends the register R, b, and (x, z) to the receiver.
3. The receiver runs the verification algorithm on the registers R and C.

It is easy to check that the two states on which the receiver applies the verification algorithm are the same. □

B Equivalence of Binding Properties

In this paper, we adopt sum-binding (Definition 3.4) as a definition of binding property of commitment schemes. On the other hand, the concurrent work by Ananth et al. [AQY21] introduces a seemingly stronger definition of binding, which we call AQY-binding, and shows that their commitment scheme satisfies it. The advantage of the AQY-binding is that it naturally fits into the security analysis of oblivious transfer in [BCKM21]. That is, a straightforward adaptation of the proofs in [BCKM21] enables us to prove that a commitment scheme satisfying AQY-binding and computational hiding implies the existence of oblivious transfer and multi-party computation (MPC). Combined with their construction of an AQY-binding and computational hiding commitment scheme from PRSGs, they show that PRSGs imply oblivious transfer and MPC.

We found that it is already implicitly shown in [FUYZ20] that the sum-binding and AQY-binding are equivalent for non-interactive commitment schemes in a certain form called the *generic form* as defined in [YWLQ15, Yan20, FUYZ20].[10] Since our commitment scheme is in the generic form, we can conclude that our commitment scheme also satisfies AQY-binding, and thus can be used for constructing oblivious transfer and MPC based on [BCKM21]. We explain this in more detail below.

Commitment Schemes in the General Form. We say that a commitment scheme is in the general form if it works as follows over registers (C, R).

1. In the commit phase, for generating a commitment to $b \in \{0, 1\}$, the sender applies a unitary Q_b on $|0...0\rangle_C \otimes |0...0\rangle_R$ and sends the C register to the receiver.
2. In the reveal phase, the sender sends the R register along with the revealed bit b. Then, the receiver applies $Q_b^\dagger$, measures both C and R in the computational basis, and accepts if the measurement outcome is $0...0$.

See [Yan20, Definition 2] for the more formal definition. Yan [Yan20, Theorem 1] showed that for commitment schemes in the general form, the sum-binding is equivalent to the *honest-binding*, which means $F(\sigma_0, \sigma_1) = \mathsf{negl}(\lambda)$, where F is the fidelity and σ_b is the honestly generated commitment to b for $b \in \{0, 1\}$, i.e., $\sigma_b := \mathrm{Tr}_R(Q_b|0...0\rangle\langle0...0|_{RC}Q_b^\dagger)$.

AQY-Binding. Roughly speaking, the AQY-binding requires that there is an (inefficient) extractor $\mathcal{E}$ that extracts a committed message from the commitment and satisfies the following: We define the following two experiments between a (possibly dishonest) sender and the honest receiver:

Real Experiment: In this experiment, the sender and receiver run the commit and reveal phases, and the experiment returns the sender's final state ρ_S and the revealed bit b, which is defined to be $\perp$ if the receiver rejects.

---

[10] We remark that it is also noted in [AQY21, Remark 6.2] that they are "probably equivalent".

Ideal Experiment: In this experiment, after the sender sends a commitment, the extractor $\mathcal{E}$ extracts b' from the commitment. After that, the sender reveals the commitment and the receiver verifiers it. Let b be the revealed bit, which is defined to be $\perp$ if the receiver rejects. The experiment returns (ρ_S, b) if $b = b'$ and otherwise $(\rho_S, \perp)$ where ρ_S is sender's final state.

Then we require that for any (unbounded-time) malicious sender, outputs of the real and ideal experiments are statistically indistinguishable. See [AQY21, Definition 6.1] for the formal definition.

Sum-Binding and AQY-Binding are Equivalent. First, it is easy to see that AQY-binding implies sum-binding. By the AQY-binding, we can see that a malicious sender can reveal a commitment to $b \in \{0, 1\}$ only if $\mathcal{E}$ extracts b except for a negligible probability. Moreover, it is clear that $\Pr[\mathcal{E} \text{ extracts } 0] + \Pr[\mathcal{E} \text{ extracts } 1] \leq 1$ for any fixed commitment. Thus, the sum-binding follows.

We observe that the other direction is implicitly shown in [FUYZ20] as explained below. As already mentioned, the sum-binding is equivalent to honest-binding. For simplicity, we start by considering the case of perfectly honest-binding, i.e., $F(\sigma_0, \sigma_1) = 0$.

First, as shown in [FUYZ20, Corollary 4], there is an (inefficient) measurement (Π_0, Π_1) that perfectly distinguishes σ_0 and σ_1 since we assume $F(\sigma_0, \sigma_1) = 0$. Then, we can define the extractor $\mathcal{E}$ for the AQY-binding as an algorithm that just applies the measurement (Π_0, Π_1) and outputs the corresponding bit b. It is shown in [FUYZ20, Lemma 6] that the final joint state over sender's and receiver's registers does not change even if we apply the measurement (Π_0, Π_1) to the commitment before the reveal phase conditioned on that the receiver accepts. In the case of rejection, note that the revealed bit is treated as $\perp$ in the experiment for the AQY-binding. Moreover, the measurement on the commitment register does not affect sender's final state since no information is sent from the receiver to the sender. By combining the above observations, the joint distribution of the sender's final state and the revealed bit does not change even if we measure the commitment in (Π_0, Π_1). This means that the AQY-binding is satisfied.

For the non-perfectly honest-binding case, i.e., $F(\sigma_0, \sigma_1) = \mathsf{negl}(\lambda)$, we can rely on the perturbation technique. It is shown in [FUYZ20, Lemma 8] that for a non-perfectly honest-binding commitments characterized by unitaries (Q_0, Q_1), there exist unitaries $(\tilde{Q}_0, \tilde{Q}_1)$ that characterize a perfectly honest-binding commitment scheme and are close to (Q_0, Q_1) in the sense that replacing (Q_0, Q_1) with $(\tilde{Q}_0, \tilde{Q}_1)$ in any experiment only negligibly changes the output as long as the experiment calls (Q_0, Q_1) or $(\tilde{Q}_0, \tilde{Q}_1)$ polynomially many times. By using this, we can reduce the AQY-binding property of non-perfectly honest-binding commitment schemes to that of perfectly honest-binding commitment schemes with a negligible security loss.

References

[AQY21]   Ananth, P., Qian, L., Yuen, H.: Cryptography from pseudorandom quantum states. IACR Cryptol. ePrint Arch. **2021**, 1663 (2021)

[BB84]   Bennett, C.H., Brassard, G.: Quantum cryptography: public key distribution and coin tossing. In: IEEE International Conference on Computers Systems and Signal Processing, pp. 175–179. IEEE (1984)

[BB21]   Bitansky, N., Brakerski, Z.: Classical binding for quantum commitments. In: Nissim, K., Waters, B. (eds.) TCC 2021. LNCS, vol. 13042, pp. 273–298. Springer, Cham (2021). https://doi.org/10.1007/978-3-030-90459-3_10

[BBCS92] Bennett, C.H., Brassard, G., Crépeau, C., Skubiszewska, M.-H.: Practical quantum oblivious transfer. In: Feigenbaum, J. (ed.) CRYPTO 1991. LNCS, vol. 576, pp. 351–366. Springer, Heidelberg (1992). https://doi.org/10.1007/3-540-46766-1_29

[BCKM21] Bartusek, J., Coladangelo, A., Khurana, D., Ma, F.: One-way functions imply secure computation in a quantum world. In: Malkin, T., Peikert, C. (eds.) CRYPTO 2021. LNCS, vol. 12825, pp. 467–496. Springer, Cham (2021). https://doi.org/10.1007/978-3-030-84242-0_17

[Blu81]   Blum, M.: Coin flipping by telephone. In: CRYPTO 1981, volume ECE Report 82–04, pp. 11–15 (1981)

[BS19]   Brakerski, Z., Shmueli, O.: (Pseudo) random quantum states with binary phase. In: Hofheinz, D., Rosen, A. (eds.) TCC 2019, Part I. LNCS, vol. 11891, pp. 229–250. Springer, Cham (2019). https://doi.org/10.1007/978-3-030-36030-6_10

[BS20]   Brakerski, Z., Shmueli, O.: Scalable pseudorandom quantum states. In: Micciancio, D., Ristenpart, T. (eds.) CRYPTO 2020, Part II. LNCS, vol. 12171, pp. 417–440. Springer, Cham (2020). https://doi.org/10.1007/978-3-030-56880-1_15

[CK88]   Crépeau, C., Kilian, J.: Achieving oblivious transfer using weakened security assumptions (extended abstract). In: 29th FOCS, pp. 42–52 (1988)

[CLS01]   Crépeau, C., Légaré, F., Salvail, L.: How to convert the flavor of a quantum bit commitment. In: Pfitzmann, B. (ed.) EUROCRYPT 2001. LNCS, vol. 2045, pp. 60–77. Springer, Heidelberg (2001). https://doi.org/10.1007/3-540-44987-6_5

[DFL+09] Damgård, I., Fehr, S., Lunemann, C., Salvail, L., Schaffner, C.: Improving the security of quantum protocols via commit-and-open. In: Halevi, S. (ed.) CRYPTO 2009. LNCS, vol. 5677, pp. 408–427. Springer, Heidelberg (2009). https://doi.org/10.1007/978-3-642-03356-8_24

[DH76]   Diffie, W., Hellman, M.E.: New directions in cryptography. IEEE Trans. Inf. Theory **22**(6), 644–654 (1976)

[DMS00]   Dumais, P., Mayers, D., Salvail, L.: Perfectly concealing quantum bit commitment from any quantum one-way permutation. In: Preneel, B. (ed.) EUROCRYPT 2000. LNCS, vol. 1807, pp. 300–315. Springer, Heidelberg (2000). https://doi.org/10.1007/3-540-45539-6_21

[Dol21]   Doliskani, J.: Efficient quantum public-key encryption from learning with errors. arXiv:2105.12790 (2021)

[FUYZ20] Fang, J., Unruh, D., Yan, J., Zhou, D.: How to base security on the perfect/statistical binding property of quantum bit commitment? Cryptology ePrint Archive: Report 2020/621 (2020)

[GC01]   Gottesman, D., Chuang, I.L.: Quantum digital signatures. arXiv:quant-ph/0105032 (2001)

[GLSV21] Grilo, A.B., Lin, H., Song, F., Vaikuntanathan, V.: Oblivious transfer is in MiniQCrypt. In: Canteaut, A., Standaert, F.-X. (eds.) EUROCRYPT 2021. LNCS, vol. 12697, pp. 531–561. Springer, Cham (2021). https://doi.org/10.1007/978-3-030-77886-6_18

[HILL99] Håstad, J., Impagliazzo, R., Levin, L.A., Luby, M.: A pseudorandom generator from any one-way function. SIAM J. Comput. **28**(4), 1364–1396 (1999)

[IL89]   Impagliazzo, R., Luby, M.: One-way functions are essential for complexity based cryptography (extended abstract). In: 30th FOCS, pp. 230–235 (1989)

[ILL89]   Impagliazzo, R., Levin, L.A., Luby, M.: Pseudo-random generation from one-way functions (extended abstracts). In: 21st ACM STOC, pp. 12–24 (1989)

[IR90]   Impagliazzo, R., Rudich, S.: Limits on the provable consequences of one-way permutations. In: Goldwasser, S. (ed.) CRYPTO 1988. LNCS, vol. 403, pp. 8–26. Springer, New York (1990). https://doi.org/10.1007/0-387-34799-2_2

[JLS18]   Ji, Z., Liu, Y.-K., Song, F.: Pseudorandom quantum states. In: Shacham, H., Boldyreva, A. (eds.) CRYPTO 2018, Part III. LNCS, vol. 10993, pp. 126–152. Springer, Cham (2018). https://doi.org/10.1007/978-3-319-96878-0_5

[KKNY12] Kawachi, A., Koshiba, T., Nishimura, H., Yamakami, T.: Computational indistinguishability between quantum states and its cryptographic application. J. Cryptol. **25**(3), 528–555 (2011). https://doi.org/10.1007/s00145-011-9103-4

[KO09]   Koshiba, T., Odaira, T.: Statistically-hiding quantum bit commitment from approximable-preimage-size quantum one-way function. In: Childs, A., Mosca, M. (eds.) TQC 2009. LNCS, vol. 5906, pp. 33–46. Springer, Heidelberg (2009). https://doi.org/10.1007/978-3-642-10698-9_4

[KO11]   Koshiba, T., Odaira, T.: Non-interactive statistically-hiding quantum bit commitment from any quantum one-way function. arXiv:1102.3441 (2011)

[Kre21]   Kretschmer, W.: Quantum pseudorandomness and classical complexity. In: TQC 2021 (2021)

[LC97]   Lo, H.-K., Chau, H.F.: Is quantum bit commitment really possible? Phys. Rev. Lett. **78**, 3410–3413 (1997)

[LR86]   Luby, M., Rackoff, C.: Pseudo-random permutation generators and cryptographic composition. In: 18th ACM STOC, pp. 356–363 (1986)

[May97]   Mayers, D.: Unconditionally secure quantum bit commitment is impossible. Phys. Rev. Lett. **78**, 3414–3417 (1997)

[Mer90]   Merkle, R.C.: A certified digital signature. In: Brassard, G. (ed.) CRYPTO 1989. LNCS, vol. 435, pp. 218–238. Springer, New York (1990). https://doi.org/10.1007/0-387-34805-0_21

[MP12]   Micciancio, D., Peikert, C.: Trapdoors for lattices: simpler, tighter, faster, smaller. In: Pointcheval, D., Johansson, T. (eds.) EUROCRYPT 2012. LNCS, vol. 7237, pp. 700–718. Springer, Heidelberg (2012). https://doi.org/10.1007/978-3-642-29011-4_41

[MS94]   Mayers, D., Salvail, L.: Quantum oblivious transfer is secure against all individual measurements. In: Proceedings Workshop on Physics and Computation, PhysComp 1994, pp. 69–77. IEEE (1994)

[Nao91] Naor, M.: Bit commitment using pseudorandomness. J. Cryptol. **4**(2), 151–158 (1991). https://doi.org/10.1007/BF00196774

[NS03] Nayak, A., Shor, P.: Bit-commitment-based quantum coin flipping. Phys. Rev. A **67**, 012304 (2003)

[Unr16] Unruh, D.: Collapse-binding quantum commitments without random oracles. In: Cheon, J.H., Takagi, T. (eds.) ASIACRYPT 2016, Part II. LNCS, vol. 10032, pp. 166–195. Springer, Heidelberg (2016). https://doi.org/10.1007/978-3-662-53890-6_6

[Yan20] Yan, J.: General properties of quantum bit commitments. Cryptology ePrint Archive: Report 2020/1488 (2020)

[Yao95] Yao, A.C.-C.: Security of quantum protocols against coherent measurements. In: 27th ACM STOC, pp. 67–75 (1995)

[YWLQ15] Yan, J., Weng, J., Lin, D., Quan, Y.: Quantum bit commitment with application in quantum zero-knowledge proof (extended abstract). In: Elbassioni, K., Makino, K. (eds.) ISAAC 2015. LNCS, vol. 9472, pp. 555–565. Springer, Heidelberg (2015). https://doi.org/10.1007/978-3-662-48971-0_47

Semi-quantum Tokenized Signatures

Omri Shmueli$^{(\boxtimes)}$

Tel Aviv University, Tel Aviv, Israel
omrishmueli@mail.tau.ac.il

Abstract. Quantum tokenized signature schemes (Ben-David and Sattath, QCrypt 2017) allow a sender to generate and distribute quantum unclonable states which grant their holder a one-time permission to sign in the name of the sender. Such schemes are a strengthening of public-key quantum money schemes, as they imply public-key quantum money where some channels of communication in the system can be made classical.

An even stronger primitive is semi-quantum tokenized signatures, where the sender is classical and can delegate the generation of the token to a (possibly malicious) quantum receiver. Semi-quantum tokenized signature schemes imply a powerful version of public-key quantum money satisfying two key features:
- The bank is classical and the scheme can execute on a completely classical communication network. In addition, the bank is *stateless* and after the creation of a banknote, does not hold any information nor trapdoors except the balance of accounts in the system. Such quantum money scheme solves the main open problem presented by Radian and Sattath (AFT 2019).
- Furthermore, the classical-communication transactions between users in the system are *direct* and do not need to go through the bank. This enables the transactions to be both classical and private.

While fully-quantum tokenized signatures (where the sender is quantum and generates the token by itself) are known based on quantum-secure indistinguishability obfuscation and injective one-way functions, the semi-quantum version is not known under any computational assumption. In this work we construct a semi-quantum tokenized signature scheme based on quantum-secure indistinguishability obfuscation and the subexponential hardness of the Learning with Errors problem. In the process, we show new properties of quantum coset states and a new hardness result on indistinguishability obfuscation of classical subspace membership circuits.

1 Introduction

Quantum money schemes are one of the basis pillars in quantum cryptography, allowing a bank to distribute quantum unclonable states in a system of users, who

The full version of this work can be found at https://eprint.iacr.org/2022/228.

O. Shmueli—Supported by ISF grants 18/484 and 19/2137, by Len Blavatnik and the Blavatnik Family Foundation, by the European Union Horizon 2020 Research and Innovation Program via ERC Project REACT (Grant 756482), and by the Clore Israel Foundation.

Y. Dodis and T. Shrimpton (Eds.): CRYPTO 2022, LNCS 13507, pp. 296–319, 2022.
https://doi.org/10.1007/978-3-031-15802-5_11

can trade the states as currency. The gold standard of quantum money requires the scheme to be *public-key* [2], including two quantum algorithms, Bank and QV, with the following syntax: Bank samples a quantum token $(pk, |qt\rangle_{pk}) \leftarrow$ Bank, where $|qt\rangle_{pk}$ is a quantum state and pk is a classical public verification key. pk can be distributed in the user network and the quantum part $|qt\rangle_{pk}$ can be sent to some specific user. The copy of $|qt\rangle_{pk}$ can then be passed around between users in the system, and be publicly verified with QV using the key pk. The core security guarantee assures that tokens are unclonable by anyone but the bank, or even more tightly, no user can generate two states that both pass the quantum verification $QV(\cdot, pk)$.

By combining intrinsic properties of quantum information with cryptographic techniques, public-key quantum money holds great promise for the future of information technology. Such quantum cryptographic schemes implement functionalities that are *known to be impossible* in a world where only classical computation exists and also create a basis of techniques towards even more advanced primitives, like quantum lightning [8] and quantum copy-protection of programs [1]. Notably, public-key quantum money gives a solution to the problem of privacy in a currency system, where we want a system that is both, secure (a banknote keeps its value and cannot be counterfeited) and private (transaction's information can be kept only to the two parties involved, in particular, the bank does not have to know).

Unfortunately, by the standard definition, to execute a quantum money scheme we need quantum computation to generate and verify tokens, and quantum communication to transfer tokens between devices[1]. Ideally, however, we would like to minimize the required model, and use quantum computation and only *classical* communication - more precisely, making the communication classical while keeping the key advantages of quantum money (e.g. privacy of transactions) is a central open problem in quantum cryptography. Besides the intriguing theoretical question and the fact that there is a fundamental difference between classical and quantum communication[2], practical differences include (1) the fact that a classical communication network can be based on *information broadcasting* (which uses information cloning to execute), which in particular enables communication between mobile devices, and (2) that transactions based on classical communication has the potential to provide *proof of payment*, as the clonable classical transcript can serve as a proof.

Looking more closely on the classical communication problem, there are three directions of communication in a token system: (1) from the bank to a user,

---

[1] Note that quantum teleportation is a known technique to transfer quantum information using classical communication channels. However, assuming no available quantum channel, physical contact is required to distribute the entangled EPR pairs that are used for teleporting the quantum data.

[2] e.g. classical information is more stable and classical communication is likely to be more efficient, as a consequence of the better algorithmic efficiency and lower rate of classical error correcting codes, compared to their quantum counterparts.

(2) from a user to another user, and (3) from a user to the bank. It is a known fact that the classical communication problem can be partially solved, by getting stronger no-cloning guarantees. Specifically, there are three known levels of no-cloning security for the quantum tokens. These levels enable increased classical communication, as we will later see.

1. **No Cloning:** The most basic security level of a quantum token is unclonability. No cloning says that a quantum polynomial-time malicious receiver Rec^* that obtains a single token $(\mathsf{pk}, |\mathsf{qt}\rangle_{\mathsf{pk}})$ cannot output two quantum states $|\mathsf{qt}_1\rangle, |\mathsf{qt}_2\rangle$, such that both pass the public quantum verification $\mathsf{QV}(\cdot, \mathsf{pk})$.

2. **Classically Certifiable Destruction:** The next, stronger guarantee is classically certifiable destruction (CCD). In this version, along with Bank, QV, there are two additional algorithms; a quantum algorithm GenCert and a classical algorithm CV. While QV allows to publicly verify quantum tokens as before, GenCert allows to destroy the quantum token and output crt, a classical certificate of destruction for it. This certificate can later be verified by the classical verification algorithm CV using the public key pk.
   CCD security says that no adversary Rec^* can get a single token $(\mathsf{pk}, |\mathsf{qt}\rangle_{\mathsf{pk}})$ and output both, a quantum token $|\mathsf{qt}\rangle'$ that passes the verification of $\mathsf{QV}(\cdot, \mathsf{pk})$ and crt a classical certificate for its destruction that passes the classical verification of $\mathsf{CV}(\cdot, \mathsf{pk})$. Note that this guarantee is at least as strong as the previous no-cloning, because as part of the correctness of schemes with CCD, for any quantum token $|\mathsf{qt}\rangle'$ that passes the verification $\mathsf{QV}(\cdot, \mathsf{pk})$, a valid classical certificate of destruction crt that passes $\mathsf{CV}(\cdot, \mathsf{pk})$ can be generated (thus two copies of the quantum token imply one quantum token and one classical certificate of destruction for it).

3. **Tokenized Signing:** The third and strongest known level of no-cloning security is tokenized signing. In such scheme like before we have Bank, QV, GenCert, CV, except that now GenCert gets not only the quantum token $(\mathsf{pk}, |\mathsf{qt}\rangle_{\mathsf{pk}})$, but also a bit $b \in \{0,1\}$. The bit b acts as a target for the destruction process. Specifically, given $(\mathsf{pk}, |\mathsf{qt}\rangle_{\mathsf{pk}})$ and $b \in \{0,1\}$, the algorithm generates $\mathsf{crt}_b \leftarrow \mathsf{GenCert}(\mathsf{pk}, |\mathsf{qt}\rangle_{\mathsf{pk}}, b)$, a "certificate of destruction with respect to the bit b". The classical verification algorithm then gets, additionally to the classical certificate crt and the public key pk, a bit b, and verifies that indeed crt is a valid certificate for the bit b.
   The tokenized signatures security guarantee says that no Rec^* can get a single token $(\mathsf{pk}, |\mathsf{qt}\rangle_{\mathsf{pk}})$ and generate two classical certificates crt_0, crt_1 that pass the classical verification with the two different bits, that is, crt_0 passes for $b = 0$ and crt_1 passes for $b = 1$. This guarantee is at least as strong as the previous CCD. To see this, assume there is an adversary Rec^* that outputs a quantum token $|\mathsf{qt}\rangle'$ that passes quantum verification and a

classical receipt crt that passes classical verification. crt passes classical verification which means it passes it for some bit $b \in \{0, 1\}$ - we can find out what the bit b is by executing classical verification on crt with input target 0 and input target 1, and then use $|qt\rangle'$ to generate a targeted classical certificate of destruction for $\neg b$. In this process we obtain crt_b, $crt_{\neg b}$. The targeted destruction mechanism allows us to think of $(pk, |qt\rangle_{pk})$ as a one-time signature token to sign in the name of the bank on a single bit, and in particular, we can think of the certificate generation algorithm as a quantum signing algorithm $crt_b \leftarrow Sign(pk, |qt\rangle_{pk}, b)$, hence the name signature tokens.

User-to-Bank Classical Communication from CCD Tokens. When we move from standard unclonable tokens to CCD tokens, any user can effectively "send" tokens to the bank, using only classical communication: by destroying the token $crt \leftarrow GenCert(pk, |qt\rangle_{pk})$ and sending the classical crt to the bank, the user proves to the bank that it cannot spend the money of that token anymore in the network, and the bank can reimburse the balance of that user. Still, CCD tokens do not solve any of the other two directions of communication: from the bank to a user, and from one user to another user.

1.1   The Advantages of Quantum Signature Tokens

Having the strongest no-cloning guarantee, the power behind signature tokens emerges when the tokens are used in a sequence: We can take λ i.i.d. signature tokens $(pk_1, |qt\rangle_{pk_1}), (pk_2, |qt\rangle_{pk_2}), \cdots, (pk_\lambda, |qt\rangle_{pk_\lambda})$ as a single "string signature token" unit that can sign on any length-λ string. Along with the sequence of tokens, the bank decides on a token value $x \in \mathbb{N} \cup \{0\}$ (in the context of quantum money, this is how much money the bank assigns to that token), samples a unique (with high probability) identifier which is a random serial number $s \leftarrow \{0, 1\}^\lambda$, and a classical signature $\sigma := \sigma_{(pk_1, \cdots, pk_\lambda, x, s)}$ for the entire classical part of the token. The signature token is then

$$pk = (pk_1, \cdots, pk_\lambda, x, s, \sigma), \ |qt\rangle_{pk} = (|qt\rangle_{pk_1}, |qt\rangle_{pk_2}, \cdots, |qt\rangle_{pk_\lambda}) \ .$$

Note that σ is a signature for the entire sequence together, thus one cannot mix and match signatures of two different strings s_1, s_2 produced from two different tokens, in order to get a signature for a third string s_3. Tokens of value $x = 0$ can be regarded as "dummy tokens" - we next show how they can be used.

User-to-User Classical Communication from Signature Tokens. Like CCD tokens, string signature tokens enable the previous classical communication from user to bank (as they are only a strengthening of CCD tokens), but moreover, they enable an additional direction of classical communication, from one user to another. More elaborately, one user Rec_1 holding a token $(\mathsf{pk}_1, |\mathsf{qt}\rangle_{\mathsf{pk}_1})$ of value x_1, can transfer the value x_1 to another user Rec_2 holding a token $(\mathsf{pk}_2, |\mathsf{qt}\rangle_{\mathsf{pk}_2})$ of value of 0, by using $|\mathsf{qt}\rangle_{\mathsf{pk}_1}$ to sign on s_2, the serial number of the token $(\mathsf{pk}_2, |\mathsf{qt}\rangle_{\mathsf{pk}_2})$. After the produced signature is sent to Rec_2, the token $(\mathsf{pk}_2, |\mathsf{qt}\rangle_{\mathsf{pk}_2})$ can be considered to have the value x_1.

Additionally to enabling user-to-user classical communication, two derived abilities of string signature tokens are as follows:

- **Online token destruction:** When the bank wants a certificate of destruction for any token, it samples a random string $d \leftarrow \{0,1\}^\lambda$ and asks the user to sign on d with the signature token.
- **Token value split:** To split the value x of the token $(\mathsf{pk}_1, |\mathsf{qt}\rangle_{\mathsf{pk}_1})$ between two tokens $(\mathsf{pk}_2, |\mathsf{qt}\rangle_{\mathsf{pk}_2})$, $(\mathsf{pk}_3, |\mathsf{qt}\rangle_{\mathsf{pk}_3})$ into $u_2, u_3 \in \mathbb{N} \cup \{0\}$ such that $u_2 + u_3 = x$ (i.e. the value of $(\mathsf{pk}_2, |\mathsf{qt}\rangle_{\mathsf{pk}_2})$ is added u_2 and the value of $(\mathsf{pk}_3, |\mathsf{qt}\rangle_{\mathsf{pk}_3})$ is added u_3), we can hash the serial numbers s_2, s_3 of the two target tokens along with the partition u_2, u_3 of x to a length-λ string, $H(s_2, s_3, u_2, u_3) = y$ for a collision resistant hash function $H : \{0,1\}^* \rightarrow \{0,1\}^\lambda$, and then use $(\mathsf{pk}_1, |\mathsf{qt}\rangle_{\mathsf{pk}_1})$ to sign on y. This effectively gives a classical proof for the new values of the tokens $(\mathsf{pk}_2, |\mathsf{qt}\rangle_{\mathsf{pk}_2})$, $(\mathsf{pk}_3, |\mathsf{qt}\rangle_{\mathsf{pk}_3})$.

More Advantages of Signature Tokens for Quantum Money. Aside from direct classical transactions, we get additional unique characteristics to a public-key quantum money system that is based on string signature tokens: **(1) No token database:** When a user wants to return a token to the bank and get its bank account balance reimbursed (using only classical communication), the user and bank can execute the online destruction mechanism. In contrast, in a quantum money system based on CCD tokens, where the token return mechanism is the user simply generating a classical certificate of destruction by itself and sending it to the bank, the bank needs to maintain a database of all previously-destroyed tokens, so malicious users cannot illegally re-use the mechanism and send the same classical certificate of destruction multiple times, for the same token. **(2) Dynamic payment amounts:** The value split mechanism gives one the ability for granular payment amounts, where a user can dynamically choose the amount it wants to pay (unlike in the CCD-based scheme where the value x of a token is fixed during its creation by the bank). **(3) Provable payments:** When one user sends a direct payment to a second user, by signing on the serial number of a dummy token which the second users holds, this signature on the serial number is also a proof of payment, which we do not have in the CCD tokens setting (without going through the bank). **(4) Private classical payments:** While in a scheme based on tokenized signatures, classical user-to-user transactions are direct and thus private, the bank can still obtain information when the user returns a banknote. The online destruction mechanism enables that when the user returns the signature for d using a token that was worth x, if it wishes to hide the token's information (i.e. all information of that token except its worth) and maintain privacy, it can encrypt the classical signature for d and send the encryption together with a zero-knowledge proof that the content of the encryption is a signature for d, and the token that signed on it has a value of x. This mechanism is still secure for the bank, as with high probability, it will never sample a repeating test string d.

1.2 Semi-quantum Tokenized Signatures

We know how to construct public-key quantum money with signature tokens based on quantum-secure indistinguishability obfuscation and injective one-way functions, from a combination of the work of Ben-David and Sattath [3] with the work of Coladangelo, Liu, Liu, and Zhandry [4]. While such quantum money scheme can cover two out of three directions of communication classically (i.e. from users to the bank and from users to other users), the direction from the bank to users still needs to be quantum.

A strengthening of public-key quantum money is public-key *semi-quantum* money, where everything is the same as before (i.e. same syntax and hierarchy of no-cloning levels of the tokens), but the bank is a classical algorithm, which in particular makes the interaction from bank to users classical. More precisely, the generation of a token is by an interactive protocol between the classical bank Bank and a possibly malicious, quantum receiver Rec: $(\mathsf{pk}, |\mathsf{qt}\rangle_{\mathsf{pk}}) \leftarrow \langle \mathsf{Bank}, \mathsf{Rec}\rangle_{(\mathsf{OUT_{Bank}}, \mathsf{OUT_{Rec}})}$, i.e. the output of the bank is pk (this is the public key which the bank can now distribute), and the output of the receiver is the quantum state $|\mathsf{qt}\rangle_{\mathsf{pk}}$. Similarly to before, no-cloning guarantees (i.e. standard no-cloning, CCD or tokenized signing) apply for the state $|\mathsf{qt}\rangle_{\mathsf{pk}}$, but crucially, these guarantees now need to hold even given the fact the actual generator of the state is a possibly malicious receiver Rec^*. Radian and Sattath [5] introduced the notion of semi-quantum money, and showed a construction of public-key semi-quantum money with CCD tokens, based on quantum lightning [8] - a primitive which to this day we do not know how to construct.

Shmueli [7] later constructs a public-key semi-quantum money scheme with CCD tokens, based on quantum-secure indistinguishability obfuscation and the sub-exponential quantum hardness of the Learning With Errors problem. This means that based on these computational assumptions, we know how to construct a public-key quantum money scheme that covers two directions of communication classically: from the bank to users (because the scheme is semi-quantum and a user can execute the receiver in the token generation protocol) and from a user to the bank (because the tokens are CCD tokens, and as we have seen earlier, such tokens enable returning tokens to the bank by destroying them and sending the receipt to the bank)[3]. So, looking on what we saw until now,

- Public-key fully-quantum money with signature tokens is missing the classical direction from the bank to users, and,
- Public-key semi-quantum money with CCD tokens is missing the classical direction from one user to another.

It remains an open question to classically cover *all three directions of communication at once*. We don't know how to construct such primitive under any computational assumption.

A construction of public-key semi-quantum money with *signature tokens*, or in short, a semi-quantum tokenized signature scheme, solves the above problem, and more. Such scheme has a classical bank like the scheme from [7], but unlike the previous scheme, it also has the 4 fundamental advantages of signature tokens for quantum money (mentioned in Sect. 1.1). In particular, Radian and Sattath [5] leave two open problems in their work: One open problem of constructing a *memory-dependent* public-key semi-quantum money, and a stronger and the main open problem of constructing a *memoryless* public-key semi-quantum money (both notions are defined in their work). The public-key semi-quantum money with CCD tokens of Shmueli [7] solves the construction of a memory-dependent scheme, while constructing a semi-quantum tokenized signature scheme will resolve the main question of constructing a memoryless scheme.

Our focus in this work is to construct a semi-quantum tokenized signature scheme. On the technical side of things, such scheme will show for the first time that it is possible for a classical computer to securely delegate the generation of quantum states that maintain the tokenized signing property.

1.3 Results

We resolve the open question and construct a semi-quantum tokenized signature scheme, based on the existence of indistinguishability obfuscation (iO) for classical circuits secure against quantum polynomial-time attacks, and on that the Learning With Errors [6] problem has sub-exponential indistinguishability against quantum computers, that is, there exists some constant $\delta \in (0, 1)$ such

---

[3] A nice property of a semi-quantum CCD tokens scheme is *in-direct* classical-communication transactions from user to user: A user can return a token to the bank, and then the bank can classically send a newly-generated token with the same value to the recipient user of that transaction. Observe, however, that such in-direct transactions are always known by the bank and thus are not private, which is one of the fundamental problems that quantum money is intended to solve.

that for every quantum polynomial-time algorithm, Decisional LWE cannot be solved with advantage greater than $2^{-\lambda^\delta}$, where $\lambda \in \mathbb{N}$ is the security parameter of LWE[4].

Formally, we have the following main Theorem.

Theorem 1. *Assume that Decisional LWE has sub-exponential quantum indistinguishability and that indistinguishability obfuscation for classical circuits exists with security against quantum polynomial time distinguishers. Then, there is a semi-quantum tokenized signature scheme.*

The remaining of the paper is as follows. In Sect. 2 we explain the main ideas in our construction. The Preliminaries are omitted from this proceedings version and are given in the full version of this work. In Sect. 3 we present our construction of semi-quantum tokenized signatures with correctness proof and proof for security against sabotage. The full version of the paper also contains the security proof against signature counterfeiting.

2   Technical Overview

In this section we explain the main technical ideas in our construction and the structure of the overview is as follows. In Sect. 2.1 we review the previous works related to our goal of constructing semi-quantum tokenized signatures, and explain why a straightforward extension of these works does not work to obtain our goal. In Sect. 2.2 we describe our construction and the reasoning behind it, with no security proof. In Sect. 2.3 we explain how the security of the entire scheme is reduced to proving a new hardness property of indistinguishability obfuscation, which is captured by our main technical Lemma in the full version of this work. Finally, in Sect. 2.4 we explain the main steps of proving this Lemma.

2.1   Semi-quantum CCD Tokens and Fully-quantum Signature Tokens

Starting off based on previous work, there is a single protocol [7] where a classical Bank can delegate to a quantum Rec the generation of quantum unclonable tokens - this scheme lets the bank and receiver sample together by interaction $(\mathsf{pk}, |\mathsf{qt}\rangle_{\mathsf{pk}}) \leftarrow \langle \mathsf{Bank}, \mathsf{Rec} \rangle_{(\mathsf{OUT}_{\mathsf{Bank}}, \mathsf{OUT}_{\mathsf{Rec}})}$ a token for the receiver (the public key is the output of the bank, which the bank can then share with anyone, in particular the receiver). More precisely, the tokens in the scheme are CCD tokens. As

---

[4] Note that this assumption is weaker than assuming that Decisional LWE is hard for sub-exponential time quantum algorithms, which is considered a standard cryptographic assumption.

mentioned in the introduction, the scheme also includes public quantum verification $QV(pk, |qt\rangle_{pk}) \in \{0, 1\}$, certificate generation $crt \leftarrow GenCert(pk, |qt\rangle_{pk})$, and public classical verification $CV(pk, crt) \in \{0, 1\}$.

Our direction in this overview will be to upgrade the construction to be able to generate not only CCD, but signature tokens. This means to have a signing procedure $\sigma_b \leftarrow Sign(pk, |qt\rangle_{pk}, b)$ instead of the certificate generation $crt \leftarrow GenCert(pk, |qt\rangle_{pk})$, and the classical verification will become a classical signature verification $CV(pk, \sigma_b, b) \in \{0, 1\}$. Looking at another previous work [3,4] which uses a quantum bank but manages to build the stronger signature tokens, it makes sense to try and combine the techniques of the two works. These two works are even more so inviting to be fused, as it is the case that in both works, the tokens are *coset states* - states of the form $|S\rangle^{x,z} := \sum_{u \in S}(-1)^{\langle z,u \rangle}|x + u\rangle$ for a subspace $S \subseteq \{0,1\}^\lambda$ and two strings $x, z \in \{0,1\}^\lambda$. Let us recall the high-order bits in the two works, and then examine their possible joining.

Recap: Coset States as Fully-quantum Signature Tokens. The fully-quantum tokenized signature scheme of [3,4] is as follows: The bank samples a random $\frac{\lambda}{2}$-dimensional subspace $S \subseteq \{0,1\}^\lambda$, random strings $x, z \in \{0,1\}^\lambda$ and generates $|qt\rangle_{pk} := |S\rangle^{x,z}$ i.e. $\sum_{u \in S}(-1)^{\langle z,u \rangle}|x + u\rangle$. The public verification key of the state is $pk = (O_{S+x}, O_{S^\perp+z})$, for $O_{S+x} \leftarrow iO(C_{S+x}), O_{S^\perp+z} \leftarrow iO(C_{S^\perp+z})$, where iO is a quantum-secure indistinguishability obfuscator for classical circuits and $C_{S+x}, C_{S^\perp+z}$ are circuits that check membership in the corresponding cosets $S + x$, $S^\perp + z$. The entire token $(pk, |qt\rangle_{pk})$ is sent to the receiver.

Public quantum verification QV of the scheme is the standard procedure to verify a coset state [2]: Given input a quantum λ-qubit register QT, (1) Check that the output qubit of $O_{S+x}(QT)$ is 1, then (2) perform Quantum Fourier Transform (QFT) in base 2 i.e. $H^{\otimes \lambda}$ on QT, then (3) Check that the output qubit of $O_{S^\perp+z}(QT)$ is 1. It is a known fact in the literature that a successful verification in such procedure projects the state to be exactly $|qt\rangle_{pk} = |S\rangle^{x,z}$. Finally, regarding the signing algorithm $Sign(pk, |qt\rangle_{pk}, b)$, to sign on $b = 0$ just measure $|qt\rangle_{pk}$, and to sign on $b = 1$ measure in the Hadamard basis i.e. perform $H^{\otimes \lambda}$ and then measure. Accordingly, a valid signature for $b = 0$ is any string in $S + x$, which can be publicly verified using O_{S+x}, and a valid signature for $b = 1$ is any string in $S^\perp + z$, which can be publicly verified using $O_{S^\perp+z}$.

The main technical part of the works [3,4] is to show that it is computationally impossible, given $((O_{S+x}, O_{S^\perp+z}), |S\rangle^{x,z})$, to output both $s \in (S + x)$ and $s^\perp \in (S^\perp + z)$.

Recap: Coset States as Semi-quantum CCD Tokens. Moving to the semi-quantum setting, the scheme of [7] includes a 3-message coset state generation protocol, as follows:

1. The classical Bank samples a random $\frac{\lambda}{2}$-dimensional subspace $S \subseteq \{0,1\}^\lambda$ (represented by a matrix $\mathbf{M}_S \in \{0,1\}^{\frac{\lambda}{2} \times \lambda}$), and sends to the receiver $(\mathbf{M}_S^x, \mathsf{ct}_x)$, an encryption of the matrix $\mathbf{M}_S$ under hybrid quantum fully-homomorphic encryption (QFHE)[5].

2. The quantum receiver Rec homomorphically evaluates the circuit C_{ssg}, which is a quantum circuit that gets as input the classical description of a subspace $S \subseteq \{0,1\}^\lambda$ e.g. by a matrix, and generates a uniform superposition over S. Thus, the receiver obtains a quantum, homomorphically evaluated ciphertext,

$$\left(|S\rangle^{x',z'}, \mathsf{ct}_{(x',z')} \right) \leftarrow \mathsf{QHE.Eval}\left((\mathbf{M}_S^x, \mathsf{ct}_x), C_{\mathsf{ssg}} \right) ,$$

and sends to Bank the classical part $\mathsf{ct}_{(x',z')}$.

3. Bank decrypts $(x', z') = \mathsf{QHE.Dec}(\mathsf{ct}_{(x',z')})$ and sends obfuscations $O_{S+x'} \leftarrow \mathsf{iO}(C_{S+x'})$, $O_{S^\perp+z'} \leftarrow \mathsf{iO}(C_{S^\perp+z'})$ as the public verification key pk.

The coset state $|S\rangle^{x',z'}$ which the receiver holds is the quantum part $|\mathsf{qt}\rangle_{\mathsf{pk}}$ of the token. Accordingly, public quantum verification QV is identical to that of [3,4], the certificate generation $\mathsf{crt} \leftarrow \mathsf{GenCert}(\mathsf{pk}, |\mathsf{qt}\rangle_{\mathsf{pk}})$ is simply a standard basis measurement and the classical certificate verification is just verifying $\mathsf{CV}(\mathsf{pk}, \mathsf{crt}) := O_{S+x'}(\mathsf{crt})$.

In the security argument it is shown that it is computationally impossible to output both, the quantum state $|\mathsf{qt}\rangle'$ that passes the verification $\mathsf{QV}(\mathsf{pk}, \cdot)$ and a certificate of destruction for it i.e. any string $s \in (S + x')$. The work does not claim that the generated coset state maintains the tokenized signing property, in fact, it is not even defined what it means that a tokens signs on 0 or 1.

Attacking the Combined Scheme. As we said in the beginning of the overview, we should first try to combine the schemes. Since both schemes have the same token structure (a coset state) and public key (obfuscations of the membership functions for the primal and dual cosets), to combine the schemes, all we need to do is to take the token generation protocol of [7] and define a signature for $b = 0$ to be any $s \in (S + x')$ and a signature for $b = 1$ to be any $s^\perp \in (S^\perp + z')$. To argue that the combined scheme maintains the tokenized signing property, it is required to prove that for any quantum polynomial-time receiver Rec* that interacts with the classical Bank during the token generation protocol, it is impossible to output $(s, s^\perp)$.

As it turns out, there is a simple way for an adversary to break the tokenized signing security of the combined protocol. More elaborately, consider the follow-

---

[5] A hybrid QFHE scheme is one where every encryption of a quantum state $|\psi\rangle$ is of the form $\left(|\psi\rangle^{x,z}, \mathsf{ct}_{(x,z)} \right)$, where $|\psi\rangle^{x,z}$ is a quantum OTP encryption of $|\psi\rangle$ with keys $x, z \in \{0,1\}^\lambda$, and $\mathsf{ct}_{(x,z)}$ is a classical FHE encryption of the keys.

ing attacker Rec^* that interacts with Bank in the protocol of [7] (described in the previous paragraph):

1. Rec^* obtains $(\mathbf{M}_S^x, \mathsf{ct}_x)$, the first message from Bank.
2. Rec^* samples a random $r \in \{0,1\}^{\frac{\lambda}{2}}$ and homomorphically evaluates the following *classical* circuit $C_{r,1}$: The circuit $C_{r,1}$ takes as input the matrix $\mathbf{M}_S \in \{0,1\}^{\frac{\lambda}{2} \times \lambda}$ and outputs $s := r^T \cdot \mathbf{M}_S$, a vector in the row span. The receiver gets the ciphertext $(\mathsf{ct}_{x'}, s \oplus x')$.
3. Rec^* samples a random $r^\perp \in \{0,1\}^{\frac{\lambda}{2}}$ and homomorphically evaluates the following *classical* circuit $C_{r^\perp,2}$: The circuit $C_{r^\perp,2}$ takes as input the matrix $\mathbf{M}_S \in \{0,1\}^{\frac{\lambda}{2} \times \lambda}$, computes a basis for $S^\perp$ in the form of a matrix $\mathbf{M}_{S^\perp} \in \{0,1\}^{\frac{\lambda}{2} \times \lambda}$ and outputs $s^\perp := (r^\perp)^T \cdot \mathbf{M}_{S^\perp}$, a vector in the row span. The receiver gets the ciphertext $(\mathsf{ct}_{x''}, s^\perp \oplus x'')$.

Assume without the loss of generality that in the QFHE, the classical FHE scheme that encrypts the classical QOTP keys x, z, is a bit encryption scheme (this assumption is w.l.o.g. as we do have such QFHE schemes where the classical FHE is a bit-encryption scheme. In fact, this is true for most known constructions). This means in particular that the ciphertext $\mathsf{ct}_{x',z'}$ which the receiver sends in the second message of the protocol is comprised of two ciphertexts, $\mathsf{ct}_{x'}, \mathsf{ct}_{z'}$.

Going back to our attack, the malicious receiver Rec^* can send $(\mathsf{ct}_{x'}, \mathsf{ct}_{x''})$ as the second message in the protocol (which was originally $\mathsf{ct}_{x',z'}$) to Bank, which decrypts to get x', x'', and sends the obfuscations accordingly: $O_{S+x'}$, $O_{S^\perp + x''}$ in the third message of the protocol. Finally, note that the receiver still holds $(s \oplus x') \in (S + x')$ and thus a signature for $b = 0$, and also holds $(s^\perp \oplus x'') \in (S^\perp + x'')$ and thus a signature for $b = 1$.

2.2 Signing Coset States by Splitting

With accordance to the above attack, if we wish to stay with the classical generation protocol of [7], we need to move to a different signing procedure - this will be our first new technique. Formally, we would like to reduce the task of breaking the security of QFHE, to the task of breaking the security of the tokenized signature scheme. Note that S is a random subspace of dimension $\frac{\lambda}{2}$ and thus takes a tiny fraction of $\frac{2^{\frac{\lambda}{2}}}{2^\lambda} = 2^{-\frac{\lambda}{2}}$ inside the set of all length-λ strings $\{0,1\}^\lambda$. This means that by the security of the QFHE, it should be computationally hard to get $(\mathbf{M}_S^x, \mathsf{ct}_x)$ the classical QFHE encryption of a basis for S, and find a non-zero vector in S. Thus, what we aim for as a very first step is a *definition* of valid signatures for $b = 0$ and $b = 1$ such that given σ_0, σ_1, two signatures for 0 and 1, it is possible to efficiently derive a vector $s \in (S \setminus \{0\})$.

We suggest the following signature definitions for a bit $b \in \{0,1\}$: At the beginning of the protocol, additionally to choosing S at random, the bank randomly splits S (which has $\frac{\lambda}{2}$ dimensions) into S_0, a $\left(\frac{\lambda}{2} - 1\right)$-dimensional subspace of S, and the coset $S_0 + w$, for $w \in (S \setminus S_0)$. Note that these two parts are exactly two disjoint halves of S. If we define a signature for b to be any string in $S_0 + b \cdot w + x'$, then one can verify that the sum of any pair of signatures $\sigma_0 \in (S + x'), \sigma_1 \in (S + w + x')$ is a non-zero vector inside S. The above only opens the way for the solution, as we did not yet solve the two main technical parts:

- **Signing:** Given the generated coset state $|S\rangle^{x',z'}$, how can the honest Rec always succeed in signing on b? Simply measuring $|S\rangle^{x',z'}$ will yield the wanted signature only with probability $1/2$.
- **Security:** Given our mechanism for signing (which we did not describe yet), how can we prove security for the new scheme? This part is presented in Sects. 2.3 and 2.4 of the overview.

Projecting on Half the Coset with Overwhelming Probability. We put the security of the scheme aside for the rest of Sect. 2.2 and focus on proving correctness, that is, explaining how to sign. We show how to transform $|S\rangle^{x',z'}$ into $|S_0 + b \cdot w\rangle^{x',z'}$ given $b \in \{0,1\}$, which will suffice, as a signature can be obtained at that point with probability 1, by measurement. To enable the transformation, the first change in the protocol is that in the third and last message of the protocol, where the bank usually sends the public key $\mathsf{pk} := (O_{S+x'}, O_{S^\perp+z'})$, it now sends an expanded key: $\mathsf{pk}' := (O_{S_0+x'}, O_{S_0+w+x'}, O_{S^\perp+z'})$.

Given the state $|S\rangle^{x',z'}$ and $\mathsf{pk}' := (O_{S_0+x'}, O_{S_0+w+x'}, O_{S^\perp+z'})$, we explain how to sign on $b = 0$ (the procedure for $b = 1$ is symmetric) by getting the state $|S_0\rangle^{x',z'}$. By measuring the output bit of $O_{S_0+x'}(|S^{x',z'}\rangle)$, if we succeed (which happens with probability $1/2$) we are done, and if we fail we have $|S_0 + w\rangle^{x',z'}$. It will be enough for the procedure to make the correction and go from the faulty state $|S_0 + w\rangle^{x',z'}$ back to the original state $|S\rangle^{x',z'}$ - since the original state re-enables the experiment of obtaining the correct state $|S_0\rangle^{x',z'}$ with probability $1/2$, we can make λ consecutive iterations of trying to project $|S\rangle^{x',z'}$ to $|S_0\rangle^{x',z'}$ (and correct otherwise), and thus fail with an overall probability of $1 - 2^{-\lambda}$.

Correction of a Faulty Coset State. The correction procedure from $|S_0 + w\rangle^{x',z'}$ to $|S\rangle^{x',z'}$ is as follows: We start with performing QFT (i.e. $H^{\otimes\lambda}$) on $|S_0 + w\rangle^{x',z'}$ which gives us

$$\sum_{u \in S_0^\perp} (-1)^{\langle x'+w,u\rangle} |z' + u\rangle .$$

We can write the above state as

$$\sum_{(u \in S_0^\perp) \wedge (\langle u, w \rangle = 0)} (-1)^{\langle x'+w, u \rangle} |z' + u\rangle + \sum_{(u \in S_0^\perp) \wedge (\langle u, w \rangle = 1)} (-1)^{\langle x'+w, u \rangle} |z' + u\rangle$$

$$= \sum_{(u \in S_0^\perp) \wedge (\langle u, w \rangle = 0)} (-1)^{\langle x', u \rangle} |z' + u\rangle - \sum_{(u \in S_0^\perp) \wedge (\langle u, w \rangle = 1)} (-1)^{\langle x', u \rangle} |z' + u\rangle.$$

Notice that $u \in S^\perp$ if and only if $(u \in S_0^\perp) \wedge (\langle u, w \rangle = 0)$, also, the set of vectors u' such that $(u' \in S_0^\perp) \wedge (\langle u', w \rangle = 1)$ is exactly $S^\perp + v$, for any v such that $(v \in S_0^\perp) \wedge (\langle v, w \rangle = 1)$. We thus write the above sum as

$$\sum_{u \in S^\perp} (-1)^{\langle x', u \rangle} |z' + u\rangle - \sum_{u \in S^\perp} (-1)^{\langle x', u+v \rangle} |z' + u + v\rangle .$$

The left sum in the above state is exactly $|S^\perp\rangle^{z',x'}$, which means that if we project the above state with measuring the output bit of $O_{S^\perp + z'}(\cdot)$ and get 1, we have $|S^\perp\rangle^{z',x'}$ and by executing QFT we go back to $|S\rangle^{x',z'}$, as required.

In case we get 0 then we have $\sum_{u \in S^\perp} (-1)^{\langle x', u+v \rangle} |z' + u + v\rangle$ and we go for the last part of the correction: We can clear the global phase,

$$\sum_{u \in S^\perp} (-1)^{\langle x', u+v \rangle} |z' + u + v\rangle = (-1)^{\langle x', v \rangle} \sum_{u \in S^\perp} (-1)^{\langle x', u \rangle} |z' + u + v\rangle$$

$$\equiv \sum_{u \in S^\perp} (-1)^{\langle x', u \rangle} |z' + u + v\rangle ,$$

and execute QFT to get

$$\sum_{u \in S} (-1)^{\langle z'+v, u \rangle} |x' + u\rangle .$$

We can write the above state by splitting the sum to S_0 and $S_0 + w$,

$$\sum_{u \in S_0} (-1)^{\langle z'+v, u \rangle} |x' + u\rangle + \sum_{u \in S_0} (-1)^{\langle z'+v, u+w \rangle} |x' + u + w\rangle ,$$

and the advantage in that is, because $(v \in S_0^\perp) \wedge (\langle v, w \rangle = 1)$, the above state can be written as

$$\sum_{u \in S_0} (-1)^{\langle z', u \rangle} |x' + u\rangle - \sum_{u \in S_0} (-1)^{\langle z', u+w \rangle} |x' + u + w\rangle$$

$$= |S_0\rangle^{x',z'} - |S_0 + w\rangle^{x',z'} .$$

Finally, although we can correct the above state to be $|S\rangle^{x',z'} := |S_0\rangle^{x',z'} + |S_0 + w\rangle^{x',z'}$ (by a phase flip conditioned on the acceptance bit of the circuit $O_{S_0+w+x'}$), there is no need. This follows because the above state is again a state that enables projecting it on $|S_0\rangle^{x',z'}$ with success probability of $1/2$, and if we fail we get $-|S_0 + w\rangle^{x',z'} \equiv |S_0 + w\rangle^{x',z'}$, which were exactly the properties we needed from $|S\rangle^{x',z'}$.

2.3 Proving CCD Security Versus Proving Tokenized Signing Security

To quickly touch base on where we currently stand, our new generation protocol for signature tokens is the same as the CCD token generation from [7] (which is described in Sect. 2.1), with two differences:

- The last message from Bank to Rec in the new protocol is $\mathsf{pk}' := (O_{S_0+x'}, O_{S_0+w+x'}, O_{S^\perp+z'})$ rather than $\mathsf{pk} = (O_{S+x'}, O_{S^\perp+z'})$ from the previous.
- Instead of the certificate generation $\mathsf{crt} \leftarrow \mathsf{GenCert}(\mathsf{pk}, |S\rangle^{x',z'})$ of the previous work which just makes a measurement to the coset state (and does not really use pk), we now have a bit-signing procedure $\sigma_b \leftarrow \mathsf{Sign}(\mathsf{pk}', |S\rangle^{x',z'}, b)$, described in Sect. 2.2.

Until now we did not cover any of the security aspects of our construction, only the correctness. This following part of the overview, which explains the security argument in high-level, is constructed as follows: We recall the security arguments from previous work [7] that are still relevant for our new construction, until we arrive at the key point of difference between the current work and the previous. Next, we explain why the previous techniques do not cover this difference. Finally, we explain how our main technical Lemma covers this gap and enables us to prove that the new scheme produces signature tokens. The overview for the proof of Lemma is presented in Sect. 2.4.

Previous Techniques and Our Security Argument Outline. In our reduction setting, given a malicious Rec* that breaks the security of the semi-quantum tokenized signature scheme, we construct an adversary $\mathcal{A}_{\mathbf{QHE}}$ against the QFHE scheme, in the following manner:

1. $\mathcal{A}_{\mathbf{QHE}}$ gets the ciphertext $(\mathbf{M}_S^x, \mathsf{ct}_x)$ as input (for a random S with dimension $\frac{\lambda}{2}$) and passes it directly to Rec* as the first message of the bank in the protocol.
2. Rec* returns ct^* as the second message in the protocol.
3. $\mathcal{A}_{\mathbf{QHE}}$ computes (O_1, O_2, O_3) as the third message in the protocol and sends to Rec*.
4. Rec* outputs two signatures σ_0, σ_1. These signatures are used by $\mathcal{A}_{\mathbf{QHE}}$, which outputs the sum $\sigma_0 + \sigma_1$ as an attempt for a non-zero vector in S.

The reason why this sum is indeed a non-zero vector in S, at least when the messages of the bank are honestly generated, was explained earlier, in the beginning of Sect. 2.2.

Note that the third message (O_1, O_2, O_3) of $\mathcal{A}_{\mathbf{QHE}}$ needs to be computationally indistinguishable from $(O_{S_0+x'}, O_{S_0+w+x'}, O_{S^\perp+z'})$, the third message in the original protocol. Crucially, in the original protocol, the secret key fhek of the QFHE is used to generate this third message. Specifically, the bank obtains (x', z') by decryption. Having fhek is clearly not possible for the QFHE adversary $\mathcal{A}_{\mathbf{QHE}}$, and the reduction needs to overcome this difficulty.

We prove the reduction by a hybrid argument, and use three previously known tools in the process.

Subspace-Hiding Obfuscation: We use the well-known subspace-hiding [8] property of indistinguishability obfuscation, which says that (as long as quantum-secure injective one-way functions exist) the obfuscation $O_{S+x} \leftarrow iO(C_{S+x})$ is indistinguishable from an obfuscation $O_{T+x} \leftarrow iO(C_{T+x})$, for a random superspace $S \subseteq T$ - as long as the dimension of T is not too large[6], even if S is known to the attempting distinguisher.

Sub-Exponential Security of QFHE: Another aid we use is the assumption that the QFHE has sub-exponential security[7], which in turn implies that it should not be possible to get a non-zero vector in S with probability greater than $\approx 2^{-\lambda^{\delta'}}$. Note that since we can pick δ the parameter indicating the dimension of the subspaces T_0, T_1 to be any constant, we can take it as a function of δ', in particular, $\delta := \frac{\delta'}{2}$. Such choice of parameters implies $2^{-\lambda^\delta} >> 2^{-\lambda^{\delta'}}$.

Blind Sampling of Obfuscations: As part of the security argument in [7] it is shown that given any fixed pair T_0, T_1 of subspaces with dimension $\lambda - \lambda^\delta$ each, even if we do not know x', z', we can successfully sample from a distribution indistinguishable from $(O_{T_0+x'}, O_{T_0+w+x'}, O_{T_1+z'})$ with probability $\approx 2^{-\lambda^\delta}$.

Together, the above seemingly paves the way to finish the proof by a hybrid argument:

- Hyb_0 : In the first hybrid $\mathcal{A}_{\mathbf{QHE}}$ acts exactly like the bank and computes the third message $(O_{S_0+x'}, O_{S_0+w+x'}, O_{S^\perp+z'})$ using the secret QFHE key fhek. As we know, two valid signatures σ_0, σ_1 in this setting indeed imply that $\sigma_0 + \sigma_1$ is a non-zero vector in S.

---

[6] For any constant $\delta \in (0, 1]$, the indistinguishability holds for dimension bounded by $\lambda - \lambda^\delta$.

[7] The sub-exponential security says that there exists some constant $\delta' \in (0, 1]$ such that it is impossible for any quantum polynomial-time attacker to distinguish encryptions of differing plaintexts with advantage greater than $2^{-\lambda^{\delta'}}$.

- Hyb_1 : In the next hybrid $\mathcal{A}_{\mathbf{QHE}}$ still holds fhek, but sends $(O_{T_0+x'}, O_{T_0+w+x'}, O_{T_1+z'})$ instead. This is indistinguishable from the previous hybrid by the subspace hiding property of the iO. Recall the sub-exponential security of the QFHE where the exponent constant is $\delta' \in (0, 1]$. We take the dimension of the random superspaces $S_0 \subseteq T_0$, $S^\perp \subseteq T_1$ to be both $\lambda - \lambda^\delta$, for $\delta := \frac{\delta'}{2}$.

- Hyb_2 : In the next hybrid $\mathcal{A}_{\mathbf{QHE}}$ still holds fhek, but the subspaces T_0, T_1 are fixed by an averaging argument, to be the pair of subspaces that maximize the probability for a successful attack i.e. $\sigma_0 + \sigma_1 \in (S \setminus \{0\})$. Note that S is a random subspace of dimension $\frac{\lambda}{2}$ subjected to $S_0 \subseteq T_0$, $T_1^\perp \subseteq S$. By the sub-exponential security of the QFHE and by the fact that this restriction on S still leaves it enough entropy, it is still computationally impossible to find a non-zero vector in S with probability $>> 2^{-\lambda^{\delta'}}$.

- Hyb_3 : In this experiment $\mathcal{A}_{\mathbf{QHE}}$ does not hold fhek, and given the fixed subspaces T_0, T_1 samples from $(O_{T_0+x'}, O_{T_0+w+x'}, O_{T_1+z'})$ and still succeeds with probability $\approx 2^{-\lambda^\delta}$, by blind sampling of the obfuscated circuits.

All hybrids from Hyb_0 to Hyb_2 are indistinguishable, thus in Hyb_2 we still have $\sigma_0 + \sigma_1 \in (S \setminus \{0\})$, but the secret QFHE key fhek is still needed. Hyb_3 then successfully samples from the same output distribution of Hyb_2, without holding fhek and with probability $\approx 2^{-\lambda^\delta} >> 2^{-\lambda^{\delta'}}$, which finishes the proof as with this same probability we get a non-zero vector in S, in contradiction to the sub-exponential security of the QFHE.

Key Point of Difference - Quantumness in the Reduction. We inserted one small, but fatal inaccuracy to the above hybrid argument: When we use subspace-hiding techniques to hide S, it becomes no longer correct that getting *any* vector $s \in (S \setminus \{0\})$ is sufficient to break the QFHE security. More precisely, in the last hybrid Hyb_2 and on, the subspaces T_0, T_1 are fixed and moreover, $T_1^\perp \subseteq S$. This makes getting $s \in (S \setminus \{0\})$ not only possible, but trivial: any $s \in (T_1^\perp \setminus \{0\})$ will do. In order to break the QFHE we will need $s \in (S \setminus T_1^\perp)$.

To understand why needing $s \in (S \setminus T_1^\perp)$ rather than only $s \in (S \setminus \{0\})$ tears apart the above security proof sketch for signature tokens, let us first understand why the above argument actually holds when we want to prove that the tokens in the scheme maintain the weaker, CCD security guarantee. In a nutshell, the key difference is that in the CCD security reduction we are able to use the *quantumness* of the output of the adversary Rec^*.

A successful adversary Rec^* against CCD security manages to output not only two classical strings as signatures, σ_0, σ_1, but one certificate $\mathsf{crt} \in (S + x')$ along with the quantum state $|S\rangle^{x',z'} := \sum_{u \in S} (-1)^{\langle z', u \rangle} |x' + u\rangle$. The use of such output in the reduction is by adding crt to the superposition $|S\rangle^{x',z'}$; this only cancels the x'-pad and gets us $|S\rangle^{0^\lambda, z'}$. Now, the quantum state $|S\rangle^{0^\lambda, z'}$

does not give us just an arbitrary non-zero vector in S, but measuring it gives us a *uniform sample* from S. In particular, it is easy to get $s \in (S \setminus T_1^\perp)$ from such measurement, because the fraction of $T_1^\perp$ in S is negligible, which means that with overwhelming probability, the random sample lands outside $T_1^\perp$.

Technically, the above hybrid argument fails to prove tokenized signing already in Hyb_1; Even though the hybrids Hyb_0, Hyb_1 are indeed indistinguishable, and even though in both of them we can know S_0, w, x', z' and check whether the output of Rec^* still maintains $\sigma_0 \in (S_0 + x')$, $\sigma_1 \in (S_0 + w + x')$, it can still be the case that $\sigma_0 + \sigma_1 \in T_1^\perp$. Then, this fact that $\sigma_0 + \sigma_1 \in T_1^\perp$ is dragged for the remaining hybrids, which invalidates the proof - the reduction does not find a vector in $(S \setminus T_1^\perp)$, and thus QFHE security is unbroken.

Avoiding the Dual Subspace to Prove Tokenized Signing Security. It seems that we need a property of the indistinguishability obfuscator that is of different nature from the subspace-hiding property. We want to claim that given an obfuscation O_{T_1} of a random superspace of $S^\perp$, it is computationally hard to find a vector in the dual subspace $T_1^\perp$. Note that such hardness property will finish our proof: We can use it after moving from the above Hyb_0 to Hyb_1, claiming that in Hyb_1, the adversary cannot find vectors in $T_1^\perp$. Finally, since the adversary does find vectors in S, we know that the vector in S we found $\sigma_0 + \sigma_1$ is in $(S \setminus T_1^\perp)$. This property can then be carried for the rest of the hybrid experiments, to break the security of the QFHE in the end.

Ideally we indeed would like to prove such strong hardness property, but we do not manage to do so, in fact, it isn't even true that it is always hard: If the dimension of $T_1^\perp$, the subspace of S is big enough (which means that the randomly sampled primal superspace T_1 is not that much bigger than $S^\perp$), just by outputting a vector in S, we must be able to land inside $T_1^\perp$ with good probability.

What we do manage to show in our main technical Lemma is a *dual subspace anti-concentration* property, that says that while it may be possible to hit the dual subspace $T_1^\perp$ after getting an obfuscation $\mathsf{O}_{T_1} \leftarrow \mathsf{iO}(C_{T_1})$ (for a random high-dimensional superspace of $S^\perp$), it is hard to concentrate there exclusively. In other words, such adversary will always have to make a *near miss*, i.e. even if it tries to avoid S, if it manages to hit $T_1^\perp$ with a noticeable probability, it has to accidentally hit the background subspace S sometimes, that is, also with a noticeable probability.

2.4   Hardness of Concentration in Dual of Obfuscated Subspace

The last part remaining is to state and prove our anti-concentration Lemma. The statement roughly says the following: Assume that quantum-secure injective one-way functions exist, that iO is a quantum-secure indistinguishability obfuscator for classical circuits and that $S \subseteq \{0,1\}^\lambda$ is a subspace of dimension $\frac{\lambda}{2}$. Let $\delta \in (0,1]$ a constant, and for a quantum polynomial-time adversary $\mathcal{A}$, which is given $O_T \leftarrow iO(T)$ an obfuscation of a random $(\lambda - \lambda^\delta)$-dimensional subspace $T \subseteq \{0,1\}^\lambda$ subjected to $S \subseteq T$, denote by $s := \mathcal{A}(O(T))$ the output of $\mathcal{A}$. Then, for any quantum polynomial-time $\mathcal{A}$, if the output vector s satisfies $s \in (T^\perp \setminus \{0\})$ i.e. inside the dual of T, with a noticeable probability ε_0, then, there is a noticeable probability ε_1 such that s also satisfies $s(S^\perp \setminus T^\perp)$ i.e. it is inside $S^\perp$ but outside $T^\perp$.

Our strategy for proving the lemma is showing a hardness reduction from obfuscated subspace distinguishing (breaking subspace hiding) to obfuscated subspace dual concentration (breaking the anti-concentration Lemma). More formally, assume there is a quantum polynomial-time adversary $\mathcal{A}$ that violates our anti-concentration lemma. This means that given $O(T)$, the output $\mathcal{A}(O_T)$ is in $T^\perp \setminus \{0\}$ with a noticeable probability, but is also concentrated there (with respect to $S^\perp$), that is, the output $A(O_T)$ is in $S^\perp \setminus T^\perp$ with only a negligible probability. We aim to use this output pattern to construct a new adversary $\mathcal{A}_{\mathsf{sh}}$ that distinguishes between an obfuscation O_S of S and an obfuscation O_T of T, a random $(\lambda - \lambda^\delta)$-dimensional superspace of S. Our proof will consider two logical cases, which are split with accordance to the behavior of the output $\mathcal{A}(O_S)$ of $\mathcal{A}$ on a random obfuscation of the membership circuit for the subspace S.

First Case: $\mathcal{A}(O_S)$ is in Some Small Subspace of $S^\perp$ with Good Probability. In the first case there exists some subspace $T_\mathcal{A}$ inside $S^\perp$ such that the output $\mathcal{A}(O_S)$ of $\mathcal{A}$, for a random obfuscation $O_S \leftarrow iO(S)$, is in $T_\mathcal{A}$ with some non-negligible probability ε.

The main observation in the first case is given by three points, the combination of which gives us a way to use $\mathcal{A}$ in order to break subspace hiding:

1. The output of $\mathcal{A}$ for an obfuscation $O_S \leftarrow iO(S)$ of S is in some specific subspace $T_\mathcal{A}$ with a non-negligible probability, which means in particular that given $\mathcal{A}$, there exists a basis $B_\mathcal{A}$ for the subspace $T_\mathcal{A}$. This basis $B_\mathcal{A}$ can serve the new adversary $\mathcal{A}_{\mathsf{sh}}$ as non-uniform classical advice. This means that $\mathcal{A}_{\mathsf{sh}}$ can check membership in $T_\mathcal{A}$ efficiently by Gaussian elimination.
2. T is a random superspace of S with $\lambda - \lambda^\delta$ dimensions. This means that the dual $T^\perp$ of T is a relatively small subspace (of only λ^δ dimensions) and is random inside $S^\perp$. Combining this fact with the fact that $T_\mathcal{A}$ is a fixed and small subspace of $S^\perp$, the probability for $T^\perp$ and $T_\mathcal{A}$ to have a non-zero-vector intersection is exponentially small and in particular negligible.
3. The output $\mathcal{A}(O_T)$ of $\mathcal{A}$ for an obfuscation of T is concentrated in $T^\perp$ with respect to $S^\perp$. This means that there is at most a negligible chance that $\mathcal{A}(O_T)$ is in $S^\perp$ but outside $T^\perp$.

Recalling that T_A is inside $S^\perp$, it can be verified by the reader that the combination of 2 and 3 implies that the output $\mathcal{A}(O_T)$ hits the subspace T_A with at most a negligible probability. On the other hand, the output $\mathcal{A}(O_S)$ hits T_A with a non-negligible probability. Finally, an adversary $\mathcal{A}_{sh}$ can get an obfuscation z which is either from $O_S \leftarrow iO(S)$ or from $O_T \leftarrow iO(T)$ (for an appropriately random T), execute $\mathcal{A}(z)$ and check if the result is in T_A - this gives an adversary that breaks subspace hiding with a non-negligible advantage in quantum polynomial time.

Second Case: $\mathcal{A}(O_S)$ is Scattered. In the second case we assume the negation of the first case, that is, there is no small subspace T_A of $S^\perp$ such that the output $\mathcal{A}(O_S)$ is inside this subspace with a non-negligible probability. In first glance on the second case, it seems that the output of $\mathcal{A}$ is indistinguishable between the two input distributions O_S and O_T: while by the definition of the second case, the output $\mathcal{A}(O_S)$ is scattered in $S^\perp$ (and also outside $S^\perp$), the output $\mathcal{A}(O_T)$ is constrained to be in $T^\perp$ when inside $S^\perp$, but since the *subspace itself $T^\perp$ is scattered* in $S^\perp$, this also implies that $\mathcal{A}(O_T)$ is somewhat of a random vector.

The key to solving the second case is first asking what happens over many samples, that is, let us assume for a moment that subspace hiding is extendable to many samples, and $O_S^{(1)}$, $O_S^{(2)}$, $\cdots$, $O_S^{(\lambda)}$ is indistinguishable from $O_T^{(1)}$, $O_T^{(2)}$, $\cdots$, $O_T^{(\lambda)}$. Because $\mathcal{A}(O_S)$ is scattered, when looking on the outputs $\mathcal{A}(O_S^{(1)})$, $\mathcal{A}(O_S^{(2)})$, $\cdots$, $\mathcal{A}(O_S^{(\lambda)})$, we get random vectors with no particular pattern (at the least, with respect to small subspaces of dimension $\leq \lambda^\delta$). However, when we look at the series of outputs $\mathcal{A}(O_T^{(1)})$, $\mathcal{A}(O_T^{(2)})$, $\cdots$, $\mathcal{A}(O_T^{(\lambda)})$, since $\mathcal{A}(O_T)$ is obligated to either be in $T^\perp$ or not be in the larger $S^\perp$ at all, and $T^\perp$ has a small dimension λ^δ, we get an interesting and efficiently recognizable pattern.

Second Case: Dimension Recognition rather than Subspace Recognition and Double Obfuscation. If we are building $\mathcal{A}_{sh}$, an adversary against subspace hiding, T is unknown to $\mathcal{A}_{sh}$. However, the adversary $\mathcal{A}_{sh}$ can use $\mathcal{A}$ to recognize the *dimension* of the dual subspace $T^\perp$. Given the samples $O_T^{(1)}$, $O_T^{(2)}$, $\cdots$, $O_T^{(\lambda)}$, we can check whether $\mathcal{A}(O_T^{(i)})$ is in $S^\perp$ or not - if it is inside $S^\perp$, we put that vector v_i aside. At the end of this process, we get some set B^* of size $\leq \lambda$. Now, from the fact that $\mathcal{A}(O_T)$ is concentrated in $T^\perp$, one can verify that the dimension of B^* is bounded by λ^δ with overwhelming probability. On the other hand, the same process of building B^*, when we are given samples $O_S^{(1)}$, $O_S^{(2)}$, $\cdots$, $O_S^{(\lambda)}$ that are obfuscations of S rather than T, will yield a subspace B^* of dimension $> \lambda^\delta$. The last fact follows exactly because $\mathcal{A}(O_S)$ is scattered, and does not hit a particular subspace T_A with a non-negligible probability (unlike the behavior of $\mathcal{A}(O_S)$ in the first logical case). In conclusion, an adversary $\mathcal{A}_{sh}$ that gets $z^{(1)}, z^{(2)}, \cdots, z^{(\lambda)}$ which are either i.i.d samples from $iO(S)$ or from $iO(T)$, executes $\mathcal{A}(z^{(1)}), \cdots, \mathcal{A}(z^{(\lambda)})$, builds the basis B^* and checks if its dimension is bigger or bounded by λ^δ, can distinguish between the two extended distributions.

We saw that if the distributions $D_S := (O_S^{(1)}, O_S^{(2)}, \cdots, O_S^{(\lambda)})$ and $D_T := (O_T^{(1)}, O_T^{(2)}, \cdots, O_T^{(\lambda)}$ $\{T$ superspace of $S, \dim(T) = \lambda - \lambda^\delta\})$ are indistinguishable, we are done. However, a standard hybrid argument does not show this: a hybrid argument easily shows that subspace hiding implies that D_S is indistinguishable from $D_T' := (O_{T_1}, O_{T_2}, \cdots, O_{T_\lambda})$, that is, a distribution where in every one of the λ obfuscations T_i is sampled independently of the previous samples and is only subjected to being a superspace of S with dimension $\lambda - \lambda^\delta$. In our target distribution D_T, the superspace T is sampled *once*, and all λ obfuscations are of the same subspace T.

Finally, we show how to use *double obfuscation* in order to complete our reduction. Specifically, what we show in the body of the paper (in the proof of the anti concentration Lemma) is that given a single sample $z_T \leftarrow iO(T)$, by the standard security of indistinguishability obfuscation, λ second obfuscations $(O^{(1)} \leftarrow iO(z_T), \cdots, O^{(\lambda)} \leftarrow iO(z_T))$ of the already obfuscated once z_T are indistinguishable from D_T. It is also shown that a double obfuscation of S, that is, $O_{O_S} \leftarrow iO(iO(S))$ preserves all of the properties of a single obfuscation, in particular, the output $\mathcal{A}(O_{O_S})$ is also scattered like $\mathcal{A}(O_S)$.

The above finishes our reduction: An adversary $\mathcal{A}_{sh}$ that breaks subspace hiding will get z either from $iO(S)$ or from $iO(\{T$ superspace of $S, \dim(T) = \lambda - \lambda^\delta\})$, and sample λ i.i.d. second obfuscations $(O_z^{(1)}, \cdots, O_z^{(\lambda)})$ of z. $\mathcal{A}_{sh}$ will then execute $\mathcal{A}$ on each of the λ samples, get a vector v_i for each execution and put it aside if $v_i \in S^\perp$ - these vectors put aside are denoted with B^*. As we saw, if z is an obfuscation of S then the dimension of B^* is bounded by λ^δ with a negligible probability, and if z is an obfuscation of T then B^* has dimension $\leq \lambda^\delta$ with a non-negligible probability, which finishes our proof.

3   Semi-quantum Tokenized Signatures Construction

In this section we present our construction of a semi-quantum tokenized signatures (SQTS) scheme, proof of correctness and proof of security against quantum and classical sabotage.

Ingredients and Notation:

- A quantum hybrid fully homomorphic encryption scheme (QHE.Gen, QHE.Enc, QHE.OTP, QHE.Dec, QHE.QOTP, QHE.Eval), with sub-exponential advantage security.
- An indistinguishability obfuscation scheme iO.

In Fig. 1 we describe the token generation protocol and token quantum verification procedures. In Fig. 2 we describe the quantum signing algorithm and the classical signature verification procedures.

Protocol 1

Token Generation Protocol: Sen is classical and Rec is quantum. The joint input is the security parameter $\lambda \in \mathbb{N}$.

1. Sen samples a random $\frac{\lambda}{2}$-dimensional subspace $S \subseteq \{0,1\}^\lambda$, described by a matrix $\mathbf{M}_S \in \{0,1\}^{\frac{\lambda}{2} \times \lambda}$. Samples OTP key $p_x \leftarrow \{0,1\}^{\frac{\lambda^2}{2}}$ to encrypt $\mathbf{M}_S^{(p_x)} = \mathsf{QHE.OTP}_{p_x}(\mathbf{M}_S)$, and then $\mathsf{fhek} \leftarrow \mathsf{QHE.Gen}(1^\lambda, 1^{\ell(\lambda)})$ for some polynomial $\ell(\cdot)$, $\mathsf{ct}_{p_x} \leftarrow \mathsf{QHE.Enc}_{\mathsf{fhek}}(p_x)$. Sen sends the encryption $(\mathbf{M}_S^{(p_x)}, \mathsf{ct}_{p_x})$ to Rec.

2. Let C the quantum circuit that for an input matrix $\mathbf{M} \in \{0,1\}^{\frac{\lambda}{2} \times \lambda}$, outputs a uniform superposition of its row span. The receiver Rec homomorphically evaluates C: $(|S\rangle^{x,z}, \mathsf{ct}_{x,z}) \leftarrow \mathsf{QHE.Eval}\left((\mathbf{M}_S^{(p_x)}, \mathsf{ct}_{p_x}), C\right)$, saves the quantum part $|S\rangle^{x,z}$ and sends the classical part $\mathsf{ct}_{x,z}$ to Sen.

3. Sen decrypts $(x, z) = \mathsf{QHE.Dec}_{\mathsf{fhek}}(\mathsf{ct}_{x,z})$. If $x \in S$, the interaction is terminated. Let $\mathbf{M}_{S^\perp} \in \{0,1\}^{\frac{\lambda}{2} \times \lambda}$ a basis for $S^\perp$ (as a matrix), let w the first row in $\mathbf{M}_S$ and let $\mathbf{M}_{S_0} \in \{0,1\}^{(\frac{\lambda}{2}-1) \times \lambda}$ the rest of the matrix $\mathbf{M}_S$, without w.
   Sen computes indistinguishability obfuscations $O_{S_0+x} \leftarrow \mathsf{iO}(\mathbf{M}_{S_0}, x)$, $O_{S_0+w+x} \leftarrow \mathsf{iO}(\mathbf{M}_{S_0}, w+x)$, $O_{S^\perp+z} \leftarrow \mathsf{iO}(\mathbf{M}_{S^\perp}, z)$, all with padding $\mathsf{poly}'(\lambda)$ for some polynomial poly'.
   The output of Sen is $\mathsf{pk} := (O_{S_0+x}, O_{S_0+w+x}, O_{S^\perp+z})$, the output of Rec is $|\mathsf{qt}\rangle_{\mathsf{pk}} := |S\rangle^{x,z}$.

Quantum Token Verification:

- $\mathsf{QV}\left((O_{S_0+x}, O_{S_0+w+x}, O_{S^\perp+z}), \mathsf{QT}\right)$: Given a public key and a λ-qubit quantum register QT, the verifier checks two things:
  - Checks that the output qubit of $(O_{S_0+x} \vee O_{S_0+w+x})(\mathsf{QT})$ is 1.
  - Executes Hadamard transform $H^{\otimes\lambda}$ on QT and then checks that the output qubit of $O_{S^\perp+z}(\mathsf{QT})$ is 1.
  If both checks passed, the verifier executes $H^{\otimes\lambda}$ again on QT and accepts the signature token.

Fig. 1. Token generation protocol between the classical sender and quantum receiver, and quantum token verification procedure of our semi-quantum tokenized signature scheme.

Protocol 2

Quantum Signing Algorithm:

- Sign $\left((O_{S_0+x}, O_{S_0+w+x}, O_{S^\perp+z}), QT, b\right)$: Given a public key, a λ-qubit quantum register QT and $b \in \{0, 1\}$, the signing algorithm repeats the following procedure λ times and if the loop did not terminate in the middle, it outputs $\perp$.

  1. Measure the output qubit of $O_{S_0+b\cdot w+x}(QT)$, let $m \in \{0, 1\}$ the measurement result.

     (a) If $m = 1$, measure the register QT to get measurement σ_b, output σ_b and terminate.

     (b) If $m = 0$, execute $H^{\otimes\lambda}$ on QT, measure the output qubit of $O_{S^\perp+z}(QT)$, and execute $H^{\otimes\lambda}$ on QT once again. Restart the loop.

Classical Signature Verification:

- CV $\left((O_{S_0+x}, O_{S_0+w+x}, O_{S^\perp+z}), \sigma_b, b\right)$: To verify a classical signature candidate σ_b for the bit b, the verifier outputs the bit $O_{S_0+b\cdot w+x}(\sigma_b)$.

Fig. 2. The quantum signature algorithm and the classical signature verification procedure of our semi-quantum tokenized signature scheme.

3.1 Correctness and Security Against Sabotage

We first prove that our scheme is correct, which includes two steps: (1) If the scheme's algorithms are ran honestly then the protocol ends successfully, with the output of the honest receiver having negligible trace distance to $|S\rangle^{x,z}$. (2) We recall that $|S\rangle^{x,z}$ passes the quantum verification with probability 1, which overall means that the probability to pass the quantum verification is $1 - \text{negl}(\lambda)$.

Claim. If the token generation protocol is executed honestly, the quantum token $|qt\rangle_{pk}$ has negligible trace distance from the state $|S\rangle^{x,z} := \sum_{u \in S}(-1)^{\langle z, u\rangle}|x + u\rangle$ (the output of the protocol is defined to be $\perp$ in case the honest sender aborted the interaction), where x, z are the values obtained by the decryption executed by the sender in step 3 of the protocol.

Proof. By the statistical correctness of the QFHE, at the end of step 2 of the generation protocol, the quantum state that the honest Rec holds in its quantum-evaluated register has negligible trace distance to $|S\rangle^{x,z}$, that is, this negligible distance holds with probability 1 over the first two messages of the protocol.

Now, we claim that the probability for such honest Rec to have $x \in S$ is negligible. So, assume towards contradiction it was noticeable. Because the probability for $x \in S$ is noticeable, it has to be the case that with a noticeable probability, when we execute the honest protocol, at the end of step 2 the receiver holds a state with negligible trace distance to $|S\rangle^{x,z}$ for $x \in S$. Now, for any $x \in S$ it follows that $|S\rangle^{x,z} = |S\rangle^{0^\lambda,z}$. This means that by measuring the receiver's state we get a non-zero vector in S with overwhelming probability, and overall, with a noticeable probability we can get a non-zero vector in S without even knowing the QFHE secret key.

Getting a non-zero vector in S violates the security of the QFHE, due to the fact that S is chosen at random and it covers only a negligible fraction out of $\{0,1\}^\lambda$. So, the honest execution of the protocol terminates on with a negligible probability.

Overall, with probability $1 - \text{negl}(\lambda)$, we have $x \notin S$, the protocol ends successfully and the receiver holds a quantum state with negligible trace distance to $|S\rangle^{x,z}$.

We explain how Claim 3.1 implies the statistical correctness of our scheme.

Proposition 1. *The scheme presented in Protocol 1 has statistical correctness.*

Proof. In Claim 3.1 we saw that with probability $1 - \text{negl}(\lambda)$, the honest receiver Rec holds a quantum state with negligible trace distance to $|S\rangle^{x,z}$.

Finally, our public quantum verification QV is the standard QFT-based verification procedure of a coset state, and a well-known fact in the literature that a successful verification of such procedure is a projection of the verified state onto the subspace spanned only by the coset state [2,3]. Because the trace distance of $|\text{qt}\rangle_{\text{pk}}$ from $|S\rangle^{x,z}$ is negligible, the probability for the state to be verified is overwhelming.

Overall, with probability $1 - \text{negl}(\lambda)$ over the execution of the honest protocol, the receiver's quantum state passes the quantum verification $\text{QV}(\text{pk}, \cdot)$.

Security Against Quantum Sabotage. From the fact that the quantum verification $\text{QV}(\text{pk}, \cdot)$ is a projector on the coset state, it follows that after a single successful quantum verification, $|\text{qt}\rangle_{\text{pk}}$ is now $|S\rangle^{x,z}$, which passes the next quantum verification with probability 1.

It remains to prove the security of the scheme against classical sabotage.

Proposition 2. *The scheme presented in Protocol 1 has security against classical sabotage.*

Proof. The starting point of the algorithm is the state after passing successfully the verification $\text{QV}(\text{pk}, \cdot)$, which, as we stated above, means the state is exactly $|S\rangle^{x,z}$. After the first step of an iteration, if $m = 1$ we are done as we have $|S_0 + b \cdot w\rangle^{x,z}$ after the measurement, which means that by measuring we get $\sigma_b \in (S_0 + b \cdot w)$ with probability 1. If $m = 0$ we now have $|S_0 + (\neg b) \cdot w\rangle^{x,z}$.

Regarding the second step 1b, denote by $m' \in \{0, 1\}$ the measured output bit of $O_{S^\perp + z}(\mathsf{QT})$, that is, in step 1b of the signing procedure we execute QFT on QT, then measure the output qubit of $O_{S^\perp + z}(\mathsf{QT})$ (we denoted by m' the outcome of this 1-qubit measurement) and then execute QFT on QT again.

One can verify that if $m' = 1$ then we have $|S^\perp\rangle^{z,x}$ before the second QFT, and thus back to $|S\rangle^{x,z}$ after the second QFT. On the other hand, if $m' = 0$, after the second QFT we have $|S_0\rangle^{x,z} - |S_0 + w\rangle^{x,z}$.

In any case, regardless of the value m', at the end of step 1b of the signing procedure, the state (which is either $|S\rangle^{x,z}$ or $|S_0\rangle^{x,z} - |S_0 + w\rangle^{x,z}$) maintains the property that after measuring the the the output bit of $O_{S_0 + b \cdot w}(\mathsf{QT})$ (which will come up in upcoming step 1 of the next iteration) will project the state to be the correct $|S_0 + b \cdot w\rangle^{x,z}$ with probability $1/2$ and with the remaining probability $1/2$ it will be projected to $|S_0 + (\neg b) \cdot w\rangle^{x,z}$.

We deduce that at the beginning of each of the λ iterations we make, when we start with step 1, before the step is executed, we have a state that is projected to $|S_0 + b \cdot w\rangle^{x,z}$ with probability $1/2$ and to $|S_0 + (\neg b) \cdot w\rangle^{x,z}$ with probability $1/2$. The entire process will thus fail only if we fail consecutively λ times, where each experiment is independent from the rest and succeeds with probability $1/2$. Overall, this implies a failure probability of $1 - 2^{-\lambda}$.

Acknowledgements. We are grateful to Tamer Mour, for helpful discussions during the writing of this work.

References

1. Aaronson, S.: Quantum copy-protection and quantum money. In: 2009 24th Annual IEEE Conference on Computational Complexity, pp. 229–242. IEEE (2009)
2. Aaronson, S., Christiano, P.: Quantum money from hidden subspaces. In: Proceedings of the Forty-Fourth Annual ACM Symposium on Theory of Computing, pp. 41–60 (2012)
3. Ben-David, S., Sattath, O.: Quantum tokens for digital signatures. arXiv preprint arXiv:1609.09047 (2016)
4. Coladangelo, A., Liu, J., Liu, Q., Zhandry, M.: Hidden cosets and applications to unclonable cryptography. In: Malkin, T., Peikert, C. (eds.) CRYPTO 2021. LNCS, vol. 12825, pp. 556–584. Springer, Cham (2021). https://doi.org/10.1007/978-3-030-84242-0_20
5. Radian, R.: Semi-quantum money. In: Proceedings of the 1st ACM Conference on Advances in Financial Technologies, pp. 132–146 (2019)
6. Regev, O.: On lattices, learning with errors, random linear codes, and cryptography. J. ACM (JACM) **56**(6), 1–40 (2009)
7. Shmueli, O.: Public-key quantum money with a classical bank. Cryptology ePrint Archive (2021)
8. Zhandry, M.: Quantum lightning never strikes the same state twice. In: Ishai, Y., Rijmen, V. (eds.) EUROCRYPT 2019. LNCS, vol. 11478, pp. 408–438. Springer, Cham (2019). https://doi.org/10.1007/978-3-030-17659-4_14

Secure Multiparty Computation I

Structure-Aware Private Set Intersection, with Applications to Fuzzy Matching

Gayathri Garimella, Mike Rosulek, and Jaspal Singh$^{(\boxtimes)}$

Oregon State University, Corvallis, USA
singjasp@oregonstate.edu

Abstract. In two-party private set intersection (PSI), Alice holds a set X, Bob holds a set Y, and they learn (only) the contents of $X \cap Y$. We introduce **structure-aware PSI** protocols, which take advantage of situations where Alice's set X is publicly known to have a certain structure. The goal of structure-aware PSI is to have communication that scales with the *description size* of Alice's set, rather its *cardinality*.

We introduce a new generic paradigm for structure-aware PSI based on function secret-sharing (FSS). In short, if there exists compact FSS for a class of structured sets, then there exists a semi-honest PSI protocol that supports this class of input sets, with communication cost proportional only to the FSS share size. Several prior protocols for efficient (plain) PSI can be viewed as special cases of our new paradigm, with an implicit FSS for unstructured sets.

Our PSI protocol can be instantiated from a significantly weaker flavor of FSS, which has not been previously studied. We develop several improved FSS techniques that take advantage of these relaxed requirements, and which are in some cases exponentially better than existing FSS.

Finally, we explore in depth a natural application of structure-aware PSI. If Alice's set X is the union of many radius-δ balls in some metric space, then an intersection between X and Y corresponds to **fuzzy PSI**, in which the parties learn which of their points are within distance δ. In structure-aware PSI, the communication cost scales with the number of balls in Alice's set, rather than their total volume. Our techniques lead to efficient fuzzy PSI for ℓ_∞ and ℓ_1 metrics (and approximations of ℓ_2 metric) in high dimensions. We implemented this fuzzy PSI protocol for 2-dimensional ℓ_∞ metrics. For reasonable input sizes, our protocol requires 45–60% less time and 85% less communication than competing approaches that simply reduce the problem to plain PSI.

1 Introduction

Private Set Intersection (PSI) allows Alice with input A and Bob with input B to learn *only* the intersection $A \cap B$ of their sets and reveals no additional information. In this paper, we introduce **structure-aware private set intersection**

Authors partially supported by NSF award 2150726.

Y. Dodis and T. Shrimpton (Eds.): CRYPTO 2022, LNCS 13507, pp. 323–352, 2022.
https://doi.org/10.1007/978-3-031-15802-5_12

(PSI) where one of the parties, say Alice, has an input set A with some publicly known structure and Bob's input B is a set of unstructured points. They want to jointly compute the set of Bob's inputs that lie within Alice's input structure. An immediate approach for this problem is to enumerate or expand Alice's structured input into an unstructured set A^* and employ existing efficient plain PSI protocols. However, this is impractical because the cardinality of the expanded set can be prohibitively large, and PSI protocols have communication cost that scale with the cardinality of the input sets. We ask the question -

Can we make PSI protocols more efficient when there is publicly known structure in the parties' input sets?

In particular, is there a PSI protocol whose cost scales with the *description size* of the structured input A rather than the *cardinality* of A^*? We answer the above question affirmatively with a new framework for structure-aware PSI based on function secret sharing (FSS). We relax the constraints of standard FSS to introduce and study the notion of weak FSS. As our main result we show that for any structured input A, our framework reduces PSI to the task of designing efficient and succinct weak FSS for Alice's structured set A.

We design several novel and efficient FSS schemes for the family of sets of union of balls assuming different levels of structure. A standard boolean FSS scheme for a collection of sets S can compute "succinct" shares k_0, k_1 of any set $S \in S$ and for any input x, the individual shares k_0 or k_1 can be used to evaluate secret shares of the membership test of input $x \in S$. Formally, FSS schemes consist of algorithm Share which computes the secret-shares k_0, k_1 and algorithm Eval that can be used to compute shares of the membership test $((\text{Eval}(k_0, x) \oplus \text{Eval}(k_1, x)) = (x \in S)$.[1] PRG based FSS constructions are known for many interesting family of sets with membership functions that can be expressed as point functions, comparison functions, multi-dimensional intervals or decision trees [5,9,10].

Our work introduces weak boolean **FSS** that allows for "false positives" in the membership evaluation—i.e., when $x \notin S$, the xor of the shares evaluate $((\text{Eval}(k_0, x) \oplus \text{Eval}(k_1, x))$ to true with at least some bounded probability p. We also make another useful relaxation (the details are in Sect. 3.2) which together enable more efficient constructions compared to standard boolean FSS.

Finally, we instantiate our PSI framework with an FSS for unions of balls to obtain **fuzzy private set intersection (PSI)**. Here, Alice has a set of points A and Bob has a set of points B and they would like to learn the pairs $(a, b) \in A \times B$ satisfying $d(a, b) \leq \delta$, where d is a distance metric and δ is a public threshold. They should learn nothing about A and B, beyond this set of close pairs. We can compute this using our structure-aware PSI protocol by assigning Alice's structured input A^* as the union of many δ-balls (a δ-ball of radius δ centered at a is $\{b \mid d(a, b) \leq \delta\}$) and Bob's input is his unstructured input set B.

---

[1] The original formulation of FSS by Boyle et al. [9] is in terms of functions instead of sets, however in this work we are only interested in boolean set membership functions - hence we reframed the FSS definition.

1.1   Our Contributions

New weak FSS Constructions. We introduce the notion of **weak FSS** (parameterized by p and k), which for a family of sets consists of algorithms Share and Eval defined as:

- If $(k_0, k_1) \leftarrow \mathsf{Share}(A)$, for a set A in the family, then each k_i individually looks pseudorandom.
- If $x \in A$ then $\Pr[\mathsf{Eval}(k_0, x) \oplus \mathsf{Eval}(k_1, x) = 0^k] = 1$, where the probability is over the sampling of $(k_0, k_1) \leftarrow \mathsf{Share}(A)$.
- If $x \notin A$ then $\Pr[\mathsf{Eval}(k_0, x) \oplus \mathsf{Eval}(k_1, x) \neq 0^k] \geq p$, where the probability is over the sampling of $(k_0, k_1) \leftarrow \mathsf{Share}(A)$.

We also propose several new techniques for (weak) FSS constructions offering two significant advantages. One, our weak FSS has significantly smaller share sizes than standard FSS. Second, we achieve significantly more efficient share-evaluation cost than existing FSS.

Consider our motivating example of fuzzy PSI where the structured set is the union of balls. Existing FSS techniques can be used for this kind of structure—however, the result is an FSS where evaluating the share on a single point requires time linear in the number of balls. This cost leads to a fuzzy PSI protocol with whose computation cost scales with the *product* of the two sets' cardinalities. Our new techniques provide FSS for a union of balls, where the share-evaluation cost is independent of the number of balls.

We specifically focus on the case where the structured set is a union of n balls of radius δ under the ℓ_∞ norm in d-dimensional space $\{0, 1, \ldots, 2^u - 1\}^d$. We use the concat technique (described in Subsect. 4.2) to develop weak FSS for a d dimensional ℓ_∞ ball (which is a cross product of d intervals). This technique essentially combines the outputs of FSS for d 1-dimension intervals that make the input ball - making the output length $k = d$. We further employ the spatial-hashing technique (from Subsect. 4.3) to design weak bFSS for union of balls. Using this technique, at a high level, we divide the input space into contiguous grid cells; construct FSS keys for each grid cell that intersect with any input ball; and then pack these FSS keys into an oblivious key value data structure. In our construction we ensure that for point in a grid cell not intersecting with any input ball, the FSS outputs is a random string - setting the false positive probability $p = 1 - 1/2^k$. Hence both relaxations in our bFSS definitions are key when designing bFSS for union of l_∞ balls.

An important theme in this work is that *more structure leads to more efficient FSS/PSI.* We consider three increasing levels of structure for such sets, which result in significantly better dependence on the dimension:

- The least amount of structure is when the balls are disjoint. Existing techniques give an FSS for this case whose share size depends on the dimension as $O(\min\{u, \delta\}^d)$. In our new FSS for disjoint balls, the dependence on the dimension is $O((4 \log \delta)^d)$.
- If the balls are spaced far apart—*i.e.*, no two centers are closer than distance 4δ—then we can achieve FSS whose dependence on the dimension is $O(2^d)$.

- Finally, if the balls are *globally-axis disjoint*—meaning that the projection of the balls onto every axis is disjoint—then we can achieve FSS whose dependence on the dimension is only $O(d)$.

Our techniques can also apply to the ℓ_1 metric (and to close approximations of the ℓ_2 metric), although the dependence on the dimension changes for the three different cases above.

Structure-Aware PSI. We initiate the study of **structure-aware PSI,** which exploits known structure in Alice's input set to achieve better efficiency than a conventional, "general purpose PSI" protocol. Our primary measure of efficiency is the *communication cost* of PSI protocols. Conventional PSI protocols have communication cost $O((|A| + |B|)\kappa)$, where A and B are the input sets. A structure-aware PSI protocol should have communication cost $O((d + |B|)\kappa)$, where $d \ll |A|$. Ideally d is the *description size*, not cardinality, of A. Various different structures for A can be considered—not just the union of radius-δ balls, as in our motivating application for fuzzy PSI.

General Protocol Paradgim. Most efficient PSI protocols use the classic oblivious PRF (OPRF) paradigm of Freedman *et al.* [22]. In an OPRF, Alice has an input set A, and Bob has no input. Bob learns a PRF seed k while Alice learns $\{\mathsf{PRF}_k(a) \mid a \in A\}$. The parties can obtain a PSI protocol by having Bob send $\{\mathsf{PRF}_k(b) \mid b \in B\}$ to Alice. Our structure-aware PSI is an instance of the OPRF-to-PSI paradigm, but with a **structure-aware OPRF** that takes advantage of publicly known structure in the OPRF receiver's set A. We construct semi-honest structure-aware PSI/OPRF from any weak FSS construction for the receiver's set A. Our key theorem can be summarized as follows:

Main Theorem (Informal). *If there is a weak FSS for a family $\mathcal{S}$ of sets, with shares of length σ, then there is a semi-honest structure-aware PSI protocol (where Alice's input $A \in \mathcal{S}$) with communication $O((\sigma + |B|)\kappa)$.*

In particular, the reliance on Alice's set is reduced from $O(|A|\kappa)$ in a general-purpose PSI protocol to $O(\sigma\kappa)$. The problem of constructing structure-aware PSI therefore reduces to the simpler problem of constructing a weak FSS for the supported structure, with share size smaller than the set cardinality.

Our structure-aware PSI protocol is inspired by the IKNP OT extension protocol [30]. As such, it uses only cheap symmetric-key operations apart from a small number of base-OTs and FSS operations. Hence, if the underlying FSS is also based on symmetric-key operations, the resulting PSI protocol has high potential to be practically efficient.

Generalizing Other PSI Protocols. Our protocol generalizes several prior leading PSI/OPRF protocols [13,30,39], in the sense that these protocols are obtained by instantiating our protocol with an appropriate FSS. Since these protocols support PSI for arbitrary sets, we can interpret them as implicitly defining an FSS for arbitrary sets. These FSS schemes have share size proportional to the cardinality of the set. The real power of our paradigm is when it is used for structured sets, that have compact FSS shares that are significantly smaller than the cardinality of the set.

Fuzzy PSI Implementation. We build a prototype implementation of fuzzy PSI using our new techniques. Our implementation supports 2-dimensional balls in the ℓ_∞ norm. When Alice has roughly 2700 balls of radius 30 (covering 10 million points), and Bob has a million points, our protocol requires roughly 41 s and 156 MB of communication. In contrast, the naïve approach (plain PSI with Alice's expanded set) requires 75 s and 1180 MB of communication using the efficient semi-honest plain PSI protocol of [36].

1.2 Related Work

Conventional PSI. Over the last decade, PSI techniques have matured and become truly practical. PSI is regularly used in practice to solve some of the problems listed above, at scale. There are quite a few protocol paradigms for PSI, including circuit-based [27,42], oblivious polynomial evaluation via additively homomorphic encryption [18,34], key agreement [19,28,31], bloom filters [20,46], to name a few.

Despite many interesting protocol approaches, modern PSI is practical and scalable **thanks almost entirely to the oblivious transfer (OT) paradigm.** Using modern OT extension [30] techniques, it is possible to generate many (millions) of OT instances extremely efficiently. These OTs are then used to carry out the comparisons necessary for PSI. With OT extension, the *marginal* cost each OT instance involves only cheap symmetric-key operations (*e.g.*, calls to AES). Thus, the OT-based PSI paradigm is the **only approach** in which each of the parties' items contributes just a small constant number of fast symmetric-key operations to the overall protocol cost. Pinkas, Schneider, and Zohner [43] were the first to propose basing PSI directly on OT; their approach was later refined in a series of works [13,24,36,39–41,47,48]. The current leading OT-based 2-party PSI protocols are [13,36] in the semi-honest model and [24,40,48] for malicious security.

Note that even recent progress on so-called *silent OT* [6–8,17,49], which allows parties to generate essentially unlimited oblivious transfer instances with no communication, does **not** solve the problem of structure-aware PSI. Silent OT techniques generate only *random* OT correlations, which must be converted to chosen-input OT instances using communication [3]. Conventional PSI protocols, even based on silent OT, require a number of OT primities (and hence communication) proportional to the cardinality of sets, and do not take advantage of sets with low description size.

PSI with Sublinear Communication. It is possible to construct a PSI protocol with communication sublinear in one of the parties' sets, using RSA accumulators [1] or leveled fully homomorphic encryption [14,15]. Both of these techniques are "heavy machinery" in the sense that they imply single-server PIR.

Other works have explored the use of an one-time offline phase for PSI [33,44], especially in the context of private contact discovery [32], where a large set remains relatively static. The use of an offline phase is out of scope in our work, as we measure total communication cost.

Fuzzy PSI. Fuzzy PSI was introduced by Freedman *et al.* [23], who give a protocol for Hamming-distance (over tuples of strings). Later, Chmielewski and Hoepman [16] showed an attack against this protocol and proposed their own protocols, one of which was itself later attacked and improved upon by Ye *et al.* [54]. All of these protocols use the *oblivious polynomial evaluation* technique, in which the parties encode their input sets as roots of a polynomial and use additively homomorphic public-key encryption to manipulate these polynomials.

Indyk & Woodruff [29] describe a fuzzy PSI protocol for Hamming and ℓ_2 metrics, but their protocol requires generic MPC (*e.g.*, Yao's protocol) evaluation of a decryption circuit for a homomorphic encryption scheme, for every item. Bedő *et al.* [4] construct a fuzzy PSI protocol using homomorphic encryption. Doumen [21] gives a fuzzy PSI protocol under a non-standard security model, where the goal is to bound the loss in entropy about the input sets caused by running the protocol.

Chakraborti *et al.* [12] construct fuzzy PSI protocols (which they call *distance-aware PSI*) for Hamming distance, based on homomorphic encryption. Their protocol has false positives in the final result. They also describe a fuzzy PSI protocol for 1-dimensional integers—*i.e.*, points a and b are matched if $|a - b| \leq \delta$. This protocol is an elegant reduction to plain PSI, where parties can simply run plain PSI on sets that are larger by a factor of $O(\log \delta)$. Uzun *et al.* [51] also recently proposed a fuzzy PSI protocol for Hamming distance, based on homomorphic encryption techniques.

There are several works studying so-called *fuzzy matching* or *fuzzy handshake* protocols [2,52,53]. These protocols reveal to the participants whether the intersection of their sets has cardinality above some threshold (*i.e.*, whether $|A \cap B| \geq t$; see also [25,55]). Such a functionality can be used for applications like fingerprint matching [50] and ride-sharing [26]. For these works, the "fuzziness" is with respect to the entire sets A and B, measured by *exact* matches between items of A and B. In our setting, fuzziness refers to individual items of A and B that are similar but not necessarily equal.

Applications of Fuzzy PSI. Pal *et al.* [38] use fuzzy PSI in the context of compromised credentials checking, to check whether a user's password is *similar* to passwords that have been leaked online. They use the "naïve reduction" of fuzzy PSI to plain PSI, but set sizes in their application are small enough that this approach is practical.

2   Preliminaries

Semi-Honest Security. We rely on the *Universal Composability* (UC) framework from [11] to show that our 2-party protocols are secure against passive adversaries. Parties P_0 and P_1 with inputs x_0 and x_1 run protocol Π to learn the output of a function $f(x_0, x_1)$; P_i's view $\mathsf{View}(P_i, 1^\kappa, x_0, x_1)$ during an honest execution consists of her private input x_i, privately chosen randomness and the transcript of the protocol.

We say that protocol Π securely realizes a functionality f if there exists a simulator Sim for both parties and for all possible inputs x_0, x_1 such that:

$$\mathsf{Sim}(P_i, x_i, f(x_0, x_1), 1^\kappa) \cong \mathsf{View}(P_i, x_0, x_1, 1^\kappa)$$

the views from the simulation and honest execution are computationally indistinguishable in the security parameter κ.

2.1 Hamming Correlation Robustness

Our protocol is based on IKNP OT-extension [30]. That protocol requires a hash function with a certain security property:

Definition 1 ([30]). *Let $H : \{0,1\}^* \times \{0,1\}^\kappa \to \{0,1\}^v$ be a function and define the related function $F_s(t, x) = H(t; x \oplus s)$, where $s \in \{0,1\}^\kappa$. We say that H is **correlation robust** if F_s is indistinguishable from a random function, against distinguishers that never query with repeated t-values. Intuitively, values of the form $H(t_i; x_i \oplus s)$ look jointly pseudorandom, even with known t_i, x_i values and a common s.*

All protocols in the "IKNP family" require a hash function with a similar kind of security property; e.g., [35, 36]. The specific property we use is defined below:

Definition 2. *Let $H : \{0,1\}^* \times (\{0,1\}^k)^\ell \to \{0,1\}^v$ be a function and define the related function $F_s(t, x, \Delta) = H(t; x \oplus s \odot \Delta)$, where $s \in \{0,1\}^\ell$; x, Δ are vectors of length ℓ with components in $\{0,1\}^k$; and $\odot$ is componentwise multiplication (of a bit times a string). We say that H is **Hamming correlation robust** if F_s is indistinguishable from a random function, against distinguishers that never query with repeated t-values and always query with Δ having at least κ nonzero components.*

Intuitively, values of the form $H(t_i; x_i \oplus s \odot \Delta_i)$ look jointly pseudorandom, even with known t_i, x_i, Δ_i values and a common s, provided that each Δ_i has high Hamming weight.

This definition generalizes the one from [36] in that x and Δ are bit strings (vectors of bits) in [36], whereas in our protocol x and Δ can be vectors with components from $\{0,1\}^k$.

3 Building Blocks

3.1 2PC Ideal Functionalities

Oblivious transfer is a special case of secure two-party computation, in which a sender has a pair of input strings m_0, m_1, a receiver has input $b \in \{0,1\}$, and the receiver learns output m_b. The sender learns nothing about b, and the receiver learns nothing about m_{1-b}.

Our structure-aware PSI protocol requires the parties to perform a small number of oblivious transfers. We use $\mathcal{F}_{ot}$ to denote an ideal functionality providing an instance of oblivious transfer.

3.2   Function Secret Sharing

A 2 party FSS scheme for a class of functions $\mathcal{F}$ allows a dealer to distribute a function $f \in \mathcal{F}$ into two shares (f_1, f_2), where each share individually hides the function f. Furthermore, $f(x) = f_1(x) \oplus f_2(x)$ for all inputs x. The main efficiency measure of FSS is the size of the function shares f_1, f_2.

Boolean Function Secret Sharing. In this work we will specifically be interested in secret sharing *indicator functions* for a family of sets. The indicator function evaluates to 0 when the input belongs to the set, and otherwise it evaluates to 1. We relax the definition of FSS for indicator functions to allow for one-sided false positive error and output length being greater than a bit. We call our definition (p, k)-**Boolean Function Secret Sharing** $((p, k)$-bFSS), where p is the false positive error probability and k is the output length. Let $\mathcal{S} \subseteq 2^{\mathcal{U}}$ be a family of sets for some universe of points $\mathcal{U}$. Then we formally define the syntax and security of this relaxed FSS primitive as follows:

Definition 3 (bFSS syntax). *A 2-party (p, k)-bFSS scheme for a family of sets $\mathcal{S} \subseteq 2^{\mathcal{U}}$ with input domain $\mathcal{U}$ consists of a pair of algorithms (Share, Eval) with the following syntax:*

- *$(k_0, k_1) \leftarrow$ Share$(1^\kappa, \hat{S})$: The randomized share function takes as input the security parameter κ and (the description of) a set $S \in \mathcal{S}$ as input. It outputs two shares.*
- *$y_{idx} \leftarrow$ Eval$(1^\kappa, idx, k_{idx}, x)$: The deterministic evaluation function takes as input the security parameter, party index $idx \in \{0, 1\}$, the corresponding share k_{idx} and input $x \in \mathcal{U}$, and it outputs a string $y_{idx} \in \{0, 1\}^k$.*

Usually the security parameter 1^κ is not written as an explicit function argument.

Definition 4 (bFSS security). *A 2-party (p, k)-bFSS scheme (Share, Eval) for $\mathcal{S} \subseteq 2^{\mathcal{U}}$ is **secure** if is satisfies the following conditions:*

- *Correctness for yes-instances: For every set $S \in \mathcal{S}$, $x \in S$, and security parameter κ:*

$$\Pr\left(y_0 \oplus y_1 = 0^k \;\middle|\; \begin{array}{l} (k_0, k_1) \leftarrow \text{Share}(1^\kappa, S) \\ y_0 \leftarrow \text{Eval}(1^\kappa, 0, k_0, x) \\ y_1 \leftarrow \text{Eval}(1^\kappa, 1, k_1, x) \end{array} \right) = 1$$

- *Bounded false positive rate: For every set $S \in \mathcal{S}$, $\underline{x \in \mathcal{U} \setminus S}$, and security parameter κ:*

$$\Pr\left(y_0 \oplus y_1 \neq 0^k \;\middle|\; \begin{array}{l} (k_0, k_1) \leftarrow \text{Share}(1^\kappa, S) \\ y_0 \leftarrow \text{Eval}(1^\kappa, 0, k_0, x) \\ y_1 \leftarrow \text{Eval}(1^\kappa, 1, k_1, x) \end{array} \right) \geq p$$

– **Privacy:** *There exists a simulator Sim such that for all* $idx \in \{0,1\}$ *and all* $S \in \mathcal{S}$, *the following distributions are indistinguishable in* κ:

$$\boxed{\begin{array}{l} (k_0, k_1) \leftarrow \mathsf{Share}(1^\kappa, S) \\ \text{return } k_{\mathsf{idx}} \end{array}} \cong_\kappa \mathsf{Sim}(1^\kappa, idx)$$

In other words, each individual share leaks nothing about S. *We further say that the bFSS has* **pseudorandom keys** *if the output of Sim is a random string of some fixed length.*

Definition 5 (Strong bFSS). *A* **strong bFSS** *is a (1,1)-bFSS.*

Strong bFSS corresponds to the original FSS definition of [9]—*i.e.*, no false positives—when restricted to sharing indicator functions of sets.

Definition 6 (PRF property). *A* (p, k)*-bFSS scheme* (Share, Eval) *for a family of sets* $\mathcal{S} \subseteq 2^\mathcal{U}$ *with input domain* $\mathcal{U}$ *and key space* $\mathcal{K}$ *is said to satisfy the PRF property if for any* $idx \in \{0,1\}$, $x \in \mathcal{U}$, $\mathsf{Expt}(1^\kappa, idx, x)$ *is indistinguishable from a uniform random string, where* Expt *is defined as:*

$$\boxed{\begin{array}{l} \mathsf{Expt}(1^\kappa, \mathsf{idx}, x): \\ \hline \quad k \leftarrow \mathcal{K} \\ \quad \text{return } \mathsf{Eval}(1^\kappa, \mathsf{idx}, k, x) \end{array}}$$

3.3 Oblivious Key Value Store

An **oblivious key value store (OKVS)** [24] is a data structure that encodes a set of key-value mappings while hiding the set of keys used.

Definition 7 ([24]). *An* **oblivious key-value store (OKVS)** *consists of algorithms* Encode *and* Decode, *with an associated space* $\mathcal{K}$ *of keys and space* $\mathcal{V}$ *of values. An OKVS must satisfy the following properties:*

– **Correctness:** *For all* $A \subseteq \mathcal{K} \times \mathcal{V}$ *with distinct* $\mathcal{K}$*-values, and all* $(k, v) \in A$:

$$\Pr[\mathsf{Decode}(\mathsf{Encode}(A), k) = v] \text{ is overwhelming}$$

One may call Decode *with any* $k \in \mathcal{K}$, *and indeed, someone who holds* Encode(A) *may not know whether a particular* k *was included in* A.
– **Obliviousness:** *For all distinct* $\{k_1^0, \ldots, k_n^0\}$ *and distinct* $\{k_1^1, \ldots, k_n^1\}$, *the output of* $\mathcal{R}(k_1^0, \ldots, k_n^0)$ *is indistinguishable from that of* $\mathcal{R}(k_1^1, \ldots, k_n^1)$, *where:*

$$\boxed{\begin{array}{l} \mathcal{R}(k_1, \ldots, k_n): \\ \hline \quad \text{for } i \in [n]: v_i \leftarrow \mathcal{V} \\ \quad \text{return } \mathsf{Encode}(\{(k_1, v_1), \ldots, (k_n, v_n)\}) \end{array}}$$

Garimella *et al.* [24] define the properties of an OKVS and construct an efficient one based on 3-way cuckoo hashing. If values from $\in \mathcal{V}$ require v bits to write, then their construction encodes n key-value pairs with roughly $1.35nv$ bits—close to the optimal length nv.

A special class of OKVS is **boolean OKVS**, where the OKVS data structure itself is a vector of strings $D = (d_1, \ldots, d_n)$ and Eval is defined as $\mathsf{Eval}(D, x) = \bigoplus_{i \in \pi(x)} d_i = \langle \pi(x), D \rangle$ for some function π. The function π specifies which positions of the data structure to probe.

Our construction also requires the following additional property of OKVS, that we prove is satisfied by all existing OKVS constructions in full version of this paper:

Definition 8. *An OKVS satisfies the* **independence property** *if for all $A \subseteq \mathcal{K} \times \mathcal{V}$ with distinct $\mathcal{K}$-values, and any k^* not appearing in the first component of any pair in A, the output of $\mathsf{Decode}(\mathsf{Encode}(A), k^*)$ is indistinguishable from random, over the randomness in* Encode.

4 bFSS Constructions

Our high-level goal is efficient bFSS schemes for collections of ℓ_∞ balls in d dimensions. This kind of geometric structure can be viewed hierarchically: a *union* of balls, where each ball is a *Cartesian product* of *1-dimensional intervals*. Our final bFSS constructions reflect this hierarchy. At each level of the hierarchy there may be different choices of bFSS construction. A visual overview of the possibilities is provided in Fig. 1.

4.1 Existing Schemes

In this section we recall bFSS constructions from previous works that are relevant for the geometric structures that we consider. All prior work considers only **strong**, *i.e.*, $(1, 1)$-bFSS. All of which satisfy the PRF property:

Theorem 1. *Any strong bFSS F for a collection of sets S in the universe $\mathcal{U}$ with pseudo-random keys satisfies the PRF property (Definition 6).*

A proof of this theorem can be found in full version of this paper.

The simplest of all bFSS schemes is a trivial sharing of a **truth table**. We denote this construction as tt. The two parties hold additive secret shares of the truth table for the set's membership function. This bFSS construction is viable only for sets that exist in a relatively small universe of items.

What we call the sum construction is a simple method to construct bFSS for a disjoint union, from an bFSS for each term in the union. The method works only for strong, *i.e.*, $(1, 1)$-bFSS.

Theorem 2 (sum). *If F_1 is a $(1, 1)$-bFSS for S_1 with share size σ_1, and F_2 is a $(1, 1)$-bFSS for S_2 with share size σ_2, then $\mathsf{sum}[F_1, F_2]$ is a $(1, 1)$-bFSS for $\{S_1 \cup S_2 \mid S_1 \in \mathcal{S}_1, S_2 \in \mathcal{S}_2, S_1 \cap S_2 = \emptyset\}$ with share size $\sigma_1 + \sigma_2$.*

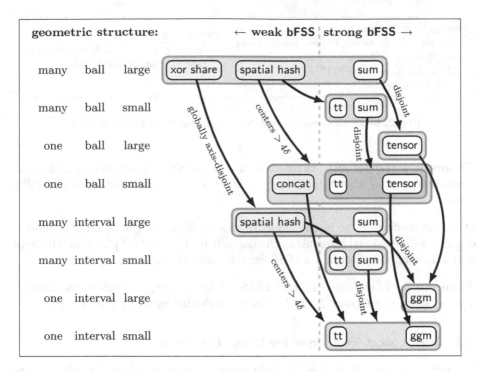

Fig. 1. Map of bFSS constructions for geometric structures. Large/small refer to whether the structure exists in a large or small geometric domain. Edges in this map represent reductions. For example, the leftmost edge means: *The "xor share" construction reduces the problem of bFSS for "many ball large" structures to the problem of bFSS for "many interval large" structures, provided that the input satisfies the "globally axis-disjoint" condition.* All weak bFSS constructions are new in this work.

A proof of this can be found in full version of this paper. Boyle *et al.* [9] construct an bFSS scheme for intervals, which we call ggm (it composes PRGs together into a GGM-style tree). Let $\mathcal{D} = \{0, 1, \ldots, 2^u - 1\}$ and define $\mathsf{INT}_u = \{[a, b] \mid a, b \in \mathcal{D}\}$—i.e., the set of all 1-dimensional intervals.

Theorem 3 (ggm [9]). *There exists a $(1, 1)$-bFSS for INT_u satisfying the PRF property with pseudorandom keys of share size $O(\kappa u)$ and Eval cost containing $O(u)$ PRG calls.*

Boyle *et al.* [9] also introduce a technique, which we call tensor, for decision trees and cross-products of bFSS schemes. This technique can be combined with the ggm construction to realize bFSS for d-dimensional intervals. Define multi-$\mathsf{INT}_{u,d} = \{I_1 \times I_2 \times \cdots \times I_d \mid I_1, I_2, \ldots, I_d \in \mathsf{INT}u\}$—i.e., the set of all d-dimensional intervals. Note that an ℓ_∞ ball is a d-dimensional interval with sides of equal length.

$\text{Share}_n^{\mathcal{S}}(1^\kappa, S_1 \times S_2)$:
  Initialize k_0, k_1 as empty associated arrays
  $(k_0[0], k_1[0]) \leftarrow \text{Share}^{\mathcal{S}_1}(1^\kappa, S_1)$
  $(k_0[1], k_1[1]) \leftarrow \text{Share}^{\mathcal{S}_2}(1^\kappa, S_2)$
  return (k_0, k_1)

$\text{Eval}_n^{\mathcal{S}}(1^\kappa, \text{idx}, \text{FSSkey}, x)$:
  return $\text{Eval}^{\mathcal{S}_1}(1^\kappa, \text{idx}, \text{FSSkey}[0], x)\|$
    $\text{Eval}^{\mathcal{S}_2}(1^\kappa, \text{idx}, \text{FSSkey}[1], x)$

Fig. 2. bFSS for cross product $S_1 \times S_2$ given bFSS for S_1 and S_2

Theorem 4 (tensor [9]). *There exists a $(1,1)$-bFSS for multi-INT$_{u,d}$ with pseudorandom keys of share size $O(\kappa u^d)$ and Eval cost dominated by $O(u^d)$ PRG calls.*

Define union-dint$_{u,d,n}$ to be the family of sets consisting of the union of at most n disjoint d-dimensional intervals in the domain $\{0, 1, \ldots, 2^u - 1\}^d$. From Theorem 2 and Theorem 4 we obtain a bFSS for this collection of sets:

Theorem 5. *There exists a $(1,1)$-bFSS for union-dint$_{u,d,n}$ with pseudorandom keys of share size $O(\kappa n u^d)$ and Eval cost dominated by $O(n u^d)$ PRG calls.*

4.2 New concat Technique for Cross Products

We now describe our new bFSS techniques. A common theme in all of these constructions is that they take advantage of the bFSS generalization to construct (p, k)-bFSS for $p < 1$ and/or $k > 1$.

concat denotes our simple new approach for cartesian product of several bFSS. We construct an bFSS for a product $S_1 \times S_2$ by simply concatenating outputs of an bFSS for S_1 and an bFSS for S_2. This gives us a secure (p, k)-bFSS construction for the cross product of sets with $p = \min_i p_i$ and $k = k_1 + k_2$, assuming we start from a (p_1, k_1)-bFSS and (p_2, k_2)-bFSS. The construction is described formally in Fig. 2. Similar to the disjoint union construction, the share size and the Eval complexity of this construction is the sum of share size and Eval cost for individual bFSS respectively.

Theorem 6. *If F_1 is a (p_1, k_1)-bFSS for S_1 with share size σ_1, and F_2 is a (p_2, k_2)-bFSS for S_2 with share size σ_2, then concat$[F_1, F_2]$ is a $(\min\{p_1, p_2\}, k_1 + k_2)$-bFSS for $\{S_1 \times S_2 \mid S_1 \in \mathcal{S}_1, S_2 \in \mathcal{S}_2\}$ with share size $\sigma_1 + \sigma_2$.*

Since the output of concat is simply the concatenation of the output of the two Eval's, we get the following property as well:

Theorem 7. *If bFSS F_1 and F_2 satisfy the PRF property, then concat$[F_1, F_2]$ satisfies the PRF property.*

A single ℓ_∞ ball in d dimensions can be represented as the cross product of d intervals along each of the dimension. Hence using the general bFSS construction rule in Subsect. 4.2 (the concat technique) and the strong bFSS for a single interval we get a $(1, d)$-bFSS for a single ℓ_∞ ball.

Theorem 8. *There exists a $(1, d)$-bFSS for $S = multi\text{-}INT_{u,d}$ in $\mathcal{U} = \{0, 1, \ldots, 2^u - 1\}^d$ satisfying the PRF property with pseudo-random keys of size $O(\kappa u d)$ and* Eval *cost $O(ud)$ PRG calls.*

4.3   New Spatial Hashing Technique

Here we describe our proposed approach for constructing bFSS keys for geometric objects. The spatial-hashing approach reduces the problem of bFSS for a geometric structure in a large domain to an easier problem of bFSS in a smaller domain.

Intuition: Partition the space $\{0, \ldots, 2^u - 1\}^d$ into regular grid cells. Call a grid cell "active" if it intersects with the input set that is being shared. We will build an bFSS that gives correct output in all active grid cells, while ensuring that the bFSS output in inactive grid cells is random. Because the inactive grid cells contain only points outside of the set, this approach can produce only false positives in the bFSS output (with bounded probability), which suffices for a (p, k)-bFSS with $p < 1$.

We require a component bFSS (let's call it GridFSS) which supports the possible structures that can exist in a single grid cell. To hide the identities of the active cells, we use an OKVS data structure to map grid cell identifiers to shares of GridFSS. This ensures two properties:

1. Decoding the OKVS at an active grid cell outputs the corresponding correct GridFSS share
2. Decoding the OKVS at a non-active grid cell outputs a uniformly random string, independent of the other values in the OKVS.

Hence we define our overall bFSS shares to each be an OKVS data structure that maps grid cells to GridFSS shares. To evaluate this share at a point x, identify that point's grid cell, query the OKVS at that grid cell, interpret the OKVS output as a share in GridFSS, and evaluate that share at x. The first property above ensures the correctness of the FSS when the input point is in an active grid cell. The second property ensures that outside the active grid cell the output of Eval is random.

This spatial-hashing technique is also illustrated on an example input geometry in Fig. 3.

Spatial hashing reduces the problem of bFSS in a large universe to bFSS in a small grid cell. The benefit of this is that bFSS in small grid cells can be extremely efficient. Specifically, there are many *asymptotically* efficient bFSS for various structures, but when the universe is small enough, they are concretely inferior to the trivial truth table (tt) construction. The reader should think of grid cells as small enough so that the tt approach has the smallest concrete share size. In practice, the threshold for this is grid cells with side length of a few hundred.

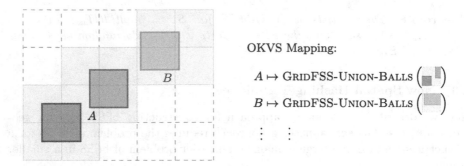

Fig. 3. Spatial hashing technique applied to an example of 3 disjoint ℓ_∞ balls in 2 dimensions. Active grid cells are shaded yellow. Contents of each active grid cell are shared using a component bFSS for union of balls. bFSS shares for each active grid cell are encoded into an OKVS (mapping grid cell ID to bFSS share).

We partition the space $\mathcal{D} = [0, 2^u - 1]^d$ into *grid cells*, which are d-dimensional cubes of side length 2δ. We can uniquely *label* each grid cell by the point contained in it that is closest to the origin. Further we define a function cell_δ (parameterized by the grid size) that maps any point in the domain $\mathcal{D}$ to its unique grid cell label. Hence the function $\mathsf{cell}_\delta^{-1}$ maps a grid cell label to the set of points contained in it. Formally we define these maps as:

Definition 9. *For any vector* $\boldsymbol{x} = (x_1, x_2, \ldots, x_d) \in \mathcal{D}$, *we define the function that maps a point to its grid cell label as:* $\mathsf{cell}_\delta(\boldsymbol{x}) = \lfloor \boldsymbol{x}/2\delta \rfloor = (\lfloor x_1/2\delta \rfloor, \ldots, \lfloor x_d/2\delta \rfloor)$. *We also define* $\mathsf{cell}_\delta^{-1}(\boldsymbol{x}) = [x_1, x_1 + 2\delta) \times [x_2, x_2 + 2\delta) \times \ldots \times [x_d, x_d + 2\delta)$, *which maps any grid cell label to the set of points contained in that grid cell.*

Definition 10. *Define* $G(\delta, u, d) = $ *set of all grid cells* $= \{\mathsf{cell}_\delta^{-1}(\boldsymbol{x}) \mid x_1, \ldots, x_d \in \{2k\delta \mid k \in [0, 2^{u-1}/\delta]\}\}$

Definition 11. *Let* S *be a family of sets over universe* $\mathcal{U} = \{0, \ldots, 2^u - 1\}^d$. *The set of all active grid cells is* $\mathsf{ActiveCells}(\delta, S) = \{C \in G(\delta, u, d) \mid C \cap S \neq \emptyset\}$. *Define* $\mathsf{MaxActiveCellCount}(\delta, \mathcal{S}) = \max_{S \in \mathcal{S}} |\mathsf{ActiveCells}(\delta, S)|$.

We propose a bFSS for the input structure S, given a bFSS GridFSS that supports the contents of each active grid cell. To take advantage of the fact that grid cells are very small, we normalize all grid cells to the origin with the following function which translates a grid cell to the origin:

Definition 12. *For any grid cell* $C \in G(\delta, u, d)$ *and any* $\boldsymbol{x} \in \mathcal{U}$ *we can define the function* $\mathsf{ShiftOrigin}(C, \boldsymbol{x}) = \{\boldsymbol{y} - \boldsymbol{x} \mid \boldsymbol{y} \in C\}$

The spatial-hashing technique is presented formally in Fig. 4 and it gives us an bFSS with the following parameters (formal proof is provided in full version of this paper):

Given a (p,k)-bFSS F for $\mathcal{S}_\delta$ and an OKVS (Encode, Decode)

$\mathsf{Share}^{\mathcal{S}}(1^\kappa, S)$:

  DummyCells $\leftarrow \emptyset$
  $\mathsf{GridKey}_0, \mathsf{GridKey}_1$ - associative arrays initialized empty
  for each $C(\boldsymbol{x}) \in \mathsf{ActiveCells}(\delta, S)$:
    $(\mathsf{GridKey}_0[\boldsymbol{x}], \mathsf{GridKey}_1[\boldsymbol{x}]) \leftarrow \mathsf{GridFSS.Share}(1^\kappa, \mathsf{ShiftOrigin}(S \cap \mathsf{cell}_\delta^{-1}(-\boldsymbol{x})))$
  do $\mathsf{MaxActiveCellCount}(\delta, \mathcal{S}) - |\mathsf{ActiveCells}(\delta, S)|$ times:
    Pick any $C'(\boldsymbol{y}) \in G(\delta, u, d) \setminus (\mathsf{ActiveCells}(\delta, S) \cup \mathsf{DummyCells})$
    DummyCells $\leftarrow$ DummyCells $\cup \{\boldsymbol{y}\}$
    $(\mathsf{GridKey}_0[\boldsymbol{y}], \mathsf{GridKey}_1[\boldsymbol{y}]) \leftarrow \mathsf{GridFSS.Share}(1^\kappa, \emptyset)$
  $k_0 \leftarrow \mathsf{OKVS.Encode}(\mathsf{GridKey}_0)$
  $k_1 \leftarrow \mathsf{OKVS.Encode}(\mathsf{GridKey}_1)$
  return (k_0, k_1)

$\mathsf{Eval}^{\mathcal{S}}(1^\kappa, \mathsf{idx}, k, \boldsymbol{x})$:

  $\mathsf{GridKey} \leftarrow \mathsf{OKVS.Decode}(k, \mathsf{cell}(\boldsymbol{x}))$
  return $\mathsf{GridFSS.Eval}(1^\kappa, \mathsf{idx}, \mathsf{GridKey}, \boldsymbol{x})$

Fig. 4. spatial-hashing$_{\delta,d}$ construction for the collection of sets $\mathcal{S}$ with grid size δ in domain $\mathcal{U} = \{0, 1, \ldots, 2^u - 1\}^d$

Theorem 9. *Let $\mathcal{S}$ be a family of sets over universe $\mathcal{U} = \{0, \ldots, 2^u - 1\}^d$. Let δ be an arbitrary integer representing the grid size. Define $\mathcal{S}_\delta = \{\mathsf{ShiftOrigin}(S \cap \mathsf{cell}_\delta^{-1}(\boldsymbol{x}), \boldsymbol{x}) \mid S \in \mathcal{S}, C(\boldsymbol{x}) \in G(\delta, u, d)\}$.*

If $\mathsf{GridFSS}$ is a (p, k)-bFSS for $\mathcal{S}_\delta$ with pseudo-random keys and satisfying the PRF property with share size σ, then $\mathsf{spatial\text{-}hashing}_{\delta,d}[\mathsf{GridFSS}]$ is a $(\min\{1 - 2^{-k}, p\}, k)$-bFSS for $\mathcal{S}$ with share size $O(\mathsf{MaxActiveCellCount}(\delta, \mathcal{S}) \cdot \sigma)$

We next employ this spatial-hashing technique to develop efficient bFSS constructions for union of ℓ_∞-balls.

bFSS for Union of Disjoint ℓ_∞ Balls. We define the collection of sets $\mathsf{union\text{-}disj}_{u,d,\delta,n}$ to contain sets, each containing at most n disjoint ℓ_∞ balls of radius δ in the $\mathcal{U} = \{0, 1, \ldots, 2^u - 1\}^d$. If we use the spatial hashing technique for the same grid size parameter δ then each active grid cell would intersect at most 2^d input balls and $\mathsf{MaxActiveCellCount}$ would be $n2^d$.

Lemma 1. *Any radius-δ ℓ_∞ ball in $\mathcal{U}$ intersects with at most 2^d disjoint ℓ_∞-balls.*

Proof. An ℓ_∞ ball with radius δ is a d dimensional cube of side length 2δ. Hence the intersection of any two overlapping ℓ_∞ δ radius balls contains at least one vertex of both the balls. The lemma follow from the fact that a d dimensional cube has at max 2^d vertices and that the input set S contain all disjoint ℓ_∞ balls.

Lemma 2. *For any $S \in$ union-disj$_{u,d,\delta,n}$ and any grid cell $C \in G(\delta, u, d)$, the cell cell$_\delta^{-1}(C)$ intersects with at max 2^d balls in S.*

Proof. cell$_\delta^{-1}(C)$ is itself a ℓ_∞ ball of radius δ. Hence this follows from the previous lemma.

Lemma 3. *For $S =$ union-disj$_{u,d,\delta,n}$, MaxActiveCellCount$(\delta, S) = n2^d$*

To construct bFSS for union-disj$_{u,d,\delta,n}$ we need a component GridFSS that can support the union of at most 2^d balls in a single grid cell. We can use the bFSS for union-dint with $\mathcal{U} = \{0, 1, \ldots, 2\delta - 1\}^d$, which gives us the following theorem:

Theorem 10. *There exists a $(0.5, 1)$-bFSS for the collection of sets union-disj$_{u,d,\delta,n}$ in $\mathcal{U} = \{0, 1, \ldots, 2^u - 1\}^d$, with key size $O(n\kappa(4\log\delta)^d)$ bits and evaluation cost dominated by $O((2\log\delta)^d)$ calls to a PRG.*

Union of ℓ_∞ Balls with Pairwise Distance Greater than 4δ. We can have a more efficient bFSS when the input balls are known to be sufficiently far apart. Suppose the set of balls have pairwise distance greater than 4δ. This collection of sets union-4delta$_{u,d,\delta,n}$ is parameterized by u (defines the universe $\mathcal{U} = \{0, 2, \ldots, 2^u - 1\}^d$), number of dimensions d, radius of balls δ and the number of balls n.

Lemma 4. *Any grid cell intersects with at most 1 ℓ_∞ balls from S, for any $S \in$ union-4delta$_{u,d,\delta,n}$.*

Proof. Suppose that an ℓ_∞ ball centered at c_0 intersects two balls in S centered at c_1 and c_2 respectively. Then we have:

$$d_\infty(c_0, c_1) \leq 2\delta \text{ and } d_\infty(c_0, c_2) \leq 2\delta$$
$$\implies d_\infty(c_1, c_2) \leq d_\infty(c_0, c_1) + d_\infty(c_0, c_1) \leq 4\delta \quad \text{(By triangle inequality)}$$

This contradicts the assumption that all balls have centers greater than 4δ apart.

If we apply spatial hashing to such a set of balls, we get that each active grid cell will intersect with at most 1 input ball. Hence, we can apply the spatial hashing construction using a simpler GridFSS—namely, we can use the bFSS for a single d-dimensional interval (multi-INT$_{2\delta,d}$). This saves a factor of $O(2^d/d)$ from the overall share size.

Theorem 11. *There exists a $(1 - 1/2^d, d)$-bFSS for the collection of sets union-4delta$_{u,d,\delta,n}$ in $\mathcal{U} = \{0, \ldots, 2^u - 1\}^d$, with key size $O(nd\kappa(2)^d \log\delta)$ and evaluation cost dominated by $O(d\log\delta)$ calls to a PRG.*

ℓ_∞ balls are the simplest objects we support, but ℓ_1 balls can also be supported. In the full version of the paper we sketch out the main differences between the ℓ_1 and ℓ_∞ balls case.

4.4   xor-share Technique

The bFSS construction for union of ℓ_∞ disjoint balls does not scale well with the number of dimensions, as its share size is proportional to 2^d. This stems from the fact that each input ball can intersect with 2^d grid cells in the worst case.

To improve the dependence on the dimension, consider the following approach. For each input ball i, generate an additive sharing of 0: $R[i,1] \oplus \cdots \oplus R[i,d] = 0$, where each share is assigned to one of the d dimensions. Now imagine projecting all balls onto the jth dimension—the result is a union of intervals. Suppose we had a bFSS for the union of 1-dimensional intervals, which would output $R[i,j]$ whenever a point is in the projection of the ith ball, and would output a random bit whenever the point is outside of all ball-projections. Then for every point x, we could evaluate one bFSS for each dimension (the jth bFSS for 1-dimensional intervals, evaluated at x_j), and xor the results.

If x is contained in input ball i, then the result yields $R[i,1] \oplus \cdots \oplus R[i,d] = 0$. If x is "hit" by the projection of ball i in all but the last dimension, say, then the resulting xor contains $R[i,1] \oplus \cdots \oplus R[i,d-1]$ which is uniformly random – even if x is "hit" by a different ball in dimension d. If x is not "hit" by any ball in the jth dimension, then its corresponding xor likewise gives a random result. No matter what, if x is not in any ball, then its xor is random, and this leads to a $(p,1) - \mathsf{bFSS}$ for $p = 1/2$. Note that the total share size for this bFSS is only d times larger than a bFSS for a union of 1-dimensional intervals. In other words, the dependence on dimension is no longer exponential.

However, there is one problem with this approach: What should we do if balls i and i' overlap when projected onto dimension j? In that case we would expect the jth component bFSS to evaluate to both $R[i,j]$ and $R[i',j]$ on some points. Hence, this general approach only works when the input set of ℓ_∞ balls are *globally axis disjoint*, meaning that the balls have disjoint projections onto each dimension. We define the collection of sets $\mathsf{union\text{-}glob\text{-}disj}_{u,d,\delta,n}$, to contain globally axis disjoint n ℓ_∞ d dimentional balls of radius δ in $\mathcal{U} = \{0,1,\ldots,2^u - 1\}^d$. This xor-share technique is illustrated in Fig. 5 and described formally in Fig. 6.

Let $\pi_i(x_1,\ldots,x_d) = x_i$ denote the projection of a point along dimension i. We extend this function to sets as: $\pi_i(S) = \{\pi_i(x) \mid x \in S\}$, and note that the projection of an ℓ_∞ ball onto any dimension is a 1-dimensional interval.

We can use our spatial hashing technique, but with one important caveat. Usually spatial hashing simply performs an bFSS share of the intersection of the input set with each active grid cell. However, our standard approach for spatial hashing causes the bFSS to always output 0 for intervals in the input set. In this construction we need the bFSS to sometimes output 0 and sometimes output 1 for these intervals, since they encode a particular secret share. To account for this we modify the spatial-hashing construction to take as input a set S and a set of grid cells $acvCells$, such that $\mathsf{ActiveCells} \subset acvCells$ and the spatial-hashing construction encodes GridFSS keys into an OKVS for each cell in $acvCells$. We use this generalized spatial-hashing construction when presenting this construction

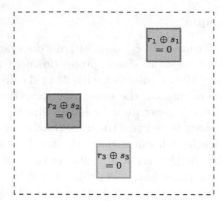

(a) Original geometric structure - globally axis disjoint

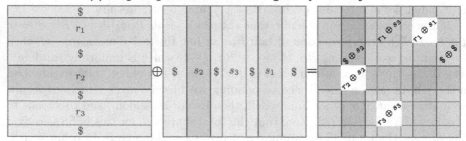

(b) Representing the original structure as the xor of two 1-dimensional structures.

Fig. 5. An illustration of our xor-share technique, applied to 3 globally axis-disjoint balls in 2 dimensions

in Fig. 6. Proof for the following theorem can be found in Its proof can be found in full version of the paper.

Theorem 12. *The construction in Fig. 6 is a (0.5, 1)-bFSS for collection of sets* union-glob-disj$_{u,d,\delta,n}$ *in* $\mathcal{U} = \{0, \ldots, 2^u - 1\}^d$, *with key size* $O(nd \log \delta)$ *bits and the evaluation cost being dominated by* $O(d \log \delta)$ *calls to a PRG.*

5   Structure-Aware PSI from bFSS

In this section we present our protocol for **structure-aware PSI**. This is a variant of PSI in which the receiver's (Alice's) input set has a known structure. The functionality details are given in Fig. 7.

Protocol Intuition. As a warmup, suppose we have a strong bFSS (*i.e.*, a (1, 1)-bFSS). Let Alice generate κ independent sharings of her structured set A, as $(k_0^{(i)}, k_1^{(i)}) \leftarrow$ Share(A). Bob chooses a random string $s \leftarrow \{0, 1\}^\kappa$ and, using the bits of s as choice bits to κ instances of oblivious transfer, he learns one share from each of the different sharings: $k_*^{(i)} = k_{s_i}^{(i)}$.

Parameters:
- $(1,1)$-bFSS F for the collection of sets union-dint$_{\lceil \log \delta \rceil,1,2}$
- An OKVS (Encode, Decode)

Share$(1^\kappa, S)$:

   for $i = 1$ to n: // *additive sharing of zero for each ball*
      $R[i,1], \ldots, R[i,d] \leftarrow_\$ \{0,1\}$, subject to $\oplus_{j=1}^{d} R[i,j] = 0$
   $S', acvCells \leftarrow \emptyset$
   for $j = 1$ to d:
      For each $C = \mathsf{cell}^{-1}(x) \in G(\delta, u, 1)$ such that $C \cap \pi_j(S) \neq \emptyset$
         Sample $r \leftarrow_\$ \{0,1\}$
         $acvCells \leftarrow acvCells \cup \{x\}$
         $S' \leftarrow S' \cup \{y \in C \mid$ if for some $i \in [1,n], y \in \pi_j(S_i)$ and $R[i,j] = 0\}$
         $S' \leftarrow S' \cup \{y \in C \mid y \notin \pi_j(S)$ and $r = 0\}$
      $(k_0[j], k_i[j]) \leftarrow \mathsf{spatial\text{-}hashing}_{\delta,1}[F](S', acvCells)$
   return $(k_0[1, \ldots, d], k_1[1, \ldots, d])$

Eval$(1^\kappa, \mathsf{idx}, k, x)$:

   Parse k as an array of d OKVS $(k[1], k[2], \ldots, k[d])$
   for $j = 1$ to d:
      $\mathsf{GridKey}[j] \leftarrow \mathsf{OKVS.Decode}(k[j], \mathsf{cell}_\delta(x_j))$
      $y[j] \leftarrow F.\mathsf{Eval}(1^\kappa, \mathsf{idx}, \mathsf{GridKey}[j], x_j)$
   return $\oplus_{j=1}^{d} y_j$

Fig. 6. A $(0.5, 1)$-bFSS for the collection of sets union-glob-disj$_{n,d,\delta}$ in the $\mathcal{U} = \{0, 1, \ldots, 2^u - 1\}^d$

Supppose Bob defines the function

$$F(x) = \mathsf{H}\Big(\mathsf{Eval}(k_*^{(1)}, x), \mathsf{Eval}(k_*^{(2)}, x), \cdots, \mathsf{Eval}(k_*^{(\kappa)}, x)\Big)$$

Bob can compute $F(x)$ for all x, but which values of $F(x)$ can Alice compute? Note that she knows all the FSS shares but does not know Bob's OT choice bits s, which determine the choice of shares used to define F.

If $x \in A$, then the correctness of the bFSS establishes that $\mathsf{Eval}(k_0^{(i)}, x) = \mathsf{Eval}(k_1^{(i)}, x)$. In this case, Bob's OT choice doesn't make a difference—both shares produce the same output. Therefore, Alice can compute $F(x)$ as

$$F(x) = \mathsf{H}\Big(\mathsf{Eval}(k_0^{(1)}, x), \mathsf{Eval}(k_0^{(2)}, x), \cdots, \mathsf{Eval}(k_0^{(\kappa)}, x)\Big) \qquad \text{(for } x \in A)$$

However, if $x \in A$ then $\mathsf{Eval}(k_0^{(i)}, x) \neq \mathsf{Eval}(k_1^{(i)}, x)$ by the properties of a strong bFSS. Intuitively, Bob's OT choice bits make a significant difference on $F(x)$. Alice would have to guess which of $(k_0^{(i)}, k_1^{(i)})$ was chosen by Bob, for *every* i simultaneously, if she is to compute $F(x)$. Equivalently, we can write $\mathsf{Eval}(k_*^{(i)}, x) = \mathsf{Eval}(k_0^{(i)}, x) \oplus s_i$, and hence:

$$F(x) = \mathsf{H}\Big(\big[\mathsf{Eval}(k_0^{(1)}, x), \mathsf{Eval}(k_0^{(2)}, x), \cdots, \mathsf{Eval}(k_0^{(\kappa)}, x)\big] \oplus s\Big) \qquad \text{(for } x \notin A)$$

Values of this form are indistinguishable from random when H is a correlation-robust hash (Definition 1) and s is uniform & secret.

In summary, Alice can learn $F(x)$ for $x \in A$, while $F(x)$ looks random for $x \notin A$. We have created an oblivious PRF (OPRF) that Alice can evaluate on a structured set A. We can then obtain a PSI protocol in the usual way [22], by having Bob send $\{F(b) \mid b \in B\}$ to Alice.

Details. The formal protocol description is given in Fig. 8. The warmup protocol above considers only $(1, 1)$-bFSS. In the general case, suppose we use a (p, k)-bFSS. The important parameter here is the false-positive probability p. When $x \notin A$, we don't always have $\mathsf{Eval}(k_0^{(i)}, x) \neq \mathsf{Eval}(k_1^{(i)}, x)$—we have it only with probability at least p.

To adjust for false positives from the bFSS, we simply increase the number of oblivious transfers (and independent bFSS sharings). We need enough bFSS instances to guarantee the following property with overwhelming probability: For all $x \notin A$, at least κ of the bFSS instances correctly satisfy $\mathsf{Eval}(k_0^{(i)}, x) \neq \mathsf{Eval}(k_1^{(i)}, x)$. These κ instances are enough to make $F(x)$ pseudorandom, if the underlying hash function H is now *Hamming* correlation robust (Definition 2).

We emphasize that even though the underlying bFSS may have false positives (with bounded probability), the resulting PSI protocol accounts for this fact and computes the intersection without error. In full version of this paper we prove the following:

Theorem 13. *The protocol in Fig. 8 securely realizes $\mathcal{F}_{\mathsf{saPSI}}$ (Fig. 7) against semi-honest adversaries, when $(\mathsf{Share}, \mathsf{Eval})$ is a secure (p, k)-bFSS and H is Hamming-correlation robust (Definition 2).*

5.1   Costs

Suppose our protocol is instantiated with a certain bFSS whose total share size is σ_{bFSS}, where $t_{\mathsf{bFSS}}^{\mathsf{Share}}$ is the time to share a set (a set from the family $\mathcal{S}$), and where $t_{\mathsf{bFSS}}^{\mathsf{Eval}}$ is the time to evaluate a share on a single input.

The communication cost of the structure-aware PSI protocol is therefore:

- From Alice to Bob: ℓ instances of OTs, in which she transfers a pair of bFSS shares—hence, $\ell \cdot \sigma_{\mathsf{bFSS}}$ bits.
- From Bob to Alice: an output of H for each of Bob's items—hence, $|B| \cdot (\lambda + \log |A| + \log |B|)$ bits.[2]

The computation cost of the protocol is:

---

[2] The presence of a $|B| \log |B|$ term here is deceptive. The protocol would be equally secure if the output of H were κ bits, in which case the length of Bob's message would be $|B|\kappa$ bits. What we have written here is an optimization, observing that shorter output of H is possible, namely $\lambda + \log |A| + \log |B|$ bits. Every PSI protocol that is based on the OPRF paradigm has communication cost of this kind—in order to achieve correctness error bounded by $2^{-\lambda}$, the OPRF outputs that Bob sends to Alice must have length at least $\lambda + \log |A| + \log |B|$.

Parameters: a family of subsets $\mathcal{S} \subseteq 2^{\mathcal{U}}$, over a universe $\mathcal{U}$ of items. A bound n on the cardinality of the unstructured set.

Functionality:
1. Receive input $A \in \mathcal{S}$ (or a concise representation of A) from Alice.
2. Receive input $B \subseteq \mathcal{U}$ of cardinality at most n from Bob.
3. Give output $A \cap B$ to Alice.

Fig. 7. Ideal functionality $\mathcal{F}_{\mathsf{saPSI}}$ for structure-aware PSI.

Parameters:
- computational security parameter κ and statistical security parameter λ
- family of sets $\mathcal{S}$ with corresponding (p, k)-bFSS scheme (Share, Eval)
- Hamming-correlation robust hash function $\mathsf{H} : \{0,1\}^* \rightarrow \{0,1\}^{\lambda + \log|A| + \log|B|}$
- oblivious transfer functionality $\mathcal{F}_{\mathsf{ot}}$
- length ℓ, chosen so that $\Pr[\mathsf{Binomial}(p, \ell) < \kappa] < 1/2^{\lambda + \log|B|}$

Inputs: Alice has (structured) set $A \in \mathcal{S}$ and Bob has (unstructured) set B.

Protocol:
1. Bob chooses a random string $s \leftarrow \{0,1\}^{\ell}$.
2. Alice generates ℓ independent FSS sharings of her input A: for $i \in [\ell]$ do
   $(k_0^{(i)}, k_1^{(i)}) \leftarrow \mathsf{Share}(1^{\kappa}, A)$.
3. The parties invoke ℓ (parallel) instances of oblivious transfer using $\mathcal{F}_{\mathsf{ot}}$. In the ith instance:
   - Alice is the sender with input $(k_0^{(i)}, k_1^{(i)})$.
   - Bob is the receiver with choice bit s_i. He obtains output $k_*^{(i)} = k_{s_i}^{(i)}$.
4. Bob computes the set
$$\widetilde{B} = \left\{ \mathsf{H}\big(b;\ \mathsf{Eval}(k_*^{(1)}, b), \mathsf{Eval}(k_*^{(2)}, b), \cdots, \mathsf{Eval}(k_*^{(\ell)}, b)\big) \ \middle|\ b \in B \right\}$$
   and sends it (randomly shuffled) to Alice.
5. Alice outputs:
$$\left\{ a \in A \ \middle|\ \mathsf{H}\big(a;\ \mathsf{Eval}(k_0^{(1)}, a), \mathsf{Eval}(k_0^{(2)}, a), \cdots, \mathsf{Eval}(k_0^{(\ell)}, a)\big) \in \widetilde{B} \right\}$$

Fig. 8. PSI protocol for structured input A and unstructured input B using bFSS.

- For Alice: she generates ℓ independent bFSS sharings of her set A, so computation $O(\ell \cdot t_{\mathsf{bFSS}}^{\mathsf{Share}})$. She also evaluates each sharing on each of her items in A, but we assume that in most bFSS this can be done as a side-effect of running the Share algorithm. We ignore the insignificant cost of the ℓ OTs.
- For Bob: he evaluates ℓ independent bFSS sharings on each of his items in B, so computation $O(\ell \cdot t_{\mathsf{bFSS}}^{\mathsf{Eval}} \cdot |B|)$.

5.2   Other Protocols as Instances of Our Framework

The PSI protocols of Pinkas *et al.* [39] (sparse OT) and of Chase-Miao [13] are actually instances of our framework, meaning that we can identify an bFSS construction that yields each of those protocols when using that bFSS construction in our protocol framework. Since these PSI protocols support arbitrary sets, their underlying bFSS constructions are for *unstructured*, arbitrary sets—the only "structure" being the cardinality of the sets. If the classic IKNP protocol [30] protocol is used for PSI (over a small universe of items) in a natural way, it also can be viewed as an instance of our protocol using a trivial bFSS (secret-shared truth table). In full version of the paper we describe these three protocols as specific instances of our approach.

5.3   bFSS Performance

In Fig. 11 we summarize the asymptotic costs of different "recipes" to build bFSS for a union of balls, under various assumptions about those balls. We also show a selection of concrete share sizes for certain parameters (ball radius and dimension), in Fig. 10.

6   Fuzzy PSI Application and Performance

We demonstrate the practicality of our structure-aware PSI protocol and bFSS constructions by exploring in-depth our original motivating example: fuzzy PSI (Fig. 9).

Our protocol requires one party to share the same set many times in a bFSS, and the other party to evaluate all bFSS shares on the same point (many times). In full version of this paper we describe how some of our bFSS constructions can be optimized for such batch operations.

6.1   Performance Comparison

The main benefit of our fuzzy PSI approach is its low communication. In this section we compare the communication costs of different fuzzy PSI protocols. Our construction for the union of balls whose centers have pairwise distance at least 4δ is concretely efficient for medium size δ and dimension d. In our implementation **we mostly focus on this bFSS construction**.

As a representative example we consider the case where Alice has a structured set A with 10 million total points, and Bob has an unstructured set B of 1.2 million points. We hold the total cardinality of Alice's set constant and consider two different ways that her points could be arranged into balls:

- 6250 balls of radius $\delta = 20$, in 2 dimensions[3]
- 2778 balls of radius $\delta = 30$, in 2 dimensions

---

[3] Our prototype implementation currently supports only 2 dimensions.

construction	(p, k)-bFSS	share size	eval cost
disjoint balls:			
spatial hash ∘ sum ∘ tensor ∘ ggm	$(0.5, 1)$	$O(n(4 \log \delta)^d \kappa)$	$O((2 \log \delta)^d)$
sum ∘ tensor ∘ ggm	$(1, 1)$	$O(n\kappa u^d)$	$O(nu^d)$
ball centers $> 4\delta$ apart:			
spatial hash ∘ concat ∘ ggm	$(1 - 1/2^d, d)$	$O(nd2^d \kappa \log \delta)$	$O(d \log \delta)$
spatial hash ∘ concat ∘ tt	$(1 - 1/2^d, d)$	$O(nd2^d \delta)$	0
globally axis-disjoint balls:			
xor share ∘ spatial hash ∘ ggm	$(0.5, 1)$	$O(nd\kappa \log \delta)$	$O(d \log \delta)$
xor share ∘ spatial hash ∘ tt	$(0.5, 1)$	$O(nd\delta)$	0
any arrangement of balls:			
bFSS for unstructured sets	$(0.5, 1)$	$O(n(2\delta)^d)$	0

Fig. 9. Asymptotic size of bFSS share for n balls (ℓ_∞ norm) of radius δ in d dimensions, over u-bit integers. Evaluation time for evaluating a share on a single point, measured in number of PRG calls. Keep in mind that each ball consists of $(2\delta)^d$ points.

bFSS construction	δ: 32 d: 2	32 10	1024 2	1024 10
disjoint balls:				
spatial hash ∘ sum ∘ tensor ∘ ggm	24.3	3.42	0.080	0.00004
sum ∘ tensor ∘ ggm [16 bit ints]	**8.0**	**0.5**	**0.008**	**5E-7**
ball centers $> 4\delta$ apart:				
spatial hash ∘ concat ∘ ggm	0.68	0.001	**0.003**	6E-9
spatial hash ∘ concat ∘ tt	**0.17**	**0.0003**	0.005	1E-8
globally axis-disjoint balls:				
xor share ∘ spatial hash ∘ ggm	0.34	0.0002	**0.002**	8E-10
xor share ∘ spatial hash ∘ tt	**0.084**	**0.00004**	0.003	1E-9
any arrangement of balls:				
bFSS for unstructured sets (amortized)	1.0	1.0	1.0	1.0

Fig. 10. Concrete size of bFSS share for n balls (ℓ_∞ norm) of radius δ in d dimensions, reported in **bits per point**. bFSS for unstructured sets refers to the polynomial-based bFSS implicit in [39], which achieves 1 bit per point only when generating many sharings of the same set.

Our Protocol. Our protocol is instantiated with computational security parameter $\kappa = 128$ and statistical security parameter $\lambda = 40$. With $d = 2$, our choice of bFSS is a $(0.75, 2)$-bFSS, and we use $\ell = 280$ base OTs so that $\Pr[\mathrm{Binomial}(0.75, \ell) < \kappa]$ is negligible (as specified in Fig. 8).

Ignoring the fixed cost of ℓ base OTs, the communication cost of our protocol is as follows. Alice sends ℓ bFSS shares encoding her set, while Bob sends $|B|$ OPRF outputs, each of length $\lambda + \log(|A| \cdot |B|)$. Using the same calculations as in Fig. 10, the cost of a single FSS share for $\delta = 20$ is 0.27 bits per item, and for $\delta = 30$ it is 0.18 bits per item. Accounting for all parameters, we obtain communication cost (in bits):[4]

$$(\delta = 20) \quad 280 \cdot 0.27|A| + 84|B| = 76|A| + 84|B| \text{ bits} = 108\mathrm{MB}$$
$$(\delta = 30) \quad 280 \cdot 0.18|A| + 84|B| = 50|A| + 84|B| \text{ bits} = 75\mathrm{MB}$$

PSI Based on Silent OT. As discussed earlier, one approach for fuzzy PSI is for Alice to simply enumerates all points with δ of her set and perform plain PSI on the result. A particularly appealing PSI protocol for this purpose is the VOLE-PSI protocol of Rindal & Schoppmann [48], because it has the lowest communication cost (to the best of our knowledge). In the VOLE-PSI protocol, Alice and Bob start by using the silent OT technique [6–8,17,49] to obtain an instance of pseudorandom vector OLE. This step requires communication that is sublinear in the size of the parties' sets, and we ignore it for the sake of simplicity.

However, a pseudorandom vector-OLE requires additional communication, so it can be derandomized for the parties' chosen PSI inputs. This derandomization takes the form of an OKVS that Alice sends to Bob, which is proportional to the size of her input set. Alice's total communication is $\rho \cdot \kappa$ bits per item, where ρ is the expansion factor of the particular OKVS (e.g., $\rho = 1.35$ in [24]). Bob sends an OPRF output of length $\lambda + \log(|A| \cdot |B|)$ bits for each item in his set, similar to our PSI protocol. The total communication cost is therefore:

$$173 \cdot |A| + 84 \cdot |B| \text{ bits} = 229\mathrm{MB}$$

Here the sizes of the balls makes no difference – only the total number of points in Alice's set, which we are holding constant. We can see that the dominant factor in the communication cost is the coefficient on $|A|$, which our protocol improves significantly (from 173 to 119 or 80). Also, the PSI sender pays less (overhead of 84 bits) than the receiver (overhead of 173 bits) per items and since Alice's set size if the dominant cost, we can get better communication if Alice is PSI sender. However, our fuzzy protocol only allows for the party with the larger set (structured) to learn the output, so we present the silent OT based PSI cost assuming that Alice is the PSI receiver.

KKRT. Another possibility for solving fuzzy PSI using plain PSI is the KKRT protocol [36], which is the fastest PSI protocol in the LAN setting. Bob's communication would be same as in our protocol except that he now needs to send

---

[4] Our actual implementation sends twice this amount of data because we do not optimize the base OTs for the case where one of the OT messages is random, as with bFSS shares.

3 hash outputs instead of a single hash output per item. Alice would send ℓ bits per hash table item, where ℓ is the parameter our protocol would use for a $(p = 0.5, k) - \mathsf{bFSS}$ ($\ell \approx 440$ for these input sizes), hash table has expansion factor $\rho = 1.35$ to number of items.[5] For the parameters considered above, this leads to total communication:

$$594 \cdot |A| + 252 \cdot |B| \text{ bits} = 780\text{MB}$$

Again, we reiterate that in our protocol we assume the receiver to have the larger input set and acknowledge that we apply this same restriction to KKRT to make our comparison.

6.2 Implementation

General Protocol Implementation. We implemented our main structure-aware fuzzy PSI protocol (Fig. 8) in C++ and our choice of parameters, input sizes and bFSS is as described in the preceding section. Our protocol Fig. 8 involves cryptographic components like (1) base oblivious transfers (2) hamming correlation hash function (3) encryption/decryption functionalities and a general communication framework. For the hamming-correlation robust hash function we use SHA256. For base OTs and general framework we use the libOTe library of Rindal [45]. We implement the bFSS recipe spatial hash ∘ concat ∘ tt, for balls of pairwise distance $> 4\delta$, and use the OKVS implementation from [37][6] for spatial hashing. Our implementation will be made available on Github upon publication.

protocol	50 Mbps time (s)	100 Mbps time (s)	150 Mbps time (s)	200 Mbps time (s)	250 Mbps time (s)	comm (MB)
KKRT [36]	218.409	131.057	101.312	81.511	75.092	1184.224
ours, $\delta = 20$ (6250 balls)	**115.49**	**87.593**	**78.404**	**73.358**	**72.27**	**319.314**
ours, $\delta = 30$ (2778 balls)	**61.675**	**48.904**	**43.573**	**42.107**	**41.198**	**156.878**

Fig. 11. Run time (in seconds) and communication (in MB) comparison of our fuzzy PSI protocol with input set sizes $|A| = 10M$ and $|B| = 1.2M$ where A consists of 2-dimensional ℓ_∞ balls We instantiate our protocol in Figure 8 with bFSS recipe spatial hash ∘ concat ∘ tt, for balls with centers $> 4\delta$ apart. We simulated a network with latency 80ms and the given bandwidth cap.

---

[5] The implementation of KKRT that we used has a large expansion factor, which accounts for the difference between this estimate and the actual communication that we measured.

[6] https://github.com/asu-crypto/mPSI.

We ran all our experiments on a single Intel Xeon processor at 2.30 GHz with 256 GB RAM over a single thread of execution. We emulate the different network settings using Linux tc command and use the same command to measure the communication cost of the protocol. We emulate a WAN-like setting assuming an average latency of 80 ms and range of bandwidth settings. For restricted network with bandwidth (including internet-like settings) {50Mbps, 100Mbps, 150Mbps, 200Mbps, 250Mbps}, our fuzzy PSI protocol has superior performance to KKRT for $\delta = \{20, 30\}$ owing largely to our communication efficiency. The vole-based PSI implementation is not publicly available to make a comparison of our run time. As discussed earlier, we believe that our communication efficiency will yield better run time on restricted bandwidths.

7   Limitation and Open Problems

The proposed OPRF-PSI framework is designed in the semi-honest model, and the malicious setting is left for future work.

In our structure-aware PSI protocol, only one input set is structured and it does not attempt to take advantage of any structure in Bob's set B. The sender in our protocol sends OPRF values for each element in its set - hence a natural question is whether we can exploit some structure in Bob's input to send this set of OPRF values more efficiently.

Alice's computation cost is still $O(|A|)$, despite A having a more concise representation. This is because she must enumerate OPRF outputs for each $a \in A$, in order to recognize them in Bob's PSI message. In order for Alice's computation to scale with the description size of A, she would need a way to efficiently "recognize" OPRF outputs that she is entitled to learn, but without explicitly enumerating them. We leave it to future work to explore how to make this possible. For now, supporting exponentially large A remains an important open problem.

Our techniques can be used to get weak bFSS for union of balls in ℓ_2 metric space by approximating each ball by a polyhedron with sufficiently good isoperimetric quotient (which is a measure of how close a shape is to a sphere). However, its still unknown if we can get symmteric key based weak bFSS for an **exact** ℓ_2 ball, which is more suited for fuzzy PSI related applications. Given a weak bFSS for a single ℓ_2 ball, we can use our spatial-hashing technique to get an efficient weak bFSS for a union of balls in ℓ_2 metric space.

References

1. Ateniese, G., De Cristofaro, E., Tsudik, G.: (If) Size matters: size-hiding private set intersection. In: Catalano, D., Fazio, N., Gennaro, R., Nicolosi, A. (eds.) PKC 2011. LNCS, vol. 6571, pp. 156–173. Springer, Heidelberg (2011). https://doi.org/10.1007/978-3-642-19379-8_10
2. Ateniese, G., Kirsch, J., Blanton, M.: Secret handshakes with dynamic and fuzzy matching. In: NDSS, vol. 7, pp. 43–54 (2007)

3. Beaver, D.: Precomputing oblivious transfer. In: Coppersmith, D. (ed.) CRYPTO 1995. LNCS, vol. 963, pp. 97–109. Springer, Heidelberg (1995). https://doi.org/10.1007/3-540-44750-4_8

4. Bedő, J., Conway, T., Ramchen, K., Teague, V.: Privately matching k-mers. Cryptology ePrint Archive, Report 2016/781 (2016). eprint.iacr.org/2016/781

5. Boyle, E., Chandran, N., Gilboa, N., Gupta, D., Ishai, Y., Kumar, N., Rathee, M.: Function secret sharing for mixed-mode and fixed-point secure computation. In: Canteaut, A., Standaert, F.-X. (eds.) EUROCRYPT 2021, Part II. LNCS, vol. 12697, pp. 871–900. Springer, Cham (2021). https://doi.org/10.1007/978-3-030-77886-6_30

6. Boyle, E., Couteau, G., Gilboa, N., Ishai, Y.: Compressing vector OLE. In: Lie, D., Mannan, M., Backes, M., Wang, X. (eds.) ACM CCS 2018, pp. 896–912. ACM Press, October 2018

7. Boyle, E., et al.: Efficient two-round OT extension and silent non-interactive secure computation. In: Cavallaro, L., Kinder, J., Wang, X., Katz, J. (eds.) ACM CCS 2019, pp. 291–308. ACM Press, November 2019

8. Boyle, E., Couteau, G., Gilboa, N., Ishai, Y., Kohl, L., Scholl, P.: Efficient pseudorandom correlation generators: silent OT extension and more. In: Boldyreva, A., Micciancio, D. (eds.) CRYPTO 2019, Part III. LNCS, vol. 11694, pp. 489–518. Springer, Cham (2019). https://doi.org/10.1007/978-3-030-26954-8_16

9. Boyle, E., Gilboa, N., Ishai, Y.: Function secret sharing. In: Oswald, E., Fischlin, M. (eds.) EUROCRYPT 2015, Part II. LNCS, vol. 9057, pp. 337–367. Springer, Heidelberg (2015). https://doi.org/10.1007/978-3-662-46803-6_12

10. Boyle, E., Gilboa, N., Ishai, Y.: Function secret sharing: Improvements and extensions. In: Weippl, E.R., Katzenbeisser, S., Kruegel, C., Myers, A.C., Halevi, S. (eds.) ACM CCS 2016, pp. 1292–1303. ACM Press, October 2016

11. Canetti, R.: Universally composable security: a new paradigm for cryptographic protocols. In: 42nd FOCS, pp. 136–145. IEEE Computer Society Press, October 2001

12. Chakraborti, A., Fanti, G., Reiter, M.K.: Distance-aware private set intersection (2021)

13. Chase, M., Miao, P.: Private set intersection in the internet setting from lightweight oblivious PRF. In: Micciancio, D., Ristenpart, T. (eds.) CRYPTO 2020, Part III. LNCS, vol. 12172, pp. 34–63. Springer, Cham (2020). https://doi.org/10.1007/978-3-030-56877-1_2

14. Chen, H., Huang, Z., Laine, K., Rindal, P.: Labeled PSI from fully homomorphic encryption with malicious security. In: Lie, D., Mannan, M., Backes, M., Wang, X. (eds.) ACM CCS 2018, pp. 1223–1237. ACM Press, October 2018

15. Chen, H., Laine, K., Rindal, P.: Fast private set intersection from homomorphic encryption. In: Thuraisingham, B.M., Evans, D., Malkin, T., Xu, D. (eds.) ACM CCS 2017, pp. 1243–1255. ACM Press, October/November 2017

16. Chmielewski, L., Hoepman, J.-H.: Fuzzy private matching. In: 2008 Third International Conference on Availability, Reliability and Security, pp. 327–334. IEEE (2008)

17. Couteau, G., Rindal, P., Raghuraman, S.: Silver: silent VOLE and oblivious transfer from hardness of decoding structured LDPC codes. In: Malkin, T., Peikert, C. (eds.) CRYPTO 2021, Part III. LNCS, vol. 12827, pp. 502–534. Springer, Cham (2021). https://doi.org/10.1007/978-3-030-84252-9_17

18. Dachman-Soled, D., Malkin, T., Raykova, M., Yung, M.: Secure efficient multiparty computing of multivariate polynomials and applications. In: Lopez, J., Tsudik, G. (eds.) ACNS 2011. LNCS, vol. 6715, pp. 130–146. Springer, Heidelberg (2011). https://doi.org/10.1007/978-3-642-21554-4_8

19. De Cristofaro, E., Tsudik, G.: Practical private set intersection protocols with linear complexity. In: Sion, R. (ed.) FC 2010. LNCS, vol. 6052, pp. 143–159. Springer, Heidelberg (2010). https://doi.org/10.1007/978-3-642-14577-3_13

20. Dong, C., Chen, L., Wen, Z.: When private set intersection meets big data: an efficient and scalable protocol. In: Sadeghi, A.-R., Gligor, V.D., Yung, M. (eds.) ACM CCS 2013, pp. 789–800. ACM Press, November 2013

21. Doumen, J.: Non-interactive fuzzy private matching. WorkingPaper TR-CTIT-07-45, Centre for Telematics and Information Technology (CTIT), Netherlands, June 2007

22. Freedman, M.J., Ishai, Y., Pinkas, B., Reingold, O.: Keyword search and oblivious pseudorandom functions. In: Kilian, J. (ed.) TCC 2005. LNCS, vol. 3378, pp. 303–324. Springer, Heidelberg (2005). https://doi.org/10.1007/978-3-540-30576-7_17

23. Freedman, M.J., Nissim, K., Pinkas, B.: Efficient private matching and set intersection. In: Cachin, C., Camenisch, J.L. (eds.) EUROCRYPT 2004. LNCS, vol. 3027, pp. 1–19. Springer, Heidelberg (2004). https://doi.org/10.1007/978-3-540-24676-3_1

24. Garimella, G., Pinkas, B., Rosulek, M., Trieu, N., Yanai, A.: Oblivious key-value stores and amplification for private set intersection. In: Malkin, T., Peikert, C. (eds.) CRYPTO 2021, Part II. LNCS, vol. 12826, pp. 395–425. Springer, Cham (2021). https://doi.org/10.1007/978-3-030-84245-1_14

25. Ghosh, S., Simkin, M.: The communication complexity of threshold private set intersection. In: Boldyreva, A., Micciancio, D. (eds.) CRYPTO 2019, Part II. LNCS, vol. 11693, pp. 3–29. Springer, Cham (2019). https://doi.org/10.1007/978-3-030-26951-7_1

26. Hallgren, P.A., Orlandi, C., Sabelfeld, A.: PrivatePool: privacy-preserving ridesharing. In: Köpf, B., Chong, S. (eds.) CSF 2017 Computer Security Foundations Symposium, pp. 276–291. IEEE Computer Society Press (2017)

27. Huang, Y., Evans, D., Katz, J.: Private set intersection: are garbled circuits better than custom protocols? In: NDSS 2012. The Internet Society, February 2012

28. Huberman, B.A., Franklin, M., Hogg, T.: Enhancing privacy and trust in electronic communities. In: ACM Conference on Electronic Commerce. ACM (1999)

29. Indyk, P., Woodruff, D.: Polylogarithmic private approximations and efficient matching. In: Halevi, S., Rabin, T. (eds.) TCC 2006. LNCS, vol. 3876, pp. 245–264. Springer, Heidelberg (2006). https://doi.org/10.1007/11681878_13

30. Ishai, Y., Kilian, J., Nissim, K., Petrank, E.: Extending oblivious transfers efficiently. In: Boneh, D. (ed.) CRYPTO 2003. LNCS, vol. 2729, pp. 145–161. Springer, Heidelberg (2003). https://doi.org/10.1007/978-3-540-45146-4_9

31. Jarecki, S., Liu, X.: Fast secure computation of set intersection. In: Garay, J.A., De Prisco, R. (eds.) SCN 2010. LNCS, vol. 6280, pp. 418–435. Springer, Heidelberg (2010). https://doi.org/10.1007/978-3-642-15317-4_26

32. Kales, D., Rechberger, C., Schneider, T., Senker, M., Weinert, C.: Mobile private contact discovery at scale. In: Heninger, N., Traynor, P. (eds.) USENIX Security 2019, pp. 1447–1464. USENIX Association, August 2019

33. Kiss, Á., Liu, J., Schneider, T., Asokan, N., Pinkas, B.: Private set intersection for unequal set sizes with mobile applications. PoPETs 2017(4), 177–197 (2017)

34. Kissner, L., Song, D.: Privacy-preserving set operations. In: Shoup, V. (ed.) CRYPTO 2005. LNCS, vol. 3621, pp. 241–257. Springer, Heidelberg (2005). https://doi.org/10.1007/11535218_15

35. Kolesnikov, V., Kumaresan, R.: Improved OT extension for transferring short secrets. In: Canetti, R., Garay, J.A. (eds.) CRYPTO 2013, Part II. LNCS, vol. 8043, pp. 54–70. Springer, Heidelberg (2013). https://doi.org/10.1007/978-3-642-40084-1_4

36. Kolesnikov, V., Kumaresan, R., Rosulek, M., Trieu, N.: Efficient batched oblivious PRF with applications to private set intersection. In: Weippl, E.R., Katzenbeisser, S., Kruegel, C., Myers, A.C., Halevi, S. (eds.) ACM CCS 2016, pp. 818–829. ACM Press, October 2016

37. Nevo, O., Trieu, N., Yanai, A.: Simple, fast malicious multiparty private set intersection. Cryptology ePrint Archive, Report 2021/1221 (2021). eprint.iacr.org/2021/1221

38. Pal, B., Islam, M., Ristenpart, T., Chatterjee, R.: Might i get pwned: a second generation password breach alerting service (2021)

39. Pinkas, B., Rosulek, M., Trieu, N., Yanai, A.: SpOT-Light: lightweight private set intersection from sparse OT extension. In: Boldyreva, A., Micciancio, D. (eds.) CRYPTO 2019, Part III. LNCS, vol. 11694, pp. 401–431. Springer, Cham (2019). https://doi.org/10.1007/978-3-030-26954-8_13

40. Pinkas, B., Rosulek, M., Trieu, N., Yanai, A.: PSI from PaXoS: fast, malicious private set intersection. In: Canteaut, A., Ishai, Y. (eds.) EUROCRYPT 2020, Part II. LNCS, vol. 12106, pp. 739–767. Springer, Cham (2020). https://doi.org/10.1007/978-3-030-45724-2_25

41. Pinkas, B., Schneider, T., Segev, G., Zohner, M.: Phasing: private set intersection using permutation-based hashing. In: Jung, J., Holz, T. (eds.) USENIX Security 2015, pp. 515–530. USENIX Association, August 2015

42. Pinkas, B., Schneider, T., Weinert, C., Wieder, U.: Efficient circuit-based PSI via cuckoo hashing. In: Nielsen, J.B., Rijmen, V. (eds.) EUROCRYPT 2018, Part III. LNCS, vol. 10822, pp. 125–157. Springer, Cham (2018). https://doi.org/10.1007/978-3-319-78372-7_5

43. Pinkas, B., Schneider, T., Zohner, M.: Faster private set intersection based on OT extension. In 23rd USENIX Security Symposium (USENIX Security 14), pp. 797–812 (2014)

44. Resende, A.C.D., Aranha, D.F.: Faster unbalanced private set intersection. In: Meiklejohn, S., Sako, K. (eds.) FC 2018. LNCS, vol. 10957, pp. 203–221. Springer, Heidelberg (2018). https://doi.org/10.1007/978-3-662-58387-6_11

45. Rindal, P.: libOTe: an efficient, portable, and easy to use Oblivious Transfer Library. github.com/osu-crypto/libOTe

46. Rindal, P., Rosulek, M.: Improved private set intersection against malicious adversaries. In: Coron, J.-S., Nielsen, J.B. (eds.) EUROCRYPT 2017, Part I. LNCS, vol. 10210, pp. 235–259. Springer, Cham (2017). https://doi.org/10.1007/978-3-319-56620-7_9

47. Rindal, P., Rosulek, M.: Malicious-secure private set intersection via dual execution. In: Thuraisingham, B.M., Evans, D., Malkin, T., Xu, D. (eds.) ACM CCS 2017, pp. 1229–1242. ACM Press, October/November 2017

48. Rindal, P., Schoppmann, P.: VOLE-PSI: fast OPRF and circuit-PSI from vector-OLE. In: Canteaut, A., Standaert, F.-X. (eds.) EUROCRYPT 2021, Part II. LNCS, vol. 12697, pp. 901–930. Springer, Cham (2021). https://doi.org/10.1007/978-3-030-77886-6_31

49. Schoppmann, P., Gascón, A., Reichert, L., Raykova, M.: Distributed vector-OLE: improved constructions and implementation. In: Cavallaro, L., Kinder, J., Wang, X., Katz, J. (eds.) ACM CCS 2019, pp. 1055–1072. ACM Press, November 2019
50. Shahandashti, S.F., Safavi-Naini, R., Ogunbona, P.: Private fingerprint matching. In: Susilo, W., Mu, Y., Seberry, J. (eds.) ACISP 2012. LNCS, vol. 7372, pp. 426–433. Springer, Heidelberg (2012). https://doi.org/10.1007/978-3-642-31448-3_32
51. Uzun, E., Chung, S.P., Kolesnikov, V., Boldyreva, A., Lee, W.: Fuzzy labeled private set intersection with applications to private real-time biometric search. In: Bailey, M., Greenstadt, R. (eds.) USENIX Security 2021, pp. 911–928. USENIX Association, August 2021
52. Wang, X.A., Xhafa, F., Luo, X., Zhang, S., Ding, Y.: A privacy-preserving fuzzy interest matching protocol for friends finding in social networks. Soft. Comput. 22(8), 2517–2526 (2017). https://doi.org/10.1007/s00500-017-2506-x
53. Wen, Y., Gong, Z.: Private mutual authentications with fuzzy matching. Int. J. High Perform. Syst. Archit. 5(1), 3–12 (2014)
54. Ye, Q., Steinfeld, R., Pieprzyk, J., Wang, H.: Efficient fuzzy matching and intersection on private datasets. In: Lee, D., Hong, S. (eds.) ICISC 2009. LNCS, vol. 5984, pp. 211–228. Springer, Heidelberg (2010). https://doi.org/10.1007/978-3-642-14423-3_15
55. Zhang, E., Chang, J., Li, Y.: Efficient threshold private set intersection. IEEE Access 9, 6560–6570 (2021)

Two-Round MPC Without Round Collapsing Revisited – Towards Efficient Malicious Protocols

Huijia Lin[1(✉)] and Tianren Liu[2]

[1] University of Washington, Seattle, USA
rachel@cs.washington.edu
[2] CFCS, Peking University, Beijing, China
trl@pku.edu.cn

Abstract. Recent works have made exciting progress on the construction of round optimal, *two-round*, Multi-Party Computation (MPC) protocols. However, most proposals so far are still complex and inefficient. In this work, we improve the simplicity and efficiency of two-round MPC in the setting with dishonest majority and malicious security. Our protocols make use of the Random Oracle (RO) and a generalization of the Oblivious Linear Evaluation (OLE) correlated randomness, called tensor OLE, over a finite field $\mathbb{F}$, and achieve the following:

- *MPC for Boolean Circuits:* Our two-round, maliciously secure MPC protocols for computing Boolean circuits, has overall (asymptotic) computational cost $O(S \cdot n^3 \cdot \log |\mathbb{F}|)$, where S is the size of the circuit computed, n the number of parties, and $\mathbb{F}$ a field of characteristic two. The protocols also make black-box calls to a Pseudo-Random Function (PRF).
- *MPC for Arithmetic Branching Programs (ABPs):* Our two-round, information theoretically and maliciously secure protocols for computing ABPs over a general field $\mathbb{F}$ has overall computational cost $O(S^{1.5} \cdot n^3 \cdot \log |\mathbb{F}|)$, where S is the size of ABP computed.

Both protocols achieve security levels inverse proportional to the size of the field $|\mathbb{F}|$.

Our construction is built upon the simple two-round MPC protocols of [Lin-Liu-Wee TCC'20], which are only semi-honest secure. Our main technical contribution lies in ensuring malicious security using simple and lightweight checks, which incur only a constant overhead over the complexity of the protocols by Lin, Liu, and Wee. In particular, in the case of computing Boolean circuits, our malicious MPC protocols have the same complexity (up to a constant overhead) as (insecurely) computing Yao's garbled circuits in a distributed fashion.

Finally, as an additional contribution, we show how to efficiently generate tensor OLE correlation in fields of characteristic two using OT.

1 Introduction

Improving efficiency is a central theme in the design of cryptographic protocols. Two important aspects are *computational efficiency* and *round efficiency*. In the

The work was partially done when Liu was a postdoctoral researcher at University of Washington.

Y. Dodis and T. Shrimpton (Eds.): CRYPTO 2022, LNCS 13507, pp. 353–382, 2022.
https://doi.org/10.1007/978-3-031-15802-5_13

context of secure Multi-Party Computation (MPC) protocols, since the seminal works in the 80s [Yao82, GMW87, BGW88, CCD88], remarkable improvements have been made on both fronts.

- In the past decade, innovative design and implementation improvements have drastically reduced the computational cost of MPC, leading to efficient protocols more and more applicable to practical situations (e.g., the SPDZ protocols [DPSZ12] and its followup works).
- Another long line of researches on minimizing the round complexity of MPC recently culminated at the construction of *two-round* MPC protocols based on the (minimal) assumption of two-round Oblivious Transfer (OT) in the Common Reference String (CRS) model [BL18, GS18]. Two rounds are optimal even for achieving only semi-honest security and with trusted setups [FKN94, IK97].

However, so far, most two-round MPC protocols are complex and inefficient, especially those achieving malicious security (even in correlated randomness and/or trusted setup model). Encouraged by the efficiency improvement in the realm of many-round MPC in the past decade, this work strives to improve the simplicity and efficiency of two-round MPC in the malicious setting with dishonest majority. Existing techniques can be broadly classified as follows:

- *Round Collapsing:* Introduced by [GGHR14] and initially relying on strong primitives such as indistinguishability obfuscation (iO) or witness encryption [GP15, CGP15, DKR15, GLS15], the round collapsing approach was improved in [GS17, BL18, GS18, GIS18, BLPV18] to rely on just malicious 2-round OT. The complexity of this approach stems from applying the *garbling technique* (e.g., [Yao82, AIK04]) to the next step function of a many-round MPC protocol to collapse the number of rounds to two. The non-black-box use of the underlying MPC protocol hurts both asymptotic and concrete efficiency.
- *Using Generic Non-Interactive Zero Knowledge (NIZK):* This approach starts with designing two-round MPC that are semi-maliciously secure[1], and then transform them to maliciously secure ones by applying generic NIZK to detect deviation from the protocol specification. Two round semi-malicious protocols can be built either via the above round collapsing approach or using primitives supporting homomorphic computation, such as, multi-key fully homomorphic encryption [AJL+12, MW16, CM15, BP16, PS16, AJJM20] or homomorphic secret sharing [BGI16, BGI17, BGI+18, BGMM20]. Using NIZK to prove about the execution of the semi-malicious MPC protocols is inefficient and leads to non-black-box use of underlying assumptions.
- *MPC-in-the-Head* [IKOS07, IPS08, IKSS21]: Another generic method for strengthening weak security to strong security is the "MPC-in-the-head" transformations [IKOS07, IPS08]. The recent work by [IKSS21] showed how to perform such transformations in just two rounds. To obtain a two-round maliciously secure protocol, the transformation uses a two-round protocol with

---

[1] These are protocols secure against corrupted parties who follow the protocol specification but may choose its input and randomness arbitrarily.

(enhanced) semi-honest security [GIS18, LLW20], to *emulate* the execution of another two-round protocol that is maliciously secure in the honest majority setting [IKP10, Pas12]. The overall complexity is the (multiplicative) compound complexity of both protocols.

We observe that existing designs of two-round malicious MPC all apply generic transformations – using garbling or NIZK or MPC – to some underlying MPC, which often leads to non-black-box constructions (with exceptions [GIS18, IKSS21]) and inefficient protocols. To improve the state-of-affairs, we consider protocols that use the Random Oracle (RO) and simple correlated randomness that can be efficiently generated in an offline phase, and aim for either information theoretic security or computational security with black-box use of simple cryptographic tools like Pseudo-Random Functions (PRFs). As seen in the literature, both the random oracle and the online-offline model are extremely successful settings for designing efficient cryptographic protocols.

Our Results: We present a ligitweight construction of 2-round malicious MPC protocols, using RO and an enhanced version of the Oblivious Linear Evaluation (OLE) correlation, called *tensor* OLE. The OLE correlation is the arithmetic generalization of the OT correlation over a finite field $\mathbb{F}$. It distributes to one party (a_1, b_1) and another (a_2, b_2) which are random elements in $\mathbb{F}$ subject to satisfying the equation $a_1 a_2 = b_1 + b_2{}^2$. The tensor OLE correlation further generalizes the OLE correlation to higher dimension: For dimension $k_1 \times k_2$,

$$P_1 \text{ holds: } \mathbf{a}_1 \in \mathbb{F}^{k_1}, \mathbf{B}_1 \in \mathbb{F}^{k_1 \times k_2}, \qquad P_2 \text{ holds: } \mathbf{a}_2 \in \mathbb{F}^{k_2}, \mathbf{B}_2 \in \mathbb{F}^{k_1 \times k_2}$$
$$\text{where } \mathbf{a}_1, \mathbf{a}_2, \mathbf{B}_1, \mathbf{B}_2 \text{ are random, subject to } \mathbf{a}_1 \mathbf{a}_2^\mathsf{T} = \mathbf{B}_1 + \mathbf{B}_2 \text{ .}$$

In our protocols, we will use pairwise tensor OLE correlation, with only small constant dimension, concretely 4×4 and 1×11. Such correlation can be generated efficiently in an offline phase using off-the-shelf OLE protocols [BCGI18, CDI+19]. We also show how to efficiently generate tensor OLE correlation for fields of characteristic two using OT, which in turn can be generated with good concrete efficiency [IKNP03, BCG+19]. We can further rely on pseudorandom correlation, which can be efficiently generated in using techniques described in [BCG+20].

Using tensor OLE correlation and RO, we obtain the following protocols, in the setting of static corruption and security with abort.

MPC FOR BOOLEAN CIRCUITS: Our first result is a construction of efficient two-round maliciously secure MPC protocols for general Boolean circuits. The protocols make use of RO and tensor OLE over a finite field $\mathbb{F}$ of characteristic two, as well as black-box calls to a PRF. (Note that we choose to not instantiate the PRF with RO, because the latter is used for a different purpose. To obtain standard-model protocols, we will employ the random oracle heuristic to replace RO with a real-life hash function. By separating PRF from RO, we reduce the use of heuristic.) When computing an n-ary circuit C, the overall computational costs of all parties is $O(|C| \cdot n^3 \cdot \log \mathbb{F})$. The security level of the protocol is inverse

---

[2] When the field is GF(2), OLE correlation coincides with the OT correlation.

proportional to the field size $|\mathbb{F}|^{-1}$; thus, $\log |\mathbb{F}|$ can be viewed as the effective security parameter. More formally,

Theorem 1 (MPC for Boolean Circuits, informal). *Let $\mathbb{F}$ be a finite field of characteristic two. Let C an n-ary Boolean circuit $C : \{0,1\}^{\ell_1} \times \cdots \times \{0,1\}^{\ell_n} \rightarrow \{0,1\}^\ell$. Assume the existence of a PRF F with security level $2^{-\kappa(\lambda)}$ where λ is the seed length.*

There exists a two-round MPC protocol Π that securely computes C, using RO *and tensor* OLE *correlated randomness, making black-box calls to the PRF, and achieving*

- *overall complexity $O(\Gamma \log \mathbb{F})$ for $\Gamma := n^3 \cdot |C|$, and*
- *ϵ-computational, malicious security with selective abort, against up to $n-1$ corruption, where the security level $\epsilon = \frac{O(\Gamma + n^2 \cdot Q_{\mathrm{RO}})}{|\mathbb{F}|} + \frac{O(n \cdot |C|)}{2^{\kappa(\log |\mathbb{F}|)}}$, and Q_{RO} is the number of random oracle queries that the adversary makes.*

More specifically, parties in our protocols communicate in total $O(\Gamma)$ elements in $\mathbb{F}$, perform in total $O(\Gamma)$ arithmetic operations in $\mathbb{F}$, use in total $O(\Gamma)$ pairs of tensor OLE correlated randomness of constant dimensions, and make in total $O(\Gamma)$ random oracle calls and $O(|C| \cdot n)$ PRF calls. In addition, we can enhance the protocol to have security with unanimous abort at the cost of increasing the complexity by an additive $\mathrm{poly}(n, \lambda)$ overhead.

Our construction follows the technique in [BMR90,DI05,LPSY15] developed in the context of constructing constant-round MPC. They showed that to securely computing a Boolean circuit C, it suffices to securely compute Yao's garbling of the circuit [Yao82]. Furthermore, the latter can be computed by a *degree three* polynomial f over a finite filed $\mathbb{F}$ of characteristic 2 – we call them the **distributed-Yao** polynomials. Therefore, designing 2-round protocols for general circuits boils down to designing 2-round protocols for computing the degree three distributed-Yao polynomials. This is indeed the approach taken by [LLW20]; however, they achieve only semi-honest security. In this work, we further achieve malicious security (see Lemma 1 below), and like [LLW20], our protocols incur only *constant overheads* – their overall asymptotically complexity is the same as the complexity of distributed-Yao polynomials.

We give slightly more detail on distributed-Yao polynomials. They compute Yao's garbled circuits in a special way: First, labels for a wire u has form $\ell_{u,b} = s_{u,b}^{(1)} \| \ldots \| s_{u,b}^{(n)}$, where $s_{u,b}^{(i)} \in \mathbb{F}$ is a PRF key sampled by party P_i. Next, the garbled table for a gate g with input wire u, v and output wire o contains entries of the form $\ell_{o,g(a,b)} \oplus (\bigoplus_i Y_{u,a}^{(i)}) \oplus (\bigoplus_i Y_{v,b}^{(i)})$, where $Y_{u,a}^{(i)}$ and $Y_{v,b}^{(i)}$ are pseudorandom one-time-pads generated via PRF using party P_i's keys $s_{u,a}^{(i)}$ and $s_{v,b}^{(i)}$ respectively (evaluating on different inputs). Hence, the output label is hidden as long as one of the PRF keys is hidden. These entries are additionally permuted using mask bits k_u, k_v which are additively shared among all parties. The important point made by [BMR90,DI05,LPSY15] is that the PRF evaluations can be done locally by each party, and given the PRF outputs as inputs to f, such a garbled circuit can be computed in just degree 3 in $\mathbb{F}$. Analyzing the distributed-Yao polynomial for a circuit C reveals that it contains $O(\Gamma) = O(|C| \cdot n^3)$ monomials over $\mathbb{F}$. In comparison, our MPC protocol implementing C has overall complexity $O(|C| \cdot n^3 \cdot \log |\mathbb{F}|)$ incurring only a constant-overhead over distributed-Yao.

MPC FOR ARITHMETIC BRANCHING PROGRAMS (ABPs): Using similar approach, we obtain efficient, two-round, MPC protocols for ABPs over field $\mathbb{F}$. Here, we compute instead the distributed version of the degree three randomized encoding of Applebaum, Ishai, and Kushilevitz (AIK) [AIK04] for ABPs. More precisely, for an ABP g, we shall compute the n-ary polynomial $f((\mathbf{x}_1, \mathbf{r}_1), \cdots, (\mathbf{x}_n, \mathbf{r}_n)) = \mathsf{AIK}_g((\mathbf{x}_1, \cdots \mathbf{x}_n); \Sigma_{i \in [n]} \mathbf{r}_i)$, where the randomness used for computing the AIK encoding is additively shared among all n parties. We refer to this polynomial the **distributed-AIK** polynomial. The complexity of the resulting MPC protocol is determined by the number of monomials in this polynomial, which is $O(\Gamma) = O(|g|^{1.5} n^2)$. However, different from the case for circuits, our two-round protocols now incur a factor $O(n)$ overhead. Constant-overhead can be retained by adding one more round. More formally,

Theorem 2 (MPC for ABPs, informal). *Let $\mathbb{F}$ be a finite field. Let g be an n-ary arithmetic branching program over $\mathbb{F}$, $g : \mathbb{F}^{l_1} \times \cdots \times \mathbb{F}^{l_n} \to \mathbb{F}$. Denote by $|g|$ the size of the matrix $M_g(\cdot)$ describing g s.t. $\det(M_g(x)) = g(x)$ for any x.*

There exists a two-round MPC protocol Π that securely computes f, using RO *and tensor* OLE *correlated randomness and achieving*

- *overall complexity $O(\Gamma \cdot n \cdot \log |\mathbb{F}|)$ for $\Gamma = |g|^{1.5} n^2$ and*
- *ϵ-statistical, malicious security with abort, against up to $n - 1$ corruption where the statistical simulation error is $\epsilon = \frac{O(\Gamma \cdot n + n^2 Q_{\mathrm{RO}})}{|\mathbb{F}|}$ and Q_{RO} is the number of random oracle queries that the adversary makes.*

Furthermore, there is a three-round protocol achieving the same as above, but with overall complexity $O(\Gamma \cdot \log |\mathbb{F}|)$.

More specifically, parties of the 3-round protocols communicate in total $O(\Gamma)$ elements in $\mathbb{F}$, perform in total $O(\Gamma)$ arithmetic operations in $\mathbb{F}$, and use in total $O(\Gamma)$ pairs of tensor OLE correlated randomness of constant dimensions.

MPC FOR DEGREE THREE POLYNOMIALS: The key that enables above theorems is our construction of, two-round, MPC protocols for computing degree *three* polynomials over an (arbitrary) sufficiently large finite field $\mathbb{F}$. Importantly, the protocol has **constant overhead** – when computing polynomials with Γ monomials over $\mathbb{F}$, our protocols have **overall complexity** $O(\Gamma \cdot \log |\mathbb{F}|)$. Furthermore, the protocol makes only black-box use to the underlying field $\mathbb{F}$.

In order to achieve constant overhead, we only require these protocols to achieve a weaker malicious security, called *security with output substitution*. Intuitively, the protocol ensures the usual privacy guarantee of honest parties inputs – that nothing about honest parties' inputs are revealed beyond the output $\mathbf{y} = f(\mathbf{x}_1, \cdots, \mathbf{x}_n)$. But the honest party may (unanimously) receive incorrect output – the adversary always learn $\mathbf{y}$, and can replace it with another output $\mathbf{y}'$ of its choice without honest parties noticing.

Lemma 1 (MPC for degree 3 polynomials, Informal). *Let $\mathbb{F}$ be a finite field. Let f be an n-ary degree three polynomial over $\mathbb{F}$, $f : \mathbb{F}^{\ell_1} \times \cdots \times \mathbb{F}^{\ell_n} \to \mathbb{F}^{\ell}$; denote by $|f|$ the number of monomials in f.*

There exists a two-round MPC protocol Π that securely computes f, using RO *and tensor* OLE *correlated randomness and achieving the following:*

- *overall complexity $O(|f|)$, and*
- *ϵ-statistical, malicious security with output substitution, against up to $n-1$ corruption, where the statistical simulation error is $\epsilon = \frac{O(|f|+n^2 Q_{\mathrm{RO}})}{|\mathbb{F}|}$ and Q_{RO} is the number of random oracle queries that the adversary makes.*

Our construction easily generalizes to computing constant degree polynomials with constant overhead, which might be of independent interests.

Using the above protocols to compute the distributed-Yao or distributed-AIK polynomials gives 2-round protocols for circuits or ABPs respectively, but achieving only security with output substitution. We complement this by a generic transformation that enhances security with output substitution to security with abort. Essentially, the transformation computes a related circuit (or ABP resp.) that computes not only the output, but also authenticates of the output using partys' private keys (supplied as part of the input). Since security with output substitution ensures the privacy of honest parties' keys, the adversary can no longer substitute the output without being detected. This transformation incurs only a small additive overhead in the case of circuits, but a multiplicative overhead $O(n)$ in the case of ABPs. That's why our two-round ABP protocols do not achieve constant overhead over the complexity of distributed-AIK. We show a different transformation that uses one more round to recover constant overhead.

TENSOR OLE OVER $\mathrm{GF}(2^\lambda)$ FROM OT: As a final contribution, we construct an efficient 4-round protocol for generating the tensor OLE correlation over $\mathrm{GF}(2^\lambda)$.

Theorem 3 (Tensor OLE over $\mathrm{GF}(2^\lambda)$ from OT, Informal). *There is a 4-round, statistically and maliciously secure two party computation protocol for sampling tensor OLE correlations, in the OT hybrid model.*

Our protocol is simple and efficient; in particular, it does not use any generic 2PC techniques such as garbling and zero-knowledge protocols. Thus, parties can run this efficient protocol to generate tensor OLE correlations in an offline stage using OT, which in turn can be generated with concrete efficiency [IKNP03, BCG+19].

Comparison with Prior Two-Round MPC. As discussed before, prior 2-round MPC constructions can be categorized into three types depending on their main technique: 1) round collapsing, 2) using NIZK, and 3) MPC-in-the-head. Almost all protocols using round collapsing and all protocols using NIZK make non-black-box use of underlying cryptographic primitive (e.g., MPC and MKFHE etc.), and many of them have poor asymptotic efficiency (e.g., [BL18, GS18]). The only black-box constructions are [GIS18, IKSS21], which as we discuss below are less efficient than our protocols.

The construction of [GIS18] is in the OT correlation model and uses the round collapsing technique. To compute a Boolean circuit f, parties need to garble the next step functions of an information theoretically and maliciously secure MPC protocol Π for f making black-box calls to OT (e.g. [IPS08]). Let C_Π be the circuit induced by Π with depth d_Π and size $|C_\Pi|$. The overall communication complexity is at least $(d_\Pi |C_\Pi| n^2 \lambda^2)$, where λ is the security parameter. Since d_Π is at least the depth d of f, and $|C_\Pi|$ at least the size of f. This leads to a dependency on $d \cdot |f|$, which is worse than our complexity.

The construction of [IKSS21] following the MPC-in-the-head approach uses a two-round protocol with (enhanced) semi-honest security such as [GIS18,LLW20], to emulate the execution of another two-round protocol that is maliciously secure in the honest majority setting [IKP10,Pas12]. Consider for instance, the complexity of [LLW20] is already $\Omega(|f|n^3\lambda)$ and a loose lower bound of the complexity of [IKP10] is $\Omega(Sn^5\lambda)$. The overall complexity is at least $\Omega(Sn^8\lambda^2)$.

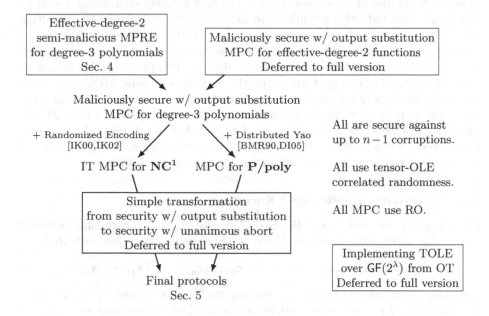

Fig. 1. Our roadmap

2   Technical Overview

Our construction follows the overall structure of the semi-honest 2-round MPC protocols of [LLW20], which uses OLE correlated randomness. However, to make LLW maliciously secure, we face two challenges:

Challenge 1: Design *simple* and *efficient* checks to detect malicious behaviours. To beat previous works, we avoid any generic transformation, such as, using generic NIZK, or even cryptographic operations. Our core protocol will be information-theoretic secure, only use black-box operations over the field. Thus the detection of malicious moves can only rely on arithmetic methods.

Challenge 2: An adversary may lie about the *correlated randomness* it received. Such malicious behavior can hardly be caught even if we allow generic NIZK proof. This is because no party can write "using proper correlated randomness" as a NP-statement, and such statement naturally involves at least 2 parties who jointly hold the correlated randomness.

To deal with these challenges, we use tensor OLE correlated randomness instead of the scalar version, so that we have more room to play with. We also use random oracle to generate challenges in the Fiat-Shamir style, so that our arithmetic proofs become non-interactive. We start with *security with output substitution*, and later transform to security with (unanimous) abort.

In the rest of the overview, we will walk through our constructions. We follow the successful paradigm of [IK00, IK02, ABT18, ABT19, LLW20]: reduce the task of securely computing a function f to the task of securely computing a simpler function $\hat{f}$. Such reduction is captured by MPRE. Section 2.1 revisits the definition of MPRE. Section 2.2 briefly presents our new MPRE, which reduces the task of computing general functions to the task of computing so-called "effective-degree-2" functions. Section 2.3 outlines 2-round malicious MPC protocols for computing effective-degree-2 functions. Composing them yields a 2-round MPC for general functions, but it only satisfies a weak notion of security. Section 2.4 outlines how to lift the security by a simple transformation. Our new constructions of MPRE and MPC are based on tensor OLE correlated randomness. In Sect. 2.5, we show how to generate such correlated randomness from OT. See Fig. 1 for a summary of the technical components and their sections in the technical body.

2.1 Multi-party Randomized Encoding

For a n-party function f, an MPRE of f consists of n preprocessing functions $h_1, \ldots, h_n$, an encoding function $\hat{f}$, and a decoding function Dec, such that,

$$\mathsf{Decode}(\hat{f}(h_1(\mathbf{x}_1, \mathbf{r}_1, \mathbf{r}_1'), \cdots, h_n(\mathbf{x}_n, \mathbf{r}_n, \mathbf{r}_n'))) = f(\mathbf{x}_1, \cdots, \mathbf{x}_n) .$$

where the preprocessing function h_i is computed locally by party P_i on its input $\mathbf{x}_i$, randomness $\mathbf{r}_i$, and correlated randomness $\mathbf{r}_i'$. A semi-honest or malicious MPRE guarantees that to securely compute f, it suffices to securely compute $\hat{f}$ against semi-honest or malicious parties. That is, the following canonical protocol computing f in the $\hat{f}$-hybrid world is semi-honestly (resp. maliciously) secure.[3]

The canonical protocol for MPRE Party P_i has input $\mathbf{x}_i$ and correlated randomness $\mathbf{r}_i'$, samples local randomness $\mathbf{r}_i$, computes $\hat{\mathbf{x}}_i = h_i(\mathbf{x}_i, \mathbf{r}_i, \mathbf{r}_i')$ and feeds $\hat{\mathbf{x}}_i$ to the functionality $F_{\hat{f}}$ computing $\hat{f}$, so that every party learns $\hat{y} := \hat{f}(\hat{\mathbf{x}}_1, \ldots, \hat{\mathbf{x}}_n)$. Then every party outputs $y = \mathsf{Dec}(\hat{y})$.

---

[3] An equivalent definition of semi-honest MPRE can be found in [ABT18], in which it is just called "MPRE". In [ABT19], malicious MPRE is called "non-interactive reduction" and the canonical protocol of a MPRE is called "$\hat{f}$-oracle-aided protocol". Both [ABT18] and [ABT19] consider the honest majority setting, so they only require the canonical protocol to be secure against a bounded number of corruptions.

In other words, MPRE is a non-interactive reduction between MPC tasks. Thanks to the composition of MPC protocols, MPRE schemes naturally composes: Given an MPRE for f as described above, and another MPRE scheme for $\hat{f}$ with preprocessing functions $h'_1, \ldots, h'_n$, the encoding function $\hat{f}'$, their composition gives an MPRE for f with encoding function $\hat{f}'$ and preprocessing functions $h'_1 \circ h_1, \cdots, h'_n \circ h_n$. As such, as demonstrated in [ABT18, ABT19, LLW20], MPRE enables a modular approach for designing round-optimal MPC: To construct a round-optimal MPC protocol Π_f for computing f, the construction of [LLW20] proceeds in three steps:

- *Step 1: Degree 3 MPRE for circuits.* First, obtain a malicious MPRE for circuits, whose encoding function g has degree 3. It turns out that the classical degree 3 (centralized) randomized encoding, given by Yao's garbled circuits, is such a MPRE, where no local preprocessing is needed (i.e., h_i is the identity function). This has been implicitly observed and leveraged in many prior works, e.g., [BMR90, IK00, IK02, DI05, LLW20].
- *Step 2: Effective degree 2 MPRE for degree 3 Polynomials.* Then, design a MPRE of g whose encoding function $\hat{g}$ has degree 2. In this step, the preprocessing functions are non-trivial and such MPRE is said to have effective degree 2.
- *Step 3: 2-round MPC for degree 2 polynomials.* Finally, design a round-optimal MPC protocol $\Pi_{\hat{g}}$ for computing $\hat{g}$.

Composing the MPRE schemes from the first two steps gives an MPRE for circuit f with encoding function $\hat{g}$. The desired protocol Π_f is then obtained by instantiating the $\hat{g}$-oracle in the canonical protocol with $\Pi_{\hat{g}}$. Note that Π_f has the same communication complexity and round complexity as $\Pi_{\hat{g}}$. The contribution of [LLW20] lies in giving efficient instantiation of Step 2 and 3 in the OLE correlated randomness model over a field $\mathbb{F}$ of characteristic 2, and their final protocol Π_f has complexity $O(|f|n^3 \log |\mathbb{F}|)$. The main drawback is that their protocols are only semi-honest secure.

Semi-Malicious MPRE. Our construction improves upon [LLW20] to achieve malicious security. Towards this, we introduce *semi-malicious* MPRE. As the name suggested, a MPRE of f is semi-maliciously secure if its canonical protocol is semi-maliciously secure, i.e., against adversaries who may choose arbitrary local randomness r_i and correlated randomness r'_i of corrupted parties, but computes the preprocessing functions correctly. Equivalently, semi-malicious MPRE means the following protocol is maliciously secure in the $\hat{f} \circ h$-hybrid world.

The canonical protocol for semi-malicious MPRE Party P_i has input $\mathbf{x}_i$, samples local randomness $\mathbf{r}_i$, and receives $\hat{\mathbf{r}}_i$, where $(\hat{\mathbf{r}}_1, \ldots, \hat{\mathbf{r}}_n)$ is the correlated randomness. Every P_i feeds $(\mathbf{x}_i, \mathbf{r}_i, \hat{\mathbf{r}}_i)$ to an oracle computing $\hat{f} \circ h$, so that every party learns

$$\hat{y} = (\hat{f} \circ h)(\mathbf{x}_1, \mathbf{r}_1, \hat{\mathbf{r}}_1, \ldots, \mathbf{x}_n, \mathbf{r}_n, \hat{\mathbf{r}}_n) := \hat{f}(h_1(\mathbf{x}_1, \mathbf{r}_1, \hat{\mathbf{r}}_1), \ldots, h_n(\mathbf{x}_n, \mathbf{r}_n, \hat{\mathbf{r}}_n)).$$

Then every party outputs $y = \mathsf{Dec}(\hat{y})$.

Now, in order to construct 2-round malicious MPC protocol for general circuits, we modify the second and third steps above to the following

- *Step 2:* **Semi-malicious** *Effective degree 2 MPRE for degree 3 Polynomials.* Design a *semi-malicious* MPRE for any degree-3 function f, whose encoding function $\hat{f}$ has degree 2;
- *Step 3: 2-round MPC for* **effective** *degree 2 polynomials.* Construct 2-round *malicious* MPC for computing $\hat{f} \circ h$, which is an effective-degree-2 function.

Composing the above two steps gives a round-optimal maliciously secure MPC protocol for degree 3 functions (Lemma 1); using it to compute the degree 3 maliciously secure MPRE for circuit f from Step 1 gives a round-optimal maliciously secure MPC protocol for f.

Next, we outline our instantiation for Step 2 in Sect. 2.2 and that for Step 3 in Sect. 2.3. The entire roadmap is illustrated in Fig. 1.

2.2   Semi-Malicious Effective-Degree-2 MPRE

This section will outline the construction of semi-malicious effective-degree-2 MPRE for any degree-3 function. We start by "canonicalizing" the degree-3 function. A degree-3 polynomial can always be written as the sum of monomials $\sum_t c_t x_{t,1} x_{t,2} x_{t,3}$, where c_t is the constant coefficient of the t-th monomial. Let the party holding $x_{t,j}$ also sample random $z_{t,j}$, then

$$\left(x_{t,1} x_{t,2} x_{t,3} + z_{t,1} + z_{t,2} + z_{z,3} \text{ for each } t, \sum_t c_t (z_{t,1} + z_{t,2} + z_{z,3}) \right), \qquad (1)$$

is (the encoding function of) a malicious MPRE for $\sum_t c_t x_{t,1} x_{t,2} x_{t,3}$, as shown in [BGI+18, GIS18, LLW20]. So it suffices to construct semi-malicious effective-degree-2 MPRE for (1). Here (1) is in what we call *canonical form*: Every coordinate of $\hat{f}$ either linear, or looks like $x_1 x_2 x_3 + z_1 + z_2 + z_3$.

As we are constructing *semi-malicious* MPRE, it is fine to construct MPRE for each coordinate of (1) separately then simply concatenate them together. That is, it suffices to consider the complete 3-party functionality

$$\mathsf{3MultPlus}((x_1, z_1), (x_2, z_2), (x_3, z_3)) := x_1 x_2 x_3 + z_1 + z_2 + z_3.$$

3MultPlus has a semi-honest effective-degree-2 MPRE (Fig. 2), which will be recalled in Sect. 4.1. For the overview, what matters is that

- This MPRE uses scalar OLE correlated randomness. That is, party P_1 receives $a_1, b_1 \in \mathbb{F}$, party P_2 receives a_2, b_2 such that a_1, a_2, b_1, b_2 are random subject to $a_1 a_2 = b_1 + b_2$.
- This MPRE has perfect semi-honest security.

Our roadmap requires a semi-malicious effective-degree-2 MPRE for 3Mult-Plus. Semi-malicious security means the corrupted parties may arbitrarily choose their local randomness or modify the correlated randomness they received.

	Party P_1	Party P_2	Party P_3
Input:	x_1, z_1	x_2, z_2	x_3, z_3
Local Randomness:	$a_{4,1}, a_{5,1}$	$a_{4,2}, a_{5,2}$	a_3
Correlated Randomness:	a_1, b_1	a_2, b_2	

$$\text{Output:} \quad \begin{bmatrix} x_1 - a_1 \left(\begin{smallmatrix} a_3 x_1 + a_1 x_3 \\ -a_1 a_3 - a_4 \end{smallmatrix} \right) & \left(\begin{smallmatrix} b_1 x_3 + b_2 x_3 + a_5 x_1 - a_1 a_5 + \\ a_4 x_2 - a_2 a_4 + z_1 + z_2 + z_3 \end{smallmatrix} \right) \\ -1 & x_3 - a_3 & a_2 x_3 - a_5 \\ & -1 & x_2 - a_2 \end{bmatrix}$$

where $a_4 := a_{4,1} + a_{4,3}$ and $a_5 := a_{5,2} + a_{5,3}$.

Fig. 2. Semi-honest MPRE for 3MultPlus [LLW20]

In standard model, semi-malicious security is implied by perfect semi-honest security, because conditional on any choice of corrupted parties' local randomness, the adversary has no advantage. But in the correlated randomness model, the semi-malicious adversary may lie about correlated randomness.

– For example, say P_1, P_2 are corrupted. If they feed a_1, b_1, a_2, b_2 as correlated randomness such that $a_1 a_2 = b_1 + b_2$, then the privacy still follows from the perfect semi-honest security. But if P_1, P_2 choose a_1, b_1, a_2, b_2 such that $a_1 a_2 \neq b_1 + b_2$, the privacy is lost (as we will show in Sect. 4.2).
– For another example, say P_1 is corrupted. If corrupted P_1 does not modify the portion of correlated randomness (a_1, b_2) it received, then the privacy still follows from the perfect semi-honest security. But if P_1 lies about (a_1, b_2), then with overwhelming probability $a_1 a_2 \neq b_1 + b_2$, and the privacy is lost (as we will show in Sect. 4.2).

In either case, if honest P_3 want to protect its privacy, it needs (and suffices) to ensure that $a_1 a_2 \neq b_1 + b_2$.

Our solution against this privacy threat is called *conditional disclosure of secrets (CDS) encoding*. Let party P_3 locally sample a random mask s. CDS encoding is a sub-module (of the final MPRE) that reveals s if and only if $a_1 a_2 \neq b_1 + b_2$. Then a candidate MPRE consists of two parts:

i) the semi-honest MPRE for 2MultPlus one-time padded by s;
ii) CDS encoding, which reveals s if and only if $a_1 a_2 = b_1 + b_2$.

But the CDS encoding resolves P_3's privacy concern at a cost: The adversary will learn a linear function in (a_1, b_1, a_2, b_2) if P_3 is corrupted. To overcome it, we have to replace the scalar OLE correlated randomness in the semi-honest MPRE by *tensor OLE correlated randomness*. That is, party P_1 receives vector $\mathbf{a}_1$, matrix $\mathbf{B}_1$; party P_2 receives vector $\mathbf{a}_2$, matrix $\mathbf{B}_2$; such that $\mathbf{a}_1, \mathbf{B}_1, \mathbf{a}_2, \mathbf{B}_2$ are random subject to $\mathbf{a}_1 \mathbf{a}_2^{\mathsf{T}} = \mathbf{B}_1 + \mathbf{B}_2^{\mathsf{T}}$. We abuse the notation and let a_1, b_1, a_2, b_2 denote the first coordinate of $\mathbf{a}_1, \mathbf{B}_1, \mathbf{a}_2, \mathbf{B}_2$ respectively. Then a_1, b_1, a_2, b_2 are random subject to $a_1 a_2 = b_1 + b_2$, i.e., their distribution is scalar OLE correlated randomness.

The next candidate MPRE is made up of:

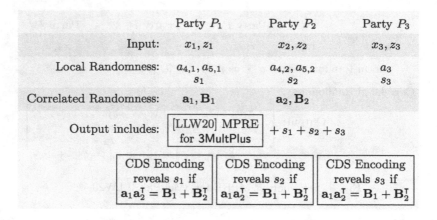

Fig. 3. Semi-Malicious MPRE for 3MultPlus

i) the semi-honest MPRE for 2MultPlus one-time padded by s;
ii) CDS encoding, which reveals s if and only if $\mathbf{a}_1\mathbf{a}_2^\mathsf{T} = \mathbf{B}_1 + \mathbf{B}_2^\mathsf{T}$.

Additionally, CDS encoding will let the adversary learn a linear leakage function in $(\mathbf{a}_1, \mathbf{B}_1, \mathbf{a}_2, \mathbf{B}_2)$ if P_3 is corrupted. But due to our careful design of CDS encoding, the leakage is one-time padded by the remaining coordinates of $\mathbf{a}_1, \mathbf{a}_2, \mathbf{B}_1, \mathbf{B}_2$, so that no information about a_1, b_1, a_2, b_2 is revealed.

So far we focus on the security concern of P_3. Party P_1, P_2 have similar concern. So in the actual semi-malicious MPRE for 3MultPlus (shown in Fig. 3), every party P_i locally sample random mask s_i, The final MPRE consists of:

i) the semi-honest MPRE for 2MultPlus one-time padded by $s_1 + s_2 + s_3$;
ii) (for each $i \in \{1, 2, 3\}$) CDS encoding that reveals s_i iff $\mathbf{a}_1\mathbf{a}_2^\mathsf{T} = \mathbf{B}_1 + \mathbf{B}_2^\mathsf{T}$.

Of course, the three instances of CDS encoding are carefully designed, so that their leakages jointly reveal no information about a_1, b_1, a_2, b_2.

In the rest of the section, we explain how CDS encoding works. W.l.o.g., we assume the secret mask is sampled by P_3.

By our discussion so far, it seems that P_3 has to sample a random matrix s_3 in order to one-time pad the [LLW20] MPRE. But as we will discover in the technical body, it is sufficient to one-time pad only the top right coordinate of the [LLW20] MPRE. So s_3 is a random scalar sampled by P_3.

We start with a simpler task, P_3 only want to verify if P_1, P_2 use legit tensor OLE correlation. Here "legit" means in the support of the distribution. A simple encoding is to let P_3 additionally sample random vectors $\mathbf{q}_1, \mathbf{q}_2$, and the encoding outputs

$$p_1 = \langle \mathbf{a}_1, \mathbf{q}_1 \rangle, \quad p_2 = \langle \mathbf{a}_2, \mathbf{q}_2 \rangle, \quad p_3 = \langle \mathbf{B}_1 + \mathbf{B}_2^\mathsf{T}, \mathbf{q}_1\mathbf{q}_2^\mathsf{T} \rangle. \quad (2)$$

Then P_3 can check whether $p_1 p_2 = p_3$. If $\mathbf{a}_1\mathbf{a}_2^\mathsf{T} = \mathbf{B}_1 + \mathbf{B}_2^\mathsf{T}$, then $p_1 p_2 = p_3$ always holds. Otherwise, $p_1 p_2 \neq p_3$ with overwhelming probability. Note that the encoding in (2) is of effective degree 2, because P_3 can locally compute $\mathbf{q}_1\mathbf{q}_2^\mathsf{T}$.

In the CDS encoding, party P_3 additionally samples random r_1, r_2. The CDS encoding outputs

$$p_1, \quad p_2, \quad p_3, \quad \text{and} \quad \mathbf{c} := \begin{bmatrix} 1 & p_2 \\ p_1 & p_3 \end{bmatrix} \begin{bmatrix} r_1 \\ r_2 \end{bmatrix} + \begin{bmatrix} 0 \\ s_3 \end{bmatrix}.$$

If $\mathbf{a}_1 \mathbf{a}_2^\mathsf{T} \neq \mathbf{B}_1 + \mathbf{B}_2^\mathsf{T}$ then $\begin{bmatrix} 1 & p_2 \\ p_1 & p_3 \end{bmatrix}$ has full-rank with overwhelming probability, and $\mathbf{c}$ is one-time padded by (r_1, r_2), thus no information about s is revealed. Otherwise when $\mathbf{a}_1 \mathbf{a}_2^\mathsf{T} = \mathbf{B}_1 + \mathbf{B}_2^\mathsf{T}$, it is easy to verify that $\langle (-p_1, 1), \mathbf{c} \rangle = s$. Note that CDS encoding is of effective degree 2, because it is a linear function in $\mathbf{a}_1, \mathbf{a}_2, \mathbf{B}_1, \mathbf{B}_2$, whose coefficient can be locally computed by P_3.

If P_3 is corrupted, the adversary chooses $\mathbf{q}_1, \mathbf{q}_2$ and learns p_1, p_2, p_3 (defined by (2)) as leakage. By enforcing some constraints on $\mathbf{q}_1, \mathbf{q}_2$ (will be discussed in the main body), the leakage will not reveal any information about a_1, b_1, a_2, b_2.

2.3   MPC for Effective-Degree-2 Functions

Given an effective-degree-2 function $g = \hat{f} \circ h$

$$g(\mathbf{x}_1, \ldots, \mathbf{x}_n) := \hat{f}(h_1(\mathbf{x}_1), \ldots, h_n(\mathbf{x}_n)),$$

we can assume w.l.o.g. that each coordinate of $\hat{f}$ has the canonical form[4]

$$\hat{f}_t(\hat{\mathbf{x}}_1, \ldots, \hat{\mathbf{x}}_n) = \mathsf{2MultPlus}((\underbrace{x_1, z_1}_{\text{owned by } P_{i_t}}), (\underbrace{x_2, z_2}_{\text{owned by } P_{j_t}})) = x_1 x_2 + z_1 + z_2$$

where x_1, z_1 are two coordinates of $\hat{\mathbf{x}}_{i_t}$ and x_2, z_2 are two coordinates of $\hat{\mathbf{x}}_{j_t}$.

As presented by [LLW20], there is a 2-round semi-honest MPC protocol for $\mathsf{2MultPlus}$ that uses scalar OLE correlated randomness (Fig. 4). Via parallel repetition, it implies 2-round semi-honest MPC for any effective-degree-2 functions that uses scalar OLE correlated randomness.

Towards malicious security, the starting point is the observation that the protocol for $\mathsf{2MultPlus}$ in Fig. 4 is maliciously secure *with output substitution*. Security with output substitution means the adversary, after learning the output y, may adaptively choose y' so that all honest parties (unanimously) output y'.

A natural idea is to compute all $\hat{f}_t$ using parallel sessions of the protocol in Fig. 4. Each session computes one coordinate. But parallelization does not meet the security requirement, because of the following two issues:

Consistency. Say two coordinates of $\hat{f}$ equal $x_1 x_2 + z_1 + z_2$ and $x_1 x_3 + z_1' + z_3$ respectively, where party P_1 owns x_1, z_1, z_1', party P_2 owns x_2, z_2, party P_3 owns x_3, z_3. We have to check whether P_1 feeds the *same* x_1 to the two corresponding sessions.

---

[4] Section 2.2 outlines how to canonicalize $\hat{f}$. Formally, canonical form allows some coordinates to be linear instead of $\mathsf{2MultPlus}$. The linear coordinates are easier to handle. We ignore them in the overview.

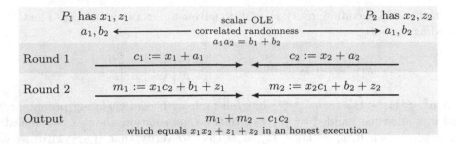

Fig. 4. 2-round semi-honest MPC for 2MultPlus

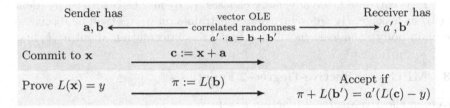

Fig. 5. commit-and-prove-linear

Well-Formedness. We have to check whether P_i computes $\hat{x}_i = h_i(x_i)$ correctly. Note that we can also assume the preprocessing functions h_i is a small arithmetic circuit that only contains multiplication gates, because such property is satisfied by our MPRE.

To resolve the well formedness issue, we introduce a commit-and-prove-linear scheme which uses vector OLE correlated randomness. It enables the sender to commit to a vector $\mathbf{x}$, then later prove $L(\mathbf{x}) = y$ for any linear function L.

As shown in Fig. 5, the scheme uses vector OLE correlated randomness between the sender and the receiver. That is, the sender receives random vectors $\mathbf{a}, \mathbf{b}$, the receiver recovers random $a', \mathbf{b}'$ subject to $a'\mathbf{a} = \mathbf{b} + \mathbf{b}'$. To commit to a vector $\mathbf{x}$, the sender simply sends $\mathbf{c} := \mathbf{x} + \mathbf{a}$ to the receiver. Later, for any linear function L, the sender can prove $L(\mathbf{x}) = y$ by sending $\pi := L(\mathbf{b})$ to the receiver; and the receiver accepts the proof iff $\pi + L(\mathbf{b}') = a'(L(\mathbf{c}) - y)$. Such scheme has

Completeness An honest proof $\pi := L(\mathbf{b})$ will always be accepted because
$\pi + L(\mathbf{b}') = L(\mathbf{b}) + L(\mathbf{b}') = a' \cdot L(\mathbf{a}) = a'(L(\mathbf{c}) - L(\mathbf{x})) = a'(L(\mathbf{c}) - y)$.

Statistical Soundness If $L(\mathbf{x}) \neq y$, any proof will be reject with overwhelming probability due to the randomness of a'.

Zero-knowledge No information about $\mathbf{x}$, other than $L(\mathbf{x})$, will be revealed to receiver, since the receiver can predict π from $\mathbf{c}, L, y$.

Reusability Given a commitment $\mathbf{c}$, the sender can prove multiple adaptively chosen linear statements $L_1(\mathbf{x}) = y_1, \ldots, L_t(\mathbf{x}) = y_t$ about the underlying message $\mathbf{x}$. The statistical soundness error is $O(t/|\mathbb{F}|)$. No information about $\mathbf{x}$ other than $L_1(\mathbf{x}), \ldots, L_t(\mathbf{x})$ will be revealed.

Then, inspired by a linear PCP scheme from [BCI+13], the sender can generate zero-knowledge proofs of more complex arithmetic statements. A particular interesting statement for ours is multiplication. Say the sender will commit to message $\mathbf{x} = (x_1, x_2, x_3, \dots)$, and then prove $x_1 x_2 = x_3$ to the receiver. We design **ProveProd** sub-protocol for such demand:

1. In order to prove $x_1 x_2 = x_3$, the sender samples random g_1, g_2 and extends its message into

$$\mathbf{x} = (x_1, g_1, x_2, g_2, x_3, x_1 g_2, x_2 g_1, g_1 g_2, \dots).$$

The dimension of the correlated randomness should be extended correspondingly. The sender commits to the extended $\mathbf{x}$ instead.

2. Random challenges q_1, q_2 are sampled.
3. The sender proves to the receiver that

$$\langle (q_1, 1), (\mathbf{x}[1], \mathbf{x}[2]) \rangle = p_1, \quad \langle (q_2, 1), (\mathbf{x}[3], \mathbf{x}[4]) \rangle = p_2,$$
$$\underset{(x_1, g_1)}{\uparrow} \qquad\qquad\qquad \underset{(x_2, g_2)}{\uparrow}$$
$$\langle (q_1 q_2, q_1, q_2, 1), (\mathbf{x}[5], \mathbf{x}[6], \mathbf{x}[7], \mathbf{x}[8]) \rangle = p_3.$$
$$\underset{(x_3, x_1 g_2, x_2 g_1, g_1 g_2)}{\uparrow}$$

The receiver accepts if $p_1 p_2 = p_3$.

$$\underset{\underset{x_1}{\downarrow}}{} \quad \underset{\underset{x_2}{\downarrow}}{} \quad \underset{\underset{x_3}{\downarrow}}{}$$

Similar to the discussion in our CDS encoding, if $\mathbf{x}[1] \cdot \mathbf{x}[3] \neq \mathbf{x}[5]$, then $p_1 p_2 \neq p_3$ with overwhelming probability due to the randomness of $q_1 q_2$. No information about x_1, x_2, x_3 are leaked if the sender is proving a true statement, as the leakage p_1, p_2 are one-time padded by g_1, g_2, and p_3 is determined by $p_3 = p_1 p_2$.

If the random challenges q_1, q_2 are sampled by the receiver, the proof will have $1/|\mathbb{F}|$ soundness error. To make the proof non-interactive, the challenges can be sampled by the random oracle, so that the soundness error becomes the number of adversary's query to random oracle divided by $|\mathbb{F}|$.

So far we can prove multiplication relation for 3 values behind a commitment. This will resolve the concern of well-formedness. To resolve the concern of consistency, we need to prove that values behind different commitments are the same. That is, say the sender will commit to messages $\mathbf{x}_1 = (x_1, \dots)$, $\mathbf{x}_2 = (x_2, \dots)$, and want to convince the receiver that $x_1 = x_2$. We design **ProveSame** sub-protocol for such proof:

1. In order to prove $x_1 = x_2$, the sender samples random g and extends its message into

$$\mathbf{x}_1 = (x_1, g, \dots), \quad \mathbf{x}_2 = (x_2, g, \dots).$$

The sender commits to the extended $\mathbf{x}_1, \mathbf{x}_2$ instead.

2. A random challenge q is sampled.
3. The sender proves to the receiver that

$$\langle (q, 1), (\mathbf{x}_1[1], \mathbf{x}_1[2]) \rangle = p_1, \quad \langle (q, 1), (\mathbf{x}_2[1], \mathbf{x}_2[2]) \rangle = p_2.$$
$$\underset{(x_1, g)}{\uparrow} \qquad\qquad\qquad \underset{(x_2, g)}{\uparrow}$$

The receiver accepts if $p_1 = p_2$.

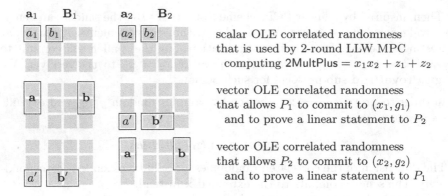

Fig. 6. Multiple roles of $\mathbf{a}_1, \mathbf{B}_1, \mathbf{a}_2, \mathbf{B}_2$

$$\overset{x_1}{\downarrow} \qquad \overset{x_2}{\downarrow}$$

Similarly, when $\mathbf{x}_1[1] \neq \mathbf{x}_2[1]$, the probability $p_1 = p_2$ is no more than $1/|\mathbb{F}|$, due to the randomness of challenge q. No information about x_1, x_2 are leaked if the sender is proving a true statement, as the leakage p_1 is one-time padded by g, and p_2 is determined by $p_2 = p_1$.

Putting Pieces Together. We develop the natural idea of using parallel sessions of the protocol for 2MultPlus. Each coordinate of $\hat{f}$ will be computed by a modified version of the 2-round LLW protocol for 2MultPlus (Fig. 4).

In the first round of the LLW protocol for 2MultPlus, party P_1 sends $c_1 := x_1 + a_1$, party P_2 sends $c_2 := x_2 + a_2$, where x_1, x_2 are their inputs, and a_1, a_2 are parts of the scalar OLE correlated randomness. Here c_i is essentially a commitment to x_i.

In the modified LLW protocol for 2MultPlus, the two parties use 3×3 tensor OLE correlated randomness. That is, party P_1 receives $\mathbf{a}_1 \in \mathbb{F}^3, \mathbf{B}_1 \in \mathbb{F}^{3 \times 3}$, party P_2 receives $\mathbf{a}_2 \in \mathbb{F}^3, \mathbf{B}_2 \in \mathbb{F}^{3 \times 3}$, where $\mathbf{a}_1, \mathbf{B}_1, \mathbf{a}_2, \mathbf{B}_2$ are random subject to $\mathbf{a}_1\mathbf{a}_2^\mathsf{T} = \mathbf{B}_1 + \mathbf{B}_2^\mathsf{T}$.[5] In the first round, P_1 broadcasts

$$\mathbf{c}_1 := (x_1, g_1) + \mathbf{a}_1[1:2],$$

where $\mathbf{a}_1[1:2]$ denotes the first two coordinates of $\mathbf{a}_1$. The choice of g_1 will be discussed later. Symmetrically, party P_2 broadcasts $\mathbf{c}_2 := (x_2, g_2) + \mathbf{a}_2[1:2]$. The two commitments $\mathbf{c}_1, \mathbf{c}_2$ will have multiple roles:

Compute 2MultPlus. Their first coordinates $\mathbf{c}_1[1], \mathbf{c}_2[1]$ are of the same form as the first message in the original LLW protocol. In the second round, P_1, P_2 will proceed with the original LLW protocol by taking $\mathbf{c}_1[1], \mathbf{c}_2[1]$ as the first round messages.

P_1 **proves consistency.** Party P_1 may need to prove that the same x_1 is used across different sessions. Note that $\mathbf{c}$ can be viewed as a commitment in

---

[5] Note the transpose of $\mathbf{B}_2$. This makes the equation remains unchanged upon exchanging subscripts.

the commit-and-prove-linear scheme. P_1 takes $\mathbf{a}_1[1{:}2], \mathbf{B}_1[1{:}2,3]$ and P_2 takes $\mathbf{a}_2[3], \mathbf{B}_2[3,1{:}2]$ as the vector OLE correlated randomness (as shown in Fig. 6). Then the ProveSame sub-protocol can prove P_1 is using a consistent value. P_1 sets g_1 according to the sub-protocol.

P_2 **proves consistency.** Symmetric to the above.

To resolve the well-formedness concern, every party has to prove that it honestly evaluates the preprocessing function. Since the preprocessing function only has multiplication gates, a party can prove well-formedness by using the ProveProd sub-protocol. (Together with ProveSame sub-protocol. Because once a party proves $x_1 x_2 = x_3$ using ProveProd, it also need to prove that the "x_1" in ProveProd is the same the "x_1" it uses in 2MultPlus sessions.)

2.4 Lift Security with Output Substitution

Security with output substitution is a weak notion of security. The adversary, after learning the function output y, may adaptively choose y' so that all honest parties (unanimously) output y'. Once we constructed MPC for **P/poly** that is secure with output substitution against malicious corruptions, we can lift its security to the standard notion of security with (unanimous) abort, with the help of *consensus MAC*, which will be introduced in the full version. We claim that the following protocol is secure with abort.

1. Party P_i has input x_i, and samples MAC key k_i.
2. Using a protocol that is secure with output substitution to compute

$$(y, \sigma) := f(x_1, \ldots, x_n), \mathsf{Sign}_{k_1, \ldots, k_n}(f(x_1, \ldots, x_n)).$$

3. Party P_i outputs y if π is a valid signature on y w.r.t. key k_i; aborts otherwise.

As the protocol suggested, consensus MAC has i) a signing algorithm Sign, which takes a message, n keys, generates a signature; and ii) a verification algorithm Verify, which takes a message, a signature and a key, outputs "accept" or "reject".

In the protocol, the adversary, after learning (y, σ), may adaptively replace the output by $(y', \sigma') \neq (y, \sigma)$. In order to achieve security with unanimous abort, all honest parties should reject (y', σ'). This hints how to define consensus MAC: the adversary wins the following game with negligible probability.

1. The adversary chooses the set of corrupted parties $C \subseteq [n]$, and chooses key k_i for each corrupted party $P_i \in C$. Every honest party $P_i \notin C$ samples k_i.
2. The adversary chooses message y and learns $\pi = \mathsf{Sign}_{k_1, \ldots, k_n}(y)$.
3. The adversary adaptively chooses $(y', \pi') \neq (y, \pi)$.
4. The adversary wins if $\mathsf{Verify}_{k_i}(y', \pi') \to$ accept for some honest party $P_i \notin C$.

Here is a simple consensus MAC scheme, whose security will be proven in the full version. Party P_i samples two random number a_i, b_i and let key $k_i := (a_i, b_i)$. The signature $\mathsf{Sign}_{k_1, \ldots, k_n}(y)$ is the degree-n polynomial π such that

$$\pi(0) = y, \quad \pi(a_1) = b_1, \quad \ldots, \quad \pi(a_n) = b_n.$$

The verification accepts a message-signature pair (y, π) w.r.t. key $k_i = (a_i, b_i)$ if and only if $\pi(0) = y$ and $\pi(a_i) = b_i$.

2.5   Tensor OLE Correlated Randomness Generation from OT

We require tensor OLE correlated randomness over a large boolean extension field $\mathbb{F} = \mathsf{GF}(2^\lambda)$, where λ is the security parameter. To generate OLE correlated randomness, it suffices to implement a protocol computing tensor OLE

$$\mathsf{TOLE}((\mathbf{a}, \mathbf{B}), \mathbf{x}) := \mathbf{a}\mathbf{x}^\mathsf{T} + \mathbf{B}$$

or random tensor OLE, and later randomize the input-output tuple.

The starting point is a semi-honest protocol [Gil99]. Say the sender has vector $\mathbf{a}$, matrix $\mathbf{B}$; the receiver has vector $\mathbf{x}$ and should learn $\mathbf{Y} = \mathbf{a}\mathbf{x}^\mathsf{T} + \mathbf{B}$. Note that $\mathbf{a}\mathbf{x}^\mathsf{T} + \mathbf{B}$, as a function in $\mathbf{x}$, is affine over $\mathsf{GF}(2)$. That is, if we let subscript $_{(2)}$ denote bit representations, there exists a binary matrix $M_{\mathbf{a}}$ such that $(\mathbf{Y})_{(2)} = (\mathbf{a}\mathbf{x}^\mathsf{T} + \mathbf{B})_{(2)} = M_{\mathbf{a}} \cdot (\mathbf{x})_{(2)} + (\mathbf{B})_{(2)}$. Thus the receiver can learn $\mathbf{Y}$ from OT.

Such protocol is not secure against a malicious sender, who can choose an arbitrary M_1 and let the receiver learn $(\mathbf{Y})_{(2)} = M_1 \cdot (\mathbf{x})_{(2)} + (\mathbf{B})_{(2)}$. To detect malicious behaviour, the receiver samples a random matrix $\mathbf{Y}^{\mathrm{shadow}}$ and let the sender learn $\mathbf{B}^{\mathrm{shadow}} = \mathbf{a}\mathbf{x}^\mathsf{T} + \mathbf{Y}^{\mathrm{shadow}}$. Formally, the sender learns

$$(\mathbf{B}^{\mathrm{shadow}})_{(2)} = M_2 \cdot (\mathbf{a})_{(2)} + (\mathbf{Y}^{\mathrm{shadow}})_{(2)}$$

from OT, where $M_2 = M_{\mathbf{x}}$ if the receiver is honest. The receiver samples a random matrix H over $\mathsf{GF}(2)$, sends H to the sender as a challenge, and asks the sender to guess $H \cdot (\mathbf{Y} + \mathbf{Y}^{\mathrm{shadow}})_{(2)}$. Note that, if both parties are honest, $H \cdot (\mathbf{Y} + \mathbf{Y}^{\mathrm{shadow}})_{(2)} = H \cdot (\mathbf{B} + \mathbf{B}^{\mathrm{shadow}})_{(2)}$. If the sender is corrupted,

$$H \cdot (\mathbf{Y} + \mathbf{Y}^{\mathrm{shadow}})_{(2)} = H \cdot \left(M_1 \cdot (\mathbf{x})_{(2)} + (\mathbf{B})_{(2)} + M_{\mathbf{a}} \cdot (\mathbf{x})_{(2)} + (\mathbf{B}^{\mathrm{shadow}})_{(2)} \right)$$
$$= H \cdot (M_1 + M_{\mathbf{a}}) \cdot (\mathbf{x})_{(2)} + H \cdot (\mathbf{B} + \mathbf{B}^{\mathrm{shadow}})_{(2)} .$$

Thus the sender will not be caught if and only if he can guess $H \cdot (M_1 + M_{\mathbf{a}}) \cdot (\mathbf{x})_{(2)}$ correctly. Let H has λ rows and assume w.l.o.g. that the receiver samples $\mathbf{x}$ at random. Then the sender will be caught will overwhelming probability if $\mathrm{rank}(M_1 + M_{\mathbf{a}}) \geq \lambda$. Because in such case, $H \cdot (M_1 + M_{\mathbf{a}}) \cdot (\mathbf{x})_{(2)}$ has large entropy conditioning on the sender's knowledge.

If $\mathrm{rank}(M_1 + M_{\mathbf{a}}) < \lambda$, say we give $(M_1 + M_{\mathbf{a}}) \cdot (\mathbf{x})_{(2)}$ to the corrupted sender, this may only help the adversary. The corrupted sender can compute $(\mathbf{B}')_{(2)} = (M_1 + M_{\mathbf{a}}) \cdot (\mathbf{x})_{(2)} + (\mathbf{B})_{(2)}$. (Honest sender simply let $\mathbf{B}' = \mathbf{B}$.) Note that $\mathbf{Y} = \mathbf{a}\mathbf{x}^\mathsf{T} + \mathbf{B}'$. The sender and receiver output $(\mathbf{a}, \mathbf{B}'), (\mathbf{x}, \mathbf{Y})$ respectively.

Such a protocol is insecure, for two reasons.

– If the sender is corrupted, he additionally knows $(M_1 + M_{\mathbf{a}}) \cdot (\mathbf{x})_{(2)}$, which is an at most λ-bit leakage of $\mathbf{x}$. If the receiver is corrupted, she additionally knows

$$H \cdot (\mathbf{B} + \mathbf{B}^{\mathrm{shadow}})_{(2)} := H \cdot (M_2 + M_{\mathbf{b}}) \cdot (\mathbf{a})_{(2)},$$

which is an at most λ-bit leakage of $\mathbf{a}$. The leakage can be removed by using randomness extractor and left-over hash lemma.
- The corrupted sender (resp. receiver) can arbitrarily choose $\mathbf{a}, \mathbf{B}$ (resp. $\mathbf{x}$). To ensure randomness, an additional re-randomization step is needed.

3   Definition of Multi-Party Randomized Encoding

Definition 1 (Multi-Party Randomized Encoding). *Let* $f : \mathcal{X}_1 \times \cdots \times \mathcal{X}_n \to \mathcal{Y}$ *be some n-party function. A* multi-party randomized encoding *(MPRE) of* f *is specified by*

- *Local randomness space* $\mathcal{R}_i$ *for* $i \in [n]$. *Correlated randomness space* $\mathcal{R}'_1 \times \cdots \times \mathcal{R}'_n$ *together with a distribution* $\mathcal{D}$ *over it.*
- *Local preprocessing function* $h_i : \mathcal{X}_i \times \mathcal{R}_i \times \mathcal{R}'_i \to \hat{\mathcal{X}}_i$.
- *Encoding function* $\hat{f} : \hat{\mathcal{X}}_1 \times \cdots \times \hat{\mathcal{X}}_n \to \hat{\mathcal{Y}}$.
- *Decoding function* $\mathsf{Dec} : \hat{\mathcal{Y}} \to \mathcal{Y}$.

Such that for any input $(x_1, \ldots, x_n)$, *the encoding*

$$\hat{y} := \hat{f}\big(h_1(x_1, r_1, r'_1), \ldots, h_n(x_n, r_n, r'_n)\big) \tag{3}$$

represents $y = f(x_1, \ldots, x_n)$ *in the following sense:*

Correctness *For any input* $(x_1, \ldots, x_n) \in \mathcal{X}_1 \times \cdots \times \mathcal{X}_n$, *randomness* $(r_1, \ldots, r_n) \in \mathcal{R}_1 \times \cdots \times \mathcal{R}_n$ *and correlated randomness* $(r'_1, \ldots, r'_n)$ *in the support of* $\mathcal{D}$, *the corresponding encoding* $\hat{y}$ *defined by* (3) *satisfies that* $f(x_1, \ldots, x_n) = \mathsf{Dec}(\hat{y})$.

Semi-Malicious Security *We say MPRE is computationally (resp. statistically) semi-malicious secure with output substitution, if the following canonical protocol computationally (resp. statistically) securely implements* $\mathcal{F}^{os}_f$:
  - *The protocol assumes ideal functionality* $\mathcal{F}^{os}_{\hat{f} \circ h}$.
  - *On input* x_i, *party* P_i *samples* $r_i \leftarrow \mathcal{R}_i$ *locally, receives* r'_i *where* $(r'_1, \ldots, r'_n)$ *is sampled from* $\mathcal{D}$, *then inputs* (x_i, r_i, r'_i) *to the ideal functionality* $\mathcal{F}^{os}_{\hat{f} \circ h}$. *Note that a corrupted party may adaptively modify its input of* $\mathcal{F}^{os}_{\hat{f} \circ h}$.
  - *Upon receiving* $\hat{y}$ *from* $\mathcal{F}^{os}_{\hat{f} \circ h}$, *party decodes* $y = \mathsf{Dec}(\hat{y})$, *and outputs* y.

Malicious Security *We say MPRE is computationally (resp. statistically) malicious secure with output substitution, if the following canonical protocol computationally (resp. statistically) securely implements* $\mathcal{F}^{os}_f$:
  - *The protocol assumes ideal functionality* $\mathcal{F}^{os}_{\hat{f}}$.
  - *On input* x_i, *party* P_i *samples* $r_i \leftarrow \mathcal{R}_i$ *locally, receives* r'_i *where* $(r'_1, \ldots, r'_n)$ *is sampled from* $\mathcal{D}$, *and locally computes* $\hat{x}_i = h_i(x_i, r_i, r'_i)$ *then inputs* $\hat{x}_i$ *to the ideal functionality* $\mathcal{F}^{os}_{\hat{f}}$.
  - *Upon receiving* $\hat{y}$ *from* $\mathcal{F}^{os}_{\hat{f}}$, *party decodes* $y = \mathsf{Dec}(\hat{y})$, *and outputs* y.

The Real Execution $\mathsf{Exec}_{C,\mathcal{A},\mathcal{Z}}(1^\lambda, \Pi)$	The Ideal Execution $\mathsf{Ideal}_{C,\mathcal{A},\mathcal{S},\mathcal{Z}}(1^\lambda, \mathcal{F}_f^{\mathrm{os}})$
1. The adversary $\mathcal{A}$ receives the corrupted parties' portions of correlated randomness $\{r_i'\}_{i \in C}$.	1. The simulator $\mathcal{S}$ receives the corrupted parties' portions of correlated randomness $\{r_i'\}_{i \in C}$, and forwards them to $\mathcal{A}$.
2. The environment $\mathcal{Z}$ chooses the input x_i for each honest party $P_i \notin C$. Every honest P_i samples local randomness r_i, receives his portion of correlated randomness r_i' and sends (x_i, r_i, r_i') to $\mathcal{F}_{\hat{f} \circ h}^{\mathrm{os}}$.	2. The environment $\mathcal{Z}$ chooses the input x_i for each honest party $P_i \notin C$. Every honest dummy P_i directly inputs x_i to $\mathcal{F}_f^{\mathrm{os}}$.
3. A corrupted party $P_i \in C$ may input any $(\bar{x}_i, \bar{r}_i, \bar{r}_i')$ to $\mathcal{F}_{\hat{f} \circ h}^{\mathrm{os}}$.	3. Any corrupted party's input to $\mathcal{F}_{\hat{f} \circ h}^{\mathrm{os}}$ is hijacked by $\mathcal{S}$. The simulator $\mathcal{S}$ extracts input x_i for each $i \in C$, and sends x_i to $\mathcal{F}_f^{\mathrm{os}}$ on behalf of dummy P_i.
4. $\mathcal{F}_{\hat{f} \circ h}^{\mathrm{os}}$ sends the output $\hat{y}$ to $\mathcal{A}$. The adversary $\mathcal{A}$ chooses and sends $\hat{y}'$ back.	4. $\mathcal{F}_f^{\mathrm{os}}$ sends the output y to $\mathcal{S}$, who generates and sends $\hat{y}$ to $\mathcal{A}$. The adversary $\mathcal{A}$ chooses and sends $\hat{y}'$ back to $\mathcal{S}$, who sends $y' = \mathsf{Dec}(\hat{y}')$ to $\mathcal{F}_f^{\mathrm{os}}$.
5. Every honest party receives $\hat{y}'$ from $\mathcal{F}_{\hat{f} \circ h}^{\mathrm{os}}$, and output $y' = \mathsf{Dec}(\hat{y}')$ to $\mathcal{Z}$.	5. Every honest dummy party receives y' from $\mathcal{F}_f^{\mathrm{os}}$, and output y' to $\mathcal{Z}$.

Fig. 7. The Security Game of Semi-Malicious MPRE.

We expand the definition of semi-malicious MPRE in more detail by describing the ideal world and real world of the security game of the canonical protocol (Fig. 7). Apparently, the adversary and the environment learn no information during the last two steps in the security game.

Effective Degree. By definition, the task of computing f against malicious corruptions is reduced to the task of computing $\hat{f}$, if MPRE is maliciously secure. To minimize the round complexity for computing $\hat{f}$, the classical approach is to reduce the arithmetic degree of $\hat{f}$. The degree of $\hat{f}$ is called the *effective degree* of this MPRE.

Formally, let $\mathbb{F}$ be a finite field. Let

$$\left(\hat{f} : \hat{\mathcal{X}}_1 \times \cdots \times \hat{\mathcal{X}}_n \to \hat{\mathcal{Y}}, h_1, \ldots, h_n \right)$$

be a MPRE for f, such that $\hat{\mathcal{X}}_1, \ldots, \hat{\mathcal{X}}_n, \hat{\mathcal{Y}}$ are vector spaces over field $\mathbb{F}$. The arithmetic degree of $\hat{f}$ over $\mathbb{F}$ is called the effective degree of the MPRE.

Arithmetic Preprocessing. By definition, the task of computing f against malicious corruptions is reduced to computing $\hat{f} \circ h$ if MPRE is semi-maliciously secure. To minimize the round complexity for computing $\hat{f} \circ h$, besides reducing the degree of $\hat{f}$, we also need the preprocessing functions $h_1, \ldots, h_n$ to be computable by poly-size arithmetic circuits.

Formally, let $(\hat{f}, h_1, \ldots, h_n)$ be a MPRE for f, who has low effective degree over a field $\mathbb{F}$. The MPRE has arithmetic preprocessing if its input spaces, local randomness spaces and correlated randomness spaces are vector spaces over $\mathbb{F}$, and the local preprocessing functions $h_1, \ldots, h_n$ are computed by poly-size arithmetic circuits over $\mathbb{F}$.

If a MPRE has effective degree 2 and arithmetic preprocessing over $\mathbb{F}$, we say $\hat{f} \circ g$ is an *effective-degree-2 function* over $\mathbb{F}$.

Definition 2 (Effective-Degree-2 Function). *A function* $g : \mathcal{X}_1 \times \cdots \times \mathcal{X}_n \to \mathcal{Y}$ *is of* effective degree 2 *over a field* $\mathbb{F}$, *if* $\mathcal{X}_1, \ldots, \mathcal{X}_n, \mathcal{Y}$ *are vector spaces over* $\mathbb{F}$ *and there exist*

- $h_i : \mathcal{X}_i \to \hat{\mathcal{X}}_i$, *an arithmetic circuit over* $\mathbb{F}$, *for each* $i \leq n$.
- $\hat{f} : \hat{\mathcal{X}}_1 \times \cdots \times \hat{\mathcal{X}}_n \to \mathcal{Y}$, *a degree-2 arithmetic function over* $\mathbb{F}$.

such that for all $(x_1, \ldots, x_n) \in \mathcal{X}_1 \times \cdots \times \mathcal{X}_n$,

$$\hat{f}(h_1(x_1), \ldots, h_n(x_n)) = g(x_1, \ldots, x_n).$$

4 MPRE for Degree-3 Functions

Let λ be the security parameter. All objects implicitly depend on λ. Most objects in this section is arithmetic over a finite field $\mathbb{F} = \mathbb{F}(\lambda)$, such that $|\mathbb{F}| = \Omega(2^\lambda)$.

Canonical Form Polynomials. Before we construct MPRE for degree-3 functions, we observe that it is w.l.o.g. to assume the degree-3 function f is of the following canonical form.

For any **canonical degree-3 function** $f : \mathbb{F}^{\ell_1} \times \cdots \times \mathbb{F}^{\ell_n} \to \mathbb{F}^\ell$, there is an index set $\mathcal{I} \subseteq [\ell]$, such that for each $t \in [\ell]$,

- If $t \notin \mathcal{I}$, the t-th coordinate of f, denoted by f_t, is of degree at most 2.
- If $t \in \mathcal{I}$, then $f_t = x_1 x_2 x_3 + z_1 + z_2 + z_3$ where x_i, z_i are from the same party. More formally, let $\mathbf{x}_i \in \mathbb{F}^{\ell_i}$ denote the i-th input of f, then

$$f_t(\mathbf{x}_1, \ldots, \mathbf{x}_n) = \mathbf{x}_{i_{t,1}}[j_{t,1}] \cdot \mathbf{x}_{i_{t,2}}[j_{t,2}] \cdot \mathbf{x}_{i_{t,3}}[j_{t,3}] + \mathbf{x}_{i_{t,1}}[j'_{t,1}] + \mathbf{x}_{i_{t,2}}[j'_{t,2}] + \mathbf{x}_{i_{t,3}}[j'_{t,3}]$$

for some $i_{t,1}, i_{t,2}, i_{t,3} \in [n]$ and $j_{t,1}, j'_{t,1} \in [\ell_{i_{t,1}}], \ldots, j_{t,3}, j'_{t,3} \in [\ell_{i_{t,3}}]$.

We assume w.l.o.g. that f is a canonical degree-3 function. It is known in the literature that (e.g. shown by [BGI+18, GIS18, LLW20]) every degree-3 function f has a semi-honest MPRE whose encoding function is canonical. The MPRE does not use correlated randomness, and is perfectly secure, thus it is also semi-maliciously secure. The MPRE does not has preprocessing (preprocessing functions are identity functions), thus semi-malicious security implies malicious security.

Moreover, such canonicalization does not increase complexity. Remind that the complexity measure we care about is its total number of monomials $\mathsf{mc}(f)$. It is not difficult to show that $\mathsf{mc}(\hat{f}) = O(\mathsf{mc}(f))$, where $\hat{f}$ is the encoding function of the MPRE for f we just discussed.

4.1   Background: Semi-honest MPRE for Degree-3 Functions

Due to canonicalization, it is sufficient to consider the minimal complete function

$$3\mathsf{MultPlus}\big((x_1, z_1), (x_2, z_2), (x_3, z_3)\big) = x_1 x_2 x_3 + z_1 + z_2 + z_3.$$

It only involves three parties P_1, P_2, P_3. Party P_i has input $x_i, z_i \in \mathbb{F}$. The output can also be presented as a $\mathbb{F}$-modular branching program:

$$x_1 x_2 x_3 + z_1 + z_2 + z_3 = \det \begin{bmatrix} x_1 & z_1 + z_2 + z_3 \\ -1 & x_3 \\ & -1 & x_2 \end{bmatrix}$$

As shown by AIK, it has a degree-3 random encoding

$$\begin{bmatrix} 1 & a_1 & a_4 \\ & 1 \\ & & 1 \end{bmatrix} \cdot \begin{bmatrix} x_1 & z_1 + z_2 + z_3 \\ -1 & x_3 \\ & -1 & x_2 \end{bmatrix} \cdot \begin{bmatrix} 1 & a_3 & a_5 \\ & 1 & a_2 \\ & & 1 \end{bmatrix}$$
$$= \begin{bmatrix} x_1 - a_1 & \begin{pmatrix} a_3 x_1 + a_1 x_3 \\ -a_1 a_3 - a_4 \end{pmatrix} & \begin{pmatrix} \boxed{a_1 a_2 x_3} + a_5 x_1 - a_1 a_5 + \\ a_4 x_2 - a_2 a_4 + z_1 + z_2 + z_3 \end{pmatrix} \\ -1 & x_3 - a_3 & a_2 x_3 - a_5 \\ & -1 & x_2 - a_2 \end{bmatrix},$$

where $a_1, \ldots, a_5 \in \mathbb{F}$ are the randomness of the encoding.

Notice that the randomized encoding only has one degree-3 monomial term $a_1 a_2 x_3$ (highlighted by a box). Assume a_1, a_2 are sampled from scalar OLE correlated randomness, that is, $a_1, b_1, a_2, b_2 \in \mathbb{F}$ are randomly sampled conditioning on $a_1 a_2 = b_1 + b_2$, then $a_1 a_2 x_3 = (b_1 + b_2) x_3$ becomes degree-2. This observation is formalized by [LLW20], there is an effective-degree-2 semi-honest MPRE for 3MultPlus using OLE correlated randomness, as presented in Fig. 8.

4.2   CDS Encoding

We observe that the MPRE presented in Fig. 8 is not semi-maliciously secure. Semi-malicious security does not follow automatically from perfect semi-honest security because of the correlated randomness. Party P_1 or P_2 can locally modify its portion of the correlated randomness. For example, if corrupted P_1 replaces b_1 by $b_1 + 1$, the decoding will output $x_1 x_2 x_3 + x_3 + z_1 + z_2 + z_3$. Similarly, if P_1 replaces a_1 by $a_1 + 1$, the decoding will output $x_1 x_2 x_3 - a_2 x_3 + z_1 + z_2 + z_3$. In either case, privacy is lost.

To prevent such attacks, we will invent a tool called *conditional disclosure of secret (CDS) encoding*, which reveals a secret only if a_1, a_2, b_1, b_2 satisfy the OLE relation $a_1 a_2 = b_1 + b_2$.

We start with protecting P_3's privacy, the cases of protecting P_1 or P_2 are similar. Party P_1 has $a_1, b_1 \in \mathbb{F}$. Party P_2 has $a_2, b_2 \in \mathbb{F}$. Party P_3 has a secret $s \in \mathbb{F}$. We would like to construct a CDS encoding that achieves three goals:

Input: P_i has $x_i, z_i \in \mathbb{F}$.

Local Randomness: P_1 samples $a_{4,1} \in \mathbb{F}$; P_2 samples $a_{5,2} \in \mathbb{F}$; P_3 samples $a_3, a_{4,3}, a_{5,3} \in \mathbb{F}$.

Correlated Randomness: $a_1, b_1, a_2, b_2 \in \mathbb{F}$ are randomly sampled under constraint $a_1 a_2 = b_1 + b_2$. P_1 receives (a_1, b_1). P_2 receives (a_2, b_2). P_3 has no correlated randomness.

Preprocessing: None. I.e., the preprocessing functions are identity functions.

Encoding Function: Outputs the following matrix

$$
\widehat{\mathsf{3MultPlus}}\Big(\big((x_1,z_1),a_{4,1},(a_1,b_1)\big),\big((x_2,z_2),a_{5,2},(a_2,b_2)\big),\big((x_3,z_3),(a_3,a_{4,3},a_{5,3}),\bot\big)\Big) =
$$

$$
\begin{bmatrix}
x_1 - a_1 & \begin{pmatrix} a_3 x_1 + a_1 x_3 \\ -a_1 a_3 - a_4 \end{pmatrix} & \begin{pmatrix} b_1 x_3 + b_2 x_3 + a_5 x_1 - a_1 a_5 + \\ a_4 x_2 - a_2 a_4 + z_1 + z_2 + z_3 \end{pmatrix} \\
-1 & x_3 - a_3 & a_2 x_3 - a_5 \\
& -1 & x_2 - a_2
\end{bmatrix}, \quad (4)
$$

where $a_4 := a_{4,1} + a_{4,3}$ and $a_5 := a_{5,2} + a_{5,3}$.

Decoding Function: Outputs the determinant of the encoding.

Fig. 8. The Effective-Degree-2 Semi-Honest MPRE for 3MultPlus

- To disclose s if $a_1 a_2 = b_1 + b_2$.
- To hide s if $a_1 a_2 \neq b_1 + b_2$.
- To reveal nothing about a_1, a_2, b_1, b_2 except whether $a_1 a_2 = b_1 + b_2$.
- The encoding function is quadratic.

We stress that the CDS encoding we are going to build *is not* a MPRE for any function, since it does not follow the same syntax. For example, the security of CDS encoding will rely on the fact that (a_1, a_2, b_1, b_2) is sampled from OLE correlated randomness. The CDS encoding will be used as a sub-module of the semi-maliciously secure MPRE in Sect. 4.3, where CDS encoding is carefully aligned with the rest of the MPRE.

It turns out that, towards building CDS encoding, we need to replace scalar OLE correlated randomness with tensor OLE correlated randomness. Let P_1 receive random $\mathbf{a}_1 \in \mathbb{F}^2$, $\mathbf{B}_1 \in \mathbb{F}^{2 \times 2}$ and let P_2 receive random $\mathbf{a}_2 \in \mathbb{F}^2$, $\mathbf{B}_2 \in \mathbb{F}^{2 \times 2}$, such that $\mathbf{a}_1 \mathbf{a}_1^\mathsf{T} = \mathbf{B}_1 + \mathbf{B}_2^\mathsf{T}$. Party P_1, P_2 use the first coordinates of the tensor-OLE correlated randomness as the original scalar OLE correlated randomness. That is, let $(a_1, b_1, a_2, b_2) := (\mathbf{a}_1[1], \mathbf{B}_1[1], \mathbf{a}_2[1], \mathbf{B}_2[1])$. The remaining coordinates will be used to hide a_1, b_1, a_2, b_2.

The CDS encoding is formally described in Fig. 9. As we emphasized, CDS encoding is not a MPRE. For correctness, the secret s can be decoded if $\mathbf{a}_1 \mathbf{a}_1^\mathsf{T} = \mathbf{B}_1 + \mathbf{B}_2^\mathsf{T}$. For privacy, the encoding can be simulated given the corrupted parties' input and the following information:

- The secret s if $\mathbf{a}_1 \mathbf{a}_1^\mathsf{T} = \mathbf{B}_1 + \mathbf{B}_2^\mathsf{T}$.
- $p_1 = \langle \mathbf{a}_1, \mathbf{q}_1 \rangle$, $p_2 = \langle \mathbf{a}_2, \mathbf{q}_2 \rangle$, $p_3 = \langle \mathbf{B}_1 + \mathbf{B}_2^\mathsf{T}, \mathbf{q}_1 \mathbf{q}_2^\mathsf{T} \rangle$, where $\mathbf{q}_1 = (q_1, 1)$, $\mathbf{q}_2 = (q_2, 1)$ are sampled by party P_3. (If the adversary corrupts P_3, it can adaptively choose q_1, q_2.)

The outer MPRE specifies 3 parties, denoted by P_1, P_2, P_3

Input: Party P_3 receives as input $s \in \mathbb{F}$. Party P_1 receives random $\mathbf{a}_1 \in \mathbb{F}^2, \mathbf{B}_1 \in \mathbb{F}^{2 \times 2}$. Party P_2 receives random $\mathbf{a}_2 \in \mathbb{F}^2, \mathbf{B}_2 \in \mathbb{F}^{2 \times 2}$. $(\mathbf{a}_1, \mathbf{a}_2, \mathbf{B}_1, \mathbf{B}_2)$ is supposed to be sampled from tensor-OLE correlated randomness.

Randomness: In addition, P_3 samples $q_1, q_2, r_1, r_2 \in \mathbb{F}$.

Preprocessing: P_3 locally computes $r_1 q_1, r_2 q_2, q_1 q_2, r_2 q_1, r_2 q_1 q_2$.

Encoding Function: Define $\mathbf{q}_1 = (q_1, 1), \mathbf{q}_2 = (q_2, 1)$. The functionality outputs $p_1 = \langle \mathbf{a}_1, \mathbf{q}_1 \rangle$, $p_2 = \langle \mathbf{a}_2, \mathbf{q}_2 \rangle$, $p_3 = \langle \mathbf{B}_1 + \mathbf{B}_2^\mathsf{T}, \mathbf{q}_1 \mathbf{q}_2^\mathsf{T} \rangle$ and

$$\mathbf{c} = \begin{bmatrix} 1 & \langle \mathbf{a}_2, \mathbf{q}_2 \rangle \\ \langle \mathbf{a}_1, \mathbf{q}_1 \rangle & \langle \mathbf{B}_1 + \mathbf{B}_2^\mathsf{T}, \mathbf{q}_1 \mathbf{q}_2^\mathsf{T} \rangle \end{bmatrix} \cdot \begin{bmatrix} r_1 \\ r_2 \end{bmatrix} + \begin{bmatrix} 0 \\ s \end{bmatrix}$$

Decoding Function: Check if $p_1 p_2 = p_3$. If so, output $\langle \mathbf{c}, (-p_1, 1) \rangle$. Otherwise, output $\perp$.

Fig. 9. CDS Encoding

Let us convey some intuitions why the three goals of CDS encoding in Fig. 9 are achieved.

- For disclosing s: If $(\mathbf{a}_1, \mathbf{a}_2, \mathbf{B}_1, \mathbf{B}_2)$ is in the support of tensor-OLE correlated randomness, then $p_1 p_2 = p_3$, thus the matrix $\begin{bmatrix} 1 & p_2 \\ p_1 & p_3 \end{bmatrix}$ is not full-rank. The secret s can still be recovered from $\mathbf{c}$.
- For hiding s: If $a_1 a_2 \neq b_1 + b_2$, it means $(\mathbf{a}_1, \mathbf{a}_2, \mathbf{B}_1, \mathbf{B}_2)$ is not tensor-OLE correlation. Then $p_1 p_2 \neq p_3$ with high probability due to the randomness of q_1, q_2. Since matrix $\begin{bmatrix} 1 & p_2 \\ p_1 & p_3 \end{bmatrix}$ is full-rank, the secret s is perfectly masked by (r_1, r_2).
- The encoding also leaks information about $\mathbf{a}_1, \mathbf{B}_1, \mathbf{a}_2, \mathbf{B}_2$, but as we will show, a_1, b_1, a_2, b_2 remain hidden. p_1, p_2 are one-time padded by $\mathbf{a}_1[2], \mathbf{a}_2[2]$. We leave the analysis of p_3 to the next section.
- The encoding function outputs $p_1 = \langle \mathbf{a}_1, \mathbf{q}_1 \rangle$, $p_2 = \langle \mathbf{a}_2, \mathbf{q}_2 \rangle$,

$$p_3 = \langle \mathbf{B}_1 + \mathbf{B}_2^\mathsf{T}, \begin{bmatrix} q_1 q_2 & q_1 \\ q_2 & 1 \end{bmatrix} \rangle, \quad \mathbf{c} = \begin{bmatrix} r_1 + \langle \mathbf{a}_2, \begin{bmatrix} r_2 q_2 \\ r_2 \end{bmatrix} \rangle \\ \langle \mathbf{a}_1, \begin{bmatrix} r_1 q_1 \\ r_1 \end{bmatrix} \rangle + \langle \mathbf{B}_1 + \mathbf{B}_2^\mathsf{T}, \begin{bmatrix} r_2 q_1 q_2 & r_2 q_1 \\ r_2 q_2 & r_2 \end{bmatrix} \rangle \end{bmatrix}$$

has degree 2 after $r_1 q_1, r_2 q_2, q_1 q_2, r_2 q_1, r_2 q_1 q_2$ are locally computed by P_3.

4.3 Semi-Malicious MPRE for Degree-3 Functions

Based on the CDS encoding (Fig. 9) we discussed in Sect. 4.2, we construct a semi-maliciously secure MPRE (Fig. 10) for canonical degree-3 functions. The MPRE has effective degree 2.

The idea is simple: Three parties P_1', P_2', P_3' need to compute $x_1 x_2 x_3 + z_1 + z_2 + z_3$. Every party P_i' samples a random mask s_i, one-time pads the output by s_i, and reveals s_i if and only if P_1' and P_2' use legit OLE correlated randomness. The last operation is allowed by our CDS encoding.

Function Input: P_i has $\mathbf{x}_i \in \mathbb{F}^{\ell_i}$

Function: A canonical degree-3 function f. By definition, there exists an index set $\mathcal{I}$. For each $t \notin \mathcal{I}$, the degree of f_t is at most 2. For each $t \in \mathcal{I}$, f_t equals $\mathbf{x}_{i_{t,1}}[j_{t,1}] \cdot \mathbf{x}_{i_{t,2}}[j_{t,2}] \cdot \mathbf{x}_{i_{t,3}}[j_{t,3}] + \mathbf{x}_{i_{t,1}}[j'_{t,1}] + \mathbf{x}_{i_{t,2}}[j'_{t,2}] + \mathbf{x}_{i_{t,3}}[j'_{t,3}]$ for some $i_{t,1}, i_{t,2}, i_{t,3} \in [n]$ and $j_{t,i}, j'_{t,i} \in [\ell_i]$.

As long as t is clear in the context, we refer to $P_{i_{t,1}}, P_{i_{t,2}}, P_{i_{t,3}}$ as P'_1, P'_2, P'_3 resp. and refer to $\mathbf{x}_{i_{t,1}}[j_{t,1}], \mathbf{x}_{i_{t,2}}[j_{t,2}], \mathbf{x}_{i_{t,3}}[j_{t,3}], \mathbf{x}_{i_{t,1}}[j'_{t,1}], \mathbf{x}_{i_{t,2}}[j'_{t,2}], \mathbf{x}_{i_{t,3}}[j'_{t,3}]$ as $x_1, x_2, x_3, z_1, z_2, z_3$ resp.

Randomness: For each $t \in \mathcal{I}$, P'_1 samples $s_{t,1}, a_{t,4,1} \in \mathbb{F}$, P'_2 samples $s_{t,2}$, $a_{t,5,2} \in \mathbb{F}$, P'_3 samples $s_{t,3}, a_{t,3}, a_{t,4,3}, a_{t,5,3} \in \mathbb{F}$. They also sample additional randomness according to the sub-module of CDS encoding (Fig. 9).

We will omit t in subscript, if there is no confusion.

Correlated Randomness: For each $t \in \mathcal{I}$, P'_1 receives $\mathbf{a}_{t,1} \in \mathbb{F}^4, \mathbf{B}_{t,1} \in \mathbb{F}^{4 \times 4}$, P'_2 receives $\mathbf{a}_{t,2} \in \mathbb{F}^4, \mathbf{B}_{t,2} \in \mathbb{F}^{4 \times 4}$ where $(\mathbf{a}_{t,1}, \mathbf{a}_{t,2}, \mathbf{B}_{t,1}, \mathbf{B}_{t,2})$ is sampled from 4×4 tensor OLE correlated randomness.

We will omit t from the subscript, if there is no confusion.

Preprocessing: Required by the sub-module of CDS encoding (Fig. 9).

Encoding Function: For each $t \notin \mathcal{I}$, output f_t.

For each $t \in \mathcal{I}$, output

$$M_t = 3\widehat{\mathsf{MultPlus}}\big(((x_1, z_1 + s_1), a_{4,1}, (a_1, b_1)),$$
$$((x_2, z_2 + s_2), a_{5,2}, (a_2, b_2)), \quad ((x_3, z_3 + s_3), (a_3, a_{4,3}, a_{5,3}), \perp)\big)$$

where $a_1 := \mathbf{a}_1[1], a_2 := \mathbf{a}_2[1], b_1 := \mathbf{B}_1[1,1], b_2 := \mathbf{B}_2[1,1]$.

P'_1, P'_2, P'_1 use CDS encoding to disclose s_1, conditioning on

$$\begin{bmatrix} \mathbf{a}_1[1] \\ \mathbf{a}_1[3] \end{bmatrix} \begin{bmatrix} \mathbf{a}_2[1] \\ \mathbf{a}_2[3] \end{bmatrix}^{\mathsf{T}} = \begin{bmatrix} \mathbf{B}_1[1,1] & \mathbf{B}_1[1,3] \\ \mathbf{B}_1[3,1] & \mathbf{B}_1[3,3] \end{bmatrix} + \begin{bmatrix} \mathbf{B}_2[1,1] & \mathbf{B}_2[1,3] \\ \mathbf{B}_2[3,1] & \mathbf{B}_2[3,3] \end{bmatrix}^{\mathsf{T}}$$

P'_1, P'_2, P'_2 use CDS encoding to disclose s_2, conditioning on

$$\begin{bmatrix} \mathbf{a}_1[1] \\ \mathbf{a}_1[4] \end{bmatrix} \begin{bmatrix} \mathbf{a}_2[1] \\ \mathbf{a}_2[4] \end{bmatrix}^{\mathsf{T}} = \begin{bmatrix} \mathbf{B}_1[1,1] & \mathbf{B}_1[1,4] \\ \mathbf{B}_1[4,1] & \mathbf{B}_1[4,4] \end{bmatrix} + \begin{bmatrix} \mathbf{B}_2[1,1] & \mathbf{B}_2[1,4] \\ \mathbf{B}_2[4,1] & \mathbf{B}_2[4,4] \end{bmatrix}^{\mathsf{T}}$$

P'_1, P'_2, P'_3 use CDS encoding to disclose s_3, conditioning on

$$\begin{bmatrix} \mathbf{a}_1[1] \\ \mathbf{a}_1[2] \end{bmatrix} \begin{bmatrix} \mathbf{a}_2[1] \\ \mathbf{a}_2[2] \end{bmatrix}^{\mathsf{T}} = \begin{bmatrix} \mathbf{B}_1[1,1] & \mathbf{B}_1[1,2] \\ \mathbf{B}_1[2,1] & \mathbf{B}_1[2,2] \end{bmatrix} + \begin{bmatrix} \mathbf{B}_2[1,1] & \mathbf{B}_2[1,2] \\ \mathbf{B}_2[2,1] & \mathbf{B}_2[2,2] \end{bmatrix}^{\mathsf{T}}$$

Decoding Function: For each $t \notin \mathcal{I}$, output f_t.

For each $t \in \mathcal{I}$, decode the CDS encoding to recover s_1, s_2, s_3. If s_1, s_2, s_3 are recovered, output $\det M_t - s_1 - s_2 - s_3$. Otherwise, output $\perp$.

Fig. 10. The Semi-Malicious MPRE For Degree-3 Functions

Lemma 2. *Figure 10 presents a semi-maliciously secure MPRE for degree-3 function f, whose effective degree is 2.*

The proof and the efficiency analysis are deferred to the full version.

	ℓ-size ABP		ℓ-gate circuit
	complexity	statistical security	complexity
2-round, security w/ output substitution	$O(n^2\ell^{1.5})$	$O(\frac{n^2\ell^{1.5}+n^2\cdot Q_{RO}}{|\mathbb{F}|})$	$O(n^3\ell)$
3-round, security w/ unanimous abort			
2-round, security w/ selective abort	$O(n^3\ell^{1.5})$	$O(\frac{n^3\ell^{1.5}+n^2\cdot Q_{RO}}{|\mathbb{F}|})$	
2-round, security w/ unanimous abort	$\text{poly}(n,\ell)$	$O(\frac{\text{poly}(n,\ell)+n^2\cdot Q_{RO}}{|\mathbb{F}|})$	$O(n^3\ell)+\text{poly}(n,\lambda)$

Complexity is measure by the number of field elements communicated.

Fig. 11. The final MPC protocols

5   Putting Pieces Together

MPC Protocols for Degree-3 Functions. Let f be a degree-3 function. By Lemma 2, there is an effective-degree-2 semi-malicious MPRE that has arithmetic preprocessing and uses tensor-OLE correlated randomness. In the full version, we present 2-round maliciously secure MPC protocol for computing any effective-degree-2 function using tensor-OLE correlated randomness (outlined in Sect. 2.3). Their composition is a 2-round statistically maliciously secure MPC protocol for computing f.

MPC Protocols for Circuits. Let f be a function that is computed by a Boolean circuit of ℓ gates. In the full version, we recall the reduction from **P/poly** to degree-3. So the tasking of computing f can be reduced to computing a degree-3 function $\hat{f}$. Therefore, there is a 2-round MPC protocol that is maliciously secure with output substitution. The protocol makes black-bow calls to PRF. The security of the protocol can be lifted by the technique presented in the full version (outlined in Sect. 2.4). So, there are, as shown in Fig. 11,

– A 3-round MPC protocol that is maliciously secure with unanimous abort and has the same complexity.
– A 2-round MPC protocol that is maliciously secure with selective abort and has the same complexity.
– A 2-round MPC protocol that is maliciously secure with unanimous abort and has an additive polynomial growth on the complexity.

MPC for Arithmetic Branching Programs. Let f be an arithmetic $\mathbf{NC^1}$ function. As we recall in the full version, there is a reduction from $\mathbf{NC^1}$ to degree-3. So the task of computing f can be reduced to computing a degree-3 function $\hat{f}$. Therefore, there is a 2-round MPC protocol that is maliciously secure with output substitution.

Similar to the case of Boolean circuits, the security can be lifted to security with selective/unanimous abort, at various costs, as shown in Fig. 11.

Acknowledgement. We thank Antigoni Polychroniadou for being our shepherd and her help, and the anonymous Crypto reviewers for their helpful comments and suggestions. We thank Hoeteck Wee for being part of the initial discussion and his suggestion of directions. Finally, we thank Stefano Tessaro for his comments.

Huijia Lin and Tianren Liu were supported by NSF grants CNS-1936825 (CAREER), CNS-2026774, a JP Morgan AI research Award, a Cisco research award, and a Simons Collaboration on the Theory of Algorithmic Fairness. In addition, Tianren Liu was supported by NSFC excellent young scientists fund program.

References

[ABT18] Applebaum, B., Brakerski, Z., Tsabary, R.: Perfect secure computation in two rounds. In: Beimel, A., Dziembowski, S. (eds.) TCC 2018, Part I. LNCS, vol. 11239, pp. 152–174. Springer, Cham (2018). https://doi.org/10.1007/978-3-030-03807-6_6

[ABT19] Applebaum, B., Brakerski, Z., Tsabary, R.: Degree 2 is complete for the round-complexity of malicious MPC. In: Ishai, Y., Rijmen, V. (eds.) EUROCRYPT 2019, Part II. LNCS, vol. 11477, pp. 504–531. Springer, Cham (2019). https://doi.org/10.1007/978-3-030-17656-3_18

[AIK04] Applebaum, B., Ishai, Y., Kushilevitz, E.: Cryptography in NC^0. In: 45th FOCS, pp. 166–175. IEEE Computer Society Press, October 2004

[AJJM20] Ananth, P., Jain, A., Jin, Z., Malavolta, G.: Multi-key fully-homomorphic encryption in the plain model. In: Pass, R., Pietrzak, K. (eds.) TCC 2020, Part I. LNCS, vol. 12550, pp. 28–57. Springer, Cham (2020). https://doi.org/10.1007/978-3-030-64375-1_2

[AJL+12] Asharov, G., Jain, A., López-Alt, A., Tromer, E., Vaikuntanathan, V., Wichs, D.: Multiparty computation with low communication, computation and interaction via threshold FHE. In: Pointcheval, D., Johansson, T. (eds.) EUROCRYPT 2012. LNCS, vol. 7237, pp. 483–501. Springer, Heidelberg (2012). https://doi.org/10.1007/978-3-642-29011-4_29

[BCG+19] Boyle, E., Couteau, G., Gilboa, N., Ishai, Y., Kohl, L., Scholl, P.: Efficient pseudorandom correlation generators: silent OT extension and more. In: Boldyreva, A., Micciancio, D. (eds.) CRYPTO 2019, Part III. LNCS, vol. 11694, pp. 489–518. Springer, Cham (2019). https://doi.org/10.1007/978-3-030-26954-8_16

[BCG+20] Boyle, E., Couteau, G., Gilboa, N., Ishai, Y., Kohl, L., Scholl, P.: Efficient pseudorandom correlation generators from ring-LPN. In: Micciancio, D., Ristenpart, T. (eds.) CRYPTO 2020, Part II. LNCS, vol. 12171, pp. 387–416. Springer, Cham (2020). https://doi.org/10.1007/978-3-030-56880-1_14

[BCGI18] Boyle, E., Couteau, G., Gilboa, N., Ishai, Y.: Compressing vector OLE. In: Lie, D., Mannan, M., Backes, M., Wang, X. (eds.) ACM CCS 2018, pp. 896–912. ACM Press, October 2018

[BCI+13] Bitansky, N., Chiesa, A., Ishai, Y., Paneth, O., Ostrovsky, R.: Succinct non-interactive arguments via linear interactive proofs. In: Sahai, A. (ed.) TCC 2013. LNCS, vol. 7785, pp. 315–333. Springer, Heidelberg (2013). https://doi.org/10.1007/978-3-642-36594-2_18

[BGI16] Boyle, E., Gilboa, N., Ishai, Y.: Function secret sharing: improvements and extensions. In: Weippl, E.R., Katzenbeisser, S., Kruegel, C., Myers, A.C., Halevi, S. (eds.) ACM CCS 2016, pp. 1292–1303. ACM Press, October 2016

[BGI17] Boyle, E., Gilboa, N., Ishai, Y.: Group-based secure computation: optimizing rounds, communication, and computation. In: Coron, J.-S., Nielsen, J.B. (eds.) EUROCRYPT 2017, Part II. LNCS, vol. 10211, pp. 163–193. Springer, Cham (2017). https://doi.org/10.1007/978-3-319-56614-6_6

[BGI+18] Boyle, E., Gilboa, N., Ishai, Y., Lin, H., Tessaro, S.: Foundations of homomorphic secret sharing. In: Karlin, A.R. (ed.) ITCS 2018, vol. 94, pp. 21:1–21:21. LIPIcs, January 2018

[BGMM20] Bartusek, J., Garg, S., Masny, D., Mukherjee, P.: Reusable two-round MPC from DDH. In: Pass, R., Pietrzak, K. (eds.) TCC 2020, Part II. LNCS, vol. 12551, pp. 320–348. Springer, Cham (2020). https://doi.org/10.1007/978-3-030-64378-2_12

[BGW88] Ben-Or, M., Goldwasser, S., Wigderson, A.: Completeness theorems for non-cryptographic fault-tolerant distributed computation (extended abstract). In: 20th ACM STOC, pp. 1–10. ACM Press, May 1988

[BL18] Benhamouda, F., Lin, H.: k-round multiparty computation from k-round oblivious transfer via garbled interactive circuits. In: Nielsen, J.B., Rijmen, V. (eds.) EUROCRYPT 2018, Part II. LNCS, vol. 10821, pp. 500–532. Springer, Cham (2018). https://doi.org/10.1007/978-3-319-78375-8_17

[BLPV18] Benhamouda, F., Lin, H., Polychroniadou, A., Venkitasubramaniam, M.: Two-round adaptively secure multiparty computation from standard assumptions. In: Beimel, A., Dziembowski, S. (eds.) TCC 2018, Part I. LNCS, vol. 11239, pp. 175–205. Springer, Cham (2018). https://doi.org/10.1007/978-3-030-03807-6_7

[BMR90] Beaver, D., Micali, S., Rogaway, P.: The round complexity of secure protocols (extended abstract). In: 22nd ACM STOC, pp. 503–513. ACM Press, May 1990

[BP16] Brakerski, Z., Perlman, R.: Lattice-based fully dynamic multi-key FHE with short ciphertexts. In: Robshaw, M., Katz, J. (eds.) CRYPTO 2016, Part I. LNCS, vol. 9814, pp. 190–213. Springer, Heidelberg (2016). https://doi.org/10.1007/978-3-662-53018-4_8

[CCD88] Chaum, D., Crépeau, C., Damgård, I.: Multiparty unconditionally secure protocols (extended abstract). In: 20th ACM STOC, pp. 11–19. ACM Press, May 1988

[CDI+19] Chase, M., et al.: Reusable non-interactive secure computation. In: Boldyreva, A., Micciancio, D. (eds.) CRYPTO 2019, Part III. LNCS, vol. 11694, pp. 462–488. Springer, Cham (2019). https://doi.org/10.1007/978-3-030-26954-8_15

[CGP15] Canetti, R., Goldwasser, S., Poburinnaya, O.: Adaptively secure two-party computation from indistinguishability obfuscation. In: Dodis, Y., Nielsen, J.B. (eds.) TCC 2015, Part II. LNCS, vol. 9015, pp. 557–585. Springer, Heidelberg (2015). https://doi.org/10.1007/978-3-662-46497-7_22

[CM15] Clear, M., McGoldrick, C.: Multi-identity and multi-key leveled FHE from learning with errors. In: Gennaro, R., Robshaw, M. (eds.) CRYPTO 2015, Part II. LNCS, vol. 9216, pp. 630–656. Springer, Heidelberg (2015). https://doi.org/10.1007/978-3-662-48000-7_31

[DI05]   Damgård, I., Ishai, Y.: Constant-round multiparty computation using a black-box pseudorandom generator. In: Shoup, V. (ed.) CRYPTO 2005. LNCS, vol. 3621, pp. 378–394. Springer, Heidelberg (2005). https://doi.org/10.1007/11535218_23

[DKR15] Dachman-Soled, D., Katz, J., Rao, V.: Adaptively secure, universally composable, multiparty computation in constant rounds. In: Dodis, Y., Nielsen, J.B. (eds.) TCC 2015, Part II. LNCS, vol. 9015, pp. 586–613. Springer, Heidelberg (2015). https://doi.org/10.1007/978-3-662-46497-7_23

[DPSZ12] Damgård, I., Pastro, V., Smart, N., Zakarias, S.: Multiparty computation from somewhat homomorphic encryption. In: Safavi-Naini, R., Canetti, R. (eds.) CRYPTO 2012. LNCS, vol. 7417, pp. 643–662. Springer, Heidelberg (2012). https://doi.org/10.1007/978-3-642-32009-5_38

[FKN94] Feige, U., Kilian, J., Naor, M.: A minimal model for secure computation (extended abstract). In: 26th ACM STOC, pp. 554–563. ACM Press, May 1994

[GGHR14] Garg, S., Gentry, C., Halevi, S., Raykova, M.: Two-round secure MPC from indistinguishability obfuscation. In: Lindell, Y. (ed.) TCC 2014. LNCS, vol. 8349, pp. 74–94. Springer, Heidelberg (2014). https://doi.org/10.1007/978-3-642-54242-8_4

[Gil99] Gilboa, N.: Two party RSA key generation. In: Wiener, M. (ed.) CRYPTO 1999. LNCS, vol. 1666, pp. 116–129. Springer, Heidelberg (1999). https://doi.org/10.1007/3-540-48405-1_8

[GIS18] Garg, S., Ishai, Y., Srinivasan, A.: Two-round MPC: information-theoretic and black-box. In: Beimel, A., Dziembowski, S. (eds.) TCC 2018, Part I. LNCS, vol. 11239, pp. 123–151. Springer, Cham (2018). https://doi.org/10.1007/978-3-030-03807-6_5

[GLS15] Dov Gordon, S., Liu, F.-H., Shi, E.: Constant-round MPC with fairness and guarantee of output delivery. In: Gennaro, R., Robshaw, M. (eds.) CRYPTO 2015, Part II. LNCS, vol. 9216, pp. 63–82. Springer, Heidelberg (2015). https://doi.org/10.1007/978-3-662-48000-7_4

[GMW87] Goldreich, O., Micali, S., Wigderson, A.: How to prove All NP statements in zero-knowledge and a methodology of cryptographic protocol design (extended abstract). In: Odlyzko, A.M. (ed.) CRYPTO 1986. LNCS, vol. 263, pp. 171–185. Springer, Heidelberg (1987). https://doi.org/10.1007/3-540-47721-7_11

[GP15]   Garg, S., Polychroniadou, A.: Two-round adaptively secure MPC from indistinguishability obfuscation. In: Dodis, Y., Nielsen, J.B. (eds.) TCC 2015, Part II. LNCS, vol. 9015, pp. 614–637. Springer, Heidelberg (2015). https://doi.org/10.1007/978-3-662-46497-7_24

[GS17]   Garg, S., Srinivasan, A.: Garbled protocols and two-round MPC from bilinear maps. In: Umans, C. (ed.) 58th FOCS, pp. 588–599. IEEE Computer Society Press, October 2017

[GS18]   Garg, S., Srinivasan, A.: Two-round multiparty secure computation from minimal assumptions. In: Nielsen, J.B., Rijmen, V. (eds.) EUROCRYPT 2018, Part II. LNCS, vol. 10821, pp. 468–499. Springer, Cham (2018). https://doi.org/10.1007/978-3-319-78375-8_16

[IK97]   Ishai, Y., Kushilevitz, E.: Private simultaneous messages protocols with applications. In: Fifth Israel Symposium on Theory of Computing and Systems, ISTCS 1997, Ramat-Gan, Israel, 17–19 June 1997, Proceedings, pp. 174–184. IEEE Computer Society (1997)

[IK00] Ishai, Y., Kushilevitz, E.: Randomizing polynomials: a new representation with applications to round-efficient secure computation. In: 41st FOCS, pp. 294–304. IEEE Computer Society Press, November 2000

[IK02] Ishai, Y., Kushilevitz, E.: Perfect constant-round secure computation via perfect randomizing polynomials. In: Widmayer, P., Eidenbenz, S., Triguero, F., Morales, R., Conejo, R., Hennessy, M. (eds.) ICALP 2002. LNCS, vol. 2380, pp. 244–256. Springer, Heidelberg (2002). https://doi.org/10.1007/3-540-45465-9_22

[IKNP03] Ishai, Y., Kilian, J., Nissim, K., Petrank, E.: Extending oblivious transfers efficiently. In: Boneh, D. (ed.) CRYPTO 2003. LNCS, vol. 2729, pp. 145–161. Springer, Heidelberg (2003). https://doi.org/10.1007/978-3-540-45146-4_9

[IKOS07] Ishai, Y., Kushilevitz, E., Ostrovsky, R., Sahai, A.: Zero-knowledge from secure multiparty computation. In: Johnson, D.S., Feige, U. (eds.) 39th ACM STOC, pp. 21–30. ACM Press, June 2007

[IKP10] Ishai, Y., Kushilevitz, E., Paskin, A.: Secure multiparty computation with minimal interaction. In: Rabin, T. (ed.) CRYPTO 2010. LNCS, vol. 6223, pp. 577–594. Springer, Heidelberg (2010). https://doi.org/10.1007/978-3-642-14623-7_31

[IKSS21] Ishai, Y., Khurana, D., Sahai, A., Srinivasan, A.: On the round complexity of black-box secure MPC. In: Malkin, T., Peikert, C. (eds.) CRYPTO 2021, Part II. LNCS, vol. 12826, pp. 214–243. Springer, Cham (2021). https://doi.org/10.1007/978-3-030-84245-1_8

[IPS08] Ishai, Y., Prabhakaran, M., Sahai, A.: Founding cryptography on oblivious transfer – efficiently. In: Wagner, D. (ed.) CRYPTO 2008. LNCS, vol. 5157, pp. 572–591. Springer, Heidelberg (2008). https://doi.org/10.1007/978-3-540-85174-5_32

[LLW20] Lin, H., Liu, T., Wee, H.: Information-theoretic 2-round MPC without round collapsing: adaptive security, and more. In: Pass, R., Pietrzak, K. (eds.) TCC 2020, Part II. LNCS, vol. 12551, pp. 502–531. Springer, Cham (2020). https://doi.org/10.1007/978-3-030-64378-2_18

[LPSY15] Lindell, Y., Pinkas, B., Smart, N.P., Yanai, A.: Efficient constant round multi-party computation combining BMR and SPDZ. In: Gennaro, R., Robshaw, M. (eds.) CRYPTO 2015, Part II. LNCS, vol. 9216, pp. 319–338. Springer, Heidelberg (2015). https://doi.org/10.1007/978-3-662-48000-7_16

[MW16] Mukherjee, P., Wichs, D.: Two round multiparty computation via multi-key FHE. In: Fischlin, M., Coron, J.-S. (eds.) EUROCRYPT 2016, Part II. LNCS, vol. 9666, pp. 735–763. Springer, Heidelberg (2016). https://doi.org/10.1007/978-3-662-49896-5_26

[Pas12] Paskin-Cherniavsky, A.: Secure computation with minimal interaction. Ph.D. thesis, Computer Science Department, Technion, Haifa, Israel (2012). Advised by Yuval Ishai and Eyal Kushilevitz

[PS16] Peikert, C., Shiehian, S.: Multi-key FHE from LWE, revisited. In: Hirt, M., Smith, A. (eds.) TCC 2016, Part II. LNCS, vol. 9986, pp. 217–238. Springer, Heidelberg (2016). https://doi.org/10.1007/978-3-662-53644-5_9

[Yao82] Yao, A.C.-C.: Protocols for secure computations (extended abstract). In: 23rd FOCS, pp. 160–164. IEEE Computer Society Press, November 1982

More Efficient Dishonest Majority Secure Computation over $\mathbb{Z}_{2^k}$ via Galois Rings

Daniel Escudero[1]([⊠]), Chaoping Xing[2], and Chen Yuan[2]

[1] J.P. Morgan AI Research, New York, USA
daniel.escudero@protonmail.com
[2] School of Electronic Information and Electrical Engineering,
Shanghai Jiao Tong University, Shanghai, China

Abstract. In this work we present a novel actively secure multiparty computation protocol in the dishonest majority setting, where the computation domain is a ring of the type $\mathbb{Z}_{2^k}$. Instead of considering an "extension ring" of the form $\mathbb{Z}_{2^{k+\kappa}}$ as in SPD$\mathbb{Z}_{2^k}$ (Cramer et al., CRYPTO 2018) and its derivatives, we make use of an actual ring extension, or more precisely, a Galois ring extension $\mathbb{Z}_{p^k}[\mathbf{X}]/(h(\mathbf{X}))$ of large enough degree, in order to ensure that the adversary cannot cheat except with negligible probability. These techniques have been used already in the context of honest majority MPC over $\mathbb{Z}_{p^k}$, and to the best of our knowledge, our work constitutes the first study of the benefits of these tools in the dishonest majority setting.

Making use of Galois ring extensions requires great care in order to avoid paying an extra overhead due to the use of larger rings. To address this, reverse multiplication-friendly embeddings (RMFEs) have been used in the honest majority setting (e.g. Cascudo et al., CRYPTO 2018), and more recently in the dishonest majority setting for computation over $\mathbb{Z}_2$ (Cascudo and Gundersen, TCC 2020). We make use of the recent RMFEs over $\mathbb{Z}_{p^k}$ from (Cramer et al., CRYPTO 2021), together with adaptations of some RMFE optimizations introduced in (Abspoel et al., ASIACRYPT 2021) in the honest majority setting, to achieve an efficient protocol that only requires in its online phase $12.4k(n-1)$ bits of amortized communication complexity and one round of communication for each multiplication gate. We also instantiate the necessary offline phase using Oblivious Linear Evaluation (OLE) by generalizing the approach based on Oblivious Transfer (OT) proposed in MASCOT (Keller et al., CCS 2016). To this end, and as an additional contribution of potential independent interest, we present a novel technique using Multiplication-Friendly Embeddings (MFEs) to achieve OLE over Galois ring extensions using black-box access to an OLE protocol over the base ring $\mathbb{Z}_{p^k}$ without paying a quadratic cost in terms of the extension degree. This generalizes the approach in MASCOT based on Correlated OT Extension. Finally, along the way we also identify a bug in a central proof in MASCOT, and we implicitly present a fix in our generalized proof.

1 Introduction

Secure multiparty computation is a set of tools and techniques that enables a group of parties, each having a private input, to jointly compute a given function

© International Association for Cryptologic Research 2022
Y. Dodis and T. Shrimpton (Eds.): CRYPTO 2022, LNCS 13507, pp. 383–412, 2022.
https://doi.org/10.1007/978-3-031-15802-5_14

while only revealing its output. Since its introduction in the late 80s by Yao in [29], several techniques for evaluating functionalities securely have been designed. These typically depend on the exact security setting, namely on how many parties are corrupted by an adversary, and whether they behave as an honest party (semi-honest/passive security) or if they operate in an arbitrary manner (active/malicious security).

One common aspect across all different constructions, however, is that they model the desired computation as an arithmetic circuit where gates are comprised of additions and multiplications over certain finite ring. Most attention has been devoted to the case in which the given arithmetic circuit is defined over a finite field, which is a natural choice due to its nice algebraic structure. However, there are other finite rings that are suitable for a wide range of highly relevant computations, which include, in particular, the ring $\mathbb{Z}_{p^k}$ of integers modulo p^k. For example, as shown in [16], computation over rings like $\mathbb{Z}_{2^k}$ with $k = 64$ or $k = 128$ may come with a series of performance benefits with respect to computation over prime fields of approximately the same size. Also, computation over arbitrary $\mathbb{Z}_{p^k}$ easily leads to efficient computation over arbitrary $\mathbb{Z}_m$ via the Chinese Remainder Theorem, leading to interesting results on the necessary assumptions to achieve efficient and "direct" MPC protocols.

Several such protocols have been proposed in the literature [1,2,14,24]. In the honest majority setting, where the adversary corrupts at most a minority of the parties, Shamir secret-sharing is the most widely used building block to design MPC protocols. Unfortunately, such construction cannot be instantiated over $\mathbb{Z}_{p^k}$, but recent works have successfully made use of the so-called *Galois ring extensions* in order to enable Shamir secret-sharing over this ring which, together with some care, leads to MPC over $\mathbb{Z}_{p^k}$.

On the other hand, if the adversary is not assumed to corrupt a minority of the parties—a setting which is also referred to as dishonest majority—a different tool, in contrast to Shamir secret-sharing, is typically used. In this case, the main building block is additive secret-sharing, another form of secret-sharing that does not provide the redundancy features of Shamir secret-sharing, although it is considerably much simpler. To deal with active adversaries, extra redundancy comes in the form of message authentication codes, or MACs, which enable parties to determine if certain reconstructed secret is correct, or if it was tampered with.

Most constructions of dishonest majority MPC [18,21,22] are designed to support arithmetic circuits defined over fields, mostly because of the limitations of their corresponding MACs, which are only secure as long as an adversary cannot design a polynomial of "low" degree with many roots. This is indeed the case if the given ring is a field, since a polynomial of degree d has at most $d - 1$ roots. However, when considering $\mathbb{Z}_{p^k}$ this does not longer hold, since there are polynomials of degree 1 such as $p^{k-1}X$ that have a large amount of roots (p^{k-1} in this case).

To deal with this, a novel MAC that is compatible with arithmetic modulo 2^k was proposed in [14]. This construction has inspired several other works for MPC over $\mathbb{Z}_{2^k}$ in the dishonest majority setting [13,24,27], and even some in the honest majority setting [1,2]. However, these techniques comes at the expense of increasing the ring size by an additive factor of κ, the statistical security parameter. Although follow-up works that introduce somewhat homomorphic encryption (SHE) improves the performance of the prepocessing phase [13,24, 27], their online phases still follow the original protocol in [14]. The instantiation of the online phase incurs in a communication complexity of $4(k + \kappa)(n - 1)$ for each multiplication gate as the parties have to open two values in $\mathbb{Z}_{2^{k+\kappa}}$.

From the discussion above, we see that it remains open to explore the benefits of using Galois ring extensions to achieve secure computation over $\mathbb{Z}_{p^k}$ in the dishonest majority setting.

1.1 Our Contribution

Computation over $\mathbb{Z}_{p^k}$. In this work, we design a highly efficient MPC protocol over $\mathbb{Z}_{p^k}$, for any prime p and integer $k \geq 1$,[1] that has a amortized communication complexity of $19.68k(n - 1)$ for each multiplication gate in the online phase. Such communication complexity can be further reduced to $12.4k(n-1)$ if the security parameter is $\kappa = 64$. Furthermore, the offline phase of our protocol requires an amortized communication complexity of $5142.5kn(n - 1)$ to prepare the shares for each multiplication gate in the online phase. We also note that we allow for a small k (possibly even $k = 1$), while the offline phase presented in SPD$\mathbb{Z}_{2^k}$ [14], which makes use of Oblivious Transfer (OT) as in [21], requires k to be as large as the security parameter.

Computation over $\mathbb{Z}_2$. For the case $p = 2$ and $k = 1$, that is, when computation is over $\mathbb{Z}_2$, the best known protocol of [9] requires $10.2\ell(n-1)$ bits of communication in implementing ℓ instances of multiplication simultaneously on the online phase while our protocol requires $12.4\ell(n - 1)$ bits of communication. However, their protocol needs 2 rounds of communication for each multiplication layer while our protocol only needs one round of communication. Furthermore, as the ratio of the best known RMFEs constructions improve, our construction can become more efficient. However, it is possible to bring down this cost to $8.2\ell(n-1)$ with a more tricky technique. We will briefly review such improvement in the Remark 1. Since the binary field is not the main focus of our protocol, we do not include this technique to optimize our online protocol.

Novel Techniques for OLE over Galois Ring Extensions. As an additional contribution of potential independent interest, as part of the preprocessing phase of our protocol we present a novel method to enable Oblivious Linear Evaluation (OLE) over a Galois ring extension $R = \mathbb{Z}_{p^k}/(f(x))$ of degree d based on *any* OLE protocol over $\mathbb{Z}_{p^k}$, while only paying a factor of $O(d)$. This makes novel use of Multiplication Friendly Embeddings (MFEs) [25], which converts an asymptotically good multiplicative secret sharing over extension field $\mathbb{F}_{2^d}$ into

---

[1] Even though our title includes $\mathbb{Z}_{2^k}$, our results are presented for the more general $\mathbb{Z}_{p^k}$.

an asymptotically good multiplicative secret sharing scheme over binary field $\mathbb{F}_2$. This must be compared to the naive approach to achieve OLE over a Galois ring extension which would consist of representing each factor in terms of a $\mathbb{Z}_{p^k}$-basis, and then calling the underlying OLE over $\mathbb{Z}_{p^k}$ a total of $O(d^2)$ times to handle all the resulting cross products. We elaborate on this in Sect. 1.2.

Fixing Bug in [21] *(and* [9]*)*. Our protocol shares certain similarities with the ones from [21] (which is for binary extension *fields*) and [9] (which is for computation over $\mathbb{Z}_2$). In particular, the way we authenticate elements in the preprocessing phase, which requires OLE and makes use of MFEs as mentioned above, shares certain resemblance with the corresponding authentication methods in [9,21] which make use of OT, or more specifically, Correlated OT Extension (COT), in order to avoid a quadratic blow-up in terms of the extension degree.

Due to the rough similarity between our preprocessing and the one from [9,21], we are able to produce a proof of authentication along the lines of the one in [21]. However, in the process of doing so, we identified a bug in the proof from [21] (which affects [9] as well), which invalidates the last part of their argument where it is shown that the values extracted by the simulator are unique. We discuss this bug, together with its fix, in the full version of this work.

1.2 Overview of Our Techniques

We present an overview of the main ideas behind the protocol introduced in this work, focusing on the high level ideas.

To get an idea of how our protocol works, consider the SPDZ-family of protocols over a field $\mathbb{F}_p$, which operates by additively secret-sharing each intermediate value $x \in \mathbb{F}_p$ as $[\![x]\!]$, together with shares of a global random key $[\![\alpha]\!]$, and shares of the Message Authentication Code (MAC) $[\![\alpha \cdot x]\!]$. Addition gates are handled locally, and multiplication gates make use of multiplication triples, which ultimately require opening some values. These openings are done without checking correctness, which is postponed to the final stage of the protocol where an aggregated check is performed.

The probability of the adversary cheating in the above protocol is $1/p$ so, if p is too small, we have to consider an extension field $\mathbb{F}_{p^d}$ so as to ensure that the adversary can not succeed with non-negligible probability. When it comes to the ring $\mathbb{Z}_{p^k}$, the failure probability of the adversary is still comparable to p^{-1} instead of p^{-k}. This is because there is only a $(1 - \frac{1}{p})$-fraction of invertible elements in $\mathbb{Z}_{p^k}$. To decrease the failure probability, we consider the Galois ring $R = \mathbb{Z}_{p^k}/(f(x))$, which is a degree-$d$ extension of the ring $\mathbb{Z}_{p^k}$, where $f(x)$ is a degree-d irreducible polynomial over $\mathbb{Z}_{p^k}$. This means that, if we run the SPDZ protocol over the Galois ring R by treating the input of each parties in $\mathbb{Z}_{p^k}$ as an element in R, we can obtain a SPDZ protocol with security parameter p^{-d}. However, the communication complexity of this protocol is d times bigger than the original one. To mitigate the blow-up of communication complexity, we resort to RMFEs, which can implement multiple instances of computation by embedding multiple inputs in $\mathbb{Z}_{p^k}$ into a single element in R, while keeping the security parameter of each instance to be d.

This technique which was defined over field was introduced in [8] to amortize the communication complexity in the honest majority setting, where a minimum size on the underlying field is needed in order to enable Shamir secret-sharing. Block et al. [6] independently proposed this technique to study two-party protocol over small fields. Then, this was used in [9] to amortize the communication complexity in the dishonest majority setting. This technique was restricted to the finite field $\mathbb{F}_2$ due to the fact that RMFEs were only known to exist over fields until very recently, when it was provided in [15] a construction of RMFEs over an arbitrary ring $\mathbb{Z}_{p^k}$, which enables us to amortize the communication complexity over this ring. The previous works that employ this technique require an extra round for multiplication gate so as to re-encode the secret. We save this extra round protocol by introducing a quintuple for the multiplication gate. This technique was first presented in [3] for the honest majority setting. As the ring is a generalization of field, our protocol can also be carried out over the field. This allows us to compare our protocol with those over fields $\mathbb{F}_p$ with small p. We defer the comparison to Sect. 1.3.

As we have mentioned before, we also introduce, as a potential contribution of independent interest, a method to obtain OLE protocols over the Galois ring extension R of degree d, having only black-box access to an OLE functionality over the base ring $\mathbb{Z}_{p^k}$, with a communication complexity that is linear in d. This is achieved by making novel use of MFEs, which enable us to represent a product over R as roughly d-many products over $\mathbb{Z}_{p^k}$. This way, and by exploiting the $\mathbb{Z}_{p^k}$-linearity of the MFEs, we can obtain the desired OLE over R by evaluating these many smaller OLEs over the base ring $\mathbb{Z}_{p^k}$. We note that this generalizes the approach introduced in [21], which uses COT in the setting of $p = 2$ and $k = 1$ in order to avoid a quadratic penalty in terms of the extension degree d.[2] Besides, our Galois ring is of size kd which is much bigger than other SPDZ protocols. Their protocol requires either $k = 1$ or $d = 1$ which is suitable for the use of COT. However, we may face the situation that both k, d are comparable to the security parameter κ. The direct use of COT will cause the quadratic penalty in κ. This MFE technique can break the Galois Ring into a direct sum of small integer ring $\mathbb{Z}_{p^k}$ and allow us to do the oblivious product evaluation over each $\mathbb{Z}_{p^k}$ separately. This will save us at least the penalty of quadratic d even with the COT-based approach.

We also introduce the quintuples instead of Beaver triple to save one round of communication for each multiplication gate. Note that the previous works applying RMFE such as [8,9] have to "re-encode" the secret. Basically speaking, all inputs $\boldsymbol{x}_i \in \mathbb{Z}_{p^k}^m$ are encoded as $\phi(\boldsymbol{x}_i)$ via the RMFE map. When two inputs $\phi(\boldsymbol{x}), \phi(\boldsymbol{y})$ enter the multiplication gate, the output should have the form $\phi(\boldsymbol{x} \star \boldsymbol{y})$

---

[2] Interestingly, our techniques do not constitute a strict generalization of the ones in [21], since they are of a different nature. We leave it as future work to analyze the potential benefits of our MFE-based techniques when $p = 2$ and $k = 1$ with respect to their COT-based approach.

where $\star$ is the component-wise product. If we use the Beaver triple to securely compute the multiplication gate, we have to re-encode the secret to meet the desired form. In this work, we resort to the quintuple to save one round of communication which was first presented in [1]. One can find the details in the Theorem 3 and online protocol.

From Amortized Execution to Single-Circuit. Making use of Galois rings and RMFEs imposes the restriction that the computation must occur in batches, that is, multiplications and additions occurs on vectors rather than individual values. This is perfect for secure computation over SIMD circuits, which carry out the exact same computation to several inputs simultaneously, but in general there is a wide range of practical circuits that do not exhibit this structure. The general case can be easily addressed in the exact same way as in [9] by preprocessing certain permutation tuples, that serve as a way to re-route data throughout the circuit evaluation. We do not include this in our work, and refer the reader to [9, Section 4] for an explanation of how this works, which adapts seamlessly to our case with little effort.

1.3   Related Work

Dishonest Majority MPC over $\mathbb{Z}_p$. The most standard case in the literature is when $k = 1$ and p is a large prime. In this case $\mathbb{Z}_p$ is a field, and there are multiple protocols designed to work in this setting, with the most notable being BeDOZa [5], SPDZ [17,18], MASCOT [21], Overdrive [22] and the more recent TopGear [4]. For the case in which p is a large prime, our protocol does not need to make use of any Galois ring extension, and in fact, our online phase becomes exactly the one from [17] (which is the same as in [4,21,22]).

In terms of the preprocessing all of the protocols above, except for MASCOT, are based on Somewhat Homomorphic Encryption (SHE), which was shown in [22] to perform better than OT-based approaches like MASCOT. We leave it as an interesting open problem to explore the benefits of basing the offline phase of our protocol in SHE, instead of OLE as done in our work.

Finally, MASCOT makes use of OT to instantiate the necessary preprocessing over $\mathbb{Z}_p$ by interpreting elements in this field as integers and representing them in base 2. Instead, in our case, our preprocessing would be based directly on an OLE primitive over $\mathbb{Z}_p$, and the concrete efficiency would depend on the concrete instantiation for the OLE.

Dishonest Majority MPC over $\mathbb{Z}_{2^k}$. In terms of computation over $\mathbb{Z}_{p^k}$ for a small p and $k > 1$, existing works focus on $p = 2$ and relatively large k.[3] The first such protocols was SPDZ$_{2^k}$, which introduced a novel technique of performing MAC checks over a larger ring $\mathbb{Z}_{2^{k+\kappa}}$ to achieve authentication over

---

[3] However, we remark that we are not aware of any limitation that would enable these works to be ported to the setting of $\mathbb{Z}_{p^k}$ for a more general prime p, and, furthermore, some of them already mention explicitly their ability to be generalized.

$\mathbb{Z}_{2^k}$ with error probability $2^{-\kappa}$ For each multiplication gate, SPD$\mathbb{Z}_{2^k}$ requires $4(k + \kappa)(n - 1)$ bits of communication since the shares are defined over $\mathbb{Z}_{2^{k+\kappa}}$.[4] Subsequent works that build on top of the same idea, most notably [10,24], suffer from the same overhead. In contrast, our online phase requires $4km(n-1)$ bits of communication for simultaneously computing ℓ instances for each multiplication gate. The amortized communication complexity is $\frac{4km}{\ell}(n-1) = 19.68k(n-1)$. This complexity does not grow with the security parameter m. This means if the security parameter in [14] is 4 times bigger than k, our online protocol is more efficient. One can cut this communication complexity to $12.4k(n-1)$ if the security parameter is 64.

In terms of the offline phase, SPD$\mathbb{Z}_{2^k}$ extends the OT-based approach proposed in MASCOT [21] to the $\mathbb{Z}_{2^{k+\kappa}}$ setting. However, due to the lack of invertibility in this ring, the protocol in [14] ends up adding quite some noticeable overhead so as to generate the Beaver triple. In their protocol, they claim that the parties communicate $2(k + 2\kappa)(9\kappa + 4k)n(n - 1)$ bits to securely generate a Beaver triple for multiplication gate. In our protocol, the amortized complexity of generating the quintuple for a multiplication gate is $5142.5kn(n-1)$ for $\kappa = 64$. In Sect. 6, we show that our prepocessing phase is more efficient than theirs if $k \leq 29$ for $\kappa = 64$ and $k \leq 114$ for $\kappa = 128$. Moreover, our communication complexity does not grow with the security parameter as we can amortize it away by computing more instances simultaneously. This implies that our protocol should be more competitive for high security parameter range.

Finally, the approaches in [10,24,27] make use of homomorphic encryption (either Additively or Somewhat HE) in order to create the necessary correlations among the parties for SPD$\mathbb{Z}_{2^k}$'s online phase. It is not clear how these techniques can be used in our current context where the correlations are over Galois rings, and as we have mentioned we leave it as an interesting future work to explore these potential relations.

To end, we remark that none of the protocols we have cited so far require multiple executions of the same circuit, unlike our case. As we have mentioned in Sect. 1.2, this can be easily overcome, as shown in [9], but nevertheless this adds a little overhead and an extra layer of complication.

Dishonest Majority MPC over $\mathbb{Z}_2$. Finally, we consider the relevant case of $p = 2$ and $k = 1$, which corresponds to the case of computation over $\mathbb{Z}_2 = \{0,1\}$. In this case, relevant protocols include [9,19,20,23]. These works share, at a high level, the general idea of making use of an extension field of $\mathbb{Z}_2$ of large enough degree as to guarantee small cheating probability, which is a pattern that our work also employs. However, our work is more closely related to that of [9], which on top of using field extensions to lower failure probability, also makes use of RMFEs to reduce the overhead cause by such extensions. By doing this, as shown

---

[4] An optimization in [14] seems to reduce this to $4k(n - 1)$ since the online phase can be modified so that only elements of $\mathbb{Z}_{2^k}$ are transmitted, while full elements over $\mathbb{Z}_{2^{k+\kappa}}$ only appear in the final check phase. However, a bug in this approach leads to this cost still being present in the offline phase (personal communication).

in [9], their work constitutes the state-of-the-art in terms of communication complexity in dishonest majority MPC over $\mathbb{Z}_2$.

Online Phase. Our protocol is very competitive with respect to that of [9]. In terms of the online phase, the communication complexity of our protocol, although not better than that of [9], is only worse by a small multiplicative factor 0.2. However, this is the only downside of our protocol with respect to that of [9]. Improvements of our protocol, which stem mostly from the different type of encoding we make use of, include the following:

- Our protocol is considerably simpler as it has less necessary "pieces". As a concrete example, the reader can compare the $\mathcal{F}_{\mathsf{MPC}}$ functionality we make use of in this work with respect to the corresponding functionality defined in [9]: here we only need to store vectors over $\mathbb{Z}_2$ (over $\mathbb{Z}_{p^k}$ in general), while the functionality in [9] needs to keep two dictionaries, one to store vectors over $\mathbb{Z}_2$ and another to store elements over certain field extension of $\mathbb{Z}_2$. In addition, among several other simplifications, our protocol does not make use of the input encoding mechanisms needed in [9], nor it requires re-encoding secret-shared values after each multiplication.
- Our online protocol, in spite of involving only the communication complexity overhead of a small factor 1.2 with respect to that of [9], requires half the amount of rounds than the protocol in [9]. This stems from the fact that, as mentioned above, we do not require the extra round needed in [9] to re-encode secret-shared values. Our input phase is also more efficient as we do not need to check that secret-shared values lie in certain subspace.

Offline Phase. Now, when comparing the offline phase of our protocol with respect to that of [9], we have to set $p^k = 2$. If we omits the cost of calls of OLE, our protocol is more efficient. However, we admit that it is not a fair comparison. We also want to emphasize that this OLE approach does save the communication cost for large k. If we replace the OLE with COT used by previous works like [9], the communication cost is quite close as we follow almost the same approach to generate the triples. The deviation is that our shares and MAC shares are defined over R while they divide them into two cases.

1.4 Organization of the Paper

This work is organized as follows. In Sect. 2 we present the necessary preliminaries, and then in Sect. 3 we present the online phase of our protocol. In Sect. 4 we present our protocol for authenticating secrets, which in particular includes our novel approach to OLE over Galois ring extensions based on OLE over $\mathbb{Z}_{p^k}$ using MFEs, and also the updated proof that shows that, in spite of the adversary being able to introduce errors in this protocol, there will be a unique set of extractable inputs the adversary is committed to. In Sect. 5 we present the full-fledged offline phase of our protocol, which includes the generation of the modified triples we use in our work. Finally, in Sect. 6 we analyze concretely the communication complexity of our resulting protocol.

2 Preliminaries

2.1 Basic Notation

We use bold letters (e.g. x, y) to denote vectors, and we use the star operator $(\star)$ to denote component-wise product of vectors. Also, in some cases we use the notation $x[i]$ to denote the i-entry of the vector x. Finally, we use $[N]$ to denote the set of integers $\{1, \ldots, N\}$. We denote by n the number of parties, and the set of parties is $\{P_1, \ldots, P_n\}$.

In this work we make use of the authenticated and homomorphic secret-sharing construction from [17], where a value $x \in R$ is secret-shared as $\langle x \rangle = (\llbracket x \rrbracket, \llbracket x \cdot \alpha \rrbracket, \llbracket \alpha \rrbracket)$, where $\alpha \xleftarrow{\$} R$ is a global uniformly random key. More precisely, this sharing contains three parts, $\llbracket x \rrbracket = (x^{(1)}, \ldots, x^{(n)})$, $\llbracket x \cdot \alpha \rrbracket = (m^{(1)}, \ldots, m^{(n)})$ and $\llbracket \alpha \rrbracket = (\alpha^{(1)}, \ldots, \alpha^{(n)})$, where party P_i holds the random share $x^{(i)}$ of the secret x, the MAC share $m^{(i)}$ and the key share $\alpha^{(i)}$. These satisfy $\sum_{i=1}^{n} m^{(i)} = (\sum_{i=1}^{n} x^{(i)})(\sum_{i=1}^{n} \alpha^{(i)})$.

2.2 Algebraic Preliminaries

Galois Rings. We denote by $\mathsf{GR}(p^k, d)$ the Galois ring over $\mathbb{Z}_{p^k}$ of degree d, which is a ring extension $\mathbb{Z}_{p^k}/(f(\mathtt{X}))$ of $\mathbb{Z}_{p^k}$, where $f(\mathtt{X}) \in \mathbb{Z}_{p^k}[\mathtt{X}]$ is a monic polynomial of degree d over $\mathbb{Z}_{p^k}$ whose reduction modulo p is irreducible over $\mathbb{Z}_p$. For details on Galois rings we refer the reader to the text [28], and also to the full version of this work.

Multiplication-Friendly Embeddings. We begin by considering the crucial notions of Multiplication-Friendly Embeddings (MFEs) and Reverse Multiplication-Friendly Embeddings (RMFEs), which act as an interface between Galois ring extensions and vectors over $\mathbb{Z}_{p^k}$, making the products defined in each of these structures (component-wise products for the vectors) somewhat "compatible". The asymptotically good multiplicative secret sharing schemes over field were already known in [11,12,25,26]. However, the similar results for asymptotically good multiplicative secret sharing scheme over ring were not known until very recently [15]. Basically speaking, they manage to show that the asymptotically good multiplicative secret sharing scheme over ring $\mathbb{Z}_{p^k}$ can achieve the same performance as the one over field $\mathbb{F}_p$. There results provide a machinery for explicitly constructing multiplication friendly embedding and reverse multiplication friendly embedding over ring. We start with MFEs below.

Definition 1. *Let $m, t \in \mathbb{N}$. A pair of $\mathbb{Z}_{p^k}$-module homomorphisms $\rho : \mathbb{Z}_{p^k}^t \to \mathsf{GR}(p^k, m)$ and $\mu : \mathsf{GR}(p^k, m) \to \mathbb{Z}_{p^k}^t$ is a multiplication-friendly embedding, or MFE for short, if, for all $x, y \in \mathsf{GR}(p^k, m)$ it holds that $xy = \rho(\mu(x) \star \mu(y))$.*

It is easy to see from the definition that ρ must be surjective and μ must be injective. Indeed, given $x \in \mathsf{GR}(p^k, m)$, we have that $x = x \cdot 1 = \rho(\mu(x) \star \mu(1))$, and if $\mu(x) = \mathbf{0}$ then $x = \rho(\mu(x) \star \mu(1)) = \rho(\mathbf{0} \star \mu(1)) = \rho(\mathbf{0}) = 0$. In particular, $t \geq m$.[5]

For the convenience of comparison with other works, we only list the results about $p = 2$ in the following theorem. If $p > 2$, the ratio will be smaller. This also holds for RMFEs.

Theorem 1 [15]. *There exists an explicit MFE family $(\rho_m, \mu_m)_{m \in \mathbb{N}}$ with $t(m)/m \to 5.12$ as $m \to \infty$.*

Reverse Multiplication-Friendly Embeddings. Now we define the notion of an RMFE.

Definition 2. *Let $m, \ell \in \mathbb{N}$. A pair of $\mathbb{Z}_{p^k}$-module homomorphisms (ϕ, ψ) with $\phi : \mathbb{Z}_{p^k}^\ell \to GR(p^k, m)$ and $\psi : GR(p^k, m) \to \mathbb{Z}_{p^k}^\ell$ is a reverse multiplication-friendly embedding, or RMFE for short, if, for every $\boldsymbol{x}, \boldsymbol{y} \in \mathbb{Z}_{p^k}^\ell$, it holds that $\boldsymbol{x} \star \boldsymbol{y} = \psi(\phi(\boldsymbol{x}) \cdot \phi(\boldsymbol{y}))$.*

Note that, if (ϕ, ψ) is an RMFE, then necessarily ϕ is injective and ψ is surjective, so in particular $\ell \leq m$. The following theorem shows the existence of RMFEs over $\mathbb{Z}_{2^k}$. The existence of RMFEs over $\mathbb{Z}_{p^k}$ can be found in [15].

Theorem 2 [15]. *There exists an explicit RMFE family $(\phi_m, \psi_m)_{m \in \mathbb{N}}$ with $m/\ell(m) \to 4.92$ as $m \to \infty$. For small value, we can optimize this ratio by choosing $(m, \ell(m)) = (65, 21)$ or $(m, \ell(m)) = (135, 42)$.*

Without loss of generality we can assume that $\phi(1) = 1$. This implies that, given $\boldsymbol{x} \in \mathbb{Z}_{p^k}^\ell$, a preimage of $\boldsymbol{x}$ under ψ is $x = \phi(\boldsymbol{x})$.

2.3   Security Model

We prove the security of our protocol under the Universal Composability (UC) framework by Canetti [7]. We let n be the number of parties, among which at most $n - 1$ can be actively corrupted. We let $\mathcal{C}, \mathcal{H} \subseteq [n]$ denote the index set of corrupted and honest parties, respectively. The adversary is static and malicious, which means that the corruption may only happen before the start of the protocols, and corrupted parties may behave arbitrarily. We say a protocol Π securely implement a functionality $\mathcal{F}$ with statistical security parameter κ,[6] if there is a simulator that interacts with the adversary (or more formally, the *environment*) so that he can distinguish the ideal/simulated world and the real worlds with probability at most $O(2^{-\kappa})$.

---

[5] In fact, one can reasonably easy prove that $t \geq 2m$.

[6] We consider only statistical security since, even though dishonest majority MPC is known to be generally impossibly to achieve without computational assumptions, we rely in this work on an OLE functionality, and do not provide any instantiation of it. This allows us to design protocols in the statistical setting.

The composability of the UC framework enables us to build our protocol in a modular fashion by defining small protocols together with the functionalities they are intended to implement, and proving the security of each of these pieces separately. Finally, we assume for simplicity and without loss of generality that the outputs to be computed are intended to be learned by all parties, i.e. there are no private outputs.

2.4   Communication Model

We assume private and authenticated channels between every pair of parties, as well as a broadcast channel. In addition, we assume the existence of what we call a *simultaneous message channel*, which allows the parties, each P_i holding a value x_i, to send these to all the other parties while guaranteeing that the corrupt parties cannot modify their values based on the messages from other parties. This is ultimately used to enable reconstruction of an additively shared secret while disallowing a rushing adversary from modifying the secret at will, restricting him to additive errors only. Such channel is implemented in practice by following the standard "commit-and-open" approach in which the parties first broadcast to each other a commitment of their messages, and then, only once this is done, they open via broadcast the commitments to the values they wanted to send in a first place.[7]

More formally, we model communication as an ideal functionality $\mathcal{F}_{\mathsf{Channels}}$. This is presented in detail in the full version of this work. Note that all of our protocols make use of $\mathcal{F}_{\mathsf{Channels}}$, but we do not write this explicitly in their descriptions or in their associated theorems.

3   Online Phase

We set $m = \lceil \kappa \log_p(2) \rceil$ so $p^m \geq 2^\kappa$, where κ is the statistical security parameter, and denote $\phi := \phi_m : \mathbb{Z}_{p^k}^{\ell(m)} \to R$ and $\psi := \psi_m : R \to \mathbb{Z}_{p^k}^{\ell(m)}$, the mappings whose existence is guaranteed by Theorem 2. Now that m is fixed, we write ℓ instead of $\ell(m)$. We also let $R = \mathsf{GR}(p^k, m)$ and $\overline{R} = \mathsf{GF}(p^m) = \{\overline{r} : r \in R\}$. Finally, we consider the $\mathbb{Z}_{p^k}$-linear map $\tau : R \to R$ given by $\tau = \phi \circ \psi$.

We begin by describing how the online phase of our protocol works. In more detail, we describe a protocol Π_{Online} that securely implements the MPC functionality $\mathcal{F}_{\mathsf{MPC}}$, that models general purpose secure computation over vectors $\mathbb{Z}_{p^k}^\ell$, in the $\mathcal{F}_{\mathsf{Prep}}$-hybrid model, where, as we will see, $\mathcal{F}_{\mathsf{Prep}}$ is a functionality that provides certain correlated randomness. Then, in following Sections we discuss how to instantiate $\mathcal{F}_{\mathsf{Prep}}$.

---

[7] This is modeled in other works with a functionality (typically denoted by $\mathcal{F}_{\mathsf{Comm}}$), but we decided to incorporate this as part of the communication channel for simplicity.

3.1 Required Functionalities

First, we present some of the essential functionalities we will need in this section. We follow a similar approach to that in [9]. We let $\mathcal{F}_{\mathsf{MPC}}$ be a functionality that enables the parties to input secret *vectors* in $\mathbb{Z}_{p^k}^{\ell}$, perform arbitrary SIMD affine combinations and multiplications on these, and open results. This is ultimately the functionality that we wish to instantiate. To achieve this, we consider a restricted functionality $\mathcal{F}_{\mathsf{Prep}}$ that acts like $\mathcal{F}_{\mathsf{MPC}}$, except it does not allow for multiplications. Instead, it can store certain correlated vectors upon request by the parties, which can be used to instantiate multiplications. Finally, we define $\mathcal{F}_{\mathsf{Auth}}$, which is a more restricted version of both $\mathcal{F}_{\mathsf{MPC}}$ and $\mathcal{F}_{\mathsf{Prep}}$ that acts exactly as these two except that, with respect to $\mathcal{F}_{\mathsf{MPC}}$, it does not allow for multiplication, and with respect to $\mathcal{F}_{\mathsf{Prep}}$ it does not generate correlated randomness.

We remark that these functionalities are essentially the same as the ones presented in [9]. However, we note that in our case they can be fully defined over one single ring (either $\mathbb{Z}_{p^k}^{\ell}$ or R), while in [9], due to the type of encoding they use, both rings appear simultaneously in these functionalities.

Authentication Functionality $\mathcal{F}_{\mathsf{Auth}}$. This functionality is the basic building block that allows parties to store secrets and perform affine combination on these. Intuitively, it corresponds to Homomorphic Authenticated Secret-Sharing. We remark that we will not make direct use of $\mathcal{F}_{\mathsf{Auth}}$ in this Section, but we include it since it is instructive to define this functionality first and describe both $\mathcal{F}_{\mathsf{MPC}}$ and $\mathcal{F}_{\mathsf{Prep}}$ in terms of $\mathcal{F}_{\mathsf{Auth}}$ later on. $\mathcal{F}_{\mathsf{Auth}}$ is defined as Functionality 1 below.

Functionality 1: $\mathcal{F}_{\mathsf{Auth}}$

The functionality maintains a dictionary Val, which it uses to keep track of authenticated elements of R. We use $\langle x \rangle$ to denote the situation in which the functionality stores $\mathsf{Val}[\mathtt{id}] = x$ for some identifier $\mathtt{id}$.

- **Input:** On input $(\mathsf{Input}, (\mathtt{id}_1, \mathtt{id}_2, \ldots \mathtt{id}_L), (x_1, x_2, \ldots, x_L), P_i)$ from P_i and $(\mathsf{Input}, (\mathtt{id}_1, \mathtt{id}_2, \ldots \mathtt{id}_L), P_i)$ from all other parties, set $\mathsf{Val}[\mathtt{id}_j] = x_j$ for $j = 1, 2, \ldots, L$.
- **Affine combination:** On input $(\mathsf{AffComb}, \mathtt{id}, (\mathtt{id}_1, \ldots, \mathtt{id}_L), (a_1, \ldots, a_L), a)$ from all parties, the functionality computes $z = a + \sum_{j=1}^{L} a_j \cdot \mathsf{Val}[\mathtt{id}_j]$ and stores $\mathsf{Val}[\mathtt{id}] = z$. We denote this by $\langle z \rangle \leftarrow a + \sum_{j=1}^{L} a_j \langle x_j \rangle$, where $x_j = \mathsf{Val}[\mathtt{id}_j]$.
- **Partial openings:** On input $(\mathsf{Open}, \mathtt{id})$ from all parties, if $\mathsf{Val}[\mathtt{id}] \neq \bot$, send $x = \mathsf{Val}[\mathtt{id}]$ to the adversary and wait for an x' back. Then send x' to the honest parties.
- **Check openings:** On input $(\mathsf{Check}, (\mathtt{id}_1, \mathtt{id}_2, \ldots, \mathtt{id}_L), (x_1, x_2, \ldots, x_L))$ from every party wait for an input from the adversary. If he inputs OK, and if $\mathsf{Val}[\mathtt{id}_j] = x_j$ for $j = 1, 2, \ldots, L$, return OK to all parties. Otherwise abort.

Preprocessing Functionality $\mathcal{F}_{\text{Prep}}$. This functionality extends $\mathcal{F}_{\text{Auth}}$ by letting the parties obtain shares $(\langle a \rangle, \langle b \rangle, \langle \tau(a) \rangle, \langle \tau(b) \rangle, \langle \tau(a)\tau(b) \rangle)$, where $a, b \xleftarrow{\$} R$ are uniformly random and unknown to any party. It also allows the parties to obtain $\langle r \rangle$ where $r \xleftarrow{\$} \psi^{-1}(\mathbf{0})$. $\mathcal{F}_{\text{Prep}}$ is defined as Functionality 2 below.

Functionality 2: $\mathcal{F}_{\text{Prep}}$

This functionality behaves exactly like $\mathcal{F}_{\text{Auth}}$, but in addition it supports the following commands:

- **Correlated randomness**: On input $(\text{CorrRand}, \text{id}_1, \text{id}_2, \text{id}_3, \text{id}_4, \text{id}_5)$ from all parties, sample $a, b \in R$ uniformly at random and store $\text{Val}[\text{id}_1] = a$, $\text{Val}[\text{id}_2] = b$, $\text{Val}[\text{id}_3] = \tau(a)$, $\text{Val}[\text{id}_4] = \tau(b)$ and $\text{Val}[\text{id}_5] = \tau(a) \cdot \tau(b)$.
- **Input**: On Input $(\text{InputPrep}, P_i, \text{id})$ from all parties, samples $\text{Val}[\text{id}] \xleftarrow{\$} R$ and output it to P_i.
- **Kernel element**: On input (Ker, id) from all parties, sample $r \in R$ uniformly at random subject to $\psi(r) = \mathbf{0}$, and store $\text{Val}[\text{id}] = r$.

Parallel MPC Functionality $\mathcal{F}_{\text{MPC}}$. Finally, we describe the functionality that we aim at implementing in this section. It takes $\mathcal{F}_{\text{Auth}}$ as a starting point, and implement the following changes/additions:

- It replaces R by $\mathbb{Z}_{p^k}^\ell$, so, instead of storing elements of R, it stores vectors over $\mathbb{Z}_{p^k}$ of dimension ℓ.
- Affine combinations now take coefficients over $\mathbb{Z}_{p^k}$.
- It implements a multiplication command that, on input $(\text{Mult}, \text{id}, (\text{id}_1, \text{id}_2))$ from all parties, computes $z = \text{Val}[\text{id}_1] \star \text{Val}[\text{id}_2]$ and stores $\text{Val}[\text{id}] = z$.

$\mathcal{F}_{\text{MPC}}$ is defined in full detail in the full version of this work.

3.2   Instantiating $\mathcal{F}_{\text{MPC}}$ in the $\mathcal{F}_{\text{Prep}}$-Hybrid Model

The protocol Π_{Online}, described as Protocol 1 later in the section, instantiates $\mathcal{F}_{\text{MPC}}$ in the $\mathcal{F}_{\text{Prep}}$-hybrid model, with statistical security parameter κ. Intuitively, the protocol consists of the parties storing vectors $x \in \mathbb{Z}_{p^k}^\ell$ by storing with $\mathcal{F}_{\text{Prep}}$ an element $x \in R$ with $\psi(x) = x$. The corresponding commands in $\mathcal{F}_{\text{Prep}}$ are used to instantiate Input, AffComb, Open and Check, and the correlated randomness is used to handle the Mult command.

We remark that the Input command can be instantiated more efficiently instead of relying on the corresponding command from $\mathcal{F}_{\text{Prep}}$, by using the standard approach of letting each party P_i broadcast its input masked with a random value of which the parties have (preprocessed) shares. A crucial observation is that we can allow this since *any* possible input in R is a valid input, while in other works like [9], a special "subspace check" is needed to ensure that this input lies in a special subset of valid inputs.

Protocol 1: Π_{Online}

– **Input:** The parties, upon receiving input $(\mathsf{Input}, \mathsf{id}, P_i)$, and P_i receiving input $(\mathsf{Input}, \mathsf{id}, \boldsymbol{x}, P_i)$, execute the following:

1. Call $\mathcal{F}_{\mathsf{Prep}}$ with the command $\mathsf{InputPrep}$. P_i takes the mask value $(r, \langle r \rangle)$.

2. P_i broadcasts $\phi(\boldsymbol{x}) - r$ and each party locally computes $\phi(\boldsymbol{x}) - r + \langle r \rangle$. As a result, the parties obtain $\langle x \rangle$, where $x = \phi(\boldsymbol{x}) \in \psi^{-1}(\boldsymbol{x})$.

– **Affine combination:** Upon receiving $(\mathsf{AffComb}, \mathsf{id}, (\mathsf{id}_1, \ldots, \mathsf{id}_L), (a_1, \ldots, a_L), \boldsymbol{a})$, the parties send $(\mathsf{AffComb}, \mathsf{id}, (\mathsf{id}_1, \ldots, \mathsf{id}_L), (a_1, \ldots, a_L), \phi(\boldsymbol{a}))$ to $\mathcal{F}_{\mathsf{Prep}}$.

– **Multiplication:** Upon receiving input $(\mathsf{Mult}, \mathsf{id}, (\mathsf{id}_1, \mathsf{id}_2))$, the parties proceed as described below. Let $\langle x \rangle$ and $\langle y \rangle$ be the values stored by $\mathcal{F}_{\mathsf{Prep}}$ in id_1 and id_2 respectively. Below, when not written explicitly, the identifiers needed for the given commands are assumed to be fresh and unique, and are only used ephemerally for the purpose of handling the multiplication command.

1. Call $\mathcal{F}_{\mathsf{Prep}}$ with the command $\mathsf{CorrRand}$ to obtain $(\langle a \rangle, \langle b \rangle, \langle \tau(a) \rangle, \langle \tau(b) \rangle, \langle \tau(a)\tau(b) \rangle)$.

2. Call $\mathcal{F}_{\mathsf{Prep}}$ with the command $\mathsf{AffComb}$ to obtain $\langle d \rangle \leftarrow \langle x \rangle - \langle a \rangle$ and $\langle e \rangle \leftarrow \langle y \rangle - \langle b \rangle$.

3. Call $\mathcal{F}_{\mathsf{Prep}}$ with the command Open to obtain $d \leftarrow \langle d \rangle$ and $e \leftarrow \langle e \rangle$.

4. Call $\mathcal{F}_{\mathsf{Prep}}$ with the command $\mathsf{AffComb}$ to obtain $\langle z \rangle \leftarrow \tau(d) \langle \tau(b) \rangle + \tau(e) \langle \tau(a) \rangle + \langle \tau(a)\tau(b) \rangle + \tau(d)\tau(e)$, indicating $\mathcal{F}_{\mathsf{Prep}}$ to store this value at the identifier id.

– **Partial openings:** Upon receiving input $(\mathsf{Open}, \mathsf{id})$, the parties execute the following. Let $\langle x \rangle$ be the value stored by $\mathcal{F}_{\mathsf{Prep}}$ at id.

1. Call $\mathcal{F}_{\mathsf{Prep}}$to with the command Ker to get $\langle r \rangle$ with $r \in \psi^{-1}(\boldsymbol{0})$.

2. Call $\mathcal{F}_{\mathsf{Prep}}$ with the command $\mathsf{AffComb}$ to get $\langle z \rangle \leftarrow \langle x \rangle + \langle r \rangle$, storing this value at id (hence overloading $\langle x \rangle$ with $\langle z \rangle$).

3. Call $\mathcal{F}_{\mathsf{Prep}}$ with the command Open so that the honest parties in $\mathbb{Z}_{p^k}$ learn z', for a value $z' \in R$ provided by the adversary to $\mathcal{F}_{\mathsf{Prep}}$. The parties store internally the pair (id, z').

4. The parties output $\boldsymbol{z}' = \psi(z')$.

– **Check openings:** Upon receiving input $(\mathsf{Check}, (\mathsf{id}_1, \mathsf{id}_2, \ldots, \mathsf{id}_L), (\boldsymbol{x}_1, \boldsymbol{x}_2, \ldots, \boldsymbol{x}_L))$, the parties fetch the internally stored pairs (id_j, x'_j) for $j = 1, \ldots, L$ and call $\mathcal{F}_{\mathsf{Prep}}$ on input $(\mathsf{Check}, (\mathsf{id}_1, \mathsf{id}_2, \ldots, \mathsf{id}_L), (x'_1, x'_2, \ldots, x'_L))$. If $\mathcal{F}_{\mathsf{Prep}}$ aborts, then the parties abort.

Theorem 3. *Protocol Π_{Online} implements $\mathcal{F}_{\mathsf{MPC}}$ in the $\mathcal{F}_{\mathsf{Prep}}$-hybrid model*

Proof (Sketch). A full-fledged simulation-based proof is presented in the full version of this work. Here we restrict ourselves to the core idea of the proof. First, notice that for every input $\boldsymbol{x} \in \mathbb{Z}_{p^k}^{\ell}$, the value stored by $\mathcal{F}_{\mathsf{Prep}}$ is $x := \phi(\boldsymbol{x}) - r + r = \phi(\boldsymbol{x}) \in R$, which satisfies $\psi(x) = \boldsymbol{x}$. We see then that, for the input phase, the values stored by $\mathcal{F}_{\mathsf{Prep}}$ are a preimage under ψ of the corresponding vectors that Π_{Online} stores. We claim that this invariant is preserved through the interaction with the $\mathsf{AffComb}$ and Mult commands.

The case of AffComb is easy since ψ is $\mathbb{Z}_{p^k}$-linear. To analyze Mult, consider two stored values $x, y \in \mathbb{Z}_{p^k}^\ell$ in Π_{Online}, and assume that the invariant holds, so the underlying stored values $x, y \in R$ in $\mathcal{F}_{\text{Prep}}$ satisfy $\psi(x) = x$ and $\psi(y) = y$. After the command Mult is issued to Π_{Online}, the parties get a tuple $(\langle a \rangle, \langle b \rangle, \langle \tau(a) \rangle, \langle \tau(b) \rangle, \langle \tau(a)\tau(b) \rangle)$, then open $d = x - a$ and $e = y - b$, and compute locally $\langle z \rangle \leftarrow \tau(d) \langle \tau(b) \rangle + \tau(e) \langle \tau(a) \rangle + \langle \tau(a)\tau(b) \rangle + \tau(d)\tau(e)$. We can verify that this is equal to $z = \tau(x)\tau(y)$, which preserves the invariant since $\psi(z) = \psi(\phi(\psi(x)) \cdot \phi(\psi(y))) = \psi(x) \star \psi(y) = x \star y$, using the definition of τ together with Definition 2. The above assumes that d and e are opened correctly, but this can be assumed to be the case since, if this does not hold, this will be detected in when the Check command is issued, and the adversary does not learn sensitive information before then since the values a and b perfectly mask the stored values x and y.

Finally, for the Open command, we see that, due to the invariant, the value returned by $\mathcal{F}_{\text{Prep}}$ is indeed a preimage under ψ of the value stored by Π_{Online}. However, one small technicality is that this preimage may contain "noise" from previous operations, or more precisely, which preimage is this may depend on previous data which is not intended to be revealed. This is fixed by adding a random element $r \in \psi^{-1}(0)$ before opening, which preserves the invariant, but guarantees that the preimage is uniformly random among all possible preimages. In formal terms, in the actual proof, this enables the simulator to simulate this value by simply sampling a uniformly random preimage of the output obtained from the ideal functionality $\mathcal{F}_{\text{MPC}}$. Once again, we refer the reader to the full version of this work for a more detailed and self-contained simulation-based proof. $\qquad\square$

Remark 1. One idea to bring these costs down at the expense of making the final MAC check more costly. When the parties partially open d and e, they open instead $\tau(d)$ and $\tau(e)$, by applying locally τ to each of their additive shares. The image of τ has the size of $|S^\ell|$. Now, to check these openings, the parties take linear combinations with coefficients over S, not over R, open the respective elements over R, and check that they map to the correct elements after applying τ. To get good soundness we need to repeat this several times, which makes the final check more expensive. Depending on the size of the circuit, this tradeoff, specifically, if the circuit is large enough, this approach will pay up.

4   Authentication

In this section we aim at instantiating $\mathcal{F}_{\text{Auth}}$. This makes use of the authenticated secret-sharing scheme briefly introduced in Sect. 1.2. However, for enabling the parties to create authenticated values, that is, for instantiating the Input command in $\mathcal{F}_{\text{Auth}}$, we need to rely on certain functionalities that, ultimately, are used to enable two-party secure multiplication. This building block will be also used to produce the necessary preprocessing material in Sect. 5. We begin by introducing the required functionalities below. However, first we introduce some notation.

Recall that $m = \lceil \kappa \log_p(2) \rceil$ and $R = \mathsf{GR}(p^k, m)$. Let $\rho := \rho_m : \mathbb{Z}_{p^k}^{t(m)} \to R$ and $\mu := \mu_m : R \to \mathbb{Z}_{p^k}^{t(m)}$ be the mappings from Theorem 1. We write t instead of $t(m)$.

4.1 Required Functionalities

Oblivious Linear Evaluation $\mathcal{F}_{\mathsf{OLE}}$. The functionality $\mathcal{F}_{\mathsf{OLE}}$ is described in detail below as Functionality 3. We remark that, even though OLE can be regarded as a generalization of OT, the functionality we are defining here is not a strict generalization of the functionality $\mathcal{F}_{\mathsf{ROT}}$ in [9,21]. In their case, where $p^k = 2$, the authors can use a short OT to generate certain correlated *keys*, which then can be extended via *OT extension* (with the help of a PRF) to an arbitrary amount of OTs, which suits very well the COPE application. Such approach, unfortunately, does not work for general p^k, although it does so partially for $p^k = 2^k$. As a matter of fact, we could have actually based our Π_{COPEe} protocol on a more elaborate version of OLE that is more aimed towards its use in COPE.

Functionality 3: $\mathcal{F}_{\mathsf{OLE}}$

Upon receiving $(\mathsf{OLE}, a, P_A, P_B)$ from P_A and $(\mathsf{OLE}, x, P_A, P_B)$ from P_B where $x, a \in \mathbb{Z}_{p^k}$, the functionality samples $b \xleftarrow{\$} \mathbb{Z}_{p^k}$, sets $y = ax + b$, and sends y to P_B and $-b$ to P_A.

Public Coins $\mathcal{F}_{\mathsf{Coin}}$. This functionality samples a uniformly random element in R and sends this to the parties. The detailed functionality is presented in the full version of this work.

4.2 Correlated Oblivious Product Evaluation

As in [9] and [21], the general idea to instantiate the Input command is to ask each party P_i to first sample their share $\alpha^{(i)}$ of the key α. Then, when P_j wants to input a value x, each party P_i interacts with P_j so that they obtain additive sharings $u^{(i,j)}$ and $v^{(j,i)}$ (held by P_i and P_j respectively) of $\alpha^{(i)} \cdot x$, i.e. $u^{(i,j)} + v^{(j,i)} = \alpha^{(i)} \cdot x$. Once this is done, each party P_i for $i \neq j$ can define $m^{(i)} = u^{(i,j)}$, while P_j sets $\alpha^{(j)} x + \sum_{i \neq j} v^{(j,i)}$. This way, it holds that $\sum_{i=1}^{n} m^{(i)} = \alpha \cdot x$.[8]

We refer to the required two-party interaction above by *correlated oblivious product evaluation*, or COPE for short. Our main idea consists of instantiating a COPE between P_i and P_j by letting the parties run t OLE instances, where P_i

---

[8] Notice that, since P_j knows x, the parties already hold trivial additive shares of x, namely all parties set their share to 0, and P_j sets it to x. However, in the actual protocol, P_j must also distribute actual random shares of x, since otherwise leakage may occur, for example, when adding and reconstructing shared values inputted by different parties.

inputs $\mu(\alpha^i)[l]$ and P_j inputs $\mu(x)[l]$ for $l \in [t]$ (recall that $z[l]$ denotes the l-th coordinate of the vector z). This way, P_i and P_j get shares $u^{(i,j)}$ and $v^{(j,i)}$ such that $u^{(i,j)} + v^{(j,i)} = \mu(\alpha^{(i)}) \star \mu(x)$, and, by using Definition 1, they can locally apply ρ to each share to obtain $u^{(i,j)} + v^{(j,i)} = \rho(\mu(\alpha^{(i)}) \star \mu(x)) = \alpha^{(i)} \cdot x$.

Consider the COPE instantiation sketched in previous paragraphs. We see that P_j is free to provide as input any vector $x^{(j,i)} \in \mathbb{Z}_{p^k}^t$ to the t OLE calls, but the protocol actually requires this vector to be $x^{(j,i)} = \mu(x)$, that is, it must lie in the image of μ.[9] Recall from Sect. 2.2 that μ is injective but not surjective, so there is no way in which we can enforce this. Hence, in the case of an actively corrupt P_j, the parties would not obtain additive shares of $\alpha^{(i)} \cdot x$, but instead $\rho(\mu(\alpha^{(i)}) \star x^{(j,i)})$ for some vector $x^{(j,i)}$ provided as input by P_j. Ultimately, this leads to the parties obtaining MAC shares $m^{(i)}$ where $\sum_{i=1}^{n} m^{(i)} = \alpha^{(j)}x + \sum_{i \neq j} \rho(\mu(\alpha^{(i)}) \star x^{(j,i)})$.

Similarly to [9,21], we do not attempt at removing the possibility of this attack at this stage, and instead model it as permissible behavior in the functionality $\mathcal{F}_{\mathsf{COPEe}}$ below.[10] Then, in Π_{Auth} we introduce a check that handles these inconsistencies.

Functionality 4: $\mathcal{F}_{\mathsf{COPEe}}$

This functionality runs with two parties P_i and P_j and the adversary $\mathcal{A}$. The **Initialize** phase is run once first. The **Multiply** phase can be run an arbitrary number of times.

- **Initialize:** On input $\alpha^{(i)} \in R$ from P_i, store this value.
- **Multiply:** On input $x \in R$ from P_j:
  - If P_j is corrupt then receive $v^{(j,i)} \in R$ and a vector $x^{(j,i)} \in \mathbb{Z}_{p^k}^t$ from $\mathcal{A}$ and compute $u^{(i,j)} = \rho(\mu(\alpha^{(i)}) \star x^{(j,i)}) - v^{(j,i)}$.
  - If P_i is corrupt then receive $\alpha^{(i,j)} \in \mathbb{Z}_{p^k}^t$ and $u^{(i,j)}$ from $\mathcal{A}$ and compute $v^{(j,i)} = \rho(\alpha^{(i,j)} \star \mu(x)) - u^{(i,j)}$
  - If both P_i and P_j are honest then sample $u^{(i,j)}$ and $v^{(j,i)}$ uniformly at random subject to $u^{(i,j)} + v^{(j,i)} = \alpha^{(i)} \cdot x$.

  The functionality sends $u^{(i,j)}$ to P_i and $v^{(j,i)}$ to P_j.

The functionality $\mathcal{F}_{\mathsf{COPEe}}$ can be instantiated as we have sketched above with the help of $\mathcal{F}_{\mathsf{OLE}}$. The corresponding protocol Π_{COPEe} is described in full detail in the full version of this work. We state the following theorem whose proof can be found in the full version of this work.

Theorem 4. *Protocol Π_{COPEe} implements $\mathcal{F}_{\mathsf{COPEe}}$ in the $\mathcal{F}_{\mathsf{OLE}}$-hybrid model.*

---

[9] Similarly, P_i's input must lie in the image of μ, but as we will see this deviation is not that harmful.

[10] Even though this functionality is named the same as its counterpart in [9,21], we remark that the errors the adversary can introduce in our setting are different.

4.3 Authenticated Secret-Sharing

Local Operations. The scheme $\langle \cdot \rangle$ is $\mathbb{Z}_{p^k}$-module homomorphic, so additions, subtractions, and in general $\mathbb{Z}_{p^k}$-affine combinations of $\langle \cdot \rangle$-shared values can be computed locally by the parties. These operations are standard and can be found for instance in [17]. However, for completeness, these are described in detail in the *procedure*[11] π_{Aff} given in the full version of this work. This operation is denoted by $\langle y \rangle \leftarrow a + \sum_{h=1}^{L} a_h \langle x_h \rangle$.

Opening and Checking. To partially reconstruct a shared value $\langle y \rangle = (\llbracket y \rrbracket, \llbracket \alpha \cdot y \rrbracket, \llbracket \alpha \rrbracket)$, the parties can all send their share of $\llbracket y \rrbracket$ to P_1, who can reconstruct and send the (possibly modified) result y' to the parties. To check the correctness of this opening, the parties locally compute $\llbracket \alpha \cdot y \rrbracket - y' \llbracket \alpha \rrbracket$, and send the shares of this value to each other using the simultaneous message channel. The parties abort if the reconstructed value is not 0. These operations are represented by the procedures $\pi_{\text{Open}}(\langle y \rangle)$ and $\pi_{\text{Check}}(\langle y \rangle, y')$, which are described in detail in the full version of this work.

4.4 Authentication Protocol

We describe our protocol Π_{Auth} implementing $\mathcal{F}_{\text{Auth}}$ as Protocol 2 below. At a high level, the protocol is very similar to the corresponding one proposed in [9,21]: allow the parties to obtain authenticated shares of their inputs by using $\mathcal{F}_{\text{COPEe}}$ followed by a check, process affine combinations locally using the homomorphic properties of the secret-sharing scheme, partially open shared values by using π_{Open} and check their correctness by using π_{Check}.

Protocol 2: Π_{Auth}

The parties collectively maintain a dictionary Val of shared values.

- **Initialize:** First the parties perform an initialization step that consists of each party P_i calling the **Initialize** step in $\mathcal{F}_{\text{COPEe}}$.
- **Input:** Once P_j receives $(\text{Input}, (\text{id}_1, \text{id}_2, \ldots \text{id}_L), (x_1, x_2, \ldots, x_L), P_j)$ and the other parties receive $(\text{Input}, (\text{id}_1, \text{id}_2, \ldots \text{id}_L), P_j)$, the parties execute the following.
  1. P_j samples $x_0 \xleftarrow{\$} R$.
  2. For $h = 0, \ldots, L$ and $i \in [n]$, P_j samples $x_h^{(i)} \in R$ uniformly at random subject to $\sum_{i=1}^{n} x_h^{(i)} = x_h$, and sends $\{x_h^{(i)}\}_{h=0}^{L}$ to each P_i.

---

[11] In this work we distinguish between *procedures* (denoted by smallcase π) and *protocols* (denoted by capital Π). Protocols are associated to ideal functionalities and have simulation-based proofs, whereas procedures, even though they also specify steps the parties must follow, are used as helpers within actual protocols and do not have functionalities or simulation-based proofs associated to them. This can be thought of being somewhat analogous to the difference between macros and actual functions in programming languages such as C/C++.

3. For every $i \in [n] \setminus \{j\}$, P_i and P_j execute the **Multiply** step of $\mathcal{F}_{\mathsf{COPEe}}$ $L + 1$ times, where P_j inputs $x_0, \ldots, x_L$. For $h = 0, \ldots, L$, P_i receives $u_h^{(i,j)}$ and P_j receives $v_h^{(j,i)}$.

4. For $i \in [n] \setminus \{j\}$, P_i defines $m^{(i)}(x_h) = u_h^{(i,j)}$ while P_j sets $m^{(j)}(x_h) = \alpha^{(j)} \cdot x_h + \sum_{i \neq j} v_h^{(j,i)}$. By setting $x_h^{(i)} = 0$ for $i \neq j$, the parties have defined $\langle x_h \rangle$ for $h = 0, \ldots, L$.

5. Parties call $\mathcal{F}_{\mathsf{Coin}}$ to get $r_1 \ldots, r_L \xleftarrow{\$} R$. Set $r_0 := 1$.

6. Parties compute locally $\langle y \rangle \leftarrow \sum_{h=0}^{L} r_h \langle x_h \rangle$ and call $y' \leftarrow \pi_{\mathsf{Open}}(\langle y \rangle)$ followed by $\pi_{\mathsf{Check}}(\langle y \rangle, y')$.

7. If the previous call did not result in abort, the parties store $\mathsf{Val}[\mathsf{id}_h] = \langle x_h \rangle$ for $h \in [L]$.

- **Affine combination:** If all parties receive input $(\mathsf{AffComb}, \mathsf{id}, (\mathsf{id}_1, \ldots, \mathsf{id}_L), (a_1, \ldots, a_L), a)$, they fetch $\langle x_h \rangle = \mathsf{Val}[\mathsf{id}_h]$ for $h \in [L]$, compute locally $\langle z \rangle \leftarrow a + \sum_{j=1}^{L} a_j \langle x_j \rangle$, and let $\mathsf{Val}[\mathsf{id}] = \langle z \rangle$.

- **Partial openings:** Once all parties receive input $(\mathsf{Open}, \mathsf{id})$, they recover $\langle x \rangle = \mathsf{Val}[\mathsf{id}]$ and call $x' \leftarrow \pi_{\mathsf{Open}}(\langle x \rangle)$.
- **Check openings:** If all the parties receive $(\mathsf{Check}, (\mathsf{id}_1, \mathsf{id}_2, \ldots, \mathsf{id}_L), (x_1', x_2', \ldots, x_L'))$, they set $\langle x_h \rangle = \mathsf{Val}[\mathsf{id}_h]$ for $h \in [L]$ and execute the following:

  1. Call $\mathcal{F}_{\mathsf{Coin}}$ to get $r_1, \ldots, r_L \xleftarrow{\$} R$.
  2. Compute locally $\langle y \rangle \leftarrow \sum_{h=1}^{L} r_h \langle x_h \rangle$ and $y' = \sum_{h=1}^{L} r_h \cdot x_h'$, and call $\pi_{\mathsf{Check}}(\langle y \rangle, y')$

Theorem 5. *Protocol Π_{Auth} implements $\mathcal{F}_{\mathsf{Auth}}$ in the $(\mathcal{F}_{\mathsf{Coin}}, \mathcal{F}_{\mathsf{COPEe}})$-hybrid model.*

Proof. Part of the proof is quite standard: the simulator extracts the inputs from the corrupt parties and sends this to the ideal functionality $\mathcal{F}_{\mathsf{Auth}}$, and it also emulates the functionalities $\mathcal{F}_{\mathsf{Coin}}$ and $\mathcal{F}_{\mathsf{COPEe}}$, and emulates virtual honest parties that behave as the real honest parties, except they do not know the real inputs. At the end of the execution the simulator adjusts[12] the honest parties' shares to be compatible with the output and the corrupt parties' shares.

The most complex and non-standard step is the extraction of the corrupt parties' inputs. It turns out that the check performed in the input phase may actually pass with non-negligible probability, even if the adversary cheats in the $\mathcal{F}_{\mathsf{COPEe}}$ calls. Our goal is to show that, in spite of this, the corrupt parties are still committed to a unique set of inputs—that is, these are the only values the adversary could open these sharings to in a posterior output phase—and these

---

[12] As we discuss in the full version of this work there is a subtlety with this "adjustment" that originates from the fact that R has zero-divisors.

inputs are extractable by the simulator. We point out that a full-fledged proof is given in the full version of this work. Here we only provide the intuition of how the inputs from the corrupt parties are extracted, and why they are unique. Furthermore, we assume that $k = 1$, so $R = \mathbb{F}_{p^m}$ and $\mathbb{Z}_{p^k} = \mathbb{F}_p$. The general case of a Galois ring with zero divisors in handled in the full version of this work, and requires a few extra technical considerations.

Let P_j be a corrupt party who is intended to provide some inputs $\{x_h\}_{h=0}^{L}$. For each P_i, in the $L+1$ calls to $\mathcal{F}_{\mathsf{COPEe}}$, P_j may use as input a vector $\boldsymbol{x}_h^{(j,i)}$, which leads to P_i and P_j obtaining $u_h^{(i,j)}$ and $v_h^{(j,i)}$ respectively, where these values add up to $\rho(\mu(\alpha^{(i)}) \star \boldsymbol{x}_h^{(j,i)})$. If P_j acts honestly, it would hold that $\boldsymbol{x}_h^{(j,i)} = \mu(x_h)$, but in the general case this may not hold. Then, the parties compute sharings $\langle y \rangle$, open this to a possibly incorrect value y, and finally each party P_i reveals $\sigma^{(i)}$.

The check passes if and only if $\sum_{i=1}^{n} \sigma^{(i)} = 0$. By computing an explicit expression of the $\sigma^{(i)}$ held by honest parties, we can verify that this check passes if and only if the key shares $\{\alpha^{(i)}\}_{i \in \mathcal{H}}$ held by honest parties satisfy

$$
\sum_{i \in \mathcal{C}} \sigma^{(i)} = \sum_{i \in \mathcal{H}} \alpha^{(i)} \cdot y - m^{(i)}(y)
$$

$$
= \sum_{i \in \mathcal{H}} \left(\alpha^{(i)} \cdot y - \sum_{h=0}^{L} r_h \cdot m^{(i)}(x_h) \right)
$$

$$
= \sum_{i \in \mathcal{H}} \left(\alpha^{(i)} \cdot y - \sum_{h=0}^{L} r_h \cdot u_h^{(i,j)} \right)
$$

$$
= \sum_{i \in \mathcal{H}} \left(\alpha^{(i)} \cdot y - \sum_{h=0}^{L} \left(r_h \cdot \rho(\mu(\alpha^{(i)}) \star \boldsymbol{x}_h^{(j,i)}) - r_h \cdot v_h^{(j,i)} \right) \right).
$$

We assume, for the sake of easing the notation, that there is only one honest party $\mathcal{H} = \{P_l\}$, and we denote $\alpha := \alpha^{(l)}$ and $\boldsymbol{x}_h := \boldsymbol{x}_h^{(j,l)}$. This way, we can write the above equation as

$$
\underbrace{\sum_{i \in \mathcal{C}} \sigma^{(i)} - \sum_{h=0}^{L} r_h v_h^{(j,l)}}_{=:z} = \alpha \cdot y - \sum_{h=0}^{L} r_h \cdot \rho(\mu(\alpha) \star \boldsymbol{x}_h). \tag{1}
$$

Notice that z above is a value provided by the adversary, as well as y and the vectors $\boldsymbol{x}_h$. Furthermore, the coefficients r_h are public, so the only unknown (from the adversary point of view) is the key α. Unfortunately, it can be the case that this equation holds with non-negligible probability even though P_j did not provide valid inputs. However, as we will see, in the event in which this equation holds, when the parties at a later point want to open the sharings produced by the input phase, there will only be one possible set of values the adversary can open these sharings to successfully.

Let us denote by $K_z \subseteq \mathbb{F}_{p^m}$ the set of all α satisfying Eq. (1). Some important observations about K_z:

- K_0 is an $\mathbb{F}_p$-vector space.
- Either $K_z = \emptyset$, or $K_z = K_0 + \xi$, for any $\xi \in K_z$.
- In particular, $|K_z| = 0$ or $|K_z| = |K_0|$.

Intuitively, $\mathcal{A}$ wants to set the values under its control so that $|K_z|$, which is either 0 or $|K_0|$, is as large as possible, since this way $\mathcal{A}$ increases the chances of $\alpha \in K_z$, and hence the more likely the input check passes. However, $\mathcal{A}$ does not fully control the values defining K_z: $\boldsymbol{x}_h$ must be chosen *before* $\{r_h\}_{h \in [L]}$, which are sampled at random.

Naturally, $\mathcal{A}$'s optimal strategy is to choose $z = 0$ (which is in fact what z equals to under honest behavior), since in this case there are no chances that $K_z = \emptyset$. To prove this intuition, we simply notice that the mapping $\alpha \mapsto \alpha \cdot y - \sum_{h=0}^{L} r_h \cdot \rho(\mu(\alpha) \star \boldsymbol{x}_h)$ is $\mathbb{F}_p$-linear, and $K_z \neq \emptyset$ if and only if z is in the range of this function, which we denote by Z. If $z \neq 0$, the probability that z is in this range is $|Z|/|R|$, and the conditional probability that $\alpha \in K_z$ is $|K_z|/|R| = |K_0|/|R|$. Furthermore, from the rank-nullity theorem we have that $|Z| \cdot |K_0| = |R|$ so the overall success probability, if $z \neq 0$, becomes $\frac{|Z|}{|R|} \cdot \frac{|K_0|}{|R|} = 1/|R|$, which is negligible. We see then that we can assume that $z = 0$.[13]

Suppose now that the Eq. (1) holds, that is, the input check passes. Imagine that at a later point in the actual circuit computation, a value $\langle x_h \rangle$ is intended to be opened (here x_h does not stand for a specific value yet—since the adversary did not input any concrete value—but instead it acts as an identifier for the sharings corresponding to the h-th input of P_j). The adversary can cause the partial opening to be a value x_h, and in the final check each party announces $\sigma_h^{(i)}$. As before, the check passes if and only if $\sum_{i=1}^{n} \sigma_h^{(i)} = 0$. We can compute what the MAC shares of $\langle x_h \rangle$ held by the honest parties are based on the input phase, and conclude, via a similar derivation to the one made above, that the check passes if and only if $z_h = \alpha \cdot x_h - \rho(\mu(\alpha) \star \boldsymbol{x}_h)$, where z_h is a value chosen by the adversary. As before, we can show that $z_h = 0$ for each h. Therefore, x_h must be equal to $(\rho(\mu(\alpha) \star \boldsymbol{x}_h))/\alpha$. It seems then that we have been able to "extract" the inputs that the corrupt party P_j has committed to, but these $\{x_h\}_h$ are defined in terms of the key α, which is unknown to the simulator. In what follows, we show that, with overwhelming probability, the same set of $\{x_h\}_h$ can be obtained from *any* possible key $\alpha \in K_0$, which enables extraction.

Putting together what we have seen above, for the adversary to pass all the checks it must be the case that the key $\alpha \in \mathbb{F}_{p^m}$ lies in K_0, that is, it must satisfy $0 = \sum_{h=0}^{L} r_h (\alpha \cdot x_h - \rho(\mu(\alpha) \star \boldsymbol{x}_h))$, and furthermore, the adversary can only open the input shares at a later stage to the values to $x_h = \rho(\mu(\alpha) \star \boldsymbol{x}_h)/\alpha$ for $h = 0, \ldots, L$.

Now, our goal is to show that, no matter what $\alpha \in K_0$ the honest party happens to choose, the values $\{x_h\}_h$ are fixed, which amounts to showing that the functions $f_{\boldsymbol{x}_h} : \mathbb{F}_{p^m} \setminus \{0\} \to \mathbb{F}_{p^m}$ given by $f_{\boldsymbol{x}_h}(\alpha) = \rho(\mu(\alpha) \star \boldsymbol{x}_h)/\alpha$ are constant. This will enable the simulator to *extract* x_h by using any element in K_0.

---

[13] We point out that in [21], this subtlety that enables us to consider $z = 0$ is not mentioned explicitly.

To show that each f_{x_h} is constant, we consider $e_1, \ldots, e_d \in \mathbb{F}_{p^m}$ a basis of K_0 over $\mathbb{F}_p$, and make the simple but powerful observation that, if $\{f_{x_h}(e_i)\}_h$ is proven to be constant as i ranges over $[d]$, then this will extend to any $\alpha \in K_0$. This is because, for any $(c_h) \in \mathbb{F}_p^{L+1}$, the set of $\alpha \in K_0 \backslash \{0\}$ such that $f_{x_h}(\alpha) = c_h$ forms a subspace of K_0 (after adding 0), so if $\{f_{x_h}(e_i)\}_h$ is equal to a constant $(c_h)_h$ as i ranges over $[d]$, then this subspace must include the $\mathbb{F}_p$-span of $\{e_1, \ldots, e_d\}$, which is equal to K_0 itself.

More precisely, we claim that the probability that there exist $i_0, i_1 \in [d]$ with $\{f_{x_h}(e_{i_0})\}_h \neq \{f_{x_h}(e_{i_1})\}_h$ is negligible. Indeed, since each $e_i \in K_0$, we have that $0 = e_i \cdot y - \sum_{h=0}^L r_h \cdot \rho(\mu(e_i) \star x_h)$, so

$$y = \sum_{h=0}^L r_h \cdot \left(\frac{\rho(\mu(e_i) \star x_h)}{e_i} \right) = \sum_{h=0}^L r_h \cdot f_{x_h}(e_i).$$

In particular, it holds that $0 = \sum_{h=0}^L r_h \cdot (f_{x_h}(e_{i_1}) - f_{x_h}(e_{i_0}))$, or, in other words, $(r_0, \ldots, r_L)$ is orthogonal to the vector $(f_{x_h}(e_{i_1}) - f_{x_h}(e_{i_0}))_{h=0}^L$, which is non-zero if $\{f_{x_h}(e_{i_0})\}_h \neq \{f_{x_h}(e_{i_1})\}_h$. However, the latter vector is chosen by the adversary *before* the former one is sampled uniformly at random, so the probability of this happening is at most $1/p^m$.

From the above we see that the probability that the ordered pair (i_0, i_1) results in $\{f_{x_h}(e_{i_0})\}_h \neq \{f_{x_h}(e_{i_1})\}_h$ is at most $1/p^m$, so in particular, since there are at most $d^2 \leq m^2$ such pairs, the probability that there exists at least one such pair is upper bounded by $m^2/p^m = 2^{-(m \log_2(p) - 2\log_2(m))}$. Now, it is easy to see that if $\alpha \in K_0$ is an $\mathbb{F}_p$-multiple of e_i then $f_{x_h}(\alpha) = f_{x_h}(e_i)$, so the result we have just obtained enables us to conclude that, except with probability $2^{-(m \log_2(p) - 2\log_2(m))}$, the values $\{f_{x_h}(\alpha)\}_h$ are constant for $\alpha \in K_0$.

Putting the pieces together, we see that if the adversary passes the input check, meaning that the key α chosen by the honest party lies in K_0, then there is only one possible set of values that the adversary can later open these sharings to, namely the values $x_h = f_{x_h}(\alpha')$ given by *any* $\alpha' \in K_0$. Since K_0 is known by the simulator, these inputs can be efficiently extracted.   □

5   Offline Phase

Recall that our the preprocessing phase requires to generate the quintuples $(\langle a \rangle, \langle b \rangle, \langle \tau(a) \rangle, \langle \tau(b) \rangle, \langle \tau(a)\tau(b) \rangle)$ with random elements $a, b \in R$. During the online phase, such quintuple will save one round of communication for each multiplication gate with respect to approaches like the one followed in [9]. To generate this quintuple, we begin by first generating authenticated pairs $(\langle a \rangle, \langle \tau(a) \rangle)$, a step that we carry out in a similar way as the "re-encode pair protocol" in [9]. We use a similar technique to process the random values $\langle r \rangle$ such that $r \in \ker \psi$. Finally, to obtain the products $\langle \tau(a)\tau(b) \rangle$, we make use of our $\mathcal{F}_{\mathsf{COPEe}}$ functionality, together with a cut-and-choose-based check that verifies no errors are introduced by the adversary.

We discuss these protocols in detail below.

Encoding Pairs. The idea to obtain certain amount T of pairs $(\langle a \rangle, \langle \tau(a) \rangle)$ is to generate $T + s$ many pairs $(\langle a_i \rangle, \langle \tau(a_i) \rangle)$ for $i = 1, \ldots, T + s$, and then sacrifice the last s of them by taking a random $\mathbb{Z}_{p^k}$-linear combinations of the first T pairs to obtain s equations for correctness check. If there is at least one of the first T pairs that is corrupted, with probability at most p^{-s}, the corrupted pair will pass all the check, which we can make negligible in κ by choosing s to be large enough. This is presented in detail in the Procedure 3 below.

Procedure 3: π_{Enc}

The procedure generates a series of T pairs $(\langle a_i \rangle, \langle \tau(a_i) \rangle)$ where $a_i \in R$ is a random element. We assume the functionalities $\mathcal{F}_{\mathsf{COPEe}}$ and $\mathcal{F}_{\mathsf{Auth}}$.

- **Construct:**
  1. P_i samples $a_j^{(i)} \in R$ uniformly at random for $j = 1, \ldots, s + T$.
  2. P_i calls $\mathcal{F}_{\mathsf{Auth}}$ to obtain $\left\langle a_j^{(i)} \right\rangle$ and $\left\langle \tau(a_j^{(i)}) \right\rangle$.
  3. All parties computes $\langle a_j \rangle = \sum_{i=1}^{n} \left\langle a_j^{(i)} \right\rangle, \langle \tau(a_j) \rangle = \sum_{i=1}^{n} \left\langle \tau(a_j^{(i)}) \right\rangle$.
- **Sacrifice:**
  1. All parties call $\mathcal{F}_{\mathsf{Coin}}$ to generate s random vectors $\boldsymbol{x}_i = (x_{i,1}, \ldots, x_{i,T}) \in \mathbb{Z}_{p^k}^T$.
  2. Compute $\langle b_i \rangle = \sum_{j=1}^{T} x_{i,j} \langle a_j \rangle + \langle a_{T+i} \rangle$ and $\langle c_i \rangle = \sum_{j=1}^{T} x_{i,j} \langle \tau(a_j) \rangle + \langle \tau(a_{T+i}) \rangle$ and partially open b_i and c_i.
  3. If $\tau(b_i) \neq c_i$ for some $i \in \{1, \ldots, s\}$, then abort.
  4. Call $\mathcal{F}_{\mathsf{Auth}}$ with the command Check on the opened values b_i and c_i.
- **Output:** Output $(\langle a_i \rangle, \langle \tau(a_i) \rangle)$ for $i = 1, \ldots, T$.

Kernel Elements. In order to generate sharings $\langle r \rangle$, where r is uniformly random in $\ker \psi$, we proceed in a similar way as the procedure π_{Enc}, except that instead of each party P_i calling $\mathcal{F}_{\mathsf{Auth}}$ to input a pair $(a^{(i)}, \tau(a^{(i)}))$, each party inputs a value $r^{(i)} \overset{\$}{\leftarrow} \ker \psi$. Then, the same correctness check as in π_{Enc} works in this case since $\ker \psi$ is $\mathbb{Z}_{p^k}$-linear. The resulting procedure, π_{Ker}, is presented in detail in the full version of this work.

Multiplication. As for generating $\langle \tau(a)\tau(b) \rangle$, the technique employed in [21] can not be applied to our quintuples. The reason is that to prevent the leakage of single bit of the input $\boldsymbol{a} = (a_1, \ldots, a_\gamma) \in R^\gamma$, the combine in the multiplication triple protocol in [21] takes the random linear combination $a' = \langle \boldsymbol{a}, \boldsymbol{r} \rangle$ for a random vector $\boldsymbol{r} = (r_1, \ldots, r_\gamma) \in R^\gamma$. In our situation, it requires that $\tau(a') = \tau(\sum_{i=1}^{\gamma} r_i a_i) = \sum_{i=1}^{\gamma} r_i \tau(a_i)$ which is clearly not the case. The same problem also arises in [9]. Therefore, we follow the approach in [9] by the committed MPC technique [20] to obtain $\langle \tau(a)\tau(b) \rangle$. There is some difference from [9], our share and MAC are defined over the same domain R, while the share and MAC in [9] lie in different spaces. This forces them to convert the sharing of a vector $\boldsymbol{x}$ into a sharing of an element x in the extension field at each opening. In our work, we do not need this extra step, which brings us closer to the original approach in [20].

Procedure 4: π_{Mult}

The procedure takes as input a set of $N = \gamma_1 + \gamma_1\gamma_2^2 T$ authenticated pairs $(\langle a_i \rangle, \langle \tau(a_i) \rangle), (\langle b_i \rangle, \langle \tau(b_i) \rangle)$ where $[\![\tau(a_i)]\!] = (\tau(a_i)^{(1)}, \dots, \tau(a_i)^{(n)})$ and $[\![\tau(b_i)]\!] = (\tau(b_i)^{(1)}, \dots, \tau(b_i)^{(n)})$. As output, the procedure produces a multiplication quintuple $(\langle a \rangle, \langle b \rangle, \langle \tau(a) \rangle, \langle \tau(b) \rangle, \langle \tau(a)\tau(b) \rangle)$ where $a, b \in R$ are random elements. We assume the functionalities $\mathcal{F}_{\mathsf{COPEe}}, \mathcal{F}_{\mathsf{Auth}}$ and $\mathcal{F}_{\mathsf{Coin}}$. Let $u = 2N$.

- **Multiply:**
  1. For $h = 1, \dots, N$
  2. For each ordered pair of parties P_i and P_j calls $\mathcal{F}_{\mathsf{COPEe}}$ with P_i's input $\tau(a_h)^{(i)}$ and P_j's input $\tau(b_h)^{(j)}$.
  3. P_i receives $u_h^{(i,j)}$ and P_i receives $v_h^{(j,i)}$ such that $u_h^{(i,j)} + v_h^{(j,i)} = \tau(a_h)^{(i)}\tau(b_h)^{(j)}$.
  4. P_i sets its share $c_h^{(i)} = \tau(a_h)^{(i)}\tau(b_h)^{(i)} + \sum_{j \neq i} u_h^{(i,j)} + v_h^{(i,j)}$.
  5. P_i call $\mathcal{F}_{\mathsf{Auth}}$ with the command Input to obtain $\left\langle c_h^{(i)} \right\rangle$.
  6. The parties locally compute $\langle c_h \rangle = \sum_{i=1}^{n} \left\langle c_h^{(i)} \right\rangle$.
- **Cut-and-Choose:**
  1. All parties call $\mathcal{F}_{\mathsf{Coin}}$ to obtain γ_1 distinct elements $1 \leq \ell_1, \dots, \ell_{\gamma_1} \leq N$.
  2. All parties open $\langle \tau(a_{\ell_i}) \rangle, \langle \tau(b_{\ell_i}) \rangle, \langle c_{\ell_i} \rangle$ for $i = 1, \dots, \gamma_1$. Abort if $\tau(a_{\ell_i})\tau(b_{\ell_i}) \neq c_{\ell_i}$.
- **Sacrifice:**
  1. Use $\mathcal{F}_{\mathsf{Coin}}$ to random divide the rest $N - \gamma_1$ triples $(\langle \tau(a_h) \rangle, \langle \tau(b_h) \rangle, \langle c_h \rangle)$ into $\gamma_2^2 T$ buckets with γ_1 triples in each. (We still record the other two sharings $\langle a_h \rangle$ and $\langle b_h \rangle$ for later use)
  2. In each bucket with γ_1 triples $(\langle \tau(a_i) \rangle, \langle \tau(b_i) \rangle, \langle c_i \rangle)_{i \in [\gamma_1]}$, all parties locally compute $\langle \alpha_h \rangle = \langle \tau(a_h) \rangle - \langle \tau(a_1) \rangle$ and $\langle \beta_h \rangle = \langle \tau(b_h) \rangle - \langle \tau(b_1) \rangle$ for $h = 2, \dots, \gamma_1$. All parties partially open α_h and β_h.
  3. Compute $\langle \rho_h \rangle = \langle c_h \rangle - \alpha_h \langle \tau(b_1) \rangle - \beta_h \langle \tau(a_1) \rangle - \alpha_h\beta_h - \langle c_1 \rangle$. Open ρ_h for $h = 2, \dots, \gamma_1$. Abort if $\rho_h \neq 0$ and otherwise call $(\langle \tau(a_1) \rangle, \langle \tau(b_1) \rangle, \langle c_1 \rangle)$ a correct triple.
- **Combine:**
  1. Combine on a: Use $\mathcal{F}_{\mathsf{Coin}}$ to randomly divide the remaining $\gamma_2^2 T$ triples $(\langle \tau(a_h) \rangle, \langle \tau(b_h) \rangle, \langle c_h \rangle)$ into $\gamma_2 T$ buckets with γ_2 triples in each. In each bucket, denote by $(\langle \tau(a_h) \rangle, \langle \tau(b_h) \rangle, \langle c_h \rangle)$ for $h = 1, \dots, \gamma_2$.
     (a) Locally compute

$$\langle a' \rangle = \sum_{i=1}^{\gamma_2} \langle a_i \rangle, \quad \langle \tau(a') \rangle = \sum_{i=1}^{\gamma_2} \langle \tau(a_i) \rangle, \quad \langle \tau(b') \rangle = \langle \tau(b_1) \rangle.$$

     (b) For $h = 2, \dots, \gamma_2$, locally compute $\langle \rho_h \rangle = \langle \tau(b_1) \rangle - \langle \tau(b_h) \rangle$ and partially open ρ_h.
     (c) Compute $\langle \sigma' \rangle = \langle c_1 \rangle + \sum_{i=2}^{\gamma_2}(\rho_h \langle \tau(a_h) \rangle + \langle c_h \rangle) = \langle \tau(a')\tau(b_1) \rangle$. Record the new quintuple $(\langle a' \rangle, \langle \tau(a') \rangle, \langle b' \rangle, \langle \tau(b') \rangle, \langle \sigma' \rangle)$.

2. Combine on b: Use $\mathcal{F}_{\mathsf{Coin}}$ to randomly divide the remaining $\gamma_2 T$ quintuples into $\gamma_2 T$ buckets with γ_2 triples in each. In each bucket, denote by $(\langle a_h \rangle, \langle \tau(a_h) \rangle, \langle b_h \rangle, \langle \tau(b_h) \rangle, \langle c_h \rangle)$ for $h = 1, \ldots, \gamma_2$.

   (a) Locally compute

$$\langle b' \rangle = \sum_{i=1}^{\gamma_2} \langle b_i \rangle, \quad \langle \tau(b') \rangle = \sum_{i=1}^{\gamma_2} \langle \tau(b_i) \rangle, \quad \langle \tau(a') \rangle = \langle \tau(a_1) \rangle.$$

   (b) For $h = 2, \ldots, \gamma_2$, locally compute $\langle \rho_h \rangle = \langle \tau(a_1) \rangle - \langle \tau(a_h) \rangle$ and partially open ρ_h.

   (c) Compute $\langle \sigma' \rangle = \langle c_1 \rangle + \sum_{h=2}^{\gamma_2}(\rho_h \langle \tau(b_h) \rangle + \langle c_h \rangle) = \langle \tau(a')\tau(b') \rangle$. Record the new quintuple $(\langle a' \rangle, \langle \tau(a') \rangle, \langle b' \rangle, \langle \tau(b') \rangle, \langle \sigma' \rangle)$.

   (d) Call $\mathcal{F}_{\mathsf{Auth}}$ with the command Check on the opened values so far. If the check succeeds, output the T quintuples.

Putting the Pieces Together. With the procedures π_{Enc}, π_{Ker} and π_{Mul} from above, we can now define the protocol Π_{Prep} that instantiates the functionality $\mathcal{F}_{\mathsf{Prep}}$. The protocol simply uses π_{Ker} to instantiate the Ker command, and π_{Enc} and π_{Mul} in conjunction to instantiate CorrRand. Π_{Prep} is described in detail in the full version of this work. Its security is stated in the following theorem, and since the proof follows in a similar way as the argument in [9,20], we postpone it to the full version of this work.

Theorem 6. Π_{Prep} *securely implements* $\mathcal{F}_{\mathsf{Prep}}$ *in the* $(\mathcal{F}_{\mathsf{COPEe}}, \mathcal{F}_{\mathsf{Coin}}, \mathcal{F}_{\mathsf{Auth}})$-*hybrid model.*

6   Communication Complexity Analysis

Our online phase can simultaneously evaluate ℓ instances of the same arithmetic circuit over the ring $\mathbb{Z}_{p^k}$. To the best of our knowledge, all known secret-sharing-based amortized SPDZ-like protocols are defined over finite fields, e.g., MiniMAC [19], Committed MPC [20] and RMFE-based MPC [9]. We choose $R = \mathrm{GR}(2^k, m)$ to analyze the communication complexity below. When we compare our performance with other works over finite fields, we assume $k = 1$.

Communication Complexity of the Online Phase. Our online phase only requires one round of communication for each multiplication gate. For each multiplication gate, we need to partially open two shared values $\langle r \rangle$ with $r \in R$. At each opening, all parties sent their shares to one selected player for opening and this player then broadcasts the opened value. This requires $4km(n-1)$ bits of communication.[14] Each input gate requires $km(n-1)$ bits of communication. For

---

[14] Like in previous works, we assume the cost of broadcast-with-abort is comparable sending the messages directly.

the output gate, the parties have to perform the MAC check on the random linear combination of previously opened values. This requires $2km(n-1)+2kmn$ bits of communication. If we take the approach from Remark 1, the communication cost for each multiplication gate can be further cut down to $(2km+2k\ell)(n-1)$.

Below we analyze the communication complexity of our protocol with respect to that from other approaches. These were taken from [9] (Fig. 1).

	MiniMac[19]	Committed MPC [20]	Cascudo et al. [9]	This work
Comm.	$(4\ell+2\ell^*)(n-1)$	$(4\ell+2\ell^*+r)(n-1)$	$(4\ell+2m)(n-1)$	$4m(n-1)$
Rounds	2	1	2	1

Fig. 1. The total number of bits and rounds communicated for *one batch* of ℓ multiplications in the online phase.

Now we instantiate the concrete parameters for the RMFE construction, and compare our *amortized* communication complexity (that is, per multiplication) with respect to previous works. To make a fair comparison, we use the same parameter set (ℓ, m) as in [9], namely $(\ell, m) = (21, 65)$, $(\ell, m) = (42, 135)$ and $(\ell, \ell^*, r) = (210, 1695, 2047)$, $(\ell, \ell^*, r) = (338, 3293, 4096)$ (in our RMFE, ℓ is the number of instances simultaneously computed) (Fig. 2).

Security	MiniMac[19]	Committed MPC [20]	Cascudo et al. [9]	This work
$s = 64$	$20.14(n-1)$	$29.89(n-1)$	$10.2(n-1)$	$12.4(n-1)$
$s = 128$	$23.48(n-1)$	$35.58(n-1)$	$10.42(n-1)$	$12.84(n-1)$

Fig. 2. The total number of bits communicated for computing each instance of a multiplication gate when the security parameter is $s = 64, 128$.

Communication Complexity of the Preprocessing Phase. The main bottleneck of our preprocessing protocol Π_{Prep} are the π_{Enc} and the π_{Mul} procedures (only one kernel element is needed for each final output, so we ignore the cost of π_{Ker}). Since Π_{Prep} uses $\mathcal{F}_{\mathsf{Auth}}$, we also take into account the costs of Π_{Auth}. Furthermore, since Π_{Auth} itself makes use of $\mathcal{F}_{\mathsf{COPEe}}$, and our protocol Π_{COPEe} uses $\mathcal{F}_{\mathsf{OLE}}$, we measure the ultimate costs in terms of the number of calls to $\mathcal{F}_{\mathsf{OLE}}$.

The Input command realized by Π_{Auth} aims at generating the authenticated input for each party. The most expensive cost of this protocol is the call to Π_{COPEe}. The parties need to send $2kt(n-1)$ bits for each element in R to be authenticated and make $t(n-1)$ calls to the functionality $\mathcal{F}_{\mathsf{OLE}}$.

The check procedure is used to check the correctness of the shares obtained from Π_{COPEe}. The cost of the check protocol can be amortized away as it can authenticate a batch of values by sacrificing one authenticated value. For the command CorrRand, we first need to prepare the authenticated pairs $(\langle a \rangle, \langle \tau(a) \rangle)$ with π_{Enc}. Assume that T is much larger than s, which will amortize away the cost of sacrificing s pairs. Thus, the cost for generating authenticated pairs $(\langle a \rangle, \langle \tau(a) \rangle)$ comes from the call of Π_{Auth} with the command Input. The total cost is $4ktn(n-1)$ bits for each authenticated pairs and $2t(n-1)$ calls of $\mathcal{F}_{\text{OLE}}$.

After generating $N = \gamma_1 + \gamma_1\gamma_2^2 T$ authenticated pairs, which requires $8ktn(n-1)N$ bits of communication and $4t(n-1)N$ calls of $\mathcal{F}_{\text{OLE}}$, we use π_{Mul} to create T authenticated quintuples $(\langle a \rangle, \langle b \rangle, \langle \tau(a) \rangle, \langle \tau(b) \rangle, \langle \tau(a)\tau(b) \rangle)$. In the following discussion, we assume T is big enough so as to amortize away the part of the communication that is independent of T. The procedure π_{Mul} calls Π_{COPEe} $n(n-1)N$ times, which requires $2ktn(n-1)N$ bits of communication and $tn(n-1)N$ calls of $\mathcal{F}_{\text{OLE}}$. Each party P_i calls Π_{Auth} to obtain the authenticated share $\left\langle c_h^{(i)} \right\rangle$. This requires $2ktn(n-1)N$ bits of communication and $tn(n-1)$ calls of $\mathcal{F}_{\text{OLE}}$. The total amount of bits communicated in the procedure π_{Mul} is $4ktn(n-1)N$ and $2tn(n-1)$ calls of $\mathcal{F}_{\text{OLE}}$. During the rest of the protocol, the communication costs mainly come from the partial opening. There are $3\gamma_1 + 3\gamma_2^2 T(\gamma_1 - 1) + \gamma_2 T(\gamma_2 - 1) + T(\gamma_2 - 1)$ openings in total such that each opening requires $2mt(n-1)$ bits of communications. We choose $\gamma_1 = \gamma_2 = 3$ suggested in [20]. The total bits of communication from the opening is $26T \times 2mt(n-1)$. This cost is relatively small if n is big enough.

From the above we see that generating one quintuple requires $12ktn(n-1)N/T = 12 \times 27ktn(n-1) = 324ktn(n-1)$ bits of communication and $6tn(n-1)N/T = 162tn(n-1)$ calls to $\mathcal{F}_{\text{OLE}}$. From Theorem 1 and Theorem 2, we can set $t = 5.12m$ and $m = 4.92\ell$. The communications now becomes $8161.6k\ell n(n-1)$. For small security parameter $s = 64$, we can set $m/\ell = 3.1$. To compare our result with that in [9], we set $k = 1$ and obtain $5142.5\ell n(n-1)$ bits of communication while their protocol requires $462.21\ell^2 n(n-1)$ bits. Our cost is smaller than theirs as ℓ has to be 21 or bigger to achieve 64 bits of statistical security.

Comparing to SPDZ$_{2^k}$ [14]. We proceed to the comparison with SPDZ$_{2^k}$ over the ring $\mathbb{Z}_{2^k}$. The prepocessing phase in [14] generates a Beaver triple by sacrificing $4k + 2\ell$ authenticated shares. The total cost of communication complexity to generate a Beaver triple is $2(k + 2s)(9s + 4k)n(n-1)$ where s is the security parameter. This is bigger than ours $5142.5kn(n-1)$ if $k \leq 29$. If we set the security parameter to be 128, then our prepocessing phase outperforms the one in [14] for $k \leq 114$. Our communication complexity does not grow with the security parameter. This gives us an advantage for larger security parameters (Fig. 3).

	Online phase	$s = 64$	$s = 128$
This work	$19.68k(n-1)$	$12.4k(n-1)$	$12.84k(n-1)$
SPDZ_{2^k}	$4(k+s)(n-1)$	$4(k+64)(n-1)$	$4(k+128)(n-1)$

Fig. 3. Comparison to SPDZ_{2^k} in the online phase. We note that SPDZ_{2^k} and its variant have the same communication complexity in the online phase

Acknowledgement. The research of C. Xing is supported in part by the National Key Research and Development Project 2021YFE0109900 and the National Natural Science Foundation of China under Grant 12031011. The research of C. Yuan is supported in part by the National Natural Science Foundation of China under Grant 12101403. This paper was prepared in part for information purposes by the Artificial Intelligence Research group of JPMorgan Chase & Co and its affiliates ("JP Morgan"), and is not a product of the Research Department of JP Morgan. JP Morgan makes no representation and warranty whatsoever and disclaims all liability, for the completeness, accuracy or reliability of the information contained herein. This document is not intended as investment research or investment advice, or a recommendation, offer or solicitation for the purchase or sale of any security, financial instrument, financial product or service, or to be used in any way for evaluating the merits of participating in any transaction, and shall not constitute a solicitation under any jurisdiction or to any person, if such solicitation under such jurisdiction or to such person would be unlawful. 2021 JP Morgan Chase & Co. All rights reserved.

References

1. Abspoel, M., et al.: Asymptotically good multiplicative LSSS over Galois rings and applications to MPC over $\mathbb{Z}/p^k\mathbb{Z}$. In: Moriai, S., Wang, H. (eds.) ASIACRYPT 2020, Part III. LNCS, vol. 12493, pp. 151–180. Springer, Cham (2020). https://doi.org/10.1007/978-3-030-64840-4_6
2. Abspoel, M., Cramer, R., Damgård, I., Escudero, D., Yuan, C.: Efficient information-theoretic secure multiparty computation over $\mathbb{Z}/p^k\mathbb{Z}$ via Galois rings. In: Hofheinz, D., Rosen, A. (eds.) TCC 2019, Part I. LNCS, vol. 11891, pp. 471–501. Springer, Cham (2019). https://doi.org/10.1007/978-3-030-36030-6_19
3. Abspoel, M., Cramer, R., Escudero, D., Damgård, I., Xing, C.: Improved single-round secure multiplication using regenerating codes. In: Tibouchi, M., Wang, H. (eds.) ASIACRYPT 2021, Part II. LNCS, vol. 13091, pp. 222–244. Springer, Cham (2021). https://doi.org/10.1007/978-3-030-92075-3_8
4. Baum, C., Cozzo, D., Smart, N.P.: Using TopGear in overdrive: a more efficient ZKPoK for SPDZ. In: Paterson, K.G., Stebila, D. (eds.) SAC 2019. LNCS, vol. 11959, pp. 274–302. Springer, Cham (2020). https://doi.org/10.1007/978-3-030-38471-5_12
5. Bendlin, R., Damgård, I., Orlandi, C., Zakarias, S.: Semi-homomorphic encryption and multiparty computation. In: Paterson, K.G. (ed.) EUROCRYPT 2011. LNCS, vol. 6632, pp. 169–188. Springer, Heidelberg (2011). https://doi.org/10.1007/978-3-642-20465-4_11

6. Block, A.R., Maji, H.K., Nguyen, H.H.: Secure computation with constant communication overhead using multiplication embeddings. In: Chakraborty, D., Iwata, T. (eds.) INDOCRYPT 2018. LNCS, vol. 11356, pp. 375–398. Springer, Cham (2018). https://doi.org/10.1007/978-3-030-05378-9_20

7. Canetti, R.: Universally composable security: a new paradigm for cryptographic protocols. In: FOCS 2001, Las Vegas, Nevada, USA, 14–17 October 2001, pp. 136–145. IEEE Computer Society (2001)

8. Cascudo, I., Cramer, R., Xing, C., Yuan, C.: Amortized complexity of information-theoretically secure MPC revisited. In: Shacham, H., Boldyreva, A. (eds.) CRYPTO 2018, Part III. LNCS, vol. 10993, pp. 395–426. Springer, Cham (2018). https://doi.org/10.1007/978-3-319-96878-0_14

9. Cascudo, I., Gundersen, J.S.: A secret-sharing based MPC protocol for Boolean circuits with good amortized complexity. In: Pass, R., Pietrzak, K. (eds.) TCC 2020. LNCS, vol. 12551, pp. 652–682. Springer, Cham (2020). https://doi.org/10.1007/978-3-030-64378-2_23

10. Catalano, D., Di Raimondo, M., Fiore, D., Giacomelli, I.: Mon $\mathbb{Z}_{2^k}$a: fast maliciously secure two party computation on $\mathbb{Z}_{2^k}$. In: Kiayias, A., Kohlweiss, M., Wallden, P., Zikas, V. (eds.) PKC 2020. LNCS, vol. 12111, pp. 357–386. Springer, Cham (2020). https://doi.org/10.1007/978-3-030-45388-6_13

11. Chen, H., Cramer, R.: Algebraic geometric secret sharing schemes and secure multi-party computations over small fields. In: Dwork, C. (ed.) CRYPTO 2006. LNCS, vol. 4117, pp. 521–536. Springer, Heidelberg (2006). https://doi.org/10.1007/11818175_31

12. Chen, H., Cramer, R., de Haan, R., Pueyo, I.C.: Strongly multiplicative ramp schemes from high degree rational points on curves. In: Smart, N. (ed.) EUROCRYPT 2008. LNCS, vol. 4965, pp. 451–470. Springer, Heidelberg (2008). https://doi.org/10.1007/978-3-540-78967-3_26

13. Cheon, J.H., Kim, D., Lee, K.: MHz2k: MPC from HE over $\mathbb{Z}_{2^k}$ with new packing, simpler reshare, and better ZKP. In: Malkin, T., Peikert, C. (eds.) CRYPTO 2021. LNCS, vol. 12826, pp. 426–456. Springer, Cham (2021). https://doi.org/10.1007/978-3-030-84245-1_15

14. Cramer, R., Damgård, I., Escudero, D., Scholl, P., Xing, C.: SPD$\mathbb{Z}_{2^k}$: efficient MPC mod 2^k for dishonest majority. In: Shacham, H., Boldyreva, A. (eds.) CRYPTO 2018. LNCS, vol. 10992, pp. 769–798. Springer, Cham (2018). https://doi.org/10.1007/978-3-319-96881-0_26

15. Cramer, R., Rambaud, M., Xing, C.: Asymptotically-good arithmetic secret sharing over $\mathbb{Z}/p^\ell\mathbb{Z}$ with strong multiplication and its applications to efficient MPC. In: Malkin, T., Peikert, C. (eds.) CRYPTO 2021, Part III. LNCS, vol. 12827, pp. 656–686. Springer, Cham (2021). https://doi.org/10.1007/978-3-030-84252-9_22

16. Damgård, I., Escudero, D., Frederiksen, T., Keller, M., Scholl, P., Volgushev, N.: New primitives for actively-secure MPC over rings with applications to private machine learning. In: 2019 IEEE Symposium on Security and Privacy (SP), pp. 1102–1120. IEEE (2019)

17. Damgård, I., Keller, M., Larraia, E., Pastro, V., Scholl, P., Smart, N.P.: Practical covertly secure MPC for dishonest majority – or: breaking the SPDZ limits. In: Crampton, J., Jajodia, S., Mayes, K. (eds.) ESORICS 2013. LNCS, vol. 8134, pp. 1–18. Springer, Heidelberg (2013). https://doi.org/10.1007/978-3-642-40203-6_1

18. Damgård, I., Pastro, V., Smart, N., Zakarias, S.: Multiparty computation from somewhat homomorphic encryption. In: Safavi-Naini, R., Canetti, R. (eds.) CRYPTO 2012. LNCS, vol. 7417, pp. 643–662. Springer, Heidelberg (2012). https://doi.org/10.1007/978-3-642-32009-5_38

19. Damgård, I., Zakarias, S.: Constant-overhead secure computation of Boolean circuits using preprocessing. In: Sahai, A. (ed.) TCC 2013. LNCS, vol. 7785, pp. 621–641. Springer, Heidelberg (2013). https://doi.org/10.1007/978-3-642-36594-2_35

20. Frederiksen, T.K., Pinkas, B., Yanai, A.: Committed MPC - maliciously secure multiparty computation from homomorphic commitments. In: Abdalla, M., Dahab, R. (eds.) PKC 2018, Part I. LNCS, vol. 10769, pp. 587–619. Springer, Cham (2018). https://doi.org/10.1007/978-3-319-76578-5_20

21. Keller, M., Orsini, E., Scholl, P.: MASCOT: faster malicious arithmetic secure computation with oblivious transfer. In: Weippl, E.R., Katzenbeisser, S., Kruegel, C., Myers, A.C., Halevi, S. (eds.) CCS 2016, Vienna, Austria, 24–28 October 2016, pp. 830–842. ACM (2016)

22. Keller, M., Pastro, V., Rotaru, D.: Overdrive: making SPDZ great again. In: Nielsen, J.B., Rijmen, V. (eds.) EUROCRYPT 2018, Part III. LNCS, vol. 10822, pp. 158–189. Springer, Cham (2018). https://doi.org/10.1007/978-3-319-78372-7_6

23. Larraia, E., Orsini, E., Smart, N.P.: Dishonest majority multi-party computation for binary circuits. In: Garay, J.A., Gennaro, R. (eds.) CRYPTO 2014. LNCS, vol. 8617, pp. 495–512. Springer, Heidelberg (2014). https://doi.org/10.1007/978-3-662-44381-1_28

24. Orsini, E., Smart, N.P., Vercauteren, F.: Overdrive2k: efficient secure MPC over $\mathbb{Z}_{2^k}$ from somewhat homomorphic encryption. In: Jarecki, S. (ed.) CT-RSA 2020. LNCS, vol. 12006, pp. 254–283. Springer, Cham (2020). https://doi.org/10.1007/978-3-030-40186-3_12

25. Cascudo, I., Chen, H., Cramer, R., Xing, C.: Asymptotically good ideal linear secret sharing with strong multiplication over *any* fixed finite field. In: Halevi, S. (ed.) CRYPTO 2009. LNCS, vol. 5677, pp. 466–486. Springer, Heidelberg (2009). https://doi.org/10.1007/978-3-642-03356-8_28

26. Cascudo, I., Cramer, R., Xing, C.: The Torsion-limit for algebraic function fields and its application to arithmetic secret sharing. In: Rogaway, P. (ed.) CRYPTO 2011. LNCS, vol. 6841, pp. 685–705. Springer, Heidelberg (2011). https://doi.org/10.1007/978-3-642-22792-9_39

27. Rathee, D., Schneider, T., Shukla, K.K.: Improved multiplication triple generation over rings via RLWE-based AHE. In: Mu, Y., Deng, R.H., Huang, X. (eds.) CANS 2019. LNCS, vol. 11829, pp. 347–359. Springer, Cham (2019). https://doi.org/10.1007/978-3-030-31578-8_19

28. Wan, Z.-X.: Lectures on Finite Fields and Galois Rings. World Scientific Publishing Company (2003)

29. Yao, A.C.: How to generate and exchange secrets (extended abstract). In: 27th Annual Symposium on Foundations of Computer Science, Toronto, Canada, 27–29 October 1986, pp. 162–167. IEEE Computer Society (1986)

Proof Systems

Parallel Repetition of $(k_1,\ldots,k_\mu)$-Special-Sound Multi-round Interactive Proofs

Thomas Attema[1,2,3(✉)] and Serge Fehr[1,2]

[1] CWI, Cryptology Group, Amsterdam, The Netherlands
serge.fehr@cwi.nl
[2] Mathematical Institute, Leiden University, Leiden, The Netherlands
[3] TNO, Cyber Security and Robustness, The Hague, The Netherlands
thomas.attema@tno.nl

Abstract. In many occasions, the knowledge error κ of an interactive proof is not small enough, and thus needs to be reduced. This can be done generically by repeating the interactive proof in parallel. While there have been many works studying the effect of parallel repetition on the *soundness error* of interactive proofs and arguments, the effect of parallel repetition on the *knowledge error* has largely remained unstudied. Only recently it was shown that the t-fold parallel repetition of *any* interactive protocol reduces the knowledge error from κ down to $\kappa^t + \nu$ for any non-negligible term ν. This generic result is suboptimal in that it does not give the knowledge error κ^t that one would expect for typical protocols, and, worse, the knowledge error remains non-negligible.

In this work we show that indeed the t-fold parallel repetition of any $(k_1,\ldots,k_\mu)$-special-sound multi-round public-coin interactive proof optimally reduces the knowledge error from κ down to κ^t. At the core of our results is an alternative, in some sense more fine-grained, measure of quality of a dishonest prover than its success probability, for which we show that it characterizes when knowledge extraction is possible. This new measure then turns out to be very convenient when it comes to analyzing the parallel repetition of such interactive proofs.

While parallel repetition reduces the knowledge error, it is easily seen to *increase* the *completeness error*. For this reason, we generalize our result to the case of s-out-of-t threshold parallel repetition, where the verifier accepts if s out of t of the parallel instances are accepting. An appropriately chosen threshold s allows both the knowledge error and completeness error to be reduced simultaneously.

Keywords: Proofs of knowledge · Knowledge soundness · Special-soundness · Knowledge extractor · Parallel repetition · Threshold parallel repetition

1 Introduction

1.1 Background

Proofs of Knowledge. Proofs of Knowledge (PoKs) are essential building blocks in many cryptographic primitives. They allow a prover $\mathcal{P}$ to convince a

© International Association for Cryptologic Research 2022
Y. Dodis and T. Shrimpton (Eds.): CRYPTO 2022, LNCS 13507, pp. 415–443, 2022.
https://doi.org/10.1007/978-3-031-15802-5_15

verifier $\mathcal{V}$ that it knows a (secret) string $w \in \{0,1\}^*$, called a *witness*, satisfying some public constraint. Typically a prover wishes to do this either in (honest-verifier) *zero-knowledge*, i.e., without revealing any information about the witness w beyond the veracity of the claim, or with communication costs smaller than the size of the witness w. Both these requirements prevent the prover from simply revealing the witness w.

A key property of PoKs is *knowledge soundness*. Informally, a protocol is said to be knowledge sound if a dishonest prover that does not know the secret witness can only succeed in convincing a verifier with some small probability κ called the *knowledge error*. This is formalized by requiring the existence of an efficient *extractor* so that for any dishonest prover that succeeds with probability $\epsilon > \kappa$, the extractor outputs a witness w with probability at least $\epsilon - \kappa$, up to a multiplicative polynomial loss (in the security parameter), when given black-box access to the prover [16].

Typical 3-round public-coin protocols satisfy the conceptually simpler notion called *special-soundness*. A 3-round protocol is said to be special-sound if there exists an efficient algorithm that given two valid prover-verifier conversations (transcripts) (a, c, z) and (a, c', z'), with common first message a and distinct second messages (challenges) $c \neq c'$, outputs a witness w. More generally, a 3-round protocol is called k-special-sound if the algorithm requires k transcripts, instead of 2, to compute w. If k is polynomial in the size of the input x, the property k-special-soundness tightly implies the standard notion of knowledge soundness by a generic reduction, with $\kappa = (k-1)/N$, where N is the number of challenges [3,20].

In recent years, *multi-round* PoKs have gained a lot of attention [1–4,8–11,22]. The notion of k-special-soundness, which is tailored to 3-round protocols, extends quite naturally to $(k_1, \ldots, k_\mu)$-special-soundness for $(2\mu+1)$-round protocols (see Definition 7 for the formal definition). Many of the considered multi-round protocols satisfy this multi-round version of the special-soundness property. Surprisingly, only recently it was shown that also this generalization tightly implies knowledge soundness [3].

Parallel Repetition. In certain occasions, the knowledge error κ of a "basic" PoK (and thereby the cheating probability of a dishonest prover) is not small enough, and thus needs to be reduced. This is particularly the case for lattice-based PoKs, where typically challenge sets are only of polynomial size resulting in non-negligible knowledge errors [5,21]. Reducing the knowledge error can be done generically by repeating the PoK. Indeed, repeating a PoK t times *sequentially*, i.e., one after the other, is known to reduce the knowledge error from κ down to κ^t [16]. However, this approach also increases the number of communication rounds by a factor t. This is often undesirable, and sometimes even insufficient, e.g., because the security loss of the Fiat-Shamir transformation, transforming interactive into non-interactive protocols, is oftentimes exponential in the number of rounds.

Therefore, it is much more attractive to try to reduce the knowledge error by *parallel* repetition. In the case of special-sound protocols, i.e., k-special-sound protocols with $k = 2$, such a parallel repetition is easy to analyze: the t-fold parallel repetition of a special-sound protocol with challenge space of cardinality N is again special-sound protocol, but now with a challenge space of size N^t, and so knowledge-soundness with $\kappa = 1/N^t$ follows immediately from the generic reduction. Unfortunately, this reasoning does not extend to k-special-sound protocols with $k > 2$: even though we still have that the t-fold parallel repetition of a k-special-sound protocol is k'-special-sound, but now with $k' = (k-1)^t + 1$, this large increase in the special-soundness parameter renders the extractor, obtained via the generic reduction, inefficient. More precisely, the run-time of a k'-special-sound protocol scales linearly in k', and therefore exponentially in t for $k' = (k-1)^t + 1$, unless $k = 2$. In case of multi-round protocols, it is not even clear that the t-fold parallel repetition of a $(k_1, \ldots, k_\mu)$-special-sound $(2\mu + 1)$-round protocol satisfies any meaningful notion of special-soundness.

Somewhat surprisingly, so far the only way to analyze the knowledge error κ of the parallel repetition of k-special-sound protocols with $k > 2$, or of $(k_1, \ldots, k_\mu)$-special-sound multi-round protocols, is by means of suboptimal *generic* parallel-repetition results — or by considering weaker notions of knowledge soundness (see the discussion below). Concretely, based on a result from [13], it was recently shown that the t-fold parallel repetition of *any* public-coin PoK reduces the knowledge error from κ down to $\kappa^t + \nu$ for any non-negligible term ν [3]. This generic result is suboptimal in that, when applied to a k-special-sound protocol for instance, it does not give the knowledge error κ^t that one expects (and that one should get when $k = 2$), and, worse, the knowledge error remains non-negligible.

Even though this generic parallel-repetition result was shown to be tight, in that there are protocols for which parallel repetition does not allow the knowledge error to be reduced down to a negligible function, we can well hope for a stronger result for certain classes of protocols. In particular, it is not too absurd to expect *strong* parallel repetition for k-special-sound protocols, and possibly for $(k_1, \ldots, k_\mu)$-special-sound protocols in the multi-round case. Here, as usual in the general context of parallel repetition, the term "strong" means that the figure of merit κ, here the knowledge error, drops from κ to κ^t under a t-fold parallel repetition.

Other Notions of a PoK. Due to the difficulty in proving the original definition in certain contexts, it has become quite customary to consider modified and/or relaxed notions of a PoK that make it then feasible to obtain positive or stronger results; it is then typically argued that the considered notion is still meaningful and useful (in the considered context).

For example, many works on multi-round protocols consider the weaker notion of *witness-extended emulation* rather than the standard notion of knowledge soundness [8,10]. In the context of quantum security, the knowledge extractor is typically allowed to have success probability $(\epsilon - \kappa)^c$ (up to a multiplicative polynomial loss) for an arbitrary constant c, instead of $\epsilon - \kappa$ [25]. Moreover, recently, tighter security guarantees for discrete logarithm based Σ-protocols were obtained under a relaxed notion of knowledge soundness in which the knowledge extractor is not only given black-box access to the (possibly dishonest) prover $\mathcal{P}^*$, but is also given the success probability ϵ of $\mathcal{P}^*$ as input [24]. Finally, some works even allow the extractor to depend arbitrarily on the prover $\mathcal{P}^*$ [14].

In our work here, we instead insist on the original standard definition of a PoK, and we aim for strong parallel-repetition results nevertheless.

1.2 Contributions

In short, we show a strong parallel repetition theorem for the knowledge error of $(k_1, \ldots, k_\mu)$-special-sound $(2\mu + 1)$-round protocols, for $k_1, \ldots, k_\mu$ such that their product $K = k_1 \cdots k_\mu$ is polynomial in the size of the input statement.[1] This in particular implies strong parallel repetition for k-special-sound protocols for arbitrary polynomial k.[2] Strong parallel repetition means that if the original protocol has knowledge error κ then the t-fold parallel repetition has knowledge error κ^t, which is optimal, matching the success probability of a dishonest prover that attacks each instance in the parallel repetition independently (and thus succeeds with independent probability κ in each instance).

We also consider a threshold parallel repetition, where the verifier accepts as soon as s out of the t parallel repetitions succeed, and we show also here that the knowledge error is what one would expect, matching the attack where the dishonest prover cheats in each of the t instances independently and hopes that he is successful in at least s of them.

Our results directly apply to the typical *computational* version of special soundness as well, where there exists an efficient algorithm that *either* computes a witness from sufficiently many transcripts *or* provides a solution to a computational problem that is assumed to be hard (like producing a commitment along with two distinct openings) from sufficiently many transcripts. Indeed, such a protocol can simply be cast as an ordinary "unconditional" special-sound protocol for proving knowledge of: a witness w *or* a solution to the considered computational problem, and then our results readily apply.

1.3 Highlevel Approach

The starting point of our (threshold) parallel-repetition results is the following observation, considering (a single execution of) a k-special-sound protocol. The default measure of quality of a dishonest prover $\mathcal{P}^*$ is its success probability

---

[1] The $(k_1, \ldots, k_\mu)$-special-soundness property states that there exists an *efficient* algorithm (i.e., polynomial in the input size) that, on input a set of $K = k_1 \cdots k_\mu$ accepting protocol transcripts (with certain properties), outputs a secret witness. Therefore, this property is only useful when K is polynomial.

[2] For didactical reasons, we actually first treat the case of k-special-sound protocols, i.e., $\mu = 1$, and then consider the more general case of multi-round protocols.

$\epsilon = \epsilon(\mathcal{P}^*)$. For instance, if ϵ is below the knowledge error κ then *in general* we cannot expect the extraction of a witness w to work. However, the crucial observation is that for a given dishonest prover $\mathcal{P}^*$, its success probability ϵ does actually not characterize (very well) whether extraction is possible or not. For instance, fixing $\mathcal{P}^*$'s first message, if $\mathcal{P}^*$ then answers correctly with probability ϵ (and fails to do so with probability $1-\epsilon$) independently *for each* possible choice of the challenge (where the randomness is over P^*'s randomness used for computing the response), then extraction is still possible even when $\epsilon < \kappa$ (yet noticeable): simply try sufficiently many times for k distinct challenges, and after an expected number of k/ϵ trials, we have k correct responses to distinct challenges, from which a witness can then be computed.

At the core of our results is a novel (and somewhat peculiar in its design) knowledge extractor for k-special-sound protocols, whose success probability can be expressed in terms of an alternative, in some sense more fine-grained, measure of quality of $\mathcal{P}^*$. In more detail, in the context of a k-special-sound 3-round protocol, we define $\delta_k(\mathcal{P}^*)$ to be the *minimal* success probability of $\mathcal{P}^*$ when up to $k-1$ challenges are *removed* from the challenge space (minimized over the choice of the removed challenges).[3] We then show (Lemma 2) existence of an extractor $\mathcal{E}$ that successfully extracts a witness from any $\mathcal{P}^*$ with probability $\delta_k(\mathcal{P}^*)/k$. A simple calculation also shows that $\delta_k(\mathcal{P}^*) \geq \epsilon(\mathcal{P}^*) - (k-1)/N$, confirming that a k-special-sound 3-round protocol has knowledge error $\kappa = (k-1)/N$. However, the crucial aspect is that this new measure $\delta_k(\mathcal{P}^*)$ turns out to be convenient to work with when it comes to parallel repetition.

Indeed, to obtain our parallel-repetition result for 3-round protocols, we first observe that a dishonest prover $\mathcal{P}^*$ against a t-fold parallel repetition naturally gives rise to t dishonest provers $\mathcal{P}_1^*, \ldots, \mathcal{P}_t^*$ against a single invocation: $\mathcal{P}_i^*$ simply mimics $\mathcal{P}^*$'s behavior in the i-th invocation in the parallel repetition. Thus, $\epsilon(\mathcal{P}_i^*)$ is then the probability that the i-th invocation in the parallel repetition is accepted. However, the core observation is that it is more convenient to consider the measure $\delta_k(\mathcal{P}_i^*)$ instead. Indeed, by basic probability theory we can show (Lemma 3) that $\delta_k(\mathcal{P}_1^*) + \cdots + \delta_k(\mathcal{P}_t^*) \geq \epsilon(\mathcal{P}^*) - \kappa^t$. This in turn immediately gives us a lower bound of $(\epsilon(\mathcal{P}^*) - \kappa^t)/t$ on the success probability of the natural way to try to extract a witness from $\mathcal{P}^*$, which is by means of running the above extractor $\mathcal{E}$ for the single invocation case with *each* of the $\mathcal{P}_i^*$'s separately, each run of $\mathcal{E}$ succeeding with probability $\delta_k(\mathcal{P}_i^*)$ by the property of $\mathcal{E}$. Using a slightly more careful argument than upper bounding the sum of the $\delta_k(\mathcal{P}_i^*)$'s by $t \cdot \max_i \delta_k(\mathcal{P}_i^*)$ shows a success probability of actually $(\epsilon(\mathcal{P}^*) - \kappa^t)/2$. Either way, this proves our strong parallel-repetition result for 3-round protocols.

In order to prove the corresponding strong parallel-repetition result for general $(k_1, \ldots, k_\mu)$-special-sound *multi-round* protocols, we follow the very same blueprint as above, but use an appropriately adjusted definition of $\delta_{k_1, \ldots, k_\mu}(\mathcal{P}^*)$ as the minimal success probability of $\mathcal{P}^*$ when, *in every challenge round i*, up

---

[3] This definition is well motivated: by k-special soundness, $\mathcal{P}^*$ can potentially prepare correct responses for up to $k-1$ challenges, so the interesting measure is the success probability when he gets *another* challenge, one for which he is not prepared.

to $k_i - 1$ challenges are removed from the challenge space. First constructing an extractor $\mathcal{E}$ for a single invocation by an appropriate recursive application of the extractor for the 3-round case, and then following the above line of reasoning to deal with the parallel repetition, we eventually obtain the existence of an extractor for the t-fold parallel repetition of any $(k_1, \ldots, k_\mu)$-special-sound protocol. The extractor requires an expected number of at most $t \cdot 2^\mu \cdot K \leq t \cdot K^2$ queries to $\mathcal{P}^*$ and succeeds with probability at least $(\epsilon - \kappa^t) / (2K)$, where $K = k_1 \cdots k_\mu$ and κ is the knowledge error of a single invocation of the protocol. Therefore, we prove that the t-fold parallel repetition has knowledge error κ^t.

1.4   Related Work

Reducing the Soundness Error (and Why *Knowledge* Soundness is Different). A related question is that of reducing the (ordinary) *soundness error* of an interactive proof (or argument) by parallel repetition. It is well known that the t-fold parallel repetition $(\mathcal{P}^t, \mathcal{V}^t)$ of an interactive *proof* (i.e., not argument) $(\mathcal{P}, \mathcal{V})$ reduces the *soundness error* from σ down to σ^t [15]. Namely, it is relatively easy to reduce an arbitrary prover against the t-fold parallel repetition, and which has success probability ϵ, into a *computationally unbounded* prover that successfully attacks a single instantiation with probability at least $\epsilon^{1/t}$.

The situation is trickier for interactive *arguments*, where the prover is required to be *efficient* and thus this reduction no longer works. Various parallel repetition theorems for interactive arguments have been established [7,12,13,18, 19,23]. As before, these results reduce an arbitrary prover $\mathcal{P}_t^*$ against the t-fold parallel repetition, and which has success probability ϵ, into a prover $\mathcal{P}^* = \mathcal{R}^{\mathcal{P}_t^*}$ attacking a single invocation of the interactive argument $(\mathcal{P}, \mathcal{V})$, but now with $\mathcal{P}^*$ being efficient — well, a subtle issue is that in these parallel repetition theorems there is an unavoidable trade-off between the *success probability* and the *run-time* of $\mathcal{P}^*$. For instance, the reduction in [12] results in a prover $\mathcal{P}^*$ with success probability $\epsilon^{1/t} \cdot (1 - \xi)$ and run-time polynomial in $1/\xi$ for arbitrary $\xi > 0$.

Such a trade off is fine in the context of the *soundness* error of interactive arguments (or proofs). Indeed, a reduction as above implies that if in a single invocation of the argument (or proof) any dishonest prover has bounded success probability, then a t-fold parallel repetition has exponentially small soundness error. Namely, arguing by contradiction, assuming a prover $\mathcal{P}_t^*$ against the t-fold parallel repetition with a too good success probability, by suitable choice of parameters the prover $\mathcal{P}_t^*$ can then be turned into a prover $\mathcal{P}^* = \mathcal{R}^{\mathcal{P}_t^*}$ that violates the bound on the success probability of a single invocation.

However, this trade-off between success probability and run time is a subtle but serious obstacle when considering the *knowledge soundness* of interactive proofs or arguments. Recall that, by standard definition [16], there much exist a *single* efficient extractor that works for *all* provers, and that must have a success probability that scales proportional to $\epsilon - \kappa$ for all provers (see Definition 4). But then, the naive approach of constructing the knowledge extractor $\mathcal{E}_t$ for the parallel repetition, which is by running the knowledge extractor $\mathcal{E}$ for the single invocation on the prover that is obtained by the generic reduction, i.e., setting $\mathcal{E}_t^{\mathcal{P}^*} := \mathcal{E}^{(\mathcal{R}^{\mathcal{P}^*})}$, runs into problems since the reduction $\mathcal{R}$, and thus the extractor $\mathcal{E}_t$, depends on certain parameters, like the desired success probability of $\mathcal{P}^* = \mathcal{R}^{\mathcal{P}^*}$, violating the definition.

One possible "solution" is to weaken the standard definition of a proof of knowedge and to allow the extractor to depend on certain parameters; for instance, the parallel repetition result for predictable arguments of knowledge presented in [14] follows this approach and allows the extractor to arbitrarily depend on the prover. Another approach, as taken in [3], is to consider $\mathcal{E}_t$ as above but then for a *fixed* choice of the reduction $\mathcal{R}$, e.g., for a fixed choice of ξ in the context of [12] discussed above. However, since the extractor needs to be efficient, ξ must be chosen to be non-negligible then, resulting in a prover $\mathcal{P}^*$ with success probability bounded away from 1 by a non-negligible amount, which in turn results in a non-negligible knowledge error. Indeed, [3] shows that parallel repetition reduces the knowledge error from κ down to $\kappa^t + \nu$ for an arbitrary but fixed non-negligible term ν.

As a consequence, in this work here where we do not want to weaken the definition of a proof of knowledge, but still wish to obtain strong parallel repetition results, i.e., show that the knowledge error κ drops exponentially as κ^t under parallel repetition, we cannot use the above generic reduction results but need to prove strong parallel repetition (for the considered class of protocols) *from scratch*.

The Case $t = 1$. The starting point of our parallel-repetition result is a new knowledge extractor for a single invocation of $(k_1, \ldots, k_\mu)$-special-sound protocols; we briefly compare this extractor with other knowledge extractors proposed for such protocols.

For instance, considering a different notion of knowledge soundness, [1] proposed an extractor for $(k_1, \ldots, k_\mu)$-special-sound protocols that has a *strict* polynomial run-time, yet a success probability that degrades exponentially in $K = k_1 \cdots k_\mu$. Thus, this notion is meaningful only when K is constant in the input size.

Full fledged and tight knowledge soundness for $(k_1, \ldots, k_\mu)$-special-sound protocols was only very recently shown in [3]. In that work, in line with the standard definition [16], the proposed extractor runs in expected polynomial time and succeeds with probability proportional to $\epsilon - \kappa$. As shown in Table 1, our extractor behaves somewhat worse in the (expected) polynomial run time, and also in the success probability when the newly introduced measure δ is bounded by $\epsilon - \kappa$; however, by exploiting the definition of δ, as we show in the technical part, we can obtain an extractor for a *parallel repetition* of the considered protocol by running the extractor individually on each instance of the parallel repetition. Thus, our extractor is well suited to show the claimed (threshold) parallel-repetition results. Nevertheless, it remains an interesting problem whether our extractor can be improved to match up with the extractor from [3] while still giving rise to our parallel-repetition results.

Table 1. Different knowledge extractors for $(k_1, \ldots, k_\mu)$-special-sound protocols. Here, $\epsilon = \epsilon(\mathcal{P}^*)$ denotes the success probability of the prover $\mathcal{P}^*$, N_i is size of the i-th challenge set, $\kappa = 1 - \prod_{i=1}^{\mu} \frac{N_i - k_i + 1}{N_i}$ is the knowledge error, and $K = k_1 \cdots k_\mu$. The refined quality measure $\delta = \delta(\mathcal{P}^*)$ will be defined in Sect. 3 and Sect. 4.

Extractor	Number of $\mathcal{P}^*$-queries Q	Success probability P
[1]	$Q \leq K$	$P \geq (\epsilon - \kappa)^K$
[3]	$\mathbb{E}[Q] \leq K$	$P \geq \epsilon - \kappa$
This work	$\mathbb{E}[Q] \leq 2^\mu \cdot K \leq K^2$	$P \geq \frac{1}{K}\delta \geq \frac{1}{K}(\epsilon - \kappa)$

1.5   Organization of the Paper

In Sect. 2, we introduce notation and recall standard definitions regarding interactive proofs. In Sect. 3, we show the parallel-repetition result for k-special-sound 3-round protocols: we first construct a new knowledge extractor for (the single execution of) a k-special-sound protocol, and then handle the parallel repetition of these protocols in a second step. In Sect. 4, we generalize the aforementioned results to multi-round protocols. Finally, in Sect. 5, we treat the s-out-of-t threshold parallel repetition of $(k_1, \ldots, k_\mu)$-special-sound protocols.

2   Preliminaries

2.1   Interactive Proofs

Following standard terminology, given a binary relation $R \subseteq \{0,1\}^* \times \{0,1\}^*$, a string $w \in \{0,1\}^*$ is called a *witness* for the *statement* $x \in \{0,1\}^*$ if $(x; w) \in R$. The set of valid witnesses for a statement x is denoted by $R(x)$, i.e., $R(x) = \{w : (x; w) \in R\}$. A statement that admits a witness is said to be a *true* or *valid* statement. The set of true statements is denoted by L_R, i.e., $L_R = \{x : \exists w \text{ s.t. } (x; w) \in R\}$. A binary relation is said to be an NP relation if the validity of a witness w can be verified in time polynomial in the size $|x|$ of the statement x. From now on we assume all relations to be NP relations.

An interactive proof for a relation R aims for a prover $\mathcal{P}$ to convince a verifier $\mathcal{V}$ that a statement x admits a witness, or even that the prover *knows* a witness $w \in R(x)$. We recall the following standard definitions.

Definition 1 (Interactive Proof). *An interactive proof $(\mathcal{P}, \mathcal{V})$ for relation R is an interactive protocol between two probabilistic machines, a prover $\mathcal{P}$ and a polynomial time verifier $\mathcal{V}$. Both $\mathcal{P}$ and $\mathcal{V}$ take as public input a statement x and, additionally, $\mathcal{P}$ takes as private input a witness $w \in R(x)$, which is denoted as $(\mathcal{P}(w), \mathcal{V})(x)$. As the output of the protocol, $\mathcal{V}$ either accepts or rejects. Accordingly, we say the corresponding transcript (i.e., the set of all messages exchanged in the protocol execution) is accepting or rejecting.*

An interactive proof $(\mathcal{P}, \mathcal{V})$ is *complete* if the verifier $\mathcal{V}$ accepts honest exe-cutions with a public-private input pair $(x; w) \in R$ with large probability. It is *sound* if the verifier rejects false statements $x \notin L_R$ with large probability. Origi-nally interactive proofs were defined to be complete and sound [17]. By contrast, we do not require interactive protocols to satisfy these properties by definition, but consider them as desirable additional security properties.

Definition 2 (Completeness). *An interactive proof* $(\mathcal{P}, \mathcal{V})$ *for relation* R *is complete with completeness error* $\rho \colon \{0,1\}^* \to [0,1]$ *if for every* $(x; w) \in R$,

$$\Pr((\mathcal{P}(w), \mathcal{V})(x) = \textit{reject}) \leq \rho(x).$$

If $\rho(x) = 0$ *for all* x, $(\mathcal{P}, \mathcal{V})$ *is said to be perfectly complete.*

Definition 3 (Soundness). *An interactive proof* $(\mathcal{P}, \mathcal{V})$ *for relation* R *is* sound *with soundness error* $\sigma \colon \{0,1\}^* \to [0,1]$, *if for every* $x \notin L_R$ *and every prover* $\mathcal{P}^*$,

$$\Pr((\mathcal{P}^*, \mathcal{V})(x) = \textit{accept}) \leq \sigma(x).$$

If an interactive proof is complete and sound, it "merely" allows a prover to convince a verifier that a statement x is true, i.e., $x \in L_R$. It does not necessarily convince a verifier that the prover "knows" a witness $w \in R(x)$. This stronger property is captured by the notion *knowledge soundness*. Infor-mally, an interactive proof $(\mathcal{P}, \mathcal{V})$ is knowledge sound if any prover $\mathcal{P}^*$ with $\Pr((\mathcal{P}^*, \mathcal{V})(x) = \mathsf{accept})$ large enough is able to compute a witness $w \in R(x)$.

Definition 4 (Knowledge Soundness). *An interactive proof* $(\mathcal{P}, \mathcal{V})$ *for rela-tion* R *is knowledge sound with knowledge error* $\kappa \colon \{0,1\}^* \to [0,1]$ *if there exists a positive polynomial* q *and an algorithm* $\mathcal{E}$, *called a* knowledge extractor, *with the following properties: The extractor* $\mathcal{E}$, *given input* x *and rewindable oracle access to a (potentially dishonest) prover* $\mathcal{P}^*$, *runs in an expected number of steps that is polynomial in* $|x|$ *and outputs a witness* $w \in R(x)$ *with probability*

$$\Pr((x; \mathcal{E}^{\mathcal{P}^*}(x)) \in R) \geq \frac{\epsilon(x, \mathcal{P}^*) - \kappa(x)}{q(|x|)},$$

where $\epsilon(x, \mathcal{P}^*) := \Pr((\mathcal{P}^*, \mathcal{V})(x) = \textit{accept})$.

Remark 1. It is straightforward to verify that in order to satisfy Definition 4 it is sufficient to show that the required property holds for *deterministic* provers $\mathcal{P}^*$. Let $\mathcal{P}^*$ be an arbitrary randomized dishonest prover, and let $\mathcal{P}^*[r]$ be the deterministic prover obtained by fixing $\mathcal{P}^*$'s randomness to r. Then $\epsilon(x, \mathcal{P}^*) = \mathbb{E}[\epsilon(x, \mathcal{P}^*[r])]$, where $\mathbb{E}$ denotes the expectation over the random choice of r. Furthermore, if $\mathcal{E}^{\mathcal{P}^*}$ is declared to run $\mathcal{E}^{\mathcal{P}^*[r]}$ for a random choice of r then the same holds for the success probability of the extractor: $\Pr((x; \mathcal{E}^{\mathcal{P}^*}(x)) \in R) = \mathbb{E}[\Pr((x; \mathcal{E}^{\mathcal{P}^*[r]}(x)) \in R)]$. It follows that in order to satisfy Definition 4 it is sufficient to show that the required property holds for *deterministic* provers $\mathcal{P}^*$. For this reason, we may assume provers to be deterministic, in particular, we will consider the prover's first message to be deterministic. This will significantly simplify our analysis.

Remark 2. Definition 4 is a *static* knowledge soundness definition, i.e., dishonest provers attack a *fixed* statement x. However, in some scenarios dishonest provers may choose the statement x adaptively. This would warrant a stronger *adaptive* knowledge soundness definition. However, it is easily seen that, for interactive proofs, static knowledge soundness implies adaptive knowledge soundness [16]. Hence, also in the aforementioned application scenarios Definition 4 is sufficient.

If $\epsilon(x, \mathcal{P}^*) = \Pr((\mathcal{P}^*, \mathcal{V})(x) = \mathsf{accept}) > \kappa(x)$, then the success probability of the knowledge extractor of Definition 4 is positive. Hence, $\epsilon(x, \mathcal{P}^*) > \kappa(x)$ implies that x admits a witness, i.e., $x \in L_R$. It therefore follows that knowledge soundness implies soundness.

Remark 3. Sometimes a slightly weaker definition for knowledge soundness is used [6,16,20]. This weaker definition decouples knowledge soundness from soundness by only requiring the extractor to run in expected polynomial time on inputs $x \in L_R$, i.e., it does not require the protocol to be sound. It can be shown that a *sound* protocol satisfying this weaker version of knowledge soundness is also knowledge sound in the stronger sense of Definition 4.

Definition 5 (Proof of Knowledge). *An interactive proof that is both complete with completeness error $\rho(\cdot)$ and knowledge sound with knowledge error $\kappa(\cdot)$ is a* Proof of Knowledge *(PoK) if there exists a polynomial q such that $1 - \rho(x) \geq \kappa(x) + 1/q(|x|)$ for all x.*

Let us consider some additional (desirable) properties of proofs of knowledge. We assume that the prover $\mathcal{P}$ sends the first and the last message in any interactive proof $(\mathcal{P}, \mathcal{V})$. If this is not the case, the interactive proof can be appended with an empty message. Hence, the number of communication rounds $2\mu + 1$ is always odd. We also say $(\mathcal{P}, \mathcal{V})$ is a $(2\mu + 1)$-round protocol. We will refer to *multi-round* protocols as a way of emphasizing that we are not restricting to 3-round protocols.

Definition 6 (Public-Coin). *An interactive proof $(\mathcal{P}, \mathcal{V})$ is public-coin if all of $\mathcal{V}$'s random choices are made public.*

If a protocol is public-coin, the verifier only needs to send its random choices to the prover. In this case, $\mathcal{V}$'s messages are also referred to as *challenges* and the set from which $\mathcal{V}$ samples its messages uniformly at random is called the challenge set.

We recall the notion of (general) *special-soundness*. It is typically easier to prove that an interactive proof is special-sound than to prove that it is knowledge sound. Note that we require special-sound protocols to be public-coin.

Definition 7 (k-out-of-N Special-Soundness). *Let $k, N \in \mathbb{N}$. A 3-round public-coin protocol $(\mathcal{P}, \mathcal{V})$ for relation R, with challenge set of cardinality $N \geq k$, is k-out-of-N special-sound if there exists a polynomial time algorithm that, on input a statement x and k accepting transcripts $(a, c_1, z_1), \ldots (a, c_k, z_k)$ with common first message a and pairwise distinct challenges $c_1, \ldots, c_k$, outputs a witness $w \in R(x)$. We also say $(\mathcal{P}, \mathcal{V})$ is k-special-sound and, if $k = 2$, it is simply said to be special-sound.*

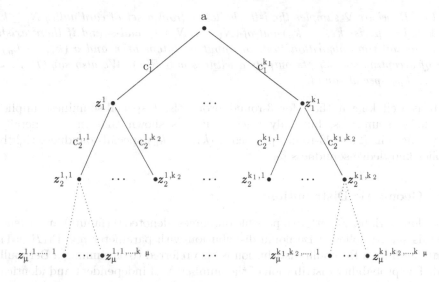

Fig. 1. $(k_1, \ldots, k_\mu)$-tree of transcripts of a $(2\mu + 1)$-round public-coin protocol [3].

We refer to a 3-round public-coin interactive proof as a *Σ-protocol*. Note that often a Σ-protocol is required to be (perfectly) complete, special-sound and special honest-verifier zero-knowledge (SHVZK) by definition. However, we do not require a Σ-protocol to have these additional properties.

Definition 8 (Σ-Protocol). *A Σ-protocol is a 3-round public-coin interactive proof.*

In order to generalize k-special-soundness to multi-round protocols we introduce the notion of a tree of transcripts. We follow the definition of [3].

Definition 9 (Tree of Transcripts). *Let $k_1, \ldots, k_\mu \in \mathbb{N}$. A $(k_1, \ldots, k_\mu)$-tree of transcripts for a $(2\mu + 1)$-round public-coin protocol $(\mathcal{P}, \mathcal{V})$ is a set of $K = \prod_{i=1}^{\mu} k_i$ transcripts arranged in the following tree structure. The nodes in this tree correspond to the prover's messages and the edges to the verifier's challenges. Every node at depth i has precisely k_i children corresponding to k_i pairwise distinct challenges. Every transcript corresponds to exactly one path from the root node to a leaf node. For a graphical representation we refer to Fig. 1. We refer to the corresponding tree of challenges as a $(k_1, \ldots, k_\mu)$-tree of challenges. The set of all $(k_1, \ldots, k_\mu)$-trees of challenges is denoted by $\mathrm{TREE}(k_1, \ldots, k_\mu)$.*

We will also write $\mathbf{k} = (k_1, \ldots, k_\mu) \in \mathbb{N}^\mu$ and refer to a $\mathbf{k}$-tree of transcripts.

Definition 10 ($(k_1, \ldots, k_\mu)$-out-of-$(N_1, \ldots, N_\mu)$ Special-Soundness). *Let $k_1, \ldots, k_\mu, N_1, \ldots, N_\mu \in \mathbb{N}$. A $(2\mu + 1)$-round public-coin protocol $(\mathcal{P}, \mathcal{V})$ for* relation R, where $\mathcal{V}$ samples the i-th challenge from a set of cardinality $N_i \geq k_i$ for $1 \leq i \leq \mu$, is $(k_1, \ldots, k_\mu)$-out-of-$(N_1, \ldots, N_\mu)$ special-sound if there exists a polynomial time algorithm that, on input a statement x and a $(k_1, \ldots, k_\mu)$-tree of accepting transcripts outputs a witness $w \in R(x)$. We also say $(\mathcal{P}, \mathcal{V})$ is $(k_1, \ldots, k_\mu)$-special-sound.

It is well known that, for 3-round protocols, k-special-soundness implies knowledge soundness, but only recently it was shown that more generally, for public-coin $(2\mu + 1)$-round protocols, $(k_1, \ldots, k_\mu)$-special-soundness tightly implies knowledge soundness [3].

2.2 Geometric Distribution

A random variable B with two possible outcomes, denoted 0 (failure) and 1 (success), is said to follow a Bernoulli distribution with parameter $p = \Pr(B = 1)$. Sampling from a Bernoulli distribution is also referred to as running a Bernoulli trial. The probability distribution of the number X of independent and identical Bernoulli trials needed to obtain a success is called the geometric distribution with parameter $p = \Pr(X = 1)$. In this case $\Pr(X = k) = (1 - p)^{k-1}p$ for all $k \in \mathbb{N}$ and we write $X \sim \mathrm{Geo}(p)$. For two independent geometric distributions we have the following lemma.

Lemma 1. Let $X \sim \mathrm{Geo}(p)$ and $Y \sim \mathrm{Geo}(q)$ be independently distributed. Then,

$$\Pr(X \leq Y) = \frac{p}{p + q - pq} \geq \frac{p}{p + q}.$$

Proof. It holds that

$$\Pr(X \leq Y) = \sum_{x=1}^{\infty} \Pr(X = x) \Pr(Y \geq x) = \sum_{x=1}^{\infty} (1 - p)^{x-1} p \cdot (1 - q)^{x-1}$$

$$= \frac{p}{1 - (1 - p)(1 - q)} \sum_{x=1}^{\infty} ((1 - p)(1 - q))^{x-1} (1 - (1 - p)(1 - q))$$

$$= \frac{p}{1 - (1 - p)(1 - q)} \sum_{x=1}^{\infty} \Pr(Z = x)$$

$$= \frac{p}{1 - (1 - p)(1 - q)} = \frac{p}{p + q - pq} \geq \frac{p}{p + q},$$

where $Z \sim \mathrm{Geo}(p + q - pq)$. This completes the proof of the lemma.   □

3   Parallel Repetition of k-Special-Sound Σ-Protocols

To simplify the exposition, we start with the simpler case of Σ-protocols; the general case of multi-round protocols will then be treated in the subsequent section. Thus, for the remainder of this section, we consider a k-special-sound public-coin interactive proof $(\mathcal{P}, \mathcal{V})$ with challenge set $\mathcal{C}$ of cardinality $N \geq k$. It is well known that such an interactive proof is a proof of knowledge with knowledge error $\kappa = (k - 1)/N$. We write $(\mathcal{P}^t, \mathcal{V}^t)$ for the t-fold parallel repetition of $(\mathcal{P}, \mathcal{V})$, which runs t instances of $(\mathcal{P}, \mathcal{V})$ in parallel and the verifier $\mathcal{V}^t$ accepts if all the parallel instances are accepted. In this section, we prove that $(\mathcal{P}^t, \mathcal{V}^t)$ is then again a proof of knowledge, but now with knowledge error κ^t, which is optimal. Thus, we show what is sometimes referred to as *strong* parallel repetition, meaning that the figure of merit decreases with power t under parallel repetition. This is well known to hold for special-sound Σ-protocols, i.e., for $k = 2$, but was open for general k.

The standard way to reason about parallel repetition for the special case $k = 2$ uses the fact that $(\mathcal{P}^t, \mathcal{V}^t)$ is ℓ-special-sound with $\ell = (k-1)^t + 1$. However, this reasoning does not apply in general, because ℓ grows exponentially in t for $k > 2$. Instead, our result crucially depends on the fact that $(\mathcal{P}^t, \mathcal{V}^t)$ is the t-fold parallel repetition of a k-special-sound protocol $(\mathcal{P}, \mathcal{V})$.

In Sect. 3.1, we first construct a novel (and somewhat peculiar) extraction algorithm for k-special-sound protocols $(\mathcal{P}, \mathcal{V})$, thereby reproving that k-special-soundness implies knowledge soundness [3]. In Sect. 3.2, we show how this extraction algorithm can be used to deduce a strong parallel repetition result for $(\mathcal{P}^t, \mathcal{V}^t)$. In Sect. 4, we then extend our results to multi-round protocols.

On a high level, the crucial ingredient in our analyses is to introduce and work with a more "fine-grained" notion of success probability of a dishonest prover, as we introduce it below.

3.1 Knowledge Soundness of a Single Invocation

Consider a dishonest prover $\mathcal{P}^*$ against the considered k-special-sound interactive proof $(\mathcal{P}, \mathcal{V})$. The goal of the extractor is to run $\mathcal{P}^*$ and rewind it sufficiently many times so as to obtain a first message a together with k correct answers $z_1, \ldots, z_k$ for k pairwise distinct challenges $c_1, \ldots, c_k \in \mathcal{C}$. The crucial question is how often $\mathcal{P}^*$ needs to be rewinded, and thus what is the (expected) running time of the extractor. Alternatively, towards satisfying Definition 4, we would like to have an extractor that runs in a fixed (expected) polynomial time, but may fail with some probability. It is quite clear that in both cases the figure of merit (i.e., the running time in the former and the success probability in the latter) depends on the *success probability* ϵ of $\mathcal{P}^*$; for instance, if ϵ is below the knowledge error κ then we cannot expect extraction to work in general. However, a crucial observation is that for a given dishonest prover $\mathcal{P}^*$, its success probability ϵ does actually not characterize (very well) whether extraction is possible or not: if in a special-sound Σ-protocol $\mathcal{P}^*$ provides the correct response with probability ϵ (and fails to do so with probability $1 - \epsilon$) *for every* possible choice of the challenge, then extraction is still possible even when $\epsilon < \kappa$ (but not negligible), simply by trying sufficiently many times for two distinct challenges. Below, we will identify an alternative, in some sense more fine-grained, "quality measure" of $\mathcal{P}^*$, and we show that this measure does characterize when extraction is possible. This will be helpful when it comes to more complicated settings, like a *parallel repetition*, or a *multi-round* protocol, or, ultimately, a *parallel repetition* of a *multi-round* protocol.

For multiple reasons, we will state and prove our core technical results in a more abstract language. One reason is that this allows us to focus on the important aspects; another reason is that we will actually exploit the considered abstraction, and thus generalization, of the considered problem. In our abstraction, we consider an arbitrary function $V: \mathcal{C} \times \{0,1\}^* \to \{0,1\}$, $(c,y) \mapsto V(c,y)$, and we consider an arbitrary (possibly probabilistic) algorithm $\mathcal{A}$ that takes as input an element $c \in \mathcal{C}$ and outputs a string $y \leftarrow \mathcal{A}(c)$. The *success probability* of $\mathcal{A}$ is then naturally defined as

$$\epsilon^V(\mathcal{A}) := \Pr\big(V(C, \mathcal{A}(C)) = 1\big),$$

where, here and below, the probability space is defined by means of the randomness of $\mathcal{A}$ and the random variable C being uniformly random in $\mathcal{C}$. If V is clear from context, we simply write $\epsilon(\mathcal{A})$.

The obvious instantiation of $\mathcal{A}$ is given by a *deterministic*[4] dishonest prover $\mathcal{P}^*$ attacking the considered k-special-sound interactive proof $(\mathcal{P}, \mathcal{V})$ on input x. More precisely, on input c, $\mathcal{A}$ runs $\mathcal{P}^*$ sending c as the challenge, and outputs $\mathcal{P}^*$'s (fixed) first message a and its response z, and the function V is defined as the verification check that $\mathcal{V}$ performs. We point out that this instantiation gives rise to a deterministic $\mathcal{A}$; however, later on it will be crucial that in our abstract treatment, $\mathcal{A}$ may be an arbitrary *randomized* algorithm that decides on its output y in a randomized manner given the input c, and that V is arbitrary.

Motivated by the k-special-soundness of the considered protocol, given (oracle access to) $\mathcal{A}$ the goal will be to find correct responses $y_1, \ldots, y_k$ for k pairwise distinct challenges $c_1, \ldots, c_k \in \mathcal{C}$, i.e., such that $V(c_i, y_i) = 1$ for all i. As we show below, the measure that captures how well this can be done is the *worst case* success probability of $\mathcal{A}$ for a random challenge when up to but less than k challenges are *removed* from the challenge space, formally given by

$$\delta_k^V(\mathcal{A}) := \min_{S \subset \mathcal{C}: |S| < k} \Pr\big(V(C, \mathcal{A}(C)) = 1 \mid C \notin S\big).$$

More precisely, we argue existence of an extraction algorithm $\mathcal{E}^{\mathcal{A}}$ with oracle access to $\mathcal{A}$, that runs in expected polynomial time and succeeds with probability at least $\delta_k^V(\mathcal{A})/k$. As before, if V is clear from context, we write $\delta_k(\mathcal{A})$.

Lemma 2 (Extraction Algorithm). *Let $k \in \mathbb{N}$ and $\mathcal{C}$ a finite set with cardinality $N \geq k$, and let $V: \mathcal{C} \times \{0,1\}^* \to \{0,1\}$. Then, there exists an algorithm $\mathcal{E}^{\mathcal{A}}$ so that, given oracle access to any (probabilistic) algorithm $\mathcal{A}: \mathcal{C} \to \{0,1\}^*$, $\mathcal{E}^{\mathcal{A}}$ requires an expected number of at most $2k-1$ queries to $\mathcal{A}$ and, with probability at least $\delta_k^V(\mathcal{A})/k$, it outputs k pairs $(c_1, y_1), (c_2, y_2), \ldots, (c_k, y_k) \in \mathcal{C} \times \{0,1\}^*$ with $V(c_i, y_i) = 1$ for all i and $c_i \neq c_j$ for all $i \neq j$.*

---

[4] Recall that, in order to prove knowledge soundness, it is sufficient to consider deterministic provers (Remark 1).

Proof. The extraction algorithm is defined recursively over k. For this reason, we add a subscript k and write $\mathcal{E}_k^{\mathcal{A}}$ for the extraction algorithm that aims to output k pairs (c_i, y_i). In this proof, we also make the set $\mathcal{D} \subseteq \mathcal{C}$, from which the extractor samples the challenges c_i, explicit by writing $\mathcal{E}_k^{\mathcal{A}}(\mathcal{D})$. This allows the extractor to be deployed on subsets $\mathcal{D}$ of the full challenge set $\mathcal{C}$, i.e., extractor $\mathcal{E}_k^{\mathcal{A}}(\mathcal{D})$ aims to output k pairs (c_i, y_i) with pairwise distinct challenges $c_i \in \mathcal{D}$ and $V(c_i, y_i) = 1$ for all i. When writing $\mathcal{E}_k^{\mathcal{A}}(\mathcal{D})$ we will always implicitly assume that $|\mathcal{D}| \geq k$. Accordingly, we also write

$$\epsilon(\mathcal{A}, \mathcal{D}) := \Pr\big(V(C, \mathcal{A}(C)) = 1\big),$$
$$\delta_k(\mathcal{A}, \mathcal{D}) := \min_{S \subseteq \mathcal{D}:|S|<k} \Pr\big(V(C, \mathcal{A}(C)) = 1 \mid C \notin S\big).$$

where the probability space is defined by means of the randomness of $\mathcal{A}$ and the random variable C being uniformly random in $\mathcal{D} \subseteq \mathcal{C}$. Note that for all $k \geq 1$,

$$\delta_{k+1}(\mathcal{A}, \mathcal{D}) \leq \delta_k(\mathcal{A}, \mathcal{D}) \leq \delta_1(\mathcal{A}, \mathcal{D}) = \epsilon(\mathcal{A}, \mathcal{D}).$$

Let us now define the extraction algorithm. Let $\mathcal{D} \subseteq \mathcal{C}$ be an arbitrary subset with cardinality at least k. For $k = 1$, the extractor $\mathcal{E}_1^{\mathcal{A}}(\mathcal{D})$ simply samples a challenge $c_1 \in \mathcal{D}$ uniformly at random and computes $y_1 \leftarrow \mathcal{A}(c_1)$. If $V(c_1, y_1) = 0$, it outputs $\perp$ and aborts. Otherwise, if $V(c_1, y_1) = 1$, it successfully outputs (c_1, y_1). This extractor queries $\mathcal{A}$ once and it succeeds with probability $\epsilon(\mathcal{A}, \mathcal{D}) = \delta_1(\mathcal{A}, \mathcal{D})$.

For $k > 1$, the extractor $\mathcal{E}_k^{\mathcal{A}}(\mathcal{D})$ first runs the extractor $\mathcal{E}_1^{\mathcal{A}}(\mathcal{D})$. If $\mathcal{E}_1^{\mathcal{A}}(\mathcal{D})$ fails, $\mathcal{E}_k^{\mathcal{A}}(\mathcal{D})$ outputs $\perp$ and aborts; otherwise, if $\mathcal{E}_1^{\mathcal{A}}(\mathcal{D})$ succeeds to output a pair (c_1, y_1), $\mathcal{E}_k^{\mathcal{A}}(\mathcal{D})$ proceeds as follows. It sets $\mathcal{D}' := \mathcal{D} \setminus \{c_1\}$ and runs $\mathcal{E}_{k-1}^{\mathcal{A}}(\mathcal{D}')$. If $\mathcal{E}_{k-1}^{\mathcal{A}}(\mathcal{D}')$ succeeds to output $k - 1$ pairs $(c_2, y_2), \ldots (c_k, y_k)$ then $\mathcal{E}_k^{\mathcal{A}}(\mathcal{D})$ successfully outputs the k pairs $(c_1, y_1), (c_2, y_2), \ldots, (c_k, y_k)$. On the other hand, if $\mathcal{E}_{k-1}^{\mathcal{A}}(\mathcal{D}')$ fails then $\mathcal{E}_k^{\mathcal{A}}(\mathcal{D})$ tosses a coin that returns heads with probability $\epsilon(\mathcal{A}, \mathcal{D})$. This coin can be implemented by running $\mathcal{E}_1^{\mathcal{A}}(\mathcal{D})$, i.e., sampling a random challenge $c \leftarrow \mathcal{D}$ and evaluating $V(c, \mathcal{A}(c))$. If the coin returns heads, $\mathcal{E}_k^{\mathcal{A}}(\mathcal{D})$ outputs $\perp$ and aborts. If the coin returns tails, $\mathcal{E}_k^{\mathcal{A}}(\mathcal{D})$ runs $\mathcal{E}_{k-1}^{\mathcal{A}}(\mathcal{D}')$ once more and performs the same steps as before. The algorithm proceeds in this manner until either it has successfully found a k pairs (c_i, y_i) or until the coin returns heads.

Let us now analyze the success probability and the expected number of $\mathcal{A}$-queries of $\mathcal{E}_k^{\mathcal{A}}$.

Success Probability. We aim to show that, for all $k \in \mathbb{N}$ and for all $\mathcal{D} \subseteq \mathcal{C}$ with $|\mathcal{D}| \geq k$, the success probability $\Delta_k(\mathcal{D})$ of the extractor $\mathcal{E}_k^{\mathcal{A}}(\mathcal{D})$ satisfies

$$\Delta_k(\mathcal{D}) \geq \delta_k(\mathcal{A}, \mathcal{D})/k.$$

The analysis goes by induction. Since

$$\Delta_1(\mathcal{D}) = \epsilon(\mathcal{A}, \mathcal{D}) = \delta_1(\mathcal{A}, \mathcal{D})/1,$$

the induction hypothesis is satisfied for the base case $k = 1$ and all $\mathcal{D} \neq \emptyset$.

Let us now consider $k > 1$ and assume that the induction hypothesis holds for $k' = k - 1$ and all $\mathcal{D}'$ with $|\mathcal{D}'| \geq k - 1$. We consider arbitrary $\mathcal{D} \subseteq \mathcal{C}$ with $|\mathcal{D}| \geq k$. Then if, in its first step, $\mathcal{E}_k^{\mathcal{A}}(\mathcal{D})$ successfully runs extractor $\mathcal{E}_1^{\mathcal{A}}(\mathcal{D})$ (outputting a pair (c_1, y_1) with $V(c_1, y_1) = 1$), it starts running two geometric experiments until one of them finishes. In the first geometric experiment the extractor aims to find an additional set of $k-1$ pairs (c_i, y_i) by running $\mathcal{E}_{k-1}^{\mathcal{A}}(\mathcal{D}')$, where $\mathcal{D}' = \mathcal{D} \setminus \{c_1\}$. By the induction hypothesis, the parameter p of this geometric distribution satisfies

$$p := \Delta_{k-1}(\mathcal{D}') \geq \delta_{k-1}(\mathcal{A}, \mathcal{D}')/(k-1) \geq \delta_k(\mathcal{A}, \mathcal{D})/(k-1).$$

In the second geometric experiment the extractor tosses a coin that returns heads with probability

$$q := \epsilon(\mathcal{A}, \mathcal{D}).$$

The second step of the extractor succeeds if the second geometric experiment does not finish before the first, and so by Lemma 1 this probability is lower bounded by

$$\Pr\big(\mathrm{Geo}(p) \leq \mathrm{Geo}(q)\big) \geq \frac{p}{p+q}$$

$$= \frac{\Delta_{k-1}(\mathcal{D}')}{\Delta_{k-1}(\mathcal{D}') + \epsilon(\mathcal{A}, \mathcal{D})}$$

$$\geq \frac{\delta_k(\mathcal{A}, \mathcal{D})/(k-1)}{\delta_k(\mathcal{A}, \mathcal{D})/(k-1) + \epsilon(\mathcal{A}, \mathcal{D})}$$

$$\geq \frac{\delta_k(\mathcal{A}, \mathcal{D})/(k-1)}{\epsilon(\mathcal{A}, \mathcal{D})/(k-1) + \epsilon(\mathcal{A}, \mathcal{D})}$$

$$= \frac{\delta_k(\mathcal{A}, \mathcal{D})}{k \cdot \epsilon(\mathcal{A}, \mathcal{D})},$$

where the second inequality follows from the monotonicity of the function $x \mapsto \frac{x}{x+q}$. Since the first step of the extractor succeeds with probability $\epsilon(\mathcal{A}, \mathcal{D})$, it follows that $\mathcal{E}_k^{\mathcal{A}}(\mathcal{D})$ succeeds with probability at least $\delta_k(\mathcal{A}, \mathcal{D})/k$.

Therefore, by induction it follows that for all k and $\mathcal{D}$ with $|\mathcal{D}| \geq k$, the extractor $\mathcal{E}_k^{\mathcal{A}}(\mathcal{D})$ succeeds with probability at least $\delta_k(\mathcal{A}, \mathcal{D})/k$. In particular, the extractor $\mathcal{E}_k^{\mathcal{A}}(\mathcal{C})$ succeeds with probability at least $\delta_k(\mathcal{A})/k$, which proves that this extractor has the desired success probability.

Expected Number of $\mathcal{A}$-Queries. For $\mathcal{D} \subseteq \mathcal{C}$ with $|\mathcal{D}| \geq k$, we let $Q_k(\mathcal{D})$ be the expected number of $\mathcal{A}$-queries made by the extractor $\mathcal{E}_k^{\mathcal{A}}(\mathcal{D})$. We will prove that $Q_k(\mathcal{D}) \leq 2k - 1$ for all $k \in \mathbb{N}$ and $\mathcal{D} \subseteq \mathcal{C}$ with $|\mathcal{D}| \geq k$. The proof of this claim goes by induction. First note that, since $Q_1(\mathcal{D}) = 1$ for all $\mathcal{D} \neq \emptyset$, this claim is clearly satisfied for the base case $k = 1$.

Let us now consider $k > 1$ and assume the claim is satisfied for $k' = k - 1$. Let $\mathcal{D} \subseteq \mathcal{C}$ be arbitrary with $|\mathcal{D}| \geq k$. Then, $\mathcal{E}_k^{\mathcal{A}}(\mathcal{D})$ first runs $\mathcal{E}_1^{\mathcal{A}}(\mathcal{D})$, which requires exactly $Q_1(\mathcal{D}) = 1$ query. Then with probability $\epsilon(\mathcal{A}, \mathcal{D})$ it continues to the second step. In each iteration of the second step $\mathcal{E}_k^{\mathcal{A}}(\mathcal{D})$ runs $\mathcal{E}_{k-1}^{\mathcal{A}}(\mathcal{D}')$, for some $\mathcal{D}' \subseteq \mathcal{C}$ with $|\mathcal{D}'| \geq k-1$, and it tosses a coin by running $\mathcal{E}_1^{\mathcal{A}}(\mathcal{D})$. Therefore, each iteration requires an expected number of at most $Q_{k-1}(\mathcal{D}') + 1 \leq 2k - 2$ queries. Moreover, the expected number of tosses until the coin returns heads is $1/\epsilon(\mathcal{A}, \mathcal{D})$. Hence, the expected number of iterations in the second step of this extraction algorithm is at most $1/\epsilon(\mathcal{A}, \mathcal{D})$. It follows that

$$Q_k(\mathcal{D}) \leq 1 + \epsilon(\mathcal{A}, \mathcal{D}) \frac{1}{\epsilon(\mathcal{A}, \mathcal{D})} (2k - 2) = 2k - 1,$$

which proves the claimed upper bound on the expected number of $\mathcal{A}$-queries and completes the proof of the lemma.   □

In the context of a deterministic dishonest prover $\mathcal{P}^*$ attacking a k-special-sound protocol, we make the following observation. First, by basic probability theory, for any $S \subseteq \mathcal{C}$ with $|S| < k$

$$\Pr\big(V(C, \mathcal{A}(C)) = 1 \mid C \notin S\big) = \frac{\Pr\big(V(C, \mathcal{A}(C)) = 1 \wedge C \notin S\big)}{\Pr\big(C \notin S\big)}$$

$$\geq \frac{\Pr\big(V(C, \mathcal{A}(C)) = 1\big) - \Pr\big(C \in S\big)}{\Pr\big(C \notin S\big)}. \tag{1}$$

Thus, the extractor $\mathcal{E}^{\mathcal{A}}$ succeeds with positive probability as soon as $\epsilon(\mathcal{A}) > \Pr\big(C \in S\big)$ for every $S \subseteq \mathcal{C}$ with $|S| < k$. More precisely,

$$\Pr\big(\mathcal{E}^{\mathcal{A}} \text{ succeeds}\big) \geq \frac{\delta_k(\mathcal{A})}{k} \geq \frac{\epsilon(\mathcal{A}) - \kappa}{k(1 - \kappa)},$$

where $\kappa = (k-1)/N$.

This observation confirms that k-special-soundness implies knowledge soundness with knowledge error κ (see also [3] for an alternative proof). This result is summarized as follows.

Theorem 1. *Let $(\mathcal{P}, \mathcal{V})$ be a k-out-of-N special-sound Σ-protocol. Then $(\mathcal{P}, \mathcal{V})$ is knowledge sound with knowledge error $\kappa = (k-1)/N$.*

Note that this is the best we can hope for, since it may be — and for typical schemes this is the case — that for any $S \subseteq \mathcal{C}$ with $|S| < k$, $\mathcal{P}^*$ can prepare a first message a for which he can correctly answer any challenge $c \in S$. Thus, $\kappa = (k-1)/N$ is the trivial cheating probability, confirming the tightness of the theorem.

3.2   Knowledge-Soundness of the Parallel Repetition

When moving to the t-fold parallel repetition $(\mathcal{P}^t, \mathcal{V}^t)$ of the k-special-sound public-coin protocol $(\mathcal{P}, \mathcal{V})$, we consider an algorithm $\mathcal{A}$ that takes as input a row $(c_1, \ldots, c_t) \in \mathcal{C}^t$ of challenges[5] and outputs a string y, and the *success probability* of $\mathcal{A}$ is then defined as

$$\epsilon^V(\mathcal{A}) = \Pr\big(V(C_1, \ldots, C_t, \mathcal{A}(C_1, \ldots, C_t)) = 1\big),$$

for some given $V \colon \mathcal{C}^t \times \{0,1\}^* \to \{0,1\}$ and where the C_i are understood to be independently and uniformly distributed over $\mathcal{C}$.

The obvious instantiation of $\mathcal{A}$ is given by a deterministic prover P^* attacking the considered t-fold parallel repetition $(\mathcal{P}^t, \mathcal{V}^t)$ of $(\mathcal{P}, \mathcal{V})$. More precisely, on input $(c_1, \ldots, c_t)$, $\mathcal{A}$ runs $\mathcal{P}^*$ sending $(c_1, \ldots, c_t)$ as the challenges for the t repetitions of $(\mathcal{P}, \mathcal{V})$, and outputs $\mathcal{P}^*$'s (fixed) first messages $(a_1, \ldots, a_t)$ and its responses $(z_1, \ldots, z_t)$, and the function V is defined as the verification procedure of $\mathcal{V}^t$, which checks each repetition independently and accepts only if all are correct.

Such an $\mathcal{A}$ naturally induces t algorithms $\mathcal{A}_1, \ldots, \mathcal{A}_t$ as considered above in the context of a single execution of a k-special-sound protocol, taking *one* challenge as input: on input c_i, the algorithm $\mathcal{A}_i$ runs $y \leftarrow \mathcal{A}(c_1, \ldots, c_t)$ with c_j chosen uniformly at random from $\mathcal{C}$ for $j \neq i$, and outputs y along with the c_j's for $j \neq i$. We can thus run the extractor from above on all of the $\mathcal{A}_i$'s individually, with the hope being that at least one of them succeeds. We know that for each $\mathcal{A}_i$ individually, the extraction succeeds with probability

$$\delta_k^V(\mathcal{A}_i) = \min_{S_i \subset \mathcal{C} : |S_i| < k} \Pr\big(V(C_i, \mathcal{A}_i(C_i)) = 1 \mid C_i \notin S_i\big), \tag{2}$$

where V is understood to appropriately reorder its inputs. The following lemma allows us to bound the probability that at least one of the extractors $\mathcal{E}^{\mathcal{A}_i}$ succeeds to produce k challenge-response pairs $((c_1, \ldots, c_t), y)$ that all verify V and for which the k choices of c_i are all distinct for the considered i.

Lemma 3. *Let $k, t \in \mathbb{N}$ and $\mathcal{C}$ a finite set with cardinality $N \geq k$. Also, let $V \colon \mathcal{C}^t \times \{0,1\}^* \to \{0,1\}$, and let $\mathcal{A}$ be a (probabilistic) algorithm that takes as input a vector $(c_1, \ldots, c_t) \in \mathcal{C}^t$ and outputs a string $y \in \{0,1\}^*$. Then*

$$\sum_{i=1}^{t} \delta_k^V(\mathcal{A}_i) \geq \frac{\epsilon^V(\mathcal{A}) - \kappa^t}{1 - \kappa},$$

where $\kappa = (k-1)/N$.

Proof. Let Λ denote the event $V(C_1, \ldots, C_t, \mathcal{A}(C_1, \ldots, C_t)) = 1$ and, for $1 \leq i \leq t$, let S_i be such that it minimizes Eq. 2. Moreover, let Γ_i denote the event $C_i \notin S_i$.

Without loss of generality, we may assume that $|S_i| = k - 1$ for all i. Then, for all i,

$$\Pr(\Gamma_i) = \Pr(C_i \notin S_i) = 1 - \Pr(C_i \in S_i) = 1 - \kappa.$$

---

[5] There is no rigorous meaning in the list of challenges forming a *row*; it is merely that later we will also consider a *column* of challenges, which will then play a different *contextual* role.

Moreover, using elementary probability theory,

$$\sum_{i=1}^{t} \delta_k^V(\mathcal{A}_i) = \sum_{i=1}^{t} \Pr\big(V(C_i, \mathcal{A}_i(C_i)) = 1 \mid C_i \notin S_i\big)$$

$$= \sum_{i=1}^{t} \Pr\big(V(C_1, \ldots, C_t, \mathcal{A}(C_1, \ldots, C_t)) = 1 \mid C_i \notin S_i\big)$$

$$= \sum_{i=1}^{t} \Pr(\Lambda \mid \Gamma_i) = \sum_{i=1}^{t} \frac{\Pr(\Lambda \wedge \Gamma_i)}{\Pr(\Gamma_i)} = \sum_{i=1}^{t} \frac{\Pr(\Lambda \wedge \Gamma_i)}{1 - \kappa}$$

$$\geq \frac{\Pr(\Lambda \wedge \exists i : \Gamma_i)}{1 - \kappa} \geq \frac{\Pr(\Lambda) - \Pr(\neg \Gamma_i \; \forall i)}{1 - \kappa} = \frac{\epsilon^V(\mathcal{A}) - \kappa^t}{1 - \kappa},$$

which completes the proof. □

Lemma 3 readily provides a lower bound on $\max_i \delta_k^V(\mathcal{A}_i) \geq \sum_i \delta_k^V(\mathcal{A}_i)/t$, and thus on the success probability of the extractor. However, we can do slightly better. For this purpose, let $\Delta = \min\big(1, \sum_{i=1}^{t} \delta_k^V(\mathcal{A}_i)/k\big)$. Then, by the inequality of the arithmetic and the geometric mean,

$$\left(\prod_{i=1}^{t}\left(1 - \frac{\delta_k^V(\mathcal{A}_i)}{k}\right)\right)^{1/t} \leq \frac{1}{t}\sum_{i=1}^{t}\left(1 - \frac{\delta_k^V(\mathcal{A}_i)}{k}\right) \leq 1 - \frac{\Delta}{t}.$$

Hence, the probability that at least one extractor $\mathcal{E}^{\mathcal{A}_i}$ succeeds equals

$$1 - \prod_{i=1}^{t}\big(1 - \delta_k^V(\mathcal{A}_i)/k\big) \geq 1 - \left(1 - \frac{\Delta}{t}\right)^t \geq 1 - e^{-\Delta} \geq (1 - e^{-1})\Delta \geq \frac{1}{2}\Delta, \quad (3)$$

where the third inequality uses that $(1 - e^{-x}) \geq (1 - e^{-1})x$ for all $0 \leq x \leq 1$, which is easily verified.[6] Hence, by Lemma 3, the probability of at least one of the extractors $\mathcal{E}^{\mathcal{A}_i}$ being successful is at least

$$\frac{\Delta}{2} \geq \frac{\epsilon^V(\mathcal{A}) - \kappa^t}{2k(1 - \kappa)}.$$

From this it follows that the t-fold parallel repetition $(\mathcal{P}^t, \mathcal{V}^t)$ of a k-special-sound protocol $(\mathcal{P}, \mathcal{V})$ is knowledge sound with knowledge error κ^t, where $\kappa = (k-1)/N$ is the knowledge error of a single execution of $(\mathcal{P}, \mathcal{V})$. This parallel repetition result for k-special-sound Σ-protocols is formalized in Theorem 2.

Theorem 2 (Parallel Repetition of k-Special-Sound Σ-Protocols). *Let $(\mathcal{P}, \mathcal{V})$ be a k-out-of-N special-sound Σ-protocol. Let $(\mathcal{P}^t, \mathcal{V}^t)$ be the t-fold parallel repetition of protocol $(\mathcal{P}, \mathcal{V})$. Then $(\mathcal{P}^t, \mathcal{V}^t)$ is knowledge sound with knowledge error κ^t for $\kappa = (k-1)/N$.*

---

[6] For instance by observing that the two sides are equal for $x = 0$ and $x = 1$, and that the left hand side is a concave function while the right hand side is linear.

Also here we have that the knowledge error κ^t matches the trivial cheating probability, which succeeds if in each instance of the parallel repetition the challenge falls into a given set of size $k - 1$.

Remark 4. The above parallel repetition result (and also the generalization of Sect. 4), directly generalize to the parallel composition of t *different* protocols, or to the parallel composition of t different instances of the same protocol. In this case, the knowledge error will be the product of the individual knowledge errors.

4   Parallel Repetition of Multi-round Protocols

We now consider the general case of multi-round protocols. The line of reasoning is quite similar to that of 3-round protocols, but with an appropriately adjusted definition of δ. So, for the remainder of this section, we consider a $(k_1, \ldots, k_\mu)$-special-sound $(2\mu+1)$-round public-coin interactive proof $(\mathcal{P}, \mathcal{V})$, where the verifier samples its j-th challenge uniformly at random from a finite set $\mathcal{C}^{[j]}$ for $1 \leq j \leq \mu$. We denote the superscript j with square brackets to distinguish the set $\mathcal{C}^{[j]}$ from the j-fold Cartesian product $\mathcal{C}^j$. Eventually, we want to analyze its t-fold parallel repetition $(\mathcal{P}^t, \mathcal{V}^t)$, but again we first consider a single invocation.

4.1   Knowledge Soundness of a Single Invocation

Here, we consider a (possibly randomized) algorithm $\mathcal{A}$ that takes as input a column $(c^1, \ldots, c^\mu) \in \mathcal{C}^{[1]} \times \cdots \times \mathcal{C}^{[\mu]}$ of challenges and outputs a string y, and we consider a function

$$V : \mathcal{C}^{[1]} \times \cdots \times \mathcal{C}^{[\mu]} \times \{0,1\}^* \to \{0,1\}.$$

The obvious instantiation is a deterministic prover $\mathcal{P}^*$ attacking the considered protocol. Formally, on input $(c^1, \ldots, c^\mu)$, $\mathcal{A}$ runs $\mathcal{P}^*$, sending c^1 in the first challenge round, c^2 in the second, etc., and eventually $\mathcal{A}$ outputs all of $\mathcal{P}^*$'s messages. Then $V : \mathcal{C}^{[1]} \times \cdots \times \mathcal{C}^{[\mu]} \times \{0,1\}^* \to \{0,1\}$ captures the verification procedure of $\mathcal{V}$, i.e., $V(c^1, \ldots, c^\mu, y) = 1$ if and only if the corresponding transcript is accepting. This instantiation results in a deterministic algorithm $\mathcal{A}$. However, again, it is crucial that in general $\mathcal{A}$ may be probabilistic, i.e., its output y is not necessarily uniquely determined by its input $(c^1, \ldots, c^\mu)$.

Syntactically identical to the previous section, the *success probability* of $\mathcal{A}$ is defined as

$$\epsilon^V(\mathcal{A}) := \Pr(V(C, \mathcal{A}(C)) = 1),$$

where here $C = (C^1, \ldots, C^\mu)$ is uniformly random in $\mathcal{C}^{[1]} \times \cdots \times \mathcal{C}^{[\mu]}$. However, here the goal of the extractor is slightly different: the goal is to find correct responses for a **k**-tree of challenges, where $\mathbf{k} = (k_1, \ldots, k_\mu)$. Generalizing the case of ordinary 3-round protocols, the figure of merit here is

$$\delta_{\mathbf{k}}^V(\mathcal{A}) := \min_{S^{[1]}, S^{[2]}(\cdot), \ldots, S^{[\mu]}(\cdot)} \Pr\left(\Lambda \,\middle|\, \begin{array}{l} C^1 \notin S^{[1]} \wedge C^2 \notin S^{[2]}(C^1) \wedge \cdots \\ \cdots \wedge C^\mu \notin S^{[\mu]}(C^1, \ldots, C^{\mu-1}) \end{array}\right), \quad (4)$$

where Λ denotes the event $V(C, \mathcal{A}(C)) = 1$ and the minimum is over all sets $S^{[1]} \in C^{[1]}|_{<k_1}$, and over all functions $S^{[2]} \colon C^{[1]} \to C^{[2]}|_{<k_2}$, $S^{[3]} \colon C^{[1]} \times C^{[2]} \to C^{[3]}|_{<k_3}$, etc. Here for any set C and $k \in \mathbb{N}$, $C|_{<k}$ denotes the set of subsets of C with cardinality smaller than k.

Indeed, the following lemma shows that there exists an expected polynomial time extractor $\mathcal{E}^{\mathcal{A}}$ with oracle access to $\mathcal{A}$ that, with probability $\delta_{\mathbf{k}}^{V}(\mathcal{A}) / \prod_{i=1}^{\mu} k_i$, succeeds to extract correct responses for a $\mathbf{k}$-tree of challenges. Exploiting the abstract notation of Lemma 2, the proof of this lemma follows by induction over the number of challenges μ sent by the verifier.

Lemma 4 (Multi-round Extraction Algorithm). *Let* $\mathbf{k} = (k_1, \ldots, k_\mu) \in \mathbb{N}^\mu$, $K = \prod_{i=1}^{\mu} k_i$, $C^{[1]}, \ldots, C^{[\mu]}$ *finite sets* $C^{[j]}$ *with cardinality* $N_j \geq k_j$, *and let* $V \colon C^{[1]} \times \cdots \times C^{[\mu]} \times \{0,1\}^* \to \{0,1\}$.

Then, there exists an algorithm $\mathcal{E}^{\mathcal{A}}$ *so that, given oracle access to any (probabilistic) algorithm* $\mathcal{A} \colon C^{[1]} \times \cdots \times C^{[\mu]} \to \{0,1\}^*$, $\mathcal{E}^{\mathcal{A}}$ *requires an expected number of at most* $2^\mu \cdot K$ *queries to* $\mathcal{A}$ *and, with probability at least* $\delta_{\mathbf{k}}^{V}(\mathcal{A})/K$, *outputs* K *pairs* $(\mathbf{c}_1, y_1), \ldots, (\mathbf{c}_K, y_K) \in C^{[1]} \times \cdots \times C^{[\mu]} \times \{0,1\}^*$ *with* $V(\mathbf{c}_i, y_i) = 1$ *for all* i *and such that the vectors* $\mathbf{c}_i \in C^{[1]} \times \cdots \times C^{[\mu]}$ *form a* $\mathbf{k}$-*tree.*

Proof. The proof goes by induction on μ. For the base case $\mu = 1$, the lemma directly follow from Lemma 2. So let us assume the lemma holds for $\mu' = \mu - 1$.

Then, for any $c \in C^{[1]}$, let $\mathcal{A}_c$ be the algorithm that takes as input a vector $(c^2, \ldots, c^\mu) \in C^{[2]} \times \cdots \times C^{[\mu]}$ and runs $\mathcal{A}(c, c^2, \ldots, c^\mu)$. The function V_c is defined accordingly, i.e.,

$$V_c \colon C^{[2]} \times \cdots \times C^{[\mu]} \times \{0,1\}^* \to \{0,1\}, \quad (c^2, \ldots, c^\mu, y) \mapsto V(c, c^2, \ldots, c^\mu, y).$$

Moreover, let $\mathbf{k}' = (k_2, \ldots, k_\mu) \in \mathbb{N}^{\mu-1}$ and $K' = \prod_{i=2}^{\mu} k_i$.

By the induction hypothesis there exists an algorithm $\mathcal{E}_{\mu-1}^{\mathcal{A}_c}$ that outputs a set $\mathcal{Y} = \{(c_i^2, \ldots, c_i^\mu, y_i)\}_{1 \leq i \leq K'}$ with

$$V(c, c_i^2, \ldots, c_i^\mu, y_i) = 1 \, \forall i \quad \text{and} \quad \{(c_i^2, \ldots, c_i^\mu)\}_i \in \mathrm{TREE}(k_2, \ldots, k_\mu).$$

Moreover, $\mathcal{E}_{\mu-1}^{\mathcal{A}_c}$ requires an expected number of at most $2^{\mu-1} \cdot K'$ queries to $\mathcal{A}_c$ (and thus to $\mathcal{A}$) and succeeds with probability at least $\delta_{\mathbf{k}'}^{V_c}(\mathcal{A}_c)/K'$. We define $W \colon C^{[1]} \times \{0,1\}^* \to \{0,1\}$, by setting $W(c, \mathcal{Y}) = 1$ if and only if $\mathcal{Y}$ is a set satisfying the above properties.

Now let $\mathcal{B}^{\mathcal{A}} \colon C^{[1]} \to \{0,1\}^*$ be the algorithm, with oracle access to $\mathcal{A}$, that takes as input an element $c \in C^{[1]}$ and runs $\mathcal{E}_{\mu-1}^{\mathcal{A}_c}$. By Lemma 2, there exists an expected polynomial time algorithm $\mathcal{E}_1^{\mathcal{B}^{\mathcal{A}}}$, with oracle access to $\mathcal{B}^{\mathcal{A}}$, that aims to output k_1 pairs $(c_1, \mathcal{Y}_1), \ldots, (c_{k_1}, \mathcal{Y}_{k_1}) \in C^{[1]} \times \{0,1\}^*$ with $W(c_i, \mathcal{Y}_i) = 1$ for all i and $c_i \neq c_j$ for all $i \neq j$. The extractor $\mathcal{E}^{\mathcal{A}}$ simply runs $\mathcal{E}_1^{\mathcal{B}^{\mathcal{A}}}$. Note that, by the associativity of the composition of oracle algorithms, $\mathcal{E}^{\mathcal{A}} = \mathcal{E}_1^{\mathcal{B}^{\mathcal{A}}} = (\mathcal{E}_1^{\mathcal{B}})^{\mathcal{A}}$ is indeed an algorithm with oracle access to $\mathcal{A}$.

Let us now analyze the success probability and the expected number of $\mathcal{A}$-queries of the algorithm $\mathcal{E}_1^{\mathcal{B}^{\mathcal{A}}}$ and therefore of $\mathcal{E}^{\mathcal{A}}$.

Success Probability. Again by Lemma 2, it follows that $\mathcal{E}_1^{\mathcal{B}^{\mathcal{A}}}$ succeeds with probability at least

$$
\begin{aligned}
\delta_{k_1}^W(\mathcal{B}^{\mathcal{A}})/k_1 &= \min_{S^{[1]} \subset \mathcal{C}^{[1]}, |S^{[1]}| < k_1} \frac{\Pr\big(W(C, \mathcal{B}^{\mathcal{A}}(C)) = 1 \mid C \notin S^{[1]}\big)}{k_1} \\
&= \min_{S^{[1]} \subset \mathcal{C}^{[1]}, |S^{[1]}| < k_1} \frac{\Pr\big(W(C, \mathcal{B}^{\mathcal{A}}(C)) = 1 \wedge C \notin S^{[1]}\big)}{k_1 \cdot \Pr(C \notin S^{[1]})} \\
&= \min_{S^{[1]} \subset \mathcal{C}^{[1]}, |S^{[1]}| < k_1} \frac{\sum_{c \notin S^{[1]}} \Pr(C = c) \cdot \Pr\big(W(c, \mathcal{B}^{\mathcal{A}}(c)) = 1\big)}{k_1 \cdot \Pr(C \notin S^{[1]})} \\
&= \min_{S^{[1]} \subset \mathcal{C}^{[1]}, |S^{[1]}| < k_1} \frac{\sum_{c \notin S^{[1]}} \Pr(C = c) \cdot \Pr\big(W(c, \mathcal{E}_{\mu-1}^{\mathcal{A}_c}) = 1\big)}{k_1 \cdot \Pr(C \notin S^{[1]})} \\
&\geq \min_{S^{[1]} \subset \mathcal{C}^{[1]}, |S^{[1]}| < k_1} \frac{\sum_{c \notin S^{[1]}} \Pr(C = c) \cdot \delta_{\mathbf{k}'}^{V_c}(\mathcal{A}_c)}{k_1 \cdot K' \cdot \Pr(C \notin S^{[1]})} \\
&= \min_{S^{[1]} \subset \mathcal{C}^{[1]}, |S^{[1]}| < k_1} \frac{\sum_{c \notin S^{[1]}} \Pr(C = c) \cdot \delta_{\mathbf{k}'}^{V_c}(\mathcal{A}_c)}{K \cdot \Pr(C \notin S^{[1]})}, \quad (5)
\end{aligned}
$$

where C is uniformly random in $\mathcal{C}$. Now note that

$$
\delta_{\mathbf{k}'}^{V_c}(\mathcal{A}_c) = \min_{S^{[2]}(\cdot), \dots, S^{[\mu]}(\cdot)} \Pr\left(\Lambda \,\middle|\, \begin{matrix} C^1 = c \wedge C^2 \notin S^{[2]}(C^1) \wedge \cdots \\ \cdots \wedge C^\mu \notin S^{[\mu]}(C^1, \dots, C^{\mu-1}) \end{matrix}\right),
$$

where Λ denotes the event $V(C, \mathcal{A}(C)) = 1$. Hence,

$$
\sum_{c \notin S^{[1]}} \Pr(C = c) \cdot \delta_{\mathbf{k}'}^{V_c}(\mathcal{A}_c) =
$$

$$
\min_{S^{[2]}(\cdot), \dots, S^{[\mu]}(\cdot)} \Pr\left(\Lambda \wedge C^1 \notin S^{[1]} \,\middle|\, \begin{matrix} C^2 \notin S^{[2]}(C^1) \wedge \cdots \\ \cdots \wedge C^\mu \notin S^{[\mu]}(C^1, \dots, C^{\mu-1}) \end{matrix}\right).
$$

Plugging this equality into Eq. 5, shows that

$$
\delta_{k_1}^W(\mathcal{B}^{\mathcal{A}})/k_1 \geq \frac{\delta_{\mathbf{k}}^V(\mathcal{A})}{K},
$$

which shows that $\mathcal{E}_1^{\mathcal{B}^{\mathcal{A}}}$ has the desired success probability.

Expected Number of $\mathcal{A}$-Queries. By Lemma 2, it follows that $\mathcal{E}_1^{\mathcal{B}^{\mathcal{A}}}$ requires an expected number of at most $2k_1$ queries to $\mathcal{B}^{\mathcal{A}}$. By the induction hypothesis it follows that $\mathcal{B}^{\mathcal{A}}$ requires an expected number of at most $2^{\mu-1} \cdot K'$ queries to $\mathcal{A}$. Hence, $\mathcal{E}^{\mathcal{A}} = \mathcal{E}_1^{\mathcal{B}^{\mathcal{A}}}$ requires an expected number of at most $2^\mu \cdot K$ queries to $\mathcal{A}$, which completes the proof of the lemma. □

Let $S^{[1]}, S^{[2]}(\cdot), \dots, S^{[\mu]}(\cdot)$ be the arguments minimizing Eq. 4. Further, let Λ denote the event $V(C, \mathcal{A}(C)) = 1$ and let Γ denote the event

$$
\Gamma = C^1 \notin S^{[1]} \wedge C^2 \notin S^{[2]}(C^1) \wedge \cdots \wedge C^\mu \notin S^{[\mu]}(C^1, \dots, C^{\mu-1}).
$$

Then, using the same kind of reasoning as in Eq. 1, we have

$$\delta_{\mathbf{k}}^V(\mathcal{A}) = \Pr(\Lambda \mid \Gamma) = \frac{\Pr(\Lambda \wedge \Gamma)}{\Pr(\Gamma)} \geq \frac{\Pr(\Lambda) - \Pr(\neg \Gamma)}{\Pr(\Gamma)} = \frac{\epsilon^V(\mathcal{A}) - \kappa}{1 - \kappa},$$

where

$$\kappa = \Pr(\neg \Gamma) = 1 - \prod_{j=1}^{\mu} \frac{N_j - k_j + 1}{N_j}.$$

This confirms that a $(k_1, \ldots, k_\mu)$-special-sound protocol is knowledge sound with knowledge error κ. See [3] for an alternative and the original proof of this statement. This result is formalized as follows.

Theorem 3. *Let $(\mathcal{P}, \mathcal{V})$ be a $(k_1, \ldots, k_\mu)$-out-of-$(N_1, \ldots, N_\mu)$ special-sound protocol. Then $(\mathcal{P}, \mathcal{V})$ is knowledge sound with knowledge error*

$$\kappa = 1 - \prod_{j=1}^{\mu} \frac{N_j - k_j + 1}{N_j}.$$

Once more, κ matches the trivial cheating probability.

4.2   Knowledge-Soundness of the Parallel Repetition

We finally move towards stating and proving our main general parallel repetition result for multi-round protocols. Thus, consider the t-fold parallel repetition $(\mathcal{P}^t, \mathcal{V}^t)$ of the given $(k_1, \ldots, k_\mu)$-special-sound $(2\mu + 1)$-round public-coin interactive proof $(\mathcal{P}, \mathcal{V})$.

We consider an algorithm $\mathcal{A}$ that takes as input a *row* $(\mathbf{c}_1, \ldots, \mathbf{c}_t)$ of *columns* $\mathbf{c}_i = (c_i^1, \ldots, c_i^\mu) \in \mathcal{C}^{[1]} \times \cdots \times \mathcal{C}^{[\mu]}$ of challenges and outputs a string y. Furthermore, we consider a verification function V, which then defines the *success probability* of $\mathcal{A}$ as

$$\epsilon^V(\mathcal{A}) = \Pr\big(V(C, \mathcal{A}(C)) = 1\big),$$

where $C = (C_1, \ldots, C_t)$ with C_i distributed uniformly and independently over $\mathcal{C}^{[1]} \times \cdots \mathcal{C}^{[\mu]}$ for all $1 \leq i \leq t$.

Again, the obvious instantiation for $\mathcal{A}$ is a deterministic dishonest prover $\mathcal{P}^*$ attacking $(\mathcal{P}^t, \mathcal{V}^t)$. More precisely, on input a row $(\mathbf{c}_1, \ldots, \mathbf{c}_t)$ of columns, $\mathcal{A}$ runs $\mathcal{P}^*$ sending $(\mathbf{c}_1, \ldots, \mathbf{c}_t)$ as the challenges, and outputs all of $\mathcal{P}^*$'s messages, and the function V is defined as the verification check that $\mathcal{V}^t$ performs.

Such an $\mathcal{A}$ naturally induces t algorithms $\mathcal{A}_1, \ldots, \mathcal{A}_t$ as considered above in the context of a single execution of a multi-round protocol, taking one challenge-column as input and outputting one string: on input $\mathbf{c}_i$, the algorithm $\mathcal{A}_i$ runs $y \leftarrow \mathcal{A}(\mathbf{c}_1, \ldots, \mathbf{c}_\mu)$ with $\mathbf{c}_j$ chosen uniformly at random from $\mathcal{C}^{[1]} \times \cdots \times \mathcal{C}^{[\mu]}$ for $j \neq i$, and outputs y along with the $\mathbf{c}_j$'s for $j \neq i$. Thus, we can run the extractor from Lemma 4 on all of the $\mathcal{A}_i$'s individually, with the goal being that at least one of them succeeds. For each $\mathcal{A}_i$ individually, the extraction succeeds with probability at least

$$\delta_{\mathbf{k}}^V(\mathcal{A}_i)/K =$$

$$\min_{S_i^{[1]}, S_i^{[2]}(\cdot), \ldots, S_i^{[\mu]}(\cdot)} \Pr\left(\Lambda_i \left| \begin{array}{c} C_i^1 \notin S_i^{[1]} \wedge C_i^2 \notin S_i^{[2]}(C_i^1) \wedge \cdots \\ \cdots \wedge C_i^\mu \notin S_i^{[\mu]}(C_i^1, \ldots, C_i^{\mu-1}) \end{array} \right.\right)/K, \quad (6)$$

where Λ_i denotes the event $V(C_i, \mathcal{A}_i(C_i)) = 1$ and V is understood to appropriately reorder its inputs and $K = \prod_{i=1}^\mu k_i$. The following lemma allows us to bound the probability that at least one of the extractors $\mathcal{E}^{\mathcal{A}_i}$ succeeds.

Lemma 5. *Let* $\mathbf{k} \in \mathbb{N}^\mu$, $t \in \mathbb{N}$, $\mathcal{C}^{[1]}, \ldots, \mathcal{C}^{[\mu]}$ *finite sets* $\mathcal{C}^{[j]}$ *with cardinality* $N_j \geq k_j$, $V: \left(\mathcal{C}^{[1]} \times \cdots \times \mathcal{C}^{[\mu]}\right)^t \times \{0,1\}^* \to \{0,1\}$, *and* $\mathcal{A}$ *a (probabilistic) algorithm that takes as input a row* $(\mathbf{c}_1, \ldots, \mathbf{c}_t)$ *of columns* $\mathbf{c}_i = (c_i^1, \ldots, c_i^\mu) \in \mathcal{C}^{[1]} \times \cdots \times \mathcal{C}^{[\mu]}$ *and outputs a string* $y \in \{0,1\}^*$. *Then*

$$\sum_{i=1}^t \delta_{\mathbf{k}}^V(\mathcal{A}_i) \geq \frac{\epsilon^V(\mathcal{A}) - \kappa^t}{1 - \kappa},$$

where

$$\kappa = 1 - \prod_{j=1}^\mu \frac{N_j - k_j + 1}{N_j}.$$

Proof. Let Λ denote the event $V(C, \mathcal{A}(C)) = 1$ and, for $1 \leq i \leq t$, let $S_i^{[1]}$ and $S_i^{[2]}(\cdot), \ldots, S_i^{[\mu]}(\cdot)$ be such that they minimize Eq. 6. Moreover, let Γ_i denote the event

$$C_i^1 \notin S_i^{[1]} \wedge C_i^2 \notin S_i^{[2]}(C_i^1) \wedge \cdots \wedge C_i^\mu \notin S_i^{[\mu]}(C_i^1, \ldots, C_i^{\mu-1}).$$

Without loss of generality, we may assume that $|S_i^{[1]}| = k_1 - 1$ and $S_i^{[j]} : \mathcal{C}^{[1]} \times \cdots \times \mathcal{C}^{[j-1]} \to \{S \subset \mathcal{C}^{[j]} : |S| = k_j - 1\}$ for all $2 \leq j \leq \mu$ and $1 \leq i \leq t$. Then, for all $1 \leq i \leq t$,

$$\Pr(\Gamma_i) = \prod_{j=1}^\mu \frac{N - k_j + 1}{N} = 1 - \kappa.$$

Moreover, using elementary probability theory,

$$\sum_{i=1}^t \delta_{\mathbf{k}}^V(\mathcal{A}_i) = \sum_{i=1}^t \Pr(\Lambda \mid \Gamma_i) = \sum_{i=1}^t \frac{\Pr(\Lambda \wedge \Gamma_i)}{\Pr(\Gamma_i)} = \sum_{i=1}^t \frac{\Pr(\Lambda \wedge \Gamma_i)}{1 - \kappa}$$

$$\geq \frac{\Pr(\Lambda \wedge \exists i : \Gamma_i)}{1 - \kappa} \geq \frac{\Pr(\Lambda) - \Pr(\neg \Gamma_i \,\forall i)}{1 - \kappa} = \frac{\epsilon^V(\mathcal{A}) - \kappa^t}{1 - \kappa},$$

which completes the proof. □

As for the parallel repetition of a 3-round protocol, it follows that the probability of at least one of the extractors $\mathcal{E}^{\mathcal{A}_i}$ being successful is at least

$$\frac{\Delta}{2} \geq \frac{\epsilon^V(\mathcal{A}) - \kappa^t}{2K(1 - \kappa)},$$

where $\Delta = \min\left(1, \sum_{i=1}^t \delta_{\mathbf{k}}^V(\mathcal{A}_i)/K\right)$ and $K = \prod_{i=1}^\mu k_i$. This gives us the following strong parallel repetition result for $(k_1, \ldots, k_\mu)$-special-sound protocols.

Theorem 4 (Parallel Repetition for Multi-Round Protocols). *Let $(\mathcal{P}, \mathcal{V})$ be a $(k_1, \ldots, k_\mu)$-out-of-$(N_1, \ldots, N_\mu)$ special-sound protocol. Let $(\mathcal{P}^t, \mathcal{V}^t)$ be the t-fold parallel repetition of protocol $(\mathcal{P}, \mathcal{V})$. Then $(\mathcal{P}^t, \mathcal{V}^t)$ is knowledge sound with knowledge error κ^t, where*

$$\kappa = 1 - \prod_{j=1}^\mu \frac{N_j - k_j + 1}{N_j},$$

is the knowledge error of $(\mathcal{P}, \mathcal{V})$.

Also here, the knowledge error κ^t coincides with the trivial cheating probability $\prod_i \Pr(\neg \Gamma_i)$, which is potentially achievable for $(k_1, \ldots, k_\mu)$-out-of-$(N_1, \ldots, N_\mu)$ special-sound protocols.

5 Threshold Parallel Repetition

The knowledge error κ^t of the t-fold parallel repetition $(\mathcal{P}^t, \mathcal{V}^t)$ of a **k**-special-sound protocol $(\mathcal{P}, \mathcal{V})$ decreases exponentially with t. However, the completeness error of $(\mathcal{P}^t, \mathcal{V}^t)$ equals $\rho' = 1 - (1 - \rho)^t$, where ρ is the completeness error of $(\mathcal{P}, \mathcal{V})$. Hence, if $\rho \notin \{0, 1\}$, the completeness error of $(\mathcal{P}^t, \mathcal{V}^t)$ increases quickly with t. In order to decrease both the knowledge and the completeness error simultaneously, we consider a *threshold parallel repetition*. The *s*-out-of-*t* threshold parallel repetition of an interactive protocol $(\mathcal{P}, \mathcal{V})$, denoted by $(\mathcal{P}^{s,t}, \mathcal{V}^{s,t})$, runs t instances of $(\mathcal{P}, \mathcal{V})$ in parallel and $\mathcal{V}^{s,t}$ accepts if at least *s*-out-of-*t* instances are accepted. In particular, it holds that $(\mathcal{P}^{t,t}, \mathcal{V}^{t,t}) = (\mathcal{P}^t, \mathcal{V}^t)$. In this section, we show that if $(\mathcal{P}, \mathcal{V})$ is **k**-special-sound then $(\mathcal{P}^{s,t}, \mathcal{V}^{s,t})$ is knowledge sound. We will immediately consider the general case of multi-round protocols.

As in Sect. 4.2, we consider an algorithm $\mathcal{A}$ that takes as input a row $\mathbf{c} = (\mathbf{c}_1, \ldots, \mathbf{c}_t)$ of columns $\mathbf{c}_i = (c_i^1, \ldots, c_i^\mu) \in \mathcal{C}^{[1]} \times \cdots \times \mathcal{C}^{[\mu]}$ of challenges and outputs a string y. However, this time we consider t different verification functions

$$V_i \colon \left(\mathcal{C}^{[1]} \times \cdots \times \mathcal{C}^{[\mu]}\right)^t \times \{0,1\}^* \to \{0,1\},$$

together with one additional *threshold* verification function defined as follows:

$$V(\mathbf{c}, y) = \begin{cases} 1 & \text{if } \sum_{i=1}^t V_i(\mathbf{c}, y) \geq s, \\ 0 & \text{otherwise}. \end{cases}$$

The obvious instantiation for $\mathcal{A}$ is a deterministic dishonest prover $\mathcal{P}^*$ attacking $(\mathcal{P}^{s,t}, \mathcal{V}^{s,t})$. This instantiation defines V_i as the verification that the i-th instance of $\mathcal{V}$ performs. The verification function V then captures the verification that $\mathcal{V}^{s,t}$ performs.

As before, such $\mathcal{A}$ induces t algorithms $\mathcal{A}_1, \ldots, \mathcal{A}_t$ as considered in the context of a single execution of $(\mathcal{P}, \mathcal{V})$, taking one challenge-column as input and outputting one string: on input $\mathbf{c}_i$, the algorithm $\mathcal{A}_i$ runs $y \leftarrow \mathcal{A}(\mathbf{c}_1, \ldots, \mathbf{c}_\ell)$ with $\mathbf{c}_j$ chosen uniformly at random from $\mathcal{C}^{[1]} \times \cdots \times \mathcal{C}^{[\mu]}$ for $j \neq i$, and outputs y along with the $\mathbf{c}_j$'s for $j \neq i$. For each $\mathcal{A}_i$, we can run the extractor from Lemma 4, which succeeds with probability at least

$$\delta_{\mathbf{k}}^{V_i}(\mathcal{A}_i) / \prod_{i=1}^{\mu} k_i =$$

$$\min_{S_i^{[1]}, S_i^{[2]}(\cdot), \ldots, S_i^{[\mu]}(\cdot)} \Pr\left(\Lambda_i \;\middle|\; \begin{matrix} C_i^1 \notin S_i^{[1]} \wedge C_i^2 \notin S_i^{[2]}(C_i^1) \wedge \\ \cdots \wedge C_i^\mu \notin S_i^{[\mu]}(C_i^1, \ldots, C_i^{\mu-1}) \end{matrix} \right) \Bigg/ \prod_{i=1}^{\mu} k_i, \quad (7)$$

where Λ_i denotes the event $V_i(C_i, \mathcal{A}_i(C_i)) = 1$ and V_i is understood to appropriately reorder its inputs. The following lemma is a generalization of Lemma 5 and it allows us to bound the probability that at least one of the extractors $\mathcal{E}^{\mathcal{A}_i}$ succeeds.

Lemma 6. *Let* $\mathbf{k} \in \mathbb{N}^\mu$, $t \in \mathbb{N}$, $\mathcal{C}^{[1]}, \ldots, \mathcal{C}^{[\mu]}$ *finite sets* $\mathcal{C}^{[j]}$ *with cardinality* $N_j \geq k_j$ *and* $\mathcal{A}$ *a (probabilistic) algorithm that takes as input a row* $(\mathbf{c}_1, \ldots, \mathbf{c}_t)$ *of columns* $\mathbf{c}_i = (c_i^1, \ldots, c_i^\mu) \in \mathcal{C}^{[1]} \times \cdots \times \mathcal{C}^{[\mu]}$ *and outputs a string* $y \in \{0,1\}^*$. *Then*

$$\sum_{i=1}^{t} \delta_{\mathbf{k}}^{V_i}(\mathcal{A}_i) \geq \frac{\epsilon^V(\mathcal{A}) - \kappa^{s,t}}{1 - \kappa},$$

where

$$\kappa^{s,t} = \sum_{\ell=s}^{t} \binom{t}{\ell} \kappa^\ell (1 - \kappa)^{t-\ell} \quad and \quad \kappa = 1 - \prod_{j=1}^{\mu} \frac{N_j - k_j + 1}{N_j}.$$

Note that $\kappa^{s,t}$ is the probability of being successful at least s times when given t trials, when each trial is successful with independent probability κ.

Proof. For $1 \leq i \leq t$, let Λ_i denote the event $V_i(C, \mathcal{A}_i(C)) = 1$ and let $S_i^{[1]}$ and $S_i^{[2]}(\cdot) \ldots, S_i^{[\mu]}(\cdot)$ such that they minimize Eq. 7. Moreover, let Γ_i denote the event

$$C_i^1 \notin S_i^{[1]} \wedge C_i^2 \notin S_i^{[2]}(C_i^1) \wedge \cdots \wedge C_i^\mu \notin S_i^{[\mu]}(C_i^1, \ldots, C_i^{\mu-1}).$$

Without loss of generality, we may assume that $|S_i^{[1]}| = k_1 - 1$ and $S_i^{[j]} : \mathcal{C}^{[1]} \times \cdots \mathcal{C}^{[j-1]} \rightarrow \{S \subset \mathcal{C}^{[j]} : |S| = k_j - 1\}$ for all $2 \leq j \leq \mu$ and $1 \leq i \leq t$. Then, for all $1 \leq i \leq t$,

$$\Pr(\Gamma_i) = \prod_{j=1}^{\mu} \frac{N - k_j + 1}{N} = 1 - \kappa.$$

Moreover, using elementary probability theory,

$$\sum_{i=1}^{t} \delta_{\mathbf{k}}^{V_i}(\mathcal{A}_i) = \sum_{i=1}^{t} \Pr(\Lambda_i \mid \Gamma_i) = \sum_{i=1}^{t} \frac{\Pr(\Lambda_i \wedge \Gamma_i)}{\Pr(\Gamma_i)} = \sum_{i=1}^{t} \frac{\Pr(\Lambda_i \wedge \Gamma_i)}{1 - \kappa}$$

$$\geq \frac{\Pr(\exists i : \Lambda_i \wedge \Gamma_i)}{1 - \kappa} \geq \frac{\Pr(|\{i : \Lambda_i\}| \geq s \wedge |\{i : \Gamma_i\}| \geq t - s + 1)}{1 - \kappa}$$

$$\geq \frac{\Pr(|\{i : \Lambda_i\}| \geq s) - \Pr(|\{i : \Gamma_i\}| \leq t - s)}{1 - \kappa} \geq \frac{\epsilon^V(\mathcal{A}) - \kappa^{s,t}}{1 - \kappa}.$$

which completes the proof.   □

As before (see Eq. 3), it follows that the probability of at least one of the extractors $\mathcal{E}^{\mathcal{A}_i}$ being successful is at least

$$\frac{\Delta}{2} \geq \frac{\epsilon^V(\mathcal{A}) - \kappa^{s,t}}{2K(1 - \kappa)},$$

where $\Delta = \min\left(1, \sum_{i=1}^{t} \delta_{\mathbf{k}}^{V_i}(\mathcal{A}_i)/K\right)$ and $K = \prod_{i=1}^{\mu} k_i$. This gives us the following threshold parallel repetition result for $(k_1, \ldots, k_\mu)$-special-sound protocols.

Theorem 5 (Threshold Parallel Repetition Theorem). *Let* $(\mathcal{P}, \mathcal{V})$ *be a* $(k_1, \ldots, k_\mu)$-*out-of-*$(N_1, \ldots, N_\mu)$ *special-sound protocol. Let* $(\mathcal{P}^{s,t}, \mathcal{V}^{s,t})$ *be the s-out-of-t threshold parallel repetition of protocol* $(\mathcal{P}, \mathcal{V})$. *Then* $(\mathcal{P}^{s,t}, \mathcal{V}^{s,t})$ *is knowledge sound with knowledge error*

$$\kappa^{s,t} = \sum_{\ell=s}^{t} \binom{t}{\ell} \kappa^\ell (1 - \kappa)^{t-\ell},$$

where

$$\kappa = 1 - \prod_{j=1}^{\mu} \frac{N_j - k_j + 1}{N_j},$$

is the knowledge error of $(\mathcal{P}, \mathcal{V})$.

As before, the knowledge error $\kappa^{s,t}$ coincides with the trivial cheating probability for $(\mathcal{P}^{s,t}, \mathcal{V}^{s,t})$, confirming the tightness of Theorem 5.

Note that the completeness error of $(\mathcal{P}^{s,t}, \mathcal{V}^{s,t})$ equals

$$\rho^{s,t} = \sum_{\ell=0}^{s-1} \binom{t}{\ell} \rho^{t-\ell} (1 - \rho)^\ell.$$

Hence, the completeness error $\rho^{s,t}$ increases and the knowledge error decreases $\kappa^{s,t}$ in s. Moreover, it is easily seen that for t large enough and $\kappa \cdot t < s < (1 - \rho)t$ the threshold parallel repetition $(\mathcal{P}^{s,t}, \mathcal{V}^{s,t})$ has a smaller knowledge and a smaller completeness error than $(\mathcal{P}, \mathcal{V})$, i.e., $\kappa^{s,t} < \kappa$ and $\rho^{s,t} < \rho$. In contrast to standard parallel repetition, threshold parallel repetition therefore allows both these errors to be reduced.

Acknowledgments. We would like to thank Michael Klooß for helpful comments and insightful discussions. The first author has been supported by EU H2020 project No. 780701 (PROMETHEUS) and the Vraaggestuurd Programma Cyber Security & Resilience, part of the Dutch Top Sector High Tech Systems and Materials program.

References

1. Attema, T., Cramer, R.: Compressed Σ-protocol theory and practical application to plug & play secure algorithmics. In: Micciancio, D., Ristenpart, T. (eds.) CRYPTO 2020, Part III. LNCS, vol. 12172, pp. 513–543. Springer, Cham (2020). https://doi.org/10.1007/978-3-030-56877-1_18
2. Attema, T., Cramer, R., Fehr, S.: Compressing proofs of k-out-of-n partial knowledge. In: Malkin, T., Peikert, C. (eds.) CRYPTO 2021, Part IV. LNCS, vol. 12828, pp. 65–91. Springer, Cham (2021). https://doi.org/10.1007/978-3-030-84259-8_3
3. Attema, T., Cramer, R., Kohl, L.: A compressed Σ-protocol theory for lattices. In: Malkin, T., Peikert, C. (eds.) CRYPTO 2021, Part II. LNCS, vol. 12826, pp. 549–579. Springer, Cham (2021). https://doi.org/10.1007/978-3-030-84245-1_19
4. Attema, T., Cramer, R., Rambaud, M.: Compressed Σ-protocols for bilinear group arithmetic circuits and application to logarithmic transparent threshold signatures. In: Tibouchi, M., Wang, H. (eds.) ASIACRYPT 2021. LNCS, vol. 13093, pp. 526–556. Springer, Cham (2021). https://doi.org/10.1007/978-3-030-92068-5_18
5. Attema, T., Cramer, R., Xing, C.: A note on short invertible ring elements and applications to cyclotomic and trinomials number fields. Math. Cryptology 1, 45–70 (2021)
6. Bellare, M., Goldreich, O.: On defining proofs of knowledge. In: Brickell, E.F. (ed.) CRYPTO 1992. LNCS, vol. 740, pp. 390–420. Springer, Heidelberg (1993). https://doi.org/10.1007/3-540-48071-4_28
7. Bellare, M., Impagliazzo, R., Naor, M.: Does parallel repetition lower the error in computationally sound protocols? In: 38th FOCS, pp. 374–383. IEEE Computer Society Press, October 1997
8. Bootle, J., Cerulli, A., Chaidos, P., Groth, J., Petit, C.: Efficient zero-knowledge arguments for arithmetic circuits in the discrete log setting. In: Fischlin, M., Coron, J.-S. (eds.) EUROCRYPT 2016, Part II. LNCS, vol. 9666, pp. 327–357. Springer, Heidelberg (2016). https://doi.org/10.1007/978-3-662-49896-5_12
9. Bootle, J., Lyubashevsky, V., Nguyen, N.K., Seiler, G.: A non-PCP approach to succinct quantum-safe zero-knowledge. In: Micciancio, D., Ristenpart, T. (eds.) CRYPTO 2020, Part II. LNCS, vol. 12171, pp. 441–469. Springer, Cham (2020). https://doi.org/10.1007/978-3-030-56880-1_16
10. Bünz, B., Bootle, J., Boneh, D., Poelstra, A., Wuille, P., Maxwell, G.: Bulletproofs: Short proofs for confidential transactions and more. In: 2018 IEEE Symposium on Security and Privacy, pp. 315–334. IEEE Computer Society Press, May 2018
11. Bünz, B., Fisch, B., Szepieniec, A.: Transparent SNARKs from DARK compilers. In: Canteaut, A., Ishai, Y. (eds.) EUROCRYPT 2020, Part I. LNCS, vol. 12105, pp. 677–706. Springer, Cham (2020). https://doi.org/10.1007/978-3-030-45721-1_24
12. Chung, K.-M., Liu, F.-H.: Parallel repetition theorems for interactive arguments. In: Micciancio, D. (ed.) TCC 2010. LNCS, vol. 5978, pp. 19–36. Springer, Heidelberg (2010). https://doi.org/10.1007/978-3-642-11799-2_2

13. Chung, K.-M., Pass, R.: Tight parallel repetition theorems for public-coin arguments using KL-divergence. In: Dodis, Y., Nielsen, J.B. (eds.) TCC 2015, Part II. LNCS, vol. 9015, pp. 229–246. Springer, Heidelberg (2015). https://doi.org/10.1007/978-3-662-46497-7_9

14. Faonio, A., Nielsen, J.B., Venturi, D.: Predictable arguments of knowledge. In: Fehr, S. (ed.) PKC 2017, Part I. LNCS, vol. 10174, pp. 121–150. Springer, Heidelberg (2017). https://doi.org/10.1007/978-3-662-54365-8_6

15. Goldreich, O.: Modern Cryptography, Probabilistic Proofs and Pseudorandomness, Algorithms and Combinatorics, vol. 17. Springer, Heidelberg (1998). https://doi.org/10.1007/978-3-662-12521-2

16. Goldreich, O.: Foundations of Cryptography: Basic Tools, vol. 1. Cambridge University Press, Cambridge (2001)

17. Goldwasser, S., Micali, S., Rackoff, C.: The knowledge complexity of interactive proof-systems (extended abstract). In: 17th ACM STOC, pp. 291–304. ACM Press, May 1985

18. Haitner, I.: A parallel repetition theorem for any interactive argument. In: 50th FOCS, pp. 241–250. IEEE Computer Society Press, October 2009

19. Håstad, J., Pass, R., Wikström, D., Pietrzak, K.: An efficient parallel repetition theorem. In: Micciancio, D. (ed.) TCC 2010. LNCS, vol. 5978, pp. 1–18. Springer, Heidelberg (2010). https://doi.org/10.1007/978-3-642-11799-2_1

20. Hazay, C., Lindell, Y.: Efficient Secure Two-Party Protocols - Techniques and Constructions. ISC, Springer, Heidelberg (2010). https://doi.org/10.1007/978-3-642-14303-8

21. Lyubashevsky, V., Seiler, G.: Short, invertible elements in partially splitting cyclotomic rings and applications to lattice-based zero-knowledge proofs. In: Nielsen, J.B., Rijmen, V. (eds.) EUROCRYPT 2018, Part I. LNCS, vol. 10820, pp. 204–224. Springer, Cham (2018). https://doi.org/10.1007/978-3-319-78381-9_8

22. Maller, M., Bowe, S., Kohlweiss, M., Meiklejohn, S.: Sonic: zero-knowledge SNARKs from linear-size universal and updatable structured reference strings. In: Cavallaro, L., Kinder, J., Wang, X., Katz, J. (eds.) ACM CCS 2019, pp. 2111–2128. ACM Press, November 2019

23. Pass, R., Venkitasubramaniam, M.: An efficient parallel repetition theorem for Arthur-Merlin games. In: Johnson, D.S., Feige, U. (eds.) 39th ACM STOC, pp. 420–429. ACM Press, June 2007

24. Rotem, L., Segev, G.: Tighter security for schnorr identification and signatures: a high-moment forking lemma for Σ-protocols. In: Malkin, T., Peikert, C. (eds.) CRYPTO 2021, Part I. LNCS, vol. 12825, pp. 222–250. Springer, Cham (2021). https://doi.org/10.1007/978-3-030-84242-0_9

25. Unruh, D.: Quantum proofs of knowledge. In: Pointcheval, D., Johansson, T. (eds.) EUROCRYPT 2012. LNCS, vol. 7237, pp. 135–152. Springer, Heidelberg (2012). https://doi.org/10.1007/978-3-642-29011-4_10

Public-Coin 3-Round Zero-Knowledge from Learning with Errors and Keyless Multi-Collision-Resistant Hash

Susumu Kiyoshima[(✉)]

NTT Research, Sunnyvale, CA, USA
susumu.kiyoshima@ntt-research.com

Abstract. We construct a public-coin 3-round zero-knowledge argument for NP assuming (i) the sub-exponential hardness of the learning with errors (LWE) problem and (ii) the existence of keyless multi-collision-resistant hash functions against slightly super-polynomial-time adversaries. These assumptions are almost identical to those that were used recently to obtain a private-coin 3-round zero-knowledge argument [Bitansky et al., STOC 2018]. (The difference is that we assume sub-exponential hardness instead of quasi-polynomial hardness for the LWE problem.)

1 Introduction

This paper concerns computational zero-knowledge (ZK) arguments, i.e., ZK proofs where soundness and zero-knowledge are both defined against polynomial-time adversaries.

A central research topic about ZK arguments is 3-round ZK arguments, which are optimal in terms of round complexity due to the impossibility of 2-round ZK arguments [25]. Obtaining 3-round ZK arguments is notoriously hard, and obtaining 3-round ZK arguments with black-box simulations is known to be impossible [23]. Until recently, 3-round ZK arguments had been obtained only under unfalsifiable knowledge-type assumptions (e.g., [4,7,9,16,27]) or under weak security definitions (e.g., [1,6,8,11,12,20,30,36,38][1]).

Recently, Bitansky, Kalai, and Paneth [10] obtained a 3-round ZK argument by relying on super-polynomial hardness of the learning with errors (LWE) assumption [39] and *keyless multi-collision-resistant hash functions*.[2] Multi-collision resistance [5,10,37] is a natural relaxation of the standard collision resistance. In the standard keyed setting, *K-collision resistance* ($K \in \mathbb{N}$) of a hash function family $\mathcal{H}$ is defined by requiring that for a random hash function $h \in \mathcal{H}$,

---

[1] Some of these works constructed even 2-round or non-interactive ZK arguments under weak security definitions.

[2] More precisely, they obtained it by relying on various cryptographic primitives that can be based on these assumptions.

The full version of this paper is available at https://ia.cr/2022/820.

Y. Dodis and T. Shrimpton (Eds.): CRYPTO 2022, LNCS 13507, pp. 444–473, 2022.
https://doi.org/10.1007/978-3-031-15802-5_16

any polynomial-time adversary cannot find a K-*collision*, i.e., any $(x_1, \ldots, x_K)$ such that $h(x_1) = \cdots = h(x_K)$. In the keyless setting, multi-collision resistance is defined by allowing K to grow with the adversary's size. That is, K-collision resistance of a keyless hash function h is defined by requiring that any polynomial-time adversary with any polynomial-size non-uniform advice z cannot find a $K(|z|)$-collision. It is unknown whether keyless multi-collision-resistant hash functions can be obtained from more standard cryptographic primitives (including keyed collision-resistant hash function families), but they have a simple falsifiable definition. Recently, they were used to obtain new results about, e.g., ZK proofs/arguments [10,12,13], succinct arguments [10], and non-malleable commitments [12]. (See [10] for more about keyless multi-collision-resistant hash functions.)

Given the result of Bitansky et al. [10], a natural question is whether we can obtain *public-coin* 3-round ZK arguments by relying on the LWE assumption and keyless multi-collision-resistant hash functions. Recall that an interactive argument is called public coin if (i) the verifier only sends the outcome of a coin toss in each round and (ii) the final output of the verifier is deterministically computed from the transcript. (Well-known examples include the classical ZK proofs of Goldreich, Micali, and Wigderson [24] and Blum [14].) In addition to being simple, public-coin ZK arguments have useful properties such as (i) they are *publicly verifiable*, i.e., verifying a proof does not require any secret information, and (ii) they can be used to achieve additional security such as *leakage-soundness* [21] and *resettable soundness* [3]. The 3-round ZK argument of Bitansky et al. [10] (as well as the subsequent 3-round statistical ZK argument of Bitansky and Paneth [13]) is not public coin.

Our result. In this paper, we give a positive result about public-coin 3-round ZK arguments.

Main Theorem (informal). Assume the existence of polynomially compressing keyless hash functions[3] that are multi-collision resistant against slightly super-polynomial-time (e.g., quasi-polynomial-time) adversaries, and additionally assume the sub-exponential hardness of the LWE assumption. Then, there exists a public-coin 3-round zero-knowledge argument for NP.

(See Theorem 2 in Sect. 7 for the formal description.) The assumptions that we use are similar to those that are used by Bitansky et al. [10] for their (private-coin) 3-round ZK argument. The difference is that we assume the sub-exponential hardness of the LWE assumption whereas Bitansky et al. [10] assume the quasi-polynomial hardness of the LWE assumption.

2   Overview of Our Techniques

Our starting point is the (private-coin) 3-round ZK argument of Bitansky, Kalai, and Paneth [10].

---

[3] e.g., those that hash length-λ^2 strings to length-λ strings.

2.1   Techniques of Bitansky et al. [10]

The main component of the 3-round ZK argument of Bitansky et al. [10] is a memory delegation scheme [6,19]. In the setting considered in [6,10], memory delegation schemes proceed in 3 rounds.

1. The prover sends the verifier a short digest of a long memory string.
2. The verifier chooses a computation to be executed on the memory, and sends the prover the description of the computation and a challenge string.
3. The prover responds with the computation output and a proof of correctness.

It is required that the verifier runs in polynomial time even when the length of the memory (and the running time of the computation to be evaluated on it) is slightly super-polynomial, such as $\lambda^{\log \lambda}$ for the security parameter λ. For security, the soundness notion given by Bitansky et al. [10] requires that no prover can generate an accepting proof for a randomly sampled output (which is sampled after a digest and a computation to be evaluated on the memory are fixed).

Bitansky et al. [10] obtained a memory delegation scheme by using a key-less multi-collision-resistant hash function and the 2-round delegation scheme of Kalai, Raz, and Rothblum [35] (the KRR delegating scheme in short). Specifically, their scheme was obtained based on the following two observations.

1. The first observation is that the KRR delegating scheme can be converted to a memory delegation scheme if there exists a keyless multi-collision-resistant hash function with a local opening property (i.e., a property that any location of a hashed string can be opened without revealing the entire string). In the KRR delegating scheme, for an input x and a Turing machine M, the verifier sends a challenge string to the prover, and the prover responds with the output $y := M(x)$ and a proof of the correctness of y. A nice property of the KRR delegating scheme is that soundness holds even when the verifier only has oracle access to (an encoding of) the input x, where the verifier only makes a small number of non-adaptive queries. Given this property, the KRR delegation scheme can be converted to a memory delegation scheme as follows. The digest is created by hashing a memory with the keyless hash function. The verifier sends a challenge string and input queries of the KRR delegation scheme.[4] The prover responds with the computation output y, a proof of the KRR delegation scheme for the correctness of y, and local opening of the queried locations of the memory. Intuitively, if local opening of the keyless hash function satisfies a sufficiently strong multi-collision-resistant property, the prover can only create accepting proofs for a small number of values of y. Thus, the prover cannot generate an accepting proof for a randomly chosen value of y.
2. The second observation is that any multi-collision-resistant hash functions can be converted to those that have a local opening property. It should be

---

[4] In Bitansky et al. [10], the input queries need to be encrypted by an FHE scheme so that the prover cannot learn the input queries. We ignite this detail in this overview.

noted that the standard tree-hashing technique cannot be used for this purpose. Indeed, in the case of multi-collision resistance, an adversary might be able to open each location to two values, and thus, it might be able to open λ locations to 2^{λ} combinations of such values. The conversion given in Bitansky et al. [10] yields a multi-collision resistant hash function for long inputs while avoiding this exponential deterioration of multi-collision resistance. (Details about this conversion, including the formal definition of multi-collision resistance of local opening, are not important to this overview.) A notable limitation is that when multiple locations are opened, they must be opened simultaneously so that the above "mixed-and-match" attack can be prevented. That is, opening each location individually as in the case of the standard tree-hashing is not allowed. Fortunately, this limitation does not cause a problem for the current purpose since the KRR delegation scheme only makes non-adaptive input queries.

The memory delegation scheme of Bitansky et al. [10] is private coin, and this is the reason why their 3-round ZK argument is private coin. Specifically, their 3-round ZK argument is obtained from a memory delegation scheme by following the idea of an earlier work [6] (roughly speaking, the idea is to reduce the round complexity of the public-coin ZK argument of Barak [2] by using a memory delegation scheme), and if the underlying memory delegation scheme is public coin, this step can be simplified straightforwardly and yields a public-coin 3-round ZK argument.

2.2 Our Techniques

We obtain a public-coin memory delegation scheme (and as a result a public-coin 3-round ZK argument) by using recent results about *succinct non-interactive arguments (SNARGs)* for deterministic computations [17,29,32].

Failed Attempt #1. First, let us consider using the result of Choudhuri, Jain, and Jin [17] that gives a SNARG for RAM computations. When their scheme is viewed as a public-coin 2-round RAM delegation scheme,[5] a memory DB is tree-hashed to a digest by using a keyed collision-resistant hash function (the key is sampled by the verifier), the verifier chooses a RAM machine R and a challenge string, and the prover responds with the output $y = R^{\mathsf{DB}}$ and a proof of correctness of y. Choudhuri et al. [17] showed that their scheme works for all polynomial-time RAM computations under the polynomial hardness of the LWE assumption, and their analysis can be trivially extended for $\lambda^{\omega(1)}$-time RAM computations under the $\lambda^{\omega(1)}$-hardness of the LWE assumption. (The verifier still runs in polynomial time.) Since the prover needs to compute a digest non-interactively in memory delegation schemes, a natural approach is to modify the RAM delegation scheme of Choudhuri et al. [17] so that it works even when the memory is hashed by a keyless multi-collision-resistant hash function.

---

[5] Their SNARG works in the common random string model and therefore can be viewed as a public-coin 2-round delegation scheme.

Unfortunately, this approach does not work (at least when naively implemented) since the scheme of Choudhuri et al. [17] requires each memory location to be locally opened individually on a locating-by-location basis as explained below. (Recall that the local opening method given by Bitansky et al. [10] for multi-collision-resistant hash functions does not allow such individual opening.) At a high level, the scheme of Choudhuri et al. [17] proves the correctness of a RAM computation by proving the correctness of multiple evaluations of a single small circuit. Intuitively, this small circuit represents a single step of the RAM computation. That is, it takes as input a local state of the RAM machine, a digest of the memory, and local opening of a single location of the memory, and it outputs an updated local state of the RAM machine along with an updated digest of the memory and a corresponding certificate. The circuit size depends on the memory length only polylogarithmically since local opening of a single location is given as input rather than the entire memory. Since this polylogarithmic dependence is essential for the verifier efficiency of the RAM delegation scheme, it is required that each location of the memory can be locally opened individually.

Failed Attempt #2. Next, let us consider using the result of Jawale, Kalai, Khurana, and Zhang [32] that obtains a SNARG from the public-coin interactive proof of Goldwasser, Kalai, and Rothblum [26] (the GKR interactive proof in short). The scheme of Jawale et al. [32], when viewed as a public-coin 2-round delegation scheme,[6] has the same syntax as the KRR delegation scheme (cf. Sect. 2.1). In addition, it has the same additional property as the KRR delegation scheme, i.e., soundness holds even when the verifier only makes a small number of non-adaptive queries to (an encoding of) the input. Therefore, just like Bitansky et al. [10] obtained a (private-coin) memory delegation scheme from the KRR delegation scheme, we can obtain a (public-coin) memory delegation scheme from the scheme of Jawale et al. [32] by combining it with a keyless multi-collision-resistant hash function. (We need to assume the sub-exponential hardness of the LWE assumption since the scheme of Jawale et al. [32] requires it.) The problem is that the scheme of Jawale et al. [32] is only shown to work for log-uniform[7] bounded-depth computations. As a result, the memory delegation scheme that we can obtain from it has the same limitation. Unfortunately, for the application to 3-round ZK arguments, memory delegation schemes for such limited computations are insufficient.

Our Approach. Given the above two failed attempts, we obtain a public-coin memory delegation scheme by using both the scheme of Choudhuri et al. [17] and the scheme of Jawale et al. [32]. We obtain our memory delegation scheme in two steps.

1. First, we obtain a public-coin *tree-hash memory delegation scheme*, i.e., a public-coin memory delegation scheme for proving the correctness of tree-hash

---

[6] Their SNARG works in the common random string model and therefore can be viewed as a public-coin 2-round delegation scheme.

[7] A computation is log-uniform if it has a circuit that can be generated by a log-space Turing machine.

computations. We obtain such a scheme by combining the scheme of Jawale et al. [32] and a keyless multi-collision-resistant hash function as suggested above. The key point is that, as already observed by Goldwasser et al. [26], the GKR interactive proof works not only for log-uniform computations but also for any computations that have a certain form of succinct descriptions. Tree-hash computations have the required form of succinct descriptions because of their simple tree structure. Thus, the GKR interactive proof can be used to prove the correctness of tree-hash computations. Then, since the scheme of Jawale et al. [32] inherits this property, the memory delegation scheme that we obtain from it also inherits this property, i.e., works for tree-hash computations.

2. Next, we use the above tree-hash memory delegation scheme to obtain a public-coin memory delegation scheme for all $\lambda^{\omega(1)}$-time computations on memories of length $\lambda^{\omega(1)}$. A key observation is that the tree-hash memory delegation scheme can be used to verify whether a digest is correctly computed for the RAM delegation scheme of Choudhuri et al. [17]. More concretely, we consider the following scheme.

   (a) The digest of a memory DB is obtained as in the tree-hash memory delegation scheme using a keyless multi-collision-resistant hash function.

   (b) The verifier sends the prover (i) a (keyed) collision-resistant hash function h together with a challenge string of the tree-hash delegation scheme and (ii) the description R of the computation to be evaluated on the memory (modeled as a RAM machine) together with a challenge string of the RAM delegation scheme of Choudhuri et al. [17].

   (c) The prover responds with (i) the tree-hash $\mathsf{rt} := \mathsf{TreeHash}_h(\mathsf{DB})$ of the memory DB w.r.t. h together with the proof of the tree-hash delegation for the correctness of rt and (ii) the output $y := R^{\mathsf{DB}}$ of the computation together with the proof of the RAM delegation scheme for the correctness of y, where rt is used as the digest in the RAM delegation scheme.

In the above scheme, the digest rt of the RAM delegation scheme is chosen adaptively after the prover learns the challenge string. Still, the tree-hash memory delegation scheme guarantees that rt is correctly computed based on the memory DB, and as a result, we can think as if rt is fixed non-adaptively. Thus, we can use the soundness of the RAM delegation scheme to show the correctness of the computation output y. (In a little more detail, we can show that a cheating prover can give accepting proofs for at most a small number of values of rt and therefore can give accepting proofs for at most a small number of values of y.)

Before concluding the technical overview, we give remarks about the actual construction given in the subsequent sections.

Remark 1 (On tree-hash memory delegation). Firstly, obtaining a tree-hash memory delegation scheme from the scheme of Jawale et al. [32] is actually not trivial. To explain the difficulty, we first note that for the soundness of the GKR interactive proof to hold, the verifier should be given oracle access to *an encoding of* the input x, and the length of the encoding is determined by various parameters of the GKR interactive proof. Now, the problem is that if we obtain a tree-hash memory delegation scheme from the scheme of Jawale et al. [32] naively, the encoding needs to be super-polynomially long since the scheme of Jawale et al. [32] uses the GKR interactive scheme with modified parameters.[8] Almost the same problem was already observed in a different context by Bronfman and Rothblum [15], and we avoid our problem as in their work. Namely, instead of directly using the result of Jawale et al. [32], we use the result of Holmgren, Lombardi, and Rothblum [29] that shows, based on Jawale et al. [32], that a SNARG can be obtained from the GKR interactive proof without modifying its parameters.

Secondly, we focus on tree-hash memory delegation schemes for tree-hash computations w.r.t. polylogarithmic-depth collision-resistant hash functions. (By doing so, we can work with the GKR interactive proof in a typical setting, i.e., for polylogarithmic-depth computations.) Such tree-hash memory delegation schemes are sufficient for our purpose since the sub-exponential hardness of the LWE assumption implies the existence of polylogarithmic-depth collision-resistant hash functions.[9]   ◇

Remark 2 (Our actual approach). Like Bitansky et al. [10], we first focus on *oracle memory delegation schemes*, which are simpler than memory delegation schemes in that the verifier publishes an encoding of the memory in the clear at the beginning. (Importantly, we do not need keyless multi-collision-resistant hash functions to construct them.) After obtaining an oracle memory delegation scheme, we upgrade it to a memory delegation scheme by using a keyless multi-collision-resistant hash function.   ◇

3   Preliminaries

We denote the security parameter by λ. Due to the space constraint, we only give a minimal set of definitions below. Additional definitions are given in the full version of this paper.

3.1   Notations for (Keyed) Hash Functions

Informally, for a hash function family $\mathcal{H}$, we use $\mathcal{H}_\lambda$ to denote the set of the hash functions that can be used for the security parameter λ. (See the full version of this paper for the formal meaning.) We usually assume that each $h \in \mathcal{H}_\lambda$ hashes a string of length 2λ to a string of length λ. For a hash function h, we use $\mathsf{TreeHash}_h$ to denote the algorithm that computes tree-hashing using h.

---

[8] If the reader is familiar with the GKR interactive proof, we note that the scheme of Jawale et al. [32] uses the GKR interactive proof with a super-polynomially large field, and as a result, the low-degree encoding of the input is super-polynomially long.

[9] For example, polylogarithmic-depth collision-resistant hash functions can be obtained by using a sub-exponentially hard collision-resistant hash function with a polylogarithmic security parameter.

3.2 Keyless Multi-Collision Resistant Hash Functions

We recall the definition of multi-collision resistant hash functions from [10], focusing on the keyless version.

Definition 1. *For any functions $K : \mathbb{N} \times \mathbb{N} \to \mathbb{N}$ and $\gamma : \mathbb{N} \to \mathbb{N}$, a keyless hash function* Hash *is said to be* weakly (K, γ)-collision-resistant *if for every probabilistic $\gamma^{O(1)}$-time adversary $\mathcal{A}$ and every sequence of polynomial-size advice $\{z_\lambda\}_{\lambda \in \mathbb{N}}$, there exists a negligible function* negl *such that for every $\lambda \in \mathbb{N}$, the following holds for $K = K(\lambda, |z_\lambda|)$.*

$$\Pr \left[\begin{matrix} y_1 = \cdots = y_K \\ \wedge\ \forall i \neq j : x_i \neq x_j \end{matrix} \middle| \begin{matrix} (x_1, \ldots, x_K) \leftarrow \mathcal{A}(1^\lambda, z_\lambda) \\ \forall i : y_i := \mathsf{Hash}(1^\lambda, x_i) \end{matrix} \right] \leq \mathsf{negl}(\gamma(\lambda)).$$

As in [10], we focus on the case that Hash is polynomially compressing in the sense that $\mathsf{Hash}(1^\lambda, \cdot)$ takes a string of length λ^2 as input and outputs a string of length λ.

3.3 Weak Memory Delegations

We recall the definition of 2-round weak memory delegation schemes [10], focusing on the keyless setting and the publicly verifiable version of the definition.

Definition 2. *We say that an efficiently samplable distribution ensemble $\{Y_\lambda\}_{\lambda \in \mathbb{N}}$ is* entropic *if $H_\infty(Y_\lambda) := -\log \max_{y \in \mathrm{supp}(Y_\lambda)} \Pr[Y_\lambda = y] = \Omega(\lambda)$.*

Definition 3. *A publicly verifiable 2-round weak memory delegation scheme consists of four algorithms* (Mem, Query, Prove, Ver) *that have the following syntax and efficiency.*

- dig := Mem$(1^\lambda, \mathsf{DB})$: Mem *is a deterministic polynomial-time algorithm that takes as input a security parameter 1^λ and a memory* DB, *and it outputs a digest* dig *of the memory.*
- $q \leftarrow$ Query(1^λ): Query *is a probabilistic polynomial-time algorithm that takes as input a security parameter 1^λ, and it outputs a query q.*
- $\pi :=$ Prove$(\mathsf{DB}, \langle M, t, y \rangle, q)$: Prove *is a deterministic algorithm that takes as input a memory* DB, *a deterministic Turing machine M (possibly with some hardwired inputs), a time bound t, an output y, and a query q, and it outputs a proof π.*
- $b :=$ Ver$(\mathsf{dig}, \langle M, t, y \rangle, q, \pi)$: Ver *is a deterministic algorithm that takes as input a digest* dig, *a deterministic Turing machine M (possibly with some hardwired inputs), a time bound t, an output y, a query q, and a proof π, and it outputs a bit b.*

Efficiency. *For any polynomial p, there exists polynomials $\mathsf{poly}_P, \mathsf{poly}_V$ such that for every $\lambda \in \mathbb{N}$, $\langle M, t, y \rangle \in \{0,1\}^{p(\lambda)}$, and $\mathsf{DB} \in \{0,1\}^*$ such that $M(\mathsf{DB})$ outputs y within t steps and $|\mathsf{DB}| \leq t \leq \lambda^{\log \lambda}$, (i) Prove$(\mathsf{DB}, \langle M, t, y \rangle, q)$ runs in time $\mathsf{poly}_P(\lambda, t)$, and (ii) Ver$(\mathsf{dig}, \langle M, t, y \rangle, q, \pi)$ runs in time $\mathsf{poly}_V(\lambda)$.*

Security. *For any function* $\bar{t} : \mathbb{N} \to \mathbb{N}$, *a publicly verifiable 2-round weak memory delegation scheme is called* sound for computation-time bound $\bar{t}$ *if it satisfies the following.*

- **Correctness.** *For every* $\lambda \in \mathbb{N}$, $\langle M, t, y \rangle \in \{0,1\}^{\mathsf{poly}(\lambda)}$, *and* $\mathsf{DB} \in \{0,1\}^*$ *such that* $M(\mathsf{DB})$ *outputs* y *within* t *steps and* $|\mathsf{DB}| \leq t \leq \bar{t}(\lambda)$,[10]

$$
\Pr \left[\mathsf{Ver}(\mathsf{dig}, \langle M, t, y \rangle, q, \pi) = 1 \,\middle|\, \begin{array}{l} \mathsf{dig} := \mathsf{Mem}(1^\lambda, \mathsf{DB}) \\ q \leftarrow \mathsf{Query}(1^\lambda) \\ \pi := \mathsf{Prove}(\mathsf{DB}, \langle M, t, y \rangle, q) \end{array} \right] = 1 \ .
$$

- **Soundness for computation-time bound** $\bar{t}$. *For every pair of* PPT *adversaries* $(\mathcal{A}_1, \mathcal{A}_2)$ *and every sequence of polynomial-size advice* $\{z_\lambda\}_{\lambda \in \mathbb{N}}$, *there exists a negligible function* negl *such that for every samplable entropic distribution ensemble* $\{Y_\lambda\}_{\lambda \in \mathbb{N}}$, *every* $\lambda \in \mathbb{N}$, *and every* $t \leq \bar{t}^{O(1)}(\lambda)$,

$$
\Pr \left[\mathsf{Ver}(\mathsf{dig}, \langle M, t, y \rangle, q, \pi) = 1 \,\middle|\, \begin{array}{l} (\mathsf{dig}, M, \mathsf{st}) \leftarrow \mathcal{A}_1(1^\lambda, z_\lambda) \\ q \leftarrow \mathsf{Query}(1^\lambda); \ y \leftarrow Y_\lambda \\ \pi \leftarrow \mathcal{A}_2(q, y, \mathsf{st}) \end{array} \right] \leq \mathsf{negl}(\lambda) \ .
$$

A publicly verifiable 2-round weak memory delegation scheme is called public coin *if the query algorithm* Query *is public coin, i.e., it just outputs a string that is sampled uniformly randomly.*

3.4   Oracle Memory Delegations

We recall the definition of 2-round oracle memory delegation schemes [10]. We use the publicly verifiable version of the definition, and for technical reasons, use a slightly modified version of the definition (see Remark 3).

Definition 4. *A publicly verifiable 2-round oracle memory delegation scheme consists of five algorithms* $(\mathsf{Mem}, \mathsf{Query}_1, \mathsf{Prove}, \mathsf{Query}_2, \mathsf{Ver})$ *that have the following syntax and efficiency.*

- $\widehat{\mathsf{DB}} := \mathsf{Mem}(1^\lambda, \mathsf{DB})$: Mem *is a deterministic polynomial-time algorithm that takes as input a security parameter* 1^λ *and a memory* DB, *and it outputs an encoding* $\widehat{\mathsf{DB}}$ *of the memory.*
- $(q, \sigma) \leftarrow \mathsf{Query}_1(1^\lambda)$: Query_1 *is a probabilistic polynomial-time algorithm that takes as input a security parameter* 1^λ, *and it outputs a query* q *and a random string* σ.
- $\pi := \mathsf{Prove}(\mathsf{DB}, \langle M, t, y \rangle, q)$: Prove *is a deterministic algorithm that takes as input a memory* DB, *a deterministic Turing machine* M *(possibly with some hardwired inputs), a time bound* t, *an output* y, *and a query* q, *and it outputs a proof* π.

---

[10] We consider a slightly weaker notion of correctness where t is at most $\bar{t}(\lambda)$. (In [10], t is at most 2^λ.)

- $I := \mathsf{Query}_2(L_{\mathsf{DB}}, \sigma, \pi)$: Query_2 *is a deterministic algorithm that takes as input a length parameter* L_{DB}, *a random string* σ, *and a proof* π, *and it outputs a set* $I \subseteq \mathbb{N}$ *of oracle queries.*
- $b := \mathsf{Ver}^{(\cdot)}(L_{\mathsf{DB}}, \langle M, t, y\rangle, q, \sigma, \pi)$: Ver *is a deterministic oracle algorithm that takes as input a length parameter* L_{DB}, *a deterministic Turing machine* M *(possibly with some hardwired inputs), a time bound* t, *an output* y, *a query* q, *a random string* σ, *and a proof* π, *and it outputs a bit* b.

Efficiency. *For any polynomial* p, *there exists polynomials* $\mathsf{poly}_P, \mathsf{poly}_V$ *such that for every* $\lambda \in \mathbb{N}$, $\langle M, t, y\rangle \in \{0,1\}^{p(\lambda)}$, *and* $\mathsf{DB} \in \{0,1\}^*$ *such that* $M(\mathsf{DB})$ *outputs* y *within* t *steps and* $|\mathsf{DB}| \le t \le \lambda^{\log \lambda}$, *(i)* $\mathsf{Prove}(\mathsf{DB}, \langle M, t, y\rangle, q)$ *runs in time* $\mathsf{poly}_P(\lambda, t)$, *and (ii)* $\mathsf{Ver}^{(\cdot)}(|\mathsf{DB}|, \langle M, t, y\rangle, q, \sigma, \pi)$ *runs in time* $\mathsf{poly}_V(\lambda)$.

Security. *For any functions* $\gamma, \bar{t} : \mathbb{N} \to \mathbb{N}$, *a publicly verifiable 2-round oracle memory delegation scheme is called* γ-*sound for computation-time bound* $\bar{t}$ *if it satisfies the following.*

- **Correctness.** *For every* $\lambda \in \mathbb{N}$, $\langle M, t, y\rangle \in \{0,1\}^{\mathsf{poly}(\lambda)}$, *and* $\mathsf{DB} \in \{0,1\}^*$ *such that* $M(\mathsf{DB})$ *outputs* y *within* t *steps and* $|\mathsf{DB}| \le t \le \bar{t}(\lambda)$,

$$\Pr\left[\mathsf{Ver}^{\widehat{\mathsf{DB}}|_I}(|\mathsf{DB}|, \langle M, t, y\rangle, q, \sigma, \pi) = 1 \;\middle|\; \begin{array}{l} \widehat{\mathsf{DB}} := \mathsf{Mem}(1^\lambda, \mathsf{DB}) \\ (q, \sigma) \leftarrow \mathsf{Query}_1(1^\lambda) \\ \pi := \mathsf{Prove}(\mathsf{DB}, \langle M, t, y\rangle, q) \\ I := \mathsf{Query}_2(|\mathsf{DB}|, \sigma, \pi) \end{array}\right] = 1 \;.$$

- γ-**soundness for computation-time bound** $\bar{t}$. *For every pair of probabilistic* $\gamma^{O(1)}$-*time adversaries* $(\mathcal{A}_1, \mathcal{A}_2)$ *and every sequence of polynomial-size advice* $\{z_\lambda\}_{\lambda \in \mathbb{N}}$, *there exists a negligible function* negl *such that for every* $\lambda \in \mathbb{N}$ *and* $t \le \bar{t}^{O(1)}(\lambda)$,

$$\Pr\left[\begin{array}{l} y \ne y' \\ \land\ \mathsf{Ver}^{\widehat{\mathsf{DB}}|_I}(L_{\mathsf{DB}}, \langle M, t, y\rangle, q, \sigma, \pi) = 1 \\ \land\ \mathsf{Ver}^{\widehat{\mathsf{DB}}|_{I'}}(L_{\mathsf{DB}}, \langle M, t, y'\rangle, q, \sigma, \pi') = 1 \end{array} \;\middle|\; \begin{array}{l} (\widehat{\mathsf{DB}}, L_{\mathsf{DB}}, M, y, y', \mathsf{st}) \leftarrow \mathcal{A}_1(1^\lambda, z_\lambda) \\ (q, \sigma) \leftarrow \mathsf{Query}_1(1^\lambda) \\ (\pi, \pi') \leftarrow \mathcal{A}_2(q, \sigma, \mathsf{st}) \\ I := \mathsf{Query}_2(L_{\mathsf{DB}}, \sigma, \pi) \\ I' := \mathsf{Query}_2(L_{\mathsf{DB}}, \sigma, \pi') \end{array}\right]$$
$$\le \mathsf{negl}(\gamma(\lambda)) \;.$$

A publicly verifiable 2-round oracle memory delegation scheme is called public coin *if the query algorithm* Query_1 *is public coin, i.e., it just outputs a string that is sampled uniformly randomly.*

Remark 3 (Differences from the original definition [10]*).* First, the syntax is slightly more general since we split the query algorithm into two, Query_1 and Query_2, so that input queries can be chosen based on the proof π. (An additional minor syntax difference is that Ver (and Query_2) is given the memory length, i.e., $|\mathsf{DB}|$.) Second, soundness is slightly stronger since we allow the adversary $\mathcal{A}_2$ to learn σ (which allows $\mathcal{A}_2$ to learn the input queries I, I'). $\diamond$

3.5 Low-Degree Extensions

Let $\mathbb{F}$ be a finite field, $\mathbb{H} \subseteq \mathbb{F}$ be a subset of $\mathbb{F}$, and $m \in \mathbb{N}$ be an integer. Any function $f : \mathbb{H}^m \to \{0,1\}$ can be extended into a (unique) function $\hat{f} : \mathbb{F}^m \to \mathbb{F}$ such that (i) $\hat{f}(z) = f(z)$ for every $z \in \mathbb{H}^m$ and (ii) $\hat{f}$ is an m-variate polynomial of degree at most $|\mathbb{H}| - 1$ in each variable. This function $\hat{f}$ (or the truth table of it) is called the *low-degree extension* (LDE) of f.

Low-Degree Extensions of Strings. The LDE of a binary string x of length N can be obtained by choosing $\mathbb{H}$ and m such that $N \leq |\mathbb{H}|^m$, identifying $\{1, \ldots, |\mathbb{H}|^m\}$ with $\mathbb{H}^m$ in the lexicographical order, and viewing x as a function $x : \mathbb{H}^m \to \{0,1\}$ such that $x(i) = x_i$ for $\forall i \in [N]$ and $x(i) = 0$ for $\forall i \in \{N+1, \ldots, |\mathbb{H}|^m\}$. We use $\mathsf{LDE}_{\mathbb{F},\mathbb{H},m}(x)$ to denote the LDE of x. We note that for any $z \in \mathbb{F}^m$, the LDE of x can be evaluated on z in time $|\mathbb{H}|^m \cdot \mathsf{poly}(m, |\mathbb{H}|)$, where we assume that we have $|\mathbb{F}| = \mathsf{poly}(|\mathbb{H}|)$ and field operations over $\mathbb{F}$ can be done in time $\mathsf{poly}(\log|\mathbb{F}|) = \mathsf{poly}(\log|\mathbb{H}|)$ (see, e.g., [26, Claim 2.3]).

4 Public-Coin Tree-Hash Oracle Memory Delegation

In this section, we construct a public-coin *tree-hash oracle memory delegation scheme*, i.e., a public-coin oracle memory delegation scheme that is focused on proving the correctness of tree-hash computations. Specifically, we consider a scheme that satisfies the following tailored soundness notion.

Definition 5. *For any hash function family $\mathcal{H}$, publicly verifiable 2-round tree-hash oracle memory delegation schemes are defined in the same way as publicly verifiable 2-round oracle memory delegation schemes (Definition 4) except for the following differences.*

1. *Correctness is defined for a statement of the form $\langle M_h, t, y \rangle$ and a memory DB of length $2^i \lambda$ for $\lambda \in \mathbb{N}, h \in \mathcal{H}_\lambda, t \in \mathbb{N}, y \in \{0,1\}^\lambda$, and $i \in [\lfloor \log^2 \lambda \rfloor]$, where M_h is a Turing machine that takes as input a string $\mathsf{DB} \in \{0,1\}^*$ and outputs $\mathsf{TreeHash}_h(\mathsf{DB})$ using the hash function h that is hardwired in it.[11]*
2. *The soundness condition is replaced with the following one.*
   - *γ-soundness. There exists a probabilistic polynomial-time algorithm Decode such that for every pair of probabilistic $\gamma^{O(1)}$-time adversaries $(\mathcal{A}_1, \mathcal{A}_2)$ and every sequence of polynomial-size advice $\{z_\lambda\}_{\lambda \in \mathbb{N}}$, there exists a negligible function negl such that for every $\lambda \in \mathbb{N}$ and $h \in \mathcal{H}_\lambda$,*

$$\Pr\left[\begin{array}{l|l} \mathsf{rt} \neq \mathsf{TreeHash}_h(\widetilde{\mathsf{DB}}) & (\widetilde{\mathsf{DB}}, L_{\mathsf{DB}}, \mathsf{st}) \leftarrow \mathcal{A}_1(1^\lambda, z_\lambda) \\ \wedge\ \mathsf{Ver}^{\widehat{\mathsf{DB}}|_I}(L_{\mathsf{DB}}, \langle M_h, t_{L_{\mathsf{DB}}}, \mathsf{rt}\rangle, & (q, \sigma) \leftarrow \mathsf{Query}_1(1^\lambda) \\ \qquad\qquad q, \sigma, \pi) = 1 & (\mathsf{rt}, \pi) \leftarrow \mathcal{A}_2(h, q, \sigma, \mathsf{st}) \\ & I := \mathsf{Query}_2(L_{\mathsf{DB}}, \sigma, \pi) \\ & \widehat{\mathsf{DB}} \leftarrow \mathsf{Decode}(\widetilde{\mathsf{DB}}, L_{\mathsf{DB}}) \end{array}\right]$$
$$\leq \mathsf{negl}(\gamma(\lambda))\ ,$$

---

[11] We assume that $h \in \mathcal{H}_\lambda$ hashes a string of length 2λ to a string of length λ. Therefore, $\mathsf{TreeHash}_h$ hashes a string of length $2^i\lambda$ to a string of length λ.

> *where $t_{L_{DB}}$ is the running time of M_h for inputs of length L_{DB}, and $\mathsf{Decode}(\cdot, L_{DB})$ always outputs a L_{DB}-bit string (or $\perp$).*

The goal of this section is to show the following lemma.

Lemma 1. *Assume the sub-exponential hardness of the LWE assumption. Then, for any polylogarithmic-depth hash function family and any sufficiently small super-polynomial functions γ (e.g., $\gamma(\lambda) = \lambda^{\log \log \lambda}$), there exists a public-coin 2-round tree-hash oracle memory delegation scheme with γ-soundness.*

4.1 Public-Coin Weak Tree-Hash Oracle Memory Delegation

As a preliminary step, we construct a scheme with a weak soundness notion (where the cheating prover is required to give a valid encoding of a memory).

Lemma 2. *Assume the sub-exponential hardness of the LWE assumption. Then, for any polylogarithmic-depth hash function family $\mathcal{H}$ and any sufficiently small super-polynomial functions γ (e.g., $\gamma(\lambda) = \lambda^{\log \log \lambda}$), there exists a public-coin 2-round tree-hash oracle memory delegation scheme with the following weaker soundness. (The differences from Definition 5 are highlighted by underlines.)*

- **Weak γ-soundness.** *There exists a deterministic polynomial-time algorithm Decode and a predicate Valid such that for every pair of probabilistic $\gamma^{O(1)}$-time adversaries $(\mathcal{A}_1, \mathcal{A}_2)$ and every polynomial-size advice $\{z_\lambda\}_{\lambda \in \mathbb{N}}$, there exists a negligible function negl such that for every $\lambda \in \mathbb{N}$ and $h \in \mathcal{H}_\lambda$,*

$$
\Pr\left[
\begin{array}{l}
\mathsf{rt} \neq \mathsf{TreeHash}_h(\widehat{\mathsf{DB}}) \\
\wedge\ \mathsf{Ver}^{\widehat{\mathsf{DB}}|_I}(L_{DB}, \langle M_h, t_{L_{DB}}, \mathsf{rt}\rangle, \\
\hspace{4em} q, \sigma, \pi) = 1 \\
\underline{\wedge\ \mathsf{Valid}(\widehat{\mathsf{DB}}, L_{DB}) = 1}
\end{array}
\;\middle|\;
\begin{array}{l}
(\widehat{\mathsf{DB}}, L_{DB}, \mathsf{st}) \leftarrow \mathcal{A}_1(1^\lambda, z_\lambda) \\
(q, \sigma) \leftarrow \mathsf{Query}_1(1^\lambda) \\
(\mathsf{rt}, \pi) \leftarrow \mathcal{A}_2(h, q, \sigma, \mathsf{st}) \\
I := \mathsf{Query}_2(L_{DB}, \sigma, \pi) \\
\widetilde{\mathsf{DB}} \leftarrow \mathsf{Decode}(\widehat{\mathsf{DB}}, L_{DB})
\end{array}
\right]
$$
$$
\leq \mathsf{negl}(\gamma(\lambda)) \ ,
$$

> *where $t_{L_{DB}}$ is the running time of M_h for inputs of length L_{DB}, and $\mathsf{Decode}(\cdot, L_{DB})$ always outputs a L_{DB}-bit string (or $\perp$).*

Furthermore, (i) $\mathsf{Mem}(1^\lambda, \mathsf{DB})$ outputs $\mathsf{LDE}_{\mathbb{F}, \mathbb{H}, m}(\mathsf{DB})$ for some $(\mathbb{F}, \mathbb{H}, m)$, where $(\mathbb{F}, \mathbb{H}, m)$ are the parameters that are determined based on $|\mathsf{DB}|$ and satisfy $2m|\mathbb{H}| < |\mathbb{F}| = \mathrm{poly}(\log \lambda)$ and $|\mathsf{DB}| \leq |\mathbb{H}|^m \leq |\mathbb{F}|^m \leq \mathrm{poly}(|\mathsf{DB}|)$, and (ii) $\mathsf{Valid}(\widehat{\mathsf{DB}}, L_{DB})$ outputs 1 if and only if $\widehat{\mathsf{DB}}$ is (the truth table of) a polynomial $\hat{x} : \mathbb{F}^m \to \mathbb{F}$ of degree at most $m(|\mathbb{H}| - 1)$.

We prove Lemma 2 by relying on recent results [29,32] about soundly applying the Fiat–Shamir transformation to the public-coin interactive proof of Gold-wasser, Kalai, and Rothblum [26] (the GKR interactive proof in short).

Preliminary 1: The GKR Interactive Proof. We recall the "bare-bones" version of the GKR interactive proof [26, Section 3], focusing on the parts that are relevant to us. (As in [32], we use a slightly modified version of it [33] so that we can use the recent results about the Fiat–Shamir transformation [29,32].)

The GKR interactive proof is a public-coin interactive proof for proving the correctness of computations. The statement consists of a circuit C and an input x, and the prover proves $C(x) = 0$. The circuit C is an arithmetic circuit over a finite field $\mathbb{F}$. The circuit C is assumed to be *layered*, i.e., the gates in C can be partitioned into layers such that (i) the starting layer consists of the input gates and the last layer consists of the output gates, and (ii) the gates in the i-th layer take their inputs from the gates in the $(i-1)$-st layer. For a circuit of depth D and W, we denote the gates in the i-th layer by $(g_{i,0}, \ldots, g_{i,W-1})$ for each $i \in \{0, \ldots, D\}$. We note that we start the index of layers from 0, i.e., the starting layer (which contains the input gates) is "the 0-th layer."

The GKR interactive proof is associated with several parameters. When the statement contains a circuit of depth D and width W, important parameters include the finite field $\mathbb{F}$ over which the circuit is defined, as well as a subset $\mathbb{H} \subset \mathbb{F}$ and an integer $m \in \mathbb{N}$. How these parameters are used in the GKR interactive proof is not important to this paper (essentially, the parameters $(\mathbb{F}, \mathbb{H}, m)$ are used to obtain the LDE of the gate values of each layer). These parameters can be set relatively freely as long as they satisfy certain constraints, such as (i) $|\mathbb{F}|$ is sufficiently larger than D, $|\mathbb{H}|$, and m and (ii) $|\mathbb{H}|^m$ is larger than the width W. When $D = \mathsf{poly}(\log W)$, a typical choice is $|\mathbb{H}| = \mathsf{poly}(\log W)$, $m = \lceil \log_{|\mathbb{H}|} W \rceil = O(\log W / \log \log W)$, and $|\mathbb{F}| = \mathsf{poly}(|\mathbb{H}|) = \mathsf{poly}(\log W)$.

Importantly, in the GKR interactive proof, the verifier does not explicitly take a statement as input. Indeed, if the verifier explicitly takes a circuit C as input, the running time of the verifier becomes $\Omega(|C|)$, and the GKR interactive proof cannot have significant efficiency benefits. In the bare-bones version of the GKR interactive proof, the verifier learns about C by making queries to certain polynomials that are guaranteed to satisfy the following conditions. Let D and W be the depth and width of C. For each $i \in [D]$, let $\mathsf{add}_i : \{0, \ldots, W-1\}^3 \to \{0,1\}$ be the function such that on input (u, v, w), it outputs 1 if and only if $g_{i,u} = g_{i-1,v} + g_{i-1,w}$, i.e., the u-th gate in the i-th layer is an addition gate such that its inputs come from the v-th and w-th gates in the $(i-1)$-st layer. Let $\{\mathsf{mult}_i\}_{i \in [D]}$ be defined similarly about multiplication gates. The functions $\{\mathsf{add}_i, \mathsf{mult}_i\}_{i \in [D]}$ are called *the functions that specify* C. Then, the verifier of the GKR interactive proof is given oracle access to *extensions* $\{\widetilde{\mathsf{add}}_i, \widetilde{\mathsf{mult}}_i\}_{i \in [D]}$ of $\{\mathsf{add}_i, \mathsf{mult}_i\}_{i \in [D]}$, where each $\widetilde{\mathsf{add}}_i, \widetilde{\mathsf{mult}}_i : \mathbb{F}^{3m} \to \mathbb{F}$ are guaranteed to satisfy the following for each $(z_u, z_v, z_w) \in \mathbb{H}^{3m}$. Let $\alpha : \mathbb{H}^m \to \{0, \ldots, |\mathbb{H}|^m - 1\}$ be the mapping that returns the lexicographic order of the input.

$$\widetilde{\mathsf{add}}_i(z_u, z_v, z_w) = \begin{cases} \mathsf{add}_i(\alpha(z_u), \alpha(z_v), \alpha(z_w)) & \text{if } \alpha(z_u), \alpha(z_v), \alpha(z_w) \leq W - 1 \\ 0 & \text{otherwise} \end{cases}.$$

$$\widetilde{\mathsf{mult}}_i(z_u, z_v, z_w) = \begin{cases} \mathsf{mult}_i(\alpha(z_u), \alpha(z_v), \alpha(z_w)) & \text{if } \alpha(z_u), \alpha(z_v), \alpha(z_w) \leq W - 1 \\ 0 & \text{otherwise} \end{cases}.$$

Extensions $\{\widetilde{\mathsf{add}}_i, \widetilde{\mathsf{mult}}_i\}_{i \in [D]}$ do not need to be the LDEs of $\{\mathsf{add}_i, \mathsf{mult}_i\}_{i \in [D]}$, but they need to be low-degree polynomials, which roughly means that the individual degree δ of each $\widetilde{\mathsf{add}}_i, \widetilde{\mathsf{mult}}_i$ is much smaller than the field size $|\mathbb{F}|$.

In [26], the bare-bones version of the GKR interactive proof is used as a stepping-stone toward their main results. For example, the bare-bones version is used to obtain an interactive proof for log-space uniform bounded-depth circuit computations. (The verifier can evaluate extensions $\{\widetilde{\mathsf{add}}_i, \widetilde{\mathsf{mult}}_i\}_{i \in [D]}$ efficiently for such computations.[12]) It is also used to obtain an interactive proof for any (not necessarily log-space uniform) bounded-depth circuit computations by considering a model where the verifier evaluates $\{\widetilde{\mathsf{add}}_i, \widetilde{\mathsf{mult}}_i\}_{i \in [D]}$ in an offline pre-processing phase. Jumping ahead, we use the bare-bones version to obtain a protocol for a circuit that is not necessarily log-space uniform. The key point is that for the circuit that we consider, the verifier can evaluate $\{\widetilde{\mathsf{add}}_i, \widetilde{\mathsf{mult}}_i\}_{i \in [D]}$ efficiently because of the simple structure of the circuit.

Below, we summarize the properties of the GKR interactive proof that we use. (It is based on [26, Theorem 3.1] and its analysis with slight adaptation. The differences are explained in footnotes.)

Lemma 3 (Soundness and efficiency of the GKR interactive proof). *There exists a constant $c_{\mathrm{GKR}} \in \mathbb{N}$ such that the GKR interactive proof is sound (with constant soundness error) when it is used with a finite field $\mathbb{F}$, an arithmetic circuit C over $\mathbb{F}$, and parameters $\mathbb{H} \subset \mathbb{F}$, $m \in \mathbb{N}$ that satisfy the following condition.*

- **GKR compatibility:** *Let W and D be the width and the depth of C. Then, there exists $\delta \in \mathbb{N}$ ($m(|\mathbb{H}| - 1) \leq \delta < |\mathbb{F}|$) for which the following hold.[13]*
  1. *The field $\mathbb{F}$ is large; concretely, $c_{\mathrm{GKR}} D m \delta \leq |\mathbb{F}| \leq \mathsf{poly}(|\mathbb{H}|)$.*
  2. *The parameters $\mathbb{H}$ and m satisfy $\max(D, \log W) \leq |\mathbb{H}| \leq \mathsf{poly}(D, \log W)$ and $W \leq |\mathbb{H}|^m \leq \mathsf{poly}(W)$.*
  3. *There exist polynomials $\{\widetilde{\mathsf{add}}_i, \widetilde{\mathsf{mult}}_i\}_{i \in [D]}$ such that (i) each $\widetilde{\mathsf{add}}_i, \widetilde{\mathsf{mult}}_i$ are of individual degree at most δ and (ii) $\{\widetilde{\mathsf{add}}_i, \widetilde{\mathsf{mult}}_i\}_{i \in [D]}$ are extensions of the functions $\{\mathsf{add}_i, \mathsf{mult}_i\}_{i \in [D]}$ that specify C.*

---

[12] More precisely, in [26], it is observed that the verifier can delegate the evaluation of $\{\widetilde{\mathsf{add}}_i, \widetilde{\mathsf{mult}}_i\}_{i \in [D]}$ to the prover, and in a subsequent work [22], it is observed that the verifier can evaluate $\{\widetilde{\mathsf{add}}_i, \widetilde{\mathsf{mult}}_i\}_{i \in [D]}$ efficiently.

[13] For convenience, we use a slightly stronger lower bound for δ. (In [26], the requirement is $|\mathbb{H}| - 1 \leq \delta < |\mathbb{F}|$.) See Footnote 14.

Furthermore, soundness holds even in a model where the verifier is not given the statement (C, x) and instead given (i) oracle access to $\{\widetilde{\mathsf{add}}_i, \widetilde{\mathsf{mult}}_i\}_{i \in [D]}$ and (ii) oracle access to a polynomial $\widehat{x} : \mathbb{F}^m \to \mathbb{F}$ that is of (total) degree at most $m(\mathbb{H}-1)$ and has x as a prefix of $\widehat{x}|_{\mathbb{H}^m}$.[14] *In such a model, the verifier runs in time $\mathsf{poly}(D, \log W)$ while the prover runs in time $\mathsf{poly}(D, W)$. The verifier queries the encoding $\widehat{x}$ at two points*[15] *(where the queries are determined by the (public) randomness of the verifier) and makes $O(D)$ queries to $\{\widetilde{\mathsf{add}}_i, \widetilde{\mathsf{mult}}_i\}_{i \in [D]}$.*

Preliminary 2: The Fiat–Shamir Transformation for the GKR Interactive Proof. We next recall a result by Holmgren et al. [29], which shows (based on an observation by Jawale et al. [32]) that we can obtain a public-coin non-interactive argument by applying the Fiat–Shamir transformation to the parallel repetition of the GKR interactive proof. The result that we use is summarized in the following lemma, which is a rephrasing of a result given in [28, Section 6.2.2] (see also [31, Corollary 6.6, Theorem 4.5]).

Lemma 4. *Let $W, D, \delta : \mathbb{N} \to \mathbb{N}$ be functions such that $W(\lambda) \le \mathsf{poly}(\lambda^{\log \lambda})$,*[16] *$D(\lambda) \le \mathsf{poly}(\log \lambda)$, and $\delta(\lambda) \le \mathsf{poly}(D(\lambda), \log W(\lambda))$. Then, under the sub-exponential hardness of the LWE assumption, there exists a public-coin hash family $\mathcal{H}_{\mathsf{FS}}$ that satisfies the following for $t(\lambda) = \mathsf{poly}(\lambda, D(\lambda), \log W(\lambda))$ and a sub-exponential function T.*

Let $\Pi = (\mathsf{Setup}, P, V)$ be the public-coin non-interactive argument that is obtained by applying the Fiat-Shamir transformation to the t-repetition of the GKR interactive proof w.r.t. the hash family $\mathcal{H}_{\mathsf{FS}}$.

1. ***Correctness.*** *For every $\lambda \in \mathbb{N}$, fix any $(C, \mathbb{F}, \mathbb{H}, m)$ such that (i) $\mathbb{F}$ is a finite field such that $|\mathbb{F}| = \mathsf{poly}(D(\lambda), \log W(\lambda))$ is sufficiently large, (ii) C is a layered arithmetic circuit over $\mathbb{F}$ with output length λ, where the width and the depth of C are at most $W(\lambda)$ and $D(\lambda)$ respectively, and (iii) $(C, \mathbb{F}, \mathbb{H}, m)$ is GKR compatible for $\delta \le \delta(\lambda)$ (cf. Lemma 3). Then, when Π is used with λ and $(C, \mathbb{F}, \mathbb{H}, m)$, the following hold for every input x and $y := C(x)$.*

$$\Pr\left[V^{\mathcal{F}}(\mathsf{crs}, x, y, \pi) = 1 \,\middle|\, \begin{array}{l} \mathsf{crs} \leftarrow \mathsf{Setup}(1^\lambda) \\ \pi \leftarrow P(\mathsf{crs}, C, x, y) \end{array}\right] = 1 \ ,$$

where $\mathcal{F} := \{\widetilde{\mathsf{add}}_i, \widetilde{\mathsf{mult}}_i\}_{i \in [D]}$ are the polynomials that are guaranteed to exist by the GKR compatibility of $(C, \mathbb{F}, \mathbb{H}, m)$.

---

[14] In [26, Theorem 3.1], the encoding $\widehat{x}$ is required to be the LDE of x. However, the only requirement that is used in the analysis of [26, Theorem 3.1] is that the individual degree of $\widehat{x}$ is upper bounded by the degree parameter δ. Since we guarantee $\delta \ge m(|\mathbb{H}| - 1)$, it suffices to require that the total degree of $\widehat{x}$ is at most $m(\mathbb{H} - 1)$ (which implies that the individual degree is at most δ).

[15] Unlike the original version [26], the version given in [33] (which is the version that we use) requires the verifier to read $\widehat{x}$ at two points.

[16] This is a super-polynomial upper bound that is sufficient for our purpose.

2. **T-soundness.** *For every probabilistic $\mathsf{poly}(T)$-time prover P^* and every sequence of polynomial-size advice $\{z_\lambda\}_{\lambda \in \mathbb{N}}$, there exists a negligible function negl such that for every $\lambda \in \mathbb{N}$, every $(C, \mathbb{F}, \mathbb{H}, m)$ as above, and every input x,*

$$\Pr\left[\begin{array}{c} y \neq C(x) \\ \wedge\ V^{\mathcal{F}}(\mathsf{crs}, x, y, \pi) = 1 \end{array} \middle| \begin{array}{c} \mathsf{crs} \leftarrow \mathsf{Setup}(1^\lambda) \\ (y, \pi) \leftarrow P^*(\mathsf{crs}, C, x, z_\lambda) \end{array} \right] \leq \mathsf{negl}(T(\lambda))\ .$$

3. **Efficiency.** *For every $\lambda \in \mathbb{N}$ and every $(C, \mathbb{F}, \mathbb{H}, m)$ as above, P runs in time $D(\lambda) \cdot \mathsf{poly}(\lambda, D(\lambda), \log W(\lambda)) + T_{\mathrm{GKR},P}$ and V runs in time $D(\lambda) \cdot \mathsf{poly}(\lambda, D(\lambda), \log W(\lambda)) + T_{\mathrm{GKR},V}$, where $T_{\mathrm{GKR},P}$ and $T_{\mathrm{GKR},V}$ are the running time of the prover and the verifier in the t-repetition of the GKR interactive proof.*

(See the full version of this paper about how we obtain Lemma 4 from [29].)

Remark 4 (On adaptive choice of y in the definition of soundness). Lemma 4 differs from what is shown in [29,32] in that (i) the output length of the circuit C is λ and (ii) the cheating prover in the definition of soundness is allowed to choose the output y adaptively. (In [29,32], the output length of C is 1, and as in the GKR interactive proof described above, the output y is fixed to be 0). Still, it is easy to see that the results in [29,32] can be used to obtain Lemma 4. Consider, for simplicity, that C outputs a binary output. (This is the case that we are interested in.) First, if the output length of C is 1 and the cheating prover adaptively chooses the output $y \in \{0, 1\}$, it suffices to consider a protocol where the verifier initiates the protocol of [29,32] twice in parallel, one for the statement $C(x) = 0$ and the other for the statement $C(x) = 1$, and the prover chooses one of them according to the actual output. Next, if the output length of C is λ, the prover and the verifier run this single-bit protocol λ times in parallel, one for each output bit. In total, the protocol of [29,32] is executed 2λ times in parallel, and it is easy to see that if there exists a cheating prover that breaks the multi-bit version with probability ϵ, there exists a cheating prover that breaks the original version with probability at least ϵ/λ. $\Diamond$

Remark 5 (On soundness when the verifier is not given (C, x) explicitly). The Fiat–Shamir transformation preserves the furthermore part of Lemma 3, i.e., soundness (and completeness) holds even when the verifier only has (i) oracle access to $\mathcal{F} = \{\widetilde{\mathsf{add}}_i, \widetilde{\mathsf{mult}}_i\}_{i \in [D]}$ and (ii) oracle access to a low-degree polynomial $\widehat{x}$ that encodes x. Also, the number of queries to $\mathcal{F}$ and $\widehat{x}$ is not increased by the Fiat–Shamir transformation.[17] Furthermore, since the queries to $\widehat{x}$ are determined by the verifier randomness in the GKR interactive proof, they are determined by the proof π after the Fiat–Shamir transformation. Thus, there is a deterministic polynomial-time algorithm $\mathsf{InpQuery}$ such that the correctness and soundness of Π hold even when we replace $V^{\mathcal{F}}(\mathsf{crs}, x, y, \pi)$

---

[17] Note that the Fiat–Shamir transformation only requires hashing the transcript (excluding x) as shown in [31, Figure 1].

with $V^{\widetilde{x}|_I, \mathcal{F}}(\mathsf{crs}, y, \pi)$, where $I := \mathsf{InpQuery}(\pi)$. Since Π is obtained from t-repetition of the GKR interactive proof for $t(\lambda) = \mathsf{poly}(\lambda, D(\lambda), \log W(\lambda))$, we have $|I| = \mathsf{poly}(\lambda, D(\lambda), \log W(\lambda))$.   ◇

Proof of Lemma 2. We are ready to give our weak tree-hash memory delegation scheme. Our approach is to use Lemma 4 for tree-hash computations. That is, we consider the GKR interactive proof for tree-hash computations and then obtain the desired protocol by applying the Fiat–Shamir transformation. By Lemma 3, we need a circuit that computes tree-hashing in a "GKR friendly" way, i.e., we need a tree-hashing circuit that satisfies properties such as having efficiently computable low-degree extensions $\{\widetilde{\mathsf{add}}_i, \widetilde{\mathsf{mult}}_i\}_{i \in [D]}$. Motivated by this observation, we show the following lemma.

Lemma 5. *Let $\mathcal{H}$ be any polylogarithmic-depth hash function family. Then, there exist polynomials $\mathsf{poly}_W, \mathsf{poly}_D, \mathsf{poly}_\delta$ such that for any $\lambda, \ell \in \mathbb{N}$ ($\ell \leq \log^2 \lambda$) and any finite field $\mathbb{F}$ of sufficiently large size $|\mathbb{F}| \leq \mathsf{poly}(\log \lambda)$, there exist a subset $\mathbb{H} \subset \mathbb{F}$ and an integer $m \in \mathbb{N}$ such that for any $h : \{0,1\}^{2\lambda} \to \{0,1\}^\lambda \in \mathcal{H}_\lambda$, there exists a layered arithmetic circuit $C : \mathbb{F}^L \to \mathbb{F}^\lambda$ that satisfies the following, where L is defined as $L := 2^\ell \lambda$.*

1. *The circuit C computes $\mathsf{TreeHash}_h$ for every input $x \in \{0,1\}^L$, and it outputs values in $\mathbb{F}^\lambda \setminus \{0,1\}^\lambda$ for inputs in $x \in \mathbb{F}^L \setminus \{0,1\}^L$. The circuit C is of width $W := \mathsf{poly}_W(\lambda, L)$ and of depth $D := \mathsf{poly}_D(\log \lambda, \ell)$.*
2. *There exist $\{\widetilde{\mathsf{add}}_i, \widetilde{\mathsf{mult}}_i\}_{i \in [D]}$ such that $(C, \mathbb{F}, \mathbb{H}, m)$ is GKR compatible for $\delta := \mathsf{poly}_\delta(D, \log W)$ and $\{\widetilde{\mathsf{add}}_i, \widetilde{\mathsf{mult}}_i\}_{i \in [D]}$. Furthermore, $\{\widetilde{\mathsf{add}}_i, \widetilde{\mathsf{mult}}_i\}_{i \in [D]}$ can be evaluated in time $\mathsf{poly}(\lambda)$ given the description of h.*

Furthermore, $(\mathbb{H}, m)$ can be obtained in polynomial time given λ and ℓ.

The proof of this lemma is straightforward. The circuit C is defined by connecting many copies of the polylogarithmic-depth circuit C_h of h in the tree structure. The key point is that, because of the tree structure of C, there exist extensions $\{\widetilde{\mathsf{add}}_i, \widetilde{\mathsf{mult}}_i\}_{i \in [D]}$ that can be evaluated almost as efficiently as the LDEs of the functions that specify C_h, which in turn can be evaluated in time $\mathsf{poly}(\lambda)$ since C_h is of size $\mathsf{poly}(\lambda)$. For a formal proof, see the full version of this paper.

Now, we proceeds to the proof of Lemma 2.

Proof (of Lemma 2). We first note that from Lemma 3, Lemma 4, Remark 5, and Lemma 5, we have the following corollary. (See the full version of this paper for the proof.)

Corollary 1. *Let $\mathcal{H}$ be any polylogarithmic-depth hash function family. Then, under the sub-exponential hardness of the LWE assumption, there exists a public-coin non-interactive argument $\Pi = (\mathsf{Setup}, P, V)$ and a deterministic polynomial-time algorithm $\mathsf{InpQuery}$ such that the following hold for a sub-exponential function T.*

1. **Parameters.** For each $\lambda, \ell \in \mathbb{N}$ such that $\ell \leq \log^2 \lambda$, the non-interactive argument Π has $(\mathbb{F}, \mathbb{H}, m)$ as parameters, where $\mathbb{F}$ is a finite field, $\mathbb{H} \subset \mathbb{F}$ is a subset, and $m \in \mathbb{N}$ is an integer such that $2m|\mathbb{H}| < |\mathbb{F}| = \mathsf{poly}(\log \lambda)$ and $L \leq |\mathbb{H}|^m \leq |\mathbb{F}|^m \leq \mathsf{poly}(L)$, where $L = 2^\ell \lambda$.

2. **Completeness.** For every $\lambda, \ell \in \mathbb{N}$ ($\ell \leq \log^2 \lambda$), $h \in \mathcal{H}_\lambda$, $x \in \{0,1\}^L$, $\widehat{x} := \mathsf{LDE}_{\mathbb{F},\mathbb{H},m}(x)$, and $y := \mathsf{TreeHash}_h(x)$,

$$
\Pr \left[V^{\widehat{x}|_I}(\mathsf{crs}, \ell, h, y, \pi) = 1 \, \middle| \, \begin{array}{l} \mathsf{crs} \leftarrow \mathsf{Setup}(1^\lambda) \\ \pi \leftarrow P(\mathsf{crs}, h, x, y) \\ I := \mathsf{InpQuery}(\pi) \end{array} \right] = 1 \ .
$$

3. **T-soundness.** For every probabilistic $\mathsf{poly}(T)$-time prover P^* and every sequence of polynomial-size advice $\{z_\lambda\}_{\lambda \in \mathbb{N}}$, there exists a negligible function negl such that for every $\lambda, \ell \in \mathbb{N}$ ($\ell \leq \log^2 \lambda$), every $h \in \mathcal{H}_\lambda$, and every polynomial $\widehat{x} : \mathbb{F}^m \to \mathbb{F}$ that is of degree at most $m(\mathbb{H} - 1)$,

$$
\Pr \left[\begin{array}{l} y \neq \mathsf{TreeHash}_h(x) \\ \wedge \ V^{\widehat{x}|_I}(\mathsf{crs}, \ell, h, y, \pi) = 1 \end{array} \, \middle| \, \begin{array}{l} \mathsf{crs} \leftarrow \mathsf{Setup}(1^\lambda) \\ (y, \pi) \leftarrow P^*(\mathsf{crs}, h, x, z_\lambda) \\ I := \mathsf{InpQuery}(\pi) \end{array} \right] \leq \mathsf{negl}(T(\lambda)) \ ,
$$

where x is the length-L prefix of $\widehat{x}|_{\mathbb{H}^m}$ if it is in $\{0,1\}^L$ and $x := \bot$ otherwise, where $L := 2^\ell \lambda$.

4. **Efficiency.** P runs in time $\mathsf{poly}(\lambda, L)$ and V runs in time $\mathsf{poly}(\lambda)$.

Given Corollary 1, the proof of Lemma 2 is trivial. Consider the delegation scheme given in Algorithm 1. The efficiency and security conditions can be verified by inspection. (We note that Mem runs in polynomial time since we have $|\mathbb{F}|^m \leq \mathsf{poly}(|\mathsf{DB}|)$.) This completes the proof of Lemma 2. □

4.2 Overview of Proof of Lemma 1

We are ready to explain how we obtain our tree-hash oracle memory delegation scheme. The idea is to upgrade the soundness of our weak tree-hash oracle memory delegation scheme (Lemma 2) by considering a verifier that additionally checks the validity of the encoded memory. Fortunately, such a check can be implemented easily by relying on well-known techniques about low-degree polynomials, namely low-degree tests and self-correction. As stated in Lemma 2, in our weak tree-hash oracle memory delegation scheme, an encoding of a memory is valid if it is a polynomial of degree at most $m(|\mathbb{H}| - 1)$. Thus, the verifier can use low-degree tests to check whether it is given an encoding $\widehat{\mathsf{DB}}$ that is close to a valid encoding $\widehat{\mathsf{DB}}'$, and then it can use self-correction to make queries to $\widehat{\mathsf{DB}}'$ through $\widehat{\mathsf{DB}}$. For a formal proof, see the full version of this paper.

5 Public-Coin Oracle Memory Delegation

In this section, we construct a public-coin oracle memory delegation scheme.

Algorithm 1 Public-coin weak oracle memory tree-hash delegation wTHDel.

Let $\Pi = (\mathsf{Setup}, P, V)$ and $\mathsf{InpQuery}$ be the public-coin non-interactive argument and the deterministic algorithm given by Corollary 1.

- $\widehat{\mathsf{DB}} := \mathsf{Mem}(1^\lambda, \mathsf{DB})$:
    1. Let ℓ^* be the integer such that $|\mathsf{DB}| = 2^{\ell^*}\lambda$, and let $(\mathbb{F}, \mathbb{H}, m)$ be the parameters that Π uses for λ and ℓ^*. Then, output $\widehat{\mathsf{DB}} := \mathsf{LDE}_{\mathbb{F}, \mathbb{H}, m}(\mathsf{DB})$.
- $(q, \sigma) \leftarrow \mathsf{Query}_1(1^\lambda)$:
    1. Run $\mathsf{crs} \leftarrow \mathsf{Setup}(1^\lambda)$.
    2. Output $q := \mathsf{crs}$ and $\sigma := \bot$.
- $\pi := \mathsf{Prove}(\mathsf{DB}, \langle M_h, t_{|\mathsf{DB}|}, \mathsf{rt} \rangle, q)$:
    1. Parse q as crs.
    2. Output $\pi \leftarrow P(\mathsf{crs}, h, \mathsf{DB}, \mathsf{rt})$, where h is the hash function that is hardwired in M_h.
- $I := \mathsf{Query}_2(|\mathsf{DB}|, \sigma, \pi)$:
    1. Output $I := \mathsf{InpQuery}(\pi)$.
- $b := \mathsf{Ver}^{\widehat{\mathsf{DB}}|_I}(|\mathsf{DB}|, \langle M_h, t_{|\mathsf{DB}|}, \mathsf{rt} \rangle, q, \sigma, \pi)$:
    1. Obtain ℓ^* as in Mem, and obtain crs from q as in Prove. (If there does not exist ℓ^* such that $|\mathsf{DB}| = 2^{\ell^*}\lambda$, output 0.)
    2. Output $b := V^{\widehat{\mathsf{DB}}|_I}(\mathsf{crs}, \ell^*, h, \mathsf{rt}, \pi)$.
- $\widetilde{\mathsf{DB}} \leftarrow \mathsf{Decode}(\widehat{\mathsf{DB}}, L_{\mathsf{DB}})$:
    1. Let $\widetilde{\mathsf{DB}}$ be the length-L_{DB} prefix of $\widehat{\mathsf{DB}}|_{\mathbb{H}^m}$.
    2. Output $\widetilde{\mathsf{DB}}$ if $\widetilde{\mathsf{DB}} \in \{0, 1\}^{L_{\mathsf{DB}}}$, and output $\bot$ otherwise.

Lemma 6. *Assume the sub-exponential hardness of the LWE assumption. Then, there exists a public-coin 2-round oracle memory delegation scheme with γ-soundness for computation-time bound γ for any (sufficiently small) super-polynomial function γ (e.g., $\gamma(\lambda) = O(\lambda^{\log \log \lambda})$).*

We prove Lemma 1 by combining our tree-hash memory delegation scheme (Lemma 1) with the RAM delegation scheme of Choudhuri et al. [17].

5.1   Preliminary: RAM Delegation

We recall the definition of publicly verifiable non-interactive RAM delegation schemes from [17,34]. (We straightforwardly generalize the definition to consider security against slightly super-polynomial-time adversaries.)

A RAM machine R with word size ℓ is modeled as a deterministic machine with random access to a memory of at most 2^ℓ bits and a local state of $O(\ell)$ bits. At every step, the machine reads or writes a single memory bit and updates its state. For simplicity, we use the security parameter λ as the word size. Also, for convenience, we consider a slightly more general model than [17,34] and think of a RAM machine that has access to a memory of at most 2^ℓ bits and additionally takes a short input. (In [17,34], a RAM machine has access to a memory of (exactly) 2^ℓ bits and takes no input other than the memory and the initial local state.) In this paper, the memory and state of a RAM machine at a given time-step are referred to as its *memory-state pair*.[18] For any RAM machine R, let U_R denote the language such that $(\ell, x, \mathsf{ms}, \mathsf{ms}', T) \in U_R$ if and only if R with word size ℓ and on input x transitions from memory-state pair ms to memory-state pair ms' in T steps.

Definition 6. *For any RAM machine R, a publicly verifiable non-interactive RAM delegation scheme for R consists of four algorithms* (Setup, Mem, Prove, Ver) *that have the following syntax.*

- (pk, vk, dk) $\leftarrow$ Setup($1^\lambda, T$): Setup *is a probabilistic algorithm that takes as input a security parameter 1^λ and a time bound T, and it outputs a triple of public keys: a prover key* pk, *a verifier key* vk, *and a digest key* dk.
- dig := Mem(dk, ms): Mem *is a deterministic algorithm that takes as input a digest key* dk *and a memory-state pair* ms, *and it outputs a digest* dig *of the memory-state pair.*
- π := Prove(pk, x, ms, ms'): Prove *is a deterministic algorithm that takes as input a prover key* pk, *an input x to R, source and destination memory-state pairs* ms, ms', *and it outputs a proof π.*
- b := Ver(vk, x, dig, dig', π): Ver *is a deterministic algorithm that takes as input a verifier key* vk, *an input x to R, source and destination digests* dig, dig', *and a proof π, and it outputs a bit b.*

Efficiency. *For any functions $T_{\mathsf{Setup}} : \mathbb{N} \times \mathbb{N} \to \mathbb{N}$ and $L_\pi : \mathbb{N} \times \mathbb{N} \times \mathbb{N} \to \mathbb{N}$, a publicly verifiable non-interactive RAM delegation scheme is said to have* setup time T_{Setup} *and* proof length L_π *if for every $\lambda, T \in \mathbb{N}$ such that $T \le 2^\lambda$ and for every $x, \mathsf{ms}, \mathsf{ms}' \in \{0,1\}^*$ such that $(\lambda, x, \mathsf{ms}, \mathsf{ms}', T) \in U_R$:*

- Setup($1^\lambda, T$) *runs in time $T_{\mathsf{Setup}}(\lambda, T)$.*
- Mem(dk, ms) *runs in time $|\mathsf{ms}| \cdot \mathsf{poly}(\lambda)$ and outputs a digest of length λ.*
- Prove(pk, x, ms, ms') *runs in time $\mathsf{poly}(\lambda, T, |x|, |\mathsf{ms}|)$ and outputs a proof of length $L_\pi(\lambda, T, |x|)$.*
- Ver(vk, x, dig, dig', π) *runs in time $O(L_\pi(\lambda, T, |x|)) + \mathsf{poly}(\lambda, |x|)$.*

Security. *For any function $\gamma : \mathbb{N} \to \mathbb{N}$, a publicly verifiable non-interactive RAM delegation scheme is called γ-sound if it satisfies the following.*

- ***Correctness.*** *For every $\lambda, T \in \mathbb{N}$ such that $T \le 2^\lambda$ and for every $x, \mathsf{ms}, \mathsf{ms}' \in \{0,1\}^*$ such that $(\lambda, x, \mathsf{ms}, \mathsf{ms}', T) \in U_R$,*

$$
\Pr\left[\mathsf{Ver}(\mathsf{vk}, x, \mathsf{dig}, \mathsf{dig}', \pi) = 1 \,\middle|\, \begin{array}{l} (\mathsf{pk}, \mathsf{vk}, \mathsf{dk}) \leftarrow \mathsf{Setup}(1^\lambda, T) \\ \mathsf{dig} := \mathsf{Mem}(\mathsf{dk}, \mathsf{ms}) \\ \mathsf{dig}' := \mathsf{Mem}(\mathsf{dk}, \mathsf{ms}') \\ \pi := \mathsf{Prove}(\mathsf{pk}, x, \mathsf{ms}, \mathsf{ms}') \end{array} \right] = 1 \ .
$$

---

[18] Unlike [17,34], we refrain from using the term "configuration" to refer to the memory and state since we allow RAM machines to additionally have inputs.

- γ-**collision resistance.** *For every probabilistic $\gamma^{O(1)}$-time adversary $\mathcal{A}$ and every sequence of polynomial-size non-uniform advise $\{z_\lambda\}_{\lambda \in \mathbb{N}}$, there exists a negligible function* negl *such that for every $\lambda \in \mathbb{N}$ and $T \leq \gamma(\lambda)$,*

$$\Pr\left[\begin{array}{l} \mathsf{ms} \neq \mathsf{ms}' \\ \wedge\ \mathsf{Mem}(\mathsf{dk}, \mathsf{ms}) = \mathsf{Mem}(\mathsf{dk}, \mathsf{ms}') \end{array} \middle| \begin{array}{l} (\mathsf{pk}, \mathsf{vk}, \mathsf{dk}) \leftarrow \mathsf{Setup}(1^\lambda, T) \\ (\mathsf{ms}, \mathsf{ms}') \leftarrow \mathcal{A}(\mathsf{pk}, \mathsf{vk}, \mathsf{dk}, z_\lambda) \end{array} \right]$$
$$\leq \mathsf{negl}(\gamma(\lambda))\ .$$

- γ-**soundness.** *For every probabilistic $\gamma^{O(1)}$-time adversary $\mathcal{A}$ and every sequence of polynomial-size non-uniform advise $\{z_\lambda\}_{\lambda \in \mathbb{N}}$, there exists a negligible function* negl *such that for every $\lambda \in \mathbb{N}$ and $T \leq \gamma(\lambda)$,*

$$\Pr\left[\begin{array}{l} \mathsf{Ver}(\mathsf{vk}, x, \mathsf{dig}, \mathsf{dig}', \pi) = 1 \\ \wedge\ (\lambda, x, \mathsf{ms}, \mathsf{ms}', T) \in U_R \\ \wedge\ \mathsf{dig} = \mathsf{Mem}(\mathsf{dk}, \mathsf{ms}) \\ \wedge\ \mathsf{dig}' \neq \mathsf{Mem}(\mathsf{dk}, \mathsf{ms}') \end{array} \middle| \begin{array}{l} (\mathsf{pk}, \mathsf{vk}, \mathsf{dk}) \leftarrow \mathsf{Setup}(1^\lambda, T) \\ (x, \mathsf{ms}, \mathsf{ms}', \mathsf{dig}, \mathsf{dig}', \pi) \leftarrow \mathcal{A}(\mathsf{pk}, \mathsf{vk}, \mathsf{dk}, z_\lambda) \end{array} \right]$$
$$\leq \mathsf{negl}(\gamma(\lambda))\ .$$

A publicly verifiable non-interactive RAM delegation scheme is called public coin *if the setup algorithm* Setup *is public coin, i.e., it just outputs a triple of strings that are sampled uniformly randomly.*

We use the following prior result [17] with straightforward adaptation.

Theorem 1. *Let γ be any (sufficiently small) super-polynomial function (e.g., $\gamma(\lambda) = \lambda^{\log \log \lambda}$), and assume the γ-hardness of the LWE assumption. Then, for any RAM machine R, there exists a publicly verifiable non-interactive RAM delegation scheme with γ-soundness, where the setup time is $T_{\mathsf{Setup}}(\lambda, T) = \mathrm{poly}(\lambda, \log T)$ and proof length is $L_\pi(\lambda, T, |x|) = \mathrm{poly}(\lambda, \log T, |x|)$. Furthermore, this scheme is public coin, and (i) the setup algorithm* Setup *outputs a hash function as a digest key, where the hash function is sampled from a collision-resistant hash function family that is independent of the computation-time bound T, and (ii) the digest algorithm* Mem*, on input a digest key* dk *and a memory-state pair* ms $= (\mathsf{DB}, \mathsf{st})$*, outputs a triple* dig $= (\mathsf{st}, \mathsf{rt}, |\mathsf{DB}|)$ *that consists of the local state* st*, the tree-hash* $\mathsf{rt} := \mathsf{TreeHash}_{\mathsf{dk}}(\mathsf{DB})$ *of the memory* DB*, and the memory length* $|\mathsf{DB}|$*, where the tree-hash is computed by using the digest key* dk *as a hash function.*

Two remarks about Theorem 1 are given below.

1. The first part of Theorem 1 differs from what is shown in [17] in that (i) RAM machines are defined in a model where a RAM machine has access to a memory of at most 2^ℓ bits (rather than exactly 2^ℓ bits) and takes a short input in addition to a local state and a memory, and (ii) soundness is required to hold for $\lambda^{\omega(1)}$-time adversaries and $\lambda^{\omega(1)}$-time RAM computations. (In [17], soundness is shown for polynomial-time adversaries and polynomial-time RAM computations under the polynomial hardness of the

LWE assumption.) Still, the first part of Theorem 1 can be easily obtained from [17]. In particular, the analysis given in [17] can be easily extended (i) for memories of at most 2^ℓ bits by appending the length $|DB|$ of the memory to the digest dig so that the verification algorithm Verify can learn $|DB|$, (ii) for RAM machines that take additional short inputs by allowing the proof length to be polynomial in the input length (but still polylogarithmic in the computation-time bound T),[19] and (iii) for $\lambda^{\omega(1)}$-time adversaries and $\lambda^{\omega(1)}$-time RAM computations by assuming the $\lambda^{\omega(1)}$-hardness of the LWE assumption.

2. Regarding the furthermore part of Theorem 1, the public-coin property is implicitly mentioned in [17]. In particular, it is mentioned that the RAM delegation scheme (or more precisely its main component) works in the common random string model rather than the common reference string model, implying that its setup algorithm Setup outputs uniformly random strings.[20] The properties of Setup and Mem can be easily verified by inspecting the scheme description given in [18, Figure 5].[21]

5.2 Proof of Lemma 6

Fix any sufficiently small super-polynomial function γ. Let R be the following RAM machine.

– R is given as input a description of a Turing machine M and given as memory a string DB. Then, R internally executes $M(DB)$.[22] When M terminates, R writes (y, t) at the beginning of the memory and terminates, where y is the output of M and t is the running time of M.

Without loss of generality, we assume that there exists a (non-decreasing) polynomial poly_R such that when the running time of $M(DB)$ is t, the running time of $R^{DB}(M)$ is $\mathsf{poly}_R(t)$, and $R^{DB}(M)$ only reads and writes the first $\mathsf{poly}_R(t)$ bits of DB (hence, we assume that DB is of length $\mathsf{poly}_R(t)$). Let $\mathsf{RDel} = (\mathsf{RDel.Setup}, \mathsf{RDel.Mem}, \mathsf{RDel.Prove}, \mathsf{RDel.Ver})$ be the public-coin non-interactive RAM delegation scheme given by Theorem 1 for the RAM machine R with γ-soundness. Recall that RDel.Setup outputs as a digest key a hash function that is sampled from a collision-resistant hash family. We

---

[19] For those who are familiar with the RAM delegation of [17], we note that we allow the statements of the batch-NP argument to contain the input of the RAM machine.

[20] Technically, the public-coin property can be verified by observing that under the LWE assumption, all the components of the scheme of [17] can be made public coin by using, e.g., an FHE scheme with pseudorandom public keys and ciphertexts.

[21] Actually, Mem in [18, Figure 5] outputs a pair dig = (st, rt), but as noted above, we consider an extended version that additionally includes $|DB|$ in dig.

[22] R emulates the working tape of M by writing it to the memory DB. (It is assumed that DB contains a padding string as a suffix so that it is long enough for the emulation of the working tape. It is also assumed that M is designed to ignore this padding part of DB.)

can assume that this hash function family is polylogarithmic depth (and secure against $\lambda^{\log \lambda}$-time adversaries) under the sub-exponential hardness of the LWE assumption (cf. Footnote 9). For this hash function family, let THDel = (THDel.Mem, THDel.Query$_1$, THDel.Query$_2$, THDel.Prove, THDel.Ver) be any public-coin 2-round tree-hash oracle memory delegation scheme with γ-soundness (e.g., the one given in Lemma 1).

Remark 6 (Simplified syntax of RDel.Setup). Without loss of generality, we can think as if RDel.Setup only takes 1^λ as input (rather than $(1^\lambda, T)$ as defined in Definition 6). This is because the output length of RDel.Setup$(1^\lambda, T)$ is bounded by $\mathsf{poly}_\mathsf{Setup}(\lambda)$ for any $T \leq 2^\lambda$ for a fixed polynomial $\mathsf{poly}_\mathsf{Setup}$. (Recall that the setup time is $T_\mathsf{Setup}(\lambda, T) = \mathsf{poly}(\lambda, \log T)$.) Indeed, in this case, we can assume without loss of generality that RDel.Setup outputs a triple of sufficiently long random strings $(\bar{\mathsf{pk}}, \bar{\mathsf{vk}}, \bar{\mathsf{dk}})$ (whose length is longer than $\mathsf{poly}_\mathsf{Setup}(\lambda)$), and RDel.Mem, RDel.Prove, and RDel.Ver use prefixes of $\bar{\mathsf{pk}}, \bar{\mathsf{vk}}$, and $\bar{\mathsf{dk}}$ as the actual keys.[23] Thus, in the following, we use this simplified syntax of RDel.Setup. Also, since RDel.Mem, RDel.Prove, and RDel.Ver need to know T to determine the lengths of the actual keys, we write them as RDel.Mem$_T$, RDel.Prove$_T$, and RDel.Ver$_T$ to make it explicit what value of T they depend on.   ◇

Our oracle memory delegation scheme ODel = (Mem, Query$_1$, Prove, Query$_2$, Ver) is given in Algorithm 2. (A high-level idea is explained in Sect. 2.) Since THDel and RDel are public coin, ODel is also public coin. Completeness holds due to the furthermore part of Theorem 1 (in particular, the part about the digest algorithm RDel.Mem).[24] The efficiency condition of ODel follows from the efficiency conditions of THDel and RDel. In the following, we focus on soundness.

Assume for contradiction that soundness does not hold, i.e., there exist a pair of probabilistic $\gamma^{O(1)}$-time adversaries $(\mathcal{A}_1, \mathcal{A}_2)$, a sequence of polynomial-size advice $\{z_\lambda\}_{\lambda \in \mathbb{N}}$, and a polynomial p such that for infinitely many $\lambda \in \mathbb{N}$, there exists $t \leq \gamma^{O(1)}(\lambda)$ such that

$$\Pr \left[\begin{array}{l} y_0 \neq y_1 \\ \wedge\ \mathsf{Ver}^{\widehat{\mathsf{DB}}|_{I_0}}(L_\mathsf{DB}, \langle M, t, y_0 \rangle, \\ \qquad\qquad q, \sigma, \pi_0) = 1 \\ \wedge\ \mathsf{Ver}^{\widehat{\mathsf{DB}}|_{I_1}}(L_\mathsf{DB}, \langle M, t, y_1 \rangle, \\ \qquad\qquad q, \sigma, \pi_1) = 1 \end{array} \middle| \begin{array}{l} (\widehat{\mathsf{DB}}, L_\mathsf{DB}, M, y_0, y_1, \mathsf{st}) \leftarrow \mathcal{A}_1(1^\lambda, z_\lambda) \\ (q, \sigma) \leftarrow \mathsf{Query}_1(1^\lambda) \\ (\pi_0, \pi_1) \leftarrow \mathcal{A}_2(q, \sigma, \mathsf{st}) \\ I_0 := \mathsf{Query}_2(L_\mathsf{DB}, \sigma, \pi_0) \\ I_1 := \mathsf{Query}_2(L_\mathsf{DB}, \sigma, \pi_1) \end{array} \right] \geq \frac{1}{p(\gamma(\lambda))} .$$

$$(1)$$

We use $(\mathcal{A}_1, \mathcal{A}_2)$ to obtain a $\gamma^{O(1)}$-time adversary $\mathcal{B}$ that breaks the soundness of RDel. A high-level strategy is as follows. As defined in Definition 6, breaking the soundness of RDel requires generating an input x, source and destination memory-state pairs $(\mathsf{ms}, \mathsf{ms}')$, source and destination digests $(\mathsf{dig}, \mathsf{dig}')$,

---

[23] Recall that RDel.Setup is public coin.

[24] Formally, completeness holds under a slightly modified definition where for each $\langle M, t, y \rangle \in \{0, 1\}^{\mathsf{poly}(\lambda)}$, we only consider a memory DB that contains a padding string as a suffix so that it is of length $T := \mathsf{poly}_R(t)$ (cf. Footnote 22).

Algorithm 2 Public-coin oracle memory delegation scheme ODel.

- $\widehat{\mathsf{DB}} := \mathsf{Mem}(1^\lambda, \mathsf{DB})$:
  1. Output $\widehat{\mathsf{DB}} := \mathsf{THDel.Mem}(1^\lambda, \mathsf{DB})$.
- $(q, \sigma) \leftarrow \mathsf{Query}_1(1^\lambda)$:
  1. Run $(q_{\mathsf{THDel}}, \sigma_{\mathsf{THDel}}) \leftarrow \mathsf{THDel.Query}_1(1^\lambda)$ and $(\mathsf{pk}, \mathsf{vk}, \mathsf{dk}) \leftarrow \mathsf{RDel.Setup}(1^\lambda)$.
  2. Output $q := (q_{\mathsf{THDel}}, \mathsf{pk}, \mathsf{vk}, \mathsf{dk})$ and $\sigma := \sigma_{\mathsf{THDel}}$.
- $\pi := \mathsf{Prove}(\mathsf{DB}, \langle M, t, y \rangle, q)$:
  1. Parse q as $(q_{\mathsf{THDel}}, \mathsf{pk}, \mathsf{vk}, \mathsf{dk})$, and let $T := \mathsf{poly}_R(t)$.
  2. Run $R^{\mathsf{DB}}(M)$. If $R^{\mathsf{DB}}(M)$ does not terminate in T steps, abort. Otherwise, let DB' denote the content of the memory at the termination of $R^{\mathsf{DB}}(M)$.
  3. Run $\pi_{\mathsf{RDel}} := \mathsf{RDel.Prove}_T(\mathsf{pk}, M, \mathsf{ms}, \mathsf{ms}')$ for $\mathsf{ms} := (\mathsf{DB}, \mathsf{st}_{\mathrm{START}})$ and $\mathsf{ms}' := (\mathsf{DB}', \mathsf{st}_{\mathrm{END}})$, where $\mathsf{st}_{\mathrm{START}}$ and $\mathsf{st}_{\mathrm{END}}$ are the initial and the terminating states of R.
  4. Run $\pi_{\mathsf{THDel}} := \mathsf{THDel.Prove}(\mathsf{DB}, \langle M_h, t_{|\mathsf{DB}|}, \mathsf{rt} \rangle, q_{\mathsf{THDel}})$, where M_h and $t_{|\mathsf{DB}|}$ are defined as in Definition 5 for the hash function $h := \mathsf{dk}$, and rt is the tree-hash that is obtained by $\mathsf{rt} := \mathsf{TreeHash}_{\mathsf{dk}}(\mathsf{DB})$.
  5. Let (y', t') be the prefix of DB' that R wrote before the termination, rt' be the tree-hash that is obtained by $\mathsf{rt}' := \mathsf{TreeHash}_{\mathsf{dk}}(\mathsf{DB}')$, and π_{TreeHash} be the local opening for (y', t') w.r.t. rt'.
  6. Output $\pi := (\mathsf{rt}, \mathsf{rt}', (y', t'), \pi_{\mathsf{RDel}}, \pi_{\mathsf{THDel}}, \pi_{\mathsf{TreeHash}})$.
- $I := \mathsf{Query}_2(|\mathsf{DB}|, \sigma, \pi)$:
  1. Parse π as $(\mathsf{rt}, \mathsf{rt}', (y', t'), \pi_{\mathsf{RDel}}, \pi_{\mathsf{THDel}}, \pi_{\mathsf{TreeHash}})$.
  2. Output $I := \mathsf{THDel.Query}_2(|\mathsf{DB}|, \sigma, \pi_{\mathsf{THDel}})$.
- $b := \mathsf{Ver}^{\widehat{\mathsf{DB}}|_I}(|\mathsf{DB}|, \langle M, t, y \rangle, q, \sigma, \pi)$:
  1. Parse q as $(q_{\mathsf{THDel}}, \mathsf{pk}, \mathsf{vk}, \mathsf{dk})$ and π as $(\mathsf{rt}, \mathsf{rt}', (y', t'), \pi_{\mathsf{RDel}}, \pi_{\mathsf{THDel}}, \pi_{\mathsf{TreeHash}})$. Also, obtain T as in Prove, and abort if $|\mathsf{DB}| \neq T$. Let $\mathsf{dig} := (\mathsf{st}_{\mathrm{START}}, \mathsf{rt}, T)$ and $\mathsf{dig}' := (\mathsf{st}_{\mathrm{END}}, \mathsf{rt}', T)$.
  2. Output 1 if all of the following hold.
     (a) $y = y'$ and $t' \leq t$.
     (b) $\mathsf{RDel.Ver}_T(\mathsf{vk}, M, \mathsf{dig}, \mathsf{dig}', \pi_{\mathsf{RDel}}) = 1$.
     (c) $\mathsf{THDel.Ver}^{\widehat{\mathsf{DB}}|_I}(|\mathsf{DB}|, \langle M_h, t_{|\mathsf{DB}|}, \mathsf{rt} \rangle, q_{\mathsf{THDel}}, \sigma, \pi_{\mathsf{THDel}}) = 1$, where $h := \mathsf{dk}$.
     (d) π_{TreeHash} is a valid local opening for (y', t') w.r.t. rt'.
     If any of the above does not hold, output 0.

---

and a proof π such that (i) π is accepting w.r.t. $(\mathsf{dig}, \mathsf{dig}')$, (ii) ms' is the correct destination memory-state pair that can be obtained by running R starting from input x and memory-state pair ms, (iii) dig is the correct digest of ms, but (iv) dig' is not the correct digest of ms'. Now, suppose the adversary pair $(\mathcal{A}_1, \mathcal{A}_2)$ generates two proofs of ODel that are accepting w.r.t. a single encoded memory $\widehat{\mathsf{DB}}$ and two different outputs as shown in (1). Then, at least one of the proofs must be accepting w.r.t. an incorrect output (i.e., an output that differs from the correct output that is obtained based on $\widehat{\mathsf{DB}}$). In that case, one of the proofs must contain a proof of RDel that is accepting w.r.t. an incorrect destination digest (i.e., a digest that differs from the correct destination digest

---

Algorithm 3 Adversary $\mathcal{B}$ against the soundness of RDel.

On input $(\mathsf{pk}, \mathsf{vk}, \mathsf{dk})$, do the following. Let $T := \mathsf{poly}_R(t)$.

1. Run $(\widehat{\mathsf{DB}}, L_{\mathsf{DB}}, M, y_0, y_1, \mathsf{st}) \leftarrow \mathcal{A}_1(1^\lambda, z_\lambda)$.
2. Run $(q_{\mathsf{THDel}}, \sigma_{\mathsf{THDel}}) \leftarrow \mathsf{THDel.Query}_1(1^\lambda)$.
3. Run $(\pi_0, \pi_1) \leftarrow \mathcal{A}_2(q, \sigma, \mathsf{st})$, where $q := (q_{\mathsf{THDel}}, \mathsf{pk}, \mathsf{vk}, \mathsf{dk})$ and $\sigma := \sigma_{\mathsf{THDel}}$.
4. For each $b \in \{0, 1\}$, parse π_b as $(\mathsf{rt}_b, \mathsf{rt}'_b, (y'_b, t'_b), \pi_{\mathsf{RDel},b}, \pi_{\mathsf{THDel},b}, \pi_{\mathsf{TreeHash},b})$, and let $\mathsf{dig}_b := (\mathsf{st}_{\mathsf{START}}, \mathsf{rt}_b, T)$ and $\mathsf{dig}'_b := (\mathsf{st}_{\mathsf{END}}, \mathsf{rt}'_b, T)$.
5. Find $b^* \in \{0, 1\}$ that satisfies all of the following.
   (a) $\mathsf{RDel.Ver}_T(\mathsf{vk}, M, \mathsf{dig}_{b^*}, \mathsf{dig}'_{b^*}, \pi_{\mathsf{RDel},b^*}) = 1$.
   (b) $\mathsf{RDel.Mem}_T(\mathsf{dk}, \mathsf{ms}) = \mathsf{dig}_{b^*}$, where $\mathsf{ms} := (\widehat{\mathsf{DB}}, \mathsf{st}_{\mathsf{START}})$ for $\widehat{\mathsf{DB}} \leftarrow \mathsf{Decode}_{\mathsf{THDel}}(\widehat{\mathsf{DB}}, L_{\mathsf{DB}})$.
   (c) $\mathsf{RDel.Mem}_T(\mathsf{dk}, \mathsf{ms}') \neq \mathsf{dig}'_{b^*}$, where ms' is the memory-state pair of R after T steps starting from input M and memory-state pair ms.
   If such b^* exists, output $(M, \mathsf{ms}, \mathsf{ms}', \mathsf{dig}_{b^*}, \mathsf{dig}'_{b^*}, \pi_{\mathsf{RDel},b^*})$. Otherwise, abort.

---

that is obtained based on $\widehat{\mathsf{DB}}$). We consider an adversary that internally runs $(\mathcal{A}_1, \mathcal{A}_2)$ and outputs such a proof.

Formally, we obtain the adversary $\mathcal{B}$ as follows. Let $\mathsf{Decode}_{\mathsf{THDel}}$ be the algorithm that is guaranteed to exist by the soundness of THDel (cf. Definition 5). Then, for any $\lambda \in \mathbb{N}$ and $t \leq \gamma^{O(1)}(\lambda)$, the adversary $\mathcal{B}$ is described in Algorithm 3. Note that $\mathcal{B}$ runs in time $\gamma^{O(1)}(\lambda)$.

Let us see that $\mathcal{B}$ indeed breaks the soundness of RDel. Fix any $\lambda \in \mathbb{N}$ and $t \leq \gamma^{O(1)}(\lambda)$ for which we have (1). Let $T := \mathsf{poly}_R(t)$. We start by giving a sequence of claims about various values that $\mathcal{B}$ computes. The first claim says that in $\mathcal{B}$, the internally emulated $(\mathcal{A}_1, \mathcal{A}_2)$ succeed with non-negligible probability as shown in (1).

Claim 1. *In an execution of* $\mathcal{B}(\mathsf{pk}, \mathsf{vk}, \mathsf{dk})$ *for* $(\mathsf{pk}, \mathsf{vk}, \mathsf{dk}) \leftarrow \mathsf{RDel.Setup}(1^\lambda)$,

$$\Pr \begin{bmatrix} y'_0 \neq y'_1 \\ \wedge\ L_{\mathsf{DB}} = T \\ \wedge\ \forall b \in \{0, 1\} : \mathsf{RDel.Ver}_T(\mathsf{vk}, M, \mathsf{dig}_b, \mathsf{dig}'_b, \pi_{\mathsf{RDel},b}) = 1 \\ \wedge\ \forall b \in \{0, 1\} : \mathsf{THDel.Ver}^{\widehat{\mathsf{DB}}|_{I_b}}(L_{\mathsf{DB}}, \langle M_{\mathsf{dk}}, t_{L_{\mathsf{DB}}}, \mathsf{rt}_b \rangle, \\ \qquad\qquad\qquad\qquad q_{\mathsf{THDel}}, \sigma, \pi_{\mathsf{THDel},b}) = 1 \\ \wedge\ \forall b \in \{0, 1\} : \pi_{\mathsf{TreeHash},b} \text{ is a valid opening for } (y'_b, t'_b), \mathsf{rt}'_b \end{bmatrix} \geq \frac{1}{p(\gamma(\lambda))},$$

where $I_b := \mathsf{THDel.Query}_2(L_{\mathsf{DB}}, \sigma, \pi_{\mathsf{THDel},b})$.

Proof. This claim follows from (1) (it suffices to rewrite (1) by inlining Query_1, Query_2, and Ver). We note that when π_0 and π_1 are accepted and $y_0 \neq y_1$, we have $y'_0 \neq y'_1$ and $L_{\mathsf{DB}} = T$ since Ver checks $y_b \stackrel{?}{=} y'_b$ and $L_{\mathsf{DB}} \stackrel{?}{=} T$. □

The second claim says that in $\mathcal{B}$, if the internally emulated $(\mathcal{A}_1, \mathcal{A}_2)$ output an accepting proof $\pi_{\mathsf{THDel},b}$ of THDel, the corresponding tree-hash rt_b is correctly computed.

Claim 2. *In an execution of* $\mathcal{B}(\mathsf{pk}, \mathsf{vk}, \mathsf{dk})$ *for* $(\mathsf{pk}, \mathsf{vk}, \mathsf{dk}) \leftarrow \mathsf{RDel.Setup}(1^\lambda)$, *for each* $b \in \{0, 1\}$,

$$\Pr\left[\begin{array}{l} \mathsf{rt} \neq \mathsf{TreeHash}_{\mathsf{dk}}(\widetilde{\mathsf{DB}}) \\ \wedge\ \mathsf{THDel.Ver}^{\widetilde{\mathsf{DB}}|_{I_b}}(L_{\mathsf{DB}}, \langle M_{\mathsf{dk}}, t_{L_{\mathsf{DB}}}, \mathsf{rt}_b \rangle, q_{\mathsf{THDel}}, \sigma, \pi_{\mathsf{THDel},b}) = 1 \end{array}\right] \leq \mathsf{negl}(\gamma(\lambda)),$$

where $I_b := \mathsf{THDel.Query}_2(L_{\mathsf{DB}}, \sigma, \pi_{\mathsf{THDel},b})$.

Proof. This claim follows immediately from the γ-soundness of THDel. $\square$

The third claim says that in $\mathcal{B}$, if the internally emulated $(\mathcal{A}_1, \mathcal{A}_2)$ output two distinct outputs y'_0, y'_1 and the corresponding openings $\pi_{\mathsf{TreeHash},0}, \pi_{\mathsf{TreeHash},1}$ are valid, the corresponding destination digests $\mathsf{dig}'_0, \mathsf{dig}'_1$ must be distinct.

Claim 3. *In an execution of* $\mathcal{B}(\mathsf{pk}, \mathsf{vk}, \mathsf{dk})$ *for* $(\mathsf{pk}, \mathsf{vk}, \mathsf{dk}) \leftarrow \mathsf{RDel.Setup}(1^\lambda)$,

$$\Pr\left[\begin{array}{l} \mathsf{dig}'_0 = \mathsf{dig}'_1 \\ \wedge\ y'_0 \neq y'_1 \\ \wedge\ \forall b \in \{0, 1\} : \pi_{\mathsf{TreeHash},b} \text{ is a valid opening for } (y'_b, t'_b), \mathsf{rt}'_b \end{array}\right] \leq \mathsf{negl}(\gamma(\lambda)).$$

Proof. Since $\mathsf{dig}'_0 = \mathsf{dig}'_1$ implies $\mathsf{rt}'_0 = \mathsf{rt}'_1$ (recall $\mathsf{dig}'_b := (\mathsf{st}_{\mathsf{END}}, \mathsf{rt}'_b, T)$), this claim follows immediately from the binding property of tree-hashing. $\square$

Now, we analyze $\mathcal{B}$. Combined with Claim 2 and Claim 3, Claim 1 implies the following when executing $\mathcal{B}(\mathsf{pk}, \mathsf{vk}, \mathsf{dk})$ for $(\mathsf{pk}, \mathsf{vk}, \mathsf{dk}) \leftarrow \mathsf{RDel.Setup}(1^\lambda)$.

$$\Pr\left[\begin{array}{l} \mathsf{dig}'_0 \neq \mathsf{dig}'_1 \\ \wedge\ L_{\mathsf{DB}} = T \\ \wedge\ \forall b \in \{0, 1\} : \mathsf{RDel.Ver}_T(\mathsf{vk}, M, \mathsf{dig}_b, \mathsf{dig}'_b, \pi_{\mathsf{RDel},b}) = 1 \\ \wedge\ \forall b \in \{0, 1\} : \mathsf{rt} = \mathsf{TreeHash}_{\mathsf{dk}}(\widetilde{\mathsf{DB}}) \end{array}\right] \geq \frac{1}{p(\gamma(\lambda))} - \mathsf{negl}(\gamma(\lambda)).$$

Note that $L_{\mathsf{DB}} = T \wedge \mathsf{rt} = \mathsf{TreeHash}_{\mathsf{dk}}(\widetilde{\mathsf{DB}})$ implies $\mathsf{RDel.Mem}_T(\mathsf{dk}, \mathsf{ms}) = \mathsf{dig}_b$ since $\mathsf{RDel.Mem}_T(\mathsf{dk}, \mathsf{ms}) = (\mathsf{st}_{\mathsf{START}}, \mathsf{rt}, |\widetilde{\mathsf{DB}}|) = (\mathsf{st}_{\mathsf{START}}, \mathsf{rt}, L_{\mathsf{DB}}) = (\mathsf{st}_{\mathsf{START}}, \mathsf{rt}, T) = \mathsf{dig}_b$ (the first equality holds due to the furthermore part of Theorem 1 and the second equality holds since $\widetilde{\mathsf{DB}}$ is obtained by $\mathsf{Decode}_{\mathsf{THDel}}(\widehat{\mathsf{DB}}, L_{\mathsf{DB}})$, which outputs an L_{DB}-bit string as stated in Definition 5). Thus, we obtain

$$\Pr\left[\begin{array}{l} \mathsf{dig}'_0 \neq \mathsf{dig}'_1 \\ \wedge\ \forall b \in \{0, 1\} : \mathsf{RDel.Ver}_T(\mathsf{vk}, M, \mathsf{dig}_b, \mathsf{dig}'_b, \pi_{\mathsf{RDel},b}) = 1 \\ \wedge\ \forall b \in \{0, 1\} : \mathsf{RDel.Mem}_T(\mathsf{dk}, \mathsf{ms}) = \mathsf{dig}_b \end{array}\right] \geq \frac{1}{p(\gamma(\lambda))} - \mathsf{negl}(\gamma(\lambda)).$$

Then, since $\mathsf{dig}'_0 \neq \mathsf{dig}'_1$ implies $\exists b^* \in \{0, 1\}$ s.t. $\mathsf{RDel.Mem}_T(\mathsf{dk}, \mathsf{ms}') \neq \mathsf{dig}'_{b^*}$, we obtain

$$\Pr\left[\begin{array}{l} \exists b^* \in \{0, 1\} : \\ \mathsf{RDel.Mem}_T(\mathsf{dk}, \mathsf{ms}') \neq \mathsf{dig}'_{b^*} \\ \wedge\ \mathsf{RDel.Ver}_T(\mathsf{vk}, M, \mathsf{dig}_{b^*}, \mathsf{dig}'_{b^*}, \pi_{\mathsf{RDel},b^*}) = 1 \\ \wedge\ \mathsf{RDel.Mem}_T(\mathsf{dk}, \mathsf{ms}) = \mathsf{dig}_{b^*} \end{array}\right] \geq \frac{1}{p(\gamma(\lambda))} - \mathsf{negl}(\gamma(\lambda)).$$

Thus, $\mathcal{B}$ does not abort with probability at least $1/p(\gamma(\lambda)) - \mathsf{negl}(\gamma(\lambda))$. Then, since the definition of ms' guarantees $(\lambda, M, \mathsf{ms}, \mathsf{ms}', T) \in U_R$ in $\mathcal{B}$ when it does not abort, we have the following about the output $(M, \mathsf{ms}, \mathsf{ms}', \mathsf{dig}_{b*}, \mathsf{dig}'_{b*}, \pi_{\mathsf{RDel},b*})$ of $\mathcal{B}$.

$$
\Pr \left[\begin{array}{l} \mathsf{RDel.Ver}_T(\mathsf{vk}, M, \mathsf{dig}_{b*}, \mathsf{dig}'_{b*}, \pi_{\mathsf{RDel},b*}) = 1 \\ \wedge\ (\lambda, M, \mathsf{ms}, \mathsf{ms}', T) \in U_R \\ \wedge\ \mathsf{RDel.Mem}_T(\mathsf{dk}, \mathsf{ms}) = \mathsf{dig}_{b*} \\ \wedge\ \mathsf{RDel.Mem}_T(\mathsf{dk}, \mathsf{ms}') \neq \mathsf{dig}'_{b*} \end{array} \right] \geq \frac{1}{p(\gamma(\lambda))} - \mathsf{negl}(\gamma(\lambda)) .
$$

Thus, $\mathcal{B}$ breaks the γ-soundness of RDel. This completes the proof of Lemma 6.

6   Public-Coin Weak Memory Delegation

In this section, we construct a public-coin memory delegation scheme.

Lemma 7. *Assume the sub-exponential hardness of the LWE assumption, and assume the existence of a keyless weakly (K, γ)-collision-resistant hash function for $K(\lambda, \zeta) = \mathsf{poly}(\lambda, \zeta)$ and $\gamma(\lambda) = \lambda^{\tau(\lambda)}$ for a super-constant function $\tau(\lambda) = \omega(1)$. Then, there exists $\bar{t}(\lambda) = \lambda^{\omega(1)}$ such that there exists a two-round memory delegation scheme with weak soundness for computation-time bound $\bar{t}$.*

We prove this lemma by following the same approach as Bitansky et al. [10] (where a private-coin memory delegation scheme is obtained from a private-coin oracle memory delegation scheme). Specifically, we obtain a public-coin memory delegation scheme by augmenting our public-coin oracle memory delegation scheme (Lemma 6) with a keyless multi-collision-resistant hash function. Roughly speaking, we modify our oracle memory delegation scheme as follows: (i) the verifier is no longer given oracle access to an encoded memory, and instead given a digest that is obtained by hashing the encoded memory with a multi-collision-resistant hash function with a local opening property (such a hash function can be obtained generically from any multi-collision-resistant hash function [10]), and (ii) the prover provides local opening of the encoded memory w.r.t. the locations that are necessary for the verification.[25] After these modifications, soundness can be shown as in Bitansky et al. [10] by relying on the multi-collision resistance of the hash function and the soundness of our oracle memory delegation scheme. (Our proof is simpler since we consider the public-coin setting.) For a formal proof, see the full version of this paper.

7   Public-Coin 3-Round Zero-Knowledge Argument

In this section, we construct a public-coin 3-round zero-knowledge argument.

Theorem 2. *Assume the sub-exponential hardness of the LWE assumption, and assume the existence of a keyless weakly (K, γ)-collision-resistant hash function for $K(\lambda, \zeta) = \mathsf{poly}(\lambda, \zeta)$ and $\gamma(\lambda) = \lambda^{\tau(\lambda)}$ for a super-constant function $\tau(\lambda) = \omega(1)$. Then, there exists a public-coin 3-round zero-knowledge argument for NP.*

---

[25] These locations can be determined based on the proof and the verifier query.

Following prior works [6,10], we prove Theorem 2 by using our weak memory delegation scheme (Lemma 7) to reduce the round complexity of Barak's public-coin zero-knowledge argument [2]. The high-level strategy is quite simple. Very roughly speaking, Barak's public-coin zero-knowledge argument uses a 4-round interactive argument to prove a statement about a digest of a long string, and the verification of this interactive argument is required to run in polynomial time even for a statement about a slightly super-polynomial computation. We reduce the round complexity of Barak's zero-knowledge argument by using our public-coin weak memory delegation scheme instead of this 4-round interactive argument. Soundness and zero-knowledge can be shown as in [6,10], and our proof is simpler since we consider the public-coin setting. For a formal proof, see the full version of this paper.

References

1. Badrinarayanan, S., Goyal, V., Jain, A., Kalai, Y.T., Khurana, D., Sahai, A.: Promise zero knowledge and its applications to round optimal MPC. In: Shacham, H., Boldyreva, A. (eds.) CRYPTO 2018, Part II. LNCS, vol. 10992, pp. 459–487. Springer, Cham (2018). https://doi.org/10.1007/978-3-319-96881-0_16
2. Barak, B.: How to go beyond the black-box simulation barrier. In: 42nd FOCS, pp. 106–115. IEEE Computer Society Press (2001). https://doi.org/10.1109/SFCS.2001.959885
3. Barak, B., Goldreich, O., Goldwasser, S., Lindell, Y.: Resettably-sound zero-knowledge and its applications. In: 42nd FOCS, pp. 116–125. IEEE Computer Society Press (2001). https://doi.org/10.1109/SFCS.2001.959886
4. Bellare, M., Palacio, A.: The knowledge-of-exponent assumptions and 3-round zero-knowledge protocols. In: Franklin, M. (ed.) CRYPTO 2004. LNCS, vol. 3152, pp. 273–289. Springer, Heidelberg (2004). https://doi.org/10.1007/978-3-540-28628-8_17
5. Berman, I., Degwekar, A., Rothblum, R.D., Vasudevan, P.N.: Multi-Collision Resistant Hash Functions and Their Applications. In: Nielsen, J.B., Rijmen, V. (eds.) EUROCRYPT 2018, Part II. LNCS, vol. 10821, pp. 133–161. Springer, Cham (2018). https://doi.org/10.1007/978-3-319-78375-8_5
6. Bitansky, N., Brakerski, Z., Kalai, Y., Paneth, O., Vaikuntanathan, V.: 3-message zero knowledge against human ignorance. In: Hirt, M., Smith, A. (eds.) TCC 2016, Part I. LNCS, vol. 9985, pp. 57–83. Springer, Heidelberg (2016). https://doi.org/10.1007/978-3-662-53641-4_3
7. Bitansky, N., et al.: The hunting of the SNARK. J. Cryptol. **30**(4), 989–1066 (2016). https://doi.org/10.1007/s00145-016-9241-9
8. Bitansky, N., Canetti, R., Paneth, O., Rosen, A.: On the existence of extractable one-way functions. In: Shmoys, D.B. (ed.) 46th ACM STOC, pp. 505–514. ACM Press (2014). https://doi.org/10.1145/2591796.2591859
9. Bitansky, N., Eizenstadt, N., Paneth, O.: Weakly extractable one-way functions. In: Pass, R., Pietrzak, K. (eds.) TCC 2020, Part I. LNCS, vol. 12550, pp. 596–626. Springer, Cham (2020). https://doi.org/10.1007/978-3-030-64375-1_21

10. Bitansky, N., Kalai, Y.T., Paneth, O.: Multi-collision resistance: a paradigm for keyless hash functions. In: Diakonikolas, I., Kempe, D., Henzinger, M. (eds.) 50th ACM STOC, pp. 671–684. ACM Press (2018). https://doi.org/10.1145/3188745.3188870

11. Bitansky, N., Khurana, D., Paneth, O.: Weak zero-knowledge beyond the black-box barrier. In: Charikar, M., Cohen, E. (eds.) 51st ACM STOC, pp. 1091–1102. ACM Press (2019). https://doi.org/10.1145/3313276.3316382

12. Bitansky, N., Lin, H.: One-message zero knowledge and non-malleable commitments. In: Beimel, A., Dziembowski, S. (eds.) TCC 2018, Part I. LNCS, vol. 11239, pp. 209–234. Springer, Cham (2018). https://doi.org/10.1007/978-3-030-03807-6_8

13. Bitansky, N., Paneth, O.: On round optimal statistical zero knowledge arguments. In: Boldyreva, A., Micciancio, D. (eds.) CRYPTO 2019, Part III. LNCS, vol. 11694, pp. 128–156. Springer, Cham (2019). https://doi.org/10.1007/978-3-030-26954-8_5

14. Blum, M.: How to prove a theorem so no one else can claim it. In: Proceedings of the International Congress of Mathematicians, vol. 2, pp. 1444–1451 (1986)

15. Bronfman, L., Rothblum, R.D.: PCPs and instance compression from a cryptographic lens. In: Braverman, M. (ed.) ITCS 2022, vol. 215, pp. 30:1–30:19. LIPIcs (2022). https://doi.org/10.4230/LIPIcs.ITCS.2022.30

16. Canetti, R., Dakdouk, R.R.: Extractable perfectly one-way functions. In: Aceto, L., Damgård, I., Goldberg, L.A., Halldórsson, M.M., Ingólfsdóttir, A., Walukiewicz, I. (eds.) ICALP 2008, Part II. LNCS, vol. 5126, pp. 449–460. Springer, Heidelberg (2008). https://doi.org/10.1007/978-3-540-70583-3_37

17. Choudhuri, A.R., Jain, A., Jin, Z.: SNARGs for $\mathcal{P}$ from LWE. In: 62nd FOCS, pp. 68–79. IEEE Computer Society Press (2022). https://doi.org/10.1109/FOCS52979.2021.00016

18. Choudhuri, A.R., Jain, A., Jin, Z.: SNARGs for $\mathcal{P}$ from LWE. Cryptology ePrint Archive, Report 2021/808, Version 20211108:181325 (2021). https://eprint.iacr.org/2021/808. An extended version of [17]

19. Chung, K.-M., Kalai, Y.T., Liu, F.-H., Raz, R.: Memory delegation. In: Rogaway, P. (ed.) CRYPTO 2011. LNCS, vol. 6841, pp. 151–168. Springer, Heidelberg (2011). https://doi.org/10.1007/978-3-642-22792-9_9

20. Deng, Y.: Individual simulations. In: Moriai, S., Wang, H. (eds.) ASIACRYPT 2020, Part III. LNCS, vol. 12493, pp. 805–836. Springer, Cham (2020). https://doi.org/10.1007/978-3-030-64840-4_27

21. Garg, S., Jain, A., Sahai, A.: Leakage-resilient zero knowledge. In: Rogaway, P. (ed.) CRYPTO 2011. LNCS, vol. 6841, pp. 297–315. Springer, Heidelberg (2011). https://doi.org/10.1007/978-3-642-22792-9_17

22. Goldreich, O.: On the doubly-efficient interactive proof systems of GKR. In: Electronic Colloquium on Computational Complexity (2017). https://eccc.weizmann.ac.il/report/2017/101

23. Goldreich, O., Krawczyk, H.: On the composition of zero-knowledge proof systems. SIAM J. Comput. **25**(1), 169–192 (1996)

24. Goldreich, O., Micali, S., Wigderson, A.: Proofs that yield nothing but their validity or all languages in NP have zero-knowledge proof systems. J. ACM **38**(3), 691–729 (1991)

25. Goldreich, O., Oren, Y.: Definitions and properties of zero-knowledge proof systems. J. Cryptol. **7**(1), 1–32 (1994). https://doi.org/10.1007/BF00195207

26. Goldwasser, S., Kalai, Y.T., Rothblum, G.N.: Delegating computation: interactive proofs for muggles. J. ACM **62**(4), 27:1-27:64 (2015)

27. Hada, S., Tanaka, T.: On the existence of 3-round zero-knowledge protocols. In: Krawczyk, H. (ed.) CRYPTO 1998. LNCS, vol. 1462, pp. 408–423. Springer, Heidelberg (1998). https://doi.org/10.1007/BFb0055744

28. Holmgren, J., Lombardi, A., Rothblum, R.D.: Fiat-Shamir via list-recoverable codes (or: Parallel repetition of GMW is not zero-knowledge). Cryptology ePrint Archive, Report 2021/286, Version: 20210307:022349 (2021). https://eprint.iacr.org/2021/286. An extended version of [29]

29. Holmgren, J., Lombardi, A., Rothblum, R.D.: Fiat-Shamir via list-recoverable codes (or: parallel repetition of GMW is not zero-knowledge). In: Khuller, S., Williams, V.V. (eds.) 53rd ACM STOC, pp. 750–760. ACM Press (2021). https://doi.org/10.1145/3406325.3451116

30. Jain, A., Kalai, Y.T., Khurana, D., Rothblum, R.: Distinguisher-dependent simulation in two rounds and its applications. In: Katz, J., Shacham, H. (eds.) CRYPTO 2017, Part II. LNCS, vol. 10402, pp. 158–189. Springer, Cham (2017). https://doi.org/10.1007/978-3-319-63715-0_6

31. Jawale, R., Kalai, Y.T., Khurana, D., Zhang, R.: SNARGs for bounded depth computations and PPAD hardness from sub-exponential LWE. Cryptology ePrint Archive, Report 2020/980, Version 20200819:035531 (2020). https://eprint.iacr.org/2020/980. An extended version of [32]

32. Jawale, R., Kalai, Y.T., Khurana, D., Zhang, R.: SNARGs for bounded depth computations and PPAD hardness from sub-exponential LWE. In: Khuller, S., Williams, V.V. (eds.) 53rd ACM STOC, pp. 708–721. ACM Press (2021). https://doi.org/10.1145/3406325.3451055

33. Kalai, Y., Paneth, O., Yang, L.: On publicly verifiable delegation from standard assumptions. Cryptology ePrint Archive, Report 2018/776 (2018). https://eprint.iacr.org/2018/776

34. Kalai, Y.T., Paneth, O., Yang, L.: How to delegate computations publicly. In: Charikar, M., Cohen, E. (eds.) 51st ACM STOC, pp. 1115–1124. ACM Press (2019). https://doi.org/10.1145/3313276.3316411

35. Kalai, Y.T., Raz, R., Rothblum, R.D.: How to delegate computations: the power of no-signaling proofs. In: Shmoys, D.B. (ed.) 46th ACM STOC, pp. 485–494. ACM Press (2014). https://doi.org/10.1145/2591796.2591809

36. Khurana, D., Sahai, A.: How to achieve non-malleability in one or two rounds. In: Umans, C. (ed.) 58th FOCS, pp. 564–575. IEEE Computer Society Press (2017). https://doi.org/10.1109/FOCS.2017.58

37. Komargodski, I., Naor, M., Yogev, E.: Collision Resistant Hashing for Paranoids: Dealing with Multiple Collisions. In: Nielsen, J.B., Rijmen, V. (eds.) EUROCRYPT 2018, Part II. LNCS, vol. 10821, pp. 162–194. Springer, Cham (2018). https://doi.org/10.1007/978-3-319-78375-8_6

38. Pass, R.: Simulation in quasi-polynomial time, and its application to protocol composition. In: Biham, E. (ed.) EUROCRYPT 2003. LNCS, vol. 2656, pp. 160–176. Springer, Heidelberg (2003). https://doi.org/10.1007/3-540-39200-9_10

39. Regev, O.: On lattices, learning with errors, random linear codes, and cryptography. J. ACM **56**(6), 1–40 (2009)

Faster Sounder Succinct Arguments and IOPs

Justin Holmgren[1(✉)] and Ron D. Rothblum[2]

[1] NTT Research, Sunnyvale, USA
justin.holmgren@ntt-research.com
[2] Technion, Haifa, Israel
rothblum@cs.technion.ac.il

Abstract. Succinct arguments allow a prover to convince a verifier that a given statement is true, using an extremely short proof. A major bottleneck that has been the focus of a large body of work is in reducing the overhead incurred by the prover in order to prove correctness of the computation. By overhead we refer to the cost of proving correctness, divided by the cost of the original computation.

In this work, for a large class of Boolean circuits $C = C(x, w)$, we construct succinct arguments for the language $\{x : \exists w \; C(x, w) = 1\}$, with $2^{-\lambda}$ soundness error, and with prover overhead $\text{polylog}(\lambda)$. This result relies on the existence of (sub-exponentially secure) linear-size computable collision-resistant hash functions. The class of Boolean circuits that we can handle includes circuits with a repeated sub-structure, which arise in natural applications such as batch computation/verification, hashing and related block chain applications.

The succinct argument is obtained by constructing *interactive oracle proofs* for the same class of languages, with $\text{polylog}(\lambda)$ prover overhead, and soundness error $2^{-\lambda}$. Prior to our work, the best IOPs for Boolean circuits either had prover overhead of $\text{polylog}(|C|)$ based on efficient PCPs due to Ben Sasson *et al.* (STOC, 2013) or $\text{poly}(\lambda)$ due to Rothblum and Ron-Zewi (STOC, 2022).

Keywords: Succinct Arguments · Proof-Systems · Zero-knowledge

1 Introduction

Succinct arguments are interactive proof systems that allow a prover to convince a verifier that a computational statement is true, using an extremely short proof. Soundness is computational—no polynomial-time cheating prover can convince the verifier to accept a false statement except with negligible probability.

Succinct arguments, especially those that are *zero-knowledge* [GMR89], originate in the pioneering theoretical works of Kilian [Kil92] and Micali [Mic00]. In recent years however they have been drawing immense interest also in practice and several different systems are being developed and deployed.[1] One of the major bottlenecks to more widespread deployment is the overhead incurred by the

---

[1] See https://zkproof.org for additional details and resources as well as the recent surveys [Ish20, Tha21].

© International Association for Cryptologic Research 2022
Y. Dodis and T. Shrimpton (Eds.): CRYPTO 2022, LNCS 13507, pp. 474–503, 2022.
https://doi.org/10.1007/978-3-031-15802-5_17

prover—the cost of proving that a statement is true is still orders of magnitude larger than directly checking that the statement is true.

The original work of Kilian [Kil92], based on PCPs and collision resistant hash functions, has a prover that has a large polynomial overhead. Since Kilian's original work, and especially in recent years, there has been significant effort in improving the prover's runtime. In particular, a recent line of works have achieved succinct arguments with a linear-size prover [BCG+17,XZZ+19, ZWZZ20,BCG20,BCL20,LSTW21,GLS+21] for arithmetic circuits over large finite fields. Even more recently, Ron-Zewi and Rothblum [RR21] constructed succinct arguments with a *strictly linear-size prover* for general Boolean circuits. However, the soundness error in their protocol is constant, rather than negligible as we would typically desire. All of these results fall short of the holy-grail in the field, which is captured by the following question:

Can we construct succinct arguments and interactive oracle proofs for size-S circuits with an $O(S) + \mathrm{poly}(\lambda)$ size prover and soundness error $2^{-\lambda}$?

We emphasize that straightforward repetition, or working over 2^λ-size finite fields, yields an $O(S \cdot \lambda)$-size prover (when implemented as a Boolean circuit). The challenge that we are faced with is therefore breaking the multiplicative dependence between the circuit size and the security parameter into an additive one.

1.1 Our Results

In this work we construct succinct arguments that come close to resolving the above question, for a large class of Boolean circuits. Our first main result is a succinct argument-system with a $|C| \cdot \mathrm{polylog}(\lambda) + \mathrm{poly}(\lambda, \log|C|)$-size prover, for the relevant class of circuits C. This result relies on the existence of linear-size computable hash functions such as those constructed by Applebaum *et al.* [AHI+17].

Theorem 1.1 (Informally Stated, see Theorem 4.6). *Assume the existence of sub-exponentially secure linear-size computable hash functions.*

Then, for any Boolean circuit $C : \{0,1\}^{n+m} \to \{0,1\}$ of size S with a "nice" succinct description of size s, there exists a succinct public-coin argument for the language $\{x \in \{0,1\}^n : \exists w \in \{0,1\}^m, C(x,w) = 1\}$, with $2^{-\lambda}$ soundness error and an $S \cdot \mathrm{polylog}(\lambda) + \mathrm{poly}(\lambda, \log S)$ size prover. The communication complexity is $\mathrm{poly}(\lambda, \log S)$, the number of rounds is $O(\log S)$ and the verifier runs in time $O(n + s \cdot \lambda)$.

We emphasize that the main novelty in Theorem 4.6 is that the prover has size roughly $S \cdot \mathrm{polylog}(\lambda)$, rather than $S \cdot \mathrm{poly}(\lambda)$. The "nice" class of circuits that we handle generalizes (modulo minor technicalities[2]) the notion of Succinct R1CS,

---

[2] Succinct R1CS was defined as a constraint system involving two types of constraints: time constraints and boundary constraints. We can always handle the time constraints, and handle natural boundary constraints, which were the motivation for the succinct R1CS definition.

introduced by Ben Sasson *et al.* [BCG+19]. Loosely speaking, this class captures computations that have some repeated sub-structure. As the precise definition is somewhat involved and quite general (see Definition 4.2) we highlight two particular examples of interest. The first is "T-iterated" circuits for $T \geq \lambda$, i.e. those which map $z = (x, w)$ to $\underbrace{(D \circ \cdots \circ D)}_{T \text{ times}}(z)$ for a small circuit D. The second is "batch" circuits, which map $(z_1, \ldots, z_T)$ to $D(z_1) \wedge \cdots \wedge D(z_T)$, again for $T \geq \lambda$. In both cases, for any $\varepsilon > 0$, we obtain a protocol where our prover has size $T \cdot |D| \cdot \text{polylog}(\lambda)$ and our verifier has size $(|D| + T^\varepsilon) \cdot \text{poly}(\lambda)$. We remark that these class of computations arise in natural scenarios involving cryptographic hashing and blockchains.

Following a body of recent works, Theorem 1.1 follows (non-trivially) from an analogous (unconditional) *interactive oracle proof* (IOP) [BCS16, RRR21]. An IOP can be thought of as an interactive version of a PCP—the prover can interact with the verifier, who in turn is allowed to read a few bits from each message sent by the prover. Our main technical result is a new efficient IOP construction for the same class of problems.

Theorem 1.2 (Informally Stated, see Theorem 4.5**).** *For the same family of Boolean circuits* $C : \{0,1\}^{n+m} \to \{0,1\}$ *of size* S *with a "nice" succinct description of size* s, *there exists an* IOP *for the language* $\{x \in \{0,1\}^n : \exists w \in \{0,1\}^m, \; C(x,w) = 1\}$, *with* $2^{-\lambda}$ *soundness error and an* $S \cdot \text{polylog}(\lambda)$ *size prover. The number of rounds is* $O(\log S)$, *the query complexity is* $s \cdot \text{poly}(\lambda)$ *and the verifier runs in time* $n \cdot \text{polylog}(\lambda) + s \cdot \text{poly}(\lambda)$.

We note that there are two aspects that make the compilation of the IOP of Theorem 1.2 into the succinct argument of Theorem 1.1 non-trivial. The first is the fact that the query complexity in Theorem 1.2 has an s dependence which may be only slightly sublinear in S, whereas the communication complexity in Theorem 1.1 has a poly-logarithmic dependence on S. This improvement is actually relatively easy to achieve—we first construct an argument-system in which the communication complexity is $s \cdot \text{poly}(\lambda)$ but then compose with an off-the-shelf argument-system (e.g., the original [Kil92] argument) to reduce the communication to be poly-logarithmic. (We remark that we leave open the question of improving the verification time and query complexity to be poly-logarithmic in the IOP of Theorem 1.2.)

A more subtle, and serious, issue is that in order to implement the standard transformation of IOPs into succinct arguments [Kil92, BCS16] the prover needs to be able to *project* its IOP messages to the specific verifier query locations. The straightforward circuit for projecting a string of length $N = S \cdot \text{polylog}(\lambda)$ to q coordinates, has size $O(N \cdot q)$ which we cannot afford. To the best of our knowledge no circuit of size $O(N) + \text{poly}(q, \log N)$ is known for the problem, which poses a serious difficulty. In [RR21] this problem was overcome by ensuring that the verifier makes only a constant number of queries to each message (or reads it entirely). In our IOP since we are aiming for $2^{-\lambda}$ soundness error, intuitively, the verifier has to make $\Omega(\lambda)$ queries and so we cannot follow the

[RR21] approach. Rather, we overcome the difficulty by ensuring a utilizing a particular query structure of our IOP verifier, see Sect. 2 for details.

1.2 Related Work

The general question of constructing cryptographic primitives with constant overhead was raised by Ishai *et al.* [IKOS08]. In particular, they asked whether we can construct zero-knowledge proofs (with negligible soundness error) and constant computational overhead for the prover.

As was previously mentioned, a recent exciting line of work [BCG+17, XZZ+19, ZWZZ20, BCG20, BCL20, LSTW21, GLS+21] has constructed succinct arguments for *arithmetic* circuits over large finite fields, with a linear-size prover (see also [GLS+21] for a more through discussion and comparison of some of these works). In the Boolean circuit regime, the best result is the recent work of [RR21] which achieves a linear-size prover, albeit with only a constant soundness error.

A separate line of work has focused on constructing zero-knowledge proofs with a linear-size prover, but where the *communication* may also grow linearly in the circuit size. (Here the aspect that makes the problem non-trivial is simply that the proof should be zero-knowledge.) Such a non-succinct zero-knowledge proof, with a linear-size prover, can be derived fairly directly from [IKOS09], using linear-size computable commitments, but the resulting proof-system has a constant soundness error.

Damgård *et al.* [DIK10] similarly construct non-succinct zero-knowledge proofs with comparable prover size to ours - namely, $|C| \cdot \mathrm{polylog}(\lambda)$. We emphasize however that the [DIK10] protocol is not succinct.

Recent works by Weng *et al.* [WYKW21] and Franzese *et al.* [FKL+21] also construct non-succinct zero-knowledge proof (with sub-constant soundness error), where the prover can be implemented as a linear-time RAM program. Concurrent to [WYKW21], and using related techniques, Dittmer *et al.* [DIO21] (see also the followup [YSWW21]) and Baum *et al.* [BMRS21] constructed zero-knowledge proofs for arithmetic circuits with constant overhead.

A separate line of work focuses on the *space efficiency* of the prover. Proof-systems achieving time *and* space efficient provers are known in the designated verifier setting [BC12, HR18] as well as in the publicly verifiable setting [BHR+20, BHR+21]. The work of [EFKP20] achieves highly efficient *parallel time*.

1.3 Organization

In Sect. 2 we give an overview of our techniques. In Sect. 3 we introduce notations and definitions that will be used throughout this work. Our main results are formally stated in Sect. 4. In Sect. 5 we introduce some tools that we be used to construct our IOPs. In Sect. 6 we give the key IOP sub-protocols that are used in our construction. In Sect. 7 we combine all of the above to prove our main results. In the full version, we include the (by now standard) definition of IOPs and concrete realizations of our tensor circuit framework.

2   Technical Overview

Multi-sumcheck with Small Error. The starting point of our work is the aforementioned recent work of Ron-Zewi and Rothblum [RR21]. One of the key technical ideas in that work is an efficient "multi-sumcheck" protocol. Generally speaking, a *multi-sumcheck* IOP is an IOP in which the verifier is given oracle access to a pair of codewords c, c', belonging to a code $C : \mathbb{F}^k \to \mathbb{F}^n$, and would like to compute the inner product $\sum_{i \in [k]} c(i) \cdot c'(i)$.[3] Ron-Zewi and Rothblum construct a linear-size encodable code C which has a multi-sumcheck protocol with a linear-size prover. Unfortunately, the protocol only has a constant soundness error.

We first discuss two common approaches for error reduction. The first is simply to repeat the protocol $O(\lambda)$ times. This indeed reduces the soundness error at an exponential rate, but naturally increases the prover's size by a λ multiplicative factor, which we would like to avoid. Another common approach is to try to work with codes with very large minimal distance, say $1 - 2^{-\lambda}$. Unfortunately, by the Plotkin bound, such codes require an exponentially-large alphabet which would again introduce a poly(λ) multiplicative factor in runtime.

Thus, our first key insight is a (simple) method for reducing the soundness error of the [RR21] protocol to $2^{-\lambda}$, but with only a polylog(λ) overhead in the prover's size.

Let $\mathbb{F}$ be a finite field of size $O(\lambda)$ and consider the Reed-Solomon code $RS_\lambda : \mathbb{F}^\lambda \to \mathbb{F}^{O(\lambda)}$ over $\mathbb{F}$ - namely, the code consisting of all degree $\lambda - 1$ polynomials over $|\mathbb{F}|$. We will use two key properties of the Reed-Solomon code: (1) that it is a *multiplication code* (since the point-wise (aka Hadamard) product of any two polynomials is a polynomial of degree at most 2λ and therefore belongs to a closely related Reed-Solomon code) *and* (2) that it can be encoded by a size $\lambda \cdot$ polylog(λ) circuit (using the Fast Fourier Transform). We remark that the parameters (in particular the field size and block length) are set so that RS_λ has a constant relative distance and further note that we could replace the Reed-Solomon code with any constant-distance multiplication code with quasi-linear time encoding.

In addition to the ubiquitous Reed-Solomon code, we will also use the code C from [RR21]. Indeed, we will combine these two codes to construct a new code D and show an efficient multi-sumcheck procedure for D with a small soundness error.

The code D is simply the tensor product of RS_λ with C, denoted $D = C \otimes RS_\lambda$. In this code, messages are viewed as $(k/\lambda) \times \lambda$ matrices and we encode them by encoding first the rows using RS_λ and encode the columns (both old and the new ones generated by the row encoding) using C (where we use C with respect to message size k/λ).[4] Observe that since RS_λ is encodable by a $\lambda \cdot$polylog(λ)-size

---

[3] For simplicity we focus here on the case of two codewords, but in general we would like to be able to handle any constant number of codewords.

[4] A minor technical inaccuracy is that the Reed-Solomon code's alphabet is $\mathbb{F}$ whereas the [RR21] code has a binary alphabet. This can be easily be resolved by a sim-

circuit, and C is encodable by a linear-size circuit, the code D is overall encodable by a circuit of size $(k/\lambda) \cdot \lambda \cdot \text{polylog}(\lambda) + O(\lambda) \cdot O(k/\lambda) = k \cdot \text{polylog}(\lambda)$. Thus, the code D maps messages of length k to codewords of length $k \cdot \text{polylog}(\lambda)$ and is encodable by a $k \cdot \text{polylog}(\lambda)$ size circuit.

Our first main step is showing a multi-sumcheck protocol for D, with soundness error $2^{-\lambda}$. Recall that the input to this protocol is two codewords $d, d' \in D$, and we would like to check that $\sum_{i \in [k/\lambda], j \in [\lambda]} d(i,j) \cdot d'(i,j) = b$, for some scalar b. The protocol is simple - the prover generates the codeword $d_{sum} \in RS_{2\lambda}$ (we use $R_{2\lambda}$ to denote the Reed-Solomon code of the same block length as RS_λ but double the degree) defined as $d_{sum} = \sum_{i \in [k]} d_i \star d'_i$, where d_i and d'_i denote the i-th rows of d and d', respectively, and $\star$ denotes a point-wise/Hadamard product. Note that by linearity, d_{sum} is indeed a codeword of $RS_{2\lambda}$ and that $\sum_j d_{sum}(j) = \sum_{i,j} d(i,j) \cdot d'(i,j)$. The prover computes d_{sum} and sends it explicitly to the verifier. The verifier in turn, after receiving the message $\tilde{d}_{sum}$ (which may or may not be equal to the intended d_{sum}) checks that $\tilde{d}_{sum} \in RS_{2\lambda}$ and that $\sum_{j \in [\lambda]} \tilde{d}_{sum}(j) = b$.

Thus, if the original claim is false, in order not to be caught already at this stage, the prover must send a false codeword $\tilde{d}_{sum} \not\equiv d_{sum}$.

At this point we observe that $\tilde{d}_{sum}$ and d_{sum} are distinct codewords and so they must disagree on a constant fraction of their coordinates. A typical "sumcheck" approach would be for the verifier to choose at random one of these coordinates and recursively check the resulting multi-sumcheck claim. This is the approach taken both in the classical sum-check as well as in [RR21].

Our approach differs here. In a nutshell, we observe that we can afford to run the [RR21] multi-sumcheck procedure for *each and every one* of the claims induced by $\tilde{d}_{sum}$, each with a constant soundness error, say $1/2$. Since *many* (i.e., $\Omega(\lambda)$) of the claims are false, the probability that the prover will successfully cheat in *all* of these invocation is $2^{-\Omega(\lambda)}$.

In more detail, denote the set of coordinates on which d_{sum} and $\tilde{d}_{sum}$ differ by $J \subseteq [O(\lambda)]$. That is,

$$J = \left\{ j : \tilde{d}_{sum}(j) \neq d_{sum}(j) = \sum_{i \in [k/\lambda]} d(i,j) \cdot d'(i,j) \right\}.$$

Recall that by the above arguments, we know that $|J| = \Omega(\lambda)$. At this point we run the [RR21] multi-sumcheck protocol, with a constant soundness error, on each and every coordinate j to check that $\sum_{i \in [k/\lambda]} d(i,j) \cdot d'(i,j) = \tilde{d}_{sum}(j)$. The cost of each invocation is $O(k/\lambda)$, and we have $O(\lambda)$ such invocations, leading to an overall cost of $O(k)$. In terms of soundness, for each $j \in J$, the probability that the verifier accepts in the underlying multi-sumcheck is at most a constant and so the probability that it accepts for *all* $j \in J$ is $2^{-\lambda}$, as desired.

---

ple extension of the [RR21] result to the larger alphabet size, while accounting for additional $\text{polylog}(|\mathbb{F}|)$ factors in efficiency, which we can afford since $|\mathbb{F}| = O(\lambda)$.

This concludes the description of the multi-sumcheck protocol. We remark that in prior works, such as [RR21], the multi-sumcheck was the key component and other protocols follows in a straightforward manner. Unfortunately, in our parameter regime this is no longer the case.

To demonstrate this, consider the following related task that arises often in the construction of IOPs. Suppose we are given access to a codeword c and want to check that the first k' bits of c are identically 0. A common approach for doing so is to have the verifier choose at random (or pseudorandomly) a vector $r \in \{0,1\}^{k'}$ and to run multi-sumcheck on the expression $\sum_{i \in [k']} r_i \cdot c_i = 0$. The point is that if the claim is false (i.e., $c_i \neq 0$ for some $i \in [k']$) then the above sum will still be zero with probability that is inversely proportional to the field size $|\mathbb{F}|$. In all prior works that we are aware of, this sufficed since the goal was to have error probability $1/|\mathbb{F}|$. In contrast, in this work we want to simultaneously work over a field of size polylog(λ) but to have soundness error $2^{-\lambda}$. We manage to solve this difficulty by taking an approach that is similar to, but somewhat more complicated than, our approach for handling the multi-sumcheck protocol.

At a high level, we again view c as a tensor codeword. Using the efficient Reed-Solomon encoding, we can transform c into a new codeword c' so that if c was non-zero in even one coordinate in $[k']$, then c' is non-zero in many of its columns. We can then check each and every one of the columns using [RR21], each with a constant error probability, to overall get a $2^{-\lambda}$ error probability.

A Difficulty with Arithmetization. With a toolkit of efficient IOP sub-protocols in hand, it now seems straightforward to use existing ideas from the literature to construct an IOP for NP. Unfortunately, this turns out to be more complicated than expected. To explain the difficulty, let us focus on a specific NP complete problem which is particularly "arithmetization friendly", called R1CS (for Rank 1 Constraint Satisfiability). We view the problem as being parameterized by three (sparse) square matrices A, B and C and a given input x belongs to the language if there exists w such that $Az \star Bz = Cz$, where $z = (x, w)$.

The typical way to arithmetize the problem is for the prover to send encodings of z, $a = Az$, $b = Bz$ and $c = Cz$ and run sub-protocols to check that:

- $a \star b = c$.
- $a = Az$, $b = Bz$ and $c = Cz$.

The first check can be handled using the multi-sumcheck and related techniques and so we do not elaborate on this point. The latter check however turns out to be more complicated.

Let us see the difficulty in trying to employ a standard approach (c.f., [BCR+19]): the verifier chooses a random (or pseudorandom) vector r to reduce checking that $a = Az$ to checking that:

$$\sum_i r_i a_i = \sum_i r_i (Az)_i = \sum_i (r^T A)_i z_i$$

and now the two sides of the equation can be computed by employing the multi-sumcheck protocol. The problem that we encounter is that a single execution of this approach only has a constant soundness error (if we are working over a small field). Our techniques for boosting the soundness that worked for multi-sumcheck seem to fail because the matrix A is arbitrary which precludes attempts at decomposing the problem into smaller sub-problems.

Rather than handling arbitrary matrices A, we restrict our attention to matrices that have a specific structure. In particular, we start by considering matrices of the form $A = I_k \otimes A_0$, where I_k is the $k \times k$ identity matrix and A_0 is a small matrix, say of size $s \times s$. Intuitively, we can think of A as acting on $k \times s$ matrices, such that if $y = A(x)$, then each row of y is obtained from the corresponding row of x by applying A_0. If x and y are column-wise encoded with a fixed linear code C, then we can say the same thing for the encodings $\hat{x}$ and $\hat{y}$ of x and y respectively: each row of $\hat{y}$ is obtained from the corresponding row of $\hat{x}$ by applying A_0.

Now if C has constant relative distance, the verifier given $\hat{x}$ and $\hat{y}$ has a way to succinctly check, with low soundness error, whether $y = Ax$: the verifier samples λ random rows of $\hat{x}$, along with the corresponding rows of $\hat{y}$, and checks that the latter are obtained from the former by applying A_0. If $y \neq Ax$, then the distance of C implies that at least a constant fraction of the rows of $\hat{y}$ are incorrectly generated, and so the verifier will reject with probability $2^{-\Omega(\lambda)}$. Note that the size of this verifier is $O(\lambda \cdot s^2)$, which can be much smaller than the number of entries of A (which is $k^2 \cdot s^2$).

We can push this simple idea quite far. Instead of viewing A as acting on matrices, we view A as acting on degree-d tensors, and instead of column-wise encodings we use tensor codes. This immediately allows us to handle matrices A of the form $A_1 \otimes \cdots \otimes A_d$. We can also handle sum of such matrices, and in fact we give a more general notion of matrices A that are computable by a new notion that we introduce called "succinct tensor circuits" (see Definition 4.2). As noted in Sect. 1.1, this notion generalizes (modulo some technicalities) the notion of succinct R1CS [BCG+19], see the full version for details.

The Projection Problem. We turn to discussing an additional subtle difficulty that we encounter when attempting to compile our IOP into an efficient argument (and which was briefly discussed in Sect. 1.1). The common approach for compiling an IOP, as proposed by [BCS16] (following [Kil92]) is for the prover to send Merkle hashes of each of its messages and, at the end of the protocol, to send authentication paths corresponding to the verifier's desired queries.

The problem is that projecting the proof string to the desired query locations may, in general, introduce overhead. This naturally raises the following question: can we construct a "multi-plexing" circuit of size $O(N) + \text{poly}(k, \log N)$ that given a string $x \in \{0,1\}^N$ (in our case the IOP string) and a set $Q \subseteq [N]$ (i.e., the verifier's queries) of size k, outputs x_Q. Note that for our purposes we cannot afford a circuit of size $\Omega(N \cdot k)$ for this task, and even a circuit of size $\Omega(N \cdot \log(N))$ would be too much.

Unfortunately, we do not know how to solve the above task in general with the desired complexity. Imagine though, that we had a promise that the query set Q has a nice structure - namely, that we can partition the input x into N/k

blocks and that the first query in Q is to block 1, the second is to block 2 and so forth. In such a case, we could just concatenate k simple multi-plexing circuits each of size $O(N/k)$ to solve the problem and get, overall, a circuit of size $O(N)$.

Unfortunately, typical IOPs have a highly random query pattern. For example, one of the tasks that we often have to do is sample some $O(\lambda)$ coordinates of a given codeword c (from a code with constant relative distance) so that we can guarantee that with probability $1 - 2^{-\lambda}$ at least one of the entries is non-zero.

Our observation, is that the random sampling of $k = O(\lambda)$ points can indeed be replaced in this case by partitioning the codeword into blocks of N/k and choosing just a single point in each block! While this distribution is far from the uniform distribution over $[n]^k$, it is easy to show that it still solves our sampling task with an exponentially small error probability. We extend this approach to all of the verifier's tests to obtain an IOP for which we can indeed efficiently project the IOP messages to the verifier's query set.

3   Preliminaries

3.1   Notation and Conventions

Throughout this paper we use the notion of a Boolean circuit. When we refer to the size of a circuit, we use the usual meaning (the number of gates).

3.2   Probability

We use the following Chernoff bound.

Fact 3.1 (Chernoff). *If $X_1, \ldots, X_n$ are independent $\{0,1\}$-valued random variables and if μ denotes the expected value of $\sum_i X_i$, then for all $0 \le \delta \le 1$,*

$$\Pr\left[\sum_i X_i \le (1 - \delta) \cdot \mu\right] \le e^{-\frac{\delta^2 \mu}{2}}.$$

3.3   Constructible Finite Fields

We will assume that all fields that we work with are *constructible*.

Definition 3.2. *A field ensemble $\mathbb{F} = (\mathbb{F}_n)_{n \in \mathbb{N}}$ is* constructible *if field elements can be represented using $O(\log(|\mathbb{F}_n|))$ bits and field operations (i.e., addition, subtraction, multiplication, inversion and sampling random elements) can be performed using a Boolean circuit of size $\mathrm{polylog}(|\mathbb{F}_n|)$.*

Fact 3.3 (See, e.g., [Sho88]). *For every $S = S(n) \ge 1$, there exists a constructible field ensemble $(\mathbb{F}_n)_{n \in \mathbb{N}}$ where each $\mathbb{F}_n$ has characteristic 2 and size $\Theta(S(n))$.*

3.4   Error-Correcting Codes

Let Σ be a finite alphabet, and k, n be positive integers (the message length and the codeword length, respectively). An (error-correcting) code is an injective map $C : \Sigma^k \to \Sigma^n$. The elements in the domain of C are called messages, and the elements in the image of C are called codewords. We say that C is systematic if the message is a prefix of the corresponding codeword, i.e., for every $x \in \Sigma^k$ there exists $z \in \Sigma^{n-k}$ such that $C(x) = (x, z)$.

The rate of a code $C : \Sigma^k \to \Sigma^n$ is the ratio $\rho := \frac{k}{n}$. The relative distance $\mathrm{dist}(C)$ of C is the maximum $\delta > 0$ such that for every pair of distinct messages $x, y \in \Sigma^k$ it holds that $\mathrm{dist}_\Sigma(C(x), C(y)) \geq \delta$.

If $\Sigma = \mathbb{F}$ for some finite field $\mathbb{F}$, and C is a linear map between the vector spaces $\mathbb{F}^k$ and $\mathbb{F}^n$ then we say that C is linear. The generating matrix of a linear code $C : \mathbb{F}^k \to \mathbb{F}^n$ is a matrix $G \in \mathbb{F}^{n \times k}$ such that $C(x) = G \cdot x$ for any $x \in \mathbb{F}^k$.

3.4.1   Multiplication Codes

Definition 3.4. *The* Hadamard *product of vectors $x, y \in \mathbb{F}^n$, denoted $x \star y$, is the vector $z \in \mathbb{F}^n$ whose i^{th} component is $z_i = x_i \cdot y_i$.*

If X and Y are subsets of $\mathbb{F}^n$, we write $X \star Y$ to denote the set $\{x \star y : x \in X, y \in Y\}$, and for integer $t \geq 0$ we define

$$X^{\star t} = \begin{cases} \{1^n\} & \text{if } t = 0 \\ X \star X^{\star(t-1)} & \text{otherwise.} \end{cases}$$

3.4.2   Tensor Codes

A main ingredient in our constructions is the tensor product operation, defined as follows (see, e.g., [Sud01, DSW06]).

Definition 3.5 (Tensor codes). *The* tensor product code *of linear codes $C : \mathbb{F}^k \to \mathbb{F}^n$ and $C' : \mathbb{F}^{k'} \to \mathbb{F}^{n'}$ is the code $C \otimes C' : \mathbb{F}^{k \times k'} \to \mathbb{F}^{n \times n'}$, where the encoding $(C \otimes C')(M)$ of any message $M \in \mathbb{F}^{k \times k'}$ is obtained by first encoding each column of M with the code C, and then encoding each of the n resulting rows with the code C'.*

Note that by linearity, the codewords of $C \otimes C'$ are $n \times n'$ matrices (over the field $\mathbb{F}$) whose columns belong to the code C, and whose rows belong to the code C'. It is also known that the converse is true: any $n \times n'$ matrix, whose columns belong to the code C, and whose rows belong to the code C', is a codeword of $C \otimes C'$.

Definition 3.6. *We say that a function $f : \{0,1\}^n \to \{0,1\}^m$ is* locally computable *by a size S circuit if there is a size-S circuit that takes as input $x \in \{0,1\}^n$ and $i \in [m]$ and outputs $f(x)_i$.*

By the definition of the tensor product code, we have the following.

Claim 3.7. *The following holds for any pair of linear codes* $C : \mathbb{F}^k \to \mathbb{F}^n$, $C' : \mathbb{F}^{k'} \to \mathbb{F}^{n'}$.

1. *If* C, C' *can be encoded by Boolean circuits of sizes* S, S' *respectively, then* $C \otimes C'$ *can be encoded by a Boolean circuit of size* $n' \cdot S + n \cdot S'$.
2. *If* C *and* C' *are locally computable by size* S_0 *and* S_0' *circuits, respectively, then:*
   (a) *There is a size* $k' \cdot S_0 + S_0'$ *circuit whose input is a message* $m \in \mathbb{F}^k \otimes \mathbb{F}^{k'}$ *and an index* $i \in [n] \times [n']$ *and whose output is* $(C \otimes C')(m)_i$.
   (b) *There is a size* $S_0 + S_0'$ *circuit that on input* $m \in \mathbb{F}^k$, $m' \in \mathbb{F}^{k'}$, *and* $i \in [n] \times [n']$, *outputs* $(C \otimes C')(m \otimes m')_i$.

For a linear code $C : \mathbb{F}^k \to \mathbb{F}^n$, let $C^{\otimes 0} := \mathbb{F} \to \mathbb{F}$ denote the identity function (i.e. the function computed by the 1×1 matrix $[1]$), and let and $C^{\otimes t}$ denote $C \otimes C^{\otimes(t-1)}$ for any $t \geq 1$.

Finally, applying iteratively the above Claim 3.7, gives the following.

Claim 3.8. *The following holds for any linear code* $C : \mathbb{F}^k \to \mathbb{F}^n$.

1. *If* $C : \mathbb{F}^k \to \mathbb{F}^n$ *can be encoded by a Boolean circuit of size* s, *then* $C^{\otimes t}$ *can be encoded by a Boolean circuit of size* $t n^{t-1} s$.
2. *If each coordinate of* C *can be computed in time* T_0, *then:*
   (a) *For every* $t \in \mathbb{Z}^+$, *there is a size* $O(k^{t-1} \cdot T_0)$ *circuit that takes as input* $m \in (\mathbb{F}^k)^{\otimes t}$ *and* $i \in [n]^t$ *and outputs* $C^{\otimes t}(m)_i$.
   (b) *For every* $t \in \mathbb{Z}^+$, *there is a size* $O(t \cdot T_0)$ *circuit that takes as input* $m_1, \ldots, m_t \in \mathbb{F}^k$ *and* $i \in [n]^t$ *and outputs* $C^{\otimes t}(m_1 \otimes \cdots \otimes m_t)_i$.

4   Main Results

Our results are most naturally stated in terms of (a slight modification to the notion of) Rank-1 Constraint Satisfaction (R1CS) relations.

Definition 4.1 (R1CS). *A Rank-1 Constraint Satisfaction (R1CS) relation over a field* $\mathbb{F}$ *is parameterized by matrices* $A, B, C \in \mathbb{F}^{M \times N}$ *and* $X \in \mathbb{F}^{n \times N}$, *and is defined as the set*

$$\mathcal{R}_{\mathsf{R1CS}}^{A,B,C,X} \stackrel{\text{def}}{=} \left\{ (x, z) \in \mathbb{F}^n \times \mathbb{F}^N : X \cdot z = x \ \wedge \ (A \cdot z) \star (B \cdot z) = C \cdot z \right\},$$

where $\star$ *denotes pointwise multiplication.*
We define $\mathcal{L}_{\mathsf{R1CS}}^{A,B,C,X}$ *as the set*

$$\left\{ x \in \mathbb{F}^n : \exists z \in \mathbb{F}^N \ s.t. \ (x, z) \in \mathcal{R}_{\mathsf{R1CS}} \right\}.$$

We remark that the standard definition of R1CS require x to be a prefix of z. Our definition can simulate the former by setting X to be the matrix that projects its length-N input to the first n coordinates.

We will focus on R1CS relations for which the matrices A, B, C, X defining the R1CS relation can be succinctly expressed as a "tensor circuit".

Definition 4.2 (Tensor Circuits). *We define a* tensor circuit over $\mathbb{F}$ *to be a triple* $C = \left((V_i)_{i\in[N]}, (L_i)_{i\in[g+1]}, (\varphi_i)_{i\in[g]}\right)$, *where each* V_i *is a vector space over* $\mathbb{F}$, *each* L_i *is a subset of* $[N]$, *and for every* $j \in [g]$, φ_j *is a linear function mapping* $\bigotimes_{i\in L_j\setminus L_{j+1}} V_i \to \bigotimes_{i\in L_{j+1}\setminus L_j} V_i$.

We associate C *with a function* $f_g \circ \cdots \circ f_1$, *where* f_i *represents a function corresponding to the* i^{th} *gate* φ_i, *and is defined as*

$$f_i : \bigotimes_{j\in L_i} V_j \to \bigotimes_{j\in L_{i+1}} V_j$$

$$f_i = \varphi_i \otimes \bigotimes_{j\in L_i\cap L_{i+1}} \mathrm{Id}_{V_j} . \tag{1}$$

Remark 4.3. In Definition 4.2, we take all tensor products to be indexed by an unordered set L. For example, each L_i is an unordered set and yet we consider the tensor product $\bigotimes_{j\in L_i} V_i$. This reflects the fact that many aspects of the "ordering" of wires in (a layer of) a circuit are arbitrary and only serve to complicate notation. For example, when applying a gate φ to the ith and j^{th} wires of a layer, it shouldn't matter whether $i = 1$ and $j = 2$, or if $i = 3$ and $j = 5$. However, if we force the usual ordered semantics, then only the former has the clean notation $\varphi \otimes \mathrm{Id}$. What we are doing with the above notation is *implicitly* specifying which wires φ is applied to via the domain of φ.

Definition 4.4 (Tensor Circuit Parameters). *If* $C = \left((V_i)_{i\in[N]}, (L_i)_{i\in[g+1]}, (\varphi_i)_{i\in[g]}\right)$ *is a tensor circuit, we define the following important parameters of* C:

- *Width:* $\max_{i\in[g+1]} \prod_{j\in L_i} \dim(V_j)$.
- *Degree:* $\max |L_i|$.
- *Number of Gates:* g
- *Total Gate Size: The sum of the circuit complexities of* φ_i.

In terms of tensor circuits, our first main result is the following IOP.

Theorem 4.5 (Main IOP Construction). *Let* $\mathcal{R} = \mathcal{R}_{R1CS}^{A,B,C,X}$ *be an* R1CS *relation, where* A, B, *and* C *are* $M \times N$ *matrices and* X *is an* $n \times N$ *matrix.*

Suppose that for some constant-dimensional integer vectors $\mathbf{k}^{(x)}, \mathbf{k}^{(y)}, \mathbf{k}^{(z)}$ *(possibly of different dimensions), there are isomorphisms* $\mathbb{F}_2^N \cong \bigotimes_i \mathbb{F}^{k_i^{(z)}}$, *and* $\mathbb{F}_2^M \cong \bigotimes_i \mathbb{F}^{k_i^{(y)}}$, *and* $\mathbb{F}_2^n \cong \bigotimes_i \mathbb{F}^{k_i^{(x)}}$, *such that when* A, B, C, *and* X *are viewed as maps between the corresponding tensor spaces, they each are computable by a constant-degree tensor circuit over* $\mathbb{F}_2$ *with* g *gates, width* W, *and total gate size* S.

Then for all $\varepsilon > 0$ *there is an* IOP *for* $\mathcal{R}$ *with soundness error* $2^{-\lambda}$ *and the following efficiency parameters:*

- *Number of rounds:* $O(\log N)$.
- *Prover size:* $W \cdot g \cdot \mathrm{polylog}(\lambda)$.
- *Verifier size:* $O(\lambda \cdot S) + \mathrm{poly}(\lambda, M^\varepsilon, \log n)$, *where the polynomial* poly *is independent of* ε, *and the verifier is given oracle access to a specific encoding of its input that is computable in time* $n \cdot \mathrm{polylog}(\lambda)$.

– **Queries:** *The verifier makes $O(\lambda \cdot S)$ queries to the messages sent by the prover, and $O(\lambda)$ queries to the encoding of its input.*

We will use the IOP of Theorem 4.5 to construct an efficient argument-system. As discussed in Sect. 2 this step is non-trivial.

Theorem 4.6 (Main Interactive Argument Construction). *Assume that there exists a sub-exponentially hard collision-resistant hash function computable by linear size circuits mapping λ bits inputs to $\lambda/2$ bit outputs.*

Let $\mathcal{R} = \mathcal{R}_{\mathsf{R1CS}}^{A,B,C,X}$ be an R1CS relation, where A, B, and C are $M \times N$ matrices and X is an $n \times N$ matrix.

Suppose that for some constant-dimensional integer vectors $\mathbf{k}^{(x)}, \mathbf{k}^{(y)}, \mathbf{k}^{(z)}$ (possibly of different dimensions), there are isomorphisms $\mathbb{F}_2^N \cong \bigotimes_i \mathbb{F}^{k_i^{(z)}}$, and $\mathbb{F}_2^M \cong \bigotimes_i \mathbb{F}^{k_i^{(y)}}$, and $\mathbb{F}_2^n \cong \bigotimes_i \mathbb{F}^{k_i^{(x)}}$, such that when A, B, C, and X are viewed as maps between the corresponding tensor spaces, they each are computable by a constant-degree tensor circuit over $\mathbb{F}_2$ with g gates, width W, and total gate size S.

Then, for every $\varepsilon > 0$, there is an interactive argument for $\mathcal{R}$ with soundness error $2^{-\lambda}$ and the following efficiency parameters:

– **Number of rounds:** $O(\log N)$.
– **Prover size:** $W \cdot g \cdot \text{polylog}(\lambda) + \text{poly}(S, \lambda) \cdot (N^\varepsilon + M^\varepsilon)$.
– **Communication complexity:** $\text{poly}(\lambda, \log(W \cdot g))$.
– **Verifier size:** $\text{poly}(\lambda) \cdot \tilde{O}(S + M^\varepsilon)$, *where the verifier is given oracle access to a specific encoding of its input that is computable by a circuit of size $n \cdot \text{polylog}(\lambda)$.*

Finally, we remark that the interactive argument of Theorem 4.6 can be made *zero-knowledge* using the standard transformation of Ben-Or *et al.* [BGG+88]. The argument can can further be *heuristically* compiled to a non-interactive argument using the Fiat-Shamir transform.

Organization. The technical heart of the proofs are in Sects. 5 and 6. Using these tools Theorems 4.5 and 4.6 are eventually proved in Sect. 7.

5   IOP Tools

5.1   Projectability

Towards constructing IOPs whose queries we can efficiently project (as discussed in Sect. 2), we state and prove some fundamental properties of projectability.

Definition 5.1 (Projectors). *If I and J are finite sets, k is a positive integer, and $\mathcal{Q}$ is a subset of I^k, we define a function $\pi_{I \times J \to \mathcal{Q}}$, called the projector from $I \times J$ to $\mathcal{Q}$, such that for all $\mathbf{x} \in \Sigma^I$ (where $\Sigma = \{0,1\}^J$) and all $\overrightarrow{\mathbf{q}} = (\mathbf{q}_1, \ldots, \mathbf{q}_k) \in \mathcal{Q}$, we have*

$$\pi_{I \times J \to \mathcal{Q}}(\mathbf{x}, \overrightarrow{\mathbf{q}}) = (\mathbf{x}_{\mathbf{q}_1}, \ldots, \mathbf{x}_{\mathbf{q}_k}) \in \Sigma^k.$$

Definition 5.2 (Projectability). *If I is a finite set and k is a positive integer, we say that a set $Q \subseteq I^k$ (with an associated $O(\log |Q|)$-bit binary representation scheme) is* projectable *if for all finite sets J, the projector from $I \times J$ to Q is computable by a Boolean circuit of size $O(|I| \cdot |J| + \log |Q|)$.*

We say that a distribution *is projectable if the support of the distribution is projectable.*

A simple example of a projectable set Q is the set of all singleton queries.

Example 5.3. For every $n \in \mathbb{N}$, the set $\{(1), \ldots, (n)\} \subseteq [n]^1$ is projectable.

Projectable sets also satisfy a "sequential composition" property.

Example 5.4. If $Q \subseteq I^N$ and $Q' \subseteq I^{N'}$ are projectable, then so is

$$(Q; Q') \stackrel{\text{def}}{=} \{(\mathbf{q}, \mathbf{q}') : \mathbf{q} \in Q, \mathbf{q}' \in Q'\} \subseteq I^{N+N'}.$$

We emphasize that when $\{Q_i\}_{i \in \mathbb{Z}^+}$ are projectable sets, Example 5.4 only implies projectability of $(Q_1; \ldots; Q_c)$ for *constant* c.

Example 5.5. If $B_1, \ldots, B_k$ are disjoint subsets of I and $Q \subseteq B_1 \times \cdots \times B_k$, then $Q \subseteq I^k$ is projectable.

Prefix Projectability. Several steps in our constructions involve generic protocol transformations that do not preserve query projectability. We formulate a stronger property called prefix projectability, which is preserved by these transformations.

Definition 5.6 (Prefixes). *Let Γ be a finite ordered set. A* prefix *of Γ is any set with the form $(-\infty, u] \stackrel{\text{def}}{=} \{x \in \Gamma : x \leq u\}$ for some $u \in \Gamma$. Similarly, a* suffix *of Γ is any set of the form $[u, \infty)$ for $u \in \Gamma$.*

Definition 5.7 (Prefix-Projectable Sets and Distributions). *Let I be a set of the form $I = \{0, 1\}^\Gamma$ where Γ is a finite ordered set.*

We say that a set $Q \subseteq I^k$ is prefix-projectable *if for any prefix P of Γ, the set Q_P is projectable, where for any subset $P \subseteq \Gamma$, we define*

$$Q_P \stackrel{\text{def}}{=} \Big\{\big((\mathbf{q}_1)_P, \ldots, (\mathbf{q}_k)_P\big) : (\mathbf{q}_1, \ldots, \mathbf{q}_k) \in Q\Big\}.$$

We say that a distribution *is prefix-projectable if the support of the distribution is prefix-projectable.*

Remark 5.8. We define *suffix projectable* sets and distributions in an analogous manner.

We now examine a few simple examples of prefix-projectable sets Q. The first example is when Q is a singleton set.

Example 5.9. For any $k, t \in \mathbb{Z}^+$ and any $Q \subseteq \left(\{0, 1\}^{[t]}\right)^k$ with $|Q| = 1$, Q is prefix-projectable.

The following proposition assists in establishing the projectability of queries to tensor codewords in which the verifier queries the entirety of the *rows* of a codeword indexed by $i_1, \ldots, i_q$. In this case the whole set of verifier's queries can be viewed as a "product" of two prefix-projectable sets: one corresponding to the set of queried rows, and the other corresponding to the set of all columns.

Definition 5.10. *Given $f : \Gamma_1 \to \{0,1\}$ and $g : \Gamma_2 \to \{0,1\}$ for disjoint sets Γ_1 and Γ_2, we define a function $f \cup g : \Gamma_1 \cup \Gamma_2 \to \{0,1\}$ such that $(f \cup g)_{\Gamma_1} = f$ and $(f \cup g)_{\Gamma_2} = g$.*

Proposition 5.11. *Suppose that Γ_1 and Γ_2 are disjoint finite sets such that $\Gamma_1 \cup \Gamma_2$ is totally ordered. Let $I_1 = \{0,1\}^{\Gamma_1}$ and $I_2 = \{0,1\}^{\Gamma_2}$.*
If $\mathcal{Q} \subseteq I_1^{k_1}$ with $k_1 \leq 2^{|\Gamma_1|}$ and $\mathcal{R} \subseteq I_2^{k_2}$ are prefix-projectable, then the set

$$(\mathcal{Q} \lhd \mathcal{R}) \stackrel{\text{def}}{=} \left\{ \left(\mathbf{q}_i \cup \mathbf{r}_j^{(i)}\right)_{\substack{i \in [k_1] \\ j \in [k_2]}} \right\}_{\substack{\vec{\mathbf{q}} \in \mathcal{Q} \\ \vec{\mathbf{r}}^{(i)} \in \mathcal{R}}} \subseteq (I_1 \times I_2)^{k_1 \cdot k_2},$$

is prefix-projectable too.

Proof. Without loss of generality suppose that $\Gamma_1 \cup \Gamma_2 = [n]$ for some integer n. We need to establish that for all $u \in [n]$ and all J, there exists a Boolean circuit $C_{\{0,1\}^{[u]} \times J \to (\mathcal{Q} \lhd \mathcal{R})_{[u]}}$ of size $O\big(2^u \cdot |J| + \log |\mathcal{Q} \lhd \mathcal{R}|\big) = O\big(2^u \cdot |J| + \log |\mathcal{Q}| + k_1 \cdot \log \mathcal{R}\big)$ such that for all $\mathbf{x} \in \{0,1\}^{\{0,1\}^{[u]} \times J}$, $\vec{\mathbf{q}} \in \mathcal{Q}$, and $\vec{\mathbf{r}}^{(1)}, \ldots, \vec{\mathbf{r}}^{(k_1)} \in \mathcal{R}$, we have

$$C_{\{0,1\}^{[u]} \times J \to (\mathcal{Q} \lhd \mathcal{R})_{[u]}}\left(\mathbf{x}, \vec{\mathbf{q}}, \vec{\mathbf{r}}^{(1)}, \ldots, \vec{\mathbf{r}}^{(k_1)}\right) = \left(\mathbf{x}_{(\mathbf{q}_i \cup \mathbf{r}_j^{(i)})_{[u]}}\right)_{\substack{i \in [k_1] \\ j \in [k_2]}}.$$

We construct $C_{\{0,1\}^{[u]} \times J \to (\mathcal{Q} \lhd \mathcal{R})_{[u]}}$ to operate as follows:

1. View $\mathbf{x}$ as an element of $\Sigma^{\{0,1\}^{[u] \cap \Gamma_1}}$, where $\Sigma = \{0,1\}^{\{0,1\}^{[u] \cap \Gamma_2} \times J}$, and use the circuit $C_{\{0,1\}^{[u] \cap \Gamma_1} \times J' \to \mathcal{Q}_{[u]}}$ where $J' = \{0,1\}^{[u] \cap \Gamma_2} \times J)$ to efficiently compute

$$\mathbf{y} \stackrel{\text{def}}{=} \left(\mathbf{x}_{\mathbf{q}_i}\right)_{i \in [k_1]} \in \Sigma^{k_1}.$$

   By the prefix-projectability of $\mathcal{Q}$, this step uses circuitry of size $O\big(2^{|\Gamma_1 \cap [u]|} \cdot |J'| + \log |\mathcal{Q}|\big) = O\big(2^u \cdot |J| + \log |\mathcal{Q}|\big)$.

2. Compute the desired output by applying the circuit $C_{\{0,1\}^{[u] \cap \Gamma_2} \times J \to \mathcal{R}_{[u]}}$ on $(\mathbf{y}_i, \vec{\mathbf{r}}^{(i)})$ for every $i \in [k_1]$. By the prefix-projectability of $\mathcal{R}$, this step uses circuitry of size $O\big(k_1 \cdot (2^{|\Gamma_2 \cap [u]|} \cdot |J| + \log |\mathcal{R}|)\big)$, which is $O\big(2^u \cdot |J| + k_1 \cdot \log |\mathcal{R}|\big)$ because $k_1 \leq 2^{|\Gamma_1|}$.

5.1.1   Projectable Samplers

One of the major building blocks in our IOPs is a method for a verifier to probabilistically query a string such that (1) the queries are projectable and (2) if the string is promised to contain many 1s, the verifier will query many of those

1s. If one simply selects a random subset of the string, then property (2) holds, but we do not know how to guarantee linear-size projectability. Thus, we will instead sample from a slightly different distribution, from which we do know how to project.

Definition 5.12 (Samplers). *We define a* (δ, λ)-*sampler for* I *as a distribution* Q *on* I^q, *where* $q = O(\lambda/\delta)$, *such that for any string* $x \in \{0, 1\}^I$ *with relative Hamming weight at least* δ, *it holds except with probability* $2^{-\lambda}$ *when sampling* $(i_1, \ldots, i_q) \leftarrow Q$ *that* $x_{i_j} = 1$ *for at least* λ *values of* $j \in [q]$.

Definition 5.13. *We say that a sampler is* prefix-projectable *or* suffix-projectable *if its queries are prefix-projectable or suffix-projectable, respectively.*

Proposition 5.14 (Prefix-Projectable Samplers). *For every constant* $t \in \mathbb{Z}^+$, *every constant* $\delta > 0$ *and every* $\lambda \in \mathbb{Z}^+$, *there is a prefix-projectable* (δ, λ)-*sampler for* $[n]^t$ *whose queries are sampleable by a circuit of size* $O(\frac{\lambda \cdot \log n}{\delta})$.
The analogous statement also holds for suffix-*projectable samplers.*

Proof. Define $\kappa = 8 \ln(2)\lambda/\delta$, assume without loss of generality that $\kappa < n^t$, and view $[\kappa]$ as $[n^d] \times [m]$ for $m < n$. Partition $[n]$ into m consecutive equal-sized intervals $S_1, \ldots, S_m$, where $S_i = [(i-1) \cdot (n/m), i \cdot n/m)$. Partition $[n]^t$ into the blocks $B_1, \ldots, B_\kappa$:

$$B_{(\mathbf{i}, \ell)} \stackrel{\text{def}}{=} \{i_1\} \times \cdots \times \{i_d\} \times S_\ell \times [n]^{t-d-1}.$$

Define Q to be the uniform distribution on $B_1 \times \cdots \times B_\kappa$.

We now argue that Q is prefix-projectable. For $j \leq d$, we have that $Q_{\leq j}$ has all its probability mass concentrated on a single tuple of queries, and so $Q_{\leq j}$ is trivially projectable. For $j > d$, the projections of the blocks $B_1, \ldots, B_\kappa$ to the first j coordinates of $[n]^d$ have disjoint supports. This implies by Example 5.5 that $Q_{\leq j}$ is projectable for $j > d$.

It is also easy to see that Q can be sampled by a circuit of size $\kappa \cdot \log n^t = O(\frac{\lambda \cdot \log n}{\delta})$.

It remains to show that Q is a (δ, λ)-sampler. Fixing an n-bit string x with relative Hamming weight at least δ, and sampling $(\mathbf{i}^{(1)}, \ldots, \mathbf{i}^{(q)}) \leftarrow Q$, let X_j denote the indicator random variable for the event that $x_{\mathbf{i}^{(j)}} = 1$.

$X_1, \ldots, X_\kappa$ are independent because Q is a product distribution, and no matter the value of x, we have that the expected value of $\sum_i X_i$ is $\delta \cdot \kappa$ (because all the blocks have equal size). It then follows from a Chernoff bound (Fact 3.1) that with all but $e^{-\delta\kappa/8} = 2^{-\lambda}$ probability, $\sum_i X_i$ is at least $\delta \cdot \kappa/2 \geq \lambda$.

Since the prefix-projectability claim used on an arbitrary ordering on $[t]$, the existence of a suffix-projectable sampler follows generically. $\square$

5.2 Encoded IOPs

We will need a variant of the IOP notion in which some messages are encoded under an error correcting code.

Definition 5.15. *An* encoded-message IOP, *wrt an error-correcting code C, is defined exactly like an* IOP *with the following modifications. As part of the protocol specification, each round is associated with a bit b_i. For rounds i for which $b_i = 1$, the honest prover must send a codeword from the code C. In the other rounds (i.e., when $b_i = 0$), the prover can send arbitrary messages. The soundness condition is relaxed and needs only hold for malicious provers who send codewords from C in every round i for which $b_i = 1$ and may send arbitrary messages in the other rounds.*

5.2.1 Projectable IOP

We say that an IOP has projectable queries if the verifier's query distribution is *projectable*. We extend this definition to prefix-projectability in the context of encoded IOPs as follows:

Definition 5.16 (Prefix-Projectable Encoded-Message IOPs). *If $C \subseteq \mathbb{F}^{[n]^t}$ is a code (e.g. if $C = D^{\otimes t}$ for $D \subseteq \mathbb{F}^n$), we say that a C-encoded IOP Π is* prefix-projectable *if for all i, the queries of the verifier to the ith encoded message are prefix-projectable. We say that Π is* prefix-projectable with respect to its input *if the verifier's input is promised to be a tuple of tensor codes, and the verifier's access to each tensor codeword is in the form of prefix-projectable queries.*

Proposition 5.17. *Let $C : \mathbb{F}^k \to \mathbb{F}^n$ be a size-S encodable code with constant relative distance and let $t \geq 3$ be a constant integer. Then any $C^{\otimes t}$-encoded prefix-projectable IOP Π can be compiled into a standard IOP Π' with the following parameters:*

- **Soundness Error:** $\varepsilon + 2^{-\lambda}$, *where ε is the soundness error of Π.*
- **Rounds:** *same as in Π.*
- **Communication:** *same as in Π.*
- **Queries:** $O(q \cdot \lambda \cdot n^2)$, *where q is the query complexity of Π.*
- **Prover Size:** *same as in Π.*
- **Verifier Size:** $S_V + \text{poly}(q, \lambda, T)$, *where T is the encoding time of C and S_V is the verifier size of Π.*
- **Query Projectability:** *The queries to each codeword are prefix-projectable.*

The proof of Proposition 5.17 uses the local testability [Vid15] and (relaxed) correctability [GRR18] of tensor codes. It requires only relatively minor adaptations to our setting (specifically to preserve projectability). We defer the proof to the full version.

6   Basic IOPs

In this section we build the key sub-protocols that will be used to construct our main IOP. We start, in Sect. 6.1 with an IOP for checking a local multiplicative relation between codewords (aka the Hadamard check) and then proceed to Sect. 6.2 in which we give an IOP for checking linear relations.

6.1   Hadamard Check

Definition 6.1. *If C is a code, we define Had^C to be the promise problem where "yes" instances are triples $\big(C(x), C(y), C(x \star y)\big)$, and "no" instances are all other triples of codewords of C.*

We first construct an IOP for the Had with constant soundness. The result basically follows from [RR21].

Proposition 6.2 (Constant Soundness Hadamard Check). *Let $\mathbb{F}$ be a constructible field extension of $\mathrm{GF}(2)$. Let $D : \mathbb{F}^k \to \mathbb{F}^n$ be a size-S encodable systematic linear code with constant rate and constant relative distance, and define $C = D^{\otimes t}$ for some constant integer t.*

There is an IOP for Had^C with constant soundness error and the following efficiency parameters:

- **Rounds:** $O(\log S)$
- **Prover size:** $S \cdot n^{t-1} \cdot \mathrm{polylog}(|\mathbb{F}|)$
- **Prover communication:** $O(n^t)$ *elements of $\mathbb{F}$.*
- **Verifier size:** $\mathrm{poly}(S, \log(|\mathbb{F}|))$ *for some polynomial poly that is independent of t.*
- **Queries:** *The verifier makes a constant number of queries to its input, and for each prover message m the verifier either reads all of m or makes a constant number of queries to symbols in m. Here we view both the input and the prover messages as strings with alphabet $\mathbb{F}$.*

Proof. The proof utilizes a code from [RR21] which supports an efficient "multi-sumcheck" protocol with constant soundness error. We use a simple extension of their construction to a larger alphabet $\mathbb{F}$. This extension incurs additional $\mathrm{polylog}(|\mathbb{F}|)$ factors in computational efficiency for both the prover and verifier, and an $O(\log(|\mathbb{F}|))$ factor in communication.

In more detail, let $\hat{C} = \hat{D}^{\otimes t}$ (where $\hat{D} : \mathbb{F}^k \to \mathbb{F}^{\hat{n}}$ is linear-size encodable) be a code that supports a "multi-sumcheck" protocol with constant soundness error (c.f., [RR21, Lemma 4.8, Proposition 4.7]).

We first describe an encoded-message IOP. Given inputs $c_x = C(x), c_y = C(y), c_z = C(z)$:

1. The prover sends re-encodings $\hat{c}_x = \hat{C}(x), \hat{c}_y = \hat{C}(y), \hat{c}_z = \hat{C}(z)$.
2. The prover and verifier invoke the consistency checking IOP of [RR21, Lemma 5.1], which has constant soundness error, on the claims

$$\Big\{ \hat{c}(i) = c(i) \text{ for all } i \in [k]^t \Big\}_{(\hat{c},c) \in \{(c_x,\hat{c}_x),(c_y,\hat{c}_y),(c_z,\hat{c}_z)\}}.$$

3. The verifier samples $r_1, \ldots, r_t \in \mathbb{F}^k$ and sends $r = r_1 \otimes \cdots \otimes r_t$ to the prover.
4. The prover and verifier invoke the multi-sumcheck protocol on the claims

$$\sum_{i \in [k]^t} \hat{c}_x(i) \cdot \hat{c}_y(i) \cdot \hat{c}_r(i) = \sum_{i \in [k]^t} \hat{c}_z(i) \cdot \hat{c}_r(i),$$

where we define $\hat{c}_r = \hat{C}(r)$.

Here the verifier needs oracle access not only to $\hat{c}_x, \hat{c}_y, \hat{c}_z : [n]^t \to \mathbb{F}$, but also to $\hat{c}_r$. Using the tensor structure of r, the verifier can emulate oracle access to $\hat{c}_r$ in size $O(t \cdot n)$ by Claim 3.8.

The constant soundness of this protocol follows from the constant soundness of the RR21 protocol, along with the fact that with all but $t/|\mathbb{F}|$ probability over the choice of r, we have $\langle v, r \rangle \neq 0$.

We compile this encoded-message IOP to a standard IOP using [RR21, Proposition 4.7].

Our Hadamard check with soundness error $2^{-\lambda}$ overhead only works for a more restricted family of codes, which we fortunately are able to construct with polylog(λ) overhead in the encoding size.

Definition 6.3 ((λ, t)-Hadamard-friendly Codes). *We say that a tensor code C over a field $\mathbb{F}$ is (λ, t)-Hadamard-friendly if it has constant rate and constant relative distance and can be written as $C = E^{\otimes t} \otimes M^{\otimes t}$, where E is any linear code and M is a multiplication code with message space $\mathbb{F}^{\lambda^{1/t}}$ and the property that $M^{\star 2}$ has constant relative distance.*

Lemma 6.4 (Improved Hadamard Check). *Let $t \in \mathbb{Z}^+$ be a constant, and let $\mathbb{F}$ be any constructible field (see Definition 3.2). Let $C \subseteq \mathbb{F}^N$ be a (λ, t)-Hadamard-friendly tensor code.*

There is an IOP for Had^C with soundness error $2^{-\lambda}$ and the following efficiency parameters:

- **Rounds:** $O(\log N)$
- **Communication:** $O(N \cdot \log |\mathbb{F}|)$
- **Prover Size:** $N \cdot \mathrm{polylog}(|\mathbb{F}|)$
- **Verifier Size:** $O\left(\lambda \cdot (\lambda + \log N) + \mathrm{poly}(N^{1/t}, \log |\mathbb{F}|)\right)$, *where we emphasize that the degree of the polynomial* poly *is independent of t.*
- **Queries:** $O(\lambda^2)$. *These queries are prefix-projectable.*

Proof. Let n_E and n_M denote the block lengths of E and M respectively. Let k_E and k_M denote the message lengths of E and M respectively. Let δ_E and δ_M denote the relative distances of E and $M^{\star 2}$ respectively. Let $\mathcal{Q}_{E^{\otimes t}}$ be a prefix-projectable (δ_E^t, λ)-sampler for $[n_E]^t$ and let $\mathcal{Q}_{M^{\otimes t}}$ be a prefix-projectable (δ_M^t, λ)-sampler for $[n_M]^t$ such that:

- $\mathcal{Q}_{E^{\otimes t}}$ and $\mathcal{Q}_{M^{\otimes t}}$ are sampleable by circuits of size $O(\lambda \cdot \log n_E)$ and $O(\lambda \cdot \log n_M)$ respectively,
- $\mathcal{Q}_{E^{\otimes t}}$ and $\mathcal{Q}_{M^{\otimes t}}$ both make $O(\lambda)$ queries.

Such $\mathcal{Q}_{E^{\otimes t}}$ and $\mathcal{Q}_{M^{\otimes t}}$ are guaranteed to exist by Proposition 5.14.

Our construction begins with an *encoded-message* IOP for Had^C, where the prover sends one message that is promised to be a codeword of $E^{\otimes t} \otimes (M^{\star 2})^{\otimes t}$. This protocol is described in Fig. 1.

Common Input: Oracle access to triple of codewords $c_x, c_y, c_z \in C = E^{\otimes t} \otimes M^{\otimes t}$

1. The prover computes and sends a codeword $c_z^\star \in E^{\otimes t} \otimes (M^{\star 2})^{\otimes t}$, defined so that $c_z^\star(\alpha, \beta) = c_x(\alpha, \beta) \cdot c_y(\alpha, \beta)$ for all $\alpha \in [k_E]^t$ and $\beta \in [n_M]^t$.
2. The verifier samples $(\alpha_1, \ldots, \alpha_{\kappa_{E \otimes t}}) \leftarrow \mathcal{Q}_{E \otimes t}$ and $(\beta_1, \ldots, \beta_{\kappa_{M \otimes t}}) \leftarrow \mathcal{Q}_{M \otimes t}$.
3. For each $j \in [\kappa_{E \otimes t}]$, and for all $\beta \in [k_M]^t$, the verifier checks that $c_z(\alpha_j, \beta) = c_z^\star(\alpha_j, \beta)$.
4. For each $j \in [\kappa_{M \otimes t}]$:
   (a) Let $\mathbf{u}_j$, $\mathbf{v}_j$, and $\mathbf{w}_j$ respectively denote the vectors $\big(c_x(\alpha, \beta_j)\big)_{\alpha \in [k_E]^t}$, $\big(c_y(\alpha, \beta_j)\big)_{\alpha \in [k_E]^t}$, and $\big(c_z^\star(\alpha, \beta_j)\big)_{\alpha \in [k_E]^t}$. Let $\hat{\mathbf{u}}_j$, $\hat{\mathbf{v}}_j$, and $\hat{\mathbf{w}}_j$ respectively denote $E^{\otimes t}(\mathbf{u}_j) = \big(c_x(\alpha, \beta_j)\big)_{\alpha \in [n_E]^t}$, $E^{\otimes t}(\mathbf{v}_j) = \big(c_y(\alpha, \beta_j)\big)_{\alpha \in [n_E]^t}$, and $E^{\otimes t}(\mathbf{w}_j) = \big(c_z^\star(\alpha, \beta_j)\big)_{\alpha \in [n_E]^t}$.
   (b) The prover and verifier, using oracle access to $\hat{\mathbf{u}}_j$, $\hat{\mathbf{v}}_j$, and $\hat{\mathbf{w}}_j$, invoke the constant soundness error IOPP of Proposition 6.2 on the claim that that $\mathbf{w}_j = \mathbf{u}_j \star \mathbf{v}_j$.

Fig. 1. Encoded-message IOP for $\mathrm{Had}^{E^{\otimes t} \otimes M^{\otimes t}}$ with soundness error $2^{-\Omega(\lambda)}$

Completeness. Follows immediately from the linearity of $E^{\otimes t}$ and $M^{\otimes t}$ and the completeness of the IOP of Proposition 6.2.

Encoded-Message Soundness. We now argue that this IOP has soundness error $2^{-\Omega(\lambda)}$ (this can then be reduced to $2^{-\lambda}$ with constant overhead by repeating in parallel. Let δ_M denote the relative distance of $M^{\star 2}$, and let δ_E denote the relative distance of E.

Case 1: We first claim that if the prover sends $c_z^\star$ that is a valid but incorrectly chosen codeword of $E^{\otimes t} \otimes (M^{\star 2})^{\otimes t}$, then the verifier rejects with all but $2^{-\Omega(\lambda)}$ probability in step 4 (if it has not already rejected in a previous step). Indeed, by the relative distance of $(M^{\star 2})^{\otimes t}$, if $c_z^\star$ is incorrect then for at least δ_M^t fraction of $\beta \in [n_M]^t$, the "column" $\big(c_z^\star(\alpha, \beta)\big)_{\alpha \in [k_E]^t}$ must be incorrect. Then by the sampling properties of $\mathcal{Q}_{M \otimes t}$, it must hold with all but $2^{-\lambda}$ probability over the choice of $\beta_1, \ldots, \beta_{\kappa_{M \otimes t}} \in [n_M]^t$ that for at least λ values of $j \in [\kappa_{M \otimes t}]$, the column $\big(c_z^\star(\alpha, \beta_j)\big)_{\alpha \in [k_E]^t}$ is incorrect (that is, for some $\alpha \in [k_E]^t$, $c_z^\star(\alpha, \beta_j) \neq c_x(\alpha, \beta_j) \cdot c_y(\alpha, \beta_j)$). Thus with all but $2^{-\Omega(\lambda)}$ probability, at least one of the invocations of the IOPP of Proposition 6.2 will cause the verifier to reject.

Case 2: Now suppose that $c_z^\star$ disagrees with c_z on some $(\alpha, \beta) \in [k_E]^t \times [k_M]^t$. We then claim that the verifier will reject with all but $2^{-\Omega(\lambda)}$ probability in Step 3. Indeed, in this case the relative distance of $E^{\otimes t}$ implies that for at least δ_E^t fraction of $\alpha \in [n_E]^t$, the "rows" $\big(c_z^\star(\alpha, \beta)\big)_{\beta \in [k_M]^t}$ and $\big(c_z(\alpha, \beta)\big)_{\beta \in [k_M]^t}$ differ. By the sampling properties of $\mathcal{Q}_{M \otimes t}$, it must hold with all but $2^{-\lambda}$ probability over the choice of $\alpha_1, \ldots, \alpha_{\kappa_{E \otimes t}} \in [n_E]^t$ that for at least $\lambda \geq 1$ values of $j \in [\kappa_{E \otimes t}]$, the rows $\big(c_z^\star(\alpha_j, \beta)\big)_{\beta \in [k_M]^t}$ and $\big(c_z(\alpha_j, \beta)\big)_{\beta \in [k_M]^t}$ differ, which causes the verifier to reject.

Finally, suppose that neither case 1 nor case 2 holds. That is, $c_z^\star$ is correctly generated and agrees with c_z on all $(\alpha, \beta) \in [k_E]^t \times [k_M]^t$. Then it must be that $z = x \star y$ as desired.

Efficiency

- **Rounds:** The round complexity is dominated by the IOPP of Step 4, which has $O\big(\log(n_E^{t-1} \cdot S_E)\big) = O(\log n_E)$ rounds.
- **Prover Size:**
  1. The computation of $c_z^\star$ in Step 1 can be done by a circuit of size $k_E^t \cdot n_M^t \cdot \text{polylog}(|\mathbb{F}|) + O\big(n_M^t \cdot n_E^{t-1} \cdot S_E\big) = O\big(N \cdot \text{polylog}(|\mathbb{F}|)\big)$.
  2. The projection of the codewords c_x, c_y, c_z, and $c_z^\star$ onto the rows and columns specified by $\{\alpha_i\}$ and $\{\beta_j\}$ can be done by a circuit of size $O\big(N \cdot \log(|\mathbb{F}|)\big)$ by the (prefix-)projectability of $\mathcal{Q}_{E^{\otimes t}}$ and $\mathcal{Q}_{M^{\otimes t}}$.
  3. In Step 4, the prover for the IOP of Proposition 6.2 is implemented by a circuit of size $n_E^t \cdot \text{polylog}(|\mathbb{F}|)$ for each of the $\kappa_{E^{\otimes t}} = O(\lambda)$ instances, making a circuit of size $\lambda \cdot n_E^t \cdot \text{polylog}(|\mathbb{F}|) = N \cdot \text{polylog}(|\mathbb{F}|)$ in total.

  Adding up these circuit sizes gives the stated bound on the prover complexity.
- **Verifier Size:**
  1. $\mathcal{Q}_{E^{\otimes t}}$ and $\mathcal{Q}_{M^{\otimes t}}$ can, by construction, be sampled by circuits of size $O\big(\lambda \cdot (\log n_E + \log n_M)\big) = O(\log N)$.
  2. In Step 3, the verifier checks equality of $O(\lambda \cdot k_M^t)$ field elements, which requires circuitry of size $O(\lambda \cdot k_M^t \cdot \log |\mathbb{F}|) = O(\lambda^2 \cdot \log |\mathbb{F}|)$.
  3. The verifier for each of the $O(\lambda)$ instances of the IOP invoked in Step 4 has size $\text{poly}(n_E, \log |\mathbb{F}|) = \text{poly}(N^{1/t}, \log |\mathbb{F}|)$ for some polynomial that does not depend on t.

  Adding everything up gives the stated bound on the size of the verifier.
- **Prefix Projectable Queries:** The verifier's queries can be partitioned into two sets of queries—the queries it makes in Step 3 and the queries it makes in Step 4. Recall that the Step 3 queries are made by selecting a prefix-projectable set of "rows" for $E^{\otimes t} \otimes M^{\otimes t}$ and querying c_z and $c_z^\star$ in each entry of these rows. The Step 4 queries are made by choosing a prefix-projectable set of "columns" for $E^{\otimes t} \otimes M^{\otimes t}$, and querying a constant number of entries independently from of each of these column. The prefix-projectability of both types of queries follows from Proposition 5.11.

Standard Model Soundness. Applying Proposition 5.17 gives an IOP in the standard model (where messages are not promised to be valid codewords).

6.2   Tensor LinCheck

Definition 6.5 (Lincheck). *If $C : \mathbb{F}^k \to \mathbb{F}^n$ and $C' : \mathbb{F}^{k'} \to \mathbb{F}^{n'}$ are linear codes and $\varphi : \mathbb{F}^k \to \mathbb{F}^{k'}$ is a linear map, we define* $\text{Lin}^{C, C', \varphi}$ *as the promise problem where:*

- *"Yes" instances consist of pairs $\big(C(x), C'(\varphi(x))\big)$,*

– *"No" instances consist of pairs $\big(C(x), C'(y)\big)$ for $y \neq \varphi(x)$.*

We start by describing a basic Lincheck IOP with poor parameters. As a matter of fact, this IOP will not involve the prover or have any interaction. Later, in Lemma 6.8 we will bootstrap this construction and get an efficient IOP.

Lemma 6.6 (Basic Lincheck). *For any constant $t \in \mathbb{Z}^+$, any finite field $\mathbb{F}$, any systematic linear codes $D : \mathbb{F}^{k_D} \to \mathbb{F}^{n_D}$, $D' : \mathbb{F}^{k_{D'}} \to \mathbb{F}^{n_{D'}}$, and $E : \mathbb{F}^{k_E} \to \mathbb{F}^{n_E}$, and any linear $\varphi : \mathbb{F}^{k_D^t} \to \mathbb{F}^{k_{D'}^t}$ that can be implemented by a size-S Boolean circuit, let $\delta_E = \Omega(1)$ denote the relative distance of E, let C denote $D^{\otimes t} \otimes E^{\otimes t}$, and let C' denote $(D')^{\otimes t} \otimes E^{\otimes t}$.*

For $\lambda \in \mathbb{Z}^+$, there is an IOP for $\mathrm{Lin}^{C,C',\varphi \otimes \mathrm{Id}}$ with soundness error $2^{-\lambda}$ and the following efficiency parameters:

- **Rounds:** 0 *(there is no prover involvement)*
- **Verifier Size:** $O(\lambda \cdot (S + \log n_E))$.
- **Verifier Randomness:** $O(\lambda \cdot \log n_E)$.
- **Query Projectability:** *The verifier makes $O\big(\lambda \cdot (k_D^t + k_{D'}^t)\big)$ queries to its input, and these queries are prefix-projectable.*

Common Input: Oracle access to a pair of codewords $c_x \in C, c_y \in C'$.

1. Let $\mathcal{Q}$ be a prefix-projectable (δ_E^t, λ)-sampler for $[n_E]^t$. The existence of such a $\mathcal{Q}$ is guaranteed by Proposition 5.14. The verifier samples $(i_1, \dots, i_\kappa) \leftarrow \mathcal{Q}$, where $\kappa = O(\lambda)$.
2. For each $j \in [\kappa]$, let $\mathbf{u}_j$ denote the vector $\big(c_x(\alpha, i_j)\big)_{\alpha \in [k_D^t]}$, let $\mathbf{v}_j$ denote the vector $\big(c_y(\alpha, i_j)\big)_{\alpha \in [k_{D'}^t]}$.
   The verifier checks that $\mathbf{v}_j = \varphi(\mathbf{u}_j)$.

Fig. 2. IOP for $\mathrm{Lin}^{C,C',\varphi \otimes \mathrm{Id}}$

Proof. The verifier is described in Fig. 2. The efficiency parameters follow immediately. Query projectability follows from Proposition 5.14.

It remains to establish that the IOP is complete and sound.

Completeness. Suppose we are given $c_x = C(x)$ and $c_y = C'\big((\varphi \otimes \mathrm{Id})(y)\big)$. Let $\mathbf{x}_j = \big(x(i,j)\big)_{i \in [k_D^t]}$ denote the jth "column" of x for $j \in [k_E]$, and similarly let $\mathbf{y}_j$ denote the jth column of y. We are promised that $\mathbf{y}_j = \varphi(\mathbf{x}_j)$ for every $j \in [k_E]$.

Now consider $\hat{y} = (\mathrm{Id} \otimes E^{\otimes t})(y)$ and $\hat{x} = (\mathrm{Id} \otimes E^{\otimes t})(x)$, both of which we can view as $k_D^t \times n_E^t$ matrices. Let $\hat{\mathbf{x}}_j$ and $\hat{\mathbf{y}}_j$ denote the jth columns of $\hat{x}$ and $\hat{y}$ respectively.

By the linearity of $E^{\otimes t}$, it holds for every $j \in [n_E]^t$ that there exist coefficients $\{\beta_{i,j}\}_{i \in [k_E]^t}$ such that

$$\hat{\mathbf{x}}_j = \sum_{i \in [k_E]^t} \beta_{i,j} \cdot \hat{\mathbf{x}}_i$$

and

$$\hat{\mathbf{y}}_j = \sum_{i \in [k_E]^t} \beta_{i,j} \cdot \hat{\mathbf{y}}_i.$$

Thus

$$\hat{\mathbf{y}}_j = \sum_{i \in [k_E]^t} \beta_{i,j} \cdot \hat{\mathbf{y}}_i$$
$$= \sum_{i \in [k_E]^t} \beta_{i,j} \cdot \mathbf{y}_i$$
$$= \sum_{i \in [k_E]^t} \beta_{i,j} \cdot \varphi(\mathbf{x}_i)$$
$$= \varphi\Big(\sum_{i \in [k_E]^t} \beta_{i,j} \cdot \mathbf{x}_i \Big)$$
$$= \varphi(\hat{\mathbf{x}}_i).$$

Since $c_x = (D^{\otimes t} \otimes \mathrm{Id})(\hat{x})$ and $c_y = (D^{\otimes t} \otimes \mathrm{Id})(\hat{y})$, completeness follows by the systematicity of $D^{\otimes t}$.

Soundness. Suppose that $c_x = C(x)$ and $\tilde{c}_y = C(\tilde{y})$ are inputs for which $\tilde{y} \neq (\varphi \otimes \mathrm{Id})(x)$. Let c_y denote what $\tilde{c}_y$ is "supposed" to be, i.e. $c_y = C\big((\varphi \otimes \mathrm{Id})(x)\big)$. Since E has constant relative distance δ_E and $\tilde{c}_y \neq c_y$, at least a δ_E fraction of the columns of $\tilde{c}_y$ must differ from c_y. Since D is systematic, these columns are determined by their first k_D entries. Finally, the fact that $\mathcal{Q}$ is a (δ_E, λ)-sampler means that at least λ of the generated claims are false. Thus the verifier rejects with all but $2^{-\Omega(\lambda)}$ probability.

Prefix-Projectability. By Proposition 5.14, we have that $(i_1, \ldots, i_\kappa)$ is prefix-projectable. Since $i_1, \ldots, i_\kappa$ are then used as indexes of rows to be queried in their entirety (or at least in their intersection with the jth column for all j in $[k_D]^t$ or $[k_{D'}]^t$), the prefix-projectability of all of the verifier's input queries follows from Proposition 5.11.

Lemma 6.6 admits a generalization to succinct tensor circuits, which is Lemma 6.8 below.

Definition 6.7. *For an integer $t \in \mathbb{Z}^+$ and a vector $\mathbf{k} = (k_1, \ldots, k_d) \in \mathbb{Z}^d$, say C is an $(\mathbb{F}, \mathbf{k}, t)$-tensor code if $C = D^{(1)} \otimes \cdots \otimes D^{(d)}$, where each $D^{(i)}$ has message space $\mathbb{F}^{k_i}$, and each $D^{(i)}$ is also a t-dimensional tensor code $D^{(i)} = (E^{(i)})^{\otimes t}$.*

Lemma 6.8. *Let $\mathbb{F}$ be any field, and for any $\mathbf{k} = (k_1, \ldots, k_d)$, let $\mathcal{M}_{\mathbf{k}}$ denote $\mathbb{F}^{k_1} \otimes \cdots \otimes \mathbb{F}^{k_d}$.*

For any constant $t \in \mathbb{Z}^+$, any $\mathbf{k}$, $\mathbf{k}'$, any $(\mathbb{F}, \mathbf{k}, t)$-tensor code C, and any $(\mathbb{F}, \mathbf{k}', t)$-tensor code C', and any linear function $\phi : \mathcal{M}_{\mathbf{k}} \to \mathcal{M}_{\mathbf{k}'}$ that is computable by a tensor circuit with width W, constant degree, and g gates with total size S, there exists an encoded-message IOP for $\mathrm{Lin}^{C, C', \phi}$ with soundness error $2^{-\lambda}$ and the following efficiency parameters:

- **Rounds:** 1 *(consisting of g encoded messages)*
- **Communication:** $O(g \cdot W)$ *elements of $\mathbb{F}$*
- **Prover Size:** $O(g \cdot W + S)$.
- **Verifier Size:** $O(\lambda \cdot (S + g \cdot \log W))$
- **Queries:** *The verifier makes $O(\lambda \cdot S)$ queries to its input and to the codewords sent by the prover, and these queries are prefix-projectable.*
- **Encoded Messages:** *For all i, the ith prover message is promised to be a codeword of a tensor code $D_i^{\otimes t}$.*

Proof. We first construct a family of codes $\{C_{\mathbf{k}}\}_{\mathbf{k}}$ where $C_{\mathbf{k}}$ is a $(\mathbf{k}, t)$-tensor code that is encodable by a circuit of size $O(|\mathcal{M}_{\mathbf{k}}|)$ and has constant rate and relative distance. For $\mathbf{k} = (k_1, \ldots, k_d)$, we define the code $C_{\mathbf{k}}$ as $(D_{k_1^{1/t}})^{\otimes t} \otimes \cdots \otimes (D_{k_d^{1/t}})^{\otimes t}$, where $\{D_k\}_{k \in \mathbb{Z}^+}$ is a family of linear-size encodable codes with constant rate and relative distance (e.g. Spielman codes), and with D_k having message space $\mathbb{F}^k$.

The tensor circuit for ϕ expresses φ as a composition of linear maps $\phi = \phi_g \circ \cdots \circ \phi_1$, where each ϕ_i can be viewed as a tensor product $\varphi_i \otimes \mathrm{Id}$. In our IOP on input $(C(x), C'(y))$, the prover computes each "intermediate state" $z^{(i)} \stackrel{\text{def}}{=} (\phi_i \circ \cdots \circ \phi_1)(x)$ (which requires circuitry of size $O(S)$), and sends encodings of these states under a "suitable" tensor code.

More specifically, the ith intermediate state $z^{(i)}$ must lie in a message space $\mathcal{M}_{\mathbf{k}^{(i)}}$ where $\mathbf{k}^{(i)} = (k_1^{(i)}, \ldots, k_d^{(i)})$ satisfies $d = O(1)$ and $\prod_j k_j^{(i)} \leq W$. The prover sends an encoding of $z^{(i)}$ under $C_{\mathbf{k}^{(i)}}$, which takes circuitry of size $O(g \cdot W)$ in total and results in $O(g \cdot W)$ field elements of communication. Adding this to the circuitry requirements for generating $z^{(1)}, \ldots, z^{(g)}$ gives the stated bound on the prover complexity.

The verifier then uses the basic lincheck (Lemma 6.6) to check consistency of every pair $(z^{(i)}, z^{(i+1)})$ for $i = 0, \ldots, g$, where we denote $z^{(0)} = x$ and $z^{(g+1)} = y$. If φ_i is computable by a circuit of size S_i, then checking consistency of $(z^{(i)}, z^{(i+1)})$ takes $O(\lambda \cdot S_i)$ queries, verifier circuitry of size $O(\lambda \cdot S_i)$, and $O(\log W)$ bits of verifier randomness. Summing this over all i gives the stated bounds on the verifier query complexity, the verifier size, and the verifier randomness. Finally, prefix-projectability follows from the prefix-projectability of the input queries in Lemma 6.6.

7   Proof of Main Results

7.1   Efficient IOP: Proof of Theorem 4.5

In this section we prove Theorem 4.5. Actually, as we will need it for our second main result, we prove the following strengthening of Proposition 4.5.

Lemma 7.1. *Theorem 4.5 holds and, moreover, the* IOP *verifier's queries are prefix-projectable.*

Proof. We start by constructing an encoded-message IOP with prefix-projectable verifier queries, and then compile it to a standard IOP using Proposition 5.17.

The main idea is simply to combine Lemmas 6.8 and 6.4. From there, it is a matter of working out what parameters are achieved.

Claim 7.2. *For every $t \in \mathbb{Z}^+$ and constant-dimensional $\mathbf{k} = (k_1, \dots, k_d)$, there is a tensor code that is simultaneously a $(\mathbf{k}, t)$-tensor code (Definition 6.7) and λ-Hadamard-friendly (Definition 6.3).*

Proof. Let $\mathbb{F}$ be a field of order $\lambda^{1/t}$, and for any $k \leq \lambda$, let $M_k : \mathbb{F}^k \to \mathbb{F}^{O(k)}$ denote an $\mathbb{F}$-linear, systematic, multiplication code that is encodable by a circuit of size $k \cdot \text{polylog}(\lambda)$, and such that $M_k^{\star 2}$ has constant relative distance. Reed-Solomon codes provide an example of such a code. For every $k \in \mathbb{Z}^+$, let $L_k : \mathbb{F}^k \to \mathbb{F}^{O(k)}$ denote an $\mathbb{F}$-linear, systematic code with constant rate and constant relative distance that is encodable by a circuit of size $O(k \cdot \log \lambda)$ (e.g. a straightforward generalization of Spielman's code [Spi96]).

Assume without loss of generality that $k_1 \geq \dots \geq k_d$. If $k_1 > \lambda$, set the code to be

$$(M_{\lambda^{1/t}})^{\otimes t} \otimes L_{(k_1/\lambda)^{1/t}}^{\otimes t} \otimes L_{k_2} \otimes \dots \otimes L_{k_d}.$$

If $k_1 \leq \lambda$, recursively let C' be a code that is simultaneously a $((k_2, \dots, k_d), t)$-tensor code and (λ/k_1)-splittable. Set our code to be $M_{k_1^{1/t}}^{\otimes t} \otimes C'$.   □

Let $D^{(x)}$ denote a $(\mathbf{k}^{(x)}, t)$-tensor code, let $D^{(z)}$ denote a $(\mathbf{k}^{(z)}, t)$-tensor code, and let $D^{(y)}$ denote a code that is simultaneously a $(\mathbf{k}^{(y)}, t)$-tensor code and λ-splittable.

The prover, given z such that $(A \cdot z) \star (B \cdot z) = (C \cdot z)$ and $X \cdot z = x$, computes and sends the following promised codewords to the verifier:

- $c_z = D^{(z)}(z)$, promised to be a codeword of $D^{(z)}$;
- $c_A = D^{(y)}(A \cdot z)$, $c_B = D^{(y)}(B \cdot z)$, and $c_B = D^{(y)}(C \cdot z)$, all promised to be codewords of $D^{(y)}$; and
- $c_x = D^{(x)}(x)$.

Upon receiving codewords $\tilde{c}_z$, $\tilde{c}_A$, $\tilde{c}_B$, $\tilde{c}_C$, and $\tilde{c}_x$, the verifier:

- Uses the generalized lincheck (Lemma 6.8) to check that if z denotes the true value encoded in $\tilde{c}_z$ under $C^{(z)}$, then $\tilde{c}_A$, $\tilde{c}_B$, and $\tilde{c}_C$ respectively encode $A \cdot z$, $B \cdot z$, and $C \cdot z$, and $\tilde{c}_x$ encodes $X \cdot z$.
- Uses the improved Hadamard check (Lemma 6.4) to check that if a, b, and c denote the values encoded in $\tilde{c}_A$, $\tilde{c}_B$, and $\tilde{c}_C$, then $c = a \star b$.

7.2   From IOPs to Arguments: Proof of Theorem 4.6

In this section we prove Theorem 4.6. To do so, we show how to compile the IOP of Lemma 7.1 into an efficient argument-system. The compiler is based on Kilian's [Kil92] PCP based construction and its extension to IOPs [BCS16] while using linear-time computable hash functions [AHI+17].

The hash functions are used to derive a succinct commitment scheme with local openings.

Definition 7.3. *A* succinct commitment with local openings *consists of a probabilistic algorithm called* setup *and three determinstic algorithms* commit, reveal *and* verify. *The setup algorithm, on input* $n, \lambda \in \mathbb{N}$ *outputs a reference string* crs. *The commit algorithm, on input* crs *and a message* $m \in \{0,1\}^n$ *outputs a commitment* c. *The algorithm* reveal, *given as input* crs, m *and an index set* $I \in [n]$ *outputs the sequence of values* $(m_i)_{i \in I} \in \{0,1\}^{|I|}$ *as well as a proof* $\pi \in \{0,1\}^{\mathrm{poly}(\log n, \lambda)}$. *The algorithm* verify *gets as input* crs, c, I, $(b_i)_{i \in I}$ *and* π *and outputs either "accept" or "reject".*

We require:

- *(Correctness:) For every* n, λ *and* $m \in \{0,1\}^n$ *and* $I \in [n]$, *it holds that* verify(crs, c, I, $(m_i)_{i \in I}, \pi$) = *accept, where* crs $\leftarrow$ setup(n, λ), $c =$ commit(crs, m) *and* $\pi \leftarrow$ reveal(crs, m, I).
- *(Succinctness:) The length of* c *is* $\mathrm{poly}(\lambda, \log n)$ *and that of* π *is* $\mathrm{poly}(\lambda, \log n, |I|)$.
- *(Binding:) For every family of polynomial-sized circuits* $\mathcal{A} = (A)_\lambda$, *the probability over the choice of* crs $\leftarrow$ setup(n, λ) *that* A_λ(crs) *outputs* (c, I, π, π') *such that* verify(crs, c, I, $(m_i)_{i \in I}, \pi_0$) = *accept and* verify(crs, c, I, $(m'_i)_{i \in I}, \pi'$) = *accept is negligible.*

The following lemma gives a construction of such a commitment scheme using a Merkle tree.

Lemma 7.4. *Assume that there exists a collision-resistant hash function computable by linear size circuits mapping* λ *bits inputs to* $\lambda/2$ *bit outputs*

Then, there exists a succinct commitment with local openings such that the commit *algorithm can be implemented by a circuit of size* $O(n + \lambda)$, *the* setup *can be implemented by a circuit of size* $\mathrm{poly}(\log n, \lambda)$, *the* verify *algorithm can be implemented by a circuit of size* $\mathrm{poly}(|I|, \log n, \lambda)$.

For any prefix-projectable set $\mathcal{Q}$, *there* reveal *algorithm, restricted to query sets* $I \in \mathcal{Q}$ *can be implemented in size* $O(n) + \mathrm{poly}(\lambda)$.

Moreover, if the collision-resistant hash is sub-exponentially strong, then the resulting commitment is also sub-exponentially small.

Proof (Proof Sketch). The construction is simply a Merkle tree hash, and using authentication paths in order to decommit.

In more detail, we use the linear-time encodable hash function, to commit to the Merkle root of the message by a linear-size circuit. To decommit to a sequence I of location, one first constructs the entire Merkle tree and then selects the relevant locations from the tree (namely those blocks corresponding to the path from the i leaf in the tree to the root, together with the corresponding siblings). Projecting to the authentication paths is done by utilizing the prefix-projectability of the query set.

Next, we use the commitment to compile the IOP into an argument-system (c.f., [BCG+17, BCG20, RR21]).

Lemma 7.5. *Assume the existence of a sub-exponentially strong* CRHF *computable by a linear-size circuit.*

Suppose that the relation $\mathcal{R}$ has an ℓ-round prefix-projectable IOP *with soundness error ε and communication complexity c. Then, $\mathcal{R}$ has an $(\ell + 2)$-round argument-system with soundness error $\varepsilon + 2^{-\lambda}$ and communication complexity $O\big((\ell + \log c) \cdot \mathrm{poly}(\lambda)\big)$.*

Furthermore, suppose that:

1. *The* IOP *prover can be implemented as a size T_P circuit, where $\mathrm{poly}(\lambda) \leq T_P$.*
2. *The* IOP *verifier has a first offline step that depends only on the input and can be implemented in size P_V and then the online step can be implemented in size T_V.*

Then, the prover of the argument-system can be implemented as a size $O(T_P) + \mathrm{poly}(\lambda)$ circuit, and the verifier can be implemented by a size P_V offline circuit followed by a size $T_V + \mathrm{poly}(\ell, \log(T_P), \lambda)$ circuit.

Proof (Sketch).
The proof is a (by now standard) extension of Kilian's [Kil92] protocol to IOPs (instead of PCPs), as proposed by Ben Sasson *et al.* [BCS16].

Lemma 7.6. *Assume that there exists a sub-exponentially hard collision-resistant hash function computable by linear size circuits mapping λ bits inputs to $\lambda/2$ bit outputs.*

Suppose that the relation $\mathcal{R}$ has an ℓ-round public-coin argument-system with soundness error ε, prover complexity T_P and verifier offline complexity P_V and online complexity T_V. Then, $\mathcal{R}$ also has an $\ell + O(1)$-round with soundness error $\varepsilon + 2^{-\lambda}$, communication complexity $\mathrm{poly}(\lambda, \log(T_V))$, prover complexity $T_P + \mathrm{poly}(T_V)$ and verifier complexity $P_V + \mathrm{poly}(\lambda, \log(T_V))$.

Proof (Proof Sketch). Loosely speaking, we simply compose the existing argument-system with Kilian's argument-system, details follow.

The prover emulates the interaction but in every round rather than sending the message in the clear, the prover sends a succinct commitment to the message. At the end of the interaction, the prover uses Kilian's [Kil92] argument-system to prove that it knows decommitments that would make the verifier accept.

Theorem 4.6 follows by combining Lemmas 7.1, 7.5 and 7.6 (where we choose ε in Lemma 7.1 to dominate the additive fixed polynomial factors in Lemmas 7.5 and 7.6).

Acknowledgements. We thank Yuval Ishai and Noga Ron-Zewi for helpful discussions.

Rothblum was supported in part by the Israeli Science Foundation (Grants No. 1262/18 and 2137/19), the Technion Hiroshi Fujiwara cyber security research center and Israel cyber directorate and by the European Union. Views and opinions expressed are however those of the author(s) only and do not necessarily reflect those of the European Union or the European Research Council. Neither the European Union nor the granting authority can be held responsible for them.

References

[AHI+17] Applebaum, B., Haramaty, N., Ishai, Y., Kushilevitz, E., Vaikuntanathan, V.: Low-complexity cryptographic hash functions. In: Papadimitriou, C.H. (ed.) ITCS 2017. LIPIcs, vol. 67. Schloss Dagstuhl - Leibniz-Zentrum für Informatik, pp. 7:1–7:31 (2017)

[BC12] Bitansky, N., Chiesa, A.: Succinct arguments from multi-prover interactive proofs and their efficiency benefits. In: Safavi-Naini, R., Canetti, R. (eds.) CRYPTO 2012. LNCS, vol. 7417, pp. 255–272. Springer, Heidelberg (2012). https://doi.org/10.1007/978-3-642-32009-5_16

[BCG+17] Bootle, J., Cerulli, A., Ghadafi, E., Groth, J., Hajiabadi, M., Jakobsen, S.K.: Linear-time zero-knowledge proofs for arithmetic circuit satisfiability. In: Takagi, T., Peyrin, T. (eds.) ASIACRYPT 2017. LNCS, vol. 10626, pp. 336–365. Springer, Cham (2017). https://doi.org/10.1007/978-3-319-70700-6_12

[BCG+19] Ben-Sasson, E., Chiesa, A., Goldberg, L., Gur, T., Riabzev, M., Spooner, N.: Linear-size constant-query IOPs for delegating computation. In: Hofheinz, D., Rosen, A. (eds.) TCC 2019. LNCS, vol. 11892, pp. 494–521. Springer, Cham (2019). https://doi.org/10.1007/978-3-030-36033-7_19

[BCG20] Bootle, J., Chiesa, A., Groth, J.: Linear-time arguments with sublinear verification from tensor codes. In: Pass, R., Pietrzak, K. (eds.) TCC 2020. LNCS, vol. 12551, pp. 19–46. Springer, Cham (2020). https://doi.org/10.1007/978-3-030-64378-2_2

[BCL20] Bootle, J., Chiesa, A., Liu, S.: Zero-knowledge succinct arguments with a linear-time prover. ePrint **2020**, 1527 (2020)

[BCR+19] Ben-Sasson, E., Chiesa, A., Riabzev, M., Spooner, N., Virza, M., Ward, N.P.: Aurora: transparent succinct arguments for R1CS. In: Ishai, Y., Rijmen, V. (eds.) EUROCRYPT 2019. LNCS, vol. 11476, pp. 103–128. Springer, Cham (2019). https://doi.org/10.1007/978-3-030-17653-2_4

[BCS16] Ben-Sasson, E., Chiesa, A., Spooner, N.: Interactive oracle proofs. In: Hirt, M., Smith, A. (eds.) TCC 2016, Part II. LNCS, vol. 9986, pp. 31–60. Springer, Heidelberg (2016). https://doi.org/10.1007/978-3-662-53644-5_2

[BGG+88] Ben-Or, M., et al.: Everything provable is provable in zero-knowledge. In: Goldwasser, S. (ed.) CRYPTO 1988. LNCS, vol. 403, pp. 37–56. Springer, New York (1990). https://doi.org/10.1007/0-387-34799-2_4

[BHR+20] Block, A.R., Holmgren, J., Rosen, A., Rothblum, R.D., Soni, P.: Public-coin zero-knowledge arguments with (almost) minimal time and space overheads. In: Pass, R., Pietrzak, K. (eds.) TCC 2020. LNCS, vol. 12551, pp. 168–197. Springer, Cham (2020). https://doi.org/10.1007/978-3-030-64378-2_7

[BHR+21] Block, A.R., Holmgren, J., Rosen, A., Rothblum, R.D., Soni, P.: Time- and space-efficient arguments from groups of unknown order. In: Malkin, T., Peikert, C. (eds.) CRYPTO 2021. LNCS, vol. 12828, pp. 123–152. Springer, Cham (2021). https://doi.org/10.1007/978-3-030-84259-8_5

[BMRS21] Baum, C., Malozemoff, A.J., Rosen, M.B., Scholl, P.: Mac'n'Cheese: zero-knowledge proofs for Boolean and arithmetic circuits with nested disjunctions. In: Malkin, T., Peikert, C. (eds.) CRYPTO 2021. LNCS, vol. 12828, pp. 92–122. Springer, Cham (2021). https://doi.org/10.1007/978-3-030-84259-8_4

[DIK10] Damgård, I., Ishai, Y., Krøigaard, M.: Perfectly secure multiparty computation and the computational overhead of cryptography. In: Gilbert, H. (ed.) EUROCRYPT 2010. LNCS, vol. 6110, pp. 445–465. Springer, Heidelberg (2010). https://doi.org/10.1007/978-3-642-13190-5_23

[DIO21] Dittmer, S., Ishai, Y., Ostrovsky, R.: Line-point zero knowledge and its applications. In: 2nd Conference on Information-Theoretic Cryptography, ITC 2021, 23–26 July 2021, Virtual Conference. LIPIcs, vol. 199. Schloss Dagstuhl - Leibniz-Zentrum für Informatik, pp. 5:1–5:24 (2021)

[DSW06] Dinur, I., Sudan, M., Wigderson, A.: Robust local testability of tensor products of LDPC codes. In: Díaz, J., Jansen, K., Rolim, J.D.P., Zwick, U. (eds.) APPROX/RANDOM -2006. LNCS, vol. 4110, pp. 304–315. Springer, Heidelberg (2006). https://doi.org/10.1007/11830924_29

[EFKP20] Ephraim, N., Freitag, C., Komargodski, I., Pass, R.: SPARKs: succinct parallelizable arguments of knowledge. In: Canteaut, A., Ishai, Y. (eds.) EUROCRYPT 2020. LNCS, vol. 12105, pp. 707–737. Springer, Cham (2020). https://doi.org/10.1007/978-3-030-45721-1_25

[FKL+21] Franzese, N., Katz, J., Lu, S., Ostrovsky, R., Wang, X., Weng, C.: Constant-overhead zero-knowledge for RAM programs. ePrint 979 (2021)

[GLS+21] Golovnev, A., Lee, J., Setty, S., Thaler, J., Wahby, R.S.: Brakedown: linear-time and post-quantum snarks for R1CS, Cryptology ePrint Archive, Report 2021/1043 (2021). https://ia.cr/2021/1043

[GMR89] Goldwasser, S., Micali, S., Rackoff, C.: The knowledge complexity of interactive proof systems. SIAM J. Comput. 18(1), 186–208 (1989)

[GRR18] Gur, T., Ramnarayan, G., Rothblum, R.D.: Relaxed locally correctable codes. In: ITCS 2018, pp. 27:1–27:11 (2018)

[HR18] Holmgren, J., Rothblum, R.: Delegating computations with (almost) minimal time and space overhead. In: Thorup, M. (ed.) FOCS 2018. IEEE Computer Society, pp. 124–135 (2018)

[IKOS08] Ishai, Y., Kushilevitz, E., Ostrovsky, R., Sahai, A.: Cryptography with constant computational overhead. In: Dwork, C. (ed.) STOC 2008. ACM, pp. 433–442 (2008)

[IKOS09] Ishai, Y., Kushilevitz, E., Ostrovsky, R., Sahai, A.: Zero-knowledge proofs from secure multiparty computation. SIAM J. Comput. 39(3), 1121–1152 (2009)

[Ish20] Ishai, Y.: Zero-knowledge proofs from information-theoretic proof systems (2020). https://zkproof.org/2020/08/12/information-theoretic-proof-systems

[Kil92] Kilian, J.: A note on efficient zero-knowledge proofs and arguments (extended abstract). In: STOC 1992, pp. 723–732 (1992)

[LSTW21] Lee, J., Setty, S., Thaler, J., Wahby, R.: Linear-time zero-knowledge snarks for R1CS. Cryptology ePrint Archive, Report 2021/030 (2021). https://eprint.iacr.org/2021/030

[Mic00] Micali, S.: Computationally sound proofs. SIAM J. Comput. **30**(4), 1253–1298 (2000)

[RR21] Ron-Zewi, N., Rothblum, R.D.: Proving as fast as computing: succinct arguments with constant prover overhead. ePrint 1673 (2021)

[RRR21] Reingold, O., Rothblum, G.N., Rothblum, R.D.: Constant-round interactive proofs for delegating computation. SIAM J. Comput. **50**(3) (2021)

[Sho88] Shoup, V.: New algorithms for finding irreducible polynomials over finite fields. In: FOCS 1988, pp. 283–290 (1988)

[Spi96] Daniel, A.: Spielman, Linear-time encodable and decodable error-correcting codes. IEEE Trans. Inf. Theory **42**(6), 1723–1731 (1996)

[Sud01] Sudan, M.: Algorithmic introduction to coding theory (lecture notes) (2001)

[Tha21] Thaler, J.: Proofs, arguments, and zero-knowledge (2021). https://people.cs.georgetown.edu/jthaler/ProofsArgsAndZK.html

[Vid15] Viderman, M.: A combination of testability and decodability by tensor products. Random Struct. Algorithms **46**(3), 572–598 (2015)

[WYKW21] Weng, C., Yang, K., Katz, J., Wang, X.: Wolverine: fast, scalable, and communication-efficient zero-knowledge proofs for Boolean and arithmetic circuits. In: SP 2021, pp. 1074–1091. IEEE (2021)

[XZZ+19] Xie, T., Zhang, J., Zhang, Y., Papamanthou, C., Song, D.: Libra: succinct zero-knowledge proofs with optimal prover computation. In: Boldyreva, A., Micciancio, D. (eds.) CRYPTO 2019. LNCS, vol. 11694, pp. 733–764. Springer, Cham (2019). https://doi.org/10.1007/978-3-030-26954-8_24

[YSWW21] Yang, K., Sarkar, P., Weng, C., Wang, X.: QuickSilver: efficient and affordable zero-knowledge proofs for circuits and polynomials over any field. ePrint 76 (2021)

[ZWZZ20] Zhang, J., Wang, W., Zhang, Y., Zhang, Y.: Doubly efficient interactive proofs for general arithmetic circuits with linear prover time. ePrint **2020**, 1247 (2020)

Succinct Interactive Oracle Proofs: Applications and Limitations

Shafik Nassar$^{(\boxtimes)}$ and Ron D. Rothblum

Technion, Haifa, Israel
{shafiknassar,rothblum}@cs.technion.ac.il

Abstract. *Interactive Oracle Proofs* (IOPs) are a new type of proof-system that combines key properties of interactive proofs and PCPs: IOPs enable a verifier to be convinced of the correctness of a statement by interacting with an untrusted prover while reading just a few bits of the messages sent by the prover. IOPs have become very prominent in the design of efficient proof-systems in recent years.

In this work we study *succinct* IOP*s*, which are IOPs in which the communication complexity is polynomial (or even linear) in the original witness. While there are strong impossibility results for the existence of succinct PCPs (i.e., PCPs whose length is polynomial in the witness), it is known that the rich class of NP relations that are decidable in small space have succinct IOPs. In this work we show both new applications, and limitations, for succinct IOPs:

- First, using one-way functions, we show how to compile IOPs into zero-knowledge *proofs*, while nearly preserving the proof length. This complements a recent line of work, initiated by Ben Sasson *et al.* (TCC, 2016B), who compile IOPs into super-succinct zero-knowledge *arguments*.
  Applying the compiler to the state-of-the-art succinct IOPs yields zero-knowledge proofs for bounded-space NP relations, with communication that is nearly equal to the original witness length. This yields the shortest known zero-knowledge proofs from the minimal assumption of one-way functions.
- Second, we give a barrier for obtaining succinct IOPs for more general NP relations. In particular, we show that if a language has a succinct IOP, then it can be decided in *space* that is proportionate only to the witness length, after a bounded-time probabilistic preprocessing. We use this result to show that under a simple and plausible (but to the best of our knowledge, new) complexity-theoretic conjecture, there is no succinct IOP for CSAT.

1 Introduction

The study of proof-systems has played an incredibly influential role in the development of theoretical computer science at large and complexity theory and cryptography in particular. Some of the most important results, concepts and

© International Association for Cryptologic Research 2022
Y. Dodis and T. Shrimpton (Eds.): CRYPTO 2022, LNCS 13507, pp. 504–532, 2022.
https://doi.org/10.1007/978-3-031-15802-5_18

open problems in this field revolve around efficient proof-systems. These include the $P \overset{?}{=} NP$ question, results such as the $IP = PSPACE$ and PCP theorems, and the notion of *zero-knowledge proofs*.

Interactive Oracle Proofs (IOP) [BCS16, RRR21], are a recently proposed type of proof-system that is playing an important role in the development of highly efficient, even practical, proofs. An IOP can be viewed as an interactive analogue of a PCP, that is, an interactive protocol in which the prover can send long messages, but the verifier only reads a few bits from each of the prover's messages. A recent exciting line of research initiated by Ben Sasson *et al.* [BCS16] (following [Kil92, Mic00]) compiles highly efficient IOPs into highly efficient zero-knowledge argument-systems that are now also being developed and deployed in practice.

One of the intriguing aspects of IOPs is that, by leveraging interaction, they allow us to circumvent some inherent efficiency barriers of PCPs (in which the interaction is just a single message). In particular, it has been known for over a decade [KR08, FS11] that SAT (the Boolean satisfiability problem) does *not* have a PCP whose length is polynomial *only* in the length of the original satisfying assignment (assuming the polynomial hierarchy does not collapse). In contrast, Kalai and Raz [KR08] showed that SAT (and more generally any bounded depth NP relation) does have a succinct IOP.[1] A more recent work of Ron-Zewi and Rothblum [RR20] gives such a succinct IOP for SAT, and more generally any bounded-space relation, in which the communication approaches the length of the unencoded witness.

In this work, we aim to better understand the limitations, and applications, of succinct IOPs. In particular we would like to understand the following two questions:

1. The results of [KR08, RR20] give succinct IOPs for either bounded-space or bounded-depth relations. But what about general[2] NP relations? For example, does the *circuit satisfiability problem* (CSAT) have a succinct IOP, or is the limitation to small depth/space in [KR08, RR20] inherent?
2. So far the applicability of succinct IOPs has been limited. This seems to mainly be due to the fact that the main bottleneck in the compilers of IOPs to efficient arguments is not the communication complexity.[3] This begs the question of what other applications can succinct IOPs be used for?

---

[1] Actually, [KR08] consider the model of *interactive* PCP, which in modern terminology, is a special-case of an IOP.

[2] Note that even though SAT is NP-complete, a succinct IOP for SAT does not automatically yield a succinct IOP for every NP relation, because the Cook-Levin theorem produces a formula whose length is polynomial in the complexity of the original NP relation, rather than just its witness.

[3] The key bottlenecks seem to be the prover's runtime and the communication complexity of the resulting argument-system. The IOP's communication complexity is a lower bound on prover runtime. The argument's communication complexity only has a logarithmic dependence on the IOPs communication.

1.1   Our Results

1.1.1   Succinct Zero-Knowledge Proofs from Succinct IOPs

As our first main result, we show how to compile IOPs into zero-knowledge *proofs*, under the minimal [OW93] assumption of one-way functions. We consider IOPs which consist of two phases: there is an *interaction phase* where the prover sends messages and the verifier only replies with random coins (without reading anything), then there is a *local computation phase* where the verifier queries the prover messages and applies a *decision predicate* on those query values (see Definitions 3 and 4). Our compiler transforms IOPs into zero-knowledge proofs in a way that preserves the communication complexity up to an additive factor which depends on the size of the verifier's decision predicate (as well as the security parameter).

Theorem 1 (Informally Stated, see Theorem 5). *Suppose the language $\mathcal{L}$ has an IOP with communication complexity cc and where the verifier's decision predicate has complexity γ. If one-way functions exist, then $\mathcal{L}$ has a zero-knowledge proof of length $cc + \mathrm{poly}(\gamma, \lambda)$, where λ is the security parameter. The zero-knowledge proof has perfect completeness and negligible soundness error.*

The proof of Theorem 1 is a relatively simple extension of the classical "notarized envelpoes" technique of Ben-Or *et al.* [BGG+88]. Indeed, our main contribution is in observing that this technique can be adapted to the IOP setting in a manner that very nearly preserves the communication complexity.

Using the compiler of Theorem 1, we are able to derive the shortest known zero-knowledge proofs that are based on one-way functions. In particular, the aforementioned work of Ron-Zewi and Rothblum [RR20] gives an IOP construction with proof length that approaches the witness length for any bounded space NP relation. This class of relations includes a large variety of natural NP relations such as SAT, k-Clique, k-Coloring, etc. We show that their IOP has very low verifier decision complexity. Applying the transformation of Theorem 1 to it we obtain a zero-knowledge proof for any bounded space NP relation, where the communication complexity in this zero-knowledge proof approaches the witness length.

Corollary 1 (Informally Stated, see Theorem 7). *Let $\mathcal{R}$ be an NP relation that can be computed in polynomial time and bounded polynomial space. If one-way functions exist, then for any constants $\beta, \gamma \in (0, 1)$, there exists a (public-coin) zero-knowledge proof for $\mathcal{R}$ with perfect completeness, negligible soundness error and proof length $(1 + \gamma) \cdot m + n^{\beta} \cdot \mathrm{poly}(\lambda)$, where n is the instance length, m is the witness length and λ is the security parameter.*

Corollary 1 constitutes the shortest known general-purpose zero-knowledge proofs under the minimal assumption of one-way functions. Prior to our work, the shortest zero-knowledge proofs, that were based on one-way functions, had communication complexity $\tilde{O}(m)$ [IKOS09, GKR15]. In contrast, under the much stronger assumption of *fully-homomorphic encryption*, Gentry *et al.* [GGI+15] constructed zero-knowledge proofs that are better than those of Corollary 1 in two ways: first, they achieve an even shorter communication complexity of $m + \text{poly}(\lambda)$ and second, the result holds for any[4] NP relation, whereas Corollary 1 is restricted to bounded-space relations.

The fact that the transformation from Theorem 1 can potentially work on other succinct IOP constructions, further motivates the study of succinct IOPs, their capabilities and limitations.

1.1.2 Limitations of Succinct IOPs

Given the succinct IOP constructions of [KR08, RR20], as well as known limitations of standard interactive proofs, it is natural to wonder whether the restriction of the [KR08, RR20] succinct IOPs to bounded depth/space relations is inherent. That is, does a succinct IOP for a given relation imply that the relation can be decided in small space?

The immediate, albeit highly unsatisfactory, answer to the above question is (most likely) negative: the class BPP has a trivial succinct IOP (in which the prover sends nothing and the verifier decides by itself) but is conjectured not to be contained in any fixed-polynomial space. So perhaps succinct IOPs are limited to relations computable in small-space or for which the corresponding language is in BPP? Unfortunately, the answer is again (likely) negative: consider the NP relation $\mathcal{R} = \{(x, w) : x \in \mathcal{L} \land (x, w) \in \mathcal{R}_{\mathsf{SAT}}\}$, where $\mathcal{L}$ is some P-complete problem.[5] Using [RR20], it is clear that $\mathcal{R}$ has a succinct IOP despite the fact that it is unlikely to be solvable in small space and the corresponding language is unlikely to be in BPP (assuming NP $\not\subseteq$ BPP).

We show that the above example essentially serves as the limit of succinct IOPs. This negative result is based on a complexity-theoretic conjecture, which, while to the best of our knowledge is new, seems quite plausible.

In more detail, we prove that if an NP relation $\mathcal{R}_{\mathcal{L}}$, corresponding to a language $\mathcal{L}$ (i.e., $\mathcal{L} = \{x : \exists w, (x, w) \in \mathcal{R}_{\mathcal{L}}\}$), has a succinct IOP, then there exists a small space algorithm *with probabilistic bounded time preprocessing* that can decide $\mathcal{L}$.

Theorem 2 (Informally stated, see Theorem 4). *If a language $\mathcal{L}$ has a k-round IOP with communication complexity cc and query complexity qc, then $\mathcal{L}$ can be decided by a $O(cc + k \log cc)$-space algorithm with probabilistic $\left(2^{qc} \cdot \text{poly}(n, 2^{k \log(cc)})\right)$-time preprocessing.*

By a s-space algorithm with t-time (probabilistic) preprocessing, we mean a (probabilistic) Turing machine that first runs in time t and outputs some intermediate state c (of size at most t). From there on a second Turing machine,

---

[4] For this result, [GGI+15] need full-fledged (rather than leveled) fully-homomorphic encryption, which are known only assuming a circular-security assumption on LWE (see, e.g., [Bra19]) or via indistinguishability obfuscation [CLTV15].

[5] As usual, by P-completeness we refer to log-space reductions. Such languages are conjectured not to be solvable in small space, see [Sma14] for further discussion.

which uses s-space, can continue the computation, viewing c as its (read-only) input tape (see Definition 12 for the formal definition). We emphasize that the restriction on the second machine is only that it runs in s space (and in particular can run for 2^s time).

Infeasibility of Succinct IOP for NP. Using Theorem 2, we argue that the existence of succinct IOPs for all of NP would have unexpected, and (arguably) unlikely, repercussions.

For example, consider the relation $\mathcal{R}_{\mathsf{CSAT}}$, consisting of all satisfiable Boolean circuits and their corresponding satisfying assignment. Given Theorem 2, the existence of a succinct IOP for $\mathcal{R}_{\mathsf{CSAT}}$ with, say, constant rounds and logarithmic query complexity, would mean that the satisfiability of a circuit of size n on m input bits, can be decided by an algorithm that first runs in time $\mathrm{poly}(n, m)$ time but from there can do arbitrary $\mathrm{poly}(m)$-space computations. We find the existence of such an algorithm unlikely and in particular point out that the straightforward decision procedure for CSAT enumerates all possible assignments, which takes space m, but also needs to check that each assignment satisfies the given circuit, which, in general, seems to require additional space n, which our $\mathrm{poly}(m)$-space algorithm does not have at this point. In other words, the straightforward algorithm needs to evaluate the circuit for each one of the candidate assignments, whereas our preprocessing model only allows for a polynomial number of evaluations (which happen a priori). Taking things a little further, we conjecture that even probabilistic quasi-polynomial time preprocessing would not be sufficient, and taking things to an extreme, it is (arguably) unlikely that $\left(2^{o(m)} \cdot \mathrm{poly}(n)\right)$-time preprocessing is sufficient. A more elaborate discussion can be found in the full version [NR22]. A parameterized version of our conjecture is stated below:

Conjecture 1. For a function class $\mathcal{T}$, the conjecture states that CSAT for circuits of size n over m input bits cannot be solved by an algorithm that uses $\mathrm{poly}(m)$ space and $t(n, m)$-time probabilistic preprocessing, for any $t \in \mathcal{T}$.

We get stronger bounds on succinct IOPs as we make the function class larger. Three interesting regimes are stated in the following corollary (ordered from the weakest bound):

Corollary 2. *Assuming Conjecture 1 we have:*

- *With $t(n, m) = \mathrm{poly}(n)$, there is no succinct IOP for $\mathcal{R}_{\mathsf{CSAT}}$ with a constant number of rounds and $O(\log n)$ query complexity.*
- *With $t(n, m) = 2^{\mathrm{polylog}(m)} \cdot \mathrm{poly}(n)$, there is no succinct IOP for $\mathcal{R}_{\mathsf{CSAT}}$ with a $\mathrm{polylog}(m)$ rounds and $\mathrm{polylog}(m) + O(\log n)$ query complexity.*
- *With $t(n, m) = 2^{o(m)} \cdot \mathrm{poly}(n)$, there is no succinct IOP for $\mathcal{R}_{\mathsf{CSAT}}$ with a $o\left(\frac{m}{\log m}\right)$ rounds and $o(m) + O(\log n)$ query complexity.*

1.2 Related Works

Lower Bounds for IPs and IOPs. Goldreich and Håstad [GH98] showed how to transform IPs to probabilistic algorithms that run in time exponential in the bits sent by the prover. Goldreich *et al.* [GVW02] showed limits on the communication complexity of interactive proofs. In particular, their results show that it is unlikely that NP-complete languages have interactive proofs with communication that is significantly shorter than the witness length. Berman *et al.* [BDRV18] showed that extremely short zero-knowledge proofs imply the existence of public-key encryption. Chiesa and Yogev [CY20] show that if a language has an IOP with very good soundness relative to its query complexity then it can be decided a by small space algorithm. This result is incomparable to Theorem 2, which shows that languages which have IOPs with short *communication* can be computed in small space (with preprocessing).

Minimizing Communication in Zero-Knowledge Proofs. Significant effort has been put into minimizing the proof length of zero-knowledge. Under the assumption of one-way functions, Ishai *et al.* [IKOS09] constructed "constant-rate" zero-knowledge proofs for all NP relations, i.e., the proof length is constant in the size of the circuit that computes the relation. For AC_0 circuits, [IKOS09] presents a zero-knowledge proof that is quasi-linear in the *witness length* and [KR08] presents a zero-knowledge proof that is polynomial in the witness length for constant depth formulas. Goldwasser *et al.* [GKR15] significantly improved the latter and showed a similar result for all of (log-space uniform) NC, again under the minimal assumption of one-way functions. As previously mentioned, using fully-homomorphic encryption, Gentry *et al.* [GGI+15] constructed zero-knowledge proofs with communication that is larger than the witness by only a small additive factor.

Another approach to minimize the proof length is to relax the notion of soundness and settle for computationally-sound proof systems, known as *arguments.* Kilian [Kil92] and Micali [Mic00] constructed extremely efficient zero-knowledge argument systems in which the communication is merely *polylogarithmic* in the witness size. Improving the latter protocol has been the focus of a major line of research in recent years. However, we stress that in this work, we focus on proof systems with statistical soundness - that is, soundness is guaranteed even against computationally unbounded cheating provers.

1.3   Our Techniques

First, in Sect. 1.3.1 we discuss our compiler for zero-knowledge proofs from IOPs. In Sect. 1.3.2, we discuss our techniques for compiling IOPs to small space algorithms with bounded time preprocessing.

1.3.1   ZKPs from IOPs

Notarized Envelopes. The zero-knowledge proof of Theorem 1 is constructed using the "notarized envelopes" technique, first introduced in [BGG+88]. We start with a high-level overview of their compiler from interactive proofs to zero-knowledge proofs. The compiler, which is applicable to any public-coin interactive proof, proceeds by emulating the original protocol but instead of having the prover send its messages in the clear (which would likely violate zero-knowledge), the prover sends (statistically binding) commitments to its messages. Leveraging the fact that the protocol is *public-coin*, the verifier does not have to read the prover messages before responding with its own random coins and so the interaction can progress.

At the end of the interaction phase, the verifier would like to actually read the messages that the prover committed to and to compute some predicate on the transcript. The key observation is that the latter is an NP statement: since the verifier is a polynomial-time machine and the computation in the end is deterministic (since the coins have been tossed already), then the commitments to the prover messages and the verifier's randomness define an NP statement, with the NP witness being the decommitments of those messages; given those decommitments, it is straightforward to decide the predicate.

At this point [BGG+88] use the fundamental zero-knowledge proof for NP [GMW86], so that the prover does not have to actually decommit (and reveal its messages) in order to prove the correctness of the NP statement. Rather can convince the verifier in *zero-knowledge* that had it indeed revealed the messages, the verifier would have accepted.

Locally Notarized Envelopes. The overhead of using the notarized envelopes technique depends on the overhead that the commitments introduce as well as the cost of the zero-knowledge proof for the final NP statement. When applied to a traditional interactive proof, this overhead depends on the total length of communication from the prover to the verifier.

For IOPs though, the overhead can be much smaller; the IOP verifier is not interested in the entire transcript but instead only in the locations of its queries. Therefore, if the prover uses a commitment that allows for a local decommitment for each bit, then, intuitively at least, the size of the NP statement should depend only on the number of queries (and the security parameter).

In the computationally-sound setting such a succinct commitment with local openings is obtained by using a Merkle tree. In our context however, we need a *statistically binding* commitment. To minimize the overhead of the commitment and achieve the desired locality, we use a pseudo-random function (PRF) as a stream cipher. In more detail, the prover first commits to the PRF seed and then uses the PRF as a pseudorandom one-time pad to all of the messages. This yields a length preserving commitment scheme that is also statistically binding, where the overhead is merely the additional commitment to the PRF seed. Although this commitment scheme does *not* support local openings, it allows us to define an NP statement that depends only on the (short) seed and the desired bits which the verifier would like to query.

IOP Compactness. The size of the NP statement depends also on the size of the computation that the verifier performs once it receives the queries. Naively, we can say that the size of the mentioned verifier computation is bounded by the running time of the verifier, and thus the NP statement is polynomially related to the running time of the verifier. However, we distinguish between the total running time of the verifier and the size of the computation it performs offline after receiving the answers to its queries. We refer to the size of the offline computation as the "compactness" of the IOP (verifier). We show that the additive overhead of using the locally notarized envelopes technique with IOPs is polynomial in the compactness of the IOP and the security parameter, thus presenting a potentially efficient transformation from IOPs to ZKPs.

We also analyze an IOP for bounded space NP relations from a previous work [RR20] and show that it is indeed very compact, thus achieving a very efficient ZKP for bounded space NP relations as per Corollary 1.

1.3.2   Infeasibility of Succinct IOPs

To show lower bounds for succinct IOPs, it is tempting to utilize existing lower bounds for either interactive proofs or PCPs. Trying to do so we run into the following difficulty. First, observe that CSAT has a very succinct interactive proof - the prover simply sends the witness! Thus, we cannot employ generic lower bounds for interactive proofs (such as IP $\subseteq$ PSPACE and similar extensions). Likewise, we cannot use the known lower bounds for succinct PCPs since, for example, the main lower bound that is known, due to Fortnow and Santhanam [FS11], also rules out a PCP for SAT, whereas by [KR08, RR20] we know that SAT has a succinct IOP.

Nevertheless, our approach is inspired by Fortnow and Santhanam [FS11], who showed that a succinct PCP for SAT collapses the polynomial hierarchy. Their proof goes through an interesting intermediate step: they show that a succinct PCP for any language implies a special kind of reduction for that language, called *instance compression*, and then prove that if SAT is instance compressible then the polynomial hierarchy collapses.

Interactive Proofs and Small Space Algorithms. There is a well established relationship between interactive proofs and small space algorithms, which stems from the fact that the optimal prover strategy can be computed in space that is proportional to the length of the transcript of the interactive proof, if given oracle access to the verifier's decision procedure.[6] This way, we can compute the probability that the verifier accepts against the optimal prover strategy and decide accordingly. Notice that this reduction does not require the interactive proof to have perfect completeness, but rather only a gap between completeness and soundness.

So the problem now boils down to bounding the space needed to emulate the verifier's decision procedure. The problem is that the verifier's decision procedure can take space that is polynomial in the instance length. This means that if we look at the overall space used, it may very well be dominated by the verifier's decision procedure (making the succinctness of the proof irrelevant).

IOPs and Small Space Algorithms. When it comes to IOPs, we can leverage the fact that the verifier queries a small number of bits from the prover messages. For simplicity, we first consider a *non-adaptive* IOP which means that after the interaction is over, the verifier generates a predicate and a set of query locations (both of which depend only on the instance and the random coins) and outputs

---

[6] See, e.g., [Gol08, Chapter 9].

the evaluation of the predicate on the query values. If we can compute the predicates and query locations for all possible random coins of the verifier, then the verifier's decision procedure can be emulated by simple oracle access to those queries and predicates - which does not add any substantial amount of space to our computation. Let's analyze the time it takes to generate all such predicates and queries: assuming the verifier uses rc random coins, we need to iterate over 2^{rc} possibilities and emulate the verifier on each of them. This takes $2^{rc} \cdot \mathrm{poly}(n)$ time. Extending this approach to general *adaptive* IOPs is not difficult: the predicates and query sets are simply replaced by *decision trees*. Computing each decision tree now requires us to iterate over all possible query values, so we get a total of $2^{rc+qc} \cdot \mathrm{poly}(n)$ time complexity, where qc is the query complexity of the IOP. This yields the following lemma:

Lemma 1 (Informally stated, see Lemma *4*). *If a language $\mathcal{L}$ can be decided by a public coin IOP where the query complexity is qc and the randomness complexity is rc. Then all of the verifier's decision trees can be computed in $2^{rc+qc} \cdot \mathrm{poly}(n)$ time.*

This approach presents another problem: computing all possible decision trees requires time that is exponential in the randomness complexity. Note that the exponential dependence on the query complexity does not bother us for two reasons: the number of queries in common IOP constructions tends to be small and, moreover, for non-adaptive IOPs this factor vanishes.

Randomness Reduction for IOPs. To address the problem of exponential dependence on the randomness complexity, we present a transformation that reduces the randomness complexity of IOPs, at the expense of having a single long verifier message at the beginning of the interaction.

We remark that a similar type of randomness reduction is known in many contexts, such as communication complexity [New91], property testing [GS10, GR18], interactive proofs [AG21], and likely many other settings as well. Nevertheless we point out the following key feature of our transformation, which to the best of our knowledge is novel: we reduce the randomness complexity during the interaction so that it does not even depend logarithmically on the input size. This is crucial in our context since a logarithmic dependence on the input size, would translate into a polynomial dependence in the reduction.

The technique, as usual in such randomness reductions is subsampling. In more detail, for a public-coin IOP, in each round, the verifier simply chooses a random string from some set U and sends it to the prover. The randomness complexity required to uniformly choose a string from U is $rc = \log|U|$. Imagine if a proper subset $S \subset U$ was chosen a priori and made known to both the prover and the verifier, such that the verifier now samples a uniform random string from S instead of U. This reduces the randomness complexity to $\log|S|$.

But does any subset S preserve the completeness and soundness properties? For perfect completeness, the answer is yes; any string that the verifier chooses would make it accept (a "yes" instance), therefore any subset S would preserve that property. Preserving soundness, on the other hand, is more challenging;

there is a prover strategy and a fraction of random strings that would make the verifier accept a "no" instance, and if S contains only such strings, then the soundness property is not preserved.

Nevertheless, we show that if the verifier generates the set S at random by choosing $\text{poly}(cc)$ strings (where cc is the prover-to-verifier communication complexity) from U, then the soundness property is preserved with overwhelming probability. The result is informally stated below.

Lemma 2 (Informally stated, see Lemma 3). *If $\mathcal{L}$ has a public-coin IOP where the prover sends cc bits in total and the verifier uses rc random coins, then $\mathcal{L}$ has a public-coin IOP where the verifier first sends a random string of length $rc \cdot \text{poly}(cc)$ and all subsequent verifier random messages are of length $O(\log cc)$. If the original IOP has perfect completeness, then so does the resulting IOP.*

At first glance, it may seem that we have not gained anything. After all, sampling a multi-set S from U requires more randomness than sampling a single string from U. However, we observe that this reduction moves up most of the randomness to the first round, while reducing the randomness complexity in all subsequent rounds.

Small Space with Probabilistic Preprocessing. Assume $\mathcal{L}$ has an IOP and assume for simplicity that the IOP has perfect completeness.[7] We sketch how we can combine Lemmas 2 and 1 to get a small space algorithm with probabilistic polynomial time preprocessing that decides $\mathcal{L}$. First, we apply Lemma 2 on the IOP and get an IOP where each verifier message, except the first one, has length $O(\log cc)$. The preprocessing algorithm starts by sampling the first verifier message S, and the computes all of the decision trees conditioned on S being the first verifier message. We note that, overall, the decision tree can be encoded using a string of length $2^{qc+k \log cc}$.

Denote by k the number of rounds in the IOP. Given all of the decision trees, the bounded space algorithm can emulate the optimal prover strategy in $O(cc + qc + k \cdot \log(cc))$ space, since the length of the remaining transcript is $O(cc + k \cdot \log(cc))$ and the queries to the decision trees can be computed in $O(qc + k \log cc)$ space. The algorithm then returns 1 if there exists a strategy that makes the verifier always accept.

Since we assume that the original IOP has perfect completeness, then so does the new IOP and specifically, for any $x \in \mathcal{L}$ and any sampled message S, there exists a prover strategy that makes the verifier accept.

We move on to analyzing soundness. By Lemma 2, the IOP produced by the randomness reduction in step is sound, so we can assume it has some constant soundness error $\varepsilon > 0$. Let x be a "no" instance. Soundness error ε implies that at most ε fraction of the possibilities for the first message might result in a "doomed state" (i.e., the verifier accepts with probability 1 after that first message). Therefore, with probability at least $1 - \varepsilon$ over the sampled S, for any residual prover strategy, there exists a strictly positive probability (over the

---

[7] This assumption is not necessary to achieve the result, see Sect. 4.

verifier's randomness) that the verifier rejects. This means that with probability $1 - \varepsilon$, the small-space algorithm would not a find a prover strategy that always makes the verifier accept and therefore would reject the instance x. This yields the desired small-space algorithm with probabilistic preprocessing as stated in Theorem 2.

1.4   Organization

Section 2 includes the preliminaries, definitions and notations. In Sect. 3, we formally state randomness reduction for IOPs. In Sect. 4, we prove that any language that has an IOP can be decided in space that is proportionate to the communication complexity after some bounded-time preprocessing. In Sect. 5, we present the compiler from IOPs to zero-knowledge proofs and apply it to the IOP of [RR20]. In addition, the full version [NR22], contains further discussion on Conjecture 1 and a proof sketch that the IOP of [RR20] is indeed compact (as per Definition 5).

2   Preliminaries

For any positive integer $n \in \mathbb{N}$, we denote by $[n]$ the set of integers $\{1, \dots, n\}$.

2.1   Basic Complexity Notations and Definitions

2.1.1   NP Relations

For a language $\mathcal{L} \in \mathsf{NP}$, we denote by $R_\mathcal{L}$ an NP *relation* of $\mathcal{L}$. The relation $R_\mathcal{L}$ consists of pairs (x, w) such that $x \in \mathcal{L}$ and w is a *witness* that allows one to verify that x is indeed in $\mathcal{L}$ in polynomial time. It holds that $x \in \mathcal{L}$ if and only if $\exists w$ such that $(x, w) \in R_\mathcal{L}$. We denote by n the instance size $|x|$, and by m the witness size $|w|$. Throughout this work, we implicitly assume that $m \leq n$.

We extend the definition of NP relations and languages to general relations and their respective languages.

Definition 1 (Languages and Relations). *Let $\mathcal{R}$ be a binary relation and assume that there exists a function $m(n)$ such that if the first element has length n, then the second element has length $m = m(n)$. We call m the* witness length *and n the* instance length *of the relation. We define $\mathcal{L}(\mathcal{R}) = \{x \; : \; \exists y \in \{0,1\}^{m(|x|)} \text{ s.t. } (x, y) \in \mathcal{R}\}$ and we call $\mathcal{L}(\mathcal{R})$ the* language of the relation $\mathcal{R}$.

2.1.2   Circuit-SAT

In the *Circuit-SAT* (CSAT) problem, the instance is a Boolean circuit and we say that it is in the language if there exists an assignment that satisfies that circuit. We define the natural relation $\mathcal{R}_{\mathsf{CSAT}}$ as the satisfiable Boolean circuits and their satisfying assignments.

2.2   Interactive Proofs and Oracle Proofs

We use the definition and notations of *interactive machines* from [Gol04].

Definition 2 *(Interactive proof). A pair of interactive machines $(\mathcal{P}, \mathcal{V})$ is called an* interactive proof system *for a language $\mathcal{L}$ if $\mathcal{V}$ is a probabilistic polynomial-time machine and the following conditions hold:*

- **Completeness:** *For every $x \in \mathcal{L}$,*

$$\Pr\left[\langle \mathcal{P}, \mathcal{V} \rangle (x) = 1\right] = 1.$$

- **Soundness:** *For every $x \notin \mathcal{L}$,*

$$\Pr\left[\langle \mathcal{P}^*, \mathcal{V} \rangle (x) = 1\right] \leq \frac{1}{2}.$$

When the language $\mathcal{L}$ is an NP *language and $x \in \mathcal{L}$, it is standard to give the prover as an input a witness w such that $(x, w) \in R_\mathcal{L}$. In this case, the completeness and soundness requirements are stated as follows:*

- **Completeness:** *For every $(x, w) \in R_\mathcal{L}$,*

$$\Pr\left[\langle \mathcal{P}(w), \mathcal{V} \rangle (x) = 1\right] = 1.$$

- **Soundness:** *For every $x \notin \mathcal{L}$ and $w^* \in \{0, 1\}^*$,*

$$\Pr\left[\langle \mathcal{P}^*(w^*), \mathcal{V} \rangle (x) = 1\right] \leq \frac{1}{2}.$$

Definition 3 *(Interactive Oracle Proof). A* public-coin *interactive oracle proof (IOP) for a language $\mathcal{L}$ is an interactive protocol between a prover $\mathcal{P}$ and a probabilistic polynomial-time machine $\mathcal{V}$. On a common input x of length $|x| = n$, the protocol consists of two phases:*

1. **Interaction:** *$\mathcal{P}$ and $\mathcal{V}$ interact for $k(n)$ rounds in the following manner: in round i, $\mathcal{P}$ sends an oracle message π_i and $\mathcal{V}$ replies with a random string r_i. Denote $r = r_1...r_k$ and $\pi = \pi_1...\pi_k$.*
2. **Query and Computation:** *$\mathcal{V}$ makes bounded number of queries to the oracles sent by the prover and accepts and rejects accordingly.*

We require:

- **Completeness:** *If $x \in \mathcal{L}$ then*

$$\Pr\left[\langle \mathcal{P}, \mathcal{V} \rangle (x) = 1\right] = 1.$$

- **Soundness:** *If $x \notin \mathcal{L}$ then for every prover $\mathcal{P}^*$ it holds that*

$$\Pr\left[\langle \mathcal{P}^*, \mathcal{V} \rangle (x) = 1\right] \leq \frac{1}{2}.$$

Parameters of IOP. We call $cc := |\pi|$ and $rc := |r|$ the *communication complexity* and *randomness complexity* of the IOP, respectively. The bound on the number of queries is denoted by qc and called the *query complexity* of the IOP. The round complexity is the total number of rounds $k = k(n)$ in the interaction phase.

Non-adaptive IOPs. Most IOP construction have the useful property of being *non-adaptive*, that is, the query locations do not depend on the answers to the previous queries. Formally:

Definition 4 (Non-adaptive IOP). *An IOP is called* non-adaptive *if the query and computation phase can be split into the two following phases:*

1. **Local Computation:** $\mathcal{V}$ *deterministically (based on r and x) produces a vector $\boldsymbol{ql}_{x,r} \in [|\pi|]^{qc}$ of qc queries and a circuit that evaluates a predicate $\phi_{x,r} : \{0,1\}^{qc} \to \{0,1\}$.*
2. **Evaluation:** $\mathcal{V}$ *queries π on the locations denoted by $\boldsymbol{ql}_{x,r}$ and plugs the values into the predicate and outputs $\phi_{x,r}\left(\pi\left[\boldsymbol{ql}_{x,r}\right]\right)$.*

Compactness. By definition, the size of the predicate (meaning the circuit that evaluates the predicate) produced by the non-adaptive IOP verifier is bounded by the running time of the verifier. However, many concrete IOP constructions have a predicate that is much shorter than the total running time of the verifier, and we leverage that property in order to construct succinct proofs. The following definition captures this property:

Definition 5 (α-*uniform γ-compact IOP*). *For any time-constructible[8] functions $\alpha(n), \gamma(n)$, we say that the IOP is α-uniform γ-compact if for every input $x \in \{0,1\}^n$ and all random coins r, the size of the circuit that evaluates the predicate $\phi_{x,r}$ is $O(\gamma(n))$. Furthermore, the circuit can be produced in time $O(\alpha(n))$ given x, r. For simplicity, if $\alpha = \mathrm{poly}(n)$, we say that the IOP is γ-compact.*

We use "the size of ϕ" and "the size of the circuit that evaluates ϕ" interchangeably, and denote that value by $|\phi|$.

IOPs for Relations. Given a binary relation $\mathcal{R}$, we define an IOP for $\mathcal{R}$ as an IOP that decides $\mathcal{L}(\mathcal{R})$, where the prover additionally receives the witness as a private input. In these constructions, the prover is usually required to be efficient, since it has the witness as an input.

Succinct IOPs. An IOP for an NP relation $\mathcal{R}_\mathcal{L}$ is called *succinct* if the communication complexity (which can be thought of as the proof length) is polynomial in the witness size, that is $cc = \mathrm{poly}(m)$. Formally:

Definition 6. *Let $\mathcal{L} \in$ NP be a language and $\mathcal{R}_\mathcal{L}$ be a corresponding NP relation with instance size n and witness size m. An IOP for $\mathcal{R}_\mathcal{L}$ is called a* succinct IOP *if the communication complexity is $\mathrm{poly}(m)$.*

---

[8] A function $f(n)$ is *time-constructible* if given there exists a Turing machine that given 1^n outputs the binary representation of $f(n)$ in $O(f(n))$ time.

2.3   Computational Indistinguishability

We say that a function $f : \mathbb{N} \to \mathbb{R}$ is negligible if for every polynomial $p(\cdot)$ it holds that $f(n) = O(1/p(n))$.

Definition 7. *Let* $\{D_n\}_{n \in \mathbb{N}}, \{E_n\}_{n \in \mathbb{N}}$ *be two distribution ensembles indexed by a security parameter* n. *We say that the ensembles are* computationally indistinguishable, *denoted* $D_n \overset{c}{\approx} E_n$, *if for any (non-uniform) probabilistic polynomial time algorithm* A, *it holds that following quantity is a negligible function in* n:

$$\left| \Pr_{x \leftarrow D_n}[A(x) = 1] - \Pr_{x \leftarrow E_n}[A(x) = 1] \right|.$$

We use some basic properties of computational indistinguishability such as the following:

Fact 1 (Concatenation). *Let* H, H', G *and* G' *be any efficiently sampleable distribution ensembles such that* $H \overset{c}{\approx} H'$ *and* $G \overset{c}{\approx} G'$. *Then* $(H, G) \overset{c}{\approx} (H', G')$.

Fact 2 (Triangle Inequality). *Let* H_1, H_2, H_3 *be any distribution ensembles. If* $H_1 \overset{c}{\approx} H_2$ *and* $H_2 \overset{c}{\approx} H_3$ *then* $H_1 \overset{c}{\approx} H_3$.

Fact 3 (Computational Data-Processing Inequality). *Let* H *and* H' *be any distribution ensembles and* A *be any PPT algorithm. If* $H \overset{c}{\approx} H'$ *then* $A(H) \overset{c}{\approx} A(H')$.

2.4   Cryptographic Primitives

2.4.1   Commitment Scheme in the CRS Model

A commitment scheme in the common reference string model is a tuple of probabilistic polynomial time algorithms (Gen, Com, Ver) where Gen outputs a common random string $r \in \{0,1\}^*$. The commit algorithm Com takes a message to be committed and the random string r and produces a commitment c and a decommitment string d. The verification algorithm takes the commitment c, the decommitment string d, an alleged committed value y and the random string r and outputs 1 if and only if it is "convinced" that c is indeed a commitment of y. We require the commitment to be computationally hiding and perfectly binding with overwhelming probability over the common random string r. All of the algorithms also take a security parameter $\lambda \in \mathbb{N}$ (in unary representation). We formally define the commitment scheme:

Definition 8 (Commitment Scheme). *A commitment scheme in the common reference string model is a tuple of probabilistic polynomial time algorithms* (Gen, Com, Ver) *that with the following semantics:*

- $r \leftarrow Gen\left(1^\lambda\right)$ *where* r *is referred to as the common reference string.*
- *For any string* $y \in \{0,1\}^*$: $(c, d) \leftarrow Com\left(1^\lambda, r, y\right)$.
- *For any strings* $c, d, y \in \{0,1\}^*$: $\{0,1\} \leftarrow Ver\left(1^\lambda, r, c, y, d\right)$.

The scheme must satisfy the following requirements:

- **Correctness:** Ver *always accepts in an honest execution, i.e., for any string y and any security λ*

$$\Pr_{\substack{r \leftarrow Gen(1^\lambda) \\ (c,d) \leftarrow Com(1^\lambda, r, y)}} \left[Ver\left(1^\lambda, r, c, y, d\right) = 1\right] = 1.$$

- **Hiding:** *For any two strings $y_1, y_2 \in \{0,1\}^*$ and any common reference string r, the distribution of the commitment of y_1 and y_2 are computationally indistinguishable, i.e., if we denote by Com_c only the commitment part of Com then: $\left\{Com_c\left(1^\lambda, r, y_1\right)\right\}_{\lambda \in \mathbb{N}} \stackrel{c}{\approx} \left\{Com_c\left(1^\lambda, r, y_2\right)\right\}_{\lambda \in \mathbb{N}}.$*
- **Binding:** *For any λ, with probability at least $1 - 2^{-\lambda}$ over the common reference string, any commitment c^* has at most one value y that can be accepted by Ver, i.e.,*

$$\Pr_{r \leftarrow Gen(1^\lambda)} \left[\exists y_1, y_2, d_1, d_2 \in \{0,1\}^* : \bigwedge_{i \in \{1,2\}} Ver\left(1^\lambda, r, c^*, y_i, d_i\right) = 1\right] < 2^{-\lambda}.$$

In this work, we refer to commitment schemes in the CRS model simply as commitment schemes. We note that due to [Nao91], we have such a commitment scheme under the standard cryptographic assumption of one-way functions.

2.4.2   Pseudorandom Function

We denote by $\mathcal{F}_n$ the set of all functions $\{0,1\}^n \to \{0,1\}$. In what follows, by a truly random function, we mean a function that is sampled uniformly at random from $\mathcal{F}_n$.

Definition 9 *(Pseudorandom Function). A function $F : \{0,1\}^\lambda \times \{0,1\}^n \to \{0,1\}$ is a pseudorandom function if for any probabilistic polynomial time oracle machine A, every polynomial $p(\cdot)$ and all sufficiently large λ it holds that*

$$\left| \Pr_{s \stackrel{\$}{\leftarrow} \{0,1\}^\lambda} \left[A^{F(s,\cdot)}\left(1^n\right) = 1\right] - \Pr_{U \stackrel{\$}{\leftarrow} \mathcal{F}_n} \left[A^{U(\cdot)}\left(1^n\right) = 1\right] \right| < \frac{1}{p(\lambda)}.$$

For convenience, we denote $F(s, x) = F_s(x)$.

Pseudorandom One-Time Pad. We mat refer to any function $f : \{0,1\}^n \to \{0,1\}$ as a string. For any collection of indices $i_1 < i_2 < ... < i_q$, we use the notation $f[I] := f(i_1) \circ ... \circ f(i_q)$ where $I = \{i_1, ..., i_q\}$. When it is clear from context, we may write $f(x)$ for any integer $x \geq 0$ and it should be understood as applying f on the binary representation of x. In this work, we will use pseudorandom functions to encrypt messages, so for any PRF F and string $y \in \{0,1\}^\ell$ (where $\ell \leq 2^n$), the expression $F_S\left[[\ell]\right] \oplus y$ represents encrypting y with a pseudorandom one-time pad obtained from F with seed S. A PRF allows us to implement a stream cipher, e.g. if we want to encrypt the messages $y_1, y_2 \in \{0,1\}^\ell$ then we can use the values $F_S(1), ..., F_S(\ell)$ to encrypt y_1 and $F_S(\ell+1), ..., F_S(2 \cdot \ell)$ to encrypt y_2.

The following fact implies that the pseudorandom one-time pad reveals no information about the encrypted string (to any computationally bounded adversary):

Fact 4. *Let $F : \{0,1\}^\lambda \times \{0,1\}^n \to \{0,1\}$ be a PRF. For any set $I \subseteq \{0,1\}^n$, the distribution ensemble $\{s \xleftarrow{\$} \{0,1\}^\lambda : F_s(I)\}_{\lambda \in \mathbb{N}}$ is computationally indistinguishable from uniform random strings of length $|I|$.*

As mentioned above, this property immediately implies that for any string y, the encryption of y using F with key/seed S yields a pseudorandom string.

2.5 Zero-Knowledge Proofs

In this section, we formally define *zero-knowledge proofs* (ZKP) for NP languages. In this paper, we focus on *computational* zero-knowledge. This notion of ZKP relies on computational indistinguishability between distribution ensembles as per Definition 7. These ensembles are indexed by a security parameter λ which is passed to the prover and verifier of the ZKP as an explicit input (in unary representation). We also require that the zero-knowledge property holds even if the verifier is given some auxiliary information. Loosely speaking, this means that any (malicious) verifier does not learn anything from the interaction with the honest prover $\mathcal{P}$ even if the verifier is given some additional a priori information. For any verifier $\mathcal{V}^*$, input $x \in \{0,1\}^*$ and auxiliary input $z \in \{0,1\}^*$ (that might depend on x), we denote by $View_{\mathcal{V}^*(z)}^{\mathcal{P}(w)}(x, \lambda)$ the *view* of $\mathcal{V}^*$ in the interaction $\langle \mathcal{P}(w), \mathcal{V}^*(z) \rangle (x, 1^\lambda)$. The view consists of the random coins tossed by $\mathcal{V}^*$ and the messages it received from the prover (alongside the inputs x, z and λ).

Definition 10 *(Zero-knowledge proofs). Let $(\mathcal{P}, \mathcal{V})$ be an interactive proof system for some language $\mathcal{L} \in$ NP with security parameter λ. The proof-system $(\mathcal{P}, \mathcal{V})$ is computational zero-knowledge w.r.t. auxiliary input if for every polynomial-time interactive machine $\mathcal{V}^*$ there exists a probabilistic polynomial-time machine Sim^*, called the simulator, such that for all $x \in \mathcal{L}$ and any auxiliary input $z \in \{0,1\}^{\mathrm{poly}(|x|)}$, the following distribution ensembles are computationally indistinguishable:*

- $\left\{ View_{\mathcal{V}^*(z)}^{\mathcal{P}(w)}(x, \lambda) \right\}_{\lambda \in \mathbb{N}}$ *where $(x, w) \in R_\mathcal{L}$.*
- $\left\{ Sim^*(z, x, 1^\lambda) \right\}_{\lambda \in \mathbb{N}}.$

Remark 1. W.l.o.g., we can assume that the malicious verifier V^* is deterministic, since coin tosses can be passed as auxiliary input.

Throughout this manuscript, we refer to computational zero-knowledge proofs w.r.t. auxiliary input simply as *zero-knowledge proofs*. When the security parameter λ is clear from context, we may omit it from the notation.

2.6   Hoeffding's Inequality

Hoeffding's inequality [Hoe63] is a classical concentration inequality which is widely used in theoretical computer science.

Theorem 3. *Let* $X_1, ..., X_n$ *be real random variables bounded by the interval* $[0, 1]$ *and denote their sum by* $S := X_1 + ... + X_n$. *If* $X_1, ..., X_n$ *are independent then for any* $\varepsilon > 0$ *it holds that*

$$\Pr\left[\left|S - \mathbb{E}\left[S\right]\right| > \varepsilon\right] < 2e^{-2\frac{\varepsilon^2}{n}}.$$

3   Randomness Reduction

In this section, we show how to reduce the randomness used by an IOP verifier. While we view this result as being of independent interest, we note that this randomness reduction will also be useful later on in Sect. 4 when we convert IOPs to bounded-space algorithms with probabilistic time preprocessing.

The procedure that we introduce achieves a relaxed notion of randomness reduction: the verifier can use a large (but still polynomial) amount of randomness only in the first round of interaction, then uses only $O(\log cc)$ random bits in each subsequent round, where cc is the communication complexity of the original IOP. Alternatively, we can view this as if before the interaction begins, a trusted setup samples a uniform random string and then the prover and verifier run an IOP, where they both have explicit access to that random string. Moreover, as shown in the full version [NR22], this common random string can also be fixed as a non-uniform advice.

The following definition captures this special type of IOP:

Definition 11. *A protocol* $(\mathcal{P}, \mathcal{V})$ *is a* IOP *in the common reference string model* (CRS IOP) *for a language* $\mathcal{L} \subseteq \{0, 1\}^*$ *with* CRS-error μ *if* $(\mathcal{P}, \mathcal{V})$ *is an* IOP *as per Definition 3 with the following modifications:*

- ***Additional Input:** In addition to the instance* $x \in \{0, 1\}^n$, *both the prover and the verifier get an input* $\rho \in \{0, 1\}^*$.
- ***Completeness:** For any* $x \in \mathcal{L}$, *with probability* $1 - \mu$ *over* $\rho \xleftarrow{\$} \{0, 1\}^*$, $\mathcal{P}$ *makes* $\mathcal{V}$ *accept with probability at least* $1 - \varepsilon_c$ *over the verifier's coin tosses:*

$$\Pr_{\rho \in \{0,1\}^*}\left[\Pr\left[\langle\mathcal{P}, \mathcal{V}\rangle(\rho, x) = 1\right] \geq 1 - \varepsilon_c\right] \geq 1 - \mu.$$

- ***Non-adaptive Soundness:** For any* $x \notin \mathcal{L}$ *and every prover strategy* $\mathcal{P}^*$, *with probability* $1 - \mu$ *over* $\rho \xleftarrow{\$} \{0, 1\}^*$, $\mathcal{P}^*$ *makes* $\mathcal{V}$ *accept with probability at most* ε_s *over the verifier's coin tosses. Formally, for every* $x \notin \mathcal{L}$ *and* $\mathcal{P}^*$

$$\Pr_{\rho \in \{0,1\}^*}\left[\Pr\left[\langle\mathcal{P}^*, \mathcal{V}\rangle(\rho, x) = 1\right] \leq \varepsilon_s\right] \geq 1 - \mu.$$

We emphasize that the external probability $1 - \mu$ is only over the choice of CRS ρ whereas the internal probabilistic statement is over all of the verifier's other coin tosses.

Remark 2. We say that the CRS IOP has *perfect completeness* if for any $x \in \mathcal{L}$ and any $\rho \in \{0,1\}^*$ it holds that $\Pr\left[\langle \mathcal{P}, \mathcal{V} \rangle(\rho, x) = 1\right] = 1$.

The following lemma shows how to transform any IOP into a CRS IOP with small randomness complexity:

Lemma 3 *(Randomness Reduction for IOPs).* *Let $\mathcal{L}$ be a language that has a k-round public-coin IOP with constant completeness and soundness errors $\varepsilon_c, \varepsilon_s$ and communication complexity cc. For any λ and constant ϵ_0 be some constant. Then $\mathcal{L}$ has a CRS IOP with CRS-error $2^{-\lambda}$, completeness error $\varepsilon_c + \epsilon_0$ and soundness error $\varepsilon_s + \epsilon_0$. The CRS length is $\mathrm{poly}(cc, rc, \lambda)$, the randomness complexity is $O\left(k \cdot \log(cc \cdot \lambda)\right)$, and the query complexity, communication complexity and number of rounds are the same as in the original IOP. Furthermore, if the original IOP has perfect completeness then the CRS IOP has perfect completeness.*

The idea that underlies the proof of Lemma 3 is to use the CRS to shrink the probability space and then argue that the resulting space is a good representative of the original space. To formalize this idea, we make use of the *game tree of a proof system* defined by Goldreich and Håstad [GH98]. The CRS defines an approximation of the tree, and both parties interact with respect to the approximated tree. Due to page constraints, the proof is deferred to the full version [NR22].

4   Limitations of Succinct IOPs

In this section, we show limitations on the expressive power of succinct IOPs. Here we consider general, *adaptive* IOPs (which only strengthens the negative result).

Loosely speaking, we show that if a language has an IOP then it can be decided by a bounded-space algorithm with bounded-time preprocessing. The amount of space used is closely related to the communication complexity of the IOP. When applying this result to a succinct IOP for an NP relation $\mathcal{R}_\mathcal{L}$ (as per Definition 6) with instance length n and witness length m we get a $\mathrm{poly}(m)$-space algorithm with $\mathrm{poly}(n)$-time preprocessing that decides the language $\mathcal{L}$.

We start by formally defining what it means for a relation to be decidable by a bounded-space algorithm with a bounded-time preprocessing:

Definition 12. *Let $\mathcal{R}$ be a relation with instance length n and witness length m and $\mathcal{L} = \mathcal{L}(\mathcal{R})$ the corresponding language (see Definition 1). We say that $\mathcal{R}$ can be decided in $s(n, m)$-space with $t(n, m)$ preprocessing with soundness error ε_s and completeness error ε_c if there exists a $t(n, m)$-time probabilistic algorithm $\mathcal{A}_1$ and a $s(n, m)$-space (deterministic) algorithm $\mathcal{A}_2$ such that:*

- If $x \in \mathcal{L}$ then $\mathrm{Pr}_{y \leftarrow \mathcal{A}_1(x)} \left[\mathcal{A}_2(y) = 1 \right] \geq 1 - \varepsilon_c$.
- If $x \notin \mathcal{L}$ then $\mathrm{Pr}_{y \leftarrow \mathcal{A}_1(x)} \left[\mathcal{A}_2(y) = 1 \right] \leq \varepsilon_s$.

In what follows we refer to $\mathcal{A}_1$ as the *preprocessor* and $\mathcal{A}_2$ as the *decider*. We also note that, as usual, the soundness error can be reduced by repetition, while increasing the time (and space) complexities accordingly. Observe that we can reduce it to negligible simply by repeating the preprocessing a polynomial number of times, while almost preserving the space used by the decider.

The main result shown in this section is the following theorem:

Theorem 4. *If a language $\mathcal{L}$ has a k-round IOP with communication complexity cc, query complexity qc and verifier run-time $T_\mathcal{V}$, then $\mathcal{L}$ can be decided in $O(cc + k \cdot \log cc)$-space with $\left(2^{qc + O(k \cdot \log cc)} \cdot T_\mathcal{V} \right)$ preprocessing with completeness and soundness errors 2^{-cc}. Furthermore, if the IOP has perfect completeness, then the algorithm has perfect completeness as well.*

As an immediate corollary, we obtain the following:

Corollary 3. *Let $\mathcal{R}_\mathcal{L}$ be an NP relation with instance size n and witness size m. If $\mathcal{R}_\mathcal{L}$ has a succinct constant-round IOP with perfect completeness and $O(\log n)$ query complexity then $\mathcal{L}$ can be decided in $\mathrm{poly}(m)$-space with $\mathrm{poly}(n)$ preprocessing. Similarly, if $\mathcal{R}_\mathcal{L}$ has a succinct $o\left(\frac{m}{\log m} \right)$-round IOP with perfect completeness and $o(m) + O(\log n)$ query complexity then $\mathcal{L}$ can be decided in $\mathrm{poly}(m)$-space with $2^{o(m)} \cdot \mathrm{poly}(n)$ preprocessing. The soundness error in both algorithms is $2^{-\mathrm{poly}(m)}$.*

4.1 Handling Small Randomness

Given an IOP and an input x, each string of random coins r defines a *decision tree* of the verifier, which dictates which queries to make and what value to output. The idea is to encode all of these decision trees, and generate a large string that represents all of them. This string can be used to implement the verifier in very small space, simply by reading a few locations of the string to determine what queries to make (to prover messages) and decide the output. This resulting verifier runs in very small space, and the final step is to convert this resulting IOP to a small-space algorithm using the following fact[9]:

Fact 5. *For any IP (P, V) there exists an algorithm $\mathcal{A}_1$ s.t. $\mathcal{A}_1(x) = \mathrm{Pr}[(P, V)(x) = 1]$ for any $x \in \{0, 1\}^*$. In addition, $\mathcal{A}_1$ runs in $O(cc + rc + S)$ space, where cc is the communication complexity, rc is the randomness complexity and S is the verifier's space complexity.*

Hence, going back to the terminology of Definition 12, the preprocessor is responsible for generating the string and the decider is simply an algorithm for computing the probability that the verifier accepts and deciding according to that probability. The following lemma captures the main property of the preprocessor:

---

[9] See, e.g., [Gol08, Chapter 9].

Lemma 4. *Let* $(\mathcal{P}, \mathcal{V})$ *be an* IOP *with communication complexity* cc, *randomness complexity* rc, *query complexity* qc *and verifier run-time* $T_\mathcal{V} > \log cc$. *Then there exists a function* $f : \{0,1\}^n \to \{0,1\}^{O(2^{rc+qc} \cdot \log cc)}$ *that can be computed in* $O\left(T_\mathcal{V} \cdot 2^{rc+qc}\right)$ *time s.t. for any* x, *the query and computation phase of* $\mathcal{V}$ *can be implemented in* $O(rc + qc + \log cc)$ *space given* $f(x)$.

Proof (of Lemma 4). Let $(\mathcal{P}, \mathcal{V})$ be an IOP as stated in the lemma. Denote by k the number of communication rounds in the IOP, and for all $i \in [k]$ let cc_i and rc_i be the length of the prover message and verifier message in round i, respectively.

Encoding a Computation Path: On input $x \in \{0,1\}^n$ and randomness $r \in \{0,1\}^{rc}$, the verifier $\mathcal{V}$ performs a local deterministic computation that depends on x, r and the values of the queries it makes. Fixing x and r, a function $f_r(x)$ computes a decision tree for the possible executions of the verifier by feeding it every possible value of each query it makes (one by one, since the verifier might be adaptive). Since there are qc binary queries, then the decision tree is a binary tree with depth qc, where each internal node contains location of the next query and each leaf contains the verifier's output given the values of the queries. Each query location can be represented using $\log cc$ bits, so the tree can be encoded using a string of length $O(2^{qc} \cdot \log cc)$. Each leaf in the tree (along with the path leading to it) takes at most $T_\mathcal{V}$ time to produce. Therefore, it can be produced in $O(2^{qc} \cdot T_\mathcal{V})$ time. In total, the function $f(x)$ computes $f_r(x)$ for each $r \in \{0,1\}^{rc}$, so the size of the string that contains all of the decision trees is $O(2^{rc+qc} \cdot \log cc)$, and it can be computed in $O(2^{rc+qc} \cdot T_\mathcal{V})$ time.

Space-Efficient Construction of the Verifier: Given this string, we can build an IOP verifier $\mathcal{V}_s$ that interacts the prover the same way that $\mathcal{V}$ does. However, in the query and computation phase, $\mathcal{V}_s$ does not have to preform any actual computation. Instead, $\mathcal{V}_s$ looks at $f(x)$ whenever it makes a query to the prover messages and finally outputs the value of the leaf it reaches in the decision tree. The total space used by $\mathcal{V}_s$ is the space required to make the queries to $f(x)$ and prover messages $\pi_1, ..., \pi_k$, which is $O(rc + qc + \log cc)$.

Correctness: For any x, it is easy to see that for any random coins r and any prover messages π, both $\mathcal{V}$ and $\mathcal{V}_s$ make the same decision: the decision tree of $\mathcal{V}$ is encoded in $f(x)$, and $\mathcal{V}_s$ simply behaves according to the instructions in $f(x)$. ∎

4.2   Handling Larger Randomness

Looking at Lemma 4, we note that the time it takes to compute $f(x)$ grows exponentially with the randomness complexity of the IOP, so for an IOP with $\omega(\log n)$ randomness complexity, the running time jumps to super polynomial. In order to solve this problem, we use the randomness reduction stated in Lemma 3. After getting the input x, we let the preprocessor sample a random CRS ρ, and then apply Lemma 4 on both of x and ρ and the IOP that takes them as an input. By setting $\lambda = cc$ in Lemma 3, we get the following properties:

1. The preprocessor that computes $f(x)$ would run in $2^{qc} \cdot T_\mathcal{V} \cdot \mathrm{poly}(cc)^k$ time.
2. The string $f(x)$ would have length $2^{qc} \cdot \mathrm{poly}(cc)^k$.
3. If the original IOP has probability $p < 1$ of accepting an input x, then with probability $1 - 2^{-cc}$ of the CRS, the new IOP has probability $p - \epsilon_0 < p' < p + \epsilon_0$ of accepting x. If $p = 1$ then the new IOP accepts x with probability 1 as well.

We are now ready to prove Theorem 4 using Lemma 4 and Fact 5.

Proof (of Theorem 4). Let $(\mathcal{P}, \mathcal{V})$ be an IOP for the language $\mathcal{L}$ as stated in the theorem, and assume without loss of generality that the completeness and soundness errors are 0.3. By applying Lemma 3 with $\lambda = cc$ and $\epsilon_0 = 0.1$, there exists a CRS IOP $(\mathcal{P}', \mathcal{V}')$ for $\mathcal{L}$ with CRS-error 2^{-cc} and completeness and soundness errors 0.4. On any input x, the preprocessor $\mathcal{A}_1$ generates a random CRS which we denote by ρ. By Lemma 4, there exists a function $f : \{0,1\}^{n+|\rho|} \rightarrow \{0,1\}^{O(2^{qc} \cdot \mathrm{poly}(cc)^k)}$ s.t. the query and computation phase of $\mathcal{V}'$ with the fixed ρ can be implemented by an oracle machine $\mathcal{V}_s$ that has oracle access to $f(x, \rho)$ and runs in $O(qc + k \cdot \log cc)$ space. The preprocessor $\mathcal{A}_1$ computes and outputs this $f(x)$. With probability $1 - 2^{-cc}$ over ρ, it holds that if $x \in \mathcal{L}$ then $\Pr[(\mathcal{P}', \mathcal{V}')(\rho, x) = 1] \geq 0.6$ and if $x \notin \mathcal{L}$ then $\Pr[(\mathcal{P}', \mathcal{V}')(\rho, x) = 1] \leq 0.4$. By Fact 5, the value $\Pr[(\mathcal{P}', \mathcal{V}')(\rho, x) = 1]$ can be computed in $O(qc + cc + k \log cc) = O(cc + k \log cc)$ space. The decider algorithm $\mathcal{A}_2$ simply computes $p = \Pr[(\mathcal{P}', \mathcal{V}')(\rho, x) = 1]$ and accepts if and only if $p \geq 0.6$. ∎

5   Succinct Zero-Knowledge Proofs from OWF

In this section we show how to construct succinct zero-knowledge proofs from succinct IOPs. Intuitively, the idea is to run an "encrypted" version of the communication phase of the IOP, where the prover sends a commitment of each oracle, instead of the oracle itself, and the verifier replies with the usual random coins. At the end of the interaction, rather than having the prover "reveal" the queries that the verifier asks, the prover proves in zero-knowledge that *if* it would have revealed the queries then the original IOP verifier would have accepted.

The technique of committing to messages in a public-coin protocol and then proving in zero-knowledge that revealing them would make the verifier accept dates back to [BGG+88]. This technique is called "notarized envelopes", where we can think that each bit of the messages is put in a secure envelope and then a "notary" proves something about the contents of those envelopes without actually opening them. But here, we leverage the fact that the verifier only cares about the values of its queries rather than the entire transcript. Therefore, the statement which the prover has to prove in zero-knowledge is much smaller than the IOP transcript and, in fact, depends mainly on the complexity of the IOP verifier.

Leveraging the small query complexity of the IOP is inspired by [Kil92, Mic00]: there, the notarized envelopes technique is applied to PCPs to achieve very efficient *computationally sound interactive proofs*, i.e., protocols that are only sound against computationally-bounded cheating provers. In Sect. 5.1, we modify this approach in two ways: we apply the notarized envelopes to IOPs instead of PCPs and we achieve *unconditional soundness* instead of computational soundness. We can think of this as a *transformation* from IOPs to ZKPs. Our contribution is implementing this transformation in a way that preserves the original communication complexity of the IOP up to an additive overhead. More precisely, the additive overhead depends on the security parameter and the complexity of the IOP verifier (or more precisely, its "compactness", see Definition 5). Furthermore, we do so under the minimal [OW93] cryptographic assumption of one-way functions.

In Sect. 5.2, we apply the transformation to the succinct IOP of [RR20]. This yields a succinct zero-knowledge proof for a rich sub-class of NP relations. Namely, for bounded-space relations, we construct zero-knowledge proofs with communication complexity that is arbitrarily close to the *witness* length - with the small additive overhead we mentioned earlier.

5.1 Communication Preserving ZKP

In this subsection, we prove the following general theorem that shows how to construct a ZKP from an IOP while nearly preserving the communication complexity, i.e., the transformation discussed above:

Theorem 5. *Assume the existence of one-way functions. Let $\mathcal{L} \in$ NP. If $(P_{\mathsf{IOP}}, V_{\mathsf{IOP}})$ is a T_V-uniform γ-compact IOP for $\mathcal{L}$, with soundness error $\varepsilon_{\mathsf{IOP}}$, communication complexity $cc = cc(n)$ and query complexity $qc = qc(n)$ where the prover runs in T_P time given the witness for x, then $\mathcal{L}$ has a public-coin zero-knowledge proof with soundness error $\varepsilon_{\mathsf{IOP}} + 2^{-\lambda}$ and proof length $cc + \mathrm{poly}(\lambda, \gamma, \log cc)$, where $\lambda > 0$ is the security parameter. Furthermore, the running time of the ZKP verifier is $T_V + \mathrm{poly}(\lambda, \gamma, \log cc)$ and the running time of the prover is $T_P + \mathrm{poly}(\lambda, \gamma)$.*

5.1.1 The Transformation

The existence of one-way functions implies the existence of the following cryptographic tools:

- A pseudorandom function $F : \{0,1\}^{\lambda} \times \{0,1\}^* \to \{0,1\}$ [GGM86, HILL99].
- A commitment scheme (Gen, Com, Ver) [Nao91, HILL99] as defined in Sect. 2.4.
- For any security parameter $\lambda > 0$, a public-coin ZKP with an efficient prover for any language $L \in$ NP with perfect completeness, soundness error $2^{-\lambda}$ and proof length $\mathrm{poly}(\lambda, n)$ [GMW86].

We describe how to use those components to transform $(P_{\mathsf{IOP}}, V_{\mathsf{IOP}})$ to a pair of interactive machines (P, V).

Let x be the input. For $\langle P_{\mathsf{IOP}}(w), V_{\mathsf{IOP}}\rangle(x)$, denote by k the number of rounds and by π_i (resp. r_i) the prover message (resp. verifier public-coins) sent in round i. Recall that at the end of the interaction phase of the IOP, the verifier V_{IOP} has an oracle access to the prover messages $\pi = (\pi_1, ..., \pi_k)$ and full access to its own random coins $r = (r_1, ..., r_k)$. In the local computation phase, V_{IOP} produces a predicate $\phi_{x,r} : \{0,1\}^{qc} \rightarrow \{0,1\}$ and query locations $Q_{x,r} \in [cc]^{qc}$ and it accepts if and only if $\phi_{x,r}(\pi[Q_{x,r}]) = 1$.

As discussed above, rather than sending π_i, the prover P sends a commitment α_i to the message π_i. The commitment is computed as follows: first, P commits to a PRF seed S, then uses F_S to encrypt each π_i using F_S as a pseudorandom one-time pad. The prover P then convinces V, in zero-knowledge, that if the query locations of the messages were revealed then V_{IOP} would have accepted. In particular, P proves that it knows some seed S such that the decryption of α w.r.t. F_S in the query locations specified by $Q_{x,r}$ would satisfy the predicate $\phi_{x,r}$.

For that purpose, we define the language $\mathcal{L}'$, consisting of tuples (ϕ, ρ, Q, y, c), where $\phi : \{0,1\}^{qc} \rightarrow \{0,1\}$ is a predicate, $\rho \in \{0,1\}^{\mathrm{poly}(\lambda)}$ is a (common reference) string, $Q \subseteq [cc]$ is a set of qc query locations, $y \in \{0,1\}^{qc}$ is a vector of *encrypted* query values (supposedly taken from the transcript) and $c \in \{0,1\}^{\mathrm{poly}(\lambda)}$ is the commitment of some seed. The tuple is in the language if and only if there exists a seed $S \in \{0,1\}^{\lambda}$ that can be revealed from c and ρ such that the decryption of y w.r.t. S and Q satisfies the predicate. For simplicity, we assume that the security parameter λ can be inferred from ρ and furthermore, is polynomially related to $|\rho|$ (which is indeed the case in [Nao91]). For simplicity, we refer to F_S as a string and use the notation $F_S[Q]$ to access the Q coordinates from F_S. Formally:

$$\mathcal{L}' = \Big\{(\phi, \rho, Q, y, c) : \exists d, S \text{ s.t. } Ver(1^\lambda, \rho, c, S, d) = 1 \text{ and } \phi(y \oplus F_S[Q]) = 1\Big\}.$$

The length of an instance (ϕ, ρ, Q, y, c) is $|\phi| + \mathrm{poly}(\lambda) + qc \cdot O(\log cc)$. The language $\mathcal{L}'$ is clearly in NP since given S and d (which have $\mathrm{poly}(\lambda)$ length), a verifier can verify that $Ver(1^\lambda, \rho, c, S, d) = 1$ in $\mathrm{poly}(\lambda)$ time, compute $y \oplus F_S[Q]$ in $\mathrm{poly}(\lambda, qc, \log cc)$ time and verify $\phi(y \oplus F_S[Q]) = 1$ in $O(|\phi|)$ time. Therefore, $\mathcal{L}'$ has a ZKP with an efficient prover which we denote by $(P_{\mathcal{L}'}, V_{\mathcal{L}'})$. Thus, the final step of the protocol is to have P and V emulate $(P_{\mathcal{L}'}, V_{\mathcal{L}'})$ to prove (in zero-knowledge) that the tuple is in $\mathcal{L}'$. Note that P can perform this step efficiently since it has the NP witness S, d. The protocol is presented in Fig. 1.

We prove the protocol is a zero-knowledge proof in two steps: first we prove that it is an interactive proof for $\mathcal{L}$ with the desired complexity properties and then we prove that it is computational zero-knowledge w.r.t. auxiliary input. This is captured by the following two lemmas:

Lemma 5. *The protocol in Fig. 1 is a public-coin interactive proof for $\mathcal{L}$. The proof length is $cc + \mathrm{poly}(\lambda, \gamma, \log cc)$, the soundness error is $\varepsilon_{\mathsf{IOP}} + 2^{-\lambda}$, the verifier runs in time $T + \mathrm{poly}(\lambda, \gamma, \log cc)$ and the prover runs in time $T_P + \mathrm{poly}(\lambda, \gamma)$.*

Communication Preserving ZK Protocol

1. V generates a reference string $\rho \leftarrow Gen\left(1^{\lambda+1}\right)$ for the commitment scheme and sends it to P.
2. P generates a random PRF seed $S \in_R \{0,1\}^\lambda$, commits to it using $(com, dec) \leftarrow Com\left(1^{\lambda+1}, \rho, S\right)$ and sends the commitment com to V.
3. P initializes $\ell \leftarrow 0$, $p = F_S([cc])$ then performs with V the following "encrypted" version of the IOP:
   For $i = 1, \ldots, k$:
   - P sends an encryption of the ith P_{IOP}'s message π_i by XORing it with fresh bits from p, i.e., sends $\alpha_i = p[\ell, .., \ell + |\pi_i| - 1] \oplus \pi_i$ and updates $\ell \leftarrow \ell + |\pi_i|$.
   - The verifier replies with the usual random coins r_i as in the IOP.
   Denote $\alpha = (\alpha_1, \ldots, \alpha_k)$ and $r = (r_1, ..., r_k)$.
4. P and V emulate $(P_{\mathcal{L}'}, V_{\mathcal{L}'})$ with $\left(\phi_{x,r}, \rho, Q_{x,r}, \alpha\left[Q_{x,r}\right], com\right)$ as common input and where $P_{\mathcal{L}'}$ further uses (S, dec) as its witness, with security parameter $\lambda + 1$ and V answers accordingly.

Fig. 1. The ZK protocol from Theorem 5

Lemma 6. *The protocol in Fig. 1 is computational zero-knowledge w.r.t. auxiliary input.*

Due to page constraints, the proof is deferred to the full version [NR22].

5.1.2 Proof of Lemma 6

We now move on to proving that the protocol (P, V) of Fig. 1 is computational zero-knowledge w.r.t. auxiliary input.

By definition of zero-knowledge, we need to show a simulator for the interaction (P, V^*), where V^* is an arbitrary (malicious) verifier. The idea is to simulate the IOP phase by replacing the honest prover messages with truly random messages and simulate the ZKP phase using the simulator for $(P_{\mathcal{L}'}, V_{\mathcal{L}'})$.

In the following discussion, for readability, we often omit the security parameter λ from the notation. However, formal claims and proofs that follow do mention the security parameter explicitly.

Let V^* be a polynomial time verifier as per Remark 1, and denote by $V_{\mathcal{L}'}^*$ the residual verifier strategy[10] that V^* uses in step 4. Let $x \in \mathcal{L}$ be an instance, $z \in \{0,1\}^{\mathrm{poly}(|x|)}$ be some auxiliary input and w be the NP witness for x. The view of V^* when interacting with the prover P on common input x and prover input w, denoted by $View_{V^*(z)}(x) := View_{V^*(z)}^{P(w)}(x)$, consists of x, z, the commitment com, the encrypted messages α and the view

---

[10] This strategy might depend on the view of V^* up to that point, but this can be passed to $V_{\mathcal{L}'}^*$ as an auxiliary input as we show later on.

of $V_{\mathcal{L}'}^*$ in step 4, denoted by $View'(\phi_{x,r}, \rho, Q_{x,r}, \alpha[Q_{x,r}], com, z_{\mathcal{L}'}, (S, dec)) := View_{V_{\mathcal{L}'}^*(z_{\mathcal{L}'})}^{P_{\mathcal{L}'}(S,dec)}(\phi_{x,r}, \rho, Q_{x,r}, \alpha[Q_{x,r}], com)$ where $z_{\mathcal{L}'} = (x, z, r, \alpha)$ is the auxiliary input for $V_{\mathcal{L}'}^*$ and S, dec are the witness for tuple being in $\mathcal{L}'$. Since $z_{\mathcal{L}'}$ contains α and the instance contains com that is, everything in the view of V^* up to that point, we can assume that

$$View_{V^*(z)}(x) = View'(\phi_{x,r}, \rho, Q_{x,r}, \alpha[Q_{x,r}], com, z_{\mathcal{L}'}).$$

By the zero-knowledge property of $(P_{\mathcal{L}'}, V_{\mathcal{L}'})$, there exists a simulator $Sim'_{V_{\mathcal{L}'}^*}$ that can simulate $View'$ with auxiliary input $z_{\mathcal{L}'}$. We observe that w.l.o.g., the input of $Sim'_{V_{\mathcal{L}'}^*}$ can simply consist of $(x, r, z, \alpha, \rho, com)$ - this is due to the fact that $Sim'_{V_{\mathcal{L}'}^*}$ can compute $\phi_{x,r}$ and $Q_{x,r}$ on its own and there is no need to pass the bits $\alpha[Q_{x,r}]$ twice. Recall that we assume $(P_{\mathsf{IOP}}, V_{\mathsf{IOP}})$ has perfect completeness, therefore for any verifier messages ρ, r and honestly generated prover messages com and α, it holds that $(\phi_{x,r}, \rho, Q_{x,r}, \alpha[Q_{x,r}], com) \in \mathcal{L}'$. Therefore, it holds that $Sim'_{V_{\mathcal{L}'}^*}(x, r, z, \alpha, \rho, com)$ and $View'(\phi_{x,r}, \rho, Q_{x,r}, \alpha[Q_{x,r}], com, z_{\mathcal{L}'})$ are computationally indistinguishable.

We now describe a simulator $Sim_{V^*}(x, z)$ that simulates $View_{V^*(z)}^{P(w)}(x)$. We start with a high-level description. Given as input x, z, the simulator emulates step 1 of of the protocol from Fig. 1 exactly as V^* would, namely, it runs $V^*(x, z)$ to generate the CRS ρ. For step 2, the simulator commits to a string of zeros and "sends" the commitment to V^*, leveraging the hiding property of the commitment scheme. For step 3, the simulator "sends" *random* messages to V^*, this time leveraging the pseudorandomness of the PRF. Finally, for step 4, the simulator simply runs $Sim'_{V_{\mathcal{L}'}^*}$ on the instance that V^* sees - which includes the commitment to zeros and the subsequent random messages. Since the output of $Sim'_{V_{\mathcal{L}'}^*}$ includes its input, specifically the auxiliary input, then Sim_{V^*} can just output the output of $Sim'_{V_{\mathcal{L}'}^*}$. The simulator Sim_{V^*} is formally described in Fig. 2.

ZK Simulator for Thoerem 5

Input: $x \in \mathcal{L}, z \in \{0,1\}^*, 1^\lambda$

1. Generate a reference string $\rho \leftarrow V^*(x, z)$.
2. Compute a commitment to zeros $(c_0, d_0) \leftarrow Com(1^\lambda, \rho, 0^\lambda)$. "Send" c_0 to V^*.
3. For $i = 1, .., k$: Generate a random β_i and "send" it to V^* and get in response r_i.
4. Output $Sim'_{V^*}(x, r, z, \beta, \rho, c_0, 1^\lambda)$.

Fig. 2. The simulator Sim_{V^*} for Theorem 5

At first glance, the zero-knowledge property of $(P_{\mathcal{L}'}, V_{\mathcal{L}'})$ does not necessarily hold in this case since the "mock" instance on which we run $Sim'_{V^*_{\mathcal{L}'}}$ is (almost definitely) not a "yes" instance. However, we observe that this "mock" instance and a "yes" instance are computationally indistinguishable; the commitment to zeros is indistinguishable from that of a randomly generated seed due to the hiding property of the commitment scheme and the truly random messages are indistinguishable from the encrypted messages used in the protocol due to the pseudorandomness of the PRF. Therefore, we can apply the computational data processing inequality (as stated in Fact 3) to deduce that the outputs of $Sim'_{V^*_{\mathcal{L}'}}$ on both instances are indistinguishable, which are in turn indistinguishable from the view $V_{\mathcal{L}'}$. This yields the following proposition:

Proposition 1. *For all $x \in \mathcal{L}$ and auxiliary input $z \in \{0,1\}^{\mathrm{poly}(|x|)}$,*

$$\left\{ Sim_{V^*}(x, z, 1^\lambda) \right\}_{\lambda \in \mathbb{N}} \stackrel{c}{\approx} \left\{ View_{V^*}(x, \lambda) \right\}_{\lambda \in \mathbb{N}}.$$

Due to page constraints, the proof is deferred to the full version [NR22].

Proof (of Lemma 6). Let $x \in \mathcal{L}$ and w be the corresponding witness. Fix some polynomial time verifier V^* and auxiliary input z. By Proposition 1, the output of the simulator Sim_{V^*} on input $(x, z, 1^\lambda)$ is computationally from the view $View_{V^*(z)}^{P(w)}(x, \lambda)$. In addition, Sim_{V^*} runs in polynomial time because it only generates random strings of polynomial size and runs the polynomial time algorithms V^*, Com and Sim'_{V^*}. This gives us the zero-knowledge property of the protocol. ∎

In total, Lemma 5 and Lemma 6 complete the proof of Theorem 5.

5.2   Constructing Succinct ZKPs

Our next step is to use Theorem 5 to construct succinct zero-knowledge proofs for NP relations that can be verified in bounded space. We rely on the following result by [RR20]:

Theorem 6 *(Extension of [RR20]).* *Let $\mathcal{L} \in$ NP with corresponding relation $\mathcal{R}_{\mathcal{L}}$ in which the instances have length m and witnesses have length n, where $m \geq n$, and such that $\mathcal{R}_{\mathcal{L}}$ can be decided in time $\mathrm{poly}(m + n)$ and space $s \geq \log m$. For any constants $\beta, \gamma \in (0, 1)$, there exists a $\beta^{-O(\frac{1}{\beta})}$-round IOP for $\mathcal{L}$ with soundness error $\frac{1}{2}$ and $(\gamma\beta)^{-O(\frac{1}{\beta})}$ query complexity. The communication consists of a first (deterministic) message sent by the prover of length $(1 + \gamma) \cdot m + \gamma \cdot n^\beta$ bits followed by $\mathrm{poly}\left(n^\beta, (\gamma\beta)^{-\frac{1}{\beta}}, s\right)$ additional communication. In addition, the IOP is $\left(\tilde{O}(n) + \mathrm{poly}\left(n^\beta, (\gamma\beta)^{-\frac{1}{\beta}}, s\right)\right)$-uniform $\mathrm{poly}\left(n^\beta, (\gamma\beta)^{-\frac{1}{\beta}}, s\right)$-compact and the prover runs in $\mathrm{poly}(n)$ time.*

Remark 3. The theorem statement in [RR20] does not include the compactness property. Nevertheless, it is relatively straightforward to show that the construction is indeed compact. In addition, [RR20] assumes that the instance length is polynomially related to the witness length and as a result, the length of the fist message only depends on the witness length, whereas we do not make that assumption and therefore Theorem 6 introduces a small dependence on the instance length. In our context, we can afford this dependence since it will anyhow appear in our ZKP construction due to the compactness property. Given these differences, for completeness, Theorem 6 is proved in the full version [NR22].

The soundness error in Theorem 6 can be reduced by parallel repetition while observing that since the first prover message is deterministic, so it does not need to be repeated. In addition, if we choose a sufficiently small β and the space s in which we can decide $\mathcal{R}_\mathcal{L}$ is sufficiently small (but still polynomially related to n), then we get the following corollary:

Corollary 4. *There exists a fixed constant $\xi > 0$ such that the following holds. Let $\mathcal{L} \in$ NP with a corresponding relation $\mathcal{R}_\mathcal{L}$ in which the instances have length n and witnesses have length m such that $m \leq n$ and $\mathcal{R}_\mathcal{L}$ can be decided in $\mathrm{poly}(n)$ time and n^ξ space. Then for any constants $\gamma \in (0,1)$ and any function $\varepsilon = \varepsilon(m) \in (0,1)$ there exists a constant β' such that for any $\beta \in (0, \beta')$ there exists an IOP for $\mathcal{L}$ with communication complexity $(1+\gamma) \cdot m + O\big(\log \frac{1}{\varepsilon}\big) \cdot \gamma \cdot n^\beta$, query complexity $O(\log \varepsilon)$ and soundness error ε. In addition, the IOP is $\tilde{O}(n)$-uniform n^β-compact and the prover runs in $\mathrm{poly}(n)$ time.*

Corollary 4 captures a rich class of NP relations (e.g. SAT or any other relation that can be decided in polynomial time and polylogarithmic space). We now apply Theorem 5 on the IOP from Corollary 4 and get a succinct ZKP for all languages in that class. This yields our main theorem:

Theorem 7. *There exists a fixed constant $\xi > 0$ such that the following holds. Let $\mathcal{R}_\mathcal{L}$ be an NP relation, in which the instances have length n and witnesses have length m such that $m \leq n$, that can be decided in $\mathrm{poly}(n)$ time and n^ξ space. Assuming one-way functions exist, then for any constant $\gamma \in (0,1)$ and security parameter $\lambda > 1$, there exists a constant β' such that for any $\beta \in (0, \beta')$ there exists a public-coin zero-knowledge proof for $\mathcal{R}_\mathcal{L}$ with $(1 + \gamma) \cdot m + \gamma \cdot n^\beta \cdot \mathrm{poly}(\lambda)$ proof length, perfect completeness and soundness error $2^{-\lambda}$. Furthermore, the verifier runs in time $\tilde{O}(n) + n^\beta \cdot \mathrm{poly}(\lambda)$ and the prover runs in $\mathrm{poly}(n)$ time.*

Due to page constraints, the proof is deferred to the full version [NR22].

Acknowledgements. We thank Yuval Filmus and Yuval Ishai for helpful discussions. We also thank the anonymous reviewers of CRYPTO 2022 for their helpful comments.

Supported in part by the Israeli Science Foundation (Grants No. 1262/18 and 2137/19), by grants from the Technion Hiroshi Fujiwara cyber security research center and Israel cyber directorate, and by the European Union. Views and opinions expressed are however those of the author(s) only and do not necessarily reflect those of the European Union or the European Research Council. Neither the European Union nor the granting authority can be held responsible for them.

References

[AG21] Applebaum, B., Golombek, E.: On the randomness complexity of interactive proofs and statistical zero-knowledge proofs. In: Tessaro, S. (ed.) 2nd Conference on Information-Theoretic Cryptography, ITC 2021, 23–26 July 2021, Virtual Conference. LIPIcs, vol. 199, pp. 4:1–4:23. Schloss Dagstuhl - Leibniz-Zentrum für Informatik (2021)

[BCS16] Ben-Sasson, E., Chiesa, A., Spooner, N.: Interactive oracle proofs. In: Hirt, M., Smith, A. (eds.) TCC 2016, Part II. LNCS, vol. 9986, pp. 31–60. Springer, Heidelberg (2016). https://doi.org/10.1007/978-3-662-53644-5_2

[BDRV18] Berman, I., Degwekar, A., Rothblum, R.D., Vasudevan, P.N.: From laconic zero-knowledge to public-key cryptography. In: Shacham, H., Boldyreva, A. (eds.) CRYPTO 2018, Part III. LNCS, vol. 10993, pp. 674–697. Springer, Cham (2018). https://doi.org/10.1007/978-3-319-96878-0_23

[BGG+88] Ben-Or, M., et al.: Everything provable is provable in zero-knowledge. In: Goldwasser, S. (ed.) CRYPTO 1988. LNCS, vol. 403, pp. 37–56. Springer, New York (1990). https://doi.org/10.1007/0-387-34799-2_4

[Bra19] Brakerski, Z.: Fundamentals of fully homomorphic encryption. In: Goldreich, O. (ed.) Providing Sound Foundations for Cryptography: On the Work of Shafi Goldwasser and Silvio Micali, pp. 543–563. ACM (2019)

[CLTV15] Canetti, R., Lin, H., Tessaro, S., Vaikuntanathan, V.: Obfuscation of probabilistic circuits and applications. In: Dodis, Y., Nielsen, J.B. (eds.) TCC 2015. LNCS, vol. 9015, pp. 468–497. Springer, Heidelberg (2015). https://doi.org/10.1007/978-3-662-46497-7_19

[CY20] Chiesa, A., Yogev, E.: Barriers for succinct arguments in the random oracle model. In: Pass, R., Pietrzak, K. (eds.) TCC 2020, Part II. LNCS, vol. 12551, pp. 47–76. Springer, Cham (2020). https://doi.org/10.1007/978-3-030-64378-2_3

[FS11] Fortnow, L., Santhanam, R.: Infeasibility of instance compression and succinct PCPs for NP. J. Comput. Syst. Sci. 77(1), 91–106 (2011)

[GGI+15] Gentry, C., Groth, J., Ishai, Y., Peikert, C., Sahai, A., Smith, A.D.: Using fully homomorphic hybrid encryption to minimize non-interative zero-knowledge proofs. J. Cryptol. 28(4), 820–843 (2015)

[GGM86] Goldreich, O., Goldwasser, S., Micali, S.: How to construct random functions. J. ACM 33(4), 792–807 (1986)

[GH98] Goldreich, O., Håstad, J.: On the complexity of interactive proofs with bounded communication. Inf. Process. Lett. 67(4), 205–214 (1998)

[GKR15] Goldwasser, S., Kalai, Y.T., Rothblum, G.N.: Delegating computation: interactive proofs for Muggles. J. ACM 62(4), 27:1–27:64 (2015)

[GMW86] Goldreich, O., Micali, S., Wigderson, A.: How to prove all NP statements in zero-knowledge and a methodology of cryptographic protocol design (extended abstract). In: Odlyzko, A.M. (ed.) CRYPTO 1986. LNCS, vol. 263, pp. 171–185. Springer, Heidelberg (1987). https://doi.org/10.1007/3-540-47721-7_11

[Gol04] Goldreich, O.: The Foundations of Cryptography - Volume 2: Basic Applications. Cambridge University Press, Cambridge (2004)

[Gol08] Goldreich, Oded: Computational Complexity - A Conceptual Perspective. Cambridge University Press, Cambridge (2008)

[GR18] Gur, T., Rothblum, R.D.: Non-interactive proofs of proximity. Comput. Complex. **27**(1), 99–207 (2016). https://doi.org/10.1007/s00037-016-0136-9

[GS10] Goldreich, O., Sheffet, O.: On the randomness complexity of property testing. Comput. Complex. **19**(1), 99–133 (2010)

[GVW02] Goldreich, O., Vadhan, S.P., Wigderson, A.: On interactive proofs with a laconic prover. Comput. Complex. **11**(1–2), 1–53 (2002)

[HILL99] Håstad, J., Impagliazzo, R., Levin, L.A., Luby, M.: A pseudorandom generator from any one-way function. SIAM J. Comput. **28**(4), 1364–1396 (1999)

[Hoe63] Hoeffding, W.: Probability inequalities for sums of bounded random variables. J. Am. Stat. Assoc. **58**(301), 13–30 (1963)

[IKOS09] Ishai, Y., Kushilevitz, E., Ostrovsky, R., Sahai, A.: Zero-knowledge proofs from secure multiparty computation. SIAM J. Comput. **39**(3), 1121–1152 (2009)

[Kil92] Kilian, J.: A note on efficient zero-knowledge proofs and arguments (extended abstract). In: Kosaraju, S.R., Fellows, M., Wigderson, A., Ellis, J.A. (eds.) Proceedings of the 24th Annual ACM Symposium on Theory of Computing, 4–6 May 1992, Victoria, British Columbia, Canada, pp. 723–732. ACM (1992)

[KR08] Kalai, Y.T., Raz, R.: Interactive PCP. In: Aceto, L., Damgård, I., Goldberg, L.A., Halldórsson, M.M., Ingólfsdóttir, A., Walukiewicz, I. (eds.) ICALP 2008. LNCS, vol. 5126, pp. 536–547. Springer, Heidelberg (2008). https://doi.org/10.1007/978-3-540-70583-3_44

[Mic00] Micali, S.: Computationally sound proofs. SIAM J. Comput. **30**(4), 1253–1298 (2000)

[Nao91] Naor, M.: Bit commitment using pseudorandomness. J. Cryptol. **4**(2), 151–158 (1991). https://doi.org/10.1007/BF00196774

[New91] Newman, I.: Private vs. common random bits in communication complexity. Inf. Process. Lett. **39**(2), 67–71 (1991)

[NR22] Nassar, S., Rothblum, R.D.: Succinct interactive oracle proofs: applications and limitations. Cryptology ePrint Archive, Paper 2022/281 (2022). https://eprint.iacr.org/2022/281

[OW93] Ostrovsky, R., Wigderson, A.: One-way functions are essential for nontrivial zero-knowledge. In: Proceedings of the Second Israel Symposium on Theory of Computing Systems, ISTCS 1993, Natanya, Israel, 7–9 June 1993, pp. 3–17. IEEE Computer Society (1993)

[RR20] Ron-Zewi, N., Rothblum, R.D.: Local proofs approaching the witness length [extended abstract]. In: 61st IEEE Annual Symposium on Foundations of Computer Science, FOCS 2020, Durham, NC, USA, 16–19 November 2020, pp. 846–857. IEEE (2020)

[RRR21] Reingold, O., Rothblum, G.N., Rothblum, R.D.: Constant-round interactive proofs for delegating computation. SIAM J. Comput. **50**(3) (2021)

[Sma14] How do we know that P != LINSPACE without knowing if one is a subset of the other? (2014). https://mathoverflow.net/questions/40770/how-do-we-know-that-p-linspace-without-knowing-if-one-is-a-subset-of-the-othe. Accessed 2 Feb 2022

Advanced Encryption Systems

Candidate Witness Encryption from Lattice Techniques

Rotem Tsabary[✉]

Google Research, Tel Aviv, Israel
rotem.ts0@gmail.com

Abstract. Witness encryption (WE), first introduced by Garg, Gentry, Sahai and Waters in [GGSW13], is an encryption scheme where messages are encrypted with respect to instances of an **NP** relation, such that in order to decrypt one needs to know a valid witness for the instance that is associated with the ciphertext.

Despite of significant efforts in the past decade to construct WE from standard assumptions, to the best of our knowledge all of the existing WE candidates either rely directly on iO or use techniques that also seem to imply iO in the same way that they seem to imply WE.

In this work we propose a new hardness assumption with regard to lattice trapdoors and show a witness encryption candidate which is secure under it. Contrary to previous WE candidates, our technique is trivially broken when one tries to convert it to iO, which suggests that the security relies on a different mechanism. We view the gap between WE and iO as an analogue to the gap between ABE and FE and thus potentially significant.

Intuitively, the assumption says that *"the best an attacker can do with a trapdoor sample is to use it semi-honestly"* – i.e. that LWE with respect to a public matrix $\mathbf{A}$, given as auxiliary information a trapdoor sample $\mathbf{K} \leftarrow \mathbf{A}^{\mathrm{TD}}(\mathbf{B})$, is as hard as LWE with respect to the public matrix $[\mathbf{A}|\mathbf{B}]$ and no auxiliary information.

In order to formally utilize the assumption we define a notion of LWE oracles with generic distributions of public matrices and auxiliary information. This model allows to bound the hardness of LWE with respect to one distribution as a function of the hardness of LWE with respect to another distribution. Repeated arguments of this flavor can be used as a sequence of hybrids in order to gradually change the challenge that an adversary is facing while keeping track on the security loss in each step of the proof. Typically security proofs of LWE-based systems implicitly make arguments of this flavor for distributions that are indistinguishable, while our model allows to make relaxed arguments that in some cases suffice for the proof requirements.

R. Tsabary—Research done while at Reichman University (IDC Herzliya), Israel, supported by ISF grant No. 1399/17.

© International Association for Cryptologic Research 2022
Y. Dodis and T. Shrimpton (Eds.): CRYPTO 2022, LNCS 13507, pp. 535–559, 2022.
https://doi.org/10.1007/978-3-031-15802-5_19

1 Introduction

Witness Encryption. Witness encryption (WE), first introduced by Garg, Gentry Sahai and Waters in [GGSW13], is an encryption scheme where messages are encrypted with respect to instances of an **NP** relation, such that in order to decrypt a ciphertext one needs to know a valid witness for the instance that is associated with the ciphertext. Despite of significant efforts in the past decade to construct witness encryption from a standard hardness assumption, to the best of our knowledge the only construction that was proven secure under an explicit assumption relies on multi-linear maps [GLW14].

WE via iO. Indisitinguishability obfuscation (iO) is known to imply WE. In the past few years there have been major breakthroughs that lead to an iO scheme with provable security from standard hardness assumptions [Lin16, LV16, Lin17, LT17, AJL+19, Agr19, JLMS19, GJLS21, JLS21]. While the result serves as a proof of feasibility, it is challenging to grasp the intuition behind the resulting construction because it consists of a long sequence of reduction steps between various notions. It is therefore natural to ask whether there exist "simple" WE and iO candidates with provable security from standard assumptions. Recently Wee and Wichs proposed in [WW21] an iO candidate from lattices, based on the framework of [BDGM20], and proved its security assuming the existence of an oblivious LWE sampler. Other LWE-based iO candidates were suggested by Wichs and Zirdelis in [WZ17] and by Chen et al. in [CVW18], however without any security proof.

1.1 Our Contribution

We propose a new hardness assumption with regard to lattice trapdoors and show a witness encryption candidate which is secure under it. Intuitively, the assumption says that *"the best an attacker can do with a trapdoor sample is to use it semi-honestly"* – i.e. that LWE with respect to a public matrix $\mathbf{A}$, given as auxiliary information a trapdoor sample $\mathbf{K} \leftarrow \mathbf{A}^{\mathsf{TD}}(\mathbf{B})$, is as hard as LWE with respect to the public matrix $[\mathbf{A}|\mathbf{B}]$ and no auxiliary information.

The assumption can be viewed as a generalization of provable cases that are widely used in the literature, where the two extreme cases are when $\mathbf{B}$ is trivially LWE-hard (e.g. uniformly random) and when $\mathbf{B}$ is trivially LWE-broken (e.g. the gadget matrix). We believe that it also captures the intuition behind other structured LWE scenarios that seem to be secure but fail to pass traditional analysis techniques, so any counter example would greatly improve our understanding of the lattice toolbox.

In order to formally state the assumption and use it in the security proof of the scheme we define a notion of LWE challenges with general distributions of public matrices and auxiliary information. This model allows us to bound the hardness of LWE with respect to one distribution as a function of the hardness of LWE with respect to another distribution. Repeated arguments of this flavor can be used as a sequence of hybrids in order to gradually change the challenge that an adversary is facing while keeping track on the security loss in each step of the proof. Typically security proofs of LWE-based systems implicitly make arguments of this flavor for distributions that are indistinguishable, while our model allows to make relaxed arguments that in some cases suffice for the proof requirements.

We note that under some circumstances a polynomial number of trapdoor samples can lead to exponentially many public matrices that are *potentially* accessible, so the model is defined such that the number of public matrices for which the adversary gets to see an LWE expression is bounded by its running time. This is enforced by modeling the LWE experiment as a game between the adversary and an oracle that has all of the accessible matrices hard-wired in it, where the oracle provides upon request LWE samples with respect to any of these matrices.

Comparison with Previous WE Candidates

WE vs. iO. To the best of our knowledge all of the existing WE candidates either rely directly on iO or use techniques that also seem to imply iO in the same way that they seem to imply WE (see the discussion above). Contrary to that, our technique is trivially broken when one tries to convert it to iO. In particular it is easy to break the underlying LWE assumption given a valid witness, which is not the case in a generic iO-based WE construction. This suggests that the differences between our technique and existing candidates are not merely technical, rather, the security is based on a different mechanism and our assumption is possibly tighter. We view the gap between WE and iO as an analogue to the gap between ABE and FE and thus potentially significant.

Number of Hybrids. The security analysis of our candidate requires $2^{\mathrm{poly}(\ell)}$ hybrids where ℓ is the witness length. This is compatible with the barriers that were discussed in [GGSW13, GLW14]. We note that the only other explicit candidate with a security proof (the MMaps-based construction of [GLW14]) requires $\mathrm{poly}(2^{\ell})$ hybrids.

2   Overview of Techniques

Our candidate conceptually consists of two layers. First, we define and show the existence of *resilient* branching programs that behave in a predicted manner when they are executed with a sequence of bits that violate the index-to-input map. This part of the work is information-theoretic in nature and relies on an iO candidate suggested by [CHVW19]. The second layer takes a branching program of this form and generates a collection of matrices and [GGH15] encodings that correspond to the nodes and edges respectively of the branching program. The matrices of the end layer are generated according to a secret-sharing access structure that is provided as part of the resilient branching program, and the ciphertext is provided as an LWE challenge with respect to the start layer.

The security analysis of the scheme takes two main steps. First, we use the security assumption about lattice trapdoors to gradually replace the GGH15 encodings with "accessible matrices" that the adversary could derive by using any sequence of trapdoors of his choice. This is done in the direction of the computation of the branching program (it is essentially a BFS over the branching program nodes). This can be interpreted as a reduction from a security game of the scheme where the trapdoor samples can be used maliciously to a security game of the scheme where the trapdoor samples can only be used as intended.

In the second part of the security analysis we prove from standard assumptions the security of the scheme in the latter game. To formalize this game, we consider an LWE experiment where the adversary can receive upon request LWE samples with respect to any accessible node in the branching program, and bound the success probability of all PPT adversaries in this experiment. In this part of the proof we use the fact that $f(x) = 0$ for all $x \in \{0,1\}^\ell$ (since security should hold only when there are no valid witnesses) and the information-theoretic properties of the resilient branching program when it is executed with corrupted sequences. This part of the proof takes $2^{\mathrm{poly}(\ell)}$ hybrids since it handles each evaluation sequence individually.

2.1 Notations

For ease of exposition we treat vectors as row vectors by default. We let $\mathbf{v}[i]$ denote the ith entry of the vector $\mathbf{v}$ and we let $\mathbf{M}[i,j]$ denote the entry in the ith row and jth column of the matrix $\mathbf{M}$. We let $\equiv_\lambda$ denote computational/statistical indistinguishability with respect to a security parameter λ.

2.2 Branching Programs with Resiliency to Corrupted Inputs

This section is based on an iO candidate suggested by [CHVW19]. The computational model that is used in this work is a generalized form of matrix branching programs. Recall that a width-w length-t matrix BP that computes a predicate $f : \{0,1\}^\ell \to \{0,1\}$ is described by a start state vector $\mathbf{v}_{start} \in \{0,1\}^w$ where $\|\mathbf{v}_{start}\|_1 = 1$, an index-to-input map $\rho : [t] \to [\ell]$ and a tuple of $2t$ evaluation matrices $\{\mathbf{M}_{j,b}\}_{j \in [t], b \in \{0,1\}}$, where the guarantee is that for all x the first entry of $\mathbf{v}_x \in \{0,1\}^w$ equals $f(x)$, where

$$\mathbf{v}_x = \mathbf{v}_{start} \prod_{j=1}^{t} \mathbf{M}_{j,x_{\rho(j)}} .$$

By Barrington's Theorem [Bar89], each $f \in \mathrm{NC}^1$ can be computed by a polynomial-sized BP whose evaluation matrices are permutations. A central problem that arises when one attempts to use branching programs in the context of witness encryption is handling evaluation sequences $z \in \{0,1\}^t$ that are inconsistent with any input string $x \in \{0,1\}^\ell$. This happens whenever there exist indices $i, i' \in [t]$ for which $\rho(i) = \rho(i')$ but $z[i] \neq z[i']$. The problem is that in a BP-based solution, for correctness we typically would provide in the ciphertext some information that allows to evaluate the BP with respect to any sequence $z \in \{0,1\}^t$, while in the security proof we can only make assumptions about the BP output when it is executed with non-corrupted sequences z.

To overcome this problem we define a generalized form of matrix BP with a related security notion, where it is required that the BP outputs 0 for any x for which $f(x) = 0$ *and also for any corrupted sequence z.* In this model we allow start vectors $\mathbf{v}_{start} \in \{0,1\}^w$ with multiple 1 entries, i.e. $\|\mathbf{v}_{start}\|_1 \geq 1$, which can be thought of as if the BP holds multiple active nodes that are being updated simultaneously according to the same sequence of input bits z. We require an additional map $F : \{0,1\}^w \to \{0,1\}$ that dictates the final output of the BP according to the active nodes in the end layer. That is, for every sequence $z \in \{0,1\}^t$ we define

$$\mathbf{v}_z = \mathbf{v}_{start} \prod_{j=1}^{t} \mathbf{M}_{j,z_j}$$

and we require that if z is consistent with some input x (according to ρ) then $F(\mathbf{v}_z) = f(x)$, and if z is corrupted then $F(\mathbf{v}_z) = 0$. This allows us in the security proof to rely on the assumption that for all $z \in \{0,1\}^t$ it holds that $F(\mathbf{v}_z) = 0$. We note that for any $f \in \mathrm{NC}^1$ there is a degenerate width-2ℓ BP of this form in which the evaluation steps simply read each input-bit once and record it in one of two possible states, and the complexity of f is pushed to F. However, in this work we impose additional restrictions about F – we require that it will be a read-once monotone CNF formula, i.e.

$$F(\mathbf{v}_z) = \bigwedge_{j \in [k]} \left(\bigvee_{i \in S_j} \mathbf{v}_z[i] \right) \tag{1}$$

where $\{S_j\}_{j \in [k]}$ are disjoint subsets of $[w]$. We also require that the evaluation matrices will be *almost* injective, where by that we mean that each evaluation matrix induces a map $[w] \to [w] \cup \{\bot\}$ where $\bot$ represents a "dead end" sink state that can have multiple pre-images, but each of the other values in $[w]$ has at most a single pre-image. Formally this translates to the requirement that every row vector and every column vector of every evaluation matrix has at most a singe entry that equals 1. We note that a Barrington's BP satisfies these structural properties and show how to compile it into a BP that is resilient to corrupted inputs.

Our compiler adds 3ℓ nodes to the width of the BP, where each triplet works as a memory cell for an input index $i \in [\ell]$. The nodes of the ith triplet represent the following possible states:

1. x_i *has not been read yet.*
2. x_i *was 0 every time it was read.*
3. x_i *was 1 every time it was read.*

The evaluation matrices can be defined naturally to maintain this information with respect to each index $i \in [\ell]$ after each evaluation step $j \in [t]$ by using a diagonal concatenation of sub-matrices that work on each index individually. In every step where the i'th bit should be read, if the received bit is inconsistent with the current state of the memory cell that corresponds to i, the BP moves to the sink state. The vector $\mathbf{v}_{start}$ is defined such that each memory cell starts at the state "x_i *has not been read yet*". The state-to-output map F consists of $k = \ell + 1$ clauses that check that each of the ℓ memory cells is in either of the three states mentioned above (i.e. that neither of the memory cells is in the sink state), and that the underlying Barrington's BP is in its accepting state.

Secret Sharing for F. Consider a simple perfect secret-sharing according to F as follows. Let F be as in Eq. (1) with respect to the subsets $\{S_j\}_{j\in[k]}$. Sample k values $\{r_j\}_{j\in[k]}$ such that each subset of size $k-1$ is uniformly random, but the sum of all of them is 0. Let each index $i \in [w]$ hold the share r_j iff $i \in S_j$. Note that since $\{S_j\}$ are disjoint each index $i \in [w]$ holds at most a single share. Each index $i \in [w]$ that does not appear in any of the sets S_j receives an independent uniformly random share $r \xleftarrow{\$} \{0,1\}$.

The properties of this secret sharing procedure that we would like to highlight are as follows. For every sequence $z \in \{0,1\}^t$ consider the subset of active indices of $\mathbf{v}_z$, i.e. $S_z = \{i : \mathbf{v}_z[i] = 1\}_{i\in[w]}$. Then according to the way we defined $\mathbf{v}_{start}$ and the evaluation matrices of the BP, it holds that:

- For $j = 1,\ldots,\ell$, if z is consistent with respect to the jth bit of the input then $|S_j \cap S_z| = 1$, otherwise $|S_j \cap S_z| = 0$.
- For $j = \ell + 1$, if the underlying Barrington's BP ends in the accepting state when it is executed with the sequence z then $|S_j \cap S_z| = 1$, otherwise $|S_j \cap S_z| = 0$.

It follows that:

- If $F(\mathbf{v}_z) = 1$ then $|S_j \cap S_z| = 1$ for all $j \in [\ell + 1]$ and therefore the sum of the shares that correspond to indices in S_z is 0.
- I $F(\mathbf{v}_z) = 0$ then there is at least one set S_{j*} for which $|S_{j*} \cap S_z| = 0$. This implies that all of the shares that correspond to the indices in S_z are uniformly random when observed together (since there are at most $k - 1$ or them). Moreover, each of the other shares that are not in S_z can be simulated as a sum of the shares that are in S_z and possibly additional random samples.

2.3 The Witness Encryption Construction

To encrypt a message $\mu \in \{0,1\}$ with respect to an **NP** relation we first generate a branching program as was described above for the verification algorithm of the relation. The encryption then proceeds as follows:

1. Sample w matrices according to the secret-sharing algorithm with respect to F that was described above. Denote these matrices by $\{\mathbf{A}_{t+1,i}\}_{i\in[w]}$. We sometimes refer to them as *the end layer*.

2. For every node of the BP, i.e. for every $i \in [w]$ and $j \in [t]$, sample a matrix $\mathbf{A}_{j,i}$ with a trapdoor.
3. For every step $j \in [t]$ sample a pair of short matrices $\mathbf{S}_{j,0}, \mathbf{S}_{j,1}$.
4. For every edge of the BP $(j, i) \rightarrow (j+1, i')$ with respect to an input bit $b \in \{0, 1\}$, if i' is not the sink state then use the trapdoor of $\mathbf{A}_{j,i}$ to sample

$$\mathbf{K} \leftarrow \mathbf{A}_{j,i}^{\mathsf{TD}}(\mathbf{S}_{j,b}\mathbf{A}_{j+1,i'}) \ .$$

5. Sample a secret vector $\mathbf{s}$. For each $i \in [w]$ for which $\mathbf{v}_{start}[i] = 1$:
   – If $\mu = 0$ then sample ct_i as a uniformly random vector.
   – If $\mu = 1$ then compute $\mathsf{ct}_i = \mathbf{s}\mathbf{A}_{1,i} + \mathbf{e}_i$ for some error vector $\mathbf{e}_i$.
   Output all of $\{\mathsf{ct}_i\}_i$ along with the trapdoor-samples from Step 4.

Note that in Step 4 the targets of the trapdoor samples do not have an error term. We *will* use an LWE assumption with respect to the secrets $\{\mathbf{S}_{j,b}\}_{j \in [t], b \in \{0,1\}}$ in intermediate hybrids during the security analysis by adding error terms $\mathbf{E}$. Intuitively, the trapdoor-targets are only accessible to the adversary as part of LWE expressions that include the error vectors $\{\mathbf{e}_i\}_i$. In the security proof we will add to the trapdoor-targets error terms $\mathbf{E}$ that are swallowed by $\{\mathbf{e}_i\}_i$ and so they do not noticeably affect the view of the adversary. We note that adding error terms $\mathbf{E}$ in the real construction would not detract from the correctness nor the security of the scheme (up to some polynomial changes in the parameters), but since it is not required we avoid it for simplicity.

Decryption. In order to decrypt a ciphertext using a valid witness $x \in \{0, 1\}^{\ell}$, apply trapdoor samples to the vectors $\{\mathsf{ct}_i\}$ according to the steps that the BP takes when it is evaluated with the input x. This should result in LWE expressions with respect to the matrices

$$\{\mathbf{S}_x\mathbf{A}_{t+1,i} \ : \ \mathbf{v}_x[i] = 1\}_{i \in [w]} \tag{2}$$

where $\mathbf{S}_x = \prod_{j=1}^{t} \mathbf{S}_{j,x_{\rho(j)}}$. Since x is a valid witness then $F(\mathbf{v}_x) = 1$ and then according to the secret sharing algorithm it should hold that

$$\sum_{i:\mathbf{v}_x[i]=1} \mathbf{A}_{t+1,i} = \mathbf{0} \ .$$

Therefore, if the sum of the LWE expressions with respect to the matrices in (2) is close to zero then output $\mu = 1$ and otherwise output $\mu = 0$.

2.4   Analysis Model

We now discuss the model that will be used in the security analysis.

Standard Decisional LWE. A standard (decisional) LWE experiment considers a distinguisher D that needs to distinguish whether it interacts with a random oracle or with an LWE oracle $\mathcal{O}^{LWE}$, where $\mathcal{O}^{LWE}$ has some secret vector $\mathbf{s}$ and error distribution χ hard-wired in it, and upon receiving a request from D the oracle samples a uniformly random matrix $\mathbf{B}$ along with an error term $\mathbf{e} \leftarrow \chi$ and replies with $(\mathbf{B}, \mathbf{sB} + \mathbf{e})$. Let us denote by Adv_D^{LWE} the advantage of D in the standard LWE experiment. The assumption that LWE is hard then can be stated as

$$\mathsf{Adv}_D^{LWE} \leq \mathrm{negl}(\lambda) \ \textit{for all} \ \text{PPT} \ \textit{distinguishers} \ D.$$

We now generalize this model so that we can make arguments about the hardness of LWE with respect to matrices $\mathbf{B}$ that are not necessarily uniform, where D might be exposed to some auxiliary information. We let aux be correlated to $\mathbf{B}$, e.g. it can be a trapdoor-sample with respect to it. We will also need to capture scenarios where D gets to *choose* matrices from an indexed domain $\{\mathbf{B}_i\}_i$.

General Public Matrices and Auxiliary Information. For any pair of (possibly correlated) distributions $\mathcal{B}$ and aux consider a distinguisher D that is provided with aux as input and needs to distinguish whether it interacts with a random oracle or with an oracle $\mathcal{O}^{LWE(\mathcal{B})}$, where $\mathcal{O}^{LWE(\mathcal{B})}$ has some secret vector $\mathbf{s}$ and error distribution χ hard-wired in it, and upon receiving a request from D the oracle samples a matrix $\mathbf{B} \leftarrow \mathcal{B}$ along with an error term $\mathbf{e} \leftarrow \chi$ and replies with $(\mathbf{B}, \mathbf{sB} + \mathbf{e})$. We denote by $\mathsf{Adv}_{D(\mathsf{aux})}^{LWE(\mathcal{B})}$ the advantage of D in an experiment of this form.

This notation allows us to make relative statements about the hardness of LWE with respect to different distributions $(\mathcal{B}, \mathsf{aux})$ and $(\mathcal{B}', \mathsf{aux}')$ before stating anything about the hardness of either of them individually. We can argue that LWE with respect to $(\mathcal{B}, \mathsf{aux})$ is at least as hard as LWE with respect to $(\mathcal{B}', \mathsf{aux}')$ as follows:

For any PPT *distinguisher* D *there exists a* PPT *distinguisher* D' *such that* (3)

$$\mathsf{Adv}_{D(\mathsf{aux})}^{LWE(\mathcal{B})} \leq \mathsf{Adv}_{D'(\mathsf{aux}')}^{LWE(\mathcal{B}')} + \mathrm{negl}(\lambda).$$

Standard proof strategies oftentimes implicitly make arguments similar to (3) for distributions $(\mathcal{B}, \mathsf{aux})$ and $(\mathcal{B}', \mathsf{aux}')$ that are indistinguishable. In fact it easy to show that whenever $(\mathcal{B}, \mathsf{aux})$ and $(\mathcal{B}', \mathsf{aux}')$ are indistinguishable then (3) indeed holds by setting $D' = D$, because the view of D remains $\mathrm{negl}(\lambda)$-close in both of the experiments.

There are also scenarios where Argument (3) holds for distributions $\mathcal{B}$ and $\mathcal{B}'$ that are clearly distinguishable. As an example, for any $\mathcal{B}$ consider $\mathcal{B}' = \mathcal{B} + \mathcal{E}$ where $\mathcal{E}$ is a distribution such that for all $\mathbf{E} \leftarrow \mathcal{E}$ the term $\mathbf{sE}$ is swallowed by the error distribution χ of the oracle $\mathcal{O}^{LWE(\mathcal{B})}$. Then $\mathcal{B}$ and $\mathcal{B}'$ might be distinguishable (e.g. if $\mathcal{B}$ is a constant), but it can be shown that (3) still holds by setting $D' = D$ because the view of D remains statistically-close in the experiments against $\mathcal{O}^{LWE(\mathcal{B})}$ and $\mathcal{O}^{LWE(\mathcal{B}+\mathcal{E})}$.

Another common scenario is when aux is efficiently sampleable and not correlated to $\mathcal{B}$. In that case Argument (3) can be proved with respect to $(\mathcal{B}, \mathsf{aux})$ and $(\mathcal{B}, 1^\lambda)$ by considering a distinguisher $\mathsf{D}'(1^\lambda)$ that locally samples aux and then works the same as $\mathsf{D}(\mathsf{aux})$.

Indexed Public Matrices. Up until now we considered an oracle $\mathcal{O}^{LWE(\mathcal{B})}$ that upon request samples a fresh instance of the form $\mathbf{B} \leftarrow \mathcal{B}$. This model does not capture cases where the distinguisher gets to choose the matrices from the domain of $\mathcal{B}$ for which he sees LWE samples. We change the definition of the oracle to support scenarios of this form. Let $\mathcal{B} = \{\mathbf{B}_i\}_{i \in [p]}$ be a collection of p matrices. The random oracle $\mathcal{O}^{LWE(\mathcal{B})}$ has a secret vector $\mathbf{s}$ and error distribution χ hard-wired in it, and upon receiving a request $i \in [p]$ it samples an error term $\mathbf{e}_i \leftarrow \chi$ and replies with $\mathbf{s}\mathbf{B}_i + \mathbf{e}_i$. Repeated queries for the same i are replied with the same error term $\mathbf{e}_i$.

Notes.

1. p can be exponentially large, but any PPT distinguisher D that interacts with $\mathcal{O}^{LWE(\mathcal{B})}$ only gets to see samples with respect to a polynomial-sized subset of $\mathcal{B}$ that it can choose adaptively upon seeing previous replies.
2. aux must be of polynomial size because it is given explicitly to D. It is also reasonable to define a model where aux can be of exponential size, such that it is hard-wired to the LWE oracle and parts of it are provided to D upon request via auxiliary queries. In this work we use the version that was discussed above because it suffices for our needs.
3. The model can capture scenarios where the oracle should sample a fresh matrix $\mathbf{B} \leftarrow \mathcal{B}'$ for each query by considering a collection $\mathcal{B} = \{\mathbf{B}_i\}_{i \in [p]}$ that consists of samples $\mathbf{B}_i \leftarrow \mathcal{B}'$ for $p \in \exp(\lambda)$.
4. The term $\mathbf{B}_i$ "in the clear" does not appear anymore in the reply of the oracle, so the model can capture cases where the matrices in $\mathcal{B}$ are not necessarily known to the attacker. Additional information about $\mathcal{B}$ can be revealed in aux if required.

Example. Consider $2t$ matrices $\{\mathbf{S}_{j,b}\}_{j \in [t], b \in \{0,1\}}$ from a Gaussian distribution and w uniformly random matrices $\{\mathbf{A}_i\}_{i \in [w]}$. Define the collection

$$\mathcal{B} = \left\{ \mathcal{B}_z = \left\{ \mathbf{B}_{z,i} = \prod_{j=1}^t \mathbf{S}_{j,z_j} \mathbf{A}_i \right\}_{i \in [w]} \right\}_{z \in \{0,1\}^t}.$$

It can be shown via a sequence of $O(t)$ hybrids that LWE with respect to $\mathcal{B}$ is hard. Consider the sequence of hybrids $\mathcal{B}^t, (\mathcal{B}^{t-1}_{temp}, \mathcal{B}^{t-1}), \ldots, (\mathcal{B}^0_{temp}, \mathcal{B}^0)$ where in each hybrid we change the way that matrices in $\mathcal{B}$ are sampled. Let $\mathcal{B}^t = \mathcal{B}$ as above and make the following inductive assumption about $\mathcal{B}^j$:

There is a collection of uniformly random matrices

$$\mathcal{A}^j = \left\{ \mathcal{A}^j_{\hat{z}} = \{ \mathbf{A}_{\hat{z},i} \}_{i \in [w]} \right\}_{\hat{z} \in \{0,1\}^{t-j}}$$

such that each $\mathbf{B}^j_{z,i} \in \mathcal{B}^j$ *is of the form*

$$\mathbf{B}^j_{z,i} = \prod_{j'=1}^{j} \mathbf{S}_{j',z_{j'}} \mathbf{A}_{\hat{z},i}$$

where $\hat{z}$ *is the length-*$(t-j)$ *suffix of* z.

Note that the assumption holds for $j = t$ by definition for the set $\mathcal{A}^t = \{ \mathbf{A}_i \}_{i \in [w]}$. For $j = t-1, \ldots, 0$, under the inductive assumption with respect to $\mathcal{B}^{j+1}$, define hybrid $\mathcal{B}^j_{temp}$ as follows:

Hybrid $\mathcal{B}^j_{temp}$. Consider the set $\mathcal{A}^{j+1}$ that satisfies the assumption for $\mathcal{B}^{j+1}$. For each $\mathbf{A}_{\hat{z},i} \in \mathcal{A}^{j+1}$ sample a pair of Gaussian matrices $\mathbf{E}^0_{\hat{z},i}, \mathbf{E}^1_{\hat{z},i}$ and define

$$\mathbf{M}^0_{\hat{z},i} := \mathbf{S}_{j,0} \mathbf{A}_{\hat{z},i} + \mathbf{E}^0_{\hat{z},i}, \qquad \mathbf{M}^1_{\hat{z},i} := \mathbf{S}_{j,1} \mathbf{A}_{\hat{z},i} + \mathbf{E}^1_{\hat{z},i} .$$

Define each $\mathbf{B}^j_{z,i} \in \mathcal{B}^j_{temp}$ as

$$\mathbf{B}^j_{z,i} = \prod_{j'=1}^{j-1} \mathbf{S}_{j',z_{j'}} \mathbf{M}^{z[j]}_{\hat{z},i}$$

where $z[j]$ is the jth bit of z and $\hat{z}$ is the length-$(t-j-1)$ suffix of z. Note that

$$\mathbf{B}^j_{z,i} = \prod_{j'=1}^{j-1} \mathbf{S}_{j',z_{j'}} \mathbf{M}^{z[j]}_{\hat{z},i}$$

$$= \prod_{j'=1}^{j-1} \mathbf{S}_{j',z_{j'}} \left(\mathbf{S}_{j,z[j]} \mathbf{A}_{\hat{z},i} + \mathbf{E}^{z[j]}_{\hat{z},i} \right)$$

$$= \underbrace{\prod_{j'=1}^{j-1} \mathbf{S}_{j',z_{j'}} \mathbf{S}_{j,z[j]} \mathbf{A}_{\hat{z},i}}_{\text{same as } \mathbf{B}^{j+1}_{z,i} \text{ in } \mathcal{B}^{j+1}} + \underbrace{\prod_{j'=1}^{j-1} \mathbf{S}_{j',z_{j'}} \mathbf{E}^{z[j]}_{\hat{z},i}}_{\mathbf{E}'} .$$

If we define the error distribution χ of the LWE oracle such that it swallows $\mathbf{E}'$ then $\mathbf{B}^j_{z,i}$ and $\mathbf{B}^{j+1}_{z,i}$ are statistically close and therefore LWE with respect to $\mathcal{B}^{j+1}$ and $\mathcal{B}^j_{temp}$ is equivalently hard.

Hybrid $\mathcal{B}^j$. The same as $\mathcal{B}^j_{temp}$, except that each matrix $\mathbf{M}^b_{\hat{z},i}$ is sampled uniformly at random. Under the standard LWE assumption, the distributions $\mathcal{B}^j_{temp}$ and $\mathcal{B}^j$ are indistinguishable and therefore LWE with respect to $\mathcal{B}^j_{temp}$ and $\mathcal{B}^j$ is equivalently hard. Moreover, the inductive assumption holds for $\mathcal{B}^j$ with respect to the set

$$\mathcal{A}^j = \left\{ \mathbf{A}_{(b,\hat{z}),i} = \mathbf{M}^b_{\hat{z},i} \right\}_{b \in \{0,1\}, \hat{z} \in \{0,1\}^{t-j-1}, i \in [w]} .$$

Lastly, from the inductive assumption Hybrid $\mathcal{B}^0$ is the uniform distribution and therefore LWE with respect to $\mathcal{B}^0$ is identical to the standard LWE experiment.

2.5 Security of the Construction

Semi-honest Security. Assume that all that the adversary can do is to evaluate the encoded BP with arbitrary sequences $z \in \{0,1\}$ of his choice. This would result in LWE challenges with respect to matrices of the form

$$\mathcal{B} = \left\{ \mathcal{B}_z = \left\{ \mathbf{B}_{z,i} = \prod_{j=1}^{t} \mathbf{S}_{j,z_j} \mathbf{A}_{t+1,i} \ : \ \mathbf{v}_z[i] = 1 \right\}_{i \in [w]} \right\}_{z \in \{0,1\}^t} . \tag{4}$$

(For simplicity of the overview we ignore here the accessible matrices in intermediate steps). In this part of the proof we show that an LWE experiment against the oracle $\mathcal{O}^{LWE(\mathcal{B})}$ is hard. Note the similarities between Eq. (4) and the example in Sect. 2.4. If all of the output matrices $\{\mathbf{A}_{t+1,i}\}_{i \in [w]}$ were uniformly random we could apply the same proof. However, here the matrices $\{\mathbf{A}_{t+1,i}\}_{i \in [w]}$ are sampled according to the secret sharing of F and therefore some subsets of these matrices are correlated. We will use the relaxed guarantee that for all sequences $z \in \{0,1\}$ it holds that $F(\mathbf{v}_z) = 0$ and therefore the output matrices $\{\mathbf{A}_{t+1,i} \ : \ \mathbf{v}_z[i] = 1\}_{i \in [w]}$ are not correlated to each other.

The proof goes via a sequence of 2^t steps iterating over $z^* \in \{0,1\}^t$, where in each step the matrices in $\mathcal{B}_{z^*}$ are replaced with independent uniformly random matrices. Each such step takes $2t$ sub-hybrids that resemble the proof in Sect. 2.4. It begins at the end layer of the BP by sampling $\{\mathbf{A}_{t+1,i} \ : \ \mathbf{v}_z[i]{=}1\}_{i \in [w]}$ uniformly at random and simulating $\{\mathbf{A}_{t+1,i} \ : \ \mathbf{v}_z[i]{\neq}1\}_{i \in [w]}$ according to the secret-sharing simulation properties that were discussed in Sect. 2.2. It then moves in t hybrids towards the start layer, in each step replacing with uniform the matrices that correspond to the length-j suffix of z^*, until all of the matrices in $\mathcal{B}_{z^*}$ are sampled uniformly at random. Lastly, it moves again in the forward direction to undo changes that affect matrices in $\mathcal{B} \backslash \mathcal{B}_{z^*}$.

In more detail, consider the sequence $\mathcal{B}^{0^t}, \dots, \mathcal{B}^{1^t}$ of length 2^t, where for $z^* \in \{0,1\}^t$ in hybrid $\mathcal{B}^{z^*} = \{\mathcal{B}^{z^*}_z\}_{z \in \{0,1\}^t}$ the matrices in $\{\mathcal{B}^{z^*}_z\}_{z<z^*}$ are sampled uniformly at random and the matrices in $\{\mathcal{B}^{z^*}_z\}_{z \geq z^*}$ are sampled as in Eq. (4). In particular $\mathcal{B}^{0^t}$ is identical to the distribution in (4) and $\mathcal{B}^{1^t}$ is identical to

the uniform distribution. For every $z^* \in \{0,1\}^t$ we show that LWE with respect to $\mathcal{B}^{z^*}$ and $\mathcal{B}^{z^*+1}$ is (almost) identically hard. The proof goes via a sequence of hybrids

$$\mathcal{B}^{z^*} = \mathcal{B}^t, (\mathcal{B}_{temp}^{t-1}, \mathcal{B}^{t-1}), \ldots, (\mathcal{B}_{temp}^0, \mathcal{B}^0), \quad (\widetilde{\mathcal{B}}^0, \widetilde{\mathcal{B}}_{temp}^0), \ldots, (\widetilde{\mathcal{B}}^{t-1}, \widetilde{\mathcal{B}}_{temp}^{t-1}), \widetilde{\mathcal{B}}^t = \mathcal{B}^{z^*+1}.$$

Make the following inductive assumption about $\mathcal{B}^j$:

There is a collection of uniformly random matrices

$$\mathcal{A}^j = \left\{ \mathcal{A}_{\hat{z}}^j = \{\mathbf{A}_{\hat{z},i} \; : \; \mathbf{v}_{z^*}[i] = 1\}_{i \in [w]} \right\}_{\hat{z} \in \{0,1\}^{t-j}}$$

such that each $\mathbf{B}_{z,i}^j \in \mathcal{B}^j$ *(for* $z \geq z^*$*) is of the form*

$$\mathbf{B}_{z,i}^j = \prod_{j'=1}^{j} \mathbf{S}_{j',z_{j'}} \mathbf{A}_{\hat{z},i}$$

where $\hat{z}$ *is the length-*$(t-j)$ *suffix of* z*, and* $\mathbf{A}_{\hat{z},i}$ *is either a matrix in* $\mathcal{A}_{\hat{z}}^j$ *(whenever* $\mathbf{v}_{z^*}[i] = 1$*), and otherwise it is a sum of up to* w *matrices in* $\mathcal{A}_{\hat{z}}^j$*.*

Note that the assumption holds for $j = t$ for the set $\mathcal{A}^t = \{\mathbf{A}_{t+1,i} \; : \; \mathbf{v}_{z^*}[i] = 1\}_{i \in [w]}$ according to the secret sharing properties in Sect. 2.2 since $F(\mathbf{v}_z) = 0$. For $j = t-1, \ldots, 0$, under the inductive assumption with respect to $\mathcal{B}^{j+1}$, define hybrid $\mathcal{B}_{temp}^j$ as follows:

Hybrid $\mathcal{B}_{temp}^j$. Consider the set $\mathcal{A}^{j+1}$ that satisfies the assumption for $\mathcal{B}^{j+1}$. For each $\mathbf{A}_{\hat{z},i} \in \mathcal{A}^{j+1}$ sample a pair of Gaussian matrices $\mathbf{E}_{\hat{z},i}^0, \mathbf{E}_{\hat{z},i}^1$ and define

$$\mathbf{M}_{\hat{z},i}^0 := \mathbf{S}_{j,0} \mathbf{A}_{\hat{z},i} + \mathbf{E}_{\hat{z},i}^0, \qquad \mathbf{M}_{\hat{z},i}^1 := \mathbf{S}_{j,1} \mathbf{A}_{\hat{z},i} + \mathbf{E}_{\hat{z},i}^1. \tag{5}$$

For each $i \in [w]$ for which $\mathbf{v}_{z^*}[i] \neq 1$ recall that $\mathbf{A}_{\hat{z},i}$ is a sum of matrices in $\mathcal{A}_{\hat{z}}^j$ and define for $b \in \{0,1\}$ the matrix $\mathbf{M}_{\hat{z},i}^b$ as a sum of the corresponding matrices in $\{\mathbf{M}_{\hat{z},i'}^b\}_{\mathbf{v}_{z^*}[i']=1}$.

Define each $\mathbf{B}_{z,i}^j \in \mathcal{B}_{temp}^j$ as

$$\mathbf{B}_{z,i}^j = \prod_{j'=1}^{j-1} \mathbf{S}_{j',z_{j'}} \mathbf{M}_{\hat{z},i}^{z[j]}$$

where $z[j]$ is the jth bit of z and $\hat{z}$ is the length-$(t-j-1)$ suffix of z. Note that

$$
\mathbf{B}^j_{z,i} = \prod_{j'=1}^{j-1} \mathbf{S}_{j',z_{j'}} \mathbf{M}^{z[j]}_{\hat{z},i}
$$

$$
= \prod_{j'=1}^{j-1} \mathbf{S}_{j',z_{j'}} \left(\mathbf{S}_{j,z[j]} \mathbf{A}_{\hat{z},i} + \mathbf{E}^{z[j]}_{\hat{z},i} \right)
$$

$$
= \underbrace{\prod_{j'=1}^{j-1} \mathbf{S}_{j',z_{j'}} \mathbf{S}_{j,z[j]} \mathbf{A}_{\hat{z},i}}_{\text{same as } \mathbf{B}^{j+1}_{z,i} \text{ in } \mathcal{B}^{j+1}} + \underbrace{\prod_{j'=1}^{j-1} \mathbf{S}_{j',z_{j'}} \mathbf{E}^{z[j]}_{\hat{z},i}}_{\mathbf{E}'} .
$$

If we define the error distribution χ of the LWE oracle such that it swallows $\mathbf{E}'$ then $\mathbf{B}^j_{z,i}$ and $\mathbf{B}^{j+1}_{z,i}$ are statistically close and therefore LWE with respect to $\mathcal{B}^{j+1}$ and $\mathcal{B}^j_{temp}$ is equivalently hard.

Hybrid $\mathcal{B}^j$. The same as $\mathcal{B}^j_{temp}$, except that each matrix $\mathbf{M}^b_{\hat{z},i}$ is sampled uniformly at random. Under the standard LWE assumption, the distributions $\mathcal{B}^j_{temp}$ and $\mathcal{B}^j$ are indistinguishable and therefore LWE with respect to $\mathcal{B}^j_{temp}$ and $\mathcal{B}^j$ is equivalently hard. Moreover, the inductive assumption holds for $\mathcal{B}^j$ with respect to the set

$$
\mathcal{A}^j = \left\{ \mathbf{A}_{(b,\hat{z}),i} = \mathbf{M}^b_{\hat{z},i} \; : \; \mathbf{v}_z[i] = 1 \right\}_{b \in \{0,1\}, \hat{z} \in \{0,1\}^{t-j-1}, i \in [w]} .
$$

From the inductive assumption in Hybrid $\mathcal{B}^0$ all of the matrices in $\mathcal{B}_{z^*}$ are sampled from the uniform distribution. However, matrices in $\mathcal{B}_z$ for $z > z^*$ are still simulated as sums of intermediate matrices that were sampled in previous hybrids according to z^*. In hybrids $(\widetilde{\mathcal{B}}^0, \widetilde{\mathcal{B}}^0_{temp}), \dots, (\widetilde{\mathcal{B}}^{t-1}, \widetilde{\mathcal{B}}^{t-1}_{temp}), \widetilde{\mathcal{B}}^t$ we undo these changes and end up with the distribution $\widetilde{\mathcal{B}}^t$ that is identical to $\mathcal{B}^{z^*+1}$.

Full Security. The security game of the construction is identical to an LWE experiment where D receives as auxiliary information all of the trapdoor samples that were generated in Step 4 of the construction, and is playing against an oracle $\mathcal{O}^{LWE(\mathcal{B}_0)}$ where

$$
\mathcal{B}_0 = \left\{ \mathbf{A}_{1,i} \; : \; \mathbf{v}_{start}[i] = 1 \right\}_{i \in [w]} .
$$

For all $j = 1, \dots, t$ we let aux_j denote the trapdoor samples that go from the jth layer to the $(j+1)$th layer of the BP, and for all $j = 0, \dots, t$ we let $\mathcal{B}_j$ denote the matrices that can be accessed via any length-j evaluation sequence:

$$
\mathcal{B}_j = \left\{ \prod_{j'=1}^{j} \mathbf{S}_{j',z'_j} \mathbf{A}_{j+1,i} \; : \; \mathbf{v}_z[i] = 1 \right\}_{z \in \{0,1\}^j, i \in [w]} .
$$

Using this notation, we prove that for any PPT D there exists a PPT D' such that:

$$\underbrace{\mathsf{Adv}_{\mathsf{D}(\mathsf{aux}_1,\ldots,\mathsf{aux}_t)}^{LWE(\mathcal{B}_0)}}_{\text{real security game}} \leq \underbrace{\mathsf{Adv}_{\mathsf{D}'(1^\lambda)}^{LWE(\mathcal{B}_0,\cdots,\mathcal{B}_t)}}_{\text{semi-honest security game}} + \mathrm{negl}(\lambda) \ . \tag{6}$$

Note that $\mathcal{B}_t$ is identical to the distribution $\mathcal{B}$ that was discussed in the previous part of the overview (Sect. 2.4), i.e. we already showed that LWE with respect to $\mathcal{B}_t$ and $\mathsf{aux} = 1^\lambda$ is hard. In the body of the paper we show that LWE with respect to $(\mathcal{B}_0,\ldots,\mathcal{B}_t)$ and $\mathsf{aux} = 1^\lambda$ is hard similarly to the proof overview that was provided here for $\mathcal{B}_t$.

The proof of (6) takes t steps, where for $j = 1,\ldots,t$ we show that

$$\mathsf{Adv}_{\mathsf{D}(\mathsf{aux}_j,\ldots,\mathsf{aux}_t)}^{LWE(\mathcal{B}_0,\ldots,\mathcal{B}_{j-1})} \leq \mathsf{Adv}_{\mathsf{D}'(\mathsf{aux}_{j+1},\ldots,\mathsf{aux}_t)}^{LWE(\mathcal{B}_0,\cdots,\mathcal{B}_j)} + \mathrm{negl}(\lambda) \tag{7}$$

via $O(w)$ reductions to our assumption.

2.6 Phrasing the Assumption

The essence of the assumption is that if there exists a successful attack on LWE with respect to $\mathbf{A}$ given a trapdoor sample $\mathbf{K} \xleftarrow{\$} \mathbf{A}^{\mathsf{TD}}(\mathbf{T})$, then there also exists a successful attack on LWE with respect to $[\mathbf{A}|\mathbf{T}]$ without $\mathbf{K}$. We make a few generalizations to this base case. First, we consider a case where the challenge is with respect to $\mathbf{CA}$ for an arbitrary matrix $\mathbf{C}$ and not necessarily $\mathbf{C} = \mathbf{I}$. More generally, we consider a challenge with respect to multiple matrices $\{\mathbf{C}_j\mathbf{A}\}_{j\in[p]}$ and a trapdoor sample $\mathbf{K} \xleftarrow{\$} \mathbf{A}^{\mathsf{TD}}(\mathbf{T})$, and assume that is not easier than a challenge with respect to $\{[\mathbf{C}_j\mathbf{A} \mid \mathbf{C}_j\mathbf{T}]\}_{j\in[p]}$ without $\mathbf{K}$. Lastly we allow additional auxiliary information and public matrices that are available to the adversary. This sums up to the following:

Main Assumption (Informal). Consider

$$(\mathbf{A}, \mathbf{A}^{\mathsf{TD}}) \leftarrow \mathsf{TrapGen}(1^n, q, m) \ .$$

Let $\mathbf{T}$ be a $n \times m'$ *target matrix*, let $\mathcal{C}$ be a collection of $n \times n$ *prefix matrices*, let aux be a poly-sized auxiliary information and let $\mathcal{B}$ be a collection of $n \times m$ matrices (where $\mathcal{B}$ and $\mathcal{C}$ are possibly of exponential size), where $\mathbf{T}, \mathcal{C}, \mathsf{aux}, \mathcal{B}$ can be correlated to each other and to $\mathbf{A}, \mathbf{A}^{\mathsf{TD}}$. Consider

$$\mathbf{K} \leftarrow \mathbf{A}^{\mathsf{TD}}(\mathbf{T}) \ .$$

Then for any PPT distinguisher D there exists a PPT distinguisher D' such that

$$\mathsf{Adv}_{\mathsf{D}(\mathsf{aux},\mathbf{K})}^{LWE(\mathcal{B},\{\mathbf{CA}\}_{\mathbf{C}\in\mathcal{C}})} \leq \mathsf{Adv}_{\mathsf{D}'(\mathsf{aux})}^{LWE(\mathcal{B},\{\mathbf{CA}\}_{\mathbf{C}\in\mathcal{C}},\{\mathbf{CT}\}_{\mathbf{C}\in\mathcal{C}})} + \mathrm{negl}(\lambda) \ .$$

Note that all of the distributions are sampled before $\mathbf{K}$ and in particular aux does not include a copy of $\mathbf{K}$ or the randomness that was used during its sampling. aux might contain another trapdoor-sample with respect to the same target $\mathbf{T}$ (or even contain $\mathbf{A}^{\mathsf{TD}}$), but in that case the assumption holds trivially because there is always a PPT D' with large advantage in the latter experiment.

Proof of (7) **via the Main Assumption.** Equation (7) considers all of the encodings that go from the j^*th layer to the $(j^* + 1)$th layer of the branching program. These are all of the encodings that are sampled with trapdoors of the nodes $\{\mathbf{A}_{j^*,i}\}_{i\in[w]}$, where each node contributes at most two encodings (one for the 0 transition and one for the 1 transition). We replace each of these encodings via a reduction to the main assumption. Let $\mathbf{K}$ be an encoding from $\mathbf{A}_{j^*,i^*}$ to $\mathbf{S}_{j^*,b}\mathbf{A}_{j^*+1,i'}$, then apply the reduction with respect to the following distributions:

- The target matrix $\mathbf{T}$ is $\mathbf{S}_{j^*,b}\mathbf{A}_{j^*+1,i'}$.
- The prefix matrices $\mathcal{C}$ are all of the possible length-$(j^* - 1)$ evaluation sequences that lead to the node $\mathbf{A}_{j^*,i^*}$:

$$\mathcal{C} = \left\{ \prod_{j=1}^{j^*} \mathbf{S}_{j,z_j} \ : \ \mathbf{v}_z[i^*] = 1 \right\}_{z\in\{0,1\}^{j^*-1}} .$$

- The auxiliary information aux consists of all of the other trapdoor samples that are available to D, i.e. $(\mathsf{aux}_{j^*+1}, \ldots, \mathsf{aux}_t)$ and the encodings in aux_{j^*} that were not replaced yet.
- The collection $\mathcal{B}$ consists of all of the matrices for which D can see an LWE sample that do not correspond to the node $\mathbf{A}_{j^*,i^*}$, i.e. $(\mathcal{B}, \ldots, \mathcal{B}_{j^*-2})$, the matrices in $\mathcal{B}_{j^*-1}$ that do not correspond to $\mathbf{A}_{j^*,i^*}$ and the matrices in $\mathcal{B}_{j^*}$ that were already added in the previous hybrids.

This sums up the technical overview of the construction and its security analysis.

2.7 Paper Structure

In Appendix A we discuss a simplified LWE scenario that resembles the security properties of our WE candidate. Due to page limit constraints we moved the information-theoretic part of the work to Appendix B. In Sect. 3 we present the generalized LWE model and our assumption. In Sect. 4 we present the witness-encryption candidate and in Appendix C we analyze its security. Appendices D and E contain supplementary materials for Sects. 3 and 4 respectively.

3   Lattice Tools

Some lattice preliminaries can be found in Appendix D.1.

3.1 LWE for General Matrices and Auxiliary Information

We now present the notation that will be used throughout this text to analyze the security of LWE with auxiliary information and public matrices from arbitrary distributions.

Definition 1 (Generalized Decisional LWE).
Let $\lambda \in \mathbb{N}$ be the security parameter, let $n, q, m \in \text{poly}(\lambda)$ be integers and let χ_e, χ_s be probability distributions over $\mathbb{Z}_q$. For every (possibly exponential) integer $p \in \mathbb{Z}$ and every distribution $\mathcal{B} = \{\mathbf{B}_i \in \mathbb{Z}_q^{n \times m}\}_{i \in [p]}$ define an LWE oracle $\mathcal{O}^{\text{LWE}(\mathcal{B})} : [p] \to \mathbb{Z}_q^m$ as follows:

1. *$\mathcal{O}^{\text{LWE}(\mathcal{B})}$ samples a secret $\mathbf{s} \leftarrow \chi_s^n$.*
2. *$\mathcal{O}^{\text{LWE}(\mathcal{B})}$ associates each $i \in [p]$ with an error vector $\mathbf{e}_i \leftarrow \chi_e^m$.*
3. *Upon receiving a query $i \in [p]$, $\mathcal{O}^{\text{LWE}(\mathcal{B})}$ returns*

$$\mathbf{u}_i := \mathbf{s}\mathbf{B}_i + \mathbf{e}_i \ .$$

In addition consider the random oracle $\mathcal{O}^{\text{rand}(\mathcal{B})} : [p] \to \mathbb{Z}_q^m$ that associates with every $i \in [p]$ a random vector $\mathbf{u}_i \xleftarrow{\$} \mathbb{Z}_q^m$.

For any distribution $\text{aux} \in \{0,1\}^{\text{poly}(\lambda)}$ we let $\text{LWE}_{n,m,q,\chi_s,\chi_e}[\mathcal{B}, \text{aux}]$ denote the challenge of distinguishing between $\mathcal{O}^{\text{LWE}(\mathcal{B})}$ and $\mathcal{O}^{\text{rand}(\mathcal{B})}$, given the auxiliary information aux.

For every distinguisher D we say that the advantage of D in the challenge $\text{LWE}_{n,m,q,\chi_s,\chi_e}[\mathcal{B}, \text{aux}]$ is

$$\text{Adv}^{\mathsf{D}}_{n,m,q,\chi_s,\chi_e}[\mathcal{B}, \text{aux}]$$
$$:= \left| Pr\left[\mathsf{D}^{\mathcal{O}^{\text{LWE}(\mathcal{B})}}(1^\lambda, \text{aux}) = 1\right] - Pr\left[\mathsf{D}^{\mathcal{O}^{\text{rand}(\mathcal{B})}}(1^\lambda, \text{aux}) = 1\right]\right| \ .$$

We sometimes omit the parameters n, m, q, χ_s, χ_e when they are clear from the context.

We also define a succinct notation for relative statements about the hardness of LWE with respect to different distributions of $\mathcal{B}, \text{aux}$:

Definition 2 (Relative Hardness of LWE).
Let $\lambda \in \mathbb{N}$ be the security parameter, let $n, q, m \in \text{poly}(\lambda)$ be integers and let χ_e, χ_s be probability distributions over $\mathbb{Z}_q$. For any pair of distributions $\mathcal{B} = \{\mathbf{B}_i \in \mathbb{Z}_q^{n \times m}\}_{i \in [p]}$, $\mathcal{B}' = \{\mathbf{B}'_i \in \mathbb{Z}_q^{n \times m}\}_{i \in [p']}$ and

$\mathsf{aux}, \mathsf{aux}' \in \{0,1\}^{\mathrm{poly}(\lambda)}$ *and any function* ϵ, *let*

$$\mathrm{LWE}[\mathcal{B}, \mathsf{aux}] \;\preccurlyeq\; \mathrm{LWE}[\mathcal{B}', \mathsf{aux}'] + \epsilon(\lambda)$$

denote that for any PPT *distinguisher* D *there exists a* PPT *distinguisher* D′ *such that*

$$\mathsf{Adv}^{\mathsf{D}}[\mathcal{B}, \mathsf{aux}] \;\leq\; \mathsf{Adv}^{\mathsf{D}'}[\mathcal{B}', \mathsf{aux}'] + \epsilon(\lambda)$$

Informally, this means that $\mathrm{LWE}[\mathcal{B}, \mathsf{aux}]$ *is at least* $(\epsilon(\lambda)$-*almost) as hard as* $\mathrm{LWE}[\mathcal{B}', \mathsf{aux}']$.

We recall the standard notion of Decisional LWE as was introduced by Regev in [Reg05], where $\mathcal{B}$ is the uniform distribution over $\mathbb{Z}_q^{n \times m}$, there is no auxiliary information and the LWE oracle sends $\mathbf{B}_i$ as a part of its response:

Definition 3 (Decisional LWE).
Let $\lambda \in \mathbb{N}$ *be the security parameter, let* $n, q, m \in \mathrm{poly}(\lambda)$ *be integers and let* χ_e, χ_s *be probability distributions over* $\mathbb{Z}_q$. *Let* $\mathcal{O}^{\mathrm{LWE}}$ *denote the oracle that works as follows:*

1. $\mathcal{O}^{\mathrm{LWE}}$ *samples a secret* $\mathbf{s} \leftarrow \chi_s^n$.
2. *Upon receiving a query,* $\mathcal{O}^{\mathrm{LWE}}$ *samples* $\mathbf{B} \xleftarrow{\$} \mathbb{Z}_q^{n \times m}$, $\mathbf{e} \leftarrow \chi_e^m$ *and returns* $(\mathbf{B}, \mathbf{sB} + \mathbf{e})$.

Let $\mathcal{O}^{\mathrm{rand}}$ *denote the oracle that upon receiving a query, samples* $\mathbf{B} \xleftarrow{\$} \mathbb{Z}_q^{n \times m}$, $\mathbf{u} \leftarrow \mathbb{Z}_q^m$ *and returns* $(\mathbf{B}, \mathbf{u})$.

We let $\mathrm{LWE}_{n,m,q,\chi_s,\chi_e}$ *denote the challenge of distinguishing between* $\mathcal{O}^{\mathrm{LWE}}$ *and* $\mathcal{O}^{\mathrm{rand}}$. *For every distinguisher* D *we say that the advantage of* D *in the challenge* $\mathrm{LWE}_{n,m,q,\chi_s,\chi_e}$ *is*

$$\mathsf{Adv}^{\mathsf{D}}_{n,m,q,\chi_s,\chi_e} := \left| Pr\left[\mathsf{D}^{\mathcal{O}^{\mathrm{LWE}}}(1^\lambda) = 1\right] - Pr\left[\mathsf{D}^{\mathcal{O}^{\mathrm{rand}}}(1^\lambda) = 1\right] \right|.$$

We sometimes omit the parameters n, m, q, χ_s, χ_e *when they are clear from the context.*

As was shown in a long sequence of works, LWE is at least as hard as the lattice problems GapSVP and SIVP under various choices of parameters. In this work we sample the LWE secret from the same distribution as the error term. [ACPS09] showed that this setting is at least as hard as when the secret is sampled uniformly form $\mathbb{Z}_q^n$.

Theorem 1 ([Reg05, Pei09, MM11, MP12, BLP+13, ACPS09]).
For all $\epsilon > 0$ there exist functions $q = q(n) \leq 2^n$, $\chi = \chi(n)$ such that χ is (B, ϵ)-bounded for some $B = B(n)$, $q/B \geq 2^{n^\epsilon}$ and such that for all $m \in \text{poly}(m)$ $\text{LWE}_{n,m,q,\chi,\chi}$ is at least as hard as the classical hardness of GapSVP_γ and the quantum hardness of SIVP_γ for $\gamma = 2^{\Omega(n^\epsilon)}$.

We now consider a number of special cases for $\mathcal{B}, \text{aux}$:

1. **Lemma 3.1.1 (Informal)** – If $\mathcal{B}$ consists of uniformly random matrices in $\mathbb{Z}_q^{n \times m}$ then $\text{LWE}[\mathcal{B}, \text{aux}]$ is at least as hard as standard decisional LWE for any efficiently samplable aux.
2. **Lemma 3.1.2 (Informal)** – For any pair of distributions $(\mathcal{B}, \text{aux})$ and $(\mathcal{B}', \text{aux}')$, if $(\mathcal{B}, \text{aux})$ and $(\mathcal{B}', \text{aux}')$ are indistinguishable then $\text{LWE}[\mathcal{B}, \text{aux}]$ and $\text{LWE}[\mathcal{B}', \text{aux}']$ are equivalently hard.
3. **Lemma 3.1.3 (Informal)** – If the error distribution χ_e swallows an error distribution $\mathcal{E}$, then $\text{LWE}[\mathcal{B}, \text{aux}]$ and $\text{LWE}[\mathcal{B} + \mathcal{E}, \text{aux}]$ are equivalently hard for any $(\mathcal{B}, \text{aux})$.

The full Lemmas and proofs can be found in Appendix D.2.

3.2   Main Assumption

Assumption 31. *Let $\lambda \in \mathbb{N}$ be the security parameter, let $n, q, m \in \text{poly}(\lambda)$ be integers and let χ_e, χ_s be probability distributions over $\mathbb{Z}_q$. Consider the following experiment:*

1. *Sample a matrix in $\mathbb{Z}_q^{n \times m}$ with a trapdoor:*

$$(\mathbf{A}, \mathbf{A}^{\text{TD}}) \leftarrow \text{TrapGen}(1^n, q, m) .$$

2. *Sample the following terms from arbitrary distributions that are possibly correlated to each other and to $\mathbf{A}, \mathbf{A}^{\text{TD}}$:*
   - *Auxiliary information $\text{aux} \in \{0,1\}^{\text{poly}(\lambda)}$.*
   - *A target matrix $\mathbf{T} \in \mathbb{Z}_q^{n \times m}$.*
   - *A collection of prefix matrices $\mathcal{S} \subseteq \mathbb{Z}_q^{n \times n}$ (possibly of exponential size).*
   - *A collection of additional public matrices $\mathcal{B} \subseteq \mathbb{Z}_q^{n \times m}$ (possibly of exponential size).*
3. *Sample*

$$\mathbf{K} \leftarrow \mathbf{A}^{\text{TD}}(\mathbf{T}) .$$

Then

$$\text{LWE}\left[\mathcal{B} \cup \{\mathbf{SA}\}_{\mathbf{S} \in \mathcal{S}} , \ (\mathbf{K}, \text{aux})\right] \preccurlyeq$$
$$\text{LWE}\left[\mathcal{B} \cup \{\mathbf{SA}, \mathbf{ST}\}_{\mathbf{S} \in \mathcal{S}} , \ \text{aux}\right] + \text{negl}(\lambda) .$$

4 Candidate Witness Encryption

The definition of witness encryption can be found in Appendix E.1.

4.1 Encodings of Matrix Branching Programs

Before proceeding to the full construction we define algorithms that create a collection of matrices and trapdoor-samples according to the nodes and edges respectively of a matrix branching program.

- EncodeEdge $\left(\mathbf{A}, \mathbf{A}^{\mathsf{TD}}, \mathbf{S}, \mathbf{A}'\right)$ takes as input a source matrix $\mathbf{A} \in \mathbb{Z}_q^{n \times m}$ along with its trapdoor $\mathbf{A}^{\mathsf{TD}}$, a secret $\mathbf{S} \in \mathbb{Z}_q^{n \times n}$ and a target matrix $\mathbf{A}' \in \mathbb{Z}_q^{n \times m}$. It computes and outputs

$$\mathbf{K} \leftarrow \mathbf{A}^{\mathsf{TD}} \left(\mathbf{S} \mathbf{A}'\right) .$$

We sometimes use the notations

$$\mathbf{K}[\mathsf{Source}] := \mathbf{A}, \qquad \mathbf{K}[\mathsf{Target}] := \mathbf{S} \mathbf{A}' .$$

- EncodeMatrix $\left(\mathbf{M}, \{\mathbf{A}_i, \mathbf{A}_i^{\mathsf{TD}}\}_{i \in [w]}, \mathbf{S}, \{\mathbf{A}_i'\}_{i \in [w]}\right)$ takes as input an evaluation matrix $\mathbf{M} \in \{0,1\}^{w \times w}$, a collection of source matrices $\{\mathbf{A}_i \in \mathbb{Z}_q^{n \times m}\}_{i \in [w]}$ along with their trapdoors $\{\mathbf{A}_i^{\mathsf{TD}} \in \mathbb{Z}_q^{n \times m}\}_{i \in [w]}$, a secret $\mathbf{S} \in \mathbb{Z}_q^{n \times n}$ and a collection of target matrices $\{\mathbf{A}_i' \in \mathbb{Z}_q^{n \times m}\}_{i \in [w]}$. It computes and outputs

$$\mathcal{K} = \left\{\mathbf{K}^{i,i'} \leftarrow \mathsf{EncodeEdge}\left(\mathbf{A}_i, \mathbf{A}_i^{\mathsf{TD}}, \mathbf{S}, \mathbf{A}_i'\right) \; : \; \mathbf{M}[i, i'] = 1\right\}_{i \in [w], i' \in [w]}$$

where $\mathbf{M}[i, i']$ denote the entry of $\mathbf{M}$ in the i'th row and i''th column.
- EncodeBP$_{\chi_S}$ $\left(\{\mathbf{M}_{j,b}\}_{j \in [t], b \in \{0,1\}}, \{\mathbf{A}_i, \mathbf{A}_i^{\mathsf{TD}}\}_{i \in [w]}, \{\mathbf{A}_i'\}_{i \in [w]}\right)$ is defined with respect to a distribution of secrets χ_S. It takes as input a collection of evaluation matrices $\{\mathbf{M}_{j,b} \in \{0,1\}^{w \times w}\}_{j \in [t], b \in \{0,1\}}$, a collection of source matrices $\{\mathbf{A}_i \in \mathbb{Z}_q^{n \times m}\}_{i \in [w]}$ along with their trapdoors $\{\mathbf{A}_i^{\mathsf{TD}}\}_{i \in [w]}$ and a collection of target matrices $\{\mathbf{A}_i' \in \mathbb{Z}_q^{n \times m}\}_{i \in [w]}$. It works as follows:
  1. For $i \in [w]$ denote $\left(\mathbf{A}_{i,1}, \mathbf{A}_{i,1}^{\mathsf{TD}}\right) := \left(\mathbf{A}_i, \mathbf{A}_i^{\mathsf{TD}}\right)$ and $\mathbf{A}_{i,t+1} := \mathbf{A}_i'$.
  2. For $j = 2, \ldots, t$ and $i \in [w]$ sample a matrix with a trapdoor

$$\left(\mathbf{A}_{i,j}, \mathbf{A}_{i,j}^{\mathsf{TD}}\right) \xleftarrow{\$} \mathsf{TrapGen}(1^n, q, m) .$$

  3. For $j \in [t]$ and $b \in \{0,1\}$ sample a secret matrix $\mathbf{S}_{j,b} \leftarrow \chi_S^{n \times n}$ and compute

$$\mathcal{K}_{j,b} \leftarrow \mathsf{EncodeMatrix}\left(\mathbf{M}_{j,b}, \{\mathbf{A}_{j,i}, \mathbf{A}_{j,i}^{\mathsf{TD}}\}_{i \in [w]}, \mathbf{S}_{j,b}, \{\mathbf{A}_{j+1,i}\}_{i \in [w]}\right) .$$

  4. Output $\{\mathcal{K}_{j,b}\}_{j \in [t], b \in \{0,1\}}$.

4.2   The Construction

Construction 4

Fix the parameters $n, m, q, \tau, B' \in \mathbb{N}$ *and the distributions* $\chi_e, \chi_s, \chi_S, \chi_E$ *as will be described later.*

- Enc$(1^\lambda, f, \mu)$:
    1. *Let*
    $$BP = \left(\ell, w, t, \rho, \mathbf{v}_{\text{start}}, \{\mathbf{M}_{i,b}\}_{i \in [t], b \in \{0,1\}}, F \right)$$

    be a BP *with resiliency to corrupted inputs that computes* f.
    2. *For* $i \in [w]$ *sample a matrix with a trapdoor*

    $$\left(\mathbf{A}_{i,1}, \mathbf{A}_{i,1}^{\text{TD}} \right) \overset{\$}{\leftarrow} \text{TrapGen}(1^n, q, m) .$$

    3. *Perform a secret sharing for the share* $\mathbf{0}^{n \times m}$ *according to* F:

    $$\text{Share}(F) \rightarrow (\mathbf{A}_{1,t+1}, \ldots, \mathbf{A}_{w,t+1})$$

    where $\mathbf{A}_{i,t+1} \in \mathbb{Z}_q^{n \times m}$ *for* $i \in [w]$.
    4. *Encode* BP *with the source matrices* $\{\mathbf{A}_{i,1}\}_i$ *and target matrices* $\{\mathbf{A}_{i,t+1}\}_i$:

    $$\{\mathcal{K}_{j,b}\}_{j \in [t], b \in \{0,1\}} \leftarrow \text{EncodeBP}_{\chi_S} \left(\{\mathbf{M}_{j,b}\}_{j \in [t], b \in \{0,1\}}, \{\mathbf{A}_{i,1}, \mathbf{A}_{i,1}^{\text{TD}}\}_{i \in [w]}, \{\mathbf{A}_{i,t+1}\}_{i \in [w]} \right) .$$

    5. *Let* $I_{start} \subseteq [w]$ *denote the indices in which the* i*'th bit of* $\mathbf{v}_{start}$ *is* 1. *That is,*
    $$I_{start} := \{i \ : \ \mathbf{v}_{start}[i] = 1\}_{i \in [w]}$$

    (where $\mathbf{v}_{start}[i]$ *denotes the* i*'th bit of* $\mathbf{v}_{start}$).
      - *If* $\mu = 1$ *then sample a secret vector* $\mathbf{s} \leftarrow \chi_s^n$ *and for* $i \in I_{start}$ *sample an error vector* $\mathbf{e}_i \leftarrow \chi_e^m$, *and compute*

        $$\mathsf{ct}_i := \mathbf{s}\mathbf{A}_{i,1} + \mathbf{e}_i .$$

      - *If* $\mu = 0$ *then for* $i \in I_{start}$ *sample*

        $$\mathsf{ct}_i \overset{\$}{\leftarrow} \mathbb{Z}_q^m .$$

    6. *Output* $\mathsf{ct} := \left(\{\mathsf{ct}_i\}_{i \in I_{start}}, BP, \{\mathcal{K}_{j,b}\}_{j \in [t], b \in \{0,1\}} \right)$.
- Dec(ct, x): *Parse*

$$\mathsf{ct} = \left(\{\mathsf{ct}_i\}_{i \in I_{start}}, BP, \{\mathcal{K}_{j,b}\}_{j \in [t], b \in \{0,1\}} \right) .$$

For every $i \notin I_{start}$ *denote* $\mathsf{ct}_i = \mathbf{0}^m$. *Consider the vector*

$$[\mathsf{ct}_1 | \ldots | \mathsf{ct}_w] \in \{\mathbb{Z}_q^m\}^w .$$

For every $j \in [t]$ *and* $b \in \{0,1\}$ *parse*

$$\mathcal{K}_{j,b} = \left\{ \mathbf{K}_{j,b}^{i,i'} \ : \ \mathbf{M}_{j,b}[i,i'] = 1 \right\}_{i \in [w], i' \in [w]}$$

and define the blocks matrix $\mathbf{K}_{j,b} \in \{\mathbb{Z}_q^{m \times m}\}^{w \times w}$ where for $i, i' \in [w]$, the block in the i th row and i' th column of $\mathbf{K}_{j,b}$ is $\mathbf{0}^{m \times m}$ if $\mathbf{M}_{j,b}[i, i'] = 0$ and otherwise it is $\mathbf{K}_{j,b}^{i,i'}$:

$$\mathbf{K}_{j,b} := \mathbf{M}_{j,b} \otimes \begin{bmatrix} \mathbf{K}_{j,b}^{1,1} & \cdots & \mathbf{K}_{j,b}^{1,w} \\ \cdots & \ddots & \cdots \\ \mathbf{K}_{j,b}^{w,1} & \cdots & \mathbf{K}_{j,b}^{w,w} \end{bmatrix}.$$

Compute

$$[\mathrm{ct}_1' | \ldots | \mathrm{ct}_w'] := [\mathrm{ct}_1 | \ldots | \mathrm{ct}_w] \prod_{j=1}^{t} \mathbf{K}_{j, x_{\rho(j)}}$$

and

$$\mathbf{v}_x := \mathbf{v}_{start}^T \cdot \prod_{j=1}^{t} \mathbf{M}_{j, x_{\rho(j)}}.$$

Let $I_x \subseteq [w]$ be the indices in which the i'th bit of $\mathbf{v}_x$ is 1, i.e.

$$I_x := \{i \ : \ \mathbf{v}_x[i] = 1\}_{i \in [w]}.$$

Compute

$$\mathrm{ct}' := \sum_{i \in I_x} \mathrm{ct}_i'$$

and output 1 iff $\|\mathrm{ct}'\|_\infty \leq B'$.

The correctness analysis can be found in Appendix E.2.

4.3 Security

Notations. The following notations will be used throughout the proof.

- For every $j = 0, \ldots, t$ and $z \in \{0, 1\}^j$ let $\mathbf{v}_z \in \{0, 1\}^w$ denote the state vector of BP after j steps when it is executed with the evaluation sequence z, i.e.

$$\mathbf{v}_z := \mathbf{v}_{start}^T \prod_{j'=1}^{j} \mathbf{M}_{j', z_{j'}}.$$

For $i \in [w]$ let $\mathbf{v}_z[i] \in \{0, 1\}$ denote the i'th bit of $\mathbf{v}_z$.

Consider the witness encryption security experiment and let $\{\mathbf{S}_{j,b}\}_{b \in \{0,1\}, j \in [t]}$ and $\{\mathbf{A}_{i,j}\}_{i \in [w], j \in [t+1]}$ be the matrices that are sampled during Enc.

- For every $j = 0, \ldots, t$ and $z \in \{0, 1\}^j$ denote

$$\mathbf{S}_z := \mathbf{I} \cdot \prod_{j'=1}^{j} \mathbf{S}_{j', z_{j'}}.$$

– For $j \in [t+1]$ define the collection:

$$\mathcal{B}^j := \{\mathbf{S}_z \mathbf{A}_{i,j} \; : \; \mathbf{v}_z[i] = 1\}_{i \in [w], z \in \{0,1\}^{j-1}} \; . \tag{1}$$

Intuitively, $\mathcal{B}^j$ consists of all of the possible states of the BP after $j-1$ evaluation steps, where $\mathbf{A}_{i,j}$ corresponds to an active BP node in the jth level and $\mathbf{S}_z$ corresponds to the evaluation sequence $z \in \{0,1\}^{j-1}$ that lead to this node.

– For $j = 1, \ldots, t$ denote $\mathsf{aux}^j := \{\mathcal{K}_{j,0}, \mathcal{K}_{j,1}\}$.

Proof Overview. Consider the security experiment and let $\mathsf{ct} = (\{\mathsf{ct}_i\}_{i \in I_{start}}, \mathsf{BP}, \{\mathcal{K}_{j,b}\}_{j \in [t], b \in \{0,1\}})$ be the challenge ciphertext with respect to a secret message $\mu \in \{0,1\}$. Recall that if $\mu = 1$ then $\{\mathsf{ct}_i\}_{i \in I_{start}}$ are of the form $\{\mathbf{sA}_{i,1} + \mathbf{e}_i\}_{i \in I_{start}}$ and if $\mu = 0$ then $\{\mathsf{ct}_i\}_{i \in I_{start}}$ are uniformly random vectors in $\mathbb{Z}_q^m$. Therefore, the security experiment is identical to an LWE challenge with respect to the public matrices $\{\mathbf{A}_{i,1}\}_{i \in I_{start}}$ and auxiliary information $(\mathsf{BP}, \{\mathcal{K}_{j,b}\}_{j \in [t], b \in \{0,1\}})$. Using the notation that was presented above, we note that

$$\mathcal{B}^1 = \{\mathbf{A}_{i,1}\}_{i \in I_{start}}, \qquad \{\mathsf{aux}^j\}_{j \in [t]} = \{\mathcal{K}_{j,b}\}_{j \in [t], b \in \{0,1\}}$$

and therefore we can say that the security experiment is identical to the LWE challenge

$$\mathrm{LWE}_{n,m,q,\chi_s,\chi_e}\left[\mathcal{B}^1, \left(\mathsf{BP}, \{\mathsf{aux}^j\}_{j \in [t]}\right)\right] \; . \tag{2}$$

The security proof goes in two main steps. Fist, we show that under Assumption 31, the challenge in Eq. (2) is at least as hard as $\mathrm{LWE}[\{\mathcal{B}^j\}_{j \in [t+1]}, \mathsf{BP}]$. In the second step we show that $\mathrm{LWE}[\{\mathcal{B}^j\}_{j \in [t+1]}, \mathsf{BP}]$ is at least as hard as standard decisional LWE by showing that $\{\mathcal{B}^j\}_{j \in [t+1]}$ are indistinguishable from uniform random matrices. The latter step requires $O(t \cdot 2^t)$ hybrids since it handles every evaluation sequence $z \in \{0,1\}^t$ individually. We now state the two main lemmas.

Lemma 1 (First Step). *Let $\{\mathcal{B}^j\}_{j \in [t+1]}, \{\mathsf{aux}^j\}_{j \in [t]}$ be as defined above, then under Assumption 31,*

$$\mathrm{LWE}_{n,m,q,\chi_s,\chi_e}\left[\mathcal{B}^1, \left(\mathsf{BP}, \{\mathsf{aux}^j\}_{j \in [t]}\right)\right] \preccurlyeq$$
$$\mathrm{LWE}_{n,m,q,\chi_s,\chi_e}\left[\{\mathcal{B}^j\}_{j \in [t+1]}, \mathsf{BP}\right] + \mathrm{negl}(\lambda) \; .$$

Lemma 2 (Second Step). *Let $\{\mathcal{B}^j\}_{j \in [t+1]}$ be as defined above and let $\mathcal{U}$ be a collection of uniformly random matrices in $\mathbb{Z}_q^{n \times m}$ such that $|\mathcal{U}| = |\{\mathcal{B}^j\}_{j \in [t+1]}|$, then under the standard decisional LWE assumption, if $f(x) = 0$ for all $x \in \{0,1\}^\ell$ then*

$$\mathrm{LWE}_{n,m,q,\chi_s,\chi_e}\left[\{\mathcal{B}^j\}_{j \in [t+1]}, \mathsf{BP}\right] \preccurlyeq$$
$$\mathrm{LWE}_{n,m,q,\chi_s,\chi_e}\left[\mathcal{U}, \mathsf{BP}\right] + 2^t \cdot \mathrm{negl}(\lambda) \; .$$

This pair of Lemmas imply the security of the scheme under standard decisional LWE:

Corollary 1 (Security of Construction 4). *Under Assumption 31 and the standard decisional LWE assumption, for any sufficiently large* λ, *for any* PPT *adversary* A *there is a negligible function* $\mathrm{negl}(\cdot)$ *such that for any* $f \in \mathcal{F}$ *where* $f : \{0,1\}^\ell \to \{0,1\}$, *if* $f(x) = 0$ *for all* $x \in \{0,1\}^\ell$ *then*

$$\left| Pr\left[A\left(\mathsf{Enc}(1^\lambda, f, 0)\right) = 1\right] - Pr\left[A\left(\mathsf{Enc}(1^\lambda, f, 1)\right) = 1\right]\right| \leq 2^t \cdot \mathrm{negl}(\lambda) .$$

In the full version of this paper we prove Lemmas 1 and 2.

References

[ABB10]   Agrawal, S., Boneh, D., Boyen, X.: Lattice basis delegation in fixed dimension and shorter-ciphertext hierarchical IBE. In: Rabin, T. (ed.) CRYPTO 2010. LNCS, vol. 6223, pp. 98–115. Springer, Heidelberg (2010). https://doi.org/10.1007/978-3-642-14623-7_6

[ACPS09] Applebaum, B., Cash, D., Peikert, C., Sahai, A.: Fast cryptographic primitives and circular-secure encryption based on hard learning problems. In: Halevi, S. (ed.) CRYPTO 2009. LNCS, vol. 5677, pp. 595–618. Springer, Heidelberg (2009). https://doi.org/10.1007/978-3-642-03356-8_35

[Agr19]   Agrawal, S.: Indistinguishability obfuscation without multilinear maps: new methods for bootstrapping and instantiation. In: Ishai, Y., Rijmen, V. (eds.) EUROCRYPT 2019. LNCS, vol. 11476, pp. 191–225. Springer, Cham (2019). https://doi.org/10.1007/978-3-030-17653-2_7

[AJL+19] Ananth, P., Jain, A., Lin, H., Matt, C., Sahai, A.: Indistinguishability obfuscation without multilinear maps: new paradigms via low degree weak pseudorandomness and security amplification. In: Boldyreva, A., Micciancio, D. (eds.) CRYPTO 2019, LNCS, vol. 11694, pp. 284–332. Springer, Cham (2019). https://doi.org/10.1007/978-3-030-26954-8_10

[Ajt96]   Ajtai, M.: Generating hard instances of lattice problems (extended abstract). In: STOC, pp. 99–108 (1996)

[Bar89]   Barrington, D.A.: Bounded-width polynomial-size branching programs recognize exactly those languages in NC1. J. Comput. Syst. Sci. **38**(1), 150–164 (1989)

[BDGM20] Brakerski, Z., Döttling, N., Garg, S., Malavolta, G.: Candidate iO from homomorphic encryption schemes. In: Canteaut, A., Ishai, Y. (eds.) EUROCRYPT 2020. LNCS, vol. 12105, pp. 79–109. Springer, Cham (2020). https://doi.org/10.1007/978-3-030-45721-1_4

[BL88]   Benaloh, J., Leichter, J.: Generalized secret sharing and monotone functions. In: Goldwasser, S. (ed.) CRYPTO 1988. LNCS, vol. 403, pp. 27–35. Springer, New York (1990). https://doi.org/10.1007/0-387-34799-2_3

[BLP+13] Brakerski, Z., Langlois, A., Peikert, C., Regev, O., Stehlé, D.: Classical hardness of learning with errors. In: Boneh, D., Roughgarden, T., Feigenbaum, J. (eds.) Symposium on Theory of Computing Conference, STOC 2013, Palo Alto, CA, USA, 1–4 June 2013, pp. 575–584. ACM (2013)

[BV16]   Brakerski, Z., Vaikuntanathan, V.: Circuit-ABE from LWE: unbounded attributes and semi-adaptive security. In: Robshaw, M., Katz, J. (eds.) CRYPTO 2016. LNCS, vol. 9816, pp. 363–384. Springer, Heidelberg (2016). https://doi.org/10.1007/978-3-662-53015-3_13

[CHKP12] Cash, D., Hofheinz, D., Kiltz, E., Peikert, C.: Bonsai trees, or how to delegate a lattice basis. J. Cryptol. **25**(4), 601–639 (2012)

[CHVW19] Chen, Y., Hhan, M., Vaikuntanathan, V., Wee, H.: Matrix PRFs: constructions, attacks, and applications to obfuscation. In: Hofheinz, D., Rosen, A. (eds.) TCC 2019. LNCS, vol. 11891, pp. 55–80. Springer, Cham (2019). https://doi.org/10.1007/978-3-030-36030-6_3

[CVW18]   Chen, Y., Vaikuntanathan, V., Wee, H.: GGH15 beyond permutation branching programs: proofs, attacks, and candidates. In: Shacham, H., Boldyreva, A. (eds.) CRYPTO 2018. LNCS, vol. 10992, pp. 577–607. Springer, Cham (2018). https://doi.org/10.1007/978-3-319-96881-0_20

[GGH15]   Gentry, C., Gorbunov, S., Halevi, S.: Graph-induced multilinear maps from lattices. In: Dodis, Y., Nielsen, J.B. (eds.) TCC 2015. LNCS, vol. 9015, pp. 498–527. Springer, Heidelberg (2015). https://doi.org/10.1007/978-3-662-46497-7_20

[GGSW13] Garg, S., Gentry, C., Sahai, A., Waters, B.: Witness encryption and its applications. In: STOC (2013)

[GJLS21] Gay, R., Jain, A., Lin, H., Sahai, A.: Indistinguishability obfuscation from simple-to-state hard problems: new assumptions, new techniques, and simplification. In: Canteaut, A., Standaert, F.-X. (eds.) EUROCRYPT 2021. LNCS, vol. 12698, pp. 97–126. Springer, Cham (2021). https://doi.org/10.1007/978-3-030-77883-5_4

[GLW14]   Gentry, C., Lewko, A., Waters, B.: Witness encryption from instance independent assumptions. In: Garay, J.A., Gennaro, R. (eds.) CRYPTO 2014. LNCS, vol. 8616, pp. 426–443. Springer, Heidelberg (2014). https://doi.org/10.1007/978-3-662-44371-2_24

[GPV08]   Gentry, C., Peikert, C., Vaikuntanathan, V.: Trapdoors for hard lattices and new cryptographic constructions. In: Dwork, C. (ed.) Proceedings of the 40th Annual ACM Symposium on Theory of Computing, Victoria, British Columbia, Canada, 17–20 May 2008, pp. 197–206. ACM (2008)

[JLMS19] Jain, A., Lin, H., Matt, C., Sahai, A.: How to leverage hardness of constant-degree expanding polynomials over $\mathbb{R}$ to build $i\mathcal{O}$. In: Ishai, Y., Rijmen, V. (eds.) EUROCRYPT 2019. LNCS, vol. 11476, pp. 251–281. Springer, Cham (2019). https://doi.org/10.1007/978-3-030-17653-2_9

[JLS21]   Jain, A., Lin, H., Sahai, A.: Indistinguishability obfuscation from well-founded assumptions. In: Khuller, S., Williams, V.V. (eds.) 53rd Annual ACM SIGACT Symposium on Theory of Computing, Virtual Event, STOC 2021, Italy, 21–25 June 2021, pp. 60–73. ACM (2021)

[Lin16]   Lin, H.: Indistinguishability obfuscation from constant-degree graded encoding schemes. IACR Cryptology ePrint Archive 2016/257 (2016)

[Lin17]   Lin, H.: Indistinguishability obfuscation from SXDH on 5-linear maps and locality-5 PRGs. In: Katz, J., Shacham, H. (eds.) CRYPTO 2017. LNCS, vol. 10401, pp. 599–629. Springer, Cham (2017). https://doi.org/10.1007/978-3-319-63688-7_20

[LT17]   Lin, H., Tessaro, S.: Indistinguishability obfuscation from trilinear maps and block-wise local PRGs. In: Katz, J., Shacham, H. (eds.) CRYPTO 2017. LNCS, vol. 10401, pp. 630–660. Springer, Cham (2017). https://doi.org/10.1007/978-3-319-63688-7_21

[LV16] Lin, H., Vaikuntanathan, V.: Indistinguishability obfuscation from DDH-like assumptions on constant-degree graded encodings. In: Dinur, I. (ed.) IEEE 57th Annual Symposium on Foundations of Computer Science, FOCS 2016, Hyatt Regency, New Brunswick, New Jersey, USA, 9–11 October 2016, pp. 11–20. IEEE Computer Society (2016)

[MM11] Micciancio, D., Mol, P.: Pseudorandom knapsacks and the sample complexity of LWE search-to-decision reductions. In: Rogaway, P. (ed.) CRYPTO 2011. LNCS, vol. 6841, pp. 465–484. Springer, Heidelberg (2011). https://doi.org/10.1007/978-3-642-22792-9_26

[MP12] Micciancio, D., Peikert, C.: Trapdoors for lattices: simpler, tighter, faster, smaller. In: Pointcheval, D., Johansson, T. (eds.) EUROCRYPT 2012. LNCS, vol. 7237, pp. 700–718. Springer, Heidelberg (2012). https://doi.org/10.1007/978-3-642-29011-4_41

[Pei09] Peikert, C.: Public-key cryptosystems from the worst-case shortest vector problem: extended abstract. In: Proceedings of the 41st Annual ACM Symposium on Theory of Computing, STOC 2009, Bethesda, MD, USA, 31 May −2 June 2009, pp. 333–342 (2009)

[Reg05] Regev, O.: On lattices, learning with errors, random linear codes, and cryptography. In: Proceedings of the 37th Annual ACM Symposium on Theory of Computing, Baltimore, MD, USA, 22–24 May 2005, pp. 84–93 (2005)

[WW21] Wee, H., Wichs, D.: Candidate obfuscation via oblivious LWE sampling. In: Canteaut, A., Standaert, F.-X. (eds.) EUROCRYPT 2021. LNCS, vol. 12698, pp. 127–156. Springer, Cham (2021). https://doi.org/10.1007/978-3-030-77883-5_5

[WZ17] Wichs, D., Zirdelis, G.: Obfuscating compute-and-compare programs under LWE. In: Umans, C. (ed.) 58th IEEE Annual Symposium on Foundations of Computer Science, FOCS 2017, Berkeley, CA, USA, 15–17 October 2017, pp. 600–611. IEEE Computer Society (2017)

Securing Approximate Homomorphic Encryption Using Differential Privacy

Baiyu Li⬛, Daniele Micciancio⬛, Mark Schultz-Wu$^{(\boxtimes)}$⬛, and Jessica Sorrell⬛

University of California, San Diego, USA
{baiyu,daniele,mdschultz,jlsorrel}@eng.ucsd.edu

Abstract. Recent work of Li and Micciancio (Eurocrypt 2021) has shown that the traditional formulation of *indistinguishability under chosen plaintext attack* (IND-CPA) is not adequate to capture the security of *approximate* homomorphic encryption against passive adversaries, and identified a stronger IND-CPA^D security definition (IND-CPA *with decryption oracles*) as the appropriate security target for approximate encryption schemes. We show how to transform any approximate homomorphic encryption scheme achieving the weak IND-CPA security definition, into one which is provably IND-CPA^D secure, offering strong guarantees against realistic passive attacks. The method works by postprocessing the output of the decryption function with a mechanism satisfying an appropriate notion of *differential privacy (DP)*, adding an amount of noise tailored to the worst-case error growth of the homomorphic computation.

We apply these results to the approximate homomorphic encryption scheme of Cheon, Kim, Kim, and Song (CKKS, Asiacrypt 2017), proving that adding Gaussian noise to the output of CKKS decryption suffices to achieve IND-CPA^D security. We precisely quantify how much Gaussian noise must be added by proving nearly matching upper and lower bounds, showing that one cannot hope to significantly reduce the amount of noise added in this post-processing step. As an additional contribution, we present and use a finer grained definition of bit security that distinguishes between a computational security parameter (c) and a statistical one (s). Based on our upper and lower bounds, we propose parameters for the counter-measures recently adopted by open-source libraries implementing CKKS.

Lastly, we investigate the plausible claim that smaller DP noise parameters might suffice to achieve IND-CPA^D-security for schemes supporting more accurate (dynamic, key dependent) estimates of ciphertext noise during decryption. Perhaps surprisingly, we show that this claim is false, and that DP mechanisms with noise parameters tailored to the error present in a given ciphertext, rather than worst-case error, are vulnerable to IND-CPA^D attacks.

Research supported by Global Research Cluster program of Samsung Advanced Institute of Technology and NSF Award 1936703.

Y. Dodis and T. Shrimpton (Eds.): CRYPTO 2022, LNCS 13507, pp. 560–589, 2022
https://doi.org/10.1007/978-3-031-15802-5_20

1   Introduction

Fully homomorphic encryption (FHE) on *approximate* numbers, proposed by Cheon, Kim, Kim and Song in [8], has attracted much attention in the past few years as a method to improve the efficiency of computing on encrypted data in a wide range of applications (like privacy preserving machine learning) where approximate results are acceptable [5–7,9,10,14,25]. The CKKS scheme [8], just like most other (homomorphic) encryption schemes based on lattices, can be proved to satisfy the well established security notion of *indistinguishability under chosen plaintext attack* (IND-CPA) [13] under widely accepted complexity assumptions, like the average-case hardness of the *Learning With Errors (LWE)* problem or the worst-case complexity of computational problems on (algebraic) point lattices [20,26,27,31].

Recently Li and Micciancio [19] have shown that the traditional formulation of IND-CPA security is inadequate to capture security of approximate encryption against passive attacks, and demonstrated that the CKKS scheme is susceptible to a very efficient total key recovery attack, mounted by a passive adversary. The problem highlighted in [19] is not with the IND-CPA security definition per se, which remains a good and well accepted definition for exact FHE schemes, but with the specifics of approximate decryption, which may inadvertently leak information about the secret key even when used by honest parties. The work [19] also proposes a new, enhanced formulation of IND-CPA security (called IND-CPA^D, or IND-CPA *with decryption oracles*), which properly captures the capabilities of a passive attacker against an *approximate* FHE scheme, and is equivalent to the standard notion of IND-CPA security for encryption schemes with exact decryption. The work [19] also suggested some practical countermeasures to avoid their attack, and all major open source libraries implementing CKKS (e.g., [15,18,24,32]) included similar countermeasures shortly after the results in [19] were made public. However, neither [19] nor any of these libraries present a solution that provably achieves the IND-CPA^D security definition proposed in [19], leaving it as an open problem.

1.1   Our Results and Techniques

In this work we show how to achieve IND-CPA^D security in a provable way. More specifically, we present a general technique to transform any approximate FHE scheme satisfying the (weak) IND-CPA security notion into one achieving the strong IND-CPA^D security definition proposed in [19]. We then demonstrate how to apply the technique to the specific case of the CKKS scheme, which is the most prominent example of approximate homomorphic encryption.

Our technique works by combining a given (approximate) FHE scheme with another fundamental tool from the cryptographers' toolbox: differential privacy. The construction is very simple and intuitive: given an approximate FHE scheme (like CKKS), we modify the decryption function by post-processing its output (the decrypted message) with a properly chosen differentially private mechanism. Using differential privacy to limit the key leakage of approximate decryption is a fairly natural idea, and it is essentially the intuition behind the practical countermeasures proposed in [19] and implemented by the libraries. But formally analyzing the method and provably achieving IND-CPA$^\mathsf{D}$ security raises a number of technical challenges:

- The Hamming metric, commonly used to define and analyze differentially private mechanisms, is not well suited to the setting of (lattice based) homomorphic encryption.
- Similarly, the Laplace noise commonly used and studied in the standard setting of differential privacy is not a good match for our target application, as it is both associated with the wrong norm (ℓ_1, rather than ℓ_2 or ℓ_∞), and has heavier tails than, e.g., the Gaussian distribution, and so will give worse bounds on the error introduced by post-processing.
- Formally proving the security of our construction requires a careful definition of what it means for an FHE scheme to be *approximate*. Previous works [8,19] simply defined approximate FHE as an encryption scheme which *does not* satisfy the correctness requirement

$$\mathsf{Dec}(\mathsf{Eval}(f, \mathsf{Enc}(m_1), \ldots, \mathsf{Enc}(m_k))) = f(m_1, \ldots, m_k) \tag{1}$$

without imposing any specific limitation on how a scheme may deviate from it.
- Perturbing the output of the decryption function with a differentially private mechanism comes at the cost of lowering the output quality, making the result of the (already approximate) decryption function even less accurate, highlighting the necessity of carefully tuning the amount of noise added.
- The minimal security level considered acceptable by applications in practice typically depends on whether the cryptographic primitive is statistically secure (against computationally unbounded adversaries) or computationally secure (in which case a higher security margin is advisable to anticipate possible algorithmic or implementation improvements in the attacks.) Our application of statistical security tools (differential privacy) to encryption seems to require the instantiation of statistical security with the high security parameters of a computational encryption scheme.

In order to address the above obstacles, we

- provide a general definition of differential privacy, parameterized by an arbitrary norm, and then instantiate it with the Euclidean norm for the case of lattice-based encryption;
- employ a differentially private mechanism (for the Euclidean norm) based on Gaussian noise, which blends well with the probability distributions used in lattice cryptography;
- give formal definitions of *approximate* FHE, which provide precise guarantees on the output quality of the (approximate) decryption function. In fact, we identify two possible definitions, based on what we call *static* and *dynamic* noise estimates, and show that they result in quite different security properties (more on this below);

- use KL-divergence and other probabilistic tools to carefully calibrate the mechanism noise to the output quality, showing that $\Theta(\kappa)$ bits of noise are required to formally achieve κ-bit IND-CPA^D security;
- present and use a finer grained definition of bit-security that distinguishes between a computational security parameter c and a statistical one s, which can be set to a lower value than c (more on this below).

We first elaborate on our definition of *approximate* FHE. Previous works [8,19] did not include a precise definition of what it means for an encryption scheme (or decryption function) to be approximate, because the quality of the approximation (and more generally, the definition of the decryption function itself) does not impact the IND-CPA security of a scheme. This is contrasted with our work, where bounding the approximation quality of the decryption function plays a critical role in our analysis. Generally speaking, an approximate FHE scheme provides a guarantee (upper bound) on how much the output of the decryption function $\mathsf{Dec}(\mathsf{Eval}(f, \mathsf{Enc}(m_1), \ldots, \mathsf{Enc}(m_k)))$ may deviate from the output of the computation $f(m_1, \ldots, m_k)$. We distinguish two types of approximate FHE:

- Approximate FHE with *static* noise estimates, where this bound can be publicly computed as a function of the homomorphic computation f performed on the input ciphertexts. This is, for example, the type of noise estimates used in the HElib library [15].
- Approximate FHE with *dynamic* noise estimates, where this bound is computed by the decryption function Dec using also the input ciphertext and the secret key. An ingenious method for dynamic noise estimation has been proposed by the PALISADE library [24].

Most of our results, like our general framework based on differential privacy and a provably IND-CPA^D secure variant of the CKKS approximate FHE scheme, are in the setting of static noise estimates. In this setting, we are able to establish the security of our generic construction (Theorem 2), and provide precise security guarantees for the modified approximate FHE scheme, showing that if the original scheme is κ-bit IND-CPA secure, then combining it with an appropriate differentially private mechanism achieves $\kappa - 8$ bits of security against the stronger IND-CPA^D security definition, losing only 8 bits of security (Theorem 2). The amount of noise required to achieve this result is quantified by the notion of ρ-KLDP (Kullback-Leibler Differential Privacy), for a sufficiently small value of ρ. Our analysis is nearly tight for the CKKS scheme, in the sense that if one uses a substantially smaller amount of noise, we are able to exhibit an attack that breaks IND-CPA^D security (Theorem 4).

When setting the parameters of a cryptosystem (or other computational cryptographic primitive), it is common to use a very conservative security level to anticipate reductions in both the hardware and operational cost of mounting an attack. A common level of security considered adequate for most applications is $c = 128$ bits of security. When applying a statistical technique (like differential privacy) to a computational primitive, this seems to require instantiating the statistical technique with the same (high) level of bit security. We propose a finer grained definition of bit-security (Definition 19) parameterized by both a *computational* parameter c and *statistical* parameter s. Technically, we say that a primitive achieves (c, s)-security if for any adversary A, either A has statistical advantage bounded by 2^{-s} (regardless of A's running time or computational assumptions), or the running time of the attack is at least 2^c times larger than the advantage achieved. Intuitively, this definition captures the notion that if c bits of security are acceptable for a computational cryptographic primitive, and s bits of security are enough for an unconditionally secure cryptographic primitive (independent of any computational assumption), then (c, s)-security is also adequate.

Still, (c, s)-security is technically easier to achieve than both c-bit computational security, and s-bit statistical security, and allows us to decrease the cost of our countermeasure (Theorem 2) by lowering the required amount of DP noise by $(c - s)/2$ bits. The standard notion of bit-security corresponds to setting $s = c$, which gives no improvement. But for typical parameter settings (e.g., $c = 128$ and $s = 64$), the refined definition allows to reduce the required amount of noise from ≈ 75 bits to ≈ 45, a substantial saving of ≈ 30 bits. As even more conservative choices, such as $s = 80$ or $s = 100$, yield savings of ≈ 24 or ≈ 14 bits of noise, we expect this refined notion of security to be concretely useful when securing CKKS against the attacks of [19].

All this is for static noise estimates. Dynamic estimates are interesting because they can provide stronger (probabilistic) guarantees on the output quality of the decryption function. Interestingly, we show that the same intuitive idea of combining approximate FHE with differential privacy, while calibrating the DP noise via dynamic error estimates, does not result in a secure scheme. In particular, we describe attacks to the IND-CPA^{D} security of CKKS using dynamic noise estimates (Theorem 6), and complete key recovery attacks for other (artificially constructed) IND-CPA-secure FHE schemes (Theorem 7).

1.2 Paper Outline

The rest of the paper is organized as follows. In Sect. 2 we present background definitions and results from cryptography, fully homomorphic encryption, and probability theory. In Sect. 3 we present our general framework to secure approximate FHE using differential privacy, for the setting of *static* error estimation. In Sect. 4 we apply the framework to the CKKS scheme, and develop our relaxed notion of bit security. In Sect. 5 we present our (negative) results for approximate FHE with *dynamic* error estimation. Section 6 concludes with a summary of our results and open problems.

2 Preliminaries

We recall some notions and known results.

2.1   Probability

We abbreviate a list of random variables $(\mathcal{X}_1, \ldots, \mathcal{X}_n)$ as $(\mathcal{X}_i)_i$. For such a list, we write $\mathcal{X}_{<i}$ to denote the prefix $(\mathcal{X}_1, \ldots, \mathcal{X}_{i-1})$. A probability ensemble $(\mathcal{P}_\theta)_\theta$ is a family of probability distributions parameterized by a variable θ, which may be a string or a vector.

Throughout this work we will use *divergences* to measure how far probability distributions are from eachother.

Definition 1. *A $\mathbb{R}$-valued function $\delta(\cdot||\cdot)$ on pairs of discrete distributions is called a* divergence *if it satisfies*

- Non-negativity: *For any discrete distributions $\mathcal{P}, \mathcal{Q}$, $\delta(\mathcal{P}||\mathcal{Q}) \geq 0$.*
- Identity of Discernibles: *If $\delta(\mathcal{P}||\mathcal{Q}) = 0$, then $\mathcal{P} = \mathcal{Q}$.*

Notably, divergences need not be symmetric, nor satisfy triangle inequality, although specific divergences will typically satisfy some additional properties than solely the above two.

Definition 2 (Statistical Distance). *Let $\mathcal{P}, \mathcal{Q}$ be discrete distributions with common support X. The* Statistical Distance *(or* Total Variation Distance*) between $\mathcal{P}$ and $\mathcal{Q}$ is $\Delta(\mathcal{P}, \mathcal{Q}) = \frac{1}{2} \sum_{x \in X} |\mathcal{P}(x) - \mathcal{Q}(x)|$.*

The statistical distance is a divergence that is symmetric and satisfies triangle inequality, *i.e.* is a metric.

Definition 3 (KL Divergence). *Let $\mathcal{P}, \mathcal{Q}$ be discrete distributions with common support X. The* Kullback-Leibler Divergence *between $\mathcal{P}$ and $\mathcal{Q}$ is $D(\mathcal{P}||\mathcal{Q}) := \sum_{x \in \mathcal{X}} \Pr[\mathcal{P} = x] \ln\left(\frac{\Pr[\mathcal{P}=x]}{\Pr[\mathcal{Q}=x]}\right)$.*

Lemma 1 (Properties of the KL Divergence, Theorem 2.2 of [29]). *The KL divergence satisfies*

1. Sub-Additivity for Joint Distributions: *If $(\mathcal{X}_0, \mathcal{X}_1)$ and $(\mathcal{Y}_0, \mathcal{Y}_1)$ are pairs of (possibly dependent) random variables, then*

$$D((\mathcal{X}_0, \mathcal{X}_1)||(\mathcal{Y}_0, \mathcal{Y}_1)) \leq \mathbb{E}_{x \sim \mathcal{X}_0}[D((\mathcal{X}_1 \mid x)||(\mathcal{Y}_1 \mid x))] + D(\mathcal{X}_0||\mathcal{Y}_0)$$
$$\leq \max_x D((\mathcal{X}_1 \mid x)||(\mathcal{Y}_1 \mid x)) + D(\mathcal{X}_0||\mathcal{X}_1),$$

2. Data Processing Inequality: *For any (potentially randomized) function f, for any two distributions $\mathcal{P}, \mathcal{Q}$, $D(f(\mathcal{P})||f(\mathcal{Q})) \leq D(\mathcal{P}||\mathcal{Q})$, and*
3. Pinsker's Inequality: *$\Delta(\mathcal{P}, \mathcal{Q}) \leq \sqrt{D(\mathcal{P}||\mathcal{Q})/2}$.*

We introduce the following notation to more compactly bound the divergence between vectors of random variables.

Definition 4. *Let $\mathcal{X} = (\mathcal{X}_i)_{i=1}^n, \mathcal{Y} = (\mathcal{Y}_i)_{i=1}^n$ be two lists of discrete random variables over the support $\prod_{i=1}^n X_i \subseteq \mathbb{R}^n$, and δ any divergence. We define the vector divergence $\hat{\delta}(\mathcal{X}||\mathcal{Y})$ to be the non-negative real vector $(v_1, \ldots, v_n) \in \mathbb{R}_{\geq 0}^n$ with coordinates $v_i = \max_a \delta([\mathcal{X}_i \mid \mathcal{X}_{<i} = a]||[\mathcal{Y}_i \mid \mathcal{Y}_{<i} = a])$.*

In this notation, sub-additivity of the KL divergence (for example) can be written as $D(\mathcal{X}||\mathcal{Y}) \leq \||\widehat{D}(\mathcal{X}||\mathcal{Y})\||_1$. Our lower bound of Sect. 4.3 will require the following bound.

Lemma 2 (Theorem 1.3 [11]). *Let $\sigma_0, \sigma_1 > 0$. Then*

$$\Delta(\mathcal{N}(0, \sigma_0^2), \mathcal{N}(0, \sigma_1^2)) \geq \frac{1}{200} \min \left\{ 1, \frac{|\sigma_0^2 - \sigma_1^2|}{\sigma_0^2} \right\}. \tag{2}$$

2.2 Bit Security

We use the notion of bit security from [22], which we briefly review below.

Definition 5 (Indistinguishability Game). *Let $\{\mathcal{D}_\theta^0\}_\theta$, $\{\mathcal{D}_\theta^1\}_\theta$ be two distribution ensembles. The indistinguishability game is defined as follows: the challenger C chooses $b \leftarrow \mathcal{U}(\{0,1\})$. At any time after that the adversary A may send (adaptively chosen) query strings θ_i to C, and obtain samples $c_i \leftarrow \mathcal{D}_{\theta_i}^b$. The goal of the adversary is to output $b' = b$.*

Definition 6 (Bit Security). *For any adversary A playing an indistinguishability game $\mathcal{G}$, we define its*

- *output probability as $\alpha^A = Pr[A \neq \bot]$, and its*
- *conditional success probability as $\beta^A = Pr[b' = b | A \neq \bot]$,*

where the probabilities are taken over the randomness of the entire indistinguishability game (including the internal randomness of A). We also define A's

- *conditional distinguishing advantage as $\delta^A = 2\beta^A - 1$, and*
- *the advantage of A as $\mathsf{adv}^A = \alpha^A(\delta^A)^2$.*

The bit security of the indistinguishability game is $\min_A \log_2 \frac{T(A)}{\mathsf{adv}^A}$, where $T(A)$ is the running time of A.

As argued in [22], this is the correct way to define bit security for decision problems. Notice quadratic scaling with δ^A, rather than the linear scaling used for search problems. For additional motivation for the quadratic dependency, we note it matches known sample complexity lower bounds for distinguishing distributions that are close in the total variation distance, see Sect. 5.2 of [3].

Lemma 3 (Lemma 2 of [22]). *Let $\mathcal{H}_i$ be k distributions and $\mathcal{G}_{i,j}$ be the indistinguishability game instantiated with $\mathcal{H}_i$ and $\mathcal{H}_j$. Let C be a fixed constant. Let $\epsilon_{i,j} = \max_A \mathsf{adv}^A$ over all adversaries A against $\mathcal{G}_{i,j}$ with $T(A) \leq C$. Then $\epsilon_{1,k} \leq 3k \sum_{i=1}^{k-1} \epsilon_{i,i+1}$.*

The two distributions to be distinguished in a game $\mathcal{G}$ sometimes both post-process samples from some other probability ensemble $\mathcal{P}_\theta$. The following theorem bounds the loss of bit security of $\mathcal{G}$ if we replace $\mathcal{P}$ with another distribution $\mathcal{Q}$.

Theorem 1 (Theorem 8 of [22]). *Let $\mathcal{G}^{\mathcal{P}}$ be an indistinguishability game with black-box access to a probability ensemble $\mathcal{P}_\theta$. If $\mathcal{G}^{\mathcal{P}_\theta}$ is κ-bit secure, and $\max_\theta D(\mathcal{P}_\theta \| \mathcal{Q}_\theta) \leq 2^{-\kappa+1}$, then $\mathcal{G}^{\mathcal{Q}_\theta}$ is $(\kappa - 8)$-bit secure.*

The aforementioned theorem is stated more generally in [22]. Our specialization of it requires that $\delta(\mathcal{P} \| \mathcal{Q}) = \sqrt{D(\mathcal{P} \| \mathcal{Q})/2}$ is what [22] calls a λ-efficient measure, which is implicit in [2, 30].

We will need a few novel bounds on the quantities previously mentioned in this sub-section. These bounds are simplest to describe in terms of the following divergence.

Definition 7 (Bit Security Divergence). *Let $\mathcal{X}, \mathcal{Y}$ be random variables supported on X. The* bit security divergence *between $\mathcal{X}$ and $\mathcal{Y}$ is the quantity*

$$\delta_{\mathsf{BS}}(\mathcal{X}, \mathcal{Y}) = \sup_{S \subseteq X} \frac{\Pr_\mathcal{X}[S] + \Pr_\mathcal{Y}[S]}{2} \Delta \left(\mathcal{X}|S, \mathcal{Y}|S \right)^2,$$

where $\mathcal{X}|S, \mathcal{Y}|S$ are the conditional distributions of $\mathcal{X}, \mathcal{Y}$, conditioned on the event S.

It is straightforward to verify that this is indeed a divergence, and moreover it is symmetric (which is why we write $\delta_{\mathsf{BS}}(\cdot, \cdot)$ rather than $\delta_{\mathsf{BS}}(\cdot \| \cdot)$). It is not a metric, as the $O(k)$ factor in Lemma 3 is known to be tight, which is incompatible with $\delta_{\mathsf{BS}}(\cdot, \cdot)$ satisfying a triangle inequality.

$\delta_{\mathsf{BS}}(\cdot, \cdot)$ captures the advantage of an optimal (potentially computationally unbounded) adversary that aborts on the set S^c, and therefore can be seen as an extension of the standard total variation distance to the framework of [22]. We will need the following novel Pinsker-like bound on this quantity.

Lemma 4. *Let $\mathcal{X}, \mathcal{Y}$ be random variables supported on X. Then $\delta_{\mathsf{BS}}(\mathcal{X}, \mathcal{Y}) \leq D(\mathcal{X} \| \mathcal{Y})/2$.*

We delay the proof of this to the full version of the paper. We can use this to bound the advantage of *computationally unbounded* adversaries in the indistinguishability game.

Lemma 5. *Let $\mathcal{G}$ be the indistinguishability game instantiated with distribution ensembles $\{\mathcal{X}_\theta\}_\theta, \{\mathcal{Y}_\theta\}_\theta$, where $\theta \in \Theta$. Let $q \in \mathbb{N}$. Then, for any (potentially computationally unbounded) adversary A making at most q queries to its oracle, we have that*

$$\mathsf{adv}^A \leq \frac{q}{2} \max_{\theta \in \Theta} D(\mathcal{X}_\theta \| \mathcal{Y}_\theta). \tag{3}$$

Proof. View an (adaptive) adversary as an arbitrary distribution on query-response pairs $\mathcal{X}_{\hat{\theta}} := ((\hat{\theta}_1, \mathcal{X}_{\hat{\theta}_1}), \ldots, (\hat{\theta}_q, \mathcal{X}_{\hat{\theta}_q}))$ (and similarly for $\mathcal{Y}_{\hat{\theta}}$). We then have that

$$\mathsf{adv}^A \leq \delta_{\mathsf{BS}}(\mathcal{X}_{\hat{\theta}}, \mathcal{Y}_{\hat{\theta}}) \leq \frac{1}{2} D(\mathcal{X}_{\hat{\theta}}, \mathcal{Y}_{\hat{\theta}}) \leq \frac{1}{2} \left\| \widehat{D}(\mathcal{X}_{\hat{\theta}}, \mathcal{Y}_{\hat{\theta}}) \right\|_1 \leq \frac{q}{2} \max_{\theta \in \Theta} D(\mathcal{X}_\theta \| \mathcal{Y}_\theta). \tag{4}$$

$\square$

2.3 Fully Homomorphic Encryption

We briefly review definitions related to FHE. For simplicity, we focus on public-key setting. In all our definitions, we denote the security parameter using κ.

Definition 8 (FHE Scheme). *A (public-key) homomorphic encryption scheme with plaintext space $\mathcal{M}$, ciphertext space $\mathcal{C}$, public key space $\mathcal{PK}$, secret-key space $\mathcal{SK}$, and space of evaluatable circuits $\mathcal{L}$ is a tuple of four probabilistic polynomial-time algorithms*

$$\mathsf{KeyGen} : 1^{\mathbb{N}} \to \mathcal{PK} \times \mathcal{SK}$$
$$\mathsf{Enc} : \mathcal{PK} \times \mathcal{M} \to \mathcal{C}$$
$$\mathsf{Dec} : \mathcal{SK} \times \mathcal{C} \to \mathcal{M}$$
$$\mathsf{Eval} : \mathcal{PK} \times \mathcal{L} \times \mathcal{C} \to \mathcal{C}$$

Typically the public key naturally splits into two components, one used by Enc and one used by Eval. This separation is used to minimize the storage requirements of encryption (as the evaluation key is often quite large), and has no impact on security, so for simplicity we model both Enc and Eval as taking as input the same public key.

Standard FHE schemes are expected to satisfy the following notion of correctness.

Definition 9 (Correctness). *An FHE scheme $\Pi = (\mathsf{KeyGen}, \mathsf{Enc}, \mathsf{Dec}, \mathsf{Eval})$ is* correct *for some class of circuits $\mathcal{L}$ if for all $m_1, \ldots, m_k \in \mathcal{M}$, for all $C \in \mathcal{L}$, for all $(\mathsf{pk}, \mathsf{sk}) \leftarrow \mathsf{KeyGen}(1^\kappa)$, we have that*

$$\mathsf{Dec}_{\mathsf{sk}}(\mathsf{Eval}_{\mathsf{pk}}(C, \mathsf{Enc}_{\mathsf{pk}}(m_1), \ldots, \mathsf{Enc}_{\mathsf{pk}}(m_k))) = C(m_1, \ldots, m_k). \tag{5}$$

One can relax the notion of correctness to *statistical* correctness, where the above identity only holds with high probability (over the random coins of Enc and Eval). We will not make a distinction between these two notions.

The work [8] introduced an "approximate" FHE scheme (CKKS), for which Eq. (5) does not hold. The security implications of this relaxation are investigated in [19], as discussed below. However, neither [8] nor [19] provide a formal definition of an "approximate" FHE scheme, and instead simply drop the correctness requirement (5) without any further restriction. This is despite the CKKS scheme satisfying an approximate version of the correctness property of Eq. (5).

The definition of *approximately correct* FHE scheme plays a fundamental role in our work. Informally, an approximately correct FHE scheme allows for meaningful, but inexact, computation on encrypted messages. To formalize the relaxed correctness requirements of an approximately correct FHE scheme, we first define the *ciphertext error*, which specifies the extent to which a homomorphic computation fails to be exact.

Definition 10 (Ciphertext Error). *Let* $\Pi = (\mathsf{KeyGen}, \mathsf{Enc}, \mathsf{Dec}, \mathsf{Eval})$ *be an FHE scheme with message space* $\mathcal{M} \subseteq \widetilde{\mathcal{M}}$, *which is a normed space with norm* $\|\cdot\| : \widetilde{\mathcal{M}} \to \mathbb{R}_{\geq 0}$. *For any ciphertext* ct, *secret key* sk, *and message* m, *the ciphertext error of* $(\mathsf{ct}, m, \mathsf{sk})$ *is defined to be*

$$\mathsf{Error}(\mathsf{ct}, m, \mathsf{sk}) = \|\mathsf{Dec}_{\mathsf{sk}}(\mathsf{ct}) - m\|. \tag{6}$$

Typically, for some circuit $C \in \mathcal{L}$, key pair $(\mathsf{pk}, \mathsf{sk}) \leftarrow \mathsf{KeyGen}(1^\kappa)$, and input values $m_1, \ldots, m_k \in \mathcal{M}$, one is interested in the quantity $\mathsf{Error}(\mathsf{ct}, m, \mathsf{sk})$ for

$$m = C(m_1, \ldots, m_k), \quad \text{and,} \quad \mathsf{ct} = \mathsf{Eval}_{\mathsf{pk}}(C, \mathsf{Enc}_{\mathsf{pk}}(m_1), \ldots, \mathsf{Enc}_{\mathsf{pk}}(m_k)),$$

i.e. where m and ct correspond to the same computation done on plaintexts and ciphertexts.

In this work we investigate two distinct correctness properties for approximate homomorphic encryption. The first is implicit in the literature on CKKS. We call this notion "static" to contrast with a later notion we investigate in Sect. 5.

Definition 11 (Static Approximate Correctness). *Let* Π *be an FHE scheme with message space* $\mathcal{M} \subseteq \widetilde{\mathcal{M}}$, *which is a normed space with norm* $\|\cdot\| : \widetilde{\mathcal{M}} \to \mathbb{R}_{\geq 0}$. *Let* $\mathcal{L}$ *be a space of circuits,* $\mathcal{L}_k \subseteq \mathcal{L}$ *the subset of parity* k *circuits, and let* $\mathsf{Estimate} : \bigsqcup_{k \in \mathbb{N}} \mathcal{L}_k \times \mathbb{R}_{\geq 0}^k \to \mathbb{R}_{\geq 0}$ *be an efficiently computable function. We call the tuple* $\widetilde{\Pi} = (\Pi, \mathsf{Estimate})$ *a statically approximate FHE scheme if for all* $k \in \mathbb{N}$, *for all* $C \in \mathcal{L}_k$, *for all* $(\mathsf{pk}, \mathsf{sk}) \leftarrow \mathsf{KeyGen}(1^\kappa)$, *if* $\mathsf{ct}_1, \ldots, \mathsf{ct}_k$ *and* $m_1, \ldots, m_k$ *are such that* $\mathsf{Error}(\mathsf{ct}_i, m_i, \mathsf{sk}) \leq t_i$, *then*

$$\mathsf{Error}(\mathsf{Eval}_{\mathsf{pk}}(C, \mathsf{ct}_1, \ldots, \mathsf{ct}_k), C(m_1, \ldots, m_k), \mathsf{sk}) \leq \mathsf{Estimate}(C, t_1, \ldots, t_k).$$

Note that the type signature $\bigsqcup_{k \in \mathbb{N}} \mathcal{L}_k \times \mathbb{R}_{\geq 0}^k \to \mathbb{R}_{\geq 0}$ encodes that $\mathsf{Estimate}$ takes as input a circuit C, and an error bound t_i for each of the k input wires to the circuit $C \in \mathcal{L}_k$. This correctness notion is "static" in the sense of static typing. In particular, $\mathsf{Estimate}$ only depends on

– the computation C to be done, and
– error bounds t_i for the inputs to the homomorphic computation.

All of these quantities are publicly computable given an abstract description of a computation, and (for non-adaptive computations) can even be precomputed (say by an FHE "compiler").

Generally $\mathsf{Estimate}(\cdot)$ either computes a (provable) worst-case bound on the error, or a (heuristic) average-case bound. Our work assumes worst-case bounds (although we discuss average-case bounds some in Sect. 6). Approximate FHE schemes often require that all $m_1, \ldots, m_k$ are of bounded norm—this can be captured in the above definition by choosing $\mathcal{M}$ to be a set of bounded norm.

Security. We use the following security definition, proposed in [19], which properly captures security of approximate FHE schemes against passive attacks.

Algorithm 1 Oracles for the IND-CPA^D game.

---

initialization
   $(\mathsf{pk}, \mathsf{sk}) \leftarrow \mathsf{KeyGen}(1^\kappa)$
global state
   $S \leftarrow \emptyset$
   $i \leftarrow 0$
$\mathsf{E}^b_{\mathsf{pk}}(m_0, m_1) :=$
   $\mathsf{ct} \leftarrow \mathsf{Enc}_{\mathsf{pk}}(m_b)$
   $S[i] \leftarrow (m_0, m_1, \mathsf{ct})$
   $i \leftarrow i + 1$
   return ct

$\mathsf{H}^b_{\mathsf{pk}}(g, \mathbf{J} = (j_1, \ldots, j_k)) :=$
   $\mathsf{ct} \leftarrow \mathsf{Eval}_{\mathsf{pk}}(g, S[j_1].\mathsf{ct}, \ldots, S[j_k].\mathsf{ct})$
   $gm_0 \leftarrow g(S[j_1].m_0, \ldots, S[j_k].m_0)$
   $gm_1 \leftarrow g(S[j_1].m_1, \ldots, S[j_k].m_1)$
   $S[i] \leftarrow (gm_0, gm_1, \mathsf{ct})$
   $i \leftarrow i + 1$
   return ct
$\mathsf{D}^b_{\mathsf{sk}}(i) :=$
   if $S[i].m_0 = S[i].m_1$
      return $\mathsf{Dec}_{\mathsf{sk}}(S[i].\mathsf{ct})$
   else
      return $\perp$

Definition 12 (IND-CPA^D Security, [19]**).** *Let* $\Pi = (\mathsf{KeyGen}, \mathsf{Enc}, \mathsf{Dec}, \mathsf{Eval})$ *be a FHE scheme. We define the IND-CPA^D game to be an indistinguishability game parameterized by distribution ensembles* $\{(\mathsf{E}^b_\theta, \mathsf{H}^b_\theta, \mathsf{D}^b_\theta)\}_\theta$ *for* $b \in \{0, 1\}$, *where these oracles are the (stateful[1]) oracles given in Algorithm 1. The scheme* Π *is* κ*-bit IND-CPA^D-secure if for any A, we have that* $\kappa \leq \log_2 \frac{T(A)}{\mathsf{adv}^A}$, *where* adv^A *is as in Definition 6.*

In [19] it is also shown that for FHE schemes satisfying the standard correctness requirement (5), IND-CPA^D security is equivalent to the traditional formulation of indistinguishability under chosen plaintext attack (IND-CPA), defined as follows.

Definition 13 (IND-CPA Security). *Let* $\Pi = (\mathsf{KeyGen}, \mathsf{Enc}, \mathsf{Dec}, \mathsf{Eval})$ *be a FHE scheme. We define the IND-CPA game to be an indistinguishability game parameterized by distribution ensembles* $\{\mathsf{E}^b_\theta\}_\theta$ *for* $b \in \{0, 1\}$ *of Algorithm 1. The scheme* Π *is* κ*-bit IND-CPA-secure if for any A, we have that* $\kappa \leq \log_2 \frac{T(A)}{\mathsf{adv}^A}$, *where* adv^A *is as in Definition 6.*

We will additionally use weaker and stronger variants of IND-CPA^D, informally defined as follows:

– q-IND-CPA^D security. This is the same as IND-CPA^D security, but restricted to adversaries that make at most $q(\kappa)$ queries to oracle D.

---

[1] As a standard convention (for this and other games defined in the paper), if at any point in a game the adversary makes an invalid query (*e.g.*, a circuit g not supported by the scheme, or indices out of range), the oracle simply returns an error symbol $\perp$.

- KR^D security, or security against key recovery attacks. Here we modify the $IND\text{-}CPA^D$ game by restricting[2] the E oracle to queries of the form $E(m, m)$, and requiring the adversary to output (at the end of the attack) a secret key sk', rather than the bit b'. The attack is successful if $sk = sk'$.

KR^D security is implied by $IND\text{-}CPA^D$ security, but it is much weaker, and it is not generally considered a satisfactory notion of security. Here (as in [19]), KR^D security is used exclusively to show that certain schemes are not secure, making the insecurity results stronger. We provide formal definitions of the above notions in the full version of the paper.

3   A Differentially Private Approach to $IND\text{-}CPA^D$ Security

In this section we investigate achieving $q\text{-}IND\text{-}CPA^D$ security for statically approximate, $IND\text{-}CPA$-secure FHE schemes $\tilde{\Pi}$. Our approach is to post-process decryptions of $\tilde{\Pi}$ with an appropriate notion of differential privacy. The noise added by this differentially private mechanism will suffice to information-theoretically hide the ciphertext error, allowing us to reduce our analysis to the case of exact FHE, where $IND\text{-}CPA$ and $q\text{-}IND\text{-}CPA^D$ security are equivalent.

3.1   Our Notion of Differential Privacy

Our notion of differential privacy is a generalization of the notion of Rényi differential privacy [23] to different norms[3]. As the tightest bounds in our setting occur in the simplest[4] case when $\alpha = 1$, we present things solely in terms of this Rényi divergence, i.e. the KL divergence.

Definition 14 (Norm KL Differential Privacy). *For $t \in \mathbb{R}_{\geq 0}$, let $M_t : B \to C$ be a family of randomized algorithms, where B is a normed space with norm $\|\cdot\| : B \to \mathbb{R}_{\geq 0}$. Let $\rho \in \mathbb{R}$ be a privacy bound. We say that the family M_t is ρ-KL differentially private (ρ-KLDP) if, for all $x, x' \in B$ with $\|x - x'\| \leq t$,*

$$D(M_t(x)\|M_t(x')) \leq \rho. \tag{7}$$

Note that our mechanism M depends on a bound on the distance $\|x - x'\| \leq t$, which it uses (internally) to set parameters to meet the desired privacy bound.

---

[2] This is without loss of generality, as the only point of general queries $E(m, m')$ is to get information correlated with the secret bit b, which the game does not depend on.

[3] In Differential Privacy, "adjacent" values are typically measured in the Hamming norm, while for our purposes the ℓ_2 and ℓ_∞ norms are of primary interest.

[4] There is an alternative simplification of the Rényi divergence when $\alpha = \infty$ known as the *max-log distance* [21] with desirable properties, for example it is a metric, similarly to the statistical distance. As our bounds degrade linearly in α as $\alpha \to \infty$, this notion is unsuitable for our situation.

In the most common case of Gaussian noise, it will use noise of standard deviation $\sigma = \Omega(2^{\kappa/2}t)$ to achieve κ-bit security (Corollary 1).

As $\|x - x'\| = \|x' - x\|$ is itself symmetric, our definition is invariant under replacing $D(\mathcal{D}_0\|\mathcal{D}_1)$ with $\max(D(\mathcal{D}_0\|\mathcal{D}_1), D(\mathcal{D}_1\|\mathcal{D}_0))$, and is therefore implicitly dependent on this larger (symmetric) measure, although we do not make this explicit in our work.

Algorithm 2 The FHE Scheme $M[\tilde{\Pi}]$

$\mathsf{Enc}'_{\mathsf{pk}}(m) :=$
 $c \leftarrow \mathsf{Enc}_{\mathsf{pk}}(m)$
 return $\mathsf{ct} = (c, t_e)$
$\mathsf{Eval}'_{\mathsf{pk}}(C, \mathsf{ct}'_1, \dots, \mathsf{ct}'_k) :=$
 $c \leftarrow \mathsf{Eval}_{\mathsf{pk}}(C, \mathsf{ct}_1.c, \dots, \mathsf{ct}_k.c)$
 $t \leftarrow \mathsf{Estimate}(C, \mathsf{ct}_1.t, \dots, \mathsf{ct}_k.t)$
 return $\mathsf{ct} = (c, t)$

$\mathsf{Dec}'_{\mathsf{sk}}(\mathsf{ct}) :=$
 return $M_{\mathsf{ct}.t}(\mathsf{Dec}_{\mathsf{sk}}(\mathsf{ct}.c))$

Definition 15. *Let* $\Pi = (\mathsf{KeyGen}, \mathsf{Enc}, \mathsf{Dec}, \mathsf{Eval})$ *be an FHE scheme with plaintext space* $\mathcal{M} \subseteq \widetilde{\mathcal{M}}$, *where* $\widetilde{\mathcal{M}}$ *is a normed space with norm* $\|\cdot\|$. *Let* $\mathsf{Estimate}$ *be such that* $\tilde{\Pi} = (\Pi, \mathsf{Estimate})$ *is statically approximate, and let* t_e *be an upper bound on ciphertext errors of all fresh encryptions* $\mathsf{Enc}_{\mathsf{pk}}(m)$ *for all* $m \in \mathcal{M}$. *Let* M_t *be a* ρ-KLDP *mechanism on* $\widetilde{\mathcal{M}}$. *Define the FHE scheme* $M[\tilde{\Pi}]$ *that has an identical* KeyGen *algorithm to* Π, *with the modified algorithms* $\mathsf{Enc}'_{\mathsf{pk}}, \mathsf{Eval}'_{\mathsf{pk}}$, *and* $\mathsf{Dec}'_{\mathsf{sk}}$ *of Algorithm 2.*

In the above definition of the scheme $M[\tilde{\Pi}]$, we use the "tagged ciphertext" notation $\mathsf{ct} = (c, t)$, where c is an ordinary ciphertext and t is an estimated ciphertext error upper bound. An initial estimation t_e is provided by the encryption algorithm, and the evaluation algorithm updates the error upper bound using $\mathsf{Estimate}(\cdot)$ such that the resulting scheme is a statically approximate FHE scheme.

Algorithm 3 The decryption oracle for the game $\mathcal{G}_1$ of Theorem 2.

$\mathsf{D}(i) :=$
 if $S[i].m_0 = S[i].m_1$
  $t_i \leftarrow S[i].\mathsf{ct}.t$
  return $M_{t_i}(S[i].m_0)$
 else
  return $\perp$

Theorem 2. *Let* $\Pi = (\mathsf{KeyGen}, \mathsf{Enc}, \mathsf{Dec}, \mathsf{Eval})$ *be an FHE scheme with plaintext space* $\mathcal{M} \subseteq \widetilde{\mathcal{M}}$, *where* $\widetilde{\mathcal{M}}$ *is a normed space with norm* $\|\cdot\|$. *Let* $\mathsf{Estimate}$ *be such* that $\tilde{\Pi} = (\Pi, \mathsf{Estimate})$ is statically approximate. Let $\kappa > 0$, let M_t be a ρ-KLDP mechanism on $\widetilde{\mathcal{M}}$ where $\rho \leq 2^{-\kappa-7}/q$, and let $q \in \mathbb{N}$. If Π is $(\kappa + 8)$-bit secure in the IND-CPA game, then $M[\tilde{\Pi}]$ is κ-bit secure in the q-IND-CPA^D game.

Proof. We defer details to the full version of the paper, and simply note that this follows from combining Lemma 5 and Theorem 1.   □

3.2   Gaussian Mechanism

In this section, we present and analyze a differentially private mechanism M_t which simply adds Gaussian noise to its input.

Definition 16. *Let $\mu \in \mathbb{Z}$, and $\sigma > 0$. The discrete Gaussian of parameters μ, σ (written $\mathcal{N}_{\mathbb{Z}}(\mu, \sigma^2)$) is the probability distribution supported on $\mathbb{Z}$ with p.m.f. $p(x) \propto \exp(-(x - \mu)^2/2\sigma^2)$.*

It is known how to (with high probability) exactly sample from this distribution in constant time [4]. We explicitly bound the impact of this on the security of our constructions in the full version of our paper.

Proposition 1 (Prop. 5 of [4]). *Let $\sigma \in \mathbb{R}_{\geq 0}$, and let $\mu, \nu \in \mathbb{Z}$. Then:*

$$D(\mathcal{N}_{\mathbb{Z}}(\mu, \sigma^2) || \mathcal{N}_{\mathbb{Z}}(\nu, \sigma^2)) = \frac{(\nu - \mu)^2}{2\sigma^2}. \tag{8}$$

Definition 17. *Let $\rho > 0$, and $n \in \mathbb{N}$. Define the (discrete) Gaussian Mechanism $M_t : \mathbb{Z}^n \to \mathbb{Z}^n$ be the mechanism that, on input $x \in \mathbb{Z}^n$, outputs a sample from $\mathcal{N}_{\mathbb{Z}^n}(x, \frac{t^2}{2\rho} I_n)$.*

Lemma 6. *For any $\rho > 0, n \in \mathbb{N}$, the Gaussian mechanism is ρ-KLDP.*

Proof. Let $\mathcal{X} = \mathcal{N}_{\mathbb{Z}^n}(x, \frac{t^2}{2\rho} I_n)$ and $\mathcal{Y} = \mathcal{N}_{\mathbb{Z}^n}(y, \frac{t^2}{2\rho} I_n)$. By sub-additivity of the KL divergence and Proposition 1, we have that $D(\mathcal{X}||\mathcal{Y}) \leq \|\widehat{D}(\mathcal{X}||\mathcal{Y})\|_1 = \frac{\rho}{t^2} \|x - y\|_2^2 \leq \rho$.   □

Corollary 1. *Let $\Pi = (\mathsf{KeyGen}, \mathsf{Enc}, \mathsf{Dec}, \mathsf{Eval})$ be an FHE scheme with plaintext space $\mathcal{M} \subseteq \widetilde{\mathcal{M}}$, where $\widetilde{\mathcal{M}} \subseteq \mathbb{Z}^n$ is a normed space with norm $\|\cdot\|$. Let $\mathsf{Estimate}$ be such that $\tilde{\Pi} = (\Pi, \mathsf{Estimate})$ is a statically approximate FHE scheme. Let M_t be the Gaussian mechanism (with $\rho := 2^{-\kappa-7}/q$). If Π is $(\kappa+8)$-bit secure in the IND-CPA game, then $M[\tilde{\Pi}]$ is κ-bit secure in the q-IND-CPA^D game.*

For $\rho := 2^{-\kappa-7}/q$, one can check that the Gaussian mechanism adds noise of standard deviation $8\sqrt{q2^\kappa}$ct.t to each coordinate, so one loses $\kappa/2 + 3 + \log_2 \sqrt{q} + \log_2$ ct.t bits of precision. As the ciphertext already contains $\log_2$ ct.t bits of noise, the *additional* precision lost by $M[\tilde{\Pi}]$ is $\kappa/2 + \log_2 \sqrt{q} + 3$ bits.

Proof. This reduces to combining Lemma 6 with Theorem 2. The size of the Gaussian noise comes from $\rho = \mathsf{ct}.t^2/2\sigma^2 \iff \sigma = \frac{1}{\sqrt{2\rho}}\mathsf{ct}.t$. As we need that $\rho \leq 2^{-\kappa-7}/q$, it follows that $\sigma \geq 8\sqrt{q}2^{\kappa/2}\mathsf{ct}.t$.   □

This transformation does not explicitly depend on the underlying parameters of the particular implementation of approximate encryption (for example, the size of the LWE moduli one is working over, the dimension of the message space, etc.), and instead only implicitly depends on these quantities via the computation of the static ciphertext error bound. We caution that to apply this result to CKKS one needs to be slightly careful about the underlying norm one is working with, which we do later in Theorem 3.

4   Application to CKKS

Prior work of [19] shows that the approximate FHE scheme of [8] does not satisfy IND-CPA^D-security, even though it satisfies IND-CPA-security. We refer the reader to [19] for additional details, but at a high level they show that publishing the results of an approximate FHE computation under CKKS leaks information about the secret key, enabling a full key recovery attack in the case of trivial computation, and an attack against IND-CPA^D-security for more general homomorphic computation. In this section, we apply Theorem 2 and Lemma 6 to give a modification of the CKKS decryption function that allows us to prove IND-CPA^D-security of the modified scheme.

We use the results of Sect. 3 to show that post-processing the results of the CKKS decryption function with the Gaussian mechanism is sufficient to achieve IND-CPA^D-security for the CKKS scheme, for large enough Gaussian noise (Sect. 4.2). We also prove a nearly matching lower bound on the Gaussian noise necessary to achieve IND-CPA^D-security for the CKKS scheme (Sect. 4.3). We then investigate a relaxed notion of security (Sect. 4.4), which may be of independent interest. With these results, we briefly examine the countermeasures adopted by some open-source implementations of CKKS, and we suggest concrete parameters (Sect. 4.5).

4.1   The CKKS Approximate FHE Scheme

We begin with a few mathematical preliminaries necessary to the CKKS scheme. For any positive integer N, let $\Phi_N(X) = \prod_{j \in \mathbb{Z}_N^*} (X - \omega_N^j)$ be the Nth cyclotomic polynomial, where $\omega_N = e^{2\pi i/N} \in \mathbb{C}$ is the complex Nth principal root of unity, and $\mathbb{Z}_N^*$ is the group of invertible integers modulo N. We recall that $\Phi_N(X) \in \mathbb{Z}[X]$ is a monic polynomial of degree $n = \varphi(N) = |\mathbb{Z}_N^*|$ with integer coefficients. We denote by $\mathcal{R}^N = \mathbb{Z}[X]/(\Phi_N(X))$ the ring of integers of the number field $\mathbb{Q}[X]/(\Phi_N(X))$, omitting the superscript when it is clear from context. We use $\mathcal{R}_Q^N = \mathbb{Z}[X]/(Q, \Phi_N(X))$ to denote the ring of elements of $\mathcal{R}^N$ reduced modulo Q.

An element $a \in \mathbb{R}[X]/(\Phi_N(X))$ may be embedded into $\mathbb{C}^n$ under the *canonical embedding* $\tau(a)$ (typically defined over $\mathbb{Q}[X]/(\Phi_N(X))$, but naturally extending to $\mathbb{R}[X]/(\Phi_N(X))$). The map $\tau(a)$ takes a to the $n = \varphi(N)$ evaluations of a at the n roots of $\Phi_N(X)$. Notice that these n values come in conjugate pairs and can be identified as a vector in $\mathbb{C}^{n/2}$ via a projection $\pi : (z, \bar{z}) \mapsto z$. So, complex vectors in $\mathbb{C}^{n/2}$ are considered as messages in CKKS, and they are encoded to plaintext polynomials in $\mathcal{R}$ by composing π^{-1} and τ^{-1} together with a scaling factor; conversely, plaintexts are decoded using $\tau \circ \pi$. We define the *canonical embedding norm* $\|\cdot\|_\infty^{\text{can}}$ of an element $a \in \mathbb{R}[X]/(\Phi_N(X))$ to be $\|a\|_\infty^{\text{can}} = \|\tau(a)\|_\infty$. We will use this norm to track the ciphertext error of CKKS ciphertexts.

We now present the relevant subroutines of the CKKS FHE scheme. We omit many details of the CKKS scheme, and refer the reader to [8] for a more complete description. The CKKS scheme is parameterized by a plaintext dimension $n/2$ (typically a power-of-two), a ciphertext modulus Q, and a discrete Gaussian error distribution χ with standard deviation σ.

- CKKS.KeyGen(1^κ): Take $w = w(\kappa)$ and $p = p(\kappa, Q)$. To generate the secret key sk, sample $s \leftarrow \{s \in \{-1, 0, 1\}^n : |s|_0 = w\}$ and take $\text{sk} = (1, s)$. To generate the public key pk, sample $a \leftarrow \mathcal{R}_Q$, $e \leftarrow \chi$, and take $\text{pk} = (b = -as + e, a)$. To generate the evaluation key ek, sample $a' \leftarrow \mathcal{R}_{pQ}$, $e' \leftarrow \chi$, and take $\text{ek} = (b', a')$ for $b' = -a's + e' + ps^2 \mod pQ$. Return $(\text{sk}, \text{pk}, \text{ek})$.
- CKKS.Encode($\mathbf{x} \in \mathbb{C}^{n/2}; \Delta$): Return $\lfloor \Delta \cdot \varphi^{-1}(\mathbf{x}) \rceil \in \mathcal{R}$.
- CKKS.Enc$_{\text{pk}}(m)$: Let T denote the distribution over $\{0, \pm 1\}^n$ induced by sampling each coordinate independently, drawing -1 with probability $1/4$, 1 with probability $1/4$, and 0 with probability $1/2$. Sample $r \leftarrow T$, $e_0, e_1 \leftarrow \chi$, and return $r \cdot \text{pk} + (m + e_0, e_1) \mod Q$.
- CKKS.Add($\mathbf{c}_0, \mathbf{c}_1 \in \mathcal{R}_Q$): Return $\mathbf{c}_0 + \mathbf{c}_1 \mod Q$.
- CKKS.Mult$_{\text{ek}}(\mathbf{c}_0, \mathbf{c}_1 \in \mathcal{R}_Q)$: For $\mathbf{c}_0 = (b_0, a_0)$ and $\mathbf{c}_1 = (b_1, a_1)$, let $(b_2, a_2) = (b_0 b_1, a_0 b_1 + a_1 b_0) + \lfloor p^{-1} \cdot a_0 a_1 \cdot \text{ek} \rceil \mod Q$. Return (b_2, a_2).
- CKKS.Decode($a \in \mathcal{R}; \Delta$): Return $\varphi(\Delta^{-1} \cdot a) \in \mathbb{C}^{n/2}$.
- CKKS.Dec$_{\text{sk}}(\mathbf{c})$: For $\mathbf{c} = (b, a) \in \mathcal{R}_Q^2$, return $b + as \mod Q$.

Note that CKKS supports encryption and decryption of floating-point inputs by pre-processing encryption with CKKS.Encode, and post-processing decryption with CKKS.Decode. All intermediate operations are then done with integer arithmetic. To simplify exposition, we focus on these intermediate operations, and therefore restrict to the case of integer arithmetic.

We will need the following (standard) expressions for how the ciphertext error transforms during addition and multiplication.

Lemma 7 (Error Growth [8]). *Let $\mathbf{c}_0$ and $\mathbf{c}_1$ denote two CKKS ciphertexts, with $\mathbf{c}_0 = \text{CKKS.Enc}_{\text{pk}}(m_0)$ and $\mathbf{c}_1 = \text{CKKS.Enc}_{\text{pk}}(m_1)$ with errors e_0 and e_1 respectively. Then the ciphertext $\mathbf{c}_{\text{Mult}} = \text{CKKS.Mult}(\mathbf{c}_0, \mathbf{c}_1)$ has error $m_0 e_1 + m_1 e_0 + e_0 e_1 + e_{\text{Mult}}$ for a term e_{Mult} that depends on the parameters of the CKKS instance (and the ciphertexts $\mathbf{c}_0, \mathbf{c}_1$). The ciphertext $\mathbf{c}_{\text{Add}} = \text{CKKS.Add}(\mathbf{c}_0, \mathbf{c}_1)$ has error $e_0 + e_1$.*

Certain authors have suggested various heuristics for analyzing e_{Mult}. We will find the following one useful for the analysis of the attack of Sect. 4.3.

Heuristic 1 (Appendix A.5 of [12]). *Let w be the hamming weight of sk. Then e_{Mult} may be modeled as a random variable with mean zero and variance $O(wn)$.*

The rest of our work will benefit from the following notation.

Definition 18. *For $\sigma > 0$, let* S-CKKS$_\sigma$ *be the CKKS encryption scheme, where one modifies decryption to compute* S-CKKS$_\sigma$.Dec$_{sk}$(ct) $=$ CKKS.Dec$_{sk}$(ct.c) $+ \mathcal{N}_{\mathbb{Z}^n}(0, \sigma^2 ct.t^2 I_n)$.

4.2   IND-CPA^D-Secure CKKS

It is straightforward to apply Corollary 1 to CKKS to obtain q-IND-CPA^D security.

Theorem 3. *For any $q \in \mathbb{N}$, if* CKKS *is $(\kappa + 8)$-bit IND-CPA-secure, and $\sigma = 8\sqrt{qn}2^{\kappa/2}$, then* S-CKKS$_\sigma$ *is κ-bit q-IND-CPA^D-secure, i.e. $\kappa/2 + \tilde{O}(1)$ additional bits of Gaussian noise suffice to achieve q-IND-CPA^D security.*

Proof. This follows immediately from Corollary 1, (using the aforementioned inequality $\|m\|_\infty^{can} \le \sqrt{n}\,\|m\|_2$, as our analysis of the Gaussian mechanism uses an ℓ_2 norm bound). □

4.3   Lower Bound for Gaussian Mechanism

Together, Lemma 6 and Theorem 2 give an upper bound on the amount of Gaussian noise required to achieve IND-CPA^D-security for an IND-CPA-secure approximate encryption scheme. In this subsection, we show that this upper bound is essentially tight for CKKS by demonstrating an attack against IND-CPA^D security for noticeably smaller Gaussian noise, *i.e.* analyzing S-CKKS$_{\sigma_s}$ for sanitization noise $\sigma_s \ll 8\sqrt{qn}2^{\kappa/2}$. In what follows, recall that $n = \varphi(N)$, and w denotes the Hamming weight of the key sk.

Algorithm 4 Adversary $A(1^\kappa, \mathsf{pk}, \mathsf{ek})$

for $i \in \{0, \dots, 44\}$ do
    $ct_i \leftarrow \mathsf{E_{pk}}(m_i^{(0)} = 0, m_i^{(1)} = B)$;
end for
for $i \in \{45, \dots, 59\}$ do
    $ct_i \leftarrow \mathsf{E_{pk}}(m_i^{(0)} = 0, m_i^{(1)} = -B)$;
end for
$ct_{60} \leftarrow \mathsf{H_{ek}}(g, \{0, \dots, 59\})$ for $g(x_0, \dots, x_{59}) = \sum_{i=0}^{29}(x_i \cdot x_{30+i})$
$m' \leftarrow \mathsf{D_{sk}}(60)$
$V_0 = 30\sigma^4 + O(wn) + \sigma_s^2$ Variance of $\tau(m')_0$ if $b = 0$
$V_1 = 30\sigma^4 + 60B^2\sigma^2 + O(wn) + \sigma_s^2$ Variance of $\tau(m')_0$ if $b = 1$
if $|\tau(m')_0| < \sqrt{\frac{\log(V_1/V_0)V_0 V_1}{V_1 - V_0}}$ then
    return 0
else
    return 1
end if

At a high level, the adversary A will exploit the message-dependence of the S-CKKS error growth (Lemma 7) to design an H query such that the expected magnitude of the ciphertext error of ct_{60} is larger when $b = 1$ than when $b = 0$. The adversary A will then query D on this ciphertext, and choose its bit based on the size of the message m' it receives.

We will next show that the aforementioned adversary will have noticeable advantage unless σ_s is larger than σ (the standard deviation of the underlying RLWE error) by a factor super-polynomial in the security parameter.

Lemma 8. *Let $\sigma_s > 0$. Then there exists an adversary A against* S-CKKS$_{\sigma_s}$ *in the* IND-CPA^D *such that* $\mathsf{adv}^A = \Omega\left(\frac{1}{\sigma_s^4 n^6}\right)$.

Proof. We first observe that the ciphertext $\mathsf{ct}_{60} = \mathsf{Eval}_{\mathsf{ek}}(g, \{0, \dots, 59\})$ is an approximate encryption of 0 both when $b = 0$ and $b = 1$ in the IND-CPA^D experiment. Therefore the decryption query made by A returns a value rather than $\perp$.

If $b = 0$, then because all ciphertexts ct_i encrypt messages $m_i = 0$, the message-dependent terms of the error growth from Lemma 7 are also 0, and so the ciphertext error of ct_{60} is $\sum_{i=0}^{29} e_{\mathsf{Mult}} + e_i e_{30+i}$, where e_i denotes the ciphertext error of ct_i. Recall that if error vectors e and e' have entries sampled from a discrete Gaussian with parameter σ, then each of the components of $\tau(ee')$ is distributed with mean 0 and variance σ^4. We can then use the Central Limit Theorem to approximate the distribution of the sum $\sum_{i=0}^{29} e_{\mathsf{Mult}} + e_i e_{30+i}$ as a Gaussian distribution with mean 0 and variance $30\sigma^4 + O(wn)$. Note that this approximation can be improved by increasing the number of terms in the sum to a larger constant. For the sake of concreteness we have designed the adversary such that there are 30 terms, as this is the value at which the Central Limit Theorem is empirically justified.

If $b = 1$, then the message-dependent terms of the error growth are significant, and the error of ct_{60} is

$$\sum_{i=0}^{14} \left(e_{\mathsf{Mult}} + e_i e_{30+i} + Be_i + Be_{30+i} \right) + \sum_{i=15}^{29} \left(e_{\mathsf{Mult}} + e_i e_{30+i} - Be_i + Be_{30+i} \right).$$

As in the case where $b = 0$, we will approximate this distribution as a Gaussian with mean 0. Though the error terms $e_i e_{30+i}$ and $Be_i + Be_{30+i}$ are not independent, they do have covariance 0, as do the terms $e_i e_{30+i}$ and $Be_{30+i} - Be_i$, and so we can approximate the sum of errors as being drawn from a discrete Gaussian distribution with mean 0 and variance $30\sigma^4 + 60B^2\sigma^2 + O(wn)$.

The adversary sees the result of post-processing the error term with the Gaussian mechanism, run with parameter σ_s, and then chooses its bit to return based on the absolute value of the first component $\tau(m')_0$ under the canonical embedding. When $b = 0$, this means the adversary sees a sample drawn from a distribution that is well-approximated by a centered Gaussian with variance $V_0 = 30\sigma^4 + O(wn) + \sigma_s^2 \mathsf{ct}.t^2$. When $b = 1$, however, the adversary sees a sample drawn from a distribution that is well-approximated by a Gaussian with the same mean, but larger variance $V_1 = 30\sigma^4 + 60B^2\sigma^2 + O(wn) + \sigma_s^2 \mathsf{ct}.t^2$. Let

$$x = \sqrt{\frac{\log(V_1/V_0)V_0V_1}{V_1 - V_0}}.$$

A straightforward calculation shows that for $|\tau(m')_0| < x$, m' is a more likely outcome when $b = 0$ than when $b = 1$, and when $|\tau(m')_0| \geq x$, m' is at least as likely when $b = 1$ as it is when $b = 0$. Then we have that the advantage of adversary A is approximately the total variation distance between a Gaussian with variance V_0 and a Gaussian with variance V_1. By Lemma 2, we have that

$$\Delta(\mathcal{N}(0, V_0), \mathcal{N}(0, V_1)) \geq \frac{1}{200} \frac{|V_0 - V_1|}{V_0} \in \Theta\left(\frac{B^2\sigma^2}{\sigma^4 + wn + \sigma_s^2 \mathsf{ct}.t^2}\right).$$

Recall that w is the hamming weight of the secret key sk, and so we have $w < n$. For security, we know that $\sqrt{n} < \sigma$, and so it follows that the advantage of our (non-aborting) adversary A against the IND-CPA^D security of CKKS is the *square* of the total variation distance, *i.e.* $\Theta\left(\frac{B^4\sigma^4}{(\sigma^4 + \sigma_s^2 \mathsf{ct}.t^2)^2}\right)$. Finally, note that for $\|e_i\|_\infty^{\mathsf{can}} < \sigma n$ holds with high probability, so $\mathsf{ct}.t \leq O(B\sigma n^{3/2})$ (where we pick up a $\sqrt{n}$ factor to convert to the ℓ_2 norm), and therefore the advantage of our adversary is $\Theta\left(\frac{B^4\sigma^4}{\sigma^8 + \sigma_s^4 \sigma^4 B^4 n^6}\right) = \Omega\left(\frac{1}{\sigma_s^4 n^6}\right)$. $\square$

Theorem 4. *If* S-CKKS$_{\sigma_s}$ *is* κ-*bit IND-CPA^D-secure, then* $\sigma_s = \Omega(2^{\kappa/4}/n^{3/2})$, *i.e. one must add at least* $\kappa/4 - \tilde{\Omega}(1)$ *bits of additional Gaussian noise.*

Proof. We have that $\kappa \leq \log_2 O\left(\frac{T(A)}{\mathsf{adv}^A}\right) \leq \log_2 O(\sigma_s^4 n^6) \implies \sigma_s \geq 2^{\kappa/4}/n^{3/2}$, and therefore $\kappa/4 - \log_2 \Omega(n^{3/2}) \leq \log_2 \sigma_s$. $\square$

We therefore see that while one can potentially improve on the concrete countermeasure of Sect. 4.5, the main (exponential) term is within a constant factor of correct.

4.4 Improved Parameters via a Relaxed Security Notion

The previous sections show that we require between $\kappa/4$ and $\kappa/2$ bits of Gaussian noise to achieve κ-bit q-IND-CPA^D-security. We next introduce a relaxed notion of security, for which we can justify a reduction in the size of Gaussians one must add to obtain a form of q-IND-CPA^D security.

Definition 19. *Let* Π *be a cryptographic primitive, and* $\mathcal{G}$ *be an indistinguishability game. Let* adv^A *be the advantage of an adversary* A *in breaking the security of* Π *in the* $\mathcal{G}$ *game. We say that* Π *has* (c, s)-*bits of* $\mathcal{G}$-*security if, for any adversary* A, *either*

$$\log_2 \frac{T(A)}{\mathsf{adv}^A} \geq c, \qquad or \qquad \log_2 \frac{1}{\mathsf{adv}^A} \geq s. \tag{9}$$

This notion may be equivalently written in a number of ways.

Definition 20. *Let $I \subseteq [0,1]$. A cryptographic primitive Π is said to be $(t(\epsilon), \epsilon)_I$-secure in an indistinguishability game $\mathcal{G}$ if, for any $\epsilon \in I$, any adversary of advantage ϵ has running time at least $t(\epsilon)$.*

Lemma 9. *Let Π be a cryptographic primitive, and $\mathcal{G}$ be an indistinguishability game. Then the following are equivalent*

1. *Π has (c, s)-bits of $\mathcal{G}$-security,*
2. *For any adversary A, $c \leq \log_2 \frac{\max(T(A), 2^{c-s})}{\mathsf{adv}^A}$, and*
3. *Π is $(2^c \epsilon, \epsilon)_{[2^{-s}, 1]}$-secure in $\mathcal{G}$.*

This second condition is a variant of Definition 6 where we implicitly pad all adversaries to have running time at least 2^{c-s}.

Note that when $s \geq c$ the second condition is equivalent to the notion of c-bit security. When $s < c$, the notion of (c, s)-bits of security is strictly weaker than the notion of c-bit security.

Lemma 10. *Let $c > 0$. Let $\mathcal{G}$ be an indistinguishability game, and Π a primitive that has c-bits of $\mathcal{G}$-security. Then for any $s < c$, there exists a primitive Π' and indisinguishability game $\mathcal{H}$ such that Π' has (c, s)-bits of $\mathcal{H}$-security, but not c-bits of $\mathcal{H}$-security.*

We next give an analogue of Theorem 2 in the setting of our relaxed notion of bit security.

Theorem 5. *Let $\Pi = (\mathsf{KeyGen}, \mathsf{Enc}, \mathsf{Dec}, \mathsf{Eval})$ be an FHE scheme with plaintext space $\mathcal{M} \subseteq \widetilde{\mathcal{M}}$, where $\widetilde{\mathcal{M}}$ is a normed space with norm $\|\cdot\|$. Let $\mathsf{Estimate}$ be such that $\widetilde{\Pi} = (\Pi, \mathsf{Estimate})$ is statically approximate. Let M_t be a ρ-KLDP mechanism. If Π is κ-bit IND-CPA-secure, then $M[\widetilde{\Pi}]$ has $(\kappa - \log_2 24, \log_2(1/\rho) - \log_2 q - \log_2 24)$-bits of q-IND-CPA^D-security.*

Proof. We defer detail to the full version of the paper, and simply note that the proof is a (relatively standard) hybrid argument. The main novelty is the relaxed notion of security we target, which allows us to bound the *statistical* advantage term $q\rho$ (corresponding to "breaking" the KLDP mechanism) by a *computational* term (corresponding to breaking IND-CPA security of $\widetilde{\Pi}$). □

Corollary 2. *Let $\sigma = \sqrt{24qn}2^{s/2}$. If CKKS is $(c + \log_2 24)$-bit IND-CPA-secure, then S-CKKS$_\sigma$ is (c, s)-bit q-IND-CPA^D-secure.*

Proof. This reduces to combining Lemma 6 with Theorem 5. The expression for ρ comes from the identity $s = \log_2(1/2\rho) - \log_2 q - \log_2 24$. The size of the Gaussian noise comes from $2^{-s}/48q = \rho = \mathsf{ct}.t^2/2\sigma^2$, which can be rewritten as $\sigma = \sqrt{24q}2^{s/2}\mathsf{ct}.t$. Note that the static estimate $\mathsf{ct}.t$ in CKKS is in the norm $\|\cdot\|_\infty^{\mathsf{can}}$, which we upper bound by $\sqrt{n}\|\cdot\|_2$ to get that $\sigma = \sqrt{24qn}2^{s/2}\mathsf{ct}.t$. Finally, we can apply Theorem 5 to achieve the result. □

Compare this result to Theorem 3, where the noise scales with the *computational* security parameter rather than the *statistical* security parameter. While choosing $s < c$ leads to a relaxed notion of security, this relaxation is precisely characterized. The non-trivial statistical attacks that we allow are

- simple to analyze (via results such as Lemma 5), and
- independent of any underlying hardware improvements (or other computational improvements, such as parallelization).

One can therefore justify a *much* smaller choice of s than the typical (computational) choice of $c = 128$. We do not suggest a particular choice for s, and instead give a variety of choices in Table 1. Note that the choice of s should be application dependent, as each time the protocol is instantiated[5] the adversary has a fresh chance to mount an attack of advantage up to 2^{-s}. For this reason, one should choose s much larger for protocols that will be instantiated many times. Note that by Lemma 9, for $s = c$ the notion of (c,s)-bits of security reduces to the notion of c-bits of security, so the top row of Table 1 equivalently states parameters to achieve 128-bits of q-IND-CPA^D-security.

A Sample Instantiation. We briefly describe a concrete instantiation of our countermeasure that achieves $(128, 64)$-bits of q-IND-CPA^D-security. Throughout, we let the number of supported decryption queries be $q = 2^{10}$. Note that one can always (later) support more decryption queries, by rekeying when one runs out. Parameterize CKKS to achieve 133-bits of IND-CPA-security, where $133 > 128 + \log_2 24$. Let n be the resulting dimension of the chosen CKKS instance. We will assume $n \leq 2^{15}$, as every choice of parameters from the Homomorphic Encryption Standard [1] satisfies this bound.

Then, by Corollary 2, if $\sigma = \sqrt{24qn}2^{s/2}$, then S-CKKS$_\sigma$ is (c,s)-bit q-IND-CPA^D-secure. In particular, this loses another $s/2 + \log_2 \sqrt{24qn}$ bits of precision compared to decrypting via returning CKKS.Dec$_{sk}$(ct.c). The particular value of $s/2 + \log_2 \sqrt{24qn}$ can be found in Table 1 as the entry labeled $(s,q) = (64, 2^{10})$, which is 46.79. Therefore, adding an additional 46.79 bits of i.i.d. Gaussian noise suffices to achieve $(128, 64)$-bits of q-IND-CPA^D-security.

4.5   Parameters for Concrete Countermeasures

As the attack in [19] was made publicly available, the major open-source implementations of the CKKS scheme adopted several different countermeasures. We briefly summarize these countermeasures in this subsection, and we propose concrete parameters for them to achieve the desired IND-CPA^D security.

---

[5] In our particular application, this includes things like re-keying, which one can do to "refresh" the number of decryptions one may release.

Table 1. Additional size of Gaussian noise (measured in bits) required by the countermeasure of Corollary 2 to achieve (c, s)-bits (Definition 19) of q-IND-CPA^D-security, where q is a bound on the number of decryption queries, and $n \leq 2^{15}$ is a bound on the ring dimension, chosen as it is the highest dimension parameter in the Homomorphic Encryption Standard [1]. This table assumes one samples Gaussians using the sampler of [4], see the full version of the paper for details.

$s \backslash q$	1	2^5	2^{10}	2^{15}
128	73.79	76.29	78.79	81.29
112	65.79	68.29	70.79	73.29
96	57.79	60.29	62.79	65.29
80	49.79	52.29	54.79	57.29
64	41.79	44.29	46.79	49.29
48	33.79	36.29	38.79	41.29
32	25.79	28.29	30.79	33.29

HElib. The decryption API implementation was modified to add pseudorandom Gaussian noise to the raw decryption result. By default, HElib implements S-CKKS$_1$, *e.g.* the size of the extra noise is equal to the size of the static error bound of the homomorphic computation. HElib also provides an optional precision parameter in its decryption API such that the extra noise is chosen to be the largest within the precision requirement (for example, if the static error bound is not tight). To achieve (c, s)-bit security against at most $q \geq 1$ decryption queries, this precision parameter should be calibrated such that sufficient (as quantified in Theorem 5 and Table 1) noise is added during decryption.

HEAAN, Lattigo. These libraries require the default decryption API to be used only by the secret key holder, and they added a specialized decryption API to share the decryption results publicly. In HEAAN, the new decryption API takes a noise size parameter, which sets the amount of Gaussian noises to be added to the raw decryption result. In Lattigo, the new decryption API takes a rounding parameter, which is used to round the raw decryption result to certain precision. For both of them, one must estimate the ciphertext error ct.t separately and set the noise parameter as in Theorem 5 and Table 1 to achieve (c, s)-bit security against q decryptions.

PALISADE. The decryption function in PALISADE also adds Gaussian noise to the raw decryption result, but the size of the noise is chosen (dynamically) in a way detailed in Sect. 5.

4.6   The Impact of Our Countermeasure

Evaluating the feasibility of our countermeasure for some application depends on both the required (application) precision, as well as the supported (library) precision. Provided the difference between these is larger than the sum of the DP noise (as measured in Table 1) with the approximation error, our countermeasure should be able to be instantiated.

32-bit applications. Concretely, many applications (say in machine learning) require 32 bits of precision. If a FHE library only supports computations with up to 64 bits of precision, this leaves at most 32 bits available for the sum of the CKKS approximation error and the DP error induced by our countermeasure. This means that at best, one will be able to choose $s \approx 32$, which is likely too low for most applications. Note that if the FHE library supports up to 128-bit precision computations[6], this problem disappears, as there are now ≈ 96 bits available for the sum of the errors, allowing the conservative choice of $s \approx 128$.

Low-precision applications. Some applications may solely require 8 or 16 bits of precision (see for example [16] or [33] for work on training ML models with low-precision computations). This leaves 48–56 bits of precision for the sum of the CKKS approximation error and the DP error. One can then choose $s \approx 64$ (16-bit required precision) or 80 (8-bit), where precise choices of s would depend on the size of the CKKS approximation error. We view either of these choices as much more reasonable than $s \approx 32$, although in all settings the particular choice of s that is appropriate is application-dependent.

5   Dynamic Error Estimation

Yuriy Polyakov [28] has recently suggested a technique to get sharper bounds on the ciphertext error of the CKKS scheme. Briefly, this is done via leveraging a special message encoding which fixes many of the coordinates of the original CKKS message space to be constantly 0. Provided one only evaluates functions which ignore these coordinates, upon decryption these coordinates will only contain the error incurred during the homomorphic computation, and one can attempt to generalize the (exact) error measurements within these coordinates to an estimate of the entirety of the error.

This notion differs from our notion of static approximate correctness in two significant ways, namely

- it depends on the particular ciphertext one is estimating the error of, *e.g.* can only be computed *dynamically* during the program "run-time", and
- it can only be computed during decryption, *e.g.* is not *publicly-computable* information about the ciphertext.

We investigate the IND-CPA^D security of applying our transformation of Definition 15 to an approximate encryption scheme that is correct in the "dynamic" sense sketched above. In this slightly modified setting, we get significantly different results. For an IND-CPA-secure, dynamic approximately correct FHE scheme $\tilde{\Pi}$, we find that $M[\tilde{\Pi}]$ is often insecure. Specifically, assuming a "non-triviality" condition on M that we define in Definition 23, we find that

---

[6] For example, Lattigo and PALISADE can both support computations of this precision.

1. for a "natural" class of IND-CPA-secure $\tilde{\Pi}$ (including CKKS), $M[\tilde{\Pi}]$ is not q-IND-CPA^D secure when one uses dynamic error estimation, and
2. there exists an IND-CPA-secure $\tilde{\Pi}$ such that $M[\tilde{\Pi}]$ is not KR^D-secure (again, when one uses dynamic error estimation).

5.1 A (Heuristic) Dynamic Estimation Procedure for CKKS

We first provide a detailed description of Yuriy Polyakov's dynamic error estimation procedure for CKKS [28], which has been implemented in PALISADE [24]. We define a variant DE-CKKS of CKKS that is modified to use this dynamic error estimation technique. The message space of DE-CKKS is the set of real vectors $\mathbb{R}^{n/2}$, which is a subset of the message space $\mathbb{C}^{n/2}$ of CKKS. We use $\Re(z)$ and $\Im(z)$ to denote the real and imaginary parts of a complex number $z \in \mathbb{C}$, respectively. We now describe the modified scheme DE-CKKS.

- DE-CKKS.KeyGen: The parameter and key generation algorithms are identical to CKKS, except that the conjugation keys are not generated anymore.
- DE-CKKS.Encode: The encoding algorithm is the same as in CKKS, except that it takes only real vectors $\mathbf{x} \in \mathbb{R}^{n/2}$.
- DE-CKKS.Enc: The encryption algorithm is identical to CKKS.
- DE-CKKS.Eval: The homomorphic evaluation algorithm is also identical to CKKS, except that homomorphic conjugation operation is no longer supported.
- DE-CKKS.Dec: The modified decryption algorithm combines the decryption and decoding algorithms of CKKS, and it works as follows given the secret key sk and a ciphertext ct.
  1. Decrypt ct and then decode the vanilla CKKS decryption result: $\mathbf{z} = $ CKKS.Decode(CKKS.Dec$_{\mathsf{sk}}$(ct)). Note that $\mathbf{z} \in \mathbb{C}^{n/2}$ is a complex vector.
  2. Let $\mathbf{x} = \Re(\mathbf{z})$, and $\mathbf{e} = \Im(\mathbf{z})$. Estimate the standard deviation $\sigma_e = $ stdev($\mathbf{e}$).
  3. Return $\mathbf{x} + \mathbf{r}$, where $\mathbf{r} \leftarrow \mathcal{N}(0, \sqrt{q+1} \cdot \sigma_e I_n)$ is a Gaussian noise vector.

In practice, since the canonical embedding is a scaled isometry with respect to the ℓ_2 norm, we can add the same amount of noise without decoding by first decrypting ct to obtain the ring element $m = $ CKKS.Dec$_{\mathsf{sk}}$(ct), computing the ℓ_2 norm of $\frac{1}{2}(m(X) - m(1/X))$ to obtain $\sigma_e' = \sqrt{n} \cdot \sigma_e$, adding $n/2$ i.i.d. Gaussians of parameter $\sqrt{q+1} \cdot \sigma_e'$ to m' and then decoding the resulting noisy ring element.

The PALISADE development team has done some experiments to validate this dynamic error estimation method, and they claimed that it provides a good estimation [28]. With optimizations described in [17], they assumed that the rescaling error dominates the ciphertext error after each rescaling operation, and that such error can be reduced in size similar to the ciphertext error in fresh encryptions. Furthermore, they assumed the adversary is non-adaptive, meaning that the input messages do not depend on any decryption result. Their experiments encrypted two random real vectors, homomorphically evaluated their component-wise product followed by a rescaling operation, and then decrypted the resulting ciphertext and compared the estimated error size with the actual ciphertext error. The results showed that the dynamically error estimation is very close to the actual ciphertext error sizes: for example, they differ by at most 2 bits when the lattice dimension is $n = 2^{13}$.

5.2 Dynamic Estimation

We next introduce the notion of a dynamically approximately correct FHE scheme $\tilde{\Pi}$. Our notion of dynamic approximate correctness depends on solely the "run-time" values of the FHE scheme, namely the secret key sk, and the ciphertext ct one wishes to bound. These suffice to instantiate the dynamic estimation scheme described in Sect. 5.1. We omit the other values (such as individual ciphertext error bounds t_i, and the circuit C itself) for simplicity—there clearly cannot be a security benefit to this omission, as an adversary can easily record or compute these values.

Definition 21 (Dynamic Approximate Correctness). *Let Π be a FHE scheme with message space $\mathcal{M} \subseteq \widetilde{\mathcal{M}}$, which is a normed space with norm $\|\cdot\| : \widetilde{\mathcal{M}} \to \mathbb{R}_{\geq 0}$. Let $\mathcal{L}$ be a space of evaluatable functions, and let $\mathsf{Estimate} : \mathcal{SK} \times \mathcal{C} \to \mathbb{R}_{\geq 0}$ be an efficiently computable function. We call the tuple of algorithms $\tilde{\Pi} = (\Pi, \mathsf{Estimate})$ a dynamically approximately correct FHE scheme if for all $m_1, \dots, m_k \in \mathcal{M}$, for all $C \in \mathcal{L}$, for all $(\mathsf{pk}, \mathsf{sk}) \leftarrow \mathsf{KeyGen}(1^\kappa)$, for all $\mathsf{ct} \leftarrow \mathsf{Eval}_{\mathsf{pk}}(C, \mathsf{Enc}_{\mathsf{pk}}(m_1), \dots, \mathsf{Enc}_{\mathsf{pk}}(m_k))$, we have that*

$$\|\mathsf{Dec}_{\mathsf{sk}}(\mathsf{ct}) - C(m_1, \dots, m_k)\| \leq \mathsf{Estimate}_{\mathsf{sk}}(\mathsf{ct}). \tag{10}$$

The above notion is a "perfect" notion of dynamic approximate correctness—there is an obvious statistical notion as well, where the desired inequality solely has to hold with high probability over all of the various sources of randomness. For simplicity of exposition we will work with the perfect notion.

We will view the notion of dynamic approximate correctness as a refinement of the notion of static approximate correctness. This can be done without loss of generality, as

- every known approximate FHE scheme is statically correct, and
- the minimum of two (correct) estimation functions is correct.

5.3 Attack Against IND-CPA$^\mathsf{D}$-Security of $M[\tilde{\Pi}]$ for "Natural" Π

We next attack the IND-CPA$^\mathsf{D}$ security of $M[\tilde{\Pi}]$ for "natural" dynamically correct schemes $\tilde{\Pi}$. We briefly summarize the attack, as it is both "obvious", and establishing it theoretically requires a few new definitions (as it fails for "unnatural" schemes). If

- dynamic error estimation is able to tightly estimate the ciphertext error,
- the growth of ciphertext error during certain operations (such as multiplication) is dependent on the input to the operation, and

– the noise the KLDP mechanism M_t adds is dependent on t in a noticable way, then

an adversary which can distinguish the smaller KLDP noise can immediately break q-IND-CPA^D-security. This is simply because one can use the aforementioned operation to construct two ciphertexts ct_0, ct_1 that encrypt the same value, but have drastically different ciphertext errors. Then, as the dynamic error estimation can detect this, the KLDP mechanism will add drastically different noise in the left and right worlds of the q-IND-CPA^D game, immediately breaking security.

The attack is straightforward to implement, which we demonstrate in Sect. 5.4. We next theoretically establish the validity of the attack, by defining the aforementioned notions of "naturality".

Definition 22 (τ-Separated Noise Estimation). *Let $\tilde{\Pi}$ be a dynamically approximately correct FHE scheme with message space $\mathcal{M}$ and space of evaluatable functions $\mathcal{L}$. Let $\tau \geq 1$, and let $C \in \mathcal{L}$ be a circuit. For $m_0, m_1 \in \mathcal{M}$, let $t(m) = \mathsf{Estimate}_{\mathsf{sk}}(\mathsf{Eval}_{\mathsf{pk}}(C, \mathsf{Enc}_{\mathsf{pk}}(m)))$. We say that C has τ-separated noise under $\tilde{\Pi}$ if there exists $m_0, m_1 \in \mathcal{M}$ such that $\tau t(m_0) = t(m_1)$ with nonnegligible probability.*

The seemingly strong condition $t_1 = \tau t_0$ can be replaced by requiring that $|t_0 - \tau t_1|$ is small, and the mechanism M_t produces larger noise as t increases. For example, the Gaussian mechanism adds noise of variance $\sigma^2 = t^2/2\rho$, which increases monotonically with t.

Definition 23 (τ-Sensitivity). *Let M_t be a ρ-KLDP mechanism on a normed space $\mathcal{M}$, and let $\tau : \mathbb{R}_{\geq 0} \to \mathbb{R}_{\geq 0}$. We say that M_t is τ-sensitive at $m \in \mathcal{M}$ if for any $t \geq 1$, the distributions $M_t(m) \not\approx_c M_{t\tau(\rho)}(m)$ are computationally distinguishable.*

The trivial 0-KLDP mechanism (which ignores its input, and returns a fixed constant) is not τ-sensitive for any τ. Note that this condition is desirable in practice—if M_t is not τ-sensitive, there is no real point in getting sharper noise estimates.

Theorem 6. *Let $\tilde{\Pi}$ be an IND-CPA-secure, dynamically approximately correct FHE scheme with message space $\mathcal{M}$ and space of evaluatable functions $\mathcal{L}$. Let $\tau : \mathbb{R}_{\geq 0} \to \mathbb{R}_{\geq 0}$, and assume that M is a ρ-KLDP mechanism which is τ-sensitive at 0. Furthermore, assume there exist $m_0, m_1 \in \mathcal{M}$ and $C \in \mathcal{L}$ such that $C(m_0) = C(m_1) = 0$ and C has τ-separated noise estimation under $\tilde{\Pi}$ with respect to inputs m_0, m_1. Then $M[\tilde{\Pi}]$ is not IND-CPA^D-secure.*

Proof. We defer details (which is simply a formalization of the attack sketched at the beginning of the section) to the full version of the paper. □

While it is not clear how to extend this attack to an attack on KR^D security (as was present in [19]), the attack still leaks information correlated with $\|m\|$.

5.4   Breaking q-IND-CPA^D-Security of PALISADE's Dynamic Error Estimation Countermeasure

We implemented the attack in Theorem 6 against the PALISADE's implementation of CKKS, which is currently the only known implementation of dynamic noise estimation. Our attack experiments use the exceedingly simple circuit $f(x_1, x_2) = x_1^2 - x_2$, as well as the circuit $g(x_0, \ldots, x_{4k-1}) = \sum_{i=0}^{2k-1}(x_i \cdot x_{2k+i})$ in Algorithm 4. Notice that both f and g evaluate to 0 on input $\mathbf{0}$. On the other hand, we chose several moderate values of $B > 0$ to set the input $\mathbf{m}$ such that $f(\mathbf{m}) = 0$ and $g(\mathbf{m}) = 0$:

- For f, let $m_1 = B$ and $m_2 = B^2$.
- For g, let $m_i = B$ for all $0 \le i \le 3k - 1$, and let $m_i = -B$ for all $3k \le i \le 4k - 1$.

Our attack homomorphically evaluates f (or g) on encryptions of both $\mathbf{0}$ and $\mathbf{m}$, then it decrypts the final ciphertexts to get z_0 and z_m. As expected, in all our experiments we see that $\|z_0\|_\infty$ and $\|z_m\|_\infty$ can be clearly distinguished. We summarize our experimental results in Table 2 with several parameter sets. We have made the source code of our experimental programs available.[7]

Table 2. The experimental results of applying the attack in Theorem 6 with circuits $f(x_1, x_2) = x_1^2 - x_2$ and $g(x_0, \ldots, x_{4k-1}) = \sum_{i=0}^{2k-1}(x_i \cdot x_{2k+i})$. For both $C \in \{f, g\}$, denote z_0 the decryption result of $\mathsf{Eval}_{\mathsf{pk}}(C, \mathsf{Enc}_{\mathsf{pk}}(\mathbf{0}))$, and z_m the decryption result of $\mathsf{Eval}_{\mathsf{pk}}(C, \mathsf{Enc}_{\mathsf{pk}}(\mathbf{m}))$ for the input $\mathbf{m}$ as defined above with parameters B and k. We set the lattice parameters (n, Q) to achieve at least 128 bit IND-CPA security, and we choose several different values for the scaling factor Δ and the slots number. For each parameter set, we run the attack 100 times and report the average and standard deviation of $\|z_0\|_\infty$ and $\|z_m\|_\infty$. As shown in the last two columns, there are clear distinctions on the estimated noise sizes between ciphertexts evaluated on $\mathbf{0}$ and $\mathbf{m}$.

Circuit	$(n, \log Q)$	$\log \Delta$	B	k	#slots	$\|z_0\|_\infty$	$\|z_m\|_\infty$
f	$(2^{13}, 100)$	40	100	-	1	$2.19 \times 10^{-8} \pm 1.83 \times 10^{-8}$	$2.75 \times 10^{-6} \pm 2.19 \times 10^{-6}$
			100	-	1024	$1.07 \times 10^{-7} \pm 1.42 \times 10^{-8}$	$1.87 \times 10^{-5} \pm 2.54 \times 10^{-6}$
			32	-	1	$1.97 \times 10^{-8} \pm 1.52 \times 10^{-8}$	$1.06 \times 10^{-6} \pm 1.06 \times 10^{-6}$
			32	-	1024	$1.08 \times 10^{-7} \pm 1.54 \times 10^{-8}$	$6.08 \times 10^{-6} \pm 8.85 \times 10^{-7}$
g	$(2^{14}, 150)$	45	32	15	1	$1.08 \times 10^{-8} \pm 4.37 \times 10^{-9}$	$2.27 \times 10^{-7} \pm 1.95 \times 10^{-7}$
			32	15	1024	$1.08 \times 10^{-8} \pm 4.14 \times 10^{-9}$	$1.40 \times 10^{-6} \pm 2.02 \times 10^{-7}$
			16	50	1	$1.07 \times 10^{-8} \pm 4.45 \times 10^{-9}$	$2.00 \times 10^{-7} \pm 1.90 \times 10^{-7}$
			16	50	1024	$1.06 \times 10^{-8} \pm 4.67 \times 10^{-9}$	$1.27 \times 10^{-6} \pm 1.70 \times 10^{-7}$

5.5   Attack Against KR^D-Security of $M[\tilde{\Pi}]$ for "Artificial" Π

We construct an (artificial) IND-CPA-secure, dynamically approximately correct FHE scheme $\tilde{\Pi}$ such that $M[\tilde{\Pi}]$ fails to be KR^D-secure.

---

[7] https://github.com/ucsd-crypto/DynamicEstimationAttack.

Theorem 7. *There exists an IND-CPA-secure, dynamically approximately correct FHE scheme $\tilde{\Pi}$ such that for any linear ρ-KLDP mechanism M that is τ-sensitive at 0, $M[\tilde{\Pi}]$ is not* KR^D-*secure.*

Proof. It suffices to (deterministically) add "noise" of the form $\tau(1, 1, \ldots, 1)$ to decryptions, where τ is (adaptively) chosen to leak bits of the secret key. We defer details to the full version.

6   Conclusion and Open Problems

In this work, we have shown that for CKKS with "static" error estimates, to obtain κ-bit IND-CPA$^\mathsf{D}$ security

– it suffices to add $\kappa/2 + \tilde{O}(1)$ bits of noise (Theorem 3), and
– it is necessary to add $\kappa/4 - \tilde{\Omega}(1)$ bits of noise (Theorem 4).

Our results therefore somewhat tightly characterize the impact on the accuracy of CKKS instantiated with a natural countermeasure to the Li-Micciancio attack [19]—$\Theta(\kappa)$ additional bits of noise are both necessary and sufficient for security. Still, it is natural to wonder if the right scaling for our countermeasures is $\kappa/4$ or $\kappa/2$.

We additionally show how one can concretely obtain smaller noise via a relaxed notion of security (Theorem 5). In particular, we show that $s/2 + \tilde{O}(1)$ bits of additional noise suffice to achieve (c, s)-bits of q-IND-CPA$^\mathsf{D}$ security, where s can plausibly be set much less than 128.

We include discussion of the concrete overhead of our countermeasure in Sect. 4.6, where find that our countermeasure is easily implementable (for general purpose computation) provided the FHE library supports 128-bit precision computations, while FHE libraries that support 64-bit precision computations may only be able to instantiate our countermeasure for certain (low-precision) applications, or with aggressive parameterizations.

Both our work and the work of [19] investigate how the *correctness* of encryption can impact the underlying *security* one attains. As correctness analysis typically leverages (unproven) heuristics for tighter noise estimates, we view formally justifying these heuristics to be important going forward, as the false heuristics may lead to security issues.

While our results on "dynamic" error estimation are negative, we have not ruled out achieving some weaker security notion with these techniques (for natural schemes). Our attack of Theorem 6 shows that dynamic error estimation can leak the norm of the input to the computation. Can the leakage be *provably* limited to this information?

Finally, our work examines *black box* modifications one can make to CKKS to attain q-IND-CPA$^\mathsf{D}$-security. It is plausible that a CKKS-specific construction could attain smaller parameters, say by randomizing homomorphic operations, choosing larger than typical scaling factors Δ, or carefully investigating the ciphertext error after bootstrapping.

References

1. Albrecht, M., et al.: Homomorphic encryption security standard. Technical report, HomomorphicEncryption.org, Toronto, Canada, November 2018. https://homomorphicencryption.org/standard/

2. Bai, S., Lepoint, T., Roux-Langlois, A., Sakzad, A., Stehlé, D., Steinfeld, R.: Improved security proofs in lattice-based cryptography: using the Rényi divergence rather than the statistical distance. J. Cryptol. **31**(2), 610–640 (2018)

3. Canonne, C.L.: A survey on distribution testing: your data is big. But is it blue? Theory of Computing, pp. 1–100 (2020)

4. Canonne, C.L., Kamath, G., Steinke, T.: The discrete gaussian for differential privacy. In: Larochelle, H., Ranzato, M., Hadsell, R., Balcan, M.F., Lin, H. (eds.) Advances in Neural Information Processing Systems, vol. 33, pp. 15676–15688. Curran Associates Inc. (2020)

5. Cheon, J.H., et al.: Toward a secure drone system: flying with real-time homomorphic authenticated encryption. IEEE Access **6**, 24325–24339 (2018)

6. Cheon, J.H., Han, K., Kim, A., Kim, M., Song, Y.: Bootstrapping for approximate homomorphic encryption. In: Nielsen, J.B., Rijmen, V. (eds.) EUROCRYPT 2018, Part I. LNCS, vol. 10820, pp. 360–384. Springer, Cham (2018). https://doi.org/10.1007/978-3-319-78381-9_14

7. Cheon, J.H., Han, K., Kim, A., Kim, M., Song, Y.: A full RNS variant of approximate homomorphic encryption. In: Cid, C., Jacobson Jr., M. (eds.) SAC 2018. LNCS, vol. 11349, pp. 347–368. Springer, Cham (2018). https://doi.org/10.1007/978-3-030-10970-7_16

8. Cheon, J.H., Kim, A., Kim, M., Song, Y.: Homomorphic encryption for arithmetic of approximate numbers. In: Takagi, T., Peyrin, T. (eds.) ASIACRYPT 2017, Part I. LNCS, vol. 10624, pp. 409–437. Springer, Cham (2017). https://doi.org/10.1007/978-3-319-70694-8_15

9. Cheon, J.H., Kim, A., Yhee, D.: Multi-dimensional packing for HEAAN for approximate matrix arithmetics. IACR Cryptology ePrint Archive, 2018:1245 (2018)

10. Cheon, J.H., Kim, D., Kim, Y., Song, Y.: Ensemble method for privacy-preserving logistic regression based on homomorphic encryption. IEEE Access **6**, 46938–46948 (2018)

11. Devroye, L., Mehrabian, A., Reddad, T.: The total variation distance between high-dimensional Gaussians with the same mean. arXiv preprint arXiv:1810.08693 (2018)

12. Gentry, C., Halevi, S., Smart, N.P.: Homomorphic evaluation of the AES circuit. In: Safavi-Naini, R., Canetti, R. (eds.) CRYPTO 2012. LNCS, vol. 7417, pp. 850–867. Springer, Heidelberg (2012). https://doi.org/10.1007/978-3-642-32009-5_49

13. Goldwasser, S., Micali, S.: Probabilistic encryption. J. Comput. Syst. Sci. **28**(2), 270–299 (1984)

14. Han, K., Hong, S., Cheon, J.H., Park, D.: Logistic regression on homomorphic encrypted data at scale. In: AAAI 2019, pp. 9466–9471. AAAI Press (2019)

15. HElib (release 2.2.0). https://github.com/homenc/HElib (2021). IBM

16. Kalamkar, D.D., et al.: A study of BFLOAT16 for deep learning training. arXiv preprint arXiv:1905.12322 (2019)

17. Kim, A., Papadimitriou, A., Polyakov, Y.: Approximate homomorphic encryption with reduced approximation error. In: Galbraith, S.D. (ed.) CT-RSA 2022. LNCS, vol. 13161, pp. 120–144. Springer, Cham (2022). https://doi.org/10.1007/978-3-030-95312-6_6

18. Lattigo 2.2.0. Online. http://github.com/ldsec/lattigo, July 2021. EPFL-LDS
19. Li, B., Micciancio, D.: On the security of homomorphic encryption on approximate numbers. In: Canteaut, A., Standaert, F.-X. (eds.) EUROCRYPT 2021. LNCS, vol. 12696, pp. 648–677. Springer, Cham (2021). https://doi.org/10.1007/978-3-030-77870-5_23
20. Lyubashevsky, V., Peikert, C., Regev, O.: On ideal lattices and learning with errors over rings. J. ACM **60**(6), 43:1–43:35 (2013)
21. Micciancio, D., Walter, M.: Gaussian sampling over the integers: efficient, generic, constant-time. In: Katz, J., Shacham, H. (eds.) CRYPTO 2017. LNCS, vol. 10402, pp. 455–485. Springer, Cham (2017). https://doi.org/10.1007/978-3-319-63715-0_16
22. Micciancio, D., Walter, M.: On the bit security of cryptographic primitives. In: Nielsen, J.B., Rijmen, V. (eds.) EUROCRYPT 2018. LNCS, vol. 10820, pp. 3–28. Springer, Cham (2018). https://doi.org/10.1007/978-3-319-78381-9_1
23. Mironov, I.: Rényi differential privacy. In: 2017 IEEE 30th Computer Security Foundations Symposium (CSF), pp. 263–275 (2017)
24. PALISADE lattice cryptography library (release 1.11.6). https://gitlab.com/palisade/ (2022). PALISADE Project
25. Park, S., Lee, J., Cheon, J.H., Lee, J., Kim, J., Byun, J.: Security-preserving support vector machine with fully homomorphic encryption. In: SafeAI@AAAI 2019, CEUR Workshop Proceedings, vol. 2301 (2019). CEUR-WS.org
26. Peikert, C.: Public-key cryptosystems from the worst-case shortest vector problem: extended abstract. In: STOC, pp. 333–342. ACM (2009)
27. Peikert, C., Regev, O., Stephens-Davidowitz, N.: Pseudorandomness of ring-LWE for any ring and modulus. In: STOC, pp. 461–473. ACM (2017)
28. Polyakov, Y.: Personal communication, October 2020
29. Polyanskiy, Y., Wu, Y.: Lecture notes on information theory. Lecture Notes for ECE563 (UIUC) and 6(2012–2016):7 (2014)
30. Pöppelmann, T., Ducas, L., Güneysu, T.: Enhanced lattice-based signatures on reconfigurable hardware. In: Batina, L., Robshaw, M. (eds.) CHES 2014. LNCS, vol. 8731, pp. 353–370. Springer, Heidelberg (2014). https://doi.org/10.1007/978-3-662-44709-3_20
31. Regev, O.: On lattices, learning with errors, random linear codes, and cryptography. J. ACM **56**(6), 34:1–34:40 (2009)
32. Microsoft SEAL (release 3.6). https://github.com/Microsoft/SEAL, November 2020. Microsoft Research, Redmond, WA
33. Wang, N., Choi, J., Brand, D., Chen, C.-Y., Gopalakrishnan, K.: Training deep neural networks with 8-bit floating point numbers. In: Advances in Neural Information Processing Systems, vol. 31 (2018)

Multi-input Attribute Based Encryption and Predicate Encryption

Shweta Agrawal[1], Anshu Yadav[1(✉)], and Shota Yamada[2]

[1] IIT Madras, Chennai, India
shweta.a@cse.iitm.ac.in, anshu.yadav06@gmail.com
[2] National Institute of Advanced Industrial Science and Technology (AIST),
Tokyo, Japan
yamada-shota@aist.go.jp

Abstract. Motivated by several new and natural applications, we initiate the study of multi-input predicate encryption (miPE) and further develop multi-input attribute based encryption (miABE). Our contributions are:

1. *Formalizing Security:* We provide definitions for miABE and miPE in the symmetric key setting and formalize security in the standard *indistinguishability* (IND) paradigm, against *unbounded* collusions.
2. *Two-input* ABE *for* NC₁ *from* LWE *and Pairings:* We provide the first constructions for two-input *key-policy* ABE for NC₁ from LWE and pairings. Our construction leverages a surprising connection between techniques recently developed by Agrawal and Yamada (Eurocrypt, 2020) in the context of succinct *single*-input *ciphertext-policy* ABE, to the seemingly unrelated problem of *two*-input *key-policy* ABE. Similarly to Agrawal-Yamada, our construction is proven secure in the bilinear generic group model. By leveraging inner product functional encryption and using (a variant of) the KOALA knowledge assumption, we obtain a construction in the standard model analogously to Agrawal, Wichs and Yamada (TCC, 2020).
3. *Heuristic two-input* ABE *for* P *from Lattices:* We show that techniques developed for succinct single-input ciphertext-policy ABE by Brakerski and Vaikuntanathan (ITCS 2022) can also be seen from the lens of miABE and obtain the first two-input key-policy ABE from lattices for P.
4. *Heuristic three-input* ABE *and* PE *for* NC₁ *from Pairings and Lattices:* We obtain the first *three*-input ABE for NC₁ by harnessing the powers of both the Agrawal-Yamada and the Brakerski-Vaikuntanathan constructions.
5. *Multi-input* ABE *to multi-input* PE *via Lockable Obfuscation:* We provide a generic compiler that lifts multi-input ABE to multi-input PE by relying on the hiding properties of Lockable Obfuscation (LO) by Wichs-Zirdelis and Goyal-Koppula-Waters (FOCS 2018), which can be based on LWE. Our compiler generalises such a compiler for single-input setting to the much more challenging setting of multiple inputs. By instantiating our compiler with our new two and three-input ABE schemes, we obtain the first constructions of two and three-input PE schemes.

© International Association for Cryptologic Research 2022
Y. Dodis and T. Shrimpton (Eds.): CRYPTO 2022, LNCS 13507, pp. 590–621, 2022.
https://doi.org/10.1007/978-3-031-15802-5_21

Our constructions of multi-input ABE provide the first improvement to the compression factor of *non-trivially exponentially efficient Witness Encryption* defined by Brakerski et al. (SCN 2018) without relying on compact functional encryption or indistinguishability obfuscation. We believe that the unexpected connection between succinct single-input ciphertext-policy ABE and multi-input key-policy ABE may lead to a new pathway for witness encryption. We remark that our constructions provide the first candidates for a nontrivial class of miFE without needing LPN or low depth PRG.

Keywords: Multi-input · Attribute Based Encryption · Predicate Encryption

1   Introduction

Attribute based encryption (ABE) is a generalization of public key encryption which enables fine grained access control on encrypted data. In an ABE scheme, the ciphertext is associated with a secret message m and a public *attribute* vector $\mathbf{x}$ while a secret key is associated with a function f. Decryption succeeds to reveal m if and only if $f(\mathbf{x}) = 1$. Security seeks ciphertext indistinguishability in the presence of *collusion* attacks, namely an adversary possessing a collection of keys $\{\mathsf{sk}_{f_i}\}_{i \in [\text{poly}]}$ should not be able to distinguish between ciphertexts corresponding to $(\mathbf{x}, m_0)$ and $(\mathbf{x}, m_1)$ unless one of the keys $\mathsf{sk}_{f_{i*}}$ is *individually* authorised to decrypt, i.e. $f_{i*}(\mathbf{x}) = 1$. ABE comes in two flavours – "key-policy" and "ciphertext-policy", depending on whether the function f is embedded in the key or the ciphertext.

The stronger notion of predicate encryption (PE) [18,29,36,49] further requires the attribute vector $\mathbf{x}$ to be hidden so that ciphertexts corresponding to $(\mathbf{x}_0, m_0)$ and $(\mathbf{x}_1, m_1)$ remain indistinguishable so long as $f_i(\mathbf{x}_0) = f_i(\mathbf{x}_1) = 0$ for all secret keys $\{\mathsf{sk}_{f_i}\}_{i \in [\text{poly}]}$ seen by the adversary.

Both ABE and PE have been widely studied, and possess elegant instantiations from a variety of assumptions [6,13,16,18,18,20,22,28,29,29,30, 32,36,36–39,46–49,51,52]. Despite all this amazing progress, however, all known constructions support the single input setting – namely, the function f embedded in the secret key sk_f has arity one, so that the secret key can be used to decrypt only a single ciphertext at a time. While the more realistic multi-input setting has been studied for other closely related notions such as fully homomorphic encryption [24,44,45] and functional encryption [1–4,7,11,23,25,27,40,50], this has not been investigated at all in the context of predicate encryption, and only sparingly [19] in the context of attribute based encryption.

Supporting Multiple Sources. We argue that the multi-input setting is important even in the context of ABE and PE and generalizing these primitives to support multiple sources enables a host of new and natural applications. At the heart of the multi-input setting, for any primitive, is the fact that data generated independently in multiple locations may be correlated in meaningful ways, and it is often pertinent to consider the input as a concatenation of these correlated partial inputs. For instance, a patient is likely to visit different medical centres for treatment of different diseases and her overall medical record is a concatenation of the medical data generated at different centers. Similarly, a company is likely to conduct research and development related to a given technology in different locations but the complete data pertaining to that technology is a concatenation of these. Moreover, to organize data logically and to benefit from cloud storage and computing, it is useful for each source to upload this encrypted data to a central server. Now, it may be desirable to provide restricted access to relevant consumers of the data, exactly as in ABE for encrypted access control (say) or PE for encrypted search (say), but with the caveat that the input was generated in a distributed manner and is encoded in multiple ciphertexts.

For concreteness, consider a doctor who is treating Covid patients and wants to understand the relation between Covid and other medical conditions such as asthma or cancer, each of which are treated at different locations. The records of a given patient are encrypted independently and stored in a central repository, and the doctor can be given a key that filters stored (encrypted) records according to criteria such as *condition = 'Covid' and condition = 'asthma' and age group =‘60–80’* and enables decryption of these. Similarly, a company (e.g. IBM) which conducts research in quantum technologies is likely to have different teams for theoretical and experimental research, and these teams are likely to work in different locations – indeed, even members of the same team may not be co-located. Data pertaining to the research could be stored encrypted in a central location where individual ciphertexts are generated independently, and the company may desire to give restricted access to a patent office. As a third example, a company may have been sued for some malpractice, and the data pertinent to the case could span multiple locations. Now the company may wish to provide restricted access to a law firm which enables decryption only of the data pertaining to the lawsuit, encrypted independently by multiple sources. A possible solution may be to gather all the information at a central entity and then use single input ABE or PE as before, but there are two problems with this approach: (i) if data is transmitted unencrypted to the central server it creates vulnerability – this can be avoided by each source encrypting to the server's public key, and the server decrypting and re-encrypting using single input schemes, but this is wasteful and cumbersome, (ii) one may desire to use an untrusted commercial cloud server to store the encrypted data, in which case the step of creating the ciphertext at a central server in step (i) is completely redundant and doubly inefficient.

Multi-input attribute based encryption (miABE) or predicate encryption (miPE) arise as natural fits to the above applications. Similarly to the single input case, the secret key corresponds to a function f but the arity of this function can now be $k > 1$ – we may have k ciphertexts generated independently encoding $(\mathbf{x}_i, m_i)_{i \in [k]}$, and decryption reveals $(m_1, \ldots, m_k)$ if and only if $f(\mathbf{x}_1, \ldots, \mathbf{x}_k) = 1$. Indeed, any application of single input ABE and PE where the underlying data is generated in multiple locations and is correlated in meaningful ways can benefit from the abstraction of multi-input ABE and PE.

Prior Work. Brakerski et al. [19] studied the notion of miABE and showed that miABE for polynomial arity implies *witness encryption* (WE). However, though they provided the first definition of miABE, they only used it as a new pathway for achieving witness encryption, not as a notion with its own applications – in their definition, only the first encryptor has any input, since this suffices for WE. They do not consider strong notions of security or provide any constructions of miABE. They also defined the notion of non-trivially exponentially efficient witness encryption (XWE), where the encryption run-time is only required to be much smaller than the trivial 2^m bound for NP relations with witness size m. They show how to construct such XWE schemes for all of NP with encryption run-time $2^{m/2}$ using the single input ABE by [28]. For encryption run-time $2^{\gamma \cdot m}$, the term γ is denoted as *compression* factor, and they explicitly left open the problem of constructing XWE schemes with an improved compression factor.

Both ABE and PE can be captured as special cases of *functional encryption* [17,48], which has been studied extensively, in both the single-input [16,17,28,48] and multi-input setting [1–4,7,11,23,25,27,40,50]. Recall that in functional encryption (FE), a secret key is associated with a function f, a ciphertext is associated with an input $\mathbf{x}$ and decryption allows to recover $f(\mathbf{x})$ and nothing else. It is easy to see that PE and ABE are both special cases of FE – in particular, both PE and ABE achieve the same functionality but restrict the security requirements of FE. In PE, we ask that the attribute $\mathbf{x}$ be hidden but only when the adversary does not see any decrypting keys, namely $f_i(\mathbf{x}) = 0$ for all function keys f_i received by the adversary. On the other hand, in FE, the attacker may request a key sk_f, so long as f does not distinguish the challenge messages $(\mathbf{x}_0, m_0), (\mathbf{x}_1, m_1)$, namely, we may have $f(\mathbf{x}_0) = f(\mathbf{x}_1) = 1$ so long as $m_0 = m_1$[1]. In the even weaker ABE, we do not ask any notion of hiding for $\mathbf{x}$, and this may be provided in the clear with the ciphertext.

Why not Functional Encryption? The informed reader may wonder what is the advantage of studying primitives like miPE or miABE when these are special cases of multi-input functional encryption (miFE), which has recently been constructed from standard assumptions [11,34]. It was shown by [11,15] that FE satisfying a certain efficiency property (known as *compactness*) implies multi-input functional encryption, which in turn implies the powerful primitive of *indistinguishability obfuscation* (iO) [14]. A long line of exciting works endeavoured to construct compact FE (and hence iO) from standard assumptions [5,12,26,33,41–43], coming ever-closer, until the very recent work of Jain, Lin and Sahai closed the last remaining gap and achieved this much sought after goal [34,35]. In [34,35], the authors provide a construction for compact FE, which in turn implies miFE for polynomial arity (albeit with exponential loss in the reduction).

Going via the route of compact FE, we obtain an exciting feasibility result for miFE and hence miABE as well as miPE. However, we argue that using something

---

[1] We note that a message m separate from attribute $\mathbf{x}$ is not required in the definition of FE, but we include it here for simpler comparison with PE and ABE.

as strong as miFE or iO to construct miABE and miPE is undesirable, and indeed an "overkill" for the following reasons:

– *Assumptions:* Compact FE of [34] is constructed via a careful combination of 4 assumptions – Learning Parity with Noise (LPN), Learning With Errors (LWE), SXDH assumption on Pairings, and pseudorandom generators computable in constant depth. In the follow-up work of [35], this set of assumptions was trimmed to exclude LWE. Therefore any construction built using compact FE must make at least this set of assumptions, which is restrictive. A major goal in the theory of cryptography is developing constructions from diverse assumptions.

– *Complexity:* The construction of compact FE is extremely complex, comprising a series of careful steps, and this must then be lifted to miFE using another complex construction [11]. Unlike FE, both PE and ABE are *much simpler, "all or nothing"* primitives and permit direct constructions in the single-input setting [16,28,29]. Do we need the full complexity of an miFE construction to get miPE or miABE? Indeed, even in the context of miFE, there is a large body of work that studies direct constructions for smaller function classes such as linear and quadratic functions [1–4,7,23,25,40,50].

– *New Techniques:* Finally and most importantly, we believe that it is extremely useful to develop new techniques for simpler primitives that are not known to be in obfustopia, and provide direct constructions. While direct constructions are likely to be more efficient, and are interesting in their own right, they may also lead to new pathways even for obfustopia primitives such as witness encryption or compact FE. Note that the only known construction of FE from standard assumptions is by [34,35], which makes crucial (and surprising) use of LPN in order to overcome a technical barrier – is LPN necessary for other primitives implied by compact FE? We believe that exploring new methods to construct weaker primitives is of central importance in developing better understanding of cryptographic assumptions, their power and limits.

1.1 Our Results

In this work, we initiate the study of multi-input predicate and attribute based encryption (miABE and miPE) and make the following contributions:

1. *Formalizing Security:* We provide definitions for miABE and miPE in the *symmetric* key setting and formalize two security notions in the standard *indistinguishability* (IND) paradigm, against *unbounded* collusions. The first (regular) notion of security assumes that the attacker does not receive any decrypting keys, as is standard in the case of PE/ABE. The second *strong* notion, allows some decrypting queries in restricted settings.

2. *Two-input* ABE *for* NC_1 *from* LWE *and Pairings:* We provide the first constructions for two-input *key-policy* ABE for NC_1 from LWE and pairings. Our construction leverages a surprising connection between techniques

recently developed by Agrawal and Yamada [10] in the context of succinct *single*-input *ciphertext-policy* ABE, to the seemingly unrelated problem of *two*-input *key-policy* ABE. Similarly to [10], our construction is proven secure in the bilinear generic group model. By leveraging inner product functional encryption and using (a variant of) the KOALA knowledge assumption, we obtain a construction in the standard model analogously to Agrawal, Wichs and Yamada [8].

3. *Heuristic two-input* ABE *for* P *from Lattices:* We show that techniques developed for succinct single-input ciphertext-policy ABE by Brakerski and Vaikuntanathan [21] can also be seen from the lens of miABE and obtain the first two-input key-policy ABE from lattices for P. Similarly to [21], this construction is heuristic.

4. *Heuristic three-input* ABE *and* PE *for* NC$_1$ *from Pairings and Lattices:* We obtain the first *three*-input ABE for NC$_1$ by harnessing the powers of both the Agrawal-Yamada [10] and the Brakerski-Vaikuntanathan [21] constructions.

5. *Multi-input* ABE *to multi-input* PE *via Lockable Obfuscation:* We provide a generic compiler that lifts multi-input ABE to multi-input PE by relying on the hiding properties of Lockable Obfuscation (LO) by Wichs-Zirdelis and Goyal-Koppula-Waters (FOCS 2018), which can be based on LWE. Our compiler generalises such a compiler for single-input setting to the much more challenging setting of multiple inputs. By instantiating our compiler with our new two and three-input ABE schemes, we obtain the first constructions of two and three-input PE schemes.

Our constructions of multi-input ABE provide the first improvement to the compression factor (from $1/2$ to $1/3$ or $1/4$) of *non-trivially exponentially efficient Witness Encryption* defined by Brakerski et al. [19] without relying on compact functional encryption or indistinguishability obfuscation. We believe that the unexpected connection between succinct single-input ciphertext-policy ABE and multi-input key-policy ABE may lead to a new pathway for witness encryption. We remark that our constructions provide the first candidates for a nontrivial class of miFE without needing LPN or low depth PRG.

1.2 Our Techniques

Modeling Multi-Input Attribute Based and Predicate Encryption. Our first contribution is to model multi-input attribute based encryption (miABE) and predicate encryption (miPE) as relevant primitives in their own right. To begin, we observe that similarly to multi-input functional encryption (miFE) [27], these primitives are meaningful primarily in the symmetric key setting where the encryptor requires a secret key to compute a ciphertext. This is to prevent the primitive becoming trivial due to excessive leakage occurring by virtue of functionality. In more detail, let us say k encryptors compute an unbounded number ciphertexts in each slot, i.e. $\{(\mathbf{x}_1^j, m_1^j), \ldots (\mathbf{x}_k^j, m_k^j)\}_{j \in [\text{poly}]}$

and the adversary obtains secret keys corresponding to functions $\{f_i\}_{i\in[\text{poly}]}$. In the multi-input setting, ciphertexts across slots can be combined, allowing the adversary to compute $f_i(\mathbf{x}_1^{j_1}, \mathbf{x}_2^{j_2}, \ldots, \mathbf{x}_k^{j_k})$ for any indices $i, j_1, \ldots, j_k \in [\text{poly}]$. In the public key setting, an adversary can easily encrypt messages for various attributes of its choice and decrypt these with the challenge ciphertext in a given slot to learn a potentially unbounded amount of information. Due to this, we believe that the primitives of miABE and miPE are meaningful in the symmetric key setting where encryption also requires a secret key.

For security, we require the standard notion of ciphertext indistinguishability in the presence of collusion attacks, as in the single-input setting. Recall that in the single-input setting, the adversary cannot request any decrypting keys for challenge ciphertexts to prevent trivial attacks. However, since we are in the symmetric key setting where the adversary cannot encrypt herself, we propose an additional notion of *strong* security which also permits the adversary to request decrypting ciphertexts in some cases. In more detail, for the case of miABE, our strong security game allows the attacker to request function keys for $\{f_i\}_{i\in[\text{poly}]}$ and ciphertexts for tuples $\{(\mathbf{x}_1^j, m_{\beta,1}^j), \ldots, (\mathbf{x}_k^j, m_{\beta,k}^j)\}_{\beta\in\{0,1\}, j\in[\text{poly}]}$ so that it may hold that $f_i(\mathbf{x}_1^{j_1}, \ldots, \mathbf{x}_k^{j_k}) = 1$ for some $i, j_1, \ldots, j_k \in [\text{poly}]$ as long as the challenge messages do not distinguish, i.e. $(m_{1,0}^{j_1} = m_{1,1}^{j_1}), \ldots, (m_{k,0}^{j_k} = m_{k,1}^{j_k})$. For the case of miPE, we analogously define a strong version of security by asking that if $f_i(\mathbf{x}_{1,\beta}^{j_1}, \ldots, \mathbf{x}_{k,\beta}^{j_k}) = 1$ holds for some $i, j_1, \ldots, j_k \in [\text{poly}]$ and $\beta \in \{0,1\}$, then it is also true that $(\mathbf{x}_{1,0}^{j_1}, \ldots, \mathbf{x}_{k,0}^{j_k}) = (\mathbf{x}_{1,1}^{j_1}, \ldots, \mathbf{x}_{k,1}^{j_k})$ and $(m_{1,0}^{j_1}, \ldots, m_{k,0}^{j_k}) = (m_{1,1}^{j_1}, \ldots, m_{k,1}^{j_k})$. For more details, please see Sect. 2.

Constructing Two Input ABE from LWE and Bilinear GGM. In constructing two input ABE (2ABE), the main difficulty is to satisfy two seemingly contradicting requirements at the same time: (1) the two ciphertexts should be created independently, (2) these ciphertexts should be combined in a way that decryption is possible. If we look at specific ABE schemes (e.g., [16,32]), it seems that these requirements cannot be satisfied simultaneously. If we want to satisfy the second requirement, the two ciphertexts should have common randomness. However to satisfy the first requirement, the randomness in the two ciphertexts needs to be sampled independently. An approach might be to fix the randomness and put it into the master secret key which is then used by both ciphertexts – but this will compromise security since fresh randomness is crucial in safeguarding semantic security.

Generating Joint Randomness: For resolving this problem, we consider a scheme that modifies two independently generated ciphertexts so that they have common randomness and then "joins" them. This common randomness is jointly generated using independently chosen randomness in each ciphertext by using a pairing operation. Specifically, we compute a ciphertext for slot 1 with randomness t_1 and encode it in $\mathbb{G}_1$ and similarly, for slot 2 with randomness t_2 in $\mathbb{G}_2$, where $\mathbb{G} : \mathbb{G}_1 \times \mathbb{G}_2 \to \mathbb{G}_T$ is a pairing group with prime order q. Then, both ciphertexts may be combined to form a new ciphertext with respect to the randomness $t_1 t_2$

on $\mathbb{G}_T$. This approach seems to be promising, because we can uniquely separate every pair of ciphertexts, since each pair (i, j) will have unique randomness $t_1^i t_2^j$. In the generic group model, this is sufficient to prohibit "mix and match" attacks that try to combine components of different ciphertexts in the same slot.

Moving Beyond Degree 2: However, since we "used up" the pairing operation here, it appears we cannot perform more than linear operations on the generated ciphertext, which would severely restrict the function class supported by our construction. In particular, pairing based ABE schemes seem not to be compatible with the above approach, because these require additional multiplication in the exponent during decryption, which cannot be supported using a bilinear map. However, at this juncture, a trick suggested by Agrawal and Yamada [10] comes to our rescue – to combine lattice based ABE with bilinear maps in a way that lets us get the "best of both".

At a high level, the Agrawal-Yamada trick rests on the observation that in certain lattice based ABE schemes [16,30], decryption is structured as follows: (i) evaluate the circuit f on ciphertext encodings of $\mathbf{x}$, (ii) compute a matrix-vector product of the ciphertext matrix and secret key vector, (iii) perform a rounding operation to recover the message. Crucially, step (i) in the above description is in fact a *linear* operation over the encodings, even for circuits in P, and the only nonlinear part of decryption is the rounding operation in step (iii). They observe that steps (i) and (ii) may be done "upstairs" in the exponent and step (iii) may be done "downstairs" by recovering the exponent brute force, when it is small enough. Importantly, the exponent is small enough when the circuit class is restricted to NC_1 using asymmetry in noise growth [28,30]. While this idea was developed in the context of a single-input ciphertext-policy ABE, it appears to be exactly what we need for *two*-input key-policy ABE!

Perspective: Connection to Broadcast Encryption: In hindsight, the application of optimal broadcast encryption requires *succinctness* of the ciphertext, which recent constructions [8,10,21] obtain by relying on the *decomposability* of specific ABE schemes [16,30] – this decomposability is also what the multi-input setting intrinsically requires, albeit for a different reason. In more detail, decomposability means that the ciphertext for a vector $\mathbf{x}$ can be decomposed into $|\mathbf{x}|$ ciphertext components each encoding a single bit $\mathbf{x}_i$, and these components can be tied together using common randomness to yield a complete ciphertext. The bit by bit encoding of the vector allows $2|\mathbf{x}|$ ciphertext components, each component encoding both bits for a given position, to together encode $2^{|\mathbf{x}|}$ possible values of $\mathbf{x}$, which leads to the succinctness of ciphertext in optimal broadcast encryption schemes [8,10,21]. In the setting of multi-input ABE, decomposability allows to morph independently generated *full* ciphertexts with distinct randomness to *components of a single* ciphertext with common randomness. The randomness is "merged" using pairings (or lattices, see below) and the resultant ciphertext can now be treated like the ciphertext of a single input scheme.

Adapting to the 2ABE *Setting:* Let us recall the structure of the ciphertext in scheme of Boneh et al. [16], which is denoted as BGG^+ hereafter. As discussed above, a ciphertext for an attribute $\mathbf{x} \in [2\ell]^2$ in BGG^+ is generated by first generating LWE encodings (their exact structure is not important for this overview) for *all possible* values of the attribute $\mathbf{x}$, namely, $\{\psi_{i,b}\}_{i \in [2\ell], b \in \{0,1\}}$ (along with other components which are not relevant here) and then selecting $\{\psi_{i,x_i}\}_{i \in [2\ell]}$ based on $\mathbf{x}$, where x_i is the i-th bit of the attribute string $\mathbf{x}$.

Given the above structure, a candidate scheme works as follows. The setup algorithm computes encodings for all possible $\mathbf{x}$, namely $\{\psi_{i,b}\}_{i,b}$ and puts them into the master secret key. The encryptor for slot 1 chooses $t_1 \leftarrow \mathbb{Z}_q$ and encodes $(t_1, \{t_1\psi_{i,x_{1,i}}\}_{i \in [\ell]})$ in the exponent of $\mathbb{G}_1$. Similarly, the encryptor for slot 2 chooses $t_2 \leftarrow \mathbb{Z}_q$ and encodes $(t_2, \{t_2\psi_{i,x_{2,i-\ell}}\}_{i \in [\ell+1,2\ell]})$ in the exponent of $\mathbb{G}_2$. In decryption, we compute a pairing of matching components of the two ciphertexts to obtain $(t_1t_2, \{t_1t_2\psi_{i,x_i}\}_{i \in [2\ell]})$ in the exponent of $\mathbb{G}_T$. Using the BGG^+ decryption procedure described above, we may perform linear operations to evaluate the circuit, apply the BGG^+ secret key and obtain the message plus noise in the exponent, which is brought "downstairs" by brute force to perform the rounding and recover the message.

Challenges in Proving Security. While the above sketch provides a construction template, security is far from obvious. Indeed, some thought reveals that the multi-input setting creates delicate attack scenarios that need care to handle. As an example, consider the strong security definition which allows the adversary to request ciphertexts that are decryptable by secret keys so long as they do not lead to a distinguishing attack. For simplicity, let us restrict to the setting where only the slot 1 ciphertext carries a message and slot 2 ciphertexts carry nothing except attributes (this restriction can be removed). Now, a slot 1 ciphertext may carry a message that depends on the challenger's secret bit as long as it is not decryptable by any key. However, slot 2 ciphertexts may participate in decryption with other slot 1 ciphertexts that do not encode the challenge bit, and decryption can (and does) lead to randomness leakage of participating ciphertexts. When such a "leaky" slot 2 ciphertext is combined with the challenge slot 1 ciphertext for decryption, security breaks down.

For concreteness, let us consider the setting where the adversary makes slot 1 ciphertext queries for $(\mathbf{x}_1, (m_0, m_1))$ and $(\mathbf{x}_1', (m_0', m_1'))$ and slot 2 ciphertext query for $(\mathbf{x}_2)$. Furthermore, the adversary makes a single key query for a circuit F such that $F(\mathbf{x}_1, \mathbf{x}_2) = 0$ (unauthorized) and $F(\mathbf{x}_1', \mathbf{x}_2) = 1$ (authorized). Note that to prevent trivial attacks, we pose the restriction that $m_0' = m_1'$, but we may have $m_0 \neq m_1$. In this setting, the 2ABE construction described above is not secure since the noise associated with the slot 2 ciphertext for $\mathbf{x}_2$ leaks during decryption of the jointly generated ciphertext for $(\mathbf{x}_1', \mathbf{x}_2)$ and this prevents using BGG^+ security for the pair $(\mathbf{x}_1, \mathbf{x}_2)$.

To resolve the above problem, we need to somehow "disconnect" randomness used in the challenge ciphertexts of slot 1 from randomness used in

---

[2] The length of the attribute is set to 2ℓ to match our two-input setting.

leaky/decrypting ciphertexts of other slots. This is tricky since the multi-input setting insists that ciphertexts be combined across slots in an unrestricted way. Fortunately, another technique developed [10] for a completely different reason comes to our assistance – we discontinue encoding the BGG^+ ciphertexts in 2ABE ciphertexts for slot 2, so that even if a slot 2 ciphertext is decrypted, this does not affect the security of the BGG^+ encoding. Instead, we encode a binary "selection vector" in the exponent of $\mathbb{G}_2$, which enables the decryptor to recover $\psi_{2,x_2,i}$ when matching positions of slot 1 and slot 2 ciphertext components are paired. In the context of broadcast encryption (i.e. succinct ciphertext-policy ABE) [10] this trick was developed because the key generator could not know the randomness used by the encryptor, and moreover this randomness is unbounded across unbounded ciphertexts. In our setting, this trick instead allows to break the leakage of correlated randomness caused by combining ciphertexts across different slots, some of which may be challenge ciphertexts and others of which may be decrypting ciphertexts. However, though we made progress we are still not done and the formal security argument still be required to address several issues – please see Sect. 3 for more details.

Constructing 2ABE in the Standard Model. We next turn to adapting the construction to the standard model – a natural starting point is the standard model adaptation of [10] by Agrawal, Wichs and Yamada [8] which is based on a non-standard knowledge type assumption KOALA on bilinear groups. Our proof begins with these ideas but again departs significantly due to the nuanced security game of the multi-input setting – indeed, we will run into subtle technical issues related to the distribution of auxiliary information which will require us to formulate a variant of KOALA.

We first outline our construction, which uses a version of inner product functional encryption (IPFE), where one can directly encrypt group elements (rather than $\mathbb{Z}_q$ elements) and can generate a secret key for group elements. Thus, a ciphertext may encrypt a vector $[\mathbf{v}]_1$ and a secret key is for $[\mathbf{w}]_2$ and the decryption result of the ciphertext using the secret key is $[\langle \mathbf{v}, \mathbf{w} \rangle]_T$. Using IPFE and ideas similar to our first construction discussed above, we encode vectors into ciphertexts and secret keys so that the decryption result ends up with the BGG^+ ciphertext randomized by a secret key specific randomness t. In more detail, a slot 1 ciphertext is an IPFE ciphertext encoding $[\mathbf{v}, 0]_2$ and a slot 2 ciphertext is an IPFE secret key encoding $[t\mathbf{w}, 0]_2$ so that $[t\langle \mathbf{v}, \mathbf{w} \rangle]_T$ is recovered upon decryption, which is a corresponding BGG^+ ciphertext randomized by t on the exponent. Here, the last 0 entries are used for the security proof. We note that compared to the solution in bilinear generic group model we explained, we dropped the randomness on the ciphertext encoding and only the secret key encoding is randomized by t. The reason why the randomness on the ciphertext encoding can be removed is that the encoding is already protected by the IPFE and this change allows to simplify the construction and proof.

In the security game, we will have $\{\mathsf{ct}^{(i)} := \mathsf{IPFE.Enc}([\mathbf{v}^{(i)}, 0]_1)\}_i$ and $\{\mathsf{sk}^{(i)} := \mathsf{IPFE.sk}([t^{(i)}\mathbf{w}^{(i)}, 0]_2)\}_i$, where $\mathsf{ct}^{(i)}$ is the i-th slot 1 ciphertext and $\mathsf{sk}^{(i)}$ is the

i-th slot 2 ciphertext. Let us say that the adversary requests Q ciphertexts in each slot. The security proof is by hybrid argument, where slot 1 ciphertexts are changed from ciphertexts for challenge bit 0 to 1 one by one. Now, to change the message in a slot 1 ciphertext i^*, we must account for its combination with *all* slot 2 ciphertexts – note that such a constraint does not arise in single input ABE/BE [8]. To handle this, we leverage the power of IPFE so that the Q second slot ciphertexts hardcode the decryption value for the chosen slot 1 ciphertext i^* and behave as before with other slot 1 ciphertexts. A bit more explicitly, the j-th secret key may be hardwired with $([t^{(j)}]_2, [t^{(j)} \mathsf{BGG}^+.\mathsf{ct}^{(j)}]_2)$, where $\mathsf{BGG}^+.\mathsf{ct}^{(j)}$ is a set of BGG^+ ciphertexts derived from $\mathbf{v}^{(i^*)}$ and $\mathbf{w}^{(j)}$. We note that since $\{\mathsf{BGG}^+.\mathsf{ct}^{(j)}\}_j$ are derived from the same vector $\mathbf{v}^{(i^*)}$, their distribution is mutually correlated.

At this stage, we have a vector of BGG^+ ciphertexts encoded in the exponent, randomized with a unique random term $t^{(j)}$ and would like to change the ciphertexts $\mathsf{BGG}^+.\mathsf{ct}^{(j)}$ into random strings using the security of BGG^+. A similar situation was dealt with by [8], who essentially showed that if $\mathsf{BGG}^+.\mathsf{ct}^{(j)}$ is individually pseudorandom given an auxiliary information aux, then by a variant of the KOALA assumption, $\{[t^{(j)}]_2, [t^{(j)} \mathsf{BGG}^+.\mathsf{ct}^{(j)}]_2\}_j$ looks pseudorandom, even if ciphertexts are mutually correlated for $j \in [Q]$. However, this idea is insufficient for our setting due to the distribution of the auxiliary information. In more detail, for the construction of [8], it sufficed to have a single BGG^+ secret key in aux, since their construction only needed a single key secure BGG^+. By applying a standard trick in lattice cryptography, they could sample the secret key first (setting other parameters accordingly) and thus regard aux as a random string. In contrast, our scheme crucially requires multiple BGG^+ secret keys, which can no longer be considered as random strings. This necessitates formulating a variant of the KOALA assumption whose distribution of the auxiliary input is structured rather than random. We do not know how to weaken this assumption using our current techniques and leave this improvement as an interesting open problem. For more details, please see full version of the paper [9, Sect. 5].

Compiling Multi-input ABE to Multi-input PE. Next, we discuss how to lift k-input miABE to k-input miPE. For the purposes of the introduction, let us focus on the case of $k = 2$. As a warm-up, we begin with the simpler setting of standard security, i.e. where there are no decrypting ciphertexts.

The natural first idea to construct miPE is to replace the single input ABE BGG^+ in our 2ABE scheme by single input PE, which has been constructed for all polynomial circuits by Gorbunov, Vaikuntanathan and Wee [29]. However, this idea quickly runs into an insurmountable hurdle – for our construction template, we need to bound the decryption noise by polynomial so that it can be recovered by brute force computation of discrete log in the final step. This is possible for ABE supporting NC_1 using asymmetric noise growth [30]. In the context of PE however, we do not know how to restrict the noise growth to polynomial – this is due to the usage of the fully homomorphic encryption in the scheme, which extends the depth of the evaluated circuit beyond what can be handled.

An alternative path to convert ABE to PE in the single input setting uses the machinery of *Lockable Obfuscation* (LO) [31,53]. Lockable obfuscation allows to obfuscate a circuit C with respect to a lock value β and a message m. The obfuscated circuit on input x outputs m if $C(x) = \beta$ and $\perp$ otherwise. For security, LO requires that if β has high entropy in the view of the adversary, the obfuscated circuit should be indistinguishable from a garbage program that does not carry any information.

Single to Multiple Inputs. The conversion in the single input setting is as follows. To encrypt a message m for an attribute $\mathbf{x}$, we first encrypt a random value β using the ABE to obtain an ABE cipheretxt ct. We then construct a circuit $C[\text{ct}]$ that hardwires ct in it, takes as input an ABE secret key and decrypts the hardwired ciphertext using it. We obfuscate $C[\text{ct}]$ with respect to the lock value β and the message m. The final PE ciphertext is the obfuscated circuit. It is easy to see that the PE scheme has correctness, since if the decryption is possible, β is recovered inside the obfuscated circuit and the lock is unlocked. By the correctness of LO, the message is revealed. In the security proof, we first change β encrypted inside ct to a zero string. This is possible using the security of ABE. Now the lock value β has high entropy from the view of the adversary. We then erase the information inside the obfuscated circuit, which includes the attribute information, using the security of LO.

Some thought reveals that the above conversion breaks down completely in the multi-input setting. For instance, if we apply the above conversion to a slot 1 ciphertext, the resulting obfuscation expects to receive slot 2 ciphertext in the clear. However, a slot 2 ciphertext of PE must also constitute an obfuscated circuit since otherwise the attribute associated with it will be leaked. But then there is no way to communicate between the two ciphertexts, both of which are obfuscated circuits!

To overcome this barrier, we develop a delicate *nested* approach which takes advantage of the fact that LO is powerful enough to handle general circuits. To restore communication between two ciphertexts while maintaining attribute privacy, we obfuscate a circuit for slot 1 that takes as input *another obfuscated circuit* for slot 2 and runs this inside itself. In more detail, the outer LO takes as input the "inner" LO circuit and the 2ABE secret key 2ABE.sk$_f$. The inner LO instance encodes the circuit for 2ABE decryption with the LO message as an SKE secret and the lock value as random tag β. It also has hardcoded in it the slot 2 2ABE ciphertext 2ABE.ct$_2$ with message β. The other piece of 2ABE, namely the slot 1 ciphertext 2ABE.ct$_1$ is hardwired in the outer LO. The outer LO encodes a circuit which runs the inner LO on inputs 2ABE.ct$_1$ and 2ABE.sk$_f$. By correctness of the inner LO, the 2ABE decryption with 2ABE.ct$_1$, 2ABE.ct$_2$ and 2ABE.sk$_f$ is executed and if the functionality is satisfied, the inner LO outputs the SKE secret key. Thus, the SKE secret key signals whether the inner LO is unlocked, and if so, uses the recovered key to decrypt an SKE ciphertext which is hardcoded in the circuit. This ciphertext encrypts some random γ which is also set as the lock value of outer LO. If the SKE decryption succeeds, the lock value matches the decrypted value and outputs the message m which is the message in the outer

LO. We note that the same SKE secret key must be used for both the inner and outer LO for them to effectively communicate.

Supporting Strong Security. This construction lends itself to a proof of security for the standard game where decrypting ciphertexts are not allowed, although via an intricate sequence of hybrids especially for the case of general k. We refer the reader to Sect. 4 for details and turn our attention to the far more challenging case of strong security. In the setting of strong security, the proof fails – note that once any slot 2 ciphertext is decrypted, we no longer have the guarantee that the message value of the inner obfuscation is hidden. Since this message is a secret key of an SKE scheme and is used to encrypt the lock values for slot 1 ciphertexts, security breaks down once more.

To overcome this hurdle, we must make the construction more complex so that the message value of the inner obfuscation is no longer a global secret and does not compromise security even if revealed. To implement this intuition, we let the inner obfuscation output a slot 2 (strong) 2ABE ciphertext when the lock is unlocked, which is then used to perform 2ABE decryption in the circuit of the outer LO. Now, even if the security of a inner obfuscated circuit is compromised, this does not necessarily mean that the security of the entire system is compromised because of the guarantees of the strong security game of 2ABE. While oversimplified, this intuition may now be formalized into a proof. For more details, please see Sect. 5.

Constructing 3ABE from Pairings and Lattices. Finally, we discuss our candidate construction for three input ABE scheme based on techniques developed by Brakerski and Vaikuntanathan [21] in conjunction with our 2ABE construction in Sect. 3. The work of Brakerski and Vaikuntanathan [21] provided a clever candidate for succinct ciphertext-policy ABE for P from lattices. Their construction also uses decomposability in order to achieve succinctness which is the starting point for the multi-input setting as discussed above. Additionally, they provide novel ways to handle the lack of shared randomness between the key generator and encryptor – while [10] use pairings to generate shared randomness, [21] use lattice ideas and it is this part which makes their construction heuristic. Here, we show that the algebraic structure of their construction not only fits elegantly to the demands of the two-input setting, but can also be made compatible with our current 2ABE construction to *amplify* arity to three! This surprising synergy between two completely different candidates of broadcast encryption, namely Agrawal-Yamada and Brakerski-Vaikuntanathan, created by decomposability and novel techniques of handling randomness, already provides an XWE of compression factor $1/4$ as against the previous best known $1/2$ [19], and may lead to other applications as well.

Recap of the Brakerski-Vaikuntanathan Construction. To dig deeper into our construction, let us first recap the core ideas of [21]. First recall the well known fact that security of BGG$^+$ encodings is lost when we have two encodings for the same position encoding a different bit, namely, $\psi_{i,0} = \mathbf{s}\mathbf{B}_i + \mathbf{e}_{i,0}$ and $\psi_{i,1} = \mathbf{s}(\mathbf{B}_i + \mathbf{G}) + \mathbf{e}_{i,1}$, where $\mathbf{s}$ is a LWE secret, $\mathbf{B}_i$ is a matrix, and $\mathbf{e}_{1,b}$ is an error vector for $b \in \{0, 1\}$. What [21] suggested is, if we augment BGG^+ encodings and mask them appropriately, then both encodings can be published and still hope to be secure. Namely, they change BGG^+ encodings to be $\psi_{i,b} = \mathbf{S}(\mathbf{B}_i + b\mathbf{G}) + \mathbf{E}_{i,b}$, where we replace the vector $\mathbf{s}$ with a matrix $\mathbf{S}$. They then mask the encodings by public (tall) matrices $\{\mathbf{C}_{i,b}\}_{i,b}$ as

$$\widehat{\psi}_{i,b} := \mathbf{C}_{i,b}\widehat{\mathbf{S}}_{i,b} + \mathbf{S}(\mathbf{B}_i + b\mathbf{G}) + \mathbf{E}_{i,b}$$

where $\{\widehat{\mathbf{S}}_{i,b}\}_{i,b}$ are random secret matrices. By releasing appropriate information, one can recover BGG^+ encodings with different LWE secrets. In more detail, we can publish a short vector $\mathbf{t_x}$ for any binary string $\mathbf{x}$ that satisfies $\mathbf{t_x}\mathbf{C}_{i,x_i} = \mathbf{0}$ (and $\mathbf{t_x}\mathbf{C}_{i,1-x_i}$ is random) for all i. This allows us to compute

$$\mathbf{t_x}\left(\mathbf{C}_{i,x_i}\widehat{\mathbf{S}}_{i,x_i} + \mathbf{S}(\mathbf{B}_i + x_i\mathbf{G}) + \mathbf{E}_{i,x_i}\right) = \mathbf{t_x}\mathbf{S}(\mathbf{B}_i + x_i\mathbf{G}) + \mathbf{t_x}\mathbf{E}_{i,x_i} = \mathbf{s_x}(\mathbf{B}_i + x_i\mathbf{G}) + \mathbf{e}_{\mathbf{x},i,x_i}$$

where we set $\mathbf{s_x} = \mathbf{t_x}\mathbf{S}$ and $\mathbf{e}_{\mathbf{x},i,b} = \mathbf{t_x}\mathbf{E}_{i,b}$. Namely, we can obtain BGG^+ samples specific to the string $\mathbf{x}$. This is similar to the idea of using pairings to choose the appropriate encoding based on the attribute string, which is used in our two-input ABE with strong security. Similarly to that case, the obtained encodings are randomized by the user specific randomness. One of the heuristic aspects of [21] is that in order for their scheme to be secure, we have to assume that there is no meaningful way to combine the BGG^+ samples obtained from different vectors $\mathbf{t_x}$ and $\mathbf{t_{x'}}$.

Let us now adapt these techniques to provide a construction of two-input ABE. In our candidate, $\{\mathbf{B}_i\}_i$ and $\{\mathbf{C}_{i,b}\}_{i,b}$ matrices are made public.[3] An encryptor for the slot 1 computes for $i \in [\ell], b \in \{0, 1\}$:

$$\left\{\psi_{i,x_{1,i}} := \mathbf{S}(\mathbf{B}_i + x_{1,i}\mathbf{G}) + \mathbf{E}_{i,x_{1,i}}\right\}_i, \ \left\{\widehat{\psi}_{i,b} := \mathbf{C}_{\ell+i,b}\widehat{\mathbf{S}}_{\ell+i,b} + \mathbf{S}(\mathbf{B}_{\ell+i} + b\mathbf{G}) + \mathbf{E}_{\ell+i,b}\right\}_{i,b}$$

where $x_{1,i}$ denotes the i-th bit of the attribute $\mathbf{x}_1$ for slot 1, ℓ denotes the length of an attribute, and $\mathbf{S}$ and $\widehat{\mathbf{S}}_{i,b}$ are freshly chosen by the encryptor. Intuitively, this is a partially stripped off version of the encodings in [21]. We believe this does not harm security, because the encryptor provides one out of two encodings for each position that is not masked by $\mathbf{C}_{i,b}\widehat{\mathbf{S}}_{i,b}$. The encryptor for slot 2 generates a vector $\mathbf{t_{x_2}}$ such that $\mathbf{t_{x_2}}\mathbf{C}_{i,x_{2,\ell+i}} = \mathbf{0}$ for all $i \in [\ell]$. The secret key for function F is simply BGG^+ secret key for the same function. In the decryption, the decryptor uses $\mathbf{t_{x_2}}$ to choose BGG^+ encodings for attribute $\mathbf{x}_2$ from $\{\widehat{\psi}_{i,b}\}_{i,b}$. The obtained encodings are with respect to the LWE secret $\mathbf{t_x}\mathbf{S}$. The decryptor can also choose BGG^+ encodings for attribute $\mathbf{x}_1$ from $\{\psi_i\}_i$. These obtained encodings constitutes a BGG^+ ciphertext for attribute $(\mathbf{x}_1, \mathbf{x}_2)$, which can be decrypted by the BGG^+ secret key. The intuition about security in [21] is that the BGG^+ encodings obtained by using $\mathbf{t_x}$ vectors cannot be combined in a meaningful way due to the different randomness.

---

[3] The construction described here is simplified. For example, we omit the additional message carrying part in the construction, which is not necessary for the overview.

Amplifying Arity. We now amplify arity by leveraging the above techniques in conjunction with our pairing based construction. Our idea is to develop the scheme so that the decryptor can recover the above partially stripped off version of the encoding in the exponent from slot 1 and slot 2 ciphertexts by using the pairing operations, where the encodings may be randomized. Then, slot 3 ciphertext corresponds to a vector $\mathbf{t}_{\mathbf{x}_3}$, which annihilates $\mathbf{C}_{i,b}$ matrices for corresponding positions to the attribute $\mathbf{x}_3$. To do so, an encryptor for the first slot encodes

$$\{t_1\psi_{i,x_i}\}_{i\in[\ell]}, \quad \{t_1\psi_{i,b}\}_{i\in[\ell+1,2\ell],b\in\{0,1\}}, \quad \{t_1\widehat{\psi_{i,b}}\}_{i\in[2\ell+1,3\ell],b\in\{0,1\}}$$

of the exponent of $\mathbb{G}_1$, where t_1 is freshly chosen randomness by the encryptor. An encryptor for the second slot encodes t_2, $t_2\mathbf{d}_{\mathbf{x}_2}$ in the exponent of $\mathbb{G}_2$, where t_2 is freshly chosen randomness by the encryptor and $\mathbf{d}_{\mathbf{x}_2}$ is a selector vector that chooses $\psi_{i,x_{2,i}}$ out of $(\psi_{i,0}, \psi_{i,1})$ by the pairing operation. Concretely, $\mathbf{d}_{\mathbf{x}_2} = \{d_{i,b}\}_{i,b}$, where $d_{i,b} = 1$ if $b = x_{2,i}$ and 0 otherwise. These vectors are randomized by position-wise randomness as is the case for our other schemes. Finally, an encryptor for slot 3 with attribute $\mathbf{x}_3$ chooses $\mathbf{t}_{\mathbf{x}_3}$ such that $\mathbf{t}_{\mathbf{x}_3}\mathbf{C}_{2\ell+i,x_{3,i}} = \mathbf{0}$.

A somewhat worrying aspect of the candidate above may be that both $t_1\psi_{i,0}$ and $t_1\psi_{i,1}$ are encoded on $\mathbb{G}_1$. However, this is also the case for [10] and as in that work, these two encodings are randomized by the position-wise randomness and cannot be combined in a meaningful way (at least in the GGM). The only way to combine them is to take a pairing product with $\mathbb{G}_2$ elements. However, after the operation, we end up with partially stripped encoding that is randomized with t_1t_2. Therefore, a successful attack against the scheme may end up with attacking a partially stripped version of [21], which we expect to be as secure as the original scheme. Please see Sect. 6 for more details.

2   Multi-input Attribute Based and Predicate Encryption

We define multi-input Attribute Based Encryption (ABE) and Predicate Encryption (PE) below. Since the only difference between the two notions is in the security game, we unify the syntax for the algorithms in what follows.

A k-input ABE/PE scheme is parametrized over an attribute space $\{(A_\lambda)^k\}_{\lambda\in\mathbb{N}}$ and function space $\{\mathcal{F}_\lambda\}_{\lambda\in\mathbb{N}}$, where each function maps $\{(A_\lambda)^k\}_{\lambda\in\mathbb{N}}$ to $\{0, 1\}$. Such a scheme is described by procedures (Setup, KeyGen, Enc$_1$, ..., Enc$_k$, Dec) with the following syntax:

Setup(1^λ) $\rightarrow$ (pp, msk): The Setup algorithm takes as input a security parameter and outputs some public parameters pp and a master secret key msk.

KeyGen(pp, msk, f) $\rightarrow$ sk$_f$: The KeyGen algorithm takes as input the public parameters pp, a master secret key msk and a function $f \in \mathcal{F}_\lambda$ and outputs a key sk$_f$.

Enc$_1$(pp, msk, α, b) $\rightarrow$ ct$_{\alpha,b,1}$: The encryption algorithm for slot 1 takes as input the public parameters pp, a master secret key msk, an attribute $\alpha \in A_\lambda$, and message $b \in \{0, 1\}$, and outputs a ciphertext ct$_{\alpha,b,1}$. For the case of ABE, the attribute string α is included as part of the ciphertext.

$\mathsf{Enc}_i(\mathsf{pp}, \mathsf{msk}, \alpha) \to \mathsf{ct}_{\alpha,i}$ for $i \geq 2$: The encryption algorithm for the ith slot where $i \in [2, k]$, takes as input the public parameters pp, a master secret key msk, and an attribute $\alpha \in A_\lambda$ and outputs a ciphertext $\mathsf{ct}_{\alpha,i}$. For the case of ABE, the attribute string α is included as part of the ciphertext.

$\mathsf{Dec}(\mathsf{pp}, \mathsf{sk}_f, \mathsf{ct}_{\alpha_1,b,1}, \mathsf{ct}_{\alpha_2,2}, \dots, \mathsf{ct}_{\alpha_k,k}) \to b'$: The decryption algorithm takes as input the public parameters pp, a key for the function f and a sequence of ciphertext of $(\alpha_1, b), \alpha_2, \dots, \alpha_k$ and outputs a string b'.

Next, we define correctness and security. For ease of notation, we drop the subscript λ in what follows.

Correctness: For every $\lambda \in \mathbb{N}, b \in \{0,1\}, \alpha_1, \dots, \alpha_k \in A, f \in \mathcal{F}$, it holds that if $f(\alpha_1, \dots, \alpha_k) = 1$, then

$$\Pr\left[\mathsf{Dec}\left(\begin{array}{c} \mathsf{pp}, \mathsf{KeyGen}(\mathsf{pp}, \mathsf{msk}, f), \\ \mathsf{Enc}_1(\mathsf{pp}, \mathsf{msk}, \alpha_1, b), \dots, \mathsf{Enc}_k(\mathsf{pp}, \mathsf{msk}, \alpha_k) \end{array} \right) = b \right] = 1 - \mathsf{negl}(\lambda)$$

where the probability is over the choice of $(\mathsf{pp}, \mathsf{msk}) \leftarrow \mathsf{Setup}(1^\lambda)$ and over the internal randomness of KeyGen and $\mathsf{Enc}_1, \dots, \mathsf{Enc}_k$.

Definition 1 (Ada-IND security for k-ABE). *For a k-ABE scheme* $\mathsf{k\text{-}ABE} = \{\mathsf{Setup}, \mathsf{KeyGen}, \mathsf{Enc}_1, \dots, \mathsf{Enc}_k, \mathsf{Dec}\}$ *for an attribute space* $\{(A_\lambda)^k\}_{\lambda \in \mathbb{N}}$, *function space* $\{\mathcal{F}_\lambda\}_{\lambda \in \mathbb{N}}$ *and an adversary* $\mathcal{A}$, *we define the* Ada-IND *security game as follows.*

1. **Setup phase:** *On input* 1^λ, *the challenger samples* $(\mathsf{pp}, \mathsf{msk}) \leftarrow \mathsf{Setup}(1^\lambda)$ *and gives* pp *to* $\mathcal{A}$.
2. **Query phase:** *The challenger samples a bit* $\beta \leftarrow \{0,1\}$. *During the game,* $\mathcal{A}$ *adaptively makes the following queries, in an arbitrary order.*
   (a) **Key Queries:** $\mathcal{A}$ *makes polynomial number of key queries, say* $p = p(\lambda)$. *As an* i-*th key query,* $\mathcal{A}$ *chooses a function* $f_i \in \mathcal{F}_\lambda$. *The challenger replies with* $\mathsf{sk}_{f_i} \leftarrow \mathsf{KeyGen}(\mathsf{pp}, \mathsf{msk}, f_i)$.
   (b) **Ciphertext Queries:** $\mathcal{A}$ *issues polynomial number of ciphertext queries for each slot, say* $p = p(\lambda)$. *As an* i-*th query for a slot* $j \in [k]$, $\mathcal{A}$ *declares*

$$\begin{cases} (\alpha_j^i, (b_0^i, b_1^i)) & \text{if } j = 1 \\ \alpha_j^i & \text{if } j \neq 1 \end{cases}$$

to the challenger, where $\alpha_j^i \in A_\lambda$ *is an attribute and* $(b_0^i, b_1^i) \in \{0,1\} \times \{0,1\}$ *is the pair of messages. Then, the challenger computes*

$$\mathsf{ct}_{j,\beta}^i = \begin{cases} \mathsf{Enc}_j(\mathsf{pp}, \mathsf{msk}, \alpha_j^i, b_\beta^i) & \text{if } j = 1 \\ \mathsf{Enc}_j(\mathsf{pp}, \mathsf{msk}, \alpha_j^i) & \text{if } j \neq 1 \end{cases}$$

and returns it to $\mathcal{A}$.
3. **Output phase:** $\mathcal{A}$ *outputs a guess bit* β' *as the output of the experiment.*

For the adversary to be admissible, *we require that for every* $f_1, \ldots, f_p \in \mathcal{F}$, *it holds that* $f_i(\alpha_1^{i_1}, \ldots, \alpha_k^{i_k}) = 0$ *for every* $i, i_1, \ldots, i_k \in [p]$.

We define the advantage $\mathsf{Adv}_{\mathsf{k\text{-}ABE},\mathcal{A}}^{\mathsf{Ada\text{-}IND}}(1^\lambda)$ *of* $\mathcal{A}$ *in the above game as*

$$\mathsf{Adv}_{\mathsf{k\text{-}ABE},\mathcal{A}}^{\mathsf{Ada\text{-}IND}}(1^\lambda) := \left| \Pr[\mathsf{Exp}_{\mathsf{k\text{-}ABE},\mathcal{A}}(1^\lambda) = 1 | \beta = 0] - \Pr[\mathsf{Exp}_{\mathsf{k\text{-}ABE},\mathcal{A}}(1^\lambda) = 1 | \beta = 1] \right|.$$

The k-ABE *scheme* k-ABE *is said to satisfy* Ada-IND *security (or simply adaptive security) if for any stateful PPT adversary* $\mathcal{A}$, *there exists a negligible function* $\mathrm{negl}(\cdot)$ *such that* $\mathsf{Adv}_{\mathsf{k\text{-}ABE},\mathcal{A}}^{\mathsf{Ada\text{-}IND}}(1^\lambda) = \mathrm{negl}(\lambda)$.

Definition 2 (Ada-IND security for k-PE). *For an* k-PE *scheme* k-PE = {Setup, KeyGen, $\mathsf{Enc}_1, \ldots, \mathsf{Enc}_k$, Dec} *for an attribute space* $\{(\mathcal{A}_\lambda)^k\}_{\lambda \in \mathbb{N}}$, *function space* $\{\mathcal{F}_\lambda\}_{\lambda \in \mathbb{N}}$ *and an adversary* $\mathcal{A}$, *we define the* Ada-IND *security game as follows.*

1. **Setup phase:** *On input* 1^λ, *the challenger samples* (pp, msk) $\leftarrow$ Setup(1^λ) *and gives* pp *to* $\mathcal{A}$.
2. **Query phase:** *The challenger samples a bit* $\beta \leftarrow \{0,1\}$. *During the game,* $\mathcal{A}$ *adaptively makes the following queries, in an arbitrary order.*
   (a) **Key Queries:** $\mathcal{A}$ *makes polynomial number of key queries, say* $p = p(\lambda)$. *For each key query* $i \in [p]$, $\mathcal{A}$ *chooses a function* $f_i \in \mathcal{F}_\lambda$. *The challenger replies with* $\mathsf{sk}_{f_i} \leftarrow$ KeyGen(pp, msk, f_i).
   (b) **Ciphertext Queries:** $\mathcal{A}$ *issues polynomial number of ciphertext queries for each slot, say* $p = p(\lambda)$. *As an* i-th *query for a slot* $j \in [k]$, $\mathcal{A}$ *declares*

$$\begin{cases} ((\alpha_{j,0}^i, \alpha_{j,1}^i), (b_0^i, b_1^i)) & \text{if } j = 1 \\ (\alpha_{j,0}^i, \alpha_{j,1}^i) & \text{if } j \neq 1 \end{cases}$$

to the challenger, where $(\alpha_{j,0}^i, \alpha_{j,1}^i)$ *is a pair of attributes and* (b_0^i, b_1^i) *is the pair of messages. Then, the challenger computes and returns to* $\mathcal{A}$

$$\mathsf{ct}_{j,\beta}^i = \begin{cases} \mathsf{Enc}_j(\mathsf{pp}, \mathsf{msk}, \alpha_{j,\beta}^i, b_\beta^i) & \text{if } j = 1 \\ \mathsf{Enc}_j(\mathsf{pp}, \mathsf{msk}, \alpha_{j,\beta}^i) & \text{if } j \neq 1 \end{cases}$$

3. **Output phase:** $\mathcal{A}$ *outputs a guess bit* β' *as the output of the experiment.*

For the adversary to be admissible, *we require that for every* $f_1, \ldots, f_p \in \mathcal{F}$, *it holds that* $f_i(\alpha_{1,\beta}^{i_1}, \ldots, \alpha_{k,\beta}^{i_k}) = 0$ *for every* $i, i_1, \ldots, i_k \in [p]$ *and* $\beta \in \{0,1\}$.

We define the advantage $\mathsf{Adv}_{\mathsf{k\text{-}PE},\mathcal{A}}^{\mathsf{Ada\text{-}IND}}(1^\lambda)$ *of* $\mathcal{A}$ *in the above game as*

$$\mathsf{Adv}_{\mathsf{k\text{-}PE},\mathcal{A}}^{\mathsf{Ada\text{-}IND}}(1^\lambda) := \left| \Pr[\mathsf{Exp}_{\mathsf{k\text{-}PE},\mathcal{A}}(1^\lambda) = 1 | \beta = 0] - \Pr[\mathsf{Exp}_{\mathsf{k\text{-}PE},\mathcal{A}}(1^\lambda) = 1 | \beta = 1] \right|.$$

The k-PE *scheme* k-PE *is said to satisfy* Ada-IND *security (or simply adaptive security) if for any stateful PPT adversary* $\mathcal{A}$, *there exists a negligible function* $\mathrm{negl}(\cdot)$ *such that* $\mathsf{Adv}_{\mathsf{k\text{-}PE},\mathcal{A}}^{\mathsf{Ada\text{-}IND}}(1^\lambda) = \mathrm{negl}(\lambda)$.

2.1 Strong Security for k-ABE and k-PE

We also consider a stronger security notion for both k-ABE as well as k-PE where
the adversary is allowed to make decrypting key requests for ciphertexts so long
as they do not distinguish the challenge bit.

Definition 3 (Strong Ada-IND security for k-ABE). *The definition for
strong Ada-IND security for k-ABE is the same as standard Ada-IND security
(Definition 1) except for the following modification. For the k-ABE adversary to
be admissible in the strong Ada-IND game, we require that*

- *If $f_i(\alpha_1^{i_1}, \ldots, \alpha_k^{i_k}) = 1$ holds for some $i, i_1, \ldots, i_k \in [p]$, then $b_0^{i_1} = b_1^{i_1}$.*

Let $(\alpha^i, (b_0^i, b_1^i))$ be the ith ciphertext query in slot 1. Then, if $b_0^i \neq b_1^i$, we call
the ciphertext returned by the challenger as a *challenge* ciphertext as it encodes
the challenge bit β. Otherwise, we refer to it as *decrypting* ciphertext, as the
adversary may potentially request a key to decrypt it.

Definition 4 (Strong Ada-IND security for k-PE). *The definition for strong
Ada-IND security for k-PE is the same as standard Ada-IND security (Definition
2) except for the following modification. For the k-PE adversary to be admissible
in the strong Ada-IND game, we require that*

- *If $f_i(\alpha_{1,\beta}^{i_1}, \ldots, \alpha_{k,\beta}^{i_k}) = 1$ holds for some $i, i_1, \ldots, i_k \in [p]$ and $\beta \in \{0,1\}$, then
  $(\alpha_{1,0}^{i_1}, \ldots, \alpha_{k,0}^{i_k}) = (\alpha_{1,1}^{i_1}, \ldots, \alpha_{k,1}^{i_k})$ and $b_0^{i_1} = b_1^{i_1}$.*

Let $((\alpha_0^i, \alpha_1^i), (b_0^i, b_1^i))$ be the ith ciphertext query in slot 1. Then, if $\alpha_0^i \neq \alpha_1^i$
or $b_0^i \neq b_1^i$, we call the ciphertext returned by the challenger as a *challenge*
ciphertext as it encodes the challenge bit β. Otherwise, we refer to it as *decrypting*
ciphertext, as the adversary may potentially request a key to decrypt it.

Definition 5 (Strong VerSel-IND security for k-ABE and k-PE). *The
definitions for strong VerSel-IND security for k-ABE and k-PE are the same as
strong Ada-IND security above except that the adversary $\mathcal{A}$ is required to submit
the challenge queries and secret key queries to the challenger before it samples
the public key.*

2.2 Generalization to Multi-Slot Message Scheme

In the above, we focus our attention on k-ABE and k-PE schemes that only
contain a message in a single slot, the remaining slots being free of messages.
We can also consider a generalized version of the notions where each slot carries
a message and all the messages are recovered in successful decryption. For k
polynomial, it is easy to extend a construction with single slot message to the
generalized version where each slot contains a message, simply by running k
instances of the scheme in parallel and rotating the slot which contains the
message in each instance to cover all k slots. Moreover we claim that since the

k message scheme is a concatenation of k one message schemes, security of the latter implies security of the former. In more detail, suppose there exists an adversary against the k message scheme with non-negligible advantage ϵ. This can be used to construct an adversary against one of the underlying one message schemes with non-negligible advantage ϵ/k.

3   Two-Input ABE for NC_1 from Pairings and LWE

In this section, we construct two input ABE for NC_1 circuits. More formally, our construction can support attribute space $A_\lambda = \{0,1\}^{\ell(\lambda)}$, and any circuit class $\mathcal{F} = \{\mathcal{F}_\lambda\}_\lambda$ that is subclass of $\{\mathcal{C}_{2\ell(\lambda),d(\lambda)}\}_\lambda$ with arbitrary $\ell(\lambda) \le \mathrm{poly}(\lambda)$ and $d(\lambda) = O(\log \lambda)$, where $\mathcal{C}_{2\ell(\lambda),d(\lambda)}$ is a set of circuits with input length $2\ell(\lambda)$ and depth at most $d(\lambda)$. We can prove that the scheme satisfies strong security as per Definition 3 assuming LWE in bilinear generic group model. Since the intuition was described in Sect. 1, we proceed directly with the construction. We refer to the full version of the paper [9] for backgrounds on lattices and pairings respectively and for description of the kpABE scheme by Boneh et al. [16] on which our construction is based.

Construction. We proceed to describe our construction.

$\mathsf{Setup}(1^\lambda)$: On input 1^λ, the setup algorithm defines the parameters $n = n(\lambda)$, $m = m(\lambda)$, noise distribution χ over $\mathbb{Z}$, $\tau_0 = \tau_0(\lambda)$, $\tau = \tau(\lambda)$, and $B = B(\lambda)$ as specified for the kpABE scheme of Boneh et al. (pl. see [9, Sect. 2.5]). It samples a group description $\mathbb{G} = (q, \mathbb{G}_1, \mathbb{G}_2, \mathbb{G}_T, e, [1]_1, [1]_2)$. Sets $L := (3\ell + 1)m + 2$ and proceeds as follows.
  1. Sample BGG^+ scheme:
     (a) Sample $(\mathbf{A}, \mathbf{A}_{\tau_0}^{-1}) \leftarrow \mathsf{TrapGen}(1^n, 1^m, q)$ such that $\mathbf{A} \in \mathbb{Z}_q^{n \times m}$.
     (b) Sample random matrix $\mathbf{B} = (\mathbf{B}_1, \dots, \mathbf{B}_{2\ell}) \leftarrow (\mathbb{Z}_q^{n \times m})^{2\ell}$ and a random vector $\mathbf{u} \leftarrow \mathbb{Z}_q^n$.
  2. Sample $\mathbf{w} \leftarrow (\mathbb{Z}_q^*)^L$.
  3. Output $\mathsf{pp} = (\mathbf{A}, \mathbf{B}, \mathbf{u})$, $\quad \mathsf{msk} = (\mathbf{A}_{\tau_0}^{-1}, \mathbf{w}, [1]_1, [1]_2)$.

$\mathsf{KeyGen}(\mathsf{pp}, \mathsf{msk}, F)$: Given input the public parameters pp, master secret key msk and a circuit F, compute BGG^+ function key for circuit F as follows:
  1. Compute $\mathbf{H}_F = \mathsf{EvalF}(\mathbf{B}, F)$ and $\mathbf{B}_F = \mathbf{B}\mathbf{H}_F$.
  2. Compute $[\mathbf{A} \| \mathbf{B}_F]_\tau^{-1}$ from $\mathbf{A}_{\tau_0}^{-1}$ and sample $\mathbf{r} \in \mathbb{Z}^{2m}$ as $\mathbf{r}^\top \leftarrow [\mathbf{A} \| \mathbf{B}_F]_\tau^{-1}(\mathbf{u}^\top)$.
  3. Output the secret key $\mathsf{sk}_F := \mathbf{r}$.

$\mathsf{Enc}_1(\mathsf{pp}, \mathsf{msk}, \mathbf{x}_1, b)$: Given input the public parameters pp, master secret key msk, attribute vector $\mathbf{x}_1$, message bit b, encryption for slot 1 is defined as follows:
  1. Sample LWE secret $\mathbf{s} \leftarrow \mathbb{Z}_q^n$ and noise terms $e_0 \leftarrow \chi$, $\mathbf{e} \leftarrow \chi^m$, $\mathbf{e}_i, \mathbf{e}_{\ell+i,b} \leftarrow \widetilde{\chi^m}$ for $i \in [\ell], b \in \{0,1\}$, where $\widetilde{\chi^m}$ is defined as in [9, Sect. 2.4].
  2. For $i \in [\ell]$, compute $\psi_i := \mathbf{s}(\mathbf{B}_i - x_{1,i}\mathbf{G}) + \mathbf{e}_i$.

3. For $i \in [\ell + 1, 2\ell]$, $b \in \{0, 1\}$, compute $\psi_{i,b} := \mathbf{s}(\mathbf{B}_i - b\mathbf{G}) + \mathbf{e}_{i,b}$.
4. Compute $\psi_{2\ell+1} := \mathbf{s}\mathbf{A} + \mathbf{e}$ and $\psi_{2\ell+2} := \mathbf{s}\mathbf{u}^\top + e_0$.
5. Set $\mu = \lceil \frac{q}{2} \rceil b$; $\mathbf{c} = (1, \{\psi_i\}_{i \in [\ell]}, \{\psi_{i,b}\}_{i \in [\ell+1, 2\ell], b \in \{0,1\}}, \psi_{2\ell+1}, \psi_{2\ell+2} + \mu)$.
6. Sample $t_1 \leftarrow \mathbb{Z}_q^*$ and output $\mathsf{ct}_1 = [t_1 \mathbf{c} \odot \mathbf{w}]_1$.

$\mathsf{Enc}_2(\mathsf{pp}, \mathsf{msk}, \mathbf{x}_2)$: Given input the public parameters pp, master secret key msk, attribute vector $\mathbf{x}_2$, encryption for slot 2 is defined as follows:

1. Let $\mathbf{1}_a := (1, \ldots, 1) \in \mathbb{Z}_q^a$ and $\mathbf{0}_a := (0, \ldots, 0) \in \mathbb{Z}_q^a$. Set

$$
\hat{\psi}_{i,b} := \begin{cases} \mathbf{1}_m \in \mathbb{Z}_q^m & \text{if } b = x_{2,i} \\ \mathbf{0}_m \in \mathbb{Z}_q^m & \text{if } b \neq x_{2,i} \end{cases} \quad \text{for } i \in [\ell+1, 2\ell] \text{ and } b \in \{0, 1\}.
$$

2. Set $\mathbf{d} = (1, \mathbf{1}_{\ell m}, \{\hat{\psi}_{i,b}\}_{i \in [\ell+1, 2\ell], b \in \{0,1\}}, \mathbf{1}_m, 1)$.
3. Sample $t_2 \leftarrow \mathbb{Z}_q^*$ and output $\mathsf{ct}_2 = [t_2 \mathbf{d} \oslash \mathbf{w}]_2$.

$\mathsf{Dec}(\mathsf{pp}, \mathsf{sk}_F, \mathsf{ct}_1, \mathsf{ct}_2)$: The decryption algorithm takes as input the public parameters pp, the secret key sk_F for circuit F and ciphertexts ct_1 and ct_2 corresponding to the two attributes $\mathbf{x}_1$ and $\mathbf{x}_2$ and proceeds as follows:

1. Take the coordinate-wise pairing between ciphertexts:
   Compute $[\mathbf{v}]_T = [t_1 t_2 \mathbf{c} \odot \mathbf{d}]_T$ as $\mathsf{ct}_1 \odot \mathsf{ct}_2$.
2. De-vectorize obtained vector:
   Expand $[\mathbf{v}]_T$ for $i \in [\ell]$, $j \in [\ell+1, 2\ell]$, $b \in \{0, 1\}$, to obtain:

   $[v_0]_T = [t_1 t_2]_T,\ [\mathbf{v}_i]_T = [t_1 t_2 \psi_i]_T,$

   $[\mathbf{v}_{j,b}]_T = [t_1 t_2 \psi'_{j,b}]_T,\ \text{where } \psi'_{j,b} = \begin{cases} (\mathbf{s}(\mathbf{B}_j - x_{2,j}\mathbf{G}) + \mathbf{e}_{j,b}), & \text{if } b = x_{2,j} \\ \mathbf{0}, & \text{if } b = 1 - x_{2,j} \end{cases},$

   $[\mathbf{v}_{2\ell+1}]_T = [t_1 t_2 \psi_{2\ell+1}]_T,\ [v_{2\ell+2}]_T = [t_1 t_2 (\psi_{2\ell+2} + \mu)]_T.$

3. Compute Evaluation function for BGG^+ ciphertexts in exponent:
   Let $\mathbf{x} = (\mathbf{x}_1, \mathbf{x}_2)$. Compute $\widehat{\mathbf{H}}_{F,\mathbf{x}} = \mathsf{EvalFX}(F, \mathbf{x}, \mathbf{B})$.

4. Perform BGG^+ decryption in the exponent:
   Form $[\mathbf{v}_{\mathbf{x}}]_T = [\mathbf{v}_1, \ldots, \mathbf{v}_\ell, \mathbf{v}_{\ell+1, x_{2,1}}, \ldots \mathbf{v}_{2\ell, x_{2,\ell}}]_T$ and parse $\mathsf{sk}_F = \mathbf{r}$ as $\mathbf{r} = (\mathbf{r}_1 \in \mathbb{Z}_q^m, \mathbf{r}_2 \in \mathbb{Z}_q^m)$. Then compute

   $$[v']_T := [(v_{2\ell+2} - (\mathbf{v}_{2\ell+1}\mathbf{r}_1^\top + \mathbf{v}_{\mathbf{x}}\widehat{\mathbf{H}}_{F,\mathbf{x}}\mathbf{r}_2^\top))]_T$$

5. Recover exponent via brute force if $F(\mathbf{x}) = 0$:
   Find $\eta \in [-B, B] \cup [-B + \lceil q/2 \rceil, B + \lceil q/2 \rceil]$ such that $[v_0]_T^\eta = [v']_T$ by brute-force search. If there is no such η, output $\perp$. To speed up the operation, one can employ the baby-step giant-step algorithm.

6. Output 0 if $\eta \in [-B, B]$ and 1 if $[-B + \lceil q/2 \rceil, B + \lceil q/2 \rceil]$.

Correctness: Due to space constraints, we argue correctness in the full version [9, Sect. 4].

Proof of Security: We prove the security via the following theorem.

Theorem 1. *Our* 2ABE *scheme for function class* NC_1 *satisfies strong* Ada-IND *security in the generic group model assuming that the* kpABE *scheme* BGG$^+$ *for function class* NC_1 *satisfies* Ada-INDr *security (please see full version [9] for definition of* Ada-INDr *security).*

The proof is provided in the full version of the paper [9, Sect. 4].

4   Compiling k-ABE to k-PE via Lockable Obfuscation

In this section we describe our compiler to lift k-input ABE to k-input PE. Namely, we construct k-input predicate encryption using k-input ABE and lockable obfuscation. The conversion preserves Ada-IND security. The extension of the conversion that preserves strong security is provided in Sect. 5.

Construction. Our construction uses the following building blocks:

1. A secret key encryption scheme SKE = (SKE.Setup, SKE.Enc, SKE.Dec).
2. A Lockable Obfuscator LO = (LO.Obf, LO.Eval) with lock space $\mathcal{L} = \{0,1\}^m$ and input space $\mathcal{X} = \{0,1\}^n$.
3. A k-input ABE scheme kABE = (kABE.Setup, kABE.KeyGen, kABE.Enc$_1$, ..., kABE.Enc$_k$, kABE.Dec) in which the message bit is associated with the last slot, kABE.Enc$_k$. We require $k = O(1)$.

   In the construction below, we require the message space of the SKE scheme to be the same as the lock space $\mathcal{L}$ of the lockable obfuscator scheme LO and the message space of kABE to be the same as the key space of SKE.

We now describe the construction of k-input predicate encryption scheme. Our k-input PE construction has the same attribute space and the function class as the underlying k-input ABE, when we consider the function class of NC_1 circuits or polynomial-size circuits.

Setup(1^λ) : On input the security parameter 1^λ, the Setup algorithm does the following:
1. Run (kABE.msk, kABE.pp) $\leftarrow$ kABE.Setup(1^λ).
2. Run SKE.Setup(1^λ) k times and obtain secret keys $K_1, K_2, \ldots, K_k$.
3. Output msk = (kABE.msk, $K_1, \ldots, K_k$) and pp = kABE.pp.

KeyGen(pp, msk, F) : On input the public parameters pp, the master secret key msk = (kABE.msk, $K_1, \ldots, K_k$) and a circuit F, the KeyGen algorithm does the following:
1. Run kABE.sk$_F$ $\leftarrow$ kABE.KeyGen(pp, kABE.msk, F).
2. Output sk$_F$ = kABE.sk$_F$.

Enc$_1$(pp, msk, $\mathbf{x}_1, m$): On input the public parameters pp, master secret key msk = (kABE.msk, $K_1, \ldots, K_k$), attribute $\mathbf{x}_1$ for position 1 and message m, the encryption algorithm does the following:

1. Sample $\gamma_1 \leftarrow \mathcal{L}$ and let $\mathsf{ct}_1^* = \mathsf{SKE.Enc}(K_1, \gamma_1)$
2. Compute $\mathsf{ct}_1 = \mathsf{kABE.Enc}_1(\mathsf{pp}, \mathsf{kABE.msk}, \mathbf{x}_1)$.
3. Define a function $f_1[\mathsf{ct}_1, \mathsf{ct}_1^*]$ as in Fig. 1.
4. Output $\mathsf{ct}_1' = \mathsf{LO.Obf}(1^\lambda, f_1[\mathsf{ct}_1, \mathsf{ct}_1^*], m, \gamma_1)$.

$\mathsf{Enc}_i(\mathsf{pp}, \mathsf{msk}, \mathbf{x}_i)$ for $2 \leq i \leq k$: On input the public parameters pp, master secret key $\mathsf{msk} = (\mathsf{kABE.msk}, K_1, \ldots, K_k)$, attribute $\mathbf{x}_i$ for position i, the encryption algorithm does the following:

1. Sample a random value $\gamma_i \leftarrow \mathcal{L}$ and let $\mathsf{ct}_i^* = \mathsf{SKE.Enc}(K_i, \gamma_i)$.
2. Compute $\mathsf{ct}_i = \begin{cases} \mathsf{kABE.Enc}_i(\mathsf{pp}, \mathsf{kABE.msk}, \mathbf{x}_i) & \text{for } 2 \leq i < k \\ \mathsf{kABE.Enc}_k(\mathsf{pp}, \mathsf{kABE.msk}, \mathbf{x}_k, K_k) & \text{for } i = k \end{cases}$.
3. Define a function $f_i[\mathsf{ct}_i, \mathsf{ct}_i^*]$ as in Fig. 1.
4. Output $\mathsf{ct}_i' = \mathsf{LO.Obf}(1^\lambda, f_i[\mathsf{ct}_i, \mathsf{ct}_i^*], K_{i-1}, \gamma_i)$.

Circuit $f_i[\mathsf{ct}_i, \mathsf{ct}_i^*]$ for $1 \leq i \leq k$

1. Parse input as $(\mathsf{ct}_1, \ldots, \mathsf{ct}_{i-1}, \tilde{G}_{i+1}, \ldots, \tilde{G}_k, \mathsf{sk}_F)$ where ct_j is regarded as a slot j ciphertext of kABE, $\tilde{G}_j$ is regarded as an obfuscated circuit of LO and sk_F is regarded as a kABE secret key.
2. Compute $K_i' = \begin{cases} \mathsf{LO.Eval}(\tilde{G}_{i+1}, (\mathsf{ct}_1, \ldots, \mathsf{ct}_i, \tilde{G}_{i+2}, \ldots, \tilde{G}_k, \mathsf{sk}_F)) & \text{for } 1 \leq i < k \\ \mathsf{kABE.Dec}(\mathsf{pp}, \mathsf{sk}_F, \mathsf{ct}_1, \ldots, \mathsf{ct}_k) & \text{for } i = k \end{cases}$
3. Outputs $\gamma_i' \leftarrow \mathsf{SKE.Dec}(K_i', \mathsf{ct}_i^*)$.

Fig. 1. Circuit Obfuscated by Slot i Encryption for $1 \leq i \leq k$

$\mathsf{Dec}(\mathsf{sk}_F, \mathsf{ct}_1', \ldots, \mathsf{ct}_k')$: On input the secret key sk_F for function F, and kPE ciphertexts $\mathsf{ct}_1', \ldots, \mathsf{ct}_k'$, do the following:
1. Parse ct_1' as an LO obfuscation.
2. Compute and output $\mathsf{LO.Eval}(\mathsf{ct}_1', (\mathsf{ct}_2', \ldots, \mathsf{ct}_k', \mathsf{sk}_F))$.

Correctness. Here, we briefly discuss the correctness of the scheme. For the full proof, we refer to the full version of the paper [9, Sect. 6]. If we run $\mathsf{LO.Eval}(\mathsf{ct}_1', (\mathsf{ct}_2', \ldots, \mathsf{ct}_k', \mathsf{sk}_F))$, we end up with running the inner most obfuscation that obfuscates $f_k[\mathsf{ct}_k, \mathsf{ct}_k^*]$ on input $(\mathsf{ct}_1, \ldots, \mathsf{ct}_{k-1}, \mathsf{sk}_F)$. Within the circuit, K_k is retrieved by the kABE decryption and thus it recovers the lock value γ_k, which unlocks the obfuscation. The circuit outputs K_{k-1} and this is then input to the second-innermost obfuscated circuit, which outputs K_{k-2} because of the similar reason. This process continues until the outermost circuit is unlocked and outputs the hardwired message m.

Security. We can prove that the above PE construction satisfies Ada-IND security if so does the underlying kABE. We refer to the full version of the paper [9, Sect. 6] for the full proof. Here, we provide an intuition. First, we replace K_k encrypted in kABE.Enc$_k$ with $\mathbf{0}$. This is possible by using the security of the underlying kABE. Then, we can use the security of SKE to change all ct$_k^*$ hardwired in the slot k ciphertexts, since K_k is not used except for the encrypting the lock value γ_k due to the change introduced in the previous step. This allows us to change the circuit ct$_k'$ into a simulated one rather than honestly obfuscated one, since the lock value γ_k is erased in the previous step. This in particular erases K_{k-1}, which allows to invoke the security of SKE to erase the lock value γ_{k-1}. This process continues until we can convert ct$_1'$ into a simulated circuit. At this point, every ciphertext is a simulated circuit and does not convey any information of attribute or message, as desired.

Applications. The conversion above can be applied to all the multi-input ABE schemes in this paper. Here, we focus on the applications to the candidate two input ABE scheme from lattices provided in the full version of the paper [9, Sect. 9] and the candidate three input ABE scheme in Sect. 6. The other schemes will be discussed in Sect. 5 because they satisfy strong (very selective) security and thus we can apply the conversion in Sect. 5. A nice property of the PE scheme obtained from the two input ABE scheme in [9, Sect. 9] is that it can handle any polynomial-size circuits. Besides, we can expect that it is post-quantum secure, because it does not use pairings and only uses lattice tools. By applying the conversion to the three input ABE scheme in Sect. 6, we can obtain a three-input PE scheme that can handle NC_1 circuits.

5   Two-Input PE with Stronger Security

In this section we describe our compiler to lift 2-input ABE to 2-input PE that preserves strong security. The conversion uses lockable obfuscation similarly to Sect. 4. Unlike the conversion in Sect. 4, we do not know how to extend it to general arity k and it is set to be $k = 2$ here. It uses the following building blocks:

1. Two instances of 2-input ABE scheme. In one instance the message is associated with encryption for position 2, while in the other instance, the message is associated with the encryption for position 1. We represent the two instances as 2ABE = (2ABE.Setup, 2ABE.KeyGen, 2ABE.Enc$_1$, 2ABE.Enc$_2$, 2ABE.Dec) and 2ABE$'$ = (2ABE$'$.Setup, 2ABE$'$.KeyGen, 2ABE$'$.Enc$_1$, 2ABE$'$.Enc$_2$, 2ABE$'$.Dec).
2. A Lockable Obfuscator Obf = (LO.Obf, LO.Eval).

Construction. Our two-input PE construction has the same attribute space and the function class as the underlying two-input ABE, when we consider the function class of NC_1 circuits or polynomial-size circuits.

Setup(1^λ) : On input 1^λ, the Setup algorithm does the following:
  1. Run (2ABE.msk, 2ABE.pp) ← 2ABE.Setup(1^λ) and (2ABE$'$.msk, 2ABE$'$.pp) ← 2ABE$'$.Setup(1^λ).

2. Output $\mathsf{msk} = (\mathsf{2ABE.msk}, \mathsf{2ABE'.msk})$ and $\mathsf{pp} = (\mathsf{2ABE.pp}, \mathsf{2ABE'.pp})$.

$\mathsf{KeyGen}(\mathsf{pp}, \mathsf{msk}, F)$: On input the public parameters pp, the master secret key msk and a circuit F, the keygen algorithm does the following:

1. Parse msk as $(\mathsf{2ABE.msk}, \mathsf{2ABE'.msk})$ and $\mathsf{pp} = (\mathsf{2ABE.pp}, \mathsf{2ABE'.pp})$.
2. Run $\mathsf{2ABE.sk}_F \leftarrow \mathsf{2ABE.KeyGen}(\mathsf{2ABE.pp}, \mathsf{2ABE.msk}, F)$ and $\mathsf{2ABE'.sk}_F \leftarrow \mathsf{2ABE'.KeyGen}(\mathsf{2ABE'.pp}, \mathsf{2ABE'.msk}, F)$.
3. Output $\mathsf{sk}_F = (\mathsf{2ABE.sk}_F, \mathsf{2ABE'.sk}_F)$.

$\mathsf{Enc}_1(\mathsf{pp}, \mathsf{msk}, \mathbf{x}_1, m)$: On input the public parameters, pp, master secret key msk, attribute $\mathbf{x}_1$ for position 1 and message m, the encryption algorithm does the following:

1. Parses msk as $(\mathsf{2ABE.msk}, \mathsf{2ABE'.msk})$ and pp as $(\mathsf{2ABE.pp}, \mathsf{2ABE'.pp})$.
2. Computes $\mathsf{ct}_1 = \mathsf{2ABE.Enc}_1(\mathsf{2ABE.pp}, \mathsf{2ABE.msk}, \mathbf{x}_1)$.
3. Sample $\alpha \leftarrow \mathcal{M}$ and compute $\mathsf{ct}'_1 = \mathsf{2ABE'.Enc}_1(\mathsf{2ABE'.pp}, \mathsf{2ABE'.msk}, \mathbf{x}_1, \alpha)$.
4. Define a function $f_1[\mathsf{ct}_1, \mathsf{ct}'_1]$, with $\mathsf{ct}_1, \mathsf{ct}'_1$ being hardwired (Fig. 2).
5. Output $\mathsf{ct}''_1 = \mathsf{LO.Obf}(1^\lambda, f_1[\mathsf{ct}_1, \mathsf{ct}'_1], m, \alpha)$.

Circuit $f_1[\mathsf{ct}_1, \mathsf{ct}'_1]$

1. Parse input as $(\tilde{G}, \mathsf{sk}, \mathsf{sk}')$ where $\tilde{G}$ is regarded as an obfuscated circuit of LO, and sk and sk' are regarded as secret keys of $\mathsf{2ABE}$ and $\mathsf{2ABE'}$ respectively.
2. Compute $r \leftarrow \mathsf{LO.Eval}(\tilde{G}, (\mathsf{ct}_1, \mathsf{sk}))$.
3. Output $\alpha' = \mathsf{2ABE'.Dec}(\mathsf{2ABE'.pp}, \mathsf{sk}', \mathsf{ct}'_1, r)$.

Fig. 2. Circuit Obfuscated by Slot 1 Encryption

$\mathsf{Enc}_2(\mathsf{pp}, \mathsf{msk}, \mathbf{x}_2)$:

1. Parse msk as $(\mathsf{2ABE.msk}, \mathsf{2ABE'.msk})$ and pp as $(\mathsf{2ABE.pp}, \mathsf{2ABE'.pp})$.
2. Compute $\mathsf{ct}_2 = \mathsf{2ABE.Enc}_2(\mathsf{2ABE.pp}, \mathsf{2ABE.msk}, \mathbf{x}_2, \beta)$, where $\beta \leftarrow \mathcal{M}$.
3. Compute $\mathsf{ct}'_2 = \mathsf{2ABE.Enc}'_2(\mathsf{2ABE'.pp}, \mathsf{2ABE'.msk}, \mathbf{x}_2)$.
4. Define a function $f_2[\mathsf{ct}_2]$, with ct_2 being hardwired, as in Fig. 3.
5. Output $\mathsf{ct}''_2 = \mathsf{LO.Obf}(1^\lambda, f_2[\mathsf{ct}_2], \mathsf{ct}'_2, \beta)$.

Circuit $f_2[\mathsf{ct}_2]$

1. Parse input as $(\mathsf{ct}_1, \mathsf{sk})$ where ct_1 is regarded as a ciphertext of $\mathsf{2ABE}$ for the first slot and sk is regarded a secret key of $\mathsf{2ABE}$.
2. Output $\beta' \leftarrow \mathsf{2ABE.Dec}(\mathsf{2ABE.pp}, \mathsf{sk}, \mathsf{ct}_1, \mathsf{ct}_2)$.

Fig. 3. Circuit Obfuscated by Slot 2 Encryption

$\mathsf{Dec}(\mathsf{sk}_F, \mathsf{ct}_1'', \mathsf{ct}_2'')$: On input the secret key sk_F for function F, and 2PE ciphertexts ct_1'' and ct_2'', do the following:

1. Parse sk_F as $(\mathsf{2ABE.sk}_F, \mathsf{2ABE'.sk}_F)$.
2. Output $\mathsf{LO.Eval}(\mathsf{ct}_1'', (\mathsf{ct}_2'', \mathsf{2ABE.sk}_F, \mathsf{2ABE'.sk}_F))$.

Correctness. Recall that $\mathsf{ct}_1'' = \mathsf{LO.Obf}(1^\lambda, f_1[\mathsf{ct}_1, \mathsf{ct}_1'], m, \alpha)$. We claim that

$$f_1[\mathsf{ct}_1, \mathsf{ct}_1'](\mathsf{ct}_2'', \mathsf{2ABE.sk}_F, \mathsf{2ABE'.sk}_F) = \alpha.$$

This may be argued via the following steps:

1. Recall that $\mathsf{ct}_2'' = \mathsf{LO.Obf}(1^\lambda, f_2[\mathsf{ct}_2], \mathsf{ct}_2', \beta)$ and $f_2[\mathsf{ct}_2](\mathsf{ct}_1, \mathsf{2ABE.sk}_F) = \mathsf{2ABE.Dec}(\mathsf{2ABE.pp}, \mathsf{2ABE.sk}_F, \mathsf{ct}_1, \mathsf{ct}_2) = \beta$. The second equality follows by correctness of 2ABE and the fact that ct_1 and ct_2 encrypt β under attributes $\mathbf{x}_1, \mathbf{x}_2$. Since ct_2'' has lock value β and message value ct_2', we have by correctness of LO that $\mathsf{LO.Eval}(\mathsf{ct}_2'', (\mathsf{ct}_1, \mathsf{2ABE.sk}_F)) = \mathsf{ct}_2'$.

2. Next, following the description of $f_1[\mathsf{ct}_1, \mathsf{ct}_1']$ (Fig. 2), we evaluate $\mathsf{2ABE'.Dec}$ $(\mathsf{2ABE'.sk}_F, \mathsf{ct}_1', \mathsf{ct}_2')$ and recover α by correctness of 2ABE' decryption and the construction of ct_1' and ct_2' as encryptions of α under attributes $\mathbf{x}_1, \mathbf{x}_2$.

Thus, we get that $f_1[\mathsf{ct}_1, \mathsf{ct}_1'](\mathsf{ct}_2'', \mathsf{2ABE.sk}_F, \mathsf{2ABE'.sk}_F) = \alpha$. Now, by correctness of LO, we have that $\mathsf{LO.Eval}(\mathsf{ct}_1'', (\mathsf{ct}_2'', \mathsf{2ABE.sk}_F, \mathsf{2ABE'.sk}_F)) = m$ as desired. This concludes the proof.

Security. We prove security via the following theorem.

Theorem 2. *Assume* LO *is a secure lockable obfuscation scheme as per Definition 2.9 in [9] and that* 2ABE *and* 2ABE' *are secure two input* ABE *schemes satisfying strong security as in Definition 3 (resp., strong very selective security as in Definition 5). Then, the* 2PE *construction presented above satisfies strong security as per Definition 4 (resp., strong very selective security as in Definition 5).*

Due to space constraints, the proof is provided in the full version [9, Sect. 7].

Applications. By applying the above conversion to two input ABE scheme with strong security in Sect. 3, we obtain a candidate construction of two input PE scheme with strong security. A caveat here is that the resulting scheme cannot necessarily be proven secure under LWE in the bilinear generic group model as one might expect. The problem here is that our conversion uses the decryption algorithm of the underlying two input ABE scheme in a non-black box way, which especially uses the code of the group operations. To claim the security of the resulting scheme, we heuristically assume that the two-input ABE scheme in Sect. 3 is strongly secure even in the standard model if we implement the bilinear generic group model with concrete well-chosen bilinear group and then apply the above conversion. We note that this kind of heuristic instantiation is widely used in the context of cryptographic hash functions and bilinear maps. We also mention that we can apply the above conversion to the two input ABE scheme in standard model provided in the full version [9, Sect. 5]. Since the scheme is proven secure in the standard model, the construction does not suffer from the above problem.

6 Three-Input ABE from Pairings and Lattices

In this section, we provide a candidate construction for 3ABE using the structure of [21] and [10] as discussed in Sect. 1. Leveraging ideas from the Brakerski-Vaikuntanathan construction [21], we also obtain a candidate for 2ABE for P – due to space constraints, we provide this construction in the full version [9]. Our 3ABE scheme supports NC_1 circuits. More formally, it supports attribute space $A_\lambda = \{0,1\}^{\ell(\lambda)}$ and any circuit class $\mathcal{F} = \{\mathcal{F}_\lambda\}_\lambda$ that is subclass of $\{\mathcal{C}_{3\ell(\lambda),d(\lambda)}\}_\lambda$ with arbitrary $\ell(\lambda) \leq \text{poly}(\lambda)$ and $d(\lambda) = O(\log \lambda)$, where $\mathcal{C}_{3\ell(\lambda),d(\lambda)}$ is a set of circuits with input length $3\ell(\lambda)$ and depth at most $d(\lambda)$.

Setup(1^λ): On input 1^λ, the setup algorithm defines the parameters $n = n(\lambda)$, $m = m(\lambda)$, $k = k(\lambda)$, noise distribution χ, $\hat{\chi}$ over $\mathbb{Z}$, $\tau_0 = \tau_0(\lambda)$, $\tau = \tau(\lambda)$, $\tau_0' = \tau_0'(\lambda)$, $\tau_t = \tau_t(\lambda)$ and $B = B(\lambda)$ as specified later. It samples a group description $\mathbb{G} = (q, \mathbb{G}_1, \mathbb{G}_2, \mathbb{G}_T, e, [1]_1, [1]_2)$. It then sets $L := (5\ell + 1)m + 1$ and proceeds as follows.

1. Samples BGG$^+$ scheme:
   (a) Samples $(\mathbf{A}, \mathbf{A}_{\tau_0}^{-1}) \leftarrow \text{TrapGen}(1^n, 1^m, q)$ such that $\mathbf{A} \in \mathbb{Z}_q^{n \times m}$.
   (b) Samples random matrix $\mathbf{B} = (\mathbf{B}_1, \ldots, \mathbf{B}_{3\ell}) \leftarrow (\mathbb{Z}_q^{n \times m})^{3\ell}$ and a random vector $\mathbf{u} \leftarrow \mathbb{Z}_q^n$.
2. Samples $w_0 \leftarrow \mathbb{Z}_q^*$, $\mathbf{W} \leftarrow (\mathbb{Z}_q^*)^{k \times L}$.
3. Samples BV scheme:
   (a) Samples $\mathbf{C}$ along with its trapdoor $\mathbf{C}_{\tau_0'}^{-1}$ as
   $$(\mathbf{C}, \mathbf{C}_{\tau_0'}^{-1}) \leftarrow \text{TrapGen}(1^{2(\ell+1)n}, 1^k, q), \text{ where}$$
   $$\mathbf{C}^\top = (\mathbf{C}_{2\ell+1,0}\|\mathbf{C}_{2\ell+1,1}\|\cdots\|\mathbf{C}_{3\ell,0}\|\mathbf{C}_{3\ell,1}\|\mathbf{C}_{3\ell+1}\|\mathbf{C}_{3\ell+2}) \in (\mathbb{Z}_q^{k \times n})^{2(\ell+1)}.$$
4. Outputs $\text{pp} = (\mathbf{A}, \mathbf{B}, \mathbf{C}, \mathbf{u})$, $\text{msk} = \left(\mathbf{A}_{\tau_0}^{-1}, \mathbf{C}_{\tau_0'}^{-1}, w_0, \mathbf{W}\right)$.

KeyGen(pp, msk, F): On input the public parameters pp, master secret key msk and a circuit F, compute BGG$^+$ function key for circuit F as follows:
1. Compute $\mathbf{H}_F = \text{EvalF}(\mathbf{B}, F)$ and $\mathbf{B}_F = \mathbf{B}\mathbf{H}_F$.
2. Compute $[\mathbf{A}\|\mathbf{B}_F]_\tau^{-1}$ from $\mathbf{A}_{\tau_0}^{-1}$ and sample $\mathbf{r} \in \mathbb{Z}^{2m}$ as $\mathbf{r}^\top \leftarrow [\mathbf{A}\|\mathbf{B}_F]_\tau^{-1}(\mathbf{u}^\top)$.
3. Output the secret key $\text{sk}_F := \mathbf{r}$.

Enc$_1$(pp, msk, $\mathbf{x}_1, \mu$): On input the public parameters pp, master secret key msk, attribute vector $\mathbf{x}_1$, message bit μ, encryption for slot 1 is defined as follows:
1. Set $\mathbf{m} = \lceil \frac{q}{K} \rceil \mu(1, \ldots, 1) \in \mathbb{Z}_q^k$. We define $K = 2\tau_t \sqrt{n}k$. .
2. Samples LWE secret $\mathbf{S} \leftarrow \mathbb{Z}_q^{k \times n}$ and error terms $\mathbf{e}_0 \leftarrow \chi^k$, $\mathbf{E} \leftarrow \chi^{k \times m}$, $\mathbf{E}_{i,x_{1,i}} \leftarrow \hat{\chi}^{k \times m}$, for $i \in [\ell]$, $\mathbf{E}_{i,b} \leftarrow \hat{\chi}^{k \times m}$, for $i \in [\ell + 1, 3\ell]$, $b \in \{0, 1\}$.
3. For $i \in [\ell]$, computes $\psi_{i,x_{1,i}} := \mathbf{S}(\mathbf{B}_i - x_{1,i}\mathbf{G}) + \mathbf{E}_{i,x_{1,i}} \in \mathbb{Z}_q^{k \times m}$.
4. For $i \in [\ell + 1, 3\ell]$, $b \in \{0, 1\}$, computes $\psi_{i,b} := \mathbf{S}(\mathbf{B}_i - b\mathbf{G}) + \mathbf{E}_{i,b} \in \mathbb{Z}_q^{k \times m}$.
5. Computes $\psi_{3\ell+1} := \mathbf{S}\mathbf{A} + \mathbf{E} \in \mathbb{Z}_q^{k \times m}$ and $\psi_{3\ell+2}^\top := \mathbf{S}\mathbf{u}^\top + \mathbf{e}_0^\top \in \mathbb{Z}_q^{k \times 1}$.
6. Sample $\hat{\mathbf{S}}_{3\ell+1} \leftarrow \mathbb{Z}_q^{n \times m}$, $\hat{\mathbf{s}}_{3\ell+2} \leftarrow \mathbb{Z}_q^n$, $\{\hat{\mathbf{S}}_{2\ell+i,b}\}_{i \in [\ell], b \in \{0,1\}} \leftarrow (\mathbb{Z}_q^{n \times m})^{2\ell}$, $\hat{\mathbf{E}} \leftarrow \chi^{k \times m}$, $\hat{\mathbf{e}}_0 \leftarrow \chi^k$, $\hat{\mathbf{E}}_{2\ell+i,b} \leftarrow \hat{\chi}^{k \times m}$ for $i \in [\ell]$, $b \in \{0, 1\}$.

7. Compute all possible "BV encodings" for slot 3 attribute $\mathbf{x}_3$ and construct $\widehat{\mathbf{C}}_1$ as follows:

$$\widehat{\mathbf{C}}_1 = (\{\psi_{i,x_{1i}}\}_{i\in[\ell]}, \{\psi_{i,b}\}_{\substack{i\in[\ell+1,2\ell], \\ b\in\{0,1\}}}, \{\mathbf{C}_{i,b}\widehat{\mathbf{S}}_{i,b} + \widehat{\mathbf{E}}_{i,b} + \psi_{i,b}\}_{\substack{i\in[2\ell+1,3\ell], \\ b\in\{0,1\}}},$$

$$\mathbf{C}_{3\ell+1}\widehat{\mathbf{S}}_{3\ell+1} + \widehat{\mathbf{E}} + \psi_{3\ell+1}, \mathbf{C}_{3\ell+2}\widehat{\mathbf{s}}_{3\ell+2}^\top + \widehat{\mathbf{e}}_0^\top + \psi_{3\ell+2}^\top + \mathbf{m}^\top) \in \mathbb{Z}_q^{k\times L}.$$

Here, we assume that the entries of $\widehat{\mathbf{C}}_1$ are vectorized in some fixed order.

8. Sample $t_{\mathbf{x}_1} \leftarrow \mathbb{Z}_q^*$ and output $\mathsf{ct}_1 = ([t_{\mathbf{x}_1} w_0]_1, [t_{\mathbf{x}_1}\widehat{\mathbf{C}}_1 \odot \mathbf{W}]_1$.

$\mathsf{Enc}_2(\mathsf{pp}, \mathsf{msk}, \mathbf{x}_2)$: On input the public parameters pp, master secret key msk, attribute vector $\mathbf{x}_2$, encryption for slot 2 is defined as follows:

1. Set $\widehat{\mathbf{C}}_2 = (\mathbf{1}_{k\times\ell m}, \{\widehat{\psi}_{\ell+i,x_{2,i}}\}_{i\in[\ell]}, \mathbf{1}_{k\times 2\ell m}, \mathbf{1}_{k\times m}, \mathbf{1}_{k\times 1})$, where

$$\widehat{\psi}_{\ell+i,b} := \begin{cases} \mathbf{1}_m \in \mathbb{Z}_q^m & \text{if } b = x_{2,i} \\ \mathbf{0}_m \in \mathbb{Z}_q^m & \text{if } b \neq x_{2,i} \end{cases} \quad \text{for } i \in [\ell] \text{ and } b \in \{0,1\}.$$

2. Sample $t_{\mathbf{x}_2} \leftarrow \mathbb{Z}_q^*$ and output $\mathsf{ct}_2 = ([t_{\mathbf{x}_2}/w_0]_2, [t_{\mathbf{x}_2}\widehat{\mathbf{C}}_2 \oslash \mathbf{W}]_2$.

$\mathsf{Enc}_3(\mathsf{pp}, \mathsf{msk}, \mathbf{x}_3)$: Given input the public parameters pp, master secret key msk, attribute vector $\mathbf{x}_3$, encryption for slot 3 is defined as follows:

1. Compute $[(\mathbf{C}_{2\ell+1,\mathbf{x}_{3,1}} \| \cdots \| \mathbf{C}_{3\ell,\mathbf{x}_{3,\ell}} \| \mathbf{C}_{3\ell+1} \| \mathbf{C}_{3\ell+2})^\top]_{\tau_t}^{-1}$ from $\mathbf{C}_{\tau_0'}^{-1}$ and sample short vector $t_{\mathbf{x}_3}$ such that
$t_{\mathbf{x}_3}\mathbf{C}_{2\ell+i,\mathbf{x}_{3,i}} = \mathbf{0}$ for all $i \in [\ell]$, $t_{\mathbf{x}_3}\mathbf{C}_{3\ell+1} = t_{\mathbf{x}_3}\mathbf{C}_{3\ell+2} = \mathbf{0}$, as
$t_{\mathbf{x}_3}^\top \leftarrow [(\mathbf{C}_{2\ell+1,\mathbf{x}_{3,1}} \| \cdots \| \mathbf{C}_{3\ell,\mathbf{x}_{3,\ell}} \| \mathbf{C}_{3\ell+1} \| \mathbf{C}_{3\ell+2})^\top]_{\tau_t}^{-1}(\mathbf{0}^\top)$.

2. Output $\mathsf{ct}_3 = t_{\mathbf{x}_3}$.

$\mathsf{Dec}(\mathsf{pp}, \mathsf{sk}_F, \mathsf{ct}_1, \mathsf{ct}_2, \mathsf{ct}_3)$: On input the public parameters pp, the secret key sk_F for circuit F and ciphertexts ct_1, ct_2 and ct_3 corresponding to the three attributes $\mathbf{x}_1$, $\mathbf{x}_2$ and $\mathbf{x}_3$, the decryption algorithm proceeds as follows:

1. Takes the coordinate-wise pairing between ciphertexts for slot 1 and slot 2:
Computes $[v_0]_T = [t_{\mathbf{x}_1}t_{\mathbf{x}_2}]_T$ and $[\mathbf{V}]_T = [t_{\mathbf{x}_1}t_{\mathbf{x}_2}\widehat{\mathbf{C}}_1 \odot \widehat{\mathbf{C}}_2]_T$ as $e(\mathsf{ct}_1, \mathsf{ct}_2)$.

2. Expands obtained matrix:
Let $\mathbf{x} = (\mathbf{x}_1, \mathbf{x}_2, \mathbf{x}_3)$. Expands $[\mathbf{V}]_T$ to obtain:
$[\mathbf{V}_i]_T = [t_{\mathbf{x}_1}t_{\mathbf{x}_2}\psi_{i,x_i}]_T$ for $i \in [\ell]$, $[\mathbf{V}_{i,b}]_T = [t_{\mathbf{x}_1}t_{\mathbf{x}_2}\psi'_{i,b}]_T$, where

$$\psi'_{i,b} = \begin{cases} \psi_{i,x_i} & \text{if } b = x_i \\ 0 & \text{if } b = 1 - x_i \end{cases}, \text{ for } i \in [\ell+1, 2\ell], b \in \{0,1\}.$$

$[\mathbf{V}_{i,b}]_T = [t_{\mathbf{x}_1}t_{\mathbf{x}_2}(\psi_{i,b} + \mathbf{C}_{i,b}\widehat{\mathbf{S}}_{i,b} + \widehat{\mathbf{E}}_{i,b})]_T$ for $i \in [2\ell+1, 3\ell], b \in \{0,1\}$,

$[\mathbf{V}_{3\ell+1}]_T = [t_{\mathbf{x}_1}t_{\mathbf{x}_2}(\mathbf{C}_{3\ell+1}\widehat{\mathbf{S}}_{3\ell+1} + \widehat{\mathbf{E}} + \psi_{3\ell+1})]_T$,

$[v_{3\ell+2}^\top]_T = [t_{\mathbf{x}_1}t_{\mathbf{x}_2}(\mathbf{C}_{3\ell+2}\widehat{\mathbf{s}}_{3\ell+2}^\top + \widehat{\mathbf{e}}_0^\top + \psi_{3\ell+2}^\top + \mathbf{m}^\top)]_T$.

3. Recovers BGG^+ ciphertext components for third slot:
Let us denote $\mathbf{V}_{i,x_i}$ as $\mathbf{V}_i$ for $i \in [2\ell+1, 3\ell]$.
Computes $[t_{\mathbf{x}_3}\mathbf{V}_i]_T = [t_{\mathbf{x}_1}t_{\mathbf{x}_2}t_{\mathbf{x}_3}(\psi_{i,x_i} + \widehat{\mathbf{E}}_{i,x_i})]_T$ for $i \in [2\ell+1, 3\ell]$,
$[t_{\mathbf{x}_3}\mathbf{V}_{3\ell+1}]_T = [t_{\mathbf{x}_1}t_{\mathbf{x}_2}t_{\mathbf{x}_3}(\psi_{3\ell+1} + \widehat{\mathbf{E}})]_T$ and $[t_{\mathbf{x}_3}v_{3\ell+2}^\top]_T = [t_{\mathbf{x}_1}t_{\mathbf{x}_2}t_{\mathbf{x}_3}(\psi_{3\ell+2}^\top + \mathbf{m}^\top + \widehat{\mathbf{e}}_0^\top)]_T$.
(because $t_{\mathbf{x}_3}\mathbf{C}_{i,x_i} = \mathbf{0}$ for $i \in [2\ell+1, 3\ell]$, $t_{\mathbf{x}_3}\mathbf{C}_{3\ell+1} = t_{\mathbf{x}_3}\mathbf{C}_{3\ell+2} = \mathbf{0}$)

4. Computes function to be applied on BGG^+ ciphertexts:

   Computes $\widehat{\mathbf{H}}_{F,\mathbf{x}} = \mathsf{EvalFX}(F, \mathbf{x}, \mathbf{B})$.

5. Performs BGG^+ decryption in the exponent:
   (a) Let us denote $\mathbf{V}_{i,x_i}$ as $\mathbf{V}_i$ for $i \in [\ell+1, 2\ell]$.
   (b) Computes $[\mathbf{t}_{\mathbf{x}_3}\mathbf{V}_i]_T$ for $i \in [2\ell]$.
   (c) Forms $[\mathbf{t}_{\mathbf{x}_3}\mathbf{V}_{\mathbf{x}}]_T = [\mathbf{t}_{\mathbf{x}_3}\mathbf{V}_1\|\dots\|\mathbf{t}_{\mathbf{x}_3}\mathbf{V}_{3\ell}]_T$, $\mathbf{r} = (\mathbf{r}_1 \in \mathbb{Z}_q^m, \mathbf{r}_2 \in \mathbb{Z}_q^m)$.
   (d) Then computes
   $$[v']_T := \left[\left(\mathbf{t}_{\mathbf{x}_3}\mathbf{v}_{3\ell+2}^\top - \left(\mathbf{t}_{\mathbf{x}_3}\mathbf{V}_{3\ell+1}\mathbf{r}_1^\top + \mathbf{t}_{\mathbf{x}_3}\mathbf{V}_{\mathbf{x}}\widehat{\mathbf{H}}_{F,\mathbf{x}}\mathbf{r}_2^\top\right)\right)\right]_T$$

6. Recover exponent via brute force if $F(\mathbf{x}) = 0$:
   After simplification, for $F(\mathbf{x}) = 0$, we get $v' = t_{\mathbf{x}_1}t_{\mathbf{x}_2}(\mathbf{t}_{\mathbf{x}_3}\mathbf{m}^\top + e')$, where e' is the combined error. Find $\eta \in [-B, B] \cup [-B - \lceil q/2\rceil, B - \lceil q/K\rceil] \cup [-B + \lceil q/K\rceil, B + \lceil q/2\rceil]$ such that $[v_0]_T^\eta = [v']_T$ by brute-force search. If there is no such η, output $\perp$. In the correctness, we show that η can be found in polynomial steps. To speed up the operation, one can employ the baby-step giant-step algorithm.

7. Output 0 if $\eta \in [-B, B]$ and 1, otherwise.

Parameters and Correctness: We choose the parameters for the 3-ABE scheme as follows (pl. refer to the full version [9] for definition of SampZ):

$$m = n^{1.1}\log q, \qquad k = \theta(n\ell \log q), \qquad q = 2^{\Theta(\lambda)}$$
$$\tau_0 = n\log q \log m, \qquad \tau = m^{3.1}\ell \cdot 2^{O(d)} \qquad \tau_0' = \omega(\sqrt{2n(\ell+1)\log q \log k}),$$
$$\chi = \mathsf{SampZ}(3\sqrt{n}), \quad \hat{\chi} = \mathsf{SampZ}(6\sqrt{n}m^2), \quad B = \ell m^5 n^3 k\tau\tau_t \cdot 2^{O(d)}.$$

We can set τ_t to be arbitrary polynomial such that $\tau_t > \tau_0'$. The parameter n may be chosen as $n = \lambda^c$ for some constant $c > 1$.

We argue correctness in the full version of the paper [9, Sect. 8].

Acknowledgements. The third author was partially supported by JST AIP Acceleration Research JPMJCR22U5 and JSPS KAKENHI Grant Number 19H01109, Japan.

References

1. Abdalla, M., Benhamouda, F., Gay, R.: From single-input to multi-client inner-product functional encryption. In: Galbraith, S.D., Moriai, S. (eds.) ASIACRYPT 2019. LNCS, vol. 11923, pp. 552–582. Springer, Cham (2019). https://doi.org/10.1007/978-3-030-34618-8_19

2. Abdalla, M., Benhamouda, F., Kohlweiss, M., Waldner, H.: Decentralizing inner-product functional encryption. In: Lin, D., Sako, K. (eds.) PKC 2019. LNCS, vol. 11443, pp. 128–157. Springer, Cham (2019). https://doi.org/10.1007/978-3-030-17259-6_5

3. Abdalla, M., Catalano, D., Fiore, D., Gay, R., Ursu, B.: Multi-input functional encryption for inner products: function-hiding realizations and constructions without pairings. In: Shacham, H., Boldyreva, A. (eds.) CRYPTO 2018. LNCS, vol. 10991, pp. 597–627. Springer, Cham (2018). https://doi.org/10.1007/978-3-319-96884-1_20

4. Abdalla, M., Gay, R., Raykova, M., Wee, H.: Multi-input inner-product functional encryption from pairings. In: Coron, J.-S., Nielsen, J.B. (eds.) EUROCRYPT 2017. LNCS, vol. 10210, pp. 601–626. Springer, Cham (2017). https://doi.org/10.1007/978-3-319-56620-7_21

5. Agrawal, S.: Indistinguishability obfuscation without multilinear maps: new techniques for bootstrapping and instantiation. In: Ishai, Y., Rijmen, V. (eds.) EUROCRYPT 2019. LNCS, vol. 11476, pp. 191–225. Springer, Cham (2019). https://doi.org/10.1007/978-3-030-17653-2_7

6. Agrawal, S., Freeman, D.M., Vaikuntanathan, V.: Functional encryption for inner product predicates from learning with errors. In: Lee, D.H., Wang, X. (eds.) ASIACRYPT 2011. LNCS, vol. 7073, pp. 21–40. Springer, Heidelberg (2011). https://doi.org/10.1007/978-3-642-25385-0_2

7. Agrawal, S., Goyal, R., Tomida, J.: Multi-input quadratic functional encryption from pairings. In: Malkin, T., Peikert, C. (eds.) CRYPTO 2021. LNCS, vol. 12828, pp. 208–238. Springer, Cham (2021). https://doi.org/10.1007/978-3-030-84259-8_8

8. Agrawal, S., Wichs, D., Yamada, S.: Optimal broadcast encryption from LWE and pairings in the standard model. In: Pass, R., Pietrzak, K. (eds.) TCC 2020. LNCS, vol. 12550, pp. 149–178. Springer, Cham (2020). https://doi.org/10.1007/978-3-030-64375-1_6

9. Agrawal, S., Yadav, A., Yamada, S.: Multi-input attribute based encryption and predicate encryption. IACR Cryptology ePrint Archive (2022)

10. Agrawal, S., Yamada, S.: Optimal broadcast encryption from pairings and LWE. In: Canteaut, A., Ishai, Y. (eds.) EUROCRYPT 2020. LNCS, vol. 12105, pp. 13–43. Springer, Cham (2020). https://doi.org/10.1007/978-3-030-45721-1_2

11. Ananth, P., Jain, A.: Indistinguishability obfuscation from compact functional encryption. In: Gennaro, R., Robshaw, M. (eds.) CRYPTO 2015. LNCS, vol. 9215, pp. 308–326. Springer, Heidelberg (2015). https://doi.org/10.1007/978-3-662-47989-6_15

12. Ananth, P., Jain, A., Lin, H., Matt, C., Sahai, A.: Indistinguishability obfuscation without multilinear maps: iO from LWE, bilinear maps, and weak pseudorandomness. In: CRYPTO (2019)

13. Attrapadung, N.: Dual system encryption via doubly selective security: framework, fully secure functional encryption for regular languages, and more. In: Nguyen, P.Q., Oswald, E. (eds.) EUROCRYPT 2014. LNCS, vol. 8441, pp. 557–577. Springer, Heidelberg (2014). https://doi.org/10.1007/978-3-642-55220-5_31

14. Barak, B., et al.: On the (Im)possibility of obfuscating programs. In: Kilian, J. (ed.) CRYPTO 2001. LNCS, vol. 2139, pp. 1–18. Springer, Heidelberg (2001). https://doi.org/10.1007/3-540-44647-8_1

15. Bitansky, N., Vaikuntanathan, V.: Indistinguishability obfuscation from functional encryption. In: FOCS (2015)

16. Boneh, D., et al.: Fully key-homomorphic encryption, arithmetic circuit ABE and compact garbled circuits. In: Nguyen, P.Q., Oswald, E. (eds.) EUROCRYPT 2014. LNCS, vol. 8441, pp. 533–556. Springer, Heidelberg (2014). https://doi.org/10.1007/978-3-642-55220-5_30

17. Boneh, D., Sahai, A., Waters, B.: Functional encryption: definitions and challenges. In: Ishai, Y. (ed.) TCC 2011. LNCS, vol. 6597, pp. 253–273. Springer, Heidelberg (2011). https://doi.org/10.1007/978-3-642-19571-6_16

18. Boneh, D., Waters, B.: Conjunctive, subset, and range queries on encrypted data. In: Vadhan, S.P. (ed.) TCC 2007. LNCS, vol. 4392, pp. 535–554. Springer, Heidelberg (2007). https://doi.org/10.1007/978-3-540-70936-7_29

19. Brakerski, Z., Jain, A., Komargodski, I., Passelègue, A., Wichs, D.: Non-trivial witness encryption and Null-iO from standard assumptions. In: Catalano, D., De Prisco, R. (eds.) SCN 2018. LNCS, vol. 11035, pp. 425–441. Springer, Cham (2018). https://doi.org/10.1007/978-3-319-98113-0_23

20. Brakerski, Z., Vaikuntanathan, V.: Circuit-ABE from LWE: unbounded attributes and semi-adaptive security. In: Robshaw, M., Katz, J. (eds.) CRYPTO 2016. LNCS, vol. 9816, pp. 363–384. Springer, Heidelberg (2016). https://doi.org/10.1007/978-3-662-53015-3_13

21. Brakerski, Z., Vaikuntanathan, V.: Lattice-inspired broadcast encryption and succinct ciphertext policy ABE. In: ITCS (2022)

22. Chen, J., Wee, H.: Semi-adaptive attribute-based encryption and improved delegation for Boolean formula. In: Abdalla, M., De Prisco, R. (eds.) SCN 2014. LNCS, vol. 8642, pp. 277–297. Springer, Cham (2014). https://doi.org/10.1007/978-3-319-10879-7_16

23. Chotard, J., Dufour Sans, E., Gay, R., Phan, D.H., Pointcheval, D.: Decentralized multi-client functional encryption for inner product. In: Peyrin, T., Galbraith, S. (eds.) ASIACRYPT 2018. LNCS, vol. 11273, pp. 703–732. Springer, Cham (2018). https://doi.org/10.1007/978-3-030-03329-3_24

24. Clear, M., McGoldrick, C.: Multi-identity and multi-key leveled FHE from learning with errors. In: Gennaro, R., Robshaw, M. (eds.) CRYPTO 2015. LNCS, vol. 9216, pp. 630–656. Springer, Heidelberg (2015). https://doi.org/10.1007/978-3-662-48000-7_31

25. Datta, P., Okamoto, T., Tomida, J.: Full-hiding (Unbounded) multi-input inner product functional encryption from the k-linear assumption. In: Abdalla, M., Dahab, R. (eds.) PKC 2018. LNCS, vol. 10770, pp. 245–277. Springer, Cham (2018). https://doi.org/10.1007/978-3-319-76581-5_9

26. Gay, R., Jain, A., Lin, H., Sahai, A.: Indistinguishability obfuscation from simple-to-state hard problems: new assumptions, new techniques, and simplification. In: Canteaut, A., Standaert, F.-X. (eds.) EUROCRYPT 2021. LNCS, vol. 12698, pp. 97–126. Springer, Cham (2021). https://doi.org/10.1007/978-3-030-77883-5_4

27. Goldwasser, S., et al.: Multi-input functional encryption. In: Nguyen, P.Q., Oswald, E. (eds.) EUROCRYPT 2014. LNCS, vol. 8441, pp. 578–602. Springer, Heidelberg (2014). https://doi.org/10.1007/978-3-642-55220-5_32

28. Gorbunov, S., Vaikuntanathan, V., Wee, H.: Attribute based encryption for circuits. In: STOC (2013)

29. Gorbunov, S., Vaikuntanathan, V., Wee, H.: Predicate encryption for circuits from LWE. In: Gennaro, R., Robshaw, M. (eds.) CRYPTO 2015. LNCS, vol. 9216, pp. 503–523. Springer, Heidelberg (2015). https://doi.org/10.1007/978-3-662-48000-7_25

30. Gorbunov, S., Vinayagamurthy, D.: Riding on asymmetry: efficient ABE for branching programs. In: Iwata, T., Cheon, J.H. (eds.) ASIACRYPT 2015. LNCS, vol. 9452, pp. 550–574. Springer, Heidelberg (2015). https://doi.org/10.1007/978-3-662-48797-6_23

31. Goyal, R., Koppula, V., Waters, B.: Lockable obfuscation. In: FOCS (2017)

32. Goyal, V., Pandey, O., Sahai, A., Waters, B.: Attribute-based encryption for fine-grained access control of encrypted data. In: ACM CCS (2006)
33. Jain, A., Lin, H., Matt, C., Sahai, A.: How to leverage hardness of constant-degree expanding polynomials over $\mathbb{R}$ to build $i\mathcal{O}$. In: Ishai, Y., Rijmen, V. (eds.) EUROCRYPT 2019. LNCS, vol. 11476, pp. 251–281. Springer, Cham (2019). https://doi.org/10.1007/978-3-030-17653-2_9
34. Jain, A., Lin, H., Sahai, A.: Indistinguishability obfuscation from well-founded assumptions. In: STOC (2021)
35. Jain, A., Lin, H., Sahai, A.: Indistinguishability obfuscation from LPN over large fields, DLIN, and constant depth PRGs. In: EUROCRYPT (2022)
36. Katz, J., Sahai, A., Waters, B.: Predicate encryption supporting disjunctions, polynomial equations, and inner products. In: Smart, N. (ed.) EUROCRYPT 2008. LNCS, vol. 4965, pp. 146–162. Springer, Heidelberg (2008). https://doi.org/10.1007/978-3-540-78967-3_9
37. Lewko, A., Okamoto, T., Sahai, A., Takashima, K., Waters, B.: Fully secure functional encryption: attribute-based encryption and (Hierarchical) inner product encryption. In: Gilbert, H. (ed.) EUROCRYPT 2010. LNCS, vol. 6110, pp. 62–91. Springer, Heidelberg (2010). https://doi.org/10.1007/978-3-642-13190-5_4
38. Lewko, A., Waters, B.: Unbounded HIBE and attribute-based encryption. In: Paterson, K.G. (ed.) EUROCRYPT 2011. LNCS, vol. 6632, pp. 547–567. Springer, Heidelberg (2011). https://doi.org/10.1007/978-3-642-20465-4_30
39. Lewko, A., Waters, B.: New proof methods for attribute-based encryption: achieving full security through selective techniques. In: Safavi-Naini, R., Canetti, R. (eds.) CRYPTO 2012. LNCS, vol. 7417, pp. 180–198. Springer, Heidelberg (2012). https://doi.org/10.1007/978-3-642-32009-5_12
40. Libert, B., Ţiţiu, R.: Multi-client functional encryption for linear functions in the standard model from LWE. In: Galbraith, S.D., Moriai, S. (eds.) ASIACRYPT 2019. LNCS, vol. 11923, pp. 520–551. Springer, Cham (2019). https://doi.org/10.1007/978-3-030-34618-8_18
41. Lin, H.: Indistinguishability obfuscation from constant-degree graded encoding schemes. In: Fischlin, M., Coron, J.-S. (eds.) EUROCRYPT 2016. LNCS, vol. 9665, pp. 28–57. Springer, Heidelberg (2016). https://doi.org/10.1007/978-3-662-49890-3_2
42. Lin, H.: Indistinguishability obfuscation from SXDH on 5-linear maps and locality-5 PRGs. In: Katz, J., Shacham, H. (eds.) CRYPTO 2017. LNCS, vol. 10401, pp. 599–629. Springer, Cham (2017). https://doi.org/10.1007/978-3-319-63688-7_20
43. Lin, H., Vaikuntanathan, V.: Indistinguishability obfuscation from DDH-like assumptions on constant-degree graded encodings. In: FOCS (2016)
44. López-Alt, A., Tromer, E., Vaikuntanathan, V.: On-the-fly multiparty computation on the cloud via multikey fully homomorphic encryption. In: STOC (2012)
45. Mukherjee, P., Wichs, D.: Two round multiparty computation via multi-key FHE. In: Fischlin, M., Coron, J.-S. (eds.) EUROCRYPT 2016. LNCS, vol. 9666, pp. 735–763. Springer, Heidelberg (2016). https://doi.org/10.1007/978-3-662-49896-5_26
46. Okamoto, T., Takashima, K.: Fully secure functional encryption with general relations from the decisional linear assumption. In: Rabin, T. (ed.) CRYPTO 2010. LNCS, vol. 6223, pp. 191–208. Springer, Heidelberg (2010). https://doi.org/10.1007/978-3-642-14623-7_11

47. Okamoto, T., Takashima, K.: Adaptively attribute-hiding (Hierarchical) inner product encryption. In: Pointcheval, D., Johansson, T. (eds.) EUROCRYPT 2012. LNCS, vol. 7237, pp. 591–608. Springer, Heidelberg (2012). https://doi.org/10.1007/978-3-642-29011-4_35

48. Sahai, A., Waters, B.: Fuzzy identity-based encryption. In: Cramer, R. (ed.) EUROCRYPT 2005. LNCS, vol. 3494, pp. 457–473. Springer, Heidelberg (2005). https://doi.org/10.1007/11426639_27

49. Shi, E., Bethencourt, J., Chan, T.H., Song, D., Perrig, A.: Multi-dimensional range query over encrypted data. In: SP (2007)

50. Tomida, J.: Tightly secure inner product functional encryption: multi-input and function-hiding constructions. In: Galbraith, S.D., Moriai, S. (eds.) ASIACRYPT 2019. LNCS, vol. 11923, pp. 459–488. Springer, Cham (2019). https://doi.org/10.1007/978-3-030-34618-8_16

51. Waters, B.: Functional encryption for regular languages. In: Safavi-Naini, R., Canetti, R. (eds.) CRYPTO 2012. LNCS, vol. 7417, pp. 218–235. Springer, Heidelberg (2012). https://doi.org/10.1007/978-3-642-32009-5_14

52. Wee, H.: Dual system encryption via predicate encodings. In: Lindell, Y. (ed.) TCC 2014. LNCS, vol. 8349, pp. 616–637. Springer, Heidelberg (2014). https://doi.org/10.1007/978-3-642-54242-8_26

53. Wichs, D., Zirdelis, G.: Obfuscating compute-and-compare programs under LWE. In: FOCS (2017)

Formal Verification of Saber's Public-Key Encryption Scheme in EasyCrypt

Andreas Hülsing[1]([⊠])(iD), Matthias Meijers[1]([⊠])(iD), and Pierre-Yves Strub[2]([⊠])(iD)

[1] Eindhoven University of Technology, Eindhoven, The Netherlands
fv-saber-pke@mmeijers.com
[2] Meta, Paris, France

Abstract. In this work, we consider the formal verification of the public-key encryption scheme of Saber, one of the selected few post-quantum cipher suites currently considered for potential standardization. We formally verify this public-key encryption scheme's IND-CPA security and δ-correctness properties, i.e., the properties required to transform the public-key encryption scheme into an IND-CCA2 secure and δ-correct key encapsulation mechanism, in EasyCrypt. To this end, we initially devise hand-written proofs for these properties that are significantly more detailed and meticulous than the presently existing proofs. Subsequently, these hand-written proofs serve as a guideline for the formal verification. The results of this endeavor comprise hand-written and computer-verified proofs which demonstrate that Saber's public-key encryption scheme indeed satisfies the desired security and correctness properties.

Keywords: Formal Verification · Saber · EasyCrypt

1 Introduction

In 1994, Shor showed how to efficiently solve the integer factorization and discrete logarithm problems on a sufficiently powerful quantum computer [17]. Consequently, since contemporary public-key cryptography is predominantly based on the hardness of these problems, the advent of such quantum computers would enable adversaries to compromise the security provided by this type of cryptography [19]. Although it is not entirely clear when the first sufficiently powerful quantum computer will be operational, the progress made hitherto, the currently remaining challenges, and the amount of interest in this topic suggest that this might well transpire in the near future [16]. As such, a timely replacement of

Andreas Hülsing and Matthias Meijers are funded by an NWO VIDI grant (Project No. VI.Vidi.193.066). At the time of writing, Pierre-Yves Strub was at Institut Polytechnique de Paris, France, and was partially supported by the ERC Advanced Grant *Procontra* (ID: 885666). Date: 2022-07-31

Y. Dodis and T. Shrimpton (Eds.): CRYPTO 2022, LNCS 13507, pp. 622–653, 2022.
https://doi.org/10.1007/978-3-031-15802-5_22

the contemporary public-key cryptography by quantum-resistant alternatives is imperative.

At the time of writing, the National Institute of Standards and Technology (NIST) is hosting a competition with the purpose of standardizing post-quantum alternatives to the current public-key cryptography; this competition is in its final stage, leaving only a selected few of the best candidates. One of these candidates is Saber, a suite of post-quantum cryptographic constructions for public-key encryption and key establishment [10]. In particular, Saber comprises an IND-CCA2 secure key encapsulation mechanism (KEM) which is the suite's principal scheme of interest due to NIST announcing that they will exclusively standardize KEMs as stand-alone constructions for key encipherment. Saber's KEM is obtained by applying a variant of the Fujisaki-Okamoto (FO) transform on an IND-CPA secure public-key encryption (PKE) scheme. Given that the FO transform has already been analyzed previously [18], this work directs its attention to Saber's PKE scheme, analyzing the claimed security and correctness properties of this PKE scheme necessary to transform it into a secure and (sufficiently) correct KEM.

Historically, (the specifications of) cryptographic constructions have been demonstrated to possess their desired properties through hand-written proofs. However, the innovation and development in the field of cryptography have led to a significant increase in the complexity of these constructions and their proofs. As a result, devising these constructions and carrying out the corresponding hand-written proofs has become substantially more challenging. Numerous examples of proofs exist that, although extensively scrutinized and universally considered correct, turned out to be faulty. Furthermore, in some of these cases, the corresponding cryptographic construction was additionally found to be insecure [14]. These instances exemplify the intricacy of contriving and verifying cryptographic constructions and their proofs. In addition, even if (the specification of) a cryptographic construction and its proof are entirely correct, implementation flaws may invalidate any of the construction's properties and guarantees. Once again, ample examples exist of this phenomenon, signifying the complexity of constructing and verifying cryptographic implementations [15].

The complexity issues associated with devising cryptographic constructions, proofs, and implementations partially induced the inception of the scientific field of computer-aided cryptography. As its name suggests, this field endeavors to devise computer-assisted methods for constructing and verifying cryptography [3]. The purpose of these computer-assisted methods is to reduce the complexity of the manual labor required in the construction and verification process while consistently enforcing a high level of rigor. This increases the confidence in the cryptographic specifications and implementations that are devised and analyzed in this manner.

Over the years, the research conducted in the field of computer-aided cryptography has produced copious tools and frameworks aimed at the construction and verification of cryptography in a multitude of different ways and contexts [3]. Furthermore, these tools and frameworks have been successfully employed in the construction and verification of increasingly prominent targets; for example, EasyCrypt and Jasmin have been used to construct and verify a functionally correct, constant-time, and efficient implementation of ChaCha20-Poly1305 [1], and Tamarin has been used to verify (the specification of) TLS 1.3 [8]. For a more comprehensive overview and discussion, see [3]. Based on the context in which Saber's PKE scheme and the considered proofs manifest themselves, the tool of choice for this work is EasyCrypt. Namely, EasyCrypt adopts the code-based approach to provable security, modeling common security-related concepts, such as security notions and hardness assumptions, as well-defined probabilistic programs [5,6]. Additionally, the tool's higher-order ambient logic, standard library, and other built-in mechanisms allow for extensive and (partially) automated mathematical reasoning. Altogether, these features facilitate a natural formalization and manageable verification of the considered proofs for the desired security and correctness properties of Saber's PKE scheme.

Our Contribution. This work considers the formal verification of the desired security and correctness properties of Saber's PKE scheme in EasyCrypt. More precisely, for security, this concerns the IND-CPA property based on the assumed computational hardness of the Module Learning With Rounding (MLWR) problem; for correctness, this concerns the δ-correctness property defined in [12]. In addition to discussing the EasyCrypt-related material, we also present the hand-written proofs devised specifically for this formal verification endeavor; indeed, compared to the currently existing hand-written proofs, these are significantly more detailed and, hence, less ambiguous.

The purpose of this work is to establish a higher level of confidence in the security and correctness of Saber's PKE scheme and, by extension, the KEM obtained from applying the relevant variant of the FO transform discussed in [12]. In accordance with the above-mentioned properties that we consider for Saber's PKE scheme, this relevant variant of the FO transform is $FO^{\perp}$, i.e., the variant that transforms an IND-CPA secure and δ-correct PKE scheme into an IND-CCA2 secure and δ-correct KEM[1]. Naturally, this ultimately serves the purpose of assisting the cryptographic community in making a well-informed decision regarding the standardization of post-quantum cryptography. Thus far, no other formal verification efforts regarding Saber's schemes have been carried out (or, at least, no such endeavors are publicly known).

As an additional contribution, we construct and extend several EasyCrypt libraries with the generic definitions and properties of multiple concepts that are used in the formal verification of Saber's PKE scheme. In particular, we create a library that generically defines the structure and behavior of polynomial quotient rings. Moreover, we extend several existing libraries with results regarding distributions over integer rings and polynomials. Due to their abstractness, these libraries are reusable and can be employed in the analysis of other cryptographic systems that use the same or similar mathematical structures, e.g., other lattice-

---

[1] Although the original paper of Saber states that Saber's KEM is constructed through this variant, the specification of Saber's KEM shows that, technically, a subtly different transform has been used [10,11].

based cryptographic systems. Although we do not explicitly present them here, these libraries can be found in the code associated with this work or in the standard library of EasyCrypt.

Full-Fledged Formal Verification of Saber-Based KEM. Albeit the work presented in this paper has merit on its own, a natural addition would be to formally verify the relevant variant of the FO transform and, thus, obtain a complete formal verification of (the specification of) a secure and (sufficiently) correct KEM based on Saber's PKE. Actually, the formal verification of this transformation has already been performed in previous independent work by Unruh [18]. While certainly contributory and valuable, Unruh's work employs the qRHL tool; indeed, this unfortunately implies that combining his work with this work requires manual reasoning about the compatibility of results obtained through different tools with vastly different syntaxes and semantics. Naturally, such reasoning might be error-prone and, therefore, not ideal. As such, a more robust alternative for extending this work would be to perform the formal verification of the FO transform in EasyCrypt, enabling the direct verification of the compatibility of the results within EasyCrypt. However, this goes beyond the scope of this work.

Overview. The remainder of this paper is structured as follows. First, Sect. 2 introduces the notation utilized throughout this paper and restates the specification of Saber's PKE scheme. Second, Sect. 3 discusses the hand-written proof and formal verification of the security property of Saber's PKE scheme. Finally, Sect. 4 is analogous to Sect. 3 but, instead of the security property, considers the correctness property of Saber's PKE scheme.

2 Preliminaries

Notation. First, for any natural number $0 < q$, we denote the ring of integers modulo q by $\mathbb{Z}_q$; correspondingly, $\mathbb{Z}_q[X]$ represents the polynomial ring with coefficients in $\mathbb{Z}_q$. Additionally, we define R_q to be $\mathbb{Z}_q[X]/(X^n+1)$, where $n = 2^{\epsilon_n}$ for some $\epsilon_n \in \mathbb{N}$. As a final extension, we let $R_q^{m \times n}$ stand for the R_q-module of $m \times n$-dimensional matrices over R_q.

Second, for any natural numbers $0 < p$ and $0 < q$, we define a "modular scaling and flooring" function $\lfloor \cdot \rceil_{q \to p} : \mathbb{Z}_q \to \mathbb{Z}_p$, based on the closely related function defined in [2]. Furthermore, we straightforwardly define coefficient-wise and entry-wise extensions of this function to polynomials and vectors/matrices, respectively. Given any $x \in \mathbb{Z}_q$, the modular scaling and flooring function (for some valid p and q) computes the image corresponding to x as follows.

$$\lfloor x \rceil_{q \to p} = \lfloor \frac{p}{q} \cdot x \rfloor \bmod p$$

Although not explicitly stated, $\frac{p}{q} \cdot x$ is computed over the field of real numbers; to this end, the function uses the obvious interpretations of p, q, and x as real numbers. Notice that when p and q are both powers of two, the modular scaling and flooring operator is equivalent to a regular bit-shift (to the left if $p > q$ and to the right if $p < q$).

Third, for any natural numbers $0 < p$ and $0 < q$, we define a "modular scaling and rounding" function $\lfloor \cdot \rceil_{q \to p} : \mathbb{Z}_q \to \mathbb{Z}_p$ that is identical to the modular scaling and flooring function (for the same p and q), except that it uses rounding instead of flooring. Moreover, this operator is extended similarly to the modular scaling and flooring operator.

Fourth, analogously to the above modular scaling functions, we extend the modular reduction function coefficient-wise and entry-wise to polynomials and vectors/matrices, respectively.

Fifth, we denote the uniform distribution by $\mathcal{U}$ and the centered binomial distribution by β_μ. Furthermore, for distribution $\chi \in \{\mathcal{U}, \beta_\mu\}$ and R_q-module $R_q^{m \times n}$ (as defined above), we use $\chi(R_q^{m \times n})$ to signify the distribution over matrices from $R_q^{m \times n}$ that arises when (each coefficient of) every entry is distributed according to χ.

Finally, we typeset regular (i.e., non-vector and non-matrix) elements with lowercase, italic letters; vectors with lowercase, boldface letters; and matrices with uppercase, boldface letters. Additionally, sampling from a distribution χ and storing the result in x is written as $x \leftarrow_\$ \chi$. Lastly, in bit strings, we denote (sub)strings of n consecutive 0 or (n consecutive) 1 bits by 0^n or 1^n, respectively.

Saber's PKE. In this work, we adopt the specification of Saber's PKE scheme that is provided in the original paper [10]. For intelligibility purposes, Algorithm 1, Algorithm 2, and Algorithm 3 respectively restate the specifications of the scheme's key generation, encryption[2], and decryption algorithms utilizing the above-introduced notation. In these specifications, identifiers gen, l, t, p, q, μ, h_1, h_2, and $\mathbf{h}$ refer to the same function, parameters, and constants as in the original specifications. Particularly, gen is a mathematical function that maps bit strings of length 256 to matrices from $R_q^{l \times l}$; certainly, l is strictly positive. Furthermore, $t = 2^{\epsilon_t}$, $p = 2^{\epsilon_p}$, and $q = 2^{\epsilon_q}$ for some $\epsilon_t, \epsilon_p, \epsilon_q \in \mathbb{N}$ such that $0 < \epsilon_t + 1 < \epsilon_p < \epsilon_q$. Lastly, $h_1 = \sum_{i=0}^{n-1} \frac{q}{2 \cdot p} \cdot X^i$ and $h_2 = \sum_{i=0}^{n-1} (\frac{p}{4} - \frac{p}{4 \cdot t}) \cdot X^i$, both elements of R_q, while $\mathbf{h}$ is defined as the l-dimensional vector with all entries equal to h_1. Crucially, as a consequence of these definitions, we have that for all $x \in \mathbb{Z}_q$, $\lfloor x \rfloor_{q \to p} = \lfloor x + h_1 \rfloor_{q \to p}$; by extension, $\lfloor \mathbf{v} \rfloor_{q \to p} = \lfloor \mathbf{v} + \mathbf{h} \rfloor_{q \to p}$ for all $\mathbf{v} \in R_q^{l \times 1}$.

Throughout the remainder, Saber's PKE scheme will be referred to by the identifier Saber.PKE; the scheme's algorithms will be denoted by their respective procedure identifiers provided in the specifications.

3   Security

In this section, we cover Saber.PKE's security property by discussing the essential parts of the hand-written proof and the corresponding formal verification

---

[2] Note that the message $m \in \{0, 1\}^n$ is implicitly encoded as an element of R_2 by dedicating a separate coefficient to each bit.

Algorithm 1 Saber's Key Generation Algorithm

1: **procedure** Saber.KeyGen()
2:     $\text{seed}_{\mathbf{A}} \leftarrow\!\!\$ \; \mathcal{U}(\{0,1\}^{256})$
3:     $\mathbf{A} \leftarrow \text{gen}(\text{seed}_{\mathbf{A}})$
4:     $\mathbf{s} \leftarrow\!\!\$ \; \beta_\mu(R_q^{l \times 1})$
5:     $\mathbf{b} \leftarrow \lfloor \mathbf{A} \cdot \mathbf{s} + \mathbf{h} \rfloor_{q \to p}$
6:     **return** $\text{pk} := (\text{seed}_{\mathbf{A}}, \mathbf{b}), \; \text{sk} := \mathbf{s}$

Algorithm 2 Saber's Encryption Algorithm

1: **procedure** Saber.Enc($\text{pk} := (\text{seed}_{\mathbf{A}}, \mathbf{b}), \; m$)
2:     $\mathbf{A} \leftarrow \text{gen}(\text{seed}_{\mathbf{A}})$
3:     $\mathbf{s}' \leftarrow\!\!\$ \; \beta_\mu(R_q^{l \times 1})$
4:     $\mathbf{b}' \leftarrow \lfloor \mathbf{A}^T \cdot \mathbf{s}' + \mathbf{h} \rfloor_{q \to p}$
5:     $v' \leftarrow \mathbf{b}^T \cdot (\mathbf{s}' \bmod p) + (h_1 \bmod p)$
6:     $c_m \leftarrow \lfloor v' + \lfloor m \rfloor_{2 \to p} \rfloor_{p \to 2 \cdot t}$
7:     **return** $c := (c_m, \mathbf{b}')$

Algorithm 3 Saber's Decryption Algorithm

1: **procedure** Saber.Dec($\text{sk} := \mathbf{s}, \; c := (c_m, \mathbf{b}')$)
2:     $v \leftarrow \mathbf{b}'^T \cdot (\mathbf{s} \bmod p) + (h_1 \bmod p)$
3:     $m' \leftarrow \lfloor v - \lfloor c_m \rfloor_{2 \cdot t \to p} + (h_2 \bmod p) \rfloor_{p \to 2}$
4:     **return** m'

---

in EasyCrypt. Due to space considerations, some less informative material is omitted from this section and provided in the extended version of the paper instead [13]. At the relevant places, we explicitly mention which material this concerns.

Notion and Assumptions. Prior to discussing the actual hand-written proof, we introduce the relevant security notion and hardness assumptions. Here, we do not yet present any formalizations in EasyCrypt; instead, we postpone this to the relevant places in the discussion concerning the formal verification.

Foremost, we reiterate that Saber.PKE attempts to achieve the IND-CPA security notion based on the assumed computational hardness of the MLWR problem; the specifications of the corresponding games are respectively provided in Fig. 1 and Fig. 2.

Then, the advantage of an adversary $\mathcal{A} = (\mathsf{P}, \mathsf{D})$ against $\text{Game}^{\text{IND-CPA}}_{\mathcal{A}, \text{Saber.PKE}}$ is defined as follows.

$$\text{Adv}^{\text{IND-CPA}}_{\text{Saber.PKE}}(\mathcal{A}) = \left| \Pr\left[\text{Game}^{\text{IND-CPA}}_{\mathcal{A}, \text{Saber.PKE}} = 1 \right] - \frac{1}{2} \right|$$

Moreover, the advantage of an adversary $\mathcal{A}$ against $\text{Game}^{\text{MLWR}}_{\mathcal{A}, m, l, \mu, q, p}(u)$ is defined as given below.

$$\text{Adv}^{\text{MLWR}}_{m, l, \mu, q, p}(\mathcal{A}) = \left| \Pr\left[\text{Game}^{\text{MLWR}}_{\mathcal{A}, m, l, \mu, q, p}(1) = 1 \right] - \Pr\left[\text{Game}^{\text{MLWR}}_{\mathcal{A}, m, l, \mu, q, p}(0) = 1 \right] \right|$$

$$\text{Game}_{\mathcal{A},\text{Saber.PKE}}^{\text{IND-CPA}}$$

1 : $u \leftarrow\!\!\$\; \mathcal{U}(\{0,1\})$

2 : $(\text{pk}, \text{sk}) \leftarrow \text{Saber.KeyGen}()$

3 : $(m_0, m_1) \leftarrow \mathcal{A}.\text{P}(\text{pk})$

4 : $c \leftarrow \text{Saber.Enc}(\text{pk}, m_u)$

5 : $u' \leftarrow \mathcal{A}.\text{D}(c)$

6 : **return** $(u' = u)$

Fig. 1. The IND-CPA Game for Saber.PKE

$$\text{Game}_{\mathcal{A},m,l,\mu,q,p}^{\text{MLWR}}(u)$$

1 : $\mathbf{A} \leftarrow\!\!\$\; \mathcal{U}(R_q^{m \times l})$

2 : $\mathbf{s} \leftarrow\!\!\$\; \beta_\mu(R_q^{l \times 1})$

3 : $\mathbf{b}_0 \leftarrow \lfloor \mathbf{A} \cdot \mathbf{s} \rceil_{q \rightarrow p}$

4 : $\mathbf{b}_1 \leftarrow\!\!\$\; \mathcal{U}(R_p^{m \times 1})$

5 : **return** $\mathcal{A}(\mathbf{A}, \mathbf{b}_u)$

Fig. 2. The MLWR Game

Rather than directly employing the MLWR game, our proof utilizes two variant games, GMLWR and XMLWR, that (partly) generate the matrix $\mathbf{A}$ through a function instead of randomly sampling it. In case this function is a random oracle, these variant games are at least as hard as the MLWR game. This approach makes for a more general security theorem that holds for all valid instantiations of the gen function (and the parameters) of Saber; additionally, this enables us to separately analyze the utilized hardness assumptions in the random oracle model while staging the security proof in the standard model. The specifications of the GMLWR and XMLWR games are respectively given in Fig. 3 and Fig. 4; notice that the gen parameter in these games is expected to be a mathematical function mapping from bit strings of length 256 to matrices from $R_q^{l \times l}$ (where q and l are two of the other parameters of the games), similar to the identically named function used in Saber.PKE. The advantages of adversaries against these games are defined analogously to the advantage of adversaries against the MLWR game.

$$\text{Game}_{\mathcal{A},\text{gen},l,\mu,q,p}^{\text{GMLWR}}(u)$$

1 : $\text{seed}_\mathbf{A} \leftarrow\!\!\$\; \mathcal{U}(\{0,1\}^{256})$

2 : $\mathbf{A} \leftarrow \text{gen}(\text{seed}_\mathbf{A})$

3 : $\mathbf{s} \leftarrow\!\!\$\; \beta_\mu(R_q^{l \times 1})$

4 : $\mathbf{b}_0 \leftarrow \lfloor \mathbf{A} \cdot \mathbf{s} \rceil_{q \rightarrow p}$

5 : $\mathbf{b}_1 \leftarrow\!\!\$\; \mathcal{U}(R_p^{l \times 1})$

6 : **return** $\mathcal{A}(\text{seed}_\mathbf{A}, \mathbf{b}_u)$

Fig. 3. The GMLWR Game

$$\text{Game}_{\mathcal{A},\text{gen},l,\mu,q,p}^{\text{XMLWR}}(u)$$

1 : $\text{seed}_\mathbf{A} \leftarrow\!\!\$\; \mathcal{U}(\{0,1\}^{256})$

2 : $\mathbf{A} \leftarrow \text{gen}(\text{seed}_\mathbf{A})$

3 : $\mathbf{s} \leftarrow\!\!\$\; \beta_\mu(R_q^{l \times 1})$

4 : $\mathbf{b}_0 \leftarrow \lfloor \mathbf{A}^T \cdot \mathbf{s} \rceil_{q \rightarrow p}$

5 : $\mathbf{b}_1 \leftarrow\!\!\$\; \mathcal{U}(R_p^{l \times 1})$

6 : $\mathbf{a} \leftarrow\!\!\$\; \mathcal{U}(R_q^{1 \times l})$

7 : $d_0 \leftarrow \lfloor \mathbf{a} \cdot \mathbf{s} \rceil_{q \rightarrow p}$

8 : $d_1 \leftarrow\!\!\$\; \mathcal{U}(R_p)$

9 : **return** $\mathcal{A}(\text{seed}_\mathbf{A}, \mathbf{b}_u, \mathbf{a}, d_u)$

Fig. 4. The XMLWR Game

Considering $\text{Game}^{\text{GMLWR}}_{\mathcal{A},\text{gen},l,\mu,q,p}(u)$ and $\text{Game}^{\text{XMLWR}}_{\mathcal{A},\text{gen},l,\mu,q,p}(u)$, we can rather easily observe that if gen is a random oracle, these (instances of) games are at least as hard as $\text{Game}^{\text{MLWR}}_{\mathcal{A},l,l,\mu,q,p}(u)$ and $\text{Game}^{\text{MLWR}}_{\mathcal{A},l+1,l,\mu,q,p}(u)$, respectively. Naturally, these observations can be formalized in random oracle model proofs. In fact, we constructed these proofs, subsequently carrying out their formal verification in EasyCrypt. Since they are relatively simple, we omit these proofs and their formal verification in this discussion; instead, we provide them in the extended version of the paper [13]. Nevertheless, here we do note that these random oracle model proofs exclusively employ history-free reductions, ensuring the validity of these proofs in the quantum setting [7]. Unfortunately, at the time of performing the formal verification, EasyCrypt did not provide the features necessary to formally verify the soundness of this argument[3].

Hand-Written Proof. Utilizing the above-introduced security notion and hardness assumptions, we devise a code-based, game-playing proof of Saber.PKE's security in the standard model. The security theorem we aim to prove is the following. Here, gen, q, p, t, l, and μ refer to the previously introduced function and parameters of Saber; as such, these are assumed to satisfy the corresponding requirements imposed by Saber.

Security Theorem. *Let $\frac{q}{p} \leq \frac{p}{2t}$. Then, for any adversary $\mathcal{A}$, there exist adversaries $\mathcal{B}_0$ and $\mathcal{B}_1$, each with approximately the same running time as $\mathcal{A}$, such that*

$$\text{Adv}^{\text{IND-CPA}}_{\text{Saber.PKE}}(\mathcal{A}) \leq \text{Adv}^{\text{GMLWR}}_{\text{gen},l,\mu,q,p}(\mathcal{B}_0) + \text{Adv}^{\text{XMLWR}}_{\text{gen},l,\mu,q,p}(\mathcal{B}_1)$$

Conceptually, the proof of the above theorem is similar to the security proof concerning Saber's key exchange scheme given in the original paper [10]; in particular, between the proofs, the structures of the game sequences are quite alike, and the justifications of the steps within the proofs are primarily based on the same reasoning. Nevertheless, as aforementioned, the security proof presented in this work is significantly more detailed and meticulous. While constructing such a proof has merit on its own, the primary rationale for this is that it facilitates the subsequent formal verification in EasyCrypt. Namely, the formal verification enforces a high level of rigorousness and granularity on the proof; already having a detailed hand-written proof as a reference eases this process substantially. Naturally, knowing this hand-written proof similarly helps comprehend the material of the corresponding formal verification. For this reason, we cover the hand-written proof that we devised before advancing to the discussion on the formal verification.

The ensuing proof consists of a sequence of five games, depicted in Fig. 5; for each game, the statements that differ from the preceding game are highlighted with a gray background. In this sequence, the first game arises from replacing the procedure identifiers in $\text{Game}^{\text{IND-CPA}}_{\mathcal{A},\text{Saber.PKE}}$ by the corresponding specifications; the remainder of the games are slight variations of this initial

---

[3] However, since then, these features have been implemented and integrated into EasyCrypt, making the formal verification of the validity of the random oracle model proofs in the quantum setting a potential objective for future work [4].

game. As such, for $\text{Game}_{\mathcal{A}}^i$ ($0 \leq i \leq 4$), the advantage of $\mathcal{A}$ is defined analogously to $\text{Adv}_{\text{Saber.PKE}}^{\text{IND-CPA}}(\mathcal{A})$; we denote this advantage by $\text{Adv}^i(\mathcal{A})$. We now bound the difference in advantages between any two consecutive games from the game sequence.

Step 1: $\text{Game}_{\mathcal{A}}^0$ - $\text{Game}_{\mathcal{A}}^1$. In the first step, we alter the way in which $\mathbf{b}$ is obtained. Specifically, rather than computing $\mathbf{b}$ by $\lfloor \mathbf{A} \cdot \mathbf{s} + \mathbf{h} \rfloor_{q \rightarrow p}$, as $\text{Game}_{\mathcal{A}}^0$ does, $\text{Game}_{\mathcal{A}}^1$ samples $\mathbf{b}$ uniformly at random from its domain. As a side effect of this change, $\text{Game}_{\mathcal{A}}^1$ does not utilize $\mathbf{s}$ anymore; for this reason, $\mathbf{s}$ is completely removed from $\text{Game}_{\mathcal{A}}^1$.

Considering the difference between $\text{Game}_{\mathcal{A}}^0$ and $\text{Game}_{\mathcal{A}}^1$, we can see that the pair $(\text{seed}_{\mathbf{A}}, \mathbf{b})$ in $\text{Game}_{\mathcal{A}}^0$ is constructed identically to the pair $(\text{seed}_{\mathbf{A}}, \mathbf{b}_0)$ in $\text{Game}_{\mathcal{A}, \text{gen}, l, \mu, q, p}^{\text{GMLWR}}(u)$; contrarily, in $\text{Game}_{\mathcal{A}}^1$, the pair $(\text{seed}_{\mathbf{A}}, \mathbf{b})$ is constructed identically to the pair $(\text{seed}_{\mathbf{A}}, \mathbf{b}_1)$ in $\text{Game}_{\mathcal{A}, \text{gen}, l, \mu, q, p}^{\text{GMLWR}}(u)$. Consequently, an adversary $\mathcal{A}$ that is able to distinguish between these two games can be used to construct an adversary $\mathcal{B}_0^{\mathcal{A}}$ against the corresponding instance of the GMLWR game. Figure 6 provides such a reduction adversary.

Based on the reduction adversary given in Fig. 6, we can deduce that for any given adversary $\mathcal{A}$ against $\text{Game}_{\mathcal{A}}^0$ and $\text{Game}_{\mathcal{A}}^1$, there exists an adversary $\mathcal{B}_0^{\mathcal{A}}$ against the corresponding instance of the GMLWR game such that $\left| \Pr\left[\text{Game}_{\mathcal{A}}^0 = 1\right] - \Pr\left[\text{Game}_{\mathcal{A}}^1 = 1\right] \right| = \text{Adv}_{\text{gen}, l, \mu, q, p}^{\text{GMLWR}}(\mathcal{B}_0^{\mathcal{A}})$. Indeed, this is a consequence of the fact that, from the perspective of $\mathcal{A}$, $\mathcal{B}_0^{\mathcal{A}}(\text{seed}_{\mathbf{A}}, \mathbf{b}_u)$ perfectly simulates $\text{Game}_{\mathcal{A}}^0$ when $u = 0$ and $\text{Game}_{\mathcal{A}}^1$ when $u = 1$.

Step 2: $\text{Game}_{\mathcal{A}}^1$ - $\text{Game}_{\mathcal{A}}^2$. For the second step, we introduce a modification that results in an adversary against $\text{Game}_{\mathcal{A}}^2$ always acquiring at least as much information as an adversary against $\text{Game}_{\mathcal{A}}^1$. Consequently, given an adversary $\mathcal{A}$ against $\text{Game}_{\mathcal{A}}^1$, we can construct an adversary $\mathcal{R}^{\mathcal{A}}$ against $\text{Game}_{\mathcal{R}^{\mathcal{A}}}^2$ such that $\text{Adv}^1(\mathcal{A}) = \text{Adv}^2(\mathcal{R}^{\mathcal{A}})$. Specifically, this can be accomplished by straightforwardly letting $\mathcal{R}^{\mathcal{A}}$ disregard any additional information it receives relative to the information provided to an adversary against the first game. Figure 7 presents this reduction adversary.

Naturally, for the desired equality of advantages to hold, the reduction adversary should, from the perspective of $\mathcal{A}$, perfectly simulate a run of $\text{Game}_{\mathcal{A}}^1$. Since the only difference between the considered games concerns the computation of $\hat{c}$, this wholly depends on the indistinguishability of $\hat{c}$ (from $\text{Game}_{\mathcal{A}}^1$) and $\hat{c}'$ (from $\text{Game}_{\mathcal{R}^{\mathcal{A}}}^2$); the remainder is trivially identical. Therefore, consider $x = v' + \lfloor m_u \rfloor_{2 \rightarrow p}$, where v' and m_u are as in $\text{Game}_{\mathcal{A}}^1$ and $\text{Game}_{\mathcal{A}}^2$. Then, because $\epsilon_t + 1 < \epsilon_p$, the modular scaling and flooring operation performed on x in $\text{Game}_{\mathcal{A}}^1$ effectively carries out a right-bit shift of $\epsilon_p - (\epsilon_t + 1)$ bits on each coefficient of x. Consequently, denoting the binary representation of a coefficient of x by $a_{\epsilon_p - 1} \ldots a_0$, the corresponding coefficient of the resulting $\hat{c}$ equals $a_{\epsilon_p - 1} \ldots a_{\epsilon_p - \epsilon_t - 1}$. Similarly, because $\epsilon_p < \epsilon_q$ (which implies $2 \cdot \epsilon_p - \epsilon_q < \epsilon_q$), $\text{Game}_{\mathcal{R}^{\mathcal{A}}}^2$ essentially performs a right-bit shift of $\epsilon_p - (2 \cdot \epsilon_p - \epsilon_q) = \epsilon_q - \epsilon_p$ bits. Certainly, for each coefficient $a_{\epsilon_p - 1} \ldots a_0$ of x, this gives a resulting coefficient $a_{\epsilon_p - 1} \ldots a_{\epsilon_q - \epsilon_p}$ of $\hat{c}$. At this point, employing the assumption stated in the secu-

$\underline{\text{Game}_{\mathcal{A}}^0}$

1 : $u \leftarrow\!\!\$\, \mathcal{U}(\{0,1\})$
2 : $\text{seed}_{\mathbf{A}} \leftarrow\!\!\$\, \mathcal{U}(\{0,1\}^{256})$
3 : $\mathbf{A} \leftarrow \text{gen}(\text{seed}_{\mathbf{A}})$
4 : $\mathbf{s} \leftarrow\!\!\$\, \beta_\mu(R_q^{l \times 1})$
5 : $\mathbf{b} \leftarrow \lfloor \mathbf{A} \cdot \mathbf{s} + \mathbf{h} \rfloor_{q \to p}$
6 : $(m_0, m_1) \leftarrow \mathcal{A}.\mathsf{P}((\text{seed}_{\mathbf{A}}, \mathbf{b}))$
7 : $\mathbf{s}' \leftarrow\!\!\$\, \beta_\mu(R_q^{l \times 1})$
8 : $\mathbf{b}' \leftarrow \lfloor \mathbf{A}^T \cdot \mathbf{s}' + \mathbf{h} \rfloor_{q \to p}$
9 : $v' \leftarrow \mathbf{b}^T \cdot (\mathbf{s}' \bmod p) + (h_1 \bmod p)$
10 : $\hat{c} \leftarrow \lfloor v' + \lfloor m_u \rfloor_{2 \to p} \rfloor_{p \to 2 \cdot t}$
11 : $u' \leftarrow \mathcal{A}.\mathsf{D}((\hat{c}, \mathbf{b}'))$
12 : $\textbf{return } (u' = u)$

$\underline{\text{Game}_{\mathcal{A}}^1}$

1 : $u \leftarrow\!\!\$\, \mathcal{U}(\{0,1\})$
2 : $\text{seed}_{\mathbf{A}} \leftarrow\!\!\$\, \mathcal{U}(\{0,1\}^{256})$
3 : $\mathbf{A} \leftarrow \text{gen}(\text{seed}_{\mathbf{A}})$
4 : Skip
5 : $\mathbf{b} \leftarrow\!\!\$\, \mathcal{U}(R_p^{l \times 1})$
6 : $(m_0, m_1) \leftarrow \mathcal{A}.\mathsf{P}((\text{seed}_{\mathbf{A}}, \mathbf{b}))$
7 : $\mathbf{s}' \leftarrow\!\!\$\, \beta_\mu(R_q^{l \times 1})$
8 : $\mathbf{b}' \leftarrow \lfloor \mathbf{A}^T \cdot \mathbf{s}' + \mathbf{h} \rfloor_{q \to p}$
9 : $v' \leftarrow \mathbf{b}^T \cdot (\mathbf{s}' \bmod p) + (h_1 \bmod p)$
10 : $\hat{c} \leftarrow \lfloor v' + \lfloor m_u \rfloor_{2 \to p} \rfloor_{p \to 2 \cdot t}$
11 : $u' \leftarrow \mathcal{A}.\mathsf{D}((\hat{c}, \mathbf{b}'))$
12 : $\textbf{return } (u' = u)$

$\underline{\text{Game}_{\mathcal{A}}^2}$

1 : $u \leftarrow\!\!\$\, \mathcal{U}(\{0,1\})$
2 : $\text{seed}_{\mathbf{A}} \leftarrow\!\!\$\, \mathcal{U}(\{0,1\}^{256})$
3 : $\mathbf{A} \leftarrow \text{gen}(\text{seed}_{\mathbf{A}})$
4 : Skip
5 : $\mathbf{b} \leftarrow\!\!\$\, \mathcal{U}(R_p^{l \times 1})$
6 : $(m_0, m_1) \leftarrow \mathcal{A}.\mathsf{P}((\text{seed}_{\mathbf{A}}, \mathbf{b}))$
7 : $\mathbf{s}' \leftarrow\!\!\$\, \beta_\mu(R_q^{l \times 1})$
8 : $\mathbf{b}' \leftarrow \lfloor \mathbf{A}^T \cdot \mathbf{s}' + \mathbf{h} \rfloor_{q \to p}$
9 : $v' \leftarrow \mathbf{b}^T \cdot (\mathbf{s}' \bmod p) + (h_1 \bmod p)$
10 : $\hat{c} \leftarrow \lfloor v' + \lfloor m_u \rfloor_{2 \to p} \rfloor_{p \to p^2/q}$
11 : $u' \leftarrow \mathcal{A}.\mathsf{D}((\hat{c}, \mathbf{b}'))$
12 : $\textbf{return } (u' = u)$

$\underline{\text{Game}_{\mathcal{A}}^3}$

1 : $u \leftarrow\!\!\$\, \mathcal{U}(\{0,1\})$
2 : $\text{seed}_{\mathbf{A}} \leftarrow\!\!\$\, \mathcal{U}(\{0,1\}^{256})$
3 : $\mathbf{A} \leftarrow \text{gen}(\text{seed}_{\mathbf{A}})$
4 : Skip
5 : $\mathbf{b} \leftarrow\!\!\$\, \mathcal{U}(R_q^{l \times 1})$
6 : $(m_0, m_1) \leftarrow \mathcal{A}.\mathsf{P}((\text{seed}_{\mathbf{A}}, \mathbf{b}))$
7 : $\mathbf{s}' \leftarrow\!\!\$\, \beta_\mu(R_q^{l \times 1})$
8 : $\mathbf{b}' \leftarrow \lfloor \mathbf{A}^T \cdot \mathbf{s}' + \mathbf{h} \rfloor_{q \to p}$
9 : $v' \leftarrow \lfloor \mathbf{b}^T \cdot \mathbf{s}' + h_1 \rfloor_{q \to p}$
10 : $\hat{c} \leftarrow v' + (\lfloor m_u \rfloor_{2 \to p^2/q} \bmod p)$
11 : $u' \leftarrow \mathcal{A}.\mathsf{D}((\hat{c}, \mathbf{b}'))$
12 : $\textbf{return } (u' = u)$

$\underline{\text{Game}_{\mathcal{A}}^4}$

1 : $u \leftarrow\!\!\$\, \mathcal{U}(\{0,1\})$
2 : $\text{seed}_{\mathbf{A}} \leftarrow\!\!\$\, \mathcal{U}(\{0,1\}^{256})$
3 : $\mathbf{A} \leftarrow \text{gen}(\text{seed}_{\mathbf{A}})$
4 : Skip
5 : $\mathbf{b} \leftarrow\!\!\$\, \mathcal{U}(R_q^{l \times 1})$
6 : $(m_0, m_1) \leftarrow \mathcal{A}.\mathsf{P}((\text{seed}_{\mathbf{A}}, \mathbf{b}))$
7 : Skip
8 : $\mathbf{b}' \leftarrow\!\!\$\, \mathcal{U}(R_p^{l \times 1})$
9 : $v' \leftarrow\!\!\$\, \mathcal{U}(R_p)$
10 : $\hat{c} \leftarrow v' + (\lfloor m_u \rfloor_{2 \to p^2/q} \bmod p)$
11 : $u' \leftarrow \mathcal{A}.\mathsf{D}((\hat{c}, \mathbf{b}'))$
12 : $\textbf{return } (u' = u)$

Fig. 5. Game Sequence of Saber.PKE's Security Proof

$$
\begin{array}{l}
\hline
\mathcal{B}_0^{\mathcal{A}}(\text{seed}_\mathbf{A}, \mathbf{b}_u) \\
\hline
1: \quad w \leftarrow\!\!\$\, \mathcal{U}(\{0,1\}) \\
2: \quad \mathbf{A} \leftarrow \mathsf{gen}(\text{seed}_\mathbf{A}) \\
3: \quad (m_0, m_1) \leftarrow \mathcal{A}.\mathsf{P}((\text{seed}_\mathbf{A}, \mathbf{b}_u)) \\
4: \quad \mathbf{s}' \leftarrow\!\!\$\, \beta_\mu(R_q^{l \times 1}) \\
5: \quad \mathbf{b}' \leftarrow \lfloor \mathbf{A}^T \cdot \mathbf{s}' + \mathbf{h} \rfloor_{q \to p} \\
6: \quad v' \leftarrow \mathbf{b}_u^T \cdot (\mathbf{s}' \bmod p) + (h_1 \bmod p) \\
7: \quad \hat{c} \leftarrow \lfloor v' + \lfloor m_w \rfloor_{2 \to p} \rfloor_{p \to 2 \cdot t} \\
8: \quad w' \leftarrow \mathcal{A}.\mathsf{D}((\hat{c}, \mathbf{b}')); \\
9: \quad \textbf{return } (w' = w); \\
\hline
\end{array}
$$

Fig. 6. Reduction Adversary $\mathcal{B}_0^{\mathcal{A}}$ Against $\text{Game}^{\text{GMLWR}}_{\mathcal{B}_0^{\mathcal{A}}, \mathsf{gen}, l, \mu, q, p}(u)$

$$
\begin{array}{l}
\hline
\mathcal{R}^{\mathcal{A}}.\mathsf{P}((\text{seed}_\mathbf{A}, \mathbf{b})) \\
\hline
1: \quad \textbf{return } \mathcal{A}.\mathsf{P}((\text{seed}_\mathbf{A}, \mathbf{b})) \\
\hline
\end{array}
\qquad
\begin{array}{l}
\hline
\mathcal{R}^{\mathcal{A}}.\mathsf{D}((\hat{c}, \mathbf{b}')) \\
\hline
1: \quad \hat{c}' \leftarrow \lfloor \hat{c} \rfloor_{p^2/q \to 2 \cdot t} \\
2: \quad \textbf{return } \mathcal{A}.\mathsf{D}((\hat{c}', \mathbf{b}')) \\
\hline
\end{array}
$$

Fig. 7. Reduction Adversary $\mathcal{R}^{\mathcal{A}}$ Against $\text{Game}^2_{\mathcal{R}^{\mathcal{A}}}$

rity theorem, i.e., $\frac{q}{p} \leq \frac{p}{2 \cdot t}$, we can see that the subsequent modular scaling and flooring operation applied by $\mathcal{R}^{\mathcal{A}}$ on $\hat{c}$ carries out an additional right-bit shift of $2 \cdot \epsilon_p - \epsilon_q - \epsilon_t - 1$ bits; in terms of the original x, this operation transforms each coefficient $a_{\epsilon_p - 1} \ldots a_{\epsilon_q - \epsilon_p}$ into $a_{\epsilon_p - 1} \ldots a_{\epsilon_p - \epsilon_t - 1}$, identical to the corresponding coefficient of $\hat{c}$ in $\text{Game}^1_{\mathcal{A}}$. Thus, the $\hat{c}'$ of $\text{Game}^2_{\mathcal{R}^{\mathcal{A}}}$ indeed is indistinguishable from the $\hat{c}$ of $\text{Game}^1_{\mathcal{A}}$; as such, the reduction adversary is correctly constructed and gives the desired equality of advantages.

Step 3: $\text{Game}^2_{\mathcal{A}}$ - $\text{Game}^3_{\mathcal{A}}$. In this step, similarly to the preceding step, we exclusively introduce changes that provide an adversary against $\text{Game}^3_{\mathcal{A}}$ with at least as much information as an adversary against $\text{Game}^2_{\mathcal{A}}$. Therefore, given any adversary $\mathcal{A}$ against $\text{Game}^2_{\mathcal{A}}$, we can construct an adversary $\mathcal{R}^{\mathcal{A}}$ against $\text{Game}^3_{\mathcal{R}^{\mathcal{A}}}$ such that $\mathsf{Adv}^2(\mathcal{A}) = \mathsf{Adv}^3(\mathcal{R}^{\mathcal{A}})$. Figure 8 provides such a reduction adversary.

$$
\begin{array}{l}
\hline
\mathcal{R}^{\mathcal{A}}.\mathsf{P}((\text{seed}_\mathbf{A}, \mathbf{b})) \\
\hline
1: \quad \mathbf{b}_p \leftarrow \mathbf{b} \bmod p \\
2: \quad \textbf{return } \mathcal{A}.\mathsf{P}((\text{seed}_\mathbf{A}, \mathbf{b}_p)) \\
\hline
\end{array}
\qquad
\begin{array}{l}
\hline
\mathcal{R}^{\mathcal{A}}.\mathsf{D}((\hat{c}, \mathbf{b}')) \\
\hline
1: \quad \hat{c}' \leftarrow \hat{c} \bmod p^2/q \\
2: \quad \textbf{return } \mathcal{A}.\mathsf{D}((\hat{c}', \mathbf{b}')); \\
\hline
\end{array}
$$

Fig. 8. Reduction Adversary $\mathcal{R}^{\mathcal{A}}$ Against $\text{Game}^3_{\mathcal{R}^{\mathcal{A}}}$

In order to substantiate that the reduction adversary in Fig. 8 perfectly simulates a run of $\text{Game}_{\mathcal{A}}^2$ (from the perspective of $\mathcal{A}$), we argue the following points.

- Sampling $\mathbf{b}$ from $\mathcal{U}(R_q^{l \times 1})$ and, subsequently, reducing it modulo p is well-defined and equivalent to sampling $\mathbf{b}$ directly from $\mathcal{U}(R_p^{l \times 1})$. That is, the $\mathbf{b}_p$ that $\mathcal{R}^{\mathcal{A}}$ provides to $\mathcal{A}$ in $\text{Game}_{\mathcal{R}^{\mathcal{A}}}^3$ is indistinguishable from, i.e., identically distributed to, the $\mathbf{b}$ that $\mathcal{A}$ receives in $\text{Game}_{\mathcal{A}}^2$.
- Utilizing the $\hat{c}$ given in $\text{Game}_{\mathcal{R}^{\mathcal{A}}}^3$, the $\hat{c}'$ that $\mathcal{R}^{\mathcal{A}}$ computes (and calls $\mathcal{A}$ with) is indistinguishable from, i.e., identically distributed to, the $\hat{c}$ provided to $\mathcal{A}$ in $\text{Game}_{\mathcal{A}}^2$.

Certainly, since $\mathbf{b}$ and $\hat{c}$ are the only artifacts provided to the adversary that differ between the considered games, the above two points are sufficient to demonstrate that the reduction adversary gives rise to the desired equality of advantages.

Regarding the first point, suppose $\mathbf{b}$ is sampled from $\mathcal{U}(R_q^{l \times 1})$ as in $\text{Game}_{\mathcal{R}^{\mathcal{A}}}^3$. Then, by definition, every coefficient of (each entry of) $\mathbf{b}$ is an element from $\mathbb{Z}_q$. Since $p \mid q$, reduction modulo p is well-defined for each of these coefficients; in turn, the extension of this modular reduction to the complete vector, i.e., $\mathbf{b} \bmod p$, is well-defined as well. Furthermore, since precisely $\frac{q}{p}$ elements from $\mathbb{Z}_q$ map to a specific $x \in \mathbb{Z}_p$ when reduced modulo p, exactly $\frac{q^{n \cdot l}}{p^{n \cdot l}}$ elements from $R_q^{l \times 1}$ map to a specific $\mathbf{v} \in R_p^{l \times 1}$ when reduced modulo p. Therefore, sampling $\mathbf{b}$ from $\mathcal{U}(R_q^{l \times 1})$ and, subsequently, reducing it modulo p is well-defined and results in an element that is uniformly distributed over $R_p^{l \times 1}$.

Concerning the second point, consider the computation of $\mathbf{b}^T \cdot \mathbf{s}' + h_1$ in $\text{Game}_{\mathcal{R}^{\mathcal{A}}}^3$. As a consequence of the previous point, reducing the result of this computation modulo p provides an identical result to the analogous computation in $\text{Game}_{\mathcal{A}}^2$; equivalently, the computation of $\mathbf{b}^T \cdot (\mathbf{s}' \bmod p) + (h_1 \bmod p)$ (from $\text{Game}_{\mathcal{A}}^2$) and $\mathbf{b}^T \cdot \mathbf{s}' + h_1$ (from $\text{Game}_{\mathcal{R}^{\mathcal{A}}}^3$) are equal in the least significant ϵ_p bits. Thus, if $a_{\epsilon_q - 1} \ldots a_{\epsilon_p - 1} \ldots a_0$ denotes the binary representation of a coefficient of the computation in $\text{Game}_{\mathcal{R}^{\mathcal{A}}}^3$, then $a_{\epsilon_p - 1} \ldots a_0$ denotes its counterpart from $\text{Game}_{\mathcal{A}}^2$. Certainly, from this follows that the corresponding coefficient of v' in $\text{Game}_{\mathcal{R}^{\mathcal{A}}}^3$ is computed as $\lfloor a_{\epsilon_q - 1} \ldots a_{\epsilon_p - 1} \ldots a_0 \rfloor_{q \to p} = a_{\epsilon_q - 1} \ldots a_{\epsilon_p - 1} \ldots a_{\epsilon_q - \epsilon_p}$. Then, denoting a coefficient of m_u by b_0, we can derive that the corresponding coefficients of $\hat{c}$ between the games are identical in their $2 \cdot \epsilon_p - \epsilon_q$ least significant bits as follows[4].

$$
\begin{aligned}
\text{Game}_{\mathcal{A}}^2 : \quad & \lfloor a_{\epsilon_p - 1} \ldots a_0 + \lfloor b_0 \rfloor_{2 \to p} \rfloor_{p \to p^2/q} = \\
& \lfloor a_{\epsilon_p - 1} \ldots a_0 + b_0 0^{\epsilon_p - 1} \rfloor_{p \to p^2/q} = \\
& \lfloor (a_{\epsilon_p - 1} + b_0) \ldots a_0 \rfloor_{p \to p^2/q} = \\
& (a_{\epsilon_p - 1} + b_0) \ldots a_{\epsilon_q - \epsilon_p}
\end{aligned}
$$

[4] Notice that in $\text{Game}_{\mathcal{R}^{\mathcal{A}}}^3$, the explicit modular reduction in $v' + (\lfloor m_u \rfloor_{2 \to p^2/q} \bmod p)$ is merely used to accentuate the interpretation of $\lfloor m_u \rfloor_{2 \to p^2/q}$ as an element of R_p; that is, the modular reduction does not affect the actual value of m_u.

$$\text{Game}^3_{\mathcal{R}^{\mathcal{A}}} : a_{\epsilon_q-1} \ldots a_{\epsilon_p-1} \ldots a_{\epsilon_q-\epsilon_p} + (\lfloor b_0 \rfloor_{2 \to p^2/q} \bmod p) =$$
$$a_{\epsilon_q-1} \ldots a_{\epsilon_p-1} \ldots a_{\epsilon_q-\epsilon_p} + 0^{\epsilon_q-\epsilon_p} b_0 0^{2 \cdot \epsilon_p - \epsilon_q - 1} =$$
$$d_{\epsilon_q-1} \ldots d_{\epsilon_p} (a_{\epsilon_p-1} + b_0) a_{\epsilon_p-2} \ldots a_{\epsilon_q-\epsilon_p}$$

Here, $(a_{\epsilon_p-1} + b_0)$ represents the (single) bit value resulting from the addition of the a_{ϵ_p-1} and b_0 bits (modulo 2); furthermore, each d_i represents a bit that might be influenced by potential carries. Finally, we see that $\mathcal{R}^{\mathcal{A}}$ indeed correctly computes (and calls $\mathcal{A}$ with) a $\hat{c}'$ that is indistinguishable from the $\hat{c}$ of $\text{Game}^2_{\mathcal{A}}$ by reducing each coefficient of the $\hat{c}$ provided in $\text{Game}^3_{\mathcal{R}^{\mathcal{A}}}$ modulo $\frac{p^2}{q} = 2^{2 \cdot \epsilon_p - \epsilon_q}$ and, hence, effectively discarding the $\epsilon_q - \epsilon_p$ most significant bits.

Step 4: $\text{Game}^3_{\mathcal{A}}$ - $\text{Game}^4_{\mathcal{A}}$. For the final step, we change the manner in which $\mathbf{b}'$ and v' are obtained. Namely, instead of computing these values by $\lfloor \mathbf{A}^T \cdot \mathbf{s}' + \mathbf{h} \rfloor_{q \to p}$ and $\lfloor \mathbf{b}^T \cdot \mathbf{s}' + h_1 \rfloor_{q \to p}$, as is done in $\text{Game}^3_{\mathcal{A}}$, they are sampled uniformly at random from their respective domains in $\text{Game}^4_{\mathcal{A}}$. As a consequence of this adjustment, $\mathbf{s}'$ becomes redundant and, for this reason, is removed from $\text{Game}^4_{\mathcal{A}}$.

In $\text{Game}^3_{\mathcal{A}}$, the tuple $(\text{seed}_{\mathbf{A}}, \mathbf{b}', \mathbf{b}^T, v')$ is constructed identically to the tuple $(\text{seed}_{\mathbf{A}}, \mathbf{b}_0, \mathbf{a}, d_0)$ in $\text{Game}^{\text{XMLWR}}_{\mathcal{A},\text{gen},l,\mu,q,p}(u)$; contrarily, the tuple $(\text{seed}_{\mathbf{A}}, \mathbf{b}', \mathbf{b}^T, v')$ in $\text{Game}^4_{\mathcal{A}}$ is constructed in the same way as the tuple $(\text{seed}_{\mathbf{A}}, \mathbf{b}_1, \mathbf{a}, d_1)$ in $\text{Game}^{\text{XMLWR}}_{\mathcal{A},\text{gen},l,\mu,q,p}(u)$. As such, any adversary $\mathcal{A}$ distinguishing between $\text{Game}^3_{\mathcal{A}}$ and $\text{Game}^4_{\mathcal{A}}$ can be used to construct an adversary against the corresponding instance of the XMLWR game. Figure 9 contains such a reduction adversary.

$\mathcal{B}^A_1(\text{seed}_{\mathbf{A}}, \mathbf{b}_u, \mathbf{a}, d_u)$
1:   $w \leftarrow_\$ \mathcal{U}(\{0,1\});$
2:   $(m_0, m_1) \leftarrow \mathcal{A}.\text{P}((\text{seed}_{\mathbf{A}}, \mathbf{a}^T))$
3:   $\hat{c} \leftarrow d_u + (\lfloor m_w \rfloor_{2 \to p^2/q} \bmod p)$
4:   $w' \leftarrow \mathcal{A}.\text{D}((\hat{c}, \mathbf{b}_u))$
5:   **return** $(w = w')$

Fig. 9. Reduction Adversary $\mathcal{B}^A_1$ Against $\text{Game}^{\text{XMLWR}}_{\mathcal{B}^A_1,\text{gen},l,\mu,q,p}(u)$

Employing the reduction in Fig. 9, we can derive a result analogous to the result of the first step. Specifically, for any adversary $\mathcal{A}$ distinguishing between $\text{Game}^3_{\mathcal{A}}$ and $\text{Game}^4_{\mathcal{A}}$, there exists an adversary $\mathcal{B}^A_1$ against $\text{Game}^{\text{XMLWR}}_{\mathcal{B}^A_1,\text{gen},l,\mu,q,p}(u)$ such that $|\Pr[\text{Game}^3_{\mathcal{A}} = 1] - \Pr[\text{Game}^4_{\mathcal{A}} = 1]| = \text{Adv}^{\text{XMLWR}}_{\text{gen},l,\mu,q,p}(\mathcal{B}^A_1)$. Certainly, this is due to the fact that, from the perspective of $\mathcal{A}$, $\mathcal{B}^A_1(\text{seed}_{\mathbf{A}}, \mathbf{b}_u, \mathbf{a}, d_u)$ perfectly simulates $\text{Game}^3_{\mathcal{A}}$ when $u = 0$ and $\text{Game}^4_{\mathcal{A}}$ when $u = 1$.

Analysis of $\text{Game}^4_{\mathcal{A}}$. Examining $\text{Game}^4_{\mathcal{A}}$, we can observe that all artifacts given to the adversary are uniformly distributed over their domain; particularly, $\hat{c}$ is uniformly distributed over R_p because the uniformity of v' is maintained under addition with (the scaled) m_u. Certainly, in this game, v' essentially constitutes a generalization of the one-time pad to the (additive) group of R_p. As such, the computed ciphertext is uniformly distributed and completely independent of all other information. This implies that an adversary against $\text{Game}_{\mathcal{A}}^4$ must randomly guess the bit u; as a result, for any adversary $\mathcal{A}$, we have $\Pr\left[\text{Game}_{\mathcal{A}}^4 = 1\right] = \frac{1}{2}$.

Final Result. Aggregating all results, we can derive the security theorem as follows.

$$\forall_{\mathcal{A}} \exists_{\mathcal{A}', \mathcal{B}_0, \mathcal{B}_1} :$$

$$\text{Adv}_{\text{Saber.PKE}}^{\text{IND-CPA}}(\mathcal{A}) = \text{Adv}^0(\mathcal{A}) = \left| \Pr\left[\text{Game}_{\mathcal{A}}^0 = 1\right] - \frac{1}{2} \right| =$$

$$\left| \Pr\left[\text{Game}_{\mathcal{A}}^0 = 1\right] - \Pr\left[\text{Game}_{\mathcal{A}'}^4 = 1\right] \right| \leq$$

$$\left| \Pr\left[\text{Game}_{\mathcal{A}}^0 = 1\right] - \Pr\left[\text{Game}_{\mathcal{A}}^1 = 1\right] \right| + \left| \Pr\left[\text{Game}_{\mathcal{A}}^1 = 1\right] - \Pr\left[\text{Game}_{\mathcal{A}'}^4 = 1\right] \right| =$$

$$\text{Adv}_{\text{gen},l,\mu,q,p}^{\text{GMLWR}}(\mathcal{B}_0) + \left| \Pr\left[\text{Game}_{\mathcal{A}}^1 = 1\right] - \Pr\left[\text{Game}_{\mathcal{A}'}^4 = 1\right] \right| =$$

$$\text{Adv}_{\text{gen},l,\mu,q,p}^{\text{GMLWR}}(\mathcal{B}_0) + \text{Adv}_{\text{gen},l,\mu,q,p}^{\text{XMLWR}}(\mathcal{B}_1)$$

In this derivation, the inequality arises from an application of the triangle in equality; the second-to-last equality follows from the result of the first step in the proof; and the last equality holds due to the results of the second, third, and fourth step, as well as the fact that $\Pr\left[\text{Game}_{\mathcal{A}'}^4 = 1\right] = \frac{1}{2}$. At last, compressing the above derivation gives the desired result.

$$\forall_{\mathcal{A}} \exists_{\mathcal{B}_0, \mathcal{B}_1} : \text{Adv}_{\text{Saber.PKE}}^{\text{IND-CPA}}(\mathcal{A}) \leq \text{Adv}_{\text{gen},l,\mu,q,p}^{\text{GMLWR}}(\mathcal{B}_0) + \text{Adv}_{\text{gen},l,\mu,q,p}^{\text{XMLWR}}(\mathcal{B}_1)$$

As a final remark, although no formal analysis is provided, it is evident that the running time for each of $\mathcal{B}_0$ and $\mathcal{B}_1$ is approximately equal to that of $\mathcal{A}$. In particular, excluding the calls to $\mathcal{A}$'s abstract algorithms, all employed reductions exclusively perform sequential operations that can straightforwardly be executed efficiently.

Formal Verification. Following the hand-written security proof, we discuss several representative parts of the corresponding formal verification in Easy-Crypt. Specifically, we examine the formalization of (part of) the fundamental specification; furthermore, we consider the formalization specific to the initial two proof steps and the final result. Notably, we do not cover the concrete proofs of the results in EasyCrypt. This is mainly because the exposition of such technical endeavors would not be meaningful to the current discussion; moreover, this does not take away from the meaningfulness of the results presented here since, assuming the utilized tool is sound, validation of a formal verification artifact merely requires validation of the formalized specification and related claims (as long as the claims are successfully verifiable in the tool). Nevertheless, all results have successfully been formally verified. The code corresponding to this formal verification is provided in the repository belonging to this work; this repository can be found at https://github.com/MM45/Saber-Formal-Verification-EasyCrypt.

Fundamental Specification. Foremost, we formalize the most rudimentary part of the considered context: Saber's parameters and the corresponding constraints. These formalizations are presented in Listing 1.1 and Listing 1.2, respectively.

```
1   const eq, ep, et: int.
2   const en: int.
3
4   const q: int = 2^eq.
5   const p: int = 2^ep.
6   const t: int = 2^et.
7   const n: int = 2^en.
8   const l: int.
```

Listing 1.1. Saber's Parameters

```
1   axiom zero_en: 0 <= en.
2   axiom one_et1: 1 <= et + 1.
3   axiom et2_ep: et + 2 <= ep.
4   axiom ep1_eq: ep + 1 <= eq.
5   axiom one_l: 1 <= l.
```

Listing 1.2. Parameter Constraints

Naturally, each constant defined in the former listing represents the similarly-named parameter of Saber; furthermore, the second, third, and fourth axioms in the latter listing together formalize $1 \leq \epsilon_t + 1 \wedge \epsilon_t + 2 \leq \epsilon_p \wedge \epsilon_p + 1 \leq \epsilon_q$, which is equivalent to the previously mentioned constraint that Saber enforces on these exponents, i.e., $0 < \epsilon_t + 1 < \epsilon_p < \epsilon_q$.

Subsequent to the parameters, we define the necessary types and operators[5]. First, most of the types we define are used to denote the algebraic structures employed in Saber; for example, we define Zq, Rq, Rq_vec, and Rq_mat to respectively denote $\mathbb{Z}_q$, R_q, $R_q^{l \times 1}$, and $R_q^{l \times l}$. The types for the remainder of the algebraic structures follow a similar identifier format, e.g., Rp represents R_p. Naturally, for each of these types, the appropriate structure is formalized and assigned. Second, the formalizations of the functions predominantly consist of operators that carry out modular reduction or modular scaling and flooring. Listing 1.3 contains the definitions for a selected few of these operators.

```
1   op Zq2Zp (z : Zq) : Zp = Zp.inzmod (Zq.asint z).
2
3   op scaleZq2Zp (z : Zq) : Zp =
4         Zp.inzmod (shr (Zq.asint z) (eq - ep)).
5   op scaleZp2Zq (z : Zp) : Zq =
6         Zq.inzmod (shl (Zp.asint z) (eq - ep)).
```

Listing 1.3. Modular Reduction and Modular Scaling and Flooring

Here, the asint operator converts from the associated integer ring type, e.g., Zp or Zq, to the integers; the inzmod operator performs the opposite conversion. In its conversion, inzmod implicitly reduces the provided argument modulo the corresponding modulus. Moreover, shr and shl respectively compute a right and left bit-shift of their first (integer) argument by a number of bits equal to their second (integer) argument. Apart from the specific operators shown in this

---

[5] In EasyCrypt, an operator denotes a mathematical function.

listing, we define variants for each type combination involved in a modular reduction or modular scaling and flooring throughout; this includes the extensions of these operators to (vectors of) polynomials. For intelligibility purposes, all of these operators share the same self-explanatory identifier format. Lastly, a single additional operator models the gen function. This operator is left rather abstract, merely mapping a seed to an element of $R_q^{l \times l}$ without other properties or requirements.

At this point, the only remaining fundamental artifacts to formalize are the required distributions. For the uniform distributions, we utilize the built-in mechanisms of EasyCrypt to construct precise formalizations; for type X, these distributions are denoted by dX. Contrariwise, instead of $\beta_\mu(R_q^{l \times 1})$, we formalize an arbitrary, generic distribution over $R_q^{l \times 1}$ that is denoted by dsmallRq_vec. Indeed, this generic distribution most definitely encompasses $\beta_\mu(R_q^{l \times 1})$. In consequence of this more abstract approach, the formal verification gives slightly stronger guarantees without requiring additional nontrivial assumptions; specifically, with this approach, the formal verification shows that the security proof is valid for any distribution (over $R_q^{l \times 1}$) in place of $\beta_\mu(R_q^{l \times 1})$, provided the MLWR game is hard with this distribution. Moreover, this approach precludes the (somewhat tedious) effort of precisely formalizing $\beta_\mu(R_q^{l \times 1})$; this is also the reason we do not formalize the μ parameter (see Listing 1.1).

Leveraging the above fundamentals, we can formalize the remainder of the necessary higher-level artifacts such as the specification of Saber.PKE, the security notion, the hardness assumptions, the game sequence, and the justifications for the steps in the game-based proof. Although we do not explicitly present every utilized artifact here, the ensuing discussion will cover several of them at the relevant places.

Step 1: Game_A^0 - Game_A^1. Before the formal verification of each step, and so also preceding the formal verification of the first step, we formalize the adversary class(es), games, and reduction adversary relevant to this step. Concerning the former, Listing 1.4 depicts the formalizations of the classes of IND-CPA adversaries and GMLWR adversaries, both utilized in the first step.

```
1   module type Adv_INDCPA = {
2     proc choose(pk : seed * Rp_vec) : R2 * R2
3     proc guess(c : R2t * Rp_vec) : bool
4   }.
5
6   module type Adv_GMLWR = {
7     proc guess(sd : seed, b : Rp_vec) : bool
8   }.
```

Listing 1.4. Classes of IND-CPA Adversaries and GMLWR Adversaries

A module type defines an abstract interface that modules may implement. EasyCrypt allows universal quantification over these types, enabling one to abstractly reason about every potential instantiation; therefore, this mechanism is well-suited to capture the concept of an adversary class[6]. Regarding the module types presented above, `Adv_INDCPA` denotes the class of IND-CPA adversaries, where `choose` and `guess` respectively represent $\mathcal{A}.P$ and $\mathcal{A}.D$; `Adv_GMLWR` denotes the class of GMLWR adversaries, where `guess` represents the only algorithm of these adversaries. Naturally, the parameters and return values of these procedures accordingly formalize the parameters and return values of the corresponding algorithms.

Employing the formalization of the adversary classes, we formalize the necessary games. First, Listing 1.5 provides the formalization of $\text{Game}_{\mathcal{A}}^0$. Here, as well as in all ensuing listings, the $(*\ldots*)$ comment represents the (uninteresting) omitted section of variable declarations.

```
1   module Game0(A : Adv_INDCPA) = {
2     proc main() : bool = {
3       (*...*)
4       u <$ dbool;
5       sd <$ dseed;
6       _A <- gen sd;
7       s <$ dsmallRq_vec;
8       b <- scaleRqv2Rpv (_A *^ s + h);
9
10      (m0, m1) <@ A.choose((sd, b));
11
12      s' <$ dsmallRq_vec;
13      b' <- scaleRqv2Rpv ((trmx _A) *^ s' + h);
14      v' <- (dotp b (Rqv2Rpv s')) + (Rq2Rp h1);
15      chat <- scaleRp2R2t (v' + (scaleR22Rp (
16                  if u then m1 else m0)));
17
18      u' <@ A.guess((chat, b'));
19      return (u = u');
20    }
21  }.
```

Listing 1.5. $\text{Game}_{\mathcal{A}}^0$

As exemplified in this listing, we formalize games through parameterized modules; specifically, the parameter provided to such modules is another module that formalizes the considered adversary. Moreover, the actual statements executed by the game are encapsulated in a procedure; however, this is merely a syntactical requirement of EasyCrypt. Statements in module procedures belong to one of several categories: regular assignment statements (using <-), sample statements (using <$), and procedure call statements (using <@). Then, noting that *^, `dotp`, `trmx`, `h1`, and `h` respectively denote matrix-vector multiplication, dot

---

[6] Nevertheless, albeit customary in hand-written cryptographic proofs, EasyCrypt currently does not provide the possibility to restrict the space or time complexity of module types.

product, transpose, h_1, and $\mathbf{h}$, we can see that GameO(A).main() is a line-by-line verbatim translation of $\text{Game}^0_{\mathcal{A}}$, where A formalizes $\mathcal{A}$. Furthermore, from this formalization of $\text{Game}^0_{\mathcal{A}}$, we can straightforwardly derive the formalization of $\text{Game}^1_{\mathcal{A}}$; indeed, we merely remove line 7 and replace line 8 with the appropriate sample statement.

The last game relevant to the first step is $\text{Game}^{\text{GMLWR}}_{\mathcal{A},\text{gen},l,\mu,q,p}(u)$; the formalization of this game is presented in Listing 1.6.

```
1   module GMLWR (A : Adv_GMLWR) = {
2     proc main (u : bool) : bool = {
3       (*...*)
4       sd <$ dseed;
5       _A <- gen sd;
6       s <$ dsmallRq_vec;
7
8       if (u) {
9         b <$ dRp_vec;
10      } else {
11        b <- scaleroundRqv2Rpv (_A *^ s);
12      }
13      u' <@ A.guess (sd, b);
14      return u';
15    }
16  }.
```

Listing 1.6. $\text{Game}^{\text{GMLWR}}_{\mathcal{A},\text{gen},l,\mu,q,p}(u)$

Here, scaleroundRqv2Rpv formalizes the extension (to polynomial vectors) of the modular scaling and rounding function employed in $\text{Game}^{\text{GMLWR}}_{\mathcal{A},\text{gen},l,\mu,q,p}(u)$. Taking this into account, we can see that GMLWR(A).main(u) is a correct formalization of $\text{Game}^{\text{GMLWR}}_{\mathcal{A},\text{gen},l,\mu,q,p}(u)$, where A and u respectively denote $\mathcal{A}$ and u[7].

Penultimately, we formalize adversary $\mathcal{B}^{\mathcal{A}}_0$ against $\text{Game}^{\text{GMLWR}}_{\mathcal{B}^{\mathcal{A}}_0,\text{gen},l,\mu,q,p}(u)$. More specifically, we formalize this reduction adversary as a parameterized module BO(A : Adv_INDCPA) of type Adv_GMLWR. Indeed, the Adv_GMLWR type enforces BO(A) to implement guess(sd, b); in this case, this procedure precisely formalizes the $\mathcal{B}^{\mathcal{A}}_0(\text{seed}_{\mathbf{A}}, \mathbf{b}_u)$ presented in Fig. 6. Due to the similarities between $\mathcal{B}^{\mathcal{A}}_0$ and the initial two games in the game sequence, BO(A).guess(sd, b) is nearly identical to the above-discussed formalizations of $\text{Game}^0_{\mathcal{A}}$ and $\text{Game}^1_{\mathcal{A}}$. For this reason, we refrain from explicitly presenting the formalization of this reduction adversary here.

Finally, we formalize the result of the security proof's first step. In particular, we do so by formulating an appropriate lemma; Listing 1.7 provides this lemma.

---

[7] Remark that the considered parameters of $\text{Game}^{\text{GMLWR}}_{\mathcal{A},\text{gen},l,\mu,q,p}(u)$ are the same as the similarly named (function and) parameters of Saber; hence, these are already formalized outside of the GMLWR module, see the foregoing discussion concerning the fundamental specification.

```
1  lemma Step_Distinguish_Game0_Game1_GMLWR &m :
2    `| Pr[Game0(A).main() @ &m : res] -
3       Pr[Game1(A).main() @ &m : res] |
4    =
5    `| Pr[GMLWR( B0(A) ).main(true) @ &m : res] -
6       Pr[GMLWR( B0(A) ).main(false) @ &m : res] |.
```

Listing 1.7. First Step in Game-Playing Security Proof

In this lemma, A is an arbitrary module of type `Adv_INDCPA`; that is, A formalizes an arbitrary IND-CPA adversary. Furthermore, `&m` signifies an arbitrary memory that, in this case, essentially formalizes the context in which the games and adversaries are executed. Then, given that `` `|x| ``, `Pr[E]`, and `res` respectively denote the absolute value of `x`, probability of `E`, and return value of the considered procedure, we can recognize the following correspondences.

$$\texttt{Pr[Game0(A).main() @ \&m : res]} \cong \Pr\left[\text{Game}_{\mathcal{A}}^0 = 1\right]$$

$$\texttt{Pr[Game1(A).main() @ \&m : res]} \cong \Pr\left[\text{Game}_{\mathcal{A}}^1 = 1\right]$$

$$\texttt{Pr[GMLWR(B0(A)).main(true) @ \&m : res]} \cong \Pr\left[\text{Game}_{\mathcal{B}_0^{\mathcal{A}},\text{gen},l,\mu,q,p}^{\text{GMLWR}}(1) = 1\right]$$

$$\texttt{Pr[GMLWR(B0(A)).main(false) @ \&m : res]} \cong \Pr\left[\text{Game}_{\mathcal{B}_0^{\mathcal{A}},\text{gen},l,\mu,q,p}^{\text{GMLWR}}(0) = 1\right]$$

This demonstrates that `Step_Distinguish_Game0_Game1_GMLWR` correctly formalizes the result of the initial step of the security proof.

Step 2: $\text{Game}_{\mathcal{A}}^1$ - $\text{Game}_{\mathcal{A}}^2$. For the formal verification of the second step, similarly to before, we first formalize the required games and reduction adversary. Concerning the games, since $\text{Game}_{\mathcal{A}}^1$ has already been formalized in the preceding step, we only need to formalize $\text{Game}_{\mathcal{A}}^2$. The formalization of $\text{Game}_{\mathcal{A}}^2$ can straightforwardly be derived from the formalization of $\text{Game}_{\mathcal{A}}^0$ presented in Listing 1.5; more precisely, this can be achieved by removing line 7, changing line 8 to the proper sampling statement, and appropriately modifying the computation of `chat` in line 15. Regarding the reduction adversary, we construct a module `A2(A1 : Adv_INDCPA)` of type `Adv_INDCPA_2`. This module type is identical to `Adv_INDCPA`, except for the fact that the parameter of its `guess` procedure is of type `Rppq * Rp_vec` instead of type `R2t * Rp_vec`; this models that the ciphertext given to the adversary in $\text{Game}_{\mathcal{A}}^2$ is an element of $R_{p^2/q} \times R_p^{l \times 1}$ instead of $R_{2 \cdot t} \times R_p^{l \times 1}$. In other words, while `Adv_INDCPA` formalizes the class of adversaries against $\text{Game}_{\mathcal{A},\text{Saber.PKE}}^{\text{IND-CPA}}$, $\text{Game}_{\mathcal{A}}^0$, and $\text{Game}_{\mathcal{A}}^1$, `Adv_INDCPA_2` formalizes the class of adversaries against $\text{Game}_{\mathcal{A}}^2$ [8]. In accordance with its module type, `A2` implements `choose(pk)` and `guess(c)`, respectively formalizing $\mathcal{R}^{\mathcal{A}}.\text{P}((\text{seed}_{\mathbf{A}}, \mathbf{b}))$ and $\mathcal{R}^{\mathcal{A}}.\text{D}((\hat{c}, \mathbf{b}'))$ as specified in Fig. 7. Indeed, `A2(A1).choose(pk)` merely returns `A1.choose(pk)`; `A2(A1).guess(c)` performs an appropriate modular scaling

---

[8] Analogously, there is a separate module type that formalizes the class of adversaries against $\text{Game}_{\mathcal{A}}^3$ and $\text{Game}_{\mathcal{A}}^4$.

and flooring operation on the first element of c before returning A1.guess(c'), where c' denotes the adjusted c.

Having constructed the necessary formalizations, we can express the lemma that formalizes the result of the security proof's second step; this lemma is presented in Listing 1.8.

```
1  lemma Step_Game1_Game2 &m :
2    `| Pr[Game1(A).main() @ &m : res] - 1%r / 2%r |
3    =
4    `| Pr[Game2( A2(A) ).main() @ &m : res] - 1%r / 2%r |.
```

Listing 1.8. Second Step in Game-Playing Security Proof

In this lemma, as in Step_Distinguish_Game0_Game1_GMLWR, A denotes an arbitrary module of type Adv_INDCPA, i.e., the formalization of an arbitrary IND-CPA adversary. Then, given the previously explained interpretation of the employed statements and the fact that 1%r / 2%r denotes $\frac{1}{2}$, we can see that Step_Game1_ Game2 accurately formalizes the result of the second step of the security proof.

Step 3, Step 4, and Analysis of $\text{Game}_{\mathcal{A}}^{4}$. Based on the preceding discussion, the formal verification process for the remaining two steps of the security proof can straightforwardly be extrapolated. Namely, the formal verification of the third step, reducing from $\text{Game}_{\mathcal{A}}^{3}$ to $\text{Game}_{\mathcal{A}}^{2}$, follows an analogous procedure to the second step; the formal verification of the fourth step, reducing from $\text{Game}_{\mathcal{A},\text{gen},l,\mu,q,p}^{\text{XMLWR}}(u)$ to distinguishing between $\text{Game}_{\mathcal{A}}^{3}$ and $\text{Game}_{\mathcal{A}}^{4}$, has a similar structure to the first step.

Regarding the formal verification of the $\frac{1}{2}$ winning probability of any adversary against $\text{Game}_{\mathcal{A}}^{4}$, we foremost formally verify the equivalence between $\text{Game}_{\mathcal{A}}^{4}$ and a contrived auxiliary game; this auxiliary game is identical to $\text{Game}_{\mathcal{A}}^{4}$, except that it samples every artifact from the appropriate uniform distribution and delays the sampling of u to the final statement (preceding the return statement). Due to its construction, contrary to $\text{Game}_{\mathcal{A}}^{4}$, the auxiliary game facilitates the formal verification of the invariable $\frac{1}{2}$ winning probability. Afterward, the fact that any adversary against $\text{Game}_{\mathcal{A}}^{4}$ has a $\frac{1}{2}$ winning probability directly follows from the equivalence between $\text{Game}_{\mathcal{A}}^{4}$ and the auxiliary game.

Final Result (Security Theorem). Finally, we consider the security theorem. Similarly to the security proof's steps, this theorem is formalized by formulating a suitable lemma; this lemma is provided in Listing 1.9.

```
1  lemma Saber_INDCPA_Security_Theorem &m :
2    exists (BG <: Adv_GMLWR) (BX <: Adv_XMLWR),
3    `| Pr[CPA(Saber_PKE_Scheme, A).main() @ &m : res] -
4       1%r / 2%r |
5    <=
6    `| Pr[GMLWR(BG).main(true) @ &m : res] -
7       Pr[GMLWR(BG).main(false) @ &m : res] |
8    +
9    `| Pr[XMLWR(BX).main(true) @ &m : res] -
10      Pr[XMLWR(BX).main(false) @ &m : res] |.
```

Listing 1.9. Security Theorem

Once again, A denotes an arbitrary module of type Adv_INDCPA. Furthermore, CPA and XMLWR are modules respectively comprising the formalizations of the IND-CPA and XMLWR games. In contrast to the modules considered hitherto, the CPA module is provided by EasyCrypt's standard library and defined with respect to a generic PKE scheme. For this reason, the CPA module needs to be instantiated with the desired concrete PKE scheme via its first parameter; naturally, in this case we use the module that formalizes Saber.PKE, Saber_PKE_Scheme, as the concrete PKE scheme. Lastly, exists (BG <: Adv_GMLWR) (BX <: Adv_XMLWR) constitutes an existential quantifier over a module of type Adv_GMLWR and a module of type Adv_XMLWR. Combining this with the foregoing material, we can see that Saber_INDCPA_Security_Theorem exactly formalizes the security theorem, as desired. This completes the formal verification of Saber.PKE's IND-CPA security property.

4 Correctness

Proceeding from the discussion on Saber.PKE's security property, we now consider the scheme's correctness property. In particular, we do so by discussing the most important parts of the devised hand-written proof and corresponding formal verification, akin to the foregoing discussion on the security property.

Alternative Specification and Correctness Notion. Before advancing to the actual hand-written proof of Saber.PKE's correctness property, we establish an alternative, yet equivalent, specification of Saber.PKE[9]; additionally, we introduce the relevant notion of correctness.

Foremost, to refer to the alternative specification of Saber.PKE, we use Saber.PKEA; furthermore, the key generation, encryption, and decryption algorithms of Saber.PKEA are respectively denoted by Saber.KeyGenA, Saber.EncA, and Saber.DecA. For the latter two algorithms, Algorithm 4 and Algorithm 5 provide the corresponding specifications; the specification of Saber.KeyGenA is identical to that of Saber.KeyGen and, therefore, not explicitly presented here.

---

[9] This alternative specification is based on the alternative specification of Saber's key exchange scheme presented in [9].

Algorithm 4 Alternative Specification of Saber's Encryption Algorithm

1: **procedure** Saber.EncA(pk := (seed$_\mathbf{A}$, $\mathbf{b}$), m)
2:     $\mathbf{A} \leftarrow$ gen(seed$_\mathbf{A}$)
3:     $\mathbf{s}' \leftarrow\$ \beta_\mu(R_q^{l \times 1})$
4:     $\mathbf{b}' \leftarrow \lfloor \mathbf{A}^T \cdot \mathbf{s}' + \mathbf{h} \rfloor_{q \to p}$
5:     $\mathbf{b}_q \leftarrow \lfloor \mathbf{b} \rfloor_{p \to q}$
6:     $v' \leftarrow \mathbf{b}_q^T \cdot \mathbf{s}' + \frac{q}{p} \cdot h_1$
7:     $c_m \leftarrow \lfloor v' + \lfloor m \rfloor_{2 \to q} \rfloor_{q \to 2 \cdot t}$
8:     **return** $c := (c_m, \mathbf{b}')$

Algorithm 5 Alternative Specification of Saber's Decryption Algorithm

1: **procedure** Saber.DecA(sk := $\mathbf{s}$, $c := (c_m, \mathbf{b}')$)
2:     $\mathbf{b}'_q \leftarrow \lfloor \mathbf{b}' \rfloor_{p \to q}$
3:     $v \leftarrow \mathbf{b}_q'^T \cdot \mathbf{s} + \frac{q}{p} \cdot h_1$
4:     $m' \leftarrow \lfloor v - \lfloor c_m \rfloor_{2 \cdot t \to q} + \frac{q}{p} \cdot h_2 \rfloor_{q \to 2}$
5:     **return** m'

As shown in Algorithm 4 and Algorithm 5, Saber.EncA and Saber.DecA ensure that all of their operations exclusively involve elements from R_q (or $R_q^{l \times 1}$). This is accomplished by carrying out the appropriate modular scaling and flooring operations on elements that do not originate from these structures. For instance, Saber.EncA performs $\lfloor \mathbf{b} \rfloor_{p \to q}$ and $\lfloor m \rfloor_{2 \to q}$; similarly, Saber.DecA performs $\lfloor \mathbf{b}' \rfloor_{p \to q}$ and $\lfloor c_m \rfloor_{2 \cdot t \to q}$[10]. Furthermore, to guarantee their equivalence to the original specifications despite these differences, Saber.EncA and Saber.DecA consistently multiply h_1 and h_2 by $\frac{q}{p} \in R_q$. These alternative encryption and decryption algorithms can intuitively be seen to be equivalent to their original counterparts by noting that Saber.EncA and Saber.DecA essentially perform the same operations as Saber.Enc and Saber.Dec, except that certain elements considered in these operations contain additional appended zero bits. The primary rationale behind adopting this alternative specification for the correctness analysis is that it provides a convenient way to describe the errors induced by some of the modular scaling and flooring operations as elements from R_q (or $R_q^{l \times 1}$); this especially simplifies the corresponding formal verification by minimizing the number of different types considered throughout.

Regarding the correctness notion, as aforementioned, we employ the definition provided in [12]. For convenience, we restate this definition for a generic PKE scheme here[11]; specifically, using the game presented in Fig. 10, we say

---

[10] Recall that $0 < \epsilon_t + 1 < \epsilon_p < \epsilon_q$ and, hence, $2 \le 2 \cdot t < p < q$; as a consequence, $\lfloor \cdot \rfloor_{2 \to q}$, $\lfloor \cdot \rfloor_{2 \cdot t \to q}$, and $\lfloor \cdot \rfloor_{p \to q}$ effectively constitute left bit-shifts.
[11] Actually, the definition we present and use is slightly different from, yet trivially equivalent to, the definition provided in [12]. Namely, the definition we utilize considers the success probability instead of the failure probability; this is the only difference with the definition from [12].

PKE is δ-correct if for all $\mathcal{A}$, the following holds.

$$\Pr\left[\text{Game}_{\mathcal{A},\text{PKE}}^{\text{FOCOR}} = 1\right] \geq 1 - \delta$$

In the concrete cases of Saber.PKE and Saber.PKEA, $\delta \neq 0$ due to the errors caused by several of the modular scaling and flooring operations; moreover, from the equivalence between Saber.PKE and Saber.PKEA, it follows that $\Pr\left[\text{Game}_{\mathcal{A},\text{Saber.PKEA}}^{\text{FOCOR}} = 1\right]$ is equal to $\Pr\left[\text{Game}_{\mathcal{A},\text{Saber.PKE}}^{\text{FOCOR}} = 1\right]$ for any $\mathcal{A}$.

$\text{Game}_{\mathcal{A},\text{PKE}}^{\text{FOCOR}}$
1 : $(\text{pk}, \text{sk}) \leftarrow \text{KeyGen}()$
2 : $m \leftarrow \mathcal{A}(\text{pk}, \text{sk})$
3 : $c \leftarrow \text{Enc}(\text{pk}, m)$
4 : $m' \leftarrow \text{Dec}(\text{sk}, c)$
5 : $\textbf{return } (m' = m)$

$\text{PProg}^{\delta\text{COR}}$
1 : $\mathbf{A} \leftarrow \mathcal{U}(R_q^{l \times l})$
2 : $\mathbf{s} \leftarrow\$ \mathcal{U}(R_q^{l \times 1})$
3 : $\mathbf{s'} \leftarrow\$ \mathcal{U}(R_q^{l \times 1})$
4 : $\textbf{return } \text{ccrng}(\text{err\_expression}(\mathbf{A}, \mathbf{s}, \mathbf{s'}))$

Fig. 10. Correctness Game

Fig. 11. Probabilistic Program For Correctness Based on Error Expression

Hand-Written Proof. As alluded to above, Saber.PKEA and, by equivalence, Saber.PKE are not perfectly correct; that is, $\Pr\left[\text{Game}_{\mathcal{A},\text{Saber.PKEA}}^{\text{FOCOR}} = 1\right] < 1$. Concerning the specification of $\text{Game}_{\mathcal{A},\text{Saber.PKEA}}^{\text{FOCOR}}$, we can see that this game essentially verifies whether m' equals m after the sequential execution of $(\text{pk}, \text{sk}) \leftarrow$ Saber.KeyGenA(), $c \leftarrow$ Saber.EncA(pk, m), and $m' \leftarrow$ Saber.DecA(sk, c). As such, given some $m \in \mathcal{M}$, we can derive the expression that determines whether $m' = m$ by considering the specifications of Saber.PKEA's algorithms. Before the derivation of this expression, we define several error terms; these error terms capture the errors introduced by the modular scaling and flooring operations. Ultimately, as the remainder will show, the expression derived for the verification of $m' = m$, henceforth referred to as "error expression", exclusively depends on these error terms[12]. In turn, because these error terms, when fully expanded, only depend on randomly sampled artifacts (and constants) from the algorithms of Saber.PKEA, one can exhaustively compute the distribution of the error expression and, hence, the probability that this expression lies within a certain range. In fact, the authors of Saber have constructed a script that performs this exact computation, (indirectly) claiming that this is equivalent to computing the correctness of Saber.PKE (independent of the message) [9,10]. Therefore, the ensuing proof aims to show that this probability computation indeed computes the δ such that $\Pr\left[\text{Game}_{\mathcal{A},\text{PKE}}^{\text{FOCOR}} = 1\right] = 1 - \delta$ holds for any $\mathcal{A}$.

---

[12] Similarly to the specification of Saber.PKEA, the definitions of these error terms are inspired by the error terms provided in [9].

The first error term we define relates to $\mathbf{A} \cdot \mathbf{s}$ and $\mathbf{b}_q$; particularly, this error term, $\mathbf{err}_{\mathbf{b}_q}$, represents the error of $\mathbf{b}_q$ relative to $\mathbf{A} \cdot \mathbf{s}$, as defined below.

$$\mathbf{err}_{\mathbf{b}_q} = \mathbf{b}_q - \mathbf{A} \cdot \mathbf{s} = \lfloor \lfloor \mathbf{A} \cdot \mathbf{s} + \mathbf{h} \rfloor_{q \to p} \rfloor_{p \to q} - \mathbf{A} \cdot \mathbf{s}$$

The second error term is similar to the previous one, except that it relates to $\mathbf{A}^T \cdot \mathbf{s}'$ and $\mathbf{b}'_q$ instead of $\mathbf{A} \cdot \mathbf{s}$ and $\mathbf{b}_q$. The definition of this error term is given below.

$$\mathbf{err}_{\mathbf{b}'_q} = \mathbf{b}'_q - \mathbf{A}^T \cdot \mathbf{s}' = \lfloor \lfloor \mathbf{A}^T \cdot \mathbf{s}' + \mathbf{h} \rfloor_{q \to p} \rfloor_{p \to q} - \mathbf{A}^T \cdot \mathbf{s}'$$

The final error term captures the error related to $v' + \lfloor m \rfloor_{2 \to q}$ and $\lfloor c_m \rfloor_{2 \cdot t \to q}$; this error term is defined below.

$$\mathrm{err}_{c_m q} = \lfloor c_m \rfloor_{2 \cdot t \to q} - (v' + \lfloor m \rfloor_{2 \to q}) + \frac{q}{4 \cdot t}$$
$$= \lfloor \lfloor v' + \lfloor m \rfloor_{2 \to q} \rfloor_{q \to 2 \cdot t} \rfloor_{2 \cdot t \to q} - (v' + \lfloor m \rfloor_{2 \to q}) + \frac{q}{4 \cdot t}$$

In contrast to the other error terms, $\mathrm{err}_{c_m q}$ adds a constant that is not present in the related modular scaling and flooring operations. This constant, i.e., $\frac{q}{4 \cdot t} \in R_q$, ensures that the coefficients of $\mathrm{err}_{c_m q}$ are centered around zero; indeed, the coefficients of $\mathbf{err}_{\mathbf{b}_q}$ and $\mathbf{err}_{\mathbf{b} g'_q}$ are already centered around zero as is.

Utilizing the above-introduced error terms, we presently derive the error expression. To this end, considering the sequential execution of Saber.PKEA's algorithms, we first rewrite $v - \lfloor c_m \rfloor_{2 \cdot t \to q} + \frac{q}{p} \cdot h_2$ as follows. At times, to prevent cluttering, we replace $\lfloor m \rfloor_{2 \to q} + \frac{q}{4 \cdot t} + \frac{q}{p} \cdot h_2$ by horizontal dots.

$$v - \lfloor c_m \rfloor_{2 \cdot t \to q} + \frac{q}{p} \cdot h_2 =$$
$$v - (\mathrm{err}_{c_m q} + v' + \lfloor m \rfloor_{2 \to q} - \frac{q}{4 \cdot t}) + \frac{q}{p} \cdot h_2 =$$
$$\mathbf{b}'^T_q \cdot \mathbf{s} - \mathbf{b}^T_q \cdot \mathbf{s}' - \mathrm{err}_{c_m q} - \lfloor m \rfloor_{2 \to q} + \frac{q}{4 \cdot t} + \frac{q}{p} \cdot h_2 =$$
$$(\mathbf{s}'^T \cdot \mathbf{A} + \mathbf{err}^T_{\mathbf{b}'_q}) \cdot \mathbf{s} - (\mathbf{s}^T \cdot \mathbf{A}^T + \mathbf{err}^T_{\mathbf{b}_q}) \cdot \mathbf{s}' - \mathrm{err}_{c_m q} - \ldots =$$
$$\mathbf{s}'^T \cdot \mathbf{A} \cdot \mathbf{s} + \mathbf{err}^T_{\mathbf{b}'_q} \cdot \mathbf{s} - \mathbf{s}^T \cdot \mathbf{A}^T \cdot \mathbf{s}' - \mathbf{err}^T_{\mathbf{b}_q} \cdot \mathbf{s}' - \mathrm{err}_{c_m q} - \ldots =$$
$$\mathbf{err}^T_{\mathbf{b}'_q} \cdot \mathbf{s} - \mathbf{err}^T_{\mathbf{b}_q} \cdot \mathbf{s}' - \mathrm{err}_{c_m q} - \ldots =$$
$$- \lfloor m \rfloor_{2 \to q} + \mathbf{err}^T_{\mathbf{b}'_q} \cdot \mathbf{s} - \mathbf{err}^T_{\mathbf{b}_q} \cdot \mathbf{s}' - \mathrm{err}_{c_m q} + \frac{q}{4} =$$
$$\lfloor m \rfloor_{2 \to q} + \frac{q}{4} + \mathbf{err}^T_{\mathbf{b}'_q} \cdot \mathbf{s} - \mathbf{err}^T_{\mathbf{b}_q} \cdot \mathbf{s}' - \mathrm{err}_{c_m q}$$

In this derivation, most equalities follow from trivial substitutions, reorderings, simplifications, and basic operator properties; however, confirming the validity of the fifth and final equality might require some more thought. Specifically, the fifth equality holds due to the fact that $\mathbf{s}'^T \cdot \mathbf{A} \cdot \mathbf{s}$ and $\mathbf{s}^T \cdot \mathbf{A}^T \cdot \mathbf{s}'$ are equal and, as such, cancel each other out. Observing that both of these terms are elements of R_q, i.e., no vectors[13], this can be deduced as shown below.

$$\mathbf{s}'^T \cdot \mathbf{A} \cdot \mathbf{s} = ((\mathbf{s}'^T \cdot \mathbf{A} \cdot \mathbf{s})^T)^T = (\mathbf{s}^T \cdot \mathbf{A}^T \cdot \mathbf{s}')^T = \mathbf{s}^T \cdot \mathbf{A}^T \cdot \mathbf{s}'$$

The final equality of the preceding derivation is valid because $\lfloor m \rfloor_{2 \to q}$ is equal to $-\lfloor m \rfloor_{2 \to q}$. Particularly, since each coefficient of m equals either 0 or 1, each coefficient of its scaled counterpart $\lfloor m \rfloor_{2 \to q}$ has value $0 \cdot \frac{q}{2} = 0$ or $1 \cdot \frac{q}{2} = \frac{q}{2}$; consequently, each coefficient of $-\lfloor m \rfloor_{2 \to q}$ equals $-0 = 0$ or $-\frac{q}{2}$. Naturally, in R_q, these corresponding coefficients of $\lfloor m \rfloor_{2 \to q}$ and $-\lfloor m \rfloor_{2 \to q}$ are equivalent.

Additionally considering the modular scaling and flooring operation that Saber.DecA applies to $v - \lfloor c_m \rfloor_{2 \cdot t \to q} + \frac{q}{p} \cdot h_2$, we can utilize the above-derived expression to determine the final value Saber.DecA assigns to m'.

$$
\begin{aligned}
m' &= \lfloor v - \lfloor c_m \rfloor_{2 \cdot t \to q} + \frac{q}{p} \cdot h_2 \rfloor_{q \to 2} \\
&= \lfloor \lfloor m \rfloor_{2 \to q} + \frac{q}{4} + \mathbf{err}_{\mathbf{b}'_q}^T \cdot \mathbf{s} - \mathbf{err}_{\mathbf{b}_q}^T \cdot \mathbf{s}' - \mathrm{err}_{c_{mq}} \rfloor_{q \to 2} \\
&= m + \lfloor \frac{q}{4} + \mathbf{err}_{\mathbf{b}'_q}^T \cdot \mathbf{s} - \mathbf{err}_{\mathbf{b}_q}^T \cdot \mathbf{s}' - \mathrm{err}_{c_{mq}} \rfloor_{q \to 2}
\end{aligned}
$$

Here, the last equality can be seen to hold by considering that m is an element of R_2, $\frac{q}{4} + \mathbf{err}_{\mathbf{b}'_q}^T \cdot \mathbf{s} - \mathbf{err}_{\mathbf{b}_q}^T \cdot \mathbf{s}' - \mathrm{err}_{c_{mq}}$ is an element of R_q, and $\lfloor \cdot \rfloor_{2 \to q}$ and $\lfloor \cdot \rfloor_{q \to 2}$ respectively perform left and right bit-shifts of $\epsilon_q - 1$ bits. Namely, this implies that both sides of the last equality add the (single) bit of each coefficient of m to the most significant bit of the corresponding coefficient of $\frac{q}{4} + \mathbf{err}_{\mathbf{b}'_q}^T \cdot \mathbf{s} - \mathbf{err}_{\mathbf{b}_q}^T \cdot \mathbf{s}' - \mathrm{err}_{c_{mq}}$.

At this point, it is rather trivial to derive that $m' = m$ if and only if $\lfloor \frac{q}{4} + \mathbf{err}_{\mathbf{b}'_q}^T \cdot \mathbf{s} - \mathbf{err}_{\mathbf{b}_q}^T \cdot \mathbf{s}' - \mathrm{err}_{c_{mq}} \rfloor_{q \to 2} = 0$. In turn, the latter is veracious if and only if each coefficient of $\frac{q}{4} + \mathbf{err}_{\mathbf{b}'_q}^T \cdot \mathbf{s} - \mathbf{err}_{\mathbf{b}_q}^T \cdot \mathbf{s}' - \mathrm{err}_{c_{mq}}$ lies in the (discrete) range $[0, \frac{q}{2})$. Finally, subtracting the $\frac{q}{4}$ constant, we obtain the desired result: $m' = m$ if and only if each coefficient of $\mathbf{err}_{\mathbf{b}'_q}^T \cdot \mathbf{s} - \mathbf{err}_{\mathbf{b}_q}^T \cdot \mathbf{s}' - \mathrm{err}_{c_{mq}}$ lies in the (discrete) range $[-\frac{q}{4}, \frac{q}{4})$. Indeed, $\mathbf{err}_{\mathbf{b}'_q}^T \cdot \mathbf{s} - \mathbf{err}_{\mathbf{b}_q}^T \cdot \mathbf{s}' - \mathrm{err}_{c_{mq}}$ constitutes the desired error expression.

As a last endeavor preceding the conclusion of this proof, we show that the error term $\mathrm{err}_{c_{mq}}$ is independent of the message m. As a result, since the other error terms do not contain m, it follows that the complete error expression is independent of the message as well. To this end, consider the part of the error term that includes m, i.e., $\lfloor \lfloor v' + \lfloor m \rfloor_{2 \to q} \rfloor_{q \to 2 \cdot t} \rfloor_{2 \cdot t \to q} - (v' + \lfloor m \rfloor_{2 \to q})$. Akin to before, interpreting the modular scaling and flooring operations as bit-shifts allows to deduce that $\lfloor \lfloor v' + \lfloor m \rfloor_{2 \to q} \rfloor_{q \to 2 \cdot t} \rfloor_{2 \cdot t \to q}$ is identical to $v' + \lfloor m \rfloor_{2 \to q}$ in its $\epsilon_q - \epsilon_t - 1$ most significant bits, but exclusively contains zero bits otherwise. Since $\lfloor m \rfloor_{2 \to q}$ can only affect the value of the most significant (ϵ_q-th) bit of $v' + \lfloor m \rfloor_{2 \to q}$, it follows that $\lfloor \lfloor v' + \lfloor m \rfloor_{2 \to q} \rfloor_{q \to 2 \cdot t} \rfloor_{2 \cdot t \to q}$ is equal to $\lfloor m \rfloor_{2 \to q} + \lfloor \lfloor v' \rfloor_{q \to 2 \cdot t} \rfloor_{2 \cdot t \to q}$. Consequently, we can rewrite $\mathrm{err}_{c_{mq}}$ as shown below, demonstrating the error

---

[13] Remark that this implies the transpose reduces to the identity function.

term's independence of m.

$$\text{err}_{c_{mq}} = \lfloor \lfloor v' + \lfloor m \rfloor_{2 \to q} \rfloor_{q \to 2 \cdot t} \rfloor_{2 \cdot t \to q} - (v' + \lfloor m \rfloor_{2 \to q}) + \frac{q}{4 \cdot t}$$

$$= \lfloor m \rfloor_{2 \to q} + \lfloor \lfloor v' \rfloor_{q \to 2 \cdot t} \rfloor_{2 \cdot t \to q} - v' - \lfloor m \rfloor_{2 \to q} + \frac{q}{4 \cdot t}$$

$$= \lfloor \lfloor v' \rfloor_{q \to 2 \cdot t} \rfloor_{2 \cdot t \to q} - v' + \frac{q}{4 \cdot t}$$

Finally, utilizing the obtained results, we can infer that for any $\mathcal{A}$, computing $\Pr \left[\text{Game}_{\mathcal{A},\text{Saber.PKEA}}^{\text{FOCOR}} = 1 \right]$ is equivalent to computing the probability that all coefficients of the corresponding error expression lie in the discrete range $[-\frac{q}{4}, \frac{q}{4})$. Furthermore, because this error expression is independent of the message, this probability does not depend on the particular m. In fact, completely unfolding the error expression, we can see that excluding any constants, it solely depends on $\mathbf{A}$, $\mathbf{s}$, and $\mathbf{s}'$ produced as in Saber.KeyGenA, Saber.KeyGenA, and Saber.EncA, respectively. As such, assuming gen's output distribution is uniformly random, we can formalize the probability computation based on the error expression as the probabilistic program defined in Fig. 11; this precisely denotes the probability computation performed by the aforementioned script constructed by Saber's authors[14] [9]. Here, err_expression$(\mathbf{A}, \mathbf{s}, \mathbf{s}')$ represents the error expression $\text{err}_{\mathbf{b}'_q}^T \cdot \mathbf{s} - \text{err}_{\mathbf{b}_q}^T \cdot \mathbf{s}' - \text{err}_{c_{mq}}$, accordingly using the provided arguments as the values for $\mathbf{A}$, $\mathbf{s}$, and $\mathbf{s}'$; moreover, for $x \in R_q$, ccrng(x) denotes the predicate that evaluates to true if and only if each of x's coefficients lies in $[-\frac{q}{4}, \frac{q}{4})$.

Using PProg$^{\delta\text{COR}}$ and the equivalence between Saber.PKE and Saber.PKEA, we can derive the following concluding sequence of equalities, assuming the uniformity of gen's output distribution; certainly, these equalities hold for any adversary $\mathcal{A}$.

$$\Pr \left[\text{Game}_{\mathcal{A},\text{Saber.PKE}}^{\text{FOCOR}} = 1 \right] = \Pr \left[\text{Game}_{\mathcal{A},\text{Saber.PKEA}}^{\text{FOCOR}} = 1 \right] = \Pr \left[\text{PProg}^{\delta\text{COR}} = 1 \right]$$

Formal Verification. Having discussed the hand-written correctness proof of Saber.PKE, we imminently cover the essential parts of the corresponding formal verification in EasyCrypt. More precisely, in the ensuing, we address the formalization of the error expression, Game$_{\mathcal{A},\text{PKE}}^{\text{FOCOR}}$, and PProg$^{\delta\text{COR}}$; furthermore, we consider the formal verification of the relevant program equivalences and the final desired equality of probabilities. As with the discussion on the formal verification of Saber.PKE's security property (and for the same reasons), we do not go over the concrete proofs of the results in EasyCrypt; however, all results have successfully been formally verified. Again, the code corresponding to this formal verification is provided in the repository belonging to this work.

Starting off, we formalize Game$_{\mathcal{A},\text{PKE}}^{\text{FOCOR}}$, i.e., the correctness game regarding a generic PKE scheme. Similarly to the formalization of the games in the security

---

[14] This suggests that the script merely approximates the actual correctness value. Nevertheless, if gen is adequately instantiated, i.e., its output distribution (closely) resembles the uniform distribution, this approximation is (almost) accurate.

proof, the formalization of this correctness game requires the formalization of the considered adversary class; the latter is given in Listing 1.10.

```
1  module type Adv_Cor = {
2      proc choose(pk : seed * Rp_vec, sk : Rq_vec) : R2
3  }.
```

Listing 1.10. Class of FOCOR Adversaries

The interpretation of `Adv_Cor` and `choose` is trivially extrapolated from the discussion surrounding Listing 1.4.

Employing the above formalization of the considered adversary class, the formalization of $\text{Game}_{\mathcal{A},\text{PKE}}^{\text{FOCOR}}$ is provided in Listing 1.11.

```
1  module Cor_Game (S : Scheme, A : Adv_Cor) = {
2      proc main() : bool = {
3          (*...*)
4          (pk, sk) <@ S.kg();
5          m <@ A.choose(pk, sk);
6          c <@ S.enc(pk, m);
7          m' <@ S.dec(sk, c);
8          return (m' = Some m);
9      }
10 }.
```

Listing 1.11. $\text{Game}_{\mathcal{A},\text{PKE}}^{\text{FOCOR}}$

Modeling the fact that $\text{Game}_{\mathcal{A},\text{PKE}}^{\text{FOCOR}}$ is defined with respect to a generic PKE scheme, `Cor_Game` takes an additional parameter of the built-in (module) type `Scheme`. This module type is designed for the formalization of PKE schemes; as such, it defines the `kg`, `enc`, and `dec` procedures, respectively representing the key generation, encryption, and decryption algorithms of PKE schemes. Taking this into account, we can see that the definition of `Cor_Game` is a verbatim translation of $\text{Game}_{\mathcal{A},\text{PKE}}^{\text{FOCOR}}$ to EasyCrypt[15].

Leveraging `Cor_Game`, we formalize the equivalence between $\text{Game}_{\mathcal{A},\text{Saber.PKE}}^{\text{FOCOR}}$ and $\text{Game}_{\mathcal{A},\text{Saber.PKEA}}^{\text{FOCOR}}$ as shown in Listing 1.12. Here, as the identifiers suggest, `Saber_PKE_Scheme` formalizes Saber.PKE and `Saber_PKE_Scheme_Alt` formalizes Saber.PKEA. Furthermore, `A` constitutes an arbitrary module of type `Adv_Cor`; that is, `A` formalizes an arbitrary adversary from the class of adversaries against the correctness game. As such, `Cor_Game(Saber_PKE_Scheme, A).main` formalizes $\text{Game}_{\mathcal{A},\text{Saber.PKE}}^{\text{FOCOR}}$ and `Cor_Game(Saber_PKE_Scheme_Alt, A).main` formalizes $\text{Game}_{\mathcal{A},\text{Saber.PKEA}}^{\text{FOCOR}}$, both for an arbitrary $\mathcal{A}$.

---

[15] The `Some` in the return statement is a technical consequence of the fact that certain PKE schemes may explicitly indicate decryption failure; nevertheless, this is irrelevant to the current discussion and, thus, can be ignored. Alternatively stated, we can regard the return statement as being `return (m' = m)`.

```
1   lemma Equivalence_Cor_Game_Orig_Alt :
2     equiv [Cor_Game (Saber_PKE_Scheme , A).main ~
3           Cor_Game (Saber_PKE_Scheme_Alt , A).main
4         : ={glob A} ==> ={res}].
```

Listing 1.12. Equivalence Between $\mathrm{Game}_{\mathcal{A},\mathrm{Saber.PKE}}^{\mathrm{FOCOR}}$ and $\mathrm{Game}_{\mathcal{A},\mathrm{Saber.PKEA}}^{\mathrm{FOCOR}}$

Substantiating that `Equivalence_Cor_Game_Orig_Alt` accurately formalizes the desired equivalence, we elaborate on the interpretation of this lemma. Foremost, an `equiv` statement consists of two primary parts, both contained within the square brackets, separated by a colon: the part preceding the colon specifies the collated procedures (separated by ~); the part succeeding the colon specifies the pre- and postconditions under which the equivalence holds (separated by ==>). So, in the `equiv` statement above, `Cor_Game(Saber_PKE_Scheme, A).main` is collated with `Cor_Game(Saber_PKE_Scheme_Alt, A).main`. Moreover, = {glob A} and ={res} respectively constitute the pre- and postconditions under which the equivalence should hold. More precisely, the precondition, ={glob A}, states that in the execution of both considered programs, the initial perspectives of A should be identical; the postcondition, ={res}, denotes that for all possible output values, the probability that one of the programs returns this value equals the probability that the other program outputs this (same) value. Thus, essentially, `Equivalence_Cor_Game_Orig_Alt` formalizes that for all $\mathcal{A}$ against $\mathrm{Game}_{\mathcal{A},\mathrm{Saber.PKE}}^{\mathrm{FOCOR}}$ and $\mathrm{Game}_{\mathcal{A},\mathrm{Saber.PKEA}}^{\mathrm{FOCOR}}$, the probability of the former game outputting a certain value equals the probability of the latter game outputting that same value. This is sufficient for this formal verification.

Following, in order to formalize the equivalence between $\mathrm{Game}_{\mathcal{A},\mathrm{Saber.PKEA}}^{\mathrm{FOCOR}}$ and $\mathrm{PProg}^{\delta\mathrm{COR}}$ (for all $\mathcal{A}$), we must first formalize $\mathrm{PProg}^{\delta\mathrm{COR}}$; in turn, this requires the formalization of, in particular, the error terms and error expression. Recall that the error terms are defined as follows, using the previously derived definition of $\mathrm{err}_{c_{mq}}$ that does not include m.

$$\mathbf{err_{b_q}} = \lfloor \lfloor \mathbf{A} \cdot \mathbf{s} + \mathbf{h} \rfloor_{q \to p} \rfloor_{p \to q} - \mathbf{A} \cdot \mathbf{s}$$

$$\mathbf{err_{b'_q}} = \lfloor \lfloor \mathbf{A}^T \cdot \mathbf{s'} + \mathbf{h} \rfloor_{q \to p} \rfloor_{p \to q} - \mathbf{A}^T \cdot \mathbf{s'}$$

$$\mathrm{err}_{c_{mq}} = \lfloor \lfloor v' \rfloor_{q \to 2 \cdot t} \rfloor_{2 \cdot t \to q} - v' + \frac{q}{4 \cdot t}$$

Then, illustrating the manner in which these error terms are formalized, we examine the formalization of $\mathbf{err_{b_q}}$; this formalization is provided in Listing 1.13.

```
1   op error_bq (_A : Rq_mat) (s : Rq_vec) : Rq_vec =
2     (scaleRpv2Rqv (scaleRqv2Rpv (_A *^ s + h))) -
3     (_A *^ s).
```

Listing 1.13. err_{b_q}

As this listing demonstrates, we formalize the error terms as parameterized operators. The parameters of these operators are intended to be instantiated with the appropriate artifacts generated by (the formalization of) $\text{PProg}^{\delta\text{COR}}$; if this is the case, the operators accurately formalize the error terms. For instance, the parameters `_A` and `s` of `error_bq` are expected to be instantiated with (the formalizations of) $\mathbf{A}$ and $\mathbf{s}$, respectively. If the parameters are instantiated as such, we can see that $(\texttt{scaleRpv2Rqv (scaleRqv2Rpv (\_A *\textasciicircum s + h))) - (\_A *\textasciicircum s)}$ precisely formalizes $\lfloor\lfloor\mathbf{A}\cdot\mathbf{s}+\mathbf{h}\rfloor_{q\to p}\rfloor_{p\to q} - \mathbf{A}\cdot\mathbf{s}$; hence, with appropriate parameter instantiations, `error_bq` accurately formalizes $\mathbf{err}_{\mathbf{b}_q}$.

Next, we reiterate that, based on the error terms, the error expression is defined as given below.

$$\mathbf{err}_{\mathbf{b}'_q}^T\cdot\mathbf{s} - \mathbf{err}_{\mathbf{b}_q}^T\cdot\mathbf{s}' - \mathrm{err}_{c_{mq}}$$

Utilizing the above-discussed formalizations of $\mathbf{err}_{\mathbf{b}_q}^T$, $\mathbf{err}_{\mathbf{b}'_q}^T$, and $\mathrm{err}_{c_{mq}}$, formalizing the error expression is relatively easy. Nevertheless, for completeness, Listing 1.14 provides the resulting formalization.

```
1  op error_expression (_A : Rq_mat) (s s': Rq_vec) =
2    dotp (error_bq' _A s') s - dotp (error_bq _A s) s' -
3    error_cmq _A s s'
```

Listing 1.14. Error Expression

Employing `error_expression`, we can construct the formalization of $\text{PProg}^{\delta\text{COR}}$; this formalization is presented in Listing 1.15.

```
1  module Delta_Cor_PProg = {
2    proc main() : bool = {
3      (*...*)
4      _A <$ dRq_mat;
5      s <$ dsmallRq_vec;
6      s' <$ dsmallRq_vec;
7      return ccrng (error_expression _A s s');
8    }
9  }.
```

Listing 1.15. $\text{PProg}^{\delta\text{COR}}$

As expected, since $\text{PProg}^{\delta\text{COR}}$ merely comprises three sampling operations and a return statement, the definition of `Delta_Cor_PProg` is rather straightforward. Specifically, the only novelty in this definition concerns the `ccrng` operator in the return statement. As its identifier suggests, this operator merely formalizes the ccrng predicate. That is, `ccrng` takes an argument of type `Rq` and evaluates to true if and only if all of the argument's coefficients lie between $-\frac{q}{4}$ (including) and $\frac{q}{4}$ (excluding).

Harnessing the formalizations of $\text{Game}_{A,\text{Saber.PKEA}}^{\text{FOCOR}}$ and $\text{PProg}^{\delta\text{COR}}$, we can formalize the equivalence between these games; Listing 1.16 provides the formalization of this equivalence.

```
1   lemma Equivalence_CorGame_DeltaCorPProg :
2     equiv[Cor_Game(Saber_PKE_Scheme_Alt , A).main ~
3           Delta_Cor_PProg.main : true ==> ={res}].
```

Listing 1.16. Equivalence Between $\mathrm{Game}_{A,\mathrm{Saber.PKEA}}^{\mathrm{FOCOR}}$ and $\mathrm{PProg}^{\delta\mathrm{COR}}$

As in preceding correctness-related listings, A constitutes an arbitrary module of type `Adv_Cor`, formalizing an arbitrary $\mathcal{A}$ against $\mathrm{Game}_{A,\mathrm{Saber.PKEA}}^{\mathrm{FOCOR}}$. Furthermore, the interpretation of `Equivalence_CorGame_DeltaCorPProg` is similar to the interpretation of the equivalence lemma provided in Listing 1.12. More precisely, `Equivalence_CorGame_DeltaCorPProg` formalizes that for all $\mathcal{A}$ against $\mathrm{Game}_{A,\mathrm{Saber.PKEA}}^{\mathrm{FOCOR}}$, the probability that $\mathrm{Game}_{A,\mathrm{Saber.PKEA}}^{\mathrm{FOCOR}}$ outputs a specific value is equal to the probability that $\mathrm{PProg}^{\delta\mathrm{COR}}$ outputs that same value; this holds for all possible output values.

Finally, albeit trivially veracious at this point, we formally verify the fact that for any $\mathcal{A}$ against $\mathrm{Game}_{A,\mathrm{Saber.PKE}}^{\mathrm{FOCOR}}$, $\mathrm{Pr}\left[\mathrm{Game}_{A,\mathrm{Saber.PKE}}^{\mathrm{FOCOR}} = 1\right]$ is equal to $\mathrm{Pr}\left[\mathrm{PProg}^{\delta\mathrm{COR}} = 1\right]$. Listing 1.17 contains the formalization of this statement. Given that, once again, A is an arbitrary module of type `Adv_Cor`, the interpretation of the lemma in this listing should be evident from previous listings and corresponding discussions.

```
1   lemma Eq_Prob_CorGameOrig_DeltaCorPProg &m :
2     Pr[Cor_Game(Saber_PKE_Scheme , A).main() @ &m : res]
3     =
4     Pr[Delta_Cor_PProg.main() @ &m : res].
```

Listing 1.17. $\mathrm{Pr}\left[\mathrm{Game}_{A,\mathrm{Saber.PKE}}^{\mathrm{FOCOR}} = 1\right] = \mathrm{Pr}\left[\mathrm{PProg}^{\delta\mathrm{COR}} = 1\right]$

Naturally, the veracity of this lemma immediately follows from the previously verified equivalences presented in Listing 1.12 and Listing 1.16 (and their transitivity). This completes the formal verification of Saber.PKE's correctness property. Combining this with the preceding security-related results, we have formally verified that Saber.PKE possesses the properties necessary to transform it into a IND-CCA2 secure and (sufficiently) correct KEM via the relevant variant of the FO transform.

References

1. Almeida, J.B., Barbosa, M., Barthe, G., Grégoire, B., Koutsos, A., Laporte, V., Oliveira, T., Strub, P.-Y.: The last mile: high-assurance and high-speed cryptographic implementations. In: 2020 IEEE Symposium on Security and Privacy, pp. 965–982. IEEE Computer Society Press, May 2020
2. Banerjee, A., Peikert, C., Rosen, A.: Pseudorandom functions and lattices. In: Pointcheval, D., Johansson, T. (eds.) EUROCRYPT 2012. LNCS, vol. 7237, pp. 719–737. Springer, Heidelberg (2012). https://doi.org/10.1007/978-3-642-29011-4_42

3. Barbosa, M., Barthe, G., Bhargavan, K., Blanchet, B., Cremers, C., Liao, K., Parno, B.: SoK: computer-aided cryptography. In: 2021 IEEE Symposium on Security and Privacy (SP), pp. 777–795. IEEE Computer Society, May 2021

4. Barbosa, M., Barthe, G., Fan, X., Grégoire, B., Hung, S.-H., Katz, J., Strub, P.-Y., Wu, X., Zhou, L.: EasyPQC: verifying post-quantum cryptography. Cryptology ePrint Archive, Report 2021/1253 (2021)

5. Barthe, G., Crespo, J.M., Grégoire, B., Kunz, C., Zanella Béguelin, S.: Computer-aided cryptographic proofs. In: Beringer, L., Felty, A. (eds.) ITP 2012. LNCS, vol. 7406, pp. 11–27. Springer, Heidelberg (2012). https://doi.org/10.1007/978-3-642-32347-8_2

6. Bellare, M., Rogaway, P.: The security of triple encryption and a framework for code-based game-playing proofs. In: Vaudenay, S. (ed.) EUROCRYPT 2006. LNCS, vol. 4004, pp. 409–426. Springer, Heidelberg (2006). https://doi.org/10.1007/11761679_25

7. Boneh, D., Dagdelen, Ö., Fischlin, M., Lehmann, A., Schaffner, C., Zhandry, M.: Random Oracles in a quantum world. In: Lee, D.H., Wang, X. (eds.) ASIACRYPT 2011. LNCS, vol. 7073, pp. 41–69. Springer, Heidelberg (2011). https://doi.org/10.1007/978-3-642-25385-0_3

8. Cremers, C., Horvat, M., Hoyland, J., Scott, S., van der Merwe, T.: A comprehensive symbolic analysis of TLS 1.3. In: Thuraisingham, B.M., Evans, D., Malkin, T., Xu, D. (eds.) ACM CCS 2017, pp. 1773–1788. ACM Press, October/November 2017

9. D'Anvers, J.-P.: Design and security analysis of lattice-based post-quantum encryption. Ph.D. dissertation, KU Leuven Arenberg Doctoral School, May 2021

10. D'Anvers, J.-P., Karmakar, A., Sinha Roy, S., Vercauteren, F.: Saber: Module-LWR based key exchange, CPA-secure encryption and CCA-secure KEM. In: Joux, A., Nitaj, A., Rachidi, T. (eds.) AFRICACRYPT 2018. LNCS, vol. 10831, pp. 282–305. Springer, Cham (2018). https://doi.org/10.1007/978-3-319-89339-6_16

11. Duman, J., Hövelmanns, K., Kiltz, E., Lyubashevsky, V., Seiler, G.: Faster Kyber and Saber via a generic Fujisaki-Okamoto transform for multi-user security in the QROM (2021)

12. Hofheinz, D., Hövelmanns, K., Kiltz, E.: A modular analysis of the Fujisaki-Okamoto transformation. In: Kalai, Y., Reyzin, L. (eds.) TCC 2017. LNCS, vol. 10677, pp. 341–371. Springer, Cham (2017). https://doi.org/10.1007/978-3-319-70500-2_12

13. Hülsing, A., Meijers, M., Strub, P.-Y.: Formal verification of Saber's public-key encryption scheme in EasyCrypt. Cryptology ePrint Archive, Paper 2022/351 (2022). https://eprint.iacr.org/2022/351

14. Koblitz, N., Menezes, A.J.: Critical perspectives on provable security: fifteen years of "another look" papers. Adv. Math. Commun. 13(4), 517–558 (2019)

15. Lazar, D., Chen, H., Wang, X., Zeldovich, N.: Why does cryptographic software fail? A case study and open problems. In: Proceedings of 5th Asia-Pacific Workshop on Systems, APSys 2014, pp. 1–7. Association for Computing Machinery (2014)

16. Mosca, M.: Cybersecurity in an era with quantum computers: will we be ready? IEEE Security & Privacy 16(5), 38–41 (2018). https://doi.org/10.1109/MSP.2018.3761723

17. Shor, P.: Algorithms for quantum computation: discrete logarithms and factoring. In: Proceedings 35th Annual Symposium on Foundations of Computer Science, pp. 124–134 (1994)

18. Unruh, D.: Post-quantum verification of Fujisaki-Okamoto. In: Moriai, S., Wang, H. (eds.) ASIACRYPT 2020. LNCS, vol. 12491, pp. 321–352. Springer, Cham (2020). https://doi.org/10.1007/978-3-030-64837-4_11
19. Yan, S.Y.: Quantum Attacks on Public-Key Cryptosystems, 1st edn. Springer, Boston (2013). https://doi.org/10.1007/978-1-4419-7722-9

Secure Multiparty Computation II

SoftSpokenOT: Quieter OT Extension from Small-Field Silent VOLE in the Minicrypt Model

Lawrence Roy[✉]

Oregon State University, Corvallis, USA
ldr709@gmail.com

Abstract. Given a small number of base oblivious transfers (OTs), how does one generate a large number of extended OTs as efficiently as possible? The answer has long been the seminal work of IKNP (Ishai et al., Crypto 2003) and the family of protocols it inspired, which only use Minicrypt assumptions. Recently, Boyle et al. (Crypto 2019) proposed the Silent-OT technique that improves on IKNP, but at the cost of a much stronger, non-Minicrypt assumption: the learning parity with noise (LPN) assumption. We present SoftSpokenOT, the first OT extension to improve on IKNP's communication cost in the Minicrypt model. While IKNP requires security parameter λ bits of communication for each OT, SoftSpokenOT only needs λ/k bits, for any k, at the expense of requiring $2^{k-1}/k$ times the computation. For small values of k, this tradeoff is favorable since IKNP-style protocols are network-bound. We implemented SoftSpokenOT and found that our protocol gives almost a $5\times$ speedup over IKNP in the LAN setting.

Our technique is based on a novel silent protocol for vector oblivious linear evaluation (VOLE) over polynomial-sized fields. We created a framework to build maliciously secure $\binom{N}{1}$-OT extension from this VOLE, revisiting and improving the existing work for each step. Along the way, we found several flaws in the existing work, including a practical attack against the consistency check of Patra et al. (NDSS 2017).

1 Introduction

Oblivious transfer (OT) is a basic building block of multi-party computation (MPC), and for many realistic problems, MPC protocols may require millions of OTs. [Bea96] introduced the concept of OT extension, where a small number of OTs called *base OTs* are processed to efficiently generate a much larger number of *extended OTs*. [IKNP03] (hereafter, IKNP) was the first OT extension protocol to make black-box use of its primitives, a significant improvement in efficiency. Because of its speed, it is still widely used for semi-honest OT extension.

However, IKNP has a bottleneck: communication. It transfers λ bits for every extended random OT. Recent works under the heading of Silent OT [BCGI18, BCG+19b, SGRR19, BCG+19a, YWL+20, CRR21] have communication complexity that grows only *logarithmically* in the number of oblivious transfers. Consequently, they are favored when communication is slow. On the other hand,

L. Roy—Supported by a DoE CSGF Fellowship.

Y. Dodis and T. Shrimpton (Eds.): CRYPTO 2022, LNCS 13507, pp. 657–687, 2022.
https://doi.org/10.1007/978-3-031-15802-5_23

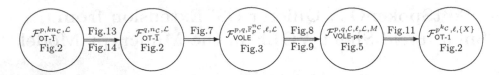

Fig. 1. Sequence of ideal functionalities and protocols used for OT extension. Here $q = p^k$ is the size of the small field VOLE, and $\mathcal{L} = \mathrm{Affine}(\mathbb{F}_p^{kn_C})$ is the set of allowed selective abort attacks against the base OT receiver. Protocols below the arrows are consistency checks needed for maliciously security.

IKNP has the advantage for computational cost: of the Silent OT protocols, only Silver [CRR21] uses a comparable amount of computation to IKNP. Additionally, while IKNP uses only Minicrypt [Imp95] assumptions (i.e. the assumptions are all provable in the random oracle model), Silent OT is based on the learning parity with noise (LPN) problem, which is not Minicrypt. Efficient instantiations depend on highly structured versions of this problem, with the most efficient protocol, Silver, owing its efficiency to a novel variant of LPN that was introduced solely for that work. Compared with a tried-and-true block cipher like AES, these assumptions are too recent to have received as much cryptanalysis.

Improvements to IKNP also benefit a number of derived protocols. For maliciously secure OT extension, the main approach [KOS15] (hereafter, KOS) is to combine IKNP with a consistency check, although Silent OT can also achieve malicious security. [KK13] achieved $\binom{N}{1}$-OT extension by noticing that part of IKNP can be viewed as encoding the OT choice bits with a repetition code. They replaced it with a more sophisticated error correcting code. [OOS17] (hereafter, OOS) and [PSS17] (hereafter, PSS) then devised more general consistency checking protocols to achieve maliciously secure $\binom{N}{1}$-OT extension. [CCG18] (hereafter, CCG) generalized OOS to work over larger fields, which have better linear codes. This allowed for fewer base OTs, but required more communication per extended OT.

1.1   Our Results

Our technique, SoftSpokenOT, makes an asymptotic improvement over IKNP's communication cost. It is the first OT extension to do so in the Minicrypt model. For any parameter $k \geq 1$, SoftSpokenOT can implement $\binom{2}{1}$-OT maliciously secure extension using only λ/k bits, compared to IKNP's λ bits. This is a communication–computation tradeoff, as the sender in our protocol must *generate* $\lambda \cdot 2^k/k$ pseudorandom bits, while IKNP only needs to generate 2λ bits. In practice, fast hardware implementations of AES make IKNP network bound, so when k is small (e.g. $k = 5$) this extra computation will have no effect on the overall protocol latency. And for $k = 2$, no extra computation is required, making it a pure improvement over IKNP. Asymptotically, setting $k = \Theta(\log(\ell))$ generates ℓ OTs with sublinear communication $\Theta\left(\frac{\lambda \cdot \ell}{\log(\ell)}\right)$, in polynomial time.

We present a sequence of protocols (Fig. 1), starting with base OTs, continuing through vector oblivious linear evaluation (VOLE), and ending at OT extension.

First, we present a novel silent protocol for VOLE over polynomial-sized fields, which may be of independent interest. A VOLE generates correlated randomness $(\vec{u}, \vec{v})$ and $(\Delta, \vec{w})$ where $\vec{w} - \vec{v} = \vec{u}\Delta$. Our next stepping stone is an ideal functionality that we call subspace VOLE, which produces correlations satisfying $W - V = UG_\mathcal{C}\text{diag}(\vec{\Delta})$. Here, $G_\mathcal{C}$ is the generator matrix for a linear code $\mathcal{C}$. Note that Δ-OT (a.k.a. correlated OT) is a special case of subspace VOLE, as is the correlation used by PaXoS [PRTY20]. Our Δ-OT works over any field of polynomial size, so it can encode the inputs for arithmetic garbling [BMR16]. Finally, we hash the subspace VOLE using a correlation robust (CR) hash to build random $\binom{N}{1}$, a correlation (x, m_x) and $(m_0, \ldots, m_{N-1})$ where the m_y are all random. These may be used directly, or to encode lookup tables representing multiple small-secret $\binom{2}{1}$-OTs [KK13].

We generalize OOS to construct a consistency checking protocol that achieves maliciously secure subspace VOLE, albeit with a selective abort attack. However, while proving our protocol secure, we found flaws (Sect. 4.1) in three existing works on consistency checks for OT extension. For OOS this is minor—just a flaw in their proof—and a special case of our new proof shows that OOS is still secure. We found two attacks on KOS which show that it is not always as secure as claimed, though it's still secure enough in practice. We leave to future research the problem of finding a sound proof of security for KOS. However, PSS's flaw is more severe, as we found a practical attack that can break their $\binom{256}{1}$-OT extension at $\lambda = 128$ security in time 2^{34} with probability 2^{-8}.

There is an existing work on OT extension consistency checking that we did not find to be flawed. CCG base their proof on [CDD+16]'s careful analysis of consistency checking for homomorphic commitments. CCG's check is similar to ours in that it works over any field. However, similarly to [CDD+16] and unlike CCG we use universal hashing to compress the random challenge of the consistency check. Additionally, we prove a tighter concrete security bound than either work, which halves the number of rows that must be consistency checked.

The final step, going from correlated randomness (i.e. subspace VOLE) to extended OTs, requires a CR hash function. For malicious security, a mechanism is needed to stop the receiver from causing a collision between CR hash inputs. [GKWY20] solve this with a tweakable CR (TCR) hash, using a tweak to stop these collisions. TCR hashes are more expensive than plain CR hashes, so Endemic OT [MR19] instead prevent the receiver from controlling the base OTs, proving that it is secure to forgo tweaks in this case. However, their proof assumes stronger properties of the consistency checking protocol than are provided by real consistency checks, allowing us to find an attack on their OT extension (see the full version). We follow [CT21] in using a universal hash to prevent collisions, only using the tweak to improve the concrete security of the TCR hash. We optimize their technique by sending the universal hash in parallel with our new consistency check—our proof shows that the receiver has few remaining choices once it learns the universal hash.

We implemented SoftSpokenOT for $\binom{2}{1}$-OT in the libOTe [Rin] library. When tested with a 1 Gbps bandwidth limit, our protocol has almost a $5\times$ speedup over

IKNP with $k = 5$, resulting from a 5× reduction in communication. The only case where SoftSpokenOT was suboptimal among the tested configurations was in the WAN setting, where it took second place to Silver. However, the assumptions needed by SoftSpokenOT are much more conservative than those used by Silver.

1.2 Technical Overview

SoftSpokenOT is a generalization of the classic oblivious transfer extension of IKNP, which at its core is based on what can be viewed as a protocol for $\mathbb{F}_2$-VOLE. This VOLE protocol starts by using a PRG to extend $\binom{2}{1}$-OT to message size ℓ. The base OT sender, P_S, gets random strings $\vec{m}_0, \vec{m}_1$ and the receiver, P_R, gets its choice bit $b \in \mathbb{F}_2$ and its chosen message $\vec{m}_b$. P_S then computes $\vec{u} = \vec{m}_0 \oplus \vec{m}_1$ and $\vec{v} = \vec{m}_1 = 0\,\vec{m}_0 \oplus 1\,\vec{m}_1$, while P_R computes $\Delta = 1 \oplus b$, and $w = \vec{m}_b = \Delta\vec{m}_0 \oplus (1 \oplus \Delta)\vec{m}_1$.[1] Then $\vec{w} \oplus \vec{v} = \Delta\vec{m}_0 \oplus \Delta\vec{m}_1 = \Delta\vec{u}$, which is a VOLE correlation: P_S gets a vector $\vec{u} \in \mathbb{F}_2^\ell$ and P_R gets a scalar $\Delta \in \mathbb{F}_2$, and they learn secret shares $\vec{v}, \vec{w}$ of the product. While $\vec{u}$ was chosen by the protocol, it possible to derandomize $\vec{u}$ to be any chosen vector. If P_S wants to use $\vec{u}'$ instead, it can send $\bar{u} = \vec{u} \oplus \vec{u}'$ to P_R, who updates its share to be $\vec{w}' = \vec{w} \oplus \Delta\bar{u}$. This preserves the VOLE correlation, $\vec{w}' \oplus \vec{v} = \Delta\vec{u} \oplus \Delta\bar{u} = \Delta\vec{u}'$, while hiding $\vec{u}'$.

The next step of the IKNP protocol is to stack λ of these $\mathbb{F}_2$-VOLEs side by side, while sending $\lambda \cdot \ell$ bits to derandomize the $\vec{u}$ vectors to all be the same. That is, for the ith VOLE, they get a correlation $W_{\cdot i} \oplus V_{\cdot i} = \Delta_i \vec{u}$, where $V_{\cdot i}$ means the ith column of a matrix V. In matrix notation, this is an outer product: $W \oplus V = \vec{u}\vec{\Delta}$, where $\vec{\Delta}$ is the row vector of all the Δ_i. Then looking at the jth row gives $W_{j \cdot} \oplus V_{j \cdot} = u_j \vec{\Delta}$, which make u_j the choice bit of a Δ-OT. That is, P_R has learned $\vec{m}_{j0} = W_{j \cdot}$ and $\vec{m}_{j1} = W_{j \cdot} \oplus \vec{\Delta}$, while P_S has its choice bit u_j and $\vec{m}_{u_j} = V_{j \cdot}$, the corresponding message. Notice that this is a correlated OT, but now the OT sender is P_R and the OT receiver is P_S –they have been reversed from what they were for the base OTs. Hashing the $\vec{m}_{jx}$ then turns them into uncorrelated OT messages.

SoftSpokenOT instead bases the OT extension on a $\mathbb{F}_{2^k}$-VOLE, where $\vec{u}$ is restricted to taking values in $\mathbb{F}_2$. We now only need λ/k of these VOLEs to get the λ bits per OT needed to make the hash secure. Derandomizing $\vec{u}$ for each OT then only needs λ/k *bits* per OT, as for each VOLE the elements of $\vec{u}$ are in $\mathbb{F}_2$, reducing a major bottleneck of IKNP. Instead of $\binom{2}{1}$-OT, our $\mathbb{F}_{2^k}$-VOLE is based on $\binom{2^k}{2^k-1}$-OT, which can be instantiated using a well known protocol [BGI17] based on a punctured PRF; see Sect. 6 for details.

In $\binom{2^k}{2^k-1}$-OT a random function $F \colon \mathbb{F}_{2^k} \to \mathbb{F}_2^\ell$ is known to P_S, while P_R has a random point Δ and the restriction F^* of F to $\mathbb{F}_{2^k} \setminus \{\Delta\}$. The earlier equations for the vectors $\vec{u}, \vec{v},$ and $\vec{w}$ were chosen to be suggestive of their generalizations:

$$\vec{u} = F(0) \oplus F(1) \qquad \Longrightarrow \qquad \vec{u} = \bigoplus_{x \in \mathbb{F}_{2^k}} F(x)$$

---

[1] Note that this is backwards from the usual description of IKNP—it's more usual to set Δ to be the b, the index of the message known to P_R. A key insight in SoftSpokenOT is that the unknown base OT message is the most important.

$$\vec{v} = 0\,F(0) \oplus 1\,F(1) \qquad\qquad \implies \vec{v} = \bigoplus_{x \in \mathbb{F}_{2^k}} x F(x)$$

$$\vec{w} = \Delta F^*(0) \oplus (1 \oplus \Delta)F^*(1) \implies \vec{w} = \bigoplus_{x \in \mathbb{F}_{2^k}} (x \oplus \Delta)F^*(x).$$

Notice that the formula for $\vec{w}$ multiplies $F^*(\Delta)$ by 0, which is good because $F(\Delta)$ is unknown to P_R. Therefore, $\vec{w} \oplus \vec{v} = \bigoplus_x \Delta F(x) = \Delta \vec{u}$.

Reducing communication by a factor of k comes at the expense of increasing computation by a factor of $2^k/k$. While there are now only λ/k VOLES, they each require both parties to evaluate F at every point (except the one that P_R does not know) in a finite field of size 2^k.

2 Preliminaries

2.1 Notation

We start counting at zero, and the set $[N]$ is $\{0, 1, \ldots, N-1\}$. The finite field with p elements is written as $\mathbb{F}_p$, the vector space of dimension n as $\mathbb{F}_p^n$, and set of all $m \times n$ matrices as $\mathbb{F}_p^{m \times n}$. The vectors themselves are written with an arrow, as $\vec{x}$, while matrices are capital letters M. Row vectors are written with a backwards arrow instead: $\overleftarrow{x}$. The componentwise product of vectors is $\vec{x} \odot \vec{y} = [x_0 y_0 \ \cdots \ x_{n-1}y_{n-1}]^\top$. Diagonal matrices are notated $\mathrm{diag}(\vec{x}) = \begin{bmatrix} x_0 & & \\ & \ddots & \\ & & x_{n-1} \end{bmatrix}$,

which makes $\vec{x} \odot \vec{y} = \mathrm{diag}(\vec{x})\vec{y}$. The ith row of a matrix M is $M_{i\cdot}$, while the jth column is $M_{\cdot j}$. The first r rows of M are $M_{[r]\cdot}$, and the first c columns are $M_{\cdot[c]}$.

There are two finite fields we will usually work with: the subfield $\mathbb{F}_p$, and its extension field $\mathbb{F}_q$, where $q = p^k$. Usually p will be prime, but that is not necessary. In a few places we will equivocate between $\mathbb{F}_q$, $\mathbb{F}_p^k$, and $[q]$, using the obvious bijections between them.

Linear Codes. Let $\mathcal{C}$ be a $[n_\mathcal{C}, k_\mathcal{C}, d_\mathcal{C}]$ linear code, that is, $\mathcal{C}$ is a $k_\mathcal{C}$-dimensional subspace of $\mathbb{F}_p^{n_\mathcal{C}}$ with minimum distance $d_\mathcal{C} = \min_{\vec{y} \in \mathcal{C} \setminus \{0\}} \|\vec{y}\|_0$, where $\|\vec{y}\|_0$ is the Hamming weight of $\vec{y}$. For a matrix A, we similarly let the Hamming weight $\|A\|_0$ be the number of nonzero columns of A. Let $G_\mathcal{C} \in \mathbb{F}_p^{k_\mathcal{C} \times n_\mathcal{C}}$ be the generator matrix of $\mathcal{C}$. We follow the convention that the messages and code words are row vectors, so a row vector $\overleftarrow{x}$ encodes to the codeword $\overleftarrow{x}G_\mathcal{C} \in \mathcal{C}$. The rows of the generator matrix must form a basis of $\mathcal{C}$, which can be completed into a basis $T_\mathcal{C}$ of $\mathbb{F}_p^{n_\mathcal{C}}$; that is, the first $k_\mathcal{C}$ rows of $T_\mathcal{C}$ are $G_\mathcal{C}$. Then $T_\mathcal{C}$ has an inverse $T_\mathcal{C}^{-1}$, the last $n_\mathcal{C} - k_\mathcal{C}$ columns of which form a parity check matrix for $\mathcal{C}$.

There are two specific codes that come up most frequently. The trivial code, $\mathbb{F}_p^n$, has all vectors as code words. That is, $G_{\mathbb{F}_p^n} = T_{\mathbb{F}_p^n} = \mathbb{1}_n$, where $\mathbb{1}_n$ is the $n \times n$ identity matrix. The repetition code, $\mathsf{Rep}(\mathbb{F}_p^n)$, consists of all vectors where all elements are the same. Its generator matrix is $G_{\mathsf{Rep}(\mathbb{F}_p^n)} = [1 \ \cdots \ 1]$.

Algorithms. We use pseudocode for our constructions. In many cases there will be two similar algorithms side by side (e.g. sender and receiver, or real and ideal), and we use whitespace to align matching lines. Sampling a value x uniformly at random in a set X is written as $x \overset{\$}{\leftarrow} X$.

2.2 Universal Hashes

We make extensive use of universal hashes [CW79], essentially as a more efficient replacement for a uniformly random matrix. We depend on the extra structure of the hash function being linear, so we give definitions specialized to that case.

Definition 2.1. *A family of matrices $\mathcal{R} \subseteq \mathbb{F}_q^{m \times n}$ is a linear ϵ-almost universal family if, for all nonzero $\vec{x} \in \mathbb{F}_q^n$, $\Pr_{R \overset{\$}{\leftarrow} \mathcal{R}}[R\vec{x} = 0] \leq \epsilon$.*

Definition 2.2. *A family of matrices $\mathcal{R} \subseteq \mathbb{F}_q^{m \times n}$ is linear ϵ-almost uniform family if, for all nonzero $\vec{x} \in \mathbb{F}_q^n$ and all $\vec{y} \in \mathbb{F}_q^m$, $\Pr_{R \overset{\$}{\leftarrow} \mathcal{R}}[R\vec{x} = \vec{y}] \leq \epsilon$.*

For characteristic 2, this is equivalent to being ϵ-almost XOR-universal. Clearly, a family that is ϵ-almost uniform is also ϵ-almost universal. We use two composition properties of universal hashes.

Proposition 2.3. *Let $\mathcal{R}$ and $\mathcal{R}'$ be ϵ and ϵ'-almost universal families, respectively. Then $R'R$ for $R \in \mathcal{R}, R' \in \mathcal{R}'$ is a $(\epsilon + \epsilon')$-universal family.*

Proposition 2.4. *Let $\mathcal{R}$ and $\mathcal{R}'$ be ϵ-almost uniform families. Then $[R\ R']$ for $R \in \mathcal{R}, R' \in \mathcal{R}'$ is a ϵ-uniform family.*

2.3 Ideal Functionalities

The protocols in this paper are analyzed in the Simplified UC model of [CCL15], so whenever an ideal functionality takes inputs or outputs, the adversary is implicitly notified and allowed to delay or block delivery of the message. The functionalities deal with three entities: the sender P_S, the receiver P_R, and the adversary $\mathcal{A}$. Instead of the usual event-driven style (essentially a state machine driven by the messages), we use a blocking call syntax for our ideal functionalities, where it stops and waits to receive a message. While we will not need to receive multiple messages at once, it would be consistent to use multiple parallel threads of execution, with syntax like $\boxed{\text{recv. } x \text{ from } P_S \parallel \text{recv. } y \text{ from } P_R}$. We omit the "operation labels" identifying the messages, instead relying on the variable names and message order to show which send corresponds to each receive. We assume the protocol messages themselves are delivered over an authenticated channel.

All of our functionalities are for different kinds of random input VOLE or OT, meaning that the protocol pseudorandomly chooses the inputs of each party. Essentially, the functionalities just generate correlated randomness. Using random VOLE or OT, the parties can still choose their inputs using derandomization, if necessary.[2] However, we cannot guarantee that a corrupted participant does not exercise partial control over the outputs of the protocols. For this reason,

---

[2] See [MR19] for details on derandomizing OT messages.

$$\mathcal{F}_{\text{OT-1}}^{N,\ell,\mathcal{L}}$$

for $i \in [\ell]$:
  if P_S is corrupted:
    recv. $F_i \in \left(\{0,1\}^\lambda\right)^{[N]}$ from $\mathcal{A}$
  else:
    $F_i \xleftarrow{\$} \left(\{0,1\}^\lambda\right)^{[N]}$
  if P_R is corrupted:
    recv. $x_i^* \in [N]$ from $\mathcal{A}$
    recv. $F_i^* \in \{0,1\}^\lambda$ from $\mathcal{A}$
    $F_i(x_i^*) := F_i^*$
  else:
    $x_i^* \xleftarrow{\$} [N]$
    $F_i^* := F_i(x_i^*)$
send $\{F_i\}_{i\in[\ell]}$ to P_S
Send/Abort$\left(\{x_i^*\}_{i\in[\ell]}, \{F_i^*\}_{i\in[\ell]}, \mathcal{L}\right)$

$$\mathcal{F}_{\text{OT-}\bar{1}}^{N,\ell,\mathcal{L}}$$

for $i \in [\ell]$:
  if P_S is corrupted:
    recv. $F_i \in \left(\{0,1\}^\lambda\right)^{[N]}$ from $\mathcal{A}$
  else:
    $F_i \xleftarrow{\$} \left(\{0,1\}^\lambda\right)^{[N]}$
  if P_R is corrupted:
    recv. $x_i^* \in [N]$ from $\mathcal{A}$
    recv. $F_i^* \in \left(\{0,1\}^\lambda\right)^{[N]\setminus\{x_i^*\}}$ from $\mathcal{A}$
    $F_i(x) := F_i^*(x), \forall x \in [N] \setminus \{x_i^*\}$
  else:
    $x_i^* \xleftarrow{\$} [N]$
    $F_i^*(x) := F_i(x), \forall x \in [N] \setminus \{x_i^*\}$
send $\{F_i\}_{i\in[\ell]}$ to P_S
Send/Abort$\left(\{x_i^*\}_{i\in[\ell]}, \{F_i^*\}_{i\in[\ell]}, \mathcal{L}\right)$

Fig. 2. Ideal functionalities for a batch of ℓ endemic OTs, with $\binom{N}{1}$-OT on the left and $\binom{N}{N-1}$-OT on the right. Differences are highlighted.

$$\mathcal{F}_{\text{VOLE}}^{p,q,\mathcal{C},\ell,\mathcal{L}}$$

if P_S is corrupted:
  recv. $U \in \mathbb{F}_p^{\ell \times k_C}, V \in \mathbb{F}_q^{\ell \times n_C}$ from $\mathcal{A}$
else:
  $U \xleftarrow{\$} \mathbb{F}_p^{\ell \times k_C}, V \xleftarrow{\$} \mathbb{F}_q^{\ell \times n_C}$
if P_R is corrupted:
  recv. $\tilde{\Delta} \in \mathbb{F}_q^{n_C}, W \in \mathbb{F}_q^{\ell \times n_C}$ from $\mathcal{A}$
  $V := -UG_C \operatorname{diag}(\tilde{\Delta}) + W$
else:
  $\tilde{\Delta} \xleftarrow{\$} \mathbb{F}_q^{n_C}$
  $W := UG_C \operatorname{diag}(\tilde{\Delta}) + V$
send U, V to P_S
Send/Abort$(\tilde{\Delta}, W, \mathcal{L})$

Send/Abort$(x \in X, y \in Y, \mathcal{L} \subseteq 2^X)$:
  if P_S is malicious:
    recv. $L \in \mathcal{L}$ from P_S
    if $x \notin L$:
      send "check failed" to P_R
      abort
  send x, y to P_R

Fig. 3. Ideal functionality for endemic subspace VOLE. $\mathcal{C}$ is a linear code.

Fig. 4. Output with leakage function. Sends x, y to P_R, after allowing P_S to do a selective abort attack on x.

we use the endemic security notion of [MR19], where any corrupted participants get to choose their protocol outputs, then the remaining honest parties receive random outputs, subject to the correlation. One difference, however, is that in our ideal functionalities an honest OT receiver doesn't get to choose its choice bits. Instead, all protocol inputs are random for honest parties.[3]

---

[3] This is similar to the pseudorandom correlation generators (PCGs) used in [BCG+19b] to build Silent OT. In fact, the small field VOLE constructed in Sect. 3.1 can be viewed as a PCG.

The ideal functionalities for length ℓ batches of $\binom{N}{1}$-OTs or $\binom{N}{N-1}$-OTs are presented in Fig. 2. In each OT, the sender P_S gets a random function $F \colon [N] \to \{0,1\}^\lambda$, which is chosen by the adversary if P_S is corrupted. If N is exponentially large, F should be thought of as an oracle, which will only be evaluated on a subset of $[N]$. The receiver P_R gets a choice element $x^* \in [N]$, as well as F^*, which is either the one point $F(x^*)$ for $\binom{N}{1}$-OT, or the restriction of F to every other point $[N]\backslash x^*$ for $\binom{N}{N-1}$-OT. Again, if P_R is corrupted then the adversary gets to choose these values.

In Fig. 3, we present subspace VOLE, a generalized notion of VOLE. Instead of a correlation of vectors $\vec{w} - \vec{v} = \vec{u}\Delta$, where $\vec{u} \in \mathbb{F}_p^\ell$ and $\vec{v} \in \mathbb{F}_q^\ell$ are given to P_S, and $\vec{w} \in \mathbb{F}_q^\ell$ and $\Delta \in \mathbb{F}_q$ to P_R [BCGI18], subspace VOLE produces a correlation of matrices $W - V = UG_\mathcal{C}\mathrm{diag}(\bar{\Delta})$, where U gets multiplied by the generator matrix $G_\mathcal{C}$ of a linear code $\mathcal{C}$. Subspace VOLE is essentially $n_\mathcal{C}$ independent VOLE correlations placed side-by-side, except that the rows of U are required to be code words of $\mathcal{C}$. For $p = q = 2$, this matches the correlation generated internally by existing $\binom{N}{1}$-OT extensions.

Selective Aborts. Our base $\binom{N}{N-1}$-OT OT and subspace VOLE protocols achieve malicious security by using a consistency check to enforce honest behavior. However, the consistency checks allow a selective abort attack where P_S can confirm a guess of part of P_R's secret outputs. This is modeled in the ideal functionality using the function Send/Abort (Fig. 4). Let $x \in X$ be the value subject to the selective abort attack, and $y \in Y$ be the rest of P_R's output. When P_S is malicious, it can guess a subset $L \subseteq X$, and if it is correct (i.e. $x \in L$) then the protocol continues as normal. But if the guess is wrong then P_R is notified of the error, and the protocol aborts.

The subset L that P_S guesses is restricted to being a member of $\mathcal{L}$, for some set of allowed guesses $\mathcal{L} \subseteq 2^X$. It is required to be closed under intersection, and contain the whole set X. For VOLE, where X is a vector space, we also require that $L - \tilde{L}_{\mathrm{off}} \in \mathcal{L}$ when $L \in \mathcal{L}$ and $\tilde{L}_{\mathrm{off}} \in X$. We use one main set of allowed guesses, $\mathrm{Affine}(\mathbb{F}_q^n)$. It is the set of all affine subspaces of $\mathbb{F}_q^n$, i.e. all subsets that are defined by zero or more constraints of the form $a_0x_0 + \cdots + a_{n-1}x_{n-1} = a_n$, for constants $a_0, \ldots, a_n \in \mathbb{F}_q$. Since $\mathbb{F}_q$ can be viewed as the vector space $\mathbb{F}_p^k$, we have a superset relationship $\mathrm{Affine}(\mathbb{F}_p^{nk}) \supseteq \mathrm{Affine}(\mathbb{F}_q^n)$. There is also $\{X\}$, the trivial guess set, which only allows a malicious P_S to guess that $x \in X$. This guess is trivially true, and so leaks no information at all.

Pre-committed Inputs. Our malicious OT extension protocol uses a universal hash to stop P_R from causing collisions between two distinct extended OTs, which is sent in parallel with the VOLE consistency check for efficiency. However, the universal hash must be chosen *after* P_R (who acts as the VOLE *sender*) picks its VOLE outputs U, V and its guess L. In Fig. 5, we modify the VOLE functionality to notify the VOLE receiver once U, V, L are almost fixed—unfortunately, the consistency check still allows U, V, L to vary somewhat. Specifically, U may have polynomially many options (which can be computationally hard to find), L can get shifted by an offset $\tilde{L}_{\mathrm{off}}$, and V can depend on the part of $\bar{\Delta}$ that is guessed.

$$\boxed{\begin{array}{l} \qquad\qquad\qquad \mathcal{F}^{p,q,\mathcal{C},\ell,\mathcal{L},M}_{\text{VOLE-pre}} \\[4pt] \hline \text{if } P_S \text{ is malicious:} \\ \quad \text{recv. } \mathcal{W}_{\text{pre}} \subseteq \{0,1\}^* \text{ from } \mathcal{A} \\ \quad \text{recv. } U_{\text{pre}} \colon \mathcal{W}_{\text{pre}} \to \mathbb{F}_p^{\ell \times k_C} \text{ from } \mathcal{A} \\ \quad \text{recv. } V_{\text{pre}} \colon \mathcal{W}_{\text{pre}} \times \mathbb{F}_q^{n_C} \to \mathbb{F}_q^{\ell \times n_C} \text{ from } \mathcal{A} \\ \quad \text{recv. } L_{\text{pre}} \colon \mathcal{W}_{\text{pre}} \to \mathcal{L} \text{ from } \mathcal{A} \\ \text{send ``commit'' to } P_R \\ \text{run } \mathcal{F}^{p,q,\mathcal{C},\ell,\mathcal{L}}_{\text{VOLE}} \\ \text{instead of Send/Abort:} \\ \quad \text{if } P_S \text{ is malicious:} \\ \qquad \text{recv. } w_{\text{pre}} \in \mathcal{W}_{\text{pre}}, \tilde{L}_{\text{off}} \in \mathbb{F}_q^{n_C} \text{ from } \mathcal{A} \\ \qquad \text{if } U \neq U_{\text{pre}}(w_{\text{pre}}) \vee V \neq V_{\text{pre}}(w_{\text{pre}}, \tilde{\Delta}) \vee \tilde{\Delta} + \tilde{L}_{\text{off}} \notin L_{\text{pre}}(w_{\text{pre}}) \\ \qquad\quad \text{send ``check failed'' to } P_R \\ \qquad\quad \text{abort} \\ \text{send } \tilde{\Delta}, W \text{ to } P_R \end{array}}$$

Fig. 5. Modification of Fig. 3 to get an ideal functionality for subspace VOLE with a pre-commitment notification. We make two additional requirements on $\mathcal{A}$. There must be a polynomial upper bound $M \geq |\mathcal{W}_{\text{pre}}|$ on the number of input choices P_S has. And, for all $\tilde{\Delta}$, $\tilde{\Delta} + \tilde{L}_{\text{off}} \in L_{\text{pre}}(w_{\text{pre}})$ must imply $V = V_{\text{pre}}(w_{\text{pre}}, \tilde{\Delta})$, to ensure that checking V_{pre} does not make the selective abort any more powerful.

To address these difficulties, we identify the possible input choices with witnesses w_{pre}, and have $\mathcal{A}$ output a witness checker, i.e. an implicitly defined set $\mathcal{W}_{\text{pre}}$ of valid witnesses. Then we require U, V, and L to be fixed in terms of w_{pre}, using functions $U_{\text{pre}}(w_{\text{pre}})$, $V_{\text{pre}}(w_{\text{pre}}, \tilde{\Delta})$, and $L_{\text{pre}}(w_{\text{pre}})$. We require a polynomial upper bound $M \geq |\mathcal{W}_{\text{pre}}|$ on the number of witnesses. Additionally, so that the correctness check for V_{pre} does not leak any information, for all $\tilde{\Delta}$ we require that $\tilde{\Delta} + \tilde{L}_{\text{off}} \in L_{\text{pre}}(w_{\text{pre}})$ implies $V = V_{\text{pre}}(w_{\text{pre}}, \tilde{\Delta})$.

These changes are behind "if P_S is malicious" checks, so in the semi-honest case $\mathcal{F}_{\text{VOLE}}$ is a equivalent to $\mathcal{F}_{\text{VOLE-pre}}$. For malicious security, $\mathcal{F}_{\text{VOLE-pre}}$ gives the adversary less power than $\mathcal{F}_{\text{VOLE}}$ because it forces some of the choices to be made early, so any protocol for $\mathcal{F}_{\text{VOLE-pre}}$ is also a protocol for $\mathcal{F}_{\text{VOLE}}$.

2.4 Correlation Robust Hashes

The final step of OT extension is to hash the output from the subspace VOLE. This requires a security assumption on the hash function H. We generalize the notion of a tweakable correlation robust (TCR) hash function [GKWY20] to our setting. While this definition will most likely be used with $p = 2$ for efficiency, there are extra theoretical difficulties associated with $p > 2$.

Definition 2.5. A function $H \in \mathbb{F}_q^{n_C} \times \mathcal{T} \to \{0,1\}^\lambda$ is a $(p, q, \mathcal{C}, \mathcal{T}, \mathcal{L})$-TCR hash if the oracles given in Fig. 6 are indistinguishable.[4] Formally, for any PPT

---

[4] Note that we do not consider multi-instance security. In fact, there is a generic attack:

TCR-real$^{H,p,q,\mathcal{C},\mathcal{L}}$
$\tilde{\Delta} \xleftarrow{\$} \mathbb{F}_q^{nc}$
QUERY($\tilde{x} \in \mathbb{F}_p^{kc} \setminus \{0\}, \tilde{y} \in \mathbb{F}_q^{nc}, \tau \in \mathcal{T}$):
$\quad$ return $H(\tilde{x}G_{\mathcal{C}} \odot \tilde{\Delta} + \tilde{y}, \tau)$
LEAK($L \in \mathcal{L}$):
$\quad$ abort if $\tilde{\Delta} \notin L$

TCR-ideal$^{H,p,q,\mathcal{C},\mathcal{L}}$
$\tilde{\Delta} \xleftarrow{\$} \mathbb{F}_q^{nc}$
QUERY($\tilde{x} \in \mathbb{F}_p^{kc} \setminus \{0\}, \tilde{y} \in \mathbb{F}_q^{nc}, \tau \in \mathcal{T}$):
$\quad z \xleftarrow{\$} \{0,1\}^\lambda$
$\quad$ return z
LEAK($L \in \mathcal{L}$):
$\quad$ abort if $\tilde{\Delta} \notin L$

(a) Real world.   (b) Ideal world.

Fig. 6. Oracles for TCR definition. Calls to QUERY must not be repeated on the same input.

adversary $\mathcal{A}$ that does not call QUERY twice on the same input $(\tilde{x}, \tilde{y}, \tau)$,

$$\mathsf{Adv}_{\mathrm{TCR}} = \left| \Pr\left[\mathcal{A}^{\mathsf{TCR\text{-}real}^{H,p,q,\mathcal{C},\mathcal{L}}}() = 1\right] - \Pr\left[\mathcal{A}^{\mathsf{TCR\text{-}ideal}^{H,p,q,\mathcal{C},\mathcal{L}}}() = 1\right] \right| \leq \mathrm{negl}.$$

Our definition is quite similar to the TCR of [GKWY20] in the special case where $\mathcal{C}$ is the repetition code. However, we explicitly include selective abort attacks in the TCR definition, while they require that the hash be secure for any distribution for $\tilde{\Delta}$ with sufficient min-entropy. Their definition has issues when instantiated from idealized primitives such as random oracles, because, when the TCR is used for OT extension, the distribution for $\tilde{\Delta}$ would have to depend on these primitives [CT21]. In the standard model, their definition is impossible to instantiate: $H(\tilde{\Delta}, 0)$ must be random by TCR security, yet restricting $\tilde{\Delta}$ so that the first bit of $H(\tilde{\Delta}, 0)$ is zero only reduces the min-entropy by approximately one bit and allows an efficient distinguisher. [CT21] fix the former issue with a definition TCR* that only applies to the ideal model, while ours allows the possibility of standard model constructions.

We now give two hash constructions, which we prove secure in the full version. Correlation robust hashes were inspired by random oracles (ROs), so it should be no surprise that a RO is a TCR hash.

Proposition 2.6. *A random oracle* RO: $\mathbb{F}_q^{nc} \times \{0,1\}^t \to \{0,1\}^\lambda$ *is a* $(p, q, \mathcal{C}, \{0,1\}^t, \mathrm{Affine}(\mathbb{F}_p^{knc}))$-*TCR hash, with distinguisher advantage at most* $\tau_{max}(\mathsf{q} + \frac{1}{2}\mathsf{q}')\mathsf{q}^{-dc}$. *Here,* τ_{max} *is the maximum number of times* QUERY *is called with the same* τ, q *is the number of RO queries made by the distinguisher, and* q' *is the number of calls to* QUERY.

The next construction comes from [GKW+20]. It is the classic $x \mapsto \pi(x) \oplus x$ permutation-based hash function, but it uses an ideal cipher so that the tweak can be the key. Changing keys in a block cipher requires recomputing the round keys, so there is a cost to changing the tweak with this method. It needs a injection ι to encode its input; when $p = 2$, ι can be the identity map.

---

given N instances, the attacker chooses an L that contains $\tilde{\Delta}$ with probability $1/N$, then brute forces $\tilde{\Delta}$ for instances where $\tilde{\Delta} \in L$. Thus, it is N-times cheaper to brute force attack H for N instances than to target a single one.

P_S		P_R
	$\xleftarrow{F} \mathcal{F}_{\mathsf{OT}\text{-}\bar{1}}^{q,1,\mathcal{L}} \xrightarrow{x^*, F^*}$	
		$\Delta := x^*$
for $x \in \mathbb{F}_q$:		for $x \in \mathbb{F}_q \setminus \{\Delta\}$:
$\vec{r}_x := \mathsf{PRG}(F(x))$		$\vec{r}_x := \mathsf{PRG}(F^*(x))$
$\vec{u} := \sum_{x\in\mathbb{F}_q} \vec{r}_x$		$\vec{w} := \sum_{x\in\mathbb{F}_q\setminus\{\Delta\}} \vec{r}_x\,(\Delta - x)$
$\vec{v} := -\sum_{x\in\mathbb{F}_q} \vec{r}_x\, x$		
output $\vec{u}, \vec{v}$		output $\Delta, \vec{w}$

Fig. 7. Protocol for small field VOLE. If $\mathcal{F}_{\mathsf{OT}\text{-}\bar{1}}^{q,1,\mathcal{L}}$ instead outputs "check failed", it should be passed straight through to P_R.

Proposition 2.7. *Let* $\mathsf{Enc}\colon \{0,1\}^t \times \{0,1\}^\lambda \to \{0,1\}^\lambda$ *be an ideal cipher, and* $\iota\colon \mathbb{F}_q^{nc} \to \{0,1\}^\lambda$ *be an injection. Then* $H(\breve{y}, \tau) = \mathsf{Enc}(\tau, \iota(\breve{y})) \oplus \iota(\breve{y})$ *is a* $(p, q, \mathcal{C}, \{0,1\}^t, \mathrm{Affine}(\mathbb{F}_p^{knc}))$*-TCR hash. The distinguisher's advantage is at most* $\tau_{max}\left((2\mathsf{q} + \frac{1}{2}\mathsf{q}')q^{-d_\mathcal{C}} + \frac{1}{2}\mathsf{q}'2^{-\lambda}\right)$*, with* q *and* q' *as in Proposition 2.6.*

3 VOLE

3.1 For Small Fields

We already presented our $\mathbb{F}_{2^k}$-VOLE in Sect. 1.2. This VOLE is generalized in Fig. 7 to work over any small field $\mathbb{F}_q$, specifically fields where q is only polynomially large, with $\vec{u}$ taking values in any subfield $\mathbb{F}_p$. It is based on a $\binom{q}{q-1}$-OT, and a pseudorandom generator $\mathsf{PRG}\colon \{0,1\}^\lambda \to \mathbb{F}_p^\ell$. While this is a VOLE protocol, we analyze it using our subspace VOLE definition by setting $\mathcal{C}$ to be the length one, dimension one code, i.e. $G_\mathcal{C} = [1]$. This makes U, V, and W all become column vectors and Δ become a scalar.

Theorem 3.1. *The VOLE given in Fig. 7 in the* $\mathcal{F}_{\mathsf{OT}\text{-}\bar{1}}^{q,1,\mathcal{L}}$ *hybrid model securely realizes* $\mathcal{F}_{\mathsf{VOLE}}^{p,q,\mathbb{F}_p,\ell,\mathcal{L}}$*, in both the semihonest and malicious models.*

Proof. The proof of correctness is simple enough. Notice that the $x = \Delta$ term of the sum for $\vec{w}$ would be multiplied by $\Delta - \Delta = 0$, so it makes no difference that it must be excluded because P_R does not know $\vec{r}_\Delta$. Therefore,

$$\vec{w} = \sum_{x\in\mathbb{F}_q\setminus\{\Delta\}} \vec{r}_x\,(\Delta - x) = \sum_{x\in\mathbb{F}_q} \vec{r}_x\,(\Delta - x) = \sum_{x\in\mathbb{F}_q} \vec{r}_x\,\Delta - \sum_{x\in\mathbb{F}_q} \vec{r}_x\, x = \vec{u}\,\Delta + \vec{v}. \quad (1)$$

Corrupt P_S. After receiving F from $\mathcal{A}$, the simulator will compute $\vec{u}, \vec{v}$ honestly and submit them to $\mathcal{F}_{\mathsf{VOLE}}^{p,q,\mathbb{F}_p,\ell,\mathcal{L}}$. If P_S is malicious, it will also forward $L \in \mathcal{L}$ to the ideal functionality. In the real world, $\mathcal{F}_{\mathsf{OT}\text{-}\bar{1}}^{q,1,\mathcal{L}}$ will generate a random $x^* = \Delta$ and send it to P_R, who will compute $\vec{w} = \vec{u}\,\Delta + \vec{v}$ by Eq. (1). In the ideal world, $\mathcal{F}_{\mathsf{VOLE}}^{p,q,\mathbb{F}_p,\ell,\mathcal{L}}$ will pick Δ randomly, receive $\vec{u}, \vec{v}$ from the simulator, and compute $\vec{w} = \vec{u}\Delta + \vec{v}$. These are identical, implying that these two worlds are indistinguishable and that this case is secure.

Corrupt P_R. After receiving F^*, x^* from $\mathcal{A}$, the simulator will compute $\Delta = x^*$ and $\vec{w}$ honestly, and submit them to $\mathcal{F}_{\mathsf{VOLE}}^{p,q,\mathbb{F}_p,\ell,\mathcal{L}}$. We do a hybrid proof, starting from the real world and going to the ideal world.

1. In the real world, $\mathcal{F}_{\mathsf{OT}\text{-}\bar{1}}^{q,1,\mathcal{L}}$ sets $F(x) = F^*(x)$ for $x \neq x^*$, generates $F(x^*)$ randomly, and sends them to P_S, who will compute $\vec{r}_x = \mathsf{PRG}(F(x))$ and $\vec{u}, \vec{v}$. By Eq. (1), $\vec{v} = \vec{w} - \vec{u}\Delta$.
2. Because $F(x^*)$ is only used to compute $\vec{r}_{x^*}$, the security of PRG implies that $\vec{r}_{x^*}$ can be replaced with a uniformly sampled value.
3. Instead of sampling $\vec{r}_{x^*}$ randomly, sample $\vec{u}$ uniformly at random and set $\vec{r}_{x^*} = \vec{u} - \sum_{x \neq x^*} \vec{r}_x$. This is an identical distribution.
4. We are now at the ideal world, where $\mathcal{F}_{\mathsf{VOLE}}^{p,q,\mathbb{F}_p,\ell,\mathcal{L}}$ will pick $\vec{u}$ randomly, receive $\Delta, \vec{w}$ from the simulator, and compute $\vec{v} = \vec{w} - \vec{u}\Delta$.

If both parties are corrupt then security is trivial, as then the simulator can just forward messages between the corrupted parties.

Efficient Computation. Let a be a generator of $\mathbb{F}_q$ over $\mathbb{F}_p$. For computation, it's convenient to represent $\vec{v}$ as a sequence of $\mathbb{F}_p$ vectors: $\vec{v} = \vec{v}_0 + a\vec{v}_1 + \cdots + a^{k-1}\vec{v}_{k-1}$. Similarly, the index x becomes $x_0 + ax_1 + \cdots + a^{k-1}x_{k-1}$. Naïve computation of $\vec{v}$ using the sum then becomes $\vec{v}_i = \sum_x x_i \vec{r}_x$, but this would require $O(kq)$ vector additions and scalar multiplications over $\mathbb{F}_p$.

This can be improved to $O(q + \frac{q}{p} + \frac{q}{p^2} + \cdots) = O(q)$ vector additions and no scalar multiplications. For all $x' \in \mathbb{F}_q$ where $x'_0 = 0$, let $\vec{r}'_{x'} = \sum_{x_0 \in \mathbb{F}_p} \vec{r}_{x'+x_0}$, and notice that all $\vec{v}_1, \ldots, \vec{v}_{k-1}$ (and $\vec{u}$) depend only on the $\vec{r}'_{x'}$. Therefore, after computing all $\frac{q}{p}$ vectors $\vec{r}'_{x'}$, the outputs $\vec{v}_1, \ldots, \vec{v}_{k-1}$ can be found by recursion on a smaller problem size. As a byproduct, computing the $\vec{r}'_{x'}$ produces sequences of partial sums $\sum_{x_0 \leq i} \vec{r}_{x'+x_0}$, and adding all of these together then gives $\sum_{x'} \sum_{x_0} (p - x_0)\vec{r}_{x'+x_0} = \vec{v}_0$. P_R can use the same algorithm to compute $\vec{w}$ by just reordering the $\vec{r}_x$ vectors at the start, because $\sum_x \vec{r}_x(\Delta - x) = \sum_x \vec{r}_{x+\Delta}(-x)$.

Concatenation. While this does not directly follow directly from the UC theorem, it should be clear that running the protocol Fig. 7 on a batch of n OTs will produce a batch of n VOLEs. The proof trivially generalizes. More precisely, it achieves $\mathcal{F}_{\mathsf{VOLE}}^{p,q,\mathbb{F}_p^n,\ell,\mathcal{L}}$ in the $\mathcal{F}_{\mathsf{OT}\text{-}\bar{1}}^{q,1,\mathcal{L}}$ hybrid model, where $\mathbb{F}_p^n$ is the trivial code with $G_{\mathbb{F}_p^n} = \mathbb{1}_n$. This will be the basis for our subspace VOLE.

3.2   For Subspaces

For $\binom{2}{1}$-OT extension, the next step would be for P_S to send a correction to make all columns of U be identical, so that each column would use the same set of choice bits. Efficient $\binom{N}{1}$-OT extension protocols like [KK13] instead must correct the rows of U to lie in an arbitrary linear code $\mathcal{C}$, rather than the repetition code. We implement subspace VOLE to handle these more general correlations.

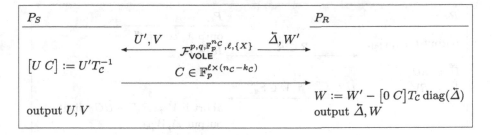

Fig. 8. Protocol for subspace VOLE.

Our protocol for subspace VOLE is presented in Fig. 8. It starts out with a VOLE correlation $W' - V = U'\text{diag}(\Delta)$. Then, P_S divides U' into parts, the message $U \in \mathbb{F}_p^{\ell \times k_C}$ and the correction syndrome $C \in \mathbb{F}_p^{\ell \times n_C - k_C}$, sending the correction to P_R. P_R then corrects W to maintain the VOLE correlation property after P_S removes C. Unfortunately, P_S can just lie when it sends C to P_R, so the protocol only achieves semi-honest security. Since the leakage set $\mathcal{L}$ only matters for malicious security, we simplify by assuming that $\mathcal{L}$ is trivial (i.e. $\{X\}$).

Theorem 3.2. *The protocol in Fig. 8 is a semi-honest realization of $\mathcal{F}_{VOLE}^{p,q,C,\ell,\{X\}}$ in the $\mathcal{F}_{VOLE}^{p,q,\mathbb{F}_p^n,\ell,\{X\}}$ hybrid model.*

Proof. First, the protocol outputs correctly satisfy the VOLE correlation:

$$W = W' - [0\ C]T_C\text{diag}(\tilde{\Delta})$$
$$= V + U'\text{diag}(\tilde{\Delta}) - [0\ C]T_C\text{diag}(\tilde{\Delta})$$
$$= V + ([U\ C]T_C - [0\ C]T_C)\text{diag}(\tilde{\Delta})$$
$$= V + UG_C\text{diag}(\tilde{\Delta}).$$

For security, notice that any $U, V, \tilde{\Delta}, W$ output by the protocol and any C that the adversary eavesdrops on (because the communication is over an authenticated, but not private, channel) corresponds to a unique $U', V, \tilde{\Delta}, W'$ from the underlying VOLE. Specifically, $U' = [U\ C]T_C$ and $W' = W + [0\ C]T_C\text{diag}(\tilde{\Delta})$. This implies the adversary does not learn anything new by corrupting either party, as they could already predict what that party knows. They only gain the power to program that the base VOLE's outputs for that party, but the simulator gains the corresponding power to program that party's protocol outputs to match. In more detail, $\mathcal{S}$ should receive from $\mathcal{A}$ the programed base VOLE outputs for the corrupted parties, simulate doing exactly what they would do in the protocol (while sampling a fake $C \xleftarrow{\$} \mathbb{F}_p^{\ell \times (n_C - k_C)}$ if P_S is honest), and program the protocol outputs to be the result.

In the ideal world, $\mathcal{S}$ generates a uniformly random consistent adversary view $U, V, \tilde{\Delta}, W$ (together with U' or W' if P_S or P_R was corrupted). In the real world, the underlying VOLE functionality picks $U', V, \tilde{\Delta}, W'$ uniformly at random subject to the constraints of the VOLE correlation and any outputs

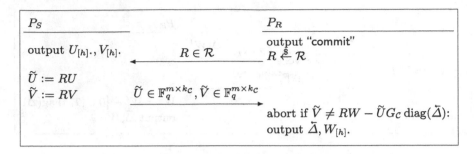

Fig. 9. Consistency checking protocol, which should be used with Fig. 8. $\mathcal{R}$ must be a ϵ-universal hash family, where all $R \in \mathcal{R}$ is $\mathbb{F}_p^h$-hiding. The "abort if" means that "check failed" is output if the check fails. If instead of giving $\tilde{\Delta}, W'$ to P_R, the base VOLE outputs "check failed", P_R should continue to play along with the protocol and only output "check failed" when it completes.

programmed by the adversary, and then the adversary gets to see the protocol run. There is a bijection between consistent adversary views and outputs of the underlying VOLE $U', V, \tilde{\Delta}, W'$, and this bijection implies that these two views are identically distributed.

4   Malicious Security

Our small field VOLE construction in Sect. 3.1 was easily proved maliciously secure. It does not involve any communication, and so there are no opportunities for any of the parties to lie. However, Sect. 3.2 requires P_S to reveal part of U, allowing a malicious P_S to lie. Following KOS and OOS, we solve this by introducing a consistency check (Fig. 9) that is run immediately afterwards, to provide a guarantee that if P_S lies then the protocol will either abort or work properly. Then the last few rows of U, V, and W are thrown away so that the values revealed in the consistency check do not leak anything. This still allows the possibility of selective abort attacks, however.

    KOS, OOS, PSS, and CCG all compute their consistency checks by multiplying each row of U with a random value—an element of an extension field for KOS or just a vector for OOS and PSS. V and W are also multiplied by random values, in a consistent way. We follow [CDD+16] in generalizing this to use linear universal hashes. Any linear ϵ-almost universal hash family $\mathcal{R} \subseteq \mathbb{F}_q^{m \times \ell}$ will work, as long as the following condition is met by every $R \in \mathcal{R}$, which guarantees that throwing away the last few rows of U is sufficient to keep the others hidden.

Definition 4.1. *A matrix $R \in \mathbb{F}_q^{m \times \ell}$ is $\mathbb{F}_p^h$-hiding if the first h inputs to R will stay hidden when the remaining inputs are secret and uniformly random. More precisely, if $\vec{x} \xleftarrow{\$} \mathbb{F}_p^\ell$ then $R\vec{x}$ must be independently random from $\vec{x}_{[h]}$*

Note that if R is $\mathbb{F}_p^h$-hiding then that it is $\mathbb{F}_q^h$-hiding, so if R is able to keep $U \in \mathbb{F}_p^{\ell \times k_c}$ hidden then it will keep $V \in \mathbb{F}_q^{\ell \times n_c}$ hidden as well.

Many useful universal hashes with elements in $\mathbb{F}_p$ satisfy this definition, including hashes based on polynomial evaluation or cyclic redundancy checks. That is, the last m columns of R will span the others, so R will be $\mathbb{F}_p^h$-hiding for $h = \ell - m$. However, this only works if the universal hash is over $\mathbb{F}_p$, rather than $\mathbb{F}_q$, as otherwise there won't be enough entropy in the last m columns to completely hide the other inputs. On the other hand, using a hash over $\mathbb{F}_q$ gives better compression. For a universal hash over $\mathbb{F}_p$, the best possible ϵ is about p^{-m}, while for $\mathbb{F}_q$ it is $q^{-m} = p^{-km}$. We believe that the best approach is to compose two universal hashes, first applying a $\mathbb{F}_p^{\ell-m'}$-hiding hash $R \in \mathcal{R} \subseteq \mathbb{F}_p^{m' \times \ell}$, then further reducing the output down to m entries with a second hash $R' \in \mathcal{R}' \subseteq \mathbb{F}_q^{m \times m'}$ where $m' \geq km$. The composed hash will be $\mathbb{F}_p^{\ell-m'}$-hiding, and will still be universal by Proposition 2.3.

Remark 4.2. P_S outputs $U_{[h]\cdot}, V_{[h]\cdot}$ in the first round, just after sending C and much before the protocol has actually completed. In applications where U will be derandomized immediately (e.g. chosen point OT extension), it is convenient to derandomize U at the same time as sending C. The protocol returning early is what allows this within the UC framework.

Remark 4.3. After sending C, P_S will not have many useful options to choose from, so the protocol notifies P_R with "commit" (as in $\mathcal{F}_{\text{VOLE-pre}}^{p,q,\mathcal{C},h,\mathcal{L},M}$) to indicate that P_S's inputs (mostly) fixed. In Sect. 5, this notification is used to send a second universal hash at the same time as R.

4.1   Flaws in Existing Consistency Checks

Given the similarity of Fig. 9 to the KOS, PSS, and OOS consistency checks, it seems natural to adapt their proofs to the subspace VOLE consistency checking protocol. However, it turns out that all three are flawed. To avoid three separate sets of notations for very similar protocols, we discuss their protocols and proofs using our notation. See the full version for a more detailed discussion of these flaws, using their original notation.

We first present the flaw in OOS, because it is most similar to our protocol.

Flaw in OOS's Proof. To get the OOS consistency check, take the protocol in Fig. 9 and set $p = q = 2$ and $R = \begin{bmatrix} X & \mathbb{1}_m \end{bmatrix}$, where $X \xleftarrow{\$} \mathbb{F}_2^{m \times \ell - m}$ is uniformly random. There are a couple of differences, but these do not affect the consistency check proper. Our sender is their receiver and vice versa, because they are implementing OT extension and we are doing subspace VOLE. And, they send a correction C for the whole of U' at once, instead of just the syndrome, because their OT choice bits are chosen rather than random.

Let $[U \; \bar{C}] = U'T_C^{-1} \oplus [0 \; C]$, so $\bar{C}$ is the error in the correction syndrome C sent by the malicious P_S. Similarly, let $\bar{U} = RU \oplus \tilde{U}$ and $\bar{V} = RV \oplus \tilde{V}$ be the errors in the consistency check messages sent by P_S. The consistency check then becomes $\bar{V} = [\bar{U} \; R\bar{C}]T_C \text{diag}(\tilde{\Delta})$ (see the proof of Theorem 4.5 for details). OOS define a set $E \subseteq [n_c]$ of column indices i where $([\bar{U} \; R\bar{C}]T_C)_{\cdot i}$ is nonzero. These are the indices i where Δ_i will have to be guessed by P_S in order to pass the consistency check. They then attempt to prove that the indices in E will be the only ones that P_S lied about. That is, their simulator tries to correct U to get P_S's real output $U^\star$, so that if $Z = [U^\star \ C]T_C \oplus U'$ then the indices of all the nonzero columns of Z are in E. This would let S update V accordingly, getting $V^\star = V \oplus Z\mathrm{diag}(\tilde{\Delta})$, which it could find because P_S must guess Δ_i for $i \in E$.

The flaw is in their proof that S can (with high probability, assuming that the check passes) extract $U^\star$. Their technique is to look at $Y = [U \ \bar{C}]T_C = U' \oplus [0 \ C]T_C$, whose rows would be in C if P_S were honest, and remove the columns in E to get a punctured matrix Y_{-E}. Then they decode the rows of Y_{-E} using the punctured code C_{-E} to get $U^\star$, since $Y \oplus Z = U^\star G_C$ and Z_{-E} should be 0. For this to work, they need the rows of Y_{-E} to be in C_{-E}. They try to prove this using the following lemma.

Lemma 4.4 (OOS, Lem. 1). *Let D be a linear code and $B \in \mathbb{F}_2^{\ell \times n_D}$ be a matrix, where not all rows of B are in D. If $X \xleftarrow{\$} \mathbb{F}_2^{m \times \ell - m}$ and $R = [X \ \mathbb{1}_m]$, then the probability that all rows of RB are in D is at most 2^{-m}.*

They apply this lemma with $D = C_{-E}$ and $B = Y_{-E}$. Note that $RY = [\bar{U} \ R\bar{C}]T_C \oplus \tilde{U}G_C$, so $RY_{-E} = \tilde{U}G_{C_{-E}}$ has all rows in C_{-E}. They conclude that with all but negligible probability, all rows of Y_{-E} are in C_{-E}. However, the lemma cannot be used in this way. The lemma requires that D and B be fixed in advance, *before* X is sampled, yet C_{-E} and Y_{-E} both depend on E. Recall that E is the set of nonzero columns of $[\bar{U} \ R\bar{C}]T_C$, which depends on both R directly, and on the consistency check message $\tilde{U}$ sent by P_S *after* it learns X.

While this shows that OOS's proof is wrong, we have not found any attacks that contradict their theorem statement. Additionally, a special case of our new proof (Theorem 4.5) shows that the OOS protocol is still secure, with statistical security only one bit less than was claimed.

Attack For PSS's Protocol. The PSS consistency checking protocol is similar to OOS's, though they only consider Walsh–Hadamard codes, and they generate $R \xleftarrow{\$} \mathbb{F}_2^{m \times \ell}$ using a coin flipping protocol. In Lemma IV.5, they have a similar proof issue to OOS, using Corollary IV.2 on dependent values when the corollary assumes they are independent. However, we focus on a more significant problem

The most important difference from OOS is that PSS attempt to compress the consistency check by summing the columns of $\tilde{V}$ to get $\tilde{v} = \tilde{V}[1 \cdots 1]^\top$. The consistency check is then that $\tilde{v}$ must equal $\left(RW \oplus \tilde{U}G_C\mathrm{diag}(\tilde{\Delta})\right)[1 \cdots 1]^\top = RW[1 \cdots 1]^\top \oplus \tilde{U}G_C\vec{\Delta}$. Let $\bar{C}, \bar{U}$, and $\bar{v}$ be defined analogously to our discussion of OOS. Then the consistency check is $\bar{v} = [\bar{U} \ R\bar{C}]T_C\vec{\Delta}$. This means that a malicious receiver only needs to guess XORs of multiple bits from $\tilde{\Delta}$, rather than the individual bits themselves.

We used this to create an attack against PSS. Have P_S lie about the bits in U' in length N intervals, where in the first OT it lies about the first N bits of $U'_{0.}$, and in the next OT the second N bits of $U'_{1.}$, and so on. Here, N is a parameter defining the tradeoff between computational cost and attack success rate. Then $[\bar{U} \ R\bar{C}]T_C$ will have rows spanned by these N bit intervals, so $[\bar{U} \ R\bar{C}]T_C\vec{\Delta}$ only depends on $\lceil \frac{n_c}{N} \rceil$ different values: $\bigoplus_{j=0}^{N-1} \Delta_{Ni+j}$ for $i \in [[\frac{n_c}{N}]]$. Therefore, the consistency check passes with probability $2^{-\lceil n_c/N \rceil}$, even though we have lied about all n_c bits. Later, having gotten away with these lies, the hashes output by the OT extension can be brute forced to solve for each N-bit chunk of $\tilde{\Delta}$ individually. This breaks the OT extension in time $\lceil \frac{n_c}{N} \rceil 2^{N-1}$. At the $\lambda = 128$ security level, $n_c = 256$, so by setting $N = 32$ we get an attack with success probability 2^{-8} that uses only 2^{34} hash evaluations.

Flaw in KOS's Proof. To turn out consistency check into KOS's, start by fixing $p = q = 2$ and $\mathcal{C} = \mathsf{Rep}(\mathbb{F}_2^\lambda)$. Let $\mathcal{R} = \mathbb{F}_2^{\lambda \times \ell}$, which means that R is $\mathbb{F}_2^{\ell - \lambda - \sigma}$-hiding with probability at least $1 - 2^{-\sigma}$. They use a coin flipping protocol to make sure that P_R cannot pick an R that is not hiding. Let α a primitive element of $\mathbb{F}_{2^\lambda}$, meaning that $\{1, \alpha, \ldots, \alpha^{\lambda-1}\}$ is a basis for $\mathbb{F}_{2^\lambda}$ over $\mathbb{F}_2$. The first half of the consistency check, $\tilde{U}$, works as normal, except that it gets encoded into a field element $u = \bigoplus_i \tilde{U}_i . \alpha^i = \vec{\alpha}^\top \tilde{U}$, where $\vec{\alpha} = [1, \alpha, \ldots, \alpha^{\lambda-1}]^\top$. The other half, $\tilde{V}$, is compressed from λ^2 bits down to λ bits by turning it into a single field element $v = \bigoplus_{ij} \tilde{V}_{ij} \alpha^{i+j} = \vec{\alpha}^\top \tilde{V} \vec{\alpha}$. Similarly, let $w = \vec{\alpha}^\top RW \vec{\alpha}$ and $\delta = \tilde{\Delta} \vec{\alpha}$. Then the consistency check becomes

$$v = \vec{\alpha}^\top RW \vec{\alpha} \oplus \vec{\alpha}^\top \tilde{U} G_\mathcal{C} \mathrm{diag}(\tilde{\Delta})\vec{\alpha}$$
$$= w \oplus u G_\mathcal{C} \mathrm{diag}(\tilde{\Delta})\vec{\alpha} = w \oplus u[1 \cdots 1]\mathrm{diag}(\tilde{\Delta})\vec{\alpha} = w \oplus u\delta.$$

Because $\mathcal{C}$ is a repetition code, U' is supposed to be derandomized so that all columns are identical to U. Let $Y = U' \oplus [0\ C]T_\mathcal{C}$ be the derandomization of U'. Then columns i and j are called *consistent* if they imply the same values of U, i.e. if $Y_{.i} = Y_{.j}$. Also let S_Δ be the set of possible Δ that cause the consistency check to succeed. KOS's proof of security for malicious P_S depends entirely on their Lemma 1, which states several properties of their consistency check. Most importantly, it implies that for any u, v sent by P_S, with probability $1 - 2^{-\lambda}$ there exists $k \in \mathbb{N}$ such that $|S_\Delta| = 2^k$ and k is at most the size of the largest group of consistent columns.

KOS gave no proof for Lemma 1, instead citing the full version of their paper, which has not been made public. However, the authors of KOS were kind enough to give an unpublished draft [KOS21]. Unfortunately, their proof has a similar flaw to OOS's, because they assume that R is sampled after S_Δ is known.

Unlike OOS, we found a counterexample to show that KOS's Lemma 1 is false, which we call a collision attack. Let the malicious P_S choose C uniformly at random (so Y will also be uniformly random) but still provide an honest v during the consistency check. Because of the correction P_R applies, W will be

$$W = V \oplus (U' \oplus [0\ C]T_\mathcal{C})\mathrm{diag}(\tilde{\Delta}) = V \oplus Y\mathrm{diag}(\tilde{\Delta})$$

Let $\bar{y} = \vec{\alpha}^\top RY$. The consistency check is then

$$v = \vec{\alpha}^\top RV\vec{\alpha} \oplus \vec{\alpha}^\top RY\mathrm{diag}(\tilde{\Delta})\vec{\alpha} \oplus u G_\mathcal{C} \mathrm{diag}(\tilde{\Delta})\vec{\alpha}$$
$$0 = (\bar{y} \oplus u[1 \cdots 1])\mathrm{diag}(\tilde{\Delta})\vec{\alpha}.$$

If u is set to be some element y_i of $\tilde{y}$, the consistency check at least won't depend on Δ_i. Since Y is uniformly random, $\tilde{y}$ will be as well, so the probability of a collision among the y_i is roughly $\lambda^2 2^{-\lambda-1}$. If there is a collision $y_i = y_j$ and P_R sets $u = y_i$, then $|S_\Delta| = 2^k = 4$. This contradicts KOS's Lemma 1 because k should be at most 1 as no two columns are consistent.

In the full version we present (using KOS's notation) a stronger attack against special parameters of KOS. Assuming that a certain MinRank problem always has a solution (and heuristically it should have $2^{\lambda/5}$ solutions on average), the attack succeeds in recovering Δ with probability $2^{-\frac{3}{5}\lambda}$ using $O(2^{\lambda/5})$ random oracle queries. While this is still not a practical attack, according to KOS's proof of their Theorem 1, an attack with this few random oracle queries should only succeed with probability $O(2^{-\frac{4}{5}\lambda})$.

4.2   Our New Proof

The biggest hurdle in the proof is the case where P_S is malicious. If P_S lies when it sends C, then it will have to guess some entries of Δ, but which entries depends on what $\tilde{U}$ it decides to send. As with OOS's flawed proof, P_S does not have to make up its mind until after seeing R, and generally speaking universal hashes are only strong when used on data that was chosen independently of the hash. We need to find some property that only depends on C and R so that we can show that it holds (with high probability) based on C being independent of R, then use it to prove security.

The property we found was that R should preserve all the lies in C. More precisely, if $\bar{C}$ is the difference between the honest C and the one P_S sent, then $R\bar{C}$ and $\bar{C}$ should have the same row space.[5] The idea is that, if R were the identity, the consistency check would clearly ensure that whatever incorrect value C that P_S provides, it can still guess matrices U, V that make the VOLE correlation hold. Although R is not the identity matrix, the check still ensures that the VOLE correlation holds for $\tilde{U}, \tilde{V}$. The lie-preserving property of R then shows that they contain enough information to correct the whole of U and V so that they do satisfy the VOLE correlation.

The proof of [CDD+16] is based on a similar lie-preserving property, but they analyze this property independently from the consistency check. This leads to a bound of $\Theta(\sqrt{\epsilon})$ on the distinguisher's advantage. We instead consider these events together, because the distinguisher only succeeds when it violates the property *and* passes the consistency check. The product of these event's probabilities is smaller than either individual probability, so we prove a much smaller distinguisher advantage bound of $\Theta(\epsilon)$.

Theorem 4.5. *The subspace VOLE protocol in Fig. 8 combined with the consistency checking protocol in Fig. 9 is a maliciously secure implementation of $\mathcal{F}_{VOLE\text{-}pre}^{p,q,C,h,\mathcal{L},M}$ if $\mathcal{L} \supseteq \text{Affine}(\mathbb{F}_q^{nc})$, assuming that $\mathcal{R} \subseteq \mathbb{F}_q^{m\times\ell}$ is a ϵ-almost universal family where all R are $\mathbb{F}_p^h$-hiding. The distinguisher has advantage at most*

---

[5] This fails if there are too many lies; however the VOLE would likely abort anyway.

$$\mathcal{S}^{p,q,\mathcal{C},\ell}_{\text{sub-VOLE-mal-R}}$$

recv. $\tilde{\Delta} \in \mathbb{F}_q^{n_c}, W' \in \mathbb{F}_q^{\ell \times n_c}$ from $\mathcal{A}$

send $\tilde{\Delta}, W'$ to P_R

$C \overset{\$}{\leftarrow} \mathbb{F}_p^{\ell \times (n_c - k_c)}$

send C to P_R

$W := W' - [0\ C] T_C \operatorname{diag}(\tilde{\Delta})$

send $\tilde{\Delta}, W_{[h]\cdot}$ to $\mathcal{F}^{p,q,\mathcal{C},h,\mathcal{L},M}_{\text{VOLE-pre}}$

recv. $R \in \mathcal{R}$ from P_R

$U_\$ \overset{\$}{\leftarrow} \mathbb{F}_q^{\ell \times k_c}$

$\tilde{U} := RU_\$$

$\tilde{V} := RW - \tilde{U} G_C \operatorname{diag}(\tilde{\Delta})$

send $\tilde{U}, \tilde{V}$ to P_R

$\underline{\operatorname{Precom}(\bar{C}, R, R^{-1}):}$

$\mathcal{W}_{\text{pre}} := \{\bar{U} \in \mathbb{F}_q^{m \times k_c} \mid t \geq \| [\bar{U}\ \ R\bar{C}] T_C \|_0\}$

$U^*_{\text{pre}}(\bar{U}) := U - R^{-1}\bar{U}$

$V^*_{\text{pre}}(\bar{U}, \tilde{\Delta}) := V + R^{-1}[\bar{U}\ \ R\bar{C}] T_C \operatorname{diag}(\tilde{\Delta})$

$L'_0 := L' - \tilde{\Delta}_0$ for some $\tilde{\Delta}_0 \in L'$

$L_{\text{pre}}(\bar{U}) := L'_0 \cap \{\tilde{\Delta} \mid 0 = [\bar{U}\ \ R\bar{C}] T_C \operatorname{diag}(\tilde{\Delta})\}$

return $\mathcal{W}_{\text{pre}}, U^*_{\text{pre}}, V^*_{\text{pre}}, L_{\text{pre}}$

$$\mathcal{S}^{p,q,\mathcal{C},\ell}_{\text{sub-VOLE-mal-S}}$$

recv. $U' \in \mathbb{F}_p^{\ell \times n_c}, V \in \mathbb{F}_q^{\ell \times n_c}$ from $\mathcal{A}$

send U', V to P_S

recv. $L' \in \mathcal{L}$ from P_S:

recv. $C \in \mathbb{F}_p^{\ell \times (n_c - k_c)}$ from P_S

$[U\ \bar{C}] := U' T_C^{-1} - [0\ C]$

$R \overset{\$}{\leftarrow} \mathcal{R}$

abort if $\operatorname{rank}(R\bar{C}) < \operatorname{rank}(\bar{C})$

find $R^{-1} \in \mathbb{F}_q^{\ell \times m}$ s.t. $R^{-1}R\bar{C} = \bar{C}$

$\mathcal{W}_{\text{pre}}, U^*_{\text{pre}}, V^*_{\text{pre}}, L_{\text{pre}} := \operatorname{Precom}(\bar{C}, R, R^{-1})$

send $\mathcal{W}_{\text{pre}}, U^*_{\text{pre}}, V^*_{\text{pre}}, L_{\text{pre}}$ to $\mathcal{F}^{p,q,\mathcal{C},h,\mathcal{L},M}_{\text{VOLE-pre}}$

send R to P_S

recv. $\tilde{U} \in \mathbb{F}_q^{m \times k_c}, \tilde{V} \in \mathbb{F}_q^{m \times n_c}$ from P_S

$\bar{U} := RU - \tilde{U};\quad U^* := U^*_{\text{pre}}(\bar{U})$

$\bar{V} := RV - \tilde{V};\quad V^* := V - R^{-1}\bar{V}$

send $U^*_{[h]\cdot}, V^*_{[h]\cdot}$ to $\mathcal{F}^{p,q,\mathcal{C},h,\mathcal{L},M}_{\text{VOLE-pre}}$

find $\tilde{L}_{\text{off}} \in -L'$ s.t. $\bar{V} = [\bar{U}\ \ R\bar{C}] T_C \operatorname{diag}(\tilde{L}_{\text{off}})$

abort if none exist

send $\bar{U}, \tilde{L}_{\text{off}}$ to $\mathcal{F}^{p,q,\mathcal{C},h,\mathcal{L},M}_{\text{VOLE-pre}}$

Fig. 10. Simulators for malicious security of Fig. 8 combined with Fig. 9, for a single corrupt party. $\mathcal{S}^{p,q,\mathcal{C},\ell}_{\text{sub-VOLE-mal-R}}$ is for corrupt P_R, while $\mathcal{S}^{p,q,\mathcal{C},\ell}_{\text{sub-VOLE-mal-S}}$ is for corrupt P_S.

$$\frac{\epsilon q}{q-1} + q^{-t-1}, \text{ where } t = \frac{d_C}{1 + \sqrt{1 + \frac{d_C}{n_C} - \frac{1}{n_C^2}}} \geq \frac{d_C}{2} \text{ and } M = n_C(d_C - t).$$

Note: when instantiated as in OOS, $\epsilon = 2^{-m}$ and $q = 2$, so our proof shows that OOS has only 1 bit less statistical security than was claimed. The q^{-t-1} term only matters for the pre-commitment property, which OOS does not consider.

Proof. There are four cases, depending on which parties are corrupted. If both parties are corrupted then the real protocol can be simulated trivially, by ignoring the ideal functionality and just passing messages between the corrupted parties. If both players are honest, the situation is very similar to the semi-honest protocol (Theorem 3.2). The only difference is the additional two rounds, which can be simulated by picking a random $R \in \mathcal{R}$, as well as sampling fake P_S values $U_\$ \overset{\$}{\leftarrow} \mathbb{F}_p^{\ell \times k_c}$ and $V_\$ \overset{\$}{\leftarrow} \mathbb{F}_p^{\ell \times n_c}$ and simulating the third round as $\tilde{U} = RU_\$, \tilde{V} = RV_\$$. Since both parties are honest, U and V are uniformly random, and so Definition 4.1 guarantees that these fakes are indistinguishable from the real consistency check.

The situation is similar when only P_R is corrupted (simulator in Fig. 10, top left). Following the same principle as for the semi-honest protocol, $\mathcal{S}$ starts by performing the computations that an honest P_R would, while randomly sampling a fake syndrome C to send. To simulate the consistency check, after receiving R, the simulator fakes $\tilde{U}$ like in the honest–honest case, then solves for $\tilde{V}$ as the only possibility that will pass the consistency check. The real protocol and the simulation are indistinguishable because the honesty of P_S implies that the consistency check will always pass, so the formula for $\tilde{V}$ must always hold, and P_R cannot tell that $\tilde{U}$ was generated from the fake $U_\$$ because R is $\mathbb{F}_p^h$-hiding.

The most interesting case is when P_S is corrupt. We present a hybrid proof, starting with the real world, where the real protocol gets executed using the underlying ideal functionality $\mathcal{F}_{\mathsf{VOLE}}^{p,q,\mathbb{F}_p^{n_C},\ell,\mathcal{L}}$, and work towards the ideal world, where the simulator (Fig. 10, right) liaises between the corrupted sender and the desired ideal functionality $\mathcal{F}_{\mathsf{VOLE\text{-}pre}}^{p,q,\mathcal{C},h,\mathcal{L},M}$.

1. Compute what P_S's honest output would be, and the difference between the honest syndrome and the one P_S provided: $[U\ \bar{C}] = U'T_C^{-1} - [0\ C]$. Add a check after P_S sends $\tilde{U}$ and $\tilde{V}$, where if $\mathrm{rank}(R\bar{C}) < \mathrm{rank}(\bar{C})$, "check failed" is sent to P_R and the protocol aborts. The environment's advantage for this step is the probability that this abort triggers and the protocol would not have aborted anyway. We bound this probability using the following lemma.

Lemma 4.6. *Let $\mathcal{R} \subseteq \mathbb{F}_q^{m \times n}$ be a linear ϵ-almost universal family, and let A be any matrix in $\mathbb{F}_q^{n \times l}$. Then, $\mathbb{E}_{R \xleftarrow{\$} \mathcal{R}}\left[q^{\mathrm{rank}(A)-\mathrm{rank}(RA)} - 1\right] \leq \epsilon(q^{\mathrm{rank}(A)} - 1)$.*

Proof. By the rank–nullity theorem, R defines an isomorphism $\mathbb{F}_q^n / \ker(R) \cong \mathrm{colspace}(R)$. Its restriction to $\mathrm{colspace}(A)$ gives an isomorphism $\mathrm{colspace}(A) / \ker(R) \cong \mathrm{colspace}(RA)$. Therefore,

$$
\begin{aligned}
\mathrm{rank}(RA) &= \dim(\mathrm{colspace}(RA)) \\
&= \dim(\mathrm{colspace}(A)) - \dim(\mathrm{colspace}(A) \cap \ker(R)) \\
&= \mathrm{rank}(A) - \dim(\mathrm{colspace}(A) \cap \ker(R)).
\end{aligned}
$$

We then want to bound the expected value of $X = q^{\dim(\mathrm{colspace}(A) \cap \ker(R))} - 1 = |\mathrm{colspace}(A) \cap \ker(R) \backslash \{0\}|$. That is, X is the number of nonzero $v \in \mathrm{colspace}(A)$ such that $Rv = 0$. By Definition 2.1, for any particular $v \neq 0$ the probability that $Rv = 0$ is at most ϵ. Since X is the sum of $|\mathrm{colspace}(A) \backslash \{0\}| = q^{\mathrm{rank}(A)} - 1$ indicator random variables, we get $\mathbb{E}[X] \leq \epsilon(q^{\mathrm{rank}(A)} - 1)$. $\square$

For the real protocol to not abort, $\tilde{V} = RW - \tilde{U}G_C\mathrm{diag}(\breve{\Delta})$ must hold. Because P_R is uncorrupted, $\breve{\Delta}$ is sampled uniformly in $\mathbb{F}_q^{n_c}$ and W' is computed as $U'\mathrm{diag}(\breve{\Delta}) + V$. Therefore,

$$
\begin{aligned}
W = W' - [0\ C]T_C\mathrm{diag}(\breve{\Delta}) &= (U' - [0\ C]T_C)\mathrm{diag}(\breve{\Delta}) + V \\
&= [U\ \bar{C}]T_C\mathrm{diag}(\breve{\Delta}) + V.
\end{aligned}
$$

Let $\bar{U} = RU - \tilde{U}$ and $\bar{V} = RV - \tilde{V}$ be the differences between the honest consistency check messages and the ones sent by P_S. Then the consistency check is equivalent to $-\bar{V} = [\bar{U}\ R\bar{C}]T_C\mathrm{diag}(\breve{\Delta})$. Next, we need to bound

$$
\begin{aligned}
P &= \Pr[\text{abort} \wedge \text{check passes}] \\
&= \Pr[\mathrm{rank}(R\bar{C}) < \mathrm{rank}(\bar{C}) \wedge -\bar{V} = [\bar{U}\ R\bar{C}]T_C\mathrm{diag}(\breve{\Delta})].
\end{aligned}
$$

Triggering this condition requires guessing $[\bar{U} \quad R\bar{C}]T_C\mathrm{diag}(\tilde{\Delta})$, i.e. guessing Δ_i for every nonzero column $([\bar{U} \quad R\bar{C}]T_C)_{.i}$. Let $N = \| [\bar{U} \quad R\bar{C}]T_C\|_0$ be the number of these nonzero columns. A lower bound for N is $\mathrm{rank}([\bar{U} \quad R\bar{C}]T_C)$, because every zero column does not contribute to the rank. T_C is invertible, so multiplying by it does not change the rank. Adding extra columns only increases rank, so $\mathrm{rank}([\bar{U} \quad R\bar{C}]) \geq \mathrm{rank}(R\bar{C})$. Up until the consistency check, the behavior of P_R has been independent of $\tilde{\Delta}$, and N is also independent of $\tilde{\Delta}$, so $\Pr[\mathrm{check} \mid N] \leq q^{-N}$. Let $r = \mathrm{rank}(\bar{C}) - \mathrm{rank}(R\bar{C})$, so $N \geq \mathrm{rank}(\bar{C}) - r$. Then $P \leq \mathbb{E}[q^{-\mathrm{rank}(\bar{C})+r} \mathbb{1}_{r\geq 1}]$, since the added abort occurs exactly when $r \geq 1$, and expectation of conditional probability is marginal probability.

Now, apply Lemma 4.6 to $\bar{C}$ to get $\mathbb{E}[q^r - 1] \leq \epsilon(q^{\mathrm{rank}(\bar{C})} - 1)$. If $r \geq 1$ then $\frac{q^r}{q^r-1} \leq \frac{q}{q-1}$. Multiply both sides by $q^r - 1$ to get

$$q^r \mathbb{1}_{r\geq 1} \leq \frac{q}{q-1}(q^r - 1).$$

$$P \leq \mathbb{E}[q^{-\mathrm{rank}(\bar{C})+r}\mathbb{1}_{r\geq 1}] \leq \epsilon\frac{q}{q-1}\frac{(q^{\mathrm{rank}(\bar{C})}-1)}{q^{\mathrm{rank}(\bar{C})}} \leq \epsilon\frac{q}{q-1}$$

2. After checking that $\mathrm{rank}(R\bar{C}) = \mathrm{rank}(\bar{C})$, find $R^{-1} \in \mathbb{F}_q^{\ell \times m}$ such that $R^{-1}R\bar{C} = \bar{C}$. To do this, find the reduced row echelon forms $F = AR\bar{C}$ and $F' = B\bar{C}$ of $R\bar{C}$ and $\bar{C}$, where $A \in \mathbb{F}_q^{m \times m}$ and $B \in \mathbb{F}_p^{\ell \times \ell}$ are invertible matrices. Because they have the same rank, $R\bar{C}$ and $\bar{C}$ must have the same row space. The uniqueness of reduced row echelon forms implies that all nonzero rows of F and F' will be identical, so

$$F' = \begin{bmatrix} F \\ 0 \end{bmatrix} \quad \text{and} \quad \bar{C} = B^{-1}F' = B^{-1}\begin{bmatrix} \mathbb{1}_m \\ 0 \end{bmatrix}F = B^{-1}\begin{bmatrix} \mathbb{1}_m \\ 0 \end{bmatrix}AR\bar{C},$$

which gives a formula for R^{-1}.

Correct P_S's VOLE correlation as $U^\star = U - R^{-1}\bar{U}$ and $V^\star = V - R^{-1}\bar{V}$. Then, assuming that the consistency check passes,

$$W = [U \quad \bar{C}]T_C\mathrm{diag}(\tilde{\Delta}) + V$$
$$= [(U^\star + R^{-1}\bar{U}) \quad \bar{C}]T_C\mathrm{diag}(\tilde{\Delta}) + V^\star + R^{-1}\bar{V}$$
$$= U^\star G_C\mathrm{diag}(\tilde{\Delta}) + V^\star + R^{-1}\left([\bar{U} \quad R\bar{C}]T_C\mathrm{diag}(\tilde{\Delta}) + \bar{V}\right)$$
$$= U^\star G_C\mathrm{diag}(\tilde{\Delta}) + V^\star.$$

3. Let $\mathcal{W}_{\mathrm{pre}} = \mathbb{F}_q^{m \times k_C}$, then run $\mathsf{Precom}(\bar{C}, R, R^{-1})$ to get the pre-commitment functions $U_{\mathrm{pre}}^\star, V_{\mathrm{pre}}^\star, L_{\mathrm{pre}}$ as in the simulator, as well as $\tilde{\Delta}_0 \in L'$ and $L'_0 = L' - \tilde{\Delta}_0$. Also, find some $\tilde{L}_{\mathrm{off}} \in -L'$ where $\bar{V} = [\bar{U} \quad R\bar{C}]T_C\mathrm{diag}(\tilde{L}_{\mathrm{off}})$. Replace the underlying guess $\tilde{\Delta} \in L'$ and the consistency check $-\bar{V} = [\bar{U} \quad R\bar{C}]T_C\mathrm{diag}(\tilde{\Delta})$ with $\tilde{\Delta} + \tilde{L}_{\mathrm{off}} \in L_{\mathrm{pre}}(\bar{U})$. When such an $\tilde{L}_{\mathrm{off}}$ exists, we need to show that this is equivalent to the consistency check. L'_0 is the linear subspace obtained by shifting L' to go through the origin, so $\tilde{\Delta} + \tilde{L}_{\mathrm{off}} \in L'_0$ if and only if $\tilde{\Delta} \in L'$

because $\tilde{\Delta} + \tilde{L}_{\text{off}}$ is the difference of two elements of the affine subspace L'. When $\tilde{\Delta} + \tilde{L}_{\text{off}} \in L'_0$, we have that $\tilde{\Delta} + \tilde{L}_{\text{off}} \in L_{\text{pre}}(\bar{U})$ is equivalent to $0 = [\bar{U} \ \ R\bar{C}]T_{\mathcal{C}}\text{diag}(\tilde{\Delta} + \tilde{L}_{\text{off}})$, which equals $[\bar{U} \ \ R\bar{C}]T_{\mathcal{C}}\text{diag}(\tilde{\Delta}) + \bar{V}$. The latter being zero is the consistency check.

We must also show that if the consistency check would pass, then a solution $\tilde{L}_{\text{off}}$ must exist. Assume that there exists some $\tilde{\Delta}_1 \in L'$ that would pass the consistency check, i.e. $-\bar{V} = [\bar{U} \ \ R\bar{C}]T_{\mathcal{C}}\text{diag}(\tilde{\Delta}_1)$. Then $-\tilde{\Delta}_1 \in -L'$ is a valid solution for $\tilde{L}_{\text{off}}$.

4. Factor out the sampling of Δ, the computation of $W_{[h]\cdot} = U^{\star}_{[h]\cdot}\text{diag}(\tilde{\Delta}) + V^{\star}_{[h]\cdot}$, and the selective abort attack $\tilde{\Delta} + \tilde{L}_{\text{off}} \in L_{\text{pre}}(\bar{U})$ into the ideal functionality $\mathcal{F}^{p,q,\mathcal{C},h,\mathcal{L},M}_{\text{VOLE-pre}}$. The ideal functionality also includes an abort if $U^{\star} \neq U^{\star}_{\text{pre}}(\bar{U})$ or $V^{\star} \neq V^{\star}_{\text{pre}}(\bar{U}, \tilde{\Delta})$, and we must show that neither will occur. The former cannot occur because that is exactly how $U^{\star}$ is calculated. For the latter, when the consistency check passes we have

$$V^{\star}_{\text{pre}}(\bar{U}, \tilde{\Delta}) = V + R^{-1}[\bar{U} \ \ R\bar{C}]T_{\mathcal{C}}\text{diag}(\tilde{\Delta}) = V - R^{-1}\bar{V} = V^{\star}.$$

5. We are now almost at the ideal world. We just need to change $\mathcal{W}_{\text{pre}}$ to be $\{\bar{U} \in \mathbb{F}^{m \times k_{\mathcal{C}}}_q \mid t \geq \| [\bar{U} \ \ R\bar{C}]T_{\mathcal{C}}\|_0\}$, as in the simulator, and show that $|\mathcal{W}_{\text{pre}}| \leq M$. Changing $\mathcal{W}_{\text{pre}}$ is only detectable if $\bar{U} \notin \mathcal{W}_{\text{pre}}$ and the consistency check still passes. Then the adversary must guess $\| [\bar{U} \ \ R\bar{C}]T_{\mathcal{C}}\|_0 \geq t + 1$ entries of $\tilde{\Delta}$, which has negligible probability q^{-t-1}. We just need to choose t to be as large as possible while keeping M small.

Finding a $\bar{U}$ such that $[\bar{U} \ \ R\bar{C}]T_{\mathcal{C}} = \bar{U}G_{\mathcal{C}} + [0 \ \ R\bar{C}]T_{\mathcal{C}}$ has few nonzero columns is equivalent to a bounded distance decoding problem over $\mathbb{F}_{q^m}$. That is, interpreting each column as an element of $\mathbb{F}_{q^m}$, $\bar{U}G_{\mathcal{C}}$ must be a code word close to $-[0 \ \ R\bar{C}]T_{\mathcal{C}}$ in Hamming weight. The simplest choice would be to set t to be the decoding radius $\lfloor \frac{d_{\mathcal{C}}-1}{2} \rfloor$ of $\mathcal{C}$, guaranteeing that there is at most a single element of $\mathcal{W}_{\text{pre}}$. To get a tighter bound, we use the Cassuto–Bruck list decoding bound [CB04], which implies $M \leq n_{\mathcal{C}}(d_{\mathcal{C}} - t)$ when $t = \dfrac{d_{\mathcal{C}}}{1 + \sqrt{1 + \frac{d_{\mathcal{C}}}{n_{\mathcal{C}}} - \frac{1}{n_{\mathcal{C}}^2}}}$.

Optimizations. There are a couple ways that the communication complexity of Fig. 9 can be improved. First, if the universal hash R contains a lot of entropy, a seed $s \in \{0,1\}^{\lambda}$ may be sent instead, so $R = \text{PRG}(s)$. The only place the randomness of R was used was to upper bound the probability that $\text{rank}(R\bar{C}) < \text{rank}(\bar{C})$. $\bar{C}$ cannot depend on s, so if using a PRG changed this probability more than negligibly then there would be an attack against the PRG.

A second optimization is to hash $\tilde{V}$ with a local random oracle Hash before sending it, because all that's needed is an equality check. The simulator (in the malicious P_S case) could then extract $\tilde{V}$ from its hash, then continue as usual. Interestingly, for concrete security it would be fine even if Hash were just an arbitrary collision resistant hash. Looking at just $\bar{C}$ and $\tilde{U}$, the simulator can see which entries of $\tilde{\Delta}$ are being guessed, though not what the guesses are. By

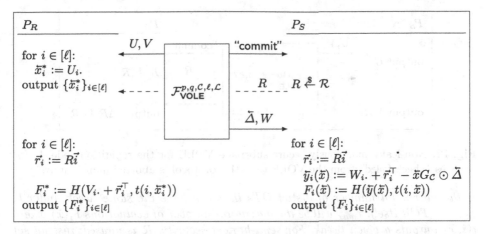

Fig. 11. $\binom{p^{kc}}{1}$-OT extension protocol. Note that the parties for the base VOLE are swapped, with P_S (instead of P_R) getting $\tilde{\Delta}$. If P_S receives "check failed" from the VOLE then the protocol is aborted immediately. For semi-honest security, the "commit" and R steps are skipped, and $\vec{r}_i := 0$.

looping through a random subset of 2^σ possible guesses (and for the usual setting of $\sigma = 40$ this is quite feasible), $\mathcal{S}$ can find the preimage of $\mathsf{Hash}(\tilde{V})$ often enough to only give the distinguisher an additional advantage of $2^{-\sigma}$.

5 OT Extension

Now that we have constructed subspace VOLE, it is time to go back to our original goal: OT extension. Like previous OT extensions, we hash our correlated randomness in order to get random OTs. For malicious security, our protocol (Fig. 11) follows [CT21] in using a universal hash to avoid collisions between extended OTs, avoiding the need for a TCR hash. However, a TCR hash allows for better concrete security (at they expense of performance) by reducing $\tau_{\max}$, which is the maximum number of queries $H(\tilde{y}, \tau)$ on the same tweak τ. We allow an arbitrary function $t(i, \tilde{x})$ to control how many different hashes use the same tweak. Unlike [CT21], our analysis allows R to be sent in parallel with the VOLE protocol, saving a round of communication.

For generality, we allow any finite field, but we expect that $p = 2$ will be most efficient in almost all cases. We equivocate between the choices U_i in $\mathbb{F}_p^{kc}$ from the VOLE, and the choices x_i^* in $[p^{kc}]$ expected for OT. This can be thought of as writing x_i^* in base p.

Theorem 5.1. *The protocol in Fig. 11 achieves $\mathcal{F}_{OT\text{-}1}^{p^{kc}, \ell, \{X\}}$ with malicious security in the $\mathcal{F}_{VOLE\text{-}pre}^{p,q,\mathcal{C},\ell,\mathcal{L},M}$ hybrid model, assuming that $H \colon \mathbb{F}_q^{nc} \times \mathcal{T} \to \{0,1\}^\lambda$ is a $(p, q, \mathcal{C}, \mathcal{T}, \mathcal{L})$-TCR hash, and $\mathcal{R} \subseteq \mathbb{F}_q^{nc \times \lceil \log_q(\ell) \rceil}$ is an ϵ-almost uniform family. $\epsilon M \ell (t_{max} - 1)/2 + \mathsf{Adv}_{TCR}$, where t_{max}*

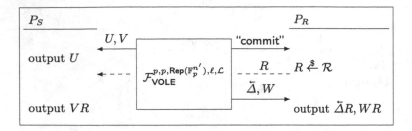

Fig. 12. Non-leaky maliciously secure subspace VOLE for the repetition code. If P_R receives "check failed" from the VOLE then the protocol is aborted immediately.

is the maximum number of distict OTs that can have the same tweak under t. For the TCR itself, τ_{max} will be the maximum number of evaluations $F_i(\tilde{x})$ where $t(i, \tilde{x})$ outputs a given tweak. For semi-honest security, $\mathcal{R}$ is unused; instead set $\epsilon = q^{-nc}$ and $M = 1$.

Proof. See the full version of this work.

5.1 Δ-OT

A common variant of OT extension is Δ-OT (a.k.a. correlated OT), where all OT messages follow the pattern $m_0, m_1 = m_0 \oplus \Delta$. It is useful for authenticated secret sharing and garbled circuits. More generally, over a larger field, it works as $m_x = m_0 + x\Delta$, and is useful for encoding the inputs to arithmetic garbling [BMR16].

Δ-OT works easily as a special case of subspace VOLE where $q = p$ and $\mathcal{C} = \mathsf{Rep}(\mathbb{F}_p^n)$,[6] except which party is called the sender and which the receiver is swapped, like with OT extension. However, in the malicious setting our subspace VOLE allows a selective abort attack, and while for some applications (such as garbling) it may be allowed to leak a few bits for Δ, in others it may not. [BLN+15] solve this problem by multiplying the Δ-OT messages by a uniformly random rectangular matrix, throwing away some of the OT message. With high probability, any correlation among the bits of Δ is also lost, resulting in a non-leaky Δ-OT. In Fig. 12, we generalize this idea to use a universal hash, which can be more computationally efficient than a random matrix.

Theorem 5.2. *The protocol in Fig. 12 achieves $\mathcal{F}_{VOLE}^{p,p,\mathsf{Rep}(\mathbb{F}_p^n),\ell,\{X\}}$ with malicious security in the $\mathcal{F}_{VOLE\text{-}pre}^{p,p,\mathsf{Rep}(\mathbb{F}_p^{n'}),\ell,\mathrm{Affine}(\mathbb{F}_p^{n'}),M}$ hybrid model, assuming that $\mathcal{R} \subseteq \mathbb{F}_p^{n' \times n}$ is a ϵ-almost uniform family and $n' \geq n$. The advantage is bounded by $\epsilon M(p^n - 1)$.*

Proof. See the full version of this work.

Note that if $\mathcal{R}$ has the optimal $\epsilon = p^{-n'}$, such as when it is a uniformly random matrix, the environment's advantage is upper bounded by $Mp^{n-n'}$. Therefore, n' should be set to $n + \log_p(2)\sigma$ for security.

---

[6] Note that subspace VOLE with $q = p^k$ and $\mathcal{C} = \mathsf{Rep}(\mathbb{F}_p^n)$ can easily be turned into VOLE for $q = p$ and $\mathcal{C} = \mathsf{Rep}(\mathbb{F}_p^{kn})$, by interpreting $\mathbb{F}_q$ as a vector space over $\mathbb{F}_p$.

P_S		P_R

$$\xleftarrow{\hspace{1.5cm} \{F_i\}_{i\in[k]} \hspace{1.5cm}}$$

$$\mathcal{F}^{p,k,\mathcal{L}}_{\mathsf{OT\text{-}\bar{1}}} \quad \xrightarrow{\hspace{0.3cm} \{x_i^*, F_i^*\}_{i\in[k]} \hspace{0.3cm}}$$

$G, t := \mathsf{BuildPPRF}(F)$

$$\xrightarrow{\hspace{1cm} \{t_x^i \in \{0,1\}^\lambda\}_{1\le i < k, x\in[p]} \hspace{1cm}}$$

output G

output $\mathsf{EvalPPRF}(x^*, F^*, t)$

$\mathsf{BuildPPRF}(F)$:	$\mathsf{EvalPPRF}(x^*, F^*, t)$:
$\quad$ for $x \in [p]$:	$\quad$ for $x \in [p] \setminus \{x_0^*\}$:
$\quad\quad s_x^1 := F_0(x)$	$\quad\quad s_x^{*\,1} := F_0^*(x)$
	$\quad\quad y_1^* := x_0^*$
$\quad$ for $i := 1$ to $k - 1$:	$\quad$ for $i := 1$ to $k - 1$:
$\quad\quad$ for $y \in [p^i]$, $x \in [p]$:	$\quad\quad$ for $y \in [p^i] \setminus \{y_i^*\}$, $x \in [p]$:
$\quad\quad\quad s_{py+x}^{i+1} := \mathsf{PRG}_x(s_y^i)$	$\quad\quad\quad s_{py+x}^{*\,i+1} := \mathsf{PRG}_x(s_y^{*\,i})$
$\quad\quad$ for $x \in [p]$:	$\quad\quad$ for $x \in [p] \setminus \{x_i^*\}$:
$\quad\quad\quad t_x^i := F_i(x) \oplus \bigoplus\limits_{y\in[p^i]} s_{py+x}^{i+1}$	$\quad\quad\quad s_{py_i^*+x}^{*\,i+1} := t_x^i \oplus F_i^*(x) \oplus \bigoplus\limits_{y\in[p^i]\setminus\{y_i^*\}} s_{py+x}^{*\,i+1}$
	$\quad\quad y_{i+1}^* := py_i^* + x_i^*$
$\quad$ return $(y \mapsto s_y^k), t$	$\quad$ return $y^*, (y \mapsto s_y^{*\,k-1})$

Fig. 13. Protocol for $\binom{q}{q-1}$-OT based on $\binom{p}{p-1}$-OT, using a punctured PRF.

6 Base OTs

Our small field VOLE (Fig. 7) is based on $\binom{q}{q-1}$-OT, yet actual base OTs are generally $\binom{2}{1}$-OT. We follow [BGI17] in using a punctured PRF to efficiently construct $\binom{N}{N-1}$-OT. Our protocol (see Fig. 13) is based on the optimized version in [SGRR19], which generates $\binom{p^k}{p^k-1}$-OT from k $\binom{p}{p-1}$-OTs.

It depends on a $\mathsf{PRG}\colon \{0,1\}^\lambda \to (\{0,1\}^\lambda)^p$. The xth block of λ bits from this PRG is written as $\mathsf{PRG}_x(s)$. The PRG is used to create a GGM tree [GGM86]. Starting at the root of the tree, P_R gets $p-1$ of the p children from $\mathcal{F}^{p,k,\mathrm{Affine}(\mathbb{F}_p^k)}_{\mathsf{OT\text{-}\bar{1}}}$, and at every level down the tree the protocol maintains the property that P_R knows all but one of the nodes at that level. Each level i of the tree is numbered from 0 to $p^i - 1$, with the yth node in the layer containing the value s_y^i. This means that the children of node s_y^i are $s_{py+x}^{i+1} = \mathsf{PRG}_x(s_y^i)$, for $x \in [p]$. P_S computes the whole GGM tree in $\mathsf{BuildPPRF}$, finds the totals $t_x^i = \bigoplus_y s_{py+x}^{i+1}$ for each x, and uses the ith base OT to send all but one of these totals to P_R. Let y_i^* be the index of the node on the active path in layer i, i.e., the layer i node that P_R cannot learn. Then P_R will know every s_y^i except for $s_{y_i^*}^i$, so it can compute $s_{py_i^*+x}^{i+1} = t_x^i \oplus \bigoplus_{y\neq y_i^*} s_{py+x}^{i+1}$. Thus, it learns s_y^{i+1} for all $y \neq y_{i+1}^*$. In the full version, we prove that the leaves becomes the messages of an $\binom{p^k}{p^k-1}$-OT.

Theorem 6.1. *Figure 13 constructs* $\mathcal{F}^{q,1,\{X\}}_{\mathsf{OT\text{-}\bar{1}}}$ *out of* $\mathcal{F}^{p,k,\{X\}}_{\mathsf{OT\text{-}\bar{1}}}$, *and is secure in the semi-honest model.*

P_S	P_R
$\tilde{s}, \tilde{t} := \mathsf{ProvePPRF}(G)$ $\quad\xrightarrow{\tilde{s},\tilde{t}\,\in\,\{0,1\}^{2\lambda}}\quad$	
	abort if $\tilde{s} \neq \mathsf{VerifyPPRF}(y^*, G^*, \tilde{t})$
output $\mathsf{PRG}_1' \circ G$	output $y^*, \mathsf{PRG}_1' \circ G^*$

$$
\begin{array}{ll}
\underline{\mathsf{ProvePPRF}(G):} & \underline{\mathsf{VerifyPPRF}(y^*, G^*, \tilde{t}):}\\[4pt]
\quad \text{for } y \in [q]: & \quad \text{for } y \in [q] \setminus \{y^*\}:\\
\qquad \tilde{s}_y := \mathsf{PRG}_0'(G(y)) & \qquad \tilde{s}_y^* := \mathsf{PRG}_0'(G^*(y))\\
\quad \tilde{t} := \bigoplus_{y\in[q]} \tilde{s}_y & \quad \tilde{s}_{y^*}^* := \tilde{t} \oplus \bigoplus_{y\in[q]\setminus\{y^*\}} \tilde{s}_y^*\\
\quad \tilde{s} := \mathsf{Hash}(\tilde{s}_0 \| \cdots \| \tilde{s}_{q-1}) & \quad \tilde{s} := \mathsf{Hash}(\tilde{s}_0^* \| \cdots \| \tilde{s}_{q-1}^*)\\
\quad \text{return } \tilde{s}, \tilde{t} & \quad \text{return } \tilde{s}
\end{array}
$$

Fig. 14. Consistency checking for $\binom{q}{q-1}$-OT. This makes Fig. 13 maliciously secure.

While the protocol only does a single $\binom{q}{q-1}$-OT from a batch of k $\binom{p}{p-1}$-OTs, it should be clear that a batch of n $\binom{q}{q-1}$-OT can be constructed from a batch of nk $\binom{p}{p-1}$-OTs. For $p = 2$, the base $\binom{p}{p-1}$-OTs are just $\binom{2}{1}$-OTs. For $p > 2$, they can be constructed from chosen message $\binom{p}{1}$-OT, by sending just the messages P_R is supposed to see.

6.1 Consistency Checking

In Fig. 14, we present the consistency check from the maliciously secure $\binom{2^k}{2^k-1}$-OT of [BCG+19a]. We prove a stronger property of their check, that P_S can only check guesses for the x_i^*s individually, not all of them together, which shows that any possible selective abort attack is in $\mathrm{Affine}(\mathbb{F}_p^k)$. This assumes that PRG is collision resistant for its whole output, so there are no $s \neq s'$ such that $\mathsf{PRG}_x(s) = \mathsf{PRG}_x(s')$ for all $x \in [p]$. As in [BCG+19a], the protocol needs a second PRG, $\mathsf{PRG}': \{0,1\}^\lambda \to \{0,1\}^{2\lambda} \times \{0,1\}^\lambda$, which must be collision resistant in its first output PRG_0'. In the consistency check, P_S sends the total of all $\tilde{s}_y^k = \mathsf{PRG}_0'(s_y^k)$ so that P_R can reconstruct $\tilde{s}_{y^*}^k$. P_R then evaluates a collision resistant hash of all the $\tilde{s}_y^k$ and checks that it matches the hash from P_S. As we prove in the full version, this commits P_S to a single possibility for each $\tilde{s}_y^k$.

Theorem 6.2. *Figure 14 (composed with Fig. 13) is a maliciously secure* $\mathcal{F}_{OT\text{-}\bar{1}}^{q,1,\mathrm{Affine}(\mathbb{F}_p^k)}$ *in the* $\mathcal{F}_{OT\text{-}\bar{1}}^{p,k,\mathrm{Affine}(\mathbb{F}_p^k)}$ *hybrid model.*

7 Implementation

We implemented[7] our $\binom{2}{1}$-OT semi-honest and malicious protocols in the libOTe library [Rin], so that we could assess efficiency and parameter choices. We focus

---

[7] Source code is at https://github.com/ldr709/softspoken-implementation.

only on the case of binary fields $(p = 2)$, as for this problem there is little benefit to using a larger p. First, we discuss the choices we made in instantiation.

For semi-honest security, our protocol depends on only a PRG and a TCR hash. We instantiate the TCR hash using Proposition 2.7, with AES as the ideal cipher. To keep τ_{max} low, we set $t(i, \tilde{x}) = \lfloor i/1024 \rfloor$, changing the tweak every 1024 OTs. We also used the hash as a PRG, evaluating it as $H(s, t(0)), H(s \oplus 1, t(1)), \ldots$ for a seed s. This allows the same AES round keys to be used across the many different PRG seeds used by OT extension, while AES-CTR would need to store many sets of round keys—too many to fit in L1 cache.

Malicious security additionally requires a universal hash for Fig. 9. As recommended in Sect. 4, we construct the universal hash in two stages. First, take each block of 64 bits from $\tilde{x}$ and interpret it as an element of $\mathbb{F}_{2^{64}}$. These blocks become the coefficients of a polynomial over $\mathbb{F}_{2^{64}}$, which is evaluated at a random point to get $R\tilde{x}$. We choose the constant term to always be zero, which makes this a uniform family (not just universal), allowing the use of Proposition 2.4 to sum multiple hashes together. Limiting each hash to 2^{20} blocks (each 64-bits long) before switching to the next (generated from a PRG seed) makes this a 2^{-44}-almost uniform family over $\mathbb{F}_2$. The second stage R' of the universal hash is over $\mathbb{F}_{2^k}$. It further compresses the output in $\mathbb{F}_{2^k}^{64}$ down to only $\mathbb{F}_{2^k}^{\lceil 40/k \rceil}$. We made the simple choice of a uniformly random matrix in $\mathbb{F}_{2^k}^{\lceil 40/k \rceil \times 64}$, which achieves the optimal $\epsilon = 2^{-k \lceil \frac{40}{k} \rceil}$ for a uniform family of this size. Figure 11 also needs a uniform hash, and we use $\mathbb{F}_{2^{128}}$-multiplication of the tweak with the hash key.

The punctured PRF (Fig. 14) requires collision resistant primitives PRG, PRG', and Hash. For PRG, we assume that it is hard to find $s \neq s'$ such that $H(s, 0) = H(s', 0)$ and $H(s, 1) = H(s', 1)$, which is true in the ideal cipher model (see full version). We use Blake2 [ANWW13] for PRG'[8] and Hash.

7.1 Performance Comparison

In Tables 1 and 2, we present benchmarks of our implementation in both the semi-honest and malicious settings, for a variety of communication settings and parameter choices. We also compare to existing OT extensions. All results were measured on an Intel i7-7500U laptop CPU, with the sender and receiver each running on a single thread. The software was compiled with GCC 11.1 with -O3 and link-time optimizations enabled, and executed on Linux. In the localhost setting, there is no artificial limit on the communication between these threads, though the kernel has overhead in transferring the data, which is why our $k = 2$ is faster than $k = 1$ even in this case. We simulated communicating over a LAN by applying a latency of 1 ms and a 1 Gbps bandwidth limit. For the WAN setting, this becomes 40 ms and 100 Mbps. Base OTs were generated using the EKE-based OT of [MRR21].[9] The choice bits of SoftSpokenOT were derandomized immediately, as were the choice bits for Ferret, to provide the most

---

[8] H would also work, assuming that PRG'$_0$ concatenates two output blocks from H.

[9] Silent OT needs more than λ base OTs, and so as an optimization it generates them using KOS, which needs only λ base OTs.

Table 1. Time and communication required to generate 10^7 OTs, averaged over 50 runs. The best entry in each column is **bolded**, and the second best is underlined. Communication costs for maliciously secure versions are within 10 KB of the semi-honest ones. The setup costs are included.

Protocol	Communication		Semi-honest Security Time (ms)			Malicious Security Time (ms)		
	KB	bits/OT	localhost	LAN	WAN	localhost	LAN	WAN
IKNP [IKNP03] / KOS [KOS15]	160010	128	391	1725	15525	443	1802	15662
SoftSpoken ($k = 1$)	160009	128	243	1590	15420	<u>298</u>	1637	15648
SoftSpoken ($k = 2$)	80009	64	**210**	815	7730	**255**	893	7985
SoftSpoken ($k = 3$)	53759	43	<u>223</u>	568	5208	322	677	5419
SoftSpoken ($k = 4$)	40008	32	261	<u>433</u>	3995	311	<u>530</u>	4114
SoftSpoken ($k = 5$)	32510	26	337	**348**	3271	454	**465**	3447
SoftSpoken ($k = 6$)	27509	22	471	488	2811	588	613	2985
SoftSpoken ($k = 7$)	23760	19	777	843	2380	899	966	<u>2554</u>
SoftSpoken ($k = 8$)	20008	16	1259	1314	<u>1916</u>	1293	1322	**2130**
SoftSpoken ($k = 9$)	18759	15	2302	2338	2439	2460	2457	2590
SoftSpoken ($k = 10$)	16259	13	3984	3983	4097	4126	4132	4223
Ferret [YWL+20]	2976	2.38	2156	2160	2825	2240	2242	3108
Silent (Quasi-cyclic) [BCG+19a]	**127**	**0.10**	7735	7736	8049			
Silent (Silver, weight 5) [CRR21]	<u>127</u>	<u>0.10</u>	613	613	**746**			

Table 2. One-time setup costs for OT protocols in Table 1. SoftSpokenOT protocols have nearly identical setup costs, and so only a range is given.

Semi-honest Security

Protocol	Comm	localhost		LAN		WAN	
	KB	P_R	P_S	P_R	P_S	P_R	P_S
IKNP [IKNP03]	4.2	27	19	32	21	94	54
SoftSpoken (k in 1–10)	8.3–9.8	27–29	28–30	32–44	33–45	86–101	127–142
Silent (Quasi-cyclic) [BCG+19a]	53.4	31	33	32	34	102	146
Silent (Silver, weight 5) [CRR21]	53.4	28	30	33	35	102	147
Ferret [YWL+20]	1166.8	65	65	70	65	552	342

Malicious Security

Protocol	Comm	localhost		LAN		WAN	
	KB	P_R	P_S	P_R	P_S	P_R	P_S
KOS [KOS15]	4.2	28	28	33	32	105	145
SoftSpoken (k in 1–10)	9.3–16.8	27–33	28–34	32–38	32–38	100–109	141–151
Ferret [YWL+20]	1175.3	73	73	75	73	608	553

direct comparison with IKNP and KOS. The choice bits for the Silent OTs were not derandomized, slightly biasing the comparison in their favor.

Although for $k = 1$ our protocol is the same as IKNP in the semi-honest setting, our implementation is significantly faster. This mainly comes from a new implementation of 128×128 bit transposition, based on using AVX2 to implement Eklundh's algorithm [TE76]. This gave a $6\times$ speedup for bit transposition, which is a significant factor of IKNP's overall runtime.

In our benchmark, Silver did not perform as well as IKNP in the localhost setting, while [CRR21] found that Silver was nearly 60% faster than IKNP. We attribute this difference to using a lower quality computer, which has less memory bandwidth than the machine used for their benchmark. This is important for

Silver's transposed encoding, a memory intensive operation. Compared to Silent OT, we achieve better concrete performance in the localhost and LAN settings, but the extremely low communication of Silent OT puts Silver in first place for the WAN setting. We claim another a benefit to our protocol over Silver, since SoftSpokenOT only needs fairly conservative assumptions about well-studied objects like block ciphers, while Silver depends on hardness of LPN for a novel family of codes that has yet to receive much cryptanalysis. More conservative versions of Silent OT, based on either quasi-cyclic codes [BCG+19a] or local linear codes [YWL+20], are slower than SoftSpokenOT across the tested settings.

For malicious security, we use a more efficient universal hash function compared to KOS, who require the additional generation of 128 bits from a PRG for every OT as part of the consistency check. We have not benchmarked maliciously secure implementations of Silent OT and Silver, but they likely have very similar performance to the semi-honest case.

References

[ANWW13] Aumasson, J.-P., Neves, S., Wilcox-O'Hearn, Z., Winnerlein, C.: BLAKE2: Simpler, Smaller, Fast as MD5. In: Jacobson, M., Locasto, M., Mohassel, P., Safavi-Naini, R. (eds.) ACNS 2013. LNCS, vol. 7954, pp. 119–135. Springer, Heidelberg (2013). https://doi.org/10.1007/978-3-642-38980-1_8

[BCG+19a] Boyle, E., et al.: Efficient two-round OT extension and silent non-interactive secure computation. In: ACM CCS, pp. 291–308 (2019)

[BCG+19b] Boyle, E., Couteau, G., Gilboa, N., Ishai, Y., Kohl, L., Scholl, P.: Efficient Pseudorandom Correlation Generators: Silent OT Extension and More. In: Boldyreva, A., Micciancio, D. (eds.) CRYPTO 2019. LNCS, vol. 11694, pp. 489–518. Springer, Cham (2019). https://doi.org/10.1007/978-3-030-26954-8_16

[BCGI18] Boyle, E., Couteau, G., Gilboa, N., Ishai, Y.: Compressing vector OLE. In: Lie, D., Mannan, M., Backes, M., Wang, X. (eds.) ACM CCS 2018, pp. 896–912. ACM Press, October 2018

[Bea96] Beaver, D.: Correlated pseudorandomness and the complexity of private computations. In: 28th ACM STOC, pp. 479–488. ACM Press, May 1996

[BGI17] Boyle, E., Gilboa, N., Ishai, Y.: Group-Based Secure Computation: Optimizing Rounds, Communication, and Computation. In: Coron, J.-S., Nielsen, J.B. (eds.) EUROCRYPT 2017. LNCS, vol. 10211, pp. 163–193. Springer, Cham (2017). https://doi.org/10.1007/978-3-319-56614-6_6

[BLN+15] Burra, S.S., et al.: High performance multi-party computation for binary circuits based on oblivious transfer. Cryptology ePrint Archive, Report 2015/472 (2015). https://eprint.iacr.org/2015/472

[BMR16] Ball, M., Malkin, T., Rosulek, M.: Garbling gadgets for Boolean and arithmetic circuits. In: ACM CCS 2016, pp. 565–577. ACM Press, October 2016

[CB04] Cassuto, Y., Bruck, J.: A combinatorial bound on the list size. Technical report, California Institute of Technology (2004)

[CCG18] Cascudo, I., Christensen, R.B., Gundersen, J.S.: Actively Secure OT-Extension from q-ary Linear Codes. In: Catalano, D., De Prisco, R. (eds.) SCN 2018. LNCS, vol. 11035, pp. 333–348. Springer, Cham (2018). https://doi.org/10.1007/978-3-319-98113-0_18

[CCL15] Canetti, R., Cohen, A., Lindell, Y.: A Simpler Variant of Universally Composable Security for Standard Multiparty Computation. In: Gennaro, R., Robshaw, M. (eds.) CRYPTO 2015. LNCS, vol. 9216, pp. 3–22. Springer, Heidelberg (2015). https://doi.org/10.1007/978-3-662-48000-7_1

[CDD+16] Cascudo, I., Damgård, I., David, B., Döttling, N., Nielsen, J.B.: Rate-1, Linear Time and Additively Homomorphic UC Commitments. In: Robshaw, M., Katz, J. (eds.) CRYPTO 2016. LNCS, vol. 9816, pp. 179–207. Springer, Heidelberg (2016). https://doi.org/10.1007/978-3-662-53015-3_7

[CRR21] Couteau, G., Rindal, P., Raghuraman, S.: Silver: Silent VOLE and Oblivious Transfer from Hardness of Decoding Structured LDPC Codes. In: Malkin, T., Peikert, C. (eds.) CRYPTO 2021. LNCS, vol. 12827, pp. 502–534. Springer, Cham (2021). https://doi.org/10.1007/978-3-030-84252-9_17

[CT21] Chen, Y.L., Tessaro, S.: Better Security-Efficiency Trade-Offs in Permutation-Based Two-Party Computation. In: Tibouchi, M., Wang, H. (eds.) ASIACRYPT 2021. LNCS, vol. 13091, pp. 275–304. Springer, Cham (2021). https://doi.org/10.1007/978-3-030-92075-3_10

[CW79] Carter, J.L., Wegman, M.N.: Universal classes of hash functions. J. Comput. Syst. Sci. **18**(2), 143–154 (1979)

[GGM86] Goldreich, O., Goldwasser, S., Micali, S.: How to construct random functions. J. ACM **33**(4), 792–807 (1986)

[GKW+20] Guo, C., Katz, J., Wang, X., Weng, C., Yu, Yu.: Better Concrete Security for Half-Gates Garbling (in the Multi-instance Setting). In: Micciancio, D., Ristenpart, T. (eds.) CRYPTO 2020. LNCS, vol. 12171, pp. 793–822. Springer, Cham (2020). https://doi.org/10.1007/978-3-030-56880-1_28

[GKWY20] Guo, C., Katz, J., Wang, X., Yu, Y.: Efficient and secure multiparty computation from fixed-key block ciphers. In: 2020 IEEE Symposium on Security and Privacy, pp. 825–841, May 2020

[IKNP03] Ishai, Y., Kilian, J., Nissim, K., Petrank, E.: Extending Oblivious Transfers Efficiently. In: Boneh, D. (ed.) CRYPTO 2003. LNCS, vol. 2729, pp. 145–161. Springer, Heidelberg (2003). https://doi.org/10.1007/978-3-540-45146-4_9

[Imp95] Impagliazzo, R.: A personal view of average-case complexity. In: Proceedings of Structure in Complexity Theory. Tenth Annual IEEE Conference (1995)

[KK13] Kolesnikov, V., Kumaresan, R.: Improved OT Extension for Transferring Short Secrets. In: Canetti, R., Garay, J.A. (eds.) CRYPTO 2013. LNCS, vol. 8043, pp. 54–70. Springer, Heidelberg (2013). https://doi.org/10.1007/978-3-642-40084-1_4

[KOS15] Keller, M., Orsini, E., Scholl, P.: Actively Secure OT Extension with Optimal Overhead. In: Gennaro, R., Robshaw, M. (eds.) CRYPTO 2015. LNCS, vol. 9215, pp. 724–741. Springer, Heidelberg (2015). https://doi.org/10.1007/978-3-662-47989-6_35

[KOS21] Keller, M., Orsini, E., Scholl, P.: Actively secure OT extension with optimal overhead. Unpublished draft of full version (2021)

[MR19] Masny, D., Rindal, P.: Endemic oblivious transfer. In: Cavallaro, L., Kinder, J., Wang, X.F., Katz, J. (eds.) ACM CCS 2019, pp. 309–326. ACM Press, November 2019

[MRR21] McQuoid, I., Rosulek, M., Roy, L.: Batching Base Oblivious Transfers. In: Tibouchi, M., Wang, H. (eds.) ASIACRYPT 2021. LNCS, vol. 13092, pp. 281–310. Springer, Cham (2021). https://doi.org/10.1007/978-3-030-92078-4_10

[OOS17] Orrù, M., Orsini, E., Scholl, P.: Actively Secure 1-out-of-N OT Extension with Application to Private Set Intersection. In: Handschuh, H. (ed.) CT-RSA 2017. LNCS, vol. 10159, pp. 381–396. Springer, Cham (2017). https://doi.org/10.1007/978-3-319-52153-4_22

[PRTY20] Pinkas, B., Rosulek, M., Trieu, N., Yanai, A.: PSI from PaXoS: Fast, Malicious Private Set Intersection. In: Canteaut, A., Ishai, Y. (eds.) EUROCRYPT 2020. LNCS, vol. 12106, pp. 739–767. Springer, Cham (2020). https://doi.org/10.1007/978-3-030-45724-2_25

[PSS17] Patra, A., Sarkar, P., Suresh, A.: Fast actively secure OT extension for short secrets. In: NDSS 2017. The Internet Society (2017)

[Rin] Rindal, P.: libOTe: an efficient, portable, and easy to use Oblivious Transfer Library. https://github.com/osu-crypto/libOTe

[SGRR19] Schoppmann, P., Gascón, A., Reichert, L., Raykova, M.: Distributed vector-OLE: improved constructions and implementation. In: ACM CCS 2019, pp. 1055–1072 (2019)

[TE76] Twogood, R.E., Ekstrom, M.P.: An extension of Eklundh's matrix transposition algorithm and its application in digital image processing. IEEE Trans. Comput. C-25(9), 950–952 (1976)

[YWL+20] Yang, K., Weng, C., Lan, X., Zhang, J., Wang, X.: Ferret: fast extension for correlated OT with small communication. In: ACM CCS 2020, pp. 1607–1626. ACM Press, November 2020

Maliciously Secure Massively Parallel Computation for All-but-One Corruptions

Rex Fernando[1]([✉]), Yuval Gelles[2], Ilan Komargodski[2,3][iD], and Elaine Shi[4]

[1] UCLA, Los Angeles, USA
rex1fernando@gmail.com
[2] Hebrew University, Jerusalem, Israel
yuval.gelles@mail.huji.ac.il, ilank@cs.huji.ac.il
[3] NTT Research, Sunnyvale, USA
[4] Carnegie Mellon University, Pittsburgh, USA

Abstract. The Massive Parallel Computing (MPC) model gained wide adoption over the last decade. By now, it is widely accepted as the right model for capturing the commonly used programming paradigms (such as MapReduce, Hadoop, and Spark) that utilize parallel computation power to manipulate and analyze huge amounts of data.

Motivated by the need to perform large-scale data analytics in a privacy-preserving manner, several recent works have presented generic compilers that transform algorithms in the MPC model into secure counterparts, while preserving various efficiency parameters of the original algorithms. The first paper, due to Chan et al. (ITCS '20), focused on the honest majority setting. Later, Fernando et al. (TCC '20) considered the dishonest majority setting. The latter work presented a compiler that transforms generic MPC algorithms into ones which are secure against *semi-honest* attackers that may control all but one of the parties involved. The security of their resulting algorithm relied on the existence of a PKI and also on rather strong cryptographic assumptions: indistinguishability obfuscation and the circular security of certain LWE-based encryption systems.

In this work, we focus on the dishonest majority setting, following Fernando et al. In this setting, the known compilers do not achieve the standard security notion called *malicious* security, where attackers can arbitrarily deviate from the prescribed protocol. In fact, we show that unless very strong setup assumptions as made (such as a *programmable* random oracle), it is provably *impossible* to withstand malicious attackers due to the stringent requirements on space and round complexity.

As our main contribution, we complement the above negative result by designing the first general compiler for malicious attackers in the dishonest majority setting. The resulting protocols withstand all-but-one corruptions. Our compiler relies on a simple PKI and a (programmable) random oracle, and is proven secure assuming LWE and SNARKs. Interestingly, even with such strong assumptions, it is rather non-trivial to obtain a secure protocol.

© International Association for Cryptologic Research 2022
Y. Dodis and T. Shrimpton (Eds.): CRYPTO 2022, LNCS 13507, pp. 688–718, 2022.
https://doi.org/10.1007/978-3-031-15802-5_24

1 Introduction

The Massively Parallel Computation (MPC[1]) model, first introduced by Karloff, Suri, and Vassilvitskii [45], is widely accepted as the *de facto* model of computation that abstracts modern distributed and parallel computation. This theoretical model is considered to best capture the computational power of numerous programming paradigms, such as MapReduce, Hadoop, and Spark, that have been developed to utilize parallel computation power to manipulate and analyze huge amounts of data.

In the MPC model, there is a huge data-set whose size is N. There are M machines connected via pairwise communication channels and each machine can only store $S = N^\varepsilon$ bits of information locally for some $\varepsilon \in (0,1)$. We assume that $M \in \Omega(N^{1-\varepsilon})$ so that all machines can jointly at least store the entire data-set. This setting is believed to capture best large clusters of Random Access Machines (RAMs), each with a somewhat considerable amount of local memory and processing power, yet not enough to store the massive amount of available data. Such clusters are operated by large companies such as Google or Meta.

The primary metric of efficiency for algorithms in the MPC model is their *round complexity*. In general, the goal is to achieve algorithms which run in $o(\log_2 N)$ rounds; Ideally, we aim for algorithms with $O(1)$ or $O(\log \log N)$ rounds. The local computation time taken by each machine is essentially "for free" in this model. By now, there is an immensely rich algorithmic literature suggesting various non-trivial efficient algorithms for tasks of interest, including graph problems [1–3,5–8,10,14,15,26,29,34,39,43,48,49,56,60], clustering [11,13,31,38,62] and submodular function optimization [32,47,53,59].

Secure MPC. The MPC framework enables the algorithmic study of the large-scale data analytics commonly performed today. From a security point of view, a natural question is whether it is possible to do so in a privacy-preserving manner. This question is of increasing importance because numerous data analytics tasks we want to perform on these frameworks involve sensitive user data, e.g., users' behavior history on websites and/or social networks, financial transaction data, medical records, or genomic data. Traditional deployment of MPC is often centralized and typically hosted by a single company such as Google or Meta. However, for various reasons, it may not be desirable for users to disclose sensitive data in the clear to centralized cloud providers.

As a concrete motivating scenario, imagine that multiple hospitals each host their own patient records, but they would like to join forces and perform some clinical study on the combined records. In this case, each hospital contributes one or more machines to the MPC cluster, and the challenge here is how the hospitals can securely compute on their joint dataset without disclosing their patient records. In this scenario, since the hospitals are mutually distrustful, it is desirable to obtain a privacy guarantee similar to that of cryptographic secure multi-party computation. That is, we would like to ensure that *nothing*

---

[1] Throughout this paper, whenever the acronym MPC is used, it means "Massively Parallel Computation" and not "Multi-Party Computation".

is leaked beyond the output of the computation. More specifically, just like in cryptographic secure computation, we consider an adversary who can observe the communication patterns between the machines and also control some fraction of the machines. Note that all machines' outputs can also be in encrypted format such that only an authorized data analyst can decrypt the result; or alternatively, secret shared such that only the authorized data analyst can reconstruct. In these cases, the adversary should not be able to learn anything at all from the computation. We call MPC algorithms that satisfy the above guarantee *secure MPC*.

Why Classical Secure Computation Techniques Fail. There is a long line of work on secure multiparty computation (starting with [16,41]), and so it is natural to wonder whether classical results can be directly applied or easily extended to the MPC model. Unfortunately, this is not the case, due to the space constraint imposed on each machine. Algorithms in the MPC model must work in as few rounds as possible while consuming small space. Note that since the number M of machines can be even larger than the space s of a machine, a single machine cannot even receive messages from all parties at once, since it would not be able to simultaneously store all such messages. This immediately makes many classical techniques unfit for the MPC model. In many classical works, a single party must store commitments or shares of all other parties' inputs [4,30,41,46,54,57]. Also, protocols that require simultaneously sending one broadcast message per party (e.g., Boyle et al. [20]) are unfit since this also implies that each party needs to receive and store a message from all other parties.[2]

State of the Art. Chan, Chung, Lin, and Shi [25] put forward the challenge of designing secure MPC algorithms. Chan et al.'s main result is a compiler that takes any MPC algorithm and outputs a secure counterpart that defends against a malicious adversary who controls up to $1/3 - \eta$ fraction of machines (for a small constant η). The round overhead of their compiler is only a constant multiplicative factor, and the space required by each machine only increases by a multiplicative factor that is a fixed polynomial in the security parameter. *Malicious* security relies on the existence of a threshold FHE (TFHE) scheme, (simulation-extractable multi-string) NIZKs, and the existence of a common random string (CRS) that is chosen *after* the adversary commits to its corrupted set. If the protocol specification can be written as a shallow circuit, then a leveled TFHE scheme would suffice, and so the construction can be based on LWE [4, 19,61]. Otherwise, we need a non-leveled scheme which we can get by relying on Gentry's bootstrapping technique [36]. This requires the TFHE scheme being "circular secure".[3]

---

[2] Some works design "communication preserving" secure computation protocols (for example, [44,50,55]) where the goal is to eliminate input/output-size dependency in communication complexity-all of these works only address the two parties setting.

[3] In a leveled scheme the key and ciphertext sizes grow with the depth of the circuit being evaluated. In contrast, in a non-leveled scheme these sizes depend only on the security parameter. Gentry's bootstrapping requires the assumption that ciphertexts

More recently, Fernando et al. [33] considered the *dishonest majority* setting and presented two compilers. The first compiler only applies to a limited set of MPC functionalities (ones with a "short" output) and the second applies to all MPC functionalities. Both their compilers rely on a public-key infrastructure (PKI) and they obtain security for a *semi-honest* attacker that controls all machines but one. The round overhead of their compilers is similarly only a constant multiplicative factor, and the space required by each machine only increases by a multiplicative factor that is a fixed polynomial in the security parameter. Their first compiler is secure assuming a TFHE scheme and the second compiler is secure assuming TFHE, LWE, and indistinguishability obfuscation [12, 35]. Both compilers require the TFHE scheme to be "circular secure". This work leaves two very natural open questions:

- Is it possible to get malicious security in the dishonest majority setting? Here, no feasibility result is known under any assumption!
- Can we avoid non-standard assumptions in the dishonest majority setting?

1.1   Our Results

We make progress towards answering both of the above problems. Our contributions can be summarized as follows (with details following):

1. We prove that it is impossible to obtain a maliciously secure compiler for MPC protocols, no matter what computational assumptions are used. Our impossibility result works even if the compiler assumes a PKI, a common reference string, or even a non-programmable random oracle.
2. We complement the above impossibility result by presenting a maliciously secure compiler for MPC protocols, assuming a *programmable* random oracle, zero-knowledge SNARKs, and LWE. This result is our main technical contribution.
3. Lastly, we make a simple observation that allows us to get rid of the circular security assumption on TFHE that was made by Fernando et al. [33], as long as the protocol specification can be written as a shallow circuit. Thus, in this case, our observation can be used to re-derive [33]'s semi-honest long output protocol, relying only on LWE and indistinguishability obfuscation. This is useful since many MPC algorithms have very low depth, usually at most poly-logarithmic in the input size (e.g., [3, 8, 39, 43] to name a few).

An Impossibility Result for Semi-malicious Compilers. We show an impossibility result for a generic compiler that results with a semi-malicious secure MPC. The impossibility result holds in the setting of Fernando et al. [33], where strong cryptographic assumptions as well as a PKI were used. In fact, the impossibility result shows that no matter what cryptographic hardness assumptions

---

remain semantically secure even when we use the encryption scheme to encrypt the secret decryption key.

are used and even if the compiler relies on a PKI, a common reference string (CRS), or a (non-programmable) random oracle, then no generic compiler can result with semi-malicious secure MPC protocols.

In more detail, we show that the restrictions imposed by the MPC model (the near constant round complexity along with the space constraint) make it impossible to implement certain functionalities in a (semi-malicious) secure manner. Specifically, we design a functionality for which there is a party whose outgoing communication complexity is roughly proportional to the number of parties. This, in turn, means that either the round blowup or the space blowup must be significant, leading to a contradiction. The functionality that we design assumes the existence of a one-way functions.

This impossibility result is inspired by a related lower bound due to Hubáček and Wichs [44] who showed that the communication complexity of any malicious secure function evaluation protocol must scale with the output size of the function. We extend their proof to the (multiparty, space constrained) MPC setting allowing various trusted setup assumptions.

A Malicious Compiler. We observe that the above impossibility result does not hold if the compiler relies on a *programmable* random oracle. To this end, as our second and more technical result, we give a compiler which takes as input any insecure MPC protocol and turns it into one that is secure against a *malicious* attacker that controls all machines but one. This compiler relies on a few assumptions: LWE, the existence of a programmable random oracle, and a *zero-knowledge succinct non-interactive arguments of knowledge* (zkSNARK). The compilation preserves the asymptotical round complexity of the original (insecure) MPC algorithm. This is the first secure MPC compiler for the malicious, all-but-one corruption setting, under any assumption.

Recall that a SNARK is a non-interactive argument system which is succinct and has a strong soundness guarantee. By succinct we mean that the proof size is very short, essentially independent of the computation time or the witness size. The strong soundness guarantee of SNARKs is knowledge-soundness that guarantees that an adversary cannot generate a new proof unless it knows a witness. This is formalized via the notion of an *extractor* which says that if an adversary manages to produce an acceptable proof, there must be an efficient extractor which is able to "extract" the witness. A SNARK is said to be *zero-knowledge* if the proof reveals "nothing" about the witness. There are many constructions of SNARKs with various trade offs between efficiency, security guarantees, and the required assumptions, for example the works of [18,42,52]. All of these constructions can be used to instantiate our compiler, resulting in a compact CRS with size independent of the number of parties and the input and output size.

From Semi-malicious to Malicious. The above result is obtained in two steps. First, we obtain a *semi-malicious* MPC compiler. This step builds on the semi-honest (long output) protocol of Fernando et al. [33] and extends it to the semi-malicious setting. Second, we *generically* transform any semi-malicious MPC algorithm into a malicious one (both for all-but-one corruptions). The transformation uses only zero-knowledge SNARKs and has only constant overhead in its round complexity.

We remark that our semi-malicious protocol does not need a random oracle if we only need semi-honest security. This result is interesting by itself since it gives a strict improvement over the result of Fernando et al. [33]. Indeed, we get the same result as that of [33] except that we use plain threshold FHE as opposed to their result which relies on a novel circular security assumption related to threshold FHE.

Recall that in semi-malicious security introduced by Asharov et al. [4], corrupt parties must follow the protocol specification, as in semi-honest security, but can use arbitrary values for their random coins. In fact, the adversary only needs to decide on the input and the random coins to use for each party in each round at the time that the party sends the first message.

Our semi-malicious to malicious compiler is essentially a GMW-type [41] compiler but for the MPC setting, and therefore is of independent interest. Interestingly, standard compilation techniques in the secure computation literature do not apply to the MPC model. For example, it is well-known that in the standard model, one can generically use non-interactive zero-knowledge proofs (NIZKs) to compile any semi-malicious protocol into a malicious one (see e.g., [4,54]) without adding any rounds. However, this transformation relies on a broadcast channel and is therefore inapplicable to the MPC model. We therefore present a relaxation of semi-malicious security, called *P2P semi-malicious security*, which fits better to a peer-to-peer communication network, and in particular, to the MPC model. We show a generic transformation from P2P semi-malicious security to malicious security, assuming LWE and a zkSNARK for NP. Our transformation is much more involved than the classical one in the broadcast model (which uses "only" zero-knowledge proofs) and requires us to design and combine several new primitives. We believe that this relaxation of semi-malicious security and the transformation themselves are of independent interest.

Paper Organization

In Sect. 2, we give an overview of the techniques used in obtaining our results. In Sect. 3 we formally defined the model and the malicious and P2P-semi-malicious security definitions. In Sect. 4 we prove the impossibility result of generic (semi-)malicious compilers even using setup assumptions. In Sect. 5 we introduce two commonly used procedures. In Sect. 6 we give a P2P-semi-malicious compiler for long-output MPC protocols. Lastly, in Sect. 7 we give our P2P-semi-malicious-to-malicious compiler.

2   Overview of Our Techniques

First, let us briefly recall the computational model. The total input size contains N bits and there are about $M \approx N^{1-\varepsilon}$ machines, each having space $S = N^{\varepsilon}$. The space of each machine is bounded by S and so in particular, in each round each machine can receive at most S bits. We are given some protocol in the MPC model that computes some functionality $f \colon (\{0,1\}^{l_{in}})^M \to (\{0,1\}^{l_{out}})^M$, where $l_{in}, l_{out} \leq S$, and we would like to compile it into a secure version that computes the same functionality. We would like to preserve the round complexity up to constant blowup, and to preserve the space complexity as much as possible. Ultimately, we want to guarantee the strong notion of security against malicious attackers that can arbitrarily deviate from the protocol specification.

Since our goal is to use cryptographic assumptions to achieve security for MPC protocols, we introduce an additional parameter λ, which is a security parameter. For a meaningful statement, one must assume that $N = N(\lambda)$ is a polynomial and that S is large enough to store $O(\lambda)$ bits.

We assume that the communication pattern, i.e., the number of messages sent by each party, the size of messages, and the recipients, do not leak anything about the parties' inputs. We call a protocol that achieves this property *communication oblivious*. This assumption can be made without loss of generality due to a result of Chan et al. [25] who showed that any MPC protocol can be made communication oblivious with constant blowup in rounds and space.

It is instructive to start by explaining where classical approaches to obtaining malicious security break down. A natural approach to bootstrap semi-honest to malicious security is by enforcing honest behavior. A semi-honest compiler was given by Fernando et al. [33] so this seems like a good starting point. Typically, such a transformation is done first letting parties commit to their (secret) inputs and running a coin-flipping protocol to choose randomness for all parties before the beginning of computations, and then together with every message they send, they attach a proof that the message is well formed and was computed correctly using the committed randomness. The proofs must be zero-knowledge so that no information is leaked about their input and randomness. This is the most common generic approach, introduced already in the original work of Goldreich, Micali, and Wigderson (GMW) [41]. It turns out that trying to adapt this approach to the MPC setting runs into many challenges.

- GMW-type compilers usually rely on a multiparty coin-flipping protocol since the underlying semi-honest protocol only guarantees security when parties use fresh and uniform randomness to generate their messages. It is not clear how to perform such a task *while respecting the constraints of the MPC model*.
- GMW-type compilers usually rely on an all-to-all communication pattern. That is, whenever a party P_i sends a message, it must prove individually to each other party P_j that it acted honestly. This, of course, is completely untenable in the MPC model, since it would mean an $O(M)$ blowup in communication. Specifically, assume party P_1 sends a message m during round 1. Even if the message is meant only for P_2, the GMW compiler requires P_1 to broadcast a commitment c_m of m to every other party too, and prove that the message committed under c_m is computed correctly. This is necessary because other parties may later on receive messages from, say, P_2, that depend on m. This approach incurs $O(M)$ communication blowup, and this blowup must be charged either to round complexity or space in the MPC model.

The impossibility result. It turns out that the above challenges are somewhat inherent in the MPC setting in the sense that *it is impossible to bypass them*, even if arbitrarily strong cryptographic assumptions are made or even if trusted setup assumptions are used (e.g., a PKI or a non-programmable random oracle). Specifically, it is impossible to obtain a maliciously-secure MPC compiler under any cryptographic assumption and even if various setup assumptions are used.

The main idea for this impossibility result is to consider the following functionality: party 1 holds as input a PRF key k and the functionality is to send to party $i \in [M]$ the value of the PRF at point i, i.e., $\mathsf{PRF}_k(i)$. The attacker will control all parties but 1. We show that any malicious compiler for this functionality must incur non-trivial overhead either in the round complexity or in the space complexity, rendering it useless in the MPC setting. More specifically, we show that the total size of outgoing communication from party 1 must be proportional to the number of machines in the system, M, which in turn means it must store this many bits in a small number of rounds, implying our result. The proof of this lower bound on the outgoing communication complexity of party 1 is inspired by a related lower bound due to Hubáček and Wichs [44] who showed that the communication complexity of any malicious secure function evaluation protocol (a 2-party functionality) must scale with the output size of the function. We extend their proof to the (multiparty, space constrained) MPC setting and also to capture various trusted setup assumptions.

The main idea of the proof is as follows. The view of the adversary in any realization of the above protocol contains about M outputs of the PRF. By security, these outputs should be efficiently simulatable. If the communication complexity from party 1 is smaller than M, we can use the simulator to efficiently compress about M PRF values. This contradicts the fact that the outputs of a PRF are incompressible. The actual argument captures protocols that might rely on setup which is chosen before the inputs, for instance, a PKI or a non-programmable random oracle. Additionally, the above argument works even if the underlying MPC is not maliciously secure but only "semi-malicious" or even our new notion "P2P-semi-malicious" (both of which will be discussed below).

2.1 Our Malicious Compiler for Short Output Protocols

To explain the main ideas underlying our compiler we first focus on a simpler setting where the given (insecure) MPC algorithm has an output that fits into the memory of a single machine. Following the terminology of Fernando et al. [33], we call such protocols *short output*. Recall that our impossibility result from above basically says that the outgoing communication complexity from some party must scale with the total output size. Since the latter is very small in our case, we conclude that the impossibility result does not apply to short output MPC protocols.

Our starting point is the semi-honest compiler of Fernando et al. [33]: execute Π under the hood of a homomorphic encryption (HE) scheme and eventually (somehow) decrypt the result. If implemented correctly, intuitively, it is plausible that such a protocol will guarantee security for any single party, even if all other ones are colluding. The main question is basically how to decrypt the result of the computation. Fernando et al. [33] relied on a threshold FHE scheme to implement the above blueprint.

At this point we would like to emphasize that it is not immediately straight-forward how to adapt existing threshold- or multi-key-based FHE [4,9,19,22,51, 54,58] solutions to the MPC model. At a high-level, using these tools, each party first broadcasts an encryption of its input. Then each party locally (homomor-phically) computes the desired function over the combined inputs of all parties, and finally all parties participate in a joint decryption protocol that allows them to decrypt the output (and nothing else). However, the classical joint decryption protocols are completely non-interactive but consume high space: each party broadcasts a "partial decryption" value so that each party who holds partial decryptions from all other parties can locally decode the final output of the pro-tocol. If the underlying MPC protocol is short output, then we can leverage the fact that for known TFHE schemes, the joint decryption process can be executed "incrementally" over a tree-like structure, making it perfectly fit into the MPC model. Specifically, it is possible to perform a joint decryption protocol in the MPC model to recover the output *as long as it fits into the memory of a single machine*.

Avoiding Coin-Flipping (or: P2P Semi-malicious Security). As men-tioned, we do not know how to directly perform a multiparty coin-flipping proto-col in the MPC model. Many previous works, such as [4,54], bypass this problem in the name of saving rounds of communication, by assuming that the underlying protocol satisfies a stronger notion of security called *semi-malicious* security.

In semi-malicious security, the guarantee is similar to semi-honest security, namely, that the attacker has to follow the protocol, except that it is free to choose its own randomness. This is formalized by the requirement that after every message the adversary sends on behalf of a corrupted party, it must *explain* all messages sent up to this point by the party by providing an input and ran-domness which is consistent with this party's messages.

We do not know if the above semi-honest protocol can be proven to satisfy semi-malicious security. This is because the classical definition of semi-malicious security seems specifically defined to work in the broadcast model, and there are subtle problems that arise when using it without broadcast. Nevertheless, we manage to define a relaxation of semi-malicious security, we term *P2P semi-malicious security*, which turns out to be easier to work with in the MPC model. With this refine notion in hand, we show that the above-mentioned semi-honest MPC compiler satisfies P2P semi-malicious security. This step is rather straightforward once the right definition is in place. The main technical contribution is a method to bootstrap this (weaker) notion of security to full-fledged malicious security.

To explain what P2P semi-malicious security is, it is instructive to be more precise about what semi-malicious security means. Specifically, in the semi-malicious corruption model the adversary is only required to give a local explanation of each corrupted party's messages. In the broadcast channel, this is not a problem because all messages are public anyway, even those *between* corrupted parties. However, absent a broadcast channel, the adversary need not explain messages between corrupt parties as they can essentially be performed by the attacker, outside of the communication model. (Recall that in the definition of secure computation, an adversary is only required to furnish messages which honest parties can see.) Thus, in the P2P semi-malicious security model, we require the adversary to explain its behavior completely by also explaining the "hidden" messages sent amongst corrupt parties. While this gives a weaker security guarantee than classical semi-malicious security it is still stronger than semi-honest security and it turns out to be sufficient for us to go all the way to malicious security.

Enforcing P2P Semi-malicious Behavior. The next challenge is how to compile our P2P semi-malicious protocol into a maliciously secure one. Recall that classical GMW-type [41] compilers do not work in the MPC model since whenever a party P_i sends a message, it must prove individually to each other party P_j that it acted honestly. This, of course, is completely untenable in the MPC model, since it would mean an $O(M)$ blowup in communication. Specifically, assume party P_1 sends a message m during round 1. Even if the message is meant only for P_2, the GMW compiler requires P_1 to broadcast a commitment c_m of m to every other party too, and prove that the message committed under c_m is computed correctly. This is necessary because other parties may later on receive messages from, say, P_2, that depend on m. This approach incurs $O(M)$ communication blowup, and this blowup must be charged either to round complexity or space in the MPC model.

First attempt. We use a strong form of zero-knowledge proofs, known as *succinct non-interactive arguments of knowledge* or zkSNARKs. These proofs have the useful property that they can be recursively composed without blowing up the size of the proofs. What this means is that if a verifier sees a proof π for some statement x, it can then compute a new proof π' that attests to knowledge of a valid proof π for x. In our setting, this means that every party P_i can prove that its (committed) new state and outgoing messages are computed correctly based on its committed previous state and random coins, as well as a set of incoming messages which themselves must carry valid zkSNARKs that vouch for their validity.

Remark 1. Note that for this to work in the MPC model, we need that the proofs are computable in space proportional to the space of the local round computation. A SNARK that preserves the space bound in this way is called a *complexity-preserving SNARK*, and generic transformations from any SNARK to a complexity-preserving one are known [18].

Unfortunately, proving the security of this scheme turns out to be problematic. In the security proof, we would need to recursively extract the composed zkSNARK proofs in order to find the "cheating" proof (as some proofs along the way could be correct). That is, we need to invoke the SNARK extractor over an adversary *that itself is an extractor*. Unfortunately, performing this recursive extraction naïvely blows up the running time of the extractor *exponentially* with the depth of the recursion, and thus the recursive composition can only be performed $O(1)$ times. This means that we would be able to support only constant-round MPC protocols. Some works bypass this problem by making the very strong, non-standard assumption that there is a highly efficient extractor (i.e., where the overhead is *additive*) and therefore recursive composition can be performed for an unbounded number of times (for example, [17,18,21,28]). We want to avoid such strong assumptions.

Remark 2. At a very high level, proofs carrying data (PCDs) [18,23,24,27] are a generalization of classical proofs that allow succinctly proving honest behavior over a distributed computation graph. While the communication underlying an MPC algorithm can be viewed as a specific distributed computation, we cannot use them directly to get malicious security. The main problem is that PCDs only exist for restricted classes of graphs, unless very strong assumptions are made. Known PCDs (e.g., the one of Bitansky et al. [18] which in turn relies on SNARKs) only support constant-depth graphs or polynomial-depth paths. Our protocol does not fit into either of these patterns. It is possible to get PCD for arbitrary graphs from SNARKs where the extractor has an *additive polynomial-time overhead*, but as mentioned we want to avoid such strong assumptions. Second, note that we require privacy when compiling a malicious-secure protocol, which PCDs alone do not guarantee.

Our solution. Our goal is however to support an arbitrary round MPC protocol. To this end, we devise a method for verifying P2P-semi-malicious behavior by ensuring consistency and synchrony of intermediate states after every round, instead of throughout the whole protocol. We want that at the end of each round, the parties collectively hold a succinct commitment to the entire current state of all parties in the protocol. Given this commitment and a commitment to the previous round's state, the parties then collectively compute a proof that the entire current-round state has been obtained via an honest execution of one round of the protocol with respect to the previous-round state. This is implemented by recursively composing succinct proofs about the *local* state of each machine (using its limited view of the protocol execution) into a conjunction of these statements which proves *global* honest behavior. We implement this sub-protocol by composing zkSNARKs in a tree-like manner so that we only have constant blow up in round complexity.

To describe our approach, we first design a few useful subprotocols:

1. CalcMerkleTree sub-protocol: every party $i \in [M]$ has an input x_i, and they run an MPC protocol such that everyone learns the root digest τ of a Merkle tree over $\{x_i\}_{i \in [M]}$, and moreover, every party learns an opening that vouches for its own input x_i w.r.t. to the Merkle root τ. We make the arity γ of the Merkle tree as large as λ, i.e., the security parameter, and therefore the depth of the tree is a constant. The protocol works in the most natural manner by aggregating the hash over the γ-fan-in Merkle tree: in every level of the tree, each group of γ parties send their current hash to a designated party acting as the parent; and the parent aggregates the hashes into a new hash. At this moment, we can propagate the opening to each party, this time in the reverse direction: from the root to all leaves. The protocol completes in constant number of rounds.

2. Agree sub-protocol: every party $i \in [M]$ has an input x_i, and they run a secure MPC protocol to decide if all of them have the same input. To accomplish this in constant number of rounds in the MPC model without blowing up the space, we use a special threshold signature scheme that allows for distributed reconstruction. We build such a signature scheme by adapting a scheme of Boneh et al. [19] to our setting. Crucially, the signature scheme of [19] has a reconstruction procedure which is essentially *linear*. In this way, the parties can aggregate their signature shares over a wide-arity, constant-depth tree (where the arity is again λ). If all parties do not have the same input, disagreement can be detected during the protocol. Otherwise, the party representing the root obtains a final aggregated signature which is succinct. It then propagates the signature in the reverse direction over the tree to all parties.

3. RecCompAndVerify subprotocol: every party $i \in [M]$ holds a zkSNARK proof π_i to some statement stmt_i. They run an MPC protocol to compute a recursively composed proof π for a statement that is the conjunction of all stmt_is. This is also performed by aggregating the proofs over a wide-arity, constant-depth tree (where the arity is again λ); and the aggregation function in this case is the recursive composition function of the zkSNARK. The aggregated proof is propagated in the reverse direction over the tree to all parties.

In the first phase, before the protocol begins, each party holds an input and randomness for the underlying protocol which is being compiled. First, the parties engage in a "commitment phase": (1) each party computes a non-interactive hiding and binding commitment to their input and randomness, and then (2) the parties collectively generate a Merkle root τ_0 which commits to these commitments. This step can be accomplished by 1) calling CalcMerkleTree subprotocol, at the end of which every party receives a Merkle root τ_0 and its own opening, and 2) calling Agree to ensure everyone agrees on τ_0.

The next phase is used to simulate the first round of the underlying protocol. Recall that at this point all parties have a consistent Merkle root τ_0 which commits to their inputs and randomnesses, so in other words, τ_0 commits to the global starting state of the protocol. Each party executes the underlying protocol to obtain a new private state $\mathsf{st}_{i,1}$ and a list $\mathsf{msg}_{i,1}^{\mathsf{out}}$ of its outgoing messages. It then sends these outgoing messages to the recipient parties, and also stores any messages it received in a list $\mathsf{msg}^{\mathsf{in}}_{i,1}$. Every party now has a combined local state $(\mathsf{st}_{i,1}, \mathsf{msg}^{\mathsf{in}}_{i,1}, \mathsf{msg}^{\mathsf{out}}_{i,1})$. All parties now collectively compute a Merkle root τ_1 of all their combined states, again by calling the CalcMerkleTree and Agree sub-protocols. The parties now need to compute a new succinct proof π_1 that the entire round-1 state committed to by τ_1 has been honestly computed with respect to τ_0. For this to be true, each party P_i must not only prove that $(\mathsf{st}_{i,1}, \mathsf{msg}^{\mathsf{out}}_{i,1})$ was honestly computed, but also that its outgoing messages have been properly received by its recipients. At this point, each party P_i replies to every party P_j that sent a message that it received with an opening in the global state τ_1 that proves that it has recorded the message correctly in its list $\mathsf{msg}^{\mathsf{in}}_{i,1}$. Now, each party P_i can compute a proof that $(\mathsf{st}_{i,1}, \mathsf{msg}^{\mathsf{out}}_{i,1})$ has been computed honestly, and in addition, that every message in $\mathsf{msg}^{\mathsf{out}}_{i,1}$ has been copied to $\mathsf{msg}_{j,1}$, where P_j is the recipient of the message. These proofs are again aggregated using a recursive composition tree into a single succinct proof, by calling RecCompAndVerify.

The rounds which follow proceed in essentially the same way. The only difference is that in successive rounds, the input to each party's local computation also includes the incoming messages $\mathsf{msg}^{\mathsf{in}}_{i,r}$. In this way, the parties incrementally verify that the protocol is being performed honestly, without ever having to store a full transcript of the execution.

In terms of efficiency, the above compiler essentially replaces each round of the underlying protocol with a constant number of rounds, therefore the round blowup is constant. Moreover, the extra local space per party needed to carry out this transformation is only $\mathsf{poly}(\lambda) \cdot S$, where λ is the security parameter and S is the space bound of the underlying protocol.

Technicalities in the proof. The most interesting challenge that arises is handling the recursive composition of the SNARKs. In particular, we are in the context of secure computation, and therefore we are required to exhibit a simulator which can replicate the behavior of an adversary in the ideal world. This means we will need to simulate the honest parties' SNARKs, so we will require SNARKs with a zero-knowledge property, or zkSNARKs. Moreover, we need to extract the corrupted parties' witnesses. Since the recursive composition tree in the simulated world will include a combination of real and simulated proofs, it is not clear how to use a standard SNARK extractor to extract in this setting. To overcome this, we use a stronger notion of extraction, known as identity-based simulation extractability, which works even in the presence of simulated proofs [21]. At a high level, in this type of SNARK, each party receives an identity and proves statements with respect to that identity. Then, during extraction, the adversary receives a restricted trapdoor which allows it to simulate any proof with an honest id. The extractor is then guaranteed to extract valid witness for any proof generated with an id that is not in the honest set. Crucially, this notion is implied by the existence of vanilla SNARKs for NP along with one-way functions, as shown by Boyle et al. [21]. (Note that the transformation of [18] for complexity preserving SNARKs also preserves the identity-based simulation extractability property).

Using the simulation-extractability property of a SNARK in the context of secure computation protocols is trickier than the analogous usage of (non-succinct) non-interactive arguments. In particular, the extractor needs to make non-black-box use of the adversary [37]. A naive way for the simulator to use this property would be to extract the witnesses used by the corrupted parties in every round, and then to verify using the witnesses that the round was computed honestly. Unfortunately, it is not clear how to run the extractor in every round without recursively composing the extractor with itself R times. This is problematic in super-constant round protocols, because the extraction time could depend double-exponentially in the number of rounds. This appears to be even more of a problem for the following reason. Since we are using recursively composable SNARKs, soundness of our proofs are only guaranteed by exhibiting an extractor, and thus it seems like extraction in every round is inevitable. However, we bypass this problem by forcing the corrupted parties to commit at the very beginning to all randomness which they use in the protocol, even the randomness used to commit to their private state in each round. This allows us to write a simulator which only extracts in the first "commit phase" round, and also allows us to guarantee soundness via a reduction which only extracts in the first round and some other arbitrarily chosen round (the reduction is to the collision-resistance of the hash function or the binding property of the commitment scheme). See details in Appendix 7.

2.2   Our Malicious Security for Long Output Protocols

Now, we consider general MPC protocols. Due to our impossibility result, obtaining an analogous result for general MPC protocols necessarily requires a new approach, even if we only want to get (P2P) semi-malicious security. To put things in context, it is useful to recall the *semi-honest* MPC compiler for general MPC protocols of Fernando et al. [33].

Recall that the main challenge is to perform joint decryption of threshold FHE ciphertexts where each party eventually wants to learn its own output. Here is where Fernando et al. [33] used indistinguishability obfuscation: they generate an obfuscated circuit that has the master secret key hardwired and only agrees to decrypt the given M ciphertexts. Ensuring that this circuit itself is succinct requires careful use of SSB hashing [44] among other techniques. Once the circuit is small enough, they invoked their short output protocol to generate it securely and then distribute to all parties.[4]

This MPC compiler provably (due to our impossibility result) does *not* result in P2P-semi-malicious MPC protocols. Moreover, it is not a matter of throwing in more cryptographic assumptions or modifying the protocol in some clever way—any such modification will still result with an insecure protocol against semi-malicious attackers. Our main observation used to bypass this is that the

---

[4] Recall that no party knows the master secret key and so an inner short-output protocol is executed. Its inputs include the shares of the master secret key and it outputs an obfuscation of the aforementioned circuit.

impossibility result fails for protocols where the simulator can program the setup *adaptively, depending on the private inputs of the parties.* To this end, we rely on a programmable random oracle to "program" a specific uniformly-looking value, tying the hands of semi-malicious attackers.

In more detail, at the end of the evaluation phase, each party holds an encryption of its output. These outputs are (homomorphically) padded, and then all of these padded ciphertexts are used in a joint protocol to compute a "restricted decryption" obfuscated circuit. Additional randomness is generated by each party by querying the random oracle and is hardwired (in a hashed manner) in the restricted decryption circuit; this randomness is generally ignored throughout the protocol. The simulator will use these random values to program the "right" values to be output by the restricted decryption circuit. Specifically, in semi-malicious security, after each party commits to its input and randomness, the simulator knows the private inputs and pads of malicious parties. At this point, it can program the random oracle at the appropriate location so that using it to mask the padded output gives the right output. We refer to Sect. 6 for the precise details.

From semi-malicious to malicious. To compile the above semi-malicious protocol into a malicious one, we essentially use the same compiler that we described in Sect. 2.1. Indeed, that compiler did not rely on the underlying MPC being short output at any point. The only technical issue is that we need to address the fact that the underlying semi-malicious MPC compiler uses a random oracle which makes it delicate in combination with SNARKs whose goal is to enforce honest behaviour. To overcome this problem, we carefully design the semi-malicious protocol in a way that allows us to separate the random oracle-related computation from the statement that is being proven via the SNARKs. Specifically, we design the semi-malicious MPC compiler so that the "important" points of the random oracle are known to all parties and so parties can locally verify that part of the computation without using a SNARK, and the SNARK will only apply to the other part of the computation which is in the plain model.

3   The MPC Model and Security Definitions

In this section we formally define the MPC model and then define appropriate security definitions. The model is defined in Sect. 3.1. The security of MPC algorithms is defined in a standard way, following the security definition in multi-party computation literature. We focus on the strongest notion of security called *malicious* security but we also define a weaker notion called *semi-malicious* security which we use as a stepping stone towards malicious security (see Sects. 3.2 and 3.3, respectively).

3.1   The Massively Parallel Computation Model

We briefly recall the massively parallel computation (MPC) model, following Chan et al. [25] and refer to their work for a more detailed description. In the

MPC model, there are M parties (also called machines) and each party has a local space of S bits. The input is assumed to be distributively stored in each party, and let N denote the total input size in bits. It is standard to assume $M \geq N^{1-\varepsilon}$ and $S = N^\varepsilon$ for some small constant $\varepsilon \in (0,1)$. Note that the total space is $M \cdot S$ which is large enough to store the input (since $M \cdot S \geq N$), but at the same time it is not desirable to "waste" space and so it is commonly further assumed that $M \cdot S \in \tilde{O}(N)$ or $M \cdot S = N^{1+\theta}$ for some small constant $\theta \in (0,1)$. Further, assume that $S = \Omega(\log M)$.

At the beginning of a protocol, each party receives an input, and the protocol proceeds in rounds. During each round, each party performs some local computation given its current state, and afterwards may send messages to some other parties through private authenticated pairwise channels. An MPC protocol must respect the space restriction throughout its execution-namely, each party may store at any point in time during the execution of the protocol at most S bits of information (which in turn implies that each party can send or receive at most S bits in each round). When the protocol terminates, the result of the computation is written down by all machines to some designated output tape, and the output of the protocol is interpreted as the concatenation of the outputs of all machines. In particular, an output of a given machine is restricted to at most S bits. An MPC algorithm may be randomized, in which case every machine has a sequential-access random tape and can read random coins from the random tape. The size of this random tape is not charged to the machine's space consumption.

In this paper, we will be compiling MPC algorithms into secure counterparts and so it will be will be convenient to make several assumptions about the underlying (insecure) MPC, denoted Π:

- In protocol Π, each party P_i takes a string x_i of size l_{in} as input and outputs a string y_i of size l_{out}, where $l_{\text{in}}, l_{\text{out}} \leq S$. It follows that $N = l_{\text{in}} \cdot M$.
- Let R be the number of rounds that the protocol takes. In each round $r \in [R]$, the behavior of party $i \in [M]$ is described as a circuit $\mathsf{NextSt}_{i,r}$. We assume that $\mathsf{NextSt}_{i,r}$ takes a string $\mathsf{st}_{i,r-1} \| \mathsf{msg}^{\text{in}}_{i,r-1}$ as an input and outputs string $\mathsf{st}_{i,r} \| \mathsf{msg}^{\text{out}}_{i,r}$, where $\mathsf{st}_{i,r}$ is the *state* of party i in round r and $\mathsf{msg}^{\text{in}}_{i,r-1}$, the incoming messages to party i in round $r-1$, and $\mathsf{msg}^{\text{out}}_{i,r}$ are the outgoing messages of party i in round r. Note that the space of each party is limited to S bits, so in particular $|\mathsf{st}_{i,r}| \leq S$ for each $i \in [M]$ and $r \in [R]$.
- The protocol is *communication-oblivious*: in round $r \in [R]$, each party P_i sends messages of a prescribed size to prescribed parties. In particular, this means that the communication pattern of the protocol is independent of the input and therefore does not leak any information about it. This assumption is without loss of generality due to a transformation from the work of Chan et al. [25] who showed that any MPC protocol can be transformed into a communication-oblivious one with only a constant multiplicative factor in the number of rounds.

3.2   Malicious Security for MPC Protocols

We now define malicious security for MPC protocols following the general real-ideal framework (given e.g., in [40]) for defining secure protocols. We consider protocols assuming a PKI and a random oracle. Security is shown by exhibiting a simulator which can generate a view that is indistinguishable from the adversary's real-world view. We want to handle adversaries which can cause the corrupted parties to deviate arbitrarily from the protocol specification. To do that, we define real-world and ideal-world executions as follows. We consider an MPC protocol Π which realizes a functionality $f(x_1, \ldots, x_M) \to (y_1, \ldots, y_M)$.

Communication model and setup. Our protocols will assume authenticated pairwise channels between parties, such that a message sent from an honest party P_i to an honest party P_j is always received by P_j at the end of the round in which it was sent. We assume that the adversary can see all messages sent between honest parties. On the other hand, we do not assume honest parties can see messages between corrupted parties. We note that since our security definition will allow aborts, it is not necessary to prevent "flooding" attacks.

Furthermore, our protocol will rely on trusted setup, i.e., a PKI and a random oracle. The public key of the PKI is denoted pk and the random oracle is denoted $\mathcal{O}$. Every party in the protocol (including the adversary) has query access to $\mathcal{O}$.

The real-world execution. In the real-world execution, the protocol Π is carried out among the M parties, where some subset $\mathcal{C}$ of corrupted parties is controlled by the adversary $\mathcal{A}$. $\mathsf{real}_{\mathcal{A}}^{\Pi}(1^\lambda, 1^M, \{x_i\}_{i \in [M]})$ a random variable whose value is the output of the execution which is described as follows. First, $\mathcal{A}$ is initialized with security parameter 1^λ. $\mathcal{A}$ first chooses an input size (the length of $x_1 || \ldots || x_M$). After receiving the public key pk and the number M of parties, $\mathcal{A}$ chooses a set $\mathcal{C}$, and then receives the set $\{(x_i, \mathsf{sk}_i)\}_{i \in \mathcal{C}}$ of the corrupted parties' inputs and secret keys. The honest parties are then initialized with the inputs $\{x_i\}_{i \in [M] \setminus \mathcal{C}}$, and then $\mathcal{A}$ performs an execution of Π with the honest parties, providing all messages on behalf of the corrupted parties. Note that $\mathcal{A}$ does not need to provide messages sent between corrupted parties, since the honest parties do not see these messages. At the end of the protocol execution, $\mathcal{A}$ may output an arbitrary function of its view. Note that throughout the experiment $\mathcal{A}$ may perform arbitrary queries to the oracle $\mathcal{O}$. The output of $\mathsf{real}_{\mathcal{A}}^{\Pi}(1^\lambda, 1^M, \{x_i\}_{i \in [M]})$ is defined to be a tuple consisting of the output of $\mathcal{A}$, a sequence of input-output pairs corresponding to the oracle queries that were made, along with the outputs of all honest parties.

The ideal-world execution with abort. The ideal-world execution is given with respect to the function f which is computed by an honest execution of Π. In the ideal world, an adversary $\mathcal{S}$, called the simulator, interacts with an ideal functionality $\mathcal{F}^f$. Denote with $\mathsf{ideal}_{\mathcal{S}}^{\mathcal{F}^f}(1^\lambda, 1^M, \{x_i\}_{i \in [M]})$ the output of the execution which is defined as follows:

- **Choosing input size and the corrupted set:** First, $\mathcal{S}$ chooses an input size. After receiving M, $\mathcal{S}$ chooses the set $\mathcal{C}$ of corrupted parties, and receives the set $\{x_i\}_{i \in \mathcal{C}}$. The honest parties $\{P_i\}_{i \in [M] \backslash \mathcal{C}}$, are each initialized with input x_i.
- **Sending inputs to the trusted party:** Every honest party sends its input x_i to $\mathcal{F}^f$, and $\mathcal{F}^f$ records $\tilde{x}_i = x_i$. $\mathcal{S}$ sends a set $\{\tilde{x}_i\}_{i \in \mathcal{C}}$ of arbitrary inputs, where each $\tilde{x}_i$ is not necessarily equal to x_i.
- **Trusted party sends the corrupted parties' outputs to the adversary:** $\mathcal{F}^f$ now computes $f(\tilde{x}_1, \ldots \tilde{x}_M) \rightarrow (y_1, \ldots, y_M)$. It sends $\{y_i\}_{i \in \mathcal{C}}$ to $\mathcal{S}$
- **Adversary chooses which honest parties will abort:** $\mathcal{S}$ now sends the set $\{\text{instr}_i\}_{i \in [M] \backslash \mathcal{C}}$ to $\mathcal{F}^f$, where for each i, instr_i is either "continue" or "abort". $\mathcal{F}^f$ then sends output y_i to each honest party P_i where instr_i is "continue", and sends output $\bot$ to each honest party P_i where instr_i is "abort".
- **Outputs:** $\mathcal{S}$ outputs an arbitrary function of its view. The output of the execution is defined to be a tuple consisting of $\mathcal{S}$'s output along with all outputs of the honest parties.

We now define malicious security for MPC protocols formally in terms of the real-world and ideal-world executions.

Definition 1. *We say that an MPC protocol Π for a functionality f is malicious secure in the PKI model and random oracle model if for every non-uniform polynomial-time adversary $\mathcal{A}$ there exists a non-uniform polynomial-time simulator $\mathcal{S}$ such that for every ensemble $\{x_i\}_{i \in [M]}$ of poly-size inputs, $\text{real}_{\mathcal{A}}^{\Pi}(1^\lambda, 1^M, \{x_i\}_{i \in [M]})$ is computationally indistinguishable from $\text{ideal}_{\mathcal{S}}^{\mathcal{F}^f}(1^\lambda, 1^M, \{x_i\}_{i \in [M]})$.*

Remark 3 (Programmability). The above definition allows the simulator $\mathcal{S}$ to "program" the random oracle answers in its simulation. To allow this, the distinguisher in Definition 1 must not have access to this oracle.

Alternatively, sometimes a non-programmable variant is used. Specifically, here the distinguisher in Definition 1 *does* have access to this oracle and so $\mathcal{S}$ cannot program answers to its choice.

3.3 P2P Semi-malicious Security for MPC Protocols

We define a variant of semi-malicious security which is designed to be more suitable for models other than the broadcast model. We first explain why the original semi-malicious definition yields subtle problems when we do not assume the existence of a broadcast channel, and then we describe our modification to the definition.

In the original definition of semi-malicious security given by [4], a semi-malicious adversary is only required to give a *local* explanation of its behavior. Namely, whenever the adversary sends a message on behalf of a corrupted party

P_i, the adversary must write to the witness tape an input-randomness pair for P_i. It must be the case that the message just sent by P_i, along with all previous messages sent from P_i, are consistent with the input and randomness given by the adversary. Note that the adversary gives such an input-randomness pair whenever any corrupted party sends a message that is visible to honest party.

If we assume all communication takes place via a broadcast channel, this means that all messages are visible to honest parties, even messages between corrupted parties. Thus, an adversary is restricted to following the protocol specification honestly, with the proviso that it can change the input/randomness pairs for the corrupted parties partway through the protocol.

In the case of point-to-point channels, adversary is not required to furnish messages between corrupted parties, because they are not assumed to be visible to the honest parties. So although the adversary must explain any message sent from a corrupted party P_i to an honest party P_j with an input/randomness pair which is consistent with P_i's message, it is not required to explain the messages which were received by P_i from other corrupted parties. Since it can lie about the messages received by P_i from corrupted parties in previous rounds, the adversary can behave very differently from the honest protocol behavior. Thus, point-to-point channels offer much more freedom to a semi-malicious adversary than the standard case of a broadcast channel.

Our variant of this definition is designed to fix this problem and to bring the adversary's behavior back to what semi-malicious security is intuitively supposed to guarantee, namely that the adversary must act according to the honest protocol specification, modulo choosing the randomness for the corrupted parties and choosing different input/randomness pairs in different rounds.

We define our variant of semi-malicious security, which we call *security against P2P semi-malicious adversaries*, or *P2P semi-malicious security* for short. Like in malicious security definition, we use the real-ideal paradigm, the "semi-malicious" real-world execution is defined below, and the ideal-world execution is the same as in the malicious security definition from Sect. 3.2. Again, as before, we consider protocols in the PKI model and also in the presence of a random oracle that all participating parties (including the adversary) can query at any point in time. (Note that Remark 3 about programmability of the random oracle applies here as well.)

The real-world execution. In the real-world execution, the protocol Π is carried out among the M parties, where some subset $\mathcal{C}$ of corrupted parties is controlled by a *P2P semi-malicious adversary* $\mathcal{A}$. Denote $\mathsf{smReal}_{\mathcal{A}}^{\Pi}(1^\lambda, 1^M, \{x_i\}_{i \in [M]})$ a random variable whose value is the output of the execution which is described as follows. The real-world execution is similar to the real-world execution in the case of malicious security, except that we restrict the set of adversaries to P2P-semi-malicious ones. Such an adversary is required to have a special output tape called the "witness tape", and after each round ℓ it must write explanation of it behavior to this tape. That is, the adversary must write to the witness tape a set $\{(x_i, r_i)\}_{i \in \mathcal{C}}$ consisting of an input and randomness for *every* corrupted party. (This is in contrast to standard semi-malicious security, where the adversary need only write the input and randomness (x_j, r_j) of each corrupted party which sent a message to an honest party.) Observe that the messages sent by any party in $\mathcal{C}$ in the honest protocol specification up to and including round ℓ are uniquely determined by $\{(x_i, r_i)\}_{i \in \mathcal{C}}$ and the setup (PKI and random oracle queries determined by the honest protocol specification) along with all messages sent from $[M] \setminus \mathcal{C}$ to $\mathcal{C}$ in previous rounds. Note that the witnesses given in different rounds not need be consistent. Also, we assume that the attacker is rushing and hence may choose the corrupted messages and the witness $\{(x_i, r_i)\}_{i \in \mathcal{C}}$ in each round adaptively, after seeing the protocol messages of the honest parties in that round. Lastly, the adversary may also choose to abort the execution on behalf of $\{P_i\}_{i \in \mathcal{C}}$ in any step of the interaction. At the end of the protocol execution, $\mathcal{A}$ may output an arbitrary function of its view. Note that throughout the experiment $\mathcal{A}$ may perform arbitrary queries to the oracle $\mathcal{O}$. The output of $\mathsf{smReal}_{\mathcal{A}}^{\Pi}(1^\lambda, 1^M, \{x_i\}_{i \in [M]})$ is defined to be a tuple consisting of the output of $\mathcal{A}$, a sequence of input-output pairs corresponding to the oracle queries that were made, along with the outputs of all honest parties.

Definition 2. *We say that an MPC protocol Π for a functionality f is P2P semi-malicious secure in the PKI model and random oracle model if for every non-uniform polynomial-time P2P semi-malicious adversary $\mathcal{A}$ there exists a non-uniform polynomial-time $\mathcal{S}$ such that for every ensemble $\{x_i\}_{i \in [M]}$ of poly-size inputs, $\mathsf{smReal}_{\mathcal{A}}^{\Pi}(1^\lambda, 1^M, \{x_i\}_{i \in [M]})$ is computationally indistinguishable from $\mathsf{ideal}_{\mathcal{S}}^{\mathcal{F}^f}(1^\lambda, 1^M, \{x_i\}_{i \in [M]})$.*

4 Impossibility of a (Semi-)Malicious Secure Compiler

In this section we prove that there is no generic compiler from insecure MPC protocol to semi-malicious secure counterparts. Our impossibility works even in the presence of various setup models. For instance, even if there is a PKI, a common reference string, and a (non-programmable) oracle, our result rules out a generic compiler.

Theorem 4.1. *Assume that there is a pseudorandom function family (PRF). Then, there is no generic compiler that takes as input an MPC protocol and outputs a P2P-semi-malicious MPC protocol that realizes the same functionality, unless the round complexity depends polynomially on the number of machines. This is true even if the compiler relies on a PKI or a (non-programmable) random oracle.*

Overview. The proof relies on the fact that a too-good-to-be-true compiler could be used to efficiently "compress" the outputs of a PRF. This is inspired by a result of Hubáček and Wichs [44] who showed that the communication complexity of any malicious secure function evaluation protocol must scale with the output size of the function. We extend their proof to the (multiparty, space constrained) multi party computation setting and also to capture various trusted setup assumptions.

More specifically, the hard functionality is one where party P_1 has, as input, a PRF key k and it wants to transmit the value of the PRF at location $i \in \{2, \ldots, M\}$ to party P_i. The insecure implementation of this functionality is obtained by sending the PRF key to each party to locally evaluate the PRF at its own index location. For $\epsilon \in (0, 1)$ and $S = M^\epsilon$, this can be implemented in constant number of rounds by distributing the PRF key in a (arity $\sqrt{S}$) tree-like manner. This protocol is clearly insecure (w.r.t any reasonable notion of security). We are going to show that in any semi-malicious implementation of this functionality, party P_1 must send $\Omega(M)$ bits of information throughout the execution.

The formal proof of the above intuition shows that any generic semi-malicious compiler must incur non-trivial overhead either in space or in the round complexity (thereby making our protocol not in the MPC model). This is formalized in the full version of our paper, and Theorem 4.1 is a direct corollary of it. The proof is an adaptation of [44] and is given for completeness.

We refer to the full version for the proof of Theorem 4.1.

5   Common Subprotocols

We introduce two common subprotocols that take $O(\log_\gamma M)$ rounds and the communication is $O(S \cdot \gamma)$ per round for each machine, implement useful functionalities.

5.1   The **Distribute** Subprotocol

Consider the simple distribution functionality: P_1 has some string x and it wants to distribute x to all the other parties. In the normal model with point-to-point channels, P_1 can just send x to every other party which can be done in a single round. However, is problematic since it requires P_1 to send messages of $\Omega(M)$ bits in a single round. The following protocol implements this functionality by delivering x along a "tree".

Protocol 1. Distribute$_\gamma(x)$

Input: P_1 holds a string x where $|x| \leq S$.
Output: Each party holds x.
  1: Let $t = \lceil \log_\gamma M \rceil$. We refer to a party P_i as being on the level k if $(i - 1)$ is a multiple of γ^k.
  2: For each round $k \in [t]$, all the parties on level $t + 1 - k$ send x to the parties on level $t - k$.

5.2   The **Combine** Subprotocol

The protocol **Combine** (described in Protocol 2) implements the following functionality. Initially, each party $i \in [M]$ has an input x_i, and they want to jointly compute $\text{op}_{i=1}^M x_i = x_1 \text{ op } x_2 \text{ op } \ldots \text{ op } x_M$, where op is some associative operator.

Note that if each party i sends x_i to the recipient P_1 in a single round, P_1 receive messages of $\Omega(M)$ bits in a single round. In protocol Combine, we use the similar trick to ask parties aggregate the values in a tree fashion and in each round, all child nodes send the values they aggregate in their own subtree to their parent nodes.

Protocol 2. Combine$_\gamma$(op, $\{x_i\}_{i\in[M]}$)

Input: Party P_i holds x_i where $\gamma \cdot |x_i| \leq S$, and the parties agree on an associative operator op.
Output: P_1 holds $\text{op}_{i=1}^{M} x_i$.
1: Let $t = \lceil \log_\gamma M \rceil$. We refer to a party P_i as being on the level k if $(i-1)$ is a multiple of γ^k. Each node P_i sets $x_{i,0} \leftarrow x_i$.
2: For each round $k \in [t]$, for each party i on level k, P_i computes $x_{i,k} = \text{op}_{j=1}^{\gamma} x_{j',k-1}$ where $j' = i + \gamma^{k-1}(j-1)$.
3: After t rounds, P_1 has $x_{1,t} = x_1 \text{ op} \dots \text{op} \, x_M$.

---

6 Semi-malicious Secure MPC for Long Output

In this section, we give a semi-malicious compiler for general MPC protocols. The compiler takes as input an arbitrary (possibly insecure) MPC protocol and transforms it into a semi-malicious counterpart.

Theorem 6.1 (Semi-Malicious Secure MPC for Long Output). *Let $\lambda \in \mathbb{N}$ be a security parameter. Assume that we are given a deterministic MPC protocol Π that completes in R rounds in which each of the M machines utilizes at most S local space. Assume that $M \in \text{poly}(\lambda)$ and $\lambda \leq S$. Further, assume that there is a (non-leveled) threshold FHE scheme.*

Then, there is a compiler that transforms Π into another protocol $\tilde{\Pi}$ which assumes a PKI and a (programmable) random oracle, and furthermore realizes Π with P2P semi-malicious security in the presence of an adversary that statically corrupts up to $M - 1$ parties. Moreover, $\tilde{\Pi}$ completes in $R + O(1)$ rounds and consumes at most $S \cdot \text{poly}(\lambda)$ space per machine.

Property of our compiler is that for every message m, that sent in the original protocol, the size of the corresponding message in compiled protocol is $|m| \cdot \text{poly}(\lambda)$, and the size of every additional message in the compiled protocol is $\text{poly}(\lambda)$.

Our compiler also support different space per machine. Specifically, let S_i be the space of the corresponding machine in the original protocol, then this machine consumes at most $S_i \cdot \text{poly}(\lambda)$ space in the compiled protocol. Similarly, the communication complexity of each machine is also preserved, up to the same multiplicative security parameter blowup.

We refer to the full version for the proof of Theorem 6.1.

7 Malicious-Secure MPC

This section is devoted to presenting and analyzing our P2P-semi-malicious to malicious compiler. The formal statement is given next.

Theorem 7.1 (P2P-Semi-malicious to malicious compiler). *Assume hardness of LWE and the existence of a SNARK scheme for NP. Let $\lambda \in \mathbb{N}$ be a security parameter. Assume that we are given a P2P-semi-malicious MPC protocol Π secure against up to $M - 1$ corruptions in the PKI model. Suppose that it consumes R rounds in which each of the M machines utilizes at most S local space. Assume that $M \in \mathsf{poly}(\lambda)$ and $\lambda \le S$.*

Then, there exists an MPC protocol which is maliciously secure against up to $M - 1$ corruptions in the PKI model which realizes the same functionality. Moreover, the compiled protocol completes in $O(R)$ rounds and consumes at most $S \cdot \mathsf{poly}(\lambda)$ space per party.

Combining Theorem 7.1 together with our short output semi-malicious compiler (which is given in the full version of the paper), we obtain a maliciously secure compiler for short output deterministic MPC protocols. Combining Theorem 7.1 together with our long output semi-malicious compiler from Theorem 6.1 we obtain a maliciously secure compiler for arbitrary deterministic MPC protocols. Full details are given in Sect. 7.3.

The rest of the section is organized as follows. In Sect. 7.1, we define several subprotocols which we will use. In Sect. 7.2, we give the formal description of the compiler and analyze its efficiency. Finally, in Sect. 7.3 we describe how to put all the pieces together to obtain a long-output malicious-secure compiler. We defer a formal proof of security to the full version of our paper.

7.1 The Subprotocols

We mention the subprotocols which will be used. These subprotocols enable the parties to compute and agree upon a Merkle root which commits to a concatenation of all parties' inputs, and to compute a succinct proof of honest behavior for each round of the underlying protocol. Note that the compiler and its subprotocols both use the Distribute and Combine subprotocols defined in Sect. 5. Due to lack of space, we briefly explain the subprotocols here and refer to the full version for full details.

The CalcMerkleTree *Subprotocol.* The purpose of this protocol is for all parties to know a Merkle root τ with respect to some hash function h which commits to their collective inputs, and for each party P_i to know an opening θ_i for its respective input. We will perform this process over a tree with arity γ. The process completes within $2\lceil \log_\gamma M \rceil$ rounds, where in each round the current layer calculates new labels and sends them to the new layer of parents, and each layer sends any opening $\theta_{i,j}$ received from its parent to all its children. At the end, each party P_i will know the root τ and an opening π_i to x_i.

The Agree *Subprotocol.* When using the CalcMerkleTree subprotocol in the malicious setting, it is not guaranteed that all honest parties will receive a consistent Merkle root τ. Indeed, the corrupted parties could cause different honest parties to receive different roots, or could prevent some honest parties from learning the openings for their inputs. Because of this, we need a way for all parties to agree on a single root, and for parties to be able to force an abort if they did not receive valid openings. To that end, we define the subprotocol **Agree**. In this subprotocol, each party P_i has as input a string x_i. The subprotocol aborts if there exists i, j where $x_i \neq x_j$. The main primitive used is a threshold signature scheme with distributed reconstruction (TSDR), see the full version of the paper for a formal definition. The distributed reconstruction property is used to achieve the required space efficiency properties.

The SNARK statements and the RecCompAndVerify *subprotocol.* The last sub-protocol, RecCompAndVerify, deals with recursive composition and verification of the zkSNARKs that prove honest behavior during the commitment phase and during each round of the underlying protocol. The subprotocol recursively composes proofs of honest behavior of each party in a given round to get a succinct joint proof of all parties' honest behavior in that round. The parties then verify the proof and abort if the proof fails to verify.

The statements used when computing zkSNARKs is $\Phi((i, r, 0, \tau_{r-1}, \tau_r), w)$. It proves that P_i's state in τ_r was computed honestly with respect to its state in τ_{r-1}, and that it sent honest messages to every party it was supposed to send messages to during round r. The security properties needed for RecCompAndVerify are defined via a game RCVSecurity. In this game, a nonuniform PPT adversary $\mathcal{A}$ invokes R sequential instances of RecCompAndVerify. The game takes two parameters r_1 and r_2; the challenger will try to extract from the proofs produced by $\mathcal{A}$ during the r_1-th and r_2-th RecCompAndVerify instances. The game is defined this way to support the extraction requirements during the proof of security of the main compiler, which is designed to only need to extract twice during the protocol.

7.2   The Compiler

We now give the formal description of the compiler.

Protocol 3. Malicious-Secure Compiler

Setup: Each party P_i knows the verification key vk along with secret key ssk_i, where $(\mathsf{vk}, \mathsf{ssk}_1, \ldots, \mathsf{ssk}_m) \leftarrow \mathsf{Sig.Setup}(1^\lambda, 1^M)$ are the setup parameters for the TSDR scheme. The parties also know a hash function h and a SNARK CRS crs. Finally, the parties know the P2P semi-malicious setup: every party knows the semi-malicious public key smpk, and each party P_i knows its semi-malicious secret key smsk_i.

Input: Party P_i has input x_i and randomness r_i to the underlying MPC protocol.

Commitment Phase:

1. Each party P_i chooses a PRF key k_i and computes a commitment
   $c_{k_i} \leftarrow$ C.Commit$(k_i; \alpha_{k_i})$. It then computes
   $c_{\mathsf{st}_{i,0}} \leftarrow$ C.Commit$((x_i, r_i); \mathsf{PRF}_{k_i}(0))$.
2. The parties run the subprotocol CalcMerkleTree$_h(\{c_{\mathsf{st}_{i,0}}||c_{k_i}\}_{i \in [n]})$, so that
   each party P_i obtains a Merkle commitment τ_0 and an opening $\theta_{i,0}$ to
   $c_{\mathsf{st}_{i,0}}||c_{k_i}$. Party P_i aborts if its opening is not valid.
3. The parties run the subprotocol Agree$_\lambda((0, \tau_0), \mathsf{vk}, \{\mathsf{ssk}_i\}_{i \in [M]})$ and abort if
   the subprotocol aborts.
4. Each party P_i calculates a SNARK $\pi_{0,r} \leftarrow \Pi.\mathsf{P}(crs, \Phi(i, 0, \bot, \tau_0),$
   $(\bot, \bot, \bot, c_{\mathsf{st}_{i,0}}, \bot, \bot, \theta_{i,0}, k_i, c_{k_i}, \alpha_{k_i}, \bot, \mathsf{st}_{i,0}, \bot), (i, 0))$.
5. All parties run RecCompAndVerify$(crs, \bot, \tau_0, \{\pi_{i,0}\}_{i \in [M]})$ to obtain and
   verify π_0, a SNARK for the statement $\Phi(0, 0, t, \bot, \tau_0)$. If the subprotocol
   aborts then all parties abort and stop responding.

Evaluation Phase: The evaluation phase is divided into steps corresponding to
the rounds of the original protocol. Each step consists of several rounds in the
new protocol. For each of the R steps, the behavior of each party P_i is as
follows:

– **For round r of the underlying protocol:** P_i starts with a state
  $(\mathsf{st}_{i,r-1}, \mathsf{msg}^{in}_{i,r-1}, \mathsf{msg}^{out}_{i,r-1})$, a Merkle root τ_{r-1} for the previous round's
  global state, and an opening $\theta_{i,r-1}$ for $c_{\mathsf{st}_{i,r-1}}||\mathsf{msg}^{in}_{i,r-1}||\mathsf{msg}^{out}_{i,r-1}||c_{k_i}$ with
  respect to τ_{r-1}, where $c_{\mathsf{st}_{i,r-1}} =$ C.Commit$(\mathsf{st}_{i,r-1}; \mathsf{PRF}_{k_i}(r-1))$.
  1. Compute $(\mathsf{st}_{i,r}, \mathsf{msg}^{out}_{i,r}) \leftarrow \mathsf{NextSt}_{i,r}(\mathsf{smpk}, \mathsf{smsk}_i, \mathsf{st}_{i,r-1}, \mathsf{msg}^{in}_{i,r-1})$.
  2. For each $(j, s_j, e_j) \in \mathsf{OutgoingMessageLocs}(i, r)$, send $\mathsf{msg}^{out}_{i,r}[s_j : e_j]$ to
     party P_j.
  3. Initialize $\mathsf{msg}^{in}_{i,r}$ as an empty string of the appropriate size.
  4. For each message m received from party j during the last step, write m
     to $\mathsf{msg}^{in}_{i,r}$ at location $\mathsf{IncomingMessageLoc}(j, i, r)$.
  5. Compute $c_{\mathsf{st}_{i,r}} \leftarrow$ C.Commit$(\mathsf{st}_{i,r}; \mathsf{PRF}_{k_i}(r))$.
  6. Run CalcMerkleTree$_h(\{c_{\mathsf{st}_{i,r}}||\mathsf{msg}^{in}_{i,r}||\mathsf{msg}^{out}_{i,r}||c_{k_i}\}_{i \in [M]})$ with all other
     parties to obtain τ_r, the Merkle root of the transcript, along with $\theta_{i,r}$,
     an opening to $\mathsf{st}_{i,r}||\mathsf{msg}^{in}_{i,r}||\mathsf{msg}^{out}_{i,r}||c_{k_i}$ with respect to τ_r. Abort if the
     opening is not valid.
  7. Run Agree$_\lambda((r, \tau_r), \mathsf{vk}, \{\mathsf{ssk}_i\}_{i \in [M]})$ and abort if the subprotocol aborts.
  8. For each party that sent a message to P_i, send $\theta_{m_{i,r}}$, an opening to
     position $\mathsf{IncomingMessageGlobalLoc}(j, i, r)$ in τ_r.
  9. Calculate a SNARK $\pi_{r,i} \leftarrow \Pi.\mathsf{P}(crs, \Phi((i, r, 0, \tau_{r-1}, \tau_r), (c_{\mathsf{st}_{i,r-1}},$
     $\mathsf{msg}^{in}_{i,r-1}, \mathsf{msg}^{out}_{i,r-1}, \theta_{i,r-1}, c_{\mathsf{st}_{i,r}}, \mathsf{msg}^{in}_{i,r}, \mathsf{msg}^{out}_{i,r}, \theta_{i,r}, k_i, c_{k_i}, \alpha_{k_i}, \mathsf{st}_{i,r-1}, \mathsf{st}_{i,r},$
     $\{(m_{j,r}, \theta_{m_{j,r}})\}_j)), (i, 0))$.
  10. All parties run RecCompAndVerify$(crs, \tau_{r-1}, \tau_r, \{\pi_{i,r}\}_{i \in [M]})$ to obtain π_r,
      a SNARK for statement $\Phi(0, r, t, \tau_{r-1}, \tau_r)$. If the subprotocol aborts,
      then all parties abort and stop responding.

Output Phase: At the end of round R, each player P_i has a state $(\mathsf{st}_{i,R}, \mathsf{msg}^{\mathsf{in}}_{i,r}, \mathsf{msg}^{\mathsf{out}}_{i,r})$. P_i does the following to compute its final output:

1. Compute $y_i \leftarrow \mathsf{NextSt}_{i,R}(\mathsf{smpk}, \mathsf{smsk}_i, \mathsf{st}_{i,R}, \mathsf{msg}^{\mathsf{in}}_{i,r})$.
2. Output y_i.

Correctness and efficiency. Correctness of the compiler follows directly from the correctness of the underlying building blocks. To analyze the efficiency of the compiler, we first recall that during the sub-protocols CalcMerkleTree, Agree, and RecCompAndVerify, each machine takes local space bounded by $S \cdot \mathsf{poly}(\lambda)$. Moreover, the complexity-preserving efficiency property of the idse-zkSNARK scheme guarantees that $\Pi.\mathsf{P}(crs, \phi, w)$ is proportional to $\mathsf{poly}(\lambda) \cdot (|\phi| + |w| + s)$, where s is the maximum space of the verification procedure for ϕ. Finally, when carrying over between rounds, the parties only need to remember the previous round's Merkle root and an opening of size $\mathsf{poly}(\lambda) \cdot S$ along with k_i and the randomness used to generate the commitment c_{k_i}. It follows from these three facts that if the total local space used by each machine during the original protocol Π is S, then the total local space used by each machine during the compiled protocol $\tilde{\Pi}$ is at most $S \cdot \mathsf{poly}(\lambda)$.

7.3 Putting It All Together

Given a *short output* MPC protocol, we can directly compile it into a P2P semi-malicious secure protocol with our short output "insecure to P2P semi-malicious secure" compiler. Then, we can compile it into a maliciously secure protocol with our "P2P semi-malicious to malicious secure" compiler from Sect. 7. The resulting maliciously secure protocol has only constant overhead in round complexity and a $\mathsf{poly}(\lambda)$ blowup in space. This lead to the following corollary:

Corollary 1. *Assume the existence of a (non-leveled) threshold FHE system, LWE, and a SNARK scheme for NP. Let $\lambda \in \mathbb{N}$ be a security parameter. Assume that we are given a (insecure) deterministic short output MPC protocol Π. Suppose that it consumes R rounds in which each of the M machines utilizes at most S local space. Assume that $M \in \mathsf{poly}(\lambda)$ and $\lambda \leq S$.*

Then, there exists an MPC protocol which realizes the same functionality as Π and which is malicious secure against up to $M - 1$ corruptions in the PKI model. Moreover, the compiled protocol completes in $O(R)$ rounds and consumes at most $S \cdot \mathsf{poly}(\lambda)$ space per party.

Given any long output protocol, we can compile it into a P2P semi-malicious secure protocol with our long output "insecure to P2P semi-malicious secure" compiler from Sect. 6. This results with a protocol in the random oracle model (which is somewhat inherent due to our lower bound). Unfortunately, we cannot directly use our "P2P semi-malicious to malicious secure" compiler since in the description of the latter we did not capture input protocols that rely on a random oracle. The reason is that SNARKs do not compose well with random oracles.

More specifically, in the long output compiled protocol all the parties calculate a shared string denoted r_{seed}, then each party calculates offline the root of a Merkle tree of the values $\{\mathcal{O}(r_{seed}||i)\}_{i\in[M]}$ which we denoted z_r. Our goal is to prove that z_r is correctly calculated.

Note that z_r is a deterministic function of r_{seed} (since the random oracle is deterministic during the execution of the protocol). So, z_r can be calculated offline and its size is $\mathsf{poly}(\lambda)$. Now, in the "P2P semi-malicious to malicious secure" compiler, after round r that corresponds to the end of in the long output compiled protocol, we perform the following steps:

1. (Recall that τ_r is the Merkle tree root of states and messages of all parties at round r.) In addition to storing τ_r, we also store z_r. Denote $\tau_r^* = (\tau_r, z_r)$ and from now on, use τ_r^* instead of τ_r.
2. The parties run $\mathsf{Agree}_\lambda(\tau_r^*, \mathsf{vk}, \{\mathsf{ssk}_i\}_{i\in[M]})$ and abort if the sub-protocol aborts.

The above steps guarantee that all of the parties use the same z_r. In round $r+1$ of the malicious compiled protocol, whenever a SNARK is computed, it proved that if we know that τ_r^* is correctly calculated, then it must also be the case that τ_{r+1} is correctly calculated. In particular, the SNARK is never applied on a statement that contains a random oracle query.

A different way to interpret the above is to imagine the statement provided to the SNARK as composed of two parts: one that depends on a short seed r_{seed} (that all parties know) and consists of random oracle queries which eventually result with a small digest z_r, and the other is a plain model computation that only depends on z_r. The point is that since z_r is deterministic function of r_{seed}, the random-oracle dependent calculation can be *locally* computed by each party (and so z_r can be verified) and the SNARK can be applied only to the plain model computation that depends on z_r. Overall, we obtain the following corollary.

Corollary 2. *Assume the existence of a (non-leveled) threshold FHE system, LWE, a SNARK scheme for NP, and iO. Let $\lambda \in \mathbb{N}$ be a security parameter. Assume that we are given a (insecure) deterministic MPC protocol Π. Suppose that it consumes R rounds in which each of the M machines utilizes at most S local space. Assume that $M \in \mathsf{poly}(\lambda)$ and $\lambda \leq S$.*

Then, there exists an MPC protocol which realizes the same functionality as Π and which is malicious secure against up to $M-1$ corruptions, in the PKI/RO model. Moreover, the compiled protocol completes in $O(R)$ rounds and consumes at most $S \cdot \mathsf{poly}(\lambda)$ space per party.

Acknowledgements. Rex Fernando is supported in part from a Simons Investigator Award, DARPA SIEVE award, NTT Research, NSF Frontier Award 1413955, BSF grant 2018393, a Xerox Faculty Research Award, a Google Faculty Research Award, and an Okawa Foundation Research Grant. This material is based upon work supported by the Defense Advanced Research Projects Agency through Award HR00112020024. Yuval Gelles and Ilan Komargodski are supported in part by an Alon Young Faculty Fellowship, by a JPM Faculty Research Award, by a grant from the Israel Science

Foundation (ISF Grant No. 1774/20), and by a grant from the US-Israel Binational Science Foundation and the US National Science Foundation (BSF-NSF Grant No. 2020643). Elaine Shi is supported in part by the US National Science Foundation (NSF awards 2044679 and 2128519).

References

1. Ahn, K.J., Guha, S.: Access to data and number of iterations: dual primal algorithms for maximum matching under resource constraints. In: TOPC (2018)
2. Andoni, A., Nikolov, A., Onak, K., Yaroslavtsev, G.: Parallel algorithms for geometric graph problems. In: STOC (2014)
3. Andoni, A., Stein, C., Zhong, P.: Log diameter rounds algorithms for 2-vertex and 2-edge connectivity. In: ICALP (2019)
4. Asharov, G., Jain, A., López-Alt, A., Tromer, E., Vaikuntanathan, V., Wichs, D.: Multiparty computation with low communication, computation and interaction via threshold FHE. In: Pointcheval, D., Johansson, T. (eds.) EUROCRYPT 2012. LNCS, vol. 7237, pp. 483–501. Springer, Heidelberg (2012). https://doi.org/10.1007/978-3-642-29011-4_29
5. Assadi, S.: Simple round compression for parallel vertex cover. CoRR abs/1709.04599 (2017)
6. Assadi, S., Bateni, M., Bernstein, A., Mirrokni, V., Stein, C.: Coresets meet EDCS: algorithms for matching and vertex cover on massive graphs. arXiv preprint arXiv:1711.03076 (2017)
7. Assadi, S., Khanna, S.: Randomized composable coresets for matching and vertex cover. In: SPAA (2017)
8. Assadi, S., Sun, X., Weinstein, O.: Massively parallel algorithms for finding well-connected components in sparse graphs. CoRR abs/1805.02974 (2018)
9. Badrinarayanan, S., Jain, A., Manohar, N., Sahai, A.: Threshold multi-key FHE and applications to round-optimal MPC. IACR Cryptology ePrint Archive, p. 580 (2018)
10. Bahmani, B., Kumar, R., Vassilvitskii, S.: Densest subgraph in streaming and mapreduce. Proc. VLDB Endowment 5(5), 454–465 (2012)
11. Bahmani, B., Moseley, B., Vattani, A., Kumar, R., Vassilvitskii, S.: Scalable K-means++. Proc. VLDB Endowment 5(7), 622–633 (2012)
12. Barak, B., et al.: On the (im)possibility of obfuscating programs. J. ACM 59, 1–48 (2012)
13. Bateni, M., Bhaskara, A., Lattanzi, S., Mirrokni, V.: Distributed balanced clustering via mapping coresets. In: NeurIPS (2014)
14. Behnezhad, S., et al.: Massively parallel computation of matching and MIS in sparse graphs. In: PODC (2019)
15. Behnezhad, S., Hajiaghayi, M., Harris, D.G.: Exponentially faster massively parallel maximal matching. In: FOCS (2019)
16. Ben-Or, M., Goldwasser, S., Wigderson, A.: Completeness theorems for non-cryptographic fault-tolerant distributed computation. In: STOC (1988)
17. Ben-Sasson, E., Chiesa, A., Tromer, E., Virza, M.: Scalable zero knowledge via cycles of elliptic curves. Algorithmica 79(4), 1102–1160 (2017)
18. Bitansky, N., Canetti, R., Chiesa, A., Tromer, E.: Recursive composition and bootstrapping for SNARKS and proof-carrying data. In: STOC (2013)

19. Boneh, D., et al.: Threshold cryptosystems from threshold fully homomorphic encryption. In: Shacham, H., Boldyreva, A. (eds.) CRYPTO 2018. LNCS, vol. 10991, pp. 565–596. Springer, Cham (2018). https://doi.org/10.1007/978-3-319-96884-1_19

20. Boyle, E., Chung, K.-M., Pass, R.: Large-scale secure computation: multi-party computation for (parallel) RAM programs. In: Gennaro, R., Robshaw, M. (eds.) CRYPTO 2015. LNCS, vol. 9216, pp. 742–762. Springer, Heidelberg (2015). https://doi.org/10.1007/978-3-662-48000-7_36

21. Boyle, E., Jain, A., Prabhakaran, M., Yu, C.: The bottleneck complexity of secure multiparty computation. In: ICALP (2018)

22. Brakerski, Z., Perlman, R.: Lattice-based fully dynamic multi-key FHE with short ciphertexts. In: Robshaw, M., Katz, J. (eds.) CRYPTO 2016. LNCS, vol. 9814, pp. 190–213. Springer, Heidelberg (2016). https://doi.org/10.1007/978-3-662-53018-4_8

23. Bünz, B., Chiesa, A., Lin, W., Mishra, P., Spooner, N.: Proof-carrying data without succinct arguments. In: Malkin, T., Peikert, C. (eds.) CRYPTO 2021. LNCS, vol. 12825, pp. 681–710. Springer, Cham (2021). https://doi.org/10.1007/978-3-030-84242-0_24

24. Bünz, B., Chiesa, A., Mishra, P., Spooner, N.: Recursive proof composition from accumulation schemes. In: Pass, R., Pietrzak, K. (eds.) TCC 2020. LNCS, vol. 12551, pp. 1–18. Springer, Cham (2020). https://doi.org/10.1007/978-3-030-64378-2_1

25. Chan, T.H., Chung, K., Lin, W., Shi, E.: MPC for MPC: secure computation on a massively parallel computing architecture. In: ITCS (2020)

26. Chang, Y., Fischer, M., Ghaffari, M., Uitto, J., Zheng, Y.: The complexity of $(\Delta+1)$ coloring in congested clique, massively parallel computation, and centralized local computation. In: PODC (2019)

27. Chiesa, A., Tromer, E.: Proof-carrying data and hearsay arguments from signature cards. In: Innovations in Computer Science - ICS, pp. 310–331 (2010)

28. Chiesa, A., Tromer, E., Virza, M.: Cluster computing in zero knowledge. In: Oswald, E., Fischlin, M. (eds.) EUROCRYPT 2015. LNCS, vol. 9057, pp. 371–403. Springer, Heidelberg (2015). https://doi.org/10.1007/978-3-662-46803-6_13

29. Czumaj, A., Łącki, J., Mądry, A., Mitrović, S., Onak, K., Sankowski, P.: Round compression for parallel matching algorithms. In: STOC (2018)

30. Dodis, Y., Halevi, S., Rothblum, R.D., Wichs, D.: Spooky encryption and its applications. In: Robshaw, M., Katz, J. (eds.) CRYPTO 2016. LNCS, vol. 9816, pp. 93–122. Springer, Heidelberg (2016). https://doi.org/10.1007/978-3-662-53015-3_4

31. Ene, A., Im, S., Moseley, B.: Fast clustering using MapReduce. In: SIGKDD (2011)

32. Ene, A., Nguyen, H.: Random coordinate descent methods for minimizing decomposable submodular functions. In: ICML (2015)

33. Fernando, R., Komargodski, I., Liu, Y., Shi, E.: Secure massively parallel computation for dishonest majority. In: Pass, R., Pietrzak, K. (eds.) TCC 2020. LNCS, vol. 12551, pp. 379–409. Springer, Cham (2020). https://doi.org/10.1007/978-3-030-64378-2_14

34. Gamlath, B., Kale, S., Mitrovic, S., Svensson, O.: Weighted matchings via unweighted augmentations. In: PODC (2019)

35. Garg, S., Gentry, C., Halevi, S., Raykova, M., Sahai, A., Waters, B.: Candidate indistinguishability obfuscation and functional encryption for all circuits. In: FOCS (2013)

36. Gentry, C.: Fully homomorphic encryption using ideal lattices. In: ACM Symposium on Theory of Computing, STOC, pp. 169–178 (2009)

37. Gentry, C., Wichs, D.: Separating succinct non-interactive arguments from all falsifiable assumptions. In: Fortnow, L., Vadhan, S.P. (eds.) STOC (2011)
38. Ghaffari, M., Lattanzi, S., Mitrović, S.: Improved parallel algorithms for density-based network clustering. In: ICML (2019)
39. Ghaffari, M., Uitto, J.: Sparsifying distributed algorithms with ramifications in massively parallel computation and centralized local computation. In: SODA (2019)
40. Goldreich, O.: Foundations of Cryptography: Volume 2. Cambridge University Press, Cambridge (2009)
41. Goldreich, O., Micali, S., Wigderson, A.: How to play any mental game or a completeness theorem for protocols with honest majority. In: STOC (1987)
42. Groth, J.: On the size of pairing-based non-interactive arguments. In: Fischlin, M., Coron, J.-S. (eds.) EUROCRYPT 2016. LNCS, vol. 9666, pp. 305–326. Springer, Heidelberg (2016). https://doi.org/10.1007/978-3-662-49896-5_11
43. Hajiaghayi, M., Seddighin, S., Sun, X.: Massively parallel approximation algorithms for edit distance and longest common subsequence. In: SODA (2019)
44. Hubáček, P., Wichs, D.: On the communication complexity of secure function evaluation with long output. In: ITCS, pp. 163–172 (2015)
45. Karloff, H.J., Suri, S., Vassilvitskii, S.: A model of computation for MapReduce. In: SODA (2010)
46. Katz, J., Ostrovsky, R., Smith, A.: Round efficiency of multi-party computation with a dishonest majority. In: Biham, E. (ed.) EUROCRYPT 2003. LNCS, vol. 2656, pp. 578–595. Springer, Heidelberg (2003). https://doi.org/10.1007/3-540-39200-9_36
47. Kumar, R., Moseley, B., Vassilvitskii, S., Vattani, A.: Fast greedy algorithms in MapReduce and streaming. TOPC 2(3), 14:1–14:22 (2015)
48. Łącki, J., Mirrokni, V.S., Wlodarczyk, M.: Connected components at scale via local contractions. CoRR abs/1807.10727 (2018)
49. Lattanzi, S., Moseley, B., Suri, S., Vassilvitskii, S.: Filtering: a method for solving graph problems in MapReduce. In: SPAA (2011)
50. Lindell, Y., Nissim, K., Orlandi, C.: Hiding the input-size in secure two-party computation. In: Sako, K., Sarkar, P. (eds.) ASIACRYPT 2013. LNCS, vol. 8270, pp. 421–440. Springer, Heidelberg (2013). https://doi.org/10.1007/978-3-642-42045-0_22
51. López-Alt, A., Tromer, E., Vaikuntanathan, V.: On-the-fly multiparty computation on the cloud via multikey fully homomorphic encryption. In: STOC (2012)
52. Micali, S.: CS proofs (extended abstracts). In: FOCS (1994)
53. Mirzasoleiman, B., Karbasi, A., Sarkar, R., Krause, A.: Distributed submodular maximization: identifying representative elements in massive data. In: NeurIPS (2013)
54. Mukherjee, P., Wichs, D.: Two round multiparty computation via multi-key FHE. In: Fischlin, M., Coron, J.-S. (eds.) EUROCRYPT 2016. LNCS, vol. 9666, pp. 735–763. Springer, Heidelberg (2016). https://doi.org/10.1007/978-3-662-49896-5_26
55. Naor, M., Nissim, K.: Communication preserving protocols for secure function evaluation. In: STOC, pp. 590–599 (2001)
56. Onak, K.: Round compression for parallel graph algorithms in strongly sublinear space. CoRR abs/1807.08745 (2018)
57. Pass, R.: Bounded-concurrent secure multi-party computation with a dishonest majority. In: Babai, L. (ed.) STOC (2004)

58. Peikert, C., Shiehian, S.: Multi-key FHE from LWE, revisited. In: TCC (2016)
59. da Ponte Barbosa, R., Ene, A., Nguyen, H.L., Ward, J.: A new framework for distributed submodular maximization. In: FOCS, pp. 645–654 (2016)
60. Rastogi, V., Machanavajjhala, A., Chitnis, L., Sarma, A.D.: Finding connected components in map-reduce in logarithmic rounds. In: ICDE (2013)
61. Regev, O.: On lattices, learning with errors, random linear codes, and cryptography. J. ACM **56**(6), 34:1–34:40 (2009)
62. Yaroslavtsev, G., Vadapalli, A.: Massively parallel algorithms and hardness for single-linkage clustering under ℓ_p-distances. In: ICML (2018)

Le Mans: Dynamic and Fluid MPC for Dishonest Majority

Rahul Rachuri and Peter Scholl$^{(\boxtimes)}$

Department of Computer Science, Aarhus University, Aarhus, Denmark
{rachuri,peter.scholl}@cs.au.dk

Abstract. Most MPC protocols require the set of parties to be active for the entire duration of the computation. Deploying MPC for use cases such as complex and resource-intensive scientific computations increases the barrier of entry for potential participants. The model of Fluid MPC (Crypto 2021) tackles this issue by giving parties the flexibility to participate in the protocol only when their resources are free. As such, the set of parties is dynamically changing over time.

In this work, we extend Fluid MPC, which only considered an honest majority, to the setting where the majority of participants at any point in the computation may be corrupt. We do this by presenting variants of the SPDZ protocol, which support dynamic participants. Firstly, we describe a *universal preprocessing* for SPDZ, which allows a set of n parties to compute some correlated randomness, such that later on, any subset of the parties can use this to take part in an online secure computation. We complement this with a *Dynamic SPDZ* online phase, designed to work with our universal preprocessing, as well as a protocol for securely realising the preprocessing. Our preprocessing protocol is designed to efficiently use pseudorandom correlation generators, thus, the parties' storage and communication costs can be almost independent of the function being evaluated.

We then extend this to support a *fluid online phase*, where the set of parties can dynamically evolve during the online phase. Our protocol achieves *maximal fluidity* and security with abort, similarly to the previous, honest majority construction. Achieving this requires a careful design and techniques to guarantee a small state complexity, allowing us to switch between committees efficiently.

1 Introduction

Secure multi-party computation (MPC) allows a set of parties to jointly compute a function on their inputs, while preserving privacy, that is, not revealing anything more about the inputs than can be deduced from the output of the function. MPC can be applied in a wide range of situations, including secure aggregation, private training or evaluation of machine learning models, threshold signing and more.

Most MPC protocols work under the assumption that the set of parties involved in the computation is fixed throughout the protocol. Although

© International Association for Cryptologic Research 2022
Y. Dodis and T. Shrimpton (Eds.): CRYPTO 2022, LNCS 13507, pp. 719–749, 2022.
https://doi.org/10.1007/978-3-031-15802-5_25

committee-based MPC and player-replaceability schemes have existed for a while, recently more practically oriented models have been proposed such as Fluid MPC [CGG+21] and YOSO [GHK+21]. These models support protocols with a *dynamically evolving* set of parties, where participants can join and leave the computation as desired, without interrupting the protocol. This enables a more flexible model, where parties can sign up to contribute their resources towards a large-scale, distributed computation, without having to commit for the duration of the entire protocol. This is particularly important for large-scale, long-running tasks such as complex scientific computations, such as Folding@home. In the *maximally fluid* setting, this concept is pushed to the limit, where each participant is only required to sign up for *a single round* of the protocol. This gives the most possible flexibility for any server who may wish to participate.

The YOSO (you only speak once) paradigm [GHK+21] also considers maximally fluid MPC protocols, with some differences in the model. Unlike Fluid MPC, they separately study the role assignment problem, where they show how to leverage a blockchain to randomly assign the committee of parties who will take part in each round. With their mechanism, the identity of any member of the current committee is only revealed after they have published their message. This allows for much stronger security guarantees, since an adversary has no way to identify which servers are involved in the computation—and hence who to corrupt—until the role played by the server has already been terminated.

Both of these works give information-theoretically secure protocols in the *honest majority* setting, where in any given round of the protocol, the majority of the computing parties should be honest. Fluid MPC achieves security with abort, where a malicious party can prevent the protocol from terminating, while YOSO achieves the stronger notion of guaranteed output delivery (but is less efficient).

1.1 Our Contributions

In this work, we study MPC with dynamically evolving parties in the *dishonest majority* setting. This gives much stronger security guarantees, since we only require that in any given round of the computation, there is at least one honest party taking part. However, it is also more challenging than honest majority. We now elaborate on our contributions and some technical background.

The challenge of fluidity and dishonest majority. In the dishonest majority setting, most practical MPC protocols are based on authenticated secret-sharing using information-theoretic MACs, such as in the SPDZ [DPSZ12] or BDOZ [BDOZ11] protocols. These protocols rely on a preprocessing phase, using more expensive, "public-key" style cryptography, to generate a large amount of correlated randomness that is consumed in a lightweight online phase. Unfortunately, this means that each party has to maintain a *large state* (the correlated randomness), the size of which grows linearly with the complexity of the function being computed. This is problematic for achieving Fluid MPC, since when changing from one committee of parties to another, the natural approach is to securely transfer the entire state to the new committee. Ideally, we want this state transfer process to be *independent* of the function being computed, to avoid the communication complexity blowing up.

Key Tool: Universal Preprocessing for Dynamic Parties. Before aiming for Fluid MPC, we look at a simpler model which allows just a single change in the set of computing parties during the protocol. We consider a *universal preprocessing* phase, where all of the parties $P_1, \ldots, P_n$ who may wish to be involved in the computation must take part. Later, any subset of the n parties can get together and run a fast, online protocol, without having to interact with anybody else. We assume the inputs to the protocol are provided by the online subset of parties (though with standard techniques such as [DDN+16], we can also support inputs from external parties).

Recall that in SPDZ, the parties need to preprocess authenticated multiplication triples, denoted $[\![a]\!]$, $[\![b]\!]$, $[\![c]\!]$, where a and b are secret, random finite field elements and $c = a \cdot b$. These values are secret-shared with MACs, given by

$$[\![x]\!] := (x^i, m^i, \Delta^i)_{i \in [n]}$$

where party P_i has the share Δ^i of the global MAC key $\Delta = \sum \Delta^i$, and also the shares x^i, m^i, satisfying $x = \sum x^i$ and $x \cdot \Delta = \sum m^i$ over the field.

Instead of producing fully authenticated triples like this, we produce a weaker form of *partial triple*, where c is unauthenticated, and not fully computed: every pair of parties (P_i, P_j) will get a two-party additive sharing of $a^i \cdot b^j$. This suffices to reconstruct a share c^i, by adding up P_i's relevant sharings of $a^i b^j$, together with $a^i b^i$.

Importantly, this also enables *any subset* of parties $\mathcal{P} \subset [n]$ to obtain a triple, by restricting to the shares a^i, b^i for $i \in \mathcal{P}$, and summing up the relevant shares of the products to get a c^i for this committee. A similar trick also works to get the MACs on a and b, since each MAC is just a secret-shared product with the fixed key Δ. Therefore, it's enough to give out two-party shares of $a^i \Delta^j$ and $b^i \cdot \Delta^j$ for every $i \neq j$.

We show how to realize this type of preprocessing using simple, pairwise correlations between every pair of parties, in the form of oblivious linear function evaluation (OLE) and vector-OLE. We ensure correctness of the authenticated $[\![a]\!]$, $[\![b]\!]$ shares using a consistency check, which we formalize via a multi-party vector-OLE functionality. However, our protocol does not guarantee correctness of the shares of cross-products $a^i \cdot b^j$. We therefore model these errors via adversarial influence in the preprocessing functionality.

PCG-Friendliness. An important feature of our preprocessing protocol is that it is *PCG-friendly*, meaning that it can be implemented using *pseudorandom correlation generators* (PCGs) [BCG+19b]. A PCG allows two parties to take a pair of short, correlated seeds, and expand them to produce a much larger quantity of correlated randomness. There are efficient PCGs for vector-OLE, based on variants of the LPN assumption [BCGI18, BCG+19a, WYKW21], and for OLE under a variant of ring-LPN [BCG+20]. By supporting PCGs in our preprocessing, we obtain communication and storage complexities as small as $O(n \log |C|)$ field elements per party, for an arithmetic circuit C. Prior to our work, we stress that even with a statically chosen online phase, there was no practical, multi-party SPDZ-like protocol[1] that could support a preprocessing phase with this feature with good concrete efficiency—ours is the first protocol to support this "silent" feature. In recent, concurrent work [BGIN22], another MPC protocol with sublinear preprocessing was given. Their preprocessing protocol also relies on PCGs, but scales with the square root of the circuit size rather than logarithmically. However, their online phase communication matches is slightly better than ours, and the communication of their preprocessing phase scales better with the number of parties.

Dynamic Variant of SPDZ Online Phase. One issue with our universal pre-processing is that, since the c terms of triples are not authenticated, we cannot use the same online phase as SPDZ. Instead, we modify the online phase so that in each multiplication, we first authenticate c before using a triple to multiply. Since a malicious party may have introduced errors in c, we then need to add a *verification phase*, to check the multiplications are correct. We do this following the approach of Chida et al. [CGH+18] (also used by the honest majority Fluid compiler of [CGG+21]). Here, as well as computing the circuit, the parties compute a randomised version of the circuit, where each wire value has been multiplied by a secret, random value $r \in \mathbb{F}_p$. At the end of the computation, the parties run a batch verification process to check consistency of the two computations. We show that this guarantees our protocol is correct, even with our weaker preprocessing protocol which allows malicious parties to introduce special types of errors into c.

Overall, the communication cost of our dynamic online protocol is only 4 field elements on top of the SPDZ online phase [DPSZ12, DKL+13], which costs 2 elements per party. However, this comes with the benefits of (1) a dynamically chosen online committee, and (2) a PCG-friendly preprocessing phase, where each party's communication and storage complexity is $O(n \log |C|)$, instead of $O(|C|)$ storage and $O(n|C|)$ communication for standard SPDZ preprocessing. Note that after locally expanding the PCG seeds, the preprocessing material for our dynamic and fluid protocols has size $O(n|C|)$ per party, which is n times larger than SPDZ. However, once the online committee is known in Dynamic SPDZ, this can be compressed down to $O(|C|)$.

Maximally Fluid Online Phase. We now turn to the harder task of obtaining an online phase where the set of computing parties can dynamically change. We

---

[1] In the two party setting, an efficient PCG-based SPDZ preprocessing protocol was given in [BCG+19b].

focus on the most challenging goal of *maximal fluidity*, where in each round, a different committee can sign up to receive one round of messages from the previous committee, before sending one round of messages and going offline.

This brings additional obstacles when it comes to preprocessing data, as well as verifying MACs on opened values during the online protocol. Since the MAC key of a committee is determined by the sum of the MAC keys of the parties in it, different committees will have different MAC keys. The issue with this is that, even though our universal preprocessing allows any committee to obtain a multiplication triple, these triples end up being authenticated under different MAC keys, depending on the committee. Hence, re-sharing state from one committee to another will lead to values that are authenticated under a different MAC key.

As a first attempt to deal with this problem, one could have the current committee, $\mathcal{P}_{\mathsf{curr}}$, securely *reshare* the current state of intermediate computation values, including their MAC key $\Delta_{\mathcal{P}_{\mathsf{curr}}}$, to the next committee, $\mathcal{P}_{\mathsf{next}}$. To proceed further, however, $\mathcal{P}_{\mathsf{next}}$ will need authenticated triples under the same MAC key. Our preprocessing phase, on the other hand, only allows them to obtain triples under a different key $\Delta_{\mathcal{P}_{\mathsf{next}}}$. To avoid this issue, $\mathcal{P}_{\mathsf{curr}}$ would instead have to reshare *all of* the triples needed for the rest of the circuit evaluation, after which, $\mathcal{P}_{\mathsf{next}}$ would use some of these, reshare to the next committee and so on. This incurs a huge blow up in communication cost, which we would like to avoid.

Our method for dealing with this is a secure *key-switching* procedure, which allows $\mathcal{P}_{\mathsf{curr}}$ to transfer a shared $[\![x]\!]$ to $\mathcal{P}_{\mathsf{next}}$ in a single round, while switching to $\mathcal{P}_{\mathsf{next}}$'s MAC key. Another constraint we have from the model is that $\mathcal{P}_{\mathsf{next}}$ cannot send any messages to $\mathcal{P}_{\mathsf{curr}}$. At first glance, it may seem impossible, since $\mathcal{P}_{\mathsf{curr}}$ should not have any information on the next key. However, we show that by leveraging the power of our universal preprocessing, key-switching can be done with just a single set of messages from $\mathcal{P}_{\mathsf{curr}}$ to $\mathcal{P}_{\mathsf{next}}$.

In addition to securely switching keys, another challenge in our maximally fluid protocol is how to check MACs on opened values. We cannot use the batched MAC check from SPDZ, since this involves storing a large state, which has to be passed around until the end of the protocol. Instead, we modify this to an incremental procedure, where only a constant-sized state needs to be transferred in each round. We adopt a similar incremental protocol to verify multiplications, where, as in our Dynamic SPDZ protocol, we use the same randomised circuit idea as [CGH+18].

1.2 Related Work

Bracha [Bra85] introduced the idea of using committees in distributed protocols with a large number of parties, which has been used in a number of MPC protocols since. One recent example is [GSY21], which constructs committee-based MPC when up to 1/3 of the parties may be corrupt, achieving a construction that scales to hundreds of thousands of parties. Although part of their protocol is based on SPDZ, they do not support the notion of a dynamically chosen subset of parties from the preprocessing set carrying out the online computation.

Concretely, their online phase for circuit evaluation costs 7x higher than SPDZ, whereas we estimate that we only suffer a 3x overhead. A detailed analysis of the costs is provided in Sect. 6.

Another relevant work is [SSW17], which outsources SPDZ preprocessing to an external set of parties. However, unlike our protocol, this requires resharing the entire preprocessing data from the external set to the online committee. We avoid this in Dynamic SPDZ, by relying on our universal preprocessing.

The area of proactive security has long considered the notion of an adversary who can corrupt different parties throughout the computation. These works typically use a proactive secret sharing scheme, where secrets are maintained by an ever-changing set of parties. Works such as [HJKY95, MZW+19] show security in the presence of a mobile adversary that can corrupt and uncorrupt parties at different points in the protocol. More recently, [BGG+20, GKM+20] construct secret-sharing protocols for the case of honest majority with active security. The model used in these papers also splits the work done by each committee into two parts, one used to do the computation with parties interacting only within the committee, and one used to perform a secure state-transfer to the committee that comes after them. The primary difference between Fluid SPDZ and proactive MPC is the motivation and the behaviour of the adversary. In proactive schemes, the adversary typically operates with a "corruption budget" that limits the adversary from being able to corrupt parties arbitrarily. We do not make such an assumption, and our motivation primarily comes from giving parties in a computation the ability to drop in and out, while minimising the minimum number of rounds they have to stay on for. In addition, we try to achieve a small *state complexity*, so that switching committees is not communication intensive.

2   Preliminaries and Security Model

2.1   Preliminaries

We use κ as the security parameter and ρ as the statistical security parameter. Bold letters such as a are used to indicate vectors, and $a[i]$ refers to the i-th element of the vector. We write $[a, b]$ to denote the set of natural numbers $\{a, \ldots, b\}$ and $[a, b) = \{a, \ldots, b - 1\}$.

Additional Functionalities. We make use of some standard functionalities in the paper, which are detailed in the full version [RS21]. These include a functionality for oblivious transfer $\mathcal{F}_{OT}$, coin-tossing $\mathcal{F}_{Rand}$, commitment $\mathcal{F}_{Commit}$, and a weak equality test $\mathcal{F}_{EQ}$, that checks equality of two private inputs, while always revealing one party's input to the adversary.

2.2   Modelling Fluid MPC in Dishonest Majority

The remainder of this subsection covers definitions pertaining to the Fluid model. Computation broadly proceeds in 4 phases – preprocessing, input, execution, and output. This is similar to that of Fluid MPC [CGG+21], with the addition of a preprocessing phase, which is used to generate data-independent information in the form of multiplication triples, to be used in the execution phase. In the preprocessing phase, we require all parties who wish to take part in the computation at some later point to be active, and after this they may go offline. The execution phase proceeds in epochs, where each epoch runs among a fixed set of parties, or committee. An epoch contains two parts, the *computation phase*, where the committee performs some computation, followed by a *hand-off phase*, used to securely transfer the current state to the next committee.

Fluidity. The computation phase of each epoch may take several rounds of interaction. Fluidity is defined as the minimum number of rounds in any given epoch of the execution phase. We say that a protocol achieves *maximal fluidity* if the epoch only lasts for one round. This means each server in the committee does some local computation, before sending a single message to the next committee in the hand-off phase. In the input and output phases, we do not measure fluidity, instead, the committee may interact for several rounds to share inputs or reconstruct the outputs.

A server is said to be "active" in the computation if it either performs computations or sends and/or receives messages. Therefore, a server participating in epoch i is active starting from the hand-off phase of epoch $i - 1$, until the end of the hand-off phase of epoch i.

Committee formation. The committees used in each epoch may be either fixed ahead of time, or chosen on-the-fly throughout the computation. Fixing them ahead of time can be useful, for instance, in a volunteer sign-up based model, where servers can volunteer to participate in any epoch, and stay on for any number of epochs depending on their resource constraints. On the other hand, choosing committees on-the-fly may be desirable in settings closer to the YOSO model [GHK+21], where a role-assignment mechanism is used to ensure that the next committee is only revealed at the last possible moment.

In this work, we do not distinguish between these two cases, and instead simply require that during the hand-off phase of epoch i, the current committee, denoted $\mathcal{P}_i$, knows the identities of the parties in the next committee $\mathcal{P}_{i+1}$. We make no assumptions or restrictions about the overlap between committees. As in [CGG+21], the formation process can be modelled with an ideal functionality that samples and broadcasts committees according to the desired mechanism.

Corruption. Our model allows all-but-one of the servers who are active at the start of any given epoch to be corrupted, where the set of corrupt parties is fixed at the beginning of the epoch. Formally, this corresponds to an R-*adaptive adversary* from [CGG+21]. Here, at the beginning of epoch i with committee $\mathcal{P}_i$, the adversary may adaptively choose a set of servers in $\mathcal{P}_i$ to be corrupted, and then learns the entire state of each corrupted server in any prior epochs. For the duration of epoch i, this set of corrupted parties is then fixed and cannot change. To rule out the adversary learning information on prior epochs, a server

S may be corrupted in epoch i only if this does not lead to any prior epoch j with committee $\mathcal{P}_j$ becoming entirely corrupt.

We use this model for the online phase of our fluid MPC protocol. Note that for our dynamic SPDZ protocol, where the online committee does not change, this corresponds to the more common notion of static security. In the preprocessing phase for both dynamic SPDZ and our fluid MPC protocol, we have only proven security against a static adversary. While for fluid MPC, we would ideally also like the preprocessing to be adaptively secure, this is particularly challenging in the dishonest majority setting, and is known to imply strong primitives like non-committing encryption. In fact, since no practical adaptively secure preprocessing protocols are even known for the standard SPDZ protocol [DPSZ12], we view this as an interesting open problem.

2.3   Security Model

To model fluid MPC, we adopt the arithmetic black box model (ABB), which is an ideal functionality $\mathcal{F}_{ABB}$ in the universal composability framework [Can01]. The functionality allows for a set of parties $P_1, \ldots, P_n$ to input their values, perform computations on them, and receive the outputs. The functionality is parameterised by a finite field $\mathbb{F}_p$, and supports native operations of addition and multiplication in the field.

We instantiate $\mathcal{F}_{ABB}$ with the Dynamic SPDZ protocol ($\Pi_{SPDZ\text{-}Online}$), which uses a preprocessing phase between a set of parties, and supports a dynamically chosen subset to perform the online phase. The preprocessing phase is used to set up partially authenticated, partially formed triples using pairwise MACs similar to BDOZ [BDOZ11] and TinyOT [HSS17]. We adapt the vector OLE from Wolverine [WYKW21], and PCGs from [BCG+19a] and use them to form the partial triples.

To model Fluid MPC, we modify $\mathcal{F}_{ABB}$ to support computations with dynamic committees, as functionality $\mathcal{F}_{DABB}$ in Fig. 1. The main difference is that now, the functionality keeps track of the currently active committee in a variable $\mathcal{P}_{curr}$. In operations which are part of the execution phase, where the committee may change, the functionality receives the identity of the next committee from the currently active parties (if it receives inconsistent inputs, we assume it aborts). In our protocol, the **Batch Multiply** command is the only part of the execution phase with interaction, so this is where any changes in committee might take place. We have $\mathcal{P}_{curr}$ provide the next committee $\mathcal{P}_{next}$ as input, and then wait for another message from $\mathcal{P}_{next}$, who will provide a subsequent committee $\mathcal{P}'_{next}$. This is because our multiplication protocol takes place over two rounds, so it inherently allows up to two committee changes whenever it is called (if we want to support maximal fluidity).

In practice, with our protocol it is possible to interleave multiplications, so that a new multiplication can be started before the old one has finished (reducing round complexity). However, for simplicity, we do not model this in $\mathcal{F}_{DABB}$.

We instantiate $\mathcal{F}_{DABB}$ with a Fluid Online ($\Pi_{Fluid\text{-}Online}$) protocol. It extends the model of Fluid MPC [CGG+21] which only works for the honest majority

---

Functionality $\mathcal{F}_{\mathsf{DABB}}$

Parameters: Finite field $\mathbb{F}_p$, and set of parties $\mathcal{P}_{\mathsf{main}} = \{P_1, \ldots, P_n\}$. The functionality assumes all parties have agreed upon public identifiers id_x, for each variable x used in the computation. For a vector $\boldsymbol{x} = (x_1, \ldots, x_m)$, we write $\mathsf{id}_{\boldsymbol{x}} = (\mathsf{id}_{x_1}, \ldots, \mathsf{id}_{x_m})$.

Initialise: On input $(\mathsf{Init}, \mathcal{P}_{\mathsf{curr}})$ from P_i, for $i \in [1, n]$, where each P_i sends the same set $\mathcal{P}_{\mathsf{curr}} \subset \mathcal{P}_{\mathsf{main}}$, initialise $\mathcal{P}_{\mathsf{curr}}$ as the first active committee.

Input: On input $(\mathsf{Input}, \mathsf{id}_x, x)$ from some $P_i \in \mathcal{P}_{\mathsf{main}}$, and $(\mathsf{Input}, \mathsf{id}_x)$ from all parties in $\mathcal{P}_{\mathsf{curr}}$, store the pair (id_x, x).

Add: On input $(\mathsf{Add}, \mathsf{id}_z, \mathsf{id}_x, \mathsf{id}_y)$ from P_i, for every $P_i \in \mathcal{P}_{\mathsf{curr}}$, compute $z = x + y$ and store (id_z, z).

Batch Multiply: On input $(\mathsf{Mult}, \mathcal{P}_{\mathsf{next}}, \mathsf{id}_{\boldsymbol{z}}, \mathsf{id}_{\boldsymbol{x}}, \mathsf{id}_{\boldsymbol{y}})$ from every $P_i \in \mathcal{P}_{\mathsf{curr}}$:

- Compute $\boldsymbol{z} = \boldsymbol{x} * \boldsymbol{y}$.
- Update $\mathcal{P}_{\mathsf{curr}} := \mathcal{P}_{\mathsf{next}}$.
- Wait to receive a message $(\mathsf{MultFinish}, \mathcal{P}'_{\mathsf{next}})$ from every $P_i \in \mathcal{P}_{\mathsf{curr}}$. Then, store the batch of products $(\mathsf{id}_{\boldsymbol{z}}, \boldsymbol{z})$ and update $\mathcal{P}_{\mathsf{curr}} := \mathcal{P}'_{\mathsf{next}}$.

Output: On input $(\mathsf{Output}, \mathsf{id}_z)$ from every $P_i \in \mathcal{P}_{\mathsf{curr}}$, where id_z has been stored previously, retrieve (id_z, z) and send it to the adversary. Wait for input from the adversary, if it is $\mathsf{Deliver}$, send the output to every $P_i \in \mathcal{P}_{\mathsf{curr}}$. Otherwise, abort.

Fig. 1. Functionality for a dynamic arithmetic black box

case, to the dishonest majority setting with active security. It uses the same preprocessing phase as Dynamic SPDZ, but the online phase supports committees switching. Parties can leave the computation by securely transferring their state to the subsequent committee, and rejoin the computation at a later point.

3 Universal Preprocessing for Dynamic Committees

In this section, we present the preprocessing phase used in our two online protocols. Our main design goals are (1) to allow a flexible and dynamic choice of participants during the online phase, and (2) to obtain a silent preprocessing phase, where the storage and communication complexities are (almost) independent of the function being computed. The section is organised in a top-down manner, where we start by describing an ideal preprocessing functionality, and then gradually explain our protocol for realising it.

Overview. In this section, we focus on realising $\mathcal{F}_{\mathsf{Prep}}$, using variants of oblivious linear function evaluation (OLE), as well as how to realise a multi-party variant of vector-OLE ($\mathcal{F}_{\text{nVOLE}}$). Some of the remaining building blocks we use to implement this are deferred to the full version [RS21].

3.1 Preprocessing Functionality

Let $\mathcal{P}_{\text{main}} = \{P_1, \ldots, P_n\}$ be the set of all parties who may want to participate in the online phase.

Authenticated Secret Sharing. For the preprocessing, we use two kinds of secret sharing. $[x]$ denotes that $x \in \mathbb{F}_p$ is additively shared between the parties, that is, $x = x^1 + \ldots + x^n$ where P_i holds x^i. We also use pairwise authenticated shares, indicated by $\langle x \rangle$. Here, in addition to an additive share of x, each party holds an information-theoretic MAC on their share with every other party, who holds a corresponding MAC key. The MAC of P_i's share x^i under P_j's key is defined as $M_j^i = K_i^j + \Delta^j \cdot x^i$, where P_i holds the MAC M_j^i and P_j holds the local key K_i^j as well as the global key Δ^j (which is fixed for all MACs). While the shares x^i lie over the field $\mathbb{F}_p$, we allow MAC keys and MACs to be in an extension field $\mathbb{F}_{p^r}$, giving a forgery probability of p^{-r}, in case p is not large enough for the desired statistical security level.

If x is only shared between a smaller committee $\mathcal{P}_C \subset \mathcal{P}_{\text{main}}$, we write $[x]^{\mathcal{P}_C}$. Similarly, for pairwise MACs, we can consider a sharing between two (possibly overlapping) committees $\mathcal{P}_A, \mathcal{P}_B \subset \mathcal{P}_{\text{main}}$, where $\mathcal{P}_A$ holds shares and MACs on x, while $\mathcal{P}_B$ holds the corresponding MAC keys:

$$\langle x \rangle^{\mathcal{P}_A, \mathcal{P}_B} = \left(\{x^i, (M_j^i)_{j \in \mathcal{P}_B}\}_{i \in \mathcal{P}_A}, \{\Delta^j, (K_i^j)_{i \in \mathcal{P}_A}\}_{j \in \mathcal{P}_B} \right)$$

When the committees are clear from context, we will sometimes omit them and simply write $\langle x \rangle$ or $[x]$.

If all the parties in $\mathcal{P}$ of size n have a sharing $\langle x \rangle^{\mathcal{P}}$, where $x = x^1 + \cdots + x^n$, any two subsets $\mathcal{P}_A, \mathcal{P}_B$ can locally convert this into a sharing $\langle x' \rangle^{\mathcal{P}_A, \mathcal{P}_B}$ of a *different* value $x' = \sum_{i \in \mathcal{P}_A} x^i$. This procedure is done by simply restricting the relevant shares and MACs to those corresponding to the two committees. We denote it as follows:

$$\mathsf{RestrictShares}(\langle x \rangle^{\mathcal{P}}, \mathcal{P}_A, \mathcal{P}_B) \to \langle x' \rangle^{\mathcal{P}_A, \mathcal{P}_B}$$

In our protocols, we rely on the fact that if the original shares of x were uniformly random, then so is the resulting value x'.

Functionality (Fig. 2). The aim of $\mathcal{F}_{\text{Prep}}$ is to allow arbitrary committees to obtain $[\cdot]$ and $\langle \cdot \rangle$-shared values, in the form of random authenticated field elements, and partial triples. The functionality begins with an initialization phase, which models the setting up of the necessary data to obtain up to m_R random values and m_T multiplication triples. Then, either the Rand or Trip command can be queried by a pair of dynamically-chosen committees $(\mathcal{P}_{\text{curr}}, \mathcal{P}_{\text{next}})$, who obtain the appropriate shares. We assume that each query uses a distinct index k, which is necessary to ensure that in our protocol, the corresponding preprocessing data is not reused when another committee produces a triple.[2]

A key difference between our functionality and previous works like SPDZ [DPSZ12, DKL+13] is that our triples are only *partially authenticated*. In a random triple (a, b, c) where $c = a \cdot b$, the values a and b are authenticated with pairwise MACs, while c is only additively shared. This is a crucial aspect which allows our protocol to support dynamically-chosen parties, and also achieving a communication overhead that is significantly less than the circuit size. One drawback of this preprocessing, compared to SPDZ, is that the size of each partial triple is $O(n)$ field elements per party, due to the pairwise MACs and products. However, once the online phase committee in which the triples will be used is known, they can be compressed to standard, constant-sized SPDZ triples.

3.2   Preprocessing Protocol

Our protocol for realising $\mathcal{F}_{\mathsf{Prep}}$ consists of two main building blocks: a 2-party OLE functionality, and an n-party vector-OLE (VOLE) functionality; we elaborate on these below, and later (in Sect. 3.3) show how they can be realized. These are used for computing the unauthenticated shares of c in multiplication triples, and authenticated shares of random values, respectively.

Programmable OLE. We use a functionality for *random, programmable oblivious linear evaluation* (OLE), $\mathcal{F}_{\mathsf{OLE}}^{\mathsf{prog}}$, shown in Fig. 3. This is a two-party functionality, which computes a batch of secret-shared products, i.e. random tuples $(u_i, v_i), (w_i, x_i)$, where $w_i = u_i x_i + v_i$, over the field $\mathbb{F}_p$. The *programmability* requirement is that, for any given instance of the functionality, the party who obtains u_i or v_i can program these to be derived from a chosen random seed. This allows e.g. the same u_i's to be used in a different instance of $\mathcal{F}_{\mathsf{OLE}}^{\mathsf{prog}}$. We model the programmability with a function $\mathsf{Expand} : S \to \mathbb{F}_{p^r}^m$, which deterministically expands the chosen seed into a vector of field elements. When instantiating the functionality, the expansion function will correspond to some kind of secure PRG.

Multi-party programmable VOLE. Vector oblivious linear evaluation (VOLE) can be seen as a batch of OLEs with the same x_i value in each tuple, that is, a vector $\boldsymbol{w} = \boldsymbol{u}x + \boldsymbol{v}$, where $x \in \mathbb{F}_p$ is a scalar given to one party. Here, while x lies in the field $\mathbb{F}_p$, the remaining values are in the extension field $\mathbb{F}_{p^r}$, since we use VOLE to generate MACs. In multi-party VOLE, shown as $\mathcal{F}_{\mathsf{nVOLE}}$ in Fig. 4, every pair of parties (P_i, P_j) is given a random VOLE instance $\boldsymbol{w}_j^i = \boldsymbol{u}^i x^j + \boldsymbol{v}_i^j$. The functionality guarantees *consistency*, in the sense that the same $\boldsymbol{u}^i$ or x^j values will be used in each of the instances involving P_i or P_j. While unlike the OLE

---

[2] In our online phases, we assume the parties have a means of agreeing upon the ordering of committees to ensure that the indices queried to $\mathcal{F}_{\mathsf{Prep}}$ are not reused.

Functionality $\mathcal{F}_{\mathsf{Prep}}$

Parameters: Finite fields $\mathbb{F}_p$ and $\mathbb{F}_{p^r}$, parties $P_1, \ldots, P_n$, adversary $\mathcal{A}$ and set of honest parties $\mathcal{P}_H$.

Functionality: Generates triples with unauthenticated c, and authenticated random values.

Init: On receiving $(\mathsf{Init}, m_T, m_R)$ from P_i, for $i \in [1, n]$, where m_T is the upper bound on the number of triples and m_R on random values, sample a MAC key $\Delta^i \leftarrow \mathbb{F}_{p^r}$, send Δ^i to P_i and ignore subsequent Init commands from P_i.

Random Value: On input $(\mathsf{Rand}, \mathcal{P}_{\mathsf{curr}}, \mathcal{P}_{\mathsf{next}}, k)$ from every $P_i \in \mathcal{P}_{\mathsf{curr}} \cup \mathcal{P}_{\mathsf{next}}$, where $k \in [1, m_R]$ and Rand has not been queried before with the same k:

1. Sample shares $r^i \leftarrow \mathbb{F}_p$, for $i \in \mathcal{P}_{\mathsf{curr}}$.
2. For each $i \in \mathcal{P}_{\mathsf{curr}}$ and $j \in \mathcal{P}_{\mathsf{next}} \setminus \{i\}$, sample $K_i^j \leftarrow \mathbb{F}_{p^r}$ and let $M_j^i = K_i^j + \Delta^j \cdot r^i \in \mathbb{F}_{p^r}$.
3. Let $\langle r \rangle^{\mathcal{P}_{\mathsf{curr}}, \mathcal{P}_{\mathsf{next}}} = \left(r^i, (M_j^i, K_i^j)_{j \in \mathcal{P}_{\mathsf{next}} \setminus \{i\}} \right)_{i \in \mathcal{P}_{\mathsf{curr}}}$, and output the relevant shares, MACs and MAC keys to the parties in $\mathcal{P}_{\mathsf{curr}}, \mathcal{P}_{\mathsf{next}}$.

Triple: On input $(\mathsf{Trip}, \mathcal{P}_{\mathsf{curr}}, \mathcal{P}_{\mathsf{next}}, k)$, from every $P_i \in \mathcal{P}_{\mathsf{curr}} \cup \mathcal{P}_{\mathsf{next}}$, where $k \in [1, m_T]$ and Trip has not been queried before with the same k:

1. Run the steps from **Random Value** twice, to create sharings $\langle a \rangle, \langle b \rangle$.
2. *Additive errors:* Wait for $\mathcal{A}$ to input $\{\delta_a^i, \delta_b^i\}_{i \in \mathcal{P}_H \cap \mathcal{P}_{\mathsf{curr}}}$, each in $\mathbb{F}_p$. Let $c = a \cdot b + \sum_{i \in \mathcal{P}_H \cap \mathcal{P}_{\mathsf{curr}}} (a^i \cdot \delta_b^i + b^i \cdot \delta_a^i)$.
3. Sample shares $c^i \in \mathbb{F}_p$, for $i \in \mathcal{P}_{\mathsf{curr}}$, such that $\sum_{i \in \mathcal{P}_{\mathsf{curr}}} c^i = c$. Let $[c]^{\mathcal{P}_{\mathsf{curr}}} := (c^i)_{i \in \mathcal{P}_{\mathsf{curr}}}$.
4. Output $\langle a \rangle^{\mathcal{P}_{\mathsf{curr}}, \mathcal{P}_{\mathsf{next}}}, \langle b \rangle^{\mathcal{P}_{\mathsf{curr}}, \mathcal{P}_{\mathsf{next}}}, [c]^{\mathcal{P}_{\mathsf{curr}}}$ to the parties in $\mathcal{P}_{\mathsf{curr}}, \mathcal{P}_{\mathsf{next}}$.

Corrupt parties: In addition to additive errors, corrupt parties may choose their own randomness for all sharings, namely r^i in Rand, a^i, b^i, c^i in Trip, as well as any MACs and MAC keys they receive. The honest parties' shares/MACs/keys are adjusted accordingly.

Fig. 2. Functionality for the preprocessing

functionality, the u^i, x^i values in $\mathcal{F}_{\mathsf{nVOLE}}$ are not programmable, we do require that the functionality outputs to P_i a short seed representing u^i, so that P_i can later use this as an input to program $\mathcal{F}_{\mathsf{OLE}}^{\mathsf{prog}}$.

Protocol. Given these building blocks, we use the preprocessing protocol Π_{Prep} (Fig. 5) to generate partially authenticated triples and authenticated random values between dynamically chosen committees. As discussed earlier, the key observation is that it suffices to generate a batch of *pairwise* secret-shared products, between every pair of parties, which can later be combined to produce preprocessing amongst an arbitrary subset of the parties.

The protocol is relatively straightforward, involving no interaction other than calling the relevant functionalities. In the Init phase of the protocol, each party

---

Functionality $\mathcal{F}_{\mathsf{OLE}}^{\mathsf{prog}}$

Parameters: Finite field $\mathbb{F}_{p^r}$, and expansion function $\mathsf{Expand} : S \to \mathbb{F}_p^m$ with seed space S and output length m.
The functionality runs between parties P_A and P_B.

On receiving s_a from P_A and s_b from P_B, where $s_a, s_b \in S$:

1. Compute $\boldsymbol{u} = \mathsf{Expand}(s_a)$, $\boldsymbol{x} = \mathsf{Expand}(s_b)$ and sample $\boldsymbol{v} \leftarrow \mathbb{F}_p^m$.
2. Output $\boldsymbol{w} = \boldsymbol{u} * \boldsymbol{x} + \boldsymbol{v}$ to P_A and $\boldsymbol{v}$ to P_B.

Corrupt parties: If P_B is corrupt, $\boldsymbol{v}$ may be chosen by $\mathcal{A}$. For a corrupt P_A, $\mathcal{A}$ can choose $\boldsymbol{w}$ (and then $\boldsymbol{v}$ is recomputed accordingly).

Fig. 3. Functionality for programmable OLE

Functionality $\mathcal{F}_{\mathsf{nVOLE}}$

Parameters: Finite field $\mathbb{F}_{p^r}$, and expansion function $\mathsf{Expand} : S \to \mathbb{F}_p^m$ with seed space S and output length m. The functionality runs between $P_1, \ldots, P_n$.

Initialise: On receiving Init from P_i, for $i \in [1, n]$, sample $\Delta^i \leftarrow \mathbb{F}_{p^r}$, send it to P_i, and ignore all subsequent Init commands from P_i.
Extend: On receiving (Extend) from every $P_i \in \mathcal{P}$:

1. Sample $\mathsf{seed}^i \leftarrow S$, for each $P_i \in \mathcal{P}$.
2. Compute $\boldsymbol{u}^i = \mathsf{Expand}(\mathsf{seed}^i)$.
3. Sample $(\boldsymbol{v}_i^j)_{j \neq i} \leftarrow \mathbb{F}_{p^r}^m$ for $i \in \mathcal{P}, j \neq i$. Retrieve Δ^j and compute $\boldsymbol{w}_j^i = \boldsymbol{u}^i \cdot \Delta^j + \boldsymbol{v}_i^j$.
4. If P_j is corrupt, receive a set I from $\mathcal{A}$. If $\mathsf{seed} \in I$, send success to P_j and continue. Else, send abort to both parties, output seed to P_j and abort.
5. Output $\left((\mathsf{seed}^i, \boldsymbol{w}_j^i), \boldsymbol{v}_j^i\right)_{j \neq i}$ to P_i, for $P_i \in \mathcal{P}$.

Corrupt parties: A corrupt P_i can choose Δ^i and seed^i. It can also choose $\boldsymbol{w}_j^i$ (and $\boldsymbol{v}_i^j$ is recomputed accordingly) and $\boldsymbol{v}_j^i$.
Global key query: If P_i is corrupted, receive (guess, Δ') from $\mathcal{A}$ with $\Delta' \in \mathbb{F}_{p^r}^n$. If $\Delta' = \Delta$, where $\Delta = (\Delta^1, \ldots, \Delta^n)$, send success to P_i and ignore any subsequent global key query. Else, send (abort, Δ) to P_i, abort to P_j and abort.

Fig. 4. Functionality for n-party VOLE

P_i initializes $\mathcal{F}_{\mathsf{nVOLE}}$, obtaining a random MAC key Δ^i. Parties use the **Extend** command of $\mathcal{F}_{\mathsf{nVOLE}}$ to authenticate their shares with every other party. Towards this, each P_i calls $\mathcal{F}_{\mathsf{nVOLE}}$ twice, which picks two random seeds s_a^i, s_b^i and expands them into the shares $\boldsymbol{a}^i, \boldsymbol{b}^i$. It outputs to P_i the pairwise MACs on its shares

---

Protocol Π_{Prep}

Parameters: Finite field $\mathbb{F}_{p^r}$, number of triples m_T, random values m_R, and expansion function $\mathsf{Expand} : S \rightarrow \mathbb{F}_p^m$ with seed space S and output length m.

Init: Run the following two stages among all the parties in $\mathcal{P}_{\mathsf{main}}$.

Triples setup: repeat the following, until $\geq m_T$ outputs have been obtained (each iteration produces m).

1. Each P_i calls $\mathcal{F}_{\mathsf{nVOLE}}$ with Init, receiving Δ^i.
2. Each P_i, for $i \in [1, n]$, calls $\mathcal{F}_{\mathsf{nVOLE}}$ twice, with input Extend and receives the seeds s_a^i, s_b^i. Use the outputs to define vectors of shares $\langle a \rangle, \langle b \rangle$ such that $\boldsymbol{a}^i = \mathsf{Expand}(s_a^i)$ and $\boldsymbol{b}^i = \mathsf{Expand}(s_b^i)$.
3. Every ordered pair (P_i, P_j) for $i, j \in [1, n]$ calls $\mathcal{F}_{\mathsf{OLE}}^{\mathsf{prog}}$ with P_i sending s_a^i and P_j sending s_b^j, and it sends back $\boldsymbol{u}^{i,j}$ to P_i and $\boldsymbol{v}^{j,i}$ to P_j, such that $\boldsymbol{u}^{i,j} + \boldsymbol{v}^{j,i} = \boldsymbol{a}^i * \boldsymbol{b}^j$.

Random values setup: repeat the following, until $\geq m_R$ outputs have been obtained.

1. Every P_i, for $i \in [1, n]$, samples a seed $s_r^i \in S$ and calls $\mathcal{F}_{\mathsf{nVOLE}}$ with input (Extend, s_r^i) from P_i, forming $\langle r \rangle$.

Triples: To get the k-th triple in committees $\mathcal{P}_{\mathsf{curr}}, \mathcal{P}_{\mathsf{next}}$:

1. Let $\langle a' \rangle, \langle b' \rangle$ be the k-th shares from $\langle a \rangle, \langle b \rangle$. The parties run $\mathsf{RestrictShares}(\langle a' \rangle, \langle b' \rangle, \mathcal{P}_{\mathsf{curr}}, \mathcal{P}_{\mathsf{next}})$ to obtain $\langle a \rangle^{\mathcal{P}_{\mathsf{curr}}, \mathcal{P}_{\mathsf{next}}}, \langle b \rangle^{\mathcal{P}_{\mathsf{curr}}, \mathcal{P}_{\mathsf{next}}}$.
2. Each $P_i \in \mathcal{P}_{\mathsf{curr}}$ computes $c^i = a^i \cdot b^i + \sum_{j \in \mathcal{P}_{\mathsf{curr}} \setminus \{i\}} (\boldsymbol{u}^{i,j}[k] + \boldsymbol{v}^{i,j}[k])$.
3. The parties output the triple $(\langle a \rangle^{\mathcal{P}_{\mathsf{curr}}, \mathcal{P}_{\mathsf{next}}}, \langle b \rangle^{\mathcal{P}_{\mathsf{curr}}, \mathcal{P}_{\mathsf{next}}}, [c]^{\mathcal{P}_{\mathsf{curr}}})$.

Random Values: To get the k-th random value in committees $\mathcal{P}_{\mathsf{curr}}, \mathcal{P}_{\mathsf{next}}$, the parties take $\langle r' \rangle$, the k-th random value from $\langle r \rangle$, and run $\mathsf{RestrictShares}$ to convert this to $\langle r \rangle^{\mathcal{P}_{\mathsf{curr}}, \mathcal{P}_{\mathsf{next}}}$.

Fig. 5. Protocol for preprocessing

of the triples, along with the seeds. Each pair (P_i, P_j) then use $\mathcal{F}_{\mathsf{OLE}}^{\mathsf{prog}}$ to obtain 2-party sharings of the products $\boldsymbol{a}^i * \boldsymbol{b}^j$, for each $j \neq i$.

Later, when a triple is required by the committees $\mathcal{P}_{\mathsf{curr}}, \mathcal{P}_{\mathsf{next}}$, every party in the committee $\mathcal{P}_{\mathsf{curr}}$ sums up its pairwise shares of the product terms corresponding to one triple, obtaining a share of $a \cdot b$, where a, b are the sum of the corresponding shares within that committee. The second committee $\mathcal{P}_{\mathsf{next}}$ does not have any shares of $a \cdot b$, but instead obtains the MAC keys on the a, b shares from the previous $\mathcal{F}_{\mathsf{nVOLE}}$ outputs. To obtain authenticated random values, a similar procedure is done using only $\mathcal{F}_{\mathsf{nVOLE}}$ to add MACs.

Note that, if a corrupt party P_i inputs an inconsistent seed s_a^i or s_b^i into $\mathcal{F}_{\mathsf{OLE}}^{\mathsf{prog}}$, the resulting triple will be incorrect. This is modelled by the additive errors that may be introduced in $\mathcal{F}_{\mathsf{Prep}}$.

In the full version [RS21], we prove the following.

Theorem 1. *Suppose that* Expand $: S \to \mathbb{F}_p^m$ *is a secure pseudorandom generator. Then, the protocol* Π_{Prep} *securely implements the functionality* $\mathcal{F}_{\mathsf{Prep}}$ *in the* $(\mathcal{F}_{\mathsf{nVOLE}}, \mathcal{F}_{\mathsf{OLE}}^{\mathsf{prog}})$*-hybrid model, when up to* $n-1$ *out of* n *parties are corrupted.*

3.3   Instantiating Multi-party VOLE

In multi-party VOLE, each party P_i runs an instance of random VOLE with every other party P_j. We model two-party random VOLE as the functionality $\mathcal{F}_{\mathsf{VOLE}}^{\mathsf{prog}}$ [RS21], and show how to realize it in Sect. 3.3. To allow parties to use the *same* random input in different VOLE instances, the functionality is also programmable, similarly to $\mathcal{F}_{\mathsf{OLE}}^{\mathsf{prog}}$.

The main challenge in realizing $\mathcal{F}_{\mathsf{nVOLE}}$ is to guarantee that each party uses the same programmed input across every instance of $\mathcal{F}_{\mathsf{VOLE}}^{\mathsf{prog}}$ with other parties. For instance, a corrupt party P_i could potentially use different Δ^i values as the sender, or different seeds for $\boldsymbol{u}^i$ as the receiver across instances. To prevent this, we use a consistency check to prevent parties from using different inputs across the instances. The check involves taking a random linear combination of the outputs of $\mathcal{F}_{\mathsf{VOLE}}^{\mathsf{prog}}$ and opening the sum, and is similar to the $\Pi_{\mathsf{TripleBucketing}}$ protocol from [HSS17], except we work over a general finite field rather than $\mathbb{F}_2$.

Another difference is that we formalize the resulting protocol and show it realizes the multi-party VOLE functionality, while in [HSS17], the check was only used as part of a larger protocol. To prove this, we had to introduce the **Global key query** command in $\mathcal{F}_{\mathsf{nVOLE}}$, which allows corrupt parties to try to guess the honest parties' global scalars (MAC keys).

The final protocol for Π_{nVOLE} appears in Fig. 6.

Consistency Check: Since $\mathcal{F}_{\mathsf{VOLE}}^{\mathsf{prog}}$ does not guarantee that each party uses the same seed s^i or scalar Δ^i with every other party, we need some sort of a consistency check to detect malicious behaviour. The high level idea is for parties to compute random linear combinations on the outputs of $\mathcal{F}_{\mathsf{VOLE}}^{\mathsf{prog}}$, securely open the sum and check that it is zero. This check is similar to the idea from [HSS17], wherein it was used to check TinyOT triples.

The protocol starts with each (P_i, P_j) running $\mathcal{F}_{\mathsf{VOLE}}^{\mathsf{prog}}$ between them twice, once with P_i as the sender and once as the receiver. Recall that for a value v, P_i holds the share $\langle v \rangle = (v^i, \{M_j^i, K_j^i\}_{j \neq i})$. Using the outputs of $\mathcal{F}_{\mathsf{VOLE}}^{\mathsf{prog}}$, each P_i can define its shares of $\langle r_1 \rangle, \ldots, \langle r_m \rangle, \langle t \rangle \in \mathbb{F}_{p^r}$ locally. To compute a random linear combination, parties call $\mathcal{F}_{\mathsf{Rand}}$ and receive $\chi_1, \ldots, \chi_m \in \mathbb{F}_{p^r}$. They can locally compute shares of $\langle C \rangle$, and reconstruct C by broadcasting the shares. We wish to check $\sum_{i=1}^{n} Z_j^i = 0$ for $j \in [1, n]$, where $\{Z_j^i\}_{i \neq j} = M_j^i$ and $Z_i^i = (C^i - C) \cdot \Delta^i - \sum_{j \neq i} K_j^i$. Parties commit and open their shares, and locally check that each $\sum_{i=1}^{n} Z_j^i = 0$. If any of them fail, they abort.

An analysis of the check is provided in the full version [RS21], along with the proof for the following theorem:

Protocol Π_{nVOLE}

Parameters: Extension field $\mathbb{F}_{p^r}$, parties $P_1, \ldots, P_n$.
Initialise: Each party P_i samples $\Delta^i \leftarrow \mathbb{F}_{p^r}$. Every ordered pair of parties (P_i, P_j) calls $\mathcal{F}_{\mathsf{VOLE}}^{\mathsf{prog}}$ with $(\mathsf{Init}, \Delta^i)$, Init respectively.
Random Values: To create m authenticated random values $\langle r_1 \rangle, \ldots, \langle r_m \rangle$,

1. Each party P_i samples a seed s^i.
2. Each ordered pair of parties (P_i, P_j) call $\mathcal{F}_{\mathsf{VOLE}}^{\mathsf{prog}}$, with P_i sending (Extend, s^i) and P_j sending Extend. P_i receives $\{r_k^i, M_j^{i,k}\}$ and P_j receives $K_i^{j,k}$ for $k \in [1, m+1]$.
3. The outputs of $\mathcal{F}_{\mathsf{VOLE}}^{\mathsf{prog}}$ define sharings $\langle r_1 \rangle, \ldots, \langle r_m \rangle, \langle t \rangle \in \mathbb{F}_{p^r}$, where each $r_j = \sum_{i=1}^n r_j^i$ and $t = \sum_{i=1}^n r_{m+1}^i$.
4. Each P_i does the following to check the consistency of inputs to $\mathcal{F}_{\mathsf{VOLE}}^{\mathsf{prog}}$:
   (a) Call $\mathcal{F}_{\mathsf{Rand}}$ together with other parties to get random values $\chi_1, \ldots, \chi_m \in \mathbb{F}_{p^r}$.
   (b) Locally compute
$$\langle C \rangle = \sum_{i=1}^m \chi_i \cdot \langle r_i \rangle + \langle t \rangle$$
   (c) P_i has a share C^i, the MACs and keys $(M_j^i, K_j^i)_{j \neq i}$ from $\langle C \rangle$.
   (d) P_i rerandomizes the share locally by sending a zero share to the other parties. Call the randomised shares $\hat{C}^i$.
   (e) Broadcasts $\hat{C}^i$ and reconstructs $C = \sum_{i=1}^n \hat{C}^i$
   (f) P_i calls $\mathcal{F}_{\mathsf{Commit}}$ with $n+1$ values:
$$C^i, \quad (Z_j^i)_{j \neq i} = M_j^i, \quad Z_i^i = (C^i - C) \cdot \Delta^i - \sum_{j \neq i} K_j^i$$

5. Parties open their commitments and check that $\sum_{i=1}^n Z_j^i = 0$, for $j \in [1,n]$. In addition, each P_i checks that $Z_i^j = K_j^i + C^j \cdot \Delta^i$. If any of the checks fail, **abort**.

Fig. 6. Protocol for Consistent VOLE

Theorem 2. *Protocol Π_{nVOLE} UC-securely computes $\mathcal{F}_{\mathsf{nVOLE}}$ in the presence of a static malicious party corruption up to $n-1$ in the $(\mathcal{F}_{\mathsf{VOLE}}^{\mathsf{prog}}, \mathcal{F}_{\mathsf{Coin}}, \mathcal{F}_{\mathsf{Commit}})$-hybrid model.*

The Missing Pieces: Programmable OLE and VOLE. We now describe how to realize the two missing building blocks used in our preprocessing protocol, namely 2-party programmable OLE and VOLE.

Realizing $\mathcal{F}_{\mathsf{OLE}}^{\mathsf{prog}}$. This can be realized in a number of ways, for instance, based on linearly homomorphic encryption [BDOZ11]. However, this would give a protocol with communication that scales *linearly* in m, the number of OLEs. Instead, we rely on the recent work of [BCG+20], which uses a variant of the ring-LPN assumption to obtain communication that is *logarithmic* in m. While the OLE functionality from [BCG+20] is not programmable, we observe that their protocol easily supports programmable inputs, so suffices for our application.

Realizing $\mathcal{F}_{\mathsf{VOLE}}^{\mathsf{prog}}$. Unlike the OLE protocol from [BCG+20], this work starts with a building block called *single-point* VOLE, where the vector $\boldsymbol{u}$ contains a single, non-zero element, which is assumed to be sampled at random. When we need programmability, however, we cannot assume this. We therefore modify the underlying single-point VOLE from [WYKW21] to support programmable inputs, and show that the resulting protocol is still secure. We show how this can then be used to build programmable VOLE, with essentially the same steps as [WYKW21]. The full details of this are given in the full version [RS21].

4   Dynamic SPDZ

We now show how to use our preprocessing to obtain a dynamic variant of the SPDZ protocol [DPSZ12,DKL+13]. The preprocessing is performed between the entire set of parties $\mathcal{P}_{\mathsf{main}} = \{P_1, \ldots, P_n\}$, and later, when an *online phase committee* $\mathcal{P}_{\mathsf{curr}} \subset \mathcal{P}_{\mathsf{main}}$ wants to run MPC, they non-interactively select the relevant preprocessing data, and run our online phase. We consider evaluating arithmetic circuits over $\mathbb{F}_p$ for a large enough (superpolynomial) p, and will use $\mathcal{F}_{\mathsf{Prep}}$ entirely over $\mathbb{F}_p$ (i.e. not using the extension field $\mathbb{F}_{p^r}$).

Since our preprocessing is significantly weaker than SPDZ—due to faulty and partially authenticated triples—we cannot use the same online phase for multiplications. Instead, in our multiplication protocol, we will first have the parties add a MAC to the 'c' component of a triple (using a preprocessed random authenticated value), and then use the fully authenticated triple to multiply. Since the triples may be faulty, to verify multiplications we take the approach of [CGH+18], where parties compute two versions of the circuit: one with the actual inputs and one with a randomised version of the inputs. At the end of the protocol, they first run a MAC Check protocol to verify correctness of the opened values in multiplication, as in SPDZ. If this check succeeds, they open the random value used to compute the randomised circuit. Using that, they take a random linear combination of wires in both circuits and check that they are the consistent. We start by describing the online phase protocol $\Pi_{\mathsf{SPDZ\text{-}Online}}$, before analysing the verification process and concluding with a cost analysis.

SPDZ Sharing, Share Conversion and Opening. A SPDZ share of $v \in \mathbb{F}_p$ contains a vector of additive shares $([v], [\Delta], [\Delta \cdot v])$, where the shares are held by each P_i within the current committee $\mathcal{P}_{\mathsf{curr}}$. We denote this by $[\![\cdot]\!]^{\mathcal{P}_{\mathsf{curr}}}$, and omit $\mathcal{P}_{\mathsf{curr}}$ when it is clear from context. Note that the MAC key Δ is fixed for every sharing in the same committee.

Given a pairwise authenticated sharing $\langle x \rangle^{\mathcal{P}_{\mathsf{curr}}, \mathcal{P}_{\mathsf{curr}}}$, the parties can *locally* convert this into a SPDZ sharing with the procedure Π_{Convert}:

$$\Pi_{\text{Convert}}(\langle x \rangle^{\mathcal{P}_{\text{curr}}, \mathcal{P}_{\text{curr}}}) : P_i \text{ outputs } \left(x^i, \Delta^i, \Delta^i \cdot x^i + \sum_{j \in \mathcal{P}_{\text{curr}}} (M_j^i - K_j^i) \right)$$

where M_j^i, K_j^i are P_i's MACs and MAC keys from the $\langle \cdot \rangle$ sharing. By inspection, this gives a consistent sharing $[\![x]\!]^{\mathcal{P}_{\text{curr}}}$.

We let Π_{Open} denote the opening protocol, which given $[\![x]\!]$ or $[x]$ has all parties send to each other their shares x^i and reconstruct $x = \sum x^i$. This procedure does not check the MACs, so it may be unreliable. To check the MAC on an opened value (after running Π_{Open}), we use the standard SPDZ MAC check protocol [DKL+13], shown in Fig. 7.

Protocol $\Pi_{\text{SPDZ-MAC}}$

Usage: Parties in $\mathcal{P}_{\text{curr}}$ want to check the MACs on opened values $(A_1, \ldots, A_m)$.

1. Parties in $\mathcal{P}_{\text{curr}}$ call $\mathcal{F}_{\text{Rand}}$ to obtain random values $\chi_1, \ldots, \chi_m \in \mathbb{F}_p$.
2. Compute $A = \sum_{j=1}^m \chi_j \cdot A_j$ and $[\gamma] = \sum_{j=1}^m \chi_j \cdot [\Delta \cdot A_j]$.
3. Compute $[\sigma] = [\gamma] - [\Delta] \cdot A$. Each $P_i \in \mathcal{P}_{\text{curr}}$ calls $\mathcal{F}_{\text{Commit}}$ with input $[\sigma]$.
4. Parties open their commitments and check that $\sum_{i=1}^n [\sigma] = 0$. If not, output **abort**, else output **continue**.

Fig. 7. Protocol to check MACs in Dynamic SPDZ

Online Protocol. $\Pi_{\text{SPDZ-Online}}$ (Fig. 8) begins with each P_i in a set of parties $\mathcal{P}_{\text{curr}} \subseteq \mathcal{P}_{\text{main}}$ querying $\mathcal{F}_{\text{Prep}}$ to receive an authenticated random value $\langle t \rangle$, where P_i knows t, and every other party has a share of the MAC. P_i uses this to generate $[\![\cdot]\!]$ sharing of its input x. This takes one round, where P_i sends $x + t$ to everyone else, along with a fresh sharing of x. The parties then use their MACs from $\langle t \rangle$ to obtain the MAC share for $[\![x]\!]$. For the randomised circuit evaluation (used to check multiplications), during initialization the parties first use $\mathcal{F}_{\text{Prep}}$ to obtain a random sharing $[\![r]\!]$. Then, whenever an input $[\![x]\!]$ is authenticated, the parties multiply it with $[\![r]\!]$, using a triple from $\mathcal{F}_{\text{Prep}}$.

Addition and multiplication by a public constant are standard operations, performed locally by every party on its shares. Multiplication is the more challenging operation as we do not have fully authenticated triples. The first step is to call $\mathcal{F}_{\text{Prep}}$ twice to get two triples $([\![a]\!], [\![b]\!], [c])$, $([\![a']\!], [\![b']\!], [c'])$, as well as two random values $[\![l]\!], [\![l']\!]$, incrementing the corresponding counter after each call. $[\![l]\!], [\![l']\!]$ are used to authenticate $[c], [c']$ of the triples. This is done by computing $[l+c], [l'+c']$ locally, and opening the values by broadcasting the shares. Parties can then locally compute the MAC on c as $\Delta^i \cdot (l+c) - [\Delta \cdot l]$ for P_i. However, since we do not check the correctness at this point, the MACs in $[\![c]\!], [\![c']\!]$ might have an additive error chosen by the adversary. In addition, the c part of the triple may have errors, since this is allowed by $\mathcal{F}_{\mathsf{Prep}}$.

Let P_i be an honest party in $\mathcal{P}_{\mathsf{curr}}$. In a triple (a, b, c), c^i can have additive errors of the form $\{\delta_a^{j,i} \cdot b^i + \delta_b^{j,i} \cdot a^i\}_{j \in \mathcal{P}_\mathcal{A}}$, where $\delta_a^{j,i}, \delta_b^{j,i}$ are chosen by a malicious P_j in $\mathcal{F}_{\mathsf{Prep}}$. We show in the full version [RS21] that these errors do not give the adversary any additional power compared to injecting additive errors to the output of multiplications in the online phase, and will be detected by our verification procedure. Using the potentially inconsistent triples, parties then compute the multiplications $x \cdot y$, $rx \cdot y$ by opening $[\![x-a]\!]$, $[\![y-b]\!]$, $[\![rx-a']\!]$, $[\![y-b']\!]$ in the standard way of using Beaver triples. To open $[\![\cdot]\!]$-shared values, parties broadcast arithmetic shares of the value and continue with the computation. At the end of the protocol, the verification phase computes a MAC Check on all the authenticated values that had been opened. The protocol for the online phase of Dynamic SPDZ appears in Fig. 8.

Note that for a multiplication $x \cdot y$, it is important that $[\![l+c]\!]$ is not opened in the same round as $[\![x-a]\!]$, $[\![y-b]\!]$. This is because if we do, a rushing adversary can perform the following attack: To make the illustration simpler, we consider only two parties P_i, P_j in the committee. Suppose the adversary P_j introduces an error $\delta_b^{j,i} \cdot a^i$ with an honest party P_i, using the errors in $\mathcal{F}_{\mathsf{Prep}}$. The adversary then waits until it receives $x-a$, and when opening $[\![l+c]\!]$, injects another additive error given by $\left((x - a) + a^j\right) \cdot \delta_b^{j,i}$. Therefore, the triple will now be:

$$[\![a]\!], [\![b]\!], [\![c]\!] = \{[c] + \delta_b^{j,i} \cdot a^i + [(x - a) + a^j] \cdot \delta_b^{j,i}, [\Delta \cdot c]\}$$
$$= \{[c] + x \cdot \delta_b^{j,i}, [\Delta \cdot c]\}$$

This results in the adversary mounting a selective failure attack, since the error now depends on the secret wire value x. It can be avoided by making the adversary add the additive error prior to learning $x - a$. A simple way of achieving this is to authenticate c one round prior to opening $x - a$. Although this costs an additional round, the authentication step of a triple for the current layer can easily be merged with the opening of $x - a$ from the previous layer. This is still secure because the triples are independent and the adversary does not gain anything by opening the independently masked c in the previous layer.

The verification phase, described in Fig. 9, is run before outputting any result of a computation. First, the parties check the MACs on all the values that were opened over the course of the computation. If the check fails, the parties abort. Otherwise, they proceed by checking correctness of multiplications, with the check from [CGH+18], which involves checking a random linear combination of the inputs and outputs, and randomised versions of them. Parties start by calling $\mathcal{F}_{\mathsf{Coin}}$ to receive random challenges $\alpha_1, \ldots, \alpha_N$ and $\beta_1, \ldots, \beta_M \in \mathbb{F}_p$. They locally compute $[\![u]\!] = \sum_{i=1}^{N} \alpha_i \cdot [\![rz_i]\!] + \sum_{i=1}^{M} \beta_i \cdot [\![av_i]\!]$ and $[\![w]\!] = \sum_{i=1}^{N} \alpha_i \cdot [\![z_i]\!] + \sum_{i=1}^{M} \beta_i \cdot [\![v_i]\!]$. If no cheating had occurred, opening $[\![u]\!] - r \cdot [\![w]\!]$ should result in zero. To check this, parties securely reconstruct $[\![r]\!]$ using Π_{Open}, locally compute $[\![u]\!] - r \cdot [\![w]\!]$. If the opened value is not zero, they reject.

Protocol $\Pi_{\text{SPDZ-Online}}$

Init: Each $P_i \in \mathcal{P}_{\text{main}}$ sends (Init, m_T, m_R) to $\mathcal{F}_{\text{Prep}}$ and receives Δ^i. Later, when $\mathcal{P}_{\text{curr}} \subseteq \mathcal{P}_{\text{main}}$ wants to run the online phase, each $P_i \in \mathcal{P}_{\text{curr}}$ sets count = 0, rcount = 0, and calls $\mathcal{F}_{\text{Prep}}$ with $(\text{Rand}, \mathcal{P}_{\text{curr}}, \mathcal{P}_{\text{curr}}, \text{rcount})$ to obtain $[\![r]\!]$.

Input: To share an input x, P_i inputs $(\text{Rand}, P_i, \mathcal{P}_{\text{curr}}, \text{rcount})$ to $\mathcal{F}_{\text{Prep}}$ to get $\langle t \rangle$, where P_i knows t. Then,

1. P_i samples shares of x such that $x = \sum_{j \in \mathcal{P}_{\text{curr}}} x^j$ and sends $(x^j, x + t)$ to each $P_j \in \mathcal{P}_{\text{curr}}$. P_i sets its share $(\Delta \cdot x)^i = \Delta^i \cdot (x + t) - (\Delta t)^i$, where $(\Delta t)^i = \Delta^i \cdot t - \sum_{j \in \mathcal{P}_{\text{curr}} \setminus \{P_i\}} M_j^i$.
2. Each $P_j \in \mathcal{P}_{\text{curr}} \setminus \{P_i\}$ sets its share to be $[\![x]\!] = (x^j, \Delta^j \cdot (x + t) - (\Delta t)^j)$, where $(\Delta t)^j = K_i^j$.
3. Each $P_i \in \mathcal{P}_{\text{curr}}$ runs **Multiplication** below on $[\![x]\!]$ and $[\![r]\!]$ to get $[\![r \cdot x]\!]$.[a]

Addition: To perform addition, $[\![z]\!] = [\![x]\!] + [\![y]\!]$, each $P_i \in \mathcal{P}_{\text{curr}}$ locally adds their shares of $[\![x]\!], [\![y]\!]$, and $[\![rx]\!], [\![ry]\!]$ to get $[\![x + y]\!], [\![r(x + y)]\!]$.

Addition by Constant: To compute $[\![z]\!] = [\![x + c]\!]$, a designated party (say P_j) adds c to its share x^j, and all parties add $\Delta^i c$ to their MAC share.

Multiplication by Constant: To compute $[\![z]\!] = k \cdot [\![x]\!]$, each $P_i \in \mathcal{P}_{\text{curr}}$ locally multiply the public constant k to shares of $[\![x]\!]$ to get $[\![kx]\!], [\![r \cdot (kx)]\!]$.

Multiplication: To compute $[\![z]\!] = [\![x]\!] \cdot [\![y]\!]$ and $[\![rz]\!] = [\![rx]\!] \cdot [\![y]\!]$, each $P_i \in \mathcal{P}_{\text{curr}}$:

1. Calls $\mathcal{F}_{\text{Prep}}$ twice with inputs $(\text{Trip}, \mathcal{P}_{\text{curr}}, \mathcal{P}_{\text{curr}}, \text{count})$, incrementing count after each call. $\mathcal{F}_{\text{Prep}}$ outputs shares of the triples $(\langle a \rangle, \langle b \rangle, [c]), (\langle a' \rangle, \langle b' \rangle, [c'])$.
2. Calls $\mathcal{F}_{\text{Prep}}$ with $(\text{Rand}, \mathcal{P}_{\text{curr}}, \mathcal{P}_{\text{curr}}, \text{rcount})$ twice to receive $\langle l \rangle, \langle l' \rangle$. Increment rcount after each call.
3. Applies Π_{Convert} on $(\langle a \rangle, \langle b \rangle, \langle a' \rangle, \langle b' \rangle, \langle l \rangle, \langle l' \rangle)$ to get $[\![\cdot]\!]$ shares.
4. Runs Π_{Open} on $[e] = [x - a], [d] = [y - b], [e'] = [rx - a']$ and $[d'] = [y - b']$).
5. Runs Π_{Open} on $[l + c], [l' + c']$ and computes the multiplications as:

$$[\Delta \cdot c] = (l + c) \cdot \Delta^j - [\Delta \cdot l], \quad [\Delta \cdot c'] = (l' + c') \cdot \Delta^j - [\Delta \cdot l]$$
$$[\![z]\!] = e \cdot d + e \cdot [\![b]\!] + d \cdot [\![a]\!] + [\![c]\!]$$
$$[\![rz]\!] = e' \cdot d' + e' \cdot [\![b']\!] + d' \cdot [\![a']\!] + [\![c']\!]$$

Reconstruction: First, run $\Pi_{\text{SPDZ-Verify}}$ to check the multiplications. Then, to output $[\![z]\!]$, run Π_{Open} on $[z]$, then use $\Pi_{\text{SPDZ-MAC}}$ to check its MAC.

---

[a] We actually only use one triple to multiply x and r, skipping the extra product in the protocol.

Fig. 8. Protocol for the online phase of Dynamic SPDZ

The analysis of the verification phase proceeds similarly to that of [CGH+18], except we also need to deal with the additional errors from our preprocessing functionality. We prove the following in the full version [RS21].

Protocol $\Pi_{\text{SPDZ-Verify}}$

Verification: Let $\{v_i, rv_i\}_{i \in [M]}$ be the input wires of the circuit, and $\{z_i, rz_i\}_{i \in [N]}$ be the output wires of multiplication gates of the circuit.

1. Parties start by running $\Pi_{\text{SPDZ-MAC}}$ to check MACs on all the values opened in multiplications and inputs previously. If $\Pi_{\text{SPDZ-MAC}}$ fails, abort, else continue.
2. Parties call $\mathcal{F}_{\text{Coin}}$ to receive $\alpha_1, \ldots, \alpha_N, \beta_1, \ldots, \beta_M \in \mathbb{F}_p$
3. Parties locally compute

$$[\![u]\!] = \sum_{i=1}^{N} \alpha_i \cdot [\![rz_i]\!] + \sum_{i=1}^{M} \beta_i \cdot [\![rv_i]\!]$$

$$[\![w]\!] = \sum_{i=1}^{N} \alpha_i \cdot [\![z_i]\!] + \sum_{i=1}^{M} \beta_i \cdot [\![v_i]\!]$$

4. Parties open $[\![r]\!]$ by broadcasting shares of $[r]$ and running $\Pi_{\text{SPDZ-MAC}}$ on it.
5. Parties locally compute $[\![u]\!] - r[\![w]\!]$, open it and run $\Pi_{\text{SPDZ-MAC}}$. If the MAC check passes and $u - rw = 0$, parties **Accept** it and go to reconstruction, else **Reject**.

Fig. 9. Protocol for the verification phase in Dynamic SPDZ

Lemma 1. *Suppose $\mathcal{A}$ introduces additive errors of the form $\delta_a^{j,i}, \delta_b^{j,i} \neq 0$, for malicious parties P_j and honest P_i in $\mathcal{F}_{\text{Prep}}$, and in $\Pi_{\text{SPDZ-Online}}$ additive errors $\delta_c, \delta_{c'} \neq 0$ when authenticating triples a, b, c and a', b', c' respectively. If any errors are non-zero, then the Verification phase in $\Pi_{\text{SPDZ-Online}}$ fails with probability less than $2/p$.*

The following theorem, proven in the full version [RS21], shows that the protocol securely realizes the standard arithmetic black-box functionality, $\mathcal{F}_{\text{ABB}}$ (recall, this is identical to $\mathcal{F}_{\text{DABB}}$ in Fig. 1, except the operations are all carried out in one committee, $\mathcal{P}_{\text{curr}}$).

Theorem 3. *Protocol $\Pi_{\text{SPDZ-Online}}$ UC-securely computes $\mathcal{F}_{\text{ABB}}$ in the presence of a static malicious adversary corrupting up to all-but-one of the parties in $\mathcal{P}_{\text{curr}}$, in the $(\mathcal{F}_{\text{Prep}}, \mathcal{F}_{\text{Coin}})$-hybrid model.*

Complexity Analysis. Compared with the standard SPDZ online phase [DKL+13], our dynamic variant is more expensive, since we need to verify multiplications. Instead of 2 openings of $[\![\cdot]\!]$-shared values per multiplication, as in SPDZ, we need 4 openings of $[\![\cdot]\!]$-shared values, plus 2 openings of $[\cdot]$ sharings. This leads the overall online communication and the storage complexity to be around 3x that of SPDZ. However, our preprocessing protocol from Sect. 3 is vastly more efficient than any SPDZ preprocessing, since it is the only protocol that is PCG-friendly, allowing N triples to be preprocessed with communication scaling in $O(\log N)$.

Furthermore, this comes with the additional flexibility of dynamically choosing the set of parties in the online phase.

5   Fluid SPDZ

In this section, we show how to run Fluid SPDZ, which is a SPDZ-like online phase that supports fluidity. We base ourselves on the universal preprocessing from Sect. 3, where the entire set of parties, $\mathcal{P}_{\mathsf{main}}$, is involved. Later, in the online phase, we start with a subset of parties $\mathcal{P}_{\mathsf{curr}} \subset \mathcal{P}_{\mathsf{main}}$, and this committee can later evolve in a dynamic way (in contrast to Dynamic SPDZ, where the committee is fixed once the online phase begins). As discussed in Sect. 2, we assume when the committee changes at the end of an epoch, the current committee is made aware of the identity of the next committee who they hand-off their state to. We show how to leverage $\mathcal{F}_{\mathsf{Prep}}$ to achieve a *maximally fluid* online phase, where each epoch may last only one round. In our protocol, we will denote the current committee in a given epoch by $\mathcal{P}_{\mathsf{curr}}$. Before going into the main online protocol, we cover some key building blocks necessary to support fluidity, and describe how we adapt the SPDZ MAC check protocol to work in this context.

Simple Resharing. We use a standard method for resharing an additively shared value $[x]^{\mathcal{P}_{\mathsf{curr}}}$ from committee $\mathcal{P}_{\mathsf{curr}}$ into committee $\mathcal{P}_{\mathsf{next}}$, as shown in Fig. 10. To reduce communication, we assume a setup where every pair of parties shares a common PRG seed. (If this is not available, note that we can still have parties in $\mathcal{P}_{\mathsf{curr}}$ sample and send the PRG seeds, which saves communication when a large batch of values is being reshared).

Protocol Π_{Reshare}

Setup: Each pair of parties $P_i, P_j \in \mathcal{P}_{\mathsf{main}}$ has a common PRG seed $s^{i,j}$.
Usage: $\mathcal{P}_{\mathsf{curr}}$ reshares $[x]^{\mathcal{P}_{\mathsf{curr}}}$ to $\mathcal{P}_{\mathsf{next}}$. Parties in $\mathcal{P}_{\mathsf{next}}$ are indexed from 1 to m.

1. Each $P_i \in \mathcal{P}_{\mathsf{curr}}$ computes $x^{i,j} \in \mathbb{F}_p$ as a fresh output of a PRG applied to $s^{i,j}$, for $j = 2, \ldots, m$. P_i defines $x^{i,1} = x^i - \sum_{j=2}^{m} x^{i,j}$.
2. Each P_i sends $x^{i,1}$ to P_1 in $\mathcal{P}_{\mathsf{next}}$. Each $P_j \in \mathcal{P}_{\mathsf{next}}$ defines its share as $x^j = \sum_{i \in \mathcal{P}_{\mathsf{curr}}} x^{i,j}$ (where if $j \neq 1$, $x^{i,j}$ is computed from the PRG).

Fig. 10. Protocol for resharing values across committees

Resharing with MACs: The Key-Switch Procedure. Since our protocol uses SPDZ $\llbracket \cdot \rrbracket$-sharing, simple resharing is not enough to securely transfer the state from one committee to another. We also need a way to securely reshare a value $[\![x]\!]$, while *switching* to a different MAC key, which is held by the second committee.

Our solution is to use the *key-switch protocol*, $\Pi_{\text{Key-Switch}}$, shown in Fig. 11. This securely transfers $[\![x]\!]$ from $\mathcal{P}_{\text{curr}}$ to $\mathcal{P}_{\text{next}}$, while switching to the appropriate MAC key. The protocol proceeds as follows: each party $P_i \in \mathcal{P}_{\text{curr}}$ starts with a random value r^i that is pairwise authenticated with every party in $\mathcal{P}_{\text{curr}} \cup \mathcal{P}_{\text{next}}$— that is, P_i holds a MAC on t^i under P_j's MAC key, for each $P_j \in \mathcal{P}_{\text{curr}} \cup \mathcal{P}_{\text{next}}$. This can easily be obtained by a call to $\mathcal{F}_{\text{Prep}}$ using the Rand command. Each P_i can then obtain $[\Delta_{\mathcal{P}_{\text{curr}}} \cdot t]$, where $t = \sum_{i \in \mathcal{P}_{\text{curr}}} t^i$, by combining the relevant MAC shares as in Π_{Convert}, thus forming $[\![t]\!]$. The idea now is for $\mathcal{P}_{\text{curr}}$ to open the masked value $x + t$, which $\mathcal{P}_{\text{next}}$ can use to obtain $[\Delta_{\mathcal{P}_{\text{next}}} \cdot x] = [\Delta_{\mathcal{P}_{\text{next}}}] \cdot (x + t) - [\Delta_{\mathcal{P}_{\text{next}}} \cdot t]$. All that remains is for parties in $\mathcal{P}_{\text{next}}$ to get $[\Delta_{\mathcal{P}_{\text{next}}} \cdot t]$. Note that $\Delta_{\mathcal{P}_{\text{next}}} \cdot t = \sum_{i \in \mathcal{P}_{\text{curr}}} \sum_{j \in \mathcal{P}_{\text{next}}} M_j^i - K_i^j$. Therefore, the parties in $\mathcal{P}_{\text{curr}}$ can reshare $M = \sum_{j \in \mathcal{P}_{\text{next}}} M_j^i$ to parties in $\mathcal{P}_{\text{next}}$, who then locally sum the shares and their keys to obtain shares of $\Delta_{\mathcal{P}_{\text{next}}} \cdot t = M - \sum_{i \in \mathcal{P}_{\text{curr}}} K_i^j$. Security of $\Pi_{\text{Key-Switch}}$ is stated in Lemma 2, and analysed in the full version [RS21].

Lemma 2. *If parties in $\mathcal{P}_{\text{curr}}$ follow the protocol, $\Pi_{\text{Key-Switch}}$ leads to a consistent sharing of $[\![x]\!]^{\mathcal{P}_{\text{curr}}}$, and its transcript is simulatable by random values.*

Protocol $\Pi_{\text{Key-Switch}}$

Input: $[\![x]\!] = ([x], [\Delta_{\mathcal{P}_{\text{curr}}} \cdot x])$ in $\mathcal{P}_{\text{curr}}$.
Output: $[\![x]\!] = ([x], [\Delta_{\mathcal{P}_{\text{next}}} \cdot x])$ in $\mathcal{P}_{\text{next}}$.

1. Each $P_i \in \mathcal{P}_{\text{curr}}$ calls $\mathcal{F}_{\text{Prep}}$ with $(\text{Rand}, \mathcal{P}_{\text{curr}}, \mathcal{P}_{\text{curr}} \cup \mathcal{P}_{\text{next}}, \text{rcount})$ to receive $t^i, \{M_j^i\}_{j \in \mathcal{P}_{\text{curr}} \cup \mathcal{P}_{\text{next}}}$, while $P_j \in \mathcal{P}_{\text{curr}} \cup \mathcal{P}_{\text{next}}$ receives K_i^j.
2. $\mathcal{P}_{\text{curr}}$ uses Π_{Convert} to form $[\![t]\!]^{\mathcal{P}_{\text{curr}}}$. Each $P_i \in \mathcal{P}_{\text{curr}}$ computes $M^i = \sum_{j \in \mathcal{P}_{\text{next}}} M_j^i$ to obtain $[M]$.
3. Parties in $\mathcal{P}_{\text{curr}}$ run $\Pi_{\text{Open}}([\![x + t]\!])$ and $\Pi_{\text{Reshare}}([M], [x])$, all to $\mathcal{P}_{\text{next}}$.
4. Each $P_j \in \mathcal{P}_{\text{next}}$ computes $K^j = \sum_{i \in \mathcal{P}_{\text{curr}}} K_i^j$ to obtain $[K]$, and then defines $[\Delta_{\mathcal{P}_{\text{next}}} \cdot t] = [M] - [K]$.
5. Finally, P_j can compute its share of the MAC $[\Delta_{\mathcal{P}_{\text{next}}} \cdot x]$ as $[\Delta_{\mathcal{P}_{\text{next}}}] \cdot (x + t) - [\Delta_{\mathcal{P}_{\text{next}}} \cdot t]$. $\mathcal{P}_{\text{next}}$ outputs $[x], [\Delta_{\mathcal{P}_{\text{next}}} \cdot x]$.

Fig. 11. Protocol to switch MAC keys

Fluid MAC Check: The MAC check protocol from SPDZ (Fig. 7) is designed to check a large batch of MACs at the end of the computation. The protocol involves computing an additively shared $[\sigma]$, which is derived from a random linear combination of all the opened values and the corresponding MACs. We call σ the *MAC check state*. If there was no cheating, σ, when opened, should be zero. In the fluid setting, however, deferring the MAC check means that parties need to keep track of all the opened values and MACs by resharing them across committees, which blows up the complexity of the protocol. An alternative would be to run the full MAC Check protocol on values as soon as they are opened over the course of the computation. Instantiating this in a maximally fluid way would run over 4 epochs. Instead, we propose an incremental version of the check that updates the MAC check state in every epoch, using a fresh random challenge to serve as the next linear combination coefficient. This essentially compresses the number of things to be checked down to a constant size. Another advantage of the incremental check is that it only runs over 2 epochs.

$\Pi_{\text{Fluid-MAC}}$, detailed in Fig. 12, has two subprotocols. During the online computation, parties run **Compute State** to incrementally update the MAC check state, the shared value $[\sigma]$ (which is initially zero). At the end of the computation, the final committee runs **Check State** to check that the $[\sigma]$ is still zero. Let $(A_1, \ldots, A_m)$ be a set of opened values that $\mathcal{P}_i$ wants to check the MACs on. We assume that $\mathcal{P}_{i+1}$ holds the shared state $[\sigma']$, from prior epochs. The protocol begins with $\mathcal{P}_i$, which opens a random challenge β from $\mathcal{F}_{\text{Prep}}$ to $\mathcal{P}_{i+1}$; since β is obtained in $\langle \cdot \rangle$ form, $\mathcal{P}_{i+1}$ can locally check the MACs on β to verify this. By taking a linear combination with powers of β, $\mathcal{P}_{i+1}$ computes $[\sigma] = [\sigma'] + \gamma^k - [\Delta_{\mathcal{P}_i}] \cdot A$, where $A = \sum_{j=1}^{m} \beta^j \cdot A_j$ and $\gamma^k = \sum_{j=1}^{m} \beta^j \cdot [\Delta_{\mathcal{P}_i} \cdot A_j]$.

At the end of the protocol, when a committee wants to complete the MAC Check, all it has to do is securely open $[\sigma]$ and check that it is zero.

Fluid Verify: In $\Pi_{\text{Fluid-Verify}}$, parties in a given committee, say $\mathcal{P}_{i+1}$, want to verify the outputs of multiplication gates using the randomised circuit outputs, similar to the verification method from Sect. 4. As in the Fluid MAC check, we carry out the check incrementally throughout the computation, where in the first phase, the parties open a random value, which is expanded into challenges $\alpha_i \in \mathbb{F}_p$, used to update the sharings $[\![u]\!]$, $[\![w]\!]$, corresponding to the tally of randomised multiplications and actual multiplications. These are maintained as state, until the final verification phase where we open $[\![r]\!]$ and check that $[\![u]\!] - r \cdot [\![w]\!] = 0$. The underlying technique is similar to the one used in [CGG+21], and the protocol appears in the full version [RS21].

Fluid Online: We now describe how the online phase works. $\Pi_{\text{Fluid-Online}}$ begins the same way as $\Pi_{\text{SPDZ-Online}}$ with a set of parties $\mathcal{P}_{\text{curr}} \subseteq \mathcal{P}_{\text{main}}$, running Input and Initialise phases. These are used to set up the preprocessing functionality, and create authenticated sharings of the inputs. During these two phases, we assume that the committee does not change. Addition and multiplication by a public constant are local operations, so they are naturally maximally fluid operations.

Multiplication needs to be spread out over multiple epochs to do it in a maximally fluid way. To evaluate one multiplication between x, y, we need to perform two multiplications: $x \cdot y$ and $rx \cdot y$. At a high level, we can think of parties doing two things in $\Pi_{\text{Fluid-Mult}}$. The first is computing output shares of

---

Protocol $\Pi_{\text{Fluid-MAC}}$

Usage: Parties in $\mathcal{P}_i$ want to check the MACs values $(A_1, \ldots, A_m)$ opened to them. We assume $\mathcal{P}_{i+1}$ gets the MAC state $[\sigma']$ from a previous run of $\Pi_{\text{Fluid-MAC}}$.

Compute State: Compute the MAC check state $[\sigma]$:

Committee i:
1. Each $P_j \in \mathcal{P}_i$ calls $\mathcal{F}_{\text{Prep}}$ with input $(\text{Rand}, \mathcal{P}_i, \mathcal{P}_{i+1}, \text{rcount})$ to receive $\langle \beta^j \rangle$.
2. **Hand-off:** Send β^j, M_k^j to each $P_k \in \mathcal{P}_{i+1}$, along with $A_1, \ldots, A_m$. Reshare $[\sigma'], [\Delta_{\mathcal{P}_i}], [\Delta_{\mathcal{P}_i} \cdot A_1], \ldots, [\Delta_{\mathcal{P}_i} \cdot A_m]$.

Committee $i+1$:
3. P_k locally checks $M_k^j = \beta^j \cdot \Delta^k + K_j^k$ for all $j \in \mathcal{P}_i$, and aborts if any of them fail. Let $\beta = \sum_{j \in \mathcal{P}_i} \beta^j$.
4. It updates $[\sigma']$ as $[\sigma] = [\sigma'] + \gamma^k - [\Delta_{\mathcal{P}_i}] \cdot A$, where $A = \sum_{j=1}^m (\beta)^j \cdot A_j$ and $\gamma^k = \sum_{j=1}^m (\beta)^j \cdot [\Delta_{\mathcal{P}_i} \cdot A_j]$ (here, $(\beta)^j$ is the j-th power of β).

Check State: (Committee $i+2$)

5. Set $\sigma^j = \sum_{k \in \mathcal{P}_{i+1}} [\sigma^k]$. Each $P_j \in \mathcal{P}_{i+2}$ calls $\mathcal{F}_{\text{Commit}}$ to commit to σ^j.
6. Open all commitments, and if they are consistent, **Accept** if $\sum_{j \in \mathcal{P}_{i+2}} \sigma^j = 0$. Else, **Reject**.

Fig. 12. MAC check protocol for a fluid committee

the multiplications $[\![z]\!], [\![rz]\!]$. The second thing is running the MAC check and the verification protocols in an incremental way, so that we retain a small state complexity throughout the computation. Both of these parts are run in parallel between the committees $\mathcal{P}_{\text{curr}-1}, \mathcal{P}_{\text{curr}}, \mathcal{P}_{\text{curr}+1}$.

The full online phase is given in Fig. 13. Below, we focus on describing the multiplication protocol, shown in the full version [RS21].

Computing the output shares. In order for the current committee $\mathcal{P}_{\text{curr}}$ to evaluate the multiplications, we start with the committee of the previous epoch $\mathcal{P}_{\text{curr}-1}$. We want to use $\mathcal{P}_{\text{curr}-1}$ to set up an authenticated triple for $\mathcal{P}_{\text{curr}}$ to use. Towards this, $\mathcal{P}_{\text{curr}-1}$ calls $\mathcal{F}_{\text{Prep}}$ to receive two triples - $(\langle a \rangle, \langle b \rangle, [c])$ and $(\langle a' \rangle, \langle b' \rangle, [c'])$. In addition, they also call it using Rand to receive authenticated shares of two random values $\langle l \rangle$ and $\langle l' \rangle$, to be used to authenticate $[c], [c']$. Parties use Π_{Convert} to locally go from $\langle \cdot \rangle$ to $[\![\cdot]\!]$ shares of the triples and the random values. To transfer the triples to $\mathcal{P}_{\text{curr}}$ such that the MACs are under their key, $\mathcal{P}_{\text{curr}-1}$ runs the $\Pi_{\text{Key-Switch}}$ protocol with $\mathcal{P}_{\text{curr}}$, on $([\![a]\!], [\![b]\!]), ([\![a']\!], [\![b']\!]), [\![l]\!], [\![l']\!]$ and opens $[l + c], [l' + c']$ to them. As a result, $\mathcal{P}_{\text{curr}}$ can locally get authenticated shares of the triples under the MAC key $\Delta_{\mathcal{P}_{\text{curr}}}$. Using shares of the triples, they locally compute $[\![x - a]\!], [\![y - b]\!], [\![x - a']\!], [\![y - b']\!]$ and open them to $\mathcal{P}_{\text{curr}+1}$. $\mathcal{P}_{\text{curr}+1}$ can compute $[\![z]\!], [\![rz]\!]$ using the standard Beaver multiplication technique.

Protocol $\Pi_{\text{Fluid-Online}}$

Init: Every $P_i \in \mathcal{P}_{\text{curr}} \subseteq \mathcal{P}_{\text{main}}$ sets $\text{count} = 0, \text{rcount} = 0$. P_i inputs $(\text{Rand}, \mathcal{P}_{\text{curr}}, \mathcal{P}_{\text{curr}}, \text{rcount})$ to $\mathcal{F}_{\text{Prep}}$ and receives $\langle r \rangle$. P_i sends (Init, m_T, m_R) to $\mathcal{F}_{\text{Prep}}$ and receives Δ^i.

Input: To form $[\![\cdot]\!]$-sharing of an input x possessed by $P_i \in \mathcal{P}_{\text{main}}$,

1. P_i along with parties in $\mathcal{P}_{\text{curr}}$ runs $\Pi_{\text{Key-Switch}}$, where P_i (acting as $\mathcal{P}_{\text{curr}}$) inputs $[\![x]\!]$ under its key and parties in $\mathcal{P}_{\text{curr}}$ (as $\mathcal{P}_{\text{next}}$) receive $[\![x]\!]$ under their key.
2. Parties in $\mathcal{P}_{\text{curr}}$ input $(\text{Trip}, \mathcal{P}_{\text{curr}}, \mathcal{P}_{\text{curr}}, \text{count})$ to $\mathcal{F}_{\text{Prep}}$ and receive $(\langle a \rangle, \langle b \rangle, [c])$.
3. Then they engage to perform the multiplication of $\{[\![x_i]\!]\}_{i \in \mathcal{P}_{\text{curr}}}$ with $[\![r]\!]$ to produce $\{[\![r \cdot x_i]\!]\}_{i \in \mathcal{P}_{\text{curr}}}$.

Addition: To perform addition, $[\![z]\!] = [\![x]\!] + [\![y]\!]$, each $P_i \in \mathcal{P}_{\text{curr}}$ locally adds their shares of $[\![x]\!], [\![y]\!], [\![rx]\!], [\![ry]\!]$ to get $[\![x + y]\!], [\![r(x + y)]\!]$.

Addition by Constant: To compute $[\![z]\!] = [\![x + c]\!]$, a designated party (say $P_j \in \mathcal{P}_{\text{curr}}$) adds c to its share x^j, and all the other parties add $\Delta^i c$ to their MAC share.

Multiplication by Constant: To compute $[\![z]\!] = k \cdot [\![x]\!]$, each $P_i \in \mathcal{P}_{\text{curr}}$ locally multiply the public constant k to shares of $[\![x]\!]$ to get $[\![kx]\!], [\![r \cdot (kx)]\!]$.

Multiplication: To compute $[\![z]\!] = [\![x]\!] \cdot [\![y]\!]$ and $[\![rz]\!] = [\![rx]\!] \cdot [\![y]\!]$ in $\mathcal{P}_{\text{curr}}$, run $\Pi_{\text{Fluid-Mult}}$ among $(\mathcal{P}_{\text{curr-1}}, \mathcal{P}_{\text{curr}}, \mathcal{P}_{\text{curr+1}})$.

Verify and Reconstruct:

1. Parties in the final committee, say $\mathcal{P}_{final}$, run **Compute State** of $\Pi_{\text{Fluid-MAC}}$. If $\Pi_{\text{Fluid-MAC}}$ fails, **Reject**, else continue.
2. Parties execute **Final Check** phase of $\Pi_{\text{Fluid-Verify}}$. If the result is **Accept**, for each output wire z, they open $[\![z]\!]$ by broadcasting their shares to the other parties and running both phases of $\Pi_{\text{Fluid-MAC}}$. If $\Pi_{\text{Fluid-MAC}}$ fails, **Reject**.

Fig. 13. Protocol for a maximally fluid online phase

Security of the Online Protocol. We now briefly discuss security of the online protocol, $\Pi_{\text{Fluid-Online}}$. As argued in the full version [RS21], the values sent in the key-switch protocol are always indistinguishable from random, and any errors in the resulting sharing will always be detected by a MAC check. Regarding $\Pi_{\text{Fluid-MAC}}$ and $\Pi_{\text{Fluid-Verify}}$, note that these protocols both follow essentially the same set of steps as the Dynamic SPDZ protocols ($\Pi_{\text{SPDZ-MAC}}$ and $\Pi_{\text{SPDZ-Verify}}$). The key differences are (1) the random challenges are obtained by opening random authenticated sharings, instead of $\mathcal{F}_{\text{Coin}}$, and (2) the final check values are computed incrementally, instead of immediately. For (1), because the sharings are authenticated and MACs immediately checked, they are still uniformly random until the time of opening. For (2), note that since each challenge is only opened after the corresponding value being checked has been made public, its randomness still contributes in the same way as Dynamic SPDZ, to prevent cheating.

Table 1. Cost estimates for various protocols (comm. in # field elements)

Protocol	Online comm	Preproc. comm	Storage
SPDZ [KPR18,KOS16]	$2\lvert C\rvert$	$O(n\lvert C\rvert)$	$O(\lvert C\rvert)$
[BGIN22]	$2\lvert C\rvert$	$O(n\sqrt{\lvert C\rvert})$	$O(\sqrt{\lvert C\rvert})$
SPDZ (with our preproc.)	$2\,\lvert C\rvert$	$O(\lvert C\rvert)+O(n\log(\lvert C\rvert))$	$O(\lvert C\rvert)+O(n\log(\lvert C\rvert))$
Dynamic SPDZ	$6\lvert C\rvert$	$O(n\log(\lvert C\rvert))$	$O(n\log(\lvert C\rvert))$
Fluid SPDZ	$O(n_c\lvert C\rvert)$	$O(n\log(\lvert C\rvert))$	$O(n\log(\lvert C\rvert))$

During the multiplication protocol, $\Pi_{\mathsf{Fluid\text{-}Mult}}$, the parties run the same computations as in Dynamic SPDZ, with the difference that in each round, the state is securely transferred using Π_{Reshare} or $\Pi_{\mathsf{Key\text{-}Switch}}$, and the MAC check and verification procedures are run in the background. Hence, security can be proven similarly to the proof of Theorem 3. We obtain the following.

Theorem 4. *Let $\mathcal{A}$ be an R-adaptive adversary in $\Pi_{\mathsf{Fluid\text{-}Online}}$. Then, the protocol UC-securely computes $\mathcal{F}_{\mathsf{DABB}}$ in the presence of $\mathcal{A}$ in the $\mathcal{F}_{\mathsf{Prep}}$-hybrid model.*

6 Cost Analysis

In Table 1 we give some efficiency estimates for our protocols, in terms of the per-party communication and storage costs. n is the number of parties, while n_c is the average committee size in the online phase. First, in the preprocessing, our dynamic and fluid protocols have significantly smaller storage and communication compared with previous SPDZ protocols (if n is small, relative to the circuit size). As mentioned in Sect. 4, we can also use our preprocessing to get a modified version of SPDZ, with the same online cost as regular SPDZ, by verifying the multiplication triples in the offline phase. This gives the best preprocessing complexity for any SPDZ-like protocol with the same online phase.

The online complexities for all protocols apart from Fluid are just $O(1)$ field elements per multiplication, while with Fluid SPDZ, we get $O(n_c)$. This is because for the other protocols, we assume the players follow the "king" approach to open values [DN07], where parties send their shares to a designated party, who sums them up and sends back the result.

Although this takes an additional round, it reduces the communication complexity of opening a value from $O(n^2)$ to $O(n)$. While the king approach is also possible in Fluid MPC, it is harder to estimate the costs of this, since the parties need to reshare part of their current state to the king.

In Table 1 we present asymptotic estimates of the cost of variants of our protocols against the current best SPDZ protocols [KPR18,KOS16]. The primary improvement comes from our preprocessing, which can be used to run a traditional SPDZ online phase without any fluidity, at the same cost as the other approaches. It has an additional factor of $O(\lvert C\rvert)$ in the preprocessing compared to Dynamic and Fluid SPDZ because we also authenticate and check the triples in the preprocessing. Comparing Dynamic SPDZ with [KPR18,KOS16] shows that we can support dynamic participants at the cost of a small overhead in the online phase, and a vastly more cheaper preprocessing phase, making it practically efficient. Compared with the recent work of [BGIN22], our preprocessing scales asymptotically better with the circuit size, although its storage costs scale worse with the number of parties, and our online phase is slightly less efficient.

To get an idea of the concrete efficiency of our universal preprocessing, we give some communication estimates based on existing VOLE and OLE protocols. For producing $N = 2^{20}$ triples, each pair of the n parties needs a VOLE of length $4N$ and an OLE of length N field elements. Using state-of-the-art LPN-based VOLE [WYKW21] and OLE [BCG+20], this can be done with a total of around 4MB of communication per pair of parties. For example, using Dynamic SPDZ with 10 parties, each party can use under 40MB of bandwidth, to gain the ability to do MPC with any subset of parties later on.

6.1   Concrete Costs and Optimizations for $\Pi_{\text{Fluid-Online}}$

In this section, we estimate the concrete communication cost per party running $\Pi_{\text{Fluid-Online}}$. Note that running the online phase in a maximally fluid way, as described in the full version [RS21], allows for multiplications to be interleaved across committees. This means that parties in a committee, say $\mathcal{P}_i$, may be involved in three multiplications in parallel. This can be seen as running three instances of $\Pi_{\text{Fluid-Online}}$ in parallel, with $\mathcal{P}_i$ playing different roles $(\mathcal{P}_{\text{curr}-1}, \mathcal{P}_{\text{curr}}, \mathcal{P}_{\text{curr}+1})$ across the three instances in parallel. In addition, we can reduce the number of random challenges that need to be opened as part of **Compute State** and **Incremental Verification** due to the interleaving.

To calculate the concrete cost, we assume that the circuit has a uniform width of m, and the committees are of size n_c. The number of elements per party per epoch can then be estimated by the following formula: $14 \cdot m \cdot n_c + 42 \cdot m + 13 \cdot n_c + 20$. If the circuit is wide, i.e. $m \gg n_c$, the amortised cost per multiplication becomes $14 \cdot n_c + 42$. The cost of adding an additional party to the computation will roughly be 14 elements.

Though we presented maximally fluid protocols, in practice one could relax the model by allowing each epoch to last more than one round. The motivation to do so is to save in terms of the concrete communication cost. For instance, assume that the fluidity is four rounds instead of one. As the multiplication in $\Pi_{\text{Fluid-Online}}$ takes three rounds (including computing **Compute State** and **Incremental Verification**), this means the committee that starts the multiplication will be the one to finish it as well. There will not be a need for state transfer during the multiplication, essentially getting rid of all the Key-Switch operations in $\Pi_{\text{Fluid-Online}}$. Transferring the state after the multiplication is also cheaper, as the committee will only have to Key-Switch output wires of the multiplication, the MAC key, and the random value $[\![r]\!]$. The cost of running the Fluid online with a fluidity of four is $6 \cdot m + 4 \cdot n_c$, where $6 \cdot m$ is the cost for authenticating $2m$ triples and opening the Beaver triple intermediate values, and the $4 \cdot n_c$ is for the random challenges that need to be opened for **Compute State** and **Incremental Verification**. With a wide enough circuit, the amortised cost per multiplication per party comes down to about 6 elements, matching the cost of Dynamic SPDZ.

Acknowledgements. This work has been supported by the European Research Council (ERC) under the European Union's Horizon 2020 research and innovation program (grant agreements No. 803096 (SPEC)), the Digital Research Centre Denmark (DIREC), and the Aarhus University Research Foundation (AUFF) and the Independent Research Fund Denmark under project number 0165-00107B.

References

[BCG+19a] Boyle, E., Couteau, G., Gilboa, N., Ishai, Y., Kohl, L., Rindal, P., Scholl, P.: Efficient two-round OT extension and silent non-interactive secure computation. In: ACM CCS 2019. ACM Press, November 2019

[BCG+19b] Boyle, E., Couteau, G., Gilboa, N., Ishai, Y., Kohl, L., Scholl, P.: Efficient pseudorandom correlation generators: silent OT extension and more. In: Boldyreva, A., Micciancio, D. (eds.) CRYPTO 2019, Part III. LNCS, vol. 11694, pp. 489–518. Springer, Cham (2019). https://doi.org/10.1007/978-3-030-26954-8_16

[BCG+20] Boyle, E., Couteau, G., Gilboa, N., Ishai, Y., Kohl, L., Scholl, P.: Efficient pseudorandom correlation generators from ring-LPN. In: Micciancio, D., Ristenpart, T. (eds.) CRYPTO 2020, Part II. LNCS, vol. 12171, pp. 387–416. Springer, Cham (2020). https://doi.org/10.1007/978-3-030-56880-1_14

[BCGI18] Boyle, E., Couteau, G., Gilboa, N., Ishai, Y.: Compressing vector OLE. In: ACM CCS 2018. ACM Press, October 2018

[BDOZ11] Bendlin, R., Damgård, I., Orlandi, C., Zakarias, S.: Semi-homomorphic encryption and multiparty computation. In: Paterson, K.G. (ed.) EURO-CRYPT 2011. LNCS, vol. 6632, pp. 169–188. Springer, Heidelberg (2011). https://doi.org/10.1007/978-3-642-20465-4_11

[BGG+20] Benhamouda, F., et al.: Can a public blockchain keep a secret? In: Pass, R., Pietrzak, K. (eds.) TCC 2020, Part I. LNCS, vol. 12550, pp. 260–290. Springer, Cham (2020). https://doi.org/10.1007/978-3-030-64375-1_10

[BGIN22] Boyle, E., Gilboa, N., Ishai, Y., Nof, A.: Secure multiparty computation with sublinear preprocessing. In: Dunkelman, O., Dziembowski, S. (eds.) EUROCRYPT 2022. LNCS, vol. 13275, pp. 427–457. Springer, Heidelberg (2022). https://doi.org/10.1007/978-3-031-06944-4_15

[Bra85] Bracha, G.: An $O(\lg n)$ expected rounds randomized byzantine generals protocol. In: 17th ACM STOC. ACM Press, May 1985

[Can01] Canetti, R.: Universally composable security: a new paradigm for cryptographic protocols. In: 42nd FOCS. IEEE Computer Society Press, October 2001

[CGG+21] Choudhuri, A.R., Goel, A., Green, M., Jain, A., Kaptchuk, G.: Fluid MPC: secure multiparty computation with dynamic participants. In: Malkin, T., Peikert, C. (eds.) CRYPTO 2021, Part II. LNCS, vol. 12826, pp. 94–123. Springer, Cham (2021). https://doi.org/10.1007/978-3-030-84245-1_4

[CGH+18] Chida, K., et al.: Fast large-scale honest-majority MPC for malicious adversaries. In: Shacham, H., Boldyreva, A. (eds.) CRYPTO 2018, Part III. LNCS, vol. 10993, pp. 34–64. Springer, Cham (2018). https://doi.org/10.1007/978-3-319-96878-0_2

[DDN+16] Damgård, I., Damgård, K., Nielsen, K., Nordholt, P.S., Toft, T.: Confidential benchmarking based on multiparty computation. In: Grossklags, J., Preneel, B. (eds.) FC 2016. LNCS, vol. 9603, pp. 169–187. Springer, Heidelberg (2017). https://doi.org/10.1007/978-3-662-54970-4_10

[DKL+13] Damgård, I., Keller, M., Larraia, E., Pastro, V., Scholl, P., Smart, N.P.: Practical covertly secure MPC for dishonest majority – or: breaking the SPDZ limits. In: Crampton, J., Jajodia, S., Mayes, K. (eds.) ESORICS 2013. LNCS, vol. 8134, pp. 1–18. Springer, Heidelberg (2013). https://doi.org/10.1007/978-3-642-40203-6_1

[DN07] Damgård, I., Nielsen, J.B.: Scalable and unconditionally secure multiparty computation. In: Menezes, A. (ed.) CRYPTO 2007. LNCS, vol. 4622, pp. 572–590. Springer, Heidelberg (2007). https://doi.org/10.1007/978-3-540-74143-5_32

[DPSZ12] Damgård, I., Pastro, V., Smart, N., Zakarias, S.: Multiparty computation from somewhat homomorphic encryption. In: Safavi-Naini, R., Canetti, R. (eds.) CRYPTO 2012. LNCS, vol. 7417, pp. 643–662. Springer, Heidelberg (2012). https://doi.org/10.1007/978-3-642-32009-5_38

[GHK+21] Gentry, C., et al.: YOSO: you only speak once. In: Malkin, T., Peikert, C. (eds.) CRYPTO 2021, Part II. LNCS, vol. 12826, pp. 64–93. Springer, Cham (2021). https://doi.org/10.1007/978-3-030-84245-1_3

[GKM+20] Goyal, V., Kothapalli, A., Masserova, E., Parno, B., Song, Y.: Storing and retrieving secrets on a blockchain. Cryptology ePrint Archive, Report 2020/504 (2020). https://eprint.iacr.org/2020/504

[GSY21] Gordon, S.D., Starin, D., Yerukhimovich, A.: The more the merrier: reducing the cost of large scale MPC. In: Canteaut, A., Standaert, F.-X. (eds.) EUROCRYPT 2021, Part II. LNCS, vol. 12697, pp. 694–723. Springer, Cham (2021). https://doi.org/10.1007/978-3-030-77886-6_24

[HJKY95] Herzberg, A., Jarecki, S., Krawczyk, H., Yung, M.: Proactive secret sharing or: how to cope with perpetual leakage. In: Coppersmith, D. (ed.) CRYPTO 1995. LNCS, vol. 963, pp. 339–352. Springer, Heidelberg (1995). https://doi.org/10.1007/3-540-44750-4_27

[HSS17] Hazay, C., Scholl, P., Soria-Vazquez, E.: Low cost constant round MPC combining BMR and oblivious transfer. In: Takagi, T., Peyrin, T. (eds.) ASIACRYPT 2017, Part I. LNCS, vol. 10624, pp. 598–628. Springer, Cham (2017). https://doi.org/10.1007/978-3-319-70694-8_21

[KOS16] Keller, M., Orsini, E., Scholl, P.: MASCOT: faster malicious arithmetic secure computation with oblivious transfer. In: ACM CCS 2016. ACM Press, October 2016

[KPR18] Keller, M., Pastro, V., Rotaru, D.: Overdrive: making SPDZ great again. In: Nielsen, J.B., Rijmen, V. (eds.) EUROCRYPT 2018, Part III. LNCS, vol. 10822, pp. 158–189. Springer, Cham (2018). https://doi.org/10.1007/978-3-319-78372-7_6

[MZW+19] Maram, S.K.D., et al.: CHURP: dynamic-committee proactive secret sharing. In: ACM CCS 2019. ACM Press, November 2019

[RS21] Rachuri, R., Scholl, P.: Le mans: dynamic and fluid MPC for dishonest majority. Cryptology ePrint Archive, Report 2021/1579 (2021). https://eprint.iacr.org/2021/1579

[SSW17] Scholl, P., Smart, N.P., Wood, T.: When it's all just too much: outsourc-
ing MPC-preprocessing. In: O'Neill, M. (ed.) IMACC 2017. LNCS, vol.
10655, pp. 77–99. Springer, Cham (2017). https://doi.org/10.1007/978-3-
319-71045-7_4

[WYKW21] Weng, C., Yang, K., Katz, J., Wang, X.: Wolverine: fast, scalable, and
communication-efficient zero-knowledge proofs for Boolean and arithmetic
circuits. In: 42nd IEEE Symposium on Security and Privacy (Oakland
2021) (2021)

Secure Messaging

Oblivious Message Retrieval

Zeyu Liu[1](✉) and Eran Tromer[1,2]

[1] Columbia University, New York, USA
zl2967@columbia.edu
[2] Tel Aviv University, Tel Aviv, Israel

Abstract. Anonymous message delivery systems, such as private messaging services and privacy-preserving payment systems, need a mechanism for recipients to retrieve the messages addressed to them without leaking metadata or letting their messages be linked. Recipients could download all posted messages and scan for those addressed to them, but communication and computation costs are excessive at scale.

We show how untrusted servers can detect messages on behalf of recipients, and summarize these into a compact encrypted digest that recipients can easily decrypt. These servers operate obliviously and do not learn anything about which messages are addressed to which recipients. Privacy, soundness, and completeness hold even if everyone but the recipient is adversarial and colluding (unlike in prior schemes).

Our starting point is an asymptotically-efficient approach, using Fully Homomorphic Encryption and homomorphically-encoded Sparse Random Linear Codes. We then address the concrete performance using bespoke tailoring of lattice-based cryptographic components, alongside various algebraic and algorithmic optimizations. This reduces the digest size to a few bits per message scanned. Concretely, the servers' cost is ~\$1 per million messages scanned, and the resulting digests can be decoded by recipients in under ~20 ms. Our schemes can thus practically attain the strongest form of receiver privacy for current applications such as privacy-preserving cryptocurrencies.

1 Introduction

End-to-end encryption of message content is well understood and widely practiced. However, metadata about which messages were sent and received by whom, and when, can yield abundant sensitive information via traffic analysis and deductions against auxiliary information. Protecting metadata is thus crucial to anonymous message delivery systems [7] such as anonymous messaging [20,42,61], privacy-preserving analytics [11], and privacy-preserving cryptocurrencies [8,48].

Yet, the problem of protecting communication metadata remains an open challenge for many applications, especially when privacy, scalability, efficiency and decentralization are all crucial. This challenge is well exemplified by metadata protection in privacy-preserving cryptocurrencies, such as Zcash [8,30] and Monero [48]. These convey digital asset transaction on a public ledger (blockchain),

© International Association for Cryptologic Research 2022
Y. Dodis and T. Shrimpton (Eds.): CRYPTO 2022, LNCS 13507, pp. 753–783, 2022.
https://doi.org/10.1007/978-3-031-15802-5_26

while keeping the contents of every transaction hidden from all but the counterparties to the transaction (and those they elect to expose it to), using cryptographic protocols utilizing encryption and zero-knowledge proofs. Moreover, the underlying ledger is permissionless, decentralized and widely replicated, allowing anyone to send transactions over the Internet while anonymizing their IP address via standard means such as the Tor network. Supposedly, metadata leaks are thus eliminated.[1]

However, a crucial point lingers. From a receiver's perspective, a transaction pertinent to them could appear anywhere in the ledger. If the receiver has a full copy of the ledger (a "full node" in blockchain parlance), then it could scan it to identify pertinent transactions, but the requisite communication, storage and computation cost may far exceed the capabilities of recipients (e.g., already today, such ledgers are many GB in size; consider, then, wallet apps running on computationally-weak mobile devices, with little storage, using slow or expensive network connections).

How, then, can recipients efficiently *detect* which messages are pertinent to them, and *retrieve* the content of these messages? In general, we consider a bulletin board consisting of numerous messages, with arbitrary application-specific content (of fixed size). Each message is *pertinent* to a single recipient (identified by their public address) to which it was sent, and *impertinent* to other recipients. A recipient, in lieu of receiving and scanning the whole ledger (*full-scan*), may enlist the help of servers, which we call *detectors*, that will help them detect their pertinent messages and retrieve the content of these messages.

One approach is for the recipient to provide the detector with a "detection key" or "incoming viewing key", that allows the detector to check, for each bulletin board message, whether it is pertinent to that recipient [30,48]. The pertinent messages can then be stored and forwarded to the client. Unfortunately, this exposes metadata to the detector, and thus also to anyone who subverted or coerced the detector, whether in real time or retroactively. Furthermore, such long-lived detection key enables devastating deanonymization attacks.[2]

The problem of *Oblivious Message Detection (OMD)* is to perform such detection without revealing any information to the detectors about which messages are pertinent. This is done today in Zcash via the ZIP-307 "light client" protocol [27], which is essentially optimized full-scan: convert each message to a compact format which contains just enough information for the recipient to check for pertinence, and then send *all* of these compacted messages to the recipient for processing. In practice, this process can take hours even for a relatively lightly-used chain, and is recognized as a severe usability and scalability issue.

---

[1] In reality, today's blockchain privacy solutions suffer from assorted metadata leaks such as variability in transaction record size, ill-defined cryptographic guarantees, inadequate network-level anonymization, exposure of amounts at the interface between transaction pools, and operational mistakes. These are outside our scope.

[2] For example, an adversary who acquired a detection key can easily ascertain whether that key belongs to a given person, by simulating a transaction to that person and seeing if it matches that detection key; if so, then all past and future transaction pertinent to that recipient become linked.

Furthermore, the full task is *Oblivious Message Retrieval (OMR)*, where the recipient also gets the content (payload) of their pertinent messages. Given just detection, the recipient would still have to retrieve every detected pertinent message by some means. Naively querying the detector (or some other server) again leaks the pertinency metadata. This could be mitigated by using Private Information Retrieval, mixnets, or decoy traffic, but at high cost or/and ill-defined security. This is recognized by practitioners as an important open problem.[3]

These problems have been studied by two recent works, which made significant headway, but still carry significant drawbacks. Fuzzy Message Detection (FMD) [7] is based on inducing false-positive decoys into detection, and presents a difficult tradeoff between security (a high decoy density is needed to foil adversarial analysis) and efficiency (these decoys all entail costs). Private Signaling (PS) [44][4] provides full privacy only if a single detector serves all recipients in the system, and moreover requires either trusted hardware such as Intel SGX, or a pair of servers that are in constant communication but trusted not to collude. Furthermore, both works assume for correctness that all senders and recipients behave honestly, and are susceptible to amplified Denial-of-Service attacks, where an adversary can induce detector and/or recipient work that is disproportional to the number of messages they place on the bulletin board. They also exhibit linkability between detection queries and identities. (See further discussion below.) We thus pose the problem:

Is it feasible to achieve oblivious message retrieval/detection that is fully private, DoS-resistant, unlinkable, trustless, and practical?

1.1 Our Contributions

In this paper, we propose schemes that fulfill all of the above requirements. Our approach is based on homomorphic encryption using lattice-based cryptography.

Strong Security Definitions. We formally define the notions of Oblivious Message Retrieval and Detection. Our definitions capture natural notions of correctness and privacy, and moreover capture two important security notions that prior works failed to capture or achieve:

- Prior works are vulnerable to *amplified Denial-of-Service* attacks in the realistic threat model where there exist malicious participants (senders or recipients) in the messaging system. Our strengthened notion says that even if arbitrary system participants are adversarial and colluding, they cannot induce more errors or costs than honest participants.
- Prior works are vulnerable to *key-linkability* attacks, which tie retrieval actions to public identities (or to each other) since public keys are themselves reused or linkable. We achieve a strong notion of key unlinkability, preventing these.

---

[3] E.g., Zcash developers [32] deem it an "action item" that the "lightwalletd [server] learns which transactions belong to the wallet", and described the popular mitigation of using decoy fetches as "security theatre" that fails to achieve unlinkability.

[4] Private Signaling [44] is a concurrent and independent work, available only as a preprint at the time of this paper's submission.

Possibility of Compact OMR and OMD. We show that Fully Homomorphic Encryption (FHE) can be used to achieve message retrieval and detection with full privacy against any (computationally-bounded) adversary. Moreover, we show that FHE can be used to distill the full bulletin board into a *compact digest* of size that is near-linear in the number of *pertinent* messages, rather than all messages in the bulletin board.

Our approach is based on annotating messages with *clues* to their pertinence, having the detector inspect these clues using FHE and pack the pertinent messages into a compact digest using homomorphically-encoded sparse random linear codes, and having the recipient algebraically reconstruct the messages from the decrypted digest. The homomorphic packing and encoding stages are reminiscent of techniques used in batch Private Stream Search [51] and Private Information Retrieval [4,5], adapted and optimized to the OMR/OMD setting.

Practical OMR/OMD. Generic use of FHE is notoriously inefficient. We tackle this by a series of optimizations to drastically improve concrete performance. Our techniques include bespoke composition of several different lattice-based schemes (specifically PVW [54] and BFV [13,24]) and extensions thereto, utilization of SIMD-like packed operations, using a tailored Sparse Random Linear Code, optimization of multiplicative depth to avoid expensive bootstrapping, and parameter tuning.

We thereby obtain several concrete schemes, with different tradeoffs, that achieve our security notions under standard lattice hardness assumptions (Ring-LWE). Security is thus plausibly postquantum. DoS-resistance holds under an additional natural conjecture about LWE-based encryption, or using zk-SNARKs.

Implementation and Evaluation. We implemented our schemes as an open-source C++ library [50] and measured their concrete performance for a variety of parameters and in comparison to prior work. Salient observations include:

- Detector-to-recipient computation: for Bitcoin-scale parameter settings, our OMR schemes have lower detector-to-recipient communication than any other known retrieval scheme: $\sim$9 bits per message for retrieval, and $\sim$4.5 bits/msg for just detection. For even larger parameters, the amortized retrieval digest size drops below 1 bit/msg.
- Recipient's computation is faster than any other known retrieval scheme, e.g., $\sim$20 ms to retrieve 50 pertinent messages out of 500,000.
- Detector's cost for full retrieval is higher than in related schemes, but still quite practical at $\sim$0.065 s/msg ($\sim$\$1.02 per million messages) on a small cloud VM. For just detection, our scheme is faster than any other known scheme, including those based on trusted hardware.

Thus, our schemes are attractive when recipients are limited in bandwidthor computation speed. The one drawback is a one-time cost of sending a key of size $\sim$129 MB to a detector.

Cryptocurrency Integration. We discuss key design points in integrating our scheme with a blockchain-based privacy-preserving cryptocurrency (exemplified by Zcash) including protocol and costs aspect. We conclude that our

Table 1. Comparison of privacy guarantees and assumptions. Here, pN-msg-anonymity means the recipient's messages are hidden among decoy (false-positive) messages which are a p fraction of the total N messages. "Partitioned across detectors" privacy means that if multiple detectors are used for scalability, then the anonymity set is just the recipients served by the same detector. "Honest S&R" means all senders are honest when generating clue for messages, and all receivers are honest when generating their clue keys. PS1 can be modified for key unlinkability (cf. Sect. 8). TEE means Trusted Execution Environment.

Scheme		Privacy			Soundness + completeness	
		Detection	Retrieval	Assumptions	Assumptions	Overflows
Full Scan	[27]	Full		ECDH + Auth Enc	None	None
FMD1	[7]	pN-msg-anonymity, fixed $p = 2^{-i}$		PKE		None
FMD2	[7]	pN-msg-anonymity, dynamic p		PKE		None
PS1	[44]	Full	N/A	TEE (SGX) + DDH + PKE	Honest S&R	Undetected
PS2	[44]	Partitioned across detectors	N/A	Communicating non-colluding servers + Garbled Circuit + Unforgeable Sigs		Undetected
OMRt1	§5.3	Full + full-key-unlinkability		FHE		Detected
OMRp1	§6.3	Full + full-key-unlinkability		Ring-LWE	Honest S&R or Conjecture 1	Detected
OMRp2	§6.4	Full + full-key-unlinkability		Ring-LWE	or zk-SNARK	Detected

scheme is compatible with existing protocols, and that the cost of detection service would be ~$1 of Cloud Computing per million messages scanned (i.e., similar magnitude to the total monthly transaction flow in all privacy-preserving cryptocurrencies).

2 Related Work

2.1 Message Detection

Privacy-preserving message detection and retrieval has been studied in several prior and concurrent works, discussed below. Table 1 summarizes the functionality and privacy aspects of these scheme, compared to our Oblivious Message Retrieval schemes presented in Sects. 5 to 8. See also Sect. 9 (e.g., Table 2) for comparison of concrete performance.[5]

The closest prior work, addressing message detection in a sense similar to ours, is Fuzzy Message Detection (FMD) [7]. In Table 1 in this section, FMD1 and FMD2 refer to Figs. 3 and 4 in [7], respectively. FMD provides the privacy we call pN-*msg-anonymity*: the detector can observe which messages were flagged as pertinent, but hidden among many intentional false-positives which are indistinguishable from the truly pertinent messages. These decoys are a p fraction of the N messages in the bulletin. Like other decoy-based privacy notions, pN-msg-anonymity introduces uncertainty into naive analysis, but still allows many privacy-violating deductions, especially given recurring traffic or an active adversary [41].

---

[5] For reference, these tables also include *full scan*, which is the straightforward linear-communication approach where the recipient scans each message (or a relevant part thereof) in the whole bulletin board (used, e.g., in the Zcash light wallet [27]).

Another closely related work (concurrent and independent) is Private Signaling (PS) [44]. Their model assumes that *signals* (analogous to our clues) are sent directly to servers (analogous to our detectors). Servers handle these signals in a privacy-preserving way, using one of two mechanisms. The *single-server (PS1)* scheme relies on a Trusted Execution Environment (Intel SGX), running on the detector server. This is a very strong trust assumption (especially given the many past attacks on SGX [44, §2.2.1]), with total privacy failure if violated. The *two-server (PS2)* scheme instead relies on secure multiparty computation between two servers, using garbled circuit. The two servers jointly serve as a detector, and (shares of) signals are sent to both of them. Privacy holds as long as these servers communicate but do not collude nor leak their secrets. Note that in this model, if either of the servers is compromised and its data leaks, then the other server can passively deduce the protected information (the recipient of every message), even retroactively.

DoS Attacks and Key Linkability. Both FMD and PS do not provide soundness guarantees if clues, or clue keys (public addresses), are generated maliciously; they are thus subject to Denial-of-Service (DoS) attacks (see Sect. 7). They also let detection queries be linked to each other, as well as to clue keys, hence to public identities (see Sect. 8).

Retrieval. FMD originally addresses only the detection problem, but it naturally extends to retrieval by attaching the full payload for each message; we use this variant when we report the performance of FMD1 and FMD2 as retrieval schemes. PS also addresses the detection problem, but we cannot directly add payloads without breaking privacy; the PS schemes would need to be nontrivially modified to collect and send the payloads in some privacy-preserving way.

2.2   Other Works

Private Retrieval. There are also works that deal with retrieval once indices are already known, i.e., *Private Information Retrieval (PIR)* [19,36]. The *keyword PIR* variant [6,18] assumes the client knows explicit plaintext keywords to search for (similarly to PSS, discussed below). Some works [39,46,62] rely on trusted hardware, such as Intel SGX, for retrieval privacy. Others offer weak decoy-based notions of privacy [27,32]. Our model does not make any of these assumptions or relaxations.

Our construction shares some techniques with state-of-the-art batch PIR protocols [4,5], namely homomorphic accumulation of messages using FHE and linear coding. However, in our case the retrieved indices are not known a priori to the recipient, so our scheme includes encoding and homomorphic decoding of suitable clues, which are then used to guide the accumulation. Furthermore, we use a different coding technique, adapted to this setting.

Other Private Messaging Aspects. The complementary problem of maintaining *sender privacy* when posting on the bulletin board is addressed by Riposte [20], Signal's Sealed Sender [42] and its improvement [45]. Alpenhorn [38] addresses privacy-preserving connection establishment. As discussed in [7],

Alpenhorn essentially uses identity-based encryption and a trusted server to reduce that problem to the privacy-preserving message retrieval problem studied by this paper. The Vuvuzela [29] mixnet offers differential privacy for sender and receiver metadata. Rather than a bulletin board model, it assumes an online model where users to remain connected at all times (lest their messages get dropped). It employs a cluster of servers, of which at least one is assumed to be honest. Bandwidth cost is high (e.g., 30 GB/month for users and 416 TB/month for servers [29]).

Private Stream Search. Private Stream Search (PSS) was introduced by Ostrovsky and Skeith [51] and followups [9,21,25]. It allows a client to search a keyword over a database of documents and download the ones with such a keyword without revealing the keyword to the server.

In terms of techniques, our use of homomorphic accumulation and linear coding is shared also with PSS. However, in PSS, the elements being sought are plaintext words, which allows for relatively simple protocols. In OMR, conversely, the analogues are "clues" which must be randomly sampled and unlinkable, to hide the identity of the recipients. Therefore, we employ FHE to compute a complicated circuit for homomorphic decryption (and amplification) before retrieval, which creates very different cost tradeoffs, optimizations and implementation details compared to PSS. Furthermore, the past PSS works mainly focused on optimizing the communication cost, at the cost of very high server-server computation (e.g., [25], using Reed-Solomon coding, has a server perform do computation superlinear in the number of pertinent messages, for every bulletin message); we use different coding techniques to attain practicality in the OMR setting.

3   Model and Definitions

System Model. In this section, we define the model and the problem of Oblivious Message Detection and Retrieval. The system components and their high-level properties are as follows. See also the high-level components of Fig. 1 (but disregard, for now, the detailed schemes like PVW or BFV; these will be introduced in Sect. 6)

A *bulletin board* (or *board* for short), denoted BB, contains N messages (e.g., blockchain transactions). Each message is sent from some sender and addressed to some recipient, whose identities are supposed to remain private.

A message is a pair (x_i, c_i) where x_i is the *payload* to convey, and c_i is a *clue* which helps notify the intended recipient (and only them) that the message is addressed to them.

We denote the payload space $\mathcal{P} = \{0,1\}^{\tilde{n}}$ for some $\tilde{n} \in \mathbb{Z}^+$, and the clue space $\mathcal{C}$ (typically ℓ number of ciphertexts in some encryption system). The whole board BB (i.e., all payloads and clues) is public. (In applications, the payloads will typically be end-to-end encrypted.)

At any time, any potential recipient p may retrieve the messages addressed to them in BB. We call these messages *pertinent* (to p), and the rest are *impertinent*.

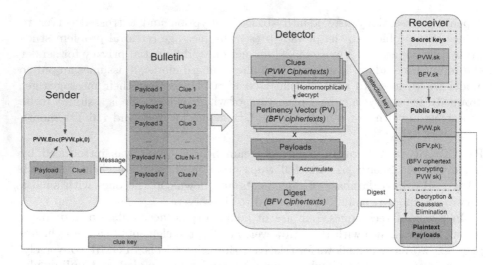

Fig. 1. System components, and major internal parts of the practical schemes.

A server, called a *detector*, helps the recipient p *detect* which message indices in BB are pertinent to them, or *retrieve* the payloads of the pertinent messages. This is done obliviously: even a malicious detector learns nothing about which messages are pertinent. The recipient gives the detector their *detection key*, and a bound $\bar{k}$ on the number of pertinent messages they expect to receive. The detector then accumulates all of the messages in BB into string M, called the *digest*, and sends it to the recipient p. The digest M should be much smaller than the board BB (ideally, proportional to $\bar{k}$).

The recipient p processes M to recover all of the pertinent messages with high probability, assuming a semi-honest detector and that the number of pertinent messages did not exceed $\bar{k}$. The *false negative rate* (probability that a pertinent message is not recovered from the digest) is denoted by ϵ_n. The *false positive rate* (probability that an impertinent message is output by the recovery procedure) is denoted by ϵ_p. Both ϵ_n and ϵ_p are small (e.g., under 10^{-9}).

There may be many detectors, and each may support many recipients. Outside our scope are application-specific aspects such as payload encryption, contact discovery and key establishment, the privacy-preserving mechanism by which messages are posted to the board, or how recipients subscribe with detectors. See related discussion in Sects. 2 and 10.

Threat Model (Non-DoS). We assume a computationally-bounded adversary that can read all public information, including all board messages, all public keys in the system, and all communication between the detector and the receiver. It can also honestly generate new messages (with any payload) and post them on the board, as well as honestly generate new clue keys and induce other parties to generate messages addressed to those keys. For soundness and completeness, we require the detectors, senders, and recipients to be honest but curious; they may collude by sharing information. In regard to privacy, we let all parties in the systems be malicious and colluding (including detectors, senders, and recipients), except of course for the sender and recipient of the message(s) whose privacy is to be protected. (A stronger Denial-of-Service (DoS) threat model will be defined in Sect. 7.1. Key unlinkability will be defined in Sect. 8.)

3.1   Definitions

Oblivious Message Retrieval. We capture the notion of an Oblivious Message Retrieval (OMR) scheme as follows.

Definition 1 (Oblivious Message Retrieval (OMR)).
An Oblivious Message Retrieval scheme has the following PPT algorithms:

- pp ← GenParams($1^\lambda, \epsilon_p, \epsilon_n$): *takes a security parameter λ, a false positive rate ϵ_p and a false negative rate ϵ_n, and outputs public parameters* pp. pp *is implicitly taken by the following algorithms.*
- (sk, pk = (pk_{clue}, pk_{detect})) ← KeyGen() : *outputs a secret key* sk *and a public key* pk *consisting of a clue key* pk_{clue} *and a detection key* pk_{detect}.
- c ← GenClue(pk_{clue}, x) : *takes a clue key and a payload $x \in \mathcal{P}$, and output a clue $c \in \mathcal{C}$.*
- M ← Retrieve(BB, $pk_{detect}, \bar{k}$) : *takes as input a board* BB $= \{(x_1, c_1), \ldots, (x_N, c_N)\}$ *for some size N, a detection key* pk_{detect}, *and an upper bound $\bar{k}$ on the number of pertinent messages addressed to that recipient; and output a digest M.*
- PL ← Decode(M, sk) : *takes the digest M and corresponding secret key* sk, *and outputs either a decoded payload list* PL $\subset \mathcal{P}^k$ *or an overflow indication* PL = overflow.

To define completeness, soundness, and privacy, we first define the notion of board generation:

Definition 2 (board generation).   *Given* pp, *and N which is the number of messages: Arbitrarily choose the number of recipients $1 \le p \le N$, and a partition of the set $[N]$ into p subsets $S_1, \ldots, S_p$ representing the indices of messages addressed to each party. Also arbitrarily choose unique payloads $(x_1, \ldots, x_N)$. For each recipient $i \in [p]$: generate keys (sk_i, pk_i) ← KeyGen(), and for each $j \in S_i$, generate c_j ← GenClue(pk_i, x_j). Then, output the board* BB $= \{(x_1, c_1), \ldots, (x_N, c_N)\}$, *the set S_1, and $(sk_1, pk_1 = (pk_{clue1}, pk_{detect1}))$.*[6]
The scheme must satisfy the following properties:

- *(Completeness) Let* pp ← GenParams($1^\lambda, \epsilon_p, \epsilon_n$). *Set any $N = $ poly(λ), and $0 < \bar{k} \le N$. Let a board* BB, *a set S of pertinent messages, and a key pair* (sk, pk = (pk_{clue}, pk_{detect})) *be generated as in Definition 2 for any choice of p, partition and payloads therein. Let M ← Retrieve(BB, $pk_{detect}, \bar{k}$) and* PL ← Decode(M, sk). *Let $k = |S|$ (the number of pertinent messages in*

---

[6] That is, S_1 is the indices of messages pertinent to the recipient whose keys are sk_1, pk_1, which wlog is the first recipient.

S). *Then either* $k > \bar{k}$ *and* PL = overflow, *or* $\Pr[x_j \in \text{PL} \mid j \in S] \geq$ $(1 - \epsilon_n - \text{negl}(\lambda))$ *for all* $j \in [N]$.

- *(Soundness) For the same quantifiers as in Completeness:* $\Pr[(x_j \in \text{PL} \mid j \notin S) \vee (x \in \text{PL} \mid x \notin (x_1, \ldots, x_N))] \leq (\epsilon_p + \text{negl}(\lambda))$ *for all* $j \in [N]$.
- *(Computational privacy) For any PPT adversary* $\mathcal{A} = (\mathcal{A}_1, \mathcal{A}_2)$: *let* pp $\leftarrow$ GenParams(ϵ_p, ϵ_n), (sk, pk $= (\text{pk}_{\text{clue}}, \text{pk}_{\text{detect}})) \leftarrow$ KeyGen() *and* (sk', pk' $= (\text{pk}'_{\text{clue}}, \text{pk}'_{\text{detect}})) \leftarrow$ KeyGen(). *Let the adversary choose a payload* x *and remember its state:* $(x, \text{st}) \leftarrow \mathcal{A}_1(\text{pp}, \text{pk}, \text{pk}')$. *Let* $c \leftarrow$ GenClue$(\text{pk}_{\text{clue}}, x)$ *and* $c' \leftarrow$ GenClue$(\text{pk}'_{\text{clue}}, x)$. *Then:* $|\Pr[\mathcal{A}_2(\text{st}, c) = 1] - \Pr[\mathcal{A}_2(\text{st}, c') = 1]| \leq$ $\text{negl}(\lambda)$.

An OMR scheme is compact *if it moreover satisfies the following:*

- *(Compactness) An* OMR *scheme is compact if for* pp $\leftarrow$ GenParams$(1^\lambda, \epsilon_p, \epsilon_n)$, (sk, pk $= (\text{pk}_{\text{clue}}, \text{pk}_{\text{detect}})) \leftarrow$ OMR.KeyGen(), *for any board* BB $= \{(x_1, c_1), \ldots, (x_N, c_N)\}$, *letting* $M \leftarrow$ Retrieve$(\text{BB}, \text{pk}_{\text{detect}}, \bar{k})$, *it always holds that:* $|M| = \text{poly}(\lambda, \log N) \cdot \log \epsilon_p^{-1} \cdot \tilde{O}(\bar{k} + \epsilon_p N)$.

Stronger Definitions. The above definition assumes that the board generation is done honestly (though possibly adaptively). For maliciously generated board (e.g., clues not form GenClue), see Sect. 7 for related attacks and a strengthening that prevents them. For simplicity, we also assume the payloads $(x_i)_{i \in [N]}$ are all unique (cf. Definition 2), but it can be naturally extended to the case of duplicate payloads.

Oblivious Message Detection. As a stepping stone towards OMR, we define a weaker functionality, *Oblivious Message Detection (OMD)*, in which the digest merely enables *detection* of the indices of the pertinent messages, but doesn't convey the corresponding payloads. Instead of a function Retrieve$(\text{BB}, \text{pk}_{\text{detect}}, \bar{k})$ that enables decoding the pertinent message *payloads*, OMD offers a function Detect$(\text{BB}, \text{pk}_{\text{detect}}, \bar{k})$ that enables decoding the pertinent message *indices*. Completeness then says that the index of each of the pertinent messages is included in PL with probability $\geq 1 - \epsilon_n - \text{negl}(\lambda)$. Soundness says that the index of each non-pertinent message is included in PL with probability $\leq \epsilon_p + \text{negl}(\lambda)$.

4 Preliminaries

Notation. All logarithms are expressed in base 2 if not indicated otherwise. Let $[n]$ denote the set $\{1., \ldots, n\}$, and let $[n, m]$ denote the set $\{n, \ldots, m\}$. We use $P(\ldots; s)$ to denote a randomized algorithm P running with randomness s. Our big-O notation, when applied to computational and communication complexity, absorbs the security parameter λ and payload size $\tilde{n}$ as a constant. When we use a pseudorandom function (PRF), we assume that its range is as implied by the context (i.e., that the PRF's outputs are computationally indistinguishable from uniform over that range). We use $\langle i \rangle_{\text{sk}}$ to denote the space of ciphertexts that decrypt to i under sk.

4.1   LWE Encryption

Our constructions will be optimized by using lattice-based encryption. We will use the PVW [54] variant of Regev's LWE-based encryption [57], defined as follows at a high level, and details in full version.   The public parameters $\mathsf{pp}_{\mathsf{LWE}} = (n, \ell, w, q, \sigma) \leftarrow \mathsf{PVW.GenParams}(1^\lambda, \ell, q, \sigma)$ contain secret key dimension n, the number of LWE samples in the public key w, noise standard deviation σ, ciphertext modulus q, and number of bits of the plaintext modulus ℓ. ($\mathsf{pp}_{\mathsf{LWE}}$ is assumed to be implicitly taken by the other algorithms.)

For key generation $(\mathsf{sk}, \mathsf{pk}) \leftarrow \mathsf{PVW.KeyGen}()$ and encryption $\mathsf{ct} = (\vec{a}, \vec{b}) \leftarrow \mathsf{PVW.Enc}(\mathsf{pk}, \vec{m}))$. Most crucial is the decryption algorithm $\vec{m} \leftarrow \mathsf{PVW.Dec}(\mathsf{sk}, ct = (\vec{a}, \vec{b}))$, which will be evaluated homomorphically. It computes ℓ inner products $\vec{d} = \vec{b} - \mathsf{sk}^T \vec{a} \in \mathbb{Z}_q^\ell$ and outputs $\vec{m} \in \mathbb{Z}_2^\ell$ where $m_i = 1$ if $\lceil q/4 \rceil \le b[i] < \lceil 3q/4 \rceil$ and $m_i = 0$ otherwise.

PVW is unconditionally correct (sound), and under the standard *Learning With Error (LWE)* hardness assumption [3,57] it fulfills the standard definitions of semantic security (IND-CPA) and key privacy.

4.2   Homomorphic Encryption

Fully Homomorphic Encryption (FHE) enables evaluation of a circuit on encrypted data, such that the resulting ciphertext (when decrypted) is the output of the circuit on the data, but the evaluator learns nothing about the data.

Formally, an (asymmetric) FHE scheme is an encryption with PPT algorithms $\mathsf{GenParams}(1^\lambda), \mathsf{KeyGen}(), \mathsf{Enc}(\mathsf{pk}, m), \mathsf{Dec}(\mathsf{sk}, c)$ fulfilling the standard definitions of semantic security, soundness, and key privacy. Moreover, it has two more PPT algorithms: $\mathsf{Eval}(\mathsf{pk}, (\mathsf{ct}_1, \ldots, \mathsf{ct}_k), C), \mathsf{Recrypt}(\mathsf{pk}, \mathsf{ct})$. Recrypt function is as defined in [26], i.e., it decrypts homomorphically using the encrypted secret key, thus yielding a fresh re-encryption of the original plaintext. These two new algorithms fulfill the following generalized correctness. Given a circuit C and plaintexts $(m_1, \ldots, m_k)$, ciphertexts $(ct_1, \ldots, ci_k)$ which are each either $\mathsf{ct}_i \leftarrow \mathsf{FHE.Enc}(\mathsf{pk}, m_i)$ or $\mathsf{ct}_i \leftarrow \mathsf{FHE.Recrypt}(\mathsf{pk}, \mathsf{FHE.Enc}(\mathsf{pk}, m_i))$, and letting $\mathsf{ct}' \leftarrow \mathsf{FHE.Eval}(\mathsf{pk}, C, (\mathsf{ct}_1, \ldots, \mathsf{ct}_k))$: $\Pr[\mathsf{FHE.Dec}(\mathsf{sk}, ct') = C(m_1, \ldots, m_k)] \ge 1 - \mathsf{negl}(\lambda)$. We require an additional property for the FHE scheme:

Definition 3 (Wrong-Key Decryption). *For an FHE scheme with plaintext space* $\mathbb{Z}_t$, *and* $t \ge 2$, *letting* $(\mathsf{sk}, \mathsf{pk}) \leftarrow \mathsf{FHE.KeyGen}(1^\lambda)$ *and* $(\mathsf{sk}', \mathsf{pk}') \leftarrow \mathsf{FHE.KeyGen}(1^\lambda)$, $\mathsf{ct} \leftarrow \mathsf{FHE.Enc}(\mathsf{pk}, 1)$, *and* $m' \leftarrow \mathsf{FHE.Dec}(\mathsf{sk}', \mathsf{FHE.Recrypt}(\mathsf{pk}', ct))$, *it holds that:* $\Pr[m' = 1] \le 1/t + \mathsf{negl}(\lambda)$.

BFV Encryption. We use the Brakerski/Fan-Vercauteran homomorphic encryption scheme [13,24], which we refer to as the BFV scheme. Given a polynomial from the cyclotomic ring $R_t = \mathbb{Z}_t[X]/(X^D + 1)$, the BFV scheme encrypts it into a ciphertext consisting of two polynomials, where each polynomial is from $R_q = \mathbb{Z}_q[X]/(X^D + 1)$ where $q > t$. We refer to t, q, and D as the plaintext modulus, the ciphertext modulus, and the ring dimension, respectively. Each ciphertext can pack D plaintext group elements $(m_1, \ldots, m_D) \in \mathbb{Z}_t^D$, and "single instruction, multiple data" (SIMD) homomorphic operations can be applied.

BFV is unconditionally correct (sound), and under the standard *Ring-LWE (RLWE)* [43,55] hardness assumption it fulfills semantic security (IND-CPA).

5   Generic OMR and OMD Using FHE

5.1   Oblivious Message Detection Using FHE

We start by constructing Oblivious Message Detection (OMD), with retrieval to be added in Sect. 5.2 This section's constructions will be based on general fully homomorphic encryption (FHE), and assume all the clues are generated honestly. This serves as a simple proof of theoretical possibility; Sect. 6 will address practicality and stronger security guarantees.

Non-compact Construction of OMD. We start by showing how pertinent messages can be *detected*, with a small digest, using any key-private public-key FHE satisfying Definition 3 (e.g., FHEW/TFHE [16,22]). For simplicity, assume the plaintext space is $\mathbb{Z}_2$.[7] Our didactic starting point is a straightforward, non-compact construction; we then improve it to achieve compactness.

High-Level Idea. Each clue c_i for $i \in [N]$ consists of ℓ ciphertexts, each encrypting the constant 1 under the public key of the party this message is addressed to. The detector, serving recipient p, will use p's FHE public key pk to recrypt all the ciphertexts in all the clues: $c_{i,j} \mapsto c'_{i,j}$ for $j \in [\ell]$. Crucially, note that each such $c'_{i,j}$ will be $\langle 1 \rangle_{\mathsf{sk}}$ if the message is addressed to p, and otherwise be 1 with probability $\leq 1/2 + \mathsf{negl}(\lambda)$ when decrypted by sk, the corresponding secret key for the recipient p (by Definition 3). Thus, for each message, The detector performs an AND gate over all $c'_{i,j}$ ($j \in [\ell]$) to get PV_i (the *Pertinency Vector*) for all $i \in [N]$. Then the detector sends PV vector to the recipient. The recipient decrypts each PV_i using its FHE secret key, and if the result is 1, deems the i-th message pertinent.

The resulting OMD algorithm $\mathsf{OMDt1}$ pseudocode and analysis is deferred to the full version.

Theorem 1. *The scheme* $\mathsf{OMDt1}$ *is an Oblivious Message Detection scheme, when instantiated with any fully homomorphic encryption scheme.*

Compact Construction of OMD. Our next step is to achieve compactness, i.e., a digest size which depends primarily on the number of *pertinent* messages k, rather than the total number of messages N. Since k itself is a private information that should not be exposed, the digest size (and detector's computation) instead

---

[7] The following naturally generalizes to plaintext space $\mathbb{Z}_t$ for any prime t. For brevity, we kept this section focused on $\mathbb{Z}_2$, which suffices for its results, and added footnotes to clarify the generalization. Section 6 will use $t > 2$.

need to depend on an *upper bound* $\bar{k}$ on the number of pertinent messages k for the particular recipient (see Definition 1). The bound $\bar{k}$ is given as a parameter to the detector.[8]

The technique used here is reminiscent of that used in [51], where homomorphic operations are used to summarize "documents" according to $0/1$ encryptions; in our case the $0/1$ encryptions are indirectly derived by homomorphic computation (as above), and the (implicit) "documents" are our message indices.

High-Level Idea. We start as above, with the detector recrypting these and computing PV_i ciphertexts which are $\langle 1\rangle_{\mathsf{sk}}$ iff the i-th message is pertinent w.h.p.

Then, we create m *buckets*, for some $m > \bar{k}$ (to be fixed later). Each bucket contains an *accumulator* Acc_i containing a value in $\mathbb{Z}_N$ encrypted under pk, represented as a vector of $\lceil\log(N)\rceil$ ciphertexts of FHE that store the bit-wise binary encoding of the $\mathbb{Z}_N$ element.[9] A bucket also contains a *counter* $\mathsf{Ctr}_{i\in[m]}$, where Ctr_i contains a value in $\mathbb{Z}_{\bar{k}}$ encrypted under pk, represented using binary encoding as well. All buckets and counters initially encrypt 0.

To add the i-th message in the board, the detector computes PV_i as in OMDt1, draws a random bucket index $\mu \in [m]$, and homomorphically adds PV_i to counter Ctr_μ in $\mathbb{Z}_{\bar{k}}$. It also homomorphically computes PV_i and adds it to the accumulator Acc_μ.

Finally, the detector sends all buckets and counters to the recipient. The recipient decrypts these and checks: if the decrypted Ctr_μ is 1, then bucket has a single pertinent message mapped to it, and the decrypted Acc_μ gives the index of that message. If any Ctr_μ decrypts to greater than 1, indicating that several pertinent messages collided in the μ-th bucket, then it outputs overflow.

This method gives us a success rate of $\rho = \prod_{i=1}^{\bar{k}-1}\frac{(m-i)}{m}$. To achieve the desired ϵ_{n}, we amplify by repeating this C times with fresh buckets and counters and re-randomized assignment of messages to buckets, such that $(1-\rho)^C < \epsilon_{\mathsf{n}}$.

Our technique is different from bloom filter as used in [17,21]. With bloom filter, the recipient runtime can easily be $O(N)$, and for $\mathsf{polylog}(N)$ cost, there is an extra false positive rate, which can be avoided using our technique.

Gathering Partial Information. The amplification can be optimized as follows. Even when a set of buckets contains collisions and thus doesn't directly decode to give all pertinent message indices, there will likely be *some* buckets in the set that do yield useful information (i.e., the corresponding counters are $\langle 1\rangle_{\mathsf{sk}}$). If we gather all such partial information together, we may get the full information. Then, the failure probability is $< 1 - \prod_{i=1}^{\bar{k}-1}(1 - (\frac{i}{m})^C)$.

Parameter Analysis. The scheme requires choice of m and C. If we choose $m = 10\bar{k}$, we can then choose the smallest integer C such that $1 - \prod_{i=1}^{\bar{k}-1}(1 - (\frac{i}{10\bar{k}})^C) \le \epsilon_{\mathsf{n}}$. We can see that $C = O(\log(\bar{k})\log(1/\epsilon_{\mathsf{n}}))$ by using union bound. We get similar results for any choice of $m > k$ that is linear in k.

---

[8] If the actual number of pertinent messages k exceeds the assumed bound $\bar{k}$, then retrieval may fail. The recipient can detect overflow and ask for the detection to be redone with a larger $\bar{k}$. Our scheme gives the exact number of k, as discussed below.

[9] For FHE over $\mathbb{Z}_t$, use $\lceil\log_t(N)\rceil$ ciphertexts per bucket.

Decoding k. We add a global counter for the total number of pertinent messages, Ttl, represented as $\lceil \log(N) \rceil$ ciphertexts of FHE containing the bit-wise binary representation of $k \in \mathbb{Z}_N$. The detector homomorphically sums all PV's into Ttl to let the recipient learn the number of pertinent messages, k.

We construct a compact OMD algorithm OMDt2 using the techniques mentioned above. Pseudocode and analysis of OMDt2 and the proof of the following theorem are deferred to the full version.

Theorem 2. *The scheme* OMDt2 *is a compact Oblivious Message Detection scheme, when instantiated with any fully homomorphic encryption scheme* FHE *and a PRF f.*

This construction satisfies the asymptotic requirements of compact OMR (completeness, soundness, privacy, and compactness). Additional asymptotic optimizations are possible and deferred to the full version. The above is still far from concrete practicality (see end of Sect. 5), as will be addressed in Sect. 6.

5.2   Payload Retrieval Using FHE

An OMD scheme, like the one above, lets the recipient learn the *indices* of the messages addressed to it in the board. It would then still need to retrieve the *content* (or *payload*) of those messages, and (in our motivating applications) do so privately without revealing which messages were of interest. As discussed in Sect. 2, retrieval with current methods *after* obtaining the indices is either inefficient or non-private.

We thus extend the above OMD scheme to Oblivious Message Retrieval, starting with a simple construction from generic FHE below, and improving it in Sect. 6. Our approach embeds techniques from PSS [9,21,25,51] and multi-query PIR [4,5] (see Sect. 2.2) into the detector's operation, without an extra round-trip to the client. Specifically, we use the encrypted 0/1 pertinency bits, derived above, to extract the pertinent payloads using homomorphic multiplication; we then compress these using homomorphically-evaluated linear codes. As discussed in Sect. 2.2, these techniques require substantial adaptations for efficiency in OMD/OMR. The generic OMR approach is detailed below, first as an inefficient construction based on generic FHE (as a didactic stepping stone), and then with major optimizations (Sect. 6).

Single Pertinent Message. Our starting point is the above OMDt1 construction. The detector's procedure OMR.Retrieve first runs PV $\leftarrow$ OMDt1.Detect$(D, \mathsf{pk}, \bar{k}, \epsilon_n)$, to obtain a pertinency vector PV of N ciphertexts, each encrypting 1 or 0. It then proceeds as follows.

Consider first the simple scenario where, throughout the board, there is a single message x_z that is pertinent for the recipient p (but z is initially unknown). Hence, PV has a single $\langle 1 \rangle_{\mathsf{sk}}$ ciphertext, and the rest are $\langle 0 \rangle_{\mathsf{sk}}$.

Let the payload space $\mathcal{P}$ be represented by a tuple of FHE's plaintext space (i.e., for $\mathcal{P} = \{0,1\}^{\tilde{n}}$ and the plaintext space $\mathbb{Z}_2$, we use $\tilde{n}$ ciphertexts to represent each payload). In the following we generalize the FHE.Enc, FHE.Eval, and $\langle \cdot \rangle_{\mathsf{sk}}$ notation to work on such tuples in the natural way, as vector operations over $\mathbb{Z}_2$. For each $i \in [N]$, multiply x_i by PV_i homomorphically to get a ciphertext tuple x_i'. Thus, $x_z' \in \langle x_z \rangle_{\mathsf{sk}}$, and $x_i' \in \langle 0 \rangle_{\mathsf{sk}}$ for $i \in [N]$ for the rest of the ciphertext tuples $(i \neq z)$. Then, homomorphically sum up all x_i' to get a ciphertext tuple M', so that $M' \in \langle x_z \rangle_{\mathsf{sk}}$. The detector sends this M' to the recipient, who decrypts it to obtain the payload x_z.

Multiple Pertinent Messages via Random Linear Coding. We generalize the above to the case of k pertinent messages, where $0 \leq k \leq \bar{k}$. The cap $\bar{k}$ is chosen by the recipient and given to the detector, but does not need to be known (or even fixed) when the board messages are generated.

The above single-message scheme fails if there are multiple pertinent messages, because the detector would output the encrypted *sum* of the k pertinent payloads, from which the individual payloads cannot be (in general) recovered. However, we can have the detector compute several encrypted combinations of the pertinent plaintexts, each one summing them with different weights, in hope of creating a linear system that the recipient can solve.

Specifically, we will choose some $m \geq \bar{k}$ and have the detector homomorphically compute encrypted payload m combinations $\mathsf{Cmb}_j \leftarrow \sum_{i \in [N]} (w_{i,j} \cdot x_i) \cdot \mathsf{PV}_i$ for $j \in [m]$, using random weights $w_{i,j}$ ($i \in [N]$, $j \in m$).[10] Letting $\mathsf{PS} \subseteq [N]$ denote the k pertinent message indices, we then have $\mathsf{Cmb}_j \in \langle \sum_{i \in \mathsf{PS}} w_{i,j} \cdot x_i \rangle_{\mathsf{sk}}$.

The combinations are realized as FHE ciphertext tuples big enough to represent $\mathcal{P}$, with element-wise operations, i.e., as a vector space over the field $\mathrm{GF}(t)$ of the plaintext space (in our case, of binary plaintext space: $\tilde{n}$ binary ciphertexts, with bitwise AND and XOR).

The OMR digest includes the aforementioned output of OMDt1.Detect, from which the recipient can recover PS. Moreover the recipient can know the weights $w_{i,j}$ (by including the seed used to pseudorandomly generate the weights in the digest). Then the recipient can decrypt the payload combinations and recover m equations over the variables $(x_i)_{i \in \mathsf{PS}}$, of the form $\sum_{i \in \mathsf{PS}} w_{i,j} x_i =$ FHE.Dec(Cmb_j) $\in \langle \sum_{i \in \mathsf{PS}} w_{i,j} \cdot x_i \rangle_{\mathsf{sk}}$ for $j \in [\bar{k}]$. If $|\mathsf{PS}| = k$ of these equations are linearly independent, then the recipient can use Gaussian elimination to recover these x_i, i.e., the pertinent messages' payloads.

For randomly-chosen weights in the field $\mathrm{GF}(t)$ (in our case $t = 2$), the probability of getting $\bar{k}$ linearly independent equations is $\prod_{i=m-\bar{k}+1}^{m}(1 - 1/t^i)$, via [58, Lemma 1]. Therefore, $m = \bar{k} + \lceil \log_t(\frac{1}{\epsilon_{\mathsf{n}}}) \rceil$ suffices.

5.3 Improved Retrieval Using SRLC

In the above attempt, the detector's computational cost for preparing the payload combinations is proportional to $\bar{k} \cdot N$. To reduce this cost, we use *Sparse*

---

[10] Here multiplication is in the field $\mathrm{GF}(2)$, for the plaintext space $\mathbb{Z}_2$, so the weights are just 0 or 1. In general, this works over $\mathrm{GF}(t)$ for prime t. From this point on we will require both multiplications and addition (to perform linear algebra), and thus consider the field $\mathrm{GF}(t)$ instead of the group $\mathbb{Z}_t$.

Random Linear Coding (SRLC) [34], encoded homomorphically. SRLC is widely studied and applied to data transmission [15, 34, 35, 60].[11]

In this approach, we create weighted linear combinations as above, but we make them sparse: each message is assigned to just a few combinations (i.e., most of the weights $w_{i,j}$ are chosen as zero). We provide the following two schemes for SRLC to ensure that the resulting combinations are still linearly independent (thus solvable by the recipient) with high probability.

SRLC1: Analytically-Bounded SRLC. For SRLC1, each weight is chosen as nonzero with probability γ/m, where γ is some SRLC parameter and m is the number of combinations. To ensure that the resulting combinations are solvable for $k < \bar{k}$ variables with probability greater than $1 - \epsilon_n$, provably $\gamma = O(\bar{k} \log^2 \bar{k} \log(\epsilon_n^{-1}))$ and $m = O(\gamma \cdot \bar{k})$ suffice.

SRLC2: Empirically-Bounded SRLC. In this scheme, we uniformly choose exactly γ nonzero weights among the m combinations. The choice of γ and m is done by an empirical estimation procedure (in the absence of tight analytical bounds), and we prove that the estimation error is negligible.

Compact OMR using SRLC. We can construct a compact OMR scheme using SRLC, following the intuition of Sects. 5.2 and 5.3. The resulting algorithm OMRt1 pseudocode is deferred to the full version. The following theorem is proven, and complexity analyzed, in the full version:

Theorem 3. *The scheme* OMRt1 *is a Oblivious Message Retrieval scheme, when instantiated with any fully homomorphic encryption scheme* FHE*, PRFs* f*, and SRLC scheme* SRLC*. Moreover, when instantiated with* SRLC1*,* OMRt1 *is also compact.*

(Im)practicality. The above establishes the asymptotic existence of compact OMR (assuming existence of FHE), but it is still impractical, e.g., due to the cost of the Recrypt algorithm in state-of-the-art FHE schemes [13, 14, 16, 22, 24]. Moreover, the clues are large (e.g., FHEW/TFHE needs 512 bytes per each of the ∼20 plaintext bits required in Sect. 5.1).

6   Practical OMR

We proceed to introduce optimizations that improve communication and computation costs to practical levels, as well as security improvements. See Sect. 9 below for implementation and quantitative evaluation.

Our starting point is the generic FHE construction of Sect. 5, generalized from plaintext space $\mathbb{Z}_2$ to $\mathbb{Z}_t$ for prime $t \geq 2$ (as discussed in footnotes whenever pertinent). The generalization immediately gives us improved concrete bounds on false positive rate, and in the SRLC-based retrieval. We then proceed to modify the scheme as follows.

---

[11] State-of-the-art batch-PIR [4, 5] uses different coding techniques, which rely on the client knowing the pertinent indices a priori.

6.1 PVW Clue Ciphertext

Instead of generating clues using encryption under an FHE scheme, we use a lighter-weight encryption scheme which can still be homomorphically decrypted and processed by the detector. Specifically, we use the PVW scheme [54], a variant of the Regev05 LWE-based encryption scheme [57]. See Sect. 4.1 for details. PVW decryption can be cheaply evaluated under FHE (we discuss in more detail later), and moreover its ciphertext size grows slowly when multiple bits are encrypted (to encrypt ℓ bits, clue size using PVW grows with $O(n + \ell)$, compared to $O(n \cdot \ell)$ in the original Regev05 scheme [57], where n is a predetermined LWE parameter to be discussed below). Choice of PVW parametersdeferred to the full version. The switch to PVW maintains the OMD/OMR privacy requirement, since PVW is IND–CPA and key-private by [28] and [54, Lemma 7.4].

6.2 BFV Leveled Homomorphic Encryption

In the detection and retrieval algorithm, we also replace FHE with leveled HE, i.e., homomorphic encryption restricted to evaluation of arithmetic circuits with predetermined multiplicative depth. This suffices since, as shown below, the multiplicative depth can be kept low and moreover, after the switch to PVW encryption, we do not need Recrypt. Specifically, we use the BFV [13,24] scheme (see Sect. 4.2).

The detection key now contains the BFV public key, and the PVW secret key PVW.sk encrypted under BFV public key. The detector uses these to homomorphically decrypt the clue, resulting in PV_i which are $\langle 0 \rangle_{sk}^{BFV}$ or $\langle 1 \rangle_{sk}^{BFV}$. It then proceed to process these into a digest as in Sect. 5, using BFV homomorphic operations, all with plaintext space $GF(t)$.

One advantage of this choice is that BFV supports "single instruction, multiple data" (SIMD) operations: each BFV ciphertext has D *slots*, each of which can convey an element of $\mathbb{Z}_t$, for some plaintext modulus t and a parameter D. When computing PV, we can thus operate on D separate messages $\{(x_i, c_i)\}$ in parallel via SIMD (see Sect. 4.2).

Specifically, the detector performs the following steps to homomorphically perform PVW.Dec (described intuitively here, and precisely in the full version). Note that for simplicity when decrypting homomorphically using BFV, we redefine our clues to be PVW encryptions of 0 instead of 1 as above (i.e. $PVW.Dec(sk_{p'}, GenClue(pk_p, \cdot)) = 0$ iff $p = p'$ w.h.p.).

- **Inner Product** (InnerProd). The detector performs the first step of PVW.Dec: inner product of the clue's PVW ciphertext with PVW.sk (that is provided by the recipient under BFV encryption).
- **Range checking** (RangeCheck). For a range $[-r, r]$ and plaintext element $u \in \mathbb{Z}_t$, this maps u to 0 if $u \in [-r, r]$, otherwise to 1. We implement this homomorphically using [33, Equation 2] as follows, using the Paterson-Stockmeyer algorithm [53] to minimize multiplicative depth. To evaluate the function $f(x)$ where $f_r(x) = 0$ for $t - r \le x \le r$, and $f(x) = 1$ otherwise, we can evaluate

the following polynomial over $\mathbb{Z}_t$:

$$\mathsf{RC}_r(X) = f_r(0) - \sum_{i=0}^{t-1} X^i \sum_{a=0}^{t-1} f_r(a)a^{t-1-i} . \tag{1}$$

We thus calculate $u' \leftarrow \mathsf{RC}_r(u)$ homomorphically, so $u' \in \langle 1 \rangle_{\mathsf{sk}}^{\mathsf{BFV}}$ iff $u \in [-r, r]$ (which is the case for pertinent messages with high probability). An exact implementation of PVW.Dec would require $r = t/4$ (by definition of PVW in Sect. 4.1), but this can be relaxed to reduce ϵ_p, since the error distribution is Gaussian.

- **PV Unpacking** (PVUnpack). Because we used SIMD evaluation, the above steps result in a single ciphertext ct whose D slots encode $u' \in \{0, 1\}$ values of D different messages. This already suffices as a digest, but to maintain a clean interface and allow further improvements below, we proceed to unpack ct's slots into separate D ciphertexts $(\mathsf{PV}_i)_{i \in [D]}$.

Between RangeCheck and PVUnpack, we flip the sign of u' ($u' \leftarrow 1 - u'$) so that after all these steps, we get PV_i ciphertexts encrypting 1 in all slots for the pertinent messages, and 0 in all slots for impertinent messages with some false positive rate. Similarly to Sect. 5, we proceed as follows.

Soundness Amplification. Analogously to in Sect. 5.1, we reduce this false positive rate by having the sender encrypt ℓ 0's to the recipient's clue key (in this case: all in a single ℓ-bit PVW ciphertext). Note that here, the probability of a clue ciphertext decrypting to 0 (so that the range-checked output is $\mathsf{PV} \in \langle 1 \rangle_{\mathsf{sk}}^{\mathsf{BFV}}$) for impertinent messages is $p = 1 - (2r + 1)/q \geq 1/2$, rather than $1/2$ as in the $\mathbb{Z}_2$ case. Therefore, using ℓ ciphertexts, we get ϵ_p of p^ℓ.

Applying all of the above, we obtain and OMD scheme analogous to OMDt2, but based on PVW clues and BFV scheme instead of generic FHE, thereby improving efficiency and size. The same technique applies toOMDt1, for more efficient *compact* detection.

Finally, compress the detection digest by one of two means.

Deterministic Digest Compression. Each BFV ciphertext can pack D elements of $\mathbb{Z}_t$, each of which can represent $\lfloor \log(t) \rfloor$ bits of plaintext information. We pack the single-bit pertinency indicators into these bits, homomorphically. This makes near-optimal use of the plaintext space; and in terms of digest size, utilization remains high: roughly **4.5 bit/msg**, for the representative parameters of Sect. 9. The recipient can sum up all these bits to get the exact number of pertinent messages, and thus robustly detects overflow.

Randomized Digest Compression. Alternatively, we can use the bucket-based method in Sect. 5.1 to achieve an compact digest, and compress D accumulators into one ciphertext to fully utilize all D slots in each ciphertext. In particular, we can achieve an amortized digest size of **less than 1 bit/msg**, including retrieval, for sufficiently large $N \gg \bar{k}$. See performance in Sect. 9.

For this methodwe could also use the summation of individual bucket counters to get k, but this may still overflow if the number of pertinent messages is huge, since each slot is computed homomorphically in the plaintext space $\mathbb{Z}_t$ (e.g. if $k \gtrsim tD$, where $tD > 10^{12}$ for typical parameters).[12]

OMD via Deterministic Digest Compression. We can use deterministic digest compression to construct a non-compact OMD, which we call OMDp1. The advantage of this method is that it does not need PVUnpack, and therefore greatly reduces the detector running time.

6.3 A Practical OMR Scheme

Figure 1 portrays the high-level components of the resulting scheme, and their invocation of different encryption schemes.

By combining all of the above detection optimizations, and adding message *retrieval* analogously to Sect. 5.3, we have a practical OMR scheme OMRp1. Here we use the aforementioned *Deterministic Digest Compression*, which is simpler than compact (randomized) detection, and offers better concrete digest size and detection time for some parameter choices (cf. Sect. 9). The resulting pseudocode is deferred to the full version. The following theorem is proven, and complexity analyzed, deferred to the full version:

Theorem 4. *The scheme* OMRp1 *is an* OMR *scheme, assuming security of* PVW *encryption (Sect. 4.2), security of* BFV *leveled HE (Sect. 4.2), when instantiated with PRF f and an SRLC scheme* SRLC.

6.4 A Practical Compact OMR Scheme

While OMRp1 above is practically efficient for many parameters of interest (cf. Sect. 9), its asymptotic digest size is still $O(N)$. An alternative approach achieves compactness, i.e., a digest size that grows only mildly with N when $\bar{k}$ is fixed and ϵ_p is small (cf. Definition 1). This can be achieved by using the *Randomized Digest Compression* approach of Sect. 6.2. The resulting practical and compact OMR algorithm, OMRp2, and the pseudocode is deferred to the full version. The following theorem is proven, and complexity analyzed, details deferred to the full version:

Theorem 5. *The scheme* OMRp2 *in* OMRp2 *is a* OMR *scheme for $N < D \cdot t/2$, assuming security of* LWE *encryption (Sect. 4.2) and security of* BFV *leveled HE (Sect. 4.2), when instantiated with PRF f and an SRLC scheme* SRLC. *Moreover when instantiated with* SRLC1, OMRp2 *is also compact.*

6.5 Additional Properties

Additional modifications improve the practicality of our algorithm. The following points are salient; further discussion is deferred to the full version.

---

[12] If such parameters are exceeded, we can avoid undetected decoding failures using a global counter that represents values in $[N]$ without overflow.

Streaming Updates. The detector can break up OMR.Retrieve into several phases and some of the phases can be done on-the-fly without receiving $\bar{k}$ from the recipient. With this process, we can greatly reduce the latency during retrieval. We defer the details to the full version. Security requires seed secrecy. For details see the paper's full version.

Handling Overflows. Retrieval may fail in case the number k of pertinent messages overflows the bound $\bar{k}$. The possibility is inherent, since information-theoretically, a compact digest for a given $\bar{k}$ cannot represent $k \gg \bar{k}$ messages. When an overflow occurs, the recipient can robustly *detect* it and sends another retrieval query to the detector, with a larger bound $\bar{k}$. To prevent the linkability of the two queries, the recipient can issue the second query from a fresh anonymized network connection, and using unlinkable keys (see Sect. 8).

Detection Key Size Reduction. The detection key includes the BFV ciphertexts $\mathsf{ct_{pvwSK}}$ encrypting $\mathsf{sk_{pvw}}$, and the BFV public keys (including encryption key, relinearization key, and rotation keys as in [37, §5.6]). Their size is $O(1)$, but concretely quite large (cf. Sect. 9). We reduce it as follows.

First, all of the aforementioned components are RLWE ciphertexts of the form $(\vec{a}, \vec{b})$, generated by the recipient who knows the corresponding RLWE secret key, and who can thus choose a pseudorandom $\vec{a}$ that is represented as a short PRG seed, thereby halving the ciphertext size. Second, we pack the $n \cdot \ell$ elements of $\mathsf{ct_{pvwSK}}$ into just ℓ BFV ciphertexts, and involve homomorphic rotation to compute the inner products. Third, the detection key size is dominated by the rotation keys in used for the homomorphic evaluation of slot rotations, and most of them can be generated for a low multiplicative level.

7   Denial-of-Service Resistance

Thus far we have assumed, as in prior works, that all clues in the board are generated honestly by the prescribed GenClue algorithm, using honestly-generated clue keys. However, clues may be generated maliciously, especially if anyone is allowed to add messages to the board in reality.

In a *Denial of Service (DoS) attack* on an OMR or OMD scheme, the adversary can maliciously generate any of the clues in board messages, in an attempt to induce false positives or false negatives in the subsequent detection/retrieval. The adversary could simply create pertinent messages for some recipient, thus trying to induce an overflow for that recipient (by exceeding their $\bar{k}$); this is inevitable and handled in Sect. 6.5. But the bigger danger is *amplified DoS*: even a single maliciously-crafted clue could cause catastrophic failure (e.g., causing false negative or positives for *many* recipients). Furthermore, the adversary may also take the role of a recipient in the system, and publish a maliciously-crafted clue key, thereby inducing honest senders to unwittingly generate harmful clues.

Attacks. OMRt1, instantiated with FHEW/TFHE, is susceptible to a *wildcard ciphertext* attack, where a malicious sender populates the clue with ciphertexts that decrypt to 1 (hence detected as pertinent) for most recipients, causing overflows. FMD [7] is also vulnerable to wildcard ciphertexts, as also observed by [40, commit `e19b99112e`]. PS [44] is likewise vulnerable to wildcard ciphertexts (in the single-server version). Moreover, in the PS model, signals are sent to servers rather than placed on the board, opens an additional DoS attack vector. For instance, a malicious sender can send many pertinent-looking signals to a server to overflow the message accumulator for recipients.

7.1   Modeling DoS Resistance

DoS Threat Model. In the DoS threat model, the computationally bounded adversary has all the power as defined in Sect. 3. Additionally, it is allowed to generate any (perhaps malformed) clues and post them on the board, as well as generate any (perhaps malformed) clue keys for other senders to use. Thus, for correctness and soundness, we assume only that the detector is honest but curious. Other parties are malicious. As before, for privacy, everyone but the message's sender and recipient are assumed malicious and colluding.

DoS Resistance Definition. We introduce a formal definition of DoS resistance, strengthening the OMR definition of Sect. 3.1. Recall that Definition 1 assumes that the clues in the board are honestly generated, using honestly generated clue keys. In that case, there is a natural ground-truth notion of pertinent messages, defined by which clue key $\mathsf{pk}_{\mathsf{clue}}$ each clue was generated for; hence soundness and completeness are defined in reference to that ground truth.

Now, however, clues may be maliciously generated and may not obviously correspond to any specific clue key (e.g., consider the wildcard ciphertext above). We thus require the existence of an *indicator* predicate $\mathcal{I}(c, \mathsf{pk}_{\mathsf{clue}})$ that serves as a ground truth for whether a given clue c is pertinent to a given user specified by their clue key $\mathsf{pk}_{\mathsf{clue}}$. This predicate should give the natural answer for honestly-generated clues and arbitrary but determined answer for otherwise-generated clues (i.e., not claiming more than one honest recipient, except with small probability, and we call this property *collision resistance*. The stronger completeness and soundness are defined w.r.t such an indicator.

Soundness and completeness are then redefined w.r.t the indicator $\mathcal{I}$, as below. Note that to facilitate tight analysis, the completeness (false negative rate) bound ϵ_n in the definition is broken up into two components: the rate ϵ_i at which the indicator fails to detect truly pertinent messages (which may be non-negligible because a indicator with high thresholds may help achieve collision resistance), and the rate $\epsilon_n - \epsilon_i$ at which the scheme fails to retrieve messages flagged by the indicator (which may be on-negligible because of error sources in the concrete scheme).

Definition 4 (DoS-resistant OMR). *Let* OMR *be an OMR scheme for error rates* ϵ_n, ϵ_p *(as in Definition 1). An* indicator *with an* indicator false negative rate $\epsilon_i \leq \epsilon_n$ *for* OMR *is a function* $b \leftarrow \mathcal{I}(\mathsf{pp}, x, c, \mathsf{pk}_{\mathsf{clue}}, \mathsf{sk})$ *on a public parameter* pp, *a message* (x, c), *a clue key* $\mathsf{pk}_{\mathsf{clue}}$, *and its corresponding secret key* sk, *outputs* $b \in \{0, 1\}$, *such that:*

- (Indicator completeness) *For* pp $\leftarrow$ GenParams($1^\lambda, \epsilon_p, \epsilon_n$), *honest-generated key pair* (sk, pk = ($pk_{clue}, \cdot$)) $\leftarrow$ KeyGen(), *for any payload* x, *and honest-generated clue* $c \leftarrow$ OMR.GenClue(pk_{clue}, x), *it holds that:*

$$\Pr[\mathcal{I}(pp, x, c, pk_{clue}, sk) = 1] \geq 1 - \epsilon_i - negl(\lambda) \ .$$

- (Collision resistance) *For any PPT adversary* $\mathcal{A}$, *let* pp $\leftarrow$ GenParams($1^\lambda, \epsilon_p, \epsilon_n$), *two honest-generated key pairs* (sk, pk = ($pk_{clue}, \cdot$)) $\leftarrow$ OMR.KeyGen() *and* (sk', pk' = ($pk'_{clue}, \cdot$)) $\leftarrow$ OMR.KeyGen(), *and adversarially-generated* $(x, c) \leftarrow \mathcal{A}(pk, pk')$, *for* $b \leftarrow \mathcal{I}(pp, x, c, pk_{clue}, sk)$ *and* $b' \leftarrow \mathcal{I}(pp, x, c, pk'_{clue}, sk')$:

$$\Pr[b = 1 \ \wedge \ b' = 1] \leq \epsilon_p + negl(\lambda) \ .$$

An OMR scheme OMR *is* DoS-resistant *for* ϵ_n *and* ϵ_p *if there exists an indicator* $\mathcal{I}$ *with an indicator false negative rate* ϵ_i *for* OMR *such that for any PPT adversary* $\mathcal{A}$, *for* pp $\leftarrow$ GenParams($1^\lambda, \epsilon_p, \epsilon_n$), (sk, pk = ($pk_{clue}, pk_{detect}$)) $\leftarrow$ OMR.KeyGen(), *and adversarially-generated board* BB $\leftarrow \mathcal{A}(pp, pk)$ *where* BB = $((x_1, c_1), \dots, (x_N, c_N))$ *and* $(x_i)_{i \in [N]}$ *are unique, for any* $0 < \bar{k} \leq N$, *letting* $M \leftarrow$ Retrieve($D, pk_{detect}, \bar{k}$), PL $\leftarrow$ Decode(M, sk):

- (DoS-completeness) *Let* $k = \sum_{i=0}^{N} \mathcal{I}(pp, x_i, c_i, pk_{clue}, sk)$. *Then either* $k > \bar{k}$ *and* PL = overflow, *or* $\Pr[x_j \in PL \mid \mathcal{I}(pp, x, c, pk_{clue}, sk) = 1] \geq 1 - (\epsilon_n - \epsilon_i) -$ negl(λ) *for all* $j \in [N]$.
- (DoS-soundness) $\Pr[x_j \in PL \mid \mathcal{I}(pp, x, c, pk_{clue}, sk) = 0] \leq$ negl(λ) *for all* $j \in [N]$.

Note that DoS-completeness implies the (weaker) completeness of Definition 1 with the same false negative rate ϵ_n, and DoS-soundness implies the (weaker) soundness of Definition 1 with false positive rate $\epsilon_p + \epsilon_n$. Completeness is trivial, and soundness is given by the following lemma (proof deferred to the full version):

Lemma 1. *Any tuple of algorithms* OMR *that is* ϵ_p-*DoS-sound by Definition 4 is* $(\epsilon_p + \epsilon_n)$-*sound by Definition 1.*

The proof of Lemma 1 is deferred to the full version.
The Oblivious Message *Detection* definition is analogously strengthened for DoS.

7.2   Attaining DoS-Resistant OMR

The OMRp1 scheme of Sect. 6 already satisfies DoS resistance (for $\epsilon_p = $ poly(λ), with a minor change, under the natural computational assumption stated in Conjecture 1 below). Intuitively, this is because PVW encryption has the property that a ciphertext that decrypts to 0 can be generated by adding up columns of the public key, but if the ciphertext is generated in any *other* way (e.g., from a different public key, or "out of the blue"), then its decryption is close to uniformly random.

Patched OMRp1. The exception to the above intuition is trivial ciphertexts (i.e., ciphertext $(\vec{a} = 0^n, \vec{b} \in \mathbb{Z}_q^\ell)$), so we redefine the clue space as $\{(\vec{a}, \vec{b}) \in \mathbb{Z}_q^{n+\ell} : \vec{a} \neq 0^n\}$. Accordingly, we change OMRp1.Retrieve to reject clues where $\vec{a} = 0^n$ and OMRp1.GenClue such that if generates a clue with $\vec{a} = 0^n$, it retries with fresh randomness (and aborts after λ attempts).

Using the patch above, our OMRp1 scheme is DoS resistance under a natural conjecture about LWE-based encryption.

Theorem 6. *For any $\epsilon_p = \text{poly}(\lambda)$, OMRp1 (patched as above) is a DoS-resistant Oblivious Message Retrieval scheme, when instantiated with any PRF f, assuming the hardness of Ring-LWE and Conjecture 1 below.*

To prove our constructions fulfill this stronger definition, we first define an indicator in a natural way: given the secret key sk and a clue $c = (\vec{u}_a, \vec{u}_b) \in \mathcal{C}$, the indicator computes $\vec{u} = \vec{u}_b - \text{sk}^T \vec{u}_a$ using the secret key and outputs 1 iff the result in range $[-r, r]$. This gives use completeness directly. The delicate part is to prove the indicator collision-resistance property. Intuitively, no matter what strategy is adopted by a PPT adversary, given two public keys it should be hard to generate a "snake-eye" ciphertext that decrypts to 0 under both keys, except with trivial probability (e.g., encrypting 0 to the first key and hoping to succeed for the second). The requisite property is formalized in the following definition[13] and conjecture:

Definition 5 (snake-eye-resistant encryption). *An encryption scheme* (KeyGen, Enc, Dec) *is δ-snake-eye-resistant if the following holds: for any PPT algorithm $\mathcal{A}$, for keys* (sk, pk) $\leftarrow$ KeyGen(1^λ) *and* (sk', pk') $\leftarrow$ KeyGen(1^λ), *for ciphertext $c \leftarrow \mathcal{A}(\text{pk}, \text{pk}')$, it holds that* $\Pr[\text{Dec}(sk, c) = 0 \wedge \text{Dec}(sk', c) = 0] \leq \delta + \text{negl}(\lambda)$.

Conjecture 1 (Patched Regev05 is snake-eye-resistant). The Regev05 scheme [57], patched such that decryption rejects any ciphertext $(\vec{a}, b)$ where $\vec{a} = \vec{0}$ and the decryption checks the result in range $[-r, r]$ as introduced in Sect. 6.2, is $\frac{2r+1}{t}$-snake-eye-resistant.

Snake-eye resistance is not generically implied by semantic security of the encryption scheme, nor by key privacy. However, Conjecture 1 can be proven under the standard (homogeneous) *Short Integer Solution (SIS)* hardness assumption [1] combined with a natural generalization of the *Knowledge of Knapsack of Noisy Inner Products* assumption [10]. We defer the high level explanation of this statement to the full version. Alternatively the latter assumption can be replaced by a zk-SNARK proof [10], appended to the ciphertext, of the statement "$(\vec{a}, b)$ was constructed as a linear combination of public-key vectors".[14]

Conjecture 1 implies a natural generalization to snake-eye resistance of PVW encryption, which implies indicator collision resistance, and thus Theorem 6 (see the full version for proofs).

---

[13] We note that for encryption schemes like El Gamal, the snake-eye-resistance is trivial, as for a ciphertext to be decrypted to the same plaintext, the secret keys must be the same as the decryption function is a one-to-one function.

[14] Such a proof fits in 192 bytes [30, §5.4.9.2] per clue regardless of ℓ, and in Zcash it can be merged into pre-existing zk-SNARK proofs in the same transaction [30].

8 Key Unlinkability

The security notions discussed thus far, and in prior works, omit another privacy consideration: linkability of the detection and clue keys. This occurs in several senses. *Detection-key to clue-key linkability* would reveal clients' identities to the detector serving them. *Detection-key to detection-key linkability* would allow detectors to link recurring clients, facilitating traffic analysis of detection queries. *Clue-key to clue-key linkability* is a concern when recipients wish to publish several addresses that are unlinkable, but (secretly) correspond to a single secret key which controls all of them (as in Zcash's "diversified address" [30]).

Linkability in Prior Work. In FMD [7], the detection keys and clue keys are a key pair in an asymmetric encryption scheme and therefore can be linked. Both PS schemes [44] link the detection key to the clue key by having a public identifying number R_i for each recipient and used in each retrieval. In both FMD and PS, the detection key and clue key are fixed for each recipient.

Defining Unlinkability. We define, in the natural way, the notion of OMR (or OMD) that is *detection-to-clue-key-unlinkable*. We also define OMR (or OMD) that is *full-key-unlinkable*: it offers algorithms $pk^*_{detect} \leftarrow$ RegenDetectKey(sk) and $pk^*_{clue} \leftarrow$ RegenClueKey(sk) that generate new public keys such that cannot be linked to other ones for the same sk. See the full version for details.

Key Unlinkability in OMRp1 and OMRp2. The OMRp1 and OMRp2 schemes are detection-to-clue-key-unlinkable, by the semantic security of BFV (applied to ct_{lweSK} in pk_{detect}). Moreover, they are full-key-unlinkable, via a key re-generation process. To resample the detection key, we generate a fresh BFV key pair (which is trivially unlinkable to prior keys) and encrypt the PVW secret key to the new BFV key (this ciphertext is also unlinkable to prior keys, by semantic security of BFV). To resample clue keys, we regenerate the PVW public keys from the PVW private key; this is indeed unlinkable. We defer the details to the full version.

Attaining Key Unlinkability for Other Schemes. Our OMRt1 scheme can be modified to achieve full-key-unlinkability similarly. We defer details to the full version. PS1 can be analogously modified to achieve detection-to-clue-key unlinkability by changing its PKE and some other modifications (deferred to the full version). It is not obvious how to achieve full-key-unlinkability, or even the weaker detection-to-clue-key-unlinkablity, for PS2, FMD1, or FMD2.

9 Performance Evaluation

We implemented the OMRp1 scheme of Sect. 6.3, and the OMRp2 scheme of Sect. 6.4 instantiated with SRLC2, in a C++ library (released as open source). We used the PALISADE library [52] for PVW encryption, and the SEAL library [47] with Intel-HEXL acceleration [12] for the BFV scheme. We benchmarked these schemes on several parameter settings, on a Google Compute Cloud c2-standard-4 instance type (4 hyperthreads of an Intel Xeon 3.10 GHz CPU with 16 GB RAM). This section reports and compares the results.

Table 2. Comparison of cost metrics, functionality and security attributes. Costs are per message, per recipient. Notation is as in Table 1. The bulletin contains $N = 500{,}000$ messages, of which $k = \bar{k} = 50$ are pertinent to the recipient. "s↔s" means server-to-server communication. For PS1/PS2, we used the times from [44, §9.2] (Intel Xeon Platinum 8259CL), and some costs are via private communication from their authors. If FMD1/FMD2 are used just for detection, the costs are essentially unchanged except that communication is ≤ 1.

	Detection schemes				Retrieval schemes (including detection)				
	ZIP-307 [23,27]	PS1 [44]	PS2 [44]	OMDp1 §6.2	Zcash full scan [23]	FMD1 [7]/[40]	FMD2 [7]	OMRp1 §6.3	OMRp2 §6.4
Communication (bytes/msg)	116	≪1	≪1 + 3M s↔s	0.56	612	42	5.3	1.13	9.03
Detector computation time (sec/msg) 1 thread	N/A	0.06	0.25	0.021	N/A	0.011 / 0.00020	0.043	0.145	0.155
2/4				0.01/0.0099				0.075/0.065	0.085/0.072
Recipient computation total time (sec) 1 thread	70	≪ 10^{-3}	≪ 10^{-3}	0.005	61	2.1	0.29	0.02	0.063
Clue size (bytes)	N/A	32	32	956	N/A	68 / 64.5	318,530	956	956
Clue key size (bytes)	N/A	32	N/A	133 k	N/A	1.5 k	1 k	133 k	133 k
Detection key size (bytes)	N/A	64	920	99 M	N/A	768	512	129 M	129 M
Retrieval privacy	Full	Full	Partitioned across detectors	Full	Full	pN-msg-anonymity $p = 2^{-5}$	pN-msg-anonymity $p = 2^{-8}$	Full	Full
Env. assumptions for privacy	None	TEE (SGX)	Non-colluding servers	None	None	None	None	None	None
Env. assumptions for Soundness+completeness	None	Honest S&R	Honest S&R	None	None	Honest S&R	Honest S&R	None	None

Parameters. We set the total number of messages to $N = 500{,}000$ (roughly the number of Bitcoin payments per day), and set the cap on the number of pertinent message to $\bar{k} = 50$. We set a false positive rate $\epsilon_p = 2^{-21}$ (including decryption failure) and a false negative rate $\epsilon_n = 2^{-30}$. The payload size is 612 bytes, as in Zcash. The internal parameter choice for PVW, BFV and other settings in OMRp1/OMRp2 are deferred to the full version of this paper.

Representative Costs. Table 2 summarizes the main cost metrics and functionality/security attributes of our scheme, compared to related ones, for the above parameters. (See also Table 1 for additional functional/security attributes and the full version for asymptotic costs,).

We see that in both communication and recipient computation, OMRp1 is better than any other scheme with retrieval functionality, thereby making it attractive for recipients that are limited in bandwidth, computation speed, or energy. Furthermore, OMRp1/OMRp2 provide the strongest form of security, and under the least assumptions.

Retrieval Scaling with #Messages. Figure 2 evaluates how the recipient's total cost of retrieval scales with increasing N, keeping $\bar{k}$ constant. As can be seen, our scheme OMRp1 outperforms all prior constructions starting at moderate bulletin sizes, in both digest size and recipient computation time.

For $N > 8 \cdot 10^6$, our compact OMR scheme OMRp2 takes the lead and achieves an amortized digest size of less than 1 bit per message. In general, the crossover point grows with k (due to the growing number of buckets in OMRp2), so OMRp2 outperforms when N is large but k is small.

The detector computation time in OMRp1/OMRp2 is worse than for FMD and full-scan. It is linear in N for all schemes, and thus follows from Table 2.

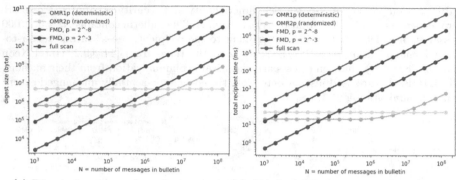

(a) Digest size vs. number of messages.   (b) Total recipient computation time vs. number of messages.

Fig. 2. Retrieval cost comparison (total digest size and recipient computation) for up to $\bar{k} = 50$ pertinent messages.

Detection Key. The detection key size is 129 MB, using the techniques of Sect. 6.5. (Without these optimizations, the detection key size is ~13.5 GB.) Note that the detection key can be sent to the detector via an insecure channel, authenticated by a hash. After the one-time cost of transmission, it can then be used to detect an arbitrary number of messages.

Memory Use. For simplicity, our implementation stores the detection key and all intermediate results in RAM, for a total memory use of ~3.5 GB per thread.

Streaming Finalization Cost. Using the streaming approach of Sect. 6.5, we can reduce the response time to recipients For OMRp1, the finalization is only ~2.1 ms/msg. It can be further reduced to ~0.35 ms/msg, since we have fixed γ. Similar results hold for OMRp2.

10   Integration and Limitations

We proceed to discuss systems aspect of integrating OMR in real-world applications, and limitations of our current constructions. For concreteness, we consider integration of OMRp1 or OMRp2 with the Zcash cryptocurrency [30] to solve the problem of receiver metadata leakage [32] from its light wallet protocol [27]. This prospective integration illustrates several hurdles and how they can be resolved. We use the same scheme parameters as in Sect. 9.

Clue Key Distribution. In our OMR approach (as for FMD [7] and single-server PS [44]), senders need to obtain the recipient's clue key to generate clues. It is natural to consider the clue key to be an extension of the public address, shared by the same trusted channels. Zcash's Unified Addresses mechanism [31] indeed allows such data to be included with public addresses in a backwards-compatible way, and payment URIs [49,59] can be similarly extended. The clue key size of 133 kB (PVW public key) has usability issues. Alternatively, the Unified Address can contain a URL from which the clue key can be fetched. Zcash diversified addresses [30] can be accompanied by different clue keys while preserving address unlinkability, using the full-key-unlinkability property.

Clue Embedding. Clues of size 956 bytes need to be attached to every payload. This is comparable to the roughly 1.3 kB of data already on-chain per such payment. The transaction format can be extended with a dedicated clue field, or clues can be embedded into OP_RETURN data or dummy output descriptions.

Detection Latency. Detectors needs to see all blockchain data, facilitating detection in several ways: in the *single-shot* model, the recipient makes a stateless query to the detector. Response latency is high: about 0.145 s/msg (cf. Table 2). The *subscribe and finalize* model utilizes a streaming version of OMRp1, as in Sect. 6.5, taking 0.0005 core-s/msg.

Detection Key. Our OMRp1 and OMRp2 schemes requires recipient to send large detection keys (~129 MB) to detectors. Conversely, OMRt1 instantiated with TFHE reduces detection key size to ~16 MB, but with much slower detection. Combining the best of these is an open problem.

Detection Cost. The detector cost is ~$1.02 per million payments scanned (per recipient), using commodity cloud computing.[15] This implies $0.02/month detection cost for Zcash's current shielded payments usage, or $1.66/month for the current usage rate of Monero (the highest-volume privacy-enhanced cryptocurrency). If all of Bitcoin's payments were instead done as Zcash shielded payments, detection cost would grow to $15.3/month ; and even higher for massive private messaging applications such as Signal. Acceleration via GPU, FPGA or ASIC can improve costs by orders of magnitudes [2,56]. For cryptocurrency applications, the recipient can directly pay the server for this anonymously.

Acknowledgements. We are grateful to Daniele Micciancio for suggesting suitable FHE schemes for Sect. 5; to Ran Canetti, Oded Regev and Noah Stephens-Davidowitz for observations on Conjecture 1; to Matthew Green, Jack Grigg, Daira Hopwood, Taylor Hornby and Madarz Virza for ideas and observations regarding Zcash integration in Sect. 10; to István András Seres and Varun Madathil for assistance in quantitative evaluation of [44] and comparisons to our work; to Miranda Christ for excellent editorial suggestions; and to Wei Dai for assistance in generating level-specific rotation keys using SEAL library.

This material is based upon work supported by DARPA under Contract No. HR001120C0085; the U.S. Department of Energy (DOE), Office of Science, Office of Advanced Scientific Computing Research under award number DE-SC-0001234, the Columbia-IBM center for Blockchain and Data Transparency; JPMorgan Chase & Co, and LexisNexis Risk Solutions. Any opinions, views, findings and conclusions or recommendations expressed in this material are those

---

[15] 0.065 s/msg (4-core, c2-standard-4 preemptible compute instance, $0.051/h). For finalization, 0.18 ms/msg, 4-core (non-preemptible instance, $0.168/h with sustained use discount). Communication cost is negligible: <10^{-9}/msg egress.

of the authors and do not necessarily reflect the views of the U.S. Government, DARPA, DOE, JPMorgan Chase & Co. or its affiliates, or other sponsors.

References

1. Ajtai, M.: Generating hard instances of lattice problems (extended abstract). In: ACM Symposium on Theory of Computing, STOC 1996, pp. 99–108. ACM (1996)
2. Al Badawi, A., Polyakov, Y., Aung, K.M.M., Veeravalli, B., Rohloff, K.: Implementation and performance evaluation of RNS variants of the BFV homomorphic encryption scheme. IEEE Trans. Emerg. Top. Comput. **9**, 941–956 (2021)
3. Albrecht, M.R., Player, R., Scott, S.: On the concrete hardness of learning with errors. J. Math. Cryptol. **9**, 169–203 (2015)
4. Ali, A., et al.: Communication-computation trade-offs in PIR. In: USENIX Security 2021, pp. 1811–1828. USENIX, August 2021
5. Angel, S., Chen, H., Laine, K., Setty, S.T.V.: PIR with compressed queries and amortized query processing. In: 2018 IEEE S&P. IEEE Computer Society Press (2018)
6. Angel, S., Setty, S.: Unobservable communication over fully untrusted infrastructure. In: OSDI 2016, pp. 551–569. USENIX, November 2016
7. Beck, G., Len, J., Miers, I., Green, M.: Fuzzy message detection. In: The ACM Conference on Computer and Communications Security, CCS 2021 (2021)
8. Ben Sasson, E., et al.: Zerocash: decentralized anonymous payments from bitcoin. In: 2014 IEEE S&P, pp. 459–474 (2014)
9. Bethencourt, J., Song, D.X., Waters, B.: New techniques for private stream searching. ACM Trans. Inf. Syst. Secur. **12**, 16:1–16:32 (2009)
10. Bitansky, N., Canetti, R., Chiesa, A., Tromer, E.: From extractable collision resistance to succinct non-interactive arguments of knowledge, and back again. In: ITCS 2012, pp. 326–349. ACM (2012)
11. Bittau, A., et al.: Prochlo: strong privacy for analytics in the crowd. In: SOSP, pp. 441–459 (2017)
12. Boemer, F., Kim, S., Seifu, G., de Souza, F.D., Gopal, V., et al.: Intel HEXL (release 1.2), September 2021. https://github.com/intel/hexl
13. Brakerski, Z.: Fully homomorphic encryption without modulus switching from classical GapSVP. In: Safavi-Naini, R., Canetti, R. (eds.) CRYPTO 2012. LNCS, vol. 7417, pp. 868–886. Springer, Heidelberg (2012). https://doi.org/10.1007/978-3-642-32009-5_50
14. Brakerski, Z., Gentry, C., Vaikuntanathan, V.: (Leveled) fully homomorphic encryption without bootstrapping. In: ITCS 2012. ACM, 8–10 January 2012
15. Brown, S., Johnson, O., Tassi, A.: Reliability of broadcast communications under sparse random linear network coding. IEEE Trans. Veh. Technol. **67**(5), 4677–4682 (2018)
16. Chillotti, I., Gama, N., Georgieva, M., Izabachène, M.: TFHE: fast fully homomorphic encryption over the torus. J. Cryptol. **33**(1), 34–91 (2020)
17. Choi, S.G., Dachman-Soled, D., Gordon, S.D., Liu, L., Yerukhimovich, A.: Compressed oblivious encoding for homomorphically encrypted search. In: CCS 2021 (2021)
18. Chor, B., Gilboa, N., Naor, M.: Private information retrieval by keywords (1998). Appeared in the Theory of Cryptography Library. http://ia.cr/1998/003

19. Chor, B., Goldreich, O., Kushilevitz, E., Sudan, M.: Private information retrieval. In: 36th FOCS, pp. 41–50. IEEE Computer Society Press, 23–25 October 1995
20. Corrigan-Gibbs, H., Boneh, D., Mazières, D.: Riposte: an anonymous messaging system handling millions of users. In: 2015 IEEE S&P, pp. 321–338 (2015)
21. Danezis, G., Diaz, C.: Space-efficient private search with applications to Rateless codes. In: Dietrich, S., Dhamija, R. (eds.) FC 2007. LNCS, vol. 4886, pp. 148–162. Springer, Heidelberg (2007). https://doi.org/10.1007/978-3-540-77366-5_15
22. Ducas, L., Micciancio, D.: FHEW: bootstrapping homomorphic encryption in less than a second. In: Oswald, E., Fischlin, M. (eds.) EUROCRYPT 2015, Part I. LNCS, vol. 9056, pp. 617–640. Springer, Heidelberg (2015). https://doi.org/10.1007/978-3-662-46800-5_24
23. Electric Coin Company: Zcash Rust crates. Commit hash: 99d877e22d58610dc43021b831a28286ef353a89. https://github.com/zcash/librustzcash
24. Fan, J., Vercauteren, F.: Somewhat practical fully homomorphic encryption. Cryptology ePrint Archive, Report 2012/144 (2012). https://ia.cr/2012/144
25. Finiasz, M., Ramchandran, K.: Private stream search at almost the same communication cost as a regular search. In: Knudsen, L.R., Wu, H. (eds.) SAC 2012. LNCS, vol. 7707, pp. 372–389. Springer, Heidelberg (2013). https://doi.org/10.1007/978-3-642-35999-6_24
26. Gentry, C.: Fully homomorphic encryption using ideal lattices. In: ACM Symposium on Theory of Computing, STOC 2009, pp. 169–178. ACM (2009)
27. Grigg, J., Hopwood, D.: Zcash improvement proposal 307: light client protocol for payment detection, September 2018. https://zips.z.cash/zip-0307
28. Halevi, S.: A sufficient condition for key-privacy. Cryptology ePrint Archive, Report 2005/005 (2005)
29. Jelle van den Hooff, J., Lazar, D., Zaharia, M., Zeldovich, N.: Vuvuzela: scalable private messaging resistant to traffic analysis. In: SOSP, pp. 137–152. ACM (2015)
30. Hopwood, D., Bowe, S., Hornby, T., Wilcox, N.: Zcash Protocol Specification Version 2021.2.14. https://github.com/zcash/zips/blob/master/protocol/protocol.pdf
31. Hopwood, D., et al.: Zcash improvement proposal 316: unified addresses and unified viewing keys, April 2021. https://zips.z.cash/zip-0316
32. Hornby, T.: Fixing privacy problems in the Zcash light wallet protocol, October 2020. https://defuse.ca/downloads/Fixing%20Privacy%20Problems%20in%20the%20Zcash%20Light%20Wallet%20Protocol.pdf
33. Iliashenko, I., Nègre, C., Zucca, V.: Integer functions suitable for homomorphic encryption over finite fields. Cryptology ePrint Archive, Report 2021/1335 (2021). WAHC 2021
34. Kaufman, T., Sudan, M.: Sparse random linear codes are locally decodable and testable. In: FOCS 2007 (2007)
35. Khan, A.S., Chatzigeorgiou, I.: Improved bounds on the decoding failure probability of network coding over multi-source multi-relay networks. IEEE Commun. Lett. 20(10), 2035–2038 (2016)
36. Kushilevitz, E., Ostrovsky, R.: Replication is not needed: single database, computationally-private information retrieval. In: FOCS 1997 (1997)
37. Laine, K.: Simple encrypted arithmetic library 2.3.1. Microsoft Research, Redmond, WA. https://www.microsoft.com/en-us/research/uploads/prod/2017/11/sealmanual-2-3-1.pdf

38. Lazar, D., Zeldovich, N.: Alpenhorn: bootstrapping secure communication without leaking metadata. In: OSDI 2016, pp. 571–586. USENIX, November 2016
39. Le, D., Tengana Hurtado, L., Ahmad, A., Minaei, M., Lee, B., Kate, A.: A tale of two trees: one writes, and other reads. In: PETS 2020, pp. 519–536, April 2020
40. Lewis, S.J.: fuzzytags. https://git.openprivacy.ca/openprivacy/fuzzytags.git
41. Lewis, S.J.: Discreet log #1: anonymity, bandwidth and fuzzytags, February 2021. https://openprivacy.ca/discreet-log/01-anonymity-bandwidth-and-fuzzytags/
42. Lund, J.: Technology preview: sealed sender for signal, October 2018. https://signal.org/blog/sealed-sender/
43. Lyubashevsky, V., Peikert, C., Regev, O.: On ideal lattices and learning with errors over rings. J. ACM **60**, 1–35 (2013)
44. Madathil, V., Scafuro, A., Seres, I.A., Shlomovits, O., Varlakov, D.: Private signaling. Cryptology ePrint Archive, Report 2021/853 (20210624:145011) (2021)
45. Martiny, I., Kaptchuk, G., Aviv, A., Roche, D., Wustrow, E.: Improving signal's sealed sender. In: NDSS 2022, January 2021
46. Matetic, S., Wüst, K., Schneider, M., Kostiainen, K., Karame, G., Capkun, S.: BITE: bitcoin lightweight client privacy using trusted execution. In: USENIX Security 2019, pp. 783–800. USENIX, August 2019
47. Microsoft SEAL (release 3.6). Microsoft Research, Redmond, WA, November 2020. https://github.com/Microsoft/SEAL
48. Noether, S.: Ring signature confidential transactions for Monero. IACR Cryptology ePrint Archive 2015/1098 (2015)
49. Nuttycombe, K., Hopwood, D.: Zcash improvement proposal 321: payment request URIs, August 2010. https://zips.z.cash/zip-0321
50. Oblivious message retrieval implementation, December 2021. https://github.com/ZeyuThomasLiu/ObliviousMessageRetrieval
51. Ostrovsky, R., Skeith, W.E.: Private searching on streaming data. In: Shoup, V. (ed.) CRYPTO 2005. LNCS, vol. 3621, pp. 223–240. Springer, Heidelberg (2005). https://doi.org/10.1007/11535218_14
52. PALISADE lattice cryptography library (release 11.2), June 2021. https://palisade-crypto.org/
53. Paterson, M., Stockmeyer, L.: On the number of nonscalar multiplications necessary to evaluate polynomials. SIAM J. Comput. **2**, 60–66 (1973)
54. Peikert, C., Vaikuntanathan, V., Waters, B.: A framework for efficient and composable oblivious transfer. In: Wagner, D. (ed.) CRYPTO 2008. LNCS, vol. 5157, pp. 554–571. Springer, Heidelberg (2008). https://doi.org/10.1007/978-3-540-85174-5_31
55. Player, R.: Parameter selection in lattice-based cryptography. Ph.D. thesis, Royal Holloway, University of London (2018)
56. Reagen, B., et al.: Cheetah: optimizing and accelerating homomorphic encryption for private inference. In: 2021 IEEE HPCA, pp. 26–39 (2021)
57. Regev, O.: On lattices, learning with errors, random linear codes, and cryptography. J. ACM **56**, 1–40 (2009)
58. Salmond, D., Grant, A.J., Grivell, I., Chan, T.: On the rank of random matrices over finite fields. CoRR (2014). http://arxiv.org/abs/1404.3250
59. Schneider, N., Corallo, M.: Bitcoin improvement proposal 21: URI scheme, January 2012. https://github.com/bitcoin/bips/blob/master/bip-0021.mediawiki
60. Tassi, A., Chatzigeorgiou, I., Lucani, D.: Analysis and optimization of sparse random linear network coding for reliable multicast services. IEEE Trans. Commun. **64**, 285–299 (2016)

61. Wolinsky, D.I., Corrigan-Gibbs, H., Ford, B., Johnson, A.: Dissent in numbers: making strong anonymity scale. In: OSDI 2012, pp. 179–182. USENIX, October 2012
62. Wüst, K., Matetic, S., Schneider, M., Miers, I., Kostiainen, K., Čapkun, S.: ZLiTE: lightweight clients for shielded Zcash transactions using trusted execution. In: Goldberg, I., Moore, T. (eds.) FC 2019. LNCS, vol. 11598, pp. 179–198. Springer, Cham (2019). https://doi.org/10.1007/978-3-030-32101-7_12

A More Complete Analysis of the Signal Double Ratchet Algorithm

Alexander Bienstock[1]($\boxtimes$), Jaiden Fairoze[2], Sanjam Garg[2,3],
Pratyay Mukherjee[4], and Srinivasan Raghuraman[5]

[1] New York University, New York, USA
abienstock@cs.nyu.edu
[2] UC Berkeley, Berkeley, USA
[3] NTT Research, Sunnyvale, USA
[4] Swirlds Labs, Dallas, USA
[5] Visa Research, Palo Alto, USA

Abstract. Seminal works by Cohn-Gordon, Cremers, Dowling, Garratt, and Stebila [EuroS&P 2017] and Alwen, Coretti and Dodis [EUROCRYPT 2019] provided the first formal frameworks for studying the widely-used Signal Double Ratchet (DR for short) algorithm.

In this work, we develop a new Universally Composable (UC) definition $\mathcal{F}_{\mathsf{DR}}$ that we show is provably achieved by the DR protocol. Our definition captures not only the security and correctness guarantees of the DR already identified in the prior state-of-the-art analyses of Cohn-Gordon *et al.* and Alwen *et al.*, but also *more* guarantees that are absent from one or *both* of these works. In particular, we construct *six* different modified versions of the DR protocol, all of which are insecure according to our definition $\mathcal{F}_{\mathsf{DR}}$, but remain secure according to one (or both) of their definitions. For example, our definition is the first to fully capture CCA-style attacks possible immediately after a compromise—attacks that, as we show, the DR protocol provably resists, but were not fully captured by prior definitions.

We additionally show that multiple compromises of a party in a short time interval, which the DR is expected to be able to withstand, as we understand from its whitepaper, nonetheless introduce a new non-trivial (albeit minor) weakness of the DR. Since the definitions in the literature (including our $\mathcal{F}_{\mathsf{DR}}$ above) do not capture security against this more nuanced scenario, we define a new stronger definition $\mathcal{F}_{\mathsf{TR}}$ that does.

Finally, we provide a *minimalistic modification* to the DR (that we call the Triple Ratchet, or TR for short) and show that the resulting protocol securely realizes the stronger functionality $\mathcal{F}_{\mathsf{TR}}$. Remarkably, the modification incurs no additional communication cost and virtually no additional computational cost. We also show that these techniques can be used to improve communication costs in other scenarios, e.g. practical Updatable Public Key Encryption schemes and the re-randomized TreeKEM protocol of Alwen *et al.* [CRYPTO 2020] for Secure Group Messaging.

The full version [8] is available as entry 2022/355 in the IACR eprint archive.

Supplementary Information The online version contains supplementary material available at https://doi.org/10.1007/978-3-031-15802-5_27.

© International Association for Cryptologic Research 2022
Y. Dodis and T. Shrimpton (Eds.): CRYPTO 2022, LNCS 13507, pp. 784–813, 2022.
https://doi.org/10.1007/978-3-031-15802-5_27

1   Introduction

Background. The Signal protocol is by far the most popular end-to-end secure messaging (SM) protocol, boasting of billions of users. Based on the Off-The-Record protocol [10], the core underlying technique of the Signal protocol is commonly known as the *Double Ratchet* (DR) algorithm. The DR is beautifully explained in the whitepaper [40] authored by the creators of Signal, Marlin-spike and Perrin. The whitepaper also outlines the desired security properties of the DR, and provides intuition on the design rationale for achieving them. Indeed, in addition to standard security against an eavesdropper who may modify ciphertexts, the DR attempts to achieve (i) *post-compromise security* (PCS) and *forward secrecy* (FS) with respect to leakages of secret state, (ii) *resilience to bad randomness*, and (iii) *immediate decryption* (all at the same time). PCS requires the conversation to naturally and quickly recover security after a leakage on one of the (or both) parties, as long as the affected parties have good randomness (and the adversary remains passive while such recovery occurs) [20]. FS requires past messages to remain secure even after a leakage on one of the (or both) parties. Resilience to bad randomness requires that as long as both parties' secret states are secure (i.e., PCS has been achieved after any corruptions), then the conversation should remain secure, even if bad randomness is used in crafting messages. Finally, immediate decryption requires parties to—immediately upon reception of ciphertexts—obtain underlying plaintexts and place them in the correct order in the conversation, even if they arrive arbitrarily out of order and if some of them are completely lost by the network (the latter is also known as *message-loss resilience*).

However, despite the elegance and simplicity of the Double Ratchet, capturing its security turned out to be not so straightforward. The first formal analysis of the DR protocol (in fact, the whole Signal protocol) was provided by Cohn-Gordon *et al.* in EuroS&P 2017 [18,19] (referred to as CCD$^+$ henceforth). However, this analysis left open several questions about the cryptographic security and correctness achieved by the DR. Following in the footsteps of CCD$^+$, a more generic and comprehensive security definition of the DR was provided by Alwen *et al.* in Eurocrypt 2019 [3] (referred to as ACD henceforth), with close focus on the immediate decryption property of the DR protocol. They provided a modular analysis with respect to game-based definitions proposed therein. Indeed, they introduced new abstract primitives and composed them into SM protocols (including the DR itself) that capture the above properties: Continuous Key Agreement (CKA), Forward-Secure Authenticated Encryption with Associated Data (FS-AEAD), and PRF-PRNGs. While the works of CCD$^+$ and ACD significantly improved our understanding of the DR, as we observe in this work, both definitional frameworks do not capture some of its security and functionality properties.

1.1   Our Contributions

In this work, our key aim is to develop a formal definitional framework that captures the security and correctness properties of the DR protocol as completely as possible. Moreover, we aspire for definitions that are simple to state and easy to build on (e.g., imagine executing a Private Set Intersection Protocol on top of the DR). More specifically:

- **New Definitional Framework for the** DR: We provide a new definition $\mathcal{F}_{DR}$ for the DR protocol, in the Universal Composability [14] (UC) framework. Our definition captures all of the security and correctness guarantees of the DR provided by ACD's and CCD⁺'s definitions, but also *more* guarantees that are absent from one or *both* of these works. To demonstrate this, we construct *six* different (albeit somewhat contrived) modified versions of the DR protocol, all of which are insecure according to our definition, but remain secure according to ACD's and/or CCD⁺'s definition. Some of these transformations are indeed based on analyzed (weaker) DR variants in the literature, while others are based on novel observations. For example, our definition is the first to fully capture CCA-style attacks that become possible on the DR immediately after a party has been compromised—attacks that, as we show, the DR provably resists, but were not fully captured by prior definitions. We provide an overview of our new definition's advantages in Sect. 1.3.

    Finally, we prove that the DR protocol, as it is described in the whitepaper [40] (in its strongest form), securely realizes our ideal functionality $\mathcal{F}_{DR}$. Our proof is modular and proceeds by expanding on ACD's modular definitional framework (see Appendix E). Note that we model part of the underlying AEAD of the DR using a programmable ideal cipher to prove security in the UC setting where an adversary can corrupt a party while a (heretofore secure) ciphertext is in transit.

- **Non-trivial (albeit minor) weakness of the** DR: We find that multiple compromises of a party in a short time interval, which the DR should be able to withstand, as we understand from its whitepaper, nonetheless introduce a new non-trivial (albeit minor) weakness of the DR. This weakness is allowed in the definitions of both ACD and CCD⁺, as well as $\mathcal{F}_{DR}$, so we provide a new stronger definition $\mathcal{F}_{TR}$ that does not allow it. We summarize this compromise scenario in Sect. 1.4.

- **Achieving stronger security:** Finally, we complement the above weakness by providing a minimalistic modification to the DR and prove the resulting protocol secure according to the stronger definition $\mathcal{F}_{TR}$. We call this new protocol the Triple Ratchet (TR) as it adds another "mini ratchet" to the public ratchet in the DR Protocol. Remarkably, the modification incurs no additional communication cost and virtually no additional computational cost. We provide an overview of the TR in Sect. 1.5.

We believe that the techniques realized here are also likely to find other applications. For instance, in Appendix F, we show that our techniques can be used to improve current practical Updatable Public Key Encryption (UPKE) constructions [4,34], reducing their communication cost by an additive factor of $|G|$, where $|G|$ is the number of bits needed to represent the size of the (CDH-hard) group used in the construction, without any additional computational cost. Furthermore, the technique yields an improvement to the communication cost of the re-randomized TreeKEM (rTreeKEM) protocol of Alwen et al. [4]—specifically, improving the communication cost by up to roughly an additive factor of $|G| \cdot n$, where n is the number of users in the group.

1.2 High-Level Summary of the Double Ratchet and Its Security Properties

Before elaborating on our results in the subsequent sections, we first give a high-level overview of the Signal Double Ratchet and its security properties which we capture in our definition. For another detailed description we refer to the Double Ratchet whitepaper [40]. Readers familiar with the Double Ratchet algorithm could easily skip this section.

We note that although we here describe the double ratchet specifically in terms of its real-world implementation [40], our paper still breaks it down into modular pieces which can be instantiated in several different ways, as in ACD. For the purpose of our paper, we assume that the two participants P_1 and P_2 share a common secret upon initialization. In Signal, this is achieved via the X3DH key exchange protocol [41], but we consider this out of scope for our study of the double ratchet. Using their initial shared secret, P_1 and P_2 can derive the initial *root key* σ which seeds the public ratchet. Furthermore, upon initialization P_2 also holds some secret exponent x_0 and P_1 holds the corresponding public value g^{x_0}. Once the initialization process completes, the ratcheting session begins.

At its core, the double ratchet has two key components: the outer public-key ratchet, and the inner symmetric-key ratchet (often referred to as simply the public and symmetric ratchets, respectively). ACD abstract out the symmetric ratchet as their FS-AEAD primitive, the update mechanism of the public ratchet as their PRF-PRNG primitive, and the means by which shared secrets are produced to update the public ratchet as their CKA primitive. The goal of the double ratchet is to provide distinct *message keys* to encrypt/decrypt each new message. For each message the same message key is derived by both parties using a symmetric *chain key* which itself is derived from the aforementioned root key. Naturally, this results in a key *hierarchy* with the root key at the top, chain keys at an intermediate layer, and message keys at the bottom. Observe a graphical depiction of this hierarchy in Fig. 1. In the Signal double ratchet, Diffie-Hellman key exchange is used to "ratchet forward" the root key, which can then be used to establish corresponding symmetric chain keys. Message keys are then derived from the current (newest) chain key, where chain keys are updated deterministically such that multiple messages can be sent in a row before a response, and no matter which of these messages is the first to arrive, the recipient can always compute its corresponding message key *immediately*. We now introduce the concept of asynchronous epochs before describing the two ratchets and the primary properties which they achieve:

Asynchronous Sending Epochs. In the double ratchet, the parties P_1 and P_2 asynchronously alternate sending messages in *epochs* (as termed in [3]): Assume that P_1 starts the conversation, sending in epoch 1 at least one message. Then once P_2 receives one of these messages, she sends messages in epoch 2. Furthermore, once P_1 receives one of these message, she starts epoch 3, and so on. We emphasize that these sending epochs are *asynchronous* – for example, even if P_2 has started sending in epoch 2, if P_1 has not yet received any such epoch 2 messages and wants to send new messages, she will still send them in epoch 1. Not until she finally receives one of P_2's epoch 2 messages will she send new messages in epoch 3.

Public Ratchet. The public ratchet forms the backbone of the double ratchet algorithm. Parties update the root key using public-key cryptography (i.e. Diffie-Hellman secrets) every time a new epoch is initiated: if P_1 wishes to start a new epoch, she must first update the root key using the Diffie-Hellman public value from P_2's latest epoch (or initialization). After deriving a new chain key from the root key, P_1 can send multiple separate messages in a row—this involves deriving a new message key for each message via the symmetric ratchet, as explained below.

We now describe the root key update process in more detail. To start a new epoch t, P_1 samples a new private exponent x_t and corresponding public value g^{x_t}. Next, she uses the public value received from P_2's latest epoch (or initialization), say $g^{x_{t-1}}$, to compute a shared secret $(g^{x_{t-1}})^{x_t} = g^{x_{t-1}x_t}$. Then, P_1 uses a two-input Key Derivation Function (KDF) to update the current root key and derive a new chain key in one go. That is, she computes $(\sigma_t, w_{t,1}) \leftarrow \text{KDF}(\sigma_{t-1}, g^{x_{t-1}x_t})$. Observe that even if P_1's state was leaked before this update, as long as the parties used good randomness in sampling their Diffie-Hellman keys, the new root key and chain key will be secure. This is the key to achieving PCS. Symmetrically, even if P_1 uses bad randomness when performing this update, as long as if σ_{t-1} was secure, then the new root key and chain key will be secure. Furthermore, root keys are clearly forward secret, from the security of the KDF and the fact that new Diffie-Hellman secrets are sampled independently of past ones.

P_1 includes in every message of the new epoch the fresh public share g^{x_t} to allow P_2 to compute the new shared secret $g^{x_{t-1}x_t}$ that is used to update the root key, no matter which message of the epoch she receives first. This in part is what provides for immediate decryption (and message loss resilience). When P_2 receives a message in P_1's new epoch, she recomputes the same above steps, i.e. she computes σ_t by first computing $(g^{x_t})^{x_{t-1}} = g^{x_{t-1}x_t}$ where x_{t-1} is P_2's own private share, followed by the same KDF computation. Once P_2 wishes to start her own new epoch, she generates another Diffie-Hellman pair $(x_{t+1}, g^{x_{t+1}})$ to

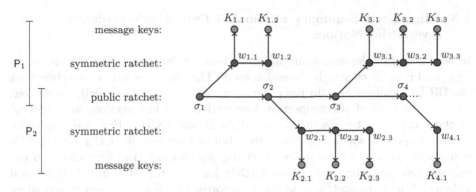

Fig. 1. Sample Double Ratchet key evolution. In this depiction, P_1 sends and P_2 receives in epoch 1, followed by P_2 sending and P_1 receiving in epoch 2, and so on. As explained in the main body, initial symmetric chain keys $w_{i,1}$ for each epoch i are derived first by the sender, then also by the receiver, using the shared root keys σ_i and asynchronously exchanged shared secrets (via DDH). Then, updated symmetric chain keys $w_{i,j}$ and message keys $K_{i,j}$ are derived deterministically from $w_{i,1}$.

ratchet the root key forward $(\sigma_{t+1}, w_{t+1,1}) \leftarrow \mathrm{KDF}(\sigma_t, g^{x_t x_{t+1}})$. Essentially, P_2 has refreshed her component of the Diffie-Hellman shared secret while reusing P_1's value from the previous epoch. Now, when P_1 receives a message for this epoch and again wishes to start a new one, she would similarly need to sample a new Diffie-Hellman share x_{t+2}. This process can continue asynchronously for as long as the session is active.

Symmetric Ratchet. The main purpose of the symmetric ratchet is to produce single-use symmetric keys for message encryption. When a party wishes to send (or receive) the next (ith) message in some epoch t, they derive a distinct message key $K_{t,i}$ from the symmetric chain key $w_{t,i}$ and simultaneously update the chain key. This is done by applying a KDF as follows: $(w_{t,i+1}, K_{t,i}) \leftarrow \mathrm{KDF}(w_{t,i})$ (if the KDF requires two inputs, a fixed value may be used to fill the other input). Observe that the symmetric ratchet is clearly forward secret from the security of the KDF. Note however that the symmetric ratchet does not have PCS due to its deterministic nature.

So, if P_1 just started a new epoch then she first computes initial symmetric chain key $w_{t,1}$ for the epoch as above. To derive a message key, P_1 puts this new chain key through the KDF to compute $(w_{t,2}, K_{t,1}) \leftarrow \mathrm{KDF}(w_{t,1})$. If P_1 wishes to send a second message, then she can derive $(w_{t,3}, K_{t,2}) \leftarrow \mathrm{KDF}(w_{t,2})$. When P_2 receives these messages from P_1, she can repeat the key derivation in the same way as P_1 and use the subsequent message keys to decrypt the messages, no matter the order in which they arrive. The deterministic nature of the symmetric ratchet, along with including the public ratchet values in every message as above, provides immediate decryption.

1.3   High-Level Summary of Our DR Definition's Strength over Prior Notions

In Sect. 2 we fully formalize our new definition for the DR in the UC framework, $\mathcal{F}_{\mathsf{DR}}$, and provide thorough discussion on it. Then in Appendix E, we show that the DR UC-realizes $\mathcal{F}_{\mathsf{DR}}$ (in the programmable ideal cipher model). Intuitively, $\mathcal{F}_{\mathsf{DR}}$ captures all of the properties described in the last section, including all of those captured by the definitions of ACD and CCD$^+$. Here we emphasize several properties which $\mathcal{F}_{\mathsf{DR}}$ guarantees, but at least one of ACD's and CCD$^+$'s definitions do not. We do so by providing *six* distinct transformations to the original DR protocol (denoted as $T_i(\mathsf{DR})$ for $i \in [6]$), showing their natural vulnerabilities here, and their insecurity according to $\mathcal{F}_{\mathsf{DR}}$, but security according to at least one of ACD's (transformations $1-4$) and CCD$^+$'s (transformations $4-6$) definitions. We show this formally in Appendix D.2. Although some of these transformations may be seen as artificial, they emphasize that our definition is stronger than those of ACD and CCD$^+$. Below we use the formalization of symmetric and public ratchets as done by ACD and also adapted by us – the symmetric ratchet is abstracted out as an *FS-AEAD* scheme and the public ratchet as a *CKA* scheme. We defer these definitions to Sect. 3 and Appendix B.

T_1: *Postponed* FS-AEAD *Key Deletion:* This transformation slightly modifies the handling of symmetric ratchet secrets. In particular, when a party receives a new message for its counterpart's next epoch, it does not immediately delete its (no longer needed) symmetric ratchet secrets from its previous sending epoch. Instead, it waits to delete these secrets until it starts its next sending epoch (i.e., sends its next message). In that case, an injection attack can be launched as follows: only focusing on the symmetric ratchet, suppose that for a sending epoch t, P_1 derives $(w_{t,2}, K_{t,1}) \leftarrow \mathsf{KDF}(w_{t,1})$ and sends an encrypted message using $K_{t,1}$, that is then received by P_2. Then P_2 sends a message in epoch $t+1$, which is received by P_1. Observe that unlike in (the strongest version of) the DR, $T_1(\mathsf{DR})$ keeps $w_{t,2}$ in P_1's memory even after receiving this epoch $t+1$ message from P_2. Now if P_1 is compromised then the attacker obtains $w_{t,2}$. Using this it can now launch an injection attack for P_1's sending epoch t (not just P_1's next sending epoch, $t+2$) by encrypting any arbitrary message of its choice using the next message key $(\cdot, K_{t,2}) \leftarrow \mathsf{KDF}(w_{t,2})$ and sending that to P_2. Note that each time a sending epoch is started in the protocol, the information about how many messages were sent in the immediately past sending epoch is included. Nonetheless, that does not thwart this attack, because it is launched even before P_1 starts the next sending epoch.

Although this transformation is perhaps artificial, one can imagine scenarios in which the relative timing of messages sent by the two parties is important. Perhaps more importantly, it is clearly less secure than the standard (most secure version of) DR, but, remarkably, the version described by ACD is indeed $T_1(\mathsf{DR})$. Furthermore, as evident by ACD's security proof, their definition therefore does not require resistance against this attack; intuitively making our (and CCD^+'s) definition stronger than theirs in this respect.

T_2: *Postponed* CKA *Key Deletion:* A similar problem arises if the keys from the public ratchet are kept for too long. The transformed protocol works as follows: suppose that in starting a new sending epoch t, P_2 samples a secret exponent x_t and combines it with the public ratchet message of P_1's prior sending epoch, $g^{x_{t-1}}$, to compute $I_t = g^{x_{t-1}x_t}$. Then, P_2 proceeds to send several messages using I_t (and the root key for the KDF, as described in Sect. 1.2) as normal. When receiving a message for the first time in sending epoch t of P_2, P_1 uses her stored secret exponent x_{t-1} and combines it with P_2's public ratchet message g^{x_t} to compute I_t. However, at this point, instead of deleting I_t (as done in the normal DR protocol), P_1 saves it in $T_2(DR)$. Now assume that P_1 receives all of P_2's epoch t messages. Then, when P_1 again switches to a new sending epoch she generates a new I_{t+1} (deleting the old I_t). An attack can be executed on $T_2(DR)$, by simply corrupting P_1 before the start of epoch $t + 1$, and then using the leaked I_t to decrypt the already delivered messages sent by P_2 in epoch t – thus breaking forward security. Note: this also requires another corruption of P_2 *before* she sends messages in the attacked epoch t, to obtain the root key for the KDF. ACD's definition explicitly prevents querying the challenge oracle immediately after corruptions, and thus does not require resistance against this attack. CCD^+'s model does explicitly require resistance against this attack. This transformation may seem artificial, but clearly allowing the adversary to decrypt old messages should not be allowed in any formal model of the DR, and in fact is not allowed in $\mathcal{F}_{DR}$.

T_3: *Eager* CKA *Randomness Sampling:* If the secret-exponent of a public-ratchet is sampled too early, then that makes the protocol vulnerable. For example, consider $T_3(DR)$ in which P_1 samples the exponent x_t for the next sending epoch t when still in receiving epoch $t - 1$. An attacker may compromise P_1 to obtain x_t (and the root key) at this stage and use that to decrypt the messages sent in the next epoch t, thereby breaking PCS. ACD's definition does not require resistance against this attack, while $\mathcal{F}_{DR}$ does, because their definition does not allow querying the challenge oracle immediately after corruptions. It is worth pointing out that the Double Ratchet whitepaper [40] and CCD^+ present $T_3(DR)$ and its early sampling as their primary description of the DR, though the whitepaper later suggests deferring randomness sampling until actually sending for better security, which we choose to model. However, the security model itself of CCD^+ only analyzes the key exchange component of the DR and we believe that it *could* indeed be composed with an AEAD scheme to avoid the weakness of $T_3(DR)$. However, this needs to be carefully done, and not according to their description of the full DR protocol.

T_4: *Malleable Ciphertexts:* If the protocol does not provide a strong non-malleability guarantee, then the DR protocol could suffer from a mauling attack according to our weaker definition $\mathcal{F}_{DR}$. More specifically, if the root key is leaked, and $T_4(\mathsf{DR})$ uses a weak mechanism to update the public ratchet (note: the DR public ratchet should provide PCS here), there may exist attacks which, for example, can successfully maul DR ciphertexts encrypting m into new ones that decrypt to $m+1$. This becomes evident when we prove the DR protocol secure according to $\mathcal{F}_{\mathsf{DR}}$, which is required to protect against such an attack, as we need to rely on such a non-malleability property. Indeed, the DR seems to require modelling the public ratchet KDF as a random oracle and that the Strong Diffie-Hellman assumption (StDH) is secure (i.e., given random and independent g^a, g^b, and oracle access to $\mathbf{ddh}(g^a, \cdot, \cdot)$ which on input group elements X, Y checks if $X^a = Y$, it is hard to compute g^{ab}), in order to realize $\mathcal{F}_{\mathsf{DR}}$. To provide evidence for this requirement: the ciphertexts and key material known to the adversary in the above scenario are almost identical to that of Hashed ElGamal encryption, for which all analyses of its CCA-security of which we are aware use the same assumptions [1,21,39]. We do not rule out a security proof from weaker assumptions, however, it seems that using a group in which only DDH is hard, and not, for example, StDH, for the public ratchet could lead to an attack like the above. ACD's definition does not require resistance against such an attack since it does not allow injections after corruptions; therefore, their security proof only relies on DDH.

CCD^{+}'s definition also does not completely cover mauling attacks, since it only analyzes the key exchange component of the DR, not any actual message transmission. Therefore, if one composes a key exchange protocol secure with respect to CCD^{+}'s definition with a non-authenticated encryption scheme, it would not provide the non-malleability guarantees required by $\mathcal{F}_{\mathsf{DR}}$.

T_5: *CKA Bad Randomness Plaintext Trigger:* The DR is very resilient to attacks against its source of randomness. However, in $T_5(\mathsf{DR})$, if a party samples a certain string of random bits, say the all-0 string, then it (rather artificially) sends the rest of its messages in the conversation as plaintext. In our (and ACD's) model, which require security even if the adversary can supply the parties with random bits each time they attempt to sample randomness, such a protocol is clearly insecure. However, CCD^{+}'s model only allows randomness *reveals* of *uniformly* sampled random bits. Thus sampling the all-0 string occurs with negligible probability (if we assume bit strings of $\mathrm{poly}(\lambda)$ length), so security in CCD^{+}'s model is retained. Although this attack is quite artificial, [5] note that attacks on randomness sources (e.g., [31]) and/or generators (e.g., [17,51]) are not captured by randomness reveals, but are captured by randomness manipulation as in our model. Furthermore, [5] show that including randomness manipulations has a concrete effect on protocol construction, particularly in Secure Messaging.

T_6: *Removed Immediate Decryption:* Finally, $T_6(\mathsf{DR})$ changes the DR to include the public ratchet message as part of only the first ciphertext of an epoch. It is thus pretty simple to violate the immediate decryption property required by our ideal functionality: First have P_1 send two messages m_1, m_2 in a new epoch t, generating ciphertexts c_1 and c_2. Then, attempt to deliver c_2 to P_2 (before c_1). Since c_2 does not include the public ratchet message of the epoch, P_2 will be unable to decrypt it to obtain m_2. While $\mathcal{F}_{\mathsf{DR}}$ does in fact require immediate decryption, CCD^+'s model does not require it (nor correctness more generally), so $T_6(\mathsf{DR})$ satisfies all formal requirements of their model. ACD's model does in fact require immediate decryption.

Although this too may be an artificial transformation, immediate decryption is an important practical property of the DR, and one of the DR's main novelties is obtaining immediate decryption at the same time as FS and PCS. Furthermore, properly modelling immediate decryption allows subsequent work to understand it, and further improve upon the DR with the requirement in mind. Indeed, many of the works which we are aware of [7,24,32,34,45], besides [3], which try to improve the DR do not consider immediate decryption in their security models or constructions, arguably thrusting these works outside of the practical realm.

1.4   High-Level Summary of the DR's Minor Weakness

Here we show a scenario that introduces a new non-trivial (albeit minor) weakness of the DR which demonstrates a gap between the security guarantees that the DR should achieve according to our understanding of its whitepaper, and those which it actually does achieve. The attack utilizes two compromises of a party in a short time interval, and stems from the fact that a party needs to hold on to the secret exponent x_t for the public ratchet that it generates in a sending epoch t until it receives a message from its counterpart's next sending epoch $t + 1$. Indeed secret exponent x_t is needed until this point because the other party uses its public component to encrypt messages in epoch $t + 1$. For example, consider a setting in that party P_1 is about to start a sending epoch t. At this point P_1's state has $g^{x_{t-1}}$ and P_2 has x_{t-1}. Now when the sending epoch commences, P_1 samples fresh secret (random) exponent x_t and combines that with $g^{x_{t-1}}$ to derive the CKA key $I_t = g^{x_{t-1}x_t}$, which she then combines with the root key σ_t to derive first the symmetric chain key $w_{t,1}$, followed by message key $K_{t,1}$. Note that if x_t is truly random, then I_t and thus $w_{t,1}$ and all subsequent message keys $K_{t,i}$ should be secure. In this epoch P_1 sends g^{x_t} to P_2, who then derives the same key I_t by computing $(g^{x_t})^{x_{t-1}}$, and subsequently $K_{t,1}$. In the next epoch, P_2 becomes a sender. Then P_2 samples a fresh x_{t+1} to derive a new CKA key $I_{t+1} = (g^{x_t})^{x_{t+1}}$ and sends $g^{x_{t+1}}$ to P_1. Now, P_1 needs to compute I_{t+1} as $(g^{x_{t+1}})^{x_t}$. To execute this step P_1 must have stored x_t throughout its sending epoch. The attack exploits this by compromising P_1 twice in a short interval:

- first compromise P_1 before starting the sending epoch t to obtain the root key σ_t;
- then compromise P_1 at any time after she sends a few messages (at least one), but before she receives any epoch $t + 1$ messages, to obtain x_t, and thus I_t;

and then combine σ_t and I_t to derive $w_{t,1}$, given which *all* messages within P_1's sending epoch t are vulnerable, including the ones that were sent between the two corruptions. Intuitively, this breaks PCS with respect to the first corruption, since as noted above, if x_t is truly random, then the corresponding message keys should be secure, as well as FS with respect to the second corruption. For more details we refer to Appendix C.2.

In Sect. 2, we provide a new ideal functionality, $\mathcal{F}_{\mathsf{TR}}$, that strengthens $\mathcal{F}_{\mathsf{DR}}$ in order to capture security against the above compromise scenario. We note that both the definitions of ACD and CCD^+ also did not capture this scenario.

1.5   High-Level Summary of the Triple Ratchet

Finally, we provide a minimalistic modification of the DR, which we call the Triple Ratchet protocol, or simply TR, with virtually no overhead over the DR. This protocol is secure against the compromise scenario provided in the previous section and thus realizes our stronger ideal functionality, $\mathcal{F}_{\mathsf{TR}}$. The TR protocol modifies the underlying public ratchet in a way that the sampled secret exponent is deterministically updated after starting a sending epoch; thus, adding a "mini ratchet" on top of Signal's public ratchet. In particular, using the notation from above, in the modified public ratchet, a party (say P_1) after sampling secret exponent x_t, and deriving $I_t = (g^{x_{t-1}})^{x_t}$, sends g^{x_t} as the public ratchet message, but stores $x'_t = x_t \cdot \mathsf{H}(I_t)$ instead of x_t. Once P_2 receives g^{x_t}, she also derives I_t and computes $g^{x'_t} = g^{x_t \cdot \mathsf{H}(I_t)}$ that she uses for the next public ratchet. In particular, in the next epoch when P_2 becomes the sender, she samples a fresh secret exponent x_{t+1}, and uses the key $I_{t+1} = g^{x'_t x_{t+1}}$. P_2 sends $g^{x_{t+1}}$, upon receiving which P_1 can compute I_{t+1} as $(g^{x_{t+1}})^{x'_t}$, but P_2 only stores $x'_{t+1} = x_{t+1} \cdot \mathsf{H}(I_{t+1})$, and so on. Assuming H to be a random oracle, or instead, circular-security of ElGamal encryption, we can show that given x'_t, I_t is completely hidden, rendering the attack of the previous section useless. Note that the communication cost remains the same for the modified protocol, that is one group element. The computation cost increases only slightly, specifically exactly once per epoch. We also note that, the alternate CKA scheme based on generic KEMs proposed by [3] seems to achieve this security too, albeit with doubling the communication cost.

Furthermore, as we show in Appendix F, our efficient modification can also be applied to practical UPKE schemes, reducing their communication by an additive factor of $|G|$, where $|G|$ is the number of bits needed to represent the size of the (CDH-hard) group used in the schemes. Using the modified UPKE scheme, we can reduce the communication of, e.g., the rTreeKEM scheme [4] used for Secure Group Messaging by an additive factor of $|G| \cdot n$, where n is the number of users in the group.

1.6   Other Related Work

Canetti, Jain, Swanberg, and Varia [16] also recently studied the security of the Signal protocol in the UC framework. Kobeissi, Bhargavan, and Blanchet [37] use automated verification tools to provide symbolic and computational proofs for a simplified variant of the Signal protocol.

Following the first formal analysis of Signal by CCD[+], researchers proposed a number of protocols that provided stronger security than the DR [5,7,25,32, 34,45]. ACD however observed that in the process of strengthening security, all such protocols suffer from steep efficiency costs and loss of *immediate decryption*, rendering these protocols impractical for real-world use.

Jost, Maurer and Mularczyk [35] analyzed ratcheting with the Constructive Cryptography framework [42]. They aimed to capture the security and composability of various sub-protocols, such as FS-AEAD, used in the construction of larger ratcheting protocols.

More recently, there has also been work on the X3DH key exchange protocol used in Signal, providing generalized frameworks that allow for post-quantum secure versions [11,13,22,30], and analyzing its offline deniability guarantees [11, 22,30,48–50].

1.7 Summary of the Rest of the Paper

In Sect. 2 we provide our UC-based ideal functionalities in Fig. 2. We put a lot of discussions around it for reader's convenience, and along the way explain why the transformations of Sect. 1.3 are insecure according to our definitions. In Sect. 3, we define the CKA primitive (capturing the public ratchet) and formally detail the two public ratchets used in the DR and TR (as described in Sect. 1.5), respectively, while only proving secure the latter.

Due to space limitations we defer the rest of the technical sections to the supplementary body. In Appendix A we provide the preliminaries containing mostly definitions borrowed from literature. In Appendix B we provide the other building blocks required for the DR (and TR), i.e., (i) we explain the (informal) properties required from the KDF used for the public ratchet (which we model as a random oracle to handle corruptions with messages in-transit; see Appendix B.1 for more discussion on this), (ii) we introduce FS-AEAD (formalizing the symmetric ratchet part), and (iii) we formally provide additional details on CKA, namely the security proof for the weaker public ratchet used in the DR. In Appendix C we detail the constructions, from the proper CKA and FS-AEAD notions, of protocols DR (Double Ratchet) and TR (Triple Ratchet), which use essentially the same presentation as ACD (fixing their error as described in $T_1(\mathsf{DR})$ and modelling the KDF as a random oracle). We also formally demonstrate the weakness of the DR with respect to our stronger functionality $\mathcal{F}_{\mathsf{TR}}$. In Appendix D we provide the full technical details of our transformations to the DR, their insecurity with respect to our functionality $\mathcal{F}_{\mathsf{DR}}$, and their security with respect to ACD's and/or CCD[+]'s notion. In Appendix E we provide the security analyses of the Double Ratchet DR and Triple Ratchet TR, formalized in Theorem 5, which are essentially the same as that presented by ACD (but also using standard non-malleability arguments and programming the random oracle to handle corruptions with messages in-transit; again, see Appendix B.1). In Appendix F, we show how the techniques used in the TR can also be used to reduce the communication costs of practical UPKE schemes. Finally, Appendix G contains technical descriptions of the UC framework, mostly borrowed from the literature, but adapted to our setting.

2　Defining Security of the Double Ratchet

In this section, we focus on obtaining an ideal functionality $\mathcal{F}_{DR}$ that captures, as completely as possible, the security provided by the Double Ratchet algorithm. We emphasize that we study the security provided by the *strongest* implementation of the DR of which we are aware. For more on this, see Appendix D. We also provide an ideal functionality $\mathcal{F}_{TR}$ that captures the security of our stronger TR protocol. Both functionalities are provided in Fig. 2.

$$\mathcal{F}_{DR} \text{ and } \boxed{\mathcal{F}_{TR}}$$

Notation: The ideal functionality interacts with two parties P_1, P_2, and an ideal adversary $\mathcal{S}$. The ideal functionality initializes lists of *used message-ids* $P_1.M$, *in-transit* messages $P_1.T$, *adversarially injected* message-ids $P_1.I$, and *vulnerable messages* $P_1.V$ sent by P_1 to P_2 to ϕ. Analogously, lists $P_2.M, P_2.T$, $P_2.I$ and $P_2.V$ are also initialized to ϕ. The ideal functionality also initializes leakage flags of both P_1 and P_2 for their corresponding (i) public ratchet secrets: $P_1.PLEK, P_2.PLEK$, (ii) current sending epoch symmetric secrets: $P_1.CUR\_SLEK$, $P_2.CUR\_SLEK$, and (iii) previous sending epoch symmetric secrets: $P_1.PREV\_SLEK$, $P_2.PREV\_SLEK$, all to 0. Further, it initializes bad-randomness flags $P_1.BAD, P_2.BAD$ and takeover possible flags $P_1.TAKEOVER\_POSS, P_2.TAKEOVER\_POSS$ to 0. Finally, it initializes the turn flag TURN as $\perp$.

- **On input** $(sid, SETUP)$ **from** P where $P \in \{P_1, P_2\}$: Send $(sid, SETUP, P)$ to $\mathcal{S}$. When $\mathcal{S}$ returns $(sid, SETUP)$ then set TURN $\leftarrow$ P, and send $(sid, INITIATED)$ to both P_1 and P_2. Ignore all future messages until this step is completed for sid. Once this happens P can send the first message.
- **On input** $(sid, mid, SEND, m)$ **from** $P \in \{P_1, P_2\}$:
  1. Ignore if mid $\in$ P.M.
  2. If $\bar{P}.CUR\_SLEK \vee (P.V \neq \emptyset)$ then $P.V \cup \{(sid, mid, m)\}$
  3. If $New(\bar{P}, TURN, P.T)^a$ then set (i) $P.PLEK \leftarrow \bar{P}.BAD$, (ii) $P.CUR\_SLEK \leftarrow \bar{P}.CUR\_SLEK \wedge (P.PLEK \vee \bar{P}.PLEK)$, and (iii) $\bar{P}.TAKEOVER\_POSS \leftarrow P.CUR\_SLEK$.
  4. Add mid to P.M; if mid $\notin$ P.I then add $(sid, mid, IN\_TRANSIT, m, P.CUR\_SLEK, TURN)$ to P.T; and pass $(sid, mid, IN\_TRANSIT, P, |m|, m')$ to $\mathcal{S}$ where $m' \leftarrow m$ if P.CUR_SLEK and $\perp$ otherwise.
- **On input** $(sid, mid, DELIVER, P, m')$ **from** $\mathcal{S}$ where $P \in \{P_1, P_2\}$:
  1. Find $(sid, mid, IN\_TRANSIT, m, \beta, \gamma) \in P.T$ and remove it from P.T. Skip rest of the steps if no such entry is found.
  2. If $\gamma = P$ then set (i) TURN $\leftarrow \bar{P}$, (ii) $P.T \leftarrow Flip(P, P.T),^b$ (iii) $P.PREV\_SLEK \leftarrow 0$, (iv) $\bar{P}.PREV\_SLEK \leftarrow \bar{P}.CUR\_SLEK$, (v) $\bar{P}.CUR\_SLEK \leftarrow 0$, (vi) $\bar{P}.PLEK \leftarrow 0$, (vii) $P.TAKEOVER\_POSS \leftarrow 0$, and (viii) $\bar{P}.V \leftarrow \emptyset$.
  3. If $\beta = 1$ then set $m \leftarrow m'$. Send $(sid, mid, DELIVER, m)$ to P.

- **On input** $(sid, LEAK, P)$ **from** $\mathcal{S}$ where $P \in \{P_1, P_2\}$:

1. If $\neg \mathsf{New}(\mathsf{P}, \mathrm{TURN}, \mathsf{P.T})$ then set $\mathsf{P.CUR\_SLEK} \leftarrow 1$, $\mathsf{P.PLEK} \leftarrow 1$, and $\bar{\mathsf{P}}.\mathsf{TAKEOVER\_POSS} \leftarrow 1$.
2. If $\neg \mathsf{New}(\bar{\mathsf{P}}, \mathrm{TURN}, \bar{\mathsf{P}}.\mathsf{T})$ then set $\bar{\mathsf{P}}.\mathsf{CUR\_SLEK} \leftarrow 1$.
3. If $\mathrm{TURN} = \bar{\mathsf{P}}$ then set $\bar{\mathsf{P}}.\mathsf{PREV\_SLEK} \leftarrow 1$.
4. If $\mathsf{New}(\mathsf{P}, \mathrm{TURN}, \mathsf{P.T}) \vee (\neg \mathsf{New}(\bar{\mathsf{P}}, \mathrm{TURN}, \bar{\mathsf{P}}.\mathsf{T}) \wedge \mathrm{TURN} = \bar{\mathsf{P}})$ then set $\mathsf{P.TAKEOVER\_POSS} \leftarrow 1$.
5. Execute $\bar{\mathsf{P}}.\mathsf{T} \leftarrow \mathsf{Unsafe}(\bar{\mathsf{P}}.\mathsf{T})^c$ ⌐and $\mathsf{P.T} \leftarrow \mathsf{Unsafe}'(\mathsf{P.T}, \mathsf{P.V}).^d$⌐ then send $\bar{\mathsf{P}}.\mathsf{T}$ ⌐and $\mathsf{P.V}$⌐ to $\mathcal{S}$.

- **On input** $(\mathsf{sid}, \mathsf{BAD\_RANDOMNESS}, \mathsf{P}, \rho)$ **from** $\mathcal{S}$ where $\rho \in \{0, 1\}$ and $\mathsf{P} \in \{\mathsf{P}_1, \mathsf{P}_2\}$: Set $\mathsf{P.BAD} \leftarrow \rho$.
- **On input** $(\mathsf{sid}, \mathsf{mid}, \mathsf{INJECT}, \mathsf{P}, m, \delta, \gamma)$ **from** $\mathcal{S}$:
  1. Skip if $(\mathsf{mid} \in \mathsf{P.I} \cup \mathsf{P.M}) \vee \neg(\mathsf{P.TAKEOVER\_POSS} \vee \mathsf{P.PREV\_SLEK} \vee \mathsf{P.CUR\_SLEK})$.
  2. If $\mathsf{P.TAKEOVER\_POSS} \wedge \delta$ then forward all subsequent incoming messages from $\bar{\mathsf{P}}$ to $\mathcal{S}$ and from $\mathcal{S}$ for $\bar{\mathsf{P}}$ directly to $\bar{\mathsf{P}}$. Also, remove from $\mathsf{P.T}$ all elements of the form $(\cdot, \cdot, \mathsf{IN\_TRANSIT}, \cdot, \cdot, \mathsf{P})$ and drop all subsequent incoming messages for $\bar{\mathsf{P}}$ generated by the ideal functionality (i.e., do not send them to $\bar{\mathsf{P}}$), except the ones generated according to the $\mathsf{DELIVER}$ command.
  3. Otherwise, add mid to $\mathsf{P.I}$ and add to $\mathsf{P.T}$ (i) if $\mathrm{TURN} = \bar{\mathsf{P}} \vee \neg \mathsf{P.CUR\_SLEK}$ then $(\mathsf{sid}, \mathsf{mid}, \mathsf{IN\_TRANSIT}, m, 1, \perp)$, (ii) if $\mathrm{TURN} = \mathsf{P} \wedge \neg \mathsf{P.PREV\_SLEK}$ then $(\mathsf{sid}, \mathsf{mid}, \mathsf{IN\_TRANSIT}, m, 1, \mathsf{P})$, and (iii) else $(\mathsf{sid}, \mathsf{mid}, \mathsf{IN\_TRANSIT}, m, 1, \gamma)$.

---

[a] $\mathsf{New}(\mathsf{P}, \mathrm{TURN}, \mathsf{P.T})$ outputs 1 if we have $\mathrm{TURN} = \mathsf{P}$ and for all $(\mathsf{sid}, \mathsf{mid}, \mathsf{IN\_TRANSIT}, m, \beta, \gamma) \in \mathsf{P.T}$ we have $\gamma \neq \mathsf{P}$; otherwise output 0.

[b] $\mathsf{Flip}(\mathsf{P}, \mathsf{P.T})$ for each $(\mathsf{sid}, \mathsf{mid}, \mathsf{IN\_TRANSIT}, m, \beta, \mathsf{P}) \in \mathsf{P.T}$ replaces it with $(\mathsf{sid}, \mathsf{mid}, \mathsf{IN\_TRANSIT}, m, \beta, \perp)$.

[c] $\mathsf{Unsafe}(\mathsf{P.T})$ for each $(\mathsf{sid}, \mathsf{mid}, \mathsf{IN\_TRANSIT}, m, \beta, \gamma) \in \mathsf{P.T}$ replaces it with $(\mathsf{sid}, \mathsf{mid}, \mathsf{IN\_TRANSIT}, m, 1, \gamma)$.

[d] $\mathsf{Unsafe}'(\mathsf{P.T}, \mathsf{P.V})$ for each $(\mathsf{sid}, \mathsf{mid}, m) \in \mathsf{P.V}$, if there is a corresponding $(\mathsf{sid}, \mathsf{mid}, \mathsf{IN\_TRANSIT}, m, \beta, \gamma) \in \mathsf{P.T}$, replaces it with $(\mathsf{sid}, \mathsf{mid}, \mathsf{IN\_TRANSIT}, m, 1, \gamma)$.

Fig. 2. The ideal functionalities $\mathcal{F}_{\mathsf{DR}}$ and $\mathcal{F}_{\mathsf{TR}}$, respectively.

2.1 Honest Execution

We start with a simplified view of the functionality where only the first three commands, namely SETUP, SEND, and $\mathsf{DELIVER}$ are executed. In other words, we consider a restricted view of the ideal functionality where leakage, bad randomness and injection attacks are not allowed. The adversary is still allowed to delay, reorder, and drop messages at will.

SETUP Command. This command can be initiated by either $\mathsf{P} = \mathsf{P}_1$ or $\mathsf{P} = \mathsf{P}_2$, and allows for initializing the communication channel between P and $\bar{\mathsf{P}}$. Looking ahead, in the real-world protocol, this initialization will involve sharing cryptographic secrets between the real-world P and real-world $\bar{\mathsf{P}}$, then properly initializing their states using these secrets. While the actual Signal protocol uses the X3DH key exchange [41] for this, the focus of our work is to analyze the security and functionality of the double ratchet algorithm, and not X3DH. Therefore, we present a simple description for the SETUP command, that may be stronger than what X3DH achieves, but nonetheless suffices for our purposes.

We note that both P_1 and P_2 must receive (sid, INITIATED) before the communication between them can proceed. Turn status flag TURN is set to the initiator P to denote that P will be the first party to send a message.

SEND Command. This command allows $P \in \{P_1, P_2\}$ to send a message m, under a unique assigned message id mid, to $\bar{P}$. Naturally, the ideal functionality only allows P to send one message under each such mid, which it ensures by aborting in Step 1 if mid is already in list P.M, and subsequently adding mid to P.M in Step 4 otherwise. Now, this message might be dropped or delayed while in transit. Thus, at this point, the message is only added to the in-transit list P.T (Step 4) and the ideal-functionality waits for the instruction from the ideal-world adversary on when this message is to be delivered (if at all).

Observe that the last element of each tuple in P.T is TURN: the turn status when P attempted to send this message (i.e., when it was added to P.T). Looking ahead, this element is used in helper function New(P, TURN, P.T) within SEND (Step 3) to determine whether P is initiating a new epoch when sending a message and, if so, the (in)security of the new epoch. When discussing the DELIVER command below, we will explain the role the last element of P.T plays in the logic of New(P, TURN, P.T) and further understand its role elsewhere in the functionality.

Finally, as typical with encryption, in the real-world the length of the encrypted message is often leaked by the ciphertext. Thus, the ideal functionality leaks the length of sent messages to the ideal adversary.

DELIVER Command. This command allows the ideal adversary to instruct the ideal functionality that a certain message, with unique message id mid, is no longer in-transit, and must be delivered to the recipient *immediately*, whether or not previously sent messages have already been delivered (thus transformation $T_6(\mathsf{DR})$ cannot realize the ideal functionality). The ideal functionality restricts the ideal adversary to delivering the message associated with this mid only once, which reflects the forward security of the DR – once a message is delivered, the recipient should no longer be able to decrypt it (in case she is leaked on afterwards). This is done by removing the entry for mid from P.T when it is delivered, so that subsequent deliveries cannot occur (Step 1).

As part of the delivery process (Step 2), the ideal functionality also checks if TURN was set to P when this message was sent. If so, the message was indeed the first of P's newest epoch that is delivered to $\bar{P}$ (out of possibly many messages that can be the first delivered in the epoch). Thus, subsequently, it will next be $\bar{P}$'s turn to start a new epoch. So, if this is the case, then TURN is flipped to $\bar{P}$. Additionally, helper function Flip(P, P.T) flips the last entry of each message from P to $\bar{P}$ in P.T to $\bot$. This is done so that subsequently, when P starts its next sending epoch, New(P, TURN, P.T) will return 1: TURN will flip back to P once a message of $\bar{\mathsf{P}}$'s next sending epoch is delivered to P for the first time, and there will be no element in P.T whose last entry is P. (Note: before P receives a message for $\bar{\mathsf{P}}$'s next sending epoch, P's sent messages will not start a new epoch, as captured by New(P, TURN, P.T), since TURN will be set to $\bar{\mathsf{P}}$.)

We also note that since UC modelling typically allows the adversary to control the communication network [14] (and thus decide when ciphertexts should be delivered), there are some *useless* protocols that may realize $\mathcal{F}_{\mathsf{DR}}$ and $\mathcal{F}_{\mathsf{TR}}$. We define *useless* protocols as those in which with any PPT environment and adversary, parties do not generate output (i.e., not even a special reject symbol, like $\bot$, representing failed authentication) for at least one ciphertext delivery, with non-negligible probability. However, we can trivially rule out such useless protocols, so that all protocols that do realize $\mathcal{F}_{\mathsf{DR}}$ or $\mathcal{F}_{\mathsf{TR}}$ and that are *not* useless indeed generate the correct output immediately upon every delivery of a ciphertext from the adversary, with all-but-negligible probability.

2.2 Execution with an Unrestricted Adversary

In addition to delaying, reordering, and dropping messages, we assume that the real-world adversary can: (i) provide bad randomness for both parties, (ii) leak their secret states; possibly multiple times at various points in the execution, (iii) tamper with in-transit messages between the parties, and (iv) attempt to inject messages on behalf of both parties. Here, we explain how the ideal functionality captures this behavior.

The Ideal Functionality's Flags. The ideal functionality uses several binary flags to properly capture adversarial behavior. The functionality initializes all of them to 0. Binary flag P.BAD captures bad randomness for party $\mathsf{P} \in \{\mathsf{P}_1, \mathsf{P}_2\}$. Naturally, P.BAD is set to 0 or 1 when the ideal-world adversary issues a (sid, $cmdBAD\_RANDOMNESS$, P, ρ) command to the ideal functionality, depending on the value of ρ. If P.BAD is set to 1 then P is provided with bad randomness (by the adversary, c.f. Appendix G) when she tries to sample some (thus rendering transformation $T_5(\mathsf{DR})$ insecure). Otherwise, P samples fresh randomness.

The ideal functionality further utilizes the following binary flags for each party $\mathsf{P} \in \{\mathsf{P}_1, \mathsf{P}_2\}$ to capture the rest of the possible adversarial behavior. We first introduce their real-world semantic meaning here before explaining (i) their evolution within the ideal functionality as a result of the ideal world adversary's behavior, then (ii) how they thus allow the ideal functionality to determine security for the session.

- P.PLEK (Public Ratchet Secrets Leakage): If P.PLEK is set to 1 then P's public ratchet secrets are leaked to the real-world adversary. Otherwise, they should be hidden from the real-world adversary.
- P.CUR_SLEK (Current Sending Symmetric Ratchet Secrets Leakage): If P.CUR_SLEK is set to 1 then the symmetric ratchet secrets of P's *current* sending epoch are leaked to the real-world adversary. Otherwise, they should be hidden from the real-world adversary

- P.PREV_SLEK (Previous Sending Symmetric Ratchet Secrets Leakage): If P.PREV_SLEK is set to 1 then the symmetric ratchet secrets of the *previous* sending epoch of P are leaked to the real-world adversary. Otherwise, they should be hidden from the real-world adversary.
- P.TAKEOVER_POSS (Takeover Possible): If P.TAKEOVER_POSS is set to 1 then the real-world adversary has the option to take over the role of P in the conversation with P̄. Otherwise, the real-world adversary should not have this option.

How the Flags are Affected by Leakages. We first describe how a leakage on one of the parties P ∈ {P_1, P_2} affects the above flags. For P.PLEK, when New(P, TURN, P.T) = 1, it is P's turn to start her next sending epoch, but she has not yet started it. Thus she does not currently have any public ratchet secret state (just P̄'s public value), so there is no effect on P.PLEK if leakage on P occurs in this case. If New(P, TURN, P.T) = 0 when leakage on P occurs, P of course does have a public ratchet secret state, as she needs to be able to receive a message for P̄'s next sending turn; thus in command LEAK, the ideal functionality sets P.PLEK to 1 (Step 1). Since P never stores P̄'s public ratchet secrets, there is never any effect on P̄.PLEK when P's state is leaked.

For P.CUR_SLEK, the functionality has similar behavior. If New(P, TURN, P.T) = 1 when leakage on P occurs, P has not yet generated the secrets for her next sending epoch, so P.CUR_SLEK is not modified. Otherwise, P has started the epoch, and so she stores the corresponding secrets in order to send new messages for the epoch; thus in command LEAK, we set P.CUR_SLEK to 1 (Step 1). Additionally, if New(P̄, TURN, P̄.T) = 1 then P̄ has not yet generated the secrets for her next sending epoch, so P̄.CUR_SLEK is not modified. Otherwise, P̄ has indeed started the epoch, in which case P must be able to derive the epoch's symmetric secrets (possibly using in-transit messages, which the adversary has), and thus in command LEAK we set P̄.CUR_SLEK to 1 (Step 2).

For P.PREV_SLEK, since in the most secure version of the DR, P only ever stores the secrets for her current sending epoch (if she has indeed started it), leakage on P has no effect on P.PREV_SLEK. However, once it is P̄'s turn to start a new sending epoch, P still stores the secrets of P̄'s previous sending epoch (in case she needs to receive messages for it; she does not yet know P̄ will never again send a message for that epoch), until she receives a message in P̄'s new epoch for the first time. Therefore, if TURN = P̄ then in command LEAK, we set P̄.PREV_SLEK to 1 (Step 3); otherwise, if TURN = P, P̄.PREV_SLEK is not modified.

Finally, for P.TAKEOVER_POSS, if it is P's turn to start a new sending epoch, then of course a leakage on P will enable the adversary to forge the first message of this new epoch and thus influence the subsequent state of P̄ upon delivery such that the adversary can take over P's role in the conversation (if it wishes). This is because the adversary will obtain the double ratchet root key, and can thus send such a message herself. Also, note that this key is derived from (i) P's previous state before she received any message for P̄'s newest epoch and (ii) any message of P̄'s newest sending epoch. Thus, additionally, if P is leaked while any message from P̄'s newest epoch is in-transit, but before P receives any such message, then the adversary can obtain the root key as above, and so will have the ability to forge the first message of P's next sending epoch. Therefore, in command LEAK, if $\text{New}(P, \text{TURN}, P.T) = 1$, or $\text{New}(\bar{P}, \text{TURN}, \bar{P}.T) = 0$ and $\text{TURN} = \bar{P}$, then we set P.TAKEOVER_POSS to 1 (Step 4). Otherwise, if P has already sent the first message of the epoch, and $\bar{P}$ has not yet started her next sending epoch, leakage on P does not reveal the root key, so P.TAKEOVER_POSS is not modified. In the former case, this is because P deletes the key after sending the message, and in the latter case, this is because the key does not yet exist. Furthermore, if P has indeed sent a message for her current sending epoch, then a leakage on P will provide the adversary with the new root key. The adversary will therefore be able to forge the first message for $\bar{P}$'s next sending epoch. So, if $\text{New}(P, \text{TURN}, P.T) = 0$ then in command LEAK, we additionally set $\bar{P}$.TAKEOVER_POSS to 1 (Step 1). Otherwise, if it is P's turn to start a new epoch, and she has not yet started it, then the new root key has not yet been generated, so $\bar{P}$.TAKEOVER_POSS is not modified.

How the Flags are Affected by Epoch Initialization. The effects on the ideal functionality's flags of epoch initialization via a SEND command are determined in Step 3 of the command. First, if P.BAD $= 1$ when starting a new epoch (i.e. P uses bad randomness to start it), then we of course set P.PLEK to 1 (In the TR we may still here have security of P's public ratchet secret state, but we choose to capture slightly weaker security for simplicity); otherwise we set P.PLEK to 0. Now, consider the privacy of the root key when $\bar{P}$.CUR_SLEK is 1 and P is initializing a new epoch:

- If $\bar{P}$.CUR_SLEK was set to 1 when $\bar{P}$ initialized her newest epoch (as we explain below), then the root key must have been leaked in addition to the corresponding symmetric ratchet secrets, since they are both part of the same KDF output.
- If $\bar{P}$.CUR_SLEK was set to 1 as a result of a leakage on P, then the root key must have been also leaked, since P needs it to start her new sending epoch.
- Finally, if $\bar{P}$.CUR_SLEK was set to 1 as a result of a leakage on $\bar{P}$, then the root key must have been also leaked, since $\bar{P}$ needs it to receive a message for P's new sending epoch.

So, if $\bar{P}$.CUR_SLEK is 1 when P initializes her new sending epoch, then it must be that the root key is leaked. Thus, only if P and $\bar{P}$ have a secure key exchange can security for the DR be recovered, which only happens if both P.PLEK and $\bar{P}$.PLEK are 0, i.e., their public ratchet secrets are both hidden from the adversary. In this case, we set P.CUR_SLEK to 0; otherwise, we set it to 1. If $\bar{P}$.CUR_SLEK is 0 at the time of initialization, then the root key must be hidden. This is because if not, then the current symmetric ratchet secrets of $\bar{P}$ would also not be hidden, since they were part of the same KDF output when $\bar{P}$ started her latest sending epoch, and there were no subsequent leakages on either party. So we set P.CUR_SLEK to 0 upon initialization, in this case.

Finally, if we do indeed set P.CUR_SLEK to 1 at this time, as we noted above, this means that the new root key is known by the adversary, and thus the adversary could forge the first message for $\bar{P}$'s next turn; otherwise the root key is hidden, and so the adversary does not have this ability. So, we set $\bar{P}$.TAKEOVER_POSS ← P.CUR_SLEK.

How the Flags are Affected by Epoch Termination. When the ideal adversary issues a **DELIVER** command for the first message of P's newest sending epoch, the ideal functionality needs to properly evolve the flags it uses to capture adversarial behavior (Step 2). First, when such a delivery occurs, $\bar{P}$'s latest sending epoch terminates, as her next message will be sent in a new epoch. To reflect this, upon such a delivery, the ideal functionality sets $\bar{P}$.PREV_SLEK ← $\bar{P}$.CUR_SLEK. Also, since $\bar{P}$ deletes her public ratchet secrets upon reception of such a message, and her newest epoch has not actually started at this point, the functionality sets $\bar{P}$.CUR_SLEK ← 0 and $\bar{P}$.PLEK ← 0.

Furthermore, in the DR, P includes in each message of an epoch the number of messages she sent in her previous epoch (see Appendix C). Thus, once $\bar{P}$ receives such a message in the DR, she knows exactly how many messages P sent in her previous epoch. So, the adversary can no longer inject messages in P's previous epoch (just modify them) and there is no more adversarial action possible for that epoch, so the functionality sets P.PREV_SLEK ← 0. Finally, since a message for P's newest sending epoch has indeed been delivered at this point, the secrets needed to start her next sending epoch are yet to be determined. Thus, the adversary cannot yet forge a message to start her next sending epoch, so the functionality sets P.TAKEOVER_POSS ← 0.

Determining New Messages' Privacy and Authenticity. We know from above that if P.CUR_SLEK = 1, then P's current symmetric ratchet secrets are leaked to the adversary. Thus, if P issues a **SEND** command for message m with id mid, and P.CUR_SLEK = 1, then the ideal functionality leaks the corresponding message to the ideal adversary (Step 4). Additionally, the ideal functionality sets the penultimate element of mid's entry in P.T to 1. This will allow the ideal adversary to modify the message associated with mid upon delivery: the adversary will issue a **DELIVER** command for mid to the functionality with input modified message m', which will then be delivered $\bar{P}$, instead of m (Step 3).

Otherwise, if P.CUR_SLEK = 0 when P issues the **SEND** command, then the ideal functionality only leaks the message length to the adversary and sets the penultimate element of the corresponding entry of P.T to 0, ensuring (for now) privacy and authenticity of m.

The Consequences of Leakages. When the adversary leaks on P in the real-world, the privacy of in-transit messages from $\bar{P}$ to P is no longer guaranteed, since P must preserve all keys that will be necessary for authenticating and decrypting them. Therefore, when the ideal adversary issues a **LEAK** command on P, the ideal functionality leaks the in-transit messages from $\bar{P}$ to P, P.T, to the ideal adversary, and allows the ideal adversary to modify them in the future (Step 5). The ideal functionality accomplishes the latter using helper function $\texttt{Unsafe}(\bar{P}.\text{T})$ which sets the penultimate element of each in-transit message of $\bar{P}.\text{T}$ to 1. As a result, the ideal adversary can modify these in-transit messages in the DELIVER command, as described above. Note that only *in-transit* messages from $\bar{\mathsf{P}}$ to P are affected (thus rendering transformation $T_2(\mathsf{DR})$ insecure).

Vulnerable Messages in the DR. As explained in Sect. 1.4, if in the DR, the root key is leaked when it is P's turn to start a new sending epoch, but P has not yet started it, then the messages of that epoch are *vulnerable*. This means that if P is leaked on before P receives a message of $\bar{\mathsf{P}}$'s next sending epoch for the first time, the messages that P sent in her own epoch become insecure.

To capture this, the ideal functionality in the SEND command adds messages to list P.V if they are indeed vulnerable (Step 2). At the start of the epoch, this is the case if $\bar{\mathsf{P}}$.CUR_SLEK $= 1$ (as explained above); in the middle of the epoch, this is the case if P.V is non-empty. Hence, if the adversary issues a LEAK command on P, in addition to the consequences of the above paragraph, the ideal functionality *also* leaks P.V and allows for future modification of its elements that are still in-transit (Step 5). The latter is accomplished via helper function $\texttt{Unsafe}'(\mathsf{P.T}, \mathsf{P.V})$, similarly as in $\texttt{Unsafe}(\bar{\mathsf{P}}.\mathsf{T})$. Note that this scenario, and the one above, are the only ones in which secure, in-transit messages are leaked to the adversary and/or subject to modification (thus transformation $T_4(\mathsf{DR})$ is insecure). Finally, if the adversary issues a DELIVER command for the first message of $\bar{\mathsf{P}}$'s next sending epoch, the ideal functionality sets P.V $= \emptyset$: P properly deletes the secrets which make those messages vulnerable at this time.

Injections and Takeovers. If P.CUR_SLEK $= 1$ or P.PREV_SLEK $= 1$, then the adversary has the secrets required to inject its own messages into P's current or previous sending epoch, respectively. Also, if P.TAKEOVER_POSS $= 1$, then the adversary can forge the first message to be delivered in P's next sending epoch to $\bar{\mathsf{P}}$. In either case, the ideal adversary issues the INJECT command to inject message m under unique message id mid on behalf of P. Of course, the ideal functionality only allows the adversary to inject one message under each such mid, which it ensures by aborting in Step 1 if mid is already in P.I, and adding it to P.I in Step 3 if not. The ideal functionality also aborts if a message with message id mid was already sent by P, i.e., it is in P.M, in which case injection of mid is not allowed, only modification. If the ideal adversary injects a message with id mid that is not a takeover forgery, then before actual delivery of the injection occurs, a corresponding entry is added to P.T.

Now, if P.TAKEOVER_POSS $= 1$, and the ideal adversary inputs $\delta = 1$ to the INJECT command, indicating that it wishes to takeover for P, then the ideal functionality thereafter directly forwards messages sent from P to the ideal adversary, and vice versa (Step 2).

If the ideal adversary injects a message with id mid that is not a takeover forgery, then before actual delivery of the injection occurs, a corresponding entry is added to P.T. However, the ideal functionality has to be careful to set the last element of this entry correctly:

- If TURN $= \bar{\mathsf{P}}$, then the first message of P's current sending epoch has already been delivered to $\bar{\mathsf{P}}$. Thus, the last element of the entry is set to $\perp$, so that if TURN is flipped to P, the entry's subsequent delivery does not prematurely flip TURN back. Moreover, if P.CUR_SLEK $= 0$, then the adversary must be injecting into P's previous sending epoch, so for the same reason as above, we set its last entry to $\perp$.

- If P.PREV_SLEK $= 0$ and TURN $=$ P, then the adversary must be injecting into P's current sending epoch, and moreover, it might be that the injected message could be the first of the epoch delivered to $\bar{P}$. Therefore, we set TURN to P.

- If neither of the above are true, i.e., TURN $=$ P, P.PREV_SLEK $= 1$, and P.CUR_SLEK $= 1$, then it could be that the adversary is injecting into *either* P's previous or current sending epoch. Therefore, the ideal adversary specifies its choice of the last element with the last input γ to the INJECT command.

Actual delivery of injections is then handled in the DELIVER command, in the same simple manner as specified in the Honest Execution Section (Sect. 2.1). Namely, delivery of injected message with message id mid is done by removing it from P.T (if such an entry exists), and sending it to $\bar{P}$. The functionality works this way in order to capture the scenario in which the real-world adversary modifies the first message of a new sending epoch for P to inform $\bar{P}$ that P's last sending epoch contains more messages than it actually does. Therefore, the real-world adversary will be able to in the future inject such additional messages whenever it wants. The ideal-world adversary thus issues an INJECT command for all of these message ids at the time of the first modification, so that later it can actually send them to $\bar{P}$ using DELIVER commands (regardless of the status of the functionality's flags at that time).

If an injected message with id mid is indeed added to P.T, then the ideal functionality needs to also make sure that P can send a message with the same mid (since it does not know about the injection), but not allow the ideal adversary to deliver two messages with the same mid (since $\bar{P}$ will only accept one such message in the DR). Therefore, in the SEND command, the ideal functionality checks if mid $\notin$ P.I and if so adds the corresponding message to P.T as in the honest execution. However, if mid is in P.I, the ideal functionality does not add the corresponding message to P.T, but still sends the length of the message (and the message itself if P.CUR_SLEK $= 1$) to the ideal adversary, mirroring that a ciphertext is still created in the real-world.

3   Continuous Key Agreement

In this section we formalize the main constructive contribution of our paper: the stronger, but virtually as efficient, public ratchet (and its mini ratchet) used by the Triple Ratchet protocol. More specifically, we first define (a version of) the *continuous key agreement* (CKA) primitive, introduced by ACD, which provides secrets for updates of the public ratchet. We provide two notions of security, that which is used by the DR and that which is used by the (stronger) TR. We also compare our definition to that of ACD. Then, we provide our CKA construction CKA^+ used in the TR and show it is secure according to the stronger definition, via the *strong-DH* (StDH) assumption [1] in the random oracle model.[1] The StDH assumption is: given random and independent group elements g^a, g^b, and access to oracle $\mathbf{ddh}(g^a, \cdot, \cdot)$, which on input X, Y returns 1 if $X^a = Y$ and 0 otherwise, it is hard to compute g^{ab}.

Defining CKA. At a high level, CKA is a synchronous two-party protocol between P_1 and P_2. Odd rounds i consist of P_1 sending and P_2 receiving a message T_i, whereas in even rounds, P_2 is the sender and P_1 the receiver. Each round i also produces a key I_i, which is output by the sender upon sending T_i and by the receiver upon receiving T_i.

Definition 1. *A* continuous-key-agreement *(CKA) scheme is a quadruple of algorithms* $\mathsf{CKA} = (\mathsf{CKA\text{-}Init\text{-}P}_1, \mathsf{CKA\text{-}Init\text{-}P}_2, \mathsf{CKA\text{-}S}, \mathsf{CKA\text{-}R})$, *where*

- $\mathsf{CKA\text{-}Init\text{-}P}_1$ *(and similarly* $\mathsf{CKA\text{-}Init\text{-}P}_2$) *takes a key k and produces an initial state* $\gamma^{\mathsf{P}_1} \leftarrow \mathsf{CKA\text{-}Init\text{-}P}_1(k)$ *(and* γ^{P_2}),
- $\mathsf{CKA\text{-}S}$ *takes a state γ, and produces a new state, message, and key* $(\gamma', T, I) \xleftarrow{\$} \mathsf{CKA\text{-}S}(\gamma)$, *and*
- $\mathsf{CKA\text{-}R}$ *takes a state γ and message T and produces new state and a key* $(\gamma', I) \leftarrow \mathsf{CKA\text{-}R}(\gamma, T)$.

Denote by $\mathcal{K}$ the space of initialization keys k and by $\mathcal{I}$ the space of CKA keys I.

Correctness. A CKA scheme is correct if in the security game in Fig. 3 (explained below), P_1 and P_2 always, i.e., with probability 1, output the same key in every round.

Security. The security property we will require a CKA scheme to satisfy is that conditioned on the transcript $T_1, T_2, \ldots$, the keys $I_1, I_2, \ldots$ are unrecoverable. An attacker against a CKA scheme is required to be passive, i.e., may not modify the messages T_i. However, it is given the power to possibly (1) control the random coins used by the sender and (2) leak the current state of either party. Given the capabilities of the adversary, it is easy to see that some keys I_i would be recoverable. The security guarantee offered by the CKA scheme would then be that even given the transcript $T_1, T_2, \ldots$, assuming certain "fine-grained" conditions around when the adversary controls the randomness used by parties and when the adversary learns the state of parties, most keys $I_1, I_2, \ldots$ are unrecoverable. It will also be the case that parties thus recover from such bad randomness and leakage issued by the adversary.

The formal security game for CKA is provided in Fig. 3. It begins with a call to the **init** oracle, which initializes the states of both parties, and defines

---

[1] We do not provide CKA schemes secure according to our definitions based on LWE or generic KEMs, as in ACD. However, we note that our stronger scheme CKA^+ is intuitively at least as strong as their construction from generic KEMs, but more efficient.

Security Games for CKA

init (t^*)
| $k \xleftarrow{\$} \mathcal{K}$
| $\gamma_0^{P_1} \leftarrow$
| CKA-Init-$P_1(k)$
| $\gamma_0^{P_2} \leftarrow$
| CKA-Init-$P_2(k)$
| $t_{P_1}, t_{P_2} \leftarrow 0$
| Recv-State$[*] \leftarrow \perp$

corr-P_1
| req allow-corr$_{P_1}$
| return $\gamma_{t_{P_1}}^{P_1}$

send-P_1
| t_{P_1} ++
| $(\gamma_{t_{P_1}}^{P_1}, T, I) \xleftarrow{\$}$
| CKA-S$(\gamma_{t_{P_1}}^{P_1})$
| Recv-State$[t_{P_1} + 1] \leftarrow$
| $\gamma_{t_{P_1}}^{P_1}$
| return (T, I)

send-P_1' (r)
| t_{P_1} ++
| req allow-bad-rand$_{P_1}$
| $(\gamma_{t_{P_1}}^{P_1}, T, I) \leftarrow$
| CKA-S$(\gamma_{t_{P_1} - 1}^{P_1}; r)$
| Recv-State$[t_{P_1} + 1] \leftarrow$
| $\gamma_{t_{P_1}}^{P_1}$
| return (T, I)

receive-P_1
| t_{P_1} ++
| $(\gamma_{t_{P_1}}^{P_1}, *) \leftarrow$ CKA-R$(\gamma_{t_{P_1} - 1}^{P_1}, T)$

chall-P_1
| t_{P_1} ++
| req $t_{P_1} = t^*$
| $(\gamma_{t_{P_1}}^{P_1}, T, I) \xleftarrow{\$}$ CKA-S$(\gamma_{t_{P_1} - 1}^{P_1})$
| return T

test (t, T, I)
| req Recv-State$[t] \neq \perp$
| if $(*, I) \leftarrow$
| CKA-R(Recv-State$[t], T)$
| | return 1
| else
| | return 0

---

allow-corr$_{P_1}$, allow-bad-rand$_{P_1}$ $:\Longleftrightarrow$
$\begin{cases} t_{P_1} \neq t^* & t^* \text{ is odd} \\ t_{P_1} \neq t^* - 1 & t^* \text{ is even} \end{cases}$

allow-corr$_{P_2}$, allow-bad-rand$_{P_2}$ $:\Longleftrightarrow$
$\begin{cases} t_{P_2} \neq t^* - 1 & t^* \text{ is odd} \\ t_{P_2} \neq t^* & t^* \text{ is even} \end{cases}$

allow-corr$_{P_1}$ $:\Longleftrightarrow$ $t_{P_1} \neq t^* - 1 \vee t^*$ is odd

allow-bad-rand$_{P_1}$ $:\Longleftrightarrow$ $t_{P_1} \neq t^* \vee t_{P_1} \neq t^* - 1$

allow-corr$_{P_2}$ $:\Longleftrightarrow$ $t_{P_2} \neq t^* - 1 \vee t^*$ is even

allow-bad-rand$_{P_2}$ $:\Longleftrightarrow$ $t_{P_2} \neq t^* \vee t_{P_2} \neq t^* - 1$

Fig. 3. Oracles corresponding to party P_1 of the CKA security game for a scheme CKA = (CKA-Init-P_1, CKA-Init-P_2, CKA-S, CKA-R); the oracles for P_2 are defined analogously. Conditions for the weaker security game, i.e., ε-security, are presented to the left of those for the stronger game, i.e., $(\varepsilon, +)$-security.

epoch counters t_{P_1} and t_{P_2}. Procedure **init** takes a value t^*, which determines in which round the challenge oracle may be called; the task of the adversary will be to recover the key I_{t^*} for that round.

Upon completion of the initialization procedure, the attacker gets to interact arbitrarily with the remaining oracles, as long as *the calls are in a "ping-pong" order*, i.e., a call to a send oracle for P_1 is followed by a receive call for P_2, then by a send oracle for P_2, etc. The attacker only gets to use the challenge oracle for epoch t^*. The attacker additionally has the capability of testing the consistency of T_t and I_t (i.e., whether the receiver in epoch t would produce key I_t on input message T_t).

The security game of ACD is parametrized by Δ_{CKA}, which stands for the number of epochs that need to pass after t^* until the states do not contain secret information pertaining to the challenge. Once a party reaches epoch $t^* + \Delta_{\mathsf{CKA}}$, its state may be revealed to the attacker (via the corresponding corruption oracle). We avoid this and define two levels of security, the former weaker than the latter. At the bottom of Fig. 3, the conditions allow-corr$_P$ and allow-bad-rand$_P$ for the weaker version are presented to the left of those of the stronger version. We define two levels of security in order to capture a stronger, more fine-grained security guarantee for CKA which will be useful in providing stronger security guarantees for the DR and TR as a whole when one considers the composition of all its building blocks, CKA being one of them. In the former, bad randomness is not allowed in the epochs t^* and $t^* - 1$, and corruptions are not allowed in the epoch t^* after invoking CKA-S (for the sender of epoch t^*) and before invoking CKA-R (for the receiver of epoch t^*). In the latter, which is used by the TR, bad randomness is not allowed in the epochs t^* and $t^* - 1$, and corruption of the receiver of epoch t^* is not allowed before invoking CKA-R (for epoch t^*). There is no other difference between the two notions.

The game ends (not made explicit) once both states are revealed after the challenge phase. The attacker wins the game if it eventually outputs the correct secret key I_{t^*} corresponding to the challenge message T_{t^*}. The advantage of an attacker $\mathcal{A}$ against a CKA scheme CKA is denoted by $\mathsf{Adv}^{\mathsf{CKA}}(\mathcal{A})$ and $\mathsf{Adv}^{\mathsf{CKA}^+}(\mathcal{A})$ for the weaker and stronger security guarantees, respectively. The attacker is parameterized by its running time t.

Definition 2. *A CKA scheme CKA is (t, ε)-secure (resp. $(t, \varepsilon, +)$-secure) if for all t-attackers $\mathcal{A}$,*

$$\mathsf{Adv}^{\mathsf{CKA}}(\mathcal{A}) \leq \varepsilon \text{ (resp. } \mathsf{Adv}^{\mathsf{CKA}^+}(\mathcal{A}) \leq \varepsilon).$$

Definition 3. *A CKA scheme CKA is simply called ε-secure (resp. $(\varepsilon, +)$-secure) if for every $t \in \mathrm{poly}(\kappa)$ and $\varepsilon \in \mathrm{negl}(\kappa)$, where κ is the security parameter,*

$$\mathsf{Adv}^{\mathsf{CKA}}(\mathcal{A}) \leq \varepsilon \text{ (resp. } \mathsf{Adv}^{\mathsf{CKA}^+}(\mathcal{A}) \leq \varepsilon).$$

Observe that since the TR uses a CKA with the latter, stronger security, the attack of Sect. 1.4 is thwarted. This is because even if the epoch t^* sender is corrupted after invoking CKA-S, I_{t^*} should remain hidden.

Remark 1. Many *natural* CKA schemes satisfy an additional property that given a CKA message T and key I for a given round, it is possible to deterministically compute the corresponding state of the receiving party after her execution of CKA-R in that round. We model this explicitly by requiring a deterministic algorithm CKA-Der-R that takes a message T and key I and produces the correct state $\gamma' \leftarrow$ CKA-Der-R(T, I). All CKA schemes in this work are required to be *natural*.

Differences from ACD

Fine-Grained Security Guarantees. Recall the "CKA from DDH" scheme from ACD (which is the public ratchet used in the DR and which we prove security for in Appendix B.3), CKA = (CKA-Init-P$_1$, CKA-Init-P$_2$, CKA-S, CKA-R), that is instantiated in a cyclic group $G = \langle g \rangle$ as follows:

- The initial shared state $k = (h, x_0)$ consists of a (random) group element $h = g^{x_0}$ and its discrete logarithm x_0. The initialization for P_1 outputs $h \leftarrow$ CKA-Init-$P_1(k)$ and that for P_2 outputs $x_0 \leftarrow$ CKA-Init-$P_2(k)$.
- The send algorithm CKA-S takes as input the current state $\gamma = h$ and proceeds as follows: It
  1. chooses a random exponent x;
  2. computes the corresponding key $I \leftarrow h^x$;
  3. sets the CKA message to $T \leftarrow g^x$;
  4. sets the new state to $\gamma \leftarrow x$; and
  5. returns (γ, T, I).
- The receive algorithm CKA-R takes as input the current state $\gamma = x$ as well as a message $T = h$ and proceeds as follows: It
  1. computes the key $I = h^x$;
  2. sets the new state to $\gamma \leftarrow h$; and
  3. returns (γ, I).

Now, let x_0 be the random exponent that is part of the initial shared state, and for $i > 0$, let x_i be the random exponent picked by CKA-S (which was run by P_1 for odd i, and P_2 for even i) in round i. Then, we have the following:

- The key for round i is $I_i = g^{x_{i-1}x_i}$.
- The message for round i is $T_i = g^{x_i}$.
- If i is odd, and P_1 has yet to invoke CKA-S, $\gamma^{P_1} = g^{x_{i-1}}$ and $\gamma^{P_2} = x_{i-1}$.
- If i is odd, and P_1 has invoked CKA-S, but P_2 has yet to invoke CKA-R, $\gamma^{P_1} = x_i$ and $\gamma^{P_2} = x_{i-1}$.
- If i is odd, and P_1 has invoked CKA-S, and P_2 has invoked CKA-R, $\gamma^{P_1} = x_i$ and $\gamma^{P_2} = g^{x_i}$.
- If i is even, and P_2 has yet to invoke CKA-S, $\gamma^{P_1} = x_{i-1}$ and $\gamma^{P_2} = g^{x_{i-1}}$.
- If i is even, and P_2 has invoked CKA-S, but P_1 has yet to invoke CKA-R, $\gamma^{P_1} = x_{i-1}$ and $\gamma^{P_2} = x_i$.
- If i is even, and P_2 has invoked CKA-S, and P_1 has invoked CKA-R, $\gamma^{P_1} = g^{x_i}$ and $\gamma^{P_2} = x_i$.

Based on the above, we make the following observations:

- If i is odd and P_1 is corrupted after invoking CKA-S, the adversary learns $\gamma^{P_1} = x_i$ and since it also has access to g^{x_j} for all $j \geq 1$, the adversary learns I_i and I_{i+1}.
- If i is even and P_1 is corrupted after invoking CKA-R, and P_2 used good randomness in picking x_i while invoking CKA-S in round i, the adversary learns $\gamma^{P_1} = g^{x_i}$, but since it only (assuming no other corruptions) has access to g^{x_j} for all $j \geq 1$, the adversary does not learn I_i (if P_1 also used good randomness in picking x_{i-1} while invoking CKA-S in round $i - 1$) or I_{i+1} (if P_1 also uses good randomness in picking x_{i+1} while invoking CKA-S in round $i + 1$).

Thus, the CKA keys for two rounds are compromised only in the case where the party that has last sent a message is corrupted, and not if the party has last received a message. This allows us to consider a more fine-grained version of the CKA security game than the one described in ACD.

Non-malleability. Consider the following scenario in the DR or TR: It is P_1's turn to start a new sending epoch, but she has not yet. Then her state is leaked, and afterwards, she sends the first message m_1 of the epoch with good randomness. Then, if P_2 started her last epoch with good randomness, and there are no other leakages, m_1 is required to remain private by $\mathcal{F}_{DR}$ and $\mathcal{F}_{TR}$, respectively. However, all authenticity for m_1 is lost—the adversary leaked on P_1 beforehand and thus could have generated the message herself. Therefore, we replace the indistinguishability definition of ACD with our recoverability definition and require non-malleability of CKA messages via the **test** oracle—the adversary should not be able to maul them in order to learn about the actual session messages sent in the DR or TR. Note that this modification makes our CKA definition incomparable in strength to that of ACD, but allows us to prove stronger security for the DR. See the full security proof of Theorem 5 for the DR and TR, as well as Appendix D.2, for more details.

Instantiating CKA^+. A CKA scheme $\mathsf{CKA}^+ = (\mathsf{CKA\text{-}Init\text{-}P_1}, \mathsf{CKA\text{-}Init\text{-}P_2}, \mathsf{CKA\text{-}S}, \mathsf{CKA\text{-}R})$ (which may be used in the TR) can be obtained assuming random oracles or circular-secure ElGamal in a cyclic group $G = \langle g \rangle$ (with exponent space $\mathcal{X}$) using a function $\mathsf{H} : \mathcal{I} \to \mathcal{X}$ as follows:

- The initial shared state $k = (h, x_0)$ consists of a (random) group element $h = g^{x_0}$ and its discrete logarithm x_0. The initialization for P_1 outputs $h \leftarrow \mathsf{CKA\text{-}Init\text{-}P_1}(k)$ and that for P_2 outputs $x_0 \leftarrow \mathsf{CKA\text{-}Init\text{-}P_2}(k)$.
- The send algorithm $\mathsf{CKA\text{-}S}$ takes as input the current state $\gamma = h$ and proceeds as follows: It
  1. chooses a random exponent x;
  2. computes the corresponding key $I \leftarrow h^x$;
  3. sets the CKA message to $T \leftarrow g^x$;
  4. sets the new state to $\gamma \leftarrow x \cdot \mathsf{H}(I)$; and
  5. returns (γ, T, I).
- The receive algorithm $\mathsf{CKA\text{-}R}$ takes as input the current state $\gamma = x$ as well as a message $T = h$ and proceeds as follows: It
  1. computes the key $I = h^x$;
  2. sets the new state to $\gamma \leftarrow h^{\mathsf{H}(I)}$; and
  3. returns (γ, I).

Note that the above scheme is *natural*, i.e., it supports a $\mathsf{CKA\text{-}Der\text{-}R}$ algorithm, namely, $\mathsf{CKA\text{-}Der\text{-}R}(T, I) = T^{\mathsf{H}(I)}$. Now we show its security in the theorem below. (We give informal details on additional security properties that we conjecture it to have in Appendix B.3)

Theorem 1. *Assume group G is (t, ε)-StDH-secure. Additionally, assume the existence of a random oracle H. Then, the above CKA scheme CKA is $(t', \varepsilon, +)$-secure for $t \approx t'$.*

Proof. Assume w.l.o.g. that t^* is *odd*, i.e., P_1 sends the challenge; the case where t^* is even is handled analogously. Let g^a, g^b be a StDH challenge. The reduction simulates the CKA protocol in the straight-forward way but embeds the challenge into the CKA as follows:

- in epoch $t^* - 1$, it uses $T_{t^*-1} = g^a$ and $I_{t^*-1} = g^{xaH(I_{t^*-2})}$, where x is the exponent used to simulate $T_{t^*-2} = g^x$.
- in epoch t^*, it uses $T_{t^*} = g^b$ and $I_{t^*} = g^{abH(I_{t^*-1})}$ which is the key the adversary is to recover, as well as sets $\gamma_{t^*}^{P_1} \leftarrow y$, for random y in $\mathcal{X}$;
- in epoch $t^* + 1$, for exponent x' (possibly generated using adversarial randomness), it uses $T_{t^*+1} = g^{x'}$ and $I_{t^*+1} = g^{yx'}$.

It is easy to verify that this correctly simulates the CKA experiment since H is a random oracle. In particular, randomly sampled y properly simulates $b \cdot H(I_{t^*})$: If $\mathcal{A}$ does not query the random oracle on I_{t^*} then y is properly distributed. Moreover, when $\mathcal{A}$ makes a random oracle query for any I, the reduction can query oracle $\mathbf{ddh}(g^a, \cdot, \cdot)$ on $(g^{bH(I_{t^*-1})}, I)$ so that if indeed $I = I_{t^*}$, the reduction will know, and then forward to its challenger $g^{ab} = I_{t^*}^{1/H(I_{t^*-1})}$ before answering the CKA$^+$ attacker's query.

Similarly, the test oracle can be perfectly simulated with the help of $\mathbf{ddh}()$: if $\mathbf{test}(t^*, T, I)$ is queried, the reduction simply queries $\mathbf{ddh}(g^a, \cdot, \cdot)$ on $(T^{H(I_{t^*-1})}, I)$; all other $\mathbf{test}()$ queries can be directly simulated. $\qquad\square$

Acknowledgements. We would like to thank Yevgeniy Dodis and Daniel Jost for helping us realize that the trick used in the CKA$^+$ construction can also be used to make UPKE more efficient (Appendix F).

This research is supported in part by DARPA under Agreement No. HR00112020026, AFOSR Award FA9550-19-1-0200, NSF CNS Award 1936826, and research grants by the Sloan Foundation, and Visa Inc. Any opinions, findings and conclusions or recommendations expressed in this material are those of the author(s) and do not necessarily reflect the views of the United States Government or DARPA.

References

1. Abdalla, M., Bellare, M., Rogaway, P.: The Oracle Diffie-Hellman assumptions and an analysis of DHIES. In: Naccache, D. (ed.) CT-RSA 2001. LNCS, vol. 2020, pp. 143–158. Springer, Heidelberg (2001). https://doi.org/10.1007/3-540-45353-9_12
2. Alwen, J., Coretti, S., Dodis, Y.: The double ratchet: security notions, proofs, and modularization for the Signal protocol. Cryptology ePrint Archive, Report 2018/1037 (2018). https://eprint.iacr.org/2018/1037
3. Alwen, J., Coretti, S., Dodis, Y.: The double ratchet: security notions, proofs, and modularization for the signal protocol. In: Ishai, Y., Rijmen, V. (eds.) EUROCRYPT 2019, Part I. LNCS, vol. 11476, pp. 129–158. Springer, Cham (2019). https://doi.org/10.1007/978-3-030-17653-2_5
4. Alwen, J., Coretti, S., Dodis, Y., Tselekounis, Y.: Security analysis and improvements for the IETF MLS standard for group messaging. In: Micciancio, D., Ristenpart, T. (eds.) CRYPTO 2020, Part I. LNCS, vol. 12170, pp. 248–277. Springer, Cham (2020). https://doi.org/10.1007/978-3-030-56784-2_9
5. Balli, F., Rösler, P., Vaudenay, S.: Determining the core primitive for optimally secure ratcheting. In: Moriai, S., Wang, H. (eds.) ASIACRYPT 2020, Part III. LNCS, vol. 12493, pp. 621–650. Springer, Cham (2020). https://doi.org/10.1007/978-3-030-64840-4_21
6. Bao, F., Deng, R.H., Zhu, H.: Variations of diffie-hellman problem. In: ICICS (2003)

7. Bellare, M., Singh, A.C., Jaeger, J., Nyayapati, M., Stepanovs, I.: Ratcheted encryption and key exchange: the security of messaging. In: Katz, J., Shacham, H. (eds.) CRYPTO 2017, Part III. LNCS, vol. 10403, pp. 619–650. Springer, Cham (2017). https://doi.org/10.1007/978-3-319-63697-9_21

8. Bienstock, A., Fairoze, J., Garg, S., Mukherjee, P., Srinivasan, R.: A more complete analysis of the signal double ratchet algorithm. Cryptology ePrint Archive, Report 2022/355 (2022)

9. Bitansky, N., Canetti, R., Halevi, S.: Leakage-tolerant interactive protocols. In: Cramer, R. (ed.) TCC 2012. LNCS, vol. 7194, pp. 266–284. Springer, Heidelberg (2012). https://doi.org/10.1007/978-3-642-28914-9_15

10. Borisov, N., Goldberg, I., Brewer, E.: Off-the-record communication, or, why not to use PGP. In: Proceedings of the 2004 ACM Workshop on Privacy in the Electronic Society, pp. 77–84 (2004)

11. Brendel, J., Fiedler, R., Günther, F., Janson, C., Stebila, D.: Post-quantum asynchronous deniable key exchange and the signal handshake. In: Hanaoka, G., Shikata, J., Watanabe, Y. (eds.) Public-Key Cryptography - PKC 2022, pp. 3–34. Springer International Publishing, Cham (2022)

12. Brendel, J., Fischlin, M., Günther, F., Janson, C.: PRF-ODH: relations, instantiations, and impossibility results. In: Katz, J., Shacham, H. (eds.) CRYPTO 2017, Part III. LNCS, vol. 10403, pp. 651–681. Springer, Cham (2017). https://doi.org/10.1007/978-3-319-63697-9_22

13. Brendel, J., Fischlin, M., Günther, F., Janson, C., Stebila, D.: Towards post-quantum security for signal's x3dh handshake. In: Selected Areas in Cryptography-SAC 2020 (2020)

14. Canetti, R.: Universally composable security: a new paradigm for cryptographic protocols. In: 42nd FOCS, pp. 136–145. IEEE Computer Society Press, Las Vegas, 14–17 October 2001

15. Canetti, R., Halevi, S., Katz, J.: Chosen-ciphertext security from identity-based encryption. In: Cachin, C., Camenisch, J.L. (eds.) EUROCRYPT 2004. LNCS, vol. 3027, pp. 207–222. Springer, Heidelberg (2004). https://doi.org/10.1007/978-3-540-24676-3_13

16. Canetti, R., Jain, P., Swanberg, M., Varia, M.: Universally composable end-to-end secure messaging. In: CRYPTO 2022 (2022)

17. Checkoway, S., et al.: On the practical exploitability of dual EC in TLS implementations. In: Fu, K., Jung, J. (eds.) USENIX Security 2014, pp. 319–335. USENIX Association, San Diego, CA, USA, 20–22 August 2014

18. Cohn-Gordon, K., Cremers, C., Dowling, B., Garratt, L., Stebila, D.: A formal security analysis of the signal messaging protocol. In: 2017 IEEE European Symposium on Security and Privacy, EuroS&P 2017, Paris, France, April 26–28, 2017, pp. 451–466. IEEE (2017). https://doi.org/10.1109/EuroSP.2017.27

19. Cohn-Gordon, K., Cremers, C., Dowling, B., Garratt, L., Stebila, D.: A formal security analysis of the signal messaging protocol. J. Cryptol. 33(4), 1914–1983 (2020). https://doi.org/10.1007/s00145-020-09360-1

20. Cohn-Gordon, K., Cremers, C.J.F., Garratt, L.: On post-compromise security. In: Hicks, M., Köpf, B. (eds.) CSF 2016 Computer Security Foundations Symposium, pp. 164–178. IEEE Computer Society Press, Lisbon, Portugal, June 27–1 2016

21. Cramer, R., Shoup, V.: Design and analysis of practical public-key encryption schemes secure against adaptive chosen ciphertext attack. SIAM J. Comput. 33(1), 167–226 (2003)

22. Dobson, S., Galbraith, S.D.: Post-quantum signal key agreement with sidh. Cryptology ePrint Archive, Report 2021/1187 (2021)

812   A. Bienstock et al.

23. Dodis, Y., Karthikeyan, H., Wichs, D.: Updatable public key encryption in the standard model (2021)

24. Durak, F.B., Vaudenay, S.: Breaking the FF3 format-preserving encryption standard over small domains. In: Katz, J., Shacham, H. (eds.) CRYPTO 2017, Part II. LNCS, vol. 10402, pp. 679–707. Springer, Cham (2017). https://doi.org/10.1007/978-3-319-63715-0_23

25. Durak, F.B., Vaudenay, S.: Bidirectional asynchronous ratcheted key agreement with linear complexity. In: Attrapadung, N., Yagi, T. (eds.) IWSEC 2019. LNCS, vol. 11689, pp. 343–362. Springer, Cham (2019). https://doi.org/10.1007/978-3-030-26834-3_20

26. FIPS, P.: 180–1. secure hash standard. National Institute of Standards and Technology 17, 45 (1995)

27. Galbraith, S.D.: Mathematics of Public Key Cryptography. Cambridge University Press, Cambridge (2012)

28. Goldreich, O.: The Foundations of Cryptography - Volume 2: Basic Applications. Cambridge University Press (2004). http://www.wisdom.weizmann.ac.il/%7Eoded/foc-vol2.html

29. Goldwasser, S., Micali, S., Rackoff, C.: The knowledge complexity of interactive proof systems. SIAM J. Comput. 18(1), 186–208 (1989). https://doi.org/10.1137/0218012

30. Hashimoto, K., Katsumata, S., Kwiatkowski, K., Prest, T.: An efficient and generic construction for signal's handshake (x3dh): post-quantum, state leakage secure, and deniable. In: Public Key Cryptography (2), pp. 410–440 (2021)

31. Heninger, N., Durumeric, Z., Wustrow, E., Halderman, J.A.: Mining your PS and QS: detection of widespread weak keys in network devices. In: Kohno, T. (ed.) USENIX Security 2012, pp. 205–220. USENIX Association, Bellevue, WA, USA, 8–10 August 2012

32. Jaeger, J., Stepanovs, I.: Optimal channel security against fine-grained state compromise: the safety of messaging. In: Shacham, H., Boldyreva, A. (eds.) CRYPTO 2018, Part I. LNCS, vol. 10991, pp. 33–62. Springer, Cham (2018). https://doi.org/10.1007/978-3-319-96884-1_2

33. Jost, D., Maurer, U.: Overcoming impossibility results in composable security using interval-wise guarantees. In: Micciancio, D., Ristenpart, T. (eds.) CRYPTO 2020, Part I. LNCS, vol. 12170, pp. 33–62. Springer, Cham (2020). https://doi.org/10.1007/978-3-030-56784-2_2

34. Jost, D., Maurer, U., Mularczyk, M.: Efficient ratcheting: almost-optimal guarantees for secure messaging. In: Ishai, Y., Rijmen, V. (eds.) EUROCRYPT 2019. LNCS, vol. 11476, pp. 159–188. Springer, Cham (2019). https://doi.org/10.1007/978-3-030-17653-2_6

35. Jost, D., Maurer, U., Mularczyk, M.: A unified and composable take on ratcheting. In: Hofheinz, D., Rosen, A. (eds.) TCC 2019. LNCS, vol. 11892, pp. 180–210. Springer, Cham (2019). https://doi.org/10.1007/978-3-030-36033-7_7

36. Kiltz, E.: A Tool box of cryptographic functions related to the Diffie-Hellman function. In: Rangan, C.P., Ding, C. (eds.) INDOCRYPT 2001. LNCS, vol. 2247, pp. 339–349. Springer, Heidelberg (2001). https://doi.org/10.1007/3-540-45311-3_32

37. Kobeissi, N., Bhargavan, K., Blanchet, B.: Automated verification for secure messaging protocols and their implementations: A symbolic and computational approach. In: 2017 IEEE European Symposium on Security and Privacy (EuroS&P), pp. 435–450 (2017)

38. Krawczyk, H., Eronen, P.: Hmac-based extract-and-expand key derivation function (hkdf). Technical report, RFC 5869, May 2010
39. Kurosawa, K., Matsuo, T.: How to remove MAC from DHIES. In: Wang, H., Pieprzyk, J., Varadharajan, V. (eds.) ACISP 2004. LNCS, vol. 3108, pp. 236–247. Springer, Heidelberg (2004). https://doi.org/10.1007/978-3-540-27800-9_21
40. Marlinspike, M., Perrin, T.: The Double Ratchet Algorithm (11 2016). https://whispersystems.org/docs/specifications/doubleratchet/doubleratchet.pdf
41. Marlinspike, M., Perrin, T.: The X3DH Key Agreement Protocol (11 2016). https://signal.org/docs/specifications/x3dh/x3dh.pdf
42. Maurer, U.: Constructive cryptography – a new paradigm for security definitions and proofs. In: Mödersheim, S., Palamidessi, C. (eds.) TOSCA 2011. LNCS, vol. 6993, pp. 33–56. Springer, Heidelberg (2012). https://doi.org/10.1007/978-3-642-27375-9_3
43. Maurer, U.M., Wolf, S.: Diffie-Hellman Oracles. In: Koblitz, N. (ed.) CRYPTO 1996. LNCS, vol. 1109, pp. 268–282. Springer, Heidelberg (1996). https://doi.org/10.1007/3-540-68697-5_21
44. Nielsen, J.B.: Separating random Oracle proofs from complexity theoretic proofs: the non-committing encryption case. In: Yung, M. (ed.) CRYPTO 2002. LNCS, vol. 2442, pp. 111–126. Springer, Heidelberg (2002). https://doi.org/10.1007/3-540-45708-9_8
45. Poettering, B., Rösler, P.: Towards bidirectional ratcheted key exchange. In: Shacham, H., Boldyreva, A. (eds.) CRYPTO 2018. LNCS, vol. 10991, pp. 3–32. Springer, Cham (2018). https://doi.org/10.1007/978-3-319-96884-1_1
46. Shoup, V.: Lower bounds for discrete logarithms and related problems. In: Fumy, W. (ed.) EUROCRYPT 1997. LNCS, vol. 1233, pp. 256–266. Springer, Heidelberg (1997). https://doi.org/10.1007/3-540-69053-0_18
47. Sipser, M.: Introduction to the theory of computation. PWS Publishing Company (1997)
48. Unger, N., Goldberg, I.: Deniable key exchanges for secure messaging. In: Ray, I., Li, N., Kruegel, C. (eds.) ACM CCS 2015, pp. 1211–1223. ACM Press, Denver, CO, USA, 12–16 October 2015
49. Unger, N., Goldberg, I.: Improved strongly deniable authenticated key exchanges for secure messaging. Proc. Priv. Enhancing Technol. 2018(1), 21–66 (2018)
50. Vatandas, N., Gennaro, R., Ithurburn, B., Krawczyk, H.: On the cryptographic deniability of the signal protocol. In: Conti, M., Zhou, J., Casalicchio, E., Spognardi, A. (eds.) ACNS 2020. LNCS, vol. 12147, pp. 188–209. Springer, Cham (2020). https://doi.org/10.1007/978-3-030-57878-7_10
51. Yilek, S., Rescorla, E., Shacham, H., Enright, B., Savage, S.: When private keys are public: results from the 2008 debian openssl vulnerability. In: Proceedings of the 9th ACM SIGCOMM Conference on Internet Measurement, IMC 2009, pp. 15–27. Association for Computing Machinery, New York (2009). https://doi.org/10.1145/1644893.1644896

Author Index

Printed in the United States
by Baker & Taylor Publisher Services